Koren Talmud Bavli

THE NOÉ EDITION

BAVA BATRA

Steinsaltz Center

KOREN

תלמוד בבלי

KOREN TALMUD BAVLI

THE NOÉ EDITION

בבא בתרא

BAVA BATRA

Daf 139b through Daf 159b

COMMENTARY BY

Rabbi Adin Even-Israel Steinsaltz

EDITOR-IN-CHIEF

Rabbi Dr Tzvi Hersh Weinreb

SENIOR CONTENT EDITOR

Rabbi Dr Shalom Z Berger

EXECUTIVE EDITOR

Rabbi Joshua Schreier

•

STEINSALTZ CENTER

KOREN PUBLISHERS JERUSALEM

Supported by the Matanel Foundation

Koren Talmud Bavli, The Noe Edition
Vol. 23g: Tractate Bava Batra, Daf 139b through Daf 159b
Paperback, ISBN, 978-965-7766-14-9

First Hebrew/English paperback edition, 2021

Koren Publishers Jerusalem Ltd.
PO Box 4044, Jerusalem 91040, ISRAEL
PO Box 8531, New Milford, CT 06776, USA
www.korenpub.com

Steinsaltz Center

Steinsaltz Center is the parent organization of institutions established by Rabbi Adin Even-Israel Steinsaltz

PO Box 45187, Jerusalem 91450 ISRAEL
Telephone: +972 2 646 0900, Fax +972 2 624 9454
www.steinsaltz-center.org

This book was published in cooperation with the Israel Institute for Talmudic Publications.

הִנֵּה יָמִים בָּאִים, נְאֻם אֲדֹנָי יֱהוִה, וְהִשְׁלַחְתִּי רָעָב בָּאָרֶץ,
לֹא־רָעָב לַלֶּחֶם וְלֹא־צָמָא לַמַּיִם, כִּי אִם־לִשְׁמֹעַ אֵת דִּבְרֵי יהוה.

Behold, days are coming – says the Lord God – I will send a hunger to the land, not a hunger for bread nor a thirst for water, but to hear the words of the Lord. (AMOS 8:11)

The Noé edition of the Koren Talmud Bavli
with the commentary of Rabbi Adin Even-Israel Steinsaltz
is dedicated to all those who open its covers
to quench their thirst for Jewish Knowledge,
in our generation of Torah renaissance.

This beautiful edition is for the young, the aged,
the novice and the savant alike,
as it unites the depth of Torah knowledge
with the best of academic scholarship.

Within its exquisite and vibrant pages,
words become worlds.

It will claim its place in the library of classics,
in the bookcases of the Beit Midrash,
the classrooms of our schools,
and in the offices of professionals and business people
who carve out precious time to grapple with its timeless wisdom.

For the Student and the Scholar

DEDICATED BY LEO AND SUE NOÉ

Steinsaltz Center

Executive Director, Steinsaltz Center
Rabbi Meni Even-Israel

Managing Editor
Rabbi Jason Rappoport

Senior Content Editor
Rabbi Dr. Shalom Z. Berger

Editors
Rabbi Dr. Joshua Amaru, *Coordinating Editor*
Rabbi Yehoshua Duker, *Final Editor*
Rabbi Avishai Magence, *Content Curator*
Yedidya Naveh, *Content Curator*
Tal Avrahami
Menucha Chwat
Rabbi Adin Krohn
Betzalel Philip Edwards
Rabbi Yonatan Shai Freedman
Raphael Friedman
Rabbi Ayal Geffon
Rabbi Uri Goldstein
Nechama Greenberg
Rabbi Tzvi Chaim Kaye
Rabbi Yonatan Kohn
Catriel Lev
Elisha Loewenstern
Adina Luber
Rabbi Simcha Mirvis
Rabbi Jonathan Mishkin
Rabbi David Sedley
Avi Steinhart
Rabbi David Strauss
Rabbi Yitzchak Twersky

Copy Editors
Aliza Israel, *Coordinator*
Ita Olesker
Debbie Ismailoff
Shira Finson
Ilana Sobel
Deena Nataf
Eliana Kurlantzick Yorav
Erica Hirsch Edvi
Nava Wieder
Sara Henna Dahan
Shalom Dinerstein

Language Consultants
Dr. Stephanie E. Binder, *Greek & Latin*
Rabbi Yaakov Hoffman, *Arabic*
Dr. Shai Secunda, *Persian*
Shira Shmidman, *Aramaic*

KOREN

Design & Typesetting
Dena Landowne Bailey, *Typesetting*
Tani Bayer, *Jacket Design*
Raphaël Freeman, *Design & Typography*

Images
Eliahu Misgav, *Illustration & Image Acquisition*
Daniel Gdalevich, *Illustration & Image Acquisition*

Introduction by the Publisher

The Talmud has sustained and inspired Jews for thousands of years. Throughout Jewish history, an elite cadre of scholars has absorbed its learning and passed it on to succeeding generations. The Talmud has been the fundamental text of our people.

Beginning in the 1960s, Rabbi Adin Even-Israel Steinsaltz שליט״א created a revolution in the history of Talmud study. His translation of the Talmud, first into modern Hebrew and then into other languages, as well the practical learning aids he added to the text, have enabled millions of people around the world to access and master the complexity and context of the world of Talmud.

It is thus a privilege to present the *Koren Talmud Bavli*, an English translation of the talmudic text with the brilliant elucidation of Rabbi Steinsaltz. The depth and breadth of his knowledge are unique in our time. His rootedness in the tradition and his reach into the world beyond it are inspirational.

Working with Rabbi Steinsaltz on this remarkable project has been not only an honor, but a great pleasure. Never shy to express an opinion, with wisdom and humor, Rabbi Steinsaltz sparkles in conversation, demonstrating his knowledge (both sacred and worldly), sharing his wide-ranging interests, and, above all, radiating his passion. I am grateful for the unique opportunity to work closely with him, and I wish him many more years of writing and teaching.

Our intentions in publishing this new edition of the Talmud are threefold. First, we seek to fully clarify the talmudic page to the reader – textually, intellectually, and graphically. Second, we seek to utilize today's most sophisticated technologies, both in print and electronic formats, to provide the reader with a comprehensive set of study tools. And third, we seek to help readers advance in their process of Talmud study.

To achieve these goals, the *Koren Talmud Bavli* is unique in a number of ways:

- The classic *tzurat hadaf* of Vilna, used by scholars since the 1800s, has been reset for great clarity, and opens from the Hebrew "front" of the book. Full *nikkud* has been added to both the talmudic text and Rashi's commentary, allowing for a more fluent reading with the correct pronunciation; the commentaries of *Tosafot* have been punctuated. Upon the advice of many English-speaking teachers of Talmud, we have separated these core pages from the translation, thereby enabling the advanced student to approach the text without the distraction of the translation. This also reduces the number of volumes in the set. At the bottom of each *daf*, there is a reference to the corresponding English pages. In addition, the Vilna edition was read against other manuscripts and older print editions, so that texts which had been removed by non-Jewish censors have been restored to their rightful place.

- The English translation, which starts on the English "front" of the book, reproduces the *menukad* Talmud text alongside the English translation (in bold) and commentary and explanation (in a lighter font). The Hebrew and Aramaic text is presented in logical paragraphs. This allows for a fluent reading of the text for the non-Hebrew or non-Aramaic reader. It also allows for the Hebrew reader to refer easily to the text alongside. Where the original text features dialogue or poetry, the English text is laid out in a manner appropriate to the genre. Each page refers to the relevant *daf*.

- Critical contextual tools surround the text and translation: personality notes, providing short biographies of the Sages; language notes, explaining foreign terms borrowed from Greek, Latin, Persian, or Arabic; and background notes, giving information essential to the understanding of the text, including history, geography, botany, archaeology, zoology, astronomy, and aspects of daily life in the talmudic era.
- Halakhic summaries provide references to the authoritative legal decisions made over the centuries by the rabbis. They explain the reasons behind each halakhic decision as well as the ruling's close connection to the Talmud and its various interpreters.
- Photographs, drawings, and other illustrations have been added throughout the text – in full color in the Standard and Electronic editions, and in black and white in the Daf Yomi edition – to visually elucidate the text.

This is not an exhaustive list of features of this edition, it merely presents an overview for the English-speaking reader who may not be familiar with the "total approach" to Talmud pioneered by Rabbi Steinsaltz.

Several professionals have helped bring this vast collaborative project to fruition. My many colleagues are noted on the Acknowledgments page, and the leadership of this project has been exceptional.

RABBI MENACHEM EVEN-ISRAEL, DIRECTOR OF THE STEINSALTZ CENTER, was the driving force behind this enterprise. With enthusiasm and energy, he formed the happy alliance with Koren and established close relationships among all involved in the work.

RABBI DR. TZVI HERSH WEINREB שליט״א, EDITOR-IN-CHIEF, brought to this project his profound knowledge of Torah, intellectual literacy of Talmud, and erudition of Western literature. It is to him that the text owes its very high standard, both in form and content, and the logical manner in which the beauty of the Talmud is presented.

RABBI JOSHUA SCHREIER, EXECUTIVE EDITOR, assembled an outstanding group of scholars, translators, editors, and proofreaders, whose standards and discipline enabled this project to proceed in a timely and highly professional manner.

RABBI MEIR HANEGBI, EDITOR OF THE HEBREW EDITION OF THE STEINSALTZ TALMUD, lent his invaluable assistance throughout the work process, supervising the reproduction of the Vilna pages.

RAPHAËL FREEMAN, EXECUTIVE EDITOR OF KOREN, created this Talmud's unique typographic design which, true to the Koren approach, is both elegant and user friendly.

It has been an enriching experience for all of us at Koren Publishers Jerusalem to work with the Steinsaltz Center to develop and produce the *Koren Talmud Bavli*. We pray that this publication will be a source of great learning and, ultimately, greater *avodat Hashem* for all Jews.

Matthew Miller, Publisher
Koren Publishers Jerusalem
Jerusalem 5772

Contents

For the vocalized Vilna Shas layout, please open as a Hebrew book.

Introduction to **Perek IX**

This chapter continues the discussion commenced in the previous chapter with regard to the *halakhot* of inheritance. It focuses on *halakhot* that are based on rabbinic decrees and local custom rather than Torah law. Four fundamental issues are addressed in the chapter.

The first issue concerns the division of an estate between the sons of the deceased, who are the heirs, and the deceased's daughters. Every marriage contract includes the following stipulation: Any female children you will have from me will live in my house and be sustained from my property until they are married (see *Ketubot* 52b). This stipulation ensures that the daughters are provided with sustenance from their father's estate until they either reach the age of majority or marry. This chapter discusses the division of the deceased's estate when it is insufficient to support both the sons and the daughters. It further discusses whether a *tumtum*, i.e., one whose sexual organs are indeterminate, is considered a male or a female with regard to this matter.

The second issue concerns a situation where the heirs enhance their inheritance before dividing the property between them. In this case it is necessary to determine how to divide the profits accrued due to the enhancement of the property. The Gemara explores several cases where the manner of dividing the enhancement is not evident, e.g., when only some of the heirs invested in the property, or when some of the heirs are adult sons and some are minor sons.

The third issue concerns instructions issued by a person on his deathbed. The Sages instituted that unlike the gift of a healthy person, the gift of a person on his deathbed does not require a formal act of acquisition, but is acquired by means of the verbal instruction of the person on his deathbed. This applies only if he transfers ownership of all his property. Furthermore, under certain circumstances he can retract the gift or transfer it to a different recipient.

The fourth issue concerns a case where two relatives die under circumstances in which it is impossible to ascertain which of them died first. It is therefore unclear who inherits from whom, and to whom the property should now be transferred. This chapter examines the manner of adjudicating these cases of uncertainty.

מתני׳ מִי שֶׁמֵּת וְהִנִּיחַ בָּנִים וּבָנוֹת, בִּזְמַן שֶׁהַנְּכָסִים מְרוּבִּין – הַבָּנִים יִירְשׁוּ וְהַבָּנוֹת יִזּוֹנוּ, נְכָסִים מוּעָטִין – הַבָּנוֹת יִזּוֹנוּ וְהַבָּנִים יִשְׁאֲלוּ עַל הַפְּתָחִים; אַדְמוֹן אוֹמֵר: בִּשְׁבִיל שֶׁאֲנִי זָכָר הִפְסַדְתִּי? אָמַר רַבָּן גַּמְלִיאֵל: רוֹאֶה אֲנִי אֶת דִּבְרֵי אַדְמוֹן.

MISHNA In the case of **one who died and left** behind both **sons and daughters,**[H] **when the estate is large the sons inherit**[N] the estate **and the daughters are provided with sustenance** from it[N] according to the stipulations of the deceased's marriage contract with their mother. With regard to **a small estate,** which is insufficient to provide for both the sons and the daughters, **the daughters are provided with sustenance. And** if **the sons,** who receive in this case neither inheritance nor sustenance, have no other means with which to support themselves, **they** go and **request** charity **at the doors.**[N] **Admon**[P] **says,** rhetorically: **I lost out** just **because I am male?** Rather, he holds that the sons also receive sustenance. **Rabban Gamliel said: I see** as correct **the statement of Admon.**

גמ׳ וְכַמָּה מְרוּבִּין? אָמַר רַב יְהוּדָה אָמַר רַב: כְּדֵי שֶׁיִּזּוֹנוּ מֵהֶן אֵלּוּ וְאֵלּוּ שְׁנֵים עָשָׂר חֹדֶשׁ. כִּי אֲמַרִיתָא קַמֵּיהּ דִּשְׁמוּאֵל, אֲמַר: זוֹ דִּבְרֵי רַבָּן גַּמְלִיאֵל בַּר רַבִּי, אֲבָל חֲכָמִים אוֹמְרִים: כְּדֵי שֶׁיִּזּוֹנוּ מֵהֶן אֵלּוּ וְאֵלּוּ עַד שֶׁיִּבָּגְרוּ.

GEMARA The Gemara asks: **And how large** must the estate be in order for the sons to inherit it? **Rav Yehuda says** that **Rav says:** Large **enough to provide sustenance from it for** both **these,** the sons, **and those,** the daughters, for **twelve months.**[N] Rav Yehuda continues: **When I said this** ruling **before Shmuel, he said: That is the statement of Rabban Gamliel bar Rabbi** Yehuda HaNasi. **But the Rabbis say:** The estate must be large **enough to provide sustenance from it for** both **these and those until** the time **that** the daughters **reach their majority,** at age twelve and six months, as indicated in the marriage contract.

אִיתְּמַר נַמִי: כִּי אֲתָא רָבִין אָמַר רַבִּי יוֹחָנָן, וְאָמְרִי לַהּ אָמַר רַבָּה בַּר בַּר חָנָה אָמַר רַבִּי יוֹחָנָן: כֹּל שֶׁיִּזּוֹנוּ מֵהֶן אֵלּוּ וְאֵלּוּ עַד שֶׁיִּבָּגְרוּ – הֵן מְרוּבִּין, פָּחוֹת מִכָּאן – הֲרֵי אֵלּוּ מוּעָטִין.

This **was also stated** by other *amora'im*: **When Ravin came** from Eretz Yisrael, he said that **Rabbi Yoḥanan says, and some say** it was **Rabba bar bar Ḥana** who says that **Rabbi Yoḥanan says: Any** estate **that** is large enough **to provide sustenance from it for** both **these and those until** the time **that** the daughters **reach their majority is a large** estate; **less than that, this is a small** estate.

וְאִי לֵיכָּא לְאֵלּוּ וְאֵלּוּ עַד שֶׁיִּבָּגְרוּ,

The Gemara asks: **And if there is not** enough to provide **for these and those until** the daughters **reach their majority,**

HALAKHA

One who died and left sons and daughters, etc. – מִי שֶׁמֵּת וְהִנִּיחַ בָּנִים וּבָנוֹת וכו׳: In the case of one who dies and leaves behind both sons and daughters, the sons inherit the estate. They are entitled to dispose of it as they wish, as long as they provide for their sisters until the latter reach their majority or are betrothed. Some hold that they may not sell the estate while they are sustaining their sisters except for the purpose of a mitzva, such as redeeming a captive (Rema, citing Mordekhai). The Rema adds that the sons are not required to be frugal in their spending. If the court notes that the sons are depleting their late father's estate, the court must ensure the welfare of the daughters by separating their due from the estate. All this applies when the estate is large enough to provide food, clothing, and accommodation for both the sons and the daughters until the daughters reach their majority, and, according to some, to pay for the daughters' marriage expenses (see *Beit Shmuel*). If the estate is not that large, the court first separates funds to provide for the daughters, and then gives the remainder to the sons. The first priority is to provide for the daughters, even if the sons must resort to begging. This is in accordance with the opinion of the unattributed mishna, and contrary to the opinion of Admon.

Nowadays, these *halakhot* apply if the father bequeathed land. If he bequeathed only movable property, both sons and daughters are provided for equally, as the daughters' right to receive sustenance from movable property is not by Torah or rabbinic law; rather it is an ordinance of the *ge'onim*, and this ordinance did not give the daughters precedence over the sons. If the estate includes both land and movable property, and together they constitute a large estate, the sons inherit the estate (Rambam *Sefer Nashim*, *Hilkhot Ishut* 19:17–18; *Shulḥan Arukh*, *Even HaEzer* 112:11–12).

PERSONALITIES

Admon – אַדְמוֹן: The Admon cited here is Admon ben Gaddai, one of the Sages of Jerusalem in the generation before the destruction of the Temple. The mishna describes Admon as one of two judges authorized to issue decrees (*Ketubot* 104b). This was presumably the highest level of judges in Jerusalem, and they had the authority to institute ordinances and issue decrees about monetary matters. The *mishnayot* in tractate *Ketubot* (108b–110a) present seven rulings made by Admon.

NOTES

The sons inherit – הַבָּנִים יִירְשׁוּ: When the estate is large, the sons acquire the property to use as they wish, and they, or the steward appointed for them if they are minors (Ramah), are then responsible for providing for their sisters. When the estate is small it is not given to the sons but is kept under the jurisdiction of the court or of a court-appointed steward, who ensures that the daughters are provided for (Ramban).

And the daughters are provided with sustenance from it – וְהַבָּנוֹת יִזּוֹנוּ: The Rashbam explains that their sustenance also includes marriage expenses, i.e., her trousseau and related expenses. Furthermore, some early commentaries understand that according to the Rashbam the daughters' sustenance includes one-tenth of the estate given as a dowry (see *Ketubot* 68b). Many early commentaries disagree with the Rashbam and hold that the dowry is not taken into account when evaluating whether the estate is designated a large or small estate (Ramban; Rashba).

They go and request charity at the doors – יִשְׁאֲלוּ עַל הַפְּתָחִים: This signifies that they have no rights in the estate. If they are unable to support themselves, they are supported by the community, as are other poor people. The daughters' sustenance takes precedence, as their right to sustenance is guaranteed by the stipulations of their mother's marriage contract, which places a lien on the estate. Rabbi Yitzḥak Karkusha adds that the Sages gave priority to the daughters' rights to sustenance over the rights of the sons to inherit, as it is more shameful for the daughters to go begging than for the sons to do so.

Twelve months – שְׁנֵים עָשָׂר חֹדֶשׁ: Some explain that the Sages defined the size of a large estate in this way in order to balance between the rabbinic ordinance protecting the daughters and the Sages' desire not to dispossess the sons of their inheritance (Ramban). The Ritva claims that the twelve-month period is based upon one opinion (*Ketubot* 97a) with regard to the amount of time for which the Sages permitted a widow to sell her husband's property after his death in order to provide sustenance for herself. She may sell property to provide sustenance for herself for twelve months, and likewise the daughters are allocated twelve months of sustenance.

שָׁקְלִי לְהוּ בָּנוֹת לְכוּלְּהוּ? אֶלָּא אֲמַר רָבָא: מוֹצִיאִין לָהֶן מְזוֹנוֹת לַבָּנוֹת עַד שֶׁיִּבָּגְרוּ, וְהַשְּׁאָר לַבָּנִים.

shall the **daughters take all** of the estate, even if it is more than is required for their sustenance? **Rather, Rava said:** The court **appropriates sustenance for the daughters until they reach their majority, and the remainder** is given **to the sons.**

פְּשִׁיטָא, מְרוּבִּין וְנִתְמַעֲטוּ – כְּבָר זָכוּ בָּהֶן יוֹרְשִׁין. מוּעָטִין וְנִתְרַבּוּ מַאי? בִּרְשׁוּת יוֹרְשִׁין קַיְימִי, הִלְכָּךְ בִּרְשׁוּת יוֹרְשִׁין שְׁבוּח, אוֹ דִּלְמָא סַלּוּקֵי מְסַלְּקִי יוֹרְשִׁין מֵהָכָא?

§ The Gemara comments: It is **obvious** that if the estate was **large and became small,**[HN] the **heirs,** i.e., the sons, **already acquired it**[N] when it was large. It remains in their possession, and they must provide for the daughters from it. The Gemara asks: If the estate was **small,** and was therefore not inherited by the sons, **and then it became large,**[H] **what** is the *halakha*? Does even a small estate **remain in the possession of the heirs,** while the court reserves it for the daughters' sustenance, and **therefore it appreciated in the possession of** the **heirs** and they receive the appreciation in the estate's value? **Or perhaps** the **heirs are** totally **removed from** possession of a small estate, and the appreciation in value is to the benefit of the daughters receiving sustenance.

תָּא שְׁמַע, דְּאָמַר רַבִּי אַסִּי אָמַר רַבִּי יוֹחָנָן: יְתוֹמִין שֶׁקָּדְמוּ וּמָכְרוּ בִּנְכָסִים מוּעָטִין – מַה שֶּׁמָּכְרוּ מָכְרוּ.

The Gemara answers: **Come** and **hear** a proof, **as Rabbi Asi says** that **Rabbi Yoḥanan says:** In the case of **orphans who preemptively sold**[HN] land **from a small estate** left to them by their father, before the court appropriated it for the daughters' sustenance, concerning **that which they sold,** the **sale** is valid, even though they acted improperly. One can infer from this that a small estate remains in the possession of the heirs even when they are not authorized to derive benefit from it, and therefore the appreciation in its value belongs to them.

יְתֵיב רַבִּי יִרְמְיָה קַמֵּיהּ דְּרַבִּי אַבָּהוּ וְקָא בָּעֵי מִינֵּיהּ: אַלְמָנָתוֹ מַהוּ שֶׁתְּמַעֵט בַּנְּכָסִים? מִי אָמְרִינַן: כֵּיוָן דְּאִית לָהּ מְזוֹנֵי – מְמַעֲטָא, אוֹ דִּלְמָא כֵּיוָן דְּאִילּוּ מִנַּסְּבָא לֵית לָהּ, הָשְׁתָּא נַמִּי לֵית לָהּ?

§ **Rabbi Yirmeya was sitting before Rabbi Abbahu and raised** the following **dilemma before him: What is** the *halakha* with regard to the sustenance to which the deceased's **widow**[HN] is entitled? Does it **reduce** the value of **the estate** when evaluating whether the estate is categorized as a large estate or a small estate? **Do we say** that **since she has** a right to receive **sustenance,** it **reduces** the value of the estate? **Or perhaps** we say that **since if she remarries she does not have** a right to sustenance, **now as well,** for the purposes of determining the value of the estate, she is considered as if **she does not have** a right to sustenance, and therefore it does not reduce the value of the estate.

HALAKHA

If the estate was large and became small – מְרוּבִּין וְנִתְמַעֲטוּ: If a large estate depreciated after its owner died, the sons nevertheless retain it, as they inherited the estate at the moment of death. The *Tur*, citing the Rashbam, rules that any shortfall is deducted equally from the sons and the daughters (Rambam *Sefer Nashim*, *Hilkhot Ishut* 19:19; *Shulḥan Arukh*, *Even HaEzer* 112:13).

If the estate was small and then it became large – מוּעָטִין וְנִתְרַבּוּ: If the estate was small at the time of the father's death and subsequently became large, the sons inherit the estate, in accordance with the Gemara's conclusion. The Rema cites an opinion that even if the matter was already settled in court and the estate was categorized as a small estate, if the estate appreciates to the point of being a large estate, the estate attains the status of a large estate. The estate retains the status of a large estate even if it then depreciates in value (Rambam *Sefer Nashim*, *Hilkhot Ishut* 19:19; *Shulḥan Arukh*, *Even HaEzer* 112:14).

Orphans who preemptively sold – יְתוֹמִין שֶׁקָּדְמוּ וּמָכְרוּ: If the sons preemptively sold property from a small estate, the sale is valid, in accordance with the opinion of Rabbi Yoḥanan. The daughters do not receive sustenance from the proceeds of the sale, since the actual property left by the father is no longer in the family's possession (*Tur*, citing Rosh). Some authorities hold that the sale is valid only if it took place prior to the court's appropriation of the daughters' sustenance from the estate (Rambam *Sefer Nashim*, *Hilkhot Ishut* 19:19; *Shulḥan Arukh*, *Even HaEzer* 112:14).

The deceased's widow, etc. – אַלְמָנָתוֹ וכו׳: If the estate is large but there is a claim upon it, which if deducted from the value of the estate would render it a small estate, it is still categorized as a large estate. This is the *halakha* with regard to a creditor's claim to money owed him, a stepdaughter's claim to sustenance, and a daughter's claim to one-tenth of the estate as a dowry. By contrast, the funds dedicated to the payment of the deceased's marriage contract, and according to the Ramban and Rashba, also those dedicated to the sustenance of the widow, are deducted before the value of the estate is determined. This ruling stems from the principle that in cases that are unresolved in the Talmud, the property remains in the possession of the last known owner. Since this is not a conclusive halakhic ruling, if one of the claimants seized property in accordance with his or her claims, it is not taken back from them (Rambam *Sefer Nashim*, *Hilkhot Ishut* 19:20; *Shulḥan Arukh*, *Even HaEzer* 112:15, and see *Beit Shmuel* there).

NOTES

If the estate was large and became small – מְרוּבִּין וְנִתְמַעֲטוּ: The value of the estate is determined as of the time of death. Later appreciation or depreciation in value discussed in the Gemara could be due to a range of factors, including a change in market value, a loss caused by actions taken by the heirs, or an increase in the cost of living.

The heirs already acquired it – כְּבָר זָכוּ בָּהֶן יוֹרְשִׁין: If, after an estate was acquired by the sons as an inheritance on the basis of its categorization as a large estate, it then depreciated to the point of becoming a small estate, it cannot then be removed from their possession and allocated to the daughters for their sustenance, as would have been the case had it been categorized as a small estate initially. Rather, the depreciation is deducted proportionally from the sons' inheritance and the daughters' sustenance (Rashbam). Rabbi Avraham *Av Beit Din* explains that this is because once the estate is categorized as a large estate, the *halakha* reverts to the Torah law of inheritance, and the rabbinic ordinance providing for the daughters does not take effect. The Ramban explains that the sons' rights to the estate stem from the *halakhot* of inheritance, which take effect at the moment of death, whereas the daughters' rights to sustenance take effect only when the property actually reaches their possession, just as a gift is acquired only when it reaches the recipient's possession.

Orphans who preemptively sold – יְתוֹמִין שֶׁקָּדְמוּ וּמָכְרוּ: The early commentaries disagree as to when this applies. The Rashbam explains that it applies only if they sold the estate before the matter came to court for adjudication and that once the court appropriated the estate for the daughters' sustenance the sons can no longer sell it. *Tosafot* maintain that even after the matter was settled in court, and the estate was appropriated for the daughters' sustenance, if the sons sold the property, their sale is valid. Some early commentaries explain that even when the sons sold the estate, the daughters do not lose their rights to sustenance and the sons must provide for them, although the property sold cannot be repossessed from the purchasers (Rav Hai Gaon; Responsa of Ri Migash). Other commentaries hold that the daughters do lose their rights to sustenance, as they are entitled to sustenance only from their father's estate directly, not from money received by the sons from the purchasers (Ramban).

The deceased's widow – אַלְמָנָתוֹ: The Sages instituted that a widow has the right to live in her late husband's house and receive sustenance from his estate until she remarries. The commentaries discuss how her sustenance is valued, as the duration of her widowhood is unknown. Some early commentaries explain that the amount is calculated based on the duration of time the Sages deemed it permitted for a widow to sell property from her husband's estate in order to provide for herself (Rabbi Avraham *Av Beit Din*; see Meiri). Others say that the widow's life expectancy is estimated and the sustenance due to her is calculated accordingly (Rabbeinu Asher of Lunel; Rashba).

אִם תִּמְצָא לוֹמַר: כֵּיוָן דְּאִילּוּ מִנַּסְבָא לֵית לָהּ הָשְׁתָּא נַמִּי לֵית לָהּ, בַּת אִשְׁתּוֹ מַהוּ שֶׁתְּמַעֵט בַּנְּכָסִים? מִי אָמְרִינַן: כֵּיוָן דְּכִי מִנַּסְבָא נַמִּי אִית לָהּ – וּמְמַעֲטָא, אוֹ דִּלְמָא כֵּיוָן דְּאִילּוּ מֵתָה לֵית לָהּ – וְלָא מְמַעֲטָא?

Furthermore, **if you say that since, if she remarries she does not have** a right to sustenance, **now as well** she is considered as if **she does not have** a right to sustenance, and it is not taken into account when evaluating the estate, then another dilemma can be raised: **What is the** *halakha* with regard to the sustenance one pledged to give, for a certain number of years, to the **daughter of his wife** from a previous marriage, i.e., his step-daughter, which is an obligation not affected by his death or by her marriage? Does it **reduce** the value of **the estate? Do we say** that **since, when she marries she also has** a right to sustenance, it **reduces** the value of the estate? **Or perhaps** we say that **since, if she dies she does not have** a right to sustenance, it **does not reduce** the value of the estate.

וְאִם תִּמְצָא לוֹמַר: כֵּיוָן דְּאִילּוּ מֵתָה לֵית לָהּ וְלָא מְמַעֲטָא, בַּעַל חוֹב מַהוּ שֶׁיְּמַעֵט בַּנְּכָסִים? מִי אָמְרִינַן: כֵּיוָן דְּכִי מָיֵית נַמִּי אִית לֵיהּ – מְמַעֵט, אוֹ דִּלְמָא כֵּיוָן דִּמְחַסְּרִי גּוּבַיְינָא לָא מְמַעֵט?

And if you say that **since, if she dies she does not have** a right to sustenance, therefore it **does not reduce** the value of the estate, **what is** the *halakha* with regard to a debt owed to the deceased's **creditor?** Does it **reduce** the value of **the estate? Do we say** that **since, when** the creditor **dies he also has** a right to the money owed him, and it is collected by his heirs, therefore it **reduces** the value of the estate? **Or perhaps** we say that **since it has not yet been collected,** it **does not reduce** the value of the estate.

וְאִיכָּא דְּבָעֵי לָהּ לְאִידָּךְ גִּיסָא: בַּעַל חוֹב מַהוּ שֶׁיְּמַעֵט בַּנְּכָסִים?

And there are those who say **that** Rabbi Yirmeya **raised the dilemmas in the opposite direction,**[N] i.e., in the reverse order: **What is** the *halakha* with regard to a debt owed to **a creditor?** Does it **reduce** the value of **the estate?**

NOTES

That he raised the dilemmas in the opposite direction – **דְּבָעֵי לָהּ לְאִידָּךְ גִּיסָא:** Although the content of the questions is identical according to both versions, the order in which the dilemmas were presented has halakhic ramifications, as the *halakha* generally follows those statements that are taken for granted in a subsequent dilemma (see Ran).

Perek **IX**
Daf **140** Amud **b**

בַּת אִשְׁתּוֹ מַהוּ שֶׁתְּמַעֵט בַּנְּכָסִים? אַלְמָנָתוֹ מַהוּ שֶׁתְּמַעֵט בַּנְּכָסִים? אַלְמָנָתוֹ וּבַת אֵי זֶה מֵהֶן קוֹדֶמֶת?

What is the *halakha* with regard to sustenance the deceased pledged to give **the daughter of his wife** from a previous marriage? Does it **reduce** the value of **the estate? What is** the *halakha* with regard to the sustenance to which **his widow** is entitled? Does it **reduce** the value of **the estate?** Furthermore, with regard to **his widow and daughter,**[N] **which of them takes precedence** if the estate is insufficient to provide sustenance for both?

אֲמַר לֵיהּ: זִיל הָאִידָּנָא וְתָא לְמָחָר. כִּי אֲתָא, אֲמַר לֵיהּ: פְּשׁוֹט מִיהַת חֲדָא, דְּאָמַר רַבִּי אַבָּא אָמַר רַבִּי אַסִּי: עָשׂוּ אַלְמָנָה אֵצֶל הַבַּת כְּבַת אֵצֶל הָאַחִין בִּנְכָסִים מוּעָטִין, מַה בַּת אֵצֶל אַחִין – הַבַּת נִיזּוֹנֶת וְהָאַחִין יִשְׁאֲלוּ עַל הַפְּתָחִים, אַף אַלְמָנָה אֵצֶל הַבַּת – אַלְמָנָה נִיזּוֹנֶת וְהַבַּת תִּשְׁאַל עַל הַפְּתָחִים.

Rabbi Abbahu **said to** Rabbi Yirmeya: **Go now and come** back **tomorrow. When he came** back, Rabbi Abbahu **said to** him: **Resolve at least one** of your questions, **as Rabbi Abba says** that **Rabbi Asi says:** The Sages **established** the status of the **widow in relation to the daughter**[H] as equivalent to the status of the **daughter in relation to the brothers in** the case of **a small estate. Just as** in the case of **a daughter in relation to** her **brothers, the daughter is sustained and the brothers** go and **request** charity **at the doors, so too** in the case of **a widow in relation to the daughter, the widow is sustained**[N] **and the daughter** goes and **requests** charity **at the doors.**

״אַדְמוֹן אוֹמֵר: בִּשְׁבִיל שֶׁאֲנִי זָכָר הִפְסַדְתִּי״? וכו׳. מַאי קָאָמַר? אָמַר אַבָּיֵי, הָכִי קָאָמַר: בִּשְׁבִיל שֶׁאֲנִי זָכָר, וְרָאוּי אֲנִי לַעֲסוֹק בַּתּוֹרָה הִפְסַדְתִּי? אֲמַר לֵיהּ רָבָא: אֶלָּא מֵעַתָּה, מַאן דְּעָסֵיק בַּתּוֹרָה הוּא דְּיָרֵית, דְּלָא עָסֵיק בַּתּוֹרָה לָא יָרֵית?! אֶלָּא אָמַר רָבָא, הָכִי קָאָמַר: בִּשְׁבִיל שֶׁאֲנִי זָכָר, וְרָאוּי אֲנִי לִירַשׁ בִּנְכָסִים מְרוּבִּין – הִפְסַדְתִּי בִּנְכָסִים מוּעָטִין?

§ The mishna teaches: **Admon says,** rhetorically: **I lost out** just **because I am male?** Rather, he holds that the sons also receive sustenance. The Gemara asks: **What is he saying? Abaye said** that **this** is what **he is saying: Because I am male, and I am fit to engage in** the study of **the Torah, I lost out** and must go begging instead of studying the Torah? **Rava said to him: If that is so,** should one conclude that **it is only one who engages in** the study of **the Torah**[N] **who inherits,** whereas one **who does not engage in** the study of **the Torah does not inherit? Rather, Rava said** that **this** is what Admon **is saying: Because I am male, and I am fit to inherit in** the case of **a large estate,** should **I lose** my inheritance entirely **in** the case of **a small estate?**

NOTES

His widow and daughter – **אַלְמָנָתוֹ וּבַת:** Rabbeinu Gershom Meor HaGola explains that this refers to his wife's daughter from her previous marriage, where he pledged to provide for her for a certain number of years. Most commentaries explain that this refers to his own daughter (see Rambam).

The widow is sustained – **אַלְמָנָה נִיזּוֹנֶת:** The reason for this is that one is presumably more concerned about preventing his wife's humiliation than that of his daughter, and he therefore would first concern himself with providing for his wife (Rabbeinu Gershom Meor HaGola).

One who engages in the study of the Torah, etc. – **מַאן דְּעָסֵיק בַּתּוֹרָה וכו׳:** The Rashbam explains that Rava is stating that it is obvious that if one has two sons and one of them does not study Torah, he does not lose his inheritance, as the rights of inheritance are not dependent upon the personal qualities of the heir; rather, they are his by right.

HALAKHA

The widow in relation to the daughter – **אַלְמָנָה אֵצֶל הַבַּת:** If one died, leaving a widow and a daughter, the widow is provided for from the estate. If the estate is too small to provide for the daughter as well, then the daughter requests charity at the doors. Even if the daughter marries, and she brings the estate into her marriage as part of her dowry, the widow is still entitled to be sustained from the estate. Furthermore, even if the daughter then dies, in which case her husband inherits from her, the widow is still entitled to be sustained from the estate. This final ruling is the *halakha* only with regard to usufruct property. With regard to guaranteed property, the husband has the status of a purchaser, and the widow cannot demand the estate from him (Rambam *Sefer Nashim, Hilkhot Ishut* 20:11; *Shulḥan Arukh Even HaEzer* 93:4, and see *Beit Shmuel* there).

מתני׳ הִנִּיחַ בָּנִים וּבָנוֹת וְטוּמְטוּם, בִּזְמַן שֶׁהַנְּכָסִים מְרוּבִּין – הַזְּכָרִים דּוֹחִין אוֹתוֹ אֵצֶל נְקֵבוֹת, נְכָסִים מוּעָטִין – הַנְּקֵבוֹת דּוֹחוֹת אוֹתוֹ אֵצֶל זְכָרִים.

MISHNA With regard to one who **left** behind **sons and daughters and a *tumtum*,**[H] whose halakhic status as male or female is indeterminate, the *halakha* is as follows: **When the estate is large the males direct** the *tumtum* **to the females** and exclude him from the inheritance, claiming that perhaps the *tumtum* is female. When the **estate is small, the females direct** the *tumtum* **to the males** and exclude him from receiving sustenance, claiming that perhaps the *tumtum* is male.

הָאוֹמֵר: ״אִם תֵּלֵד אִשְׁתִּי זָכָר יִטּוֹל מָנֶה״, יָלְדָה זָכָר – יִטּוֹל מָנֶה; ״נְקֵבָה מָאתַיִם״, יָלְדָה נְקֵבָה – נוֹטֶלֶת מָאתַיִם;

With regard to **one who says: If my wife gives birth**[N] **to a male**[H] the offspring **shall receive** a gift of **one hundred dinars,** if **she** in fact **gave birth to a male,** the offspring **receives one hundred dinars.** If he says: If my wife gives birth to **a female** the offspring shall receive a gift of **two hundred** dinars, if **she** in fact **gave birth to a female,** the offspring **receives two hundred** dinars.

״אִם זָכָר מָנֶה, אִם נְקֵבָה מָאתַיִם״, וְיָלְדָה זָכָר וּנְקֵבָה – זָכָר נוֹטֵל מָנֶה, נְקֵבָה נוֹטֶלֶת מָאתַיִם; יָלְדָה טוּמְטוּם – אֵינוֹ נוֹטֵל. אִם אָמַר ״כָּל מַה שֶּׁתֵּלֵד אִשְׁתִּי יִטּוֹל״ – הֲרֵי זֶה יִטּוֹל; וְאִם אֵין שָׁם יוֹרֵשׁ אֶלָּא הוּא – יוֹרֵשׁ אֶת הַכֹּל.

If he says: **If** my wife gives birth to **a male** the offspring shall receive a gift of **one hundred dinars** and **if** she gives birth to **a female** the offspring shall receive a gift of **two hundred** dinars, **and** in fact **she gave birth to** both **a male and a female,**[N] the **male** offspring **receives one hundred dinars** and the **female** offspring **receives two hundred** dinars. If **she gave birth to a *tumtum*,** the *tumtum* **does not receive** anything. **If he said: Whatever** offspring **my wife gives birth to shall receive** a gift of a certain sum, and she gave birth to a *tumtum*, the *tumtum* **receives** it. **And if there is no heir other than** the *tumtum*, the *tumtum* **inherits all** of the estate.

גמ׳ דּוֹחִין אוֹתוֹ, וְשָׁקֵיל כְּבַת? הָא קָתָנֵי סֵיפָא: יָלְדָה טוּמְטוּם – אֵינוֹ נוֹטֵל! אָמַר אַבַּיֵּי: דּוֹחִין אוֹתוֹ וְאֵין לוֹ.

GEMARA The mishna states that the males direct the *tumtum* to the females. The Gemara asks: Does this mean that **they direct him, and he takes** sustenance **like a daughter? Isn't it taught** in the **latter clause** of the mishna that if one said that either his male or female child will receive a certain sum once his wife gives birth, and **she gave birth to a *tumtum*,** the *tumtum* **does not receive** anything? This indicates that the *tumtum* does not have the rights of a female. **Abaye says:** The mishna means that **they direct him** to the females, **but he has no** rights to sustenance.

וְרָבָא אָמַר: דּוֹחִין אוֹתוֹ וְיֵשׁ לוֹ, וְסֵיפָא – אֲתָאן לְרַבָּן שִׁמְעוֹן בֶּן גַּמְלִיאֵל, דְּתַנְיָא יָלְדָה טוּמְטוּם וְאַנְדְּרוֹגִינוֹס – רַבָּן שִׁמְעוֹן בֶּן גַּמְלִיאֵל אוֹמֵר: אֵין קְדוּשָּׁה חָלָה עֲלֵיהֶן.

And Rava says: They direct him to the females **and he has** a right to sustenance. **And** with regard to **the latter clause** of the mishna, which grants the *tumtum* nothing at all, there **we arrive at** the opinion of **Rabban Shimon ben Gamliel,**[N] **as it is taught** in a mishna (*Temura* 24b): If one consecrates a firstborn animal while it is still a fetus, stating that if it is male it shall be a burnt-offering and if it is female it shall be a peace-offering, and the mother **gave birth to a *tumtum* or a hermaphrodite** [*androginos*],[LB] **Rabban Shimon ben Gamliel says: It is not imbued with sanctity,**[H] as it is neither male nor female. So too, in the case discussed in the mishna here, Rabban Shimon ben Gamliel maintains that the *tumtum* receives nothing, as he is considered to be a distinct entity of indeterminate sex, neither male nor female.

HALAKHA

One who left sons and daughters and a *tumtum* – הִנִּיחַ בָּנִים וּבָנוֹת וְטוּמְטוּם: With regard to one who left behind sons and daughters, and also a *tumtum* or hermaphrodite, if the estate is large, the sons inherit it and direct the *tumtum* to take his portion with the daughters, and he is provided with sustenance like them, in accordance with the opinion of Rava. If the estate is small, the daughters direct the *tumtum* to the sons, saying: You are a male and have no portion with us. The reason is that the *tumtum* is of uncertain status, and the *halakha* is that one with an uncertain claim cannot extract property from one who has a definite claim to it (Rambam *Sefer Mishpatim*, *Hilkhot Naḥalot* 5:2; *Shulḥan Arukh*, *Ḥoshen Mishpat* 280:9).

If my wife gives birth to a male, etc. – אִם תֵּלֵד אִשְׁתִּי זָכָר וכו׳: If a person on his deathbed instructs others to give a gift to his unborn son, the gift is valid. If he specifies that if his wife gives birth to a male the offspring will receive one hundred dinars, and if she gives birth to a female the offspring will receive two hundred dinars, then if she gives birth to a male, the offspring receives one hundred dinars, and if she gives birth to a female, the offspring receives two hundred dinars. If she gives birth to both a male and a female, the male receives one hundred dinars and the female receives two hundred dinars. If she gives birth to a *tumtum* or a hermaphrodite, the offspring receives the smaller of the two stipulated gifts. This is not in accordance with the ruling of the mishna, as Rava attributed it to Rabban Shimon ben Gamliel, who holds that a *tumtum* is classified as a distinct entity of indeterminate sex, i.e., neither male nor female, whereas the *halakha* is that the status of a *tumtum* is uncertain. A *tumtum* whose sex becomes apparent receives inheritance or sustenance as a male or female, respectively (Rambam *Sefer Kinyan*, *Hilkhot Zekhiya UMattana* 8:6; *Shulḥan Arukh*, *Ḥoshen Mishpat* 253:26–27).

A *tumtum* or a hermaphrodite…it is not imbued with sanctity – טוּמְטוּם וְאַנְדְּרוֹגִינוֹס...אֵין קְדוּשָּׁה חָלָה עֲלֵיהֶן: One whose animal is pregnant can state that if it gives birth to a male, the offspring shall be a burnt-offering, and if it gives birth to a female, the offspring shall be a peace-offering. If the animal gives birth to a *tumtum* or a hermaphrodite, the offspring is not imbued with sanctity at all (Rambam *Sefer Avoda*, *Hilkhot Ma'aseh HaKorbanot* 15:8 and *Hilkhot Issurei Mizbe'aḥ* 3:3, 10).

LANGUAGE

Hermaphrodite [*androginos*] – אַנְדְּרוֹגִינוֹס: From the Greek ἀνδρόγυνος, *androgunos*, which literally means man-woman, i.e., one who has both male and female reproductive organs.

BACKGROUND

A *tumtum* or a hermaphrodite – טוּמְטוּם וְאַנְדְּרוֹגִינוֹס: These are two instances in which both the primary and secondary sexual characteristics of an individual are irregular, and their sex is unclear both biologically and halakhically. The sexual organs of a *tumtum* are concealed. The sex of a *tumtum* might become apparent later in life when certain developmental changes take place. A hermaphrodite has both male and female sexual organs.

NOTES

If my wife gives birth, etc. – אִם תֵּלֵד אִשְׁתִּי וכו׳: This is halakhically problematic, as a gift to one who has not yet come into the world has no validity. The Rashbam explains that the mishna is referring to the gift of a person on his deathbed, or to one who transfers ownership to a fetus through the agency of a third party. According to the statement of Rabbi Yoḥanan (see 142b), even though one generally cannot transfer ownership of property to a fetus, the reason for this is that he may not sincerely intend to transfer it to the fetus. Therefore, one can transfer ownership of property to his own unborn son, since a person is favorably inclined toward his son and it is assumed that he is fully sincere.

And she gave birth to both a male and a female – וְיָלְדָה זָכָר וּנְקֵבָה: The Rashbam understands the ruling of the mishna to be that if the wife gave birth to either a male or a female child, that child receives what the father stipulated. By contrast, if she gave birth to both a male and a female, neither receives anything, as it did not occur to the father that she might give birth to twins, and his intention was to give a gift to a single child. Most commentaries explain that the mishna is referring to the birth of twins, and he is obligated to give the sums he mentioned both to the male and to the female.

We arrive at the opinion of Rabban Shimon ben Gamliel – אֲתָאן לְרַבָּן שִׁמְעוֹן בֶּן גַּמְלִיאֵל: Rabban Shimon ben Gamliel maintains that the status of a *tumtum* is not that of one about whom it is uncertain if the sex is male or female. Rather, a *tumtum* is classified as a distinct entity of indeterminate sex (Rashbam; Ri Migash; Rid). Others reject this interpretation, as the Gemara elsewhere (*Bekhorot* 42a) concludes that everyone agrees that a *tumtum* is one whose status is uncertain. They explain that Rabban Shimon ben Gamliel holds that whenever a person specifies a male or a female, both with regard to a gift and with regard to consecrating an animal, he is referring only to one who is clearly male or clearly female and not to a *tumtum* (*Tosafot Yeshanim*; Rabbi Avraham *Av Beit Din*; Rabbeinu Yona).

מֵיתִיבֵי: טוּמְטוּם יוֹרֵשׁ כְּבֵן וְנִיזּוֹן כְּבַת; בִּשְׁלָמָא לְרָבָא, יוֹרֵשׁ כְּבֵן – בִּנְכָסִים מוּעָטִין, וְנִיזּוֹן כְּבַת – בִּנְכָסִים מְרוּבִּין,

The Gemara **raises an objection** from a *baraita*: **A *tumtum* inherits as a son and is sustained as a daughter. Granted, according to Rava,** the *baraita* can be explained to mean that the clause: **Inherits as a son,** is **in** the case of **a small estate,** as the daughters direct the *tumtum* to the sons, and just as there is no inheritance for the sons, there is none for the *tumtum* either. And the clause: **And is sustained as a daughter,** is **in** the case of a **large estate,** as the sons direct the *tumtum* to the daughters, and the *tumtum* receives sustenance along with them.

Perek **IX**
Daf **141** Amud **a**

אֶלָּא לְאַבָּיֵי מַאי נִיזּוֹן כְּבַת? וּלְטַעְמִיךְ, לְרָבָא מַאי יוֹרֵשׁ כְּבֵן? אֶלָּא רָאוּי לִירַשׁ וְאֵין לוֹ, הָכָא נַמִי – רָאוּי לִזּוֹן וְאֵין לוֹ.

But according to the opinion of **Abaye, what** does it mean that the *tumtum* **is sustained as a daughter,** since Abaye maintains that the *tumtum* does not have the rights of a daughter? The Gemara responds: **And according to your reasoning,** even **according to Rava, what** does it mean that a *tumtum* **inherits as a son,** since Rava concedes that the *tumtum* and sons do not actually inherit anything? **Rather,** the *baraita* means that it is **fitting** for the *tumtum* **to inherit but he does not** actually inherit. **Here too,** with regard to sustenance, according to Abaye, the *baraita* means that it is **fitting** for the *tumtum* **to be sustained, but he is not** actually sustained.

״הָאוֹמֵר אִם יָלְדָה אִשְׁתִּי זָכָר״ וכו׳. לְמֵימְרָא, דְּבַת עֲדִיפָא לֵיהּ מִבֵּן, וְהָא אָמַר רַבִּי יוֹחָנָן מִשּׁוּם רַבִּי שִׁמְעוֹן בֶּן יוֹחַאי: כׇּל שֶׁאֵינוֹ מַנִּיחַ בֵּן לְיוֹרְשׁוֹ – הַקָּדוֹשׁ בָּרוּךְ הוּא מָלֵא עָלָיו עֶבְרָה, שֶׁנֶּאֱמַר: ״וְהַעֲבַרְתֶּם אֶת נַחֲלָתוֹ לְבִתּוֹ״, וְאֵין הַעֲבָרָה אֶלָּא עֶבְרָה, שֶׁנֶּאֱמַר: ״יוֹם עֶבְרָה הַיּוֹם הַהוּא״!

§ The mishna teaches: With regard to **one who says: If my wife gives birth to a male** the offspring shall receive one hundred dinars, if she in fact gave birth to a male, the offspring receives one hundred dinars. If he says: If my wife gives birth to a female the offspring shall receive two hundred dinars, if she in fact gave birth to a female, the offspring receives two hundred dinars. The Gemara asks: **Is this to say that for him a daughter is preferable to a son? But** this seems to contradict what **Rabbi Yoḥanan says in the name of Rabbi Shimon ben Yoḥai:** With regard to **anyone who does not leave** behind **a son to inherit** from **him, the Holy One, Blessed be He, is filled with wrath upon him, as it is stated:** "If a man dies, and has no son, **then you shall cause his inheritance to pass** [*veha'avartem*] **to his daughter**" (Numbers 27:8). The term *ha'avara* means **nothing other** than **wrath, as it is stated: "That day is a day of wrath** [*evra*]" (Zephaniah 1:15).

לְעִנְיַן יְרוּשָּׁה – בֵּן עֲדִיף לֵיהּ, לְעִנְיַן הַרְוָוחָה – בִּתּוֹ עֲדִיפָא לֵיהּ.

The Gemara resolves the contradiction: **With regard to the matter of inheritance, for him a son is preferable** to a daughter, as a son bears his name and retains his ancestral heritage within his father's tribe, but **with regard to the matter of** providing for his offspring's **comfort,**[N] **for him his daughter is preferable** to his son, as a son is more capable of coping for himself and the daughter needs more support.

וּשְׁמוּאֵל אָמַר: הָכָא בִּמְבַכֶּרֶת עָסְקִינַן, וּכְדְרַב חִסְדָּא, דְּאָמַר רַב חִסְדָּא: בַּת תְּחִלָּה – סִימָן יָפֶה לְבָנִים. אִיכָּא דְּאָמְרִי: דִּמְרַבְּיָא לַאֲחַהָא, וְאִיכָּא דְּאָמְרִי: דְּלָא שָׁלְטָא בֵּיהּ עֵינָא בִּישָׁא. אֲמַר רַב חִסְדָּא: וּלְדִידִי בְּנָתָן עֲדִיפָן לִי מִבְּנֵי.

And Shmuel said: Here we are dealing with a mother who is **giving birth for the first time, and** this is **in accordance with** the statement **of Rav Ḥisda, as Rav Ḥisda says:** If one gives birth to **a daughter first,** it **is a good sign for sons. There are** those **who** say that this is because **she raises her brothers,** i.e., helps in their upbringing, **and there are** those **who say** that this is **because the evil eye**[N] **does not have dominion over** the father. **Rav Ḥisda said: And as for myself, I prefer daughters to sons.**[N]

וְאִיבָּעֵית אֵימָא: הָא מַנִּי? רַבִּי יְהוּדָה הִיא.

The Gemara adds: **And if you wish, say:** In accordance with **whose** statement **is this** mishna in which preference is given to the daughter? **It is** in accordance with the statement of **Rabbi Yehuda.**

NOTES

With regard to the matter of his offspring's comfort – לְעִנְיַן הַרְוָוחָה: A father prefers to give more sustenance to his daughter because she is less capable of supporting herself by asking for charity (Rashbam). Rabbi Avraham *Av Beit Din* explains this differently: It is not the manner of a woman to seek out a man to marry, and therefore the father needs to provide her with a large dowry so that men will seek to marry her.

The evil eye – עֵינָא בִּישָׁא: Some explain that people envy the father because he has a firstborn son. The Maharsha explains that the envy is directed toward the firstborn son, as he receives a double portion of the inheritance, and this also causes some hostility between him and his brothers. By contrast, when the firstborn is a daughter, all of the sons inherit equally and there is no tension in the family.

I prefer daughters to sons – בְּנָתָן עֲדִיפָן לִי מִבְּנֵי: The Rashbam suggests that perhaps Rav Ḥisda said this because his sons died during his lifetime. By contrast, *Tosafot* prove that Rav Ḥisda did have surviving sons. They explain that Rav Ḥisda said this because his sons-in-law were among the greatest Sages of their generation and were greater than his sons. The Maharal explains that Rav Ḥisda's daughters were pious and wise, and were more exceptional than his sons.

That he did not have a daughter – שֶׁלֹּא הָיָה לוֹ בַּת: This is in light of the statement in *Sefer Ben Sira* concerning the many worries a father has with regard to his daughter, both before and after she marries. By not having a daughter, Abraham was spared these tribulations (see 16b).

Property of uncertain ownership – מָמוֹן הַמּוּטָּל בְּסָפֵק: Some commentaries explain that this ruling is in accordance with the opinion of Sumakhos, that property of uncertain ownership is divided among the litigants. According to the majority opinion, the son, as heir to the estate, is considered to be in possession of all of it, and the burden of proof rests upon the claimant, i.e., the daughter (Ramban). The Ramah explains that Rav Kahana's ruling accords with the majority opinion. The principle that the burden of proof rests upon the claimant is inapplicable here, since neither is considered to be in possession of the gift and their claims are of equal merit.

הֵי רַבִּי יְהוּדָה? אִילֵימָא רַבִּי יְהוּדָה דְּ״בַכֹּל״, דְּתַנְיָא: ״וַה׳ בֵּרַךְ אֶת אַבְרָהָם בַּכֹּל״ – רַבִּי מֵאִיר אוֹמֵר: שֶׁלֹּא הָיָה לוֹ בַּת, רַבִּי יְהוּדָה אוֹמֵר: שֶׁהָיְתָה לוֹ בַּת וּ״בַכֹּל״ שְׁמָהּ; אֵימוּר דְּשָׁמְעַתְּ לֵיהּ לְרַבִּי יְהוּדָה – בְּרַתָּא נַמִּי לָא חַסְּרֵיהּ רַחֲמָנָא לְאַבְרָהָם, דַּעֲדִיפָא מִבֵּן מִי שָׁמְעַתְּ לֵיהּ?

The Gemara asks: **Which** statement of **Rabbi Yehuda** is this referring to? **If we say** it is referring to the statement of **Rabbi Yehuda with regard to** the term **"with everything [*bakkol*],"** that is difficult. The Gemara cites Rabbi Yehuda's statement. **As it is taught** in a *baraita*: "And Abraham was old, well stricken in age; **and the Lord had blessed Abraham with everything [*bakkol*]**" (Genesis 24:1). **Rabbi Meir says:** The blessing was **that he did not have a daughter.**[N] **Rabbi Yehuda says:** The blessing was **that he had a daughter, and her name** was **Bakkol.** Evidently, Rabbi Yehuda understands the birth of a daughter to be a blessing. The Gemara explains the difficulty: **Say that you heard Rabbi Yehuda** explain that the blessing was that **the Merciful One did not even deprive Abraham** of **a daughter,** in addition to his sons. **Did you hear him** say **that** a daughter is **preferable to a son?**

אֶלָּא הָא רַבִּי יְהוּדָה, דְּתַנְיָא: מִצְוָה לָזוּן אֶת הַבָּנוֹת, וְקַל וָחוֹמֶר לְבָנִים דְּעָסְקִי בַּתּוֹרָה, דִּבְרֵי רַבִּי מֵאִיר; רַבִּי יְהוּדָה אוֹמֵר: מִצְוָה לָזוּן אֶת הַבָּנִים, וְקַל וָחוֹמֶר לְבָנוֹת דְּלָא לִיתְזְלָן.

The Gemara proposes another of Rabbi Yehuda's statements: **Rather,** it is referring to **this** other statement of **Rabbi Yehuda, as it is taught** in a *baraita*: One is not halakhically obligated to provide sustenance for his children beyond the age of six. Nevertheless, it is **a mitzva to provide sustenance for the daughters.**[H] **And** one can infer ***a fortiori*** that it is certainly a mitzva to provide **for sons, who are engaged in** the study of **the Torah;** this is **the statement of Rabbi Meir. Rabbi Yehuda says:** It is **a mitzva to provide sustenance for the sons. And** one can infer ***a fortiori*** that it is certainly a mitzva to provide **for daughters,** so **that they not be disgraced** by having to beg for their livelihood. This indicates that with regard to providing sustenance for one's children, Rabbi Yehuda gives preference to the daughters.

אֶלָּא הָא דְּתַנְיָא: יָלְדָה זָכָר וּנְקֵבָה – הַזָּכָר נוֹטֵל שִׁשָּׁה דִּינָרִין, וְהַנְּקֵבָה נוֹטֶלֶת שְׁנֵי דִּינָרִין, בְּמַאי?

§ The mishna discusses a case where one stipulated that if his wife gives birth to a male the offspring shall receive one hundred dinars, and if she gives birth to a female the offspring shall receive two hundred dinars. The mishna states that if she gave birth to both a male and a female, the male receives one hundred dinars and the female receives two hundred. The Gemara asks: **But** with regard to **that which is taught** in a *baraita* (*Tosefta* 9:4): If she **gave birth to a male and a female, the male receives six dinars** of gold, which are equivalent to one hundred fifty dinars of silver, **and the female receives two dinars** of gold, equivalent to fifty dinars of silver, **with what** situation is this *baraita* dealing?

אֲמַר רַב אַשִׁי, אֲמַרִיתָהּ לִשְׁמַעְתָּא קַמֵּיהּ דְּרַב כָּהֲנָא: בִּמְסָרֵס, דַּאֲמַר: ״זָכָר תְּחִלָּה – מָאתַיִם, נְקֵבָה אַחֲרָיו – וְלֹא כְלוּם. נְקֵבָה תְּחִלָּה – מָנֶה, זָכָר אַחֲרֶיהָ – מָנֶה״, וְיָלְדָה זָכָר וּנְקֵבָה, וְלָא יָדְעִינַן הֵי מִינַּיְיהוּ נְפַק בְּרֵישָׁא; זָכָר שָׁקֵיל מָנֶה מִמַּה נַּפְשָׁךְ, אִידָךְ מָנֶה הֲוָה מָמוֹן הַמּוּטָּל בְּסָפֵק וְחוֹלְקִין.

Rav Ashi said: I said this *halakha* before Rav Kahana, and he explained it as teaching **about one who inverted** the stipulations of his gift. The *baraita* is referring to one **who said:** If **a male** is born **first** he will receive **two hundred** dinars, and if **a female** is born **after him** she will receive **nothing.** And if **a female** is born **first** she will receive **one hundred dinars,** and if **a male** is born **after her** he will receive **one hundred dinars. And** the mother **gave birth to a male and a female, but we do not know which of them emerged** from the womb **first.** In this case, the **male takes one hundred dinars,** as **whichever way you** look at it, this sum is due to him. **The other one hundred dinars are property of uncertain ownership**[N] **and are divided** equally between the male and female.

וְהָא דְּתַנְיָא: יָלְדָה זָכָר וּנְקֵבָה – אֵין לוֹ אֶלָּא מָנֶה, הֵיכִי מַשְׁכַּחַתְּ לַהּ? אָמַר רָבִינָא: בִּ״מְבַשְּׂרֵנִי״;

The Gemara asks: **And** with regard to **that which is taught** in another *baraita*: If **she gave birth to a male and a female, he** receives **only one hundred dinars, how can you find these** circumstances? **Ravina said:** This is referring **to** one who said: I shall give a certain sum to whoever **informs me.**

HALAKHA

It is a mitzva to provide sustenance for the daughters, etc. – מִצְוָה לָזוּן אֶת הַבָּנוֹת וכו׳: One is not required, even by rabbinic law, to provide sustenance for his children beyond the age of six. Even so, if one is financially able to support his children, and they are unable to support themselves (*Beit Shmuel*), it is incumbent upon him to support them. This is part of one's obligation to give charity, enabling his sons to study Torah and his daughters to behave virtuously and not be disgraced, and the court coerces one to fulfill this charitable obligation (Rambam *Sefer Zera'im*, *Hilkhot Mattenot Aniyyim* 10:16 and *Sefer Nashim*, *Hilkhot Ishut* 12:14–15; *Shulḥan Arukh*, *Yoreh De'a* 251:3 and *Even HaEzer* 71:1).

דְּתַנְיָא: ״הַמְבַשְּׂרֵנִי בַּמֶּה נִפְטַר רַחְמָהּ שֶׁל אִשְׁתִּי, אִם זָכָר יִטּוֹל מָנֶה״ – יָלְדָה זָכָר נוֹטֵל מָנֶה, ״אִם נְקֵבָה מָנֶה״ – יָלְדָה נְקֵבָה נוֹטֵל מָנֶה, יָלְדָה זָכָר וּנְקֵבָה – אֵין לוֹ אֶלָּא מָנֶה.

This is **as it is taught** in a *baraita* (*Tosefta* 9:5): In a case where one said: **Whoever informs me** as **to what opened my wife's womb,** i.e., what the sex of her child is, **if it is a male,** the one who informs me **shall receive one hundred dinars.** Therefore, if the wife **gave birth to a male,** the one who informed him **receives one hundred dinars.** If he also said: **If it is a female** he shall receive **one hundred dinars, if she gave birth to a female,** he **receives one hundred dinars. If she gave birth to a male and a female, he** receives **only one hundred dinars.**

וְהָא ״זָכָר וּנְקֵבָה״ לָא אָמַר! דְּאָמַר נָמֵי ״אִם זָכָר וּנְקֵבָה נָמֵי יִטּוֹל מָנֶה״. אֶלָּא לְמַעוּטֵי מַאי? לְמַעוּטֵי נֵפֶל.

The Gemara challenges: **But** since **he did not say** anything about **a male and a female,** if she gave birth to a male and a female, he should not receive anything. Why does the *baraita* state that he receives one hundred dinars? The Gemara answers: This is referring to **where he also said:** If she gives birth to **a male and a female** he shall **also receive one hundred dinars.** The Gemara asks: **But** if he stated all of the possibilities, **what** did his stipulations serve **to exclude?** The Gemara answers: They serve **to exclude** a case where she gives birth to **a non-viable newborn,** in which case he receives nothing.

הַהוּא דַּאֲמַר לָהּ לִדְבֵיתְהוּ: נִכְסַי לְהַאי דִּמְעַבַּרְתְּ; אָמַר רַב הוּנָא: הָוֵי מְזַכֶּה לְעוּבָּר, וְהַמְזַכֶּה לְעוּבָּר לֹא קָנָה.

§ The Gemara relates: There was **a certain** man **who said to his wife: My property** is given **to the one with whom you are pregnant. Rav Huna said: This is** a case of **one who transfers ownership** of an item **to a fetus, and** in the case of **one who transfers ownership** of an item **to a fetus,**[H] the fetus **does not acquire** the item.

אֵיתִיבֵיהּ רַב נַחְמָן לְרַב הוּנָא: הָאוֹמֵר ״אִם יָלְדָה אִשְׁתִּי זָכָר יִטּוֹל מָנֶה״ – יָלְדָה זָכָר נוֹטֵל מָנֶה! אֲמַר לֵיהּ: מִשְׁנָתֵינוּ אֵינִי יוֹדֵעַ מִי שְׁנָאָהּ.

Rav Naḥman raised an objection to the opinion of **Rav Huna** opinion from the mishna, which states: With regard to **one who says: If my wife gives birth to a male** the offspring **shall receive one hundred dinars,** if **she** in fact **gave birth to a male,** the offspring **receives one hundred dinars.** This indicates that the fetus did acquire the money. Rav Huna **said to him: I do not know who taught our mishna.** It is not identifiable with a known opinion, and presumably the text has been corrupted.

וְלֵימָא לֵיהּ: רַבִּי מֵאִיר הִיא, דְּאָמַר: אָדָם מַקְנֶה דָּבָר שֶׁלֹּא בָּא לָעוֹלָם!

The Gemara asks why Rav Huna replied in this manner: **But let him say to** Rav Naḥman: **It is** in accordance with the opinion of **Rabbi Meir,**[N] **who says: A person can transfer ownership** of **an entity that has not** yet **come into the world,** e.g., produce that has not yet grown. Just as he maintains that one can transfer ownership of an entity that has not yet come into the world, so too, he maintains that one can transfer ownership of an item to a fetus, who has not yet been born.

אֵימוֹר דִּשְׁמַעַתְּ לֵיהּ לְרַבִּי מֵאִיר – לְדָבָר שֶׁיֶּשְׁנוֹ בָּעוֹלָם, לְדָבָר שֶׁאֵינוֹ בָּעוֹלָם מִי שְׁמַעַתְּ לֵיהּ?

The Gemara rejects this explanation: **Say that you heard Rabbi Meir** express this opinion with regard to transferring ownership of an entity that has not yet come into the world **to an entity that is in the world. Did you hear him** speak of transferring ownership **to an entity that has not** yet **come into the world,** e.g., a fetus?

וְלֵימָא לֵיהּ: רַבִּי יוֹסֵי הִיא, דְּאָמַר: עוּבָּר קָנֵי! דִּתְנַן: עוּבָּר פּוֹסֵל וְאֵינוֹ מַאֲכִיל, דִּבְרֵי רַבִּי יוֹסֵי!

The Gemara proposes another resolution to Rav Naḥman's objection: **But let** Rav Huna **say to** Rav Naḥman: **It is** in accordance with the opinion of **Rabbi Yosei, who says: A fetus acquires** ownership, **as we learned** in a mishna (*Yevamot* 67a): With regard to an Israelite woman who married a priest and he died and left her pregnant, the **fetus disqualifies** its father's Canaanite slaves from partaking of *teruma,*[B] because until it is born the fetus is not considered a priest, and the slaves, who are part of its inheritance, are not the slaves of a priest. **And** the fetus **does not enable** its mother **to partake** of *teruma,*[HN] even though it is the child of a priest. This is **the statement of Rabbi Yosei.** It is evident from this mishna that Rabbi Yosei holds that a fetus inherits its father's property.

HALAKHA

One who transfers ownership of an item to a fetus – הַמְזַכֶּה לְעוּבָּר: One cannot transfer ownership of an item to one who has not yet come into the world. Therefore, if one transfers ownership to an unborn child, the fetus does not acquire it, even if the giver says that the transfer of ownership should take effect only when the child is born (Rambam *Sefer Kinyan, Hilkhot Mekhira* 22:10 and *Hilkhot Zekhiya UMattana* 8:5; *Shulḥan Arukh, Ḥoshen Mishpat* 210:1, 253:26).

The fetus disqualifies its father's slaves from *teruma* and does not enable its mother to partake of *teruma* – עוּבָּר פּוֹסֵל וְאֵינוֹ מַאֲכִיל: A fetus causes its mother to be disqualified from partaking of *teruma* but does not enable its mother to partake of *teruma*. How so? It is prohibited for a priest's daughter who is pregnant from an Israelite man to partake of *teruma*, as she is the mother of an Israelite. In addition, if the daughter of a non-priest married a priest, and her husband died and left her pregnant, she does not partake of *teruma* as the mother of a priest, even though the child is of priestly lineage (Rambam *Sefer Zera'im, Hilkhot Terumot* 8:1–2).

NOTES

It is in accordance with Rabbi Meir – רַבִּי מֵאִיר הִיא: The early commentaries ask why the Gemara suggests this to Rav Huna, as even if he attributed the mishna to Rabbi Meir, it would still contradict Rav Huna's ruling that one cannot transfer ownership of an item to a fetus, as Rav Huna himself holds in accordance with the opinion of Rabbi Meir that one can transfer ownership of an entity that has not yet come into the world. Some say that the Gemara is not attempting to resolve the objection to Rav Huna's statement but is just seeking the source of the opinion in the mishna.

The Rashba maintains that the Gemara's suggestion could resolve the objection to Rav Huna's ruling. The Gemara at first assumes that just as Rabbi Meir holds that one can transfer ownership of an entity that has not yet come into the world, he also maintains that one can transfer ownership to an entity that has not yet come into the world. Rav Huna agrees with Rabbi Meir's opinion with regard to the first point, but not with regard to the second point.

The fetus disqualifies its father's slaves from *teruma* and does not enable its mother to partake of *teruma* – עוּבָּר פּוֹסֵל וְאֵינוֹ מַאֲכִיל: Once the fetus inherits his father's property he is considered the slaves' owner, and since he is classified as an Israelite until he is born, he disqualifies them from partaking of *teruma*. *Tosafot* note that Rashi (*Yevamot* 67a) understands this discussion as pertaining only to the mother, i.e., the fetus disqualifies its mother from partaking of *teruma*. According to this interpretation, the discussion is not relevant to the laws of inheritance at all.

BACKGROUND

The fetus disqualifies its father's slaves from *teruma* – עוּבָּר פּוֹסֵל: *Teruma* is eaten by priests, in a state of ritual purity, and by Torah law it is prohibited for non-priests to partake of *teruma*. Certain relatives or dependents of priests may partake of *teruma*, even though they themselves are not priests. These include a priest's wife, his sons, his unmarried daughters, and his Canaanite slaves. In addition, a priest may feed *teruma* to his animals. It is permitted for a priest's widow to partake of *teruma* if she has children or grandchildren from her deceased husband, even if she herself is not the daughter of a priest. Since the fetus is not considered a priest until he is born, he does not enable his mother, or the Canaanite slaves he inherits, to partake of *teruma*.

NOTES

A person who is fit to inherit from him – מִי שֶׁרָאוּי לְיוֹרְשׁוֹ: The Gemara here understands that the phrase: Who is fit to inherit from him, includes a fetus (Rashbam).

שָׁאנֵי יְרוּשָּׁה הַבָּאָה מֵאֵילֶיהָ.

The Gemara rejects this explanation: **Inheritance is different,** since, unlike a gift, **it comes** into the possession of the heir **by itself,** without a formal act of acquisition. Therefore, a fetus can acquire an inheritance, but not a gift.

וְלֵימָא לֵיהּ: רַבִּי יוֹחָנָן בֶּן בְּרוֹקָה הִיא, דְּאָמַר: לָא שְׁנָא יְרוּשָּׁה וְלָא שְׁנָא מַתָּנָה! דִּתְנַן, רַבִּי יוֹחָנָן בֶּן בְּרוֹקָה אוֹמֵר: אִם אָמַר עַל מִי שֶׁרָאוּי לְיוֹרְשׁוֹ – דְּבָרָיו קַיָּימִין!

The Gemara proposes another resolution to Rav Naḥman's objection: **But let** Rav Huna **say to** Rav Naḥman: **It is** in accordance with the opinion of **Rabbi Yoḥanan ben Beroka, who says:** The case of **an inheritance is not different, and** the case of **a gift** one gives to his heir **is not different,** i.e., the same *halakhot* apply to both. **As we learned** in a mishna (130a): **Rabbi Yoḥanan ben Beroka says: If one said about** a person **who is fit to inherit** from **him,**[N] e.g., one of his sons: This person will inherit all of my property, **his statement stands.**

אֵימוּר דִּשְׁמַעְתְּ לֵיהּ לְרַבִּי יוֹחָנָן בֶּן בְּרוֹקָה – לְדָבָר שֶׁיֶּשְׁנוֹ בָּעוֹלָם, לְדָבָר שֶׁאֵינוֹ בָּעוֹלָם מִי אָמַר?

The Gemara rejects this explanation: **Say that you heard Rabbi Yoḥanan ben Beroka** express this opinion with regard to a gift given **to an entity that** already **exists in the world,** but **does he say** anything with regard to a gift given **to an entity that has not** yet **come into the world?**

וְלֵימָא לֵיהּ: רַבִּי יוֹחָנָן בֶּן בְּרוֹקָה הִיא, וְסָבַר לַהּ כְּרַבִּי יוֹסֵי! מִי יֵימַר דְּסָבַר לַהּ.

The Gemara proposes another resolution to Rav Naḥman's objection: **But let** Rav Huna **say to** Rav Naḥman: **It is** in accordance with the opinion of **Rabbi Yoḥanan ben Beroka,** who compares a gift to an inheritance, **and he holds in accordance with** the opinion of **Rabbi Yosei,** that a fetus is fit to inherit. The Gemara rejects this explanation: **Who says that** Rabbi Yoḥanan ben Beroka **holds** in accordance **with** the opinion of Rabbi Yosei?

וְלֵימָא לֵיהּ: בִּ״מְבַשְּׂרֵנִי״! אִי הָכִי, דְּקָתָנֵי סֵיפָא: וְאִם אֵין שָׁם יוֹרֵשׁ אֶלָּא הוּא – יוֹרֵשׁ הַכֹּל; אִי בִּ״מְבַשְּׂרֵנִי״, יוֹרֵשׁ מַאי עֲבִידְתֵּיהּ?

The Gemara proposes another resolution to Rav Naḥman's objection: **But let** Rav Huna **say to** Rav Naḥman that the mishna is referring not to one who gave a gift to the fetus, but **to** one who said: I shall give a certain sum to whoever **informs me.** This person is in the world. The Gemara rejects this explanation as well: **If that is so,** then concerning **that** which **the last clause** of the mishna **teaches: And if there is no heir other than** the *tumtum*, the *tumtum* **inherits all** of the estate, **if** the mishna is referring **to** one who said: I shall give a certain sum to whoever **informs me, what is the purpose of** mentioning **an heir,** since the mishna is not discussing a gift to the heir at all?

וְלֵימָא לֵיהּ: בְּשֶׁיָּלְדָה! אִי הָכִי, דְּקָתָנֵי סֵיפָא: וְאִם אָמַר ״כָּל מַה שֶּׁתֵּלֵד אִשְׁתִּי יִטּוֹל״ – הֲרֵי זֶה יִטּוֹל; ״כָּל שֶׁתֵּלֵד״? ״כָּל שֶׁיָּלְדָה״ מִיבָּעֵי לֵיהּ!

The Gemara proposes another resolution to Rav Naḥman's objection: **But let** Rav Huna **say to** Rav Naḥman: The mishna is referring **to** a case **where** the gift was made after his wife had already **given birth** but he did not yet know the sex of the baby. The Gemara rejects this explanation as well: **If that is so,** then concerning **that** which **the latter clause** of the mishna **teaches: Whatever** offspring **my wife gives birth to shall receive** a certain sum, and she gave birth to a *tumtum*, the *tumtum* **receives** it, there is a difficulty. According to this explanation, the phrase: **Whatever** offspring my wife **gives birth to,** is incorrect. The mishna **should have said: Whatever** offspring my wife **gave birth to.**

Perek **IX**
Daf **142** Amud **a**

וְלֵימָא לֵיהּ: דְּאָמַר ״לִכְשֶׁתֵּלֵד״! רַב הוּנָא לְטַעְמֵיהּ, דְּאָמַר רַב הוּנָא: אַף ״לִכְשֶׁתֵּלֵד״ – לֹא קָנָה,

The Gemara proposes another resolution to Rav Naḥman's objection: **But let** Rav Huna **say to** Rav Naḥman that the mishna is referring to one **who says** that the transfer of ownership should take effect **when she gives birth,** at which point the child already exists. The Gemara rejects this resolution: Rav Huna does not interpret the mishna in this way, because **Rav Huna** conforms **to his** line of **reasoning, as Rav Huna says: Even** if one says that the transfer of ownership should take effect **when she gives birth,** the fetus **does not acquire** it.

דְּאָמַר רַב נַחְמָן: הַמְזַכֶּה לְעוּבָּר לֹא קָנָה, ״לִכְשֶׁתֵּלֵד״ – קָנָה; וְרַב הוּנָא אָמַר: אַף ״לִכְשֶׁתֵּלֵד״ – לֹא קָנָה; וְרַב שֵׁשֶׁת אָמַר: אֶחָד זֶה וְאֶחָד זֶה – קָנָה.

The Gemara clarifies: **As Rav Naḥman says:** With regard to **one who transfers ownership** of an item **to a fetus,** the fetus **does not acquire** it. But if he says that the transfer of ownership of the item should take effect **when she gives birth,** the fetus **acquires** it.[N] **And Rav Huna says:**[N] **Even** if he says that the transfer of ownership of the item should take effect **when she gives birth,** the fetus **does not acquire** it, because the fetus did not exist in the world when he transferred ownership. **And Rav Sheshet says:** In **both this** case **and that** case, the fetus **acquires** the item.

אֲמַר רַב שֵׁשֶׁת: מְנָא אָמִינָא לָהּ? דְּתַנְיָא: גֵּר שֶׁמֵּת וּבִזְבְּזוּ יִשְׂרָאֵל נְכָסָיו, וְשָׁמְעוּ שֶׁיֵּשׁ לוֹ בֵּן אוֹ שֶׁהָיְתָה אִשְׁתּוֹ מְעוּבֶּרֶת – חַיָּיבִין לְהַחֲזִיר. הֶחֱזִירוּ הַכֹּל, וְאַחַר כָּךְ שָׁמְעוּ שֶׁמֵּת בְּנוֹ אוֹ שֶׁהִפִּילָה אִשְׁתּוֹ, הֶחֱזִיק בַּשְּׁנִיָּה – קָנָה, וּבָרִאשׁוֹנָה – לֹא קָנָה;

Rav Sheshet said: From where do I say that the fetus acquires the item? **As it is taught** in a *baraita*: With regard to **a convert who died,** apparently without offspring, **and Jews plundered** [*uvizbezu*][NL] **his property,**[H] assuming that he had no heirs and his property was therefore ownerless, **and** subsequently **they heard that he had a son or that his wife was pregnant, they are obligated to return** the property.[N] If **they returned it all, and then they heard that his son died or that his wife miscarried,** if one **took possession at the second** time, after hearing about the death or the miscarriage, he **acquired** the property, **but** if one took possession only **at the first** time, before it was known there was an heir at all, he **did not acquire** the property.

וְאִי סָלְקָא דַּעְתָּךְ עוּבָּר לָא קָנֵי, לָמָּה לְהוּ אַחְזוּקֵי בַּשְּׁנִיָּה? הָא אַחֲזִיקוּ לְהוּ חֲדָא זִימְנָא!

Rav Sheshet explains: **And if it enters your mind** that **a fetus does not acquire** property, **why do they need** to **take possession** again **the second** time? **Didn't they** already **take possession one time?** Evidently, the miscarried fetus had acquired ownership in the meantime.

אֲמַר אַבָּיֵי: יְרוּשָּׁה הַבָּאָה מֵאֵילֶיהָ שָׁאנֵי. רָבָא אֲמַר: שָׁאנֵי הָתָם, דְּרַפּוּיֵי מְרַפְּיָאן בִּידַיְיהוּ מֵעִיקָּרָא.

Abaye said in reply to Rav Sheshet: **Inheritance, which comes** into the possession of the heir **by itself** without a formal act of acquisition,[N] **is different.** Even if a fetus inherits property, it may not be able to acquire property in any other manner, e.g., receiving a gift. **Rava said:** It **is different there,** in the case where they plundered the property of the convert, **as the** property **was initially** only **loosely held in their hands,** as they did not clearly know whether or not the deceased convert had heirs. Therefore, the first time they took possession was not sufficient, and they needed to take possession again in order to acquire the property.

LANGUAGE

Plundered [*bizbezu*] – בִּזְבְּזוּ: Here *bizbezu* is used in the sense of plundered [*bazezu*], the difference between these terms being only that the latter stems from the three-letter root *beit*, *zayin*, *zayin*, whereas the former stems from the similar four-letter root *beit*, *zayin*, *beit*, *zayin*. The usual meaning of the term *bizbez*, i.e., wasting resources, is related to the concept of plundering, as both are acts hastily performed with property.

HALAKHA

A convert who died without offspring and Jews plundered his property, etc. – גֵּר שֶׁמֵּת וּבִזְבְּזוּ יִשְׂרָאֵל נְכָסָיו וכו׳: If a convert presumed to be childless died and Jews plundered his property, and then they heard that he was not yet dead, or that he had a son, or that his wife was pregnant, they are obligated to return the property. If they return it and then hear that their original information was correct, and they had in fact plundered the property after the convert had died, or after the convert's son had died, or after his wife had miscarried, they can take possession of the property again. Whoever takes possession the second time acquires the property. Those who took possession only the first time do not acquire it (Rambam *Sefer Kinyan, Hilkhot Zekhiya UMattana* 2:18; *Shulḥan Arukh, Ḥoshen Mishpat* 275:30).

NOTES

But if he says when she gives birth, the fetus acquires it – לִכְשֶׁתֵּלֵד קָנָה: The commentaries raise a difficulty with regard to Rav Naḥman's opinion: When the transaction took place there was no recipient in existence in the world. Therefore, even if he stipulated that the gift should take effect when the child will be born, the transaction should not be valid. Rabbeinu Yona explains that the father transferred ownership by means of a deed, which was still in existence at the time of birth. Therefore, the transaction can take effect then. Alternatively, the property was transferred to a third party on behalf of the child and the third party was in possession of the property when the child was born. *Tosefot HaRosh* notes that since the child acquires the property only once it is born, the giver can revoke the gift until that time.

As Rav Naḥman says…and Rav Huna says, etc. – דְּאָמַר רַב נַחְמָן...וְרַב הוּנָא אָמַר וכו׳: The early commentaries note that according to the Gemara elsewhere (see *Bava Metzia* 66b), Rav Huna holds that one can transfer ownership of an entity that has not yet come into the world, even though he cannot transfer ownership of an item to an entity that has not yet come into the world. Conversely, Rav Naḥman holds that one cannot transfer ownership of an entity that has not yet come into the world, even though one can transfer ownership of an item to a fetus if he stipulates that the transaction will take effect once the fetus is born. The Rosh understands that Rav Huna and Rav Naḥman disagree as to what constitutes a more substantial impediment to the completion of the transaction: The fact that the recipient is not yet in existence, or the fact that the item in question is not yet in existence. The Rid explains that Rav Huna considers the fetus as one who does not yet exist at all, whereas Rav Naḥman considers the fetus as one who is in existence but is not a legal person, and therefore he cannot acquire property. Once he is born the transaction is effective.

And…plundered – וּבִזְבְּזוּ: Any born Jew, by definition, has heirs. Even if he does not have close family, he has relatives at some level who become his heirs. A convert is considered a newborn person upon conversion. His gentile family does not inherit from him. If he did not father children after he converted, he has no heirs, and when he dies his property becomes ownerless; whoever takes possession of it first acquires it.

They are obligated to return the property – חַיָּיבִין לְהַחֲזִיר: The fact that their acquisition is nullified when it becomes known that the convert's wife is pregnant indicates that the fetus inherits the property (Rashbam).

Inheritance which comes by itself without acquisition – יְרוּשָּׁה הַבָּאָה מֵאֵילֶיהָ: The heir is considered the direct continuation of the deceased. Inheritance is not defined as a transaction, and there is consequently no need for a formal act of acquisition. By contrast, a formal act of acquisition is required in order to acquire a gift, and this cannot be performed with regard to a fetus, which according to *halakha* is not considered a legal person.

HALAKHA

A one-day-old child inherits his mother's property – נוֹחֵל בְּנִכְסֵי הָאֵם: With regard to a son who predeceases his mother without leaving behind any progeny, when his mother dies, her inheritance reverts to her father's household. If the mother predeceases the son, even if he is only one day old, he inherits from her, and his heirs from his father's family inherit from him. The Rema writes that if she dies while pregnant, the fetus does not inherit from her and the inheritance does not pass to the fetus's heirs from its father's family, because it is assumed that the fetus died before its mother, as stated by Rav Sheshet. When it is known that the mother died first, the fetus inherits from its mother and the inheritance passes to the fetus's heirs from its father's family (Rambam *Sefer Mishpatim*, *Hilkhot Naḥalot* 1:13, 5:7; *Shulḥan Arukh*, *Ḥoshen Mishpat* 276:5, and *Sma* and *Netivot HaMishpat* there).

מַאי בֵּינַיְיהוּ? אִיכָּא בֵּינַיְיהוּ: שֶׁשָּׁמְעוּ בּוֹ שֶׁמֵּת וְלֹא מֵת, וְאַחַר כָּךְ מֵת.

The Gemara asks: **What is** the difference **between** Abaye's refutation and Rava's refutation? The practical difference **between them** is in a case **where they** initially **heard** with regard **to** the fetus **that he** had **died,** and they then took possession of the property. **But** in reality, he had **not died, and then** he **died.** According to Abaye, a fetus inherits property. Therefore, the property was not ownerless, and the plunderers did not acquire it. According to Rava, since the plunderers heard that the fetus had died, they took a firm hold upon the property, and they acquired it the first time.

תָּא שְׁמַע: תִּינוֹק בֶּן יוֹם אֶחָד נוֹחֵל וּמַנְחִיל; בֶּן יוֹם אֶחָד – אִין, עוּבָּר – לָא! הָא אָמַר רַב שֵׁשֶׁת: נוֹחֵל בְּנִכְסֵי הָאֵם לְהַנְחִיל לָאַחִין מִן הָאָב. וְדַוְקָא בֶּן יוֹם אֶחָד, אֲבָל עוּבָּר – לָא, מַאי טַעְמָא?

The Gemara offers another refutation of the opinion of Rav Sheshet: **Come** and **hear** a proof from a mishna (*Nidda* 43b–44a): **A one-day-old child inherits** property **and bequeaths** property. One can infer that if the child is **one day old, yes,** he inherits property; but **a fetus** does **not.** The Gemara replies: **Doesn't Rav Sheshet say** that the mishna teaches a different *halakha*? The mishna teaches that a one-day-old child **inherits his mother's property**[H] the moment he is born, so that he is able **to bequeath** it, if he then dies, **to** his heirs who are not the mother's heirs, e.g., his **paternal brothers.** This *halakha* **specifically** applies from when he is **one day old, but a fetus** whose mother died **does not** inherit from her. **What is the reason** for this?

Perek IX
Daf 142 Amud b

BACKGROUND

Lizard [*leta'a*] – לְטָאָה: The *leta'a* is likely one or more species of lizard from the family Lacertidae. These lizards range in length from 15 to 25 cm, and they have developed limbs that allow them to run quickly. Their skin is generally so soft that it wrinkles, although in some species the skin is tight on the body.

Small-spotted lizard

NOTES

That a one-day-old child reduces the portion of the firstborn – שֶׁמְּמַעֵט בְּחֵלֶק בְּכוֹרָה: A fetus inherits from his father just as a one-day-old child does. The difference between them is with regard to how they affect the portion of the firstborn. If the son was not yet born at the time of the father's death, and in addition to him there were a firstborn and an ordinary son, the firstborn first receives one-third of the inheritance as his firstborn portion, as if the fetus did not exist, and the remainder is divided into three portions, i.e., for the firstborn, the fetus, and the other brother. If he was a one-day-old child, he reduces the portion of the firstborn: The firstborn receives one-fourth as his firstborn portion, and the remainder is divided equally among the three brothers.

דְּהוּא מָיֵית בְּרֵישָׁא, וְאֵין הַבֵּן יוֹרֵשׁ אֶת אִמּוֹ בַּקֶּבֶר לְהַנְחִיל לָאַחִין מִן הָאָב.

The reason is **that** we presume that the fetus **died first,** before its mother died, **and the son does not inherit from his mother** while **in the grave,** in order **to bequeath** the inheritance **to his paternal brothers.** The *halakha* is that if a son dies, and afterward his mother dies, the deceased son does not inherit from his mother and subsequently bequeath the inheritance to his paternal brothers, who are not related to the mother. But in other cases, where it is not his mother's estate, a fetus inherits property.

לְמֵימְרָא, דְּהוּא מָיֵית בְּרֵישָׁא? וְהָא הֲוָה עוּבְדָא וּפִרְכֵּס תְּלָתָא פִּרְכּוּסֵי! אֲמַר מָר בַּר רַב אַשִׁי: מִידֵּי דַּהֲוָה אַזְנַב הַלְּטָאָה שֶׁמְּפַרְכֶּסֶת.

The Gemara asks: **Is this to say that** it is certain that the fetus **died first? But there was an incident** where the mother died **and** the fetus **made three spasmodic motions** afterward. Apparently, a fetus can die after the mother. **Mar bar Rav Ashi said:** That incident was **just as it is with the tail of the lizard,**[B] **which jerks** after being severed from the lizard, but it is just a spasmodic motion which does not indicate that it is still alive.

מָר בְּרֵיהּ דְּרַב יוֹסֵף מִשְּׁמֵיהּ דְּרָבָא אָמַר: לוֹמַר, שֶׁמְּמַעֵט בְּחֵלֶק בְּכוֹרָה. וְדַוְקָא בֶּן יוֹם אֶחָד, אֲבָל עוּבָּר – לָא, מַאי טַעְמָא? ״וְיָלְדוּ לוֹ״ אָמַר רַחֲמָנָא;

Mar, son of Rav Yosef, says in the name of Rava: The mishna comes **to say that** a one-day-old child **reduces the portion of the firstborn.**[N] The firstborn is entitled to a double portion of the inheritance, and this is calculated taking into account the portion due to his dead brother. **And** it is in this context that **specifically** the portion of **a one-day-old** child is taken into account, **but** the portion of **a fetus is not** taken into account,[H] even though a fetus also inherits property. **What is the reason** for this? **The Merciful One states** concerning the portion of the firstborn: "If a man has two wives, the one beloved, and the other hated, **and they bore him children,** both the beloved and the hated; and if the firstborn son be hers that was hated" (Deuteronomy 21:15). The term "children" excludes a fetus.

HALAKHA

That a one-day-old child reduces the portion of the firstborn…but the portion of a fetus is not taken into account – שֶׁמְּמַעֵט בְּחֵלֶק בְּכוֹרָה...אֲבָל עוּבָּר לָא: A one-day-old child is a full-fledged heir, and he reduces the portion of the firstborn. Therefore, if a newborn had two brothers, one of whom was the firstborn, and the newborn died even when one day old, the inheritance is divided into fourths. The firstborn receives two-fourths, the remaining brother receives one-fourth, and the one-fourth which would have been the inheritance of the deceased brother is divided equally between them. If it was a non-viable newborn, the inheritance is divided into thirds, the firstborn receives two-thirds, and the remaining brother receives one-third. This is in accordance with Rava's opinion as cited by Mar, son of Rav Yosef, and in accordance with the conclusion of the Gemara (Rambam *Sefer Mishpatim*, *Hilkhot Naḥalot* 2:5; *Shulḥan Arukh*, *Ḥoshen Mishpat* 277:5, and see *Sma* there).

דְּאָמַר מָר בְּרֵיהּ דְּרַב יוֹסֵף מִשְּׁמֵיהּ דְּרָבָא: בֵּן שֶׁנּוֹלַד לְאַחַר מִיתַת אָבִיו – אֵינוֹ מְמַעֵט בְּחֵלֶק בְּכוֹרָה, מַאי טַעְמָא? ״וְיָלְדוּ לוֹ״ אָמַר רַחֲמָנָא, וְהָא לֵיכָּא.

This is similar to another *halakha*, **as Mar, son of Rav Yosef, says in the name of Rava: A son who was born after his father's death**[H] **does not reduce the firstborn's portion. What is the reason** for this? **The Merciful One states** in the Torah: **"And they bore him children,"** and this term "children" **does not** apply to a fetus.

בְּסוּרָא מַתְנוּ הָכִי. בְּפוּמְבְּדִיתָא מַתְנוּ הָכִי, אָמַר מָר בְּרֵיהּ דְּרַב יוֹסֵף מִשְּׁמֵיהּ דְּרָבָא: בְּכוֹר שֶׁנּוֹלַד לְאַחַר מִיתַת אָבִיו – אֵינוֹ נוֹטֵל פִּי שְׁנַיִם, מַאי טַעְמָא? ״יַכִּיר״ אָמַר רַחֲמָנָא, וְהָא לֵיתָא דְּיַכִּיר. וְהִלְכְתָא כְּכָל הָנֵי לִישָּׁנֵי דְּאָמַר מָר בְּרֵיהּ דְּרַב יוֹסֵף מִשְּׁמֵיהּ דְּרָבָא.

The Gemara notes: **In Sura they taught** Mar's statement **that** way, but **in Pumbedita they taught** it **this** way: **Mar, son of Rav Yosef, says in the name of Rava: A firstborn who was born after his father's death**[HN] **does not receive a double** portion. **What is the reason** for this? **The Merciful One states** in the Torah: "But **he shall acknowledge** the firstborn, the son of the hated, by giving him a double portion" (Deuteronomy 21:17), **and** in this case the father **is not** there **that** he can **acknowledge** him. The Gemara concludes: **And the *halakha* is in accordance with all these versions** of that **which Mar, son of Rav Yosef, says in the name of Rava.** Accordingly, a one-day-old child reduces the portion of the firstborn, a son born after his father's death does not reduce the firstborn's portion, and a firstborn born after his father's death does not receive a double portion.

אָמַר רַבִּי יִצְחָק אָמַר רַבִּי יוֹחָנָן: הַמְזַכֶּה לְעוּבָּר – לֹא קָנָה. וְאִם תֹּאמַר: מִשְׁנָתֵינוּ – הוֹאִיל וְדַעְתּוֹ שֶׁל אָדָם קְרוֹבָה אֵצֶל בְּנוֹ.

§ **Rabbi Yitzḥak says** that **Rabbi Yoḥanan says:** With regard to **one who transfers ownership** of an item **to a fetus,** the fetus **does not acquire** the item. **And if you say** that the statement of **our mishna** (140b), with regard to one who gives a gift to his unborn child, indicates that an item can be transferred to a fetus, the circumstances there are unique. **Since the disposition of a person** is to be **inclined toward his son,**[HN] the Sages validated such a transfer, but one cannot transfer an item to the unborn child of another.

אֲמַר לֵיהּ שְׁמוּאֵל לְרַב חָנָא בַּגְדָּתָאָה: פּוֹק אַיְיתִי לִי בֵּי עַשְׂרָה, וְאֵימַר לָךְ בְּאַפַּיְיהוּ: הַמְזַכֶּה לְעוּבָּר – קָנָה. וְהִלְכְתָא: הַמְזַכֶּה לְעוּבָּר – לֹא קָנָה.

Shmuel said to Rav Ḥana of Baghdad: Go out and **bring me an assembly of ten** men, **and I will say** a *halakha* **to you in their presence,** so that it will be well publicized. The *halakha* was: With regard to **one who transfers ownership** of an item **to a fetus,** the fetus **acquires** the item. The Gemara concludes: **And the *halakha*** is that with regard to **one who transfers ownership** of an item **to a fetus,** the fetus **does not acquire** the item.

HALAKHA

A son who was born after his father's death – בֵּן שֶׁנּוֹלַד לְאַחַר מִיתַת אָבִיו: A son who was born after his father's death does not reduce the firstborn's share, in accordance with Rava's opinion as cited by Mar, son of Rav Yosef, and in accordance with the conclusion of the Gemara (Rambam *Sefer Mishpatim, Hilkhot Naḥalot* 2:5; *Shulḥan Arukh, Ḥoshen Mishpat* 277:5).

A firstborn who was born after his father's death – בְּכוֹר שֶׁנּוֹלַד לְאַחַר מִיתַת אָבִיו: A firstborn who was born after his father's death does not receive a double portion, in accordance with Rava's opinion as cited by Mar, son of Rav Yosef, and in accordance with the conclusion of the Gemara. Some say that even if he was born when his father was on his deathbed, he does not receive a double portion, as this is also a case where the father is unable to acknowledge him (Rambam *Sefer Mishpatim, Hilkhot Naḥalot* 2:2; *Shulḥan Arukh, Ḥoshen Mishpat* 277:3, and in the comment of Rema).

One who transfers ownership to a fetus…the disposition of a person is to be inclined toward his son, etc. – הַמְזַכֶּה לְעוּבָּר לֹא קָנָה...דַּעְתּוֹ שֶׁל אָדָם קְרוֹבָה אֵצֶל בְּנוֹ וכו׳: One cannot transfer ownership of property to one who has not yet come into the world. Therefore, if one transfers an item to another's unborn child, the fetus does not acquire the item, even if the giver says that the transfer of the item should take effect when the child is born. By contrast, if one transfers an item to his own unborn child, the fetus acquires the item, even if the giver does not state that the transfer of the item should take effect when the child is born. This ruling is in accordance with the opinion of Rabbi Yoḥanan. Rav Hai Gaon rules that only a person on his deathbed can transfer ownership of property to his unborn child, but the *halakha* is not in accordance with this opinion. One can transfer ownership of property to his unborn child only if it is at least forty days into gestation (Rambam *Sefer Kinyan, Hilkhot Mekhira* 22:10 and *Hilkhot Zekhiya UMattana* 8:5; *Shulḥan Arukh, Ḥoshen Mishpat* 210:1 and *Sma* there, 253:26).

NOTES

A firstborn who was born after his father's death – בְּכוֹר שֶׁנּוֹלַד לְאַחַר מִיתַת אָבִיו: There are two ways in which a firstborn born after his father's death might have a brother. One possibility is that he has a twin brother. Alternatively, his father had several wives who all gave birth after the father's death.

Since the disposition of a person is inclined toward his son – הוֹאִיל וְדַעְתּוֹ שֶׁל אָדָם קְרוֹבָה אֵצֶל בְּנוֹ: According to this explanation, the reason a fetus cannot generally acquire items is not because of an intrinsic lack of the ability to do so. Rather, since it is as yet unborn, the one transferring the item has not completely resolved to give it to him. This is not the case with one's son, since his disposition is inclined toward him, and his resolve to transfer the item is wholehearted (Rashbam; Rabbi Yitzḥak Karkusha). Others say that this refers specifically to a person on his deathbed. Since his disposition is inclined toward his son, there is concern lest he become dangerously agitated if he is unable to give his property to his unborn son; therefore, the Sages instituted a special provision for this circumstance enabling him to transfer the property to his unborn son. In other cases this provision does not apply, and a fetus cannot acquire an item, as a fetus is not yet in the world and lacks the ability to acquire property (Rav Hai Gaon; Rif; Ramban; Ritva).

The Ramah notes that although Rabbi Yoḥanan employs the term: Toward his son, the same applies with regard to his daughter, as indicated by the mishna. The early commentaries disagree as to whether the stage of gestation is a factor. Rabbi Yitzḥak Karkusha holds that this does not apply to a first-trimester fetus; Rabbi Avraham *Av Beit Din* says that it does not apply to a fetus of less than forty days, as until then the fetus is considered as mere water. The *Sefer HaIttur* maintains that this concept applies at any stage of gestation.

LANGUAGE

Young man [*talya*] – טַלְיָא: The Aramaic term *talya* is related to the Hebrew word for lamb, *taleh*. It does not refer to any specific age range, and may be used for a newborn baby as well as for a youth (see 91b).

Youngsters [*dardekei*] – דַּרְדְּקֵי: From the Aramaic word meaning youth. It appears in the Aramaic translation of the book of Job, where the word *tze'irim* is rendered as *dardakin*. From there it was incorporated into Hebrew and Arabic.

הַהוּא דַּאֲמַר לִדְבֵיתְהוּ: נְכָסַי לִבְנֵי דְּיֶהֱווּ לִי מִינֵּיךְ, אֲתָא בְּרֵיהּ קַשִּׁישָׁא אֲמַר לֵיהּ: הַהוּא גַּבְרָא מַאי תֶּיהֱוֵי עֲלֵיהּ? אֲמַר לֵיהּ: זִיל קְנֵי כְּחַד מִבְּרָא; הָנָךְ – וַדַּאי לָא קָנוּ, דְּאַכַּתִּי לֵיתְנְהוּ.

§ The Gemara relates: There was **a certain** man **who said to his wife,** before she conceived: **My property** is given **to the sons that I will have from you.**[H] **His older son** from a previous marriage **came and said to him: That man,** i.e., me, **what will become of him,** i.e., will I receive nothing? **He said to** his son: **Go and acquire** a portion **like one of the sons** who will be born, i.e., you will receive a share as well. The Gemara comments: **Those** sons who were not yet born **certainly did not acquire** the property, and do not receive more than their share as heirs, **as they are not yet** in existence.

הַאי, אִית חוּלַק לְטַלְיָא בִּמְקוֹם בְּנַיָּא, אוֹ לֵית לֵיהּ חוּלַק לְטַלְיָא בִּמְקוֹם בְּנַיָּא? רַבִּי אָבִין וְרַבִּי מְיָישָׁא וְרַבִּי יִרְמְיָה דְּאָמְרִי: אִית חוּלַק לְטַלְיָא בִּמְקוֹם בְּנַיָּא; רַבִּי אַבָּהוּ וְרַבִּי חֲנִינָא בַּר פַּפִּי וְרַבִּי יִצְחָק נַפָּחָא דְּאָמְרִי: לֵית חוּלַק לְטַלְיָא בִּמְקוֹם בְּנַיָּא.

The Gemara asks: With regard to **this** son, **does the young man** [*letalya*][L] receive an additional **share**[N] of the inheritance in a case **where** there are other **sons** from the second wife, since his father gave him an additional share, **or does the young man not** receive an additional **share** of the inheritance **where** there are other **sons?** There are **Rabbi Avin, and Rabbi Meyasha, and Rabbi Yirmeya, who** all **say: The young man does** receive an additional **share** of the inheritance **where** there are other **sons.** And there are **Rabbi Abbahu, and Rabbi Ḥanina bar Pappi, and Rabbi Yitzḥak Nappaḥa, who** all **say: The young man does not** receive an additional **share**[H] of the inheritance **where** there are other **sons.**

אֲמַר לֵיהּ רַבִּי אַבָּהוּ לְרַבִּי יִרְמְיָה: הִלְכְתָא כְּוָותָן אוֹ הִלְכְתָא כְּוָתַיְיכוּ? אֲמַר לֵיהּ: פְּשִׁיטָא דְּהִלְכְתָא כְּוָותָן, דְּקַשִּׁישְׁנָא מִינַּיְיכוּ, וְלָאו הִלְכְתָא כְּוָותַיְיכוּ, דְּדַרְדְּקֵי אַתּוּן. אֲמַר לֵיהּ: מִידֵי בְּקַשִּׁישׁוּתָא תַּלְיָא מִילְּתָא? בְּטַעֲמָא תַּלְיָא מִילְּתָא. וְטַעֲמָא מַאי? זִיל לְגַבֵּיהּ דְּרַבִּי אָבִין דְּאַסְבַּרְתָּה נִיהֲלֵיהּ,

Rabbi Abbahu said to Rabbi Yirmeya: Is **the *halakha* in accordance with our** opinion, **or is the *halakha* in accordance with your** opinion? Rabbi Yirmeya **said to** Rabbi Abbahu: It is **obvious that the *halakha*** is **in accordance with our** opinion, **as we are older than you,**[N] **and the *halakha*** is **not in accordance with your** opinion, **as you are youngsters** [*dardekei*].[L] Rabbi Abbahu **said to** Rabbi Yirmeya in reply: **Does the matter depend upon age? The matter depends upon the reason**[N] behind the ruling. Rabbi Yirmeya asked him: **And what is your reason?** Rabbi Abbahu replied: **Go to Rabbi Avin, as I explained** this *halakha* **to him,**

HALAKHA

My property is given to the sons that I will have from you – נְכָסַי לִבְנֵי דְּיֶהֱווּ לִי מִינֵּיךְ: If one says to his wife: My property is given to the sons that I will have from you, they do not acquire any property. Since his wife is not yet pregnant at the time of the gift, they are not in existence even to the extent that the father's disposition would be inclined toward them (Rambam *Sefer Kinyan*, *Hilkhot Mekhira* 22:11; *Shulḥan Arukh*, *Ḥoshen Mishpat* 210:1).

The young man does not receive an additional share – לֵית חוּלַק לְטַלְיָא: If one transfers ownership of his property to an animal or to a person who has not yet come into the world, and then he says to another person: Acquire the property as this animal did, or Acquire the property as this person who has not yet come into the world did, the recipient does not acquire any property. This is as Rabbi Avin explained to Rabbi Yirmeya, and as indicated by the statements of the Gemara in the continuation of the discussion (Rambam *Sefer Kinyan*, *Hilkhot Mekhira* 22:12; *Shulḥan Arukh*, *Ḥoshen Mishpat* 210:2).

NOTES

Does the young man receive an additional share – אִית חוּלַק לְטַלְיָא: The father included his son in the gift he made to his as-yet-unconceived sons. The sons who had not yet been conceived do not acquire any property by means of this gift. Since the gifts seem to be dependent upon each other, the young man's gift might be invalidated by the association. Yet, it is possible that the gift to the first son stands on its own, as though he had said to him that he should receive a portion as he would were he one of the other sons, and had they actually received the gift. If that is the case, if three sons were subsequently born, the oldest son would claim a fourth of the inheritance on the basis of his father's promise, and then all four of them would divide the remainder. If he was also a firstborn, he would likewise receive a firstborn's share.

As we are older than you – דְּקַשִּׁישְׁנָא מִינַּיְיכוּ: Since there is no decisive proof with which to resolve the dispute, the question is whose judgment is more reliable, and one should follow the judgment of the older Rabbis, who are more experienced.

The matter depends upon the reason – בְּטַעֲמָא תַּלְיָא מִילְּתָא: The younger Rabbis had a considered reason behind their statement, whereas the older Rabbis merely expressed their judgment without substantive proof.

וְכַרְכֵּישׁ בָּהּ רֵישֵׁיהּ בֵּי מִדְרָשָׁא. אֲזַל לְגַבֵּיהּ, אֲמַר לֵיהּ: אִילּוּ אָמַר לֵיהּ ״קְנִי כַּחֲמוֹר״, מִי קָנֵי?

and he nodded [***vekharkeish***][L] **his head** in **the study hall** in approval **of this** explanation. Rabbi Yirmeya **went to** Rabbi Avin, who **said to him:** Rabbi Abbahu's reasoning is that **if** a father **said to** his son: **Acquire** an item **as a donkey** does, **does he acquire** it? In the same manner that the son would not acquire anything if his acquisition were likened to that of a donkey, which possesses no ability to acquire an item, so too, since the father compared the son's acquisition to the acquisition effected by his unborn children, who possess no ability to acquire property, the son did not acquire any property.

דְּאִיתְּמַר: ״קְנִי כַּחֲמוֹר״ – לֹא קָנָה. ״אַתְּ וַחֲמוֹר״ – רַב נַחְמָן אָמַר: קָנָה מֶחֱצָה, וְרַב הַמְנוּנָא אָמַר: לֹא אָמַר כְּלוּם, וְרַב שֵׁשֶׁת אָמַר: קָנָה הַכֹּל.

This is **as it was stated:** With regard to one who says to another: **Acquire** an item **as a donkey** does, he **does not acquire** any property, as a donkey cannot acquire property. But with regard to one who says: **You and a donkey**[H] shall both acquire my property, there is a disagreement. **Rav Naḥman says:** The person **acquires** his **half** of the property, **and Rav Hamnuna says:** It is as though the giver **does not say anything.** Since the beneficiary was included with the donkey in the same acquisition, he does not acquire any property, just as the donkey does not acquire any property. **Rav Sheshet says:** The person **acquires all** the property. As the giver knew that a donkey cannot acquire property, he intended for the person, who was capable of acquiring property, to acquire all the property.

אָמַר רַב שֵׁשֶׁת: מְנָא אָמֵינָא לַהּ? דְּתַנְיָא, רַבִּי יוֹסֵי אוֹמֵר: אֵין לְךָ מַר בְּקִישּׁוּת אֶלָּא פְּנִימִי שֶׁבּוֹ, לְפִיכָךְ כְּשֶׁהוּא תּוֹרֵם – מוֹסִיף עַל הַחִיצוֹן שֶׁבּוֹ וְתוֹרֵם;

Rav Sheshet said: From where do I say this? As it is taught in a *baraita*: **Rabbi Yosei says: There is nothing bitter in the cucumber**[B] **other than its inner** part, which is sometimes bitter and inedible and unfit to be separated as *teruma*. **Therefore,** since one does not know if the cucumber he separates as *teruma* is bitter inside, **when he separates *teruma*,** he **adds** part of another cucumber as *teruma*, in addition **to the outer** part **of** the cucumber, which is edible. **And he separates** both **as *teruma*,** thereby ensuring that the *teruma* consists of sufficient edible cucumber.

אַמַּאי? ״אַתְּ וַחֲמוֹר״ הוּא!

Rav Sheshet asks: **Why** does the separation of *teruma* take effect? **Is it** not analogous to one who states: **You and a donkey** shall acquire an item, since he designated as *teruma* both the outer part of the cucumber, which is fit to become *teruma*, and the inedible inner part, which is not fit to become *teruma*? Since this does not invalidate the separation of *teruma* with regard to the edible outer part, one can infer that although the donkey cannot acquire property, this does not prevent the person from acquiring the property.

שָׁאנֵי הָתָם, דְּמִדְּאוֹרַיְיתָא תְּרוּמָה מְעַלְּיְיתָא הִיא;

The Gemara replies: **It is different there, as by Torah law** the bitter inner part **is** also **properly** considered ***teruma***, even though by rabbinic law if one separated inferior produce as *teruma* he must again separate produce of superior quality as *teruma*. Therefore, when one designates the entire cucumber as *teruma*, he is not designating both fit and unfit produce.

דְּאָמַר רַבִּי אִילְעָא: מִנַּיִן לַתּוֹרֵם מִן הָרַע עַל הַיָּפֶה שֶׁתְּרוּמָתוֹ תְּרוּמָה? שֶׁנֶּאֱמַר: ״וְלֹא תִשְׂאוּ עָלָיו חֵטְא בַּהֲרִימְכֶם אֶת חֶלְבּוֹ מִמֶּנּוּ״, וְאִם אֵינוֹ קָדוֹשׁ – נְשִׂיאוּת חֵטְא לָמָּה? מִכָּאן לַתּוֹרֵם מִן הָרַע עַל הַיָּפֶה שֶׁתְּרוּמָתוֹ תְּרוּמָה.

This is **as Rabbi Ile'a says: From where** is it derived **that** the *halakha* **with regard to one who separates *teruma* from poor**-quality produce **for superior**-quality produce is **that his *teruma*** is valid ***teruma***? It is **as it is stated** with regard to *teruma*: **"And you shall bear no sin by reason of it, seeing that you have set apart from it the best thereof"** (Numbers 18:32). By inference, this indicates that it is a transgression to separate the inferior part of the produce as *teruma*. Rabbi Ile'a explains the proof: **And if** the inferior produce **is not sanctified** as *teruma*, **why** does it involve the **bearing of sin,** as it is a meaningless act? **From here** one can derive that **that** the *halakha* with regard to **one who separates *teruma* from poor**-quality produce **for superior**-quality produce is **that** although he acted improperly, **his *teruma*** is valid ***teruma***.

LANGUAGE

Nodded [*karkeish*] – **כַּרְכֵּישׁ:** This term is similar in meaning to the Hebrew word *kishkesh*, which denotes moving or shaking something. Some hold that the word originates from the Greek **κερκίς**, *kerkis*, meaning a weaving shuttle, which moves from side to side between the threads on the loom. The nodding of the head or the movement of other body parts can resemble the movement of a weaver's shuttle.

HALAKHA

You and a donkey, etc. – אַתְּ וַחֲמוֹר: If one said to another: Both you and this animal shall acquire my property, the person acquires half of the property. This is in accordance with the opinion of Rav Naḥman, as the *halakha* generally follows his opinion in cases of monetary law (Rambam *Sefer Kinyan*, *Hilkhot Mekhira* 22:12; *Shulḥan Arukh*, *Ḥoshen Mishpat* 210:3).

BACKGROUND

The bitter part of the cucumber – מַר בְּקִישּׁוּת: The cucumber, *Cucumis chate*, is a summer fruit of the Cucurbitaceae family, and a species of gourd. It is called *melafefon* in modern Hebrew. The fruit is up to 80 cm long, is narrow, and can be bent or twisted. The fruit may be eaten raw or cooked, but it becomes bitter or sour when it is overripe.

אֲמַר לֵיהּ רַב מָרְדְּכַי לְרַב אַשִׁי, מְתִיב רַב אַוְיָא תְּיוּבְתָּא: מַעֲשֶׂה בְּחָמֵשׁ נָשִׁים וּבָהֶן שְׁתֵּי אֲחָיוֹת, וְלִיקֵּט אֶחָד כַּלְכָּלָה שֶׁל תְּאֵנִים, וְשֶׁלָּהֶן הָיְתָה, וְשֶׁל שְׁבִיעִית הָיְתָה, וְאָמַר: "הֲרֵי כּוּלְּכֶן מְקוּדָּשׁוֹת לִי בְּכַלְכָּלָה זוֹאת", וְקִבְּלָה אַחַת מֵהֶן עַל יְדֵי כּוּלָּן – אָמְרוּ חֲכָמִים: אֵין אֲחָיוֹת מְקוּדָּשׁוֹת;

§ The Gemara cited Rav Hamnuna's opinion that if one says: You and a donkey shall acquire my property, he did not say anything. **Rav Mordekhai said to Rav Ashi: Rav Avya raises an objection** to Rav Hamnuna's opinion from a mishna (*Kiddushin* 50b): **An incident** occurred **involving five women,**[H] **and among them** were **two sisters, and one person gathered a basket**[B] **of figs that belonged to them, and** the fruit **was of the Sabbatical Year,**[B] **and he said: You are hereby all betrothed to me with this basket, and one of them accepted it on behalf of all of them. The Sages said: The sisters are not betrothed,**[N] as it is prohibited to marry the sister of one's wife during her lifetime.

אֲחָיוֹת הוּא דְּאֵין מְקוּדָּשׁוֹת, הָא נָכְרִיּוֹת מְקוּדָּשׁוֹת; וְאַמַּאי? "אַתְּ וַחֲמוֹר" הִיא!

One can infer from the mishna: **It is** only the **sisters who are not betrothed, but** the **unrelated women** are **betrothed. But why** is that so? **It is** analogous to one who states: **You and a donkey** shall acquire an item. Since he tried to betroth two women ineligible for betrothal together with the eligible women, the betrothal should not take effect even with regard to the eligible women.

אֲמַר לֵיהּ: הַיְינוּ דַּחֲזַאי רַב הוּנָא בַּר אַוְיָא בְּחֶלְמָא דְּמוֹתִיב רַב אַוְיָא תְּיוּבְתָּא, לָאו מִי אוֹקִימְנָא דְּאָמַר: "הָרְאוּיָה מִכֶּם לְבִיאָה תִּתְקַדֵּשׁ לִי"?

Rav Ashi **said to** Rav Mordekhai: **This is why I saw Rav Huna bar Avya in a dream, because** you were going to tell me that **Rav Avya raised an objection** to Rav Hamnuna's opinion. But as for this objection, **didn't we interpret** the mishna in *Kiddushin* as referring to **where he says: Those of you who are eligible for** engaging in **sexual intercourse** with me **shall be betrothed to me?** Since the sisters were forbidden to him, they were not included in the betrothal in the first place, and there was no impediment to the betrothal of the eligible women taking effect. The case is therefore not comparable to the case discussed by Rav Hamnuna.

הַהוּא דַּאֲמַר לָהּ לִדְבֵיתְהוּ: "נִכְסַיי לִיךְ וּלְבָנַיִךְ", אָמַר רַב יוֹסֵף: קָנְתָה מֶחֱצָה. וַאֲמַר רַב יוֹסֵף: מְנָא אָמִינָא לַהּ? דְּתַנְיָא, רַבִּי אוֹמֵר: "וְהָיְתָה לְאַהֲרֹן וּלְבָנָיו" – מֶחֱצָה לְאַהֲרֹן מֶחֱצָה לְבָנָיו.

§ The Gemara relates: There was **a certain** man **who said to his wife: My property is given to you and to your sons. Rav Yosef says:** In such a case, the wife **acquires half** of the property,[H] even though the man did not specify how much of his property he was giving her. **And Rav Yosef said: From where do I say this? As it is taught** in a *baraita*: **Rabbi** Yehuda HaNasi **says:** The verse states with regard to the shewbread: **"And it shall be for Aaron and his sons"** (Leviticus 24:9). This means **half for Aaron** and **half for his sons.**[H] One can infer from the *baraita* that when it is specified that a gift is to be divided between an individual and a group, the intention is that the individual receives half.

אֲמַר לֵיהּ אַבַּיֵי: בִּשְׁלָמָא הָתָם – אַהֲרֹן בַּר חֲלוּקָה הוּא, לְהָכִי פָּרֵט בֵּיהּ רַחֲמָנָא לְמִשְׁקַל פַּלְגָּא, אִשָּׁה לָאו בַּת יְרוּשָּׁה הִיא, דַּיָּהּ שֶׁתִּטּוֹל כְּאֶחָד מִן הַבָּנִים!

Abaye said to Rav Yosef: **Granted, there,** in the case of the shewbread, **Aaron is eligible to receive a share** of the shewbread as a priest; it is **for this** reason that **the Merciful One specified him** separately, so **that he should take** more than other priests, i.e., **half.** But with regard to **a woman, who is not eligible to inherit** her husband's property, **it is sufficient for her to receive** a portion of the inheritance **as one of the sons,** not half of all the property.

BACKGROUND

Basket – כַּלְכָּלָה: Baskets were usually woven from willow branches or palm fronds but could also be made from other materials. They had wide openings and vertical sides, and were apparently not deep. They were used mainly to hold soft fruit, e.g., figs and grapes.

Detail of a basket of figs from a Roman fresco

Sabbatical Year – שְׁבִיעִית: The Sabbatical Year is the last year in the seven-year Sabbatical cycle. The first such cycle began after the conquest of Eretz Yisrael by Joshua. The *halakhot* of the Sabbatical Year are based on Torah law (see Leviticus 25:1–7), but most authorities maintain that the conditions enabling performance of the mitzva by Torah law do not currently exist, and therefore present-day observance is based on rabbinic ordinance. The Hebrew term for the Sabbatical Year, *shemitta*, means abandonment or release.

During the Sabbatical Year all agricultural land must lie fallow. It is prohibited to work the land, except for that which is necessary to keep existing crops alive. All produce that does grow is ownerless and must be left unguarded in the fields so that any creature, including wild animals and birds, can have ready access to it. As long as produce can still be found in the fields it may be eaten, although it may not be bought and sold in the normal manner or used for purposes other than food. After the last remnants of a crop have been removed from the field, that crop may no longer be eaten.

NOTES

The sisters are not betrothed, etc. – אֵין אֲחָיוֹת מְקוּדָּשׁוֹת: The prohibition against marrying the sister of one's wife's during her lifetime is punishable by *karet*. If one betroths a woman who is prohibited to him by a prohibition that is punishable by *karet*, the betrothal does not take effect. In the case discussed here, the man cannot betroth both sisters, for if the betrothal takes effect with regard to one, the other is prohibited to him, and her betrothal would not take effect. Since it is not clear which of them is betrothed, these are betrothals that cannot be consummated, which are not valid betrothals.

HALAKHA

An incident involving five women – מַעֲשֶׂה בְּחָמֵשׁ נָשִׁים: In the case of one who betroths several women in a single act, and among those women are two sisters, or a mother and daughter, the *halakha* is as follows: If he says: Those of you who are eligible for engaging in intercourse shall be betrothed to me, then all of them are betrothed to him, except for the sisters or the mother and daughter. Similarly, if he says: You are all betrothed to me, then the unrelated women are betrothed to him, but the sisters are not, as the *halakha* is in accordance with the opinion of Rav Naḥman. Some authorities say that in this case even Rav Naḥman concedes that the unrelated women are not betrothed. Since the *halakha* is uncertain in this case, the unrelated women are considered betrothed due to the uncertainty (Rambam *Sefer Nashim*, *Hilkhot Ishut* 9:2, and see *Maggid Mishne* there; *Shulḥan Arukh*, *Even HaEzer* 41:3).

The wife acquires half of the property – קָנְתָה מֶחֱצָה: If one says: My property is given to so-and-so and to my sons, the person he names receives half, and the sons divide the other half among themselves. Similarly, if he says: My property is given to so-and-so and so-and-so, and to the sons of a third person, the sons of the third receive half and the first two receive the other half. Even if those who are specifically named are numerous and those who are grouped together are few, those named receive half. This is in accordance with the principle stated by Rav Yosef (Rambam *Sefer Kinyan*, *Hilkhot Zekhiya UMattana* 11:5–6; *Shulḥan Arukh*, *Ḥoshen Mishpat* 247:5, 253:24).

Half for Aaron and half for his sons – מֶחֱצָה לְאַהֲרֹן מֶחֱצָה לְבָנָיו: The High Priest always takes half of the shewbread from each priestly watch, as the verse states: "And it shall be for Aaron and his sons" (Leviticus 24:9). This means half for Aaron and half for his sons. The High Priest also receives one of the two loaves made from the new wheat, offered on *Shavuot* (Rambam *Sefer Avoda*, *Hilkhot Temidin UMusafin* 4:14, 8:1).

אִינִי? וְהָא עוּבְדָא הֲוָה בִּנְהַרְדְּעָא וְאַגְבְּיֵהּ שְׁמוּאֵל פַּלְגָא, בִּטְבֶרְיָא – וְאַגְבְּיֵהּ רַבִּי יוֹחָנָן פַּלְגָא! וְתוּ, כִּי אֲתָא רַב יִצְחָק בַּר יוֹסֵף אֲמַר: הַהוּא דְּמֵי כְּלִילָא דְּשַׁדּוּ דְּבֵי מַלְכָּא אַאֲבוּלֵי וְאַאִיסְטְרוּגֵי, אֲמַר רַבִּי: נֵיתְבוּ אֲבוּלֵי פַּלְגָא וְאִיסְטְרוּגֵי פַּלְגָא!

The Gemara raises an objection: **Is that so? But there was an incident in Neharde'a** where a man gave a gift to an individual and to a group of people, **and Shmuel collected half** the sum for the individual. There was a similar case **in Tiberias, and Rabbi Yoḥanan collected half** the sum for the individual. **And furthermore, when Rav Yitzḥak bar Yosef came** from Eretz Yisrael **he said:** There was **a certain coronation tax that was placed by the royal house on the city councilmen** [*a'abulei*][L] **and on the prominent citizens** [*ve'a'isterugei*].[LN] **Rabbi** Yehuda HaNasi **said: Let the city councilmen give half and the prominent citizens half.** This indicates that when two groups are mentioned together, the intent is that each one represents half.

הָכִי הָשְׁתָּא? הָתָם מֵעִיקָּרָא כִּי הָווּ כָּתְבִי – אַאֲבוּלֵי הָווּ כָּתְבִי, וְאִיסְטְרוּגֵי הָווּ מְסַיְּיעִי בַּהֲדַיְיהוּ, וְיָדַע מַלְכָּא דְּהָווּ קָא מְסַיְּיעִי; הָשְׁתָּא, מַאי דְּקָא כָּתְבֵי אַאֲבוּלֵי וְאַאִיסְטְרוּגֵי – לְמֵימְרָא דְּהָנֵי פַּלְגָא וְהָנֵי פַּלְגָא.

The Gemara rejects this argument: **How can** the case concerning the tax **be compared** to the other cases? **There, initially, when they would write** the writ of assessment, **they would write** that it was placed **on the city councilmen**[N] alone. **And the prominent citizens would assist them** in raising the sum, **and the king knew that they were assisting** them. Therefore, **now,** the meaning of **what they wrote:** It is placed **on the city councilmen and on the prominent citizens, is to say that these** should give **half** of the tax, **and those** should give **half.**

מְתִיב רַבִּי זֵירָא: הָאוֹמֵר ״הֲרֵי עָלַי מִנְחָה מֵאָה עִשָּׂרוֹן לְהָבִיא בִּשְׁנֵי כֵלִים״ – מֵבִיא שִׁשִּׁים בִּכְלִי אֶחָד וְאַרְבָּעִים בִּכְלִי אֶחָד,

Rabbi Zeira raises an objection to Rav Yosef's ruling from a *baraita* (*Tosefta, Menaḥot* 12:7): With regard to **one who says: It is** incumbent **upon me** to bring **a meal-offering of one hundred tenths** of an ephah[B] **in two vessels,**[H] **he brings sixty**-tenths **in one vessel,** and the remaining **forty**-tenths **in one vessel,** as no more than sixty-tenths may be brought in a single vessel.

HALAKHA

It is upon me to bring a meal-offering of one hundred tenths in two vessels – הֲרֵי עָלַי מִנְחָה מֵאָה עִשָּׂרוֹן לְהָבִיא בִּשְׁנֵי כֵלִים: An individual does not bring a meal-offering of more than sixty-tenths of an ephah in a single vessel, as no more than this amount can be properly mixed in a single vessel. If he vowed to bring more than sixty-tenths, he brings sixty in one vessel and the remainder in another vessel (Rambam *Sefer Avoda, Hilkhot Ma'aseh HaKorbanot* 17:6).

LANGUAGE

City councilmen [*abulei*] – אֲבוּלֵי: From the Greek βουλή, *boulē*, meaning council. In most of the instances where this term is employed in the Talmud, it refers to the city council, a form of local senate that governed the city's affairs.

Prominent citizens [*isterugei*] – אִיסְטְרוּגֵי: From the Greek στρατηγός, *stratēgos*, which has several related meanings, including an army general. The Roman consuls were referred to as *strategoi*. In this context it apparently refers to prominent, wealthy people.

NOTES

On the city councilmen [*abulei*] and on the prominent citizens [*isterugei*] – אַאֲבוּלֵי וְאַאִיסְטְרוּגֵי: The commentaries explain the term *abulei* as referring to the wealthy (see *Gittin* 37a). The term *isterugei* is explained in various ways: The Ritva explains that it refers to the poor, whereas the Rashbam says it refers to ministers. Rabbeinu Gershom Meor HaGola explains that *abulei* are the townspeople and *isterugei* are people who dwell outside the town.

They would write that it was on the city councilmen – אַאֲבוּלֵי הָווּ כָּתְבִי: Initially the assessment would mention only the city councilmen as responsible for paying the tax. Even though it was well known that there were prominent citizens who assisted the councilmen in raising the funds, they were not specifically mentioned in the document. When the prominent citizens were specifically mentioned, this was considered notification that they would be held responsible for half of the tax. This is similar to the case of Aaron, as in both cases the party specifically mentioned would have been considered part of the group even without specific mention. Therefore, one cannot adduce proof from this case to the case of the widow, who would not receive any of her husband's property were it not for the husband's specific mention of her.

BACKGROUND

Tenths of an ephah – עִשָּׂרוֹן: An ephah is a measure of dry volume. It contains 28.88 ℓ according to the calculations of Rabbi Ḥayyim Na'e, and 43.2 ℓ according to the calculations of the *Ḥazon Ish*.

Perek **IX**
Daf **143** Amud **b**

וְאִם הֵבִיא חֲמִשִּׁים בִּכְלִי אֶחָד וַחֲמִשִּׁים בִּכְלִי אֶחָד – יָצָא; אִם הֵבִיא – אִין, לְכַתְּחִלָּה לָא; וְאִי סָלְקָא דַּעְתָּךְ כׇּל כִּי הַאי גַּוְונָא פַּלְגָא וּפַלְגָא הוּא, אֲפִילּוּ לְכַתְּחִלָּה נַמִי!

And if he brought fifty-tenths **in one vessel and fifty in one vessel, he fulfilled** his obligation. One can infer from the *baraita* that after the fact, **if he** had **brought** fifty-tenths in each vessel, **yes,** he fulfilled his obligation, but he may **not** do so ***ab initio*. And if it should enter your mind** to say that **every case like this is** divided **half and half,** it should be permitted to divide the meal-offering into equal halves **even *ab initio*.**

הָכִי הָשְׁתָּא? הָתָם אֲנַן סָהֲדֵי דְּהַאי גַּבְרָא מֵעִיקָּרָא לְקׇרְבָּן גָּדוֹל קָא מְכַוֵּין, וְהַאי דְּקָאָמַר בִּשְׁנֵי כֵלִים – דְּיָדַע דְּלָא אֶפְשָׁר לְאַתּוּיֵי בִּכְלִי אֶחָד, כַּמָּה דְּאֶפְשָׁר לְאִיתּוּיֵי מַיְיתִינַן.

The Gemara dismisses Rabbi Zeira's objection: **How can** these cases **be compared? There,** in the case of the meal-offering, **it is clear to us that this person initially intended to** bring **a large offering, and** the reason **that he said** he will bring the offering **in two vessels** was **that he knew that it is not possible to bring** the entire offering **in a single vessel.** Therefore, **we bring,** in a single vessel, **as much as** it **is possible to bring,** which is sixty-tenths. In any other case it is possible that the division should be into two equal portions.

וְהִלְכְתָא כְּוָותֵיהּ דְּרַב יוֹסֵף בְּשָׂדֶה, עִנְיָן, וּמֶחֱצָה.

The Gemara concludes: **And the *halakha* is in accordance with** the opinion **of Rav Yosef**[N] in three matters where he disagreed with Rabba: **In** the matter of dividing **a field** between brothers (see 12b); in the matter of whether certain actions are limited by the court session or by the **topic** of discussion in the court (see 114a); **and** in the matter of **half,** i.e., this matter, whether an unspecified division into two parts is divided into two equal halves.

NOTES

And the *halakha* is in accordance with the opinion of Rav Yosef, etc. – וְהִלְכְתָא כְּוָותֵיהּ דְּרַב יוֹסֵף וכו׳: The *halakha* is in accordance with the opinion of Rav Yosef in many instances; this mnemonic refers only to those cases where he was in disagreement with Rabba. Although Rabba does not appear in the discussion here, the Gemara knew that the objection Abaye raised to Rav Yosef's ruling was cited in the name of Rabba, and therefore this *halakha* fits into the same category as the other two instances where Rabba and Rav Yosef were in disagreement (Ritva, citing one of the *ge'onim*).

BACKGROUND

Silk – שִׁירָאֵי: From the Greek σηρικόν, *sērikon*, meaning silk or a particular variety of silk. Due to the complexity of the production process, natural silk is an expensive textile even today. It was even more expensive in the talmudic period, when it was imported from China, an enormous distance considering the methods of transportation available at the time. Consequently, the division of silk between the household members was liable to be a matter of contention. The discussion here refers to swaths of silk that were already cut into certain shapes or were of different colors, and therefore it was possible to distinguish between swaths suitable for women's garments and those suitable for men.

NOTES

I leave my property to my sons [*levanai*] – נִכְסַיי לְבָנַיי: This dilemma is based on the fact that *levanai* can mean either: To my sons, or: To my children.

He had a son and a grandson, do people call a grandson a son – הֲוָה לֵיהּ בְּרָא וּבַר בְּרָא, קָרוּ אִינָשֵׁי לְבַר בְּרָא בְּרָא: This refers either to the son of that same son, to whom he wished to give a separate share in the inheritance, or to the son of a different son who had died (Rashbam). The Gemara's discussion pertains only to a person who has a son in addition to the grandson. In the case of one who has a grandson but no sons, the term son is clearly intended to refer to the grandson (Ramah; Ritva).

הַהוּא דְּשַׁדַּר פִּיסְקֵי דְּשִׁירָאֵי לְבֵיתֵיהּ, אָמַר רַבִּי אַמִי: הָרְאוּיִין לְבָנִים – לְבָנִים, רְאוּיִין לְבָנוֹת – לְבָנוֹת. וְלָא אֲמַרַן אֶלָּא דְּלֵית לֵיהּ כַּלָּתָא, אֲבָל אִית לֵיהּ כַּלָּתָא – לְכַלָּתֵיהּ שָׁדַר; וְאִי בְּנָתֵיהּ לָא נְסִיבָן, לָא שָׁבֵק בְּנָתֵיהּ וּמְשַׁדַּר לְכַלָּתֵיהּ.

§ The Gemara cites additional incidents concerning a gift whose method of division was not specified: There was **a certain** man **who sent swaths of silk**[B] **to his home** as a gift. **Rabbi Ami says** that in such a case, **those** swaths that are **suitable**[H] for the sons' garments are given **to the sons,** and those that are **suitable for** the **daughters'** garments are given **to the daughters.** The Gemara comments: **We said this only when he does not have daughters-in-law, but if he has daughters-in-law,** it is presumed that **he sent** it **for his daughters-in-law. And if his daughters are not married,** it is presumed that **he does not forsake his daughters and send to his daughters-in-law,** so the silk is given to his daughters.

הַהוּא דַּאֲמַר לְהוּ: ״נִכְסַיי לְבָנַיי״, הֲוָה לֵיהּ בְּרָא וּבְרַתָּא; מִי קָרוּ אִינָשֵׁי לִבְרָא ״בְּנַיי״, וּלְסַלּוּקֵי לִבְרַתָּא מֵעִישּׂוּר קָאָתֵי. אוֹ דִּלְמָא לָא קָרוּ אִינָשֵׁי לִבְרָא ״בְּנַיי״, וּלְמוֹשְׁכָה לִבְרַתָּא בְּמַתָּנָה קָאָתֵי?

There was **a certain** man **who said to** those surrounding him: I leave **my property to my sons** [*levanai*],[NH] and **he had** only **a son and a daughter.** The question was raised: **Do people call** a single **son** in the plural: **My sons, and** in his will **he came to remove his daughter** even **from the tenth** of his property that would rightfully be her dowry? **Or perhaps people do not call** a single **son: My sons, and he came to include** his **daughter in the gift?**

אָמַר אַבָּיֵי, תָּא שְׁמַע: ״וּבְנֵי דָן חֻשִׁים״. אָמַר לֵיהּ רָבָא, דִּלְמָא כִּדְתָנָא דְּבֵי חִזְקִיָּה: שֶׁהָיוּ מְרוּבִּין כְּחוּשִׁים שֶׁל קָנֶה! אֶלָּא אָמַר רָבָא: ״וּבְנֵי פַלּוּא אֱלִיאָב״. רַב יוֹסֵף אָמַר: ״וּבְנֵי אֵיתָן עֲזַרְיָה״.

Abaye said: Come and **hear** a proof that one does refer to a single son using the plural term sons, as it is written: **"And the sons of Dan: Hushim"** (Genesis 46:23). **Rava said to** Abaye: **Perhaps** this verse should be understood **as the school of Ḥizkiyya taught,** that Hushim is not the name of Dan's son but **that they,** Dan's sons, **were as numerous as** the **groups** [*ḥushim*] **of reeds. Rather, Rava said:** One can prove this usage of the term sons in the verse: **"And the sons of Pallu: Eliab"** (Numbers 26:8). **Rav Yosef said:** This can be proven from another verse: **"And the sons of Ethan: Azariah"** (I Chronicles 2:8).

הַהוּא דַּאֲמַר לְהוּ: ״נִכְסַאי לְבָנַאי״, הֲוָה לֵיהּ בְּרָא וּבַר בְּרָא; קָרוּ אִינָשֵׁי לְבַר בְּרָא ״בְּרָא״, אוֹ לָא? רַב חֲבִיבָא אָמַר: קָרוּ אִינָשֵׁי לְבַר בְּרָא ״בְּרָא״; מָר בַּר רַב אָשֵׁי אָמַר: לָא קָרוּ אִינָשֵׁי לְבַר בְּרָא ״בְּרָא״. תַּנְיָא כְּוָותֵיהּ דְּמָר בַּר רַב אָשֵׁי: הַמּוּדָּר הֲנָאָה מִבָּנִים – מוּתָּר בִּבְנֵי בָנִים.

There was **a certain** man **who said to** those surrounding him: I leave **my property to my sons,** and **he had a son and a grandson,**[H] i.e., his son's son. The question was raised: Do **people call a grandson a son,**[N] or do they **not? Rav Ḥaviva said: People call a grandson a son. Mar bar Rav Ashi said: People do not call a grandson a son.** The Gemara comments: **It is taught** in a *baraita* **in accordance with** the opinion **of Mar bar Rav Ashi:** With regard to **one prohibited by a vow from deriving benefit from** a certain person's **sons,**[H] it is **permitted** for him to derive benefit **from the sons of** that person's **sons,** as they are not included in the term sons.

HALAKHA

Those that are suitable, etc. – הָרְאוּיִין וכו׳: If one sent garments to his home without specifying for whom they were intended, and he has both sons and daughters, if there are among them garments suitable for women, the daughters receive them, as he probably intended them for his daughters. If he has no daughters, or if his daughters are married, his sons' wives receive them, as it is reasonable to presume that the garments were intended for them. The Ramah states that this applies only if the one who sent the garments is unmarried. If he is married and his wife dwells in his home, the garments are assumed to be intended for his wife. The reason for this is that one's wife is as oneself. One therefore concerns himself about his wife's welfare more than the welfare of anyone else (Rambam *Sefer Kinyan*, *Hilkhot Zekhiya UMattana* 6:14; *Shulḥan Arukh*, *Ḥoshen Mishpat* 247:2, and see 247:1).

I leave my property to my sons – נִכְסַיי לְבָנַיי: In the case of a person on his deathbed who says: I leave my property to my sons, when he has one son and several daughters, the son inherits all of the property. This is because one might refer to one son using the plural term sons, and the daughters are not included in his statement. If he explicitly states that he leaves his property to his sons and daughters, then whatever is suitable for men is given to the sons, and whatever is suitable for women is given to the daughters (Rambam *Sefer Kinyan*, *Hilkhot Zekhiya UMattana* 11:1; *Shulḥan Arukh Ḥoshen Mishpat* 247:3, and in the comment of Rema).

A son and a grandson – בְּרָא וּבַר בְּרָא: In the case of one who had two sons, and one son died and left a surviving son, leaving his father a grandson, and the father said: I leave my property to my sons, the grandson is not included, in accordance with the opinion of Mar bar Rav Ashi. The Ramah writes that if he had no surviving sons, but only the grandson, and he said: I leave my property to my sons, then he clearly intended the grandson, even if he also had daughters (Rambam *Sefer Kinyan*, *Hilkhot Zekhiya UMattana* 11:1; *Shulḥan Arukh*, *Ḥoshen Mishpat* 247:3, and in the comment of Rema).

One prohibited by a vow from deriving benefit from a certain person's sons – הַמּוּדָּר הֲנָאָה מִבָּנִים: If one vows not to derive benefit from a certain person's sons, it is permitted for him to derive benefit from the sons of that person's sons (Rambam *Sefer Hafla'a*, *Hilkhot Nedarim* 9:23; *Shulḥan Arukh*, *Yoreh De'a* 217:46).

מתני׳ הִנִּיחַ בָּנִים גְּדוֹלִים וּקְטַנִּים, הִשְׁבִּיחוּ גְדוֹלִים אֶת הַנְּכָסִים – הִשְׁבִּיחוּ לָאֶמְצַע; אִם אָמְרוּ: ״רְאוּ מַה שֶּׁהִנִּיחַ אַבָּא, הֲרֵי אָנוּ עוֹשִׂין וְאוֹכְלִים״ – הִשְׁבִּיחוּ לְעַצְמָן. וְכֵן הָאִשָּׁה שֶׁהִשְׁבִּיחָה אֶת הַנְּכָסִים – הִשְׁבִּיחָה לָאֶמְצַע; אִם אָמְרָה: ״רְאוּ מַה שֶּׁהִנִּיחַ לִי בַּעְלִי, הֲרֵי אֲנִי עוֹשָׂה וְאוֹכֶלֶת״ – הִשְׁבִּיחָה לְעַצְמָהּ.

MISHNA In the case of **one who** died and **left** behind **adult and minor sons,**[N] if **the adult** sons **enhanced the property,**[H] **they enhanced** it so that the profit goes **to the middle,** i.e., it is distributed among all the heirs. **If** the adult sons **said** from the outset: **See that which our father left** behind;[N] **we are** going to **engage** in business with our share of the property **and profit** from it, then **they enhanced** the property **for themselves.**[N] **And similarly,** with regard to **a wife who enhanced the property** of her deceased husband,[H] **she enhanced** it so that the profit goes **to the middle,** i.e., it is divided between her and the heirs. **If she said: See that which my husband left me; I am** going to **engage** in business with my share **and profit** from it, then **she enhanced** the property **for herself.**

גמ׳ אָמַר רַב חֲבִיבָא בְּרֵיהּ דְּרַב יוֹסֵף בְּרֵיהּ דְּרָבָא מִשְּׁמֵיהּ דְּרָבָא: לֹא שָׁנוּ אֶלָּא שֶׁשָּׁבְחוּ נְכָסִים מֵחֲמַת נְכָסִים, אֲבָל שָׁבְחוּ נְכָסִים מֵחֲמַת עַצְמָן – הִשְׁבִּיחוּ לְעַצְמָן.

GEMARA **Rav Ḥaviva, son of Rav Yosef, son of Rava, says in the name of Rava: They taught** this *halakha* **only** with regard to **where the property was enhanced on account of the property,**[N] i.e., the heirs invested money from the common inheritance in order to enhance the property, and their input was only in the management of its investment. **But** if **the property was enhanced on their account,** i.e., on account of the efforts or expenditure of the adult sons, the *halakha* is that **they enhanced** it **for themselves.**

אִינִי? וְהָא אָמַר רַבִּי חֲנִינָא: אֲפִילּוּ לֹא הִנִּיחַ לָהֶם אֲבִיהֶם אֶלָּא

The Gemara asks: **Is that so? But doesn't Rabbi Ḥanina say: Even if their father left them nothing but**

NOTES

Adult and minor sons, etc. – בָּנִים גְּדוֹלִים וּקְטַנִּים וכו׳: The majority of the early commentaries hold that the *halakha* is the same in a case where all the sons were adults, as usually brothers do not charge a fee for efforts they make to invest for one another (*Tosafot*). In fact, there is even more reason for this *halakha* to apply to adult brothers, as the brothers who enhance the property expect that any effort they invest will be reciprocated by their brothers in turn (Rabbeinu Yona). The mishna emphasizes that this principle applies even in a case where there are also minor sons, who the adults do not expect will reciprocate. By contrast, the Meiri holds that this principle applies only in the case where there are also minor sons, whereas in the case of adult brothers the brothers who enhance the property do forgo compensation for their efforts.

See that which our father left behind – רְאוּ מַה שֶּׁהִנִּיחַ אַבָּא: The intent of their declaration is that they are not relinquishing their rights in their investment. The Rashbam writes that this declaration can be issued in any manner that publicizes it, whether before the court, before witnesses, or in some public forum.

They enhanced for themselves – הִשְׁבִּיחוּ לְעַצְמָן: The early commentaries disagree as to whether the profits from the enhancement of the entire property belong to the adult brothers, including the profits from the portion in the property of the minor brothers, as suggested by the incident involving Rav Safra (see 144a; *Tosafot*), or whether they receive only the profits that accrue from the enhancement of their own portion.

Where the property was enhanced on account of the property – שֶׁשָּׁבְחוּ נְכָסִים מֵחֲמַת נְכָסִים: The Rashbam explains that this refers to a case where they did not invest their own assets or physical efforts. Rather, they invested from the inheritance in order to improve it, e.g., they hired workers. Others explain that it is referring to a case where the property was improved without any investment at all, as in the case of produce that grew without any investment (see Ritva). Some say that even if they invested physical effort in the property, as long as they did not invest their own money it is considered enhancement on account of the property (Rivam). Rabbeinu Tam distinguishes between a case where the brothers enhanced an entity already in existence and where they manufactured an entirely new entity from the inheritance, as in a case where they fashioned implements from metal (*Haggahot Asheri*).

HALAKHA

If the adult sons enhanced the property – הִשְׁבִּיחוּ גְדוֹלִים אֶת הַנְּכָסִים: According to the Rambam, if the adult sons enhanced the property before it was divided, the profit from the enhancement is divided among all the heirs, even if they invested their own money in the property (*Sma*). If the adults said to the minors: See that which our father left behind; we are going to engage in business with our share of the property and profit from it, then if the enhancement was due to the investment made by those who enhanced the property, the profit goes to them. If the property was enhanced on its own account, the profit is divided equally. This ruling is apparently based on a different version of the Gemara's text, according to which Rav Ḥaviva's statement refers to the second case in the mishna (*Kesef Mishne*).

Other early authorities rule that in the case where they did not declare in advance that they are not relinquishing their rights in the profit, if the property was enhanced on its own account, the profit is divided evenly. If the property was enhanced on account of their investment, the profit goes to them. If they declared their intentions in advance, the profit goes to them regardless (Ra'avad; Rosh; Rashbam). This ruling is in accordance with the standard version of the text (Rambam *Sefer Mishpatim*, *Hilkhot Naḥalot* 9:2; *Shulḥan Arukh*, *Ḥoshen Mishpat* 287:1).

A wife who enhanced the property of her deceased husband – הָאִשָּׁה שֶׁהִשְׁבִּיחָה אֶת הַנְּכָסִים: In the case of one who died and his wife inherited from him together with her sisters or her cousins (see *Sma*), and she enhanced the property, the profit is divided equally. If she said: See that which my husband left me; I am going to enhance it and profit from it, then if the property was enhanced due to her own investment, the profit is hers. If the property was enhanced on its own account, they divide the profit equally. This is the Rambam's ruling, in accordance with his version of the Gemara's text. Conversely, according to the Ra'avad and the Rosh, this applies only if she enhanced the property without declaring her intentions in advance. If she declared in advance that she is not waiving her rights to the profit, the profit is entirely hers regardless (Rambam *Sefer Mishpatim*, *Hilkhot Naḥalot* 9:3; *Shulḥan Arukh*, *Ḥoshen Mishpat* 287:1, and see *Even HaEzer* 95:7).

אוּדַיְינֵי – הַשָּׂכָר לָאֶמְצַע; וְהָא אוּדַיְינֵי דִּמְחֲמַת עַצְמוֹ הוּא! שָׁאנֵי אוּדַיְינֵי, דִּלְנְטִירוּתָא הוּא דַּעֲבִידָא, וַאֲפִילּוּ קְטַנִּים נַמִּי מָצוּ מְנַטְרִי לָהּ.

a mortar [*udaini*],[NL] which people pay to use,[H] **the rent** goes **to the middle? But isn't** the profit accruing from **a mortar** considered profit accruing **on his,** i.e., the adult son's, **own account,** as the adult son must supervise its operation, and there is no outlay from the property? The Gemara dismisses this objection: **A mortar is different, as for** its **typical use** it can suffice **with supervision,**[N] **and even minors are able to supervise its** use. Since the adults do not contribute anything more than the minors, they cannot demand a greater share of the profits.

״אָמְרוּ: רְאוּ מַה שֶּׁהִנִּיחַ אַבָּא, הֲרֵי אָנוּ עוֹשִׂין וְאוֹכְלִין – הִשְׁבִּיחוּ לְעַצְמָן״. רַב סָפְרָא שְׁבַק אֲבוּהּ זוּזֵי, שְׁקַלִינְהוּ, עֲבַד בְּהוּ עִיסְקָא; אֲתוּ אַחֵי תְּבָעוּהוּ בְּדִינָא קַמֵּיהּ דְּרָבָא, אֲמַר לְהוּ: רַב סָפְרָא גַּבְרָא רַבָּה הוּא, לָא שָׁבֵיק גִּירְסֵיהּ וְטָרַח לְאַחֲרִינֵי.

§ The mishna teaches: If the adult sons **said** from the outset: **See that which** our **father left** behind; **we are** going to **engage** in business with our share of the property **and profit** from it, then **they enhanced** the property **for themselves.** The Gemara relates: **Rav Safra's father left** him **dinars.** Rav Safra **took them** and **entered** into **a business venture with them.**[N] **His brothers came** and **charged him in** a court of **law before Rava,** claiming their share of the profits. Rava **said to them: Rav Safra is a great man;**[H] **he does not abandon his studies and toil for others.** It is therefore clear that if he invested the money, it was for his own profit, even if he did not explicitly declare so at the outset.

״הָאִשָּׁה שֶׁהִשְׁבִּיחָה אֶת הַנְּכָסִים – הִשְׁבִּיחָה לָאֶמְצַע״. אִשָּׁה בְּנִכְסֵי יַתְמֵי מַאי עֲבִידְתָּהּ? אֲמַר רַבִּי יִרְמְיָה: בְּאִשָּׁה יוֹרֶשֶׁת.

§ The mishna teaches: With regard to **a wife who enhanced the property** of her deceased husband, **she enhanced** it so that the profit goes **to the middle.** The Gemara asks: **What is** the deceased's **wife doing with the orphans' property?** What rights does she have to the property? **Rav Yirmeya said:** The mishna is referring **to a wife** who is **an heiress,** e.g., if she were the daughter of her husband's brother, and both brothers died without leaving sons, in which case she inherits in her father's stead.

פְּשִׁיטָא! מַהוּ דְּתֵימָא: כֵּיוָן דְּלָאו דַּרְכָּהּ לְמִטְרַח, אַף עַל גַּב דְּלָא פָּרֵישׁ – כְּמוֹ דְּפָרֵישׁ דָּמֵי, קָמַשְׁמַע לַן.

The Gemara asks: Isn't it **obvious** that the *halakha* in this case is the same as with regard to any other heir? The Gemara replies: It is necessary to state this, **lest you say** that **since it is not** a woman's **way to toil** to enhance property, then **even though she did not expressly state** that she is toiling for herself, **it is considered as though** she **had expressly stated** this. The mishna **teaches us** that only if she expressly stated this do the profits accrue to her.

״וְאִם אָמְרָה: רְאוּ מַה שֶּׁהִנִּיחַ לִי בַּעְלִי, הֲרֵינִי עוֹשָׂה וְאוֹכֶלֶת – הִשְׁבִּיחָה לְעַצְמָהּ״. פְּשִׁיטָא! מַהוּ דְּתֵימָא: כֵּיוָן דְּשְׁבִיחָא לָהּ מִילְּתָא, דְּאָמְרִי: קָא טָרְחָא קַמֵּי יַתְמֵי – אַחוּלֵי אַחְלָה, קָא מַשְׁמַע לַן.

The mishna teaches: **And if she said: See that which my husband left me;**[N] **I am** going to **engage** in business with my share **and profit** from it, then **she enhanced** the property **for herself.** The Gemara asks: Isn't this **obvious?** The Gemara explains: It is necessary to state this, **lest you say** that **since** it **is praiseworthy for her** to enhance the property on behalf of the orphans, as people will **say:** See how **she toils for the orphans, she relinquishes** her right to the profits and they should divide them equally. The mishna **teaches us** that this is not the case.

NOTES

Mortar [*udaini*] – אוּדַיְינֵי: The commentaries disagree as to the meaning of the word *udaini*. The Rashbam and Rabbeinu Gershom Meor HaGola define it as a cistern cover, and explain that the Gemara is referring to a cistern that is rented to others from which to draw water. *Tosafot* and the Ramah explain that it is a kind of raised seat erected in the fields in order to keep watch over them. Rabbeinu Ḥananel and Rabbi Avraham *Av Beit Din* explain that it is a mortar and pestle.

As for its typical use it can suffice with supervision – דִּלְנְטִירוּתָא הוּא דַּעֲבִידָא: According to Rabbeinu Ḥananel, the mortar requires supervision to ensure that it does not break or get stolen. According to those who explain *udaini* as a cistern, it requires safeguarding so that no one takes water without payment (Rashbam), or so that dirt does not enter and muddy the water (Rabbeinu Gershom Meor HaGola). According to *Tosafot*, who say that it is a raised seat, it is clear that safeguarding the fields is its entire purpose. The Rashba writes that with regard to work that can be done by minors, the Sages made no further distinctions by age, and even if the brothers were only infants they receive a share of the profits.

Entered into a business venture with them – עֲבַד בְּהוּ עִיסְקָא: Rav Safra entered into partnership with another, with Rav Safra investing the money and his partner managing the business, and afterward they split the profits. This is considered enhancement on account of the property, since he did not need to exert himself further once he had arranged the partnership (Rashbam).

That which my husband left me – מַה שֶּׁהִנִּיחַ לִי בַּעְלִי: The Rashbam explains that although the previous clause of the mishna discusses an heiress, this clause discusses a widow whose husband did not leave sufficient property to cover the value of her marriage contract. As long as she declines to receive sustenance from her husband's estate, her earnings do not belong to the orphans, and therefore if she declared in advance that she intends to profit by enhancing the property, the profits belong to her. Many commentaries disagree with this explanation, as in that case the property which she enhanced belongs not to her but to the orphans, and while she has a claim upon the property, she does not have any actual ownership thereof.

LANGUAGE

Mortar [*udaini*] – אוּדַיְינֵי: Several different versions of this word exist, and there are also many different interpretations as to its meaning. Some say that it is related to the Aramaic *udna*, meaning handle or ear, and that in this context it refers to a vessel or a lid with a handle.

HALAKHA

A mortar which people pay to use, etc. – אוּדַיְינֵי וכו׳: If the adult brothers enhanced the property in a manner that the minors were also capable of performing, e.g., they rented out an item that requires only supervision of its use, and they did not declare in advance that they wish to invest their efforts only on their own account, the profit is divided among all the brothers equally. This applies even if the adult brothers toiled personally. This is the *halakha* even if the particular minors in question were incapable of these actions, as long as other minors are capable of them (*Sma*). This ruling is in accordance with the Gemara's conclusion (*Shulḥan Arukh*, *Ḥoshen Mishpat* 287:1).

Rav Safra is a great man, etc. – רַב סָפְרָא גַּבְרָא רַבָּה הוּא וכו׳: In a case where one brother took money from the estate and invested it in a business venture, if he was a great Torah scholar who does not set aside his Torah study for even an hour, the profit accrues solely to him. The reason for this is that it is clearly not his practice to set aside his Torah study and engage in business for his brothers' profit, and therefore it is considered as if he had explicitly stated so at the outset. This applies with regard to Torah scholars even nowadays (Rambam *Sefer Shofetim*, *Hilkhot Naḥalot* 9:5; *Shulḥan Arukh*, *Ḥoshen Mishpat* 287:2).

אָמַר רַבִּי חֲנִינָא: הַמַּשִּׂיא אִשָּׁה לִבְנוֹ גָּדוֹל בְּבַיִת – קְנָאוֹ. וְדַוְקָא גָּדוֹל, וְדַוְקָא בְּתוּלָה, וְדַוְקָא אִשְׁתּוֹ רִאשׁוֹנָה, וְדַוְקָא שֶׁהִשִּׂיאוֹ רִאשׁוֹן.

Rabbi Ḥanina says: In the case of **one who marries a woman to his eldest son**[H] and arranges the wedding feast **in a house** that he designated for the purpose of the wedding canopy and the wedding feast, the son **acquires** the house as a gift. The Gemara notes: **And** this is the *halakha* **specifically** in the case of the **eldest** son, **and specifically** if he is marrying **a virgin, and specifically** when this woman is **his first wife, and specifically when** the father **married him off first** among his sons. When all these conditions exist, it is presumed that the father has a particular fondness toward the son, due to which he gave him the house.

פְּשִׁיטָא, יִיחֵד לוֹ אָבִיו בַּיִת וַעֲלִיָּיה – בַּיִת קָנָה, עֲלִיָּיה לֹא קָנָה; בַּיִת וְאַכְסַדְרָה, מַהוּ? שְׁנֵי בָתִּים זֶה לִפְנִים מִזֶּה, מַהוּ? תֵּיקוּ.

The Gemara clarifies the details of this *halakha*: It is **obvious** that if **his father designated a house for** the son's nuptials[H] **and** there is **an upper story** above the house, the son **acquired the house,** but **he did not acquire the upper story.** If he designated **a house** for the son, **and** there is **a portico** [*ve'akhsadra*][L] in front of the house, **what is the** *halakha*? If there were **two houses, one within the other,**[N] and the inner one was designated for the son's nuptials, **what is the** *halakha*? The Gemara concludes: These questions **shall stand** unresolved.

מֵיתִיבִי: יִיחֵד לוֹ אָבִיו בַּיִת וּכְלֵי בַיִת – כְּלֵי בַיִת קָנָה, בַּיִת לֹא קָנָה! אָמַר רַבִּי יִרְמְיָה: כְּגוֹן שֶׁהָיָה אוֹצָרוֹ שֶׁל אָבִיו מוּנָּח שָׁם. נְהַרְדָּעֵי אָמְרִי: אֲפִילּוּ שׁוֹבְכָא דְיוֹנֵי. רַב יְהוּדָה וְרַב פַּפֵּי אָמְרִי: אֲפִילּוּ עֲצִיצָא דְהַרְסְנָא. מָר זוּטְרָא אַנְסְבֵיהּ לִבְרֵיהּ, וּתְלָא לֵיהּ סַנְדְּלָא. רַב אָשֵׁי נַסְבֵיהּ לִבְרֵיהּ, וּתְלָא לֵיהּ אַשִּׁישָׁא דְמִשְׁחָא.

The Gemara **raises an objection** from a *baraita*: If **his father designated a house and furniture**[H] **for his** son's nuptials, the son **acquired the furniture,** but **he did not acquire the house. Rabbi Yirmeya says:** This is referring to a case **where his father's storeroom was placed there.** It is clear that just as his father did not intend to give him the storeroom, neither did he intend to give him the house. The Sages **of Neharde'a say: Even** if there is only **a dovecote**[B] in the house that belongs to the father, the son does not acquire the house. **Rav Yehuda and Rav Pappi say: Even** if there is only **a pot** [*atzitza*][L] **of small fried fish,**[B] the son does not acquire the house. **Mar Zutra married off his son, and hung a sandal** in the house, to indicate that he did not intend to give the house as a gift. **Rav Ashi married off his son, and hung a jug** [*ashisha*][L] **of oil** in the house.

אָמַר מָר זוּטְרָא: הָנֵי תְּלָת מִילֵּי שַׁוְינְהוּ רַבָּנַן כְּהִלְכְתָא בְּלָא טַעְמָא: חֲדָא – הָא; אִידָךְ – דְּאָמַר רַב יְהוּדָה אָמַר שְׁמוּאֵל: הַכּוֹתֵב כׇּל נְכָסָיו לְאִשְׁתּוֹ – לֹא עֲשָׂאָהּ אֶלָּא אַפּוֹטְרוֹפָּא; אִידָךְ – דְּאָמַר רַב: "מָנֶה לִי בְּיָדְךָ, תְּנֵהוּ לִפְלוֹנִי", בְּמַעֲמַד שְׁלׇשְׁתָּן – קָנָה.

Mar Zutra says: These three matters were instituted by the Sages as a *halakha* without any explanation of their process, i.e., they instituted these enactments despite the fact that the mechanism by which they function is unclear: **One** is **this** *halakha* with regard to the son acquiring the house designated for his nuptials. **Another** is that **which Rav Yehuda says** that **Shmuel says: One who writes** a deed granting **all of his property to his wife**[H] **renders her only a steward** of his property, i.e., he intends only to put her in charge of the property and she does not acquire it. **Another** is that **which Rav says:** With regard to one who says to another: **I have one hundred dinars in your possession; give it to so-and-so,** if this occurred **in the presence of** all **three parties,**[H] that third person **acquires** it, without need of witnesses or a formal act of acquisition.

LANGUAGE

Portico [*akhsadra*] – אַכְסַדְרָה: From the Greek ἐξέδρα, *exedra*, or the Latin exedra, meaning an entrance room or sitting room.

Pot [*atzitza*] – עֲצִיצָא: Similar to the Arabic اصيص, *'aṣīṣ*, which has the same meaning. Apparently the word is derived from the Hebrew term *etz*, which means tree, and refers to the pot's use as a receptacle for potted trees and plants.

Jug [*ashisha*] – אַשִּׁישָׁא: In talmudic Aramaic, this refers to a kind of drinking vessel, a type of vial with a narrow neck.

NOTES

Two houses, one within the other – שְׁנֵי בָתִּים זֶה לִפְנִים מִזֶּה: The wedding was held in the inner house. Since the only way to enter and exit the inner house is through the outer house, the outer house might be considered ancillary to the inner house (Rid), or it might be considered as though it were also used for the wedding (Rabbeinu Gershom Meor HaGola; Rabbi Yitzḥak Karkusha). Nevertheless, it is possible that the son acquires only that which was specifically designated for the wedding.

BACKGROUND

Dovecote – שׁוֹבְכָא דְיוֹנֵי:

Dovecote built into a house

A pot [*atzitza*] of small fried fish – עֲצִיצָא דְהַרְסְנָא: It appears from various sources that these pots were usually not finely worked. They were generally fashioned from clay and only partially fired in the kiln, and they were occasionally fashioned even from wood. They were used for purposes that required a mere receptacle rather than highly refined work, mainly as planters or chamber pots, or, as in the reference here, for storing certain foodstuffs.

HALAKHA

One who marries a woman to his eldest son, etc. – הַמַּשִּׂיא אִשָּׁה לִבְנוֹ גָּדוֹל וכו׳: If one marries his eldest son to a virgin in a house, the son acquires the house. This applies specifically to the first son the father is marrying off, when this is the son's first marriage, and only if the father did not leave any items in the house. If the father left any items in the house, even a single pot, the son does not acquire the house, in accordance with the opinion of Rav Pappi. Some state that the son acquires the house only if the father has another house to live in (Rema, citing *Tur*). The Rambam writes that the Sages based this ruling on an assessment of the father's state of mind, understanding that under these circumstances, the father, out of his great joy and his love for his son, decided to transfer ownership of the house to him. This ruling applies even nowadays (Rambam *Sefer Kinyan, Hilkhot Zekhiya UMattana* 6:15; *Shulḥan Arukh, Even HaEzer* 59:1 and *Beit Shmuel* there).

If his father designated a house for the son's nuptials, etc. – יִיחֵד לוֹ אָבִיו בַּיִת וכו׳: If one designated a house for his son's nuptials and the house had an upper story, the son acquired the house but not the upper story. Similarly, if he designated a house with a portico, the son acquired the house but not the portico. If he designated two houses, one within the other, the son acquired only the house in which the wedding was held. The reason for this is that these cases stand unresolved, and as with all cases in the Talmud that stand unresolved, the court does not remove assets that are in someone's possession (Rambam *Sefer Kinyan, Hilkhot Zekhiya UMattana* 6:16; *Shulḥan Arukh, Even HaEzer* 59:3–4).

A house and furniture – בַּיִת וּכְלֵי בַיִת: If one designated a house and furniture for his son's nuptials, the son acquires the furniture even if his father left an item in the house for himself or had a storeroom there. He does not acquire the house itself, in accordance with the *baraita* as interpreted by Rabbi Yirmeya (Rambam *Sefer Kinyan, Hilkhot Zekhiya UMattana* 6:15; *Shulḥan Arukh, Even HaEzer* 59:2).

One who writes a deed granting all of his property to his wife – הַכּוֹתֵב כׇּל נְכָסָיו לְאִשְׁתּוֹ: If a person on his deathbed writes a deed granting all his property to his wife, he has merely rendered her a steward in charge of the property for his heirs. The Rambam maintains that this is the *halakha* even if an act of acquisition was performed. Other authorities disagree. If he left any part of his property for his heirs, whether land or movable property, the wife acquires the property that he gave her (Rambam *Sefer Kinyan, Hilkhot Zekhiya UMattana* 6:4; *Shulḥan Arukh, Even HaEzer* 107:1 and *Ḥoshen Mishpat* 246:7, 12).

In the presence of all three parties – בְּמַעֲמַד שְׁלׇשְׁתָּן: If three people were standing together, and one said to another of the three: I have one hundred dinars in your possession; give it to the third person standing here with us, the third person acquires the money thereby and the first party cannot renege (Rambam *Sefer Kinyan, Hilkhot Zekhiya UMattana* 3:3 and *Hilkhot Mekhira* 6:8; *Shulḥan Arukh, Ḥoshen Mishpat* 66:19–20, 126:1).

מתני׳ אַחִין הַשּׁוּתָּפִין שֶׁנָּפַל אֶחָד מֵהֶן לְאוּמָּנוּת – נָפַל לָאֶמְצַע; חָלָה וְנִתְרַפֵּא – נִתְרַפֵּא מִשֶּׁל עַצְמוֹ.

MISHNA With regard to **brothers who were** also **partners,** and it occurred **that one of them was summoned to** public **service,**[BH] which is assessed per family, **he was summoned from the middle,** i.e., the profits or expenses of his service are divided among them. If one of the brothers **became sick and sought treatment, the** cost of the **treatment is** paid **from his own** resources.[N]

גמ׳ תָּנָא: הַאי אוּמָּנוּת – לְאוּמָּנוּת הַמֶּלֶךְ. תָּנוּ רַבָּנַן: אֶחָד מִן הָאַחִין שֶׁמִּינּוּהוּ גַּבַּאי אוֹ פּוֹלְמוֹסְטוֹס, אִם מֵחֲמַת הָאַחִין – לָאַחִין, אִם מֵחֲמַת עַצְמוֹ – לְעַצְמוֹ.

GEMARA The Sages **taught: This service** mentioned in the mishna is referring **to** forced **imperial service,** but if one of the brothers engaged in a trade of his own volition, the profits are his alone. **The Sages taught** in a *baraita* (*Tosefta* 10:5): In the case of **one of the brothers who was appointed as a tax collector**[B] **or a military commander** [***polmustos***],[L] a position with the potential for profit, **if** he was appointed **on account of** all **the brothers,**[B] as the procedure was to impress a representative from each family for this purpose, any profit accrues **to** all **the brothers. If** he was appointed **on account of himself,**[N] the profit accrues **to himself.**

אִם מֵחֲמַת אַחִין לָאַחִין, פְּשִׁיטָא! לָא צְרִיכָא, דְּחָרִיף טְפֵי. מַהוּ דְּתֵימָא: חוּרְפֵּיהּ גָּרֵים לֵיהּ, קָא מַשְׁמַע לָן.

The Gemara asks: Isn't it **obvious** that **if** he was appointed **on account of** all **the brothers,** then the profit accrues **to** all **the brothers?** The Gemara responds: **No,** it is **necessary** to state this *halakha* in a case **where** the brother appointed was **sharper,** i.e., more capable, than the other brothers. **Lest you say** that **his sharpness caused him** to be selected for the position, and he should receive all the profits, the *baraita* **teaches us** that his talent notwithstanding, since he was selected as a representative of the family, the profit accrues to all the brothers.

תָּנוּ רַבָּנַן: אֶחָד מִן הָאַחִין שֶׁנָּטַל מָאתַיִם זוּז לִלְמוֹד תּוֹרָה אוֹ לִלְמוֹד אוּמָּנוּת, יְכוֹלִין הָאַחִין לוֹמַר לוֹ: אִם אַתָּה אֶצְלֵנוּ – יֵשׁ לְךָ מְזוֹנוֹת, אִם אֵין אַתָּה אֶצְלֵנוּ – אֵין לְךָ מְזוֹנוֹת.

The Sages taught: With regard to **one of the brothers, who took two hundred dinars**[N] from the common inheritance to support himself when he went to another place **to study Torah**[H] **or to learn a trade, the brothers can say to him: If you are** here **with us, you are entitled to sustenance** along with us. **If you are not** here **with us, you are not entitled to sustenance.**

וְלֵיתְבוּ לֵיהּ כׇּל הֵיכָא דְּאִיתֵיהּ! מְסַיַּיע לֵיהּ לְרַב הוּנָא, דְּאָמַר רַב הוּנָא: בִּרְכַּת הַבַּיִת בְּרוּבָּהּ. וְלֵיתְבוּ לֵיהּ לְפִי בִּרְכַּת הַבַּיִת! הָכִי נַמִּי.

The Gemara asks: **But shouldn't they give him** his sustenance **wherever he is?** The Gemara answers: This ruling **supports** the opinion **of Rav Huna, as Rav Huna says: The blessing of the house is in its abundance.** This means that the extent to which blessing permeates a home is proportionate to the number of people who live there, and when many people live together the expenses per capita decrease. The Gemara asks: **But shouldn't they give him** his sustenance **according to the blessing of the house,** i.e., the expenses he would incur even if he were in the house? The Gemara responds: **Indeed,** they are required to provide for those expenses that he would incur in any event.

BACKGROUND

That one of them was summoned to public service – שֶׁנָּפַל אֶחָד מֵהֶן לְאוּמָּנוּת: It was the practice in the Roman Empire in talmudic times, and to some extent also the practice in the Persian Empire, to press people into imperial service. Sometimes this was forced labor, e.g., building roads or other similar forms of labor, either for a small wage or for no wage at all. They would also appoint people to public office against their will. Some of these positions required a significant investment of time, or were undesirable because of ethical or other considerations, but they could also be lucrative.

Tax collector – גַּבַּאי: This position was usually an appointed one, and the tax collector was expected to submit a certain sum to the government. It was common for tax collectors to assess the tax shares in an unequitable manner, and they were generally considered wicked.

If he was appointed on account of the brothers – אִם מֵחֲמַת הָאַחִין: The government authorities would appoint one person from a certain family, or sometimes from every family in turn, to fill the office. Sometimes the authorities would choose a capable member of the family, but the appointment was dependent primarily upon one's family affiliation rather than upon one's character.

NOTES

Became sick and sought treatment, the treatment is paid from his own resources – חָלָה וְנִתְרַפֵּא, נִתְרַפֵּא מִשֶּׁל עַצְמוֹ: According to the *Tosefta* (10:6) this refers only to treatment that is of fixed cost, whereas ongoing treatment for a chronic condition is considered as sustenance, and the cost is paid from the common inheritance (*Tosafot*).

On account of himself – מֵחֲמַת עַצְמוֹ: The brother was appointed tax collector because of his abilities, and therefore the profit accrues to him (Rabbeinu Gershom Meor HaGola).

Who took two hundred dinars, etc. – שֶׁנָּטַל מָאתַיִם זוּז וכו׳: He took the money claiming that he is entitled to sustenance from the common inheritance, but his brothers contend that this sum should be deducted from his portion of the inheritance (Rabbi Avraham *Av Beit Din*; Ramah).

LANGUAGE

Military commander [*polmustos*] – פּוֹלְמוֹסְטוֹס: From the Greek πολεμιστής, *polemistēs*, meaning a soldier or warrior.

HALAKHA

Brothers…that one of them was summoned to public service – אַחִין...שֶׁנָּפַל אֶחָד מֵהֶן לְאוּמָּנוּת: In the case of brothers who inherited their father's estate and are still holding the property in partnership, and the authorities appointed one of them to a position handling government finances, the *halakha* is as follows: If he was appointed due to his father's merit, even if he was himself worthy of the appointment, any profit accruing from the appointment is divided among the brothers. The same is true with regard to any loss that ensued, e.g., if the authorities confiscated assets from him on account of the family's prosperity, the loss is divided between all of them. If his assets were confiscated on his own account, e.g., where he was wealthy independent of the inheritance, he sustains the loss on his own. Some authorities hold that the same principle applies with regard to any partnership and not only in the case of brothers (Rema, citing *Tur*). There are those who say that this principle applies only if he was appointed to the imperial service, but if he was appointed to any other position and he profited or lost thereby, any profit or loss accrues to him alone (Ri Migash; Ramban). The *Tur*, citing Rabbeinu Yona, says that even in the case of imperial service, the profit accrues to all the brothers only after he deducts the equivalent of his daily wages for each day he worked (Rambam *Sefer Mishpatim*, *Hilkhot Naḥalot* 9:6 and *Sefer Kinyan*, *Hilkhot Sheluḥin VeShutafin* 8:7; *Shulḥan Arukh*, *Ḥoshen Mishpat* 177:1).

One of the brothers who took…to study Torah – אֶחָד מִן הָאַחִין שֶׁנָּטַל...לִלְמוֹד תּוֹרָה: In the case of two partners, e.g., brothers who inherited their father's estate and are still holding the property in partnership, if one of them wishes to go elsewhere in order to study Torah or learn a trade, they assess the expenses he would incur were he to remain at home and give him this amount, even if his actual expenses are greater. This ruling is in accordance with the *baraita* and the statement of Rav Huna (Rambam *Sefer Mishpatim*, *Hilkhot Naḥalot* 9:11, and see *Sefer Nashim*, *Hilkhot Ishut* 18:4; *Shulḥan Arukh*, *Ḥoshen Mishpat* 177:4 and *Sma* there, and see *Even HaEzer* 94:6).

"חָלָה וְנִתְרַפֵּא – נִתְרַפֵּא מִשֶּׁל עַצְמוֹ". שְׁלַח רָבִין מִשְּׁמֵיהּ דְּרַבִּי אֶלְעָא: לֹא שָׁנוּ אֶלָּא שֶׁחָלָה בִּפְשִׁיעָה, אֲבָל בְּאוֹנֶס – נִתְרַפֵּא מִן הָאֶמְצַע. הֵיכִי דָּמֵי בִּפְשִׁיעָה? כִּדְרַבִּי חֲנִינָא, דְּאָמַר רַבִּי חֲנִינָא: הַכֹּל בִּידֵי שָׁמַיִם חוּץ מִצִּנִּים פַּחִים, שֶׁנֶּאֱמַר: "צִנִּים פַּחִים בְּדֶרֶךְ עִקֵּשׁ שׁוֹמֵר נַפְשׁוֹ יִרְחַק מֵהֶם".

§ The mishna teaches: If one of the brothers **became sick and sought treatment,**[H] the cost of the **treatment is paid from his own** resources. **Ravin sent** a ruling **in the name of Rabbi Ela: They taught** this **only** in a case **where he became ill through negligence. But** if he became ill **through circumstances beyond his control,** the cost of **the treatment is paid from the middle,**[N] i.e., from the common inheritance. The Gemara asks: **What are the circumstances** in which it is considered **negligence?** This is **in accordance with** the statement **of Rabbi Ḥanina, as Rabbi Ḥanina says: All** occurrences that befall man **are in the hand of Heaven**[N] **except for colds** and **obstacles** [*paḥim*],[N] from which one is able to protect himself, **as it is stated: "Colds and snares are on the path of the crooked; he who guards his soul shall keep far from them"** (Proverbs 22:5).

מתני׳ הָאַחִין שֶׁעָשׂוּ מִקְצָתָן שׁוֹשְׁבִינוּת בְּחַיֵּי הָאָב, חָזְרָה שׁוֹשְׁבִינוּת – חָזְרָה לָאֶמְצַע, שֶׁהַשּׁוֹשְׁבִינוּת נִגְבֵּית בְּבֵית דִּין. אֲבָל הַשּׁוֹלֵחַ לַחֲבֵירוֹ כַּדֵּי יַיִן וְכַדֵּי שֶׁמֶן – אֵין נִגְבִּין בְּבֵית דִּין, מִפְּנֵי שֶׁהֵן גְּמִילוּת חֲסָדִים.

MISHNA It was common practice for friends of a groom to give him gifts in order to help cover the expenses of the wedding feast. These gifts are known as gifts of groomsmen, and would be reciprocated in turn. While the groom and the groomsman were at times the recipient and the giver of the gifts, respectively, the gifts were at times provided by the father of the groomsman and received by the father of the groom. In the case of **brothers, some of whom brought gifts of groomsmen**[HB] **in their father's lifetime,** which were provided by their father, when **the gifts of groomsmen are reciprocated** after the father's death, when one of the brothers gets married, **they are reciprocated to the middle,** i.e., the gift is divided among the brothers. This is **because gifts of groomsmen are** a legal debt owed to the father, **collectible in court.**[NH] **But** with regard to **one who sends his friend jugs of wine**[N] **or jugs of oil,**[H] a reciprocal gift **is not collectible in court, because they are** considered **acts of kindness.**

NOTES

If he became ill through circumstances beyond his control the treatment is from the middle – בְּאוֹנֶס נִתְרַפֵּא מִן הָאֶמְצַע: Rabbi Avraham *Av Beit Din* cites an opinion that this principle also applies with regard to costs incurred due to any circumstances beyond his control, but concludes that it applies only in the case of illness. Some of the early commentaries explain that since anyone is liable to become ill the brothers forgive each other the expenses involved (*Tosafot Yeshanim*). Other commentaries maintain that this ruling applies only to one who became sick while serving in the imperial service (Rid).

All occurrences are in the hand of Heaven – הַכֹּל בִּידֵי שָׁמַיִם: The Gemara does not mean that a person cannot cause harm to himself intentionally, as this refers only to incidents that happen to a person against his will (*Tosafot*).

Except for colds and obstacles [*paḥim*] – חוּץ מִצִּנִּים פַּחִים: The Rashbam's version of the text reads: All occurrences that befall man are in the hand of Heaven except for a cold. Rabbeinu Gershom Meor HaGola explains that the word *paḥim* is similar to the word *yafuaḥ*, which means to blow, i.e., one can protect himself from drafts, which cause a chill. The commentaries add that this also applies to other types of illnesses that a person brings upon himself, e.g., by eating harmful foods (Rambam's Commentary on the Mishna; Ritva).

Collectible in court – נִגְבֵּית בְּבֵית דִּין: The gift was provided by the father. Therefore, when it is reciprocated it is considered repayment of a debt to the father and it becomes part of the common inheritance, rather than being considered a gift to the brother to whom it was sent (Rashbam).

Jugs of wine, etc. – כַּדֵּי יַיִן וכו׳: The Rashbam explains that these gifts were sent not for the friend's wedding but for a different feast. Therefore the *halakhot* governing gifts of groomsmen do not apply. Alternatively, the Rashbam suggests that these *halakhot* apply only to gifts of groomsmen that are brought when the friends of the groom rejoice with him. In this case, since the gifts were sent to the groom and the friend did not personally participate in the wedding feast, they are not considered a loan. Other commentaries explain that the *halakhot* governing gifts of groomsmen apply only to money that is sent to defray the wedding expenses, but not to foodstuffs (Rambam; Rabbeinu Yona).

BACKGROUND

Gifts of groomsmen [*shushevinut*] – שׁוֹשְׁבִינוּת: This word is apparently derived from the Assyrian *shusapino* or *shusabino*, meaning friend and companion of the betrothed man. It was the custom of the time for the friends of the betrothed man to rejoice with him, bringing gifts and banquet provisions for their friend's wedding, and these gifts were reciprocated at the time of the friends' own weddings. In the course of time these gifts acquired the status of a formal custom with set guidelines, and they were usually considered a kind of loan, which could be claimed in court if they were not reciprocated. Although similar to standard loans, they differed in several regards: They were reciprocated only at the time of the friend's wedding, it was not prohibited to reciprocate with a larger gift than the one received, and the Sabbatical Year did not cancel the debt.

HALAKHA

If one of the brothers became sick and sought treatment, etc. – חָלָה וְנִתְרַפֵּא וכו׳: If one of the brothers became sick, his treatment is paid for from his own resources, as stated by the mishna. This *halakha* applies only if he became sick due to negligence, e.g., if he failed to protect himself from extreme weather while outdoors, and only if the treatment is of fixed cost, as stated in the *Tosefta* (10:6). If the treatment does not have a fixed cost, or if he became sick through circumstances beyond his control, his treatment is paid for from the common inheritance. The Rema writes that according to some authorities, the *halakha* is the opposite: If he became sick due to negligence, in any event his treatment is paid for from the common inheritance. If he became sick through circumstances beyond his control, then only if the treatment has a fixed cost is it paid for from the common inheritance. According to the *Shakh* the *halakha* is in accordance with the first opinion, which is the opinion cited in the *Shulḥan Arukh* (Rambam *Sefer Kinyan*, *Hilkhot Sheluḥin VeShutafin* 8:7; *Shulḥan Arukh*, *Ḥoshen Mishpat* 177:2).

Brothers some of whom brought gifts of groomsmen, etc. – הָאַחִין שֶׁעָשׂוּ מִקְצָתָן שׁוֹשְׁבִינוּת וכו׳: If a father sent gifts of groomsmen for another's wedding in the name of one of his sons, when the gifts are reciprocated after the father's death at the son's wedding, they belong solely to that son. If the father sent them in the name of his sons without mentioning a specific son, when they are reciprocated, the gifts are divided among the brothers. This is in accordance with the opinion of Rabbi Asi. The friend to whom the original gifts of groomsmen were sent is not obligated to reciprocate fully until all the brothers wed, since the gifts of groomsmen were sent in the name of all of them. When each brother weds, the friend reciprocates that brother's share, and the gift is divided among all the brothers (Rambam *Sefer Mishpatim*, *Hilkhot Naḥalot* 9:14; *Shulḥan Arukh*, *Ḥoshen Mishpat* 286:4–5).

Because gifts of groomsmen are a legal debt collectible in court – שֶׁהַשּׁוֹשְׁבִינוּת נִגְבֵּית בְּבֵית דִּין: Gifts of groomsmen that one sends for his friend's wedding feast are not completely considered gifts, as they are sent under the expectation that they will be reciprocated in full at the time of one's own wedding. Therefore, if the giver of the gift marries and the gift is not reciprocated, he can sue for it in court. Nowadays it is not the custom to claim these gifts in court (Rambam *Sefer Kinyan*, *Hilkhot Zekhiya UMattana* 7:2, 13; *Shulḥan Arukh*, *Even HaEzer* 60:1).

One who sends his friend jugs of wine or jugs of oil, etc. – הַשּׁוֹלֵחַ לַחֲבֵירוֹ כַּדֵּי יַיִן וְכַדֵּי שֶׁמֶן וכו׳: If one sends jugs of wine, jugs of oil, or other foodstuffs as gifts of groomsmen, and the recipient does not reciprocate, one cannot sue for them in court, as they were sent as acts of kindness, and the *halakhot* governing gifts of groomsmen apply only to gifts of money. The Rashbam and the Ra'avad disagree and hold that these *halakhot* also apply to foodstuffs. According to these commentaries, the mishna and Gemara here are referring to gifts that were sent at a different time than that of the wedding, or to gifts that were sent at the time of a wedding where the giver of the gift did not personally attend the wedding feast (Rambam *Sefer Kinyan*, *Hilkhot Zekhiya UMattana* 7:15; *Tur*, *Even HaEzer* 60:1).

NOTES

If his father was sent – **נִשְׁתַּלְּחָה לְאָבִיו:** Although the gift was sent to one of the sons, it was sent primarily to honor the father (Ri Migash). Rabbeinu Gershom Meor HaGola explains that the gift was sent to the father in honor of his second marriage.

Here he sent gifts of groomsmen without specifying – **כָּאן בִּסְתָם:** The mishna is referring either to where the father did not specify which son should take the gifts to the groom, or to where he instructed one of the sons to take the gifts to the groom but did not state that he would be the one to receive the reciprocal gift (Rashbam).

If his father sent gifts of groomsmen on his behalf – **שָׁלַח לוֹ אָבִיו:** Literally translated, the *baraita* appears to be referring to gifts of groomsmen that the father sent to his son. The intent is that the father sent the gifts with his son (Rashbam; see Rabbeinu Yona).

With a man whose married brother died childless – **בְּיָבָם:** The Ritva notes that Shmuel does not disagree with the *halakha* stated by Rav Asi, since there is a *baraita* supporting Rav Asi's opinion. He is merely proposing an alternative explanation for the mishna.

Give me my groomsman – **תְּנוּ לִי שׁוֹשְׁבִינִי:** A gift of groomsmen is not an ordinary debt. It is repaid only to a specific individual, and only at the time of his wedding. This is because the purpose of the gifts of groomsmen is to enable the betrothed man to rejoice with his friends at his wedding (Rashbam). If the friend who originally brought the gift dies, the obligation to reciprocate is nullified.

גמ׳ וּרְמִינְהִי: שָׁלַח לוֹ אָבִיו שׁוֹשְׁבִינוּת, כְּשֶׁהִיא חוֹזֶרֶת – חוֹזֶרֶת לוֹ; נִשְׁתַּלְּחָה לְאָבִיו שׁוֹשְׁבִינוּת, כְּשֶׁהִיא חוֹזֶרֶת – חוֹזֶרֶת מִן הָאֶמְצַע! אָמַר רַבִּי אַסִּי אָמַר רַבִּי יוֹחָנָן: כִּי תְּנַן נַמִּי מַתְנִיתִין, נִשְׁתַּלְּחָה לְאָבִיו תְּנַן.

GEMARA **And** the Gemara **raises a contradiction** between the mishna's ruling that the gifts of groomsmen are reciprocated to the middle, and the first clause of a *baraita*: **If a father sent** his son with **gifts of groomsmen, when they are reciprocated** when that son gets married, **they are reciprocated to** that son. If **his father was sent**[N] **gifts of groomsmen**[H] for the wedding of one of his sons, **when they are reciprocated** from the father's estate, **they are reciprocated from the middle,** i.e., the cost of the gift is divided among the brothers. **Rabbi Asi says** that **Rabbi Yoḥanan says: When we learned the mishna as well, we learned** it as teaching the *halakha* with regard to gifts of groomsmen that **were sent to** the **father** for the wedding of one of his sons, not with regard to gifts of groomsmen sent by the father.

וְהָא ״אַחִין שֶׁעָשׂוּ מִקְצָתָן שׁוֹשְׁבִינוּת״ קָתָנֵי! תְּנֵי: ״לְמִקְצָתָן״. וְהָא ״חָזְרָה שׁוֹשְׁבִינוּת״ קָתָנֵי! הָכִי קָאָמַר: חָזְרָה לִגְבּוֹת – נִגְבֵּית מֵאֶמְצַע.

The Gemara objects: **But** the mishna **teaches** the *halakha* with regard to **brothers, some of whom brought gifts of groomsmen.** The Gemara responds: Emend the text of the mishna and **teach** it as saying: With regard to brothers, **to some of whom** gifts of groomsmen were brought. The Gemara objects: **But** the mishna explicitly **teaches** the *halakha* if **the gifts of groomsmen are reciprocated.** The Gemara responds: **This is** what the mishna **is saying: When it is collected** from the brothers **in return, it is collected from** the **middle.**

רַבִּי אַסִּי אָמַר, לָא קַשְׁיָא: כָּאן בִּסְתָם, כָּאן בִּמְפָרֵשׁ; כִּדְתַנְיָא: שָׁלַח לוֹ אָבִיו שׁוֹשְׁבִינוּת, כְּשֶׁהִיא חוֹזֶרֶת – חוֹזֶרֶת לוֹ; שָׁלַח אָבִיו שׁוֹשְׁבִינוּת סְתָם, כְּשֶׁהִיא חוֹזֶרֶת – חוֹזֶרֶת לָאֶמְצַע.

Rabbi Asi says: Even if the text of the mishna is not emended, it is **not difficult** and can be reconciled with the *baraita*. **Here** in the mishna it is referring to where the father sent the gifts of groomsmen **without specifying**[N] which son should be ascribed credit for bringing the gifts. **There** in the *baraita*, it is referring to **where** the father **specified** that the credit for the gifts of groomsmen should be ascribed to a specific son, who receives gifts in return, **as it is taught** in another *baraita*: If **his father sent gifts of groomsmen on his,** i.e., the son's, behalf,[N] then **when** the gift **is reciprocated, it is reciprocated to him,** i.e., to that specific son. If **his father sent gifts of groomsmen without specification,** then **when** the gift **is reciprocated, it is reciprocated to the middle.**

וּשְׁמוּאֵל אָמַר: הָכָא בְּיָבָם עָסְקִינַן, שֶׁאֵינוֹ נוֹטֵל בְּרָאוּי כִּבְמוּחְזָק.

And Shmuel says: Here in the mishna **we are dealing with a man whose married brother died childless** [*yavam*].[N] The son who brought the gifts of groomsmen died childless, his brother entered into levirate marriage with the widow, and the gifts of groomsmen were reciprocated at the wedding of the *yavam*. Although the *yavam* inherits the property of his brother, since the reciprocal gifts were not extant when his brother died, they do not belong solely to him; rather, they are divided among the brothers. This is because the *yavam* **does not take** in inheritance the property **due** the deceased **as** he does the property the deceased already **possessed.**

מִכְּלַל דְּאִידָךְ מְשַׁלֵּם? לֵימָא: ״תְּנוּ לִי שׁוֹשְׁבִינִי וְאֶשְׂמַח עִמּוֹ״!

The Gemara asks: Is it possible to conclude **by inference** from Shmuel's statement **that the other** side, i.e., a friend who had received gifts of groomsmen from the deceased, is obligated to **repay** the gifts of groomsmen he received from the deceased? Why should this be so? **Let him say: Give me my groomsman**[N] **and I will rejoice with him.** Since the one who gave him the gifts is deceased, he is not obligated to reciprocate.

מִי לָא תַּנְיָא: מָקוֹם שֶׁנָּהֲגוּ לְהַחֲזִיר קִדּוּשִׁין – מַחֲזִירִין, מָקוֹם שֶׁנָּהֲגוּ שֶׁלֹּא לְהַחֲזִיר – אֵין מַחֲזִירִין; וְאָמַר רַב יוֹסֵף בַּר אַבָּא אָמַר מָר עוּקְבָא אָמַר שְׁמוּאֵל: לֹא שָׁנוּ אֶלָּא שֶׁמֵּתָה הִיא, אֲבָל מֵת הוּא – אֵין מַחֲזִירִין, מַאי טַעְמָא? יְכוֹלָה הִיא שֶׁתֹּאמַר:

Isn't it taught in a *baraita* (*Tosefta, Pesaḥim* 3:1) with regard to similar circumstances: In **a place where** people **are accustomed to return the betrothal** money when the betrothed man or woman dies, **they return** it; in **a place where** people **are accustomed not to return it, they do not return** it. **And Rav Yosef bar Abba says** that **Mar Ukva says** that **Shmuel says: They taught** this **only** with regard to **when** the woman **dies,** in which case one follows the local custom. **But if** the man **dies,** all agree that **they do not return** the money. **What is the reason** for this? Since **she can say:**

HALAKHA

If his father was sent gifts of groomsmen – **נִשְׁתַּלְּחָה לְאָבִיו שׁוֹשְׁבִינוּת:** In the case of a father who married off his son and provided the son's wedding feast, and the son received gifts of groomsmen, when the gifts of groomsmen are reciprocated after the father's death, they are reciprocated from the common inheritance. This ruling is in accordance with the *baraita* cited by the Gemara, as interpreted by the Ri Migash. If the son provided for his own wedding feast, gifts of groomsmen that he gives are reciprocated from his share of the inheritance (Rambam *Sefer Mishpatim, Hilkhot Naḥalot* 9:13; *Shulḥan Arukh, Ḥoshen Mishpat* 286:4).

״תְּנוּ לִי בַּעְלִי וְאֶשְׂמַח עִמּוֹ״, הָכָא נַמִּי נֵימָא: ״תְּנוּ לִי שׁוֹשְׁבִינִי וְאֶשְׂמַח עִמּוֹ״!

Give me my husband and I will rejoice with him, i.e., it is not my fault that we are not getting married, she is not required to return the betrothal money. **Here too, let him say: Give me my groomsman and I will rejoice with him.**[H]

אָמַר רַב יוֹסֵף: הָכָא בְּמַאי עָסְקִינַן – כְּגוֹן שֶׁשָּׂמַח עִמּוֹ שִׁבְעָה יְמֵי מִשְׁתֶּה, וְלֹא הִסְפִּיק לְפוֹרְעוֹ עַד שֶׁמֵּת.

Rav Yosef said: With what are we dealing here? Shmuel's statement is referring to a case **where** the original recipient, in reciprocation, **rejoiced with** the brother who brought the gifts of groomsmen during the **seven days of** the wedding **feast, but did not suffice to repay him before** the brother **died.** Since it was the usual practice to send the gifts of groomsmen after the groomsman rejoiced with the betrothed man for seven days, he is obligated to reciprocate the gifts of groomsmen, and the *yavam* cannot claim them for himself.

לֵימָא: ״תְּנוּ לִי בַּעְלִי וְאֶשְׂמַח עִמּוֹ״ תַּנָּאֵי הִיא? דְּתַנְיָא: הַמְאָרֵס אֶת הָאִשָּׁה – בְּתוּלָה גּוֹבָה מָאתַיִם, וְאַלְמָנָה מָנֶה; מָקוֹם שֶׁנָּהֲגוּ לְהַחֲזִיר קִדּוּשִׁין – מַחֲזִירִין, מָקוֹם שֶׁנָּהֲגוּ שֶׁלֹּא לְהַחֲזִיר קִדּוּשִׁין – אֵין מַחֲזִירִין, דִּבְרֵי רַבִּי נָתָן. רַבִּי יְהוּדָה הַנָּשִׂיא אוֹמֵר, בֶּאֱמֶת אָמְרוּ: מָקוֹם שֶׁנָּהֲגוּ לְהַחֲזִיר – מַחֲזִירִין, מָקוֹם שֶׁנָּהֲגוּ שֶׁלֹּא לְהַחֲזִיר – אֵין מַחֲזִירִין.

The Gemara suggests: **Shall we say** that Shmuel's statement that a betrothed woman can claim: **Give me my husband and I will rejoice with him, is** a dispute between ***tanna'im*? As it is taught** in a *baraita*: With regard to **one who betrothed a woman**[H] and then he divorces her or dies, if she is **a virgin,** she **collects two hundred** dinars in payment of her marriage contract. **And** if she is **a widow,** she collects **one hundred dinars.** In **a place where** people **were accustomed to return the betrothal** money when the betrothed man or woman died, **they return** it. In **a place where** people **were accustomed not to return the betrothal** money, **they do not return** it. This is **the statement of Rabbi Natan. Rabbi Yehuda HaNasi says: Actually they said:** In **a place where** people **were accustomed to return it, they return** it; in **a place where** people **were accustomed not to return** it, **they do not return** it.

רַבִּי יְהוּדָה הַנָּשִׂיא הַיְינוּ תַּנָּא קַמָּא! אֶלָּא לָאו, ״תְּנוּ לִי בַּעְלִי וְאֶשְׂמַח עִמּוֹ״ אִיכָּא בֵּינַיְיהוּ,

The Gemara clarifies: The opinion of **Rabbi Yehuda HaNasi is** identical to the opinion of **the first *tanna*,** i.e., Rabbi Natan. **Rather, is it not** that the difference **between them** concerns the validity of the claim: **Give me my husband and I will rejoice with him?**

וְחַסּוּרֵי מִיחַסְּרָא וְהָכִי קָתָנֵי: הַמְאָרֵס אֶת הָאִשָּׁה – בְּתוּלָה גּוֹבָה מָאתַיִם, וְאַלְמָנָה מָנֶה; בַּמֶּה דְּבָרִים אֲמוּרִים – דַּהֲדַר בֵּיהּ אִיהוּ. אֲבָל מֵתָה, מָקוֹם שֶׁנָּהֲגוּ לְהַחֲזִיר – מַחֲזִירִין, מָקוֹם שֶׁנָּהֲגוּ שֶׁלֹּא לְהַחֲזִיר – אֵין מַחֲזִירִין; וְדַוְקָא שֶׁמֵּתָה הִיא, אֲבָל מֵת הוּא – אֵין מַחֲזִירִין, מַאי טַעְמָא? יְכוֹלָה הִיא שֶׁתֹּאמַר: ״תְּנוּ לִי בַּעְלִי וְאֶשְׂמַח עִמּוֹ״.

And the statement in the *baraita* **is incomplete and this** is what **it is teaching:** With regard to **one who betrothed a woman** and then the betrothal is terminated, if she is **a virgin,** she **collects two hundred** dinars in payment of her marriage contract, **and** if she is **a widow,** she collects **one hundred dinars. In what case is this statement said?** It is said **where he retracted,** i.e., he died or divorced her. **But** with regard to where **she died,** the *halakha* is as follows: In **a place where** people **were accustomed to return** the betrothal money, **they return** it; in **a place where** people **were accustomed not to return** the betrothal money, **they do not return** it. **And** this applies **specifically** to **where she died; but if he died, they do not return it.**[N] **What is the reason** for this? It is because **she can say: Give me my husband and I will rejoice with him.** This is the statement of Rabbi Natan.

וַאֲתָא רַבִּי יְהוּדָה הַנָּשִׂיא לְמֵימַר, בֶּאֱמֶת אָמְרוּ: בֵּין מֵת הוּא וּבֵין מֵתָה הִיא, מָקוֹם שֶׁנָּהֲגוּ לְהַחֲזִיר – מַחֲזִירִין, מָקוֹם שֶׁנָּהֲגוּ שֶׁלֹּא לְהַחֲזִיר – אֵין מַחֲזִירִין, וְלָא מָצְיָא אָמְרָה: ״תְּנוּ לִי בַּעְלִי וְאֶשְׂמַח עִמּוֹ״!

And Rabbi Yehuda HaNasi came to say: Actually they said: Whether he died or whether she died, in **a place where** people **were accustomed to return it, they return** it; in **a place where** people **were accustomed not to return** it, **they do not return** it, **and she cannot say: Give me my husband and I will rejoice with him.**

NOTES

If he died they do not return it – מֵת הוּא אֵין מַחֲזִירִין: If the betrothed man dies, the betrothed woman does not return the betrothal money, since she can claim that she is not the party preventing the marriage. If she dies, the obligation of her family to return the betrothal money is dependent upon custom, even though the betrothed man claims that it is not he who is preventing the marriage. The difference between the two cases stems from the fact that the betrothed woman's family is in possession of the betrothal money. The claim that one is not preventing the marriage is sufficient in order to retain possession of the money, but not in order to extract money from the other party (Rabbeinu Gershom Meor HaGola; Rabbi Avraham *Av Beit Din*).

HALAKHA

Give me my groomsman and I will rejoice with him – תְּנוּ לִי שׁוֹשְׁבִינִי וְאֶשְׂמַח עִמּוֹ: If one sent gifts of groomsmen to another and died before his own marriage or during the seven days of his own wedding feast, the recipient is not obligated to repay the gifts he received from the deceased. This is because the recipient can say to the heirs: Give me my groomsman and I will rejoice with him. If he rejoiced with him, he is obligated to give the reciprocal gifts to the heirs. Some authorities write that in this latter case, if the brother of the deceased entered into levirate marriage with the widow, he does not receive the entire gift. Rather, it is reciprocated to the common inheritance, in accordance with the opinion of Rav Yosef (Rambam *Sefer Kinyan, Hilkhot Zekhiya UMattana* 7:9–10; *Tur, Even HaEzer* 60).

One who betrothed a woman, etc. – הַמְאָרֵס אֶת הָאִשָּׁה וכו׳: If one betrothed a woman and wrote her a marriage contract but did not bring her under the marriage canopy, the marriage contract does not effect marriage, and she is only betrothed, not married. If he dies or divorces her, she collects the main sum of the marriage contract, but not the additional sum. The Rosh writes that she can collect payment of the marriage contract even from liened property sold to others, but according to the *Shulḥan Arukh* she collects payment only from unsold property. If he betrothed her and did not write her a marriage contract, and he dies or divorces her, she does not receive even the main sum of the marriage contract, since the Sages instituted payment of the marriage contract only when the woman was married or when her husband wrote her a marriage contract while she was betrothed. The Rema notes that although the Rosh, the Ran, and the *Tur* all hold that a betrothed woman is entitled to payment of her marriage contract, the accepted practice is in accordance with the first opinion, that she is not entitled (Rambam *Sefer Nashim, Hilkhot Ishut* 10:11; 11:1; *Shulḥan Arukh, Even HaEzer* 55:6).

לָא, דְּכוּלֵּי עָלְמָא – יְכוֹלָה שֶׁתֹּאמַר: ״תְּנוּ לִי בַּעֲלִי וְאֶשְׂמַח עִמּוֹ״, וּדְמִית הוּא – כּוּלֵּי עָלְמָא לָא פְּלִיגִי. כִּי פְּלִיגִי – שֶׁמֵּתָה הִיא, וְהָכָא בְּקִדּוּשִׁין לְטִיבּוּעִין נִיתְּנוּ קָא מִיפַּלְגִי, רַבִּי נָתָן סָבַר: קִדּוּשִׁין לָאו לְטִיבּוּעִין נִיתְּנוּ, וְרַבִּי יְהוּדָה הַנָּשִׂיא סָבַר: קִדּוּשִׁין לְטִיבּוּעִין נִיתְּנוּ.

The Gemara rejects this explanation: **No, everyone** agrees that **she can say: Give me my husband and I will rejoice with him, and** in a case **where he died, everyone agrees** that she does not have to return the betrothal money. **They disagree** in a case **where she died, and here** it is **with regard to** the question of whether **betrothal** money **is given as a sunk** cost,[N] i.e., that it is not returned even if the betrothal is not consummated, that **they disagree. Rabbi Natan holds** that **betrothal** money **is not given as a sunk** cost, and in a place where people were accustomed to return it, they return it. **And Rabbi Yehuda HaNasi holds** that **betrothal** money **is given as a sunk** cost.

וְהָא מָקוֹם שֶׁנָּהֲגוּ לְהַחֲזִיר – מַחֲזִירִין קָתָנֵי! הָכִי קָאָמַר: וְסִבְלוֹנוֹת, וַדַּאי מָקוֹם שֶׁנָּהֲגוּ לְהַחֲזִיר – מַחֲזִירִין.

The Gemara asks: **But doesn't** the *baraita* **teach** that according to Rabbi Yehuda HaNasi, in **a place where** people **were accustomed to return** it, **they return** it? This indicates that Rabbi Yehuda HaNasi does not hold that the betrothal money was given as a sunk cost. The Gemara replies: This is not referring to the betrothal money, which is not returned in any event. **This is** what the *baraita* **is saying: But** with regard to **presents,** which the betrothed man sent his betrothed following the betrothal, **certainly** in **a place where** people **were accustomed to return** them, **they return** them.

וְהָנֵי תַּנָּאֵי כְּהָנֵי תַּנָּאֵי; דְּתַנְיָא: קִדְּשָׁהּ בְּכִכָּר – בְּתוּלָה גּוֹבָה מָאתַיִם, וְאַלְמָנָה מָנֶה, דִּבְרֵי רַבִּי מֵאִיר; רַבִּי יְהוּדָה אוֹמֵר: בְּתוּלָה גּוֹבָה מָאתַיִם, וְאַלְמָנָה מָנֶה, וּמַחֲזֶרֶת לוֹ אֶת הַשְּׁאָר; רַבִּי יוֹסֵי אוֹמֵר: קִדְּשָׁהּ בְּעֶשְׂרִים – נוֹתֵן לָהּ שְׁלֹשִׁים חֲצָאִין, קִדְּשָׁהּ בִּשְׁלֹשִׁים – נוֹתֵן לָהּ עֶשְׂרִים חֲצָאִין.

The Gemara notes: The dispute between **these *tanna'im*,** in the following *baraita*, **is like** the dispute between **those *tanna'im*** just mentioned, **as it is taught** in a *baraita*: In a case where the man **betrothed** a woman **with a talent** of silver, equivalent to six thousand dinars, if she was **a virgin** she **collects** in payment of her marriage contract **two hundred** dinars over and above this amount, **and** if she was **a widow** she collects **one hundred dinars** over and above this amount. This is **the statement of Rabbi Meir. Rabbi Yehuda says: A virgin collects two hundred** dinars **and a widow one hundred dinars, and she returns the rest** of the betrothal money **to him. Rabbi Yosei says:** If **he betrothed her with twenty, he gives her thirty halves;** if **he betrothed her with thirty, he gives her twenty halves,** as the Gemara will explain.

בְּמַאי עָסְקִינַן? אִילֵימָא שֶׁמֵּתָה, מִי אִית לָהּ כְּתוּבָּה? וְאֶלָּא שֶׁמֵּת הוּא, אַמַּאי מַחֲזֶרֶת לוֹ אֶת הַשְּׁאָר? וְנֵימָא: ״תְּנוּ לִי בַּעֲלִי וְאֶשְׂמַח עִמּוֹ״! וְאֶלָּא בְּאֵשֶׁת יִשְׂרָאֵל שֶׁזִּינְּתָה; וּבְמַאי? אִי בְּרָצוֹן, מִי אִית לָהּ כְּתוּבָּה? וְאֶלָּא בְּאוֹנֶס, מִישְׁרָא שַׁרְיָא לֵיהּ!

The Gemara clarifies the *baraita*: **With what are we dealing? If we say** the *baraita* is referring to **when she died, is she entitled** to receive payment of her **marriage contract?**[B] **Rather,** perhaps the *baraita* is referring to **where he died,** in which case **why** does Rabbi Yehuda state that **she returns the rest** of the betrothal money **to him? Let her say: Give me my husband and I will rejoice with him. Rather,** perhaps the *baraita* is referring to the case **of the wife,** i.e., the betrothed, **of an Israelite, who committed adultery,** who cannot claim that she is available to marry her betrothed, as it is prohibited for her to engage in intercourse with him. The Gemara challenges: This is also difficult, as **with what** circumstance is the *baraita* dealing? **If** it is referring to **where** she committed adultery **willingly, is she entitled** to receive payment of her **marriage contract?**[H] **Rather,** it is referring **to** a case of **rape.** But in that case, she **is permitted to him.**[H] Why should she return the betrothal money?

NOTES

Betrothal money is given as a sunk cost – קִדּוּשִׁין לְטִיבּוּעִין נִיתְּנוּ: According to this opinion, it is understood at the time of the betrothal that the money remains in the betrothed woman's possession, irrespective of whether or not the marriage is effected. The opposing opinion holds that the betrothal money was given only for the purpose of betrothal, and it must be returned if the marriage is not effected. Some of the early commentaries note that even according to the opinion that the betrothal money is not given as a sunk cost, the woman in any case retains the value of a *peruta*, as in order for the betrothal to take effect, the woman must receive the value of a *peruta* unconditionally (Ritva; see Rashba).

BACKGROUND

Marriage contract – כְּתוּבָּה: The marriage contract is a legal document that the betrothed man gives the betrothed woman when the marriage is effected. The marriage contract states the sum of money that the wife is entitled to receive should she be divorced or widowed, and places a lien for that amount on the husband's estate. The minimal sum is two hundred dinars if the betrothed woman is a virgin, and one hundred dinars if the betrothed woman is a widow or divorcée. The contract also lists the husband's obligations toward his wife during their marriage. The main stipulations of the marriage contract are detailed in tractate *Ketubot*. The particulars of the contract are often dependent on local custom and may also include personal stipulations agreed to by the husband and wife. The marriage contract gives the marriage legitimacy and without one, the relationship is considered licentious.

HALAKHA

Where she committed adultery willingly is she entitled to receive her marriage contract – בְּרָצוֹן מִי אִית לָהּ כְּתוּבָּה: A woman who committed adultery loses her right to the main sum of the marriage contract, as well as to the additional sum and to any other stipulation of her marriage contract. She receives only that which remains intact from the property she brought with her as part of her dowry (Rambam *Sefer Nashim, Hilkhot Ishut* 24:6, 10 and *Hilkhot Sota* 1:20; *Shulḥan Arukh, Even HaEzer* 115:5).

It is referring to a case of rape, she is permitted to him – בְּאוֹנֶס, מִישְׁרָא שַׁרְיָא לֵיהּ: If a woman who was married to an Israelite was raped, she is not forbidden to her husband, and if afterward she is divorced or widowed she is entitled to receive the sum of her marriage contract like any other woman (Rambam *Sefer Nashim, Hilkhot Ishut* 24:19–21 and *Hilkhot Geirushin* 11:14; *Shulḥan Arukh, Even HaEzer* 6:11).

וְאֶלָּא, בְּאֵשֶׁת כֹּהֵן שֶׁנֶּאֶנְסָה, וּבְקִדּוּשִׁין לְטִיבוּעִין נִיתְּנוּ קָמִיפַּלְגִי, רַבִּי מֵאִיר סָבַר: קִדּוּשִׁין לְטִיבוּעִין נִיתְּנוּ, וְרַבִּי יְהוּדָה סָבַר: לָאו לְטִיבוּעִין נִיתְּנוּ. וְרַבִּי יוֹסֵי מְסַפְּקָא לֵיהּ אִי לְטִיבוּעִין נִיתְּנוּ אִי לָא,

Rather, the *baraita* is referring **to the wife,** i.e., the betrothed, **of a priest, who was raped**[H] and is prohibited from engaging in intercourse with her betrothed. She therefore cannot claim: Give me my husband and I will rejoice with him, yet she is entitled to receive payment of her marriage contract, **and the** *tanna'im* **disagree with regard to** whether **betrothal** money **is given as a sunk cost: Rabbi Meir holds that betrothal** money **is given as a sunk cost. Rabbi Yehuda holds** that it **is not given as a sunk** cost. **And Rabbi Yosei is uncertain if it is given as a sunk cost or not.**

וְהִלְכָּךְ, קִדְּשָׁהּ בְּעֶשְׂרִים – נוֹתֵן לָהּ שְׁלֹשִׁים חֲצָאִין, קִדְּשָׁהּ בִּשְׁלֹשִׁים – נוֹתֵן לָהּ עֶשְׂרִים חֲצָאִין.

The Gemara explains Rabbi Yosei's opinion: **And** since it is uncertain whether or not she is required to return the betrothal money, **therefore,** she returns only half the money: If **he betrothed her with twenty**[N] *sela*, which are equivalent to eighty dinars, she owes him forty dinars. Yet, if she is widowed or divorced, she is entitled to one hundred dinars in payment of her marriage contract, so he or his estate **gives her thirty halves** of a *sela*, which are equivalent to sixty dinars, so that she receives one hundred dinars in all. If **he betrothed her with thirty** *sela*, which are equivalent to one hundred twenty dinars, she owes him sixty dinars. Since she is entitled to one hundred dinars in payment of her marriage contract, he **gives her twenty halves** of a *sela*, equivalent to forty dinars.

אָמַר רַב יוֹסֵף בַּר מִנְיוּמִי אָמַר רַב נַחְמָן: בְּכָל מָקוֹם שֶׁנָּהֲגוּ לְהַחֲזִיר – מַחֲזִירִין, וְתַרְגּוּמָא: נְהַרְדְּעָא. שְׁאָר בָּבֶל מַאי? רַבָּה וְרַב יוֹסֵף דְּאָמְרִי תַּרְוַיְיהוּ: מוֹהֲרֵי הָדְרִי, קִדּוּשֵׁי לָא הָדְרִי. אֲמַר רַב פַּפָּא, הִלְכְתָא: בֵּין שֶׁמֵּת הוּא בֵּין שֶׁמֵּתָה הִיא וַהֲדַר בֵּיהּ הוּא – מוֹהֲרֵי הָדְרִי, קִדּוּשֵׁי לָא הָדְרִי; הָדְרָא בָּהּ אִיהִי – אֲפִילּוּ קִדּוּשֵׁי נַמִי הָדְרִי.

Rav Yosef bar Minyumi says that **Rav Naḥman says: In every place where they were accustomed to return** the betrothal money, **they return** it. **And the interpretation** of this statement is that it is referring to **Neharde'a.** The Gemara asks: With regard to **the rest of Babylonia, what** is the *halakha*? **Rabba and Rav Yosef both say:** The **presents are returned** and the **betrothal** money **is not returned. Rav Pappa said: The** *halakha* is that **whether he died** or **whether she died or** whether **he retracted** his agreement to the betrothal and divorced her, the **presents are returned**[H] and the **betrothal** money **is not returned. If she retracted** her agreement to the betrothal and requested a divorce, **even** the **betrothal** money **is returned.**

אַמֵימָר אֲמַר: קִדּוּשֵׁי לָא הָדְרִי, גְּזֵירָה שֶׁמָּא יֹאמְרוּ קִדּוּשִׁין תּוֹפְסִין בַּאֲחוֹתָהּ. רַב אַשִׁי אָמַר: גִּיטָּהּ מוֹכִיחַ עָלֶיהָ. וְהָא דְּרַב אַשִׁי בְּדוּתָא הִיא, דְּאִיכָּא דְּשָׁמַע בְּהָא וְלָא שָׁמַע בְּהָא.

Ameimar said: The **betrothal** money **is not returned.**[H] This is a rabbinic **decree, lest** people **say** that **betrothal takes effect with her sister.** If the betrothal money is returned, people are likely to think that the betrothal is retroactively nullified and that the man can betroth her sister, whereas in fact the betrothal was not retroactively nullified and he cannot betroth her. **Rav Ashi said: Her bill of divorce proves for her** that she was betrothed, so this concern is not in effect. The Gemara comments: **And this statement of Rav Ashi is a mistake, since there are those who heard about this,** i.e., the return of the betrothal money, **but did not hear about that,** i.e., the bill of divorce.

"שֶׁהַשּׁוֹשְׁבִינוּת נִגְבֵּית בְּבֵית דִּין". תָּנוּ רַבָּנַן, חֲמִשָּׁה דְּבָרִים נֶאֶמְרוּ בְּשׁוֹשְׁבִינוּת: נִגְבֵּית בְּבֵית דִּין, וְחוֹזֶרֶת בְּעוֹנָתָהּ, וְאֵין בָּהּ מִשּׁוּם רִבִּית,

§ The mishna teaches: If the gifts of groomsmen are reciprocated after the father's death, they are reciprocated to the middle, **because gifts of groomsmen are** a legal debt owed to the father, **collectible in court. The Sages taught** (*Tosefta* 10:8): **Five statements were said with regard to gifts of groomsmen:** They are **collectible in court; and** they are **reciprocated** only **at their** relevant **time,**[N] i.e., at the time of the groomsman's own wedding; **and they are not subject to** the prohibition of **interest,** i.e., it is permitted to reciprocate with a gift of greater value than the original gift;

HALAKHA

The wife of a priest who was raped – אֵשֶׁת כֹּהֵן שֶׁנֶּאֶנְסָה: If the wife of a priest was raped, she is forbidden to her husband, and he must divorce her. She is entitled to receive payment of her marriage contract (Rambam *Sefer Nashim, Hilkhot Ishut* 24:21–22 and *Sefer Kedusha, Hilkhot Issurei Bia* 18:6; *Shulḥan Arukh, Even HaEzer* 6:10; 115:6).

Presents are returned – מוֹהֲרֵי הָדְרִי: If one sent presents to the father of his betrothed and then either he or his betrothed dies, or he retracts his agreement to the betrothal, the presents are returned in their entirety, except for food and drink. This is the *halakha* irrespective of whether there are numerous presents or few, and irrespective of whether the betrothed man ate a betrothal feast at his father-in-law's house or not. The Rema holds that the food and drink are not returned only if the betrothed man ate at his father-in-law's house, in which case even food which is still intact is not returned. If the betrothed man did not eat there, everything is returned (Rambam *Sefer Kinyan, Hilkhot Zekhiya UMattana* 6:21–22; *Shulḥan Arukh, Even HaEzer* 50:3).

Betrothal money is not returned – קִדּוּשֵׁי לָא הָדְרִי: If one betroths a woman, the betrothal money is never returned. This *halakha* applies in all cases, both if she retracts her agreement to the betrothal and requests a divorce or he retracts his agreement and divorces her, both if he dies or she dies, and if he divorces her after marriage. Even if he betroths her with one thousand dinars, they are considered an unconditional gift, which is not returned. This is a rabbinic decree, lest people say that she was never betrothed. The Rema cites the Maharil, who says that if the betrothed woman retracts her agreement to the betrothal and requests a divorce after the marriage is effected, the betrothal money is returned, since people will not think that she was never betrothed. Some of the later authorities disagree (Rambam *Sefer Kinyan, Hilkhot Zekhiya UMattana* 6:18; *Shulḥan Arukh, Even HaEzer* 50:1, and *Beit Shmuel* and *Pitḥei Teshuva* there).

NOTES

And therefore if he betrothed her with twenty, etc. – וְהִלְכָּךְ קִדְּשָׁהּ בְּעֶשְׂרִים וכו׳: The Gemara elsewhere (*Bava Kamma* 35b) states that according to the opinion of Sumakhos, property of uncertain ownership is divided between the two parties, whereas according to the opinion of the Rabbis, the burden of proof rests upon the claimant. The Ritva writes that Rabbi Yosei holds in accordance with the opinion of Sumakhos, and therefore he rules that due to the uncertainty with regard to whether the betrothal money is given to be lost, the woman is required to return half the money. *Tosafot* explain that the aforementioned dispute does not apply in this case, since there is no uncertainty with regard to the facts of the case, but only with regard to the *halakha*, and in cases where the ruling is uncertain, the Rabbis sometimes concede that the sum is divided between the two parties. Furthermore, the Ramah points out that in this case, it is unclear which party should be defined as the claimant, whether it is the husband, since he is in possession of the money, or the wife, since she is in possession of the marriage contract. Therefore, the money must be divided between the two parties.

NOTES

And they are reciprocated only at their relevant time – וְחוֹזֶרֶת בְּעוֹנָתָהּ: Some of the early commentaries state that according to the Rashbam, if one did not reciprocate the gifts of groomsmen after the seven days of the wedding feast, he is no longer obligated to reciprocate. Other early commentaries reject this understanding, and prove that gifts of groomsmen are considered a loan in all respects. The stipulation that they are reciprocated only at the relevant time means that one may refuse to reciprocate the gifts before the time of the groomsman's wedding, and the groomsman may refuse to accept them before that time. Furthermore, one is required to reciprocate only when the groomsman's wedding is held in a manner similar to the wedding of the first man (Ramban; Rashba).

NOTES

That it was not with that in mind that he gave him – דְּלָאו אַדַּעְתָּא דְּהָכִי יְהַב לֵיהּ: The gifts of groomsmen are given out of friendship, not as a financially motivated loan, and the recipient is not obligated to reciprocate with a larger gift. If he does reciprocate with a larger gift, it is only out of generosity, and not intended as interest (Rashbam; Ritva).

He shall not exact it – לֹא יִגּשׂ: The Rashbam explains that the prohibition "He shall not exact it" does not apply here, as in any case one cannot demand payment of gifts of groomsmen until the time of the recipient's marriage. Rabbeinu Tam concludes that the *halakha* is the same with regard to any loan that is due only after the Sabbatical Year; since it cannot be exacted at the time the Sabbatical Year abrogates debts, the loan is not abrogated (*Tosafot*). Others explain that only gifts of groomsmen are not subject to the prohibition "He shall not exact it," because unlike ordinary loans, there is no certainty that they will ever be exacted. If the recipient dies, or remains unwed, or if the conditions stated in the Gemara subsequently are not fulfilled, the gifts are not reciprocated (*Tosafot*; Ri Migash; Ramban).

BACKGROUND

Drum – טַבְלָא:

Roman mosaic depicting musician with a tympanum, an instrument common in talmudic times

וְאֵין הַשְּׁבִיעִית מְשַׁמַּטְתָּה, וְאֵין הַבְּכוֹר נוֹטֵל בָּהּ פִּי שְׁנַיִם.

and the Sabbatical Year **does not abrogate them;**[H] **and the firstborn does not take a double** portion **of them.**

נִגְבֵּית בְּבֵית דִּין, מַאי טַעֲמָא? כְּמִלְוֶה דָּמְיָא. וְאֵין בָּהּ מִשּׁוּם רִבִּית – דְּלָאו אַדַּעְתָּא דְּהָכִי יְהַב לֵיהּ. וְאֵין הַשְּׁבִיעִית מְשַׁמַּטְתָּהּ – דְּלָא קָרֵינָא בֵּיהּ "לֹא יִגּשׂ".

The *baraita* states that gifts of groomsmen **are collectible in court. What is the reason** for this? It is that they are considered **similar to a loan.** The *baraita* states: **And they are not subject to** the prohibition of **interest.** The reason is **that** it was **not** with **that in mind** that he gave him[N] a larger gift. Rather, he did so on account of his joy at his friend's wedding. The *baraita* states: **And the Sabbatical** Year **does not abrogate them.** The reason is **that one cannot read** the verse concerning the abrogation of debts during the occurrence of the Sabbatical Year: **"He shall not exact it**[N] of his neighbor and his brother, because the Lord's release has been proclaimed" (Deuteronomy 15:2), **with regard to** gifts of groomsmen. Since one cannot choose to exact the gifts until the time of one's own wedding, they are not addressed by this verse.

וְאֵין הַבְּכוֹר נוֹטֵל פִּי שְׁנַיִם – דַּהֲוָה לֵיהּ רָאוּי, וְאֵין הַבְּכוֹר נוֹטֵל בְּרָאוּי כִּבְמוּחְזָק.

The *baraita* states: **And the firstborn does not take a double** portion from them. The reason is **that they constitute potential** inheritance, **and the firstborn does not take** in inheritance the property **due** the deceased **as** he does the property the deceased **possessed.**

אָמַר רַב כָּהֲנָא, כְּלָלָא דְשׁוּשְׁבִינוּתָא: הֲוָה בְּמָתָא – אִיבָּעֵי לֵיהּ לְמֵיתָא. שְׁמַע קַל טַבְלָא – אִיבָּעֵי לֵיהּ לְמֵיתָא. לָא שְׁמַע קַל טַבְלָא – אִיבָּעֵי לֵיהּ לְאוֹדוּעֵיהּ, תַּרְעוֹמֶת אִית לֵיהּ, שַׁלּוֹמֵי מְשַׁלֵּם.

§ **Rav Kahana said: The principle with regard to** the reciprocation of **gifts of groomsmen**[H] is: If the recipient **was in town** when his groomsman wed, **he should have come** to the wedding, and even if he did not come, he is obligated to send the gifts of groomsmen. If he was not in town, but **he** was nearby and he **heard the sound of the drum**[B] announcing the wedding, **he should have come.** If **he** was far away and **did not hear the sound of the drum,** the betrothed man **should have informed him.** If he did not inform him, the recipient **has a grievance** against the betrothed man because he did not inform him about the wedding, but **he** still **repays** the gifts of groomsmen.

HALAKHA

And the Sabbatical Year does not abrogate them, etc. – וְאֵין הַשְּׁבִיעִית מְשַׁמַּטְתָּה וכו׳: When a man gets married, it is customary for his friends and acquaintances to send him money in order to help him cover the expenses of the wedding feast. These gifts are known as gifts of groomsmen. The Sages stated five *halakhot* that distinguish these gifts from other gifts and loans: First, they are considered a loan, and are therefore collectible in court. Second, they are reciprocated only at the relevant time, i.e., when the original groomsman gets married, and only if his wedding is similar to the first groom's wedding. Third, they are not subject to the prohibition of interest, and it is therefore permitted to reciprocate with a larger gift than one received. Fourth, the Sabbatical Year does not abrogate the obligation to reciprocate the gifts of groomsmen. Fifth, if the gifts are reciprocated to the heirs of the gift giver, the firstborn does not receive a double portion from them, as they constitute potential inheritance, and the firstborn does not take a double portion in the inheritance of property due the deceased (Rambam *Sefer Kinyan*, *Hilkhot Zekhiya UMattana* 7:13; see *Shulḥan Arukh*, *Even HaEzer* 60:1).

The principle with regard to the reciprocation of gifts of groomsmen, etc. – כְּלָלָא דְשׁוּשְׁבִינוּתָא וכו׳: If one sends gifts of groomsmen for his friend's wedding feast, and he participates in the feast and eats and drinks with the groom, if he subsequently gets married, the recipient is obligated to reciprocate the gifts. If he invites his friend to the wedding, or if his friend is in town and it is not the custom there to invite people personally and the wedding is publicly announced, then the friend is obligated to reciprocate with the entire value of the gifts of groomsmen, even if he does not participate in the wedding feast. If the friend is not in town, he is still obligated to reciprocate the gifts, but the original recipient may deduct the cost of the food the original groomsman consumed at his wedding. If he is in town but the original groomsman does not personally invite him although it is the custom there to issue personal invitations, then he has a cause for grievance against the betrothed man for failing to inform him, but he is still obligated to reciprocate the gifts. In this case, the friend may make the aforementioned deduction. This ruling is in accordance with the statement of Rav Kahana, as interpreted by the Ri Migash. Nowadays it is not the custom to sue for reciprocation of gifts of groomsmen, irrespective of the circumstances (Rambam *Sefer Kinyan*, *Hilkhot Zekhiya UMattana* 7:5–6; *Shulḥan Arukh*, *Even HaEzer* 60:1).

וְעַד כַּמָּה? אֲמַר אַבַּיֵי: נָהֲגוּ בְּנֵי גִּנְנָא, עַד זוּזָא – אַיְיתָא בְּכַפֵּיהּ אָכְלֵיהּ בִּכְרֵיסֵיהּ, עַד אַרְבָּעָה – מְשַׁלֵּם פַּלְגָא, מִכָּאן וְאֵילָךְ – אִינִישׁ אִינִישׁ כַּחֲשִׁיבוּתֵיהּ.

In this case, since he did not partake of the wedding feast, he is entitled to deduct a sum from the reciprocal gift. The Gemara asks: **And up to how much** can he deduct? **Abaye said:**[H] The **members of a wedding** feast **were accustomed** to deduct according to the following principle: If the gift of groomsmen that the reciprocal giver received was **up to a dinar,** he now pays nothing, because what a person **brings in his hand he consumes in his stomach.** If the gift of groomsmen was **up to four** dinars, he now **pays half.**[N] **From that** sum **onward, each person** deducts **according to his prominence,** i.e., in accordance with the outlay that would have been required to honor the reciprocal giver properly, had he participated in the wedding feast.

תָּנוּ רַבָּנַן: עָשָׂה עִמּוֹ בְּפוּמְבֵּי, וּבִקֵּשׁ לַעֲשׂוֹת עִמּוֹ בְּצִנְעָא – יָכוֹל לוֹמַר לוֹ: בְּפוּמְבֵּי אֶעֱשֶׂה עִמְּךָ, כְּדֶרֶךְ שֶׁעָשִׂיתָ עִמִּי; עָשָׂה עִמּוֹ בִּבְתוּלָה, וּבִקֵּשׁ לַעֲשׂוֹת עִמּוֹ בְּאַלְמָנָה – יָכוֹל לוֹמַר לוֹ: בִּבְתוּלָה אֶעֱשֶׂה עִמְּךָ, כְּדֶרֶךְ שֶׁעָשִׂיתָ עִמִּי.

The Sages taught (*Tosefta* 10:9): If one **served** as groomsman **for** his friend **at a public** [*pumbei*][L] wedding,[H] **and** when the groomsman himself wed, he **requested** that his friend reciprocate **by serving** as a groomsman **for him at a private** wedding, the friend **can say to him:** I am willing to reciprocate and **serve** as groomsman **for you** only **at a public** wedding, where the rejoicing is greater, **in the manner you served** as a groomsman **for me.** If one **served** as a groomsman **for** his friend **when** he married **a virgin,**[H] **and** he **requested** that his friend reciprocate **by serving** as a groomsman **for him when** he marries **a widow,** the friend **can say to him: I shall serve** as a groomsman **for you** only **when** you marry **a virgin, in the manner you served** as a groomsman **for me.**

עָשָׂה עִמּוֹ בִּשְׁנִיָּה, וּבִקֵּשׁ לַעֲשׂוֹת עִמּוֹ בָּרִאשׁוֹנָה – יָכוֹל לוֹמַר לוֹ: לִכְשֶׁתִּשָּׂא אִשָּׁה אַחֶרֶת אֶעֱשֶׂה עִמְּךָ. עָשָׂה עִמּוֹ בְּאַחַת, וּבִקֵּשׁ לַעֲשׂוֹת עִמּוֹ בִּשְׁתַּיִם – יָכוֹל לוֹמַר לוֹ: בְּאַחַת אֶעֱשֶׂה עִמְּךָ, כְּדֶרֶךְ שֶׁעָשִׂיתָ עִמִּי.

If one **served** as a groomsman **for** his friend **when** he married **a second** wife,[N] **and** he **requested** that his friend reciprocate **by serving** as a groomsman **for him when** he marries **a first** wife, the friend **can say to him: When you marry another woman I will serve** as a groomsman **for you.** If one **served** as a groomsman **for** his friend **when** he married **one** woman, **and** he **requested** that his friend reciprocate **by serving** as a groomsman **for him when** he marries **two** women,[N] the friend **can say to him: I will serve** as a groomsman **for you when** you marry **one** woman, **in the manner you served** as a groomsman **for me.**

NOTES

Up to four dinars he pays half – **עַד אַרְבָּעָה מְשַׁלֵּם פַּלְגָא**: The Rashbam explains that a groomsman who brings a sum of up to a dinar is given a portion worth a dinar. One who brings a greater sum is honored with a larger portion. The Ra'avad explains that the groomsman brings food and drink with him. If he brings more than a dinar's worth, he needs to bring another person with him in order to help him carry the provisions. Since that person also partakes of the wedding feast, the cost of the groomsman's participation is consequently greater.

If one served as groomsman for his friend when he married a second wife, etc. – **עָשָׂה עִמּוֹ בִּשְׁנִיָּה וכו׳**: The Rashbam maintains that the groomsman can claim that he wishes to reciprocate only at the more modest celebration of a second marriage, and not at the celebration of a first marriage, which usually involves greater rejoicing. According to this understanding, the groomsman can insist that he will reciprocate only at a wedding that is similar to his own wedding, neither more ostentatious nor less. The Ramah says that one can refuse to reciprocate only if the wedding involves less rejoicing. Accordingly, he explains that a second wedding involves more rejoicing than a first wedding, as the husband is more relaxed and is able to rejoice with his friends to a greater extent than during his first wedding.

By serving as groomsman for him when he marries two women – **לַעֲשׂוֹת עִמּוֹ בִּשְׁתַּיִם**: *Tosafot* explain that the betrothed man intended to marry a second wife later on, and he asked his friend to divide the gift of groomsmen between the two weddings. Rabbeinu Gershom Meor HaGola and the Ri Migash explain that he intended to marry both wives at once. The friend can claim that he wishes to reciprocate only at a wedding with one woman, as it is more joyous.

LANGUAGE

Public [*pumbei*] – **פּוּמְבֵּי**: From the Greek πομπή, *pompē*, meaning a festive procession or public celebration. It is used to refer to a matter that is performed publicly and conspicuously.

HALAKHA

And up to how much can he deduct, Abaye said, etc. – **וְעַד כַּמָּה, אֲמַר אַבַּיֵי וכו׳**: When the cost of the food is deducted from the reciprocal gift of groomsmen, it is customary to deduct according to the following principle: If one receives one dinar as a gift of groomsmen, he does not reciprocate the gift at all, since the gift covers only the cost of the food the groomsman ate at the wedding feast. If one receives more than one dinar but less than one *sela*, he deducts half of the sum. If he receives one *sela* or more, one must assess the intent of the giver of the gift: If the giver is a prominent person, half of the sum is deducted from the reciprocal gift. If the giver is miserly and punctilious in his expenses, only the cost of the food he ate is deducted, and the rest of the gift must be reciprocated. This ruling is in accordance with the statement of Abaye, as interpreted by the Ri Migash (Rambam *Sefer Kinyan*, *Hilkhot Zekhiya UMattana* 7:7–8; *Tur*, *Even HaEzer* 60).

If one served as groomsman for his friend at a public wedding, etc. – **עָשָׂה עִמּוֹ בְּפוּמְבֵּי וכו׳**: If one sends gifts of groomsmen for his friend's wedding feast, which is held publicly, and when he himself subsequently gets married he holds a private wedding feast, the giver cannot demand reciprocation of the gift of groomsmen, since his friend can say to him: I am willing to reciprocate and serve as groomsman for you only in the manner you served as groomsman for me. According to the Rambam, the *halakha* is the same if the recipient held a private wedding feast and that giver subsequently holds a public wedding feast. The Ramah holds that one can refuse to reciprocate only if the wedding involves less rejoicing, but not if the first giver holds a wedding that involves great rejoicing (Rambam *Sefer Kinyan*, *Hilkhot Zekhiya UMattana* 7:4; *Tur*, *Even HaEzer* 60).

If one served as groomsman for his friend when he married a virgin, etc. – **עָשָׂה עִמּוֹ בִּבְתוּלָה וכו׳**: If one marries a virgin, and his groomsman subsequently marries a widow, the recipient is not obligated to reciprocate the gift of groomsmen he received, since he can say to the groom: I am willing to reciprocate and serve as groomsman for you only in the manner you served as groomsman for me. According to the Rambam, the *halakha* is the same if the recipient married a widow and the giver subsequently marries a virgin. According to the Ramah, since the wedding of a virgin involves greater rejoicing, the recipient is required to reciprocate (Rambam *Sefer Kinyan*, *Hilkhot Zekhiya UMattana* 7:3; *Tur*, *Even HaEzer* 60).

תנו רבנן: עתיר נכסין עתיר פומבי – זה הוא בעל הגדות, עתיר סלעים עתיר תקוע – זהו בעל פלפול, עתיר משח עתיר כמס – זהו בעל שמועות, הכל צריכין למרי חטיא – תלמוד.

§ **The Sages taught** in a *baraita*: There are different types of Torah scholars. There is a scholar who is **wealthy** in figurative **property** and **wealthy** in **public** renown; **this is the master of homiletics.**[N] There is a scholar who is **wealthy** in **coins** and **wealthy** in **houses; this is the master of dialectics.**[N] There is one who is **wealthy** in oil and **wealthy** in **hidden** stores; **this is the master of** halakhic **traditions.**[N] **Everyone is dependent on the owner of wheat;** this is the master of **Talmud,**[N] who understands the reasons behind the rulings and traditions.

אמר רבי זירא אמר רב, מאי דכתיב: "כל ימי עני רעים" זה בעל תלמוד, "וטוב לב משתה תמיד" – זה בעל משנה.

Rabbi Zeira says that **Rav says: What** is the meaning of that **which is written: "All the days of the poor are terrible;** and for the good-hearted it is always a feast" (Proverbs 15:15)? "All the days of the poor are terrible"; **this** is referring to the **master of Talmud,** who is wearied by the difficulty of his Talmud study. **"And for the good-hearted it is always a feast";**[N] **this** is referring to the **master of Mishna,** who recites the *mishnayot* by rote and is not wearied thereby.

רבא אמר: איפכא. והיינו דאמר רב משרשיא משמיה דרבא, מאי דכתיב: "מסיע אבנים יעצב בהם בוקע עצים יסכן בם"? "מסיע אבנים יעצב בהן" – אלו בעלי משנה, "בוקע עצים יסכן בם" – אלו בעלי תלמוד.

Rava says: The opposite is true.[N] **And this is** consistent with that **which Rav Mesharshiyya says in the name of Rava: What is** the meaning of that **which is written: "He who quarries stones shall be hurt by them; and he that chops wood shall be warmed thereby"** (Ecclesiastes 10:9). **"He who quarries stones shall be hurt by them"; these are the masters of Mishna.** They exert themselves to memorize the *mishnayot*, but since one cannot reach practical conclusions from the mishna, they are comparable to one who carries a heavy load without benefiting from it. **"He that chops wood shall be warmed thereby"; these are the masters of Talmud,** who attain the benefit of their exertions in the form of practical conclusions.

רבי חנינא אמר: "כל ימי עני רעים" – זה שיש לו אשה רעה, "וטוב לב משתה תמיד" – זה שיש לו אשה טובה. רבי ינאי אמר: "כל ימי עני רעים" – זה איסטנים, "וטוב לב משתה תמיד" – זה שדעתו יפה.

The Gemara cites other interpretations of this verse. **Rabbi Ḥanina says: "All the days of the poor are terrible"; this is** referring to one **who has a wicked wife. "And for the good-hearted it is always a feast"; this is** referring to one **who has a good wife. Rabbi Yannai says: "All the days of the poor are terrible"; this is** referring to **one who is delicate** [*istenis*][L] and overly sensitive, because he constantly encounters unpleasant situations. **"And for the good-hearted it is always a feast"; this** is referring to one **who is relaxed** and not particular with regard to his food or his surroundings.

רבי יוחנן אמר: "כל ימי עני רעים" – זה רחמן, "וטוב לב משתה תמיד" – זה אכזרי. ורבי יהושע בן לוי אמר: "כל ימי עני רעים" – זה שדעתו קצרה, "וטוב לב משתה תמיד" – זה שדעתו רחבה.

Rabbi Yoḥanan says: "All the days of the poor are terrible"; this is referring to **an empathetic person,** because he is constantly affected by the suffering in the world. **"And for the good-hearted it is always a feast"; this** is referring to **a cruel person,** who is not pained by the suffering of others. **And Rabbi Yehoshua ben Levi says: "All the days of the poor are terrible"; this** is referring to a person **of impatient disposition. "And for the good-hearted it is always a feast"; this** is referring to a person **of patient disposition.**

NOTES

Wealthy in property and wealthy in public renown, this is the master of homiletics – עתיר נכסין עתיר פומבי זה הוא בעל הגדות: The master of homiletics speaks in a style that is pleasant and easily understood, and he addresses a wide audience. He can speak anywhere, on any occasion, and his reputation spreads easily. He is therefore compared to a person whose wealth includes property, i.e., houses, fields, and orchards, as well as assets that are noticeable by all, e.g., cattle and sheep, which graze in public (Rabbeinu Gershom Meor HaGola; Rashbam). Some of the early commentaries write that the *baraita* belittles the importance of the master of homiletics, stressing that although he is well known, his merchandise is not of great value or importance (*Arukh*). Similarly, the Meiri explains that the term: Wealthy in property, describes one who owns a great deal of land that yields only small profits.

Wealthy in coins and wealthy in houses [*tekoa*], this is the master of dialectics – עתיר סלעים עתיר תקוע זהו בעל פלפול: Some early commentaries explain that *tekoa* denotes houses and is derived from the verb *taka*, meaning to pitch a tent (see Genesis 31:25). One who owns many houses always has money available from their rental (Rabbeinu Gershom Meor HaGola; Rashbam). The Meiri adds that the income from his houses accrues daily. Others explain that *tekoa* means oil and is derived from the name of the town of Tekoa, which was renowned for the quality of its oil (Rashbam). The Rid explains that *tekoa* means embedded, and it refers to someone who is so wealthy that he is embedded in piles of money.

The intent of the *baraita* is that just as this wealthy man constantly attains new coins, or different varieties of oil, so too, the master of dialectics constantly attains new insights in his studies (Rashbam). Alternatively, the comparison can be understood as indicating that the explanations of the master of dialectics are as solid and well established as houses (Rabbi Avraham *Av Beit Din*).

Wealthy in oil [*meshah*] and wealthy in hidden stores, this is the master of halakhic traditions – עתיר משח עתיר כמס זהו בעל שמועות: Some early commentaries hold that the term *meshah* means oil (Rid; Rabbi Avraham *Av Beit Din*). The Meiri explains that the term hidden stores refers to pearls or gems, and adds that both oil and gems are liable to become damaged if moved from their place of storage. The Rashbam, who maintains that the earlier term *tekoa* refers to oil, explains that the term *meshah* does not refer to oil, but is derived from *mashḥa*, which means a measure. It refers to merchandise that is measured and then hidden away in storerooms until it is sold.

According to some commentaries, this phrase is derogatory, likening the master of halakhic traditions to someone who possesses large stores of wine and oil but does not use them. Similarly, the master of halakhic traditions is extremely knowledgeable but is unable to apply his knowledge (Rabbeinu Gershom Meor HaGola; Rabbi Avraham *Av Beit Din*). The Meiri says that just as oil and gems are valuable but might become damaged if moved from their place of storage, so too, the knowledge of the master of halakhic traditions is valuable, but when he is challenged, he is unable to uphold the traditions he cites. Conversely, the Rashbam understands this phrase as a positive depiction. The master of legal traditions is compared to someone whose wealth consists of merchandise which, although usually hidden, is ultimately needed by everyone. Although the master of halakhic traditions does not derive new insights from his sources, his knowledge of the *halakhot* and amoraic traditions is needed by all the Torah scholars.

LANGUAGE

One who is delicate [*istenis*] – איסטנים: From the Greek ἀσθενής, *asthenēs*, meaning one who is weak, delicate, or sickly.

NOTES

On the owner of wheat, this is the master of Talmud – למרי חטיא תלמוד: A master of Talmud is one who is able to explain the *mishnayot* and discuss them (see 130b). Just as everyone depends on the owner of wheat to provide them with bread as a staple of their diet, so too, everyone is dependent on the master of Talmud, as it is impossible to derive halakhic conclusions from the *mishnayot* without knowledge of the talmudic explanations (Rashbam). The Maharal explains that this refers to one who possesses knowledge of oral traditions that cannot be deduced through dialectics (see *Horayot* 14a).

All the days of the poor are terrible…and for the good-hearted it is always a feast – כל ימי עני רעים...וטוב לב משתה תמיד: The Maharsha asks: Why do none of the Sages explain that "days of the poor" is referring to actual poor people? He writes that since the latter clause of the verse is not referring to one's financial situation, it is reasonable to understand the first clause of the verse, which serves as a contrast to the latter clause, in a similar manner.

The opposite is true – איפכא: The master of Mishna is likened to a poor person, as he does not understand the *mishnayot* and is therefore unable to make use of his knowledge. Conversely, the master of Talmud comprehends everything he learns (Rabbeinu Gershom Meor HaGola). Furthermore, the task of reciting the *mishnayot* without comprehension is onerous, whereas the master of Talmud is able to enjoy his studies (Maharal).

וְאָמַר רַבִּי יְהוֹשֻׁעַ בֶּן לֵוִי: כׇּל יְמֵי עָנִי רָעִים? וְהָא אִיכָּא שַׁבָּתוֹת וְיָמִים טוֹבִים! כִּדְשְׁמוּאֵל, דְּאָמַר שְׁמוּאֵל: שִׁנּוּי וֶסֶת – תְּחִלַּת חוֹלִי.

And Rabbi Yehoshua ben Levi says: Is it so that **all the days of the poor are terrible? But aren't there** ***Shabbatot*** **and Festivals,** when even the poor enjoy their meals and rest? Rather, explain this **in accordance with** the statement **of Shmuel, as Shmuel says: A change of regimen** [*veset*][HL] causes **the onset of** intestinal **disease,** and as a result the poor suffer even from a change for the good.

כְּתִיב בְּסֵפֶר בֶּן סִירָא: כׇּל יְמֵי עָנִי רָעִים, בֶּן סִירָא אוֹמֵר: אַף לֵילוֹת. בְּשֵׁפֶל גַּגִּים גַּגּוֹ, מִמְּטַר גַּגִּים לְגַגּוֹ; בְּרוּם הָרִים כַּרְמוֹ, מֵעֲפַר כַּרְמוֹ לִכְרָמִים.

It **is written in the book of ben Sira:**[B] **All the days of the poor are terrible. Ben Sira says: The nights as well. His roof is at the lowest point of the roofs; the rain of roofs go onto his roof. His vineyard is at the height of the mountains; the soil of his vineyard goes onto other vineyards.**

מתני׳ הַשּׁוֹלֵחַ סִבְלוֹנוֹת לְבֵית חָמִיו, שָׁלַח שָׁם מֵאָה מָנֶה וְאָכַל שָׁם סְעוּדַת חָתָן אֲפִילּוּ בְּדִינָר – אֵינָן נִגְבִּין, לֹא אָכַל שָׁם סְעוּדַת חָתָן – הֲרֵי אֵלּוּ נִגְבִּין. שָׁלַח סִבְלוֹנוֹת מְרוּבִּין שֶׁיַּחְזְרוּ עִמָּהּ לְבֵית בַּעְלָהּ – הֲרֵי אֵלּוּ נִגְבִּין, סִבְלוֹנוֹת מוּעָטִין שֶׁתִּשְׁתַּמֵּשׁ בָּהֶן בְּבֵית אָבִיהָ – אֵין נִגְבִּין.

MISHNA With regard to **one who sends presents** [*sivlonot*][L] **to his father-in-law's house**[H] following his betrothal, even if **he sent there** the sum of **ten thousand dinars** and subsequently **ate there a groom's feast even** worth the value **of** a single **dinar,** if for any reason the marriage is not effected, the presents **are not collected** in return by the formerly betrothed man. If he **did not eat a groom's feast there,** the presents **are collected,** as they were not an unconditional gift. If he **sent many presents**[N] with the stipulation **that they return with her to her husband's house,** i.e., to his own house, after the wedding, **these are collected** if the marriage is not effected. If he sent **a few presents for her to use while in her father's house, they are not collected.**

גמ׳ אָמַר רָבָא: דַּוְקָא דִּינָר, אֲבָל פָּחוֹת מִדִּינָר – לָא. פְּשִׁיטָא, דִּינָר תְּנַן! מַהוּ דְּתֵימָא, הוּא הַדִּין דַּאֲפִילּוּ פָּחוֹת מִדִּינָר, וְהַאי דְּקָתָנֵי דִּינָר – אוֹרְחָא דְּמִילְּתָא קָתָנֵי, קָא מַשְׁמַע לַן.

GEMARA The mishna states that if the betrothed man ate food worth even a single dinar at his father-in-law's house, the presents are not returned. **Rava says:** This applies **specifically** to the value of **a dinar, but** if he ate food worth **less than** the value of **a dinar,** it is **not** so. The Gemara asks: Isn't that **obvious,** as **we learned** the *halakha* in the mishna with reference to the value of **a dinar?** The Gemara answers: It is stated **lest you say** that **the same is true even** in the case of **less than a dinar, and** the reason **that** the mishna **teaches** the *halakha* with reference to **a dinar** is that it **teaches the matter in the manner in which it** typically occurs, and one does not usually eat less than that. Rava therefore **teaches us** that the formulation of the mishna is precise; the mishna is not referring to the value of less than a dinar.

HALAKHA

A change of regimen, etc. – שִׁנּוּי וֶסֶת וכו׳: One who has been accustomed for many years to a certain diet or other regimen, due to illness or to any other reason, should not institute a change in his regimen, as this can cause the onset of disease (Rambam *Sefer HaMadda*, *Hilkhot Deot* 4:21).

One who sends presents to his father-in-law's house – הַשּׁוֹלֵחַ סִבְלוֹנוֹת לְבֵית חָמִיו: If one sent presents to his father-in-law's house and then either he or his betrothed died, or if he retracted his agreement to the betrothal, the presents return in their entirety to him, except for food and drink. This is the *halakha* irrespective of whether there are numerous presents or few, and irrespective of whether the betrothed man ate a betrothal feast at his father-in-law's house or not. If he sent monetary gifts, or a few vessels for the betrothed woman to use in her father's house, and they were used, worn out, or lost, she is not required to return to him items or money of equivalent value. If they are still intact, they are returned to him. If they are not returned, he may sue for them in court, as it is evident that he sent them only as a courtesy. This ruling is in accordance with the statement of Ravin the Elder (see 146b), who disagrees with the ruling of the mishna (Ri Migash; Rambam). The Rema adds that the food, drink, and small gifts are kept by the betrothed woman's family only if the betrothed man ate at his father-in-law's house, in which case even those presents that are still intact are not returned. If the betrothed man did not eat there, everything is returned, in accordance with the mishna (Rambam *Sefer Kinyan*, *Hilkhot Zekhiya UMattana* 6:21–22; *Shulḥan Arukh*, *Even HaEzer* 50:3, and see *Beit Shmuel* there).

LANGUAGE

Regimen [*veset*] – וֶסֶת: From the Greek ἔθος, *ethos*, meaning custom or habit. The term *veset* is used here in the sense of a custom or routine.

Presents [*sivlonot*] – סִבְלוֹנוֹת: The majority of the commentaries explain that this term is derived from the root *samekh*, *beit*, *lamed*, which means to bear, and it is used to denote gifts. The etymology of the word is similar to the derivation of the term *masot*, which means portions (see Genesis 43:34), from the root *nun*, *sin*, *alef*, which also means to bear. Others say that the term *sivlonot* is derived from the Greek συμβολή, *sumbolē*, which can be used in the sense of a down payment, a concept that could apply in the context of an agreement between two parties.

BACKGROUND

Book of ben Sira – סֵפֶר בֶּן סִירָא: The book of ben Sira was one of the first composed after the canonization of the Bible. It was written by Shimon ben Yehoshua ben Sira, a resident of Jerusalem in the time before the Hasmonean period and a younger contemporary of Shimon HaTzaddik. The book was held in high regard. It was translated into Greek by the author's grandson in Alexandria in 132 BCE, which facilitated its circulation among those who were unfamiliar with Hebrew. Excerpts from the book of ben Sira in the original Hebrew have been found in excavations at Masada and in the Judean desert.

The Septuagint includes the book of ben Sira among the books of the Bible, leading many other translations to do the same. Although the Sages considered the book apocryphal, they did not refrain from quoting it in a most respectful manner. Occasionally they even considered it as if it were part of the Bible. The work was later banned, perhaps because it was frequently confused with a different book, the *Alphabet of ben Sira*, a popular work containing many dubious statements. The passage cited here is not found either in the translations or in the Hebrew manuscripts of the book. It does appear as an addendum in one of the manuscripts as a maxim that was transmitted verbally.

NOTES

If he sent many presents, etc. – שָׁלַח סִבְלוֹנוֹת מְרוּבִּין וכו׳: The Rashbam explains that there is no essential difference between sending many presents and sending few presents. The only distinction made is between when the betrothed man stipulates that the presents should return with her to her husband's house, and when he does not state this stipulation. The mishna refers to many presents as opposed to few presents because typically, when one sends many presents, he states an explicit stipulation that the presents should return to him after the marriage. The Rashbam also notes that the first clause in the mishna refers to a case where the betrothed man did not state this stipulation.

״אָכַל״ תְּנַן, שָׁתָה מַאי? הוּא תְּנַן, שְׁלוּחוֹ מַאי? ״שָׁם״ תְּנַן, שִׁגֵּר לוֹ מַאי?

§ The Gemara asks: **We learned** the *halakha* in the mishna with regard to a betrothed man who **ate** at his father-in-law's house. **What is** the *halakha* **if he drank** there? **We learned** the *halakha* in the mishna with regard to a case where **he,** the betrothed, ate there. **What is** the *halakha* **if his agent** ate there? **We learned** the *halakha* in the mishna with regard to a case where the betrothed man ate **there,** at his father-in-law's house. **What is** the *halakha* if his father-in-law **sent him** a feast to his home?

תָּא שְׁמַע, דְּאָמַר רַב יְהוּדָה אָמַר שְׁמוּאֵל: מַעֲשֶׂה בְּאָדָם אֶחָד שֶׁשִּׁגֵּר לְבֵית חָמִיו מֵאָה קְרוֹנוֹת שֶׁל כַּדֵּי יַיִן וְשֶׁל כַּדֵּי שֶׁמֶן וְשֶׁל כְּלֵי כֶסֶף וְשֶׁל כְּלֵי זָהָב וְשֶׁל כְּלֵי מִילַת, וְרָכַב בְּשִׂמְחָתוֹ, וְהָלַךְ וְעָמַד עַל פֶּתַח בֵּית חָמִיו, וְהוֹצִיאוּ כּוֹס שֶׁל חַמִּין וְשָׁתָה, וּמֵת.

The Gemara answers: **Come** and **hear** a proof concerning one these matters, as **Rav Yehuda says** that **Shmuel says:** There was **an incident involving one man who sent to his father-in-law's house one hundred wagons full of jars of wine and of jars of oil, and** one hundred wagons full **of silver vessels, and** one hundred wagons full **of gold vessels, and** one hundred wagons full **of garments of fine wool** [*milat*].[L] **And he rode** over **in his** state of **joy and went and stood by the entrance to his father-in-law's house. And they brought out** to him **a cup of hot** drink **and he drank** it, **and he** subsequently **died.**

וְזוֹ הֲלָכָה הֶעֱלָה רַבִּי אַחָא שַׂר הַבִּירָה לִפְנֵי חֲכָמִים לְאוּשָׁא, וְאָמְרוּ: סִבְלוֹנוֹת הָעֲשׂוּיִן לִיבָּלוֹת – אֵין נִגְבִּין, וְשֶׁאֵין עֲשׂוּיִן לִיבָּלוֹת – נִגְבִּין; שְׁמַע מִינָּהּ אֲפִילּוּ שָׁתָה.

The question arose as to whether the presents must be returned to the betrothed's heirs. **And Rabbi Aḥa Sar HaBira**[P] **raised this** *halakha* **before the Sages in Usha, and they said: Presents that are typically consumed**[N] **are not collected,** and those **that are not typically consumed are collected.** One can **conclude from** this incident that **even** if the betrothed only **drank,** some of the presents cannot be reclaimed.

שָׁמְעַתְּ מִינָּהּ אֲפִילּוּ פָּחוֹת מִדִּינָר? אָמַר רַב אַשִׁי: מַאן לֵימָא לָן דְּלָא שָׁחְקִי לֵיהּ מַרְגָּנִיתָא דְּשַׁוְיָא אַלְפָּא זוּזֵי וְאַשְׁקְיֵיהּ? שָׁמְעַתְּ מִינָּהּ אֲפִילּוּ שִׁגְּרוּ לוֹ? דִּלְמָא כָּל פֶּתַח בֵּית חָמִיו כְּבֵית חָמִיו דָּמֵי.

The Gemara asks: **Can you learn from this** incident that the presents cannot be claimed **even** if he ate or drank **less than** the value of **a dinar,** since a cup of hot drink is not worth a dinar? **Rav Ashi said: Who shall say to us that they did not grind a pearl worth one thousand dinars and serve it to him to drink?** The Gemara asks: **Can you learn from this** incident that **even** if **they sent** the feast **to him** the presents cannot be claimed, as he drank at the entrance and did not enter inside? The Gemara rejects this conclusion: **Perhaps the entire entrance of his father-in-law's house is considered as his father-in-law's house.**

אִיבַּעֲיָא לְהוּ: מַהוּ שֶׁיְּשַׁלֵּשׁ? שֶׁבַח סִבְלוֹנוֹת, מַהוּ? כֵּיוָן דְּאִי אִיתְנְהוּ לְדִידֵיהּ הָדְרִי – בִּרְשׁוּתֵיהּ שְׁבוּח, אוֹ דִּלְמָא כֵּיוָן דְּאִי אָבְדִי אוֹ מִגַּנְבִי בָּעֵי שַׁלּוֹמֵי לֵיהּ – בִּרְשׁוּתָא דִּידָהּ שְׁבוּח? תֵּיקוּ.

A dilemma was raised before the Sages: Rava states that if the betrothed man ate less than the value of a dinar at his father-in-law's house, and the marriage is not effected, he can collect the presents he sent. **What is** the *halakha* concerning **whether he must divide** the value[N] of the presents, and claim only part of the value, in proportion to the amount he ate? And **what is** the *halakha* concerning **the enhancement of** the value of **the presents?**[N] Does one say that **since** the *halakha* is that **if they are** extant **they are returned to him,** therefore **they were enhanced under his ownership? Or perhaps, since** the *halakha* is that **if they are lost or stolen,** the betrothed woman's family is **required to repay him,** therefore **they were enhanced under her ownership.** The Gemara concludes: These dilemmas **shall stand** unresolved.

בָּעֵי רָבָא: סִבְלוֹנוֹת הָעֲשׂוּיִן לִיבָּלוֹת וְלֹא בָּלוּ, מַהוּ? תָּא שְׁמַע: וְזוֹ הֲלָכָה הֶעֱלָה רַבִּי אַחָא שַׂר הַבִּירָה לִפְנֵי חֲכָמִים בְּאוּשָׁא, וְאָמְרוּ: סִבְלוֹנוֹת הָעֲשׂוּיִן לִיבָּלוֹת – אֵין נִגְבִּין, וְשֶׁאֵין עֲשׂוּיִן לִיבָּלוֹת – נִגְבִּין; מַאי לָאו אַף עַל גַּב דְּלֹא בָּלוּ? לָא, דְּבָלוּ.

Rava raises a dilemma: What is the *halakha* with regard to **presents that are typically consumed, but were not consumed?** The Gemara replies: **Come** and **hear** a proof: **And Rabbi Aḥa Sar HaBira raised this** *halakha* **before the Sages at Usha, and they said: Presents that are typically consumed are not collected,** and those **that are not typically consumed are collected. What, is it not** referring to presents that are typically consumed **even though they were not consumed?** The Gemara rejects this: **No,** the mishna is referring to presents **that were** actually **consumed.**

תָּא שְׁמַע: סִבְלוֹנוֹת מוּעָטִין שֶׁתִּשְׁתַּמֵּשׁ בָּהֶן וְהִיא בְּבֵית אָבִיהָ – אֵין נִגְבִּין! תַּרְגְּמַהּ רָבָא: בְּיֵיבָא וְסִבְכְתָא.

The Gemara replies: **Come** and **hear** a proof from the mishna: If he sent a **few presents for her to use while she is in her father's house,** they **are not collected.** This indicates that they cannot be collected in any event, irrespective of whether they were used or not. **Rava interpreted** the mishna as referring **to a snood or hairnet,** which are insignificant items that the betrothed man sends without any intention of later collecting them.

LANGUAGE

Fine wool [*milat*] – מִילַת: Some explain that this term is derived from the Greek μηλωτή, *mēlotē*, which means sheepskin. Others explain that it is derived from the name of the ancient Greek town Miletus, Μίλητος, which was known for the quality of its woolen garments. The Talmud describes *milat* as wool of the finest quality, which was obtained primarily from the fleece of sheep and lambs that were kept specifically for this purpose.

PERSONALITIES

Rabbi Aḥa Sar HaBira – רַבִּי אַחָא שַׂר הַבִּירָה: This Rabbi Aḥa was a fifth-generation *tanna*. It appears that there was a third-generation *amora* of the same name (see *Yevamot* 45a), who may have been one of his descendants. Both lived in Eretz Yisrael. The title Sar HaBira could be rendered: Master of the Temple. It is possible that this was a hereditary title that stemmed from the fact that one of his ancestors had been appointed to supervise the Temple Mount.

NOTES

Presents that are typically consumed – סִבְלוֹנוֹת הָעֲשׂוּיִן לִיבָּלוֹת: Food is considered a present that is typically consumed, as a present of food is likely to be consumed before the wedding, whereas presents of jewelry, for example, are not typically consumed (Rashbam). Rabbeinu Yona adds that clothing and monetary gifts are also considered presents that are typically consumed, since the money is likely to be spent and the clothes are likely to wear out before the wedding.

Whether he must divide the value – שֶׁיְּשַׁלֵּשׁ: If, for example, he ate half a dinar's worth of food, perhaps he may claim only half of the value of the presents, and if he ate one-third of a dinar's worth, perhaps he may claim only two-thirds of their value. Or perhaps, whenever he ate less than a dinar's worth, he collects the presents in their entirety (Rashbam; see *Tosafot*).

The enhancement of the presents – שֶׁבַח סִבְלוֹנוֹת: For example, if the betrothed man sent cattle and sheep to his father-in-law's house, and the animals gave birth, are the offspring also claimed by the betrothed man in the event that the wedding is canceled, or do the offspring belong to the betrothed woman's family? (Rashbam).

אָמַר רַב יְהוּדָה אָמַר רַב: מַעֲשֶׂה בְּאָדָם אֶחָד שֶׁשִּׁגֵּר לְבֵית חָמִיו יַיִן חָדָשׁ וְשֶׁמֶן חָדָשׁ וּכְלֵי פִשְׁתָּן חָדָשׁ בָּעֲצֶרֶת. מַאי קָא מַשְׁמַע לָן? אִיבָּעֵית אֵימָא: חֲשִׁיבוּתָא דְּאֶרֶץ יִשְׂרָאֵל קָא מַשְׁמַע לָן; וְאִיבָּעֵית אֵימָא: דְּאִי טָעֵין – טַעֲנָתֵיהּ טַעֲנָה.

§ **Rav Yehuda says** that **Rav says: There was an incident involving one man who sent new wine, and new oil, and new linen garments to his father-in-law's house at the** time of ***Shavuot*.** The Gemara asks: **What is this** incident **teaching us?** The Gemara answers: **If you wish, say** that it **teaches us the importance,** i.e., the greatness, **of Eretz Yisrael,** where there is new wine, oil, and linen already available at the time of *Shavuot*. **And if you wish, say** instead that it teaches **that if** the betrothed man **claims** that he sent these items at the time of *Shavuot*, **his claim is** a plausible **claim,** and there is no reason to question it.

אָמַר רַב יְהוּדָה אָמַר רַב: מַעֲשֶׂה בְּאָדָם אֶחָד שֶׁאָמְרוּ לוֹ אִשְׁתּוֹ תּוֹתְרָנִית הִיא, וְנִכְנַס אַחֲרֶיהָ לְחוּרְבָה לְבוֹדְקָהּ; אָמַר לָהּ: רֵיחַ צְנוֹן אֲנִי מֵרִיחַ בַּגָּלִיל,

Rav Yehuda says that **Rav says: There was an incident involving one man who was told** that **his wife,** i.e., his betrothed, **was one whose sense of smell was impaired,**[NB] **and he followed her into a ruin,** carrying a date with him, **to check her** to see if she could correctly identify the smell. **He said to her: I smell** the **scent of radish in the Galilee.**

NOTES

His wife was one whose sense of smell was impaired – אִשְׁתּוֹ תּוֹתְרָנִית הִיא: He wished to check whether she suffered from this ailment, because one betroths a woman on condition that she has no blemishes, and if it is subsequently discovered that she does have blemishes, the betrothal is null (Rabbeinu Ḥananel).

BACKGROUND

One whose sense of smell was impaired – תּוֹתְרָנִית: If a woman suffers from an ailment that diminishes or blocks her sense of smell, this is considered a hidden blemish, and it can serve as grounds for divorce or for the nullification of the betrothal. This is because the defect prevents her from properly fulfilling her duty to cook for her husband (*Pitḥei Teshuva*).

Perek **IX**
Daf **146** Amud **b**

אֲמַרָה לֵיהּ: מַן יָהֵיב לָן מִכּוֹתָבוֹת דִּירִיחוֹ וְאָכְלִינָא בֵּיהּ! נְפַל עֲלָהּ חוּרְבָה וּמֵתָה; אָמְרוּ חֲכָמִים: הוֹאִיל וְלֹא נִכְנַס אַחֲרֶיהָ אֶלָּא לְבוֹדְקָהּ, מֵתָה – אֵינוֹ יוֹרְשָׁהּ.

She said to him: Who will give us of the dates of Jericho that I shall eat them, hinting that she smelled the date he had brought with him. **The ruin collapsed upon her and she died. The Sages said: Since he went into** the ruin **after her only to check her** sense of smell, and not for the purpose of consummating their marriage, if **she dies, he does not inherit** from **her,**[N] as the marriage was not effected, and a man does not inherit from his betrothed.

״סִבְלוֹנוֹת מוּעָטִין שֶׁתִּשְׁתַּמֵּשׁ בָּהֶן בְּבֵית אָבִיהָ״ וכו׳. יָתֵיב רָבִין סָבָא קַמֵּיהּ דְּרַב פַּפָּא וְיָתֵיב וְקָאָמַר: בֵּין שֶׁמֵּתָה הִיא וּבֵין שֶׁמֵּת הוּא, הֲדַר הוּא – סִבְלוֹנוֹת הָדְרִי, מַאֲכָל וּמִשְׁתֶּה לָא הָדַר; הֲדָרָא בָּהּ אִיהִי – הֲדָרָא אֲפִילּוּ כִּישָׁא דְּיַרְקָא. אָמַר רַב הוּנָא בְּרֵיהּ דְּרַב יְהוֹשֻׁעַ: וְשָׁמִין לָהֶן דְּמֵי בָשָׂר בְּזוֹל. עַד כַּמָּה בְּזוֹל? עַד תִּילְתָּא.

§ The mishna teaches: If he sent **a few presents for her to use while in her father's house,** they are not collected. **Ravin the Elder was sitting before Rav Pappa**[N] **and he was sitting and saying: Whether she died, or whether he died,** or whether **he retracted** his agreement to the betrothal and divorced her, the **presents return** to the betrothed man or his heirs, but **food and drink do not return. If she retracted** her agreement to the betrothal[H] and requested a divorce, **even a bundle of vegetables returns** to the betrothed man. **Rav Huna, son of Rav Yehoshua, said:** When the presents are returned, the court **appraises for** the betrothed woman's family the sum that they must repay for any meat he gave her, according **to a reduced** assessment of the **value of** the **meat**[N] and not according to the price the betrothed man paid. **How much** less is the **reduced** assessment? **Up to one-third** less than he paid.

HALAKHA

If she retracted her agreement to the betrothal – הֲדָרָא בָּהּ אִיהִי: If one sends presents to his father-in-law's house and the betrothed woman retracts her agreement to the betrothal, the presents are all returned to the betrothed man, in accordance with the opinion of Ravin the Elder. Even if he sent food, the betrothed woman repays the value of the food according to the less expensive market price, which is calculated as one-third less than the standard price. If it is the custom in that place for the betrothed man to hold a betrothal feast for all his friends and acquaintances, or to pay for additional items, and he brings witnesses attesting that he spent that money according to the local custom, the betrothed woman's family pays all his expenses, since she was the cause of these expenditures. The Ra'avad disagrees with this latter ruling (see *Maggid Mishne* and *Leḥem Mishne*). The Rema adds that according to some authorities, if one sends presents after preliminary arrangements are made for the betrothal but before the betrothal and the betrothed woman retracts her agreement to the betrothal, all the presents are returned (*Nimmukei Yosef*; Ritva). Other authorities disagree (Rambam *Sefer Kinyan*, *Hilkhot Zekhiya UMattana* 6:23–24; *Shulḥan Arukh*, *Even HaEzer* 50:3, and see *Taz* and *Beit Shmuel* there).

NOTES

He does not inherit from her – אֵינוֹ יוֹרְשָׁהּ: Since she entered the ruin with him, which is a place of seclusion, this could be considered consummation of the marriage, in which case he would inherit from her. Nevertheless, since he entered the ruin with her only in order to test her and not in order to seclude himself with her, their seclusion was not considered consummation of the marriage and therefore he does not inherit from her (*Tosafot*; Rabbeinu Ḥananel; Ramah).

Ravin the Elder was sitting before Rav Pappa, etc. – יָתֵיב רָבִין סָבָא קַמֵּיהּ דְּרַב פַּפָּא וכו׳: According to most of the commentaries, Ravin the Elder is elaborating on the *halakha* stated in the mishna. When he states that the presents return to the betrothed man, he is referring either to a situation where the betrothed man sent many presents or a situation where he sent presents that are not typically consumed (Rashbam; Rashba). Similarly, the Ramah explains that Ravin is referring to a situation where the betrothed man did not eat in his father-in-law's house at all. By contrast, the Ri Migash, the Rambam, and the Meiri explain that Ravin is referring to a situation where the betrothed man sent few presents, in which case the mishna states that the presents cannot be claimed by the betrothed man. Ravin holds that whether or not the betrothed man ate in his father-in-law's house, or whether he sent many presents or few, everything is returned to the betrothed man except for food and drink. The Ritva states that this explanation is difficult, as it is unclear how Ravin the Elder can rule contrary to the mishna.

The court appraises for them according to a reduced assessment of the value of the meat – וְשָׁמִין לָהֶן דְּמֵי בָשָׂר בְּזוֹל: When the cost of the food they ate at the groom's feast is appraised, it is not appraised according to the food's common market value; rather, it is appraised according to the least expensive price at which it can be purchased, which is one-third less than the standard price. The main reason for this is that the betrothed woman's family can claim that had they known that they would have to repay the cost, they would have searched for less expensive food.

מתני׳ שְׁכִיב מְרַע שֶׁכָּתַב כָּל נְכָסָיו לַאֲחֵרִים וְשִׁיֵּיר קַרְקַע כָּל שֶׁהוּא – מַתְּנָתוֹ קַיֶּימֶת, לֹא שִׁיֵּיר קַרְקַע כָּל שֶׁהוּא – אֵין מַתְּנָתוֹ קַיֶּימֶת.

MISHNA With regard to **a person on his deathbed**[H] **who wrote** a deed granting **all of his property to others, and he reserved** for himself **any amount of land, his gift stands** even if he subsequently recovers. If **he did not reserve** for himself **any amount of land,**[H] and he recovered, **his gift does not stand,** as the gift was conditional upon his death, since is it evident that he did not intend to leave himself without means of support.

גמ׳ מַאן תַּנָּא דְּאָזְלִינַן בָּתַר אוּמְדָּנָא? אֲמַר רַב נַחְמָן: רַבִּי שִׁמְעוֹן בֶּן מְנַסְיָא הִיא; דְּתַנְיָא: הֲרֵי שֶׁהָלַךְ בְּנוֹ לִמְדִינַת הַיָּם, וְשָׁמַע שֶׁמֵּת בְּנוֹ וְעָמַד וְכָתַב כָּל נְכָסָיו לְאַחֵר, וְאַחַר כָּךְ בָּא בְּנוֹ – מַתְּנָתוֹ מַתָּנָה; רַבִּי שִׁמְעוֹן בֶּן מְנַסְיָא אוֹמֵר: אֵין מַתְּנָתוֹ מַתָּנָה, שֶׁאִלְמָלֵא הָיָה יוֹדֵעַ שֶׁבְּנוֹ קַיָּים – לֹא הָיָה כּוֹתְבָן.

GEMARA Who is the *tanna* who **taught that we follow** the principle of **assessing** a person's intentions,[N] even when he did not expressly state them? **Rav Naḥman said: This is** the opinion of **Rabbi Shimon ben Menasya, as it is taught** in a *baraita* (*Tosefta*, *Ketubot* 5:9): In a case **where one's son went overseas and he heard that his son died,** and then he **arose and wrote** a document granting **all of his property to another, and then his son came** back, **his gift** to the other people is a valid **gift. Rabbi Shimon ben Menasya says: His gift is not** a valid **gift, as had he known that his son** was **alive he would not have written** a document granting **them** his property.

רַב שֵׁשֶׁת אֲמַר: רַבִּי שִׁמְעוֹן שְׁזוּרִי הִיא; דְּתַנְיָא, בָּרִאשׁוֹנָה הָיוּ אוֹמְרִים: הַיּוֹצֵא בְּקוֹלָר וְאָמַר ״כִּתְבוּ גֵּט לְאִשְׁתִּי״ – הֲרֵי אֵלּוּ יִכְתְּבוּ וְיִתְּנוּ. חָזְרוּ לוֹמַר: אַף הַמְפָרֵשׁ וְהַיּוֹצֵא בְּשַׁיָּירָא; רַבִּי שִׁמְעוֹן שְׁזוּרִי אוֹמֵר: אַף הַמְסוּכָּן.

Rav Sheshet said: This is the opinion of **Rabbi Shimon Shezuri, as it is taught** in a mishna (*Gittin* 65b): **Initially** the Sages **would say:** With regard to **one who was taken out in a collar**[B] to be executed **and said: Write a bill of divorce for my wife, these** people **should write and give** her the document. Although he did not explicitly say the word give, this is understood to have been his intention, to release her from the necessity to perform levirate marriage or *ḥalitza*. **They** then **said** that this *halakha* applies **even to one who sets sail and one who departs with a caravan** to a far-off place. A bill of divorce is given to his wife under these circumstances even if her husband said just: Write. **Rabbi Shimon Shezuri says: Even** in the case of **one who is dangerously ill**[H] who gives that instruction, they write the bill of divorce and give it to his wife.

וְרַב נַחְמָן מַאי טַעְמָא לָא מוֹקִים לָהּ כְּרַבִּי שִׁמְעוֹן שְׁזוּרִי? שָׁאנֵי הָתָם, דַּאֲמַר ״כִּתְבוּ״. וְרַב שֵׁשֶׁת מַאי טַעְמָא לָא מוֹקִים לָהּ כְּרַבִּי שִׁמְעוֹן בֶּן מְנַסְיָא? אוּמְדָּנָא דְּמוּכָח שָׁאנֵי.

The Gemara asks: **And what is the reason** that **Rav Naḥman does not interpret** the mishna as being **in accordance with** the opinion of **Rabbi Shimon Shezuri?** The Gemara answers: Rav Naḥman holds that it **is different there, as he said: Write** a bill of divorce, thereby partially stating his intention to divorce her, whereas in the case of the mishna here, he did not express his intention at all. The Gemara asks: **And what is the reason** that **Rav Sheshet does not interpret** the mishna as being **in accordance with** the opinion of **Rabbi Shimon ben Menasya?** The Gemara answers: **An assessment** of a person's intentions **that is** clearly **proven**[N] **is different,** and it is possible that Rabbi Shimon ben Menasya does not apply this principle where the person's intentions are less evident.

מַאן תַּנָּא לְהָא דְּתָנוּ רַבָּנַן: הֲרֵי שֶׁהָיָה חוֹלֶה וּמוּטָּל בַּמִּטָּה, וְאָמְרוּ לוֹ: נְכָסֶיךָ לְמִי? וְאָמַר לָהֶן:

The Gemara asks: **Who is the** *tanna* who **taught that which the Sages taught** (*Tosefta*, *Ketubot* 4:15): If one **was ill and bedridden, and those present said to him: To whom shall your property** be given? **And he said to them:**

HALAKHA

A person on his deathbed, etc. – שְׁכִיב מְרַע וכו׳: In the case of a person on his deathbed who gives all of his property to another but reserves for himself even a small amount of his property, the *halakhot* that apply to the gift of a healthy person are applied to his gift: It is valid only if a formal act of acquisition is performed, in which case the gift cannot be retracted even if the giver recovers. If an act of acquisition is not performed, the gift is invalid even if the giver subsequently dies. According to the *Shulḥan Arukh*, this *halakha* applies if he reserves for himself literally any amount of property, whether land or movable property. The Rema adds that according to some authorities, this *halakha* applies only if he reserves for himself sufficient means to provide for himself (Rambam *Sefer Kinyan*, *Hilkhot Zekhiya UMattana* 8:15; *Shulḥan Arukh*, *Ḥoshen Mishpat* 250:4).

If he did not reserve for himself any amount of land – לֹא שִׁיֵּיר קַרְקַע כָּל שֶׁהוּא: In the case of a person on his deathbed who writes a deed granting all of his property to others without reserving anything for himself, if he recovers completely, the gift is invalid. This is the *halakha* even if an act of acquisition is performed, and even if the gift comes into the receiver's possession before the giver recovers (*Shakh*). The Rema adds that if the giver recovers he can retract the gift even if he explicitly stipulated that he would not be able to retract it. If he stipulates that he will be unable to retract the gift even if he recovers, and an act of acquisition is performed, he cannot retract the gift if he recovers (Rambam *Sefer Kinyan*, *Hilkhot Zekhiya UMattana* 8:14; *Shulḥan Arukh*, *Ḥoshen Mishpat* 250:2).

One who sets sail and one who departs with a caravan… even one who is dangerously ill – הַמְפָרֵשׁ וְהַיּוֹצֵא בְּשַׁיָּירָא... אַף הַמְסוּכָּן: If one who is dangerously ill or who is setting sail or departing with a caravan says to those present: Write a bill of divorce for my wife, they should write the bill of divorce and give it to his wife. This is because it was clearly his intention that they should write and deliver the bill of divorce (Rambam *Sefer Nashim*, *Hilkhot Geirushin* 2:12; *Shulḥan Arukh*, *Even HaEzer* 141:16).

BACKGROUND

Collar – קוֹלָר:

Collar of Roman slave

NOTES

That we follow the principle of assessing a person's intentions – דְּאָזְלִינַן בָּתַר אוּמְדָּנָא: The sick person did not state that it was only because he believed that he was dying that he was giving away his property. Despite this, the mishna rules that if he recovers, he can retract his gifts. The reason for this is that it is possible to assume that a person does not give all of his property to others if he expects to continue living, and it is therefore considered as though he expressly stipulated that the gift is conditional upon his death.

An assessment that is proven – אוּמְדָּנָא דְּמוּכָח: In the case discussed by Rabbi Shimon ben Menasya, the situation itself is indicative of the father's intentions, as he did not transfer his property to another until he heard that his son had died. In the case of a sick person, the situation in itself is not indicative, since in most cases of illness one recovers, and it is less obvious that his actions were due to the belief that he was dying (Rashbam).

דּוֹמֶה שֶׁיֵּשׁ לִי בֵּן, עַכְשָׁיו שֶׁאֵין לִי בֵּן – נְכָסַי לִפְלוֹנִי; הָיָה חוֹלֶה וּמוּטָל בְּמִטָּה, וְאָמְרוּ לוֹ: נְכָסָיו לְמִי? אָמַר לָהֶן: דּוֹמֶה שֶׁאִשְׁתִּי מְעוּבֶּרֶת, עַכְשָׁיו שֶׁאֵין אִשְׁתִּי מְעוּבֶּרֶת – נְכָסַי לִפְלוֹנִי, וְנוֹדַע שֶׁיֵּשׁ לוֹ בֵּן אוֹ שֶׁהָיְתָה אִשְׁתּוֹ מְעוּבֶּרֶת – אֵין מַתְּנָתוֹ מַתָּנָה;

Previously, I **thought that I had a son. Now** that I have been informed **that I do not have a son, my property** shall be given **to so-and-so.** Or if he **was ill and bedridden, and** those present **said to him: To whom** shall **his property** be given? And **he said to them:** Previously, I **thought that my wife was pregnant. Now** that I have been informed **that my wife is not pregnant, my property** shall be given **to so-and-so. And if it** then **became known,** in either of those cases, **that he had a son or that his wife was pregnant, his gift is not** a valid **gift,**[H] since he clearly indicated that he bestowed the gift on that recipient only because he thought he had no heir.

לֵימָא, רַבִּי שִׁמְעוֹן בֶּן מְנַסְיָא הִיא וְלָא רַבָּנַן? אֲפִילּוּ תֵּימָא רַבָּנַן, ״דּוֹמֶה״ שָׁאנֵי.

The Gemara asks: **Shall** we **say** that **this is** the opinion of **Rabbi Shimon ben Menasya and not** the opinion of **the Rabbis?** The Gemara rejects this: **You** can **even say** that this is the opinion of **the Rabbis,** as the case where he said: I **thought** that I had a son, **is different,** since he stated the reason for his actions.

וּדְקָאָרֵי לָהּ מַאי קָאָרֵי לָהּ? מַהוּ דְּתֵימָא: צַעֲרֵיהּ הוּא דְּקָא מַדְכַּר, קָא מַשְׁמַע לַן.

Since the difference between the cases is obvious, the Gemara asks: **He who asked it, why did he ask it?** The Gemara replies: **Lest you say** that when the bedridden man mentioned that he does not have a son, **he is mentioning it** only as an expression of **his sorrow,** since the matter of the disposal of his estate brings it to mind, but he is not mentioning this as the reason for the gift, the *baraita* therefore **teaches us** that the reference to his son indicates that had he known that he had a son, he would not have given his property to others.

אָמַר רַבִּי זֵירָא אָמַר רַב: מִנַּיִן לְמַתְּנַת שְׁכִיב מְרַע שֶׁהִיא מִן הַתּוֹרָה? שֶׁנֶּאֱמַר: ״וְהַעֲבַרְתֶּם אֶת נַחֲלָתוֹ לְבִתּוֹ״, יֵשׁ לְךָ הַעֲבָרָה אַחֶרֶת שֶׁהִיא כָּזוֹ, וְאֵי זוֹ? זוֹ מַתְּנַת שְׁכִיב מְרַע.

§ Unlike the gifts of a healthy person, the gifts of a person on his deathbed do not require a formal act of acquisition. **Rabbi Zeira says** that **Rav says: From where** is it derived **that** this *halakha* with regard to **the gift of a person on his deathbed is by Torah law?**[N] **As it is stated** in the passage delineating the laws of inheritance: "If a man dies, and he does not have a son, **then you shall cause his inheritance to pass to his daughter**" (Numbers 27:8). The term "you shall cause…to pass" is superfluous, as the verse could have stated: His inheritance shall go to his daughter. One can therefore derive from this term that **you have another** case of **causing** property **to pass** to another, **which is comparable to this** case of inheritance, which does not require an act of acquisition. **And what is this** case? **This is** the case of **the gift of a person on his deathbed.**

רַב נַחְמָן אָמַר רַבָּה בַּר אֲבוּהּ, מֵהָכָא: ״וּנְתַתֶּם אֶת נַחֲלָתוֹ לְאֶחָיו״, יֵשׁ לְךָ נְתִינָה אַחֶרֶת שֶׁהִיא כָּזוֹ, וְאֵי זוֹ? זוֹ מַתְּנַת שְׁכִיב מְרַע.

Rav **Naḥman** says that **Rabba bar Avuh says:** The *halakha* with regard to the gift of a person on his deathbed is derived **from here:** "And if he has no daughter, **then you shall give his inheritance to his brothers**" (Numbers 27:9). The verse could have stated: His inheritance shall go to his brothers, as inheritance is transferred by itself, without any intervention. One can therefore derive from the term "you shall give" that **you have another** case of **giving that is comparable to this** case. **And what is this** case? **This is** the case of **the gift of a person on his deathbed.**

וְרַב נַחְמָן, מַאי טַעֲמָא לָא אֲמַר מִ״וְהַעֲבַרְתֶּם״? הַהוּא מִיבָּעֵי לֵיהּ לְכִדְרַבִּי; דְּתַנְיָא, רַבִּי אוֹמֵר: בְּכוּלָּן נֶאֶמְרָה בָּהֶן נְתִינָה וְכָאן נֶאֶמְרָה הַעֲבָרָה, אֵין לְךָ שֶׁמַּעֲבִיר נַחֲלָה מִשֵּׁבֶט לְשֵׁבֶט אֶלָּא בַּת, הוֹאִיל וּבְנָהּ וּבַעְלָהּ יוֹרְשִׁין אוֹתָהּ.

The Gemara asks: **And** with regard to **Rav Naḥman, what is the reason** that he **did not say** that this *halakha* can be derived **from** the term **"you shall cause…to pass"?** The Gemara answers: **He requires that** verse **for that** which is taught **by Rabbi** Yehuda HaNasi, **as it is taught** in a *baraita*: **Rabbi** Yehuda HaNasi **says: With regard to all of** the heirs, the term **giving was stated** in the Torah, **and here,** with regard to the daughter, the term **causing to pass was stated.** One can derive from this that **there is no** heir **who** can **cause** one's **inheritance to pass from** one **tribe to** another **tribe except** for the **daughter, since her son and her husband inherit** from **her,** and they may be of a different tribe.

וְרַבִּי זֵירָא, מַאי טַעֲמָא לָא אֲמַר מִ״וּנְתַתֶּם״? אוֹרְחֵיהּ דִּקְרָא הוּא.

The Gemara asks: **And** with regard to **Rabbi Zeira, what is the reason** that **he did not say** that this *halakha* can be derived **from** the term **"Then you shall give"?** The Gemara answers: Rabbi Zeira maintains that **this** usage **is the** usual **manner of the verse,** and one cannot derive anything from this term.

HALAKHA

And it became known that he had a son or that his wife was pregnant, his gift is not a valid gift – **וְנוֹדַע שֶׁיֵּשׁ לוֹ בֵּן אוֹ שֶׁהָיְתָה אִשְׁתּוֹ מְעוּבֶּרֶת אֵין מַתְּנָתוֹ מַתָּנָה**: In the case of a person on his deathbed who is asked to whom his property shall be given, who says: Previously, I thought that I had a son or that my wife was pregnant, but now that I have been informed that I do not have a son and my wife is not pregnant, my property shall go to so-and-so, the *halakha* is as follows: If it becomes known that he has a son or that his wife was pregnant, his gift is not a valid gift, even if subsequently his son dies or his wife miscarries (Rambam *Sefer Kinyan, Hilkhot Zekhiya UMattana* 8:7; *Shulḥan Arukh, Ḥoshen Mishpat* 253:5).

NOTES

That the gift of a person on his deathbed is by Torah law – **לְמַתְּנַת שְׁכִיב מְרַע שֶׁהִיא מִן הַתּוֹרָה**: *Tosafot* explain that actually, everyone agrees that this *halakha* is a rabbinic ordinance and not Torah law, although the Sages reinforced their ordinance, treating it with the force of Torah law. The verses mentioned here are cited as a mere support.

רַב מְנַשְּׁיָא בַּר יִרְמְיָה אָמַר, מֵהָכָא: ״בַּיָּמִים הָהֵם חָלָה חִזְקִיָּהוּ לָמוּת וַיָּבֹא אֵלָיו יְשַׁעְיָהוּ בֶן אָמוֹץ הַנָּבִיא וַיֹּאמֶר אֵלָיו כֹּה אָמַר ה׳ צַו לְבֵיתְךָ כִּי מֵת אַתָּה וְלֹא תִחְיֶה״ – בְּצַוָּאָה בְּעָלְמָא.

Rav Menashya bar Yirmeya says: The *halakha* with regard to the gift of a person on his deathbed is derived **from here: "In those days Hezekiah became deathly ill, and Isaiah ben Amoz the prophet came to him, and said to him: So says the Lord: Instruct your household, for you will die, and you will not live"** (II Kings 20:1). This indicates that **merely by** issuing **an instruction,** a person on his deathbed can transfer ownership of his property.

רָמִי בַּר יְחֶזְקֵאל אָמַר, מֵהָכָא: ״וַאֲחִיתוֹפֶל רָאָה כִּי לֹא נֶעֶשְׂתָה עֲצָתוֹ וַיַּחֲבֹשׁ אֶת הַחֲמוֹר וַיֵּלֶךְ אֶל בֵּיתוֹ אֶל עִירוֹ וַיְצַו אֶל בֵּיתוֹ וַיֵּחָנַק״ – בְּצַוָּאָה בְּעָלְמָא.

Rami bar Yeḥezkel says: The *halakha* with regard to the gift of a person on his deathbed is derived **from here: "And when Ahithophel saw that his counsel was not followed, he saddled his ass,** and he arose, **and went to his home, to his city; and he instructed his household, and strangled himself"** (II Samuel 17:23). This indicates that **merely by** issuing **an instruction,** a person on his deathbed can transfer ownership of his property.

תָּנוּ רַבָּנַן, שְׁלֹשָׁה דְּבָרִים צִוָּה אֲחִיתוֹפֶל אֶת בָּנָיו: אַל תִּהְיוּ בְּמַחֲלוֹקֶת, וְאַל תִּמְרְדוּ בְּמַלְכוּת בֵּית דָּוִד, וְיוֹם טוֹב שֶׁל עֲצֶרֶת בָּרוּר – זִרְעוּ חִטִּים. מָר זוּטְרָא אֲמַר: בָּלוּל אִיתְּמַר. אָמְרִי נְהַרְדְּעֵי מִשְּׁמֵיהּ דְּרַבִּי יַעֲקֹב: לֹא בָּרוּר – בָּרוּר מַמָּשׁ, וְלֹא בָּלוּל – בָּלוּל מַמָּשׁ, אֶלָּא אֲפִילּוּ בָּלוּל וְרוּחַ צְפוֹנִית מְנַשַּׁבְתּוֹ – זֶה הוּא בָּרוּר.

The Sages taught: Before his death, when he saw that Absalom's rebellion against King David had failed, **Ahithophel instructed**[N] **his sons** with regard to **three matters: Do not be** participants **in a dispute. And do not rebel against the kingship of the house of David.**[N] **And if the festival of *Shavuot* is a clear day, sow wheat,** as it is a sign that the wheat crop will thrive. **Mar Zutra said: It was stated** that the wheat crop will thrive if *Shavuot* **is a cloudy** day, not if it is a clear day. The Sages **of Neharde'a say in the name of Rabbi Ya'akov:** According to both opinions, **a clear** day does **not literally** mean **a clear** day, **nor** does **a cloudy** day **literally** mean **a cloudy** day. **Rather, even** if the day is **cloudy but a north wind is blowing** the clouds away, **this is** considered **a clear** day.

אֲמַר לֵיהּ רַבִּי אַבָּא לְרַב אַשִׁי: אֲנַן אַדְּרַב יִצְחָק בַּר אַבְדִּימִי מַתְנִינַן לָהּ, דְּאָמַר רַב יִצְחָק בַּר אַבְדִּימִי: מוֹצָאֵי יוֹם טוֹב הָאַחֲרוֹן שֶׁל חַג הַכֹּל צוֹפִין לַעֲשַׁן הַמַּעֲרָכָה, נָטָה כְּלַפֵּי צָפוֹן – עֲנִיִּים שְׂמֵחִים וּבַעֲלֵי בָתִּים עֲצֵבִין, מִפְּנֵי שֶׁגִּשְׁמֵי שָׁנָה מְרוּבִּין וּפֵירוֹת מַרְקִיבִין;

Rabbi Abba said to Rav Ashi: We teach this matter of signs concerning crops **with regard to** the statement of **Rav Yitzḥak bar Avdimi, as Rav Yitzḥak bar Avdimi says:** At **the conclusion of the final day of the festival** of *Sukkot,* **everyone looked upon the smoke** rising from **the arrangement** of wood on the altar. If the smoke **inclined toward** the **north**[N] due to a south wind, **the poor** were **glad and the homeowners** were **sad, because** this was a sign that the **year's rainfall** would be **plentiful, and** although the rain would produce an abundant crop, the **produce** would **decay** due to the humidity. The humidity would make it difficult to store the abundant harvest, forcing the homeowners to sell the produce quickly at a lower price.

נָטָה כְּלַפֵּי דָּרוֹם – עֲנִיִּים עֲצֵבִים וּבַעֲלֵי בָתִּים שְׂמֵחִין, מִפְּנֵי שֶׁגִּשְׁמֵי שָׁנָה מוּעָטִין וּפֵירוֹת מִשְׁתַּמְּרִין; נָטָה כְּלַפֵּי מִזְרָח – הַכֹּל שְׂמֵחִין; כְּלַפֵּי מַעֲרָב – הַכֹּל עֲצֵבִין.

If the smoke **inclined toward** the **south** due to a north wind, **the poor** were **sad and the homeowners** were **glad, because** this indicated that the **year's rainfall** would be **sparse and** the **produce** would be meager and would **store** well. If the smoke **inclined toward** the **east** due to a west wind, **everyone** was **glad,** because this indicated that there would be sufficient rainfall to ensure a substantial crop, and at the same time, the produce would store well. If the smoke inclined **toward** the **west** due to an east wind, **everyone** was **sad,** because the east wind does not bring rain, and this indicated that there would be a drought.

וּרְמִינְהִי: מִזְרָחִית – לְעוֹלָם יָפָה, מַעֲרָבִית – לְעוֹלָם קָשָׁה, רוּחַ צְפוֹנִית – יָפָה לַחִטִּים בְּשָׁעָה שֶׁהֵבִיאוּ שְׁלִישׁ, וְקָשָׁה לַזֵּיתִים בְּשָׁעָה שֶׁיָּנֵיצוּ, וְרוּחַ דְּרוֹמִית – קָשָׁה לַחִטִּין בְּשָׁעָה שֶׁהֵבִיאוּ שְׁלִישׁ, וְיָפָה לַזֵּיתִים בְּשָׁעָה שֶׁיָּנֵיצוּ;

The Gemara **raises a contradiction** from a *baraita*: **An east** wind is **always beneficial,** and **a west** wind is **always harmful. A north wind** is **beneficial to the wheat when it has reached one-third** of its growth **and harmful to the olives when they are blossoming. And a south wind is harmful to the wheat when it has reached one-third** of its growth **and beneficial to the olives when they are blossoming.**

NOTES

Ahithophel instructed – צִוָּה אֲחִיתוֹפֶל: The Rashbam notes that Ahithophel's instructions were a tradition held by the Sages, as the details of his will are not stated in the verse.

And do not rebel against the kingship of the house of David – וְאַל תִּמְרְדוּ בְּמַלְכוּת בֵּית דָּוִד: Ahithophel instructed his sons not to rebel against the house of David, since he rebelled and failed (Rashbam).

If the smoke inclined toward the north – נָטָה כְּלַפֵּי צָפוֹן: The Gemara asks elsewhere (*Yoma* 21b) why this does not contradict the *baraita* that states that the wind never dispersed the smoke of the arrangement of wood on the altar. The Gemara answers that the smoke was not dispersed by the wind, but the wind did cause it to incline somewhat to the side, like a palm tree swaying in the wind.

וְאָמַר רַב יוֹסֵף, וְאִיתֵּימָא מָר זוּטְרָא, וְאִיתֵּימָא רַב נַחְמָן בַּר יִצְחָק, וְסִימָנָךְ: שֻׁלְחָן בַּצָּפוֹן וּמְנוֹרָה בַּדָּרוֹם, הַאי מְרַבֵּי דִּידֵיהּ וְהַאי מְרַבֵּי דִּידֵיהּ!

And Rav Yosef says, and some say it is Mar Zutra who says this, and some say it is Rav Naḥman bar Yitzḥak who says this: The following is your mnemonic to remember which wind is beneficial to which crop: The Table is in the north of the Sanctuary, and the Candelabrum is in the south. This one increases its own, and that one increases its own, i.e., the Table, upon which the shewbread made from wheat is placed, is in the north, and the north wind is beneficial to the wheat. The Candelabrum, which is lit with olive oil, is in the south, and the south wind is beneficial to the olives. In any event, the *baraita* contradicts the statement of Rav Yitzḥak bar Avdimi with regard to the effect of the western and eastern winds.

לָא קַשְׁיָא: הָא לָן וְהָא לְהוּ.

The Gemara answers: This is **not difficult. This,** the east wind, is **for us,** in Babylonia, **and that,** the west wind, is **for them,** in Eretz Yisrael. In Babylonia the east wind is beneficial, because water is plentiful there, and the dry east wind does not harm the crops. In Eretz Yisrael the east wind is harmful, because water is scarce, and the east wind ruins the crops, whereas the west wind brings the necessary rain.

תַּנְיָא, אַבָּא שָׁאוּל אוֹמֵר: יוֹם טוֹב שֶׁל עֲצֶרֶת בָּרוּר – סִימָן יָפֶה לְכָל הַשָּׁנָה כּוּלָּהּ. אֲמַר רַב זְבִיד: הַאי יוֹמָא קַמָּא דְּרֵישׁ שַׁתָּא, אִי חֲמִים – כּוּלָּהּ שַׁתָּא חֲמִימָא, אִי קְרִיר – כּוּלָּהּ שַׁתָּא קְרִירָא. לְמַאי נָפְקָא מִינָּהּ?

It **is taught** in a *baraita*: **Abba Shaul says: If the festival of** ***Shavuot*** is **a clear** day, this is **a good sign for the entire year. Rav Zevid said:** With regard to **this first day of Rosh HaShana, if** it is **warm, the entire year** will be **warm,** but **if it is cold, the entire year** will be **cold.** The Gemara asks: **What difference is there** whether one knows this or not?

Perek **IX**
Daf **147** Amud **b**

לִתְפִלָּתוֹ שֶׁל כֹּהֵן גָּדוֹל.

The Gemara answers: The difference is **with regard to the prayer of the High Priest,**[N] who would pray on Yom Kippur for beneficial weather, and this knowledge enabled him to formulate his prayers accordingly.

וְרָבָא אָמַר רַב נַחְמָן: מַתְּנַת שְׁכִיב מְרַע מִדְּרַבָּנַן בְּעָלְמָא הִיא, שֶׁמָּא תִּטָּרֵף דַּעְתּוֹ עָלָיו.

The Gemara resumes the discussion with regard to the gifts of a person on his deathbed: **And Rava says** that **Rav Naḥman says:** The *halakha* that the **gift of a person on his deathbed** does not require an act of acquisition **is merely by rabbinic law,**[H] and it is instituted **lest** he see that his will is not being carried out and **he lose control of his mind** due to his grief, exacerbating his physical state.

וּמִי אֲמַר רַב נַחְמָן הָכִי? וְהָא אָמַר רַב נַחְמָן, אַף עַל גַּב דְּאָמַר שְׁמוּאֵל: הַמּוֹכֵר שְׁטַר חוֹב לַחֲבֵירוֹ וְחָזַר וּמְחָלוֹ – מָחוּל, וַאֲפִילּוּ יוֹרֵשׁ מוֹחֵל, מוֹדֶה שְׁמוּאֵל, שֶׁאִם נְתָנוֹ בְּמַתְּנַת שְׁכִיב מְרַע דְּאֵינוֹ יָכוֹל לְמוֹחֲלוֹ;

The Gemara asks: **And did Rav Naḥman** actually **say this? But doesn't Rav Naḥman say: Even though Shmuel says** that with regard to **one who sells a promissory note to another and then forgives** the debt,[H] the debt **is forgiven**[N] and the note is nullified, **and even the heir** of the creditor can **forgive** the debt, **Shmuel concedes that if** the creditor **gave** the promissory note **as the gift of a person on his deathbed,**[NH] his heir **cannot forgive** the debt?[N]

HALAKHA

Is merely by rabbinic law – מִדְּרַבָּנַן בְּעָלְמָא הִיא: The gift of a person on his deathbed does not require an act of acquisition. Although this *halakha* is by rabbinic law, the Sages reinforced their ordinance, treating it with the force of Torah law so that the sick person would not become agitated upon seeing that his will is not being carried out and consequently lose control of his mind (Rambam *Sefer Kinyan, Hilkhot Zekhiya UMattana* 8:2; see 10:2).

One who sells a promissory note to another and then forgives the debt – הַמּוֹכֵר שְׁטַר חוֹב לַחֲבֵירוֹ וְחָזַר וּמְחָלוֹ: If one sells a promissory note to another and then forgives the debt, the debt is forgiven. If the creditor subsequently dies, his heir can also forgive the debt (Rambam *Sefer Kinyan, Hilkhot Mekhira* 6:12 and *Sefer Nezikin, Hilkhot Ḥovel UMazik* 7:10; *Shulḥan Arukh, Ḥoshen Mishpat* 66:23; 386:1).

If he gave the promissory note as the gift of a person on his deathbed – אִם נְתָנוֹ בְּמַתְּנַת שְׁכִיב מְרַע: If a person on his deathbed gave a promissory note to another and died, his heir cannot forgive the debt. While the creditor lives he can still forgive the debt (Rambam *Sefer Kinyan, Hilkhot Zekhiya UMattana* 10:2; *Shulḥan Arukh, Ḥoshen Mishpat* 66:27, and see *Shakh* there, 253:20).

NOTES

With regard to the prayer of the High Priest – לִתְפִלָּתוֹ שֶׁל כֹּהֵן גָּדוֹל: The High Priest would recite a prayer after he emerged from the Holy of Holies, in which he prayed for rain and beneficial weather, among other matters. If he saw that the first day of Rosh HaShana was warm, he would pray for ample rainfall to prevent the heat from causing harm (Rabbeinu Gershom Meor HaGola).

One who sells a promissory note to another and then forgives the debt, it is forgiven – הַמּוֹכֵר שְׁטַר חוֹב לַחֲבֵירוֹ וְחָזַר וּמְחָלוֹ מָחוּל: The early commentaries dispute the reason for this *halakha*, and this dispute carries halakhic ramifications. The Rif writes that one can acquire a document from another only by rabbinic law, and therefore the seller retains the right to forgive the debt. The Rif cites the Gemara here as proof, as the Gemara states that were the gift of a person on his deathbed valid by Torah law, the debt could not be forgiven. Rabbeinu Tam maintains that the sale of promissory notes is valid by Torah law. He explains that the creditor can still forgive the debt because only the lien on the debtor's property can be transferred to another, but the personal obligation of the debtor is not transferable. Since the lien on the debtor's property stems from his personal obligation to repay the debt, once the debtor's personal obligation is forgiven by the creditor, the lien is also abrogated (see Rashba). The Ra'avad explains that the debtor has a right to say to the buyer of the document that he never agreed to obligate himself to anyone other than the one who lent him the money. Consequently, the original creditor is still considered to be the one entitled to the payment, and he may forgive the debt if he so chooses.

The early commentaries state that although the creditor can forgive the debt and nullify the promissory note, he must compensate the buyer (see Rashbam). *Tosafot* state that he must compensate the buyer only for the sum he paid for the promissory note, and not for the entire amount of the loan.

If he gave the promissory note as the gift of a person on his deathbed – אִם נְתָנוֹ בְּמַתְּנַת שְׁכִיב מְרַע: The Rashbam explains that this refers either to a situation where he distributed all of his property, in which case he can confer the gift by means of verbal instruction, or to a situation where an act of acquisition was performed.

His heir cannot forgive the debt – דְּאֵינוֹ יָכוֹל לְמוֹחֲלוֹ: The creditor himself can forgive the debt either during his illness or after he recovers (Rashbam; Rabbeinu Gershom Meor HaGola).

אִי אָמְרַתְּ בִּשְׁלָמָא דְּאוֹרָיְיתָא – מִשּׁוּם הָכִי אֵינוֹ יָכוֹל לִמְחוֹל, אֶלָּא אִי אָמְרַתְּ דְּרַבָּנַן הִיא, אַמַּאי אֵינוֹ יָכוֹל לִמְחוֹל? אֵינָהּ שֶׁל תּוֹרָה וַעֲשָׂאוּהָ כְּשֶׁל תּוֹרָה.

Granted, if you say that the gift of a person on his deathbed is valid **by Torah law** without an act of acquisition, **due to that** reason the heir **cannot forgive** the debt, as the debt was acquired by another. **But if you say** that **it is** valid **by rabbinic law,**[N] **why is** the heir **unable to forgive** the debt? The Gemara replies: Rav Naḥman maintains that although this gift **is not** effective **by Torah law,** nevertheless, the Sages **made it** a *halakha* **with** the force **of Torah law.**

אָמַר רָבָא אָמַר רַב נַחְמָן: שְׁכִיב מְרַע שֶׁאָמַר ״יָדוּר פְּלוֹנִי בְּבַיִת זֶה״, ״יֹאכַל פְּלוֹנִי פֵּירוֹת דֶּקֶל זֶה״ – לֹא אָמַר כְּלוּם, עַד שֶׁיֹּאמַר: ״תְּנוּ בַּיִת זֶה לִפְלוֹנִי וְיָדוּר בּוֹ״, ״תְּנוּ דֶּקֶל זֶה לִפְלוֹנִי וְיֹאכַל פֵּירוֹתָיו״.

Rava says that Rav Naḥman says: With regard to **a person on his deathbed who says: So-and-so shall reside in this house,**[H] or who says: **So-and-so shall eat** the **fruit of this palm tree,** he has **not said anything,** as one cannot give that which is not tangible, such as the right to use property, or the right to consume fruit that has not yet grown. His statement is ineffective **until he says: Give this house to so-and-so and he shall reside there,** or: **Give this palm tree to so-and-so and he shall eat its fruit.**

לְמֵימְרָא, דְּסָבַר רַב נַחְמָן: מִילְּתָא דְּאִיתָא בִּבְרִיא אִיתָא בִּשְׁכִיב מְרַע, דְּלֵיתָא בִּבְרִיא לֵיתָא בִּשְׁכִיב מְרַע? וְהָא אָמַר רָבָא אָמַר רַב נַחְמָן:

The Gemara asks: **Is this to say that Rav Naḥman maintains** that only **a matter that can be** conferred as a gift **by a healthy person** with an act of acquisition **can be** conferred as a gift **by a person on his deathbed** by means of verbal instruction, but a matter **that cannot be** conferred as a gift **by a healthy person cannot be** conferred as a gift **by a person on his deathbed?**[N] Consequently, a person on his deathbed cannot transfer ownership of an intangible right, just as a healthy person cannot do so. **But doesn't Rava say** that **Rav Naḥman says:**

NOTES

Granted if you say the gift is valid by Torah law…but if you say it is valid by rabbinic law, etc. – אִי אָמְרַתְּ בִּשְׁלָמָא דְּאוֹרָיְיתָא...אֶלָּא אִי אָמְרַתְּ דְּרַבָּנַן הִיא וכו׳: If the gift of a person on his deathbed is valid by Torah law, it is possible that the halakhic status of the recipient is equal to that of an inheritor. Consequently, just as one heir cannot relinquish the rights of another heir to his inheritance, one heir cannot forgive a debt that another acquired by means of the gift of a person on his deathbed (Ri Migash). By contrast, if the validity of the gift is due to a rabbinic ordinance, there is no reason the gift of a promissory note should accord the recipient greater rights than are accorded in the sale of a promissory note (Rabbeinu Gershom Meor HaGola). Even though by rabbinic law the gift of a person on his deathbed is equivalent to the gift a healthy person confers by an act of acquisition, a healthy person who sells a promissory note can still forgive the debt (Ramah).

A matter that cannot be conferred by a healthy person cannot be conferred by a person on his deathbed – דְּלֵיתָא בִּבְרִיא לֵיתָא בִּשְׁכִיב מְרַע: The Sages ordained that the verbal instruction of a person on his deathbed effects a transaction only in a case where a healthy person could effect a transaction even by symbolic exchange (Rashbam).

HALAKHA

A person on his deathbed who says, so-and-so shall reside in this house – שְׁכִיב מְרַע שֶׁאָמַר יָדוּר פְּלוֹנִי בְּבַיִת זֶה: If a person on his deathbed said: So-and-so shall reside in this house, or: So-and-so shall eat the fruit of this palm tree, his words carry no halakhic weight. This is because he did not transfer ownership of a tangible object, as the right to reside in a place or to eat the fruit of a tree is comparable to speech and sleep, which are not objects that can be acquired. If he said: Give this house to so-and-so for him to reside in until such and such time, or: Give this palm tree to so-and-so for him to eat its fruit, his gift is valid, as the recipient acquires the object itself for the sake of its use (Rambam *Sefer Kinyan, Hilkhot Zekhiya UMattana* 10:15; *Shulḥan Arukh, Ḥoshen Mishpat* 253:21).

Perek **IX**
Daf **148** Amud **a**

שְׁכִיב מְרַע שֶׁאָמַר ״תְּנוּ הַלְוָאָתִי לִפְלוֹנִי״ – הַלְוָאָתוֹ לִפְלוֹנִי, וְאַף עַל גַּב דְּלֵיתֵיהּ בִּבְרִיא! רַב פַּפָּא אֲמַר: הוֹאִיל וְיוֹרֵשׁ יוֹרְשָׁהּ.

With regard to **a person on his deathbed who says: Give** the **loan** owed **to me to so-and-so**[H] as a gift, the **loan** owned to **him** is acquired **by so-and-so. And** this is the *halakha* **despite** the fact **that this does not** apply **in** the case of **a healthy person,**[N] as one cannot transfer a loan to a third party without a promissory note. **Rav Pappa says:** In this case the *halakha* of transferring loans differs with regard to a person on his deathbed, **since an heir inherits** loans without a promissory note,[N] and the Sages accorded the gift of a person on his deathbed the halakhic status of an inheritance.

HALAKHA

Give the loan owed to me to so-and-so – תְּנוּ הַלְוָאָתִי לִפְלוֹנִי: If a person on his deathbed says: Give the loan owed to me by a certain person, or the money that I deposited with a certain person, to so-and-so, his statement is valid even if was not stated in the presence of all three parties (Rambam *Sefer Kinyan, Hilkhot Zekhiya UMattana* 10:2; *Shulḥan Arukh, Ḥoshen Mishpat* 253:20, and in the comment of Rema).

NOTES

That this does not apply in the case of a healthy person – דְּלֵיתֵיהּ בִּבְרִיא: The reason that a loan cannot be transferred through the ordinary methods of acquisition is that it is not a tangible object. Once the borrower receives the money, the creditor retains only the right to collect the loan, not the actual ownership of the money, even if the money is still extant (Rabbi Avraham *Av Beit Din*).

Since an heir inherits loans without a promissory note – הוֹאִיל וְיוֹרֵשׁ יוֹרְשָׁהּ: The Rashbam explains that the Sages accorded the gift of a person on his deathbed the halakhic status of inheritance (149a). Since a loan can be inherited, it can also be given as the gift of a person on his deathbed.

רַב אַחָא בְּרֵיהּ דְּרַב אִיקָא אֲמַר: הַלְוָאָה אִיתָא בְּבָרִיא, וְכִדְרַב הוּנָא אָמַר רַב. דְּאָמַר רַב הוּנָא אָמַר רַב: ״מָנֶה לִי בְּיָדְךָ תְּנֵהוּ לִפְלוֹנִי״, בְּמַעֲמַד שְׁלָשְׁתָּן – קָנָה.

Rav Aḥa, son of Rav Ika, said: A loan without a promissory note **can be** conferred as a gift **by a healthy person. And** this is **in accordance with** that which **Rav Huna says** that **Rav says, as Rav Huna says** that **Rav says:** With regard to one who said to another: **I have one hundred dinars in your possession, give it to so-and-so,** if this was stated **in the presence of** all **three of the** parties,[H] the third party **acquires** the money without an act of acquisition and without the need for witnesses.

אִיבַּעְיָא לְהוּ: דֶּקֶל לְאֶחָד וּפֵירוֹתָיו לְאַחֵר, מַהוּ? מִי שַׁיֵּיר מְקוֹם פֵּירֵי, אוֹ לָא שַׁיֵּיר? אִם תִּמְצֵי לוֹמַר: לְאַחֵר לָא הָוֵי שִׁיּוּר, לְעַצְמוֹ חוּץ מִפֵּירוֹתָיו, מַהוּ?

§ **A dilemma was raised before** the Sages: With regard to one who gave **a palm tree to one** person **and its fruit to another,**[HN] **what is** the *halakha*? **Did** he **reserve the place of the fruit** on the tree for the second person in order to give him a tangible object, and therefore the second person acquires the fruit, **or did he not reserve** it, and the second person does not acquire the fruit? Furthermore, **if you say** that giving the palm tree to one person and giving the fruit **to another is not** considered **reserving** the place of the fruit unless this is explicitly stipulated, then if he reserves the fruit **for himself,** stating that the tree is given to another **except for its fruit, what is** the *halakha*?

אֲמַר רָבָא אֲמַר רַב נַחְמָן, אִם תִּמְצֵי לוֹמַר: דֶּקֶל לְאֶחָד וּפֵירוֹתָיו לְאַחֵר לָא הָוֵי שִׁיּוּר מְקוֹם פֵּירֵי, דֶּקֶל לְאֶחָד וְשִׁיֵּיר פֵּירוֹתָיו לְפָנָיו – שִׁיֵּיר מְקוֹם פֵּירֵי, מַאי טַעֲמָא? כָּל לְגַבֵּי נַפְשֵׁיהּ בְּעַיִן יָפָה מְשַׁיֵּיר.

Rava said that **Rav Naḥman said:** Even **if you say** that giving the **palm tree to one** person **and its fruit to another is not** considered **reserving the place of the fruit** for the second person, if he gave the **palm tree to one** person **and reserved the fruit for himself,** he also **reserved the place of the fruit** for himself.[H] **What is the reason** for this distinction? The reason is that **anything** that one reserves **with regard to himself, he reserves generously,** and therefore he reserves for himself not only the fruit itself, but also the place of the fruit.

אֲמַר לֵיהּ רַבִּי אַבָּא לְרַב אַשִׁי: אֲנַן אַדְּרַבִּי שִׁמְעוֹן בֶּן לָקִישׁ מַתְנִינַן לָהּ. דְּאָמַר רַבִּי שִׁמְעוֹן בֶּן לָקִישׁ: הַמּוֹכֵר בַּיִת לַחֲבֵירוֹ, וְאָמַר לוֹ ״עַל מְנָת שֶׁדְּיוֹטָא הָעֶלְיוֹנָה שֶׁלִּי״ – דְּיוֹטָא הָעֶלְיוֹנָה שֶׁלּוֹ.

Rabbi Abba said to Rav Ashi: We learned the aforementioned statement of Rav Naḥman **with regard to** the statement **of Rabbi Shimon ben Lakish**[N] concerning a different matter, **as Rabbi Shimon ben Lakish says:** In the case of **one who sells a house to another and says to him:** I am selling the house **on the condition that the upper story** [*deyota*][L] remains **mine, the upper story** remains **his.**

LANGUAGE

Story [*deyota*] – דְּיוֹטָא: From the Greek δίαιτα, *diaita*, meaning a room or dwelling. By extension, this can refer to the upper story of a house or an attic.

HALAKHA

In the presence of all three of the parties – בְּמַעֲמַד שְׁלָשְׁתָּן: If one lent money to another, or deposited money with another, he can transfer the money to a third party by issuing an instruction in the presence of all three parties. How so? If he says to the borrower or bailee: I have one hundred dinars in your possession, as a loan or a deposit; give it to this third person, the third person acquires the money, and the giver cannot retract his gift (Rambam *Sefer Kinyan, Hilkhot Zekhiya UMattana* 3:3 and *Hilkhot Mekhira* 6:8; *Shulḥan Arukh, Ḥoshen Mishpat* 66:19–20, 126:1).

One who gave a palm tree to one and its fruit to another – דֶּקֶל לְאֶחָד וּפֵירוֹתָיו לְאַחֵר: If one sells or gives a palm tree to one person and gives its fruit to another, he does not reserve the place of the fruit for the second person. Therefore, the first person acquires both the tree and its fruit, whereas the second person acquires nothing, in accordance with the statement of Rav Naḥman (Rambam *Sefer Kinyan, Hilkhot Mekhira* 23:4; *Shulḥan Arukh, Ḥoshen Mishpat* 209:9).

He also reserved the place of the fruit for himself – שִׁיֵּיר מְקוֹם פֵּירֵי: If one sells a palm tree to another, stating that the tree is sold except for its fruit, he reserves for himself the place of the fruit, i.e., the branches, as well as the fruit. The buyer acquires only the trunk of the tree, which he can use when the tree withers, in accordance with the statement of Rav Naḥman (Rambam *Sefer Kinyan, Hilkhot Mekhira* 23:4; *Shulḥan Arukh, Ḥoshen Mishpat* 209:10).

NOTES

One who gave a palm tree to one and its fruit to another – דֶּקֶל לְאֶחָד וּפֵירוֹתָיו לְאַחֵר: According to the Rashbam, the dilemma here pertains to the *halakha* in the mishna (146b), which distinguishes between a case where a person on his deathbed transferred ownership of his entire estate and a case where he reserved any amount of land for himself. The discussion refers to a person on his deathbed who gave his palm tree to one person and then reconsidered the matter and gave the fruit of the tree to another. The Gemara's question is whether one should assume that the giver reserved for himself the place of the fruit, i.e., the branches, which is equivalent to reserving for himself any amount of land, or whether when he gave the first recipient the palm tree he intended to give him the entire tree and reserved nothing for himself (see Rabbeinu Gershom Meor HaGola).

We learned with regard to the statement of Rabbi Shimon ben Lakish – אֲנַן אַדְּרַבִּי שִׁמְעוֹן בֶּן לָקִישׁ מַתְנִינַן לָהּ: Rav Naḥman initially made a distinction between one who reserves for himself certain rights in the property he sells or gives away and one who reserves them for another with regard to the statement of Rabbi Shimon ben Lakish. Nevertheless, one can infer the *halakha* with regard to one who gives a palm tree to another from the discussion concerning the statement of Rabbi Shimon Ben Lakish.

איבעיא להו: בית לאחד ודיוטא לאחד, מהו? מי הוי שיור או לא? אם תמצא לומר: בית לאחד ודיוטא לאחד לא הוי שיור, ״חוץ מדיוטא״ מהו?

A dilemma was raised before the Sages with regard to the statement of Rabbi Shimon ben Lakish: If one sold **a house,** i.e., a lower story, **to one** person **and** stated that the upper **story** will be sold **to one** other person, **what is** the *halakha*? **Is this** considered **reserving** additional rights for the second person apart from the upper story, **or not?**[N] **If you say** that in a case where one sells his **house to one and** the upper **story to one,** his stipulation **is not** considered **reserving** rights for the second person, there is another dilemma. If one sold a house **except for** the upper **story,** reserving the upper story for himself, **what is** the *halakha*?[N] Is this considered reserving additional rights for himself?

אמר רבא אמר רב נחמן, אם תמצא לומר: בית לאחד ודיוטא לאחד לא הוי שיור – ״חוץ מדיוטא״ הוי שיור; ואליבא דרב זביד, דאמר: שאם רצה להוציא בה זיזין – מוציא;

Rava said that **Rav Naḥman said:** Even **if you say** that where one sells the **house to one** person **and** the upper **story to one** other person, he **is not** considered to be **reserving** rights for the second person, if one sold a house **except for** the upper **story,**[H] he **is** considered to be **reserving** additional rights for himself. **And** this is **in accordance with** the opinion **of Rav Zevid, who says** that the reason the seller reserves additional rights is **that if** he **wants to extend projections from** the upper story into the space of the courtyard, **he may extend** them.

אלמא, כיון דשייר דיוטא – מקום זיזין נמי שייר. הכא נמי, כיון דאמר ״חוץ מפירותיו״ – מקום פירי שייר.

The Gemara concludes: **Evidently, since he reserved** the upper **story, he also reserved the place of the projections. Here too,** with regard to the one who gave a palm tree to another and reserved the fruit for himself, **since he said** that the tree is given to another **except for its fruit, he reserved the place of the fruit** for himself as well.

אמר רב יוסף בר מניומי אמר רב נחמן: שכיב מרע שכתב כל נכסיו לאחרים – רואין: אם במחלק, מת – קנו כולן, עמד – חוזר בכולן;

§ The mishna (146b) states that if a person on his deathbed granted all of his property to others but reserved for himself any amount of land, his gift is valid even if he recovers. If he did not reserve for himself any amount of land, his gift is not valid if he recovers. **Rav Yosef bar Minyumi says** that **Rav Naḥman says:** In the case of **a person on his deathbed who wrote** a deed granting **all of his property to others,** the manner in which he divided his property **is examined. If** it appears **that he was** intending **to divide** his entire estate among various recipients, then if **he dies, all** the recipients **acquire** their gifts. If **he recovers,** he can **retract all** of the gifts, in accordance with the ruling of the mishna.

אם בנמלך, מת – קנו כולן, עמד – אינו חוזר אלא באחרון. ודלמא עיוני קא מעיין והדר יהיב! סתמיה דשכיב מרע מידק דייק והדר יהיב.

But **if** it appears **that he was reconsidering** the matter,[H] initially intending to give away only a portion of his property, and then reconsidering and distributing the rest, then if **he dies, all** of the recipients **acquire** their gifts. If **he recovers, he can retract only the last** gift, as the previous gifts were given with the intent to reserve part of the property for himself, and they are valid even if he recovers. The Gemara asks: **Perhaps** he was not reconsidering; rather, he initially intended to transfer ownership of all of his property, and **he was considering** to whom to give each portion **and then giving** it. The Gemara answers: **The usual** way **of a person on his deathbed is to consider** the matter **carefully** first **and** only **then** to **confer** his gifts. Therefore, if he pauses to consider in the interim, it appears that he did not initially intend to transfer ownership of his entire estate.

NOTES

Is this considered reserving additional rights or not – מי הוי שיור או לא: In the case of one who sells his house to one person and the upper story to another, the second person certainly acquires the upper story, as it is tangible property. The seller's stipulation that he is selling the upper story to another person is superfluous, as in any case the upper story is not included in the sale of the lower story. The dilemma here is whether the unnecessary stipulation indicates that the seller also reserves the additional right to extend projections from the upper story into the space of the courtyard, which he sells together with the house (Rashbam). Many early commentaries disagree with this explanation, as the Gemara does not state that the buyer bought the courtyard as well. Rabbeinu Tam explains that in order to extend projections from the upper story one requires additional rights because the projections constitute an increased burden upon the walls of the house (*Tosafot* 64a).

If one sold a house except for the upper story what is the *halakha* – חוץ מדיוטא מהו: *Tosafot* note that the dilemma here is unclear, as Rabbi Shimon ben Lakish explicitly states that if one stipulates that he reserves the upper story for himself, his stipulation is effective. *Tosafot* explain that Rabbi Shimon ben Lakish is referring to one who reserves the upper story for himself using the formulation: On the condition that the upper story remains mine, whereas the dilemma here concerns one who uses the formulation: Except for the upper story. The Gemara asks whether the formulation: Except for, is effective in the same way as is the formulation: On the condition.

HALAKHA

Except for the upper story [*deyota*] – חוץ מדיוטא: If one sells a house to another and says: I am selling the house on the condition that the upper story remains mine, the upper story remains his. Even if the buyer acquires the courtyard as well, the seller may extend projections from the upper story into the space of the courtyard, in accordance with the statement of Rav Zevid (see 63b). The Rashbam writes that a roof four cubits wide enclosed by a parapet ten handbreadths high is considered an upper story. Rabbeinu Tam (see *Tosafot* 64a) explains that the term *deyota* refers to the uppermost row of stones, which protrudes above the walls of a house, upon which people would often build an additional story (Rambam *Sefer Kinyan*, *Hilkhot Mekhira* 24:16; *Shulḥan Arukh*, *Ḥoshen Mishpat* 212:3, 214:8).

HALAKHA

If it appears that he was reconsidering the matter, etc. – אם בנמלך וכו׳: If a person on his deathbed distributes all of his property to two or three people without pausing in the interim, saying that this portion shall go to so-and-so, this portion to so-and-so, and this portion to so-and-so, and he then dies, all of the recipients acquire their portions of the property, even without an act of acquisition. If he recovers, he can retract all of the gifts, even if an act of acquisition was performed. This is because these gifts have the halakhic status of a gift given by a person on his deathbed without reserving anything for himself.

If he pauses between his statements of giving one gift and another, as though considering each one in turn, all of the gifts except the last one have the halakhic status of a gift given by a person on his deathbed with the intent to reserve part of the property for himself. If an act of acquisition was performed, the gifts are valid even if he recovers. If an act of acquisition was not performed, the gifts are not valid even if he dies. The last gift is considered a gift given without reserving anything for himself. Therefore, if the giver dies, the gift is valid even if an act of acquisition was not performed. If he recovers, he can retract the gift (Rambam *Sefer Kinyan*, *Hilkhot Zekhiya UMattana* 8:21; *Shulḥan Arukh*, *Ḥoshen Mishpat* 250:11).

אמר רב אחא בר מניומי אמר רב נחמן: שכיב מרע שכתב כל נכסיו לאחרים ועמד – אינו חוזר, חיישינן שמא יש לו נכסים במדינה אחרת.

§ **Rav Aḥa bar Minyumi says that Rav Naḥman says:** With regard to **a person on his deathbed who wrote** a deed granting **all of his** generally known **property to others, and** he then **recovered, he cannot retract** it, as **we are concerned that perhaps he has property**[N] **in another province**[H] that he reserved for himself, in which case the gift is valid even if he recovered.

ואלא מתניתין דקתני: לא שייר קרקע כל שהוא – אין מתנתו קיימת, היכי משכחת לה? אמר רב חמא: באומר "כל נכסי". מר בר רב אשי אמר: במוחזק לן דלית ליה.

The Gemara asks: **But as for the mishna, which teaches:** If he **did not reserve** for himself **any amount of land,** and he recovered, **his gift is not valid, how can you find these** circumstances? **Rav Ḥama said:** The mishna is referring to a case **where he says: All my property** is given to so-and-so, in which case he clearly reserved nothing for himself. **Mar bar Rav Ashi said:** The mishna is referring to a case **where our presumption is that he does not have** property elsewhere.

איבעיא להו: חזרה במקצת הוי חזרה בכולה או לא? תא שמע: כולן לראשון ומקצתן לשני – שני קנה, ראשון לא קנה; מאי לאו בשמת?

§ **A dilemma was raised before** the Sages: With regard to the gift of a person on his deathbed, **is a partial retraction** of the gift considered **a retraction of the entire** gift, **or** it is **not** considered a retraction of the entire gift? The Gemara suggests: **Come** and **hear** a proof from a *baraita*: If one gave **all** of his property **to the first** recipient **and** then he partially retracted his gift and gave **part** of his property **to the second** recipient, **the second acquired** his gift, but **the first did not acquire** anything. **What, is it not** referring to a case **where** the giver **died,** and the reason that the first recipient does not acquire anything is that a partial retraction is considered a retraction of the entire gift?

לא, בשעמד.

The Gemara rejects this explanation: **No,** the *baraita* is referring to a case **where** the giver **recovered.** The first gift was invalidated, because he left nothing for himself, whereas the second gift remained valid, since he gave only part of his property. Had he died, the first recipient would have received the remainder, as the giver retracted only part of the first gift, which he gave to the second recipient.

הכי נמי מסתברא, מדקתני סיפא: מקצתן לראשון וכולן לשני – ראשון קנה, שני לא קנה; אי אמרת בשלמא בשעמד – משום הכי שני לא קנה. אלא אי אמרת בשמת, תרווייהו ליקנו!

The Gemara comments: **So too, it is reasonable** to understand the *baraita* in this manner. **From** the fact **that the last clause** of the *baraita* **teaches:** If he gave **part** of his property **to the first** recipient, **and** then he gave **all** of his property **to the second** recipient,[N] **the first** recipient **acquired** his gift, but **the second did not acquire** anything. **Granted, if you say** that the *baraita* is referring **to** a case **where** the giver **recovered, due to that** reason **the second** recipient **did not acquire** the gift. **But if you say** that the *baraita* is referring **to** a case **where he died, both of them should acquire** their gifts.[N]

אמר ליה רב יימר לרב אשי: ותהוי נמי בשעמד; אי אמרת בשלמא חזרה במקצת הויא חזרה בכולה – היינו דשני מיהת קנה. אלא אי אמרת חזרה במקצת לא הויא חזרה בכולה – ניהוי כמחלק, ולחד מינייהו לא ליקנו!

Rav Yeimar said to Rav Ashi: And even if the first clause of the *baraita* **is referring to** a case **where he recovered,** one can prove that a partial retraction is considered a retraction of the entire gift. **Granted, if you say** that **a partial retraction** is considered **a retraction of the entire** gift, **this is** the reason **that at least the second** recipient **acquired** the gift, as the giver reserved part of his property for himself. **But if you say** that **a partial retraction is not** considered **a retraction of the entire** gift, the giver **should be** considered **as one who was dividing** all of his property between the two recipients, **and neither of them should acquire** their gifts.

NOTES

Perhaps he has property – שמא יש לו נכסים: The early commentaries raise a difficulty: It is a principle that the burden of proof rests upon the claimant. Therefore, the property should remain under the presumptive ownership of the owner unless the claimant proves otherwise. Why, then, does the Gemara state that the gift is valid due to an unknown and unproven possibility? Rabbi Avraham *Av Beit Din* explains that the Gemara here is referring to a case where the giver specified which assets are included in the gift. This indicates that it is likely that he owns additional assets not included in the gift.

Part of his property to the first and all of his property to the second – מקצתן לראשון וכולן לשני: The Rashbam explains that the person on his deathbed gave part of his property to the first recipient and subsequently gave all of his property to the second recipient, thereby retracting the first gift. Rabbeinu Gershom Meor HaGola and the Ri Migash explain that he gave part of his property to the first recipient and all of the remainder to the second recipient. According to both explanations, after giving the second gift the giver was not left with anything, and therefore if he recovers the second gift is invalid.

Both of them should acquire their gifts – תרווייהו ליקנו: The person on his deathbed divided all of his property between the two recipients. The gifts are therefore gifts given by a person on his deathbed without reserving anything for himself, which are valid if the giver dies (Rabbeinu Gershom Meor HaGola).

HALAKHA

Perhaps he has property in another province – שמא יש לו נכסים במדינה אחרת: Even if a person on his deathbed transfers ownership of all his known property, this is still considered a gift given with the intent to reserve part of the property for himself, as he may have additional property in another province. The gift requires an act of acquisition and if the giver recovers he cannot retract the gift. If he says: All my property, which is such and such, is given to so-and-so, this is considered a gift given without reserving anything for himself, and if he recovers, he can retract the gift. Furthermore, if he transfers all his known property, and it is generally presumed that he does not own additional property, even if no one can testify to that fact, his gift is considered a gift given without reserving anything for himself (Rambam *Sefer Kinyan, Hilkhot Zekhiya UMattana* 8:20; *Shulḥan Arukh, Ḥoshen Mishpat* 250:10, and in the comment of Rema, and *Sma* there).

וְהִלְכְתָא: חֲזָרָה בְּמִקְצָת הָוְיָא חֲזָרָה בְּכוּלָּהּ; רֵישָׁא – מַשְׁכַּחַת לָהּ בֵּין שֶׁמֵּת בֵּין שֶׁעָמַד, סֵיפָא – לָא מַשְׁכַּחַת לָהּ אֶלָּא כְּשֶׁעָמַד.

The Gemara concludes: **And the *halakha* is that a partial retraction is considered a retraction of the entire gift.**[H] **You find** the *halakha* that is stated in **the first clause** of the *baraita* **both** in a case **where** the giver **died and** in a case **where he recovered.**[N] **You find** the *halakha* that is stated in **the last clause**[H] **only** in a case **where he recovered.**

אִיבַּעְיָא לְהוּ: הִקְדִּישׁ כָּל נְכָסָיו וְעָמַד, מַהוּ? מִי אָמְרִינַן: כָּל לְגַבֵּי הֶקְדֵּשׁ גָּמַר וּמַקְנֵי, אוֹ דִּלְמָא כָּל לְגַבֵּי נַפְשֵׁיהּ לָא גָּמַר וּמַקְנֵי?

§ A series of **dilemmas were raised before** the Sages: If a person on his deathbed **consecrated all of his property**[H] to the Temple treasury **and** subsequently **recovered, what is the** ***halakha***? **Do we say** that in **any** case **that concerns consecrated** property the assumption is that he **resolves to transfer** the property unconditionally, and therefore the consecration is valid even if he recovers? **Or perhaps** in **any** matter **that concerns himself** he **does not resolve to transfer** the property unconditionally.

הִפְקִיר כָּל נְכָסָיו, מַהוּ? מִי אָמְרִינַן: כֵּיוָן דְּאַף לַעֲנִיִּים כַּעֲשִׁירִים גָּמַר וּמַקְנֵי, אוֹ דִּלְמָא כָּל לְגַבֵּי נַפְשֵׁיהּ לָא גָּמַר וּמַקְנֵי?

Furthermore, if a person on his deathbed **declared all of his property ownerless, what is** the *halakha*? **Do we say** that **since** declaring his property ownerless is **for** the benefit of **the poor as well as the rich,** it involves the potential mitzva of providing for the poor, and therefore the assumption is that **he resolves to transfer** the property, i.e., declare it ownerless, unconditionally? **Or perhaps** in **any** matter **that concerns himself he does not resolve to transfer** the property unconditionally.

חִילֵּק כָּל נְכָסָיו לַעֲנִיִּים, מַאי? מִי אָמְרִינַן: צְדָקָה וַדַּאי מִגְמַר גָּמַר וּמַקְנֵי, אוֹ דִּלְמָא כָּל לְגַבֵּי נַפְשֵׁיהּ לָא גָּמַר וּמַקְנֵי? תֵּיקוּ.

Furthermore, if a person on his deathbed **divided all of his property to** be distributed to **the poor, what** is the *halakha*? **Do we say** that with regard to **charity** the assumption is that **he certainly resolves to transfer** the property unconditionally? **Or perhaps** in **any** matter **that concerns himself he does not resolve to transfer** the property unconditionally. The Gemara concludes: These dilemmas **shall stand** unresolved.

לִישָּׁנָא אַחֲרִינָא: הִקְדִּישׁ כָּל נְכָסָיו, מַהוּ? הִפְקִיר כָּל נְכָסָיו, מַהוּ? חִילֵּק כָּל נְכָסָיו לַעֲנִיִּים, מַהוּ? תֵּיקוּ.

The Gemara presents **another version** of this series of dilemmas: If a person on his deathbed **consecrated all of his property** to the Temple treasury, **what is** the *halakha*? If he **declared all of his property ownerless, what is** the *halakha*? If he **divided all of his property to** be distributed to **the poor, what is** the *halakha*? These dilemmas **shall stand** unresolved.

אָמַר רַב שֵׁשֶׁת: ״יִטּוֹל״, וְ״יִזְכֶּה״, וְ״יַחֲזִיק״ וְ״יִקְנֶה״ – כּוּלָּן לְשׁוֹן מַתָּנָה הֵן. בְּמַתְנִיתָא תָּנָא: אַף ״יַחֲסִין״ וְ״יֵרֵת״ בְּרָאוּי לְיוֹרְשׁוֹ, וְרַבִּי יוֹחָנָן בֶּן בְּרוֹקָא הִיא.

Rav Sheshet says: If one says: So-and-so **shall take** my property, **or:** So-and-so **shall gain possession** of my property, **or:** So-and-so **shall take possession**[N] of my property, **or: He shall acquire** my property, **all of** these **are terms** that denote the bestowal **of gifts. It was taught in a** ***baraita***: If one says: So-and-so **shall receive as an inheritance, or:** So-and-so **shall inherit,**[H] these are **also** valid terms denoting inheritance **in the case of one who is fit to inherit from him. And this** ***baraita*** **is** in accordance with the opinion of **Rabbi Yoḥanan ben Beroka,** who holds that one can bequeath all of his property to one of his sons using terms that denote inheritance, not only using terms that denote the bestowal of a gift.

אִיבַּעְיָא לְהוּ:

A series of **dilemmas were raised before** the Sages:

HALAKHA

A partial retraction is a retraction of the entire gift – חֲזָרָה בְּמִקְצָת הָוְיָא חֲזָרָה בְּכוּלָּהּ: If a person on his deathbed transfers all of his property to another, and he then retracts a part of his gift, he is presumed to have retracted the entire gift. The Rema writes that even if the property is given to two people with a single deed and the person on his deathbed retracts only one of the gifts, both gifts are considered to have been retracted. But if he explicitly states that he is retracting only a part of the gifts, the first recipient acquires the property the giver has not reserved for himself, despite the fact that an act of acquisition was not performed. This is because the gift initially had the status of a gift given by a person on his deathbed without reserving any property for himself, which does not require an act of acquisition. The Rema adds that according to some authorities, this is the *halakha* only if the person on his deathbed retracts a part of his gift and gives it to another. By contrast, if he reserves it for himself, the rest of the gift is invalid unless an act of acquisition is performed. If he gives part of his property to his heirs and part of it to others, and he subsequently retracts the portion that he gave to his heirs, the gift made to others is valid, as the portion given to the heirs is considered inheritance and not a gift (Rambam *Sefer Kinyan, Hilkhot Zekhiya UMattana* 9:17; *Shulḥan Arukh, Ḥoshen Mishpat* 250:12).

You find the first clause…you find the last clause, etc. – רֵישָׁא מַשְׁכַּחַת לָהּ...סֵיפָא לָא מַשְׁכַּחַת לָהּ וכו׳: If a person on his deathbed gives all of his property to one recipient, and he subsequently reconsiders and gives part of his property to a second recipient, the first person does not acquire the property even if the giver dies. The gift to the second recipient has the halakhic status of a gift given by a person on his deathbed with the intent to reserve part of the property for himself. Therefore, if an act of acquisition was performed, the gift is valid even if he recovers. If an act of acquisition was not performed, the gift is not valid even if he dies.

If a person on his deathbed gives part of his property to one recipient, performing an act of acquisition, and then gives the remainder of his property to a second recipient, the first recipient acquires the property even if the giver recovers. The gift to the second recipient has the halakhic status of a gift given by a person on his deathbed without reserving anything for himself. Therefore, if the giver dies, the gift is valid, even if an act of acquisition was not performed. If the giver recovers, the gift is invalid, even if an act of acquisition was performed (Rambam *Sefer Kinyan, Hilkhot Zekhiya UMattana* 9:17–18; *Shulḥan Arukh, Ḥoshen Mishpat* 250:12).

He consecrated all of his property, etc. – הִקְדִּישׁ כָּל נְכָסָיו וכו׳: If a person on his deathbed consecrates all of his property to the Temple treasury, or declares all of his property ownerless, or apportions all of his property to the poor, and he subsequently recovers, the gift is invalid. Even if the poor took possession of the property, it is repossessed by the original owner (Rema, citing Rivash). Some of the early authorities disagree. They maintain that even if the poor did not take possession of the property, the gift cannot be retracted (Rosh; *Tur*; Mordekhai). The *halakha* is not in accordance with their opinion. If the person on his deathbed reconsiders and wishes to retract the consecration or the declaration of his property as ownerless or the gift to the poor, and he wishes to distribute his property in another manner, he may do so (Rambam *Sefer Kinyan, Hilkhot Zekhiya UMattana* 9:19; *Shulḥan Arukh, Ḥoshen Mishpat* 250:3, and in the comment of Rema, and see *Sma*, *Shakh*, and *Netivot HaMishpat* there).

Shall take or shall gain possession…shall receive as an inheritance or shall inherit, etc. – יִטּוֹל וְיִזְכֶּה...יַחֲסִין וְיֵרֵת וכו׳: If a person on his deathbed states any of the following expressions: So-and-so shall take all of my property or a portion thereof, so-and-so shall take possession of my property, so-and-so shall gain possession of my property, so-and-so shall acquire my property, the expression denotes that he is bestowing a gift. The Mabit adds that the phrase: This item shall be for so-and-so, also denotes a gift (*Shakh*). If one says with regard to an individual who is fit to inherit from him: So-and-so shall receive this as an inheritance, or: So-and-so shall inherit this, that person acquires the gift (Rambam *Sefer Kinyan, Hilkhot Zekhiya UMattana* 9:3; *Shulḥan Arukh, Ḥoshen Mishpat* 253:2, and see 281:8).

NOTES

Both where he died and where he recovered – בֵּין שֶׁמֵּת בֵּין שֶׁעָמַד: Since a partial retraction is considered a retraction of the entire gift, the giver is considered to have retracted the gift to the first recipient, rendering it invalid. The second gift was not retracted, and since the giver reserved a portion of his property for himself, the gift is valid even if he recovers.

Shall gain possession or shall take possession, etc. – יִטּוֹל וְיִזְכֶּה וכו׳: Some of the early commentaries maintain that these terms effect acquisition only in the case of a person on his deathbed. They are ineffective in the case of a healthy person, as they merely indicate a future acquisition, not an actual transaction (Ri Migash; Rambam). Others maintain that these terms are effective also in the case of a healthy person (Ramban).

״יֶהֱנֶה בָּהֶן״, מַהוּ? דְּנֶיהֱוֵי כּוּלְּהוּ מַתָּנָה קָאָמַר, אוֹ דִּלְמָא לִיתְהַנֵּי מִינַּיְיהוּ מִידֵּי קָאָמַר? ״יֵרָאֶה בָּהֶן״, מַהוּ? ״יַעֲמוֹד בָּהֶן״, מַהוּ? ״יִשָּׁעֵן בָּהֶן״, מַהוּ? תֵּיקוּ.

If a person on his deathbed says: So-and-so **shall benefit from** my property,[H] **what is** the *halakha*? Is he **saying that all** of the property **shall be a gift? Or perhaps** he is saying that the recipient **shall derive some benefit from** the property. If he says: So-and-so **shall be seen in** my property, **what is** the *halakha*? If he says: So-and-so **shall stand in** my property, **what is** the *halakha*? If he says: So-and-so **shall rely on** my property, **what is** the *halakha*? The Gemara concludes: All these dilemmas **shall stand** unresolved.

אִיבַּעְיָא לְהוּ: מָכַר כׇּל נְכָסָיו, מַהוּ? אָמַר רַב יְהוּדָה אָמַר רַב: אִם עָמַד אֵינוֹ חוֹזֵר. וְזִימְנִין אָמַר רַב יְהוּדָה אָמַר רַב: אִם עָמַד חוֹזֵר. וְלָא פְּלִיגִי: הָא דְּאִיתְנְהוּ לְזוּזֵי בְּעֵינַיְיהוּ, הָא דְּפָרְעִינְהוּ בְּחוֹבוֹ.

A dilemma was raised before the Sages: If a person on his deathbed **sold all of his property,**[H] **what is** the *halakha*? **Rav Yehuda says** that **Rav says: If he recovers, he cannot retract** the sale. **And** at **times, Rav Yehuda said** that **Rav said: If he recovers, he can retract** the sale. **And** these statements **do not disagree. This** statement, that he can retract the sale, applies in a case **where the dinars** he received as payment **are** still **extant,**[N] i.e., in his possession. **That** statement, that he cannot retract the sale, applies in a case **where he paid his debt with** those dinars.

אִיבַּעְיָא לְהוּ: שְׁכִיב מְרַע שֶׁהוֹדָה, מַהוּ? תָּא שְׁמַע: דְּאִיסּוּר גִּיּוֹרָא הֲוָה לֵיהּ תְּרֵיסַר אַלְפֵי זוּזֵי בֵּי רָבָא. רַב מָרִי בְּרֵיהּ, הוֹרָתוֹ שֶׁלֹּא בִּקְדוּשָּׁה וְלֵידָתוֹ בִּקְדוּשָּׁה הֲוַאי, וּבֵי רַב הֲוָה.

§ **A dilemma was raised before** the Sages: In the case of **a person on his deathbed who admitted**[N] that he owed money to a certain person, where it was possible that he did not actually owe him money, **what is** the *halakha*? Does his admission qualify as the gift of a person on his deathbed? The Gemara answers: **Come** and **hear** a proof, **as Issur the convert had twelve thousand dinars** deposited in **the house of Rava. Rav Mari,**[P] Issur's **son, whose conception was not in** the **sanctity** of the Jewish people, i.e., he was conceived before his father converted, **but his birth was in** the **sanctity** of the Jewish people, i.e., he was born after his father converted, **was in** a **study hall** elsewhere when his father was on his deathbed.

NOTES

This applies where the dinars are still extant, etc. – הָא דְּאִיתְנְהוּ לְזוּזֵי בְּעֵינַיְיהוּ וכו׳: Most of the commentaries explain that if the money is still in the possession of a person on his deathbed, he can retract the sale, as one does not sell all of his property in order to replace it with money, which can be stolen (see Ramah). It is therefore evident that he sold the property because he believed his death to be imminent and he wished to relieve his heirs of the burden of selling the property (Rosh of Lunel). Alternatively, the fact that he retained the money indicates that he intended to retract the sale in the event that he would recover (Rabbeinu Gershom Meor HaGola). Once he used the money to pay his debts, it became evident that he sold the property in order to pay his debts, and he cannot retract the sale (Rashbam).

A person on his deathbed who admitted – שְׁכִיב מְרַע שֶׁהוֹדָה: The discussion here concerns a case where a person on his deathbed admits that certain possessions that are presumed to be his actually belong to another person.

HALAKHA

So-and-so shall benefit from my property, etc. – יֶהֱנֶה בָּהֶן וכו׳: If a person on his deathbed states one of the following expressions, the recipient does not acquire the property, even if an act of acquisition was performed: So-and-so shall benefit from my property, so-and-so shall stand in my property, so-and-so shall be seen in my property, so-and-so shall rely on my property. This is in accordance with the principle that in cases where the dilemma stands unresolved, the burden of proof rests upon the claimant (Rambam *Sefer Kinyan, Hilkhot Zekhiya UMattana* 9:4; *Shulḥan Arukh, Ḥoshen Mishpat* 253:2).

If a person on his deathbed sold all of his property – מָכַר כׇּל נְכָסָיו: If a person on his deathbed sells a portion of his property and an act of acquisition is performed (*Sma*), the sale is valid, as it would be were he in full health. If he sells all of his property and then recovers, if the money he received as payment is still in his possession, he can retract the sale. If he has spent the money, he cannot retract the sale (Rambam *Sefer Kinyan, Hilkhot Zekhiya UMattana* 9:21; *Shulḥan Arukh, Ḥoshen Mishpat* 250:3).

PERSONALITIES

Rav Mari – רַב מָרִי: Rav Mari, the son of Issur the convert, is apparently Rav Mari the son of Raḥel, daughter of the great *amora* Shmuel. Shmuel's daughters were captured or kidnapped, probably in a war that involved the town of his residence, Neharde'a, and one of them married a gentile named Issur, who eventually converted to Judaism and became a widely respected figure in the Jewish community. Since Rav Mari was conceived before Issur converted, he was referred to by his mother's name rather than his father's name. Rav Mari became one of the Sages of his generation, and he is mentioned in halakhic discussions together with Abaye and Rava, the leading scholars of the time. He was apparently a man of great wealth and influence, and several anecdotes are recounted concerning his virtuous personality and behavior. His sons, Mar Zutra and Rav Adda the Elder, were among the Sages of Rav Ashi's generation.

אֲמַר רָבָא: הֵיכִי נִיקְנִינְהוּ רַב מָרִי לְהָנֵי זוּזֵי? אִי בִּירוּשָּׁה – לָאו בַּר יְרוּשָּׁה הוּא; אִי בְּמַתָּנָה – מַתְּנַת שְׁכִיב מְרַע כִּירוּשָּׁה שַׁוְיוּהָ רַבָּנַן, כָּל הֵיכָא דְּאִיתֵיהּ בִּירוּשָּׁה אִיתֵיהּ בְּמַתָּנָה, כָּל הֵיכָא דְּלֵיתֵיהּ בִּירוּשָּׁה לֵיתֵיהּ בְּמַתָּנָה;

Rava reasoned that he would acquire possession of the deposit for himself, as he **said: How can Rav Mari acquire these dinars?** If he attempts to acquire the money **as inheritance, he is not fit to inherit**[HN] from Issur. Since he was conceived before his father converted, he is therefore not halakhically considered his son. **If** he attempts to acquire it **as a gift, the Sages equated** the halakhic status of the **gift of a person on his deathbed with** that of **inheritance.** Therefore, **anywhere that** the property **can be** acquired **as inheritance, it can** also **be** acquired **as a gift,** and **anywhere that** the property **cannot be** acquired **as inheritance, it cannot be** acquired **as a gift.**[HN]

אִי בִּמְשִׁיכָה – לֵיתְנְהוּ גַּבֵּיהּ; אִי בַּחֲלִיפִין – אֵין מַטְבֵּעַ נִקְנֶה בַּחֲלִיפִין; אִי אַגַּב קַרְקַע – לֵית לֵיהּ אַרְעָא; אִי בְּמַעֲמַד שְׁלָשְׁתָּן – אִי שָׁלַח לִי לָא אָזֵילְנָא.

If he attempts to acquire the dinars **by pulling** them, which is a formal act of acquisition, he will not be able to do this, as the dinars **are not with him. If** he attempts to acquire them **by** means of symbolic **exchange,**[B] a pro forma act of acquisition effecting the transfer of ownership of an article, **money cannot be acquired by** means of symbolic **exchange.**[H] **If** he attempts to acquire them **by means of** the acquisition of **land,**[B] Issur **does not have** any **land. If** he attempts to acquire them by means of verbal instruction made by his father **in the presence of** all **three** parties, i.e., the giver, the recipient, and the bailee, **if he sends for me,** the bailee, **I shall not go,** as without the presence of the bailee he cannot transfer ownership of the money.

מַתְקִיף לָהּ רַב אִיקָא בְּרֵיהּ דְּרַב אַמִי: אַמַּאי? וְלוֹדֵי אִיסּוּר דְּהָלֵין זוּזֵי דְּרַב מָרִי נִינְהוּ, וְלִיקְנִינְהוּ בְּאוֹדִיתָא! אַדְּהָכִי נְפַק אוֹדִיתָא מִבֵּי אִיסּוּר. אִיקְפַּד רָבָא, אֲמַר: קָא מַגְמְרִי טַעֲנָתָא לְאֱינָשֵׁי וּמַפְסְדִי לִי.

Rav Ika, son of Rav Ami, objected to this: Why is Rav Mari unable to acquire the money? **But** why not **let Issur admit**[HN] **that these dinars are** owned **by Rav Mari, and he shall transfer** ownership **of them** to Rav Mari **by** means of a document of **admission? In the meantime,** a document of **admission** stating that the dinars belonged to Rav Mari **emerged from Issur's house. Rava became angry,** and **said: They are teaching people** legal **claims**[N] **and causing me loss.** In any event, this incident proves that the admission of a person on his deathbed is a valid means of transferring ownership.

NOTES

He is not fit to inherit – לָאו בַּר יְרוּשָּׁה הוּא: When Rav Mari was conceived, his father was a gentile and his mother was a Jew. Therefore, he is not considered to be a son of his father (see Rashbam here and on *Tosafot*, *Bekhorot* 46a).

Anywhere that it cannot be acquired as inheritance, it cannot be acquired as a gift – כָּל הֵיכָא דְּלֵיתֵיהּ בִּירוּשָּׁה לֵיתֵיהּ בְּמַתָּנָה: Most of the early commentaries explain that since it was only due to exigent circumstances that the Sages instituted that the gift of a person on his deathbed is valid without a formal act of acquisition, they applied this ordinance only with regard to those individuals to whom the *halakhot* of inheritance apply (*Tosafot Yeshanim*). The reason for this is that the Sages instituted the ordinance of the gift of a person on his deathbed as a parallel to inheritance by Torah law. This is apparent in the *halakhot* that the gift does not require an act of acquisition and takes effect only after the person's death, as the *halakha* is the same with regard to inheritance. According to the Ramah, this means that a person who is unfit to inherit from his father cannot acquire the gift of a person on his deathbed from anyone (see Ra'avad). *Tosafot* explain that it is the person on his deathbed to whom the *halakhot* of inheritance must be applicable in order for his gift to be valid. Therefore, the gift of a convert on his deathbed who has no heirs is not valid.

But let Issur admit – וְלוֹדֵי אִיסּוּר: Many of the commentaries maintain that one's admission to financial obligations does not constitute an act of acquisition, but his admission to financial obligations is accepted (see *Nimmukei Yosef*). Others maintain that one's admission to financial obligations constitutes an act of acquisition (*Ketzot HaḤoshen*).

They are teaching people claims, etc. – קָא מַגְמְרִי טַעֲנָתָא לְאֱינָשֵׁי וכו׳: The Gemara (*Kiddushin* 17b) cites a *baraita* which states that if one borrows money from a convert and after his death returns the money to the convert's sons who converted with him, the Sages are displeased with him. The Gemara explains that this applies only with regard to a son who was born before the father converted, whereas in the case of a son who was conceived before the father converted and born after he converted, it is desirable to return the money to the son. Since Rav Mari was born after Issur converted, the commentaries question why Rava did not wish to return the money to him. Rabbeinu Tam explains that if one receives the money as a loan, one should return the money to the convert's sons so that he should not seem to be repaying good with evil. Rava received the money as a deposit, not a loan, and he did not owe Issur a debt of gratitude. He was therefore under no obligation to return the money to Rav Mari.

Others explain that the Gemara in *Kiddushin* should be understood differently: If the convert's son was born before the father converted, it is desirable to return the money to the son. But if he was conceived before the father converted and born after he converted, there exists no requirement to return the money to the son. The reason for this distinction is that the Sages ruled that it is desirable to return the loan to the convert's son, lest the loss of the money cause him to return to a gentile lifestyle. This concern is not applicable in the case of a son who was born into the sanctity of the Jewish people (Ritva, citing Rabbeinu Yona and Ramban).

Rabbeinu Yehonatan of Lunel offers a completely different explanation. He says that Rava did not wish to keep the money for himself. Rather, he intended to return it to Rav Mari. He desired to return the money as an act of piety and not as an obligation.

HALAKHA

He is not fit to inherit – לָאו בַּר יְרוּשָּׁה הוּא: By rabbinic law, a convert inherits from his gentile father, lest he return to his gentile lifestyle. He does not inherit from his father if his father is a convert, neither by Torah law nor by rabbinic law. Even if he was born after his parents converted, if his conception was not in the sanctity of the Jewish people, he does not inherit from his father nor does his father inherit from him. Therefore, if a convert dies without leaving a son whose conception and birth were in the sanctity of the Jewish people, all his property becomes ownerless, and whoever takes possession of it first acquires it (Rambam *Sefer Kinyan*, *Hilkhot Zekhiya UMattana* 1:6 and *Sefer Mishpatim*, *Hilkhot Naḥalot* 6:10; *Shulḥan Arukh*, *Ḥoshen Mishpat* 275:1, 283:1).

Anywhere that it cannot be acquired as inheritance it cannot be acquired as a gift – לֵיתֵיהּ בִּירוּשָּׁה לֵיתֵיהּ בְּמַתָּנָה: With regard to a convert whose son was not conceived in the sanctity of the Jewish people, since the son does not inherit from his father, he also cannot receive his property as the gift of a person on his deathbed. The reason for this is that a gift that a person on his deathbed bestows upon his heir has the halakhic status of inheritance. If a convert bestows such a gift upon another convert who is not his heir, the gift is valid (Rav Hai Gaon; Rif; Rambam). According to other authorities, a convert cannot give anyone such a gift, since the *halakhot* of inheritance do not apply to a convert (Rashba; Rosh), and the Rema maintains that this is the *halakha*. Some say that although a convert cannot bequeath his property by means of such a gift, his will should be fulfilled in accordance with the principle that it is a mitzva to fulfill the statement of the dead (Mordekhai; Ran), but others disagree (Rosh). This principle applies only if the inheritance was entrusted to a third party for that purpose (Rambam *Sefer Kinyan*, *Hilkhot Zekhiya UMattana* 1:6–7; *Shulḥan Arukh*, *Ḥoshen Mishpat* 256:1, and see *Sma* there).

Money cannot be acquired by symbolic exchange – אֵין מַטְבֵּעַ נִקְנֶה בַּחֲלִיפִין: Money cannot be acquired by means of symbolic exchange (Rambam *Sefer Kinyan*, *Hilkhot Mekhira* 6:1; *Shulḥan Arukh*, *Ḥoshen Mishpat* 203:1).

But let Issur admit – וְלוֹדֵי אִיסּוּר: If a person on his deathbed admits that his property belongs to another, and there is no suspicion of artifice, that person acquires the property. Even if the person on his deathbed recovers, he cannot retract his admission. The *halakha* is the same with regard to an admission pertaining to money owed to the person on his deathbed, or deposited by him with another. The admission is effective even in the case of a convert who admits that his property belongs to his son, whose conception was not in the sanctity of the Jewish people (Rambam *Sefer Kinyan*, *Hilkhot Zekhiya UMattana* 9:9; *Shulḥan Arukh*, *Ḥoshen Mishpat* 250:3, and see *Sma* and *Shakh* there, 255:2, and see 256:1).

BACKGROUND

Symbolic exchange – חֲלִיפִין: Symbolic exchange is a formal act of acquisition. If two parties agree on the exchange of one item for another, then when one of the items is acquired by an act of acquisition, e.g., by pulling, the second item is acquired by the other party. This principle is the basis for the transfer of ownership by means of a cloth. Since there is no requirement for the items exchanged to be of equal value, both movable property and land can be acquired by means of the symbolic transfer of a cloth or other small article from the buyer to the seller. The seller acquires the cloth by lifting it, and consequently, the buyer acquires the item being sold. The seller may then return the cloth to the buyer. The Gemara elsewhere (*Bava Metzia* 45b) discusses at length whether or not money can be acquired by means of symbolic exchange.

By means of acquisition of land – אַגַּב קַרְקַע: According to the mishna (*Kiddushin* 26a), movable property can be acquired together with land, and the act of acquisition performed with regard to the land also effects the acquisition of the movable property.

״שִׁיֵּיר קַרְקַע כׇּל שֶׁהוּא – מַתְּנָתוֹ קַיֶּימֶת״. וְכַמָּה ״כׇּל שֶׁהוּא״? אָמַר רַב יְהוּדָה אָמַר רַב: קַרְקַע כְּדֵי פַּרְנָסָתוֹ, וְרַב יִרְמְיָה בַּר אַבָּא אָמַר: מִטַּלְטְלִין כְּדֵי פַּרְנָסָתוֹ.

§ The mishna teaches (146b): If a person on his deathbed **reserved** for himself **any amount of land, his gift stands** even if he subsequently recovers. The Gemara asks: **And how much** is meant by the term: **Any amount?**[H] **Rav Yehuda says** that **Rav says:** This means **land** that is **sufficient** to provide **for his livelihood.**[N] Since he reserved this land for himself, one can assume that he wished to transfer the rest of his property in any event. **And Rav Yirmeya bar Abba says:** Even if he reserved for himself **movable property** that is **sufficient** to provide **for his livelihood,** his gift is valid.

אֲמַר רַבִּי זֵירָא: כַּמָּה מְכַוְּונָן שְׁמַעֲתָתָא דְּסָבֵי! קַרְקַע טַעֲמָא מַאי? דְּאִי קָאֵי סָמֵיךְ עֲלֵיהּ, מִטַּלְטְלֵי נַמִי, אִי קָאֵי סָמֵיךְ עִילָּוַיְהוּ.

Rabbi Zeira said: How meticulous[N] are **the halakhic statements of the elders** Rav Yehuda and Rav Yirmeya. With regard to **land, what is the reason** that he must have reserved enough for his livelihood? The reason is **that if he recovers** he will **rely on that** land for his livelihood. With regard to **movable property as well, if he recovers** he will **rely on it** for his livelihood.

מַתְקִיף לַהּ רַב יוֹסֵף: וּמַאי כַּוְּונְתָא? מַאן דְּאָמַר: מִטַּלְטְלִין – קַרְקַע תְּנַן! מַאן דְּאָמַר: כְּדֵי פַּרְנָסָתוֹ – כׇּל שֶׁהוּא תְּנַן!

Rav Yosef objects to Rabbi Zeira's statement: **What is meticulous** about these statements? The statement of the **one who says** the gift is valid even if he reserved for himself **movable property** is difficult, as **we learn** in the mishna that he must leave himself **land.** The statement of the **one who says** that he must leave himself an amount **sufficient** to provide **for his livelihood** is difficult, as **we learn** in the mishna that his gift is valid if he reserved for himself **any amount.**

אֲמַר לֵיהּ אַבָּיֵי: וְכׇל הֵיכָא דְּתָנֵי קַרְקַע, קַרְקַע דַּוְקָא? וְהָא תְּנַן: הַכּוֹתֵב כׇּל נְכָסָיו לְעַבְדּוֹ – יָצָא בֶּן חוֹרִין, שִׁיֵּיר קַרְקַע כׇּל שֶׁהוּא – לֹא יָצָא בֶּן חוֹרִין; רַבִּי שִׁמְעוֹן אוֹמֵר: לְעוֹלָם הוּא בֶּן חוֹרִין, עַד שֶׁיֹּאמַר: ״כׇּל נְכָסַי נְתוּנִין לִפְלוֹנִי עַבְדִּי חוּץ מֵאֶחָד מֵרִבּוֹא שֶׁבָּהֶן״;

Abaye said to Rav Yosef: **And anywhere that** the term **land is taught,** does it mean **specifically land? But didn't we learn** in a mishna (*Pe'a* 3:8): With regard to **one who writes,** i.e., gives via a document, **all of his property to his** Canaanite **slave,**[HN] the slave **has been emancipated,** but if he **reserved** for himself **any amount of land,**[N] then he **has not been emancipated,** as perhaps he reserved the slave for himself as well. **Rabbi Shimon says: He always** becomes **a freeman** regardless of the wording of the document, even if the owner reserved land for himself, **unless it says** in the document: **All of my property is given to so-and-so my slave, except for one ten-thousandth of it,**[N] as in that case it is possible that the master meant to include the slave in the portion that he is not giving away. Consequently, the slave is not emancipated.

HALAKHA

And how much is any amount, etc. – וְכַמָּה כׇּל שֶׁהוּא וכו׳: If a person on his deathbed gave all of his property to another and reserved for himself any amount of property, whether land or movable property, his gift has the halakhic status of the gift of a healthy person. The gift requires an act of acquisition, and it cannot be retracted even if he recovers. This is in accordance with the opinion of Rav Yirmeya bar Abba with regard to movable property, and in accordance with the opinion of Rav Naḥman and Rava on 150a with regard to the amount of property reserved (Rif; Rambam). The Rema adds that some say that he must reserve for himself sufficient property to sustain himself, in accordance with the opinion of Rav Yehuda (Rambam *Sefer Kinyan, Hilkhot Zekhiya UMattana* 8:15; *Shulḥan Arukh, Ḥoshen Mishpat* 250:4, and see *Sma* there, and see 250:2).

One who writes all of his property to his slave – הַכּוֹתֵב כׇּל נְכָסָיו לְעַבְדּוֹ: If one writes a deed granting all of his property to his Canaanite slave, the slave is emancipated, as the slave is part of the property, and he acquires himself in the process. If the owner reserves some of the property for himself, the slave is not emancipated and he does not acquire the property. This is so irrespective of whether the owner reserves for himself land or movable property, whether he does or does not specify which part of the property he reserves for himself, and whether he does or does not possess any other property. Even if he wrote in the deed that he gave to his slave: You shall acquire ownership of yourself and of all my property except for a certain item, the slave is not emancipated and he does not acquire the property. In this case, some of the early authorities disagree and maintain that the slave is emancipated (Rambam *Sefer Kinyan, Hilkhot Zekhiya UMattana* 3:15 and *Hilkhot Avadim* 7:1; *Shulḥan Arukh, Yoreh De'a* 267:57, and see *Shakh* there).

NOTES

Land sufficient for his livelihood – קַרְקַע כְּדֵי פַּרְנָסָתוֹ: The amount of land reserved must grow enough produce to provide the giver with a sufficient yearly income. Similarly, according to Rav Yirmeya, the amount of movable property reserved, when invested in a business, must provide him with sufficient yearly income (Rabbi Yitzḥak Karkusha, citing *Tosafot*; Rosh). Others maintain that it is sufficient if he can sustain himself from the property for one year (*Sefer HaIttur*).

How meticulous – כַּמָּה מְכַוְּונָן: Rabbi Zeira praises the accuracy of the statements of Rav Yehuda and Rav Yirmeya bar Abba, who both explain that if the person on his deathbed recovers, his gift is valid only if he left himself sufficient property to sustain himself. They disagree only with regard to the type of property that he must reserve for himself (Rashbam). Others explain that according to Rabbi Zeira, there is no disagreement between Rav Yehuda and Rav Yirmeya. Rather, each cites a different case where the gift is valid even if he recovers (*Tosafot Yeshanim*).

One who writes all of his property to his slave – הַכּוֹתֵב כׇּל נְכָסָיו לְעַבְדּוֹ: Since the slave is part of the property, the transaction results in the slave acquiring ownership of himself, and consequently he becomes a freeman.

If he reserved any amount of land – שִׁיֵּיר קַרְקַע כׇּל שֶׁהוּא: The Rashbam explains that the owner reserved for himself an unspecified part of his land. Since the halakhic status of Canaanite slaves is, in some respects, like that of land, it is possible that the unspecified land is a reference to the slave. If the owner specifies which land is not included in the gift, the fact that the owner reserved that land for himself does not preclude the slave's emancipation (see Rabbeinu Ḥananel).

Except for one ten-thousandth of it – חוּץ מֵאֶחָד מֵרִבּוֹא שֶׁבָּהֶן: In this case one may assume that his intention is to exclude the slave (Rashbam; Ri Migash). Rashi (*Gittin* 9a) explains that even if the slave is worth more than one ten-thousandth of the property, the owner is understood to have used the term disparagingly, indicating that he considers the slave worth no more than that. Alternatively, the Rambam explains that since the slave is part of the property, if the owner reserves one ten-thousandth of the property, he is considered to have reserved ownership of part of the slave as well, and since the deed does not completely emancipate the slave, it does not emancipate him at all (Rambam's Commentary on the Mishna). In any event, since the slave is not emancipated, the deed has no validity, and it was written only in order to honor the slave (Rashbam).

וְאָמַר רַב דִּימִי בַּר יוֹסֵף אָמַר רַבִּי אֶלְעָזָר: עָשׂוּ מִטַּלְטְלִין שִׁיּוּר אֵצֶל עֶבֶד, וְלֹא עָשׂוּ מִטַּלְטְלִין שִׁיּוּר אֵצֶל כְּתוּבָּה!

And Rav Dimi bar Yosef says that **Rabbi Elazar says:** The Sages **deemed movable property** to be considered a significant **reserving** of property for oneself **with regard to** the emancipation of **a slave,**[N] so that a slave is not emancipated when his owner gives him all of his other property. **But they did not deem movable property** that one withheld from his sons and earmarked for his wife to be considered a significant **reserving** of property **with regard to** her **marriage contract.**[HN] If one granted all of his property to his sons but reserved any amount of land for his wife, she forfeits her marriage contract. By not protesting the gift, she has conceded that she will collect her marriage contract only from the land he reserved for her. Nevertheless, if he reserved only movable property for his wife, she does not forfeit her marriage contract. Rabbi Elazar's ruling with regard to a slave indicates that the expression: Reserves any amount of land, does not necessarily exclude movable property.

הָתָם בְּדִין הוּא דְּלָא לִיתְנֵי קַרְקַע, וְאַיְּידֵי דִּתְנָא רֵישָׁא, רַבִּי עֲקִיבָא אוֹמֵר: קַרְקַע כׇּל שֶׁהוּא חַיֶּיבֶת בְּפֵאָה וּבְבִכּוּרִים, וְלִכְתּוֹב עֲלֵיהֶם פְּרוֹזְבּוֹל, וְלִקְנוֹת עִמָּהֶם נְכָסִים שֶׁאֵין לָהֶם אַחֲרָיוּת בְּכֶסֶף וּבִשְׁטָר וּבַחֲזָקָה, מִשּׁוּם הָכִי קָתָנֵי קַרְקַע.

Rav Yosef replies: **There,** with regard to the slave, **by right** the mishna **should not** have **taught** the *halakha* with regard to **land,** but it should have taught the *halakha* with regard to all property. **But since** the **former clause** of the mishna **teaches** a *halakha* with regard to land, the mishna mentions land in the subsequent clause as well. The Gemara cites the former clause (*Pe'a* 3:6): **Rabbi Akiva says:** The owner of **any amount of land is obligated in** ***pe'a***[B] **and in first fruits;**[B] **and** if the debtor possesses any amount of land the creditor **can write a document that prevents the Sabbatical Year from abrogating an outstanding debt** [***prosbol***][L] **for it**[BN] so that his loans will not be canceled in the seventh year; **and he can acquire property that does not serve as a guarantee** along **with it by** means of **money, by a deed, or by taking possession**[B] of it. Rav Yosef concludes: **Due to this** reason, the mishna **teaches** the *halakha* with regard to **land.**

NOTES

A reserving of property with regard to a slave – שִׁיּוּר אֵצֶל עֶבֶד: If one writes a deed granting all of his property to his slave except for a small part of his movable property, the slave is not emancipated. The Rashbam explains that this is because people refer to a slave as movable property, and therefore the exception may have referred to the slave.

With regard to her marriage contract – אֵצֶל כְּתוּבָּה: The Rashbam explains that this refers to the *halakha* stated previously (see 132a–132b). If one writes a deed granting all of his property to his sons, and he reserves any amount of land for his wife, it is assumed that she thereby releases the lien on her husband's property created by her marriage contract, and she forfeits payment of her marriage contract. This does not apply if he leaves his wife nothing except movable property, because the lien of the marriage contract applies only to land, and therefore, if the woman is left nothing but movable property it is considered as if nothing were reserved for her, and she does not release the lien on her husband's property.

Others explain that the Gemara here is referring to property that one reserves for himself, apart from the property one grants to his sons and to his wife. If one reserves any amount of land for himself, it is assumed that his wife does not release the lien on her husband's property. Even if she does not object to the arrangement, one may assume that this is only because she relies on collecting payment of her marriage contract from the land that her husband reserves for himself. If he reserves only movable property for himself and his wife does not object to the arrangement, it is assumed that she releases her lien upon the property, since payment of the marriage contract is not collected from movable property (Rabbeinu Gershom Meor HaGola; Rambam; *Tosafot Yeshanim*).

Despite the fact that by rabbinic law payment of the marriage contract is not collected from movable property, the *ge'onim* instituted that it can be collected from movable property. The authorities disagree with regard to the ramifications of this ordinance in the case of one who grants all of his property to his sons and reserves any amount of property for his wife. Some authorities maintain that as a result of this ordinance, movable property is considered equivalent to land both with regard to the *halakha* that if one reserves any amount of movable property for his wife it is assumed that she releases the lien on her husband's property, and with regard to the *halakha* that if one reserves any amount of movable property for himself, it is assumed that his wife does not release the lien on her husband's property (*Beit Yosef*). Others maintain that despite this ordinance, if one reserves for his wife nothing except movable property, she does not forfeit payment of her marriage contract. The reason for this is that the ordinance was enacted in order to enhance a woman's ability to collect payment of her marriage contract, not to weaken it (Meiri). Furthermore, in this case one cannot assume that the wife releases her lien on her husband's property (*Darkhei Moshe*).

And can write a ***prosbol*** **for it – וְלִכְתּוֹב עֲלֵיהֶם פְּרוֹזְבּוֹל:** A *prosbol* is effective only if the debtor owns land. If the debtor does not own any land, the lender gives him an amount of land sufficient to grow a stalk of cabbage (Rambam). The early commentaries offer different explanations for this *halakha*. Rashi explains elsewhere that loans commonly involve a lien on land, and the Sages instituted the *prosbol* only for typical cases. Others explain that when the debtor possesses land it is considered as though the debt had already been collected, since land cannot be hidden or removed, and therefore the debt is not abrogated by the Sabbatical Year (*Tosefot Yom Tov*).

HALAKHA

But they did not deem movable property a reserving of property with regard to her marriage contract – וְלֹא עָשׂוּ מִטַּלְטְלִין שִׁיּוּר אֵצֶל כְּתוּבָּה: If one writes a deed granting all of his property to his sons, except for one portion that he reserves for his wife, she forfeits payment of her marriage contract. If he grants her movable property, or if he reserves for himself a portion of land from which she can collect payment of her marriage contract, she does not forfeit her marriage contract. The *ge'onim* instituted that payment of the marriage contract can be collected from movable property. Consequently, if one reserves for himself any amount of movable property, his wife's marriage contract remains valid. The authorities disagree with regard to one who grants all of his land to his sons, leaving nothing for himself, and grants his wife only movable property. Some authorities maintain that she forfeits payment of her marriage contract (*Beit Yosef*), and others maintain that she does not forfeit payment of her marriage contract (Rambam *Sefer Kinyan, Hilkhot Zekhiya UMattana* 6:10; *Shulḥan Arukh, Even HaEzer* 106:1–2, and see *Beit Shmuel* there).

BACKGROUND

Pe'a **– פֵּאָה:** The term *pe'a* literally means corner, and it refers to the produce left in the corner of the field. The Torah prohibits the owner of a field from harvesting this produce. One must leave this produce for the poor to collect themselves (Leviticus 19:9, 23:22). The Sages instituted that the area of the corner must be at least one-sixtieth of the field.

First fruits – בִּכּוּרִים: The Torah requires one to bring to the Temple the first fruits that grow each year on his land (see Deuteronomy 26:1–11). The first fruits are brought only from the seven species for which Eretz Yisrael is praised.

Can write a ***prosbol*** **for it – לִכְתּוֹב עֲלֵיהֶם פְּרוֹזְבּוֹל:** The Torah states that the Sabbatical Year abrogates any debts that are due to be collected at the end of the Sabbatical Year (see Deuteronomy 15:1–11). The *prosbol* is a document that prevents outstanding debts from being abrogated by the Sabbatical Year. The principle behind the *prosbol* is that if the loan contract has been given to the court for collection, the loan is not abrogated. When Hillel the Elder saw that many people were refraining from lending money in the years preceding the Sabbatical Year because they were concerned that they would not get their money back, he instituted a process whereby the lender authorizes the court to collect all of his debts. The *prosbol* formalizes this transfer of authority to the court.

Taking possession – חֲזָקָה: This is one of the modes of acquisition applicable to land. The buyer acquires the property by performing an action that demonstrates his ownership of the property, e.g., by locking the door of the property, by building a fence around the property, or by making a breach in the fence.

LANGUAGE

Prosbol **– פְּרוֹזְבּוֹל:** Although this word is clearly Greek in origin, the exact source is unclear. Some suggest that it is derived from προβολή, *probolē*, which can refer to the delivery of a declaration before a court or an assembly of people, and can also refer to a loan. Among other explanations, it has been suggested that it is related to προσβολή, *prosbolē*, the completion of a sale.

וְכָל הֵיכָא דְּתָנֵי "כָּל שֶׁהוּא" לֵית לֵיהּ שִׁיעוּרָא? וְהָא תְּנַן, רַבִּי דּוֹסָא בֶּן הָרְכִּינָס אוֹמֵר: חָמֵשׁ רְחֵלוֹת גּוֹזְזוֹת מָנֶה מָנֶה וּפְרָס – חַיָּיבוֹת בְּרֵאשִׁית הַגֵּז, וַחֲכָמִים אוֹמְרִים: חָמֵשׁ רְחֵלוֹת גּוֹזְזוֹת כָּל שֶׁהֵן; וְאָמְרִינַן, וְכַמָּה כָּל שֶׁהֵן? אָמַר רַב: מָנֶה וּפְרָס, וּבִלְבַד שֶׁיְּהוּ מְחוּמָּשׁוֹת!

Abaye raises an objection to Rav Yosef's statement that the term any amount should be understood literally: **And anywhere that** the term: **Any amount, is taught,** does the amount **not have a measure? But didn't we learn** in a mishna (*Ḥullin* 135a): **Rabbi Dosa ben Harkinas says:** When shearing **five sheep,** the **sheared** wool of each sheep, with the wool weighing **one hundred dinars and half of one hundred dinars,**[B] i.e., one hundred and fifty dinars, renders the owner **obligated in** the mitzva to give **the first sheared** wool to the priests. **And the Rabbis say: Five sheep,** each of whose **sheared** wool yields wool weighing **any amount.**[H] **And we say: And how much** is signified by the term: **Any amount? Rav says:** A total weight of **one hundred dinars and half** of one hundred dinars, **provided that** the one hundred and fifty dinars **are divided** equally **between the five** sheep.[N] This indicates that the term any amount can denote a certain minimal amount.

הָתָם בְּדִין הוּא דְּלָא לִיתְנֵי כָּל שֶׁהוּא, וְאַיְּידֵי דְּקָאָמַר תַּנָּא קַמָּא שִׁיעוּרָא רַבָּה אָמַר אִיהוּ נַמִי שִׁיעוּרָא זוּטְרָא, קָרֵי לָהּ "כָּל שֶׁהוּא".

Rav Yosef replies: **There,** with regard to the first sheared wool, **by right** the mishna **should not** have **taught** the *halakha* with regard to **any amount. But since the first *tanna*,** Rabbi Dosa ben Harkinas, **states a large measure,** the Rabbis **also state** that they require **a small measure,** and therefore they **call** this measure **any amount.** But with regard to the gift of a person on his deathbed, the term any amount should be understood literally.

פְּשִׁיטָא, אֲמַר "מִטַּלְטְלַי לִפְלָנְיָא" – כָּל מָאנֵי תַּשְׁמִישְׁתֵּיהּ קָנֵי, לְבַר מֵחִטֵּי וְשַׂעֲרֵי. "כָּל מִטַּלְטְלַי לִפְלָנְיָא" – אֲפִילּוּ חִטֵּי וְשַׂעֲרֵי, וַאֲפִילּוּ רֵיחַיִם הָעֶלְיוֹנָה קָנָה, לְבַר מֵרֵיחַיִם הַתַּחְתּוֹנָה. "כָּל דְּמִטַּלְטֵל" – אֲפִילּוּ רֵיחַיִם הַתַּחְתּוֹנָה קָנֵי.

§ It is **obvious** that if one **said:** I give **my movable property**[N] **to so-and-so,**[H] then that person **acquires all of his utensils, excluding** his **wheat and barley.**[N] If one said: I give **all my movable property**[N] **to so-and-so,** then that person acquires **even** the **wheat and barley, and he acquires even the upper millstone,** since it is occasionally removed from its place. He acquires all the property that is not land or houses, **except for the lower millstone,** which is never moved. If he said: I give **everything that can be moved** to so-and-so, that person **acquires even the lower millstone,** as it is possible to move it.

אִיבַּעְיָא לְהוּ: עַבְדָּא כְּמִקַּרְקְעָא אוֹ כְּמִטַּלְטְלָא דָּמֵי? אֲמַר לֵיהּ רַב אַחָא בְּרֵיהּ דְּרַב אַוְיָא לְרַב אַשִׁי, תָּא שְׁמַע: הַמּוֹכֵר אֶת הָעִיר – מָכַר בָּתִּים, שִׁיחִין וּמְעָרוֹת, וּמֶרְחֲצָאוֹת, וּבֵית הַבַּדִּין, וּבֵית הַשְּׁלָחִין, אֲבָל לֹא אֶת הַמִּטַּלְטְלִין; וּבִזְמַן שֶׁאָמַר: "הִיא וְכָל מַה שֶּׁבְּתוֹכָהּ", אֲפִילּוּ הָיוּ בָּהּ בְּהֵמָה אוֹ עֲבָדִים – הֲרֵי כּוּלָּן מְכוּרִין; אִי אָמְרַתְּ בִּשְׁלָמָא כְּמִטַּלְטְלָא דָּמֵי, מִשּׁוּם הָכִי לָא מִיזְדַּבַּן בְּרֵישָׁא, אֶלָּא אִי אָמְרַתְּ כְּמִקַּרְקְעָא דָּמֵי, אַמַּאי לָא מִיזְדַּבַּן?

A dilemma was raised before the Sages: Is the legal status of a Canaanite **slave like** that of **land, or** is his status **like** that of **movable property?**[N] **Rav Aḥa, son of Rav Avya, said to Rav Ashi: Come** and **hear** a proof from a mishna (68a): A landowner **who sells the city has sold** with it the **houses,** and the **ditches and caves, and** the **bathhouses,** and **the olive presses and the irrigated fields, but not the movable property. But when** the seller **said** to the buyer: I am selling **it and everything that is in it,** then **even if there were animals or** Canaanite **slaves in** the city, **they are all sold.** Rav Aḥa, son of Rav Avya, explains the proof: **Granted, if you say** that the legal status of a Canaanite slave **is like** that of **movable property, due to that reason he is not sold in the first** case. **But if you say** that the legal status of a Canaanite slave **is like** that of **land, why is he not sold** with the city?

BACKGROUND

Sheared wool one hundred dinars and half of one hundred dinars – גּוֹזְזוֹת מָנֶה מָנֶה וּפְרָס: One hundred and fifty dinars is about 700 g. Nowadays sheep yield more wool than this. It seems that Rabbi Dosa was not stating the approximate yield of wool. Rather, his intention was to establish a minimum standard below which the yield is not defined as sheared wool with regard to this *halakha*.

HALAKHA

Five sheep each of whose sheared wool yields any amount, etc. – חָמֵשׁ רְחֵלוֹת גּוֹזְזוֹת כָּל שֶׁהֵן וכו׳: One is not obligated to separate the wool from the first sheared wool unless he owns at least five sheep. The total yield of their sheared wool must be no less than the weight of sixty *sela*, and each sheep must yield wool weighing at least twelve *sela*, in accordance with the Gemara's conclusion in tractate *Ḥullin* (137a). If one of the sheep yields less than twelve *sela* the owner is exempt from separating the wool from the first sheared wool, even when the total yield weighs sixty *sela* (Rambam *Sefer Zera'im, Hilkhot Bikkurim* 10:13; *Shulḥan Arukh, Yoreh De'a* 333:9).

I give my movable property to so-and-so, etc. – מִטַּלְטְלַי לִפְלָנְיָא וכו׳: If a person on his deathbed states that he gives his movable property to so-and-so, the recipient receives all of his utensils, but not his wheat or barley. The recipient also does not acquire the giver's merchandise (*Sma*). If he says: All my movable property shall be given to so-and-so, the recipient acquires all of his movable property, including his Canaanite slaves, which in this case are also considered movable property (see 128b). He does not acquire a lower millstone, which is set in the ground. If he says: Everything that can be moved shall be given to so-and-so, the recipient acquires even the lower millstone. This *halakha* also applies in the case of a healthy person who gives these gifts by means of an act of acquisition (Rambam *Sefer Kinyan, Hilkhot Zekhiya UMattana* 11:12–14; *Shulḥan Arukh, Ḥoshen Mishpat* 248:10 and *Beur HaGra* there).

NOTES

Provided that the dinars are divided equally between the five sheep – וּבִלְבַד שֶׁיְּהוּ מְחוּמָּשׁוֹת: Each sheep must yield wool weighing no less than thirty dinars. If a sheep yields less than this amount, it is not included among the five sheep (Rashbam; see Ritva).

If one said, I give my movable property – אֲמַר מִטַּלְטְלַי: The discussion here applies both in the case of a person on his deathbed, whose statement effects the transfer of ownership without an act of acquisition, and in the case of a healthy person, who performs an act of acquisition (Rashbam).

Excluding wheat and barley – לְבַר מֵחִטֵּי וְשַׂעֲרֵי: Wheat and barley are not included when using the term movable property, since they are referred to as produce (Rabbeinu Yehonatan of Lunel; Ra'ah).

All my movable property – כָּל מִטַּלְטְלַי: Since the word all is unnecessary, it is regarded as an indication that he desires to expand the gift to include anything that can be considered movable property.

Is the status of a slave like land or like movable property – עַבְדָּא כְּמִקַּרְקְעָא אוֹ כְּמִטַּלְטְלָא דָּמֵי: The early commentaries explain that with regard to matters of Torah law and matters of Torah terminology, the legal status of a Canaanite slave is like that of land. The discussion here pertains to the status of a Canaanite slave in common parlance. Since the intent of a document is interpreted according to the standard usage of the terms appearing in the document, it is necessary to ascertain which term is commonly used with regard to Canaanite slaves (see Rashbam and *Tosafot*).

וְאֶלָּא מַאי? כִּמְטַלְטְלָא דָּמֵי, מַאי "אֲפִילּוּ"? [אֶלָּא] מַאי אִית לָךְ לְמֵימַר? שָׁאנֵי מְטַלְטְלָא דְּנָיֵיד מִמְּטַלְטְלָא דְּלָא נָיֵיד; אֲפִילּוּ תֵּימָא כִּמְקַרְקְעָא דָּמֵי, שָׁאנֵי מְקַרְקְעָא דְּנָיֵיד מִמְּקַרְקְעָא דְּלָא נָיֵיד.

Rav Ashi replied: **Rather, what** do you say? Do you maintain that his legal status **is like** that of **movable property?** If there is no difference in legal status between Canaanite slaves and movable property, **what** is the reason that the mishna emphasizes in the second case that **even** the Canaanite slaves are sold? **Rather, what have you to say** to explain this? One must explain that **movable property that moves** by itself **is different from movable property that does not move** by itself, and therefore one might have thought that although the sale includes movable property, Canaanite slaves are not included in the sale. In the same manner, **even** if **you say** that the legal status of a Canaanite slave **is like** that of **land, land that moves is different from land that does not move.** Therefore, the legal status of Canaanite slaves cannot be proved from this mishna.

אֲמַר לֵיהּ רָבִינָא לְרַב אַשִׁי, תָּא שְׁמַע: הַכּוֹתֵב לְעַבְדּוֹ כָּל נְכָסָיו – יָצָא בֶּן חוֹרִין, שִׁיֵּיר קַרְקַע כָּל שֶׁהוּא – לֹא יָצָא בֶּן חוֹרִין; רַבִּי שִׁמְעוֹן אוֹמֵר: לְעוֹלָם הוּא בֶּן חוֹרִין – עַד שֶׁיֹּאמַר "כָּל נְכָסַי נְתוּנִין לִפְלוֹנִי עַבְדִּי חוּץ מֵאֶחָד מֵרִבּוֹא שֶׁבָּהֶן";

Ravina said to Rav Ashi: Come and **hear** a proof from a mishna (*Pe'a* 3:8): With regard to **one who writes,** i.e., gives via a document, **all of his property to his** Canaanite **slave,** the slave **has been emancipated,** but if he **reserved** for himself **any amount of land,** then he **has not been emancipated,** as perhaps he reserved the slave for himself as well. **Rabbi Shimon says: He always** becomes **a freeman** regardless of the wording of the document, even if the owner reserved land for himself, **unless it says** in the document: **All of my property is given to so-and-so my slave, except for one ten-thousandth of it.**

וְאָמַר רַב דִּימִי בַּר יוֹסֵף אָמַר רַבִּי אֶלְעָזָר: עָשׂוּ מְטַלְטְלִין שִׁיּוּר אֵצֶל עֶבֶד, וְלֹא עָשׂוּ מְטַלְטְלִין שִׁיּוּר אֵצֶל כְּתוּבָּה; וַאֲמַר לֵיהּ רָבָא לְרַב נַחְמָן: מַאי טַעְמָא? עַבְדָּא מְטַלְטְלָא הוּא, וּמְטַלְטְלָא לִמְטַלְטְלָא הָוֵי שִׁיּוּר, וּכְתוּבַּת אִשָּׁה מְקַרְקְעָא הוּא, וּמְטַלְטְלָא לִמְקַרְקְעָא לָא הָוֵי שִׁיּוּר.

And Rav Dimi bar Yosef says that **Rabbi Elazar says:** The Sages **deemed movable property** to be considered a significant **reserving** of property for oneself **with regard to a slave,** so that the slave is not emancipated when the owner gives him all of his other property. **But they did not deem movable property** that one withheld from his sons and earmarked for his wife to be considered a significant **reserving** of property **with regard to** her **marriage contract. And Rava said to Rav Naḥman: What is the reason** for this? Rav Naḥman explained: A Canaanite **slave is** considered **movable property, and** reserving **movable property is** considered a significant **reserving with regard to movable property. But a woman's marriage contract is** a document concerning **land,** since the payment of the marriage contract is collected from land, **and** reserving **movable property is not** considered a significant **reserving with regard to land.** Rav Naḥman states that a Canaanite slave is considered movable property.

אֲמַר לֵיהּ: אֲנַן מִשּׁוּם דְּלָאו כְּרוּת גִּיטָּא מַתְנֵינַן לָהּ.

Rav Ashi **said to** Ravina: The reason the slave is not emancipated if the master reserved part of the property for himself is not that the slave is included in the property that the owner reserved for himself. Rather, **we teach this** *halakha* as being **due to** the fact **that** the document is **not a bill** of manumission **that** completely **severs**[N] the bond between the slave and the master.

NOTES

That it is not a bill of manumission that severs – **דְּלָאו כְּרוּת גִּיטָּא:** The Torah refers to a woman's bill of divorce as a scroll of severance (see Deuteronomy 24:1), from which the Sages derive that it is valid only if it completely severs the bond between husband and wife. It is derived by means of a verbal analogy that this *halakha* applies to a slave's bill of manumission.

The early authorities disagree with regard to the explanation of this Gemara. The Rashbam explains that a slave is not generally considered movable property. But if the master reserves an unspecified part of the property for himself, the possibility still exists that he intends to reserve the slave as part of his movable property, and therefore the bill does not completely sever the bond between the slave and the master. The Rashba explains that the flaw is in the wording of the phrase: All of my property is given to you except for one part of the property. The term property includes both the slave and that part of the property that the master reserves for himself, and therefore it does not constitute complete severance. Accordingly, if one writes in the bill of manumission: You shall acquire ownership of yourself and of all my property except for a certain field or a certain item, the slave is emancipated.

אָמַר רָבָא אָמַר רַב נַחְמָן: חֲמִשָּׁה – עַד שֶׁיִּכְתְּבוּ כׇּל נִכְסֵיהֶם, וְאֵלּוּ הֵן: שְׁכִיב מְרַע, עַבְדּוֹ, אִשְׁתּוֹ, וּבָנָיו, מַבְרַחַת.

§ **Rava says that Rav Naḥman says:** There are **five** types of gifts to which specific *halakhot* apply, but the *halakhot* do not apply **until** the owners **write** a deed granting **all of their property** to another without reserving anything for themselves, **and they are as follows:** The gift of **a person on his deathbed,**[N] a gift to one's Canaanite **slave,** a gift to one's **wife,** a gift to one's **sons,** and the gift of **a woman who shelters** her property from her prospective husband[NH] by transferring her property to another before her marriage. In this latter case the Sages instituted that if her husband dies or divorces her she can reclaim the property.

שְׁכִיב מְרַע, דִּתְנַן: שְׁכִיב מְרַע שֶׁכָּתַב כׇּל נְכָסָיו לַאֲחֵרִים וְשִׁיֵּיר קַרְקַע כׇּל שֶׁהוּא – מַתְּנָתוֹ קַיֶּימֶת, לֹא שִׁיֵּיר קַרְקַע כׇּל שֶׁהוּא – אֵין מַתְּנָתוֹ קַיֶּימֶת.

The Gemara explains each of these cases: In the case of a gift of **a person on his deathbed,** this is **as we learned** in the mishna (146b): With regard to **a person on his deathbed who wrote** a deed granting **all of his property to others, and he reserved** for himself **any amount of land, his gift stands** even if he subsequently recovers. If **he did not reserve** for himself **any amount of land,** and he recovered, **his gift does not stand,** as the gift was conditional upon his death, since evidently he did not intend to leave himself without means of support if he survived.

עַבְדּוֹ, דִּתְנַן: הַכּוֹתֵב כׇּל נְכָסָיו לְעַבְדּוֹ – יָצָא בֶּן חוֹרִין, שִׁיֵּיר קַרְקַע כׇּל שֶׁהוּא – לֹא יָצָא בֶּן חוֹרִין.

In the case of a gift to one's **slave,** this is **as we learned** in a mishna (*Pe'a* 3:8): With regard to **one who writes** a deed granting **all of his property to his** Canaanite **slave,** the slave **has been emancipated,** but if he **reserved** for himself **any amount of land,** then he **has not been emancipated,** as perhaps he reserved the slave for himself as well.

אִשְׁתּוֹ, דְּאָמַר רַב יְהוּדָה אָמַר שְׁמוּאֵל: הַכּוֹתֵב כׇּל נְכָסָיו לְאִשְׁתּוֹ – לֹא עֲשָׂאָהּ אֶלָּא אַפּוֹטְרוֹפָּא.

In the case of a gift to one's **wife,** this is **as Rav Yehuda says** that **Shmuel says: One who writes** a deed granting **all of his property to his wife**[H] **renders her only a steward** of his property, i.e., he intends only to place her in charge of the property and she does not acquire it. According to Rav Naḥman, this applies only if he did not reserve any part of the property for himself.

בָּנָיו, דִּתְנַן: הַכּוֹתֵב כׇּל נְכָסָיו לְבָנָיו, וְכָתַב לְאִשְׁתּוֹ קַרְקַע כׇּל שֶׁהוּא – אִבְּדָה כְּתוּבָּתָהּ.

In the case of a gift to one's **sons,** this is **as we learned** in a mishna (*Pe'a* 3:7): With regard to **one who writes** a deed granting **all of his property to his sons, and he writes** in the deed that he grants **any amount of land to his wife, she forfeits** payment of **her marriage contract.**[N] If he reserves any amount of land for himself, his wife does not forfeit payment of her marriage contract.

מַבְרַחַת, דְּאָמַר מָר: מַבְרַחַת צְרִיכָה שֶׁתִּכְתּוֹב כׇּל נְכָסֶיהָ.

In the case of a gift of **a woman who shelters** her property from her intended husband, this is **as the Master says:** In the case of **a woman who** wishes to **shelter** her property from her prospective husband, **she must write** a deed granting **all of her property** to another. If she reserves for herself any amount of property, she cannot reclaim the property if she is widowed or divorced.

וּבְכוּלְּהוּ – מִטַּלְטְלֵי הָוֵי שִׁיּוּר, לְבַר מִכְּתוּבָּה, דְּאַמְּקַרְקְעֵי תַּקִּינוּ רַבָּנַן, מִמִּטַּלְטְלֵי לָא תַּקּוּן רַבָּנַן.

The Gemara concludes: **With regard to all of these** cases, reserving **movable property is** considered a significant **reserving** of property, **except with regard to** a woman's **marriage contract.** If one grants all of his property to his sons except for any amount of land, which he gives to his wife, and he reserves for himself only movable property, his wife forfeits payment of her marriage contract, as nothing remains in the husband's possession from which she is entitled to collect payment. This is **because the Sages instituted** that the lien on the marriage contract is placed **on land, and the Sages did not institute** that the marriage contract can be collected **from movable property.**

אַמֵּימָר אָמַר: מִטַּלְטְלֵי דִּכְתִיבִי בִּכְתוּבָּה וְאִיתְנְהוּ בְּעֵינַיְהוּ – הָוֵי שִׁיּוּר.

Ameimar said: With regard to **movable property that is** explicitly **written in the marriage contract** as property from which the debt may be collected **and is still extant,** if the husband reserves this property for himself, this **is** considered a significant **reserving** of property, and his wife does not forfeit payment of her marriage contract.

NOTES

The gift of a person on his deathbed – שְׁכִיב מְרַע: The Rosh writes that according to the statement of Rav Yehuda (149b), this case differs from the other cases cited here, as even if a person on his deathbed reserves for himself a part of his property, if he does not leave himself sufficient property to provide for his livelihood, his gift is valid (*Tosefot HaRosh*). The Rif writes that Rav Naḥman disagrees with Rav Yehuda, and the *halakha* is in accordance with the opinion of Rav Naḥman.

A woman who shelters her property from her prospective husband – מַבְרַחַת: One does not generally transfer ownership of all of one's property to another. Therefore, if a woman transfers ownership of all of her property to another prior to her marriage, one may assume that she does so only in order to prevent her husband from acquiring ownership of the property, and she does not intend to fully relinquish her rights to the property. Consequently, the Sages instituted that if her husband dies or divorces her she may reclaim the property. If she retains ownership of part of her property, this assumption does not apply and she cannot reclaim the property if she is widowed or divorced.

She forfeits payment of her marriage contract – אִבְּדָה כְּתוּבָּתָהּ: This *halakha* is discussed in detail earlier in the tractate (see 132a–132b). If one writes a deed granting all of his property to his sons except for any amount of land that he grants to his wife, and she does not object to the arrangement, it is assumed that she thereby releases the lien on her husband's property created by her marriage contract, and she forfeits her right to receive the payment of the marriage contract. If her husband reserves any amount of land for himself, one cannot assume that her acquiescence signifies that she releases the lien on her husband's property. Even if she does not object to the arrangement, this might be because she relies on collecting the payment of her marriage contract from the land that her husband reserves for himself. Consequently, she does not forfeit payment of her marriage contract. Payment of the marriage contract is not collected from movable property, and therefore, in a case where the husband reserves only movable property for himself, this possibility does not apply, and if the wife does not object to the arrangement, it is assumed that she releases the lien on her husband's land.

HALAKHA

A woman who shelters her property from her prospective husband – מַבְרַחַת: If a woman writes a deed prior to her marriage granting all of her property to another and she is subsequently widowed or divorced, the gift is nullified. This is because it is assumed that she gave the gift only in order to shelter the property from her husband. If she explicitly writes that the gift is absolute and will never revert to her, the gift is not nullified (*Maggid Mishne*, citing Ri Migash). If she reserves any of the property for herself, even movable property (*Maggid Mishne*), her gift is valid, and if she is later divorced, ownership of the property does not revert to her. If she dies during her husband's lifetime, the recipient acquires the property irrevocably (Rambam *Sefer Kinyan, Hilkhot Zekhiya UMattana* 6:12 and *Sefer Nashim, Hilkhot Ishut* 22:9; *Shulḥan Arukh, Even HaEzer* 90:7, and see *Ḥoshen Mishpat* 99:6).

One who writes all of his property to his wife, etc. – הַכּוֹתֵב כׇּל נְכָסָיו לְאִשְׁתּוֹ וכו׳: If a person on his deathbed writes a deed granting all of his property to his wife, he has rendered her a steward in charge of the property for his heirs. According to the Rambam, this is the *halakha* even if an act of acquisition was performed. Other authorities disagree. If he left any part of his property for his heirs, whether land or movable property, the wife acquires the property that he gave her (Rambam *Sefer Kinyan, Hilkhot Zekhiya UMattana* 6:4; *Shulḥan Arukh, Even HaEzer* 107:1 and *Ḥoshen Mishpat* 246:7, 12).

אֲמַר "נְכָסַי לִפְלָנְיָא" – עַבְדָּא אִיקְּרֵי נִכְסֵי, דִּתְנַן: הַכּוֹתֵב כׇּל נְכָסָיו לְעַבְדּוֹ – יָצָא בֶּן חוֹרִין. אַרְעָא אִיקְּרֵי נִכְסֵי, דִּתְנַן: נְכָסִים שֶׁיֵּשׁ לָהֶן אַחְרָיוּת נִקְנִין בְּכֶסֶף וּבִשְׁטָר וּבַחֲזָקָה. גְּלִימָא אִיקְּרֵי נִכְסֵי, דִּתְנַן: וְשֶׁאֵין לָהֶן אַחְרָיוּת – אֵין נִקְנִין אֶלָּא בִּמְשִׁיכָה.

§ If one **said: My property** shall go **to so-and-so,**[NH] anything that is referred to as property is included in the gift. A Canaanite **slave is called property, as we learned** in a mishna (*Pe'a* 3:8): With regard to **one who writes,** i.e., gives via a document, **all of his property to his** Canaanite slave, the slave **has been emancipated. Land is called property, as we learned** in a mishna (*Kiddushin* 26a): **Property that serves as a guarantee,** i.e., land, **can be acquired by** means of **money, by** means of **a deed, or by taking possession** of it. **A cloak,** as well as other garments and movable property, **is called property, as we learned** in that same mishna: **And** property **that does not serve as a guarantee,** i.e., movable property, **can be acquired only by pulling.**

זוּזֵי אִיקְּרֵי נִכְסֵי, דִּתְנַן: וְשֶׁאֵין לָהֶן אַחְרָיוּת נִקְנִין עִם נְכָסִים שֶׁיֵּשׁ לָהֶן אַחְרָיוּת, בְּכֶסֶף וּבִשְׁטָר וּבַחֲזָקָה. כִּי הָא דְּרַב פַּפָּא הֲווֹ לֵיהּ תְּרֵיסַר אַלְפֵי זוּזֵי בֵּי חוֹזַאי, אַקְנִינְהוּ נִיהֲלֵיהּ לְרַב שְׁמוּאֵל בַּר אַחָא אַגַּב אַסִּיפָּא דְּבֵיתֵיהּ, כִּי אֲתָא, נְפַק לְאַפֵּיהּ עַד תָּוָךְ.

Money [*zuzei*][L] **is called property, as we learned** in that same mishna: **And** property **that does not serve as a guarantee can be acquired** together **with property that serves as a guarantee by** means of **money, by** means of **a deed, or by taking possession** of it. Money is among the types of property that can be acquired by means of the acquisition of land, as is evident from **this** incident **involving Rav Pappa,**[N] who **had twelve thousand dinars** loaned to the people of **Bei Ḥozai.** Rav Pappa **transferred** ownership of the money **to Rav Shmuel bar Aḥa,** who was traveling to Bei Ḥozai, **by means of** transferring ownership of **the threshold of his house,** so that Rav Shmuel bar Aḥa could collect the money. **When** Rav Shmuel bar Aḥa **came** back with the money, Rav Pappa was so pleased that he **went out as far as Tavakh to meet him.**

שְׁטָרָא אִיקְּרֵי נִכְסֵי, דְּאָמַר רַבָּה בַּר יִצְחָק: שְׁנֵי שְׁטָרוֹת הֵן, אָמַר "זְכוּ בְּשָׂדֶה זֶה לִפְלוֹנִי וְכִתְבוּ לוֹ אֶת הַשְּׁטָר" – חוֹזֵר בַּשְּׁטָר וְאֵינוֹ חוֹזֵר בַּשָּׂדֶה, "עַל מְנָת שֶׁתִּכְתְּבוּ לוֹ אֶת הַשְּׁטָר" – חוֹזֵר בֵּין בַּשְּׁטָר בֵּין בַּשָּׂדֶה;

A deed is called property, as Rabba bar Yitzḥak says: There are two types of **deeds** with regard to the acquisition of land. If one **said** to the witnesses: **Acquire this field on behalf of so-and-so and write the deed for him**[N] as proof of the sale, the giver **can retract the deed but he cannot retract the** transfer of ownership of the **field** once the other party has taken possession of it. If one said: Acquire this field on behalf of so-and-so **on the condition that you write the deed for him,** the giver **can retract both the deed and** the transfer of **the field,** as he stipulated that the acquisition of the field is dependent on the writing of the deed.

וְרַב חִיָּיא בַּר אָבִין אָמַר רַב הוּנָא: שְׁלֹשָׁה שְׁטָרוֹת הֵן, תְּרֵי – הָנֵי דַּאֲמַרַן, אִידָךְ – אִם קָדַם מוֹכֵר וְכָתַב אֶת הַשְּׁטָר, כְּאוֹתָהּ שֶׁשָּׁנִינוּ:

And Rav Ḥiyya bar Avin says that **Rav Huna says: There are three** types of **deeds. Two** are **those that we stated** above, and **the other** is as follows: **If the seller wrote the deed in advance** and kept it until the buyer would come and pay him. The Gemara adds parenthetically: This is **like that** *halakha* **that we learned** in a mishna (167b):

NOTES

My property shall go to so-and-so – נְכָסַי לִפְלָנְיָא: Rabbeinu Gershom Meor HaGola explains that the discussion here pertains to the gift of a person on his deathbed (see Rashba). The Rashbam writes that it also pertains to the gift of a healthy person that is acquired by means of an act of acquisition. The Rashbam notes further that these *halakhot* apply not only with regard to the specific term property [*nekhes*], but also to any similar term denoting property, whether in Hebrew or in other languages.

As this incident involving Rav Pappa – כִּי הָא דְּרַב פַּפָּא: This incident illustrates the fact that although money cannot be acquired by symbolic exchange, and it differs in this regard from movable property, it can be acquired by means of the acquisition of land (Rashbam).

Acquire this field on behalf of so-and-so and write the deed for him, etc. – זְכוּ בְּשָׂדֶה זֶה לִפְלוֹנִי וְכִתְבוּ לוֹ אֶת הַשְּׁטָר וכו׳: This statement separates the acquisition of the field from the writing of the deed. Consequently, if the deed has not yet been received the seller can retract his decision to provide the buyer with a deed. Once an act of acquisition has been performed, the buyer acquires the field, and the seller cannot cancel the sale.

HALAKHA

My property shall go to so-and-so – נְכָסַי לִפְלָנְיָא: If a person on his deathbed says: My property shall go to so-and-so, the recipient receives all of his movable property, land, garments, money, and deeds (see *Leḥem Mishne*). The principle is that the term property includes anything that one would sell when in need of money in ordinary circumstances (Rambam *Sefer Kinyan, Hilkhot Zekhiya UMattana* 11:15; *Shulḥan Arukh, Ḥoshen Mishpat* 248:11, and see *Sma* there, and see 66:4, 248:13).

LANGUAGE

Money [*zuzei*] – זוּזֵי: A *zuz* is one dinar. The source of this term is unclear, although the midrash explains homiletically that it is connected to the meaning of the word *zuz*, which means move. It teaches: Why are they called *zuzim*? Since they move, i.e., they are transferred, from one person to another (*Bemidbar Rabba*).

כּוֹתְבִין שְׁטָר לַמּוֹכֵר וְאַף עַל פִּי שֶׁאֵין לוֹקֵחַ עִמּוֹ; כֵּיוָן שֶׁהֶחֱזִיק זֶה בַּקַּרְקַע – נִקְנָה שְׁטָר כׇּל מָקוֹם שֶׁהוּא; וְזוֹ הִיא שֶׁשָּׁנִינוּ: נְכָסִים שֶׁאֵין לָהֶן אַחְרָיוּת נִקְנִין עִם הַנְּכָסִים שֶׁיֵּשׁ לָהֶן אַחְרָיוּת בְּכֶסֶף וּבִשְׁטָר וּבַחֲזָקָה.

A scribe may **write a deed** of sale **for the seller** of property at the seller's request, **even if the buyer is not with him** when he presents his request, as the deed obligates only the seller. In this case, **once this one,** the buyer, **has taken possession of the land, the deed is acquired,**[N] **wherever it is. And this is** as it is stated in the mishna **that we learned** (*Kiddushin* 26a): **Property that does not serve as a guarantee can be acquired** together **with the property that serves as a guarantee by** means of **money, by** means of **a deed, or by taking possession** of it. One can learn from this that a deed is included in the term: Property that does not serve as a guarantee.

NOTES

The deed is acquired – נִקְנָה שְׁטָר: Since the deed is already written for the buyer, even if the seller does not deliver it to him, the buyer acquires it together with the property.

בְּהֵמָה אִיקְּרֵי נִכְסֵי, דִּתְנַן: הַמַּקְדִּישׁ נְכָסָיו וְהָיְתָה בָּהֶן בְּהֵמָה רְאוּיָה לְגַבֵּי מִזְבֵּחַ – זְכָרִים עוֹלוֹת, וּנְקֵבוֹת יִמָּכְרוּ לְצָרְכֵי זִבְחֵי שְׁלָמִים. עוֹפוֹת אִיקְּרֵי נִכְסֵי, דִּתְנַן: הַמַּקְדִּישׁ נְכָסָיו וְהָיוּ בָּהֶן דְּבָרִים הָרְאוּיִין לְגַבֵּי מִזְבֵּחַ: יֵינוֹת, שְׁמָנִים וְעוֹפוֹת.

An animal is called property, as we learned in a mishna (*Shekalim* 12a): In a case of **one who consecrated his property, and on the** property **there were animals**[H] fit to be sacrificed **upon the altar, male** animals are sacrificed as **burnt-offerings, and female** animals **are sold for the purpose of** being sacrificed as **peace-offerings. Birds are called property, as we learned** in a mishna (*Shekalim* 12a): In a case of **one who consecrated his property, and on the** property **there were items that were fit to** be sacrificed **upon** the **altar, e.g., wines, oils, and birds,**[H] Rabbi Eliezer says: They are sold for the needs of that kind of item, i.e., to individuals who will use them as such.

תְּפִלִּין אִיקְּרֵי נִכְסֵי, דִּתְנַן: הַמַּקְדִּישׁ נְכָסָיו – מַעֲלִין לוֹ תְּפִלִּין. אִיבַּעְיָא לְהוּ: סֵפֶר תּוֹרָה מַאי? כֵּיוָן דְּלָא מִזְדַּבַּן, דְּאָסוּר לְזַבּוּנֵיהּ – לָאו נִכְסֵי הוּא, אוֹ דִּלְמָא כֵּיוָן דְּמִזְדַּבַּן לִלְמוֹד תּוֹרָה וְלִישָּׂא אִשָּׁה – נִכְסֵי הוּא? תֵּיקוּ.

Phylacteries are called property,[H] **as we learned** in a mishna (*Arakhin* 23b): With regard to **one who consecrates his property,** the value of his **phylacteries is assessed for him**[H] and he redeems them by paying their value to the Temple treasury. **A dilemma was raised before** the Sages: With regard to **a Torah scroll,**[H] **what is** the *halakha*? Is it considered property or not? Does one say that **since it is not sold, as it is prohibited to sell** a Torah scroll,[H] **it is** therefore **not** considered **property? Or perhaps** one says that **since it may be sold** in order to enable one **to study Torah or to marry a woman, it is** considered **property.** The Gemara concludes: The dilemma **shall stand** unresolved.

(סִימָן: זוּטְרָא אִימֵּיהּ דְּעַמְרָם מִתַּרְתֵּי אַחְוָותָא רַב טוֹבִי וְרַב דִּימִי וְרַב יוֹסֵף)

§ The Gemara presents **a mnemonic**[B] for the series of incidents stated below: **Zutra, the mother, of Amram, from two sisters, Rav Tovi, and Rav Dimi and Rav Yosef.**

אִימֵּיהּ דְּרַב זוּטְרָא בַּר טוֹבִיָּא כְּתַבִינְהוּ לְנִכְסָהּ לְרַב זוּטְרָא בַּר טוֹבִיָּא, דְּבָעְיָא לְאִנְסוּבֵי לֵיהּ לְרַב זְבִיד. אִינְּסִיבָא וְגֵירְשָׁהּ, אָתְיָא לְקַמֵּיהּ דְּרַב בֵּיבָי בַּר אַבַּיֵי, אֲמַר: מִשּׁוּם אִנְסוּבֵי, וְהָא אִינְּסִיבָא.

The mother of Rav Zutra bar Toviyya wrote a deed granting **her property to Rav Zutra bar Toviyya,** explaining that she was doing so **because she wanted to get married to Rav Zevid,**[P] and she did not want him to acquire her property. **She married** Rav Zevid, **and he divorced her. She came before Rav Beivai bar Abaye**[P] to claim her property from her son. Rav Beivai **said:** She transferred her property **because** she wanted **to get married, and she married.** Since her intentions were fulfilled, even though she subsequently was divorced, the gift is a valid gift.

BACKGROUND

Mnemonic – סִימָן: The Talmud was studied orally for many generations, and therefore mnemonic devices were employed in order to help students remember a series of *halakhot* and the order in which they were taught.

PERSONALITIES

Rav Zevid – רַב זְבִיד: Rav Zevid was a fifth-generation Babylonian *amora*. He was a preeminent disciple of Abaye and Rava, and he cites numerous statements of theirs. It appears that he devoted considerable time to explaining the *baraitot* taught in Rabbi Oshaya's study hall. After Rava's death his yeshiva was divided, and Rav Zevid succeeded Rav Ḥama as head of the Pumbedita branch, a position which he held for about ten years. It is recorded that he was poisoned by servants of the Exilarch because they were upset by his stringent halakhic rulings (*Avoda Zara* 38b).

Rav Beivai bar Abaye – רַב בֵּיבָי בַּר אַבַּיֵי: Rav Beivai was a fifth-generation Babylonian *amora*. Presumably, he was the son of Abaye, Rava's friend and colleague. There is no available information with regard to the identity of his teachers, although he probably studied with his father and the other Sages of the previous generation. He engaged in halakhic discussions primarily with Rav Pappa and Rav Huna, son of Rav Yehoshua. Apparently, he lived in Pumbedita and worked with his father as a farmer. His statements appear throughout the Talmud, although he never headed his own yeshiva. Rav Beivai engaged in the study of esoterica, and many of his statements in that field of study are found in the Talmud.

HALAKHA

One who consecrated his property and on it there were animals – הַמַּקְדִּישׁ נְכָסָיו וְהָיְתָה בָּהֶן בְּהֵמָה: If one consecrates all of his property without specifying whether it is consecrated for the altar or for Temple maintenance, and included in his property are unblemished animals fit for sacrificing on the altar, the male animals are sold to those who need to sacrifice burnt-offerings and the buyers then sacrifice them as burnt-offerings. The female animals are sold to those who need to sacrifice peace-offerings, and the buyers then sacrifice them as peace-offerings. The money received for them is allocated for Temple maintenance (Rambam *Sefer Hafla'a*, *Hilkhot Arakhin VaḤaramim* 5:7).

One who consecrated…wines, oils, and birds, etc. – הַמַּקְדִּישׁ...יֵינוֹת שְׁמָנִים וְעוֹפוֹת: If one consecrates all of his property without specifying whether it is consecrated for the altar or for Temple maintenance, and included in his property are wines, oils, fine flour, and birds, those items that are fit to be sacrificed on the altar should be sold to people who are required to bring offerings of that kind, and the buyers then sacrifice them accordingly. The proceeds of the sale are used to purchase male animals, which are sacrificed as burnt-offerings (Rambam *Sefer Hafla'a*, *Hilkhot Arakhin VaḤaramim* 5:8).

An animal is called property…phylacteries are called property, etc. – בְּהֵמָה אִיקְּרֵי נִכְסֵי...תְּפִלִּין אִיקְּרֵי נִכְסֵי וכו׳: If a person on his deathbed said: My property shall go to so-and-so, his domesticated and undomesticated animals (*Tur*), his birds, and even his phylacteries are all included in the term property. The principle is that the term property includes anything that is typically sold and that is permitted for one to sell when one requires money (Rambam *Sefer Kinyan*, *Hilkhot Zekhiya UMattana* 11:15; *Shulḥan Arukh*, *Ḥoshen Mishpat* 248:11, and see *Sma* there).

One who consecrates his property, the value of his phylacteries is assessed for him – הַמַּקְדִּישׁ נְכָסָיו מַעֲלִין לוֹ תְּפִלִּין: If one consecrates or dedicates to the Temple all of his property, everything he owns is collected by the Temple treasury, even his phylacteries. The value of his phylacteries is assessed and he then redeems them (Rambam *Sefer Hafla'a*, *Hilkhot Arakhin VaḤaramim* 6:3, and see Radbaz there).

Torah scroll – סֵפֶר תּוֹרָה: If a person on his deathbed says: My property shall go to so-and-so, and among his possessions is a Torah scroll, it is uncertain whether or not the Torah scroll is included in the term property. Therefore, the recipient does not receive it. But if he seizes possession of it, it is not appropriated from him, in accordance with the *halakha* with regard to all unresolved dilemmas in the Talmud. Other sacred books are included in the term property (Rambam *Sefer Kinyan*, *Hilkhot Zekhiya UMattana* 11:15; *Shulḥan Arukh*, *Ḥoshen Mishpat* 248:11, 12).

A Torah scroll…as it is prohibited to sell it – סֵפֶר תּוֹרָה...דְּאָסוּר לְזַבּוּנֵיהּ: One may not sell a Torah scroll that is designated for public reading (*Shakh*), even if he has numerous Torah scrolls. It is prohibited to sell it even if he barely has enough to eat (Rema). One may not sell an old Torah scroll even in order to purchase a new one (see *Shakh*). It is permitted to sell a Torah scroll only in order to finance Torah study, to marry a woman, to redeem captives, to provide for Torah students, or to marry off orphans (Rambam *Sefer Ahava*, *Hilkhot Sefer Torah* 10:2; *Shulḥan Arukh*, *Oraḥ Ḥayyim* 153:6 and *Yoreh De'a* 270:1).

PERSONALITIES

Rami bar Ḥama – רמי בר חמא: The name Rami is an abbreviated form of Rav Ami. Rami bar Hama was an important Babylonian *amora* of the fourth generation. In his youth he was already considered the outstanding disciple of Rav Ḥisda, and he and his brother, Rav Ukva bar Ḥama, married the daughters of Rav Ḥisda. Rami bar Ḥama also studied in the academies of Rav Naḥman and Rav Sheshet, even engaging them in halakhic debate. He was known for his sharp intellect and his masterful memory of the oral tradition. He sought to resolve any dilemma posed to him by employing logical reasoning rather than by citing *mishnayot* and *baraitot*, in contrast to the approach of his teacher, Rav Sheshet. Rami bar Ḥama maintained a close relationship with his younger friend and colleague Rava, and after his death Rava married his widow.

אמר ליה רב הונא בריה דרב יהושע: משום דאתו ממולאי אמריתו מילי מולייתא? אפילו למאן דאמר מברחת קני, הני מילי היכא דלא גליא דעתה, אבל הכא – גליא דעתה דמשום אינסובי הוא, והא אינסיבא ואיגרשה.

Rav Huna, son of Rav Yehoshua, said to Rav Beivai: Is it **because you come from** a line of **truncated** [***mula'ei***] **people,**[N] from the house of the High Priest Eli, whose descendants were condemned to premature death (see I Samuel 2:31), that **you say truncated** [***mulyata***] and unsound **matters? Even according to the one who says** that the deed of **a woman who shelters** her property from her intended husband **effects acquisition,**[N] and the woman cannot reclaim the property, **this matter** applies **where she did not reveal her intentions** in transferring ownership of her property. **But here, she revealed her intentions that** she transferred the property **because** she wanted **to marry; and she married, but was divorced.** Therefore, since she is no longer married, she can reclaim the property.

אימיה דרמי בר חמא באורתא כתבתינהו לנכסה לרמי בר חמא, בצפרא כתבתינהו לרב עוקבא בר חמא. אתא רמי בר חמא לקמיה דרב ששת, אוקמיה בנכסי; אזל רב עוקבא בר חמא קמיה דרב נחמן, אוקמיה בנכסי.

The mother of Rami bar Ḥama wrote a deed **in the evening** granting **her property to Rami bar Ḥama.**[P] **In the morning** of the following day, **she wrote** a deed granting her property **to** his brother, **Rav Ukva bar Ḥama. Rami bar Ḥama came before Rav Sheshet,** who **established him** as the owner **of the property,** as the deed transferring the property to him preceded the gift to his brother. **Rav Ukva bar Ḥama came before Rav Naḥman,** who **established him** as the owner **of the property.**

אתא רב ששת לקמיה דרב נחמן, אמר ליה: מאי טעמא אוקמיה מר לרב עוקבא בר חמא? אי משום דהדרא בה – והא שכיבא! אמר ליה, הכי אמר שמואל: כל שאילו עמד חוזר, חוזר במתנתו.

Rav Sheshet came before Rav Naḥman and **said to him: What is the reason** that the **Master established Rav Ukva bar Ḥama** as the owner of the property? **If** it is **because she retracted** her gift, **but didn't she die?** Since the gift of a person on his deathbed is considered valid, Rami bar Ḥama already acquired the property in the evening. Rav Naḥman **said to** Rav Sheshet: **This** is what **Shmuel says:** With regard to the gift of a person on his deathbed, in **any** case **where he could retract** his gift **if he were to recover,**[H] i.e., if he transferred ownership of all of his property, even if he does not recover, **he can retract his gift.**

NOTES

You come from truncated [*mula'ei*] people – אתו ממולאי: Various explanations have been offered for this expression, which appears in several places with regard to Rav Beivai bar Abaye. Rabbeinu Gershom Meor HaGola says that the term *mula'ei* means truncated, as Eli's descendants were condemned to die prematurely. Elsewhere, Rashi explains that *mula'ei* is related to *umlalim*, miserable ones. Alternatively, he suggests that *mula'ei* is related to *ba'alei mumim*, blemished ones or hunchbacks. The Rashbam and *Tosafot* assert that the descendants of Eli were called *mula'ei* because they came from a place called Mamla. The *ge'onim* understand that the expression is derived from the root *mem*, *lamed*, *alef*, which means full, and refers to a person of distinction. According to this interpretation, Rav Huna retorted that because he comes from a distinguished family, Rav Beivai permits himself to speak haughtily, without examining his words carefully (*Arukh*).

According to the one who says that the deed of a woman who shelters her property effects acquisition – למאן דאמר מברחת קני: This is subject to a tannaitic dispute (see Rashbam and *Ketubot* 79a). *Tosafot* explain that the dispute concerns a case where a woman transferred ownership of only a portion of her property, in which case it is possible that she intended to irrevocably give it away and did not expect it to be returned in the future. If she transferred ownership of all of her property, all agree that the recipient does not acquire ownership. The early commentaries note that according to the Gemara's conclusion, even if the woman did not explicitly state her reasons for transferring ownership of the property, she can retract the gift if her husband dies or divorces her. If she stated that the gift shall always belong to the recipient, she cannot retract the gift (Ri Migash; Ramah).

HALAKHA

In any case where he could retract his gift if he were to recover, etc. – כל שאילו עמד חוזר וכו׳: A person on his deathbed who gives his property to another can retract his gift, either partially or completely, whether in order to retain it for himself or to give the gift to another. The Rema adds that with regard to a gift of part of one's property, this *halakha* applies only if he specifies that the gift is the gift of a person on his deathbed. If the gift is acquired by means of an act of acquisition, he cannot retract the gift, neither part of the gift nor all of the gift, neither in order to retain it for himself nor to transfer it to another (Rambam *Sefer Kinyan*, *Hilkhot Zekhiya UMattana* 9:15; *Shulḥan Arukh*, *Ḥoshen Mishpat* 250:13, and see *Sma* there).

אֵימוּר דַּאֲמַר שְׁמוּאֵל – לְעַצְמוֹ, לְאַחֵר מִי אֲמַר? אֲמַר לֵיהּ, בְּפֵירוּשׁ אֲמַר שְׁמוּאֵל: בֵּין לְעַצְמוֹ בֵּין לְאַחֵר.

Rav Sheshet responded: **Say that Shmuel said** that he can retract his gift if he wants to retain the property **for himself,** but if he wants to retract his gift in order to give it **to another, did he** also **say** that he can do so? Rav Naḥman **said to** Rav Sheshet: **Shmuel explicitly said** that he can retract his gift **both** in order to retain the property **for himself and** to grant it **to another.**

אִימֵּיהּ דְּרַב עַמְרָם חֲסִידָא הֲוָה לָהּ מְלוֹגָא דִּשְׁטָרָאֵי, כִּי קָא שָׁכְבָא אֲמַרָה: לֶיהֱוֵי לְעַמְרָם בְּרִי; אָתֵי אֲחוּהּ לְקַמֵּיהּ דְּרַב נַחְמָן, אֲמַרוּ לֵיהּ: וְהָא לָא מְשַׁךְ! אֲמַר לְהוּ: דִּבְרֵי שְׁכִיב מְרַע כִּכְתוּבִין וְכִמְסוּרִין דָּמוּ.

The mother of Rav Amram the Pious[P] **had a bundle** [*meloga*][L] of promissory **notes. When she was dying, she said: Let** these promissory notes **be for Amram, my son. His brothers came before Rav Naḥman. They said to** Rav Naḥman: **But** Rav Amram **did not pull**[N] the bundle of documents, and since an act of acquisition was not performed he did not acquire them. Rav Naḥman **said to them:** An act of acquisition was not required, because **the statement of a person on his deathbed is considered as written and as** though the documents were **delivered**[H] to the recipient.

אַחְתֵּיהּ דְּרַב טוֹבִי בַּר רַב מַתָּנָה כְּתַבְתִּינְהוּ לְנִכְסָהּ לְרַב טוֹבִי בַּר רַב מַתָּנָה בְּצַפְרָא, לְפַנְיָא אֲתָא רַב אַחַדְבוֹי בַּר רַב מַתָּנָה בָּכָה לָהּ, אֲמַר לָהּ, הָשְׁתָּא אָמְרִי: מָר צוּרְבָא מֵרַבָּנַן וּמָר לָאו צוּרְבָא מֵרַבָּנַן! כְּתַבְתִּינְהוּ נִיהֲלֵיהּ; אֲתָא לְקַמֵּיהּ דְּרַב נַחְמָן, אֲמַר לֵיהּ, הָכִי אָמַר שְׁמוּאֵל: כׇּל שֶׁאִילּוּ עָמַד חוֹזֵר, חוֹזֵר בְּמַתְּנָתוֹ.

The sister of Rav Tovi bar Rav Mattana[P] **wrote** a deed **in the morning** granting **her property to Rav Tovi bar Rav Mattana. In the evening** another brother, **Rav Aḥadvoi bar Rav Mattana, came** and **cried to her.** Rav Aḥadvoi **said to her: Now** people **will say** that you gave your property to Rav Tovi because this **Master,** Rav Tovi, is **a Torah scholar, and** that **Master,** Rav Aḥadvoi, **is not a Torah scholar. She wrote** a deed granting the property **to him.** Rav Tovi **came before Rav Naḥman.** Rav Naḥman **said to** Rav Tovi: **This** is what **Shmuel says:** With regard to the gift of a person on his deathbed, in **any** case **where he could retract** his gift **if he were to recover,** even if he does not recover, **he can retract his gift,** and therefore the property belongs to Rav Aḥadvoi.

אַחְתֵּיהּ דְּרַב דִּימִי בַּר יוֹסֵף הֲוָה לָהּ פִּיסְקְתָא דְּפַרְדֵּיסָא, כׇּל אֵימַת דַּהֲוָת חָלְשָׁא הֲוָה מַקְנְיָא לֵיהּ נִיהֲלֵיהּ,

The sister of Rav Dimi bar Yosef had a tract of land in **an orchard. Whenever she was sick** and thought that she was dying, **she would transfer** ownership of the orchard **to** Rav Dimi,

LANGUAGE

Bundle [*meloga*] – מְלוֹגָא: Apparently from the Greek μολγός, *molgos*, which in a certain dialect refers to a leather bag used to hold various items. The etymology of this word is unclear.

PERSONALITIES

Rav Amram the Pious – רַב עַמְרָם חֲסִידָא: Rav Amram the Pious was a Babylonian *amora* of the third generation. It is unclear whether he should be identified as Rav Amram, who appears in the Talmud as Rav Amram without the appellation the Pious. He apparently served as a judge in his town and as the halakhic authority for the house of the Exilarch. He was meticulous in the mitzva of attaching sky blue wool to his ritual fringes. He may have sold sky blue wool to the public, which is a trade that requires a high level of credibility.

Rav Tovi bar Rav Mattana – רַב טוֹבִי בַּר רַב מַתָּנָה: Rav Tovi bar Rav Mattana was a Babylonian *amora* of the fourth generation. The incident recounted here apparently occurred in his youth. He is later mentioned as an important Sage, whose statements are cited by Rav Yosef and with whom Rav Yosef engages in halakhic discourse. He was apparently a judge in his town. Of his brother, Rav Aḥadvoi, nothing is known beyond the incident recounted here, apart from a single halakhic statement. This would explain why he wept before his sister: Compared to his more important brother, people would not regard him as a Torah scholar.

NOTES

But Rav Amram did not pull – וְהָא לָא מְשַׁךְ: The Ritva notes that this term is inaccurate, as the sale of promissory notes is effected by the formal act of lifting or passing and not by the formal act of pulling. In any event, the brothers' claim is clear: Rav Amram did not perform an act of acquisition, and therefore the gift is invalid.

The Rashba writes that according to the *halakha*, the content of a promissory note is not acquired by merely transferring the document (see 77a). Therefore, even a person on his deathbed must state that he transfers the promissory note together with all liens pertaining to it. This is because the rabbinic ordinance eliminates only the necessity to perform an act of acquisition, but not the requirement to state what is included in the gift. The Rambam disagrees with the Rashba on this matter.

HALAKHA

A bundle of promissory notes…the statement of a person on his deathbed is considered as written and as delivered – מְלוֹגָא דִּשְׁטָרָאֵי...דִּבְרֵי שְׁכִיב מְרַע כִּכְתוּבִין וְכִמְסוּרִין דָּמוּ: If a person on his deathbed says: Let this promissory note concerning the debt owed to me by so-and-so be given to another, the recipient acquires the right to collect the debt stated in the promissory note. The recipient acquires the debt even though the giver did not state that he transfers the promissory note together with all liens pertaining to it (*Shakh*), and the recipient acquires it even if he did not perform an act of acquisition. This is because the statement of a person on his deathbed is considered as written and as though the document were delivered to the recipient (Rambam *Sefer Kinyan, Hilkhot Zekhiya UMattana* 10:2; *Shulḥan Arukh, Ḥoshen Mishpat* 253:20, and see 66:42).

וְכִי קָיְימָא הֲוַת הָדְרָא בָּהּ. זִימְנָא חֲדָא חֲלַשָׁא, שְׁלַחָה לֵיהּ: תָּא קְנֵי, שְׁלַח: לָא בָּעֵינָא. שְׁלַחָה לֵיהּ: תָּא קְנֵי כָּל הֵיכָא דְּבָעֵית. אֲזַל שַׁיְּירַהּ וְקָנוּ מִינַּהּ. כִּי קָיְימָא הֲדָרָא בָּהּ,

and when she recovered she would retract her gift. **On one occasion she was sick. She sent** a message to Rav Dimi: **Come** and **acquire** my property. **He sent** a message back to her: **I do not want** to come. **She sent** a message **to him: Come and acquire** my property in **any manner that you want. He went and reserved** for her part of the orchard, **and** he **acquired** the rest of the property **from her**[N] with an act of acquisition. **When she recovered she retracted** the gift.

אֲתַאי לְקַמֵּיהּ דְּרַב נַחְמָן. שָׁלַח לֵיהּ: תָּא. לָא אֲתָא, אֲמַר: מַאי אֵיתֵי? הָא שַׁיְּירַהּ וְקָנוּ מִינַּהּ. שְׁלַח לֵיהּ: אִי לָא אָתֵית, מָחֵינָא לָךְ בְּסִילְוָא דְּלָא מַבַּע דָּמָא.

She came before Rav Naḥman to reclaim it. Rav Naḥman **sent** a message **to** Rav Dimi: **Come** to court. Rav Dimi **did not come. He said: What** reason is there for **me to come? Didn't I reserve** part of the property for her, **and** I **acquired** the rest of the property **from her** with an act of acquisition? Therefore, the acquisition is complete. Rav Naḥman **sent** a message **to** Rav Dimi: **If you do not come, I will strike you with a thorn** [*besileva*][L] **that does not draw blood,** i.e., I will excommunicate you.

אֲמַר לְהוּ לְסָהֲדֵי: הֵיכִי הֲוָה מַעֲשֶׂה? אֲמַרוּ לֵיהּ, אֲמַרָה הָכִי: וַוי דְּקָא מִיתָה הַךְ אִיתְּתָא! אֲמַר לְהוּ: אִם כֵּן הֲוָה מְצַוֶּה מֵחֲמַת מִיתָה, וּמְצַוֶּה מֵחֲמַת מִיתָה – חוֹזֵר.

Inquiring into the matter, Rav Naḥman **said to the witnesses: How did the act** of transferring the property take place? The witnesses **said to** Rav Naḥman: **This** is what **she said: Woe, that woman is dying!**[N] Rav Naḥman **said to them: If so, this is** a case of **one who issues directives** with regard to his property **due to** his expectation of his imminent **death.**[HN] **And one who issues directives due to** his expectation of his imminent **death can retract** his gift even if he did not transfer all of his property, as he evidently granted the gift only because he expected to die.

אִיתְּמַר: מַתְּנַת שְׁכִיב מְרַע בְּמִקְצָת – אֲמַרוּהָ רַבָּנַן קַמֵּיהּ דְּרָבָא מִשְּׁמֵיהּ דְּמָר זוּטְרָא בְּרֵיהּ דְּרַב נַחְמָן דַּאֲמַר מִשְּׁמֵיהּ דְּרַב נַחְמָן: הֲרֵי הִיא כְּמַתְּנַת בָּרִיא, וַהֲרֵי הִיא כְּמַתְּנַת שְׁכִיב מְרַע; הֲרֵי הִיא כְּמַתְּנַת בָּרִיא – שֶׁאִם עָמַד אֵינוֹ חוֹזֵר, וַהֲרֵי הִיא כְּמַתְּנַת שְׁכִיב מְרַע – דְּלָא בָּעֲיָא קִנְיָן.

§ **It was stated** that the *amora'im* disagreed with regard to **a gift of a person on his deathbed** that includes only **a part** of his property.[H] **The Sages said** the following **before Rava in the name of Mar Zutra, son of Rav Naḥman, who said it in the name of Rav Naḥman: This** type of gift **is** in some respects **like the gift of a healthy person,** and in other respects **it is like the gift of a person on his deathbed. It is like the gift of a healthy person,** as, **if he recovers he cannot retract** it, as stated in the mishna. **And it is like** the **gift of a person on his deathbed, as it does not require** an act of **acquisition.**[N] Rather, it is acquired by means of verbal instruction alone.

אֲמַר לְהוּ רָבָא: לָאו אָמִינָא לְכוּ, לָא תִּיתְלוּ בּוּקֵי סְרִיקֵי בְּרַב נַחְמָן? הָכִי אָמַר רַב נַחְמָן: הֲרֵי הִיא כְּמַתְּנַת בָּרִיא וּבָעֲיָא קִנְיָן.

Rava said to the Sages: **Did I not say to you: Do not hang empty pitchers** [*bukei*][L] **upon Rav Naḥman,** i.e., do not attribute incorrect statements to him? **This is what Rav Naḥman says:** A gift of a person on his deathbed that includes only a part of his property **is like the gift of a healthy person and requires** an act of **acquisition.** If an act of acquisition is not performed, the acquisition of the gift is not effective even if the owner dies.

LANGUAGE

Thorn [*sileva*] – סִילְוָא: Similar to the term *sol* in mishnaic Hebrew, this word may be related to the biblical term *salon*, which also means a thorn (see Ezekiel 2:6, 28:24). A similar Arabic term, سلاء, *sullā'*, means the thorn of a palm tree. These are the small leaves on the palm branches that become hard and thorny over time and that cause great pain if one is pricked with one.

Pitchers [*bukei*] – בּוּקֵי: Probably derived from the Greek βῖκος, *bikos*, which is also a kind of container used for drinking. The phrase: Do not hang empty pitchers, may refer to the practice of hanging empty pitchers on trees in order to scare away birds.

HALAKHA

One who issues directives due to imminent death – מְצַוֶּה מֵחֲמַת מִיתָה: If a person on his deathbed bestows a gift and states that the bestowal of the gift is due to his expectation of his imminent death, even if he reserves part of his property for himself, the gift is acquired upon his death by means of the verbal instruction and an act of acquisition is not required. If he recovers, he can retract the gift even if he transferred part of his property and reserved part of it for himself. This *halakha* applies even if he does not explicitly state that he is bestowing the gift due to his expectation of his imminent death, but it appears from the manner of his speech that he is bestowing the gift due to his expectation of his imminent death, e.g., if he laments his impending demise. According to some authorities, this *halakha* applies even if he merely mentions the matter of death in his statement (Rambam *Sefer Kinyan*, *Hilkhot Zekhiya UMattana* 8:23; *Shulḥan Arukh*, *Ḥoshen Mishpat* 250:7).

A gift of a person on his deathbed that includes only a part of his property, etc. – מַתְּנַת שְׁכִיב מְרַע בְּמִקְצָת וכו׳: If a person on his deathbed gives part of his property to another, the legal status of his gift is equivalent to that of the gift of a healthy person, and it requires an act of acquisition. Therefore, even if he recovers, if an act of acquisition has been performed he cannot retract the gift. If an act of acquisition is not performed the gift is not valid, even if he subsequently dies (Rambam *Sefer Kinyan*, *Hilkhot Zekhiya UMattana* 8:15; *Shulḥan Arukh*, *Ḥoshen Mishpat* 250:4).

NOTES

He went and reserved part of it and acquired the rest from her – אֲזַל שַׁיְּירַהּ וְקָנוּ מִינַּהּ: This doubly reinforced the transaction, as the gift now had the status of a gift of a person on his deathbed of only a part of the giver's property, and an act of acquisition was performed.

Woe that woman is dying – וַוי דְּקָא מִיתָה הַךְ אִיתְּתָא: The Rashbam explains that she exclaimed: Woe is me that I am dying and will not see my brother again before my death. Rabbeinu Gershom Meor HaGola explains that she said this because she was so sick that she thought she was going to die, and therefore she wished to transfer her property to her brother.

One who issues directives due to imminent death – מְצַוֶּה מֵחֲמַת מִיתָה: The definition of a person on his deathbed includes any sick person who is bedridden and too weak to leave his home (see 154a). If such a person did not transfer all of his property, his gift is not considered the gift of a person on his deathbed. In addition, if one's words indicate that he believes he is dying, he is considered one who issues directives due to his expectation of his imminent death, and any gift that he bestows has the status of the gift of a person on his deathbed.

Rav Shmuel ben Ḥofni Gaon writes that whenever the sick person mentions his death his gift is considered the gift of one who issues directives due to his expectation of his imminent death. Some early commentaries write that according to the Jerusalem Talmud, during the first three days of sickness, the sick person is considered a person on his deathbed, whereas beyond that time, he is considered one who issues directives due to his expectation of his imminent death, even if he does not mention his death. One who suddenly becomes dangerously ill is also assumed to be instructing his household due to his expectation of his imminent death (see *Tur*, citing *Sefer Halttur* and Rosh). According to the Rif and the Rambam, if one who departs on a long journey by caravan or by sea first transfers his property, he also has the status of one who issues directives due to his expectation of his imminent death, as he transfers his property only out of fear that he will not return from the journey. Other early commentaries disagree (*Tosafot*; Rabbeinu Yona).

And it is like the gift of a person on his deathbed as it does not require acquisition – וַהֲרֵי הִיא כְּמַתְּנַת שְׁכִיב מְרַע דְּלָא בָּעֲיָא קִנְיָן: The reasoning behind this opinion is that the Sages instituted that the gift of a person on his deathbed is valid lest his anxiety that his wishes will not be carried out cause him grief and exacerbate his poor physical state (147b). Therefore, there is no reason to differentiate between a case where he transferred all of his property and a case where he transferred only part of his property (Ra'avad).

אֵיתִיבֵיהּ רָבָא לְרַב נַחְמָן: שִׁיֵּיר קַרְקַע כׇּל שֶׁהוּא – מַתְּנָתוֹ קַיֶּימֶת; מַאי לָאו דְּלָא קָנוּ מִינֵּיהּ? לָא, דְּקָנוּ מִינֵּיהּ. אִי הָכִי, אֵימָא סֵיפָא: לֹא שִׁיֵּיר קַרְקַע כׇּל שֶׁהוּא – אֵין מַתְּנָתוֹ קַיֶּימֶת; וְאִי דְּקָנוּ מִינֵּיהּ, אַמַּאי אֵין מַתְּנָתוֹ קַיֶּימֶת?

Rava raised an objection to Rav Naḥman from the mishna (146b): If **he reserved** for himself **any amount of land, his gift stands. What, is it not** referring even to a case **where** the gift **was not acquired from him** by means of an act of acquisition? **No,** it is referring to a case **where** the gift **was acquired from him** by means of an act of acquisition. Rava asks: **If that is so, say the last clause** of the mishna: If **he did not reserve** for himself **any amount of land,** and he recovered, **his gift does not stand. And if** the mishna is referring to a case **where** the gift **was acquired from him** by means of an act of acquisition, **why does his gift not stand?**

אֲמַר לֵיהּ, הָכִי אָמַר שְׁמוּאֵל: שְׁכִיב מְרַע שֶׁכָּתַב כׇּל נְכָסָיו לַאֲחֵרִים, אַף עַל פִּי שֶׁקָּנוּ מִיָּדוֹ – עָמַד חוֹזֵר, בְּיָדוּעַ שֶׁלֹּא הָיָה מְצַוֶּה אֶלָּא מֵחֲמַת מִיתָה.

Rav Naḥman **said to** Rava: **This is what Shmuel says:** With regard to **a person on his deathbed who wrote** a deed granting **all of his property to others** without reserving anything for himself, **even though** the gift **was acquired from his possession** by means of an act of acquisition,[H] if **he recovers, he can retract** his gift. The reason for this is that **it is known that he was issuing directives** with regard to his property **only due to** his expectation of his imminent **death.**

אֵיתִיבֵיהּ רַב מְשַׁרְשְׁיָא לְרָבָא: מַעֲשֶׂה בְּאִמָּן שֶׁל בְּנֵי רוֹכֵל שֶׁהָיְתָה חוֹלָה, וְאָמְרָה: תִּנָּתֵן כְּבֵינָתִי לְבִתִּי, וְהוּא בִּשְׁנֵים עָשָׂר מָנֶה, וּמֵתָה, וְקִיְּימוּ דְּבָרֶיהָ! הָתָם בִּמְצַוָּה מֵחֲמַת מִיתָה.

Rav Mesharshiyya raised an objection to Rava: There was an **incident involving the mother of the sons of Rokhel, who was sick, and she said: My brooch** [*keveinati*][L] **shall be given to my daughter, and it is** valued **at twelve hundred dinars. And** this woman subsequently **died, and** the Sages **upheld her statement** even though the gift included only a part of her property and an act of acquisition was not performed. Rava replied: That incident is different, as the case **there** is referring **to one who issues directives due to** his expectation of his imminent **death.**

אֵיתִיבֵיהּ רָבִינָא לְרָבָא: הָאוֹמֵר ״תְּנוּ גֵּט זֶה לְאִשְׁתִּי וּשְׁטַר שִׁחְרוּר זֶה לְעַבְדִּי״ וּמֵת – לֹא יִתְּנוּ לְאַחַר מִיתָה, ״תְּנוּ מָנֶה לִפְלוֹנִי״ וּמֵת – יִתְּנוּ לְאַחַר מִיתָה;

Ravina raised an objection to Rava from a mishna (*Gittin* 13a): In the case of **one who says: Give this bill of divorce to my wife,**[H] **or:** Give **this bill of manumission to my slave,**[H] **and** then he **dies, one should not give it after** his **death.** But if one says: **Give one hundred dinars to so-and-so, and** then he **died,**[H] **one does give** the recipient the money **after** his **death.** This indicates that a gift of a person on his deathbed that includes only a part of his property does not require an act of acquisition.

וּמִמַּאי דְּלָא קָנוּ מִינֵּיהּ? דּוּמְיָא דְּגֵט, מָה גֵּט לָאו בַּר קִנְיָן, אַף הַאי נָמֵי דְּלָא קָנוּ מִינֵּיהּ! הָתָם נָמֵי בִּמְצַוֶּה מֵחֲמַת מִיתָה.

And from where can one learn **that** the money **was not acquired from him** by means of an act of acquisition? This is learned from the fact that this *halakha* was juxtaposed to the *halakha* with regard to a bill of divorce, indicating that this case is **similar to a bill of divorce. Just as a bill of divorce is not subject to** the standard *halakhot* of an act of acquisition, **so too,** in **this** case of the gift of one hundred dinars, the mishna is referring to a case **where** the money **was not acquired from him** by means of an act of acquisition. Rava replied: **There, too,** the mishna is referring **to one who issues directives** with regard to his property **due to** his imminent **death.**

רַב הוּנָא בְּרֵיהּ דְּרַב יְהוֹשֻׁעַ אָמַר: מְצַוֶּה מֵחֲמַת מִיתָה בְּעָלְמָא בָּעֵיא קִנְיָן, וְכִי תַּנְיָא הָנֵי מַתְנְיָיתָא – בִּמְחַלֵּק כׇּל נְכָסָיו, דְּהַהִיא מַתְּנַת שְׁכִיב מְרַע שַׁוְיוּהָ.

Rav Huna, son of Rav Yehoshua, said: The gift of **one who issues directives** with regard to his property **due to** his expectation of his imminent **death generally requires** an act of **acquisition.**[N] **And when it is taught** in **these** *baraitot* that an act of acquisition is not required, the *baraitot* are referring **to one who divides all of his property** between different recipients, **as in that** case, the Sages **accorded** the gift the legal status of **a gift of a person on his deathbed.**

וְהִלְכְתָא: מַתְּנַת שְׁכִיב מְרַע בְּמִקְצָת בָּעֲיָא קִנְיָן, וְאַף עַל גַּב דְּמֵית; מְצַוֶּה מֵחֲמַת מִיתָה לָא בָּעֲיָא קִנְיָן, וְהוּא דְּמֵית; עָמַד חוֹזֵר, וְאַף עַל גַּב דְּקָנוּ מִינֵּיהּ.

The Gemara concludes: **And the *halakha*** is that **a gift of a person on his deathbed** that includes only **a part** of his property **requires** an act of **acquisition;** otherwise it is invalid **even though he** subsequently **died,** and the gift is inherited by his heirs instead. The gift of **one who issues directives** with regard to his property **due to** his expectation of his imminent **death does not require** an act of **acquisition. And this** applies only **when** he subsequently **died.** If he **recovered,** he can **retract** his gift **even though it was acquired from him** by means of an act of acquisition.

HALAKHA

Even though it was acquired from his possession by an act of acquisition, etc. – אַף עַל פִּי שֶׁקָּנוּ מִיָּדוֹ וכו׳: If a person on his deathbed writes a deed granting all of his property to others and reserves nothing for himself, if he subsequently recovers completely the gift is null and void, even if an act of acquisition was performed. If he granted all of his property to others and also forgave a debt, if he recovers, the debt is not forgiven (*Sma*). If he stipulates when bestowing the gift that he will not be able to retract it, he can still retract it if he recovers, unless it is acquired from him by means of an act of acquisition (Rambam *Sefer Kinyan, Hilkhot Zekhiya UMattana* 8:14, 9:16; *Shulḥan Arukh, Ḥoshen Mishpat* 250:2, and in the comment of Rema).

Give this bill of divorce to my wife – תְּנוּ גֵּט זֶה לְאִשְׁתִּי: If one sends a bill of divorce to his wife and it enters her possession after his death, she is not divorced, as a bill of divorce is not valid after the husband's death (*Shulḥan Arukh, Even HaEzer* 141:58).

Or give this bill of manumission to my slave – וּשְׁטַר שִׁחְרוּר זֶה לְעַבְדִּי: If one instructs another to give a bill of manumission to his slave, the slave is not emancipated until the bill comes into the slave's possession. Therefore, it should not be given to him after the death of his master. The Rema adds that some authorities say that if the master gives the bill of manumission to an agent and says: Give this bill to my slave, it is considered as though he had said: Acquire it on his behalf, and the slave is immediately emancipated (Rambam *Sefer Kinyan, Hilkhot Avadim* 6:1; *Shulḥan Arukh, Yoreh De'a* 267:76).

If one says, give one hundred dinars to so-and-so, and he died, etc. – תְּנוּ מָנֶה לִפְלוֹנִי וּמֵת וכו׳: If a person on his deathbed says: Give one hundred dinars to so-and-so, it is given in accordance with his instructions, whether he specifies or does not specify which one hundred dinars he is referring to. This applies in the case of one who issues directives with regard to his property due to his expectation of imminent death and in the case of one who transfers ownership of all of his property, dividing it between numerous people and stating that so-and-so should receive one hundred dinars.

If a person on his deathbed does not transfer all of his property, but only grants a certain individual one hundred dinars without specifying which dinars, his gift has the legal status of the gift of a person on his deathbed that includes only a part of the giver's property. Such a gift can be acquired only by an act of acquisition, and only if the giver indicates that his intention is to enhance the legal power of the recipient (see 152a). Since money cannot be acquired by means of symbolic exchange, he must transfer the money by means of the acquisition of land, or by entrusting the money to a third party before his death (Rambam *Sefer Kinyan, Hilkhot Zekhiya UMattana* 10:1; *Shulḥan Arukh, Ḥoshen Mishpat* 253:18).

LANGUAGE

Brooch [*keveina*] – כְּבֵינָה: The Rashbam explains that this is a decorated clasp used to secure the collar of a garment (see Rashi on *Gittin* 15a). Others explain that the term refers to a type of scarf or mantle. This explanation is based on the Aramaic translation of Song of Songs, which translates the term *redidi* (Song of Songs 5:7), my mantle, as *keveintaya*.

NOTES

One who issues directives due to his imminent death generally requires acquisition – מְצַוֶּה מֵחֲמַת מִיתָה בְּעָלְמָא בָּעֵיא קִנְיָן: Rav Huna, son of Rav Yehoshua, disagrees with the aforementioned *amora'im*.

אִיתְּמַר: מַתְּנַת שְׁכִיב מְרַע שֶׁכָּתוּב בָּהּ קִנְיָן – בֵּי רַב מִשְּׁמֵיהּ דְּרַב אָמְרִי: אַרְכְּבֵיהּ אַתְּרֵי רִיכְשֵׁי, וּשְׁמוּאֵל אֲמַר: לָא יָדַעְנָא מַאי אָדוּן בָּהּ.

§ **It was stated** that the *amora'im* disagreed with regard to a deed pertaining to the **gift of a person on his deathbed in which** it **is written** that an act of **acquisition** was also performed.[NH] In **the study hall of Rav they say in the name of Rav:** The person on his deathbed **caused** the recipient **to mount two steeds,** i.e., he strengthened the validity of his gift in two different ways. **And Shmuel said: I do not know what I should rule with regard to this** gift, as it may not be a valid gift.

בֵּי רַב מִשְּׁמֵיהּ דְּרַב אָמְרִי: אַרְכְּבֵיהּ אַתְּרֵי רִיכְשֵׁי, הֲרֵי הִיא כְּמַתְּנַת בָּרִיא, הֲרֵי הִיא כְּמַתְּנַת שְׁכִיב מְרַע; הֲרֵי הִיא כְּמַתְּנַת בָּרִיא – שֶׁאִם עָמַד אֵינוֹ חוֹזֵר, הֲרֵי הִיא כְּמַתְּנַת שְׁכִיב מְרַע – שֶׁאִם אָמַר הַלְוָאָתוֹ לִפְלוֹנִי – הַלְוָאָתוֹ לִפְלוֹנִי.

The Gemara explains: In **the study hall of Rav they say in the name of Rav** that **he caused him to mount two steeds.** On the one hand, **it is like** the **gift of a healthy person,** but on the other hand, **it is like** the **gift of a person on his deathbed. It is like** the **gift of a healthy person,** as, **if he recovers he cannot retract** the gift, because an act of acquisition was performed. **It is like** the **gift of a person on his deathbed,** as, **if he said** that the **loan** owed to **him** should be given **to so-and-so,**[N] the **loan** owed to **him** is acquired **by so-and-so,** whereas a healthy person cannot transfer his right to collect a debt except in the presence of all three parties.

וּשְׁמוּאֵל אֲמַר: לָא יָדַעְנָא מַאי אָדוּן בָּהּ, שֶׁמָּא לֹא גָּמַר לְהַקְנוֹתוֹ אֶלָּא בִּשְׁטָר, וְאֵין שְׁטָר לְאַחַר מִיתָה.

And Shmuel said: I do not know what I should rule with regard to this gift. **Perhaps** the fact that an act of acquisition was performed indicates that **he resolved to transfer it** to him **only with a deed.** The gift of a person on his deathbed takes effect only after he dies, **and a deed is not** effective if it is delivered **after** the **death** of the owner.

וְרָמֵי דְּרַב אַדְּרַב, וְדִשְׁמוּאֵל אַדִּשְׁמוּאֵל; דִּשְׁלַח רָבִין מִשְּׁמֵיהּ דְּרַבִּי אַבָּהוּ, הֱווּ יָדְעִי שֶׁשָּׁלַח רַבִּי אֶלְעָזָר לַגּוֹלָה מִשּׁוּם רַבֵּינוּ: שְׁכִיב מְרַע שֶׁאָמַר "כִּתְבוּ וּתְנוּ מָנֶה לִפְלוֹנִי" וּמֵת – אֵין כּוֹתְבִין וְנוֹתְנִין, שֶׁמָּא לֹא גָּמַר לְהַקְנוֹתוֹ אֶלָּא בִּשְׁטָר, וְאֵין שְׁטָר לְאַחַר מִיתָה. וְאָמַר רַב יְהוּדָה אָמַר שְׁמוּאֵל, הִלְכְתָא: כּוֹתְבִין וְנוֹתְנִין;

The Gemara **raises a contradiction between** this statement **of Rav and** another statement **of Rav, and between** this statement **of Shmuel and** another statement **of Shmuel.** This is **as Ravin sent in the name of Rabbi Abbahu: You should know that Rabbi Elazar sent** a ruling **to the Diaspora,** i.e., Babylonia, **in the name of our teacher,**[N] Rav: With regard to **a person on his deathbed who says: Write** a deed **and give** with it **one hundred dinars**[N] **to so-and-so,**[H] **and** he **died** before the deed was written, **it is not written and given** to that person. The reason for this is that **perhaps he resolved to transfer** the gift to him **only** with the **deed, and a deed is not** effective if it is delivered **after** the **death** of the owner. **And Rav Yehuda says** that **Shmuel says:** The *halakha* is that the deed **is written and given** to the recipient.

NOTES

The gift of a person on his deathbed in which it is written that acquisition was also performed – מַתְּנַת שְׁכִיב מְרַע שֶׁכָּתוּב בָּהּ קִנְיָן: This dispute pertains to the gift of a person on his deathbed who transfers all his property, as such a gift does not require an act of acquisition. In the case of a person on his deathbed who transfers only some of his property to another, all agree that an act of acquisition is required (Rashbam). Others add that the dispute also pertains to one who gives only some of his property to another in a case where he is issuing directives with regard to his property due to the expectation of imminent death, as an act of acquisition is not required in that case either (Rabbi Avraham *Av Beit Din*; Rambam; Ramah).

As if he said that the loan owed to him should be given to so-and-so – שֶׁאִם אָמַר הַלְוָאָתוֹ לִפְלוֹנִי: The discussion here pertains to a loan by oral agreement, which cannot be transferred by a healthy person to another individual, except in the presence of all three parties, i.e., the lender, the borrower, and the recipient. In the case of the gift of a person on his deathbed, the Sages instituted that a loan can be transferred to another by verbal instruction (see 148a).

In the name of our teacher – מִשּׁוּם רַבֵּינוּ: Rabbeinu Gershom Meor HaGola explains that this refers to Rav. In his youth, Rabbi Elazar was a disciple of Rav in Babylonia, and afterward he ascended to Eretz Yisrael.

Write a deed and give one hundred dinars – כִּתְבוּ וּתְנוּ מָנֶה: The Rashba notes that this refers to land worth one hundred dinars, since money cannot be acquired by means of a deed.

HALAKHA

The gift of a person on his deathbed in which it is written that acquisition was performed – מַתְּנַת שְׁכִיב מְרַע שֶׁכָּתוּב בָּהּ קִנְיָן: If a person on his deathbed gives all of his property to another by means of an act of acquisition, or even if he gives only some of his property to another, but he states that it is the gift of a person on his deathbed, the gift is not acquired even if he dies. Even if he writes a deed and delivers the deed to the recipient before he dies, the recipient does not acquire the gift. The reason for this is that he may have resolved to transfer ownership of the property only with an act of acquisition, and an act of acquisition is not effective after the death of the owner. If he specifies in the deed that the act of acquisition is performed only in order to enhance the legal power of the recipient, e.g., if he writes: And we, the witnesses, acquired it from him by means of an act of acquisition in addition to this gift, then the recipient acquires the gift. The Rema adds that if he writes that the deed should be understood in any way that validates it, the recipient acquires the gift (Maharam Padua). This ruling is in accordance with the opinion of Shmuel, as the *halakha* is in accordance with Shmuel in monetary matters, and also in accordance with the statement of Rava and Rav Naḥman (Rambam *Sefer Kinyan, Hilkhot Zekhiya UMattana* 8:10–11; *Shulḥan Arukh, Ḥoshen Mishpat* 250:9, 17).

Write a deed and give one hundred dinars to so-and-so, etc. – כִּתְבוּ וּתְנוּ מָנֶה לִפְלוֹנִי וכו׳: If a person on his deathbed gives his property to another and issues a directive that a deed should be written for the recipient together with the gift, and he dies, the deed is not written and given to the intended recipient. Even if the document is written before he dies, it is not given to the recipient after his death. The reason for this is that perhaps he resolved to transfer the gift to him only with the deed, and a deed is not effective after the death of the owner. If the giver clearly intends to enhance the legal power of the recipient by writing a deed for the recipient, e.g., if he says: Give him the property and also write a deed for him, then the deed is written and given to the recipient even after the death of the giver. This ruling is in accordance with the opinion of Shmuel, as the *halakha* is in accordance with Shmuel in matters of monetary law (Rambam *Sefer Kinyan, Hilkhot Zekhiya UMattana* 8:12–13; *Shulḥan Arukh, Ḥoshen Mishpat* 250:18).

קַשְׁיָא דְּרַב אַדְּרַב, קַשְׁיָא דִּשְׁמוּאֵל אַדִּשְׁמוּאֵל!

The Gemara concludes: The first statement **of Rav is difficult,** as it is apparently contradicted **by** the other statement **of Rav,** and the first statement **of Shmuel is difficult,** as it is apparently contradicted **by** the other statement **of Shmuel.**

דְּרַב אַדְּרַב לָא קַשְׁיָא: הָא דְּקָנוּ מִינֵּיהּ, הָא דְּלָא קָנוּ מִינֵּיהּ; דִּשְׁמוּאֵל אַדִּשְׁמוּאֵל לָא קַשְׁיָא: בִּמְיַפֶּה אֶת כֹּחוֹ.

The Gemara replies: The apparent contradiction **between** the first statement **of Rav** and the other statement **of Rav** is **not difficult. This** statement, that the gift is valid, is referring to a case **where** the gift **was acquired from** the person on his deathbed by means of an act of acquisition.[N] **That** other statement is referring to a case **where** the gift **was not acquired from him** by means of an act of acquisition, but only by verbal instruction, and therefore the deed is not written after his death. The apparent contradiction **between** the first statement **of Shmuel** and the other statement **of Shmuel** is **not difficult,** as Shmuel's statement that the deed is written after his death is referring to a case **where** the giver was clearly **enhancing the** legal **power** of the recipient[N] by providing him with a deed, and he was not making the gift contingent upon the delivery of a deed.

יָתֵיב רַב נַחְמָן בַּר יִצְחָק אֲחוֹרֵיהּ דְּרָבָא, וִיתֵיב רָבָא קַמֵּיהּ דְּרַב נַחְמָן קָא בָּעֵי מִינֵּיהּ, מִי אֲמַר שְׁמוּאֵל: שֶׁמָּא לֹא גָּמַר לְהַקְנוֹתוֹ אֶלָּא בִּשְׁטָר וְאֵין שְׁטָר לְאַחַר מִיתָה? וְהָא אָמַר רַב יְהוּדָה אָמַר שְׁמוּאֵל: שְׁכִיב מְרַע שֶׁכָּתַב כָּל נְכָסָיו לַאֲחֵרִים, אַף עַל פִּי שֶׁקָּנוּ מִיָּדוֹ – עָמַד חוֹזֵר,

Rav Naḥman bar Yitzḥak was sitting behind Rava, and Rava was sitting before Rav Naḥman, and Rava **asked** Rav Naḥman: **Did Shmuel** actually **say** that **perhaps** the fact that an act of acquisition was performed indicates that the person on his deathbed **resolved to transfer** ownership of the gift **only with** the **deed, and** therefore the gift is invalid, as **a deed is not** effective if it is delivered **after** the **death** of the owner? **But doesn't Rav Yehuda say** that **Shmuel says:** With regard to **a person on his deathbed who wrote** a deed granting **all of his property to others, even though** they **performed an act of acquisition,** if **he recovers he can retract** his gift?

NOTES

This is where the gift was acquired from him by acquisition – **הָא דְּקָנוּ מִינֵּיהּ:** If a person on his deathbed performs an act of acquisition despite the fact that this is unnecessary, this indicates that he is enhancing the legal power of the recipient beyond the status of the recipient of the gift of a person on his deathbed. Therefore, if he recovers, he cannot retract the gift.

Where the giver was clearly enhancing the legal power of the recipient – **בִּמְיַפֶּה אֶת כֹּחוֹ:** The giver stated in the deed that it is not intended to limit the validity of the gift. Rather, the deed is meant to strengthen the recipient's claim to the property. Some commentaries write that Rav probably agrees that in this case the gift stands, and there is no dispute between Rav and Shmuel on this matter (Ramban; Ritva). Others maintain that according to Rav there is no difference between a case where the giver was clearly enhancing the validity of the recipient's claim or a case where he was not (Rashba).

Perek **IX**
Daf **152** Amud **b**

בְּיָדוּעַ שֶׁלֹּא הָיָה קִנְיָן אֶלָּא מֵחֲמַת הַמִּיתָה! וְאַחֲוֵי לֵיהּ בִּידֵיהּ, וְאִשְׁתִּיק.

The reason for Shmuel's ruling is that **it is known that** an act of **acquisition** was performed **only due to** his expectation of imminent **death.** This ruling indicates that if the giver does not recover, the recipient acquires the gift, and the performance of an act of acquisition does not indicate that the giver intended to transfer the property only after his death. Rav Naḥman **indicated** the answer **to** Rava **with** a gesture of **his hand,**[N] **and** Rava **was silent.**

כִּי קָם, אֲמַר רַב נַחְמָן בַּר יִצְחָק לְרָבָא: מַאי אַחֲוֵי לָךְ? אֲמַר לֵיהּ: בִּמְיַפֶּה אֶת כֹּחוֹ.

When Rav Naḥman **arose** from his place, **Rav Naḥman bar Yitzḥak said to Rava: What did he indicate to you** with that gesture? Rava **said to him:** He indicated that the statement of Rav Yehuda is referring to a case **where** the giver was clearly **enhancing the** legal **power** of the recipient by requiring an act of acquisition to be performed in addition to bestowing the gift.

הֵיכִי דָּמֵי מְיַפֶּה אֶת כֹּחוֹ? אֲמַר רַב חִסְדָּא: ״וְקָנֵינָא מִינֵּיהּ מוֹסִיף עַל מַתַּנְתָּא דָא״.

The Gemara asks: **What is considered** an act of acquisition that **enhances the** legal **power** of the recipient? **Rav Ḥisda said:** An act of acquisition is clearly intended only to reinforce the legal power of the recipient when, for example, the following phrase is written in the deed: **And we,** the witnesses, **acquired** it **from him** by means of an act of acquisition **in addition to this gift.** This indicates that the act of acquisition was not performed in order to effect the actual acquisition.

NOTES

Rav Naḥman indicated to Rava with his hand – **וְאַחֲוֵי לֵיהּ בִּידֵיהּ:** Rav Naḥman communicated his answer by gesturing in a manner representative of an act that enhanced or reinforced something. Alternatively, Rav Naḥman merely indicated that he knew an answer to Rava's question (Rashbam; see Rashash).

פְּשִׁיטָא, כָּתַב לְזֶה וְכָתַב לְזֶה – הַיְינוּ דְּכִי אֲתָא רַב דִּימִי אֲמַר: דַּיְיתִיקֵי מְבַטֶּלֶת דַּיְיתִיקֵי; כָּתַב וְזִיכָּה לְזֶה, כָּתַב וְזִיכָּה לְזֶה – רַב אָמַר: רִאשׁוֹן קָנָה, וּשְׁמוּאֵל אָמַר: שֵׁנִי קָנָה;

§ It is **obvious** that if a person on his deathbed **wrote** a deed of transfer granting his property **to this** individual, **and** he then **wrote** a deed granting the same property **to that** individual, i.e., a second recipient, **this is** the case discussed by Rav Dimi. **As when Rav Dimi came** from Eretz Yisrael to Babylonia he **said:** A later **will** [*dayetikei*][L] **nullifies** an earlier **will.**[H] The *amora'im* disagree with regard to a case where one **wrote** a deed of transfer **and** also **conferred possession**[N] of the property **on this** individual,[H] and then he **wrote** a deed of transfer **and conferred possession** of the same property **on that** second individual. **Rav says:** The **first** recipient **acquires** the gift, **and Shmuel says:** The **second** recipient **acquires** the gift.[N]

רַב אָמַר רִאשׁוֹן קָנָה – הֲרֵי הִיא כְּמַתְּנַת בָּרִיא. וּשְׁמוּאֵל אָמַר שֵׁנִי קָנָה, הֲרֵי הִיא כְּמַתְּנַת שְׁכִיב מְרַע.

The Gemara explains: **Rav says** that the **first** recipient **acquires** the gift. Since an additional act of conferring possession of the property was performed, the gift **is** considered **like** the **gift of a healthy person,** which cannot be retracted. **Shmuel says** that the **second** recipient **acquires** the gift because **it is** considered **like** the **gift of a person on his deathbed,** which can be retracted.

וְהָא אִפְּלִיגוּ בָּהּ חֲדָא זִימְנָא, בְּמַתְּנַת שְׁכִיב מְרַע שֶׁכָּתוּב בָּהּ קִנְיָן!

The Gemara asks: **But didn't** Rav and Shmuel already **disagree about this** matter **once? With regard to** a deed pertaining to the **gift of a person on his deathbed in which** it **is written** that an act of **acquisition** was also performed, Rav maintained that the gift cannot be retracted, whereas Shmuel maintained that the acquisition was not effective. Why is it necessary to record another disagreement with regard to the same principle?

צְרִיכָא, דְּאִי אִיתְּמַר בְּהָא – בְּהָא קָאָמַר רַב, מִשּׁוּם דְּקָנוּ מִינֵּיהּ, אֲבָל בְּהָא דְּלָא קָנוּ מִינֵּיהּ – אֵימָא מוֹדֶה לֵיהּ לִשְׁמוּאֵל; וְאִי אִיתְּמַר בְּהָא – בְּהָא קָאָמַר שְׁמוּאֵל, אֲבָל בְּהַךְ – אֵימָא מוֹדֶה לֵיהּ לְרַב, צְרִיכָא.

The Gemara replies: It **is necessary** to cite both cases. This is **because if it were stated** only **with regard to that** case, where an act of acquisition was recorded in the deed, one might say that only **in that** case **Rav says** that the gift cannot be retracted, **because an act of acquisition was** performed. **But in this** case, **where an act of acquisition was not** performed,[N] one might **say** that **he concedes to Shmuel. And if it was stated** only **with regard to this** case, where he conferred possession of the property on the recipient through a deed alone, one might say that only **in this** case **Shmuel says** that he can retract the gift. **But in the other** case, where an act of acquisition was recorded in the deed, one might **say** that Shmuel **concedes to Rav** that he cannot retract it. Therefore, it **is necessary** to cite both cases.

בְּסוּרָא מַתְנוּ הָכִי. בְּפוּמְבְּדִיתָא מַתְנוּ הָכִי: אָמַר רַב יִרְמְיָה בַּר אַבָּא, שְׁלַחוּ לֵיהּ מִבֵּי רַב לִשְׁמוּאֵל: יְלַמְּדֵנוּ רַבֵּינוּ, שְׁכִיב מְרַע שֶׁכָּתַב כׇּל נְכָסָיו לַאֲחֵרִים וְקָנוּ מִיָּדוֹ, מַהוּ? שְׁלַח לְהוּ: אֵין אַחַר קִנְיָן כְּלוּם.

In Sura they taught the statements of Rav and Shmuel **that** way, as stated above. **In Pumbedita they taught** their statements **like this:**[N] **Rav Yirmeya bar Abba says:** After the death of Rav, the following question **was sent from the study hall of Rav to Shmuel: Let our teacher teach us:** With regard to **a person on his deathbed who wrote** a deed of transfer granting **all of his property to others, and they performed an act of acquisition, what is** the *halakha*? Shmuel **sent to them** in reply: **After** an act of **acquisition** is performed, **nothing** can effect a retraction of the gift.[H]

LANGUAGE

Will [*dayetikei*] – דייתיקי: From the Greek διαθήκη, *diathēkē*, meaning a will. The Sages expound upon the term homiletically as though it were Aramaic: *Da tehei lemeikam*, which means: This will stand (see Rashbam). Rabbeinu Tam explains that the person writing the will declares that he is writing it with the intention of recovering and continuing to live, and not out of an expectation that he will soon die.

NOTES

And also conferred possession – וְזִיכָּה: The intent of the term conferred possession is not entirely clear, and the early commentaries explain the term in various ways. Some state that in addition to writing the deed he instructed the recipient to take possession of the property in his presence (Rabbeinu Gershom Meor HaGola; *Ge'onim*). Others say that he conferred possession on the recipient by instructing another person to acquire the property on behalf of the recipient (Ri Migash; Ramah). The Rashbam maintains that in addition to writing the deed of transfer, the giver delivered the deed to the recipient.

The second recipient acquires the gift – שֵׁנִי קָנָה: The early commentaries ask: Shmuel states (152a) that if the gift of a person on his deathbed is acquired by an act of acquisition, it is uncertain whether the gift is valid. If so, why does Shmuel maintain that in this case the second recipient certainly acquires the gift? The commentaries explain that the Gemara here is referring to a case where the giver was clearly enhancing the legal power of the recipient by conferring possession of the property upon him (see Ritva).

Where an act of acquisition was not performed – דְּלָא קָנוּ מִינֵּיהּ: An act of acquisition refers to acquisition by means of symbolic exchange. One might have thought that although an act of acquisition strengthens the validity of the gift, the act of conferring possession does not.

In Pumbedita they taught their statements like this – בְּפוּמְבְּדִיתָא מַתְנוּ הָכִי: The Rashbam writes that some explain that this is referring to the opinion of Shmuel with regard to the gift of a person on his deathbed, which is accompanied by an act of acquisition. According to the version of Shmuel's statement that was taught in Pumbedita, Shmuel does not disagree with Rav's opinion in this matter (see *Piskei HaRid*). The Rashbam does not accept this explanation, and he maintains that the Gemara is referring to the dispute with regard to one who wrote a deed and conferred possession of his property on the recipient. According to the Pumbedita version of Shmuel's statement, Shmuel is referring to a case where in addition to writing a deed of transfer and conferring possession of the property on the recipient, an act of acquisition was also performed. Since the giver strengthened the validity of his gift both by conferring possession of the property upon the recipient and by performing an act of acquisition, even Shmuel concedes that the giver clearly intended to enhance the legal power of the recipient, and he was not making the gift conditional upon the delivery of the deed. Therefore, the acquisition takes effect at once, and the giver cannot retract the gift.

HALAKHA

A later will nullifies an earlier will – דַּיְיתִיקֵי מְבַטֶּלֶת דַּיְיתִיקֵי: If a person on his deathbed writes a will granting his property to one person, and he then retracts his gift and writes a second will granting his property to another, the second recipient acquires the property. The giver can change his mind several times before he dies, whether he gives all or only some of his property to others. If he gives only some of his property to others he must state explicitly that he is giving the property as the gift of a person on his deathbed (*Maggid Mishne*; Rema). He can retract his gift both in order to reserve it for himself and in order to bequeath it to another. But once he gives the will to an agent, he cannot retract the gift in order to bequeath it to another unless he instructs the agent to transfer the will to the first recipient only after his death (Rambam *Sefer Kinyan*, *Hilkhot Zekhiya UMattana* 9:15; *Shulḥan Arukh*, *Ḥoshen Mishpat* 250:13, and see *Sma* there).

Wrote a deed of transfer and conferred possession on this individual, etc. – כָּתַב וְזִיכָּה לְזֶה וכו׳: If a person on his deathbed writes a deed of transfer granting his property to one person, and he also gifts the property by means of an act of acquisition performed by a third party, he can still retract his gift and give the property to another, in accordance with the opinion of Shmuel, as the *halakha* is in accordance with Shmuel in matters of monetary law. The Rosh explains that with regard to movable property, one confers it upon another by having a third party pull the property on behalf of the recipient. With regard to land, the giver must instruct the third party to take possession of the property on behalf of the recipient and thereby acquire it for him (Rambam *Sefer Kinyan*, *Hilkhot Zekhiya UMattana* 9:15; *Shulḥan Arukh*, *Ḥoshen Mishpat* 250:13, and see *Sma* there).

After acquisition is performed nothing can effect a retraction of the gift – אֵין אַחַר קִנְיָן כְּלוּם: With regard to a person on his deathbed who wrote a deed of transfer granting his property to another, if he conferred possession of the property on the recipient and an act of acquisition was also performed, nothing can effect a retraction of the gift. This applies whether he gave all or only some of his property to another. He cannot retract the gift either in order to retain the property for himself or in order to transfer it to another. This ruling is in accordance with the version of Shmuel's statement that was taught in Pumbedita and with the statement of Rav Huna (Rambam *Sefer Kinyan*, *Hilkhot Zekhiya UMattana* 9:16; *Shulḥan Arukh*, *Ḥoshen Mishpat* 250:13).

סְבוּר מִינֵּיהּ: הָנֵי מִילֵּי לְאַחֵר, אֲבָל לְעַצְמוֹ לָא; אֲמַר לְהוּ רַב חִסְדָּא, כִּי אֲתָא רַב הוּנָא מִכּוּפְרֵי פֵּירְשָׁהּ: בֵּין לְעַצְמוֹ בֵּין לַאֲחֵרִים.

Rav's disciples **understood from this** that **this statement** applies only when the person on his deathbed wishes to retract his gift and transfer it **to another. But** if he recovers and wishes to retract the gift and retain it **for himself,** Shmuel's statement **does not apply.**[N] **Rav Ḥisda said to them: When Rav Huna came from Kufrei, he explained** that Shmuel's statement applies **both** to retaining the property **for himself and** to transferring it **to others.**

הַהוּא דְּקָנוּ מִינֵּיהּ, אֲתָא לְקַמֵּיהּ דְּרַב הוּנָא, אֲמַר: מַאי אִיעֲבִיד לָךְ, דְּלָא אַקְנֵית כִּדְמַקְנוּ אֱינָשֵׁי.

The Gemara relates: There was **a certain** person on his deathbed who wrote a deed of transfer granting his property to another, and **it was acquired from him** by means of an act of acquisition.[N] He subsequently recovered and wanted to retract the gift, and **he came before Rav Huna.** Rav Huna **said** to him: **What can I do for you?** You cannot retract the gift, **as you did not transfer** the gift **in the manner that people** on their deathbed **transfer** ownership of gifts, and you enhanced the legal power of the recipient by performing an act of acquisition.

הַהִיא מַתַּנְתָּא דַּהֲוָה כָּתוּב בָּהּ ״בַּחַיִּים וּבַמָּוֶת״ – רַב אָמַר: הֲרֵי הִיא כְּמַתְּנַת שְׁכִיב מְרַע, וּשְׁמוּאֵל אָמַר: הֲרֵי הִיא כְּמַתְּנַת בָּרִיא.

§ The Gemara relates: There was a deed pertaining to **a certain gift** of a person on his deathbed, **in which it was written** that the gift is given both **in life and in death.**[NH] In such a case, **Rav says: It is like** the **gift of a person on his deathbed,** and if he recovers he can retract it. **And Shmuel says: It is like** the **gift of a healthy person,** and he cannot retract it.

רַב אָמַר: הֲרֵי הִיא כְּמַתְּנַת שְׁכִיב מְרַע; מִדִּכְתִיב בָּהּ ״בַּמָּוֶת״ – אַחַר מִיתָה קָאָמַר לֵיהּ, וְהַאי דִּכְתִיב ״בַּחַיִּים״ – סִימָן בְּעָלְמָא, דְּחַיֵּי.

The Gemara explains: **Rav says: It is like** the **gift of a person on his deathbed.** This can be inferred **from** the fact **that it is written in** the deed that the gift is given **in death.** This means that the giver **is saying to him** that the gift should take effect **after** his **death, and that which is written** in the deed, that the gift is given **in life,** is **merely** an auspicious **omen,** expressing hope **that** the giver **will live.**

וּשְׁמוּאֵל אָמַר: הֲרֵי הִיא כְּמַתְּנַת בָּרִיא; מִדִּכְתִיב בָּהּ ״בַּחַיִּים״ – מֵחַיִּים קָאָמַר, וְהַאי דִּכְתַב ״וּבַמָּוֶת״ – כְּמַאן דְּאָמַר ״מֵעַתָּה וְעַד עוֹלָם״. אָמְרִי נְהַרְדְּעֵי: הִלְכְתָא כְּוָותֵיהּ דְּרַב.

And Shmuel says: It is like the **gift of a healthy person.** This can be inferred **from** the fact **that it is written in** the deed that the gift is given **in life.** This means that the giver **is saying** that the gift takes effect **during** his **life,** i.e., immediately. **And that which he wrote,** that the gift is given **in death, is like one who says: From now and for evermore,** i.e., that the gift is not retractable. The Sages **of Neharde'a say: The** ***halakha*** **is in accordance with** the opinion **of Rav.**

אֲמַר רָבָא: וְאִי כְּתִיב בָּהּ ״מֵחַיִּים״ – קָנָה.

Rava said: And if it was written in the deed that the gift is given **during life** and in death, the recipient **acquires** the gift and it cannot be retracted, as this term indicates that the gift takes effect while the giver still lives.

אֲמַר אַמֵימָר: לֵית הִלְכְתָא כְּוָותֵיהּ דְּרָבָא. אֲמַר לֵיהּ רַב אַשִׁי לְאַמֵימָר: פְּשִׁיטָא, דְּהָא אָמְרִי נְהַרְדְּעֵי הִלְכְתָא כְּוָותֵיהּ דְּרַב! מַהוּ דְּתֵימָא ״מֵחַיִּים״ מוֹדֵי רַב, קָא מַשְׁמַע לָן.

Ameimar said: The ***halakha*** **is not in accordance with** the opinion **of Rava. Rav Ashi said to Ameimar:** Isn't that **obvious, as** the Sages **of Neharde'a say** that **the** ***halakha*** **is in accordance with** the opinion **of Rav?** Ameimar replied: **Lest you say** that with regard to the term: **During life, Rav concedes**[N] that the giver intends for the gift to take effect immediately, Ameimar **teaches us** that since the giver also mentioned death, he intended the gift as the gift of a person on his deathbed and he can retract it.

הַהוּא דַּאֲתָא לְקַמֵּיהּ דְּרַב נַחְמָן לִנְהַרְדְּעָא, שַׁדְרֵיהּ לְקַמֵּיהּ דְּרַבִּי יִרְמְיָה בַּר אַבָּא לְשׁוּם טַמְיָא, אֲמַר: הָכָא אַתְרָא דִּשְׁמוּאֵל, הֵיכִי נַעֲבֵיד כְּוָותֵיהּ דְּרַב!

The Gemara relates: There was **a certain** person who wrote in the deed that the gift is given in life and in death. When he recovered he wanted to retract the gift. He **came before Rav Naḥman in Neharde'a.** Rav Naḥman **sent him to** appear **before Rabbi Yirmeya bar Abba in Shum Tamya.** Rav Naḥman **said** in explanation of his actions: **Here,** Neharde'a, **is the place of Shmuel.** Consequently, Shmuel's rulings should be followed, and therefore **how can we act in accordance with** the opinion **of Rav?**[N]

NOTES

This statement applies to another but for himself it does not apply – **הָנֵי מִילֵּי לְאַחֵר אֲבָל לְעַצְמוֹ לָא**: Rav's disciples thought that the gift cannot be retracted in order to give it to another, as the recipient acquires the gift by means of the act of acquisition. But if the giver recovers he can retract the gift, as the gift is conditional upon his death (Rashbam). The Ri Migash explains, in accordance with a different version of the text here, that Rav's disciples thought that the giver cannot retract the gift in order to retain the property for himself, since he completely removes himself from ownership of the property by performing an act of acquisition. Nevertheless, since the gift of a person on his deathbed is acquired only after death, the recipient has not yet acquired it, and therefore the giver can transfer the property to another.

A certain person who wrote a deed and it was acquired from him by an act of acquisition – **הַהוּא דְּקָנוּ מִינֵּיהּ**: The Rashbam understands this case as follows: The giver wrote a deed of transfer, conferred possession of the property on the recipient, and an act of acquisition was also performed. Rav Huna told him that although a person on his deathbed who recovers is usually able to retract his gift, in this case even Shmuel concedes that he cannot do so, since he enhanced the legal power of the recipient by both conferring possession on him and performing an act of acquisition.

A certain gift in which it was written that it is given in life and in death – **הַהִיא מַתַּנְתָּא דַּהֲוָה כָּתוּב בָּהּ בַּחַיִּים וּבַמָּוֶת**: The gift was the gift of a person on his deathbed involving only some of the giver's property, and an act of acquisition was performed (Rashbam).

With regard to the term, during life, Rav concedes – **מֵחַיִּים מוֹדֵי רַב**: Even if the term: During life, is understood merely as an auspicious omen, it appears to indicate more clearly that the giver intended the gift to take effect while he still lives.

How can we act in accordance with the opinion of Rav – **הֵיכִי נַעֲבֵיד כְּוָותֵיהּ דְּרַב**: Although the *halakha* is in accordance with the opinion of Rav, it would be disrespectful to rule contrary to the opinion of Shmuel in Neharde'a, where Shmuel was the accepted authority. Rav Naḥman therefore sent the person to Shum Tamya to appear before Rabbi Yirmeya bar Abba, who was a disciple of Rav, to rule in the case.

HALAKHA

In life and in death – **בַּחַיִּים וּבַמָּוֶת**: If a person on his deathbed gives his property to others, and he writes in the deed that the gift is given in life and in death, whether he gives all of his property or only a part of his property, his gift is considered the gift of a person on his deathbed, even if an act of acquisition is performed (*Sma*). He can therefore retract his gift irrespective of whether or not he recovers. This also applies if he writes that the gift is given during life and in death. Some authorities say that this also applies if he writes that the gift is given in death and in life (see *Shakh*). The reason for this is that the term: In death, indicates that the giver's intention is that the recipient should acquire the property only after his death, and the term: In life, is added only as an auspicious omen in order to allay his anxiety and strengthen his hope of recovery. This ruling is in accordance with the opinion of Rav, as stated in the Gemara (Rambam *Sefer Kinyan, Hilkhot Zekhiya UMattana* 8:19; *Shulḥan Arukh*, *Ḥoshen Mishpat* 251:1).

HALAKHA

If one did not write in it that he was on his deathbed – לֹא כָּתַב בָּהּ שְׁכִיב מְרַע: In the case of a deed in which there is no reference to whether the person bestowing the gift was a healthy person or a person on his deathbed, the *halakha* is as follows: If the giver claims that he was on his deathbed, and since he recovered he can retract the gift, but the recipient claims that the giver was a healthy person and he cannot retract the gift, the recipient must bring proof that the giver was a healthy person. If he does not bring proof to that effect, he receives nothing, as the burden of proof rests upon the claimant, in accordance with the opinion of the Rabbis (Rambam *Sefer Kinyan, Hilkhot Zekhiya UMattana* 9:22; *Shulḥan Arukh, Ḥoshen Mishpat* 251:2, and in the comment of Rema).

And from his sickness…was not written in it, etc. – וְלָא כָּתַב בָּהּ וּמִגּוֹ מַרְעֵיהּ וכו׳: In the case of a deed pertaining to the gift of a person on his deathbed in which it is not stated that the giver died from his sickness, and the witnesses are not available to testify on this matter, the gift is invalid even though the giver died. This is because his death does not prove that he did not recover and retract the gift, as he might have recovered and subsequently contracted a different sickness and died. Therefore, the property remains in the presumptive ownership of the heirs unless the recipient brings proof that the giver died from the sickness that he had when he gave the gift. This ruling is in accordance with the opinion of Abaye, whose opinion is supported by the opinion of Rabbi Ya'akov (153b), and in accordance with the opinion of the Rabbis in the mishna (Rambam *Sefer Kinyan, Hilkhot Zekhiya UMattana* 8:27; *Shulḥan Arukh, Ḥoshen Mishpat* 251:2).

הַהִיא דַּאֲתַאי לְקַמֵּיהּ דְּרָבָא, עֲבַד לָהּ רָבָא כִּשְׁמַעֲתֵיהּ, הֲוָה קָא טָרְדָא לֵיהּ,

The Gemara relates: There was **a certain** woman who wrote in the deed that the gift is given during life and in death. She **came before Rava. Rava acted with regard to her** case **in accordance with his halakhic** ruling, and he ruled that she cannot retract the gift. She did not accept the ruling, and **she** constantly **troubled him,** saying that he had not judged her case properly.

אֲמַר לֵיהּ לְרַב פַּפָּא בְּרֵיהּ דְּרַב חָנָן סַפְרֵיהּ: זִיל כְּתוֹב לָהּ, וּכְתוֹב בָּהּ: שׂוֹכֵר עֲלֵיהֶן אוֹ מַטְעָן. אָמְרָה: לִיטְבַּע אַרְבֵּיהּ! אַטְעוּיֵי קָא מַטְעֵית לִי! אַמְשִׁינְהוּ לְמָנֵיהּ דְּרָבָא בְּמַיָּא, וַאֲפִילּוּ הָכִי לָא אִיפְּרַק מִטִּיבְעָא.

Rava **said to Rav Pappa, his scribe, son of Rav Ḥanan: Go, write for her** a ruling in her favor, **and write in** the ruling the phrase: He may **hire** replacements **at their** expense, **or deceive them** to get them to return to work. This is a phrase from the mishna (*Bava Metzia* 75b) that discusses the ruling in the case of one who hired laborers to perform a task that cannot be delayed, and they quit. Rava intended this phrase to indicate to the court that the ruling was merely a ruse in order to persuade the woman to leave. The woman understood the ruse. **She said: May his ship sink; you are deceiving me. Rava had his clothes immersed in water** so that the curse should be fulfilled in this alternative manner, **but even so he was not saved from** the **sinking** of his ship.[N]

מתני׳ לֹא כָּתַב בָּהּ שְׁכִיב מְרַע, הוּא אוֹמֵר שְׁכִיב מְרַע הָיִיתִי, וְהֵן אוֹמְרִים בָּרִיא הָיִיתָ – צָרִיךְ לְהָבִיא רְאָיָה שֶׁשְּׁכִיב מְרַע הָיָה, דִּבְרֵי רַבִּי מֵאִיר; וַחֲכָמִים אוֹמְרִים: הַמּוֹצִיא מֵחֲבֵירוֹ עָלָיו הָרְאָיָה.

MISHNA If one **did not write in** the deed that he was **on his deathbed,**[H] and he then recovered and wished to retract the gift, and **he says: I was on my deathbed,** and since I recovered, I can retract the gift, **but** the recipients **say: You were healthy,**[N] and the gift cannot be retracted, the giver **must bring proof that he was on his deathbed** in order to retract the gift. This is **the statement of Rabbi Meir. And the Rabbis say: The burden of proof rests upon the claimant,** and since the property is in the possession of the giver, the recipients must bring proof that they have the right to receive it.

גמ׳ הַהוּא מַתַּנְתָּא דַּהֲוָה כְּתַב בָּהּ: ״כַּד הֲוָה קָצִיר וְרָמֵי בְּעַרְסֵיהּ״, וְלָא כָּתַב בָּהּ ״וּמִגּוֹ מַרְעֵיהּ אִיפְּטַר לְבֵית עוֹלָמֵיהּ״,

GEMARA There was a deed pertaining to **a certain gift** of a person on his deathbed, **in which it was written** that the gift was bestowed **when** the giver **was sick and lying in his bed, but** the continuation of the standard formula: **And from his sickness he departed to his eternal home, was not written in it.**[HN] The giver's heirs claimed that although he was ill when he wrote the deed, he later recovered, and his gift is not valid.

NOTES

He was not saved from the sinking of his ship – לָא אִיפְּרַק מִטִּיבְעָא: The Rashbam says that this is in accordance with the aphorism of the Sages: The curse of an ordinary person should not be light in your eyes (*Megilla* 15a), as even such a curse may be fulfilled. The Ritva explains that the curse was fulfilled because Rava ruled incorrectly in this matter when issuing his first ruling, since his colleagues disagreed with him, and the *halakha* is not in accordance with his opinion. Although he inadvertently ruled incorrectly, he should have taken more care before issuing his ruling, as an unwitting misinterpretation of the Talmud is tantamount to an intentional transgression (*Avot* 4:13). The Meiri writes that Rava was punished because he made light of the woman, which was inappropriate behavior, particularly for Rava, who was a great scholar and a judge.

You were healthy – בָּרִיא הָיִיתָ: The early commentaries ask why this claim should be effective, as the gift of a healthy person requires an act of acquisition. Some commentaries understand that the mishna is referring to a case where it was stated in the deed that an act of acquisition was performed (see Ritva). Rabbeinu Yona and the Meiri explain that the deed stated only that so-and-so had given his property to so-and-so. The giver claimed that since the deed did not mention an act of acquisition, this indicates that it was the gift of a person on his deathbed, which is acquired by verbal instruction. The recipients claimed either that the deed was written only as proof of the transaction, which was effected with a valid act of acquisition, or that the deed itself effected the acquisition, as land can be acquired by means of a deed of transfer.

And from his sickness…was not written in it, etc. – וְלָא כָּתַב בָּהּ וּמִגּוֹ מַרְעֵיהּ וכו׳: The witnesses would write this formula in the document they composed after his death, in which they recorded the instructions the deceased issued verbally while he was on his deathbed. In this case, the person died, but his heirs claimed that he had recovered after writing the deed, and it should be assumed that he had retracted the gift. *Tosafot* note that if a person on his deathbed recovers completely, he does not have to explicitly retract his gift, as the recovery itself nullifies his gift.

אֲמַר רַבָּה: הֲרֵי מֵת, וַהֲרֵי קִבְרוֹ מוֹכִיחַ עָלָיו. אֲמַר לֵיהּ אַבַּיֵי: הַשְׁתָּא, וּמָה סְפִינָה שֶׁרוּבָּן לְאַבֵּד – נוֹתְנִין עֲלֵיהֶן חוּמְרֵי חַיִּים וְחוּמְרֵי מֵתִים, חוֹלִין, שֶׁרוֹב חוֹלִין לְחַיִּים – לֹא כׇּל שֶׁכֵּן!

Rabba said: He is dead,[N] **and his grave proves** that **he** died. It may therefore be assumed that he did not recover from his sickness, and his gift remains valid. **Abaye said to him: And now, if** in the case of **a ship** that sank, **where** the fate of **most of** the passengers of sunken ships is **to perish,** the **stringencies of** the **living and** the **stringencies of** the **dead are applied to them**[HN] due to the uncertainty as to whether they are alive or dead, in the case of **sick people, where** the fate of **most sick people** is **to return to life, all the more so** is it **not** clear[N] that one should assume that he recovered from the illness and his gift is invalid?

אֲמַר רַב הוּנָא בְּרֵיהּ דְּרַב יְהוֹשֻׁעַ: כְּמַאן אָזְלָא הָא שְׁמַעְתָּא דְּרַבָּה? כְּרַבִּי נָתָן; דְּתַנְיָא: מִי מוֹצִיא מִיַּד מִי? הוּא מוֹצִיא מִידֵיהֶן בְּלֹא רְאָיָה, וְהֵן אֵין מוֹצִיאִין מִיָּדוֹ אֶלָּא בִּרְאָיָה, דִּבְרֵי רַבִּי יַעֲקֹב;

Rav Huna, son of Rav Yehoshua, said: In accordance with whose opinion **is that** ***halakha*** **of Rabba?** It is **in accordance with** the opinion of **Rabbi Natan, as it is taught** in a *baraita*: With regard to a case where one who gave his property to others claims that since he was on his deathbed at the time he can retract the gifts, and the recipients claim that he was healthy and cannot retract it, **who removes** the property **from whose possession?** The giver **can remove** it **from** the recipients' **possession without proof,**[N] as the property was previously established to be in his possession, **but** the recipients **can remove** it **from** the giver's **possession only with proof.** This is **the statement of Rabbi Ya'akov.**

רַבִּי נָתָן אוֹמֵר: אִם בָּרִיא הוּא – עָלָיו לְהָבִיא רְאָיָה שֶׁהָיָה שְׁכִיב מְרַע, אִם שְׁכִיב מְרַע הוּא – עֲלֵיהֶן לְהָבִיא רְאָיָה שֶׁבָּרִיא הָיָה.

Rabbi Natan says: The presumption is that the current situation reflects the situation at the time the gift was bestowed. Therefore, **if he is** currently **healthy,** the obligation **is upon him to bring proof that he was on his deathbed** when he gave his property to others. **If he is** currently **on his deathbed,** the obligation **is upon** the recipients **to bring proof that he was healthy** then.

אָמַר רַבִּי אֶלְעָזָר: וּלְטוּמְאָה – כְּמַחְלוֹקֶת; דִּתְנַן: בִּקְעָה, בִּימוֹת הַחַמָּה – רְשׁוּת הַיָּחִיד לְשַׁבָּת וּרְשׁוּת הָרַבִּים לְטוּמְאָה,

Rabbi Elazar says: And with regard to a case of uncertain **ritual impurity,** the *halakha* depends **on the** same **dispute.** This is **as we learned** in a mishna (*Teharot* 6:7): The *halakha* is that a case where it is uncertain if something or someone became impure in the public domain, the item or person is deemed pure. With regard to **an expanse of fields, in the summer,** when many people pass through the fields, it is considered **the private domain with regard to** the *halakhot* of **Shabbat, but** it is considered **the public domain with regard to** the *halakhot* of **ritual impurity,**[N] and if one is uncertain as to whether he was rendered impure there, he is deemed pure.

HALAKHA

The stringencies of the living and the stringencies of the dead are applied to them – נוֹתְנִין עֲלֵיהֶן חוּמְרֵי חַיִּים וְחוּמְרֵי מֵתִים: In the case of a ship that sank at sea, the stringencies of the living and the stringencies of the dead are applied to the passengers. Their wives are prohibited from remarrying, and if a passenger entrusted to an agent a bill of divorce that was not yet delivered to his wife, it is not delivered to her. If the agent delivered the bill of divorce to the wife, there is uncertainty whether or not she is divorced. If one of the passengers was an Israelite married to the daughter of a priest or a priest married to an Israelite woman, his wife may not partake of *teruma* (Rambam *Sefer Nashim*, *Hilkhot Geirushin* 6:28 and *Sefer Zera'im*, *Hilkhot Terumot* 9:2; *Shulḥan Arukh*, *Even HaEzer* 141:69).

NOTES

He is dead – הֲרֵי מֵת: The presumption is that the current situation is indicative of the former situation. Since the giver is dead, it is presumed that he died from that sickness, and the recipient retains his presumptive ownership (see Rabbeinu Yona).

The stringencies of the living and the stringencies of the dead are applied to them – נוֹתְנִין עֲלֵיהֶן חוּמְרֵי חַיִּים וְחוּמְרֵי מֵתִים: The wives of passengers on a ship that sank may not remarry, and their heirs cannot take possession of their estates, as those passengers may still be living. If one of the travelers was an Israelite married to the daughter of a priest, she cannot partake of *teruma* on the assumption that her husband died, as her husband might still be alive. Conversely, if one of the passengers was a priest married to an Israelite woman, his wife may not partake of *teruma*, as her husband might have died.

All the more so is it not clear – לֹא כׇּל שֶׁכֵּן: The Gemara does not report Rabba's reply to Abaye. The Rosh writes that the Gemara (154a) indicates that Rabba retracted his opinion. Conversely, the Rid explains that Rabba did not consider it necessary to reply to Abaye, as Rabba's opinion is supported by the statement of Rabbi Natan. Rabba maintains that one cannot compare the case of a person on his deathbed who died to the case of a ship that sank, since in the case of the person on his deathbed it is known what happened to him afterward. Furthermore, one may presume that the witnesses would not transfer the deed to the recipient unless they knew that the giver had died from the sickness that had afflicted him at the time (Ramban).

He can remove it from the recipients' possession without proof – הוּא מוֹצִיא מִידֵיהֶן בְּלֹא רְאָיָה: The principle is that property retains its previous ownership status unless proven otherwise. Therefore, although the recipient possesses a deed to the property, he is at a disadvantage (Rashbam; see Jerusalem Talmud 9:6).

The private domain with regard to Shabbat but the public domain with regard to ritual impurity – רְשׁוּת הַיָּחִיד לְשַׁבָּת וּרְשׁוּת הָרַבִּים לְטוּמְאָה: The distinction between a public domain and a private domain pertains to the *halakhot* of Shabbat, monetary law, and ritual impurity, and the classification of these domains depends on the context. With regard to Shabbat, a private domain is an area delineated by partitions at least ten handbreadths high, and the public domain is an area sixteen cubits wide that is frequented daily by a multitude of people. With regard to monetary law, a public domain and a private domain are defined primarily according to the ownership of the area. With regard to ritual impurity, a private domain is defined as a secluded area that is not usually frequented by people, whereas the public domain is a place that is frequented by people. The Sages derived from the Torah passage concerning the *halakhot* of a *sota* that in a case of uncertainty with regard to impurity, the *halakha* depends on the place where the uncertainty arose. If the uncertainty arose in a private domain, the item or person is deemed impure, but if it arose in a public domain, the item or person is deemed pure (see *Sota* 28b).

בִּימוֹת הַגְּשָׁמִים – רְשׁוּת הַיָּחִיד לְכָאן וּלְכָאן.

In the rainy season, when not many people pass through the fields, an expanse of fields is considered **the private domain** both **with regard to this,** Shabbat, **and with regard to that,**[HN] ritual impurity. Therefore, if one is uncertain whether he was rendered impure there, he is deemed impure. If one does not know whether the day he entered the expanse of fields was considered part of the summer or the rainy season, and he is uncertain whether he was rendered impure there, Rabbi Ya'akov maintains that he retains the status of purity that he held before entering the fields. According to Rabbi Natan, it is presumed that he entered the fields during the same season in which he came to ask whether he was rendered impure.

אָמַר רָבָא: לֹא שָׁנוּ אֶלָּא שֶׁלֹּא עָבְרוּ עָלָיו יְמוֹת הַגְּשָׁמִים, אֲבָל עָבְרוּ עָלָיו יְמוֹת הַגְּשָׁמִים – רְשׁוּת הַיָּחִיד לְכָאן וּלְכָאן.

Rava disagrees with Rabbi Elazar and **says: They taught** the ruling of the mishna **only** with regard to a case **where the rainy season has not** yet **passed over** the fields[N] after the possibility arose that the fields contained impurity. **But if the rainy season has** already **passed over** the fields, it is considered **the private domain** both **with regard to this,** Shabbat, **and with regard to that,** ritual impurity. Even though the one who passed through the fields came to ask about his status in the summer, when the fields should be considered the public domain, he is nevertheless deemed impure even according to Rabbi Natan, and there is no parallel dispute with regard to uncertain ritual impurity.

"וַחֲכָמִים אוֹמְרִים: הַמּוֹצִיא מֵחֲבֵירוֹ עָלָיו הָרְאָיָה" וכו'.

§ The mishna teaches: **And the Rabbis say: The burden of proof rests upon the claimant,** and since the property is in the possession of the giver, the recipients must bring proof that they have the right to receive it.

HALAKHA

An expanse of fields is considered the private domain with regard to this and with regard to that – רְשׁוּת הַיָּחִיד לְכָאן וּלְכָאן: With regard to an expanse of fields that is enclosed by a fence, during the rainy season it is considered a private domain both with regard to Shabbat and with regard to the *halakhot* of ritual impurity. If it is not enclosed by a fence it is considered a private domain only with regard to ritual impurity. Once the rainy season has passed, the fields are considered a private domain with regard to ritual impurity even during the summer (Rambam *Sefer Tahara, Hilkhot She'ar Avot HaTumot* 20:6).

NOTES

In the rainy season it is the private domain with regard to this and with regard to that – בִּימוֹת הַגְּשָׁמִים רְשׁוּת הַיָּחִיד לְכָאן וּלְכָאן: The Rashbam and *Tosafot* explain that in the rainy season the fields are sown, and the owners object to people entering, as they might trample the seeds. Rabbeinu Ḥananel and the Ra'avad say that in the rainy season people do not walk through the fields due to the accumulation of rainwater and mud (see *Tosafot*).

Where the rainy season has not passed over the fields – שֶׁלֹּא עָבְרוּ עָלָיו יְמוֹת הַגְּשָׁמִים: The Rashbam explains that Rava's statement does not refer to the previous statement of Rabbi Elazar, and it is cited here in order to clarify the mishna. Rava says that an expanse of fields is considered the public domain during the summer only if the rainy season has not happened since they were fenced in. Once the rainy season has happened, they permanently maintain the status of a private domain with regard to ritual impurity. The reason for this is either because of the stringency of the *halakhot* of ritual impurity, or in order to avoid confusion and causing the words of the Sages to become a subject of mockery. Although elsewhere the mishna states that the status of an expanse of fields with regard to ritual impurity is subject to change, this refers only to a case where the fields were noticeably changed, e.g., by the removal of a fence surrounding them (Ra'avad).

Perek **IX**
Daf **154** Amud **a**

רְאָיָה בְּמַאי? רַב הוּנָא אָמַר: רְאָיָה בְּעֵדִים; רַב חִסְדָּא וְרַבָּה בַּר רַב הוּנָא אָמְרִי: רְאָיָה בְּקִיּוּם הַשְּׁטָר.

The Gemara asks: With regard to the **proof** that the recipients must bring, **in what** manner is it brought? **Rav Huna says:** The **proof** is presented **by** bringing **witnesses** who testify that the giver was healthy. **Rav Ḥisda and Rabba bar Rav Huna say:** The **proof** is presented **by** the **ratification of the deed,** i.e., the recipients are required only to ascertain that the signatures of the witnesses on the deed are authentic in order to prove that it is not forged.

רַב הוּנָא אָמַר רְאָיָה בְּעֵדִים, קָא מִיפַּלְגִי בִּפְלוּגְתָּא דְּרַבִּי יַעֲקֹב וְרַבִּי נָתָן,

The Gemara explains: **Rav Huna says** that the **proof** is presented **by** bringing **witnesses.** He maintains that Rabbi Meir and the Rabbis **disagree with regard to** the issue that is the subject of **the dispute of Rabbi Ya'akov and Rabbi Natan** in the *baraita* (153b).

(סִימָן: מַנִּיחַ) רַבִּי מֵאִיר כְּרַבִּי נָתָן, וְרַבָּנַן כְּרַבִּי יַעֲקֹב;

The Gemara notes **a mnemonic** device that indicates which tannaitic opinions are correlated: ***Manniaḥ,*** which represents the letters *mem, nun, yod, ḥet,* stands for Meir, Natan, Ya'akov, and the Rabbis [*ḥakhamim*]. This indicates that **Rabbi Meir,** who says that the giver must bring proof that he was on his deathbed, holds **in accordance with** the opinion of **Rabbi Natan,** who maintains that one presumes that the current situation reflects the situation at the time the gift was bestowed. **And the Rabbis,** who say that the recipients must bring proof that the giver was healthy, hold **in accordance with** the opinion of **Rabbi Ya'akov.**[N]

NOTES

And the Rabbis hold in accordance with Rabbi Ya'akov – וְרַבָּנַן כְּרַבִּי יַעֲקֹב: This can be proved only by the testimony of witnesses, as the mishna is referring to a case where the deed does not indicate the physical condition of the giver.

רַב חִסְדָּא וְרַבָּה בַּר רַב הוּנָא אָמְרִי רְאָיָה בְּקִיּוּם הַשְּׁטָר, קָא מִיפַּלְגִי בְּמוֹדֶה בִּשְׁטָר שֶׁכְּתָבוֹ צָרִיךְ לְקַיְּימוֹ, דְּרַבִּי מֵאִיר סָבַר: מוֹדֶה בִּשְׁטָר שֶׁכְּתָבוֹ – אֵינוֹ צָרִיךְ לְקַיְּימוֹ, וְרַבָּנַן סָבְרִי: מוֹדֶה בִּשְׁטָר שֶׁכְּתָבוֹ – צָרִיךְ לְקַיְּימוֹ.

Rav Ḥisda and Rabba bar Rav Huna say that the **proof** is presented **by the ratification of the deed.** The Gemara explains: Rav Ḥisda and Rabba bar Rav Huna maintain that Rabbi Meir and the Rabbis **disagree with regard to** whether when there is a debtor **who admits that he wrote** a promissory **note,**[H] the creditor **must ratify it**[N] in court in order to collect payment. The same ruling would apply to a case where the person on his deathbed admits that he wrote the deed granting the gift. They explain **that Rabbi Meir holds** that when there is a debtor **who admits that he wrote** a promissory **note,** the creditor **need not ratify it** in court in order to collect payment, and in this case the giver cannot invalidate the deed by claiming that he was on his deathbed. **But the Rabbis hold** that even when there is a debtor **who admits that he wrote** a promissory **note,** the creditor **must ratify it** in court in order to collect payment.

וְהָא אִיפְּלִיגוּ בַּהּ חֲדָא זִימְנָא! דְּתַנְיָא: אֵין נֶאֱמָנִין לְפוֹסְלוֹ, דִּבְרֵי רַבִּי מֵאִיר, וַחֲכָמִים אוֹמְרִים: נֶאֱמָנִין!

The Gemara asks: **But didn't they** already **disagree with regard to this** matter **once? As it is taught** in a *baraita*: With regard to witnesses who ratified their signatures but claimed that at the time they signed the document they were not fit to bear witness, their testimony is **not deemed credible to invalidate** the document; this is **the statement of Rabbi Meir. And the Rabbis say:** Their testimony is **deemed credible.**[H]

צְרִיכָא, דְּאִי אִיתְּמַר הַהִיא, בְּהַהִיא קָאָמְרִי רַבָּנַן, מִשּׁוּם דְּאַלִּימֵי עֵדִים וּמָרְעִי שְׁטָרָא, אֲבָל הָכָא, הוּא דְּלָאו כֹּל כְּמִינֵּיהּ – אֵימָא לָא;

The Gemara answers: It **is necessary** to state both cases, **because if** only **that** case with regard to witnesses who disqualified their testimony **was stated,** one might think that **the Sages say** that their testimony is accepted only **in that** case, **due to** the fact **that** the testimony of **witnesses is powerful**[N] **and they can impair** the validity of the **document, but here,** with regard to **him,** the giver, **who** admitted that he wrote the deed but it **is not in his** power to impair the validity of the deed, **I would say** that his claim is **not** accepted.

וְאִי אִיתְּמַר בְּהָא, בְּהָא קָאָמַר רַבִּי מֵאִיר, אֲבָל בְּהַךְ אֵימָא מוֹדֶה לְהוּ לְרַבָּנַן, צְרִיכָא.

And if only **this** case, with regard to a debtor who admits that he wrote a promissory note, **was stated,** one might think that **Rabbi Meir says** that the giver cannot invalidate the deed only **with regard to this** case, **but with regard to that** case, where the witnesses ratified their signatures, **I would say** that Rabbi Meir **concedes to the Rabbis** that witnesses can invalidate the deed. Therefore, it **is necessary** to state the dispute in both cases.

HALAKHA

A debtor who admits that he wrote a promissory note – מוֹדֶה בִּשְׁטָר שֶׁכְּתָבוֹ: A creditor who claims that he is owed money and produces a promissory note is required to first ratify the document. If he does not bring witnesses to ratify it, the debtor can claim that he has repaid the debt, even if he admits that the document is authentic (Rambam *Sefer Mishpatim, Hilkhot Malve VeLoveh* 14:5; *Shulḥan Arukh, Ḥoshen Mishpat* 82:1).

And the Rabbis say their testimony is deemed credible – וַחֲכָמִים אוֹמְרִים נֶאֱמָנִין: If witnesses ratify their signatures on a promissory note but claim that at the time they signed the document they were minors or otherwise disqualified from bearing witness, their testimony is deemed credible. This is the *halakha* only if their signatures cannot be ratified by comparing them with their signatures on another document, and only if they stated this immediately after ratifying the document, within the amount of time it takes to greet one's teacher (Rambam *Sefer Shofetim, Hilkhot Edut* 3:6; *Shulḥan Arukh, Ḥoshen Mishpat* 46:37).

NOTES

With regard to whether when there is a debtor who admits that he wrote a promissory note, the creditor must ratify it – בְּמוֹדֶה בִּשְׁטָר שֶׁכְּתָבוֹ צָרִיךְ לְקַיְּימוֹ: According to Rav Ḥisda and Rabba bar Rav Huna, both Rabbi Meir and the Rabbis maintain that the current situation reflects the situation at the time the gift was bestowed. Since the giver is currently healthy, he is presumed to have been healthy at the time of the gift, and once the deed is ratified all agree that the recipient can collect the gift. Rabbi Meir and the Rabbis disagree with regard to whether the recipient is required to first ratify the deed, i.e., to bring witnesses who can certify that the signatures of the witnesses on the deed are authentic. According to the opinion of Rabbi Meir, a document is presumed valid unless the giver claims that it is forged. If the giver admits that the document is authentic, it is not necessary to ratify it. According to the opinion of the Rabbis, as long as the document is not ratified by the testimony of witnesses, the giver can invalidate it. The reason for this is that if the validity of the document is based only on the statement of the giver, he can invalidate it through any other claim. This is in accordance with the principle that the mouth that prohibited it is the mouth that permitted it, in this case, the very person who ratified the document is the one who invalidated it. It is therefore necessary for the recipient to ratify the deed by means of the testimony of witnesses.

That the testimony of witnesses is powerful – דְּאַלִּימֵי עֵדִים: The Ritva explains that witnesses can invalidate even a document that has already been ratified. One might therefore have thought that only witnesses can invalidate a document with a different claim, e.g., that at the time they were not fit to bear witness. By contrast, one might have thought that the giver, who cannot invalidate a ratified document, cannot invalidate even a document that he himself ratified.

וְכֵן אָמַר רַבָּה: רְאָיָה בְּעֵדִים. אֲמַר לֵיהּ אַבַּיֵי: מַאי טַעֲמָא? אִי נֵימָא, מִדְּכוּלְּהוּ כְּתִיב בְּהוּ "כַּד הֲוָה מְהַלֵּךְ עַל רַגְלוֹהִי בְּשׁוּקָא", וּבְהָא לָא כְּתִיב בָּהּ – שְׁמַע מִינָּהּ שְׁכִיב מְרַע הֲוֵי. אַדְּרַבָּה, מִדְּכוּלְּהוּ כְּתִיב בְּהוּ: "כַּד קְצִיר וּרְמִי בְּעַרְסֵיהּ", וְהָא לָא כְּתִיב בָּהּ – שְׁמַע מִינָּהּ בָּרִיא הֲוֵי!

And Rabba also says: With regard to the **proof** that the recipients must present, it is presented **by** bringing **witnesses**[N] who testify that the giver was healthy. **Abaye said to him: What is the reason** for this? **If we say** that **due to** the fact **that in all** deeds of gift the following formulation **is written: When he was walking on his feet in the marketplace,** which indicates that the gift was the gift of a healthy person, **and in this** deed this **was not written,** therefore one may **conclude** from the deed that the giver **was on his deathbed,** that is not correct. **On the contrary,** one could say that **due to** the fact **that in all** deeds concerning the gifts of a person on his deathbed the following **is written: When he was sick and lying in his bed, and in this** deed this **was not written,** therefore one may **conclude from** the deed that the giver **was healthy.**

אִיכָּא לְמֵימַר הָכִי וְאִיכָּא לְמֵימַר הָכִי, אוֹקֵי מָמוֹנָא בְּחֶזְקַת מָרֵיהּ.

Rabba replied: Since one **can say this and** one **can say that,** nothing can be concluded from the formulation of the deed. Therefore, due to the uncertainty, **establish the property in the possession of its** last known **owner.**

וּבִפְלוּגְתָּא, דְּרַבִּי יוֹחָנָן אָמַר: רְאָיָה בְּעֵדִים, וְרַבִּי שִׁמְעוֹן בֶּן לָקִישׁ אָמַר: רְאָיָה בְּקִיּוּם הַשְּׁטָר.

And this dispute with regard to the statement of the Rabbis is also the subject **of a dispute** between other *amora'im*, **as Rabbi Yoḥanan says:** The **proof** is presented **by** bringing **witnesses, and Rabbi Shimon ben Lakish says:** The **proof** is presented **by** the **ratification of the deed.**

אֵיתִיבֵיהּ רַבִּי יוֹחָנָן לְרַבִּי שִׁמְעוֹן בֶּן לָקִישׁ: מַעֲשֶׂה בִּבְנֵי בְרַק בְּאֶחָד שֶׁמָּכַר בְּנִכְסֵי אָבִיו וּמֵת, וּבָאוּ בְּנֵי מִשְׁפָּחָה וְעִרְעֲרוּ לוֹמַר: קָטָן הָיָה בִּשְׁעַת מִיתָה, וּבָאוּ וְשָׁאֲלוּ אֶת רַבִּי עֲקִיבָא: מַהוּ לְבוֹדְקוֹ? אָמַר לָהֶם: אִי אַתֶּם רַשָּׁאִים לְנַוְּולוֹ; וְעוֹד, סִימָנִין עֲשׂוּיִין לְהִשְׁתַּנּוֹת לְאַחַר מִיתָה;

Rabbi Yoḥanan raised an objection to Rabbi Shimon ben Lakish from a *baraita*: There was **an incident in Bnei Brak involving one who sold** some **of his father's property**[H] that he had inherited, **and he died, and the members of his family came and contested** the sale, **saying: He was a minor**[N] **at the time of** his **death,** and therefore the sale was not valid. **And they came and asked Rabbi Akiva: What is the** *halakha*? Is it permitted to exhume the corpse in order **to examine it** and ascertain whether or not the heir was a minor at the time of his death? Rabbi Akiva **said to them:** It is **not permitted for you to disgrace him** for the sake of a monetary claim. **And furthermore, signs** indicating puberty **are likely to change**[N] **after death,** and therefore nothing can be proved by exhuming the body.

NOTES

And Rabba also says proof is presented by bringing witnesses – וְכֵן אָמַר רַבָּה רְאָיָה בְּעֵדִים: The early commentaries raise a difficulty: The Gemara (153b) cites Rabba as maintaining that one presumes that the current situation reflects the situation at the time the gift was bestowed, in accordance with the opinion of Rabbi Natan. Accordingly, the giver should not be required to bring witnesses, but only to ratify the deed. The Rosh maintains that Rabba retracted his opinion, accepting the objection of Abaye (153b). Other commentaries write that in one instance the Gemara is referring to Rabba, and in the other it is referring to Rava (see Ritva).

He was a minor – קָטָן הָיָה: One cannot sell the property he inherited from his father until he is twenty years old and has developed signs of puberty. In this case, the heir had reached the age of twenty, but his relatives claimed that he had not yet developed the signs of puberty, and therefore his sale was invalid.

Signs indicating puberty are likely to change – סִימָנִין עֲשׂוּיִין לְהִשְׁתַּנּוֹת: The signs indicating puberty are two pubic hairs. These hairs are not considered a sign of puberty if they grow on a mole. Rabbi Akiva told the buyers that even if they exhumed the body and discovered hairs that were not growing on a mole, it is possible that there had been a mole but it is no longer visible due to changes in the skin of the deceased (Ramah).

HALAKHA

Involving one who sold some of his father's property, etc. – בְּאֶחָד שֶׁמָּכַר בְּנִכְסֵי אָבִיו וכו׳: If one sells either his own property or property he inherited from his father and dies, and his relatives contest the sale, claiming that he was a minor at the time of the sale and that they wish to exhume the body in order to examine it and prove their claim, their request is denied. This is because it involves disgracing the corpse of the deceased, and furthermore, the signs indicating puberty are likely to change after death. It is also presumed that witnesses do not sign a bill of sale unless they know with certainty that the seller has reached majority (Rambam *Sefer Kinyan*, *Hilkhot Mekhira* 29:16; *Shulḥan Arukh*, *Yoreh De'a* 363:7 and *Ḥoshen Mishpat* 235:13, and in the comment of Rema).

Perek **IX**
Daf **154** Amud **b**

בִּשְׁלָמָא לְדִידִי דְּאָמִינָא רְאָיָה בְּעֵדִים, כֵּיוָן דַּאֲמַר לְלָקוֹחוֹת אַיְיתוּ עֵדִים וְלָא אַשְׁכָּחוּ – הַיְינוּ דְּקָא אָתוּ וְאָמְרוּ לֵיהּ: מַהוּ לְבוֹדְקוֹ; אֶלָּא לְדִידָךְ דְּאָמְרַתְּ רְאָיָה בְּקִיּוּם הַשְּׁטָר, לָמָּה לְהוּ לְבוֹדְקוֹ? לִקַיְּימוּ שְׁטָרַיְיהוּ וְלוֹקְמוּ בְּנִכְסֵי!

Rabbi Yoḥanan explains: **Granted, according to my** explanation of the mishna, **that I say** that the **proof** must be presented **by** bringing **witnesses,** I can explain the *baraita*. **Since** Rabbi Akiva **said to the buyers: Bring witnesses, and they did not find** witnesses, **this is** the reason **that they came and said to him: What is the** *halakha*? Is it permitted **to examine him? But according to you, that you say** that the **proof** is presented **by ratification of the deed, why do they** need **to examine him? Let them ratify their deed and they shall be established** as owners **of the property.**

מִי סָבְרַתְּ: נִכְסֵי בְּחֶזְקַת בְּנֵי מִשְׁפָּחָה קַיְימִי, וְקָא אָתוּ לָקוֹחוֹת וּמְעַרְעֲרִי? נִכְסֵי בְּחֶזְקַת לָקוֹחוֹת קַיְימִי, וְקָא אָתוּ בְּנֵי מִשְׁפָּחָה וְקָא מְעַרְעֲרִי.

Rabbi Shimon ben Lakish replies: **Do you maintain** that **the property stood in the possession of** the **members of** his **family and the buyers came and contested** their possession of the property? Rather, **the property stood in the possession of** the **buyers,**[N] and the **members of** his **family came and contested** the sale. Since they claimed that the deed was invalid, they could not prove their claim by ratifying the deed, but only by bringing witnesses or examining the body.

NOTES

The property stood in the possession of the buyers – נִכְסֵי בְּחֶזְקַת לָקוֹחוֹת קַיְימִי: This is because the bill of sale establishes the buyer as the owner, regardless of its prior status (Ritva, citing Ramban).

הָכִי נַמִּי מִסְתַּבְּרָא, מִדְּקָאָמַר לְהוּ: אִי אַתֶּם רַשָּׁאִים לְנַוְּולוֹ, וְאִישְׁתִּיקוּ; אִי אָמְרַתְּ בִּשְׁלָמָא בְּנֵי מִשְׁפָּחָה קָא מְעַרְעֲרֵי, מִשּׁוּם הָכִי אִישְׁתִּיקוּ, אֶלָּא אִי אָמְרַתְּ לָקוֹחוֹת קָא מְעַרְעֲרֵי, אַמַּאי שָׁתְקֵי? לֵימְרוּ לֵיהּ: אֲנַן זוּזֵי יָהֲבִינַן לֵיהּ, לִינַּוֵּול וְלִינַּוֵּול!

This, too, stands to reason, as Rabbi Akiva **said to** the claimants: **You are not permitted to disgrace him, and they were silent. Granted, if you say** that the **members of** his **family were contesting** the sale, **due to that** reason **they were silent,** as they accepted that they should not disgrace their relative. **But if you say** that the **buyers were contesting** the claim of the relatives, **why were they silent? They should have said to** Rabbi Akiva: **We gave him money,** and if our right to the property cannot be proven without disgracing him, **let him be disgraced.**

אִי מִשּׁוּם הָא לָא אִירְיָא, הָכִי קָאָמַר לְהוּ: חֲדָא, דְּאִי אַתֶּם רַשָּׁאִים לְנַוְּולוֹ; וְעוֹד, וְכִי תֵּימְרוּ זוּזֵי שְׁקַל, לִינַּוֵּול וְלִינַּוֵּול – סִימָנִים עֲשׂוּיִין לְהִשְׁתַּנּוֹת לְאַחַר מִיתָה.

The Gemara rejects this argument: **If it is due to that** reason, i.e., this claim they could have said, **there is no** conclusive **argument. This is what** Rabbi Akiva **said to them: One** reason to prohibit exhuming the body is **that you are not permitted to disgrace him. And furthermore, if you should say: He took** the **money; let him be disgraced,** in any event nothing can be proved by exhuming the body, as **signs** indicating puberty **are likely to change after death.**

תָּא שְׁמַע, שָׁאַל רַבִּי שִׁמְעוֹן בֶּן לָקִישׁ אֶת רַבִּי יוֹחָנָן, זוֹ שֶׁשְּׁנוּיָה בְּמִשְׁנַת בַּר קַפָּרָא: הֲרֵי שֶׁהָיָה אוֹכֵל שָׂדֶה וּבָא בְּחֶזְקַת שֶׁהִיא שֶׁלּוֹ, וְקָרָא עָלָיו אֶחָד עַרְעָר לוֹמַר: "שֶׁלִּי הִיא", וְהוֹצִיא זֶה אֶת אוֹנוֹ לוֹמַר: "שֶׁמְּכַרְתָּהּ לִי" אוֹ "שֶׁנְּתַתָּהּ לִי בְּמַתָּנָה", אִם אָמַר: "אֵינִי מַכִּיר בִּשְׁטָר זֶה מֵעוֹלָם" – יִתְקַיֵּים הַשְּׁטָר בְּחוֹתְמָיו.

The Gemara suggests: **Come and hear** a proof: **Rabbi Shimon ben Lakish asked**[N] **Rabbi Yoḥanan** about **that which is taught in the Mishna of bar Kappara:**[B] There was one **who was continually enjoying** the profits from **a field,**[H] and it was the **presumption that it was his, and someone contested his claim, saying: It is mine. And that** person, who was profiting from the field, **produced a deed,** in order **to say:** It is mine, **as you sold** this field **to me, or:** It is mine, **as you gave me** this field **as a gift. If** the one who protested his claim **said: I do not recognize that deed** as one that I have **ever** written, **the deed** must **be ratified through its signatures.**

אִם אָמַר: "שְׁטַר פַּסִּים הוּא זֶה". אוֹ "שְׁטַר אֲמָנָה, שֶׁמָּכַרְתִּי לְךָ וְלֹא נָתַתָּ לִי דָּמִים", אִם יֵשׁ עֵדִים – הַלֵּךְ אַחַר עֵדִים, וְאִם לָאו – הַלֵּךְ אַחַר הַשְּׁטָר;

If the one who protested his claim **said: This is a document of appeasement** [*shtar passim*],[L] a document written only so that the holder should appear wealthy, **or a document of trust,**[N] which means **that I sold** the field **to you** and provided you with the deed, trusting you to provide payment, **and** since **you did not give me** the **money** the sale is void, then **if there are witnesses, follow** the testimony of the **witnesses, and if not, follow the deed.**

לֵימָא, רַבִּי מֵאִיר הִיא, דְּאָמַר: מוֹדֶה בִּשְׁטָר שֶׁכְּתָבוֹ אֵינוֹ צָרִיךְ לְקַיְּימוֹ, וְלֹא רַבָּנַן?

Rabbi Shimon ben Lakish concludes: According to your explanation, the Rabbis maintain that even if the deed is ratified the claimant cannot take possession of the property without bringing witnesses. If so, **shall we say** that **this** *baraita* **is** in accordance with the opinion of **Rabbi Meir, who says** that when there is a debtor **who admits that he wrote** a promissory **note,** the creditor **is not required to ratify it** in court in order to collect payment, **and** it is **not** in accordance with the opinion of **the Rabbis?**

אֲמַר לֵיהּ: לָא, שֶׁאֲנִי אוֹמֵר: דִּבְרֵי הַכֹּל – מוֹדֶה בִּשְׁטָר שֶׁכְּתָבוֹ אֵינוֹ צָרִיךְ לְקַיְּימוֹ. וְהָא מִיפְלַג פְּלִיגִי! דִּתְנַן: אֵין נֶאֱמָנִין לְפוֹסְלוֹ, דִּבְרֵי רַבִּי מֵאִיר, וַחֲכָמִים אוֹמְרִים: נֶאֱמָנִין!

Rabbi Yoḥanan **said to** Rabbi Shimon ben Lakish: **No,** it is not so. **As I say** that **everyone agrees** that in the case of a debtor **who admits that he wrote** a promissory **note,** the creditor **is not required to ratify it** in court in order to collect payment. Rabbi Shimon ben Lakish asked: **But don't they disagree, as we learned** in a *baraita*: With regard to witnesses who ratified their signatures but claimed that they were not fit to bear witness when they signed the deed, their testimony is **not deemed credible to invalidate** the document; this is **the statement of Rabbi Meir. And the Rabbis say:** Their testimony is **deemed credible.**

NOTES

Come and hear, Rabbi Shimon ben Lakish asked – תָּא שְׁמַע שָׁאַל רַבִּי שִׁמְעוֹן בֶּן לָקִישׁ: According to some of the early commentaries, the term come and hear does not appear in the text of the Gemara. Accordingly, the exchange cited here is a continuation of the aforementioned discussion between Rabbi Yoḥanan and Reish Lakish with regard to whether the mishna is referring to presenting proof by the testimony of witnesses or by ratifying the deed (see Ramban). The Ri Migash explains the version of the text that includes the term: Come and hear. According to this version, the Gemara cites this exchange in order to demonstrate that in fact Rabbi Yoḥanan maintains that the mishna is referring to presenting proof by ratifying the deed (see Maharsha).

Document of trust – שְׁטַר אֲמָנָה: The sale of land is not effected by a deed until payment has been made. The seller claimed that since the buyer did not provide payment, the sale was nullified.

BACKGROUND

The Mishna of bar Kappara – מִשְׁנַת בַּר קַפָּרָא: Bar Kappara was one of the Sages of Eretz Yisrael in the transitional generation between the *tanna'im* and the *amora'im*. His first name is unknown, though some say it was Shimon. Bar Kappara was one of the more important students of Rabbi Yehuda HaNasi, and he was a colleague of Rabbi Ḥiyya. He assembled a unique collection of *baraitot* known as the Mishna of bar Kappara. These *baraitot* are usually introduced with the words: Bar Kappara taught. His halakhic statements are mentioned many times in the Talmud. His aggadic statements and expositions appear in both the Babylonian Talmud and the Jerusalem Talmud.

HALAKHA

One who was continually enjoying the profits from a field – הֲרֵי שֶׁהָיָה אוֹכֵל שָׂדֶה: The Gemara describes a case where one is in possession of a field and enjoying the profits thereof, and another person comes and claims that the field is his. The one in possession of the field claims that he purchased the field by means of a deed, which he produces, but the other litigant claims that the deed is forged, or that it was a document of trust. The *halakha* is that the holder of the deed must ratify it in order to retain possession of the field, and if he does not ratify his deed, the field is repossessed, as even when the seller admits that he wrote the deed, the recipient is required to ratify it (Rambam *Sefer Mishpatim, Hilkhot Malve VeLoveh* 14:5, 14; *Shulḥan Arukh, Ḥoshen Mishpat* 46:1, 82:1, 140:3 and *Beur HaGra* there).

LANGUAGE

Document of appeasement [*shtar passim*] – שְׁטַר פַּסִּים: The commentaries explain that the word *passim* comes from the term *piyyusim*, which is rabbinic Hebrew and means appeasement. This refers to a situation where one persuades another to accede to his request to write a false deed, according to which he ostensibly sold him a field, so that he can appear wealthy, for the purpose of marriage, or in order to obtain a loan. According to the Jerusalem Talmud, it appears that the term is: A document of *pistis*. The term is derived from the Greek πίστις, *pistis*, meaning trustworthiness. This indicates that the document is similar to a document of trust.

אֲמַר לֵיהּ: אִי עֵדִים אַלִּימֵי וּמַרְעִי שְׁטָרָא, אִיהוּ כָּל כְּמִינֵּיהּ? אֲמַר לֵיהּ, וַהֲלֹא מִשְּׁמְךָ אָמְרוּ: יָפֶה עִרְעֲרוּ בְּנֵי מִשְׁפָּחָה! אֲמַר לֵיהּ: זוֹ אֶלְעָזָר אֲמָרָהּ, אֲנִי לֹא אָמַרְתִּי דָּבָר זֶה מֵעוֹלָם.

Rabbi Yoḥanan **said to** Rabbi Shimon ben Lakish: Even **if** the testimony of **witnesses is powerful and they impair** the validity of the **deed,** which they admit to have written, with regard to **him,** the giver, **is it in his** power to impair the validity of a deed that he admits to have written? Rabbi Shimon ben Lakish **said to** Rabbi Yoḥanan: **But wasn't it stated in your name** with regard to the aforementioned incident in Bnei Brak: The **members of** his **family contested** the claim **correctly,** even though they admitted that the deed was authentic? This means that the claimant is required to ratify the deed. Rabbi Yoḥanan **said to** Rabbi Shimon ben Lakish: **That** statement **was stated** in my name by Rabbi **Elazar,**[N] my disciple, but **I never said that statement.**

אָמַר רַבִּי זֵירָא: אִם יִכְפּוֹר רַבִּי יוֹחָנָן בְּרַבִּי אֶלְעָזָר תַּלְמִידוֹ, יִכְפּוֹר בְּרַבִּי יַנַּאי רַבּוֹ? דְּאָמַר רַבִּי יַנַּאי אָמַר רַבִּי: מוֹדֶה בִּשְׁטָר שֶׁכְּתָבוֹ אֵינוֹ צָרִיךְ לְקַיְּימוֹ, וְאָמַר לֵיהּ רַבִּי יוֹחָנָן: רַבִּי, לֹא מִשְׁנָתֵנוּ הִיא זוֹ? וַחֲכָמִים אוֹמְרִים: הַמּוֹצִיא מֵחֲבֵירוֹ עָלָיו הָרְאָיָה, אֵין רְאָיָה אֶלָּא בְּקִיּוּם הַשְּׁטָר!

Rabbi Zeira says: If Rabbi Yoḥanan denies the statement **of Rabbi Elazar, his disciple, will** Rabbi Yoḥanan also **deny that** which he said to **Rabbi Yannai, his teacher?** This is **as Rabbi Yannai says** that **Rabbi** Yehuda HaNasi **says:** When there is a debtor **who admits that he wrote** a promissory **note,** the creditor **is not required to ratify it** in court in order to collect the payment. **And Rabbi Yoḥanan said to** Rabbi Yannai: **My teacher, is this not** the case discussed in **our mishna,** which states to the contrary: **And the Rabbis say: The burden of proof rests upon the claimant?** Rabbi Yoḥanan concludes: The **proof** mentioned in this mishna **is nothing other** than **ratification of the deed.** This indicates that Rabbi Yoḥanan maintains that according to the opinion of the Rabbis, the recipient is required to ratify the deed. If so, why does he state that everyone agrees that the recipient is not required to ratify the deed?

בְּרַם נְרָאִין דִּבְרֵי רַבֵּינוּ יוֹסֵף, דְּאָמַר רַבֵּינוּ יוֹסֵף אָמַר רַב יְהוּדָה אָמַר שְׁמוּאֵל: זוֹ דִּבְרֵי חֲכָמִים, אֲבָל רַבִּי מֵאִיר אוֹמֵר: מוֹדֶה בִּשְׁטָר שֶׁכְּתָבוֹ שֶׁצָּרִיךְ לְקַיְּימוֹ. וּמַאי "דִּבְרֵי הַכֹּל"? דְּרַבָּנַן לְגַבֵּי רַבִּי מֵאִיר דִּבְרֵי הַכֹּל הִיא.

Rabbi Zeira explains: **Indeed, the statement of our teacher,** Rav **Yosef, appears** to be correct, **as our teacher** Rav **Yosef says** that **Rav Yehuda says** that **Shmuel says:** The opinions here should be reversed. **This,** the *baraita* taught by bar Kappara, according to which the deed does not require ratification, **is the statement of the Rabbis. But Rabbi Meir says** that when there is a debtor **who admits that he wrote** a promissory **note,** the creditor **is not required to ratify it** in court in order to collect payment. **And what** is the meaning of Rabbi Yoḥanan's statement that **everyone agrees** that in this case, the recipient is not required to ratify the deed? Rabbi Yoḥanan means that this is the statement of the Rabbis, and a statement **of the Rabbis that** is disputed only **by Rabbi Meir is** tantamount to **a statement** accepted **by all.**

וְהָא אִיפְּכָא תְּנַן, וַחֲכָמִים אוֹמְרִים: הַמּוֹצִיא מֵחֲבֵירוֹ עָלָיו הָרְאָיָה! אֵיפּוֹךְ. וְהָא תַּנְיָא: אֵין נֶאֱמָנִין לְפוֹסְלוֹ, דִּבְרֵי רַבִּי מֵאִיר, וַחֲכָמִים אוֹמְרִים: נֶאֱמָנִין! אֵיפּוֹךְ.

The Gemara asks: **But didn't we learn the opposite** in the mishna: **And the Rabbis say** that **the burden of proof rests upon the claimant?** This means that the recipient is required to ratify the deed. The Gemara replies: **Reverse** the opinions in the mishna. The Gemara asks: **But isn't it taught** in a *baraita*: With regard to witnesses who ratified their signatures but claimed that they were not fit to bear witness, their testimony is **not deemed credible to invalidate** the document; this is **the statement of Rabbi Meir. And the Rabbis say:** Their testimony is **deemed credible.** This indicates that according to the Rabbis the document requires ratification. The Gemara answers: Here too, **reverse** the opinions.

וְהָא רַבִּי יוֹחָנָן רְאָיָה בְּעֵדִים קָאָמַר! אֵיפּוֹךְ. לֵימָא, לֵיפּוֹךְ נָמֵי תְּיוּבְתָּא? לָא,

The Gemara asks: **But doesn't Rabbi Yoḥanan say** with regard to the proof that the recipient is required to bring, that the **proof** is presented **by** bringing **witnesses**[N] who testify that the giver was healthy, and not by ratifying the deed? The Gemara answers: **Reverse** the opinions of Rabbi Yoḥanan and Rabbi Shimon ben Lakish. Rabbi Yoḥanan maintains that the recipient is required to prove his claim only by ratifying the deed, whereas Rabbi Shimon ben Lakish maintains that the recipient is required to bring witnesses. The Gemara asks: **Shall we say** that we should **also reverse the objection** that Rabbi Yoḥanan raised to Rabbi Shimon ben Lakish previously, and say that Rabbi Shimon ben Lakish raised the objection to Rabbi Yoḥanan? The Gemara answers: **No,** that is unnecessary.

NOTES

That statement was stated by Rabbi Elazar – **זוֹ אֶלְעָזָר אֲמָרָהּ**: Rabbi Elazar was the preeminent disciple of Rabbi Yoḥanan. Rabbi Yoḥanan explained that Rabbi Elazar may have erred and attributed the statement to him. Alternatively, Rabbi Elazar may have stated this as his own opinion, but since many of his statements derived from what he had learned from Rabbi Yoḥanan, the listeners were under the impression that he was citing Rabbi Yoḥanan (Ri Migash; Ramah).

But doesn't Rabbi Yoḥanan say the proof is presented by witnesses – **וְהָא רַבִּי יוֹחָנָן רְאָיָה בְּעֵדִים קָאָמַר**: According to the Rashbam, Rabbi Zeira reversed the opinions in the mishna in order to explain the opinion of Rabbi Yoḥanan. Rabbi Yoḥanan himself holds in accordance with the opinion of the Rabbis, that when the giver admits that he wrote the deed, the recipient is not required to ratify it. According to the majority of the commentaries, although Rabbi Zeira maintains that the opinions in the mishna should be reversed, Rabbi Yoḥanan does not. According to this explanation, the Gemara here reverts to the understanding that the opinions in the mishna do not need to be reversed in order to discuss the contradicting statements of Rabbi Yoḥanan: Rabbi Yoḥanan says to Rabbi Yannai that the proof is presented by ratification of the deed, whereas Rabbi Yoḥanan previously stated that the proof is presented by bringing witnesses (see Rabbeinu Gershom Meor HaGola).

הָכִי קָאָמַר לֵיהּ רַבִּי יוֹחָנָן לְרַבִּי שִׁמְעוֹן בֶּן לָקִישׁ: בִּשְׁלָמָא לְדִידִי דְּאָמִינָא רְאָיָה בְּקִיּוּם הַשְּׁטָר, הַיְינוּ דְּמַשְׁכַּחַתְּ לָהּ דְּנָחְתִּי לָקוֹחוֹת לַנְּכָסִים, אֶלָּא לְדִידָךְ דְּאָמְרַתְּ רְאָיָה בְּעֵדִים, הֵיכִי מַשְׁכַּחַתְּ לָהּ דְּנָחְתִּי לָקוֹחוֹת בַּנְּכָסִים?

This is what Rabbi Yoḥanan said to Rabbi Shimon ben Lakish: Granted, according to my explanation of the mishna, **that I say** that presenting **proof through** the **ratification of the deed** is sufficient in order to enable the recipient to claim the gift, **this is** the reason **that** with regard to the incident in Bnei Brak **you find** the possibility **that the buyers take possession of the property**[N] by ratifying the deed. It is therefore possible that the buyers held the property, and the relatives were claiming it from them. **But according to you, that you say** that the **proof** must be presented **by** bringing **witnesses, how can you find** circumstances in **which the buyers take possession of the property,** since they have no proof?

אֲמַר לֵיהּ: מוֹדֵינָא לָךְ בְּעַרְעָר דִּבְנֵי מִשְׁפָּחָה דְּלָאו עַרְעָר הוּא, מַאי קָאָמְרִי? קָטָן הָיָה – חֲזָקָה אֵין הָעֵדִים חוֹתְמִין עַל הַשְּׁטָר אֶלָּא אִם כֵּן נַעֲשָׂה גָּדוֹל.

Rabbi Shimon ben Lakish **said to** Rabbi Yoḥanan: **I concede to you with regard to** a case **where the members of** the deceased's **family contested** the legality of the buyers' claim **that** their **contesting** the legality of that claim **is not** taken into consideration, since they are contesting the deed held by the buyers. It is therefore possible for the buyers to take possession of the property, as in this case **what do** the relatives **say?** They say that the seller **was a minor.** But there is a **presumption** that **witnesses do not sign the document unless** the seller **has become an adult.**[H] In the mishna, by contrast, there is no presumption that counters the giver's claim that he was on his deathbed. The recipient is therefore required to bring proof that the giver was healthy.

אִיתְּמַר: קָטָן מֵאֵימָתַי מוֹכֵר בְּנִכְסֵי אָבִיו? רָבָא אָמַר רַב נַחְמָן: בֶּן שְׁמֹנֶה עֶשְׂרֵה שָׁנָה, וְרַב הוּנָא בַּר חִינָּנָא אָמַר רַב נַחְמָן: מִבֶּן עֶשְׂרִים שָׁנָה. וְהָא דְּרָבָא לָאו בְּפֵירוּשׁ אִיתְּמַר אֶלָּא מִכְּלָלָא אִיתְּמַר.

§ **It was stated** that there was a dispute with regard to the following matter: **From when,** i.e., from what age, **can a minor sell his** deceased **father's property?**[NH] **Rava** says that **Rav Naḥman says:** From the time he is **eighteen years old, and Rav Huna bar Ḥinnana** says that **Rav Naḥman says: From** the time he is **twenty years old.** The Gemara notes: **And this** statement **of Rava was not stated explicitly; rather, it was stated by inference.**

מְתִיב רַבִּי זֵירָא: מַעֲשֶׂה בִּבְנֵי בְּרַק בְּאֶחָד שֶׁמָּכַר בְּנִכְסֵי אָבִיו וּמֵת, וּבָאוּ בְּנֵי מִשְׁפָּחָה וְעִרְעֲרוּ לוֹמַר קָטָן הָיָה בִּשְׁעַת מִיתָה, וּבָאוּ וְשָׁאֲלוּ אֶת רַבִּי עֲקִיבָא: מַהוּ לְבוֹדְקוֹ? אָמַר לָהֶם: אִי אַתֶּם רַשָּׁאִין לְנַוְּולוֹ; וְעוֹד, סִימָנִין עֲשׂוּיִין לְהִשְׁתַּנּוֹת לְאַחַר מִיתָה; בִּשְׁלָמָא לְמַאן דְּאָמַר בֶּן שְׁמֹנֶה עֶשְׂרֵה שָׁנָה,

Rabbi Zeira raises an objection from the aforementioned *baraita*: There was **an incident in Bnei Brak involving one who sold** some **of his father's property,** which he had inherited, **and he died,** and the **members of** his **family came and contested** the sale, **saying: He was a minor at the time of** his **death,** and therefore the sale was not valid. **And they came and asked Rabbi Akiva: What is** the *halakha*? Is it permitted to exhume the corpse in order **to examine it** and ascertain whether or not the heir was a minor at the time of his death? Rabbi Akiva **said to them:** It is **not permitted** for **you to disgrace him** for the sake of a monetary claim. **And furthermore, signs** indicating puberty **are likely to change after death,** and therefore nothing can be proved by exhuming the body. Rabbi Zeira explains the objection: **Granted, according to the one who says** that the heir can sell the property once he is **eighteen years old,**

NOTES

That the buyers take possession of the property – **דְּנָחְתִּי לָקוֹחוֹת לַנְּכָסִים**: According to the majority of commentaries, the buyers take possession of the property by ratifying the deed (Rabbeinu Gershom Meor HaGola). According to the Rashbam, Rabbi Yoḥanan holds that the deed does not require ratification, and the deed enables the buyers to take possession of the property without further proof of their claim.

From when can a minor sell his deceased father's property – **קָטָן מֵאֵימָתַי מוֹכֵר בְּנִכְסֵי אָבִיו**: According to some of the *ge'onim*, this *halakha* applies to any property owned by a minor. The Gemara refers to inheritance only because this is the most common way for a minor to acquire property. This is also the opinion of Rabbeinu Tam and the Rid. Other commentaries maintain that this restriction pertains only to property that a minor inherits from his father. It does not apply to property that he purchased or even to property that his father transferred to him as a gift during his lifetime (Rif; Rashbam; Meiri). The Ritva adds that this restriction also applies to inheritance received by a minor from other relatives.

The Ra'ah and the Rashba explain that the restriction applies only to the inheritance that a minor receives from his father. According to their opinion, the Sages instituted that a minor cannot sell his inheritance because they wished to ensure that he would not squander it. They instituted this ordinance only with regard to inheritance from one's father, which is common, but not with regard to other forms of inheritance, which are less common.

HALAKHA

A presumption that witnesses do not sign the document unless he has become an adult – **חֲזָקָה אֵין הָעֵדִים חוֹתְמִין עַל הַשְּׁטָר אֶלָּא אִם כֵּן נַעֲשָׂה גָּדוֹל**: There is a presumption that witnesses do not sign a bill of sale or a promissory note unless they know with certainty that the person incurring liability by means of the deed has reached his majority. Even if the witnesses claim that they signed the document when that person was a minor, their claim is not accepted, as they are claiming to have signed the document illegally, and if the testimony of a witness renders him wicked, his testimony in inadmissible (Rambam *Sefer Kinyan, Hilkhot Mekhira* 29:9 and *Sefer Mishpatim, Hilkhot Malve VeLoveh* 24:5; *Shulḥan Arukh, Ḥoshen Mishpat* 46:38, 235:3).

From when can a minor sell his deceased father's property – **קָטָן מֵאֵימָתַי מוֹכֵר בְּנִכְסֵי אָבִיו**: One cannot sell land inherited from one's father or from other relatives, or land received as the gift of a person on his deathbed, until he is twenty years old and has developed signs of puberty. He cannot sell the property before this time even if he has developed signs of puberty, and even if he understands the nature of business negotiations, lest he sell the property for less than its value, as a child is by nature attracted to money and does not yet comprehend the ways of the world. Once he has reached this age he can sell the property even if he does not understand the nature of business negotiations. This ruling is in accordance with the Gemara's conclusion (Rambam *Sefer Mishpatim, Hilkhot Malve VeLoveh* 14:13; *Shulḥan Arukh, Ḥoshen Mishpat* 235:9).

הַיְינוּ דְּקָאָתוּ וְאָמְרוּ לֵיהּ: מַהוּ לְבוֹדְקוֹ; אֶלָּא אִי אָמְרַתְּ מִבֶּן עֶשְׂרִים, כִּי בָּדְקוּ לֵיהּ מַאי הָוֵי? וְהָא תְּנַן: בֶּן עֶשְׂרִים שֶׁלֹּא הֵבִיא שְׁתֵּי שְׂעָרוֹת – יָבִיאוּ רְאָיָה שֶׁהוּא בֶּן עֶשְׂרִים, וְהוּא הַסָּרִיס לֹא חוֹלֵץ וְלֹא מְיַיבֵּם!

this is the reason **that they came and said to** Rabbi Akiva: **What is the** *halakha*? Is it permitted **to examine** the corpse? **But if you say** that he can sell the property **from** the time he is **twenty** years **old, even if they examine him, what of it? But didn't we learn** in a mishna (*Nidda* 47b): With regard to **a twenty-year-old** man **who did not develop two** pubic **hairs,**[HB] **proof must be brought that he is twenty** years **old,** and then he is no longer considered a minor. **And he is the sexually underdeveloped man,** who is excluded from the mitzva of levirate marriage. Therefore, if his married brother dies childless, **he neither performs *ḥalitza* nor enters into levirate marriage**[H] with his widow. Since a twenty-year-old is considered an adult even if he has not developed signs of puberty, there is no reason to examine the body.

לָאו אִיתְּמַר עֲלָהּ, אָמַר רַבִּי שְׁמוּאֵל בַּר רַב יִצְחָק אָמַר רַב: וְהוּא שֶׁנּוֹלְדוּ בּוֹ סִימָנֵי סָרִיס? אֲמַר רָבָא: דַּיְקָא נַמִּי, דְּקָתָנֵי: וְהוּא הַסָּרִיס, שְׁמַע מִינָּהּ.

The Gemara replies: **Wasn't it stated with regard to that** mishna: **Rabbi Shmuel bar Rav Yitzḥak says** that **Rav says: And** is **this** the *halakha* only **where he developed the signs of a sexually underdeveloped man?** Otherwise, a twenty-year-old who has not developed two pubic hairs is still considered a minor. The examination of the deceased could therefore be effective to see if he has other signs of being sexually underdeveloped. **Rava said:** The language of the mishna **is also precise, as it teaches: And he is the sexually underdeveloped man.** The usage of the definitive article indicates that the mishna is referring to one who is clearly a sexually underdeveloped man. The Gemara affirms: One can **conclude from** the mishna that the mishna is speaking of one who developed the signs of a sexually underdeveloped man.

וְכִי לֹא נוֹלְדוּ לוֹ סִימָנֵי סָרִיס, עַד כַּמָּה? תָּנֵי רַבִּי חִיָּיא: עַד רוֹב שְׁנוֹתָיו. כִּי אֲתָא לְקַמֵּיהּ דְּרַבִּי חִיָּיא, אִי כְּחִישׁ – אֲמַר לְהוּ: לִיבְרֵי, וְאִי אַבְרֵי – אֲמַר לְהוּ: לִיכְחוֹשׁ, דְּהָנֵי סִימָנֵי זִמְנִין דְּאָתוּ מֵחֲמַת כְּחִישׁוּתָא, זִמְנִין דְּאָתוּ מֵחֲמַת בְּרִיּוּתָא.

The Gemara asks: **And if he did not develop the signs of a sexually underdeveloped man,**[H] **until when** is he considered a minor if he does not develop two pubic hairs? **Rabbi Ḥiyya teaches** in a *baraita*: He is considered a minor **until most of his years** have elapsed,[N] i.e., until he is thirty-five years old. **When** the case of one who had not developed pubic hair **would come before Rabbi Ḥiyya,** he would offer the following advice: **If** the person was **thin, he** would **say to** those appearing in court: Cause him **to become fat, and if he was fat,** he would **say to them:** Cause him **to become thin.** This is **because these signs** indicating puberty **sometimes develop due to** excessive **thinness,** and **sometimes they develop due to corpulence.**[B]

אִיבַּעְיָא לְהוּ: תּוֹךְ זְמַן כְּלִפְנֵי זְמַן, אוֹ כִּלְאַחַר זְמַן? (אָמַר) רָבָא אָמַר רַב נַחְמָן: תּוֹךְ זְמַן כְּלִפְנֵי זְמַן; רָבָא בַּר רַב שֵׁילָא אָמַר רַב נַחְמָן: תּוֹךְ זְמַן כִּלְאַחַר זְמַן.

§ **A dilemma was raised before** the Sages: **During** the **time,** i.e., the year, when a minor comes of age with regard to selling his deceased father's property, i.e., during his eighteenth or twentieth year, is this year considered **as before** the **time** that he comes of age **or** is it considered **as after the time?** Does one come of age at the beginning or end of that year? **Rava says** that **Rav Naḥman says: During** that **time** is considered **as before** the **time,**[H] and he does not come of age until the year has elapsed. **Rava bar Rav Sheila** says that **Rav Naḥman says: During** that **time** is considered **as after** the **time,** and he is considered as having come of age during that year.

HALAKHA

A twenty-year-old man who did not develop two pubic hairs – בֶּן עֶשְׂרִים שֶׁלֹּא הֵבִיא שְׁתֵּי שְׂעָרוֹת: With regard to one who has not developed two pubic hairs by his twentieth year, if he has developed one of the signs of a sexually underdeveloped man, he assumes the status of a sexually underdeveloped man. He is retroactively considered to have become an adult from the age of thirteen and one day. If he sold land from that age onward, the sale is valid (see Ramah). One is considered to have reached his twentieth year from the time that he is nineteen years and thirty days old (*Tur*). Others maintain that he must be twenty years old less thirty days (Rambam). If he has not developed one of the signs of a sexually underdeveloped man, he assumes neither the status of a sexually underdeveloped man nor that of an adult. This pertains both to the *halakhot* of *ḥalitza* and to the validity of his sale. If one develops two facial hairs, even though he has not developed two pubic hairs, he does not assume the status of a sexually underdeveloped man. He retains the status of a minor until he develops all of the signs of a sexually underdeveloped man (Rambam *Sefer Nashim, Hilkhot Ishut* 2:11; *Shulḥan Arukh, Even HaEzer* 172:4, 6, 155:12 and *Ḥoshen Mishpat* 235:11–12).

The sexually underdeveloped man, he neither performs *ḥalitza* nor enters into levirate marriage – הַסָּרִיס לֹא חוֹלֵץ וְלֹא מְיַיבֵּם: One who is sexually underdeveloped due to natural causes is not eligible to perform *ḥalitza* or to enter into levirate marriage, nor is *ḥalitza* performed for his widow. If he did perform *ḥalitza*, or *ḥalitza* was performed for his widow, this is a meaningless act. The Rema cites the Rivash, who states that nowadays, even if one develops the signs of a sexually underdeveloped man, his status is uncertain. This is because today no one possesses the expertise to determine this status, and it is possible that he developed pubic hairs but they fell out. Therefore, it is correct to require that he perform *ḥalitza* (Rambam *Sefer Nashim, Hilkhot Yibbum VaḤalitza* 6:2; *Shulḥan Arukh, Even HaEzer* 172:1, 6, and in the comment of Rema).

He did not develop the signs of a sexually underdeveloped man – לֹא נוֹלְדוּ לוֹ סִימָנֵי סָרִיס: With regard to one who has not developed two pubic hairs and who has not developed the signs of a sexually underdeveloped man, when he reaches the age of thirty-five years and one day he assumes the status of a sexually underdeveloped man, and he is considered to have reached adulthood (Rambam *Sefer Nashim, Hilkhot Yibbum VaḤalitza* 6:11–12 and *Sefer Kinyan, Hilkhot Mekhira* 29:14; *Shulḥan Arukh, Even HaEzer* 155:12, 172:6 and *Ḥoshen Mishpat* 235:11).

During that time is considered as before the time – תּוֹךְ זְמַן כְּלִפְנֵי זְמַן: One cannot sell property that he inherited from his father until he is twenty years old, in accordance with the opinion of Rava (Rambam *Sefer Kinyan, Hilkhot Mekhira* 29:17; *Shulḥan Arukh, Ḥoshen Mishpat* 235:9).

NOTES

Most of his years have elapsed – רוֹב שְׁנוֹתָיו: The verse states: "The days of our years are seventy years" (Psalms 90:10). Once one reaches the age of thirty-five and one day he or she acquires the status of one who has reached majority, even without having developed signs of puberty or the signs of a sexually underdeveloped man or woman (Rashbam; Rambam).

BACKGROUND

A twenty-year-old man who did not develop two pubic hairs – בֶּן עֶשְׂרִים שֶׁלֹּא הֵבִיא שְׁתֵּי שְׂעָרוֹת: Delayed puberty is a known medical phenomenon that can occur both in males and in females. It is caused by insufficient hormonal secretions, which prevent the development of secondary sexual characteristics, e.g., pubic hair. Sometimes the delay is temporary, and the individual reaches complete sexual maturity a few years after the typical time. In some cases, sexual development ceases, causing a permanent state of sexual underdevelopment.

Thinness, corpulence – כְּחִישׁוּת, בְּרִיּוּתָא: Delayed puberty may be congenital, but it may also be caused by other factors. Malnutrition is known to delay the onset of puberty, sometimes by several years. Obesity can lead to hormonal imbalances, which may also delay the onset of puberty. Furthermore, hormonal imbalances may themselves cause weight problems.

וְהָא דְּרָבָא לָאו בְּפֵירוּשׁ אִיתְּמַר אֶלָּא מִכְּלָלָא אִיתְּמַר, דְּהַהוּא תּוֹךְ זְמַן דַּאֲזַל זַבֵּין נִכְסֵי וַאֲתָא לְקַמֵּיהּ דְּרָבָא, אֲמַר לְהוּ: לֹא עָשָׂה וְלֹא כְּלוּם; מַאן דַּחֲזָא סָבַר: מִשּׁוּם דְּתוֹךְ זְמַן כִּלְפְנֵי זְמַן, וְלָא הִיא, הָתָם שְׁטוּתָא יְתֵירְתָּא חֲזָא בֵּיהּ, דַּהֲוָה קָא מְשַׁחְרֵר לְהוּ לְעַבְדֵּיהּ.

The Gemara notes: **And this statement of Rava was not stated explicitly; rather, it was stated by inference. As** there was **a certain** person who was **during the time,** i.e., the year, when one comes of age **who went** and **sold** his father's **property, and** the case **came before Rava.** Rava **said to** the litigants: **He did not do anything,** and the sale is not valid. **One who observed** Rava's ruling **assumed** that he ruled in this manner **because** he maintained **that during** the **time** when he comes of age is considered **as before** the **time. But** that **is not so.** The reason for Rava's ruling was that **there,** Rava **observed excessive mental incompetence in** the behavior of that individual, **as he was emancipating his slaves.**[N] Since Rava saw that he was mentally incompetent, he invalidated the sale.

שְׁלַח לֵיהּ גִּידֵּל בַּר מְנַשְׁיָא לְרָבָא, יְלַמְּדֵנוּ רַבֵּינוּ: תִּינוֹקֶת בַּת אַרְבַּע עֶשְׂרֵה שָׁנָה וְיוֹם אֶחָד יוֹדַעַת בְּטִיב מַשָּׂא וּמַתָּן, מַהוּ? שְׁלַח לֵיהּ: אִם יוֹדַעַת בְּטִיב מַשָּׂא וּמַתָּן – מִקָּחָהּ מִקָּח וּמִמְכָּרָהּ מִמְכָּר.

§ **Giddel bar Menashya sent** an inquiry **to Rava: Let our teacher instruct us:** With regard to **a girl** who is **fourteen years and one day old**[H] who **understands**[N] **the nature of business** negotiations, **what is** the *halakha*? Can she sell property that she inherited from her father? Rava **sent** a reply **to** Giddel bar Menashya: **If she understands the nature of business** negotiations **her purchase is** a valid **purchase**[N] **and her sale is** a valid **sale.**

וְלִישְׁלַח לֵיהּ: תִּינוֹק! מַעֲשֶׂה שֶׁהָיָה כָּךְ הָיָה. וְלִישְׁלַח לֵיהּ: תִּינוֹקֶת בַּת שְׁתֵּים עֶשְׂרֵה שָׁנָה וְיוֹם אֶחָד! מַעֲשֶׂה שֶׁהָיָה כָּךְ הָיָה.

The Gemara asks: **But** Giddel **could have sent** this question **to** Rava with regard to **a boy.** Why did he not do so? The Gemara answers: **The incident that took place, took place in this way.** The Gemara asks: **But he could have sent** this question **to** Rava with regard to **a girl** who is **twelve years and one day old,** at which age a girl reaches her majority. Why did he not do so? The Gemara answers: **The incident that took place, took place in this way.**

וְהָא דְּרָבָא לָאו בְּפֵירוּשׁ אִיתְּמַר אֶלָּא מִכְּלָלָא אִיתְּמַר, דְּהַהוּא פָּחוֹת מִבֶּן עֶשְׂרִים דַּאֲזַל זַבֵּין נִכְסֵי אֲבוּהּ, כְּגִידֵּל בַּר מְנַשְׁיָא, אֲתָא לְקַמֵּיהּ דְּרָבָא. אֲמַרוּ לֵיהּ קְרוֹבֵיהּ: זִיל אֱכוֹל תַּמְרֵי וּשְׁדֵי בֵּיהּ קַשְׁיָיתָא בֵּי רָבָא, עֲבַד הָכִי; אֲמַר לְהוּ: זְבִינֵיהּ לָאו זְבִינֵי.

The Gemara notes: **And this statement of Rava was not stated explicitly; rather, it was stated by inference,** as it was inferred from the following incident. There was **a certain** person who was **under twenty** years **old** and understood business negotiations **who went** and **sold his father's property, in accordance with** the ruling that Rava sent to **Giddel bar Menashya,** and the case **came before Rava.** The seller's **relatives said to** the one who sold the property: **Go eat dates and throw** the **pits into Rava's house,** in order to prove to Rava that their relative was not mentally competent. **He did so.** Rava **said to them: His sale** is **not** a valid **sale.**

HALAKHA

A girl fourteen years and one day old, etc. – **תִּינוֹקֶת בַּת אַרְבַּע עֶשְׂרֵה שָׁנָה וְיוֹם אֶחָד וכו׳**: A minor cannot sell land. With regard to a boy of thirteen and a girl of twelve who have developed two pubic hairs, they can sell land only if they understand the nature of business negotiations. This pertains only to land that they purchased or received as the gift of a healthy person. With regard to land inherited from one's father or from other relatives, or land bequeathed to him as the gift of a person on his deathbed, he cannot sell it until he reaches the age of twenty years and develops two pubic hairs. This ruling is in accordance with the explanation of the majority of the early commentaries that the inquiry sent to Rava was not referring to inherited property (Rambam *Sefer Kinyan, Hilkhot Mekhira* 29:12; *Shulḥan Arukh, Ḥoshen Mishpat* 235:1, 8, 9).

NOTES

As he was emancipating his slaves – **דַּהֲוָה קָא מְשַׁחְרֵר לְהוּ לְעַבְדֵּיהּ**: He was squandering his property without reason (Rashbam). Rabbeinu Yona notes that actions of this kind are not listed among the signs of mental incompetence (see *Ḥagiga* 3b). He explains that this pertains only to the matter of selling property. The sale of one who squanders his property without reason is not valid, since this indicates that he does not understand the nature of business. Despite this, he does not have the status of one who is mentally incompetent, who is exempt from the obligation to perform mitzvot. According to the Rosh this applies only with regard to one who has not yet reached the age of twenty. The sale of one who has come of age is valid provided that he is not shown to be completely mentally incompetent.

A girl fourteen years and one day old who understands, etc. – **בַּת אַרְבַּע עֶשְׂרֵה שָׁנָה וְיוֹם אֶחָד יוֹדַעַת וכו׳**: The discussion here clearly pertains to the sale of land, since movable property can be sold by a girl of twelve and a boy of thirteen. The Rashbam explains that the Gemara is referring to a girl who sold property that she inherited from her father. A girl of twelve and a boy of thirteen can sell land if they are astute and understand the nature of business negotiations. If they are not demonstrably astute, they cannot sell land until they reach the age of either eighteen or twenty. Many of the early commentaries maintain that in any event one cannot sell property inherited from one's father until he is twenty. The discussion here pertains to property that one purchased or received as a gift and did not inherit from his father. This property can be sold by an individual who has reached majority if he understands the nature of business negotiations (Rif; Ramah; Rabbeinu Yona).

Her purchase is a valid purchase – **מִקָּחָהּ מִקָּח**: *Tosafot* write that this phrase is superfluous, as anyone who has reached majority can purchase land. Conversely, the Ri Migash maintains that a person who cannot sell land because he does not understand the nature of business negotiations also cannot purchase land.

NOTES

We said it is valid only with regard to movable property – **לָא אֲמָרַן אֶלָּא לְמִטַּלְטְלֵי**: The presumption is that any person who has reached majority possesses sufficient understanding to conduct transactions with regard to movable property. Therefore, his testimony with regard to movable property is accepted, as it is presumed to be accurate (see Rabbeinu Gershom Meor HaGola and Ritva). *Tosafot* write that with regard to testimony, there is no difference between movable property and land. The Gemara is referring only to testimony with regard to the value of the land. In this case the testimony of one who is not old enough to sell property is not accepted, as it is possible that he did not assess the value of the land correctly.

כִּי קָא כָּתְבוּ לֵיהּ שְׁטָרָא, אֲמַרוּ לֵיהּ לָקוֹחוֹת, זִיל אֵימָא לֵיהּ לְרָבָא: מְגִלַּת אֶסְתֵּר בְּזוּזָא, שְׁטָרָא דְּמָר בְּזוּזָא? אֲזַל אֲמַר לֵיהּ; אֲמַר לְהוּ: זְבִינֵיהּ זְבִינֵי. אֲמַרוּ לֵיהּ קְרוֹבֵיהּ: לָקוֹחוֹת אַגְמַרוּהוּ! אֲמַר לְהוּ: מַסְבְּרִי לֵיהּ סָבַר, כֵּיוָן דְּמַסְבְּרִי לֵיהּ וְסָבַר – מֵידַע יָדַע, וְהַאי דַּעֲבַד הָכִי – חוּצְפָּא יְתֵירָא הוּא דַּהֲוָה בֵּיהּ.

When they were writing for him a writ containing the decision, **the buyers said to** the seller, in order to prove that he was mentally competent: **Go and say to Rava: The scroll of Esther,** which is a large scroll, is bought **for a dinar.** Why then does **the** short **writ** containing **Master's** ruling also cost **a dinar,** which was the scribe's fee? The seller **went and said** this **to** Rava. Rava **said to them: His sale** is a valid **sale. The** boy's **relatives said to** Rava: **The buyers taught him** to say that. Rava **said to them:** Even so, when **they explain** the matter **to him he understands. Since, when they explain** a matter **to him he understands, he knows** what he is doing. **And** the reason **that he acted in this** manner, throwing the pits into Rava's house, was because of **excessive impudence that was in him,** not mental incompetence.

אָמַר רַב הוּנָא בְּרֵיהּ דְּרַב יְהוֹשֻׁעַ: וּלְעֵדוּת – עֵדוּתוֹ עֵדוּת. אֲמַר מָר זוּטְרָא: לָא אֲמָרַן אֶלָּא לְמִטַּלְטְלֵי, אֲבָל לְמִקַּרְקְעֵי לָא.

§ **Rav Huna, son of Rav Yehoshua, says: And with regard to** the **testimony** of one who is not old enough to sell property that he inherits from his father, **his testimony** is valid **testimony. Mar Zutra said: We said** that his testimony is valid **only with regard to movable property,**[NH] **but not with regard to land.**

אֲמַר לֵיהּ רַב אַשִׁי לְמָר זוּטְרָא: מַאי שְׁנָא מִטַּלְטְלֵי? דִּזְבִינֵיהּ זְבִינֵי; אֶלָּא מֵעַתָּה, הָא דִּתְנַן: הַפָּעוֹטוֹת – מִקָּחָן מִקָּח וּמִמְכָּרָן מִמְכָּר בְּמִטַּלְטְלִין, הָכִי נַמִי דְּעֵדוּתָן עֵדוּת! אֲמַר לֵיהּ: הָתָם בָּעֵינָא ״וְעָמְדוּ שְׁנֵי הָאֲנָשִׁים״, וְלֵיכָּא.

Rav Ashi said to Mar Zutra: In **what** way **is movable property different** from land? It is different **because** with regard to movable property **his sale is** a valid **sale. But if that is so,** consider **that which we learned** in a mishna (*Gittin* 59a): **A purchase** made **by young children** is a valid **purchase,**[H] **and a sale** made by them is a valid **sale.** These *halakhot* apply **to** transactions involving **movable property.** Is it possible **that also** in the case of young children **their testimony** is valid **testimony?** Isn't it an established *halakha* that minors are disqualified from bearing witness? Mar Zutra **said to** Rav Ashi: **There,** with regard to testimony, **I require** the witnesses to be men, as the verse states: **"Then the two men shall stand"** (Deuteronomy 19:17),[H] which is interpreted as referring to witnesses, **and** this requirement is **not** fulfilled in the case of young children.

אָמַר אַמֵימָר: וּמַתְּנָתוֹ מַתָּנָה. אֲמַר לֵיהּ רַב אַשִׁי לְאַמֵימָר: הָשְׁתָּא, וּמָה זְבִינֵי דִּמְקַבֵּל זוּזֵי אָמְרַתְּ דְּלָא, דִּלְמָא מוֹזִיל וּמְזַבֵּין – כׇּל שֶׁכֵּן מַתָּנָה דְּלָא מָטֵי לֵיהּ וְלָא מִידֵּי! אֲמַר לֵיהּ:

§ **Ameimar says:** With regard to one who is not old enough to sell property that he inherits from his father, if he gave a gift from the property, **his gift** is a valid **gift.**[H] **Rav Ashi said to Ameimar: Now,** if with regard to **a sale,** in **which he receives money, you say that** the Sages instituted an ordinance **that** he is **not** authorized to sell, **lest he reduce** the price of the property and deplete his father's estate, **all the more so** in the case of **a gift** he is not authorized to give a gift, **as nothing at all comes into his** possession in exchange. Ameimar **said to** Rav Ashi:

HALAKHA

And with regard to testimony…with regard to movable property, etc. – **וּלְעֵדוּת...לְמִטַּלְטְלֵי וכו׳**: A boy who is thirteen years and one day old and has developed two pubic hairs but does not understand the nature of business negotiations cannot provide testimony with regard to land. The commentaries explain that this applies only to testimony pertaining to the value of the land (*Shakh*, citing *Tosafot*). With regard to movable property, his testimony is accepted (Rambam *Sefer Shofetim, Hilkhot Edut* 9:8; *Shulḥan Arukh, Ḥoshen Mishpat* 35:3).

A purchase made by young children is a valid purchase, etc. – **הַפָּעוֹטוֹת מִקָּחָן מִקָּח וכו׳**: A child up to the age of six cannot transfer property to another, although he can acquire property for himself (*Sma*). From the age of six until he reaches majority, although his transaction is not valid by Torah law, it is valid by rabbinic ordinance, provided that he is found to understand the nature of business negotiations (Rema). This applies both to his purchases, to his sales, and to his gifts, whether large or small, whether the gift of a healthy person or the gift of a person on his deathbed. These *halakhot* apply only with regard to movable property. Some authorities maintain that from the age of ten his sale is valid even if he does not understand the nature of business negotiations, provided that he is not mentally incompetent (Rambam *Sefer Kinyan, Hilkhot Mekhira* 29:6; *Shulḥan Arukh, Ḥoshen Mishpat* 235:1, and in the comment of Rema).

Then the two men shall stand – **וְעָמְדוּ שְׁנֵי הָאֲנָשִׁים**: A minor is disqualified from bearing witness, even if he is intelligent, until he is thirteen years old and has developed two pubic hairs. If he is examined sometime after reaching the age of thirteen and is found to have developed two pubic hairs, he is retroactively considered as having reached majority from the age of thirteen. If his beard is fully grown, he does not require examination (Rambam *Sefer Shofetim, Hilkhot Edut* 9:7; *Shulḥan Arukh, Ḥoshen Mishpat* 35:1).

His gift is a valid gift – **וּמַתְּנָתוֹ מַתָּנָה**: If one who has reached the age of thirteen years and one day gives of his deceased father's property to another, his gift is a valid gift. This applies whether the gift is land or movable property, whether it is the gift of a healthy person or the gift of a person on his deathbed, and even if a steward has been appointed for him (*Haggahot Maimoniyyot*). The reason for this is that a person does not give a gift unless he derives significant benefit from the recipient, and even then this is not a common occurrence. The Sages therefore instituted that his gift should be valid, so that people will perform beneficial matters for him (Rambam *Sefer Kinyan, Hilkhot Mekhira* 29:14; *Shulḥan Arukh, Ḥoshen Mishpat* 235:10).

וּלְטַעֲמֵיךְ, זַבֵּין שָׁוֵי חַמְשָׁא בְּשִׁיתָּא, הָכִי נַמִי דִּזְבִינֵיהּ זְבִינֵי?

And according to your reasoning, that the money he receives in exchange for the property is a reason one could consider his sale valid, if **he sold** property **worth five** dinars **for six** dinars, would **his sale also be** a valid **sale?**

אֶלָּא, קִים לְהוּ לְרַבָּנַן דְּיָנוֹקָא מִקַּרְבָא דַּעְתֵּיהּ גַּבֵּי זוּזֵי, וְאִי אָמְרַתְּ זְבִינֵיהּ זְבִינֵי, זִמְנִין דִּמְקַרְקְשִׁי לֵיהּ זוּזֵי, אָזֵיל מְזַבֵּין לְכוּלְּהוּ נִכְסֵי דַּאֲבוּהּ; אֲבָל גַּבֵּי מַתָּנָה, אִי לָאו דַּהֲוָה לֵיהּ הֲנָאָה מִינֵּיהּ לָא הֲוָה יָהֵיב לֵיהּ מַתָּנָה, אָמְרוּ רַבָּנַן: תֶּיהֱוֵי מַתְּנָתוֹ מַתָּנָה, דְּלַעֲבִידוּ לְהוּ מִילֵּי.

Rather, the Sages maintain that a child's inclination is to be **attracted to money. And if you say that his sale is** a valid **sale,** there may be **times** that there are potential buyers **who rattle the dinars** before **him** in order to tempt him to sell, and **he will go and sell all of his father's property.** That is why the Sages ruled that all of his sales are not valid. **But with regard to a gift, if he did not** derive **benefit from** the recipient, **he would not give him a gift. The Sages** therefore **said: Let the gift** of an orphan **be** a valid **gift, so** that people **will perform** beneficial **matters for** the orphans, as the orphan can reciprocate by giving gifts.

אָמַר רַב נַחְמָן אָמַר שְׁמוּאֵל: בּוֹדְקִין לְקִדּוּשִׁין, לְגֵירוּשִׁין, וְלַחֲלִיצָה וּלְמֵיאוּנִין. וְלִמְכּוֹר בְּנִכְסֵי אָבִיו – עַד שֶׁיְּהֵא בֶּן עֶשְׂרִים.

§ **Rav Naḥman says** that **Shmuel says:** Children who have reached the age of majority, i.e., a boy who is thirteen years old and a girl who is twelve years old, **are examined** for signs indicating puberty if it is necessary to determine their adulthood **for** the purpose of **betrothal,**[NH] **for** the purpose of **divorce, for** the purpose of ***ḥalitza*****, and** for the purpose of stating a girl's **refusal**[B] to remain married. **But** in order **to sell from the property that** one inherited from **his father,** the seller must be older, and one cannot sell this property **until** the seller **is twenty** years **old.**

וְכֵיוָן דִּבְדַקְנָא לְקִדּוּשִׁין, לְגֵירוּשִׁין לָמָּה לִי? לָא נְצִרְכָא אֶלָּא לְיִבּוּם, דִּתְנַן: בֶּן תֵּשַׁע שָׁנִים וְיוֹם אֶחָד שֶׁבָּא עַל יְבִמְתּוֹ – קְנָאָהּ, וְאֵין נוֹתֵן גֵּט עַד שֶׁיַּגְדִּיל.

The Gemara asks: **But once I examined** the boy **for** the purpose **of betrothal, why do I** need to examine him again **for** the purpose of **divorce?** The Gemara answers: This **is necessary only with regard to** the **levirate marriage**[N] of a minor, **as we learned** in a mishna (*Nidda* 45a): A boy who is **nine years and one day old who engaged in intercourse**[B] **with his *yevama*****,**[H] i.e., his brother's widow, **acquired her** as his wife by means of engaging in the act of intercourse. Although a minor cannot betroth a woman under ordinary circumstances, in the case of levirate marriage the act of intercourse of a nine-year-old with his *yevama* effects acquisition. **But he cannot give** her **a bill of divorce until he reaches his majority.** It is therefore necessary to examine him at the time of the divorce.

NOTES

Are examined for betrothal, etc. – בּוֹדְקִין לְקִדּוּשִׁין וכו׳: Once a child reaches the age of majority, it is presumed that he or she has developed signs indicating puberty. This presumption is not always relied upon. In certain cases where it is important to determine whether the child has reached majority, an examination is performed in order to determine whether the child has developed two pubic hairs. In cases where a Torah prohibition is involved, the examination is relied upon only in order to determine whether it is necessary to be stringent. If the examination does not reveal evidence of two pubic hairs, it is not possible to be lenient and rule that the child has definitively not reached majority, as it is possible that the hairs have fallen out. In cases that involve rabbinic law, e.g., refusals, the examination is relied upon also in order to be lenient (Rid; Rif).

Only with regard to levirate marriage – אֶלָּא לְיִבּוּם: In the case of levirate marriage, the *yavam* performs an act of betrothal only by rabbinic ordinance. The actual acquisition of the *yevama*, his brother's widow, as his wife is effected by Torah law only through intercourse. The act of sexual intercourse of a boy who is nine years and one day old is considered an act of consequence in every way, e.g., if he engages in forbidden sexual intercourse with an adult woman, she is liable to receive the death penalty due to this act, although he is exempt because he is a minor. Therefore, his intercourse effects acquisition of his *yevama*. He cannot divorce her with a bill of divorce, as a bill of divorce can be written and delivered only by one who has reached majority.

BACKGROUND

Refusal – מֵיאוּן: A girl under the age of twelve can be married off by her father. If her father is no longer alive, she cannot get married by Torah law until she reaches her majority. Nevertheless, the Sages instituted that her mother or brothers can marry her off with her consent. The girl can terminate this marriage before she reaches the age of twelve by stating her refusal, i.e., by declaring that she does not want to remain married to this man. In this case a bill of divorce is not required, and the marriage is nullified retroactively. Most of the *halakhot* of refusal are discussed in tractate *Yevamot*.

A boy nine years and one day old who engaged in intercourse – בֶּן תֵּשַׁע שָׁנִים וְיוֹם אֶחָד שֶׁבָּא: Although most boys do not experience a significant bodily change at the age of nine, the development of the testicles begins to accelerate at around this time, with the attendant increase in the capacity for intercourse. Although it roughly corresponds to the average age of this development, this specification, like other specific ages the Sages established for different levels of maturity, is somewhat arbitrary, as nothing necessarily happens on that specific day per se.

HALAKHA

Are examined for betrothal – בּוֹדְקִין לְקִדּוּשִׁין: If a minor betroths or marries a woman, his action is of no consequence. The woman does not require a bill of divorce, and if he dies she does not require levirate marriage or *ḥalitza*. The definition of a minor is one who has not reached the age of thirteen or one who has reached the age of thirteen but has not developed two pubic hairs. One who has neither developed two pubic hairs nor developed the signs of a sexually underdeveloped man is considered a minor even if he is twenty years old, until he is thirty-five years and one day old (Rambam *Sefer Nashim, Hilkhot Ishut* 4:7, 2:10; *Shulḥan Arukh, Even HaEzer* 43:1, and see 167:1).

A boy nine years and one day old who engaged in intercourse with his *yevama* – בֶּן תֵּשַׁע שָׁנִים וְיוֹם אֶחָד שֶׁבָּא עַל יְבִמְתּוֹ: The sexual intercourse of a minor who is not yet nine years old is not considered an act of consequence. With regard to a boy who is nine years and one day old who engages in intercourse with his *yevama*, his act effects acquisition by rabbinic law like the levirate betrothal of an adult, although one who is that age cannot betroth any other woman. Although he acquires the *yevama* as his wife, he cannot divorce her with a bill of divorce until he reaches majority and then engages in intercourse with her. If he does not engage in intercourse with her after reaching majority and he wishes to divorce her, she requires a bill of divorce and *ḥalitza*. If he engaged in intercourse with her as a minor and died before reaching majority, or if he died after reaching majority but did not engage in intercourse with her after reaching majority, she performs *ḥalitza* and may not enter into levirate marriage with his brother (see *Beit Shmuel* and *Taz*). If he did not engage in intercourse with his *yevama* after reaching majority and he married another woman and then died, both women perform *ḥalitza* and may not enter into levirate marriage (Rambam *Sefer Nashim, Hilkhot Yibbum VaḤalitza* 1:16; *Shulḥan Arukh, Even HaEzer* 167:1–2).

NOTES

Teaches us that a woman is juxtaposed to a man – קָא מַשְׁמַע לָן דְּמַקְּשִׁינַן אִשָּׁה לְאִישׁ: Rav Naḥman does not need to teach the *halakha* that a man needs to have reached majority in order to perform *ḥalitza*, as this is derived from the *halakhot* of divorce. Rather, this is referring to the requirement for a woman who performs *ḥalitza* to have reached majority (Rashbam). Furthermore, the Gemara assumes that the case of *ḥalitza* is similar to the cases of divorce and betrothal, which were also mentioned by Rav Naḥman. Just as in these cases both the man and the woman must have reached majority, so too in the case of *ḥalitza* (*Tosafot*).

לַחֲלִיצָה – לְאַפּוּקֵי מִדְּרַבִּי יוֹסֵי, דְּאָמַר: "אִישׁ" כָּתוּב בַּפָּרָשָׁה, אֲבָל אִשָּׁה – בֵּין גְּדוֹלָה וּבֵין קְטַנָּה, קָא מַשְׁמַע לָן דְּמַקְּשִׁינַן אִשָּׁה לְאִישׁ, דְּלָא כְּרַבִּי יוֹסֵי.

The Gemara explains why it is necessary to mention examining a boy **for the purpose of** ***ḥalitza***:[H] This is mentioned **to the exclusion of that which Rabbi Yosei** says, as Rabbi Yosei **says: "Man,"** i.e., an adult man, **is written in the** Torah **passage** with regard to *ḥalitza*, as the verse states: "And if the man does not wish to take his brother's wife" (Deuteronomy 25:7). **But a woman, whether** she is **an adult or a minor,** can be released by *ḥalitza*, as the verse does not indicate her age. To counter this, Rav Naḥman **teaches us that a woman is juxtaposed to a man**[N] in this passage, indicating that the *yevama* must also have reached adulthood, and the *halakha* is **not in accordance with** the opinion of **Rabbi Yosei.**

וּלְמֵיאוּנִין – לְאַפּוּקֵי מִדְּרַבִּי יְהוּדָה, דְּאָמַר: עַד שֶׁיִּרְבֶּה שָׁחוֹר, קָא מַשְׁמַע לָן דְּלָא כְּרַבִּי יְהוּדָה.

The Gemara explains why it is necessary to mention examining a person **for** the purpose of stating her **refusal.**[H] This is mentioned **to the exclusion of that which Rabbi Yehuda** says, **as** Rabbi Yehuda **says** that a girl whose mother or brother married her off while she was a minor can nullify her marriage by refusing to remain married, and she can state this refusal **until** she reaches complete maturity, i.e., **when** the area covered by **black** pubic hairs **is greater** than the skin of the genital area. Rav Naḥman therefore **teaches us that** the *halakha* is **not in accordance with** the opinion of **Rabbi Yehuda,** and once a girl has developed two pubic hairs she cannot state her refusal.

וְלִמְכּוֹר בְּנִכְסֵי אָבִיו עַד שֶׁיְּהֵא בֶּן עֶשְׂרִים – לְאַפּוּקֵי מִמַּאן דְּאָמַר בֶּן שְׁמוֹנֶה עֶשְׂרֵה.

Rav Naḥman states: **But** in order **to sell from the property that** one inherited from **his father,** the seller must be older, and he cannot sell the property **until he is twenty** years **old.** This is mentioned **to the exclusion of** the opinion of the **one who says** that the seller can be **eighteen** years **old.**

וְהִלְכְתָא: תּוֹךְ זְמַן כְּלִפְנֵי זְמַן. וְהִלְכְתָא כְּגִידֵּל בַּר מְנַשֶּׁה.

The Gemara concludes: **And the** ***halakha*** is that with regard to the age when a minor can sell property inherited from his father, **during** the **time,** i.e., during his twentieth year, is considered **as before** the **time** when it is permitted, and he cannot sell until the end of his twentieth year. **And the** ***halakha*** **is in accordance with** the ruling that Rava sent to **Giddel bar Menashe,** that a child who has reached his majority and understands the nature of business negotiations can sell land.

וְהִלְכְתָא כְּמָר זוּטְרָא. וְהִלְכְתָא כְּאַמֵּימָר. וְהִלְכְתָא כְּרַב נַחְמָן אָמַר שְׁמוּאֵל בְּכוּלְּהוּ.

The Gemara continues: **And the** ***halakha*** **is in accordance with** the statement of **Mar Zutra,** that one who is not fit to sell land is also not fit to bear witness with regard to land. **And the** ***halakha*** **is in accordance with** the statement of **Ameimar,** that an orphan under the age of twenty can bestow gifts from the property he inherited from his father. **And the** ***halakha*** **is in accordance with** the statement that **Rav Naḥman** says that **Shmuel says with regard to all** the matters that he mentioned.

HALAKHA

For *ḥalitza* – לַחֲלִיצָה: A minor cannot perform *ḥalitza* until he reaches the age of thirteen years and one day. He is then examined, and if he is found to have developed two pubic hairs, he can perform *ḥalitza*. Similarly, a minor girl cannot perform *ḥalitza* until she reaches the age of twelve years and one day, and if she is then examined and found to have developed two pubic hairs, she can perform *ḥalitza*, in accordance with the opinion of the Rabbis. Before this time, even if she performs *ḥalitza* it is ineffective (Rambam *Sefer Nashim, Hilkhot Yibbum VaḤalitza* 1:16–18, and see *Maggid Mishne* there; *Shulḥan Arukh, Even HaEzer* 167:3–4).

For refusal – וּלְמֵיאוּנִין: There are circumstances in which a minor girl is not under her father's authority. This occurs if her father dies, or if her father betroths her to another and she is widowed or divorced while still a minor. In these circumstances, if she is subsequently betrothed to another and does not wish to remain married to him, the *halakha* is as follows: If the minor girl is between the ages of six and ten, she is examined. If she is found to be unable to safeguard her betrothal money she does not need to state her refusal. Rather, she returns to her mother's house as though she were never betrothed. If she is found to be able to safeguard her betrothal money, she must state her refusal to remain married in order to nullify the betrothal. If she is less than six years old, she does not need to state her refusal, even if she demonstrates intellectual acumen. If she is ten years old, she must state her refusal to remain married in order to nullify the betrothal, even if she is particularly unintelligent, as long as she does not demonstrate mental incompetence (*Beit Shmuel*). Some say that all this applies only if her mother or brothers married her off. If she married without their consent, she does not need to state her refusal (Rema, citing *Haggahot Alfasi*). Others say that even if she has not reached the age of six, if she has reached the age at which the transactions of young children are valid, she is required to state her refusal in order to nullify the betrothal (Ritva). This is so even if she married without the consent of her mother or brothers (Rambam *Sefer Nashim, Hilkhot Ishut* 4:7 and *Hilkhot Geirushin* 11:7; *Shulḥan Arukh, Even HaEzer* 43:2, and see *Beit Shmuel* there, 155:2).

מתני׳ הַמְחַלֵּק נְכָסָיו עַל פִּיו – רַבִּי אֶלְעָזָר אוֹמֵר: אֶחָד בָּרִיא וְאֶחָד מְסוּכָּן, נְכָסִים שֶׁיֵּשׁ לָהֶן אַחְרָיוּת – נִקְנִין בְּכֶסֶף וּבִשְׁטָר וּבַחֲזָקָה, וְשֶׁאֵין לָהֶן אַחְרָיוּת – אֵין נִקְנִין אֶלָּא בִּמְשִׁיכָה.

MISHNA With regard to **one who divides his property** between various recipients **by** means of **verbal** instruction, **Rabbi Elazar says:** Both in the case of **one** who is **healthy and** in the case of **one** who is **dangerously ill,**[N] the *halakha* is as follows: **Property that serves as a guarantee,** i.e., land, **is acquired by** means of **money, by a deed** of transfer, **or by taking possession** of it. **And that which does not serve as a guarantee,** i.e., movable property, **can be acquired only by pulling.**

NOTES

Rabbi Elazar says one who is healthy and one who is dangerously ill, etc. – רַבִּי אֶלְעָזָר אוֹמֵר אֶחָד בָּרִיא וְאֶחָד מְסוּכָּן וכו׳: Rabbi Elazar disagrees with all the aforementioned *halakhot* with regard to a person on his deathbed. He maintains that the Sages did not institute that the statement of a person on his deathbed is considered as written and as though the document were delivered to the recipient. Any gift, in any situation, must be acquired by an act of acquisition, as must the gift of a healthy person. The Rashbam and the Rashba conclude from Rabbi Elazar's statement that he maintains that the gift of a person on his deathbed cannot be retracted, as it is acquired in the same manner as the gift of a healthy person. The Ramah and the Meiri note that even according to the opinion of Rabbi Elazar, this applies only in a case where the gift is bestowed upon one who is not fit to inherit from the giver. With regard to one who divides his property between his sons, he can increase or decrease their allotted portions of the inheritance by verbal instruction, as stated in the previous chapter (130a).

Perek **IX**
Daf **156** Amud **b**

אָמְרוּ לוֹ: מַעֲשֶׂה בְּאִמָּן שֶׁל בְּנֵי רוֹכֵל שֶׁהָיְתָה חוֹלָה, וְאָמְרָה: תְּנוּ כְּבֵינָתִי לְבִתִּי, וְהִיא בִּשְׁנֵים עָשָׂר מָנֶה, וּמֵתָה, וְקִיְּימוּ אֶת דְּבָרֶיהָ! אָמַר לָהֶן: בְּנֵי רוֹכֵל תְּקַבְּרֵם אִמָּן.

The Rabbis **said to** Rabbi Elazar: There was **an incident involving the mother of the sons of Rokhel, who was sick, and who said: My brooch shall be given to my daughter, and it is** valued **at twelve hundred dinars. And** this woman subsequently **died, and** the Sages **upheld her statement.**[H] This indicates that a person on his deathbed can gift property without an act of acquisition. Rabbi Elazar **said to them:** That case was different; **the sons of Rokhel should be buried by their mother,** i.e., he cursed them. It is not possible to bring a proof from this incident, as these sons were wicked people. Consequently, when ruling in this matter the Sages did not act in accordance with the *halakha*, but allowed the mother of the sons of Rokhel to give this valuable piece of jewelry to their sister without an act of acquisition having been performed.

גמ׳ תַּנְיָא, אָמַר לָהֶן רַבִּי אֱלִיעֶזֶר לַחֲכָמִים: מַעֲשֶׂה בְּמָרוֹנִי אֶחָד שֶׁהָיָה בִּירוּשָׁלַיִם, וְהָיוּ לוֹ מִטַּלְטְלִין הַרְבֵּה וּבִיקֵּשׁ לִיתְּנָם בְּמַתָּנָה, אָמְרוּ לוֹ: אֵין לָהֶם תַּקָּנָה עַד שֶׁיַּקְנֶה עַל גַּב קַרְקַע.

GEMARA **It is taught** in a *baraita*: **Rabbi Eliezer said to the Rabbis:** There was **an incident involving a certain** man **of Meron**[N] **who was in Jerusalem, and he had a lot of movable property. And he desired to give** the movable property **as gifts** to various individuals, but they could not be acquired by pulling. The Rabbis **said to him: There is no remedy for** transferring the property **unless he transfers** the movable property **by means of** transferring the ownership of **land.**

הָלַךְ וְלָקַח בֵּית סֶלַע אֶחָד סָמוּךְ לִירוּשָׁלַיִם, וְאָמַר: צְפוֹנוֹ לִפְלוֹנִי וְעִמּוֹ מֵאָה צֹאן וּמֵאָה חָבִיּוֹת, וּדְרוֹמוֹ לִפְלוֹנִי וְעִמּוֹ מֵאָה צֹאן וּמֵאָה חָבִיּוֹת. וּמֵת, וְקִיְּימוּ חֲכָמִים אֶת דְּבָרָיו! אָמְרוּ לוֹ: מִשָּׁם רְאָיָה? מָרוֹנִי בָּרִיא הָיָה.

He went and acquired one plot of **rocky** land **adjacent to Jerusalem, and he said:** I give **the north** part **of** this area **to so-and-so, and with it one hundred sheep and one hundred barrels. And** I give **the south** part of the area **to so-and-so, and with it one hundred sheep and one hundred barrels. And he died, and the Sages upheld his statement.** This indicates that a person on his deathbed cannot transfer property without an act of acquisition. The Rabbis **said to** Rabbi Eliezer: Do you bring **proof from there?** The man **of Meron was healthy** at the time. This was not the gift of a person on his deathbed, and it could not be acquired by verbal instruction.

NOTES

Involving…of Meron – בְּמָרוֹנִי: This incident is also cited in tractate *Kiddushin* (26b). The version of the text there reads *Madoni*. This could refer to an inhabitant of the Galilean town of Madon (see Joshua 12:19), or to one who came from Media.

HALAKHA

And the Sages upheld her statement – וְקִיְּימוּ אֶת דְּבָרֶיהָ: The gifts of a person on his deathbed do not require an act of acquisition to be valid, as the Sages instituted that the statement of a person on his deathbed is considered as written and as though the document were delivered to the recipient. The reason for this ordinance is to prevent him from losing control of his mind due to his grief upon seeing that his will is not being carried out, exacerbating his illness. The Sages accorded this ordinance the force of Torah law. This applies both on weekdays and on Shabbat, and it applies even with regard to land (see *Sma*). There is no difference between a case where the giver instructs that the gift should be given immediately upon his death and a case where he states that it should be given later (Rema, citing *Nimmukei Yosef*; *Beit Yosef*, citing Ritva). The *halakhot* of the gifts of a person on his deathbed apply only if he gave all of his property to others, indicating that he is bestowing the gift in expectation of death, or if he stated explicitly that he is dividing up his property due to his imminent death (Rambam *Sefer Kinyan*, *Hilkhot Zekhiya UMattana* 8:2; *Shulḥan Arukh*, *Ḥoshen Mishpat* 250:1, and see *Sma* there).

”אָמַר לָהֶן: בְּנֵי רוֹכֵל תִּקְבְּרֵם אִמָּן“ וכו׳. מַאי טַעֲמָא קָא לָיֵיט לְהוּ? אָמַר רַב יְהוּדָה אָמַר שְׁמוּאֵל: מְקַיְּימֵי קוֹצִים בְּכֶרֶם הָיוּ, וְרַבִּי אֱלִיעֶזֶר לְטַעְמֵיהּ, דִּתְנַן: הַמְקַיֵּים קוֹצִים בְּכֶרֶם – רַבִּי אֱלִיעֶזֶר אוֹמֵר: קִדֵּשׁ, וַחֲכָמִים אוֹמְרִים: לֹא קִדֵּשׁ אֶלָּא דָּבָר שֶׁכָּמוֹהוּ מְקַיְּימִין.

§ The mishna teaches: Rabbi Elazar **said to them:** That case was different; **the sons of Rokhel should be buried by their mother.** The Gemara asks: **What is the reason** that **he was cursing them? Rav Yehuda says** that **Shmuel says: They were maintaining thorns in a vineyard**[N] and did not uproot them, **and Rabbi Eliezer** conforms **to his** line of **reasoning,**[N] as we **learned** in a mishna (*Kilayim* 5:8): With regard to **one who maintains thorns in a vineyard,**[H] **Rabbi Eliezer says: He has proscribed** the vineyard, rendering it forbidden due to the prohibition against diverse kinds. **And the Rabbis say: Only** growing **a matter,** i.e., a crop, **the like of which** people usually **maintain, proscribes**[N] a vineyard and renders it forbidden.

בִּשְׁלָמָא כַּרְכּוֹם חֲזֵי, אֶלָּא קוֹצִים לְמַאי חֲזֵי? אָמַר רַבִּי חֲנִינָא: מַאי טַעֲמָא דְּרַבִּי אֱלִיעֶזֶר? שֶׁכֵּן בַּעֲרַבְיָא מְקַיְּימִין קוֹצִים בַּשָּׂדוֹת לִגְמַלֵּיהֶן.

The Gemara asks: **Granted,** if it were **saffron** that grew in the vineyard, it **is useful** for seasoning and other uses, and therefore it proscribes the vineyard. **But** with regard to **thorns, for what are they useful? Rabbi Ḥanina said: What is the reasoning of Rabbi Eliezer?** It is **because in Arabia**[B] **they maintain thorns in the fields for their camels.**[B] Rabbi Eliezer holds that since thorns are maintained in one place, they are considered useful everywhere.

אָמַר רַבִּי לֵוִי: קוֹנִין קִנְיָן מִשְּׁכִיב מְרַע אֲפִילּוּ בְּשַׁבָּת, וְלֹא לָחוּשׁ לְדִבְרֵי רַבִּי אֱלִיעֶזֶר, אֶלָּא שֶׁמָּא תִּטְרוֹף דַּעְתּוֹ עָלָיו.

Rabbi Levi says: An act of **acquisition may be performed** in order to effect acquisition of property **from a person on his deathbed even on Shabbat,**[HN] even though transactions are not performed on Shabbat. **And** this, that an act of acquisition must be performed, is **not** stated in order **to take into consideration the statement of Rabbi Eliezer**[N] that the gifts of any person on his deathbed require an act of acquisition. **Rather,** the reason for this is that if a person on his deathbed requests the performance of an act of acquisition, his request is fulfilled, **lest** his anxiety upon seeing that his will is not being carried out cause him to **lose control of his mind** due to his grief, exacerbating his poor physical state.

HALAKHA

One who maintains thorns in a vineyard – הַמְקַיֵּים קוֹצִים בְּכֶרֶם: If one finds weeds of a kind not usually cultivated in his vineyard, they do not render the vineyard forbidden due to the prohibition of diverse kinds even if he desires to maintain them as fodder or for medicinal purposes. A vineyard is rendered forbidden only if one maintains in it a species that the majority of the populace is accustomed to cultivate. Therefore, in regions where it is the practice to allow thorns to grow as camel fodder, one who maintains thorns in his vineyard has proscribed the vineyard, in accordance with the opinion of the Rabbis (Rambam *Sefer Zera'im, Hilkhot Kilayim* 5:18; *Shulḥan Arukh, Yoreh De'a* 296:14).

Acquisition may be performed from a person on his deathbed even on Shabbat – קוֹנִין קִנְיָן מִשְּׁכִיב מְרַע אֲפִילּוּ בְּשַׁבָּת: The gifts of a person on his deathbed do not require an act of acquisition, provided that one transfers ownership of all of his property. Nevertheless, if the person on his deathbed requests to transfer ownership through an act of symbolic exchange, this is performed even on Shabbat. The reason for this is that the act of acquisition is unnecessary, and therefore the Sages permitted the act of acquisition to be performed on Shabbat, lest the sick person become agitated, adversely affecting his condition (*Leḥem Mishne*). Some authorities rule that an act of acquisition can be performed on Shabbat even when the act of acquisition is not superfluous, e.g., where the giver states that he will not retract the gift if he recovers (*Tur*, citing Rosh). The Rema adds that with regard to the gift of a person on his deathbed involving only some of the giver's property, which requires an act of acquisition, the authorities disagree. The Rashbam says that although the gift does not appear to be given in expectation of imminent death, an act of acquisition may be performed, while the *Tur*, citing Rosh, disagrees (Rambam *Sefer Kinyan, Hilkhot Zekhiya UMattana* 8:3; *Shulḥan Arukh, Ḥoshen Mishpat* 254:1).

BACKGROUND

Arabia – עֲרַבְיָא: This probably does not refer to the Arabian Peninsula, but to the Roman province of Arabia, which included Transjordan, the Sinai Peninsula, and part of northern Arabia.

Thorns…for their camels – קוֹצִים...לִגְמַלֵּיהֶן: The camel's palate consists of particularly tough skin, which enables it to eat thorny plants that other animals are unable to eat. These have nutritional value, and in regions where camels were commonly bred it was commonplace to leave them in the fields as camel fodder.

NOTES

They were maintaining thorns in a vineyard – מְקַיְּימֵי קוֹצִים בְּכֶרֶם הָיוּ: According to the Ramah this is referring to a specific kind of thorn that is fit for animal consumption. The Gemara here is in accordance with those who hold that one who maintains diverse kinds in his vineyard receives lashes even if he did not sow or plant them (Rashbam). Alternatively, Rabbi Eliezer holds that one who maintains diverse kinds in his vineyard transgresses a prohibition, and even if he is not liable to receive lashes the court penalizes him.

And Rabbi Eliezer conforms to his line of reasoning – וְרַבִּי אֱלִיעֶזֶר לְטַעְמֵיהּ: *Tosafot* write that the correct version of the text refers here to Rabbi Elazar, whose opinion is cited in the mishna (156a).

Only a matter the like of which people usually maintain proscribes – לֹא קִדֵּשׁ אֶלָּא דָּבָר שֶׁכָּמוֹהוּ מְקַיְּימִין: The verse states: "You shall not sow your vineyard with two kinds of seed" (Deuteronomy 22:9). This indicates that the prohibition applies only to those kinds of plants that it is typical to plant.

Acquisition may be performed from a person on his deathbed even on Shabbat – קוֹנִין קִנְיָן מִשְּׁכִיב מְרַע אֲפִילּוּ בְּשַׁבָּת: The Rashbam explains that this is permitted both in a situation where an act of acquisition is unnecessary, e.g., where one transfers all of his property, and where it is required, as in the case of the gift of a person on his deathbed of only some of his property. Despite the fact that the gift of a person on his deathbed of only some of his property is bestowed upon the assumption that he will recover, there is still reason for concern lest the inability to transfer the property cause the sick person anxiety and grief (see *Tosafot*). Conversely, the Rosh maintains that when one transfers only some of his property, his gift is considered the gift of a healthy person. There is therefore no reason for concern lest the inability to transfer it cause him anxiety and grief.

And not to take into consideration the statement of Rabbi Eliezer – וְלֹא לָחוּשׁ לְדִבְרֵי רַבִּי אֱלִיעֶזֶר: The Gemara's statement here apparently indicates that according to the opinion of Rabbi Eliezer the gifts of a person on his deathbed require an act of acquisition even on Shabbat. Yet the mishna later on in this *amud* cites Rabbi Eliezer's opinion to the contrary. *Tosafot* therefore write that the correct version of the text refers to Rabbi Elazar, whose opinion is cited in the mishna (156a).

מתני׳ רַבִּי אֱלִיעֶזֶר אוֹמֵר: בְּשַׁבָּת – דְּבָרָיו קַיָּימִין, מִפְּנֵי שֶׁאֵין יָכוֹל לִכְתּוֹב, אֲבָל לֹא בַּחוֹל; רַבִּי יְהוֹשֻׁעַ אוֹמֵר: בְּשַׁבָּת אָמְרוּ, קַל וָחוֹמֶר בַּחוֹל.

MISHNA **Rabbi Eliezer says: On Shabbat, the** verbal **statement** of a person on his deathbed **stands,** as he **cannot write,** and the Sages instituted that he can effect the transaction verbally lest the inability to do so exacerbate his condition. **But** a verbal instruction does **not** stand if stated **on a weekday. Rabbi Yehoshua says: With regard to Shabbat,** the Sages **stated** that his verbal instruction is sufficient, even though writing is prohibited. One can infer ***a fortiori*** that the same applies **with regard to a weekday,** when writing is permitted.

כֵּיוֹצֵא בּוֹ, זָכִין לְקָטָן וְאֵין זָכִין לְגָדוֹל, דִּבְרֵי רַבִּי אֱלִיעֶזֶר; רַבִּי יְהוֹשֻׁעַ אוֹמֵר: לְקָטָן אָמְרוּ, קַל וָחוֹמֶר לְגָדוֹל.

Similarly, one can acquire property **on behalf of a minor,**[N] **but one cannot acquire** property **on behalf of an adult,** since he can perform the act of acquisition himself; this is **the statement of Rabbi Eliezer. Rabbi Yehoshua says:** The Sages **stated** this ***halakha*** **with regard to a minor,** and one may infer ***a fortiori*** that this also applies **with regard to an adult,**[H] who is able to perform the act of acquisition himself.

גמ׳ מַתְנִיתִין מַנִּי? רַבִּי יְהוּדָה הִיא; דְּתַנְיָא: רַבִּי מֵאִיר אוֹמֵר, רַבִּי אֱלִיעֶזֶר אוֹמֵר: בַּחוֹל – דְּבָרָיו קַיָּימִין, מִפְּנֵי שֶׁיָּכוֹל לִכְתּוֹב, אֲבָל לֹא בְּשַׁבָּת;

GEMARA The Gemara asks: **Whose** opinion is expressed in the **mishna?** The Gemara answers: **This is** the opinion of **Rabbi Yehuda.** This is **as it is taught** in a *baraita*: **Rabbi Meir says** that **Rabbi Eliezer says:** With regard to a person on his deathbed who distributes his property by verbal instruction, **on a weekday, his statements stand, because he can write, but** his statement does **not** stand **on Shabbat,** because he cannot write.

רַבִּי יְהוֹשֻׁעַ

Rabbi Yehoshua

אוֹמֵר: בַּחוֹל אָמְרוּ, וְקַל וָחוֹמֶר לְשַׁבָּת. כֵּיוֹצֵא בּוֹ, זָכִין לְגָדוֹל וְאֵין זָכִין לְקָטָן, דִּבְרֵי רַבִּי אֱלִיעֶזֶר; רַבִּי יְהוֹשֻׁעַ אוֹמֵר: בְּגָדוֹל אָמְרוּ, קַל וָחוֹמֶר לְקָטָן.

says: With regard to weekdays the Sages **stated** that the verbal instruction of a person on his deathbed is valid, even though it is permitted to write. **And** one may infer ***a fortiori*** that the same applies **with regard to Shabbat,** when writing is prohibited. **Similarly, one can acquire** property **on behalf of an adult,** as he is able to effect acquisition himself, **but one cannot acquire** property **on behalf of a minor;** this is **the statement of Rabbi Eliezer. Rabbi Yehoshua says:** The Sages **stated** this *halakha* **with regard to an adult,** even though he can effect acquisition himself. One may infer ***a fortiori*** that this also applies **with regard to a minor,** who cannot effect acquisition himself.

רַבִּי יְהוּדָה אוֹמֵר, רַבִּי אֱלִיעֶזֶר אוֹמֵר: בְּשַׁבָּת – דְּבָרָיו קַיָּימִין, מִפְּנֵי שֶׁאֵינוֹ יָכוֹל לִכְתּוֹב, אֲבָל לֹא בַּחוֹל; רַבִּי יְהוֹשֻׁעַ אוֹמֵר: בְּשַׁבָּת אָמְרוּ, קַל וָחוֹמֶר בַּחוֹל. כֵּיוֹצֵא בּוֹ, זָכִין לְקָטָן וְאֵין זָכִין לְגָדוֹל, דִּבְרֵי רַבִּי אֱלִיעֶזֶר; רַבִּי יְהוֹשֻׁעַ אוֹמֵר: לְקָטָן אָמְרוּ, קַל וָחוֹמֶר לְגָדוֹל.

Rabbi Yehuda says that Rabbi Eliezer says: On Shabbat, the verbal **statement of** a person on his deathbed **stands due to** the fact **that he cannot write. But** a verbal instruction does **not stand on a weekday. Rabbi Yehoshua says: With regard to Shabbat** the Sages **stated** that his verbal instruction stands, even though writing is prohibited. One may infer ***a fortiori*** that the same applies **with regard to a weekday,** when writing is permitted. **Similarly, one can acquire** property **on behalf of a minor, but one cannot acquire** property **on behalf of an adult,** since he can effect the acquisition himself; this is **the statement of Rabbi Eliezer. Rabbi Yehoshua says:** The Sages **stated** this *halakha* **with regard to a minor,** and one may infer ***a fortiori*** that this also applies **with regard to an adult.**

מתני׳ נָפַל הַבַּיִת עָלָיו וְעַל אָבִיו, אוֹ עָלָיו וְעַל מוֹרִישָׁיו, וְהָיְתָה עָלָיו כְּתוּבַּת אִשָּׁה וּבַעַל חוֹב, יוֹרְשֵׁי הָאָב אוֹמְרִים: הַבֵּן מֵת רִאשׁוֹן וְאַחַר כָּךְ מֵת הָאָב, וּבַעֲלֵי הַחוֹב אוֹמְרִים: הָאָב מֵת רִאשׁוֹן וְאַחַר כָּךְ מֵת הַבֵּן.

MISHNA **A house collapsed on** a son **and upon his father, or upon** a certain person **and upon those** from **whom he stands to inherit,** and it is unknown who died first. If the son **bore** the responsibility to pay the **marriage contract** of his **wife and** to pay **a creditor,** and the son had no money with which to pay them except that which he might inherit from his father, and **the father's heirs say: The son died first and afterward the father died,** and therefore the son did not inherit property from his father, **and the creditors say: The father died first and afterward the son died,** resulting in the son's inheriting his father's property, enabling the creditors to collect payment from the property even after the son's death, there is a dispute with regard to how to rule.

NOTES

One can acquire property on behalf of a minor – זָכִין לְקָטָן: A minor less than six years old cannot acquire property himself, as he does not possess the power to perform an effective act of acquisition. Rabbi Eliezer therefore maintains that an adult can acquire property on his behalf (Rashbam; *Sefer HaYashar*).

HALAKHA

Stated with regard to a minor and *a fortiori* with regard to an adult – לְקָטָן אָמְרוּ קַל וָחוֹמֶר לְגָדוֹל: One can transfer ownership of a gift to another by means of a third party, whether in the presence of the recipient or not, even if the recipient is one day old. This ruling is in accordance with the statement of Rabbi Yehoshua, following the principle that in cases where there is a dispute between Rabbi Yehoshua and Rabbi Eliezer, the *halakha* is in accordance with the opinion of Rabbi Yehoshua (Rambam *Sefer Kinyan, Hilkhot Zekhiya UMattana* 4:2, 8; *Shulḥan Arukh, Ḥoshen Mishpat* 243:1, 18).

בֵּית שַׁמַּאי אוֹמְרִים: יַחֲלוֹקוּ, וּבֵית הִלֵּל אוֹמְרִים: נְכָסִים בְּחֶזְקָתָן.

Since it cannot be determined who died first, **Beit Shammai say: They divide** the property[N] between them so that the father's heirs receive half of his property and the son's creditors receive the other half. **And Beit Hillel say:** The **property** retains **its** previous ownership **status.**[NH] Since the last known owner of the property was the father, the property is given to the father's heirs.

גמ׳ תְּנַן הָתָם: הַמַּלְוֶה אֶת חֲבֵירוֹ בִּשְׁטָר – גּוֹבֶה מִנְּכָסִים מְשׁוּעְבָּדִים, עַל יְדֵי עֵדִים – גּוֹבֶה מִנְּכָסִים בְּנֵי חוֹרִין.

GEMARA **We learned** in a mishna **elsewhere** (175a): **One who lends** money **to another with a** promissory **note can collect** the debt even **from liened property** that has been sold. If one lends money only **with witnesses, he can collect** the debt only **from unsold property.**

בָּעֵי שְׁמוּאֵל: ״דְּאִיקְנֵי״ וְקָנָה, מַהוּ? אַלִּיבָּא דְּרַבִּי מֵאִיר דְּאָמַר: אָדָם מַקְנֶה דָּבָר שֶׁלֹּא בָּא לָעוֹלָם – לָא תִּיבְּעֵי לָךְ, דְּוַדַּאי קָנָה, אֶלָּא כִּי תִּיבְּעֵי לָךְ – אַלִּיבָּא דְּרַבָּנַן דְּאָמְרִי: אֵין אָדָם מַקְנֶה דָּבָר שֶׁלֹּא בָּא לָעוֹלָם.

Shmuel raises a dilemma: If the borrower wrote in the promissory note: The property **that I will acquire** in the future shall be liened to this debt, **and he** subsequently **acquired** property, **what is** the *halakha*? Is the property liened or not? The Gemara clarifies the dilemma: **According to** the opinion **of Rabbi Meir, who says: A person can transfer** ownership of **an entity that has not** yet **come into the world, you should not raise the dilemma,** as the lender **certainly acquires,** i.e., places a lien, on the property. **Rather, when should you raise the dilemma?** Raise it **according to** the opinion **of the Rabbis,**[N] **who say: A person cannot transfer** ownership of **an entity that has not** yet **come into the world.**

אָמַר רַב יוֹסֵף: תָּא שְׁמַע, וַחֲכָמִים אוֹמְרִים: זֶה הָיָה פִּיקֵּחַ שֶׁמָּכַר לוֹ אֶת הַקַּרְקַע, מִפְּנֵי שֶׁהוּא יָכוֹל לְמַשְׁכְּנוֹ עָלָיו.

Rav Yosef said: Come and **hear** proof from a mishna (*Ketubot* 110a): If one produces a promissory note against another, and the borrower produced a bill of sale dated after the promissory note that states that the lender sold him a field of his, Admon says that the borrower can say: Were I really indebted to you, you should have collected the loan when you sold me the field. **And the Rabbis say:** This does not prove anything. It is possible that **this** lender **was perspicacious, as he sold** the borrower **the land** for a good reason, **because** now **he can take** the field **as collateral from him** in lieu of the outstanding loan. This mishna indicates that even property acquired by the borrower after the promissory note is written is liened.

NOTES

They divide the property – יַחֲלוֹקוּ: Rabbeinu Gershom Meor HaGola explains that the property is divided in accordance with the principle that property of uncertain ownership is divided between the claimants. The Rashbam says that Beit Shammai conform to their line of reasoning that a promissory note that stands to be collected is considered already collected (see *Sota* 25a). In this case, therefore, the claims of the creditors and of the heirs are of equal merit, and consequently, the property is divided between them.

The property retains its previous ownership status – נְכָסִים בְּחֶזְקָתָן: Even if the father died first, when the son died the property came into the possession of the heirs. Beit Hillel maintain that a promissory note that stands to be collected is not considered to be already collected. The property is therefore presumed to be in the possession of the heirs, and the creditors are considered claimants (*Tosafot*).

According to the opinion of the Rabbis – אַלִּיבָּא דְּרַבָּנַן: The commentaries discuss the reason it might be possible to place a lien on property that one has not yet acquired, even if one holds that one cannot transfer ownership of an entity that has not yet come into the world. The Rashbam and Rabbeinu Gershom Meor HaGola explain that there is a difference between acquiring ownership of an entity that does not yet exist at all and placing a lien on property that exists but is not yet in the possession of the borrower. Rabbi Avraham *Av Beit Din* says that there is a difference between acquiring a gift and placing a lien upon property. In the case of a gift, the acquisition is effected only at the moment of the transaction. In the case of a loan, any property that the borrower subsequently acquires is placed under a lien at the moment it is acquired, as Rava states that the creditor can collect the debt from anything currently in the debtor's possession. He is therefore not entitled to sell the property, and it is possible that if he sells it, the lien is not released.

HALAKHA

And Beit Hillel say the property retains its previous ownership status – וּבֵית הִלֵּל אוֹמְרִים נְכָסִים בְּחֶזְקָתָן: Consider the case where a house collapses upon a son and upon his father, or upon a certain person and upon those from whom he stands to inherit, and it is unknown who died first. If the son bore the responsibility to pay the marriage contract of his wife and other debts and he had no money with which to pay them except that which he might inherit from his father, the following claims arise: The father's heirs claim that the son died first without leaving any property from which the debt can be collected, and the debt will not be paid. The creditors claim that the father died first and the son inherited his father's property, and therefore they can collect their debt from the deceased son's share in his father's inheritance. The *halakha* is that the property remains in the presumptive ownership of the heirs, and neither the wife not the other creditors receive any payment (see *Sma* and *Shakh*). This ruling is in accordance with the statement of Beit Hillel (Rambam *Sefer Mishpatim*, *Hilkhot Naḥalot* 5:8; *Shulḥan Arukh*, *Ḥoshen Mishpat* 104:16, 280:12).

אֲמַר לֵיהּ רָבָא: מִינֵּיהּ קָאָמַר? מִינֵּיהּ – אֲפִילּוּ מִגְּלִימָא דְּעַל כַּתְפֵּיהּ! כִּי קָא מִיבַּעְיָא לָן "דְּאִיקְנֵי" – קָנָה וּמָכַר, "דְּאִיקְנֵי" – קָנָה וְהוֹרִישׁ, מַאי?

Rava said to Rav Yosef: **Do** you **speak** of a case where the debt is collected **from** the debtor? With regard to collecting the debt **from him,** the debt is collected from any property currently in his possession, **even from the cloak that is upon his shoulders.**[NH] **When the dilemma was raised to us,** it was with regard to a case where the borrower wrote: The property **that I will acquire** shall be liened, and he subsequently **acquired** property **and sold it**[H] to others. The dilemma also pertains to a case where the borrower wrote: The property **that I will acquire** shall be liened, and he subsequently **acquired** property **and bequeathed** it to his heirs. In these cases, **what** is the *halakha*? Can the lender repossess the property from the buyer or heir?

אֲמַר רַב חָנָא, תָּא שְׁמַע: נָפַל הַבַּיִת עָלָיו וְעַל אָבִיו, עָלָיו וְעַל מוֹרִישָׁיו, וְהָיְתָה עָלָיו כְּתוּבַּת אִשָּׁה וּבַעַל חוֹב, יוֹרְשֵׁי הָאָב אוֹמְרִים: הַבֵּן מֵת רִאשׁוֹן וְאַחַר כָּךְ מֵת הָאָב, וּבַעֲלֵי חוֹבוֹת אוֹמְרִים: הָאָב מֵת רִאשׁוֹן כו׳;

Rav Ḥana said: Come and **hear** a proof from the mishna: In a case where **the house collapsed on** a son **and upon his father, or upon** a certain person **and upon those** from **whom he stands to inherit,** and it is unknown who died first, the *halakha* depends on the circumstances. If the son **bore** the responsibility to pay the **marriage contract of** his **wife and** to pay **a creditor,** and the son had no money with which to pay them except that which he might inherit from his father, and **the father's heirs say: The son died first and afterward the father died,** and therefore the son did not inherit property from his father, **and the creditors say: The father died first** and afterward the son died, there is a dispute with regard to how to rule. In this case, the creditors claim that the son inherited his father's property, and therefore they have a lien upon the property.

וְאִי סָלְקָא דַּעְתָּךְ "דְּאִיקְנֵי" קָנָה וּמָכַר, "דְּאִיקְנֵי" קָנָה וְהוֹרִישׁ – לָא מִשְׁתַּעְבֵּד, נְהִי נַמִי דְּאָב מִית בְּרֵישָׁא, "דְּאִיקְנֵי" הוּא!

The Gemara explains: **And if it enters your mind** to say that when the borrower writes: The property **that I will acquire** shall be liened, and he **acquires** property **and sells** it to others, it is not liened, and that when he writes: The property **that I will acquire** shall be liened, and he **acquires** property **and bequeaths** it to his heirs, **it is not liened,** then the mishna is difficult. **Although the father indeed died first,** this case **is** comparable to one where the borrower writes: The property **that I will acquire** shall be liened, as the son acquired the property after receiving the loan. This indicates that a lien can be placed upon property that one will acquire in the future.

אֲמַר לְהוּ רַב נַחְמָן: זְעֵירָא חַבְרִין תַּרְגְּמָהּ – מִצְוָה עַל הַיְתוֹמִים לִפְרוֹעַ חוֹבַת אֲבִיהֶן. מַתְקִיף לָהּ רַב אַשִׁי: מִלְוֶה עַל פֶּה הוּא, וְרַב וּשְׁמוּאֵל דְּאָמְרִי תַּרְוַיְיהוּ: מִלְוֶה עַל פֶּה – אֵינוֹ גּוֹבֶה לֹא מִן הַיּוֹרְשִׁין וְלֹא מִן הַלָּקוֹחוֹת!

Rav Naḥman said to the Sages: Rabbi **Zeira, our colleague, interpreted** the mishna as follows: In this case, the creditors do not claim the property because it is liened. Rather, they claim it because it is **a mitzva** incumbent **upon the orphans to repay their father's debt.**[H] **Rav Ashi objects to this:** If the promissory note does not place a lien on the property, **this is** considered **a loan by oral** agreement, **and Rav and Shmuel both say: A loan by oral** agreement **cannot be collected, neither from the heirs nor from the buyers.**

NOTES

From him, even from the cloak that is upon his shoulders – **מִינֵּיהּ אֲפִילּוּ מִגְּלִימָא דְּעַל כַּתְפֵּיהּ:** The creditor can collect payment from property currently in the debtor's possession, even if the debtor did not state that the property that he will acquire shall be liened (Rabbeinu Gershom Meor HaGola). A lien is placed upon anything the debtor acquires because the debtor is himself responsible toward the creditor, as the verse states: "The borrower is servant to the lender" (Proverbs 22:7; see *Sanhedrin* 31b), and this responsibility extends to anything in the debtor's possession.

HALAKHA

Even from the cloak that is upon his shoulders – **אֲפִילּוּ מִגְּלִימָא דְּעַל כַּתְפֵּיהּ:** A creditor can collect money owed to him from any property currently in the debtor's possession, both from land and from movable property, and even from the clothes that the debtor is wearing. He can collect even from property that the debtor acquired after receiving the loan (Rambam *Sefer Mishpatim, Hilkhot Malve VeLoveh* 18:1; *Shulḥan Arukh, Ḥoshen Mishpat* 111:1, 112:1).

He wrote, the property that I will acquire shall be liened, and he acquired property and sold it, etc. – **דְּאִיקְנֵי קָנָה וּמָכַר וכו׳:** If the borrower writes in the promissory note that even property that he will subsequently acquire will be liened, the lender can collect from property subsequently acquired by the borrower even if the property was then sold or bequeathed to a third party. This ruling is in accordance with the conclusion of the Gemara (157b). If this is not explicitly stated in the promissory note, the creditor cannot repossess the property from buyers or heirs (Rambam). The Rema adds that some authorities say that the failure to record this stipulation is merely a scribal error, and even if it is not stated in the promissory note, the creditor can repossess the property from buyers or heirs (*Tur*, citing Rosh and Rashba; *Shakh*). Nevertheless, some authorities maintain that if some form of guarantee is mentioned in the note but there is no reference to property that the borrower will subsequently acquire, then this is not presumed to be a scribal error (Rambam *Sefer Mishpatim, Hilkhot Malve VeLoveh* 18:1; *Shulḥan Arukh, Ḥoshen Mishpat* 111:20, 112:1, and in the comment of Rema).

A mitzva upon the orphans to repay their father's debt – **מִצְוָה עַל הַיְתוֹמִים לִפְרוֹעַ חוֹבַת אֲבִיהֶן:** It is a mitzva for orphans to repay their father's debt in order to preserve his honor. The court enforces their obligation to repay the debt just as the father's obligation would be enforced. This applies if the orphans inherited land. If they inherited only movable property, although it is a mitzva incumbent upon them to repay the debt, according to the Gemara this obligation is not enforced. The *ge'onim* instituted an ordinance that the father's creditor has a lien on the movable property inherited by the orphans, and therefore repayment from the father's movable property is also enforced by the court (see *Sma* and *Shakh*). This applies even if the father's debt resulted from a loan by oral agreement. Furthermore, this applies even if the father acquired the property after receiving the loan and did not explicitly state in the promissory note that the loan should be collected even from property that he will subsequently acquire (Rambam *Sefer Mishpatim, Hilkhot Malve VeLoveh* 11:8; 18:10; *Shulḥan Arukh, Ḥoshen Mishpat* 107:1).

אֶלָּא הָא מַנִּי? רַבִּי מֵאִיר הִיא, דְּאָמַר: אָדָם מַקְנֶה דָּבָר שֶׁלֹּא בָּא לָעוֹלָם.

Rather, in accordance with **whose** opinion **is this** mishna? This mishna **is** in accordance with the opinion of **Rabbi Meir, who says: A person can transfer** ownership of **an entity that has not** yet **come into the world.** Similarly, Rabbi Meir maintains that one can place a lien on property that the borrower will subsequently acquire.

אָמַר רַב יַעֲקֹב מִנְּהַר פְּקוֹד מִשְּׁמֵיהּ דְּרָבִינָא, תָּא שְׁמַע: שְׁטָרֵי חוֹב הַמּוּקְדָּמִין פְּסוּלִין, וְהַמְּאוּחָרִין כְּשֵׁרִין;

Rav Yaakov from Nehar Pekod says in the name of Ravina: Come and **hear** proof from a mishna (*Shevi'it* 10:5): **Promissory notes that are antedated,**[H] i.e., that are dated prior to the date on which the loan actually was given, **are invalid.** This is because the promissory note places a lien on the borrower's property. By dating the document earlier than the loan itself, the lender appears to have a lien on property that the borrower sold prior to taking out the loan, enabling the lender to fraudulently repossess it from the buyer. **But** promissory notes **that are postdated**[H] **are valid,** as this does not enable the lender to defraud a buyer.

וְאִי סָלְקָא דַּעְתָּךְ "דְּאִיקְנֵי" קָנָה וּמָכַר, "דְּאִיקְנֵי" קָנָה וְהוֹרִישׁ – לָא מִשְׁתַּעְבֵּד, מְאוּחָרִין אַמַּאי כְּשֵׁרִין? "דְּאִיקְנֵי" הוּא!

The Gemara explains: **And if it enters your mind** to say that property that the borrower acquires after receiving the loan **is not liened** even when he writes: The property **that I will acquire** shall be liened, and he **acquires** property **and sells** it to others, or when he writes: The property **that I will acquire** shall be liened, and he **acquires** property **and bequeaths** it to his heirs, **why,** then, **are postdated** promissory notes **valid?** They should be invalid, as in some instances they enable the creditor to fraudulently repossess property that is not liened, e.g., if the borrower acquires property after receiving the loan but before the date on the promissory note, and he sells it after that date. This case **is** comparable to one where the borrower writes: The property **that I will acquire** shall be liened.[N]

הָא מַנִּי? רַבִּי מֵאִיר הִיא, דְּאָמַר: אָדָם מַקְנֶה דָּבָר שֶׁלֹּא בָּא לָעוֹלָם.

The Gemara answers: In accordance with **whose** opinion **is this** mishna? This mishna **is** in accordance with the opinion of **Rabbi Meir, who says: A person can transfer** ownership of **an entity that has not** yet **come into the world.**

אָמַר רַב מְשָׁרְשִׁיָּא מִשְּׁמֵיהּ דְּרָבָא, תָּא שְׁמַע: לְשֶׁבַח קַרְקָעוֹת כֵּיצַד? הֲרֵי שֶׁמָּכַר שָׂדֶה לַחֲבֵירוֹ וְהִשְׁבִּיחָהּ, וּבָא בַּעַל חוֹב וּטְרָפָהּ, כְּשֶׁהוּא גּוֹבֶה – גּוֹבֶה אֶת הַקֶּרֶן מִנְּכָסִים מְשׁוּעְבָּדִין, וְאֶת הַשֶּׁבַח מִנְּכָסִים בְּנֵי חוֹרִין;

Rav Mesharshiyya says in the name of Rava: Come and **hear** proof from a *baraita*: With regard to collecting a debt **in** a case of **enhancement of land, how** does it happen that the debt cannot be collected from liened property that has been sold? This question arises in a case **where** a debtor **sold a field to another and** the buyer **enhanced it, and a creditor came and repossessed it** from the buyer. **When** the buyer **collects** the value of the land from the seller, he **collects the principal** even **from liened property** that was sold to others, **but** he collects the value of **the enhancement** only **from unsold property.**[N]

וְאִי סָלְקָא דַּעְתָּךְ "דְּאִיקְנֵי" קָנָה וּמָכַר, "דְּאִיקְנֵי" קָנָה וְהוֹרִישׁ – לָא מִשְׁתַּעְבֵּד, בַּעַל חוֹב אַמַּאי גּוֹבֶה שִׁבְחָא?

And if it enters your mind to say that property that the borrower acquires after receiving the loan **is not liened** even when he writes: The property **that I will acquire** shall be liened, and he **acquires** property **and sells** it to others, or when he writes: The property **that I will acquire** shall be liened, and he **acquires** property **and bequeaths** it to his heirs, **why does the creditor collect** his debt by repossessing the **enhancement** from the buyer? Since the enhancement was not extant at the time of the loan, it is not liened.

HALAKHA

Promissory notes that are antedated – שְׁטָרֵי חוֹב הַמּוּקְדָּמִין: Antedated promissory notes might enable a creditor to fraudulently repossess property from a buyer. The Sages therefore penalized the creditor who wrote such a note and ruled that an antedated promissory note enables the creditor to collect his debt only from unsold property, but not from liened property that has been sold. The promissory note is not invalid. If the debtor claims that the loan has been repaid, his claim is adjudicated as it would be in the case of any other promissory note. If he claims that he never borrowed the money, the antedated promissory note is considered evidence to the contrary, and the debtor assumes the presumptive status of one who falsely denies his debt. The Rema adds that some authorities say that an antedated promissory note is invalid (*Tur*, citing Rabbeinu Yitzḥak, Rosh, and Rivash). The debtor can therefore claim that the loan has been repaid, but he cannot claim that he never borrowed the money (*Sma*). Others maintain that an antedated promissory note is completely invalid, and the debtor is able to claim that he never borrowed the money. Even according to the Rema, who says that the promissory note is invalid, the debt nevertheless remains. Therefore, if witnesses testify to the loan or the debtor admits that he owes the money, the lender collects the debt from any property in the debtor's possession (*Shakh*). If the witnesses signed an antedated promissory note intentionally, all agree that the witnesses are disqualified from bearing witness in the future, as they testified falsely. The note is therefore invalid, and the creditor cannot use it even in order to collect payment from unsold property (Rambam *Sefer Mishpatim, Hilkhot Malve VeLoveh* 23:1 and *Sefer Shofetim, Hilkhot Edut* 19:3; *Shulḥan Arukh, Ḥoshen Mishpat* 34:9, and in the comment of Rema, 43:7–8).

But promissory notes that are postdated – וְהַמְּאוּחָרִין: A postdated promissory note is valid even if the note does not indicate that it is postdated. The reason for this is that postdating a promissory note only diminishes the ability of the creditor to collect his debt, as he cannot repossess property that was sold by the debtor prior to the date written in the note. This applies when the promissory note states that property that the borrower acquires after receiving the loan is also liened. If this is not stated in the postdated promissory note, it is invalid unless the promissory note states explicitly that it is postdated. According to some authorities, a creditor can repossess property that the borrower acquires after receiving the loan even if this is not stated in the promissory note, as the omission of this clause is considered a scribal error (*Tur*, citing Rosh and Rashba; *Shakh*). According to these authorities, a postdated promissory note is valid even if it does not state that property that the borrower acquires after receiving the loan is also liened, as the creditor is entitled to repossess this property (Rambam *Sefer Mishpatim, Hilkhot Malve VeLoveh* 23:2; *Shulḥan Arukh, Ḥoshen Mishpat* 43:12, and see *Shakh* there, and see 43:13).

NOTES

Is comparable to where he writes, the property that I will acquire shall be liened – דְּאִיקְנֵי הוּא: The postdated promissory note makes it appear that the property was in the borrower's possession at the time he received the loan, whereas he actually acquired it only after receiving the loan. If one cannot place a lien upon property that the borrower will acquire after receiving the loan, then the postdated promissory note enables the creditor to fraudulently repossess the property from the buyer.

But he collects the enhancement from unsold property – וְאֶת הַשֶּׁבַח מִנְּכָסִים בְּנֵי חוֹרִין: This is one of the ordinances enacted for the betterment of the world (see *Gittin* 48b).

הָא מַנִּי? רַבִּי מֵאִיר הִיא, דְּאָמַר: אָדָם מַקְנֶה דָּבָר שֶׁלֹּא בָּא לָעוֹלָם.

The Gemara answers: In accordance with **whose** opinion **is this** mishna? This mishna **is** in accordance with the opinion of **Rabbi Meir, who says: A person can transfer** ownership of **an entity that has not** yet **come into the world.** The dilemma of Shmuel is raised according to the opinion of the Rabbis.

אִם תִּמְצָא לוֹמַר: ״דְּאִיקְנֵי״ קָנָה וּמָכַר, ״דְּאִיקְנֵי״ קָנָה וְהוֹרִישׁ, לָא מִשְׁתַּעְבֵּד – הָא לָא מִשְׁתַּעְבֵּד. אִם תִּמְצָא לוֹמַר: מִשְׁתַּעְבֵּד, לָוָה וְלָוָה וְחָזַר וְקָנָה, מַהוּ? לְקַמָּא מִשְׁתַּעְבֵּד אוֹ לְבַתְרָא מִשְׁתַּעְבֵּד?

The Gemara comments: **If you say** that when the borrower writes: The property **that I will acquire** shall be liened, and he **acquires** property **and sells** it to others, it is not liened, and that when he writes: The property **that I will acquire** shall be liened, and he **acquires** property **and bequeaths** it to his heirs, **it is not liened,** then **it is not liened** and the following question will not arise. **If you say** that **it is liened, what is** the *halakha* with regard to one who **borrowed** money from one lender **and** then **borrowed** money from another lender, stating in both cases that the property that he will acquire shall be liened, **and** he **then acquired** land?[H] Does **the first** lender **have a lien upon** the property **or** does **the last** lender **have a lien upon** the property?[N]

אֲמַר רַב נַחְמָן: הָא מִילְּתָא אִיבַּעְיָא לָן, וּשְׁלַחוּ מִתָּם: רִאשׁוֹן קָנָה. רַב הוּנָא אָמַר: יַחֲלוֹקוּ. וְכֵן תָּנֵי רַבָּה בַּר אֲבוּהּ: יַחֲלוֹקוּ. אֲמַר רָבִינָא, מַהֲדוּרָא קַמָּא דְּרַב אַשִׁי אֲמַר לָן: רִאשׁוֹן קָנָה, מַהֲדוּרָא בַּתְרָא דְּרַב אַשִׁי אֲמַר לָן: יַחֲלוֹקוּ. וְהִלְכְתָא: יַחֲלוֹקוּ.

Rav Naḥman said: This matter was raised before us, and the Sages **sent** a response **from there,** from Eretz Yisrael: **The first** lender **acquires** the property, since his lien came first. **Rav Huna says:** The lenders **divide** the property between them. **And so teaches Rabba bar Avuh:** The lenders **divide** the property between them. **Ravina said: The first time Rav Ashi** taught this matter **he said to us: The first** lender **acquires** the property. **The last time Rav Ashi** taught this[B] matter **he said to us:** The lenders **divide** the property between them. **And the *halakha*** is that **they divide** the property between them.[N]

מֵיתִיבֵי: לְשֶׁבַח קַרְקָעוֹת כֵּיצַד? הֲרֵי שֶׁמָּכַר שָׂדֶה לַחֲבֵירוֹ וְהִשְׁבִּיחָהּ, וּבָא בַּעַל חוֹב וּטְרָפָהּ, כְּשֶׁהוּא גּוֹבֶה – גּוֹבֶה אֶת הַקֶּרֶן מִנְּכָסִין מְשׁוּעְבָּדִין, וְאֶת הַשֶּׁבַח מִנְּכָסִין בְּנֵי חוֹרִין; וְאִם אִיתָא, חֲצִי שֶׁבַח מִבְּעֵי לֵיהּ!

The Gemara **raises an objection** from the aforementioned *baraita*: With regard to collecting a debt **in** a case of **enhancement of land, how** does it occur that the debt cannot be collected from liened property that has been sold? This question arises in a case **where** one **sold a field to another, and** the buyer **enhanced it, and a creditor came and repossessed it**[H] from the buyer. **When** the buyer **collects** the value of the land from the seller, he **collects the principal** even **from liened property** that was sold to others, **but** he collects the value of **the enhancement** only **from unsold property. And if it is so** that in general, the property is divided between the creditors, then, since both the creditor and the buyer have a lien upon the enhancement of the property, the buyer **should** collect only **half of** the value of **the enhancement.**

מַאי גּוֹבֶה נַמִי דְּקָתָנֵי – חֲצִי שֶׁבַח.

The Gemara answers: **What** does the *baraita* mean, **as well,** when **it teaches** that the buyer **collects** the enhancement? The *baraita* means that he collects **half of** the value of **the enhancement.**

NOTES

Does the first…or does the last lender have a lien upon the property – לְקַמָּא...אוֹ לְבַתְרָא מִשְׁתַּעְבֵּד: On the one hand, the first lender places a lien upon the debtor's property first, and therefore he is entitled to be repaid first. On the other hand, it is possible that property that a debtor acquires after receiving a loan is not liened until he acquires it, at which time he has already taken out a loan from the second lender, who also placed a lien upon the debtor's property. Since the lien of the second lender was created closer to the time that the debtor acquired the property, it is possible that the lien of the second lender takes precedence (Rashbam; Rabbeinu Gershom Meor HaGola).

They divide the property between them – יַחֲלוֹקוּ: According to the Gemara's conclusion, the liens of both creditors take effect simultaneously. The property is therefore divided between the creditors in proportion to the debts owed to them (Rashbam; see Rambam).

BACKGROUND

The first time Rav Ashi taught this…the last time Rav Ashi taught this – מַהֲדוּרָא קַמָּא דְּרַב אַשִׁי...מַהֲדוּרָא בַּתְרָא דְּרַב אַשִׁי: Rav Ashi taught for sixty years. During the *kalla*, the gatherings for Torah study during Nisan and Tishrei, he would teach material that he had previously taught. He reviewed the entire Talmud during the first thirty years, and he then reviewed the Talmud a second time during the second thirty years. The first time he taught this matter refers to when he originally taught it during the first thirty years, and the last time refers to his second review of it during the last thirty years (Rashbam, citing Rav Hai Gaon and Rabbeinu Ḥananel; *Nimmukei Yosef*).

HALAKHA

One who borrowed and then borrowed from another and then acquired land – לָוָה וְלָוָה וְחָזַר וְקָנָה: If one borrows money from several individuals and subsequently acquires land, although each creditor places a lien upon property that the borrower subsequently acquires, none of the creditors has a claim that takes precedence over the claims of the others. They therefore divide the property between them in the following manner: If an equal division of the property will enable the creditor to whom the smallest sum is owed to receive the entire amount he is owed, then each creditor receives the sum of the smallest loan, and the remainder is divided equally between the remaining creditors. If an equal division of the property will not enable the creditor to whom the smallest sum is owed to receive the entire amount he is owed, then the property is divided equally between the creditors. If one of the creditors collected his debt before the others, he keeps whatever he collected, even if he was the last creditor (Rambam *Sefer Mishpatim, Hilkhot Malve VeLoveh* 20:4; *Shulḥan Arukh, Ḥoshen Mishpat* 104:6, 10, and see 104:5).

Where one sold a field to another and the buyer enhanced it and a creditor came and repossessed it – הֲרֵי שֶׁמָּכַר שָׂדֶה לַחֲבֵירוֹ וְהִשְׁבִּיחָהּ וּבָא בַּעַל חוֹב וּטְרָפָהּ: Consider a case where the borrower writes that the property that he will acquire shall be liened, and he subsequently sells his property, which is then enhanced by the buyer. When the lender repossesses the property from the buyer he also repossesses half of the enhancement of the property. According to the Rambam and the *Shulḥan Arukh*, this applies only with regard to a case where the property is enhanced by the buyer's efforts. In the case where the property was enhanced, but not by the buyer, the lender collects all of the value of the enhancement. The Rema adds that some authorities say that in the case of any enhancement the lender collects only half of the value of the enhancement (*Tur*, citing Rosh and *Maggid Mishne*). The Rema maintains that this is the authoritative *halakha*. Others maintain that the *halakha* is in accordance with the opinion of the Rambam (*Shakh*). If the property was enhanced due to the buyer's investment in the property, the buyer's expenses are deducted before calculating the half of the value of the enhancement that the lender can repossess. The Rema adds that some authorities say that even if the buyer invested in the property, the lender does not deduct his expenses, as the debt owed to him is equal to the value of the principal and the enhancement together (*Tur*, citing Rosh; *Shakh*). The buyer can subsequently collect the principal owed to him even from liened property that has been sold. He collects the value of the enhancement only from the lender himself (Rambam *Sefer Mishpatim, Hilkhot Malve VeLoveh* 21:1; *Shulḥan Arukh, Ḥoshen Mishpat* 115:1).

מתני׳ נָפַל הַבַּיִת עָלָיו וְעַל אִשְׁתּוֹ, יוֹרְשֵׁי הַבַּעַל אוֹמְרִים: אִשָּׁה מֵתָה רִאשׁוֹן וְאַחַר כָּךְ מֵת הַבַּעַל, יוֹרְשֵׁי אִשָּׁה אוֹמְרִים: בַּעַל מֵת רִאשׁוֹן וְאַחַר כָּךְ מֵתָה אִשָּׁה.

MISHNA If **the house collapsed upon** a husband **and upon his wife,**[HN] and it is unknown who died first, if the wife did not have any children from her husband, then the following claims arise: **The husband's heirs say:** The **wife died first** and was inherited by her husband, **and afterward the husband died,** and therefore the husband's heirs inherit both his and her property. The **wife's heirs say:** The **husband died first and afterward** the **wife died,** and her heirs inherit the property that she brought with her to the marriage and the payment of her marriage contract.

בֵּית שַׁמַּאי אוֹמְרִים: יַחֲלוֹקוּ; וּבֵית הִלֵּל אוֹמְרִים: נְכָסִים בְּחֶזְקָתָן, כְּתוּבָּה – בְּחֶזְקַת יוֹרְשֵׁי הַבַּעַל, נְכָסִים הַנִּכְנָסִין וְהַיּוֹצְאִין עִמָּהּ – בְּחֶזְקַת יוֹרְשֵׁי הָאָב.

Beit Shammai say: They divide the property[N] under dispute between them. **And Beit Hillel say:** The guaranteed **property** that the wife brought with her to the marriage retains **its** previous ownership **status.**[N] The sum of the **marriage contract** remains **in the possession of the husband's heirs,** since the marriage contract is collected from the husband's property. **Property that is brought into and taken out** of the marriage **with her,**[B] i.e., usufruct property that remains in the wife's possession during her marriage, remains **in the possession of the heirs of the** woman's **father.**

HALAKHA

If the house collapsed upon a husband and upon his wife – נָפַל הַבַּיִת עָלָיו וְעַל אִשְׁתּוֹ: Consider a case where a house collapsed on a husband and wife, and the husband did not have any children from his wife, and it is unknown who died first. In this case, the husband's heirs inherit the main sum and the additional sum stated in the marriage contract, even if the husband had set aside specific property for the payment of her marriage contract (*Ḥelkat Meḥokek*). The wife's heirs inherit the usufruct property that she brought to the marriage (Rambam *Sefer Mishpatim, Hilkhot Naḥalot* 5:6; *Shulḥan Arukh, Even HaEzer* 90:6).

NOTES

Upon a husband and upon his wife – עָלָיו וְעַל אִשְׁתּוֹ: The mishna is referring to a case where the wife does not have any children from her husband. The wife's heirs are her father's relatives, whereas the husband's heirs are either his sons from another wife, or his father's relatives (see Rashbam).

They divide the property – יַחֲלוֹקוּ: Beit Shammai maintain that since the uncertainty cannot be resolved, the property is divided in accordance with the principle that property of uncertain ownership is divided between the claimants. According to Beit Hillel, the matter is adjudicated according to the principles of presumptive ownership, as the burden of proof rests upon the claimant (Rabbi Yitzḥak Karkusha). The Rashbam notes that according to the Gemara elsewhere (*Yevamot* 38b), some say that with regard to the marriage contract Beit Shammai agree with Beit Hillel, and they concede that it remains in the possession of the husband's heirs.

The property retains its previous ownership status – נְכָסִים בְּחֶזְקָתָן: Some of the early commentaries say that this phrase presents the basic principle, the details of which are subsequently explained in the Gemara. Beit Hillel state that the property retains its previous ownership status, which in the case of the marriage contract means that it remains in the possession of the husband's heirs, and in the case of usufruct property means that it remains in the possession of the wife's heirs (Ba'al HaMaor; see Meiri). By contrast, the Rashbam and the majority of the early commentaries maintain that the discussion in the Gemara (158b) indicates that this phrase teaches a separate *halakha*, that with regard to property the woman brought to the marriage whose value is assessed at the time of the marriage, the woman is guaranteed to receive that sum upon termination of the marriage. Beit Hillel maintain that this property retains its previous ownership status. The ownership of property the woman brought to the marriage is discussed on the following *amud*.

BACKGROUND

Property that is brought into and taken out with her – נְכָסִים הַנִּכְנָסִין וְהַיּוֹצְאִין עִמָּהּ: There are two types of property a wife may bring into a marriage, guaranteed property and usufruct property. In the context of a marriage, guaranteed property is property that the wife brings with her as a dowry and for which the husband bears full responsibility. He may make use of the property as he sees fit. If he dies or divorces his wife, the property must be returned to the wife according to its value at the time of the wedding. Property brought to and taken out of the marriage with her refers to usufruct property. This is property that the wife brings to the marriage from her father's home, and from which her husband is entitled to derive benefit. It remains the wife's property, and it is not permitted for her husband to sell it. Although he is required to take care of this property, he is not responsible if it decreases in value. If the husband dies or divorces his wife, usufruct property is returned to the wife at its current value.

גמ׳ בְּחֶזְקַת מִי? רַבִּי יוֹחָנָן אָמַר: בְּחֶזְקַת יוֹרְשֵׁי הַבַּעַל, וְרַבִּי אֶלְעָזָר אָמַר: בְּחֶזְקַת יוֹרְשֵׁי הָאִשָּׁה,

GEMARA The mishna teaches that according to Beit Hillel, the guaranteed property that the wife brought with her to the marriage retains its previous ownership status. The Gemara asks: **In whose possession** does the guaranteed property remain? **Rabbi Yoḥanan says:** It remains **in the possession of the husband's heirs,** since the husband is liable to compensate his wife for guaranteed property in the event of loss. **And Rabbi Elazar says:**[N] It remains **in the possession of the wife's heirs,** as the property came from her father's house and belongs to her.

וְרַבִּי שִׁמְעוֹן בֶּן לָקִישׁ מִשּׁוּם בַּר קַפָּרָא אָמַר: יַחֲלוֹקוּ. וְכֵן תָּנֵי בַּר קַפָּרָא: הוֹאִיל וְהַלָּלוּ בָּאִין לִירַשׁ וְהַלָּלוּ בָּאִין לִירַשׁ – יַחֲלוֹקוּ.

And Rabbi Shimon ben Lakish says in the name of bar Kappara: They divide the property between them.[N] **And likewise bar Kappara teaches** in a *baraita*: **Since these** heirs **come to inherit and those** heirs **come to inherit,** and neither can prove his claim, **they divide** the property[H] between them.

מתני׳ נָפַל הַבַּיִת עָלָיו וְעַל אִמּוֹ – אֵלּוּ וָאֵלּוּ מוֹדִין שֶׁיַּחֲלוֹקוּ. אָמַר רַבִּי עֲקִיבָא: מוֹדֶה אֲנִי בְּזוֹ שֶׁהַנְּכָסִים בְּחֶזְקָתָן. אָמַר לוֹ בֶּן עַזַּאי: עַל חֲלוּקִין אָנוּ מִצְטַעֲרִין, אֶלָּא שֶׁבָּאתָ לְחַלֵּק עָלֵינוּ אֶת הַשָּׁוִין?!

MISHNA If **the house collapsed on** a son **and upon his mother,** and it is unknown who died first, the following claims arise: The mother's paternal family claims that the son died first, and therefore they inherit from the mother, and the son's heirs claim that the mother died first and her son inherited from her, and therefore they inherit from the son. In this case, both **these** Sages **and those** Sages, Beit Shammai and Beit Hillel, **concede that they divide** the property between them.[N] **Rabbi Akiva said: In this case I concede**[N] **that the property** retains **its** previous ownership **status.**[H] **Ben Azzai said to** Rabbi Akiva: **We are** already **troubled by** those cases where Beit Shammai and Beit Hillel **are in disagreement. But** do **you come to bring upon us a disagreement** with regard to **the** case where they **agree?**

NOTES

In whose possession, Rabbi Yoḥanan says…and Rabbi Elazar says, etc. – בְּחֶזְקַת מִי רַבִּי יוֹחָנָן אָמַר...וְרַבִּי אֶלְעָזָר אָמַר וכו׳: Rabbi Avraham *Av Beit Din* asks why the mishna states merely that the property retains its previous ownership status, leaving the question of who keeps the property open to different interpretations. He suggests that perhaps the *tanna* did not wish to decide this matter, and intentionally worded the mishna in an ambiguous manner, leaving the matter open for the Sages of a later generation to resolve.

And Rabbi Shimon ben Lakish says…they divide the property between them – וְרַבִּי שִׁמְעוֹן בֶּן לָקִישׁ...אָמַר יַחֲלוֹקוּ: According to this ruling, Beit Hillel do not state in the mishna merely that the property retains its previous ownership status. Rather, it is possible to translate the statement of Beit Hillel as saying: The guaranteed property remains in the possession of both of them, i.e., both the husband's heirs and the wife's heirs (Rashbam).

Concede that they divide the property between them – מוֹדִין שֶׁיַּחֲלוֹקוּ: In this case neither party can prove their claim, and neither party can claim that the property is in their possession more than it is in the possession of the other party. This is because the property was previously owned by the mother, and it is unknown whether it was inherited by the son or by the other heirs of the mother. The property is therefore divided between them.

In this case I concede, etc. – מוֹדֶה אֲנִי בְּזוֹ וכו׳: The term concede is anomalous here. In this case, no other *tanna* maintains that the property retains its previous ownership status, and it is therefore unclear to whom Rabbi Akiva concedes. The Rashbam explains that although this term is imprecise, since the first *tanna* uses this term, Rabbi Akiva also expresses his opinion using the same term. Rashi elsewhere writes that Rabbi Akiva was a disciple of Beit Shammai, who maintain in the previous mishna (158a) that the property is divided between the claimants. He therefore states that in this case, he concedes to Beit Hillel, who maintain in the previous mishna that the property retains its previous ownership status.

HALAKHA

Since these come to inherit and those come to inherit, they divide the property – הוֹאִיל וְהַלָּלוּ בָּאִין לִירַשׁ וְהַלָּלוּ בָּאִין לִירַשׁ יַחֲלוֹקוּ: Consider a case where a house collapsed on a husband and wife, and he did not have any children from her, and it is unknown who died first. With regard to the guaranteed property, the husband's heirs and the wife's heirs divide it between them equally, in accordance with the statement of bar Kappara, who was Rabbi Yoḥanan's teacher (Rambam *Sefer Mishpatim, Hilkhot Naḥalot* 5:6; *Shulḥan Arukh, Even HaEzer* 90:6).

In this case I concede that the property retains its previous ownership status – מוֹדֶה אֲנִי בְּזוֹ שֶׁהַנְּכָסִים בְּחֶזְקָתָן: Consider a case where a house collapsed on a son and his mother. The son's heirs, e.g., his paternal brothers, claim that the mother died first. The mother's heirs claim that the son died first, and since a son does not inherit from his mother while in the grave in order to bequeath the inheritance to his paternal brothers, the mother's heirs inherit from the mother. In this case the property is considered to be under the presumptive ownership of the mother's heirs, whose status as heirs is certain. This ruling is in accordance with the opinion of Rabbi Akiva, as explained by Rabbi Ila (Rambam *Sefer Mishpatim, Hilkhot Naḥalot* 5:6; *Shulḥan Arukh, Ḥoshen Mishpat* 280:10).

גמ׳ בְּחֶזְקַת מִי? רַבִּי אִילָא אָמַר: בְּחֶזְקַת יוֹרְשֵׁי הָאֵם; רַבִּי זֵירָא אָמַר: בְּחֶזְקַת יוֹרְשֵׁי הַבֵּן. כִּי סְלֵיק רַבִּי זֵירָא, קָם בְּשִׁיטָתֵיהּ דְּרַבִּי אִילָא, קָם רַבָּה בְּשִׁיטָתֵיהּ דְּרַבִּי זֵירָא. אָמַר רַבִּי זֵירָא, שְׁמַע מִינַּהּ: אֲוִירָא דְּאֶרֶץ יִשְׂרָאֵל מַחְכִּים.

GEMARA The mishna states that according to Rabbi Akiva, the property retains its previous ownership status. The Gemara asks: **In whose possession** does the property remain? **Rabbi Ila says:** It remains **in the possession of the mother's heirs. Rabbi Zeira,**[P] when he was still in Babylonia, **said:** It remains **in the possession of the son's heirs.**[N] **When Rabbi Zeira ascended** to Eretz Yisrael, **he adopted the opinion of Rabbi Ila,** whereas **Rabba,** in Babylonia, **adopted the opinion** stated **by Rabbi Zeira. Rabbi Zeira said: Conclude from** this incident **that the air of Eretz Yisrael makes** one **wise,** as when I ascended to Eretz Yisrael I accepted the opinion of Rabbi Ila, who was also from Eretz Yisrael, whereas Rabba, who remained in Babylonia, accepted my former opinion.

וְטַעְמָא מַאי? אָמַר אַבָּיֵי: הוֹאִיל וְהוּחְזְקָה נַחֲלָה בְּאוֹתוֹ שֵׁבֶט.

The Gemara asks: **And what is the reason** that the property remains in the possession of the mother's heirs? **Abaye says: Since the inheritance was** initially **in the possession of that tribe** of the mother,[N] it is not removed from their possession in order to transfer it to the son's heirs, who are from a different tribe.

״אָמַר לוֹ בֶּן עַזַּאי: עַל הַחֲלוּקִין אָנוּ מִצְטַעֲרִין״ וכו׳. אָמַר רַבִּי שַׂמְלַאי, עֲדָא אָמְרָה: בֶּן עַזַּאי תַּלְמִיד חָבֵר דְּרַבִּי עֲקִיבָא הֲוָה, דְּקָאָמַר לֵיהּ: ״שֶׁבָּאתָ״.

The mishna teaches: **Ben Azzai said to** Rabbi Akiva: **We are** already **troubled by** those cases where Beit Shammai and Beit Hillel **are in disagreement.** But do you come to bring upon us a disagreement with regard to the case where they agree? **Rabbi Shamlai said: That is to say** that **ben Azzai was a disciple-colleague of Rabbi Akiva**[N] and not just a disciple, **since he said to him:** Do **you come,** in the second person, rather than using the more formal third person.

שְׁלַחוּ מִתָּם: בֵּן שֶׁלָּוָה בְּנִכְסֵי אָבִיו בְּחַיֵּי אָבִיו, וּמֵת – בְּנוֹ מוֹצִיא מִיַּד הַלָּקוֹחוֹת, וְזוֹ הִיא שֶׁקָּשָׁה בְּדִינֵי מָמוֹנוֹת. לָוָה מַאי מַפֵּיק? וְעוֹד, לָקוֹחוֹת מַאי עֲבִידְתַּיְיהוּ? אֶלָּא אִי אִיתְּמַר הָכִי

§ The Sages **sent** a ruling **from there,** Eretz Yisrael: With regard to **a son who borrowed** money based **on** the security of **his father's property during his father's lifetime, and** whose father subsequently **died, his son repossesses** the property **from the buyers. And this is the** most **difficult** *halakha* to understand **with regard to monetary law.** The Gemara clarifies the ruling: If the son **borrowed, what does he repossess?** He needs to repay a debt, not to collect payment. **Moreover, what is the relevance of the buyers** in this matter? There is no mention of them in the premise. **Rather, if** this matter **was stated,** it is in **this** manner

Perek **IX**
Daf **159** Amud **a**

אִיתְּמַר: בֵּן שֶׁמָּכַר בְּנִכְסֵי אָבִיו בְּחַיֵּי אָבִיו, וּמֵת – בְּנוֹ מוֹצִיא מִיַּד הַלָּקוֹחוֹת. וְזוֹ הִיא שֶׁקָּשָׁה בְּדִינֵי מָמוֹנוֹת, וְלֵימְרוּ לֵיהּ: אֲבוּךְ מְזַבֵּין וְאַתְּ מַפֵּיק?!

that **it was stated:** With regard to **a son who sold** some **of his father's property**[NH] **during his father's lifetime, and** the son **died,** the son's **son repossesses** the property **from the buyers. And this is a difficult** *halakha* **with regard to monetary law,** as the buyers **can say to** the son's son: Does **your father sell** the property to us **and you repossess** it?

וּמַאי קוּשְׁיָא? דִּלְמָא מָצֵי אָמַר: מִכֹּחַ אֲבוּהּ דְּאַבָּא קָאָתֵינָא; תֵּדַע, דִּכְתִיב: ״תַּחַת אֲבֹתֶיךָ יִהְיוּ בָנֶיךָ תְּשִׁיתֵמוֹ לְשָׂרִים בְּכָל הָאָרֶץ״!

The Gemara asks: **And what is the difficulty? Perhaps he can say: I come** to repossess the property **on the basis of** the right of my **father's father** to the property, as I inherit directly from him. **Know** that this is so, **as it is written: "In the place of your fathers shall be your sons; you shall make them into princes throughout the land"** (Psalms 45:17). The phrase "In the place of your fathers shall be your sons" indicates that a grandson inherits from his grandfather directly, and he does not inherit through his father.

PERSONALITIES

Rabbi Zeira – רַבִּי זֵירָא: Born in Babylonia, Rabbi Zeira, known in the Jerusalem Talmud as Rabbi Ze'eira, became one of the most prominent third-generation *amora'im* of Eretz Yisrael. His father, a tax collector for the Persian government, was praised as one of the few who performed that function honestly. When Rabbi Zeira ascended to Eretz Yisrael, he decided to identify himself entirely with the Torah of Eretz Yisrael. The Gemara relates that he undertook one hundred fasts in order to forget the Torah that he had studied in Babylonia.

NOTES

In the possession of the son's heirs – בְּחֶזְקַת יוֹרְשֵׁי הַבֵּן: With regard to inheritance, the deceased's son always precedes any other heir. It is therefore possible to maintain that the presumption of ownership of the son is stronger than the presumption of ownership of the mother's heirs.

Since the inheritance was initially in the possession of that tribe of the mother – הוֹאִיל וְהוּחְזְקָה נַחֲלָה בְּאוֹתוֹ שֵׁבֶט: This reason cannot be understood literally, as the *halakha* applies even if the mother belongs to the same tribe as her husband and son. Rather, the Gemara's intent is to illustrate that the property was already in the possession of the mother, and consequently in the possession of the mother's family (Ramah).

Ben Azzai was a disciple-colleague of Rabbi Akiva – בֶּן עַזַּאי תַּלְמִיד חָבֵר דְּרַבִּי עֲקִיבָא הֲוָה: Rabbeinu Gershom Meor HaGola explains that initially ben Azzai and Rabbi Akiva were both disciples of Rabbi Eliezer, and afterward ben Azzai became a disciple of Rabbi Akiva. The Rashbam says that initially ben Azzai was a disciple of Rabbi Akiva. When he subsequently became a great scholar, he became Rabbi Akiva's colleague. The Rambam writes that a disciple-colleague is one who learned Torah from his colleague but did not acquire most of his wisdom from him.

NOTES

A son who sold some of his father's property – בֵּן שֶׁמָּכַר בְּנִכְסֵי אָבִיו: The Gemara is apparently referring to a case where the son sold property that he would inherit from his father. He then died during his father's lifetime. The Gemara states that after the father's death, the seller's son repossesses the property from the buyers (see Rashbam). This explanation is difficult, because if the son sold property that did not belong to him, the sale is not effective, and he himself could repossess the property after his father's death were he alive. Rabbeinu Tam explains that this is referring to a case where the seller states explicitly to the buyer that he is selling property that he will inherit when his father dies. Rabbeinu Tam maintains that although one cannot sell property that has not yet come into the world, in this case the sale is effective (see *Shita Mekubbetzet*). Others say that the Gemara is referring to one who sells property for the purpose of paying for the burial of his dying father, as in this case the Sages instituted that the sale is valid. Many of the early commentaries state that the discussion here pertains not to the property itself, but to the money the buyers paid for the property. The seller himself was obligated to return the money to the buyers, as the sale was invalid. His son is not obligated to return the money, as he did not inherit the property from his father (see *Tosafot*).

HALAKHA

A son who sold some of his father's property, etc. – בֵּן שֶׁמָּכַר בְּנִכְסֵי אָבִיו וכו׳: Consider the case of one who was dying and did not have the means to pay for his burial, and his son sold part of his father's property in order to pay for the burial, saying to the buyer: I hereby sell to you that which I will inherit from my father today, at such and such a price. Then, the son died first, and afterward the father died. In this case, the son's son can repossess the property from the buyers, and he is not required to reimburse them (see *Sma*). This is because his father sold property that had not yet come into his possession. The property therefore remained in the possession of the grandfather, and the grandson inherited it from his grandfather (Rambam *Sefer Kinyan, Hilkhot Mekhira* 22:7; *Shulḥan Arukh, Ḥoshen Mishpat* 211:3).

אֶלָּא אִי קַשְׁיָא הָא קַשְׁיָא: בֵּן בְּכוֹר שֶׁמָּכַר חֵלֶק בְּכוֹרָה בְּחַיֵּי אָבִיו וּמֵת בְּחַיֵּי אָבִיו – בְּנוֹ מוֹצִיא מִיַּד הַלָּקוֹחוֹת, וְזוֹ הִיא שֶׁקָּשָׁה בְּדִינֵי מָמוֹנוֹת: אֲבוּהּ מְזַבֵּין אִיהוּ מַפֵּיק?! וְכִי תֵּימָא, הָכָא נַמִי אָמַר: מִכֹּחַ אֲבוּהּ דְּאַבָּא קָאָתֵינָא; אִי מִכֹּחַ אֲבוּהּ דְּאַבָּא קָא אָתְיָא, בְּחֵלֶק בְּכוֹרָה מַאי עֲבִידְתֵּיהּ?

Rather, if there is a *halakha* with regard to monetary law that poses **a difficulty,**[N] **this is the difficult** *halakha*: With regard to **a firstborn son who sold, during his father's lifetime,** the **portion of the firstborn** that he was set to inherit, **and he died in his father's lifetime, his son can repossess** the portion of the firstborn **from the buyers. And this is a difficult** *halakha* **with regard to monetary law,** as **his father sells** the property and **he repossesses** it. **And if you would say: Here too, he says: I come** to repossess the property **on the basis of** the right of my **father's father** to the property, this is not a valid claim, as, **if he comes** to repossess the property **on the basis of** the right of his **father's father, what is the relevance** of the **portion of the firstborn,** since he is not his grandfather's firstborn?

וּמַאי קוּשְׁיָא? דִּלְמָא מָצֵי אָמַר: מִכֹּחַ אֲבוּהּ דְּאַבָּא קָאָתֵינָא וּבִמְקוֹם אָב קָאֵימְנָא!

The Gemara rejects this: **And what is the difficulty? Perhaps he can say: I come** to repossess the property **on the basis of** the right of my **father's father** to the property, **and** yet I receive the portion of the firstborn, as **I stand in** my **father's stead.**[N]

אֶלָּא אִי קַשְׁיָא הָא קַשְׁיָא: הָיָה יוֹדֵעַ לוֹ עֵדוּת בִּשְׁטָר עַד שֶׁלֹּא נַעֲשָׂה גַּזְלָן, וְנַעֲשָׂה גַּזְלָן – הוּא אֵינוֹ מֵעִיד עַל כְּתַב יָדוֹ, אֲבָל אֲחֵרִים מְעִידִין; הָשְׁתָּא אִיהוּ לָא מְהֵימַן, אַחֲרִינֵי מְהֵימְנֵי? וְזוֹ הִיא שֶׁקָּשָׁה בְּדִינֵי מָמוֹנוֹת.

Rather, if there is a *halakha* with regard to monetary law that poses **a difficulty, this is the difficult** *halakha*: One **knew testimony supporting** another, and his testimony was written **in a document before he became a robber,**[H] **and** then **he became a robber** and was disqualified from bearing witness. In this case, **he may not testify as to** the legitimacy of **his handwriting. But others may testify** that it is his handwriting on the document. The difficulty is that **now** that **his** testimony **is not deemed credible,**[N] although he knows of the matter with certainty, is it logical that **others are deemed credible** and his signature is ratified according to their testimony? **And this is a difficult** *halakha* **with regard to monetary law.**

מַאי קוּשְׁיָא? דִּלְמָא כְּגוֹן שֶׁהוּחְזַק כְּתַב יָדוֹ בְּבֵית דִּין!

The Gemara rejects this: **What is the difficulty? Perhaps** this *halakha* is referring to a case **where** the signature **was** already **presumed by** the **court** to be **his handwriting**[N] before he was disqualified, and the witnesses testify merely that the document was already ratified.

אֶלָּא אִי קַשְׁיָא הָא קַשְׁיָא: הָיָה יוֹדֵעַ לוֹ עֵדוּת בִּשְׁטָר עַד שֶׁלֹּא תִּפּוֹל לוֹ בִּירוּשָּׁה – הוּא אֵינוֹ יָכוֹל לְקַיֵּים כְּתַב יָדוֹ, אֲבָל אֲחֵרִים יְכוֹלִין לְקַיֵּים כְּתַב יָדוֹ. וּמַאי קוּשְׁיָא? דִּלְמָא הָכָא נַמִי, כְּגוֹן שֶׁהוּחְזַק כְּתַב יָדוֹ בְּבֵית דִּין!

Rather, if there is a *halakha* with regard to monetary law that poses **a difficulty, this is the difficult** *halakha*: One **knew testimony supporting** another concerning the latter's ownership of a plot of land, and his testimony was written **in a document before** the land **came into** the witness's possession **as an inheritance,** which caused the witness to become an interested party. In this case, the witness **may not ratify his handwriting. But others may ratify his handwriting.** The Gemara rejects this: **And what is the difficulty? Perhaps here too,** the *halakha* is referring to a case **where** the signature **was** already **presumed by** the **court** to be **his handwriting** before he became an interested party, and the witnesses testify merely that the document was already ratified.

NOTES

Rather if there is a *halakha* that poses a difficulty – אֶלָּא אִי קַשְׁיָא: The Rashbam says that the *halakha* sent from Eretz Yisrael was not the aforementioned *halakha*; rather, a different *halakha* was sent. *Tosafot* explain that all of these *halakhot* were sent from Eretz Yisrael, yet only one of them was referred to as a difficult *halakha* with regard to monetary law.

And I stand in my father's stead – וּבִמְקוֹם אָב קָאֵימְנָא: The grandson inherits the property directly from his grandfather, not from his father, who sold the property. He is still entitled to receive the portion of the firstborn, because the sons of the firstborn are entitled to receive a double portion in their inheritance even after their father's death. Although the firstborn does not receive a double portion in the case of potential inheritance, this is not considered potential inheritance, as the property was already in the father's possession at the time of his death (Ra'avad).

His testimony is not deemed credible, etc. – אִיהוּ לָא מְהֵימַן וכו׳: Rabbeinu Gershom Meor HaGola explains that the difficulty is that those who testify to ratify the signature of the witness come to uphold his testimony. Yet his actual testimony is no longer deemed credible. The Rashbam writes that even if his signature is ratified, since the witness is no longer deemed credible, the possibility exists that he signed the document after he was disqualified from bearing witness.

Where it was already presumed by the court to be his handwriting – שֶׁהוּחְזַק כְּתַב יָדוֹ: In other words, the witnesses testify that the court had already examined the document and the signatures of the witnesses and found everything satisfactory. The witnesses are therefore not upholding the testimony of the witness. Rather, they are upholding the ratification of a previous court (Rabbeinu Gershom Meor HaGola). The Rashbam explains that the current witnesses themselves ratified the document in court and signed the ratification before the original witness was disqualified from bearing witness, and now they are only ratifying their own signatures.

HALAKHA

One knew testimony supporting another in a document before he became a robber – הָיָה יוֹדֵעַ לוֹ עֵדוּת בִּשְׁטָר עַד שֶׁלֹּא נַעֲשָׂה גַּזְלָן: If one signed a document before he became a robber, and then he became a robber, he cannot testify to ratify his signature on a document. If there are others who recognize his signature and saw his signature on the document before he became a robber, they can testify that it is his signature. If they saw his signature on the document only after he became a robber, they cannot testify, as the possibility exists that he falsified his signature on the document after he was disqualified. The Rema adds that if there are no witnesses who recognize the robber's signature, but there are witnesses who saw the signed deed before the signatory became a robber (*Sma*), he signs his signature on another document, and this is then used in order to ratify his signature on the document in question (Rambam *Sefer Shofetim, Hilkhot Edut* 14:5; *Shulḥan Arukh, Ḥoshen Mishpat* 46:34, and see *Pitḥei Teshuva* there).

HALAKHA

One knew testimony with regard to another before he became his son-in-law – הָיָה יוֹדֵעַ לוֹ בְּעֵדוּת עַד שֶׁלֹּא נַעֲשָׂה חֲתָנוֹ: If one signed a document as a witness before he became the son-in-law of one of the parties, and then he became the son-in-law of one of the parties, he cannot testify to ratify his signature. Others can testify that they recognize his signature even if they did not see the document before he became the son-in-law of one of the parties. Some authorities say that the document is valid only if it is produced by another. If it is produced by the witnesses, they are disqualified from bearing witness with regard to the document (Rambam *Sefer Shofetim, Hilkhot Edut* 14:5; *Shulḥan Arukh, Ḥoshen Mishpat* 46:35).

It is the King's edict – גְּזֵירַת מֶלֶךְ הוּא: The Torah disqualifies relatives from bearing witness for one another. This is not because they are presumed to love one another; rather, it is a Torah edict. This is evidently so, as they are also disqualified from bearing witness against one another, and even Moses and Aaron are disqualified from bearing witness for one another (Rambam *Sefer Shofetim, Hilkhot Edut* 13:15; *Shulḥan Arukh, Ḥoshen Mishpat* 33:10).

NOTES

Even though it was not previously presumed by the court to be his handwriting – אַף עַל פִּי שֶׁלֹּא הוּחְזַק כְּתַב יָדוֹ בְּבֵית דִּין: The early commentaries explain that there is an essential difference between the case of a witness who became a robber and the case of a witness who became a relative. The robber is suspected of falsifying his testimony, and the possibility exists that he signed the document after he was disqualified, falsifying the date. According to some commentaries, this also applies in the previous case, with regard to one who became an interested party. By contrast, a relative is not suspected of falsifying his testimony, although he is disqualified from bearing witness with regard to his relative (Ri Migash). The Ritva adds that it is not possible to explain that a relative is disqualified from bearing witness due to the concern that he may testify falsely out of love of his relative, as one is disqualified from testifying against the interests of his relative as well.

That verse is written as a blessing – הַהוּא בִּבְרָכָה כְּתִיב: The verse teaches that the righteous are blessed with sons and grandsons who inherit from them. This explanation is indicated by the continuation of the verse: "You shall make them into princes throughout the land" (Rashbam).

אֶלָּא אִי קַשְׁיָא הָא קַשְׁיָא: הָיָה יוֹדֵעַ לוֹ בְּעֵדוּת עַד שֶׁלֹּא נַעֲשָׂה חֲתָנוֹ, וְנַעֲשָׂה חֲתָנוֹ – הוּא אֵינוֹ מֵעִיד עַל כְּתַב יָדוֹ, אֲבָל אֲחֵרִים מְעִידִין; הוּא לָא מְהֵימַן, אַחֲרִינֵי מְהֵימְנֵי?

Rather, if there is a *halakha* with regard to monetary law that poses **a difficulty, this is the difficult** *halakha*: **One knew testimony with regard to** another, and his testimony was written in a document **before he became** that person's **son-in-law,**[H] **and** then **he became his son-in-law.** In this case, the son-in-law **may not testify as to his handwriting,** since one cannot bear witness for his relative. **But others may testify** that it is his handwriting. Is it logical that **his** testimony **is not deemed credible,** yet **others are deemed credible** and may ratify his signature?

וְכִי תֵימָא, הָכָא נַמִי כְּגוֹן שֶׁהוּחְזַק כְּתַב יָדוֹ בְּבֵית דִּין; וְהָא אָמַר רַב יוֹסֵף בַּר מִנְיוּמִי אָמַר רַב נַחְמָן: אַף עַל פִּי שֶׁלֹּא הוּחְזַק כְּתַב יָדוֹ בְּבֵית דִּין!

And if you would say: Here too, the *halakha* is referring to a case **where** the signature **was** already **presumed by** the **court** to be **his handwriting** before he became a relative, this is difficult. **But doesn't Rav Yosef bar Minyumi say that Rav Naḥman says:** Others may testify as to the validity of his handwriting **even though** the signature **was not** previously **presumed by** the **court** to be **his handwriting?**[N]

וּמַאי קוּשְׁיָא? דִּלְמָא גְּזֵירַת מֶלֶךְ הִיא דְּאִיהוּ לָא מְהֵימַן וְאַחֲרִינֵי מְהֵימְנֵי, וְלָאו מִשּׁוּם דִּמְשַׁקֵּר! דְּאִי לָא תֵימָא הָכִי, מֹשֶׁה וְאַהֲרֹן לְחוֹתְנָם מִשּׁוּם דְּלָא מְהֵימְנֵי הוּא? אֶלָּא גְּזֵירַת מֶלֶךְ הוּא שֶׁלֹּא יָעִידוּ לָהֶם, הָכָא נַמִי גְּזֵירַת מֶלֶךְ הוּא שֶׁלֹּא יָעִיד עַל כְּתַב יָדוֹ לְחוֹתְנוֹ!

The Gemara rejects this: **And what is the difficulty? Perhaps it is the King's edict,** i.e., a divine decree, **that** the testimony of a son-in-law **is not deemed credible, and** yet the testimony of **others is deemed credible, and** the reason he is disqualified is **not that he is** suspected of **lying.** This must be so, **as if you do not say so,** why are **Moses and Aaron** disqualified from bearing witness **for their father-in-law?** Could this be **because their** testimony **is not deemed credible? Rather, it is the King's edict that** even Moses and Aaron **shall not bear witness for** their relatives. **Here too, it is the King's edict**[H] **that** a son-in-law **shall not testify as to** the validity of **his handwriting for his father-in-law.**

אֶלָּא, לְעוֹלָם כְּדַאֲמַרִינַן מֵעִיקָּרָא, וּדְקָא קַשְׁיָא לָךְ: "תַּחַת אֲבֹתֶיךָ יִהְיוּ בָנֶיךָ" – הַהוּא בִּבְרָכָה כְּתִיב.

Rather, the difficulty is **actually as we said initially,** with regard to the *halakha* that if a son sold some of his father's property and then died, the son's son repossesses the property from the buyers. **And** with regard to the verse **that** posed **a difficulty for you: "In the place of your fathers shall be your sons"** (Psalms 45:17), which apparently indicates that a grandson inherits from his grandfather directly, this is not difficult. **That** verse **is written as a blessing.**[N] The verse does not indicate the halakhic status of the grandson's inheritance, and the reason he can repossess the property is still difficult.

וּמִי מָצֵית אָמְרַתְּ בִּבְרָכָה כְּתִיב,

The Gemara asks: **But can you say that** the verse **is written as a blessing,**

Perek **IX**
Daf **159** Amud **b**

אֲבָל לְעִנְיַן דִּינָא לָא?

but with regard to the *halakha* it does **not** indicate anything?

וְהָתַנְיָא: נָפַל הַבַּיִת עָלָיו וְעַל אָבִיו, עָלָיו וְעַל מוֹרִישָׁיו, וְהָיְתָה עָלָיו כְּתוּבַּת אִשָּׁה וּבַעַל חוֹב, יוֹרְשֵׁי הָאָב אוֹמְרִים: הַבֵּן מֵת רִאשׁוֹן וְאַחַר כָּךְ מֵת הָאָב, וּבַעַל חוֹב אוֹמֵר: הָאָב מֵת רִאשׁוֹן וְאַחַר כָּךְ מֵת הַבֵּן;

But isn't it taught in the mishna (157a): **A house collapsed on** a son **and upon his father, or upon** a certain person **and upon those** from **whom he stands to inherit,** and it is unknown who died first. If the son **bore** the responsibility to pay the **marriage contract of** his **wife and** to pay **a creditor,** and the son had no money with which to pay them except that which he might inherit from his father, and **the father's heirs say: The son died first and afterward the father died,** and therefore the son did not inherit property from his father, **and the creditor says: The father died first and afterward the son died,** there is a dispute as to the *halakha*. The son therefore inherited his father's property, and his creditor has a lien upon the property, enabling him to collect payment from the property even after the son's death.

מַאי לָאו יוֹרְשֵׁי הָאָב – בְּנֵי, מוֹרִישָׁיו – אַחֵי; וְאִי סָלְקָא דַּעְתָּךְ לָא מָצֵי אָמַר "מִכֹּחַ אֲבוּהּ דְּאַבָּא קָאָתֵינָא", דִּכְתִיב "תַּחַת אֲבֹתֶיךָ יִהְיוּ בָנֶיךָ" – בִּבְרָכָה כְּתִיב, כִּי מֵת הַבֵּן וְאַחַר כָּךְ מֵת הָאָב מַאי הָוֵי? נֵימָא לְהוּ בַּעַל חוֹב: יְרוּשַּׁת אֲבוּהוֹן קָא שָׁקֵילְנָא!

What, is it not correct to explain that **the father's heirs** are the son's **sons,** and the term: Those from **whom he stands to inherit,** is referring to the deceased son's **brothers?**[N] **And if it enters your mind** to maintain that the grandson **cannot say: I come** to repossess the property **on the basis of** the right of my **father's father** to the property, **as when it is written** in the verse in Psalms: **"In the place of your fathers shall be your sons,"** this **is written as a blessing,** then the mishna is difficult. According to this understanding, grandsons inherit from their grandfather only through their father. If so, even **if the son died** first **and afterward the father died, what of it? Let the creditor say to** the son's sons: It is **their father's inheritance** that **I am taking,** as the grandsons inherit from their grandfather only through their father.

לָא, יוֹרְשֵׁי הָאָב – אֶחָיו, מוֹרִישָׁיו – אַחֵי דַּאֲבוּהּ.

The Gemara rejects this explanation: **No, the father's heirs are** the deceased son's **brothers,** who certainly inherit from their father directly, and the term: **Those** from **whom he stands to inherit,** is referring to the deceased son's **father's brothers.** Therefore, one cannot derive from the mishna that a grandson inherits from his grandfather directly.

בָּעוּ מִינֵּיהּ מֵרַב שֵׁשֶׁת: בֵּן מַהוּ שֶׁיִּירַשׁ אֶת אִמּוֹ בַּקֶּבֶר לְהַנְחִיל לָאַחִין מִן הָאָב? אֲמַר לְהוּ רַב שֵׁשֶׁת, תְּנֵיתוּהָ: הָאָב שֶׁנִּשְׁבָּה וּמֵת בְּנוֹ בַּמְּדִינָה, וּבֵן שֶׁנִּשְׁבָּה וּמֵת אָבִיו בַּמְּדִינָה – יוֹרְשֵׁי הָאָב וְיוֹרְשֵׁי הַבֵּן יַחֲלוֹקוּ;

§ The Sages **raised a dilemma before Rav Sheshet: What is** the *halakha* **with regard to a son inheriting from his mother** while he is **in the grave, in order to bequeath** that inheritance **to his paternal brothers?** If a son dies, and afterward his mother dies, does the deceased son inherit from his mother, and subsequently bequeath the inheritance to his paternal brothers, who are not related to the mother? **Rav Sheshet said to them: You learned it** in a *baraita*: Consider **the** case of a **father who was taken captive** and died in captivity, **and his son died in the province,** i.e., at home, **and** consider the case of **a son who was taken captive** and died, **and his father died in the province.** Since it is not known who died first, **the father's heirs and the son's heirs divide** the inheritance.

הֵיכִי דָּמֵי? אִילֵימָא כִּדְקָתָנֵי – הֵי נִינְהוּ יוֹרְשֵׁי הָאָב וְהֵי נִינְהוּ יוֹרְשֵׁי הַבֵּן? אֶלָּא לָאו הָכִי קָאָמַר: אָב שֶׁנִּשְׁבָּה וּמֵת בֶּן בִּתּוֹ בַּמְּדִינָה, וּבֶן בִּתּוֹ שֶׁנִּשְׁבָּה וּמֵת אֲבִי אִמּוֹ בַּמְּדִינָה, וְלָא יָדְעִינַן הֵי מִינַּיְיהוּ מִית בְּרֵישָׁא – יוֹרְשֵׁי הָאָב וְיוֹרְשֵׁי הַבֵּן יַחֲלוֹקוּ;

The Gemara asks: **What are the circumstances** of the case? **If we say** that the case **is as the** *baraita* **teaches,** the *baraita* is difficult. **Who are the father's heirs**[N] **and who are the son's heirs?** The same individuals inherit from both of them. **Rather, is it not** so that **this** is what the *baraita* **is saying:** Consider the case of **a father who was taken captive** and died in captivity, **and his daughter's son died**[H] **in the province, and** consider the case of the **son of his daughter who was taken captive** and died, **and the father of** the captive's **mother died in the province, and we do not know which of them died first.** If the father died first, his daughter's son inherits from him, and the son's paternal relatives subsequently inherit from the son. If the son died first, the father's heirs inherit the father's estate. Since it is unknown which of them died first, **the father's heirs and the son's heirs divide** the inheritance.

וְאִם אִיתָא, נְהִי נַמִי דְּבֵן מֵת בְּרֵישָׁא, לֵירְתֵיהּ לַאֲבוּהּ דְּאִמֵּיהּ בְּקִבְרֵיהּ וְלֵירְתִינְהוּ לַאֲחוּהּ מִן אֲבוּהּ! אֶלָּא לָאו שְׁמַע מִינָּהּ: אֵין הַבֵּן יוֹרֵשׁ אֶת אִמּוֹ בַּקֶּבֶר לְהַנְחִיל לָאַחִין מֵאָב.

And if it is so that a son inherits from his mother while in the grave, **although the son indeed died first, he should inherit** from **his mother's father** while **in his grave and bequeath** his inheritance **to his paternal brothers,** and the son's heirs should receive the entire inheritance. **Rather, isn't it** correct to **conclude from** the *baraita* that **the son does not inherit from his mother** while **in the grave in order to bequeath** that inheritance **to his paternal brothers?**

אֲמַר לֵיהּ רַב אַחָא בַּר מִנְיוּמִי לְאַבַּיֵי, אַף אֲנַן נַמִי תָּנֵינָא: נָפַל הַבַּיִת עָלָיו וְעַל אִמּוֹ – אֵלּוּ וָאֵלּוּ מוֹדִים שֶׁיַּחֲלוֹקוּ; וְאִם אִיתָא, נְהִי נַמִי דְּבֵן מֵת בְּרֵישָׁא, לֵירְתֵיהּ לְאִמֵּיהּ בְּקִבְרֵיהּ וְלֵירְתוּ אִינְהוּ לַאֲחֵי מֵאֲבוּהּ! אֶלָּא לָאו שְׁמַע מִינָּהּ: אֵין הַבֵּן יוֹרֵשׁ אֶת אִמּוֹ בַּקֶּבֶר לְהַנְחִיל לָאַחִין מִן הָאָב, שְׁמַע מִינָּהּ.

Rav Aḥa bar Minyumi said to Abaye: We learn this *halakha* in the mishna (158b) **as well:** If **the house collapsed on** a son **and upon his mother,** both **these** Sages **and those** Sages, Beit Shammai and Beit Hillel, **concede that** the son's heirs and the mother's heirs **divide** the property between them. **And if it is so** that a son inherits from his mother while in the grave, **although** the **son indeed died first, he should inherit** from **his mother** while **in his grave and they should inherit** from him, i.e., he should bequeath his inheritance **to his paternal brothers. Rather, isn't it** correct to **conclude from** that mishna that **the son does not inherit from his mother** while **in the grave in order to bequeath** that inheritance **to his paternal brothers?** The Gemara affirms: **Conclude from** the mishna that this is so.

NOTES

Those from whom he stands to inherit is referring to the deceased son's brothers – מוֹרִישָׁיו אַחֵי: The Gemara here tries to infer from the mishna that a grandson inherits from his grandfather directly, and not through his father. Furthermore, the Gemara understands that this principle also applies to other cases of inheritance, e.g., when a house collapses on a debtor and his brother. In this case, the debtor's sons inherit from their uncle directly, not through their father (Rabbeinu Gershom Meor HaGola; see Meiri). By contrast, the Ra'avad maintains that even if a grandson inherits from his grandfather directly, this principle does not apply in other cases of inheritance. According to this understanding, the case where the house collapsed on a certain person and those from whom he stands to inherit must be explained differently (see *Sefer Hashlama*).

Who are the father's heirs, etc. – הֵי נִינְהוּ יוֹרְשֵׁי הָאָב וכו׳: The son's heirs are the son's sons, or, if has no sons, his brothers or his father's brothers. If the son died first, the same heirs inherit the son's portion of the inheritance from his father.

HALAKHA

A father who was taken captive and died, and his daughter's son died, etc. – אָב שֶׁנִּשְׁבָּה וּמֵת בֶּן בִּתּוֹ וכו׳: Consider the case of one who died in captivity while his daughter's son died at home, or one who died at home while his daughter's son died in captivity. Since it is not known which of them died first, the heirs of the father and the heirs of the daughter's son divide the father's property between them. The Rema adds that some authorities say that all of the property is under the presumptive ownership of the father's heirs, in accordance with Rabbi Akiva's ruling (158b) that the property retains its previous ownership status (Rambam *Sefer Mishpatim, Hilkhot Naḥalot* 5:7; *Shulḥan Arukh, Ḥoshen Mishpat* 280:11).

וְטַעְמָא מַאי? אָמַר אַבַּיֵי: נֶאֶמְרָה סִיבָּה בְּבֵן וְנֶאֶמְרָה סִיבָּה בְּבַעַל, מַה סִיבָּה הָאֲמוּרָה בְּבַעַל – אֵין הַבַּעַל יוֹרֵשׁ אֶת אִשְׁתּוֹ בַּקֶּבֶר, אַף סִיבָּה הָאֲמוּרָה בְּבֵן – אֵין הַבֵּן יוֹרֵשׁ אֶת אִמּוֹ בַּקֶּבֶר לְהַנְחִיל לָאַחִין מִן הָאָב.

And what is the reason[N] that a son does not inherit from his mother while in the grave? **Abaye says:** The term **transfer,** concerning the transfer of inheritance from one tribe to another, **was stated with regard to** the inheritance of **a son** (see Numbers 36:7), **and** the term **transfer was stated with regard to** the inheritance of **a husband** (see 111b–113a and Numbers 36:9). **Just as** in the case categorized as **transfer that was stated with regard to** the inheritance **of a husband,**[N] **the husband does not inherit**[N] from **his wife** while he is **in the grave**[H] in order to bequeath that inheritance to his heirs, **so too,** in the case categorized as **transfer that was stated with regard to** the inheritance of **a son, the son does not inherit from his mother** while **in the grave**[H] **in order to bequeath** that inheritance **to his paternal brothers.**

הַהוּא דַּאֲמַר לֵיהּ לְחַבְרֵיהּ: ״נִכְסֵי דְּבַר סִיסִין מְזַבְּנִינָא לָךְ״. הֲוַאי חֲדָא אַרְעָא דַּהֲוָה מִיקַּרְיָא ״דְּבֵי בַּר סִיסִין״, אֲמַר לֵיהּ: הָא לָאו דְּבֵי בַּר סִיסִין הִיא, וְאִיקַּרוּיֵי הוּא דְּמִיקַּרְיָא ״דְּבֵי בַּר סִיסִין״.

§ There was **a certain** person **who said to another: I am selling to you** all of **the property** that I own **of bar Sisin.**[H] **There was one** parcel of **land that was called** the tract **of the house of bar Sisin.** The seller **said to** the buyer: **This** latter parcel of land **is** actually **not** the property **of the house of bar Sisin, and it is** merely **called: Of the house of bar Sisin,** and therefore it is not included in the sale.

אֲתָא לְקַמֵּיהּ דְּרַב נַחְמָן, אוֹקְמָהּ בִּידָא דְּלוֹקֵחַ. אֲמַר לֵיהּ רָבָא לְרַב נַחְמָן: דִּינָא הָכִי? הַמּוֹצִיא מֵחֲבֵירוֹ עָלָיו הָרְאָיָה! וְרָמֵי דְּרָבָא אַדְּרָבָא, וּדְרַב נַחְמָן אַדְּרַב נַחְמָן;

The matter **came before Rav Naḥman,** and **he placed** the land **in the possession of the buyer. Rava said to Rav Naḥman:** Is **this the** ***halakha***? The *halakha* is that **the burden of proof rests upon the claimant,** which in this case is the buyer. **And** the Gemara **raises a contradiction between** this statement **of Rava** and another statement **of Rava, and between** this statement **of Rav Naḥman** and another statement **of Rav Naḥman.**

דְּהַהוּא דַּאֲמַר לֵיהּ לְחַבְרֵיהּ: מַאי בָּעֵית בְּהַאי בֵּיתָא? אֲמַר לֵיהּ: מִינָּךְ זְבִינְתַּהּ וַאֲכָלִית שְׁנֵי חֲזָקָה. אֲמַר לֵיהּ: אֲנָא בִּשְׁכוּנֵי גַּוָּאֵי הֲוַאי;

The Gemara explains the contradictions. There was **a certain** man **who said to another: What do you want,** i.e., what are you doing, **with this house** of mine? **He said to** the claimant: **I purchased it from you and I** worked and **profited** from it for **the years** necessary for establishing the **presumption** of **ownership.** The claimant **said to him: I was** traveling **among the settlements** in a distant location, and I was unaware that you were residing in my house, which is why I did not lodge a protest.

NOTES

And what is the reason – וְטַעְמָא מַאי: The principle that a son does not inherit from his mother while in the grave is an exception to the rule with regard to the *halakhot* of inheritance. Generally, one can come into possession of his inheritance even if one of the relatives from which one inherits is deceased. This is because inheritance is unlike other modes of transferring property. It enters the heir's possession according to the order of precedence of kinship, and there is no need for an act of acquisition. Since it does not involve the will of the one bequeathing the inheritance, there is no need for the one bequeathing the inheritance to be alive and conscious of the transfer.

Just as in the case of transfer that was stated with regard to a husband – מַה סִיבָּה הָאֲמוּרָה בְּבַעַל: A husband inherits from his wife due to the legal bond of their marriage. Since his death ends the marriage, it is obvious that he no longer inherits her property. Conversely, a son inherits from his mother due to his filial kinship. He remains her kin even after his death, and therefore it is not necessarily apparent that he does not inherit from her while in the grave (Rivam; Rid).

The husband does not inherit, etc. – אֵין הַבַּעַל יוֹרֵשׁ וכו׳: The Rashbam explains that the husband does not inherit from his wife after her death. If she predeceases her relatives, the husband does not inherit their property through his deceased wife. Rather, the property is inherited by her own relatives. According to this explanation, there is a dissimilarity between the two phrases. In the case of the son, the term: In the grave, refers to the deceased son, whereas in the case of the husband it refers to his deceased wife.

HALAKHA

The husband does not inherit from his wife while in the grave – אֵין הַבַּעַל יוֹרֵשׁ אֶת אִשְׁתּוֹ בַּקֶּבֶר: A husband's right to inherit from his wife precedes the rights of all other heirs. This applies only during his lifetime. If the husband dies, and afterward his wife dies, he does not inherit from her while in the grave in order to bequeath her property to his next of kin. Rather, the wife's next of kin from her father's family inherit from her. This ruling is in accordance with the explanation of the Ri Migash (see 114b). If the wife dies during her husband's lifetime, and afterward her father or another relative from whom she inherits dies, the husband does not inherit from them through his wife. Rather, her offspring inherit from her. If she has no offspring, the inheritance returns to her father's family, as the husband inherits only property already in his wife's possession at the time of her death, not property due to her. This ruling is in accordance with the explanation of the Rashbam (Rambam *Sefer Mishpatim, Hilkhot Naḥalot* 1:11–12; *Shulḥan Arukh, Even HaEzer* 90:1).

The son does not inherit from his mother in the grave – אֵין הַבֵּן יוֹרֵשׁ אֶת אִמּוֹ בַּקֶּבֶר: In a case where a son dies during his mother's lifetime without leaving any offspring, when his mother dies her inheritance returns to her father's family. Although the son would inherit from his mother were he alive, he does not inherit from her while in the grave in order to bequeath the inheritance to his paternal brothers (Rambam *Sefer Mishpatim, Hilkhot Naḥalot* 1:13, and see 5:6; *Shulḥan Arukh, Ḥoshen Mishpat* 276:5, and see 280:10).

The property that I own of bar Sisin – נִכְסֵי דְּבַר סִיסִין: Consider the case of one who says to another that he is selling the field of so-and-so to him. Subsequently, when the buyer wishes to take possession of the field, the seller claims that although the field is generally known as so-and-so's field, it did not actually belong to that person, and the sale did not refer to that field. Rather, the sale referred to a different field that the seller purchased from so-and-so. In this case the seller must prove his claim. Otherwise, since the field is known as so-and-so's field, the buyer can take possession of the field, in accordance with the opinion of Rav Naḥman (Rambam *Sefer Kinyan, Hilkhot Mekhira* 21:21; *Shulḥan Arukh, Ḥoshen Mishpat* 218:25).

אֲתָא לְקַמֵּיהּ דְּרַב נַחְמָן, אֲמַר לֵיהּ: זִיל בְּרוֹר אֲכִילָתָךְ. אֲמַר לֵיהּ רָבָא לְרַב נַחְמָן: דִּינָא הָכִי? הַמּוֹצִיא מֵחֲבֵירוֹ עָלָיו הָרְאָיָה! קַשְׁיָא דְּרָבָא אַדְּרָבָא, וּדְרַב נַחְמָן אַדְּרַב נַחְמָן!

The one residing in the house **came before Rav Naḥman** for a judgment. Rav Naḥman **said to him: Go clarify your profiting,**[H] i.e., prove that you really resided there for three years, and then the case can be judged. **Rava said to** Rav Naḥman: Is **this the** correct **judgment?** The *halakha* is that **the burden of proof rests upon the claimant.** Therefore, the claimant should have to prove that the possessor did not reside in the house. The first statement **of Rava is difficult,** as it is contradicted **by** the second statement **of Rava,**[N] **and** the first statement **of Rav Naḥman** is difficult, as it is contradicted **by** the second statement **of Rav Naḥman.** In the first case, Rav Naḥman ruled in favor of the buyer, and Rava ruled in favor of the seller, whereas in the second case their rulings were reversed.

דְּרָבָא אַדְּרָבָא לָא קַשְׁיָא: הָכָא מוֹכֵר קָאֵי בְּנִכְסֵיהּ, הָתָם לוֹקֵחַ קָאֵי בְּנִכְסֵיהּ.

The Gemara answers: The apparent contradiction **between** the first statement **of Rava** and the second statement **of Rava is not difficult. Here,** with regard to the property of bar Sisin, the **seller stands in** possession of **his property,** and the buyer claims the parcel of land from him. **There,** the **buyer stands in** possession of **his property,** since he dwells in the house, and the seller wishes to evict him.

דְּרַב נַחְמָן אַדְּרַב נַחְמָן לָא קַשְׁיָא: הָכָא, כֵּיוָן דַּאֲמַר לֵיהּ ״דְּבֵי בַר סִיסִין״ וּמִיקְּרְיָא ״דְּבֵי בַר סִיסִין״ – עֲלֵיהּ דִּידֵיהּ רְמָיָא לְגַלּוֹיֵי דְּלָאו דְּבֵי בַר סִיסִין הִיא. הָכָא, לֹא יְהֵא אֶלָּא דְּנָקֵיט שְׁטָרָא, מִי לָא אָמְרִינַן לֵיהּ: קַיֵּים שְׁטָרָךְ וְקוּם בְּנִכְסֵי?

The contradiction between one statement **of Rav Naḥman and** the other statement **of Rav Naḥman** is **not difficult as well,** because there, **since** the seller **said to him:** I am hereby selling you all of the property that I own **of the house of bar Sisin, and** this parcel of land is **called: Of the house of bar Sisin,** it is **incumbent on him to reveal that it is not of the house of bar Sisin. But here,** in the case where the claimant states that he had been in a distant location, it **should not be** considered as any case **other** than one **where** the possessor is **holding a document** as evidence that he purchased the house. **Wouldn't we** then **say to him:** First **ratify your document, and** only then be **established** as the owner of the **property?**[N] In this case as well, since his presumptive ownership is in place of a document, he needs to clarify the matter by means of witnesses.

הדרן עלך מי שמת

HALAKHA

Go clarify your profiting – זִיל בְּרוֹר אֲכִילָתָךְ: Consider the case of one who is in possession of a field, and he claims that he acquired it from its owner and occupied it in the manner necessary to establish the presumption of ownership. The former owner contests his claim, stating that he was not in the province during that time, and therefore the person in possession of the field could not have acquired it from him. In this case, the person in possession of the field is required to prove that the former owner was in the province at least one day during the time in question. This ruling is in accordance with the opinion of Rav Naḥman and in accordance with the Rif's explanation of the Gemara. Some authorities say that this applies only when the person in possession of the field claims to have acquired it during a time of crisis, when travel is perilous. If the conditions of travel at the time were normal, he is not required to prove that the former owner was in the vicinity, as he might have sold the field by means of an agent (*Tur*, citing Ramah and Rosh). Some authorities say that if the person in possession of the field did not state the day or month when he acquired the field, he is required only to produce witnesses who can testify that he occupied the property for the years necessary to establish the presumption of ownership (Rambam *Sefer Mishpatim*, *Hilkhot To'en VeNitan* 15:10; *Shulḥan Arukh*, *Ḥoshen Mishpat* 146:11–12).

NOTES

The first statement of Rava is difficult as it is contradicted by the second statement of Rava, etc. – קַשְׁיָא דְּרָבָא אַדְּרָבָא וכו׳: In the first case Rava maintains that the property is under the presumptive ownership of the seller, whereas in the second case he maintains that the property is under the presumptive ownership of the buyer. In the first case Rav Naḥman rules that the seller must prove his claim, whereas in the second case he maintains that the buyer must prove his claim.

Ratify your document and be established as owner of the property – קַיֵּים שְׁטָרָךְ וְקוּם בְּנִכְסֵי: The Gemara resolves the apparent contradictions by explaining the fundamental logic of each Sage. Rava maintains that the one who is in actual possession of the property is presumed to be its owner, whereas Rav Naḥman maintains that the property is under the presumptive ownership of the party whose claim appears to be more solid.

Summary of **Perek IX**

Several fundamental issues were discussed in this chapter. With regard to the division of the estate of the deceased between the sons and the daughters, the Gemara says that when the estate is large, the sons inherit it, and they are required to provide the daughters with sustenance out of their inheritance. If the estate is insufficiently large to provide for both the sons and the daughters, the daughters' claim takes precedence over the sons' claim, since their right to sustenance is based on the stipulations of the marriage contract. The daughters are therefore provided with sustenance from the estate, while the sons are required to provide for themselves.

A *tumtum*, whose sexual organs are indeterminate, is unable to prove his claim either to the rights of a son or to the rights of a daughter. The *tumtum* is therefore excluded from receiving the inheritance of the sons in the case of a large estate and the sustenance of the daughters in the case of a small estate. The *tumtum* is still a child of the deceased and inherits from the father if there is no other child.

The Gemara examined the related issue of the legal status of a fetus. It concluded that a fetus is not considered a legal person and cannot acquire property. There is one exception to this principle: One can transfer ownership of his property to his own unborn child.

When some of the heirs are adults and others are minors, the income from and expenditures spent due to the inheritance are divided equally between the heirs until the property is divided. This also applies to profits or losses incurred by one of the brothers due to the honor of the family and social obligations such as the gifts of groomsmen. The adult sons may declare at the outset that they intend to engage in business, enhancing the property for themselves. Furthermore, if the property was enhanced due to the efforts or expenditure of the adult sons, in any event the enhancement belongs entirely to the adult sons. The same applies with regard to a wife who inherited her husband's property.

The Sages instituted that a person on his deathbed can transfer ownership of his property by verbal instruction, without performing a formal act of acquisition. This was instituted due to the concern that the sick person's condition might be exacerbated by the anxiety and anguish caused by his inability to ensure the implementation of his will. The Gemara's conclusion is that the gift of a person on his deathbed bestowed by verbal instruction is valid whether it was bestowed on a weekday or on Shabbat. With regard to several matters the gifts of a person on his deathbed have the legal status of inheritance, e.g., the transfer of ownership is effected only when the giver dies.

The Sages distinguish between several forms of gifts of a person on his deathbed. If a person on his deathbed transfers the ownership of all his property, his gift has the legal status of a gift of a person on his deathbed, and if he recovers he can retract the

gift. Furthermore, during his illness he can retract the gift or transfer it to another, and the last instruction that he issues takes effect. If a person on his deathbed transfers the ownership of only some of his property, reserving part of his property for himself, his gift does not have the status of the gift of a person on his deathbed, and he cannot retract the gift even if he recovers. If the person on his deathbed clearly indicates that he is bestowing the gift due to his expectation of imminent death, his gift has the status of the gift of a person on his deathbed, even if he transfers ownership of only some of his property.

The chapter concluded with several discussions pertaining to the division of inheritance in cases where two relatives died under circumstances that rendered it impossible to ascertain which of them died first. If a son and his father died under such circumstances, the father's heirs inherit the property, even if the son owed money to creditors. If the heirs of the two relatives are not the same individuals, e.g., in the case of a mother and son who died, the property is inherited by the heirs whose status is certain. If a husband and wife died under such circumstances, the sum of the marriage contract is inherited by the husband's heirs, the usufruct property is inherited by the wife's heirs, and the guaranteed property is divided between them.

Image **Credits**

עין משפט
נר מצוה

קסח א מיי' פ"ה מהל' נחלות הלכה ז סמג עשין נו טוש"ע ח"מ סי' רפ סעיף יח:

אֲבָל לְעִנְיַן דִּינָא לָא? *וְהָתַנְיָא: *נָפַל הַבַּיִת עָלָיו וְעַל אָבִיו, עָלָיו וְעַל מוֹרִישָׁיו, וְהָיְתָה עָלָיו כְּתוּבַּת אִשָּׁה וּבַעַל חוֹב, יוֹרְשֵׁי הָאָב אוֹמְרִים: הַבֵּן מֵת רִאשׁוֹן וְאח"כ מֵת הָאָב, וּבַעַל חוֹב אוֹמֵר: הָאָב מֵת רִאשׁוֹן וְאַחַר כָּךְ מֵת הַבֵּן; מַאי לָאו יוֹרְשֵׁי הָאָב — בָּנֵי, מוֹרִישָׁיו — אַחֵי; וְאִי סָלְקָא דַּעְתָּךְ לָא מָצֵי אָמַר "מִכֹּחַ אֲבוּהּ דְּאַבָּא קָאָתֵינָא", דְּכִי כְּתִיב "תַּחַת אֲבוֹתֶיךָ יִהְיוּ בָנֶיךָ" — בִּבְרָכָה כְּתִיב, כִּי מֵת הַבֵּן וְאח"כ מֵת הָאָב מַאי הָוֵי? נֵימָא לְהוּ בע"ח: יְרוּשַּׁת אֲבוּהוֹן קָא שָׁקֵילְנָא! לָא, יוֹרְשֵׁי הָאָב — אֶחָיו, מוֹרִישָׁיו — אַחֵי דַּאֲבוּהּ. בָּעוּ מִינֵּיהּ מֵרַב שֵׁשֶׁת: בֵּן מַהוּ שֶׁיִּירַשׁ אֶת אִמּוֹ בַּקֶּבֶר לְהַנְחִיל לָאַחִין מִן הָאָב? אֲמַר לְהוּ רַב שֵׁשֶׁת, תְּנֵיתוּהָ: הָאָב שֶׁנִּשְׁבָּה וּמֵת בְּנוֹ בַּמְּדִינָה, וּבֵן שֶׁנִּשְׁבָּה וּמֵת אָבִיו בַּמְּדִינָה — יוֹרְשֵׁי הָאָב וְיוֹרְשֵׁי הַבֵּן יַחֲלוֹקוּ; הֵיכִי דָּמֵי? אִילֵימָא כְּדְקָתָנֵי — הֵי נִינְהוּ יוֹרְשֵׁי הָאָב וְהֵי נִינְהוּ יוֹרְשֵׁי הַבֵּן? אֶלָּא לָאו הָכִי קָאָמַר: אאָב שֶׁנִּשְׁבָּה וּמֵת בֶּן בִּתּוֹ בַּמְּדִינָה, וּבֶן (א) בִּתּוֹ שֶׁנִּשְׁבָּה וּמֵת אֲבִי אִמּוֹ בַּמְּדִינָה, וְלָא יָדְעִינַן הֵי מִינַּיְיהוּ מִית בְּרֵישָׁא — יוֹרְשֵׁי הָאָב וְיוֹרְשֵׁי הַבֵּן יַחֲלוֹקוּ; וְאִם אִיתָא, נְהִי נַמִי דְּבֵן מֵת בְּרֵישָׁא, לֵירְתֵיהּ לַאֲבוּהּ דְּאִמֵּיהּ בְּקִבְרֵיהּ וְלֵירְתִינְהוּ לַאֲחוּהּ מִן אֲבוּהּ! אֶלָּא לָאו שְׁמַע מִינָּהּ: אֵין הַבֵּן יוֹרֵשׁ אֶת אִמּוֹ בַּקֶּבֶר לְהַנְחִיל לָאַחִין מֵאָב. אֲמַר לֵיהּ רַב אַחָא בַּר מַנְיוּמֵי לְאַבַּיֵי, אַף אֲנַן נַמִי תְּנֵינָא: *נָפַל הַבַּיִת עָלָיו וְעַל אִמּוֹ — אֵלּוּ וְאֵלּוּ מוֹדִים שֶׁיַּחֲלוֹקוּ; וְאִם אִיתָא, נְהִי נַמִי דְּבֵן מֵת בְּרֵישָׁא, לֵירְתֵיהּ לְאִמֵּיהּ בְּקִבְרֵיהּ וְלֵירְתוּ אִינְהוּ לַאֲחֵי מֵאֲבוּהּ! אֶלָּא לָאו שְׁמַע מִינָּהּ: *אֵין הַבֵּן יוֹרֵשׁ אֶת אִמּוֹ בַּקֶּבֶר לְהַנְחִיל לָאַחִין מִן הָאָב, שְׁמַע מִינָּהּ. וְטַעְמָא מַאי? אָמַר אַבַּיֵי: נֶאֶמְרָה סִיבָּה בְּבֵן וְנֶאֶמְרָה סִיבָּה בְּבַעַל, מַה סִיבָּה הָאֲמוּרָה בְּבַעַל — *אֵין הַבַּעַל יוֹרֵשׁ אֶת אִשְׁתּוֹ בַּקֶּבֶר, אַף סִיבָּה הָאֲמוּרָה בְּבֵן — אֵין הַבֵּן יוֹרֵשׁ אֶת אִמּוֹ בַּקֶּבֶר לְהַנְחִיל לָאַחִין מִן הָאָב. *הַהוּא דַּאֲמַר לֵיהּ לְחַבְרֵיהּ: "נִכְסֵי דְּבַר סִיסִין מְזַבְּנִינָא לָךְ". הֲוַאי חֲדָא אַרְעָא דַּהֲוָה מִיקַּרְיָא "דְּבֵי בַּר סִיסִין", אֲמַר לֵיהּ: הָא לָאו דְּבֵי בַּר סִיסִין הִיא, וְאִיקַּרוּיֵי הוּא דְּמִיקַּרְיָא "דְּבֵי בַּר סִיסִין". אֲתָא לְקַמֵּיהּ דְּרַב נַחְמָן, אוֹקְמָהּ בִּידָא דְּלוֹקֵחַ. אֲמַר לֵיהּ רָבָא לְרַב נַחְמָן: דִּינָא הָכִי? הַמּוֹצִיא מֵחֲבֵירוֹ עָלָיו הָרְאָיָה! וְרָמֵי דְּרָבָא אַדְּרָבָא, וּדְרַב נַחְמָן אַדְּרַב נַחְמָן; *דְּהַהוּא דְּא"ל לְחַבְרֵיהּ: מַאי בָּעֵית בְּהַאי בֵּיתָא? אֲמַר לֵיהּ: מִינָּךְ זְבִינְתָּהּ וַאֲכָלִית שְׁנֵי חֲזָקָה. אֲמַר לֵיהּ: אֲנָא בִּשְׁכוּנֵי גַּוָּאֵי הֲוַאי; אֲתָא לְקַמֵּיהּ דְּרַב נַחְמָן, אֲמַר לֵיהּ: זִיל בְּרוֹר אֲכִילָתָךְ. אֲמַר לֵיהּ רָבָא לְרַב נַחְמָן: דִּינָא הָכִי? הַמּוֹצִיא מֵחֲבֵירוֹ עָלָיו הָרְאָיָה! קַשְׁיָא דְּרָבָא אַדְּרָבָא, וּדְרַב נַחְמָן אַדְּרַב נַחְמָן! דְּרָבָא אַדְּרָבָא לָא קַשְׁיָא: הָכָא מוֹכֵר קָאֵי בְּנִכְסֵיהּ, הָתָם לוֹקֵחַ קָאֵי בְּנִכְסֵיהּ. דְּרַב נַחְמָן אַדְּרַב נַחְמָן לָא קַשְׁיָא: הָכָא, כֵּיוָן דַּאֲמַר לֵיהּ "דְּבֵי בַּר סִיסִין" וּמִיקַּרְיָא "דְּבֵי בַּר סִיסִין" — עֲלֵיהּ דִּידֵיהּ רַמְיָא לְגַלּוּיֵי דְּלָאו דְּבֵי בַּר סִיסִין הִיא. (ב) הָכָא, לָא יְהֵא אֶלָּא דְּנָקֵיט שְׁטָרָא, מִי לָא אָמְרִינַן לֵיהּ: קַיֵּים שְׁטָרָךְ וְקוּם בְּנִכְסֵי?§

הדרן עלך מי שמת

אמר ליה רב אחא בר מניומי תא שמע נפל הבית עליו ועל אמו כו'. תימה: רב ששת אמאי לא מייתי לה למתני'? והלא פשוט הוא! ועוד, דאיהו גופיה אמר לעיל בפרק "יש נוחלין" (דף קיד:): האשה את בנה, הא קמ"ל אשה את בנה דומיא דאשה את בעלה, מה אשה את בעלה כו' אף אשה את בנה אין הבן יורש את אמו בקבר להנחיל לאחין מן האב! ואומר רבי: דמשום דהך ברייתא משבשתא היא, הביאה והיה רוצה לתרצה. מ"ר.

אשה את בעלה אין הבעל יורש את אשתו כשהיא בקבר. לעיל בפ' "יש נוחלין" (דף קיד: ד"ה מה אשה) פי' להך מילתא, מנין דבעל אינו יורש את אשתו כשהיא בקבר.

ההוא דא"ל לחבריה נכסי דבר סיסין כו'. משום דאיירי הכא בנכסים בחזקת מי הם, אייתי ההיא עובדא דמיירי בה נמי לאוקומה נכסי בחזקת לוקח ובחזקת מוכר. מיהו, תימה היא שמביאו הגמרא שני פעמים במסכת אחת, כאן ו"בחזקת הבתים" (לעיל דף ל.).

הדרן עלך מי שמת

אֲבָל לְעִנְיַן דִּינָא לָא. בִּתְמִיָּה, מִי לָא אַשְׁכְּחַן בְּמַתְנִי' דִּין זֶה? וְאַמַּאי אָמְרִינַן "וְזוֹ הִיא שֶׁקָּשֶׁה", דְּמַשְׁמַע שֶׁאֵין מוֹצְאִין רְאָיָה לְדִבְרֵיהֶם, וּמִתּוֹךְ כָּךְ מַקְשִׁין עַל סְבָרַת שְׁמוּעָתָם! ה"ג: מַאי לָאו יוֹרְשֵׁי הָאָב בְּנֵי מוֹרִישָׁיו אַחֵי [וכו'] לֹא יוֹרְשֵׁי הָאָב אַחֵי מוֹרִישָׁיו אַחֵי דַּאֲבוּהּ. וּפֵירוּשׁוֹ: מַאי לָאו "יוֹרְשֵׁי הָאָב" הַיְינוּ בְּנֵי דְּהַהוּא בֵּן שֶׁנָּפַל הַבַּיִת עָלָיו וְעַל אָבִיו. [לעיל קנז.] כְּגוֹן שֶׁנָּפַל הַבַּיִת עַל רְאוּבֵן וְעַל יַעֲקֹב אָבִיו, וְהָיְתָה עָלָיו כְּתוּבַּת אִשָּׁה וּבַעַל חוֹב, יוֹרְשֵׁי הָאָב כְּגוֹן חֲנוֹךְ בֶּן רְאוּבֵן, אוֹמֵר: רְאוּבֵן מֵת רִאשׁוֹן, וְאַחַר כָּךְ מֵת הָאָב דְּהַיְינוּ יַעֲקֹב, וּמִכֹּחַ יַעֲקֹב אֲנִי בָּא לִירַשׁ, וְלֹא מִכֹּחוֹ שֶׁל רְאוּבֵן. אַלְמָא לְעִנְיַן דִּינָא אָמְרִינַן מִכֹּחַ אֲבוּהּ דְּאָב. וּמְשַׁנֵּי: לֹא יוֹרְשֵׁי הָאָב אֶחָיו. שֶׁל רְאוּבֵן, שֶׁאוֹמֵר: רְאוּבֵן מֵת רִאשׁוֹן וְאַחֲרָיו מֵת יַעֲקֹב אָבִיו, וְיָרַשְׁנוּ כָּל נְכָסָיו שֶׁל אָבִינוּ, וְאֵין לִרְאוּבֵן אָחִינוּ חֵלֶק בָּהֶן, שֶׁהֲרֵי הוּא מֵת תְּחִלָּה וּבֵן אֵין לוֹ. דְּהָכָא וַדַּאי לָאו מִכֹּחַ רְאוּבֵן בָּאִין לִירַשׁ, שֶׁהֲרֵי גַּם הֵם רְאוּיִין לִירַשׁ אֶת יַעֲקֹב כָּמוֹהוּ. וּמוֹרִישָׁיו — אַחֵי דַּאֲבוּהּ, אַחֵי יַעֲקֹב — עֵשָׂו, דּוֹד רְאוּבֵן. וּכְשֶׁנָּפַל הַבַּיִת עָלָיו וְעַל מוֹרִישָׁיו — דְּהַיְינוּ עֵשָׂו אֲחִי יַעֲקֹב אָבִיו, יוֹרְשֵׁי מוֹרִישָׁיו — כְּגוֹן אֲחֵי עֵשָׂו, אוֹמְרִים: רְאוּבֵן מֵת תְּחִלָּה, וְעֵשָׂו מֵת אַחֲרוֹן, וְאָנוּ יוֹרְשִׁין כָּל נְכָסָיו, כִּי לֹא יִירַשׁ רְאוּבֵן בֶּן יַעֲקֹב בְּנִכְסֵי עֵשָׂו דּוֹדוֹ תַּחַת יַעֲקֹב (*אָבִינוּ) [נ"ל אביו] שֶׁמֵּת כְּבָר, שֶׁהֲרֵי רְאוּבֵן מֵת תְּחִלָּה, וְאַחַר כָּךְ מֵת עֵשָׂו. וּבַעַל חוֹב אוֹמֵר: עֵשָׂו מֵת [לעיל קנח:] תְּחִלָּה, וּרְאוּבֵן מֵת אַחֲרוֹן. וַהֲרֵי יִירַשׁ רְאוּבֵן נִכְסֵי יַעֲקֹב אָבִיו שֶׁמֵּת בְּנִכְסֵי לעיל קיד: עֵשָׂו עִמָּכֶם (ג) וְנָטַל חֶלְקוֹ. דְּהַשְׁתָּא לֵיכָּא הָכָא "תַּחַת אֲבוֹתֶיךָ יִהְיוּ בָנֶיךָ", [שם] דִּלְעִנְיַן דִּינָא לָא אַשְׁכְּחַן בְּמַתְנִי' שׁוּם רְאָיָה לְמִילְּתָא דִּשְׁלָחוּ מִתָּם, וְהִלְכָּךְ קָשֶׁה הוּא בְּדִינֵי מָמוֹנוֹת. וּמִיהוּ, הָכִי לעיל ל. הִלְכְתָא כִּדְשָׁלְחוּ מִתָּם, דְּהָכִי סְבִירָא לְהוּ, אֶלָּא דְּלָא אַשְׁכַּחַן רְאָיָה מְפוֹרֶשֶׁת. וְכֵן כָּל הָנֵי דַּאֲמָרַן לְעֵיל — הָכִי הִלְכְתָא. בָּעוּ מִינֵּיהּ מֵרַב שֵׁשֶׁת. [לעיל כט:] יוֹסֵף בֶּן רָחֵל שֶׁמֵּת בְּחַיֵּי אִמּוֹ, וְאַחַר כָּךְ מֵתָה רָחֵל אִמּוֹ, מַהוּ שֶׁיִּירַשׁ אֶת אִמּוֹ כְּשֶׁהוּא בַּקֶּבֶר כְּאִילּוּ הוּא חַי, לְהַנְחִיל לְאֶחָיו שֶׁלּוֹ מִן אָבִיו. כְּגוֹן לִרְאוּבֵן בֶּן יַעֲקֹב מִלֵּאָה, שֶׁהוּא אָחִיו מֵאָבִיו. בַּמְּדִינָה. בְּאֶרֶץ מוֹלַדְתּוֹ. הֵי נִיהוּ יוֹרְשֵׁי הָאָב כו'. וַהֲלֹא אִם אֵין לוֹ בָּנִים לֹא לָאָב וְלֹא לַבֵּן — קְרוֹבֵי הָאָב יוֹרְשִׁין אֶת שְׁנֵיהֶם. אוֹ אִם יֵשׁ בָּנִים לְאוֹתוֹ בֵּן — הֲרֵי הֵן יוֹרְשִׁין אֶת הָאָב וְאֶת הַבֵּן. וּמֵת בֶּן בִּתּוֹ בַּמְּדִינָה. וְיוֹרְשֵׁי הַבֵּן הֵם קְרוֹבֵי אָבִיו, שֶׁהוּא בַּעַל אִמּוֹ. וְאִם אִיתָא. דְּבֵן יוֹרֵשׁ אֶת אִמּוֹ בַּקֶּבֶר. נְהִי נַמִי דְּבֵן מָיֵית בְּרֵישָׁא. אַמַּאי יַחֲלוֹקוּ יוֹרְשֵׁי הָאָב וְיוֹרְשֵׁי הַבֵּן? לֵירְתוּ יוֹרְשֵׁי הַבֵּן אֶת הַכֹּל, שֶׁהֲרֵי יִירַשׁ אֶת אֲבִי אִמּוֹ תַּחַת אִמּוֹ אַף עַל פִּי שֶׁהוּא בַּקֶּבֶר, וְלֵירְתִינְהוּ לְאֶחָיו מִן הָאָב שֶׁהֵן יוֹרְשֵׁי הַבֵּן, וְאַמַּאי יַחֲלוֹקוּ עִמָּהֶן יוֹרְשֵׁי הָאָב? לֵירְתֵיהּ לְאִמֵּיהּ בַּקֶּבֶר. דִּכְמִי שֶׁמֵּת אַחֲרוֹן דָּמֵי. אָמַר אַבַּיֵי נֶאֱמַר סִיבָּה בְּבַעַל כו'. הַמִּקְרָאוֹת מְפוֹרָשִׁין בְּ"יֵשׁ נוֹחֲלִין" (לעיל דף קיד:). אֵין הַבַּעַל יוֹרֵשׁ אֶת אִשְׁתּוֹ. כְּשֶׁהִיא (ד) מֵתָה בַּקֶּבֶר. אֵין הַבֵּן יוֹרֵשׁ אֶת אִמּוֹ כְּשֶׁהוּא בַּקֶּבֶר כו'. הַאי "בַּקֶּבֶר" לָא דָּמֵי לְהַהוּא קֶבֶר דְּבַעַל. הַהוּא דַּאֲמַר לֵיהּ לְחַבְרֵיהּ כו'. הַכֹּל פֵּירַשְׁנוּ בְּ"חֶזְקַת הַבָּתִּים" בְּרֹאשׁוֹ, וְאַגַּב גְּרָרָא דְּמַיְירֵי מַתְנִיתִין בִּנְכָסִים בְּחֶזְקָתָן, נָקַט לֵיהּ הָכָא.

הדרן עלך מי שמת

הגהות הב"ח

(א) גמ' ובן שנשבה ומת אבי אמו כנ"ל ותיבת בתו נמחק: (ב) שם לגלויי דלאו דבי בר סיסין היא התם לא יהא אלא: (ג) רשב"ם ד"ה ומשני לא וכו' בנכסי עשו עמכם ואטול חלקו דהשתא וכו' ולענין דינא: (ד) ד"ה אין הבעל וכו' כשהיא בקבר כנ"ל ותיבת מתה נמחק:

רבינו גרשום

אבל לענין דינא לא דיינינן הכי דמצי אמר להו מכח אבוה דאבא קא אתינא. ולא והתנן נפל הבית עליו ועל אביו עליו ועל מורישיו והיה עליו כתובה ובעל חוב יורשי האב וכו'. מאי לאו יורשי האב בני בניו של מת כגון שנפל הבית על אליפז ועל עשו אביו והיו טוענים יורשי האב בני אליפז על אליפז נפל תחלה ולא באו הנכסים לידו ואנו מכח אבוה דאבא אתינן בנכסים ולא מכח אליפז אבינו ואין עלינו לפרוע מחובו כלום אלמא דלגבי דינא אמרינן תחת אבותיך יהיו בניך דאמרי' מכח אבוה דאבא אתינן: עליו ועל מורישיו אחי. שהיו ראובן ושמעון אחים ולא הי' לשמעון בנים אלא ראובן היה יורש שלו ולא היו לראובן נכסים כלל והיה על ראובן כתובת אשה ובעל חוב ולשמעון הי' נכסים ונפל הבית על ראובן ועל שמעון וטענו יורשי מורישיו דהיינו בן ראובן ואמר ראובן מת תחלה ולא אתו נכסי ליד ראובן ואנו לאו מכח ראובן אתינן אלא מכח שמעון אחי דאבא אלמא דלגבי דינא אמרינן תחת אבותיך דהוה לך לירש יהיו בניך. ומשני לעולם (לא) אימא לך דלא אמרי' תחת אבותיך יהיו בניך לגבי דינא. ומתני' לא שמעי' לה כדפרישית אלא הכי פירושא יורשי האב הן אחי. כגון שנפל הבית על עשו ועל אליפז ולא היו לאליפז בנים והיה על אליפז כתובה ובעל חוב וטענו אחי אליפז על אליפז נפל תחלה ולא בא נכסי אבינו ליד אליפז ואנו מכח אבינו אתינן. ובעלי חוב אמרו על עשו נפל תחלה ואית ליה לאליפז חלק בנכסי אביו וחייבין אתם לפרוע שאתם יורשי' אליפז כפי חלקו המגיעו בירושת אביו. וה"נ מפרשי' מורישיו אחי דאבוה כגון שנפל על ראובן ועל עשו ולא היה לעשו בנים ויעקב היה מת וראובן לא היו לו בנים ועשו היה לו עוד אחים בעלי חוב אומרים עשו מת תחילה וראובן ירש במקום יעקב בנכסי עשו והיו לו נכסים לראובן ירושת דודו עשו ויורשי מורישיהן אחי עשו אומרים לא כי אלא ראובן מת תחלה ולא ירש כלום מעשו ואנו יורשין של עשו ולא של ראובן ואין לכם עלינו כלום: בן מהו שיורש את אמו בקבר (או) אם נפלה ירושה לאמו אחר שמת אם מתה שוב אמו מהו שיורש כדי להנחיל לאחין מן האב. דלא הוי להאי בן של קבר שום יורש אלא אחיו מאביו: אב שנשבה. במקום רחוק ומת שם ומת בנו במדינה בארץ מולדתו ולא היה לו בן לאותו [בן] ואין ידוע איזה מת תחלה אי האב אי הבן יורשי האב ויורשי הבן יחלוקו. ומקשי' הי ניהו יורשי האב והי ניהו יורשי הבן. והלא יורשי הבן הן הן יורשי האב ויורשי האב הן הן יורשי הבן אלא לאו הכי קאמר האב שנשבה ולא היה לו בן כי אם בן בתו ומת בן בתו במדינה או בן בתו נשבה ומת אבי אמו במדינה וזה שנשא בתו יש לו בנים מאשה אחרת הן הן יורשי הבן שהן אחין מאביו ולאב שנשבה יש לו אחין והן יורשי האב שאמר יחלוקו דממון המוטל בספק הוא. ויורשי אב קאמרי בן מת תחלה א) ובאו נכסים ליד בנו ואנו יורשים בני אחינו. בן שנשבה ומת אבי אמו במדינה היינו נמי בן בתו ומהכא איכא למשמע אם יורש אמו בקבר אי לא. נהי נמי דבן מיית ברישא ושוב מת האב אם איתא דיורש את אביו בקבר אמאי יחלוקו בין יורשי האב ובין יורשי הבן לירתו יורשי הבן כולהו אע"ג דמית הבן ואמאי יחלוקו אלא לאו ש"מ כו': נפל הבית עליו ועל אמו יורשי הבן אחים מן האב אומרים האם מתה תחלה ונכסים לידא דבן נפלו ויורשי האם אחיה אומרים בן מת ראשון ונכסים לא נפלו לבן וקתני מודים דיחלוקו ואם איתא דהבן יורש את אמו בקבר נהי דבן מיית ברישא כו': טעמא מאי. אין הבן יורש את אמו בקבר: נאמר הסיבה בבעל ונאמר הסיבה בבן. כדאוקימנא לקראי בפרק יש נוחלין: ואין הבעל יורש את אשתו בקבר. לאחר שהוא מת אינו [יורש] להנהו נכסים דנפלו לאשתו לאחר כן אע"ג דמתה היא. אף הבן נמי אין הבן יורש את אמו בקבר: נכסי דבי בר סיסין. לאותן שקניתי הנכסים מבר סיסין אני מוכר לך והוה ליה חדא ארעא דמקריא דבי בר סיסין ולא קנאה מבר סיסין אלא כך היו קורין לה. והיה רוצה הלוקח לטורפה בשביל שמכר לו כל נכסי דבי בר סיסין ואמר לו מוכר הא לאו דבי בר סיסין היא ולא מכרתי אותה: אוקמה רב נחמן לנכסי בידא דלוקח. דסבירא ליה דזבין ניהליה להההיא קרקע דמתקרי דבי בר סיסין: אמר ליה רבא. וכי דינא הכי בידא דמוכר הוה ליה לאוקמינהו דהוה מוחזק בהו וליהוי איהך מוציא מחבירו עליו הראיה: ורמי דרבא אדרבא. דלעיל סבירא ליה דבידא דמוכר הוה ליה לאוקמה והוה לוקח המוציא מחבירו והכא סבירא ליה בידא דלוקח הוה ליה לאוקמה והוה ליה המוכר המוציא מחבירו: קשיא דרב נחמן אדרב נחמן. דלעיל אוקים לנכסי בידא דלוקח והוה מוכר מוציא מחבירו עליו הראיה והכא אוקמינהו בידא דמוכר דמוחזק הוא והוה ליה לוקח המוציא מחבירו עליו הראיה. התם קסבר רבא מוכר קאי בנכסי להכי קאמר דלוקח הוה צריך להביא ראיה. אבל היכא דאכלה שני חזקה הלוקח מוחזק הוא בקרקע וקאי להכי קאמר המוכר הוה צריך להביא ראיה ואידי ואידי חד טעמא הוא: התם משום הכי אוקמיה רב נחמן בידא דלוקח דכיון דכולי עלמא קרו להאי קרקע דבי בר סיסין והוא מכר לו כל נכסי דבי בר סיסין ואמר האי קרקע לאו דבי בר סיסין היא עליה דידיה דמוכר רמיא לגלויי ולמיתי ראיה דלא דבי בר סיסין היא כדאמר הוא והיכא דלא מייתי ראיה איהו הוא דאפסיד אנפשיה משום הכי אוקמה בידא דלוקח אבל הכא דינא הוא דאיהו מייתי ראיה הלוקח הואיל ואכלה שני חזקה. והא מוכר אמר אנא בשכוני גואי הואי לא יהא דינה פחות מהדוא דנקיט שטרא בידיה ונפיק עליה ערער מי לא אמרינן ללוקח קיים שטרך וקום בנכסך ולא קשיין אהדדי. לא איתפרש לן אמאי מייתי הכא מעשה דבי בר סיסין:

הדרן עלך מי שמת

א) אולי צ"ל בא ולא באו נכסים לידו ולא יורשים לנכסי אחיו.

איתמר: [א]בֵּן שֶׁמָּכַר בְּנִכְסֵי אָבִיו בְּחַיֵּי אָבִיו, וּמֵת — בְּנוֹ מוֹצִיא מִיַּד הַלָּקוֹחוֹת. וְזוֹ הִיא שֶׁקָּשָׁה בְּדִינֵי מָמוֹנוֹת, וְלֵימְרוּ לֵיהּ: אֲבוּךְ מְזַבֵּין וְאַתְּ מַפֵּיק?! וּמַאי קוּשְׁיָא? [ב]דִּלְמָא מָצֵי אָמַר: מִכֹּחַ אֲבוּהּ דְּאַבָּא קָאָתֵינָא; תֵּדַע, דִּכְתִיב: (תהלים מה) "תַּחַת אֲבוֹתֶיךָ יִהְיוּ בָנֶיךָ תְּשִׁיתֵמוֹ לְשָׂרִים בְּכָל הָאָרֶץ"! אֶלָּא אִי קַשְׁיָא הָא קַשְׁיָא: בֵּן בְּכוֹר שֶׁמָּכַר חֵלֶק בְּכוֹרָה בְּחַיֵּי אָבִיו, וּמֵת בְּחַיֵּי אָבִיו — בְּנוֹ מוֹצִיא מִיַּד הַלָּקוֹחוֹת, וְזוֹ הִיא שֶׁקָּשָׁה בְּדִינֵי מָמוֹנוֹת: אֲבוּהּ מְזַבֵּין אִיהוּ מַפֵּיק?! וְכִי תֵּימָא, הָכָא נַמִּי אָמַר: מִכֹּחַ אֲבוּהּ דְּאַבָּא קָאָתֵינָא; אִי מִכֹּחַ אֲבוּהּ דְּאַבָּא קָא אָתְיָא, בְּחֵלֶק בְּכוֹרָה מַאי עֲבִידְתֵּיהּ? וּמַאי קוּשְׁיָא? דִּלְמָא מָצֵי אָמַר: מִכֹּחַ אֲבוּהּ דְּאַבָּא קָאָתֵינָא וּבִמְקוֹם אָב קָאֵימְנָא! אֶלָּא אִי קַשְׁיָא הָא קַשְׁיָא: (נ"ל מלוה) [ג]הָיָה יוֹדֵעַ לוֹ עֵדוּת בִּשְׁטָר עַד שֶׁלֹּא נַעֲשָׂה גַּזְלָן, וְנַעֲשָׂה גַּזְלָן — הוּא אֵינוֹ מֵעִיד עַל כְּתַב יָדוֹ, אֲבָל אֲחֵרִים *מְעִידִין; הַשְׁתָּא אִיהוּ לָא מְהֵימַן, אַחֲרִינֵי מְהֵימְנֵי? וְזוֹ הִיא שֶׁקָּשָׁה בְּדִינֵי מָמוֹנוֹת. מַאי קוּשְׁיָא? דִּלְמָא [ד]כְּגוֹן שֶׁהוּחְזַק כְּתַב יָדוֹ בְּבֵ"ד! אֶלָּא אִי קַשְׁיָא הָא קַשְׁיָא: הָיָה יוֹדֵעַ לוֹ עֵדוּת בִּשְׁטָר עַד שֶׁלֹּא תִּפּוֹל לוֹ בִּירוּשָּׁה — הוּא אֵינוֹ יָכוֹל לְקַיֵּים כְּתַב יָדוֹ, אֲבָל אֲחֵרִים יְכוֹלִין לְקַיֵּים כְּתַב יָדוֹ. (א) וּמַאי קוּשְׁיָא? דִּלְמָא הָכָא נַמִּי, כְּגוֹן שֶׁהוּחְזַק כְּתַב יָדוֹ בְּבֵ"ד! אֶלָּא אִי קַשְׁיָא הָא קַשְׁיָא: *[ה]הָיָה יוֹדֵעַ לוֹ בְּעֵדוּת עַד שֶׁלֹּא נַעֲשָׂה חֲתָנוֹ, וְנַעֲשָׂה חֲתָנוֹ — הוּא אֵינוֹ מֵעִיד עַל כְּתַב יָדוֹ, אֲבָל אֲחֵרִים מְעִידִין; הוּא לָא מְהֵימַן, אַחֲרִינֵי מְהֵימְנֵי? וְכִי תֵּימָא, הָכָא נַמִּי כְּגוֹן שֶׁהוּחְזַק כְּתַב יָדוֹ בְּבֵ"ד; וְהָא אָמַר רַב יוֹסֵף בַּר מַנְיוּמֵי אָמַר רַב נַחְמָן: [ו]אַף עַל פִּי שֶׁלֹּא הוּחְזַק כְּתַב יָדוֹ בְּבֵית דִּין! וּמַאי קוּשְׁיָא? דִּלְמָא גְּזֵירַת מֶלֶךְ הִיא דְּאִיהוּ לָא מְהֵימַן וְאַחֲרִינֵי מְהֵימְנֵי, וְלָאו מִשּׁוּם דִּמְשַׁקֵּר! דְּאִי לָא תֵּימָא הָכִי, מֹשֶׁה וְאַהֲרֹן לְחוֹתְנָם מִשּׁוּם דְּלָא מְהֵימְנֵי הוּא? אֶלָּא גְּזֵירַת מֶלֶךְ הוּא שֶׁלֹּא יָעִידוּ לָהֶם, ה"נ [ז]גְּזֵירַת מֶלֶךְ הוּא שֶׁלֹּא יָעִיד עַל כְּתַב יָדוֹ לְחוֹתְנוֹ! אֶלָּא, לְעוֹלָם כִּדַאֲמַרִינַן מֵעִיקָּרָא, וּדְקָא קַשְׁיָא לָךְ: "תַּחַת אֲבוֹתֶיךָ יִהְיוּ בָנֶיךָ" — הַהוּא בִּבְרָכָה כְּתִיב. וּמִי מָצֵית אָמְרַתְּ בִּבְרָכָה כְּתִיב, אֲבָל

רש"י

וְלֵימְרוּ לֵיהּ. לָקוֹחוֹת: אֲבוּךְ זַבֵּין וְאַתְּ מַפְּקַתְּ, שֶׁאַתָּה יוֹרֵשׁ מִמֶּנּוּ? וַהֲלֹא אֵין אָדָם יוֹרֵשׁ מַה שֶּׁמָּכַר אָבִיו! דִּלְמָא. דְּאָמַר לְהוּ חֲנוֹךְ בֶּן רְאוּבֵן: מִכֹּחַ יַעֲקֹב דְּהוּא אֲבוּהּ דְּאַבָּא קָא אָתֵינָא, דִּבְנֵי בָנִים הֲרֵי הֵן כְּבָנִים, וְכִי הֵיכִי דִּרְאוּבֵן אָבִי הָיָה יָכוֹל לִירַשׁ אֶת יַעֲקֹב אָבִיו אִילּוּ [הָיָה] חַי אַחֲרֵי מוֹת אָבִיו — כָּךְ אֲנִי יוֹרֵשׁ אֶת יַעֲקֹב מִגְּזֵירַת הַכָּתוּב, וְלֹא מִכֹּחַ רְאוּבֵן אָבִי אֲנִי יוֹרֵשׁ. וְאֵין בַּנְּכָסִים הַלָּלוּ שׁוּם זְכוּת לִרְאוּבֵן, וּמְכִירָתוֹ לָאו כְּלוּם הִיא. תֵּדַע. דַּחֲנוֹךְ בֶּן רְאוּבֵן יוֹרֵשׁ אֶת יַעֲקֹב זְקֵנוֹ שֶׁלֹּא מִכֹּחַ רְאוּבֵן, דִּכְתִיב: "תַּחַת אֲבוֹתֶיךָ יִהְיוּ בָנֶיךָ", לִרְאוּבֵן קָאָמַר: תַּחַת אֲבוֹתֶיךָ — דְּהַיְינוּ יַעֲקֹב, יִהְיוּ בָנֶיךָ — דְּהַיְינוּ חֲנוֹךְ, מִדְּלָא כְּתִיב: "תַּחְתֶּיךָ יִהְיוּ בָנֶיךָ". אֶלָּא אִי קַשְׁיָא הָא קַשְׁיָא. אִי אִיכָּא לְמֵימַר דְּשָׁלְחוּ מִתָּם "זוֹ הִיא שֶׁקָּשָׁה בְּדִינֵי מָמוֹנוֹת" — לָאו כִּי הַאי גַּוְונָא שָׁלְחוּ כִּדְלְעֵיל, דְּהָא לָאו קָשֶׁה הוּא. אֶלָּא הָכִי שָׁלְחוּ מִתָּם: בְּכוֹר שֶׁמָּכַר חֵלֶק בְּכוֹרָתוֹ בְּחַיֵּי אָבִיו, וּמֵת הַבְּכוֹר. כְּגוֹן רְאוּבֵן שֶׁמָּכַר חֵלֶק בְּכוֹרָתוֹ הָרָאוּי לְהַגִּיעוֹ בְּנִכְסֵי אָבִיו, וּמֵת רְאוּבֵן, וְאַחַר כָּךְ מֵת יַעֲקֹב — בָּא חֲנוֹךְ וּמוֹצִיא מִיַּד הַלָּקוֹחוֹת חֵלֶק בְּכוֹרַת רְאוּבֵן אָבִיו, וְנוֹטְלָהּ לְעַצְמוֹ, כְּאִילּוּ לֹא מְכָרָהּ רְאוּבֵן. שֶׁחֲנוֹךְ יוֹרֵשׁ חֵלֶק בְּכוֹרַת אָבִיו בְּנִכְסֵי זְקֵנוֹ אָבִיו, וְאע"פ שֶׁמֵּת הַבְּכוֹר בְּחַיֵּי אָבִיו. כִּדְתְנַן לְעֵיל (דף קטז:): בְּנוֹת צְלָפְחָד נָטְלוּ שְׁלֹשָׁה חֲלָקִים, חֵלֶק שֶׁהָיָה רָאוּי לַאֲבִיהֶן שֶׁהָיָה מִיּוֹצְאֵי מִצְרַיִם, (ב) וְשֶׁהָיָה בְּכוֹר וְנוֹטֵל שְׁנֵי חֲלָקִים. (ג) חֵלֶק בְּכוֹרָה מַאי עֲבִידְתֵּיהּ. וַהֲלֹא אֵינְךָ בְּכוֹר! וּמַאי קוּשְׁיָא. בְּדִינֵי מָמוֹנוֹת. דִּלְמָא מָצֵי אָמַר. חֲנוֹךְ: מִכֹּחַ יַעֲקֹב אֲבִי אַבָּא קָאָתֵינָא, כִּדְכְתִיב: "תַּחַת אֲבוֹתֶיךָ יִהְיוּ בָנֶיךָ", וְיַעֲקֹב אֲנִי יוֹרֵשׁ כְּאִילּוּ אֲנִי רְאוּבֵן, דִּבִמְקוֹם רְאוּבֵן אָבִי אֲנִי עוֹמֵד כְּאִילּוּ אֲנִי בְּכוֹר, מִגְּזֵירַת הַכָּתוּב, וּכְדִתְנַן: בְּנוֹת צְלָפְחָד כו'. אֶלָּא אִי קַשְׁיָא בְּדִינֵי מָמוֹנוֹת הָא קַשְׁיָא. וְהָכִי שְׁלַחוּ (ד) לֵיהּ מִתָּם. הָיָה יוֹדֵעַ לוֹ בְּעֵדוּת. רְאוּבֵן לְשִׁמְעוֹן, עַד שֶׁלֹּא נַעֲשָׂה רְאוּבֵן גַּזְלָן, וְהָיָה שְׁמוֹ חָתוּם בִּשְׁטַר הַלְוָאָתוֹ שֶׁל שִׁמְעוֹן. וְאַחַר כָּךְ נַעֲשָׂה גַּזְלָן. וְנִפְסַל לְעֵדוּת, כִּדְכְתִיב (שמות כג): "אַל תָּשֶׁת יָדְךָ עִם רָשָׁע לִהְיוֹת עֵד חָמָס". וְאע"פ שֶׁנֶּאֱמָן אָדָם לוֹמַר "זֶה כְּתַב יָדִי", כִּדְתְנַן בִּכְתוּבּוֹת (דף כ:), מֵעַתָּה אֵינוֹ מֵעִיד עַל כְּתַב יָדוֹ, שֶׁהֲרֵי כָּל דְּבָרָיו אָנוּ מַחֲזִיקִין שֶׁקֶר מִשֶּׁנַּעֲשָׂה גַּזְלָן, וְשֶׁמָּא עֵד אֶחָד פָּסוּל זִיְּיפוֹ, אוֹ (ה) עַצְמוֹ כְּתָבוֹ וְחָתַם בּוֹ הַיּוֹם שֶׁקֶר. אֲבָל אֲחֵרִים מְעִידִין. כִּדִמְפָרֵשׁ בַּמַּסְקָנָא. וְהַשְׁתָּא לְפוּם מַאי דְּקס"ד הָכִי קָשֶׁה בְּדִינֵי מָמוֹנוֹת: דְּאִיהוּ לָא מְהֵימַן אַחֲרִינֵי מְהֵימְנֵי? בִּתְמִיָּה. וַהֲלֹא שֶׁמָּא הוּא עַצְמוֹ חָתַם בּוֹ הַיּוֹם שֶׁקֶר, שֶׁהֲרֵי גַּזְלָן הוּא, וּכְשֶׁמַּכִּירִין חֲתִימָתוֹ מָה אָנוּ מַרְוִיחִין בְּכָךְ? וַהֲלֹא שֶׁמָּא פָּסוּל הוּא! כְּגוֹן שֶׁהוּחְזַק. בְּהֶנְפֵּק בְּבֵית דִּין בְּטֶרֶם הֱיוֹתוֹ גַּזְלָן, דְּהַשְׁתָּא לֵיכָּא לְמֵימַר הָכִי. אֶלָּא אֵלּוּ מְעִידִין שֶׁחֲתָמוֹ בְּהֶנְפֵּק זֶה וְקִיְּימוּ הַשְּׁטָר מִקַּמֵּי דְּהָוֵי הַאי גַּבְרָא גַּזְלָן, וְהַהִיא שַׁעְתָּא הָיָה הוּא עַצְמוֹ נֶאֱמָן לוֹמַר "זֶה כְּתַב יָדִי". וְהַשְׁתָּא לֵיכָּא לְמִיפְרַךְ "אִיהוּ לָא מְהֵימַן אַחֲרִינֵי מְהֵימְנֵי", דְּהָא הָנֵי אַחֲרִינֵי אַכְּתַב יָדָן הֵן מְעִידִין, וְלֹא אַכְּתַב יָדוֹ, וּשְׁטָרָא מְקַיְּימָא וְקָאֵי מִמֵּילָא. אע"פ שֶׁלֹּא הוּחְזַק כו'. דִּגְזֵירַת הַכָּתוּב הִיא דַּחֲתָנוֹ אֵינוֹ נֶאֱמָן, וְלֹא מִשּׁוּם דְּמַחֲזִיקִין לֵיהּ כִּמְזַיֵּיף וְכוֹתֵב. הִלְכָּךְ, אַחֲרִינֵי מְהֵימְנֵי, דְּלֵיכָּא לְמֵימַר מִשֶּׁנַּעֲשָׂה חֲתָנוֹ זַיֵּיף וְכָתַב. לְעוֹלָם כְּדַאֲמָרַן מֵעִיקָּרָא. בֵּן שֶׁמָּכַר בְּנִכְסֵי אָבִיו כו'. בִּבְרָכָה הוּא דִּכְתִיב. שֶׁהַצַּדִּיקִים יֵשׁ לָהֶם בָּנִים וּבְנֵי בָנִים לְיוֹרְשָׁם, כִּדְכְתִיב בְּסֵיפֵיהּ: "תְּשִׁיתֵמוֹ לְשָׂרִים בְּכָל הָאָרֶץ". אֲבָל

תוספות

ולימרו ליה אבוך זבין ואת אמאי מפקת. ותימה: למה לא יוכל להוציא מיד הלקוחות? אפילו למ"ד אדם מקנה דבר שלא בא לעולם — היינו כגון שלא מת הבן בחיי האב, אלא שנתנו לו דמים קודם שמת האב. אבל כשנפלו לו כשהוא גוסס — אמרו לעיל (דף קמז:) דאפילו לר"מ, דאמר אדם מקנה דבר שלא בא לעולם — לא מהני מידי לקנות בנכסים (ו) כשהוא גוסס! ופי' הר"ר יצחק בר' מאיר: דודאי המכר אינו מכר, אלא לענין חזרת מעות איירי הכא, שבנו מוציא השעבוד שהיה להם ללקוחות מן הדין מהם, כי אין להם אפי' שעבוד בקרקע בשביל מעותיהם. ולפי זה צריך לומר דס"ל: אדם משעבד דבר שלא בא לעולם. דאי לא משעבד — מאי מקשי: לימרו ליה אבוך זבין ואת מאי מפקת? והלא אין אדם משעבד דבר שלא בא לעולם! ואע"ג דאמרן לעיל "דאיקני" קנה והוריש לא משתעבד — היינו משום דשמואל לטעמיה, דאית ליה מלוה על פה אינו גובה מן היורשין. אבל לדידן דאית לן גובה מן היורשין — הויא כמו (נ"ל מלוה) (מלוה) ומשתעבד, אע"פ שלא בא לעולם. ואם תאמר: אכתי מאי פריך: ולימרו ליה אבוך זבין ואת מאי מפקת? דלמא היינו טעמא — משום (ז) דאין בעל חוב נוטל בראוי, כמו כתובת אשה, דתנן בבכורות פרק "יש בכור" (דף נב.) דאינה נוטלת בראוי! ושמא יש לומר: דוקא כתובת אשה, אבל בע"ח נוטל בראוי. מיהו, קשה: דא"כ כי קא חשיב בכתובות ריש פרק אע"פ (דף נד: ושם) דתנאי כתובה ככתובה דמי לענין כמה דברים — אמאי לא חשיב נמי לענין ראוי דאינה ככתובה ואיתא בבע"ח? אבל אי ליתא בבעל חוב — אתי שפיר. אבל אין להביא ראיה מדאמר בסמוך: מאי לאו, יורשי האב — בניס, מורישין — אחין. פירוש: בני הבן, וקאמר: אין בע"ח נוטל. לאו היינו משום דאינו נוטל בראוי, אלא טעמא משום דאמרי מכח (ח) דאבי אבא קאתי. אבל אין להביא ראיה מדאמר ר"נ: יתומים שגבו בחובת אביהן — בע"ח חוזר וגובה אותה מהם, אלמא נוטל בראוי. שהרי אין זה ראוי, אלא משעבדי ליה מדר' נתן. מיהו, קשה: דהל"ל "בן שלוה", ולא "בן שמכר". ולא לימא "בנו מוציא מיד הלקוחות"! ועוד קשה: למה יש לו להיות ללקוחות שעבוד על אביו? מי עדיף ממלוה על פה, דאין לך מלוה על פה גדול מזה! על כן נראה לר"י: דאלו נכסים כתב האב לבנו מהיום ולאחר מיתה, דהיינו גופא מהיום ופירות לאחר מיתה, כמו ששנינו לעיל בפרק "יש נוחלין" (דף קלו.): (ט) מכר האב או הבן בחיי האב. וסבירא להו ל"שלחו מתם" דהכא כר' יוחנן, דאמר לעיל בפ' "יש נוחלין" דלא קנה לוקח. מ"מ זו היא שקשה בדיני ממונות, דלימרו ליה: אבוך זבין כו'. ***אלא** אי קשיא הא קשיא בן שמכר כו'. ולא גרסי' (י) "אי איתמר הכי איתמר", שהרי כל הדברים הללו שלחו מתם. ומה ששלחו "זו היא שקשה בדיני ממונות" ולא ידעו על איזה דבר שלחו כו'. **כגון** שהוחזק כתב ידן בב"ד. פירש רבינו שמואל: שכתוב בו הנפק. ואין נראה לר"י, דאיך דיינים גופייהו מי לא מצי למיטעי בההוא גברא אי גזלן הוא אי לא? שהרי אין חותמין אלא על חתימת העדים, ואפי' מה שבשטר אין צריכין הדיינים לקרות! אלא ה"פ: הוחזק כתב ידו בב"ד — שרא ב"ד כתב ידו קודם שנעשה גזלן, דליכא למימר שלאחר כך חתם. כמו הוחזק שטר כתובה בשוק דפ"ב דקדושין (דף נ:), וכגון הואיל דאיתחזק בב"ד לא אמרי' בפ' "זה בורר" (סנהדרין דף לא. ושם ד"ה וכיון) דהיינו שראו ב"ד את השטר כבר, וכדפרישית בספ"ק דב"מ (דף יח:). **ואע"פ** שלא הוחזק כתב ידו בב"ד. מכאן יש ללמוד שאם היו שנים מעידים ואח"כ נעשו קרובים, שאחר מעיד על כתב ידן שמכירין אותו, ולא חיישינן שמא היום חתם. **ההוא** בברכה הוא דכתיב. דאשמועינן קרא שיזכה הצדיק לבנים כמותו, דכתיב בתריה "תשיתמו לשרים בכל הארץ". אמר

רבינו גרשום

בן שמכר בנכסי אביו בחיי אביו ומת הבן בחיי אביו ואחר כך מת אביו והחזיק הלוקח כמו שמכר לו הבן. בנו של בן מוציא מיד הלקוחות וזו היא שקשה [בדיני ממונות] שדבר תימה הוא: אבוהו מזבין ואיהו אמאי מצי מפיק. מאי קושיא להכי מוציא מיד הלקוחות דמצי למימר כשמכר נכסים הללו לא היה עדיין מוחזק בהן לפי שאביו היה קיים והוא מת קודם לאביו ולא באו נכסים לידו ואנו יורשין מכח אבי אבינו להכי מוציא מיד הלקוחות דאבוה לא מזבין: וממאי דמצי למימר הכי דמכח אבוה דאבא אתינא. דהכי כתיב קרא תחת אבותיך יהיו בניך אלמא דבמקום אבי אביו מצי מפיק דכי היכי דאבי אביו מוציא מיד הלקוחות הכי נמי מוציא הבן: אלא אי קשיא בדיני ממונות הא קשיא. בן שמכר בחלק בכורה בחיי אביו ומת הבן בחיי אביו דלא הוה מוחזק בנו מוציא כו'. אי מכח אבוה דאבא קא אתי האי בן הבן בחלק בכורה מאי עבידתיה הא אבי אביו לא היה בכור דלירת האי חלק בכורתו: והיינו קשה בדיני ממונות אמאי מוציא מיד הלקוחות. ומאי קושיא כלומר אמאי זו קשה הא מצי למימר מכח אבוה דאב' קא אתינא בכולהו נכסי דאיהו היה יורש את בנו ובמקום אב קא אתינא לירש בכורתו ולתבוע מה שמכר בחלק בכורתו דלא מצי מזבין דראוי הוה ולא מוחזק ומשום הכי מוציא מן הלקוחות: אלא הא קשה בדיני ממונות. איהו גופיה לא מהימן להעיד על כתב יד עצמו ואחריני מהימני על כתב ידו להעיד. ומאי קושיא דלמא אחריני נמי לא מהימני להעיד על כתב ידו. ומאי האי דקאמר אבל אחרים מעידים כגון שהוחזק כתב ידו של שטר זה בבית דין שהעידו אחרים לפני בית דין שזה כתב ידו והללו אומרים יודעים אנו שזה השטר הוחזק בעדים לפני בית דין שזה חתימת של פלוני. או שאמרו יודעים אנו שחתימה כזו הוחזקה לפני ב"ד שהיא של פלוני דהואיל דאתחזק בבית דין יכולין להעיד מכח בית דין אבל מחמת עצמן אינן נאמנין להעיד הואיל דאיהו לא מהימן: והאמר רב יוסף בר מניומי אע"פ שלא הוחזקה כתב ידו שלזה חתן בב"ד נאמנים להעיד על חתימת ידו וזו היא קשה. מאי קושיא משום הכי הוא אינו מעיד מפני שגזירת מלך הקב"ה הוא שפוסל קרוביו להעיד עדות ולא משום דלא הוי נאמן דודאי נאמן הוא דלא דמי לגזלן דפסול לכולי עלמא. הלכך הואיל ונאמן הוא לכולי עלמא אע"ג דהוא אינו נאמן מחמת קריבות אבל אחרים מעידין. דאי לא תימא הכי דגזירת מלך היא אלא קבעית למימר דכל קרוב פסול משום דמשקר הוא בנין אהבת קרובו. אלא מעתה משה ואהרן דפסילי אהדדי או לקרובים מי לא מהימני בדיבורם אצל קרוביהן והא קי"ל דצדיקים גמורים הוו ולא משקרי אבל חללי דעלמא אלא גזירת מלך היא דמשה ואהרן לא מסהדי לקרובין הכי נמי גזירת מלך היא דכיון דנעשה חתנו דאין מעיד לו ולא משום דלא מהימן וכיון דנאמן א) אבל אחרים מעידים לו ואכתי אין זו קושיא: לעולם כדאמרינן מעיקרא בן שמכר בנכסי אביו ומת בנו מוציא מיד הלקוחות זו היא קשה בדיני ממונות ודקא קשיא לך מאי קושיא כו' מתרצת תחת אבותך יהיו בניך התם בברכה הוא כדכתיב תשיתמו לשרים בכל הארץ. ומקשינן מי מצית אמרת בברכה כתיב אבל

א) נראה דצ"ל וכיון דנאמן הוא אינו מעיד אבל אחרים וכו'.

עין משפט נר מצוה

קסג א מיי' פכ"ב מהל' מכירה הל' ז סמג עשין פב טוש"ע חו"מ סי' ריא סעיף ג:

קסד ב מיי' שם טוש"ע שם סעיף ד:

קסה ג ד מיי' פי"ח מהל' עדות הלכה ה סמג לאוין ריד רעו טוש"ע חו"מ סי' מו סעיף לד [וברב אלפס סנהדרין פ"ג דף רסג.]:

קסו ה ו מיי' שם טוש"ע שם סעיף לה:

קסז ז מיי' שם פי"א הל' טו סמג שם טוש"ע ח"מ סי' לג סעיף י:

מסורת הש"ס

גי' רש"ל יכולים לקיים כתב ידו

[תוספתא סנהדרין פ"ה]

הגהות הב"ח

(א) גמ' אחרים יכולין לקיים כתב ידו השתא איהו לא מהימן אחריני מהימני ומאי קושיא: (ב) רשב"ם ד"ה אלא אי קשיא וכו' שהיה מיוצאי מצרים וחלקו עם אחיו בנכסי חפר ושהיה בכור נוטל ב' חלקים: (ג) ד"ה בחלק וכו' והלא אינו בכור: (ד) ד"ה אלא וכו' שלחו מתם כצ"ל ותיבת ליה נמחק: (ה) ד"ה ואח"כ וכו' או הוא עצמו: (ו) תוס' ד"ה ולימרו וכו' בנכסים שנפלו לו כשהוא גוסס וכו' ואת אמאי מפקת: (ז) בא"ד דאין בעל חוב נוטל. נ"ב כלומר הני לקוחות שהוא מוציא מהן בלא דמים לא הוו אלא כבע"ח: (ח) בא"ד מכח מדאמר רב נחמן לעיל דף קכה יתומים שגבו קרקע בחובת אביהן: (ט) בא"ד כמו ששנינו לעיל בפרק יש נוחלין וסבירא להו לשלחו מתם דהכא כר' יוחנן דאמר לעיל בפ' יש נוחלין מכר הבן בחיי האב ומת הבן לוקח מ"מ: (י) ד"ה אלא וכו' ולא גרסי' אלא אי איתמר וכו' שלחו מתם אלא שמה ששלחו זו היא.

קמא א מיי' פ"ה מהל' נחלות הל' ו סמג עשין ע טוש"ע אה"ע סי' צ סעיף ו:

קמב ב ג מיי' שם וסמג שם טוש"ע ח"מ סי' רפ סעיף ו:

גמ' בְּחֶזְקַת מִי? ר' (א) יוֹחָנָן אָמַר: בְּחֶזְקַת יוֹרְשֵׁי הַבַּעַל, וְר' אֶלְעָזָר אָמַר: בְּחֶזְקַת יוֹרְשֵׁי הָאִשָּׁה, וְר' שִׁמְעוֹן בֶּן לָקִישׁ מִשּׁוּם בַּר קַפָּרָא אָמַר: יַחֲלוֹקוּ. וְכֵן תָּנֵי בַּר קַפָּרָא: אהוֹאִיל וְהַלָּלוּ בָּאִין לִירַשׁ וְהַלָּלוּ בָּאִין לִירַשׁ – יַחֲלוֹקוּ.§ מתני' *נָפַל הַבַּיִת עָלָיו וְעַל אִמּוֹ – אֵלּוּ וְאֵלּוּ מוֹדִין שֶׁיַּחֲלוֹקוּ. אָמַר ר"ע: במוֹדֶה אֲנִי בְּזוֹ שֶׁהַנְּכָסִים בְּחֶזְקָתָן. אָמַר לוֹ בֶּן עַזַּאי: עַל (ב) חֲלוּקִין אָנוּ מִצְטַעֲרִין, אֶלָּא שֶׁבָּאתָ לְחַלֵּק עָלֵינוּ אֶת הַשָּׁוִין?!§ גמ' בְּחֶזְקַת מִי? ר' אִילָא אָמַר: גבְּחֶזְקַת יוֹרְשֵׁי הָאֵם; ר' זֵירָא אָמַר: בְּחֶזְקַת יוֹרְשֵׁי הַבֵּן. כִּי סְלֵיק רַבִּי זֵירָא, קָם בְּשִׁיטָתֵיהּ דְּרַבִּי אִילָא, (ג) קָם רַבָּה בְּשִׁיטָתֵיהּ דְּרַבִּי זֵירָא. אֲמַר רַבִּי זֵירָא, שְׁמַע מִינָּהּ: אֲוִירָא דְּאֶרֶץ יִשְׂרָאֵל מַחְכִּים. וְטַעְמָא מַאי? אָמַר אַבַּיֵי: הוֹאִיל וְהוּחְזְקָה נַחֲלָה בְּאוֹתוֹ שֵׁבֶט.§ "אָמַר לוֹ בֶּן עַזַּאי: עַל הַחֲלוּקִין אָנוּ מִצְטַעֲרִין" וכו'.§ אָמַר ר' שַׂמְלַאי, עֲדָא אָמְרָה: בֶּן עַזַּאי תַּלְמִיד חָבֵר דְּרַבִּי עֲקִיבָא הֲוָה, דְּקָאָמַר לֵיהּ: "שֶׁבָּאתָ". שָׁלְחוּ מִתָּם: בֵּן שֶׁלָּוָה בְּנִכְסֵי אָבִיו בְּחַיֵּי אָבִיו, וּמֵת – בְּנוֹ מוֹצִיא מִיַּד הַלָּקוֹחוֹת, וְזוֹ הִיא שֶׁקָּשָׁה בְּדִינֵי מָמוֹנוֹת. לֹוֶה מַאי מַפֵּיק? וְעוֹד, לָקוֹחוֹת מַאי עֲבִידְתַיְיהוּ? אֶלָּא *אִי אִיתְּמַר הָכִי אִיתְּמַר

גמ' בחזקת מי. הנכסים דקאמרי בית הלל "נכסים בחזקתן", בחזקת מי קאמרי בית הלל? בחזקת יורשי האשה. הוא דקאמרי לה, דהיא הנעלת ליה מבית אבוה. בחזקת יורשי הבעל. שאם פיחתו פיחתו לו, ואם הותירו הותירו לו, ויכול היה למוכרן, הלכך לא דמי לנכסי מלוג. יחלוקו. כדמפרש לקמן: הואיל והללו באין לירש הכל, והללו באין לירש הכל – יחלוקו, שהרי לשניהם יש טענת חזקה, כדפרישית: היא הנעלת ליה מבית אבוה, והוא מתוך שקיבל אחריות עליו קנאן, והרי הן כממונו. והאי דאמרי בית הלל "נכסים בחזקתן" – היינו בחזקת שניהן, ויחלוקו. מתני' נפל הבית עליו ועל אמו. כגון שנפל הבית על רחל אשת יעקב באלמנותה, ועל יוסף בנה מיעקב, ולא היה לה עוד בן מיעקב ולא מאיש אחר. שעכשיו טענותיהן שוות, שיורשי האם, כגון אחיה מאביה, (ד) אומרים: הבן מת ראשון והיא מתה אחרונה, וירשנו כל נכסיה. ויורשי הבן, כגון ראובן בן יעקב מלאה, טוען כל הנכסים, ואומר: רחל מתה תחלה, וירש יוסף את כל נכסיה, ואח"כ מת הוא, וירשנו כל הנכסים. אלו ואלו מודים שיחלוקו. דשניהם באין מכח טענת ירושת נכסים שהוחזקה בהן האשה לבדה בחייה באלמנותה בלא בעל. ולא דמי לנפל הבית עליו ועל אביו דלעיל, דהתם זה בא מכח ירושה וזה בא בטענת שטר חוב. וגם נפל הבית עליו ועל אשתו – יש שם נכסים שמוחזק בהן בעלה, ויש שם נכסים שמוחזקת האשה בחזקת אביה. אבל הכא – כל הנכסים הוחזקה בהן וקנאתן לאחר מות בעלה, ואבד כח בעלה וזכותו מהן. וכיון ששניהן באין בחזקת ירושה, ותובע כל אחד כל הנכסים – הוי ספק וספק, וחולקין. הלכך לא מיתוקמא אלא כגון שלא נשאר לרחל שום זרע, אבל אם יש לה עוד בן, כגון שיש לה שני בנים לרחל, יוסף מיעקב, ובנימין בנה מאיש אחר שהוא אחי יוסף מאמו, וראובן בן יעקב מלאה אומר: רחל מתה תחלה וירש יוסף חצי נכסיה, ואתה החצי, ואחר כך מת יוסף וירשתי חלקו. ובנימין אומר: לא כי, אלא יוסף מת תחלה ואחר כך מתה אמי, וירשתי כל נכסי'. על זאת נשאלתי מרבותי שבלותי"ר, ותשובותיי להם בסוף הספר לרפואות ובחוגות. ואומר אני שאין לראובן כאן כלום, משום דהוי בנימין יורש ודאי במקלת, וראובן ספק, ואין ספק מוציא מידי ודאי. שכל מקום ששנים באים מכח ירושה ויודעין לטעון (ה) מכח מי הן באין לירש, וכל אחד תובע כל הנכסים – יחלוקו, דהוי ספק וספק וחולקין, כגון במתני' שנפל הבית עליו ועל אמו, ואין לרחל עוד בן אחר אלא זה המת בלבד. וכל היכא שהאחד תובע את הכל והאחד תובע החצי – הנה זה שתובע הכל קרוי ודאי, הואיל והוי ודאי במקלת, ואידך ספק – ואין ספק מוציא מידי ודאי. והנני מביא ראיה מן השמועות הפסוקות בפרק "החולץ" (יבמות דף לה:), דתנן: ספק בן תשעה לראשון ספק בן שבעה לאחרון – יוציא והולד כשר, וחייבין עליו אשם תלוי. ואמרינן בגמרא (שם דף לח.): ספק ויבם שבאו לחלוק בנכסי סבא שהוא אביו של יבם, ספק אמר: אנא בר מינקא חנא, ופלגא דידי, ויבם אמר ליה: את ברא דידי את, ולית לך ולא מידי – הוי יבם ודאי, וספק הוי ספק, ואין ספק מוציא מידי ודאי. מינה שמעינן דכ"מ שהאחד יורש במקלת והשני ספק אם יש לו חלק בנכסים או לא – דודאי יורש את הכל. הלכך, מתני' דנפל הבית עליו ועל אמו דאמרי' יחלוקו – לא מתוקמא אלא כגון שאין לאם בן אחר אלא זה המת, שעכשיו טענותיהן שוות, שיורשי האם תובעין כל הנכסים ויורשי הבן תובעין כל הנכסים, הוו להו ספק וספק, וחולקין. דומיא דסבא ויבם בנכסי ספק, או סבא וספק בנכסי יבם שחולקין, כדאמרינן ב"החולץ". אבל אם יש לה בן שני קיים – יזכה בכל הנכסים, דהוי איהו ודאי במקלת, ויורשי הבן ספק, ואין ספק מוציא מידי ודאי. אמר ר"ע מודה אני בזו כו'. משום דנקט תנא קמא לישנא דמודים, אמר איהו נמי "מודה אני", כלומר: ואני מודה וחולק עליך, דלדברי ב"ה נמי אמרינן הכא נכסים בחזקתם. ובגמרא מפרש בחזקת מי, וטעמא נמי מפרש. אמר ליה בן עזאי על חלוקין (וכו'). דבית שמאי [ובית] הלל דלעיל, אנו מצטערין על שלא הושוו לדעת אחת, ואתה באתה לחלוק ולומר חולקין היו בית שמאי ובית הלל במה שחביריך אומרים שהן שוין?! גמ' בחזקת מי. אדר' עקיבא קאי. בחזקת יורשי האם. (ו) כדמפרש לקמיה, הואיל והוחזקה נחלה לאותו השבט. שכל ימי חיי האשה לאחר שמת בעלה היה כל ממונה בחזקתה, והרי היא משבט אביה, ואפילו כתובתה ותוספתה שנכנסה תחת בעלה, משבאו לידה הרי הן בחזקת שבט אביה, שהיא מתייחסת אחר שבט אביה. בחזקת יורשי הבן. דמשמת בעלה היה בן לאו יורש, קודם לכל קרוביה מצד האב. "קם רבה בשיטתיה דרבי זירא" לא גרסינן ליה. ובפר"ח נמי לא גרס ליה. אמר ר' זירא שמע מינה: אוירא דארץ ישראל מחכים. שמשעליתי לא"י נתתי את לבי לצאת משיטתי הראשונה, ולעמוד על אמיתת דברים. (ז) מאי טעמא. הדר ביה ר' זירא. באותו השבט. של אם. יש גורסין כאן: בעו מיניה מרב ששת בן מהו שיירש כו'. ולקמיה מפרשינן לה. עדא אמרה. וזו אומרת, עדא – כמו: הדא. תלמיד חבר. פשיטא לן דמתחלה היה תלמידו, והדא אמרה דלבסוף היה חבירו, דקאמר ליה "שבאת", ולא קאמר "שבא רבינו". שלחו מתם בן שלוה כו'. משבשתא היא, ולקמן מתרץ לה. ומשום דבמסקנא דייק לה ממתניתין נפל הבית עליו ועל אביו נקט ליה הכא. ונראית גירסת רבינו חננאל דגרס לה מקמי נפל הבית עליו ועל אשתו, דהא על נפל הבית עליו ועל אביו הוקבעה בגמרא, דמינה מייתי לה ראיה להך מילתא. ומתמה גמרא: לוה מאי מפיק. וכי בשביל שלוה ממון בחיי אביו יוציא מיד הלקוחות מה שמכר להן אביו או הוא?! אלא אי איתמר הכי איתמר בן שמכר בנכסי אביו כו'. כגון ראובן שמכר חלקו הראוי (ח) לירש בנכסי יעקב אביו, ומת ראובן בחיי יעקב אביו ואח"כ מת יעקב. בא חנוך בן ראובן ומוציא הנכסים שמכר ראובן מנכסי יעקב מיד הלקוחות, מפני שהן ראוי ולא באו ליד ראובן מעולם שיזכו בהן לקוחות מכחו. וכשם שהראוי אינו משתעבד – כך אינו נמכר, כדתנן בבכורות בפרק "יש בכור לנחלה" (דף נב:): ולא האשה בכתובתה ולא הבנות במזונותם ולא היבם – כולם אין נוטלין בראוי כבמוחזק. וכן הלכה. ולא חיישינן להאי, דדחי במסקנא ומוקי למתני' ביורשי אחוזה, דההיא קשיא והאי פירוקא אינו אלא להקשות על מה שאמר "וזו היא שקשה בדיני ממונות", והתלמוד מפרק דלא תסייעה ממתניתין, ולעולם קשה בדיני ממונות. ומכל מקום, עכשיו שקשה בדיני ממונות – כן הלכה, כדשלחו מתם קשה היא וכן הלכה כמותה, אפס דין קשה הוא בלא טעם כדמפרש ואזיל.

ולימרו

שחלקו ובא בע"ח ונטל חלקו של אחד מהם כו' (ט) כי אמר רב אסי נוטל רביע בקרקע ורביע במעות, ומסיק דמספקא ליה אי הוו לקוחות שלא באחריות. (י) פי': דאי כיורשים הוו — אז יחזרו על האחין, אי כלקוחות [שלא] באחריות הוו — אז [לא] יחזרו על האחין, ולכך נוטלין רביע. ואמאי נוטלו? הא הוו להם אחים ודאי בפלגא, והם ספק בחלקם, ואין ספק מוציא מידי ודאי! וע"ק: דהלכתא בלא טעמא הוא, שבשביל שהוא ודאי בחלק זה יהא ודאי בחלק אחר? ע"כ נראה לר"י כמו שתירץ ריב"א, דהכא מיירי שפיר שיש לה בנים אחרים לאם. והא דקרי ליהם ודאי — לפי שהוא יורש הסבא ודאי, אבל הספק אינו יורש ודאי הסבא. אבל הכא, הוי אלו ספק כמו אלו בחלק המגיע לבן, ולא שייך כאן כלל ספק ודאי. **אמר** ר"ע מודה אני בזה שהנכסים בחזקתן. אין לפרש כמו שפירש"י בב"מ פרק "המפקיד" (דף לז: וכס) דר"ע שמותי הוה, מתלמידי ב"ש, דהא הלכה כמותו מחבירו. וגם בפ"ק דיבמות (דף טו.) פליג ר"ע בצרת הבת על בית שמאי. ועוד: מאי "באת (כ) לנו לחלק את השוין"? הלא כיון דב"ש מודו בהא דנכסים בחזקתם — כ"ש ב"ה! ע"כ נראה לפרש "מודה אני בזו": למאן דמפרש בגמרא בחזקת יורשי האם הוו, מודה אני בזה, אע"ג דס"ל כבית הלל דכתובה הוי בחזקת יורשי הבעל — אלו הוי בחזקת האם. ולמאן דאמר בחזקת יורשי הבן הוי — מודה אני בזה, אע"ג דנכסי מלוג הוו בחזקת יורשי האשה — הכא מודינא דהוו בחזקת יורשי הבן.

הואיל והוחזקה נחלה באותו שבט. וא"ת: בנפל הבית עליו ועל אשתו, אמאי לא אמר בחזקת יורשי האשה מהאי טעמא? וי"ל: כיון דהכניסתם לו, אם פיחתו פיחתו לו, ואם הותירו הותירו לו — הוי כמוחזק. ולמ"ד בחזקת יורשי האשה, סובר: כיון דתטלם כשתלא, וגם הכניסתם לו — הוו (ל) בחזקתן. מ"ר.

לוה מאי מפיק. הלא לא לקחו מאביו כלום, ואינם בחזקתן! ולימרו

רבינו גרשום

בחזקת מי. אמרי ב"ה דהיינו צאן ברזל מה שהכניסה לו בכתובה דקבל עליו הבעל אחריות: א) אמר ר' אילא בחזקת יורש הבעל הואיל דבאחריות הבעל קיימי: ור' זירא אמר בחזקת יורשי האשה. הואיל והיא הכניסתן לו: אמר ר' זירא אוירא דארעא דישראל מחכים. כלומר מאחר שעליתי לארץ ישראל הבנתי בדעתי שכן הוא עיקר כדאמר ר' אילא בחזקת יורשי הבעל: וטעמא מאי אמר אביי הואיל והוחזקה נחלה באותו שבט. של בעל כלומר מאחר שהיא הכניסתן לו והוא קבל עליו אחריותן דמי כמו שלו הן הנכסים שאם נאבדו עליו לפורעו הרי הן חשובין כמו משבט אביו הוו שעליו אחריותן: נפל הבית עליו ועל אמו. יורשי הבן כגון אחין מן האב אומרים האם מתה ראשונה ואחר כך הבן ונפלו הנכסים ביד הבן והרי אנו יורשים. ויורשי האם אומרים הבן מת ראשון ולא באו נכסים לידו והרי אנו יורשין של אם: אלו ואלו. ב"ש וב"ה מודים שיחלוקו. הואיל דהללו באין בכח ירושה והללו באין בכח ירושה. אבל התם הללו באין לירש והללו בעל חוב וכתובה. הואיל ובאה בתורת חוב פליגי ב"ש דנכסים בחזקתן: אמר ר' עקיבא מודה אני בזה שהנכסים בחזקתן שאין כאן אלא ממון אחד בלבד ולא בעלי חוב: בחזקת מי. ר' אלעזר אומר בחזקת יורשי האם. שברשות האם היו תחלה: ר' יוחנן אמר בחזקת יורשי הבן. משום דמה מצינו בכל מקום הבן קודם לכל שאר יורש אף כאן יורש הבן קודם והרי הן בחזקתן: אמר לו בן עזאי על החלוקין במקום שחולקין ב"ש וב"ה: אנו מצטערין. דאיכא מחלוקת דלא מצינו להם למיקם אליבא דהלכתא מפני מחלוקתם אלא שבאת לחלוק עלינו את השוין דלא סבירא לך כוותיהו דיחלוקו: אמר ר' שמלאי מדקאמר ליה בן עזאי כך לר' עקיבא בלשון הטוב ולא אמר ליה בלשון כבוד ש"מ דבן עזאי תלמיד חבר היה של ר' עקיבא משום הכי לא חלק לו כבוד כל כך שהלכו שניהן ללמוד תורה לפני ר' אליעזר הגדול ולא פלוג שהיה בן עזאי בחור לא היה יכול לסבור סברא כר' עקיבא בתלמוד וגמר גמרא והדר הלך בן עזאי לפני ר' עקיבא להסביר: שלחו מתם בן שלוה בנכסי אביו. כלומר על נכסי אביו בחיי אביו ומת הבן בחיי אביו ואחר כך מת האב: בנו של בן. מוציא מיד הלקוחות. ומקשי' בן שלוה בנו ממאן מפיק. מי היה כאן לוקח. אלא הכי שלחו מתם. בן

ב"מ קד לו: ע"ש ולקמן קנט:]

[עי' תוס' לקמן קנט. ד"ה אלא אי קשיא]

הגהות הב"ח

(א) גמ' בחזקת מי ר' אלעזר אמר בחזקת יורשי האשה רבי יוחנן אמר בחזקת יורשי הבעל ורבי שמעון: (ב) שם במשנה על החלוקין: (ג) גמ' בשיטתיה דרבי זירא אלא קם רבה כצ"ל ותיבות קם רבה בשיטתיה דרבי זירא נמחק: (ד) רשב"ם ד"ה נפל וכו' כגון אחיה מאביה לבן אומרים הבן: (ה) ד"ה אלו ואלו וכו' מכח מי הן באין. נ"ב כלומר לאתופקי ספק ובני יבם דפ' החולץ ע"ש: (ו) ד"ה בחזקת יורשי האם כדפרשינן אביי הואיל: (ז) ד"ה וטעמא מאי הכי: (ח) ד"ה אלא אי איתמר וכו' כגון ראובן שמכר חלקו הראוי לירש: (ט) תוס' ד"ה (בבא) נפל כו' של אחד מהם כו' אמר (רבא) [רב אסי] כצ"ל ותיבת כי נמחק: (י) בא"ד שלא באחריות אם לאו פירוש דאי כיורשים וכו' אי כלקוחות שלא באחריות הוו אז לא יחזרו: (כ) ד"ה אמר וכו' מאי באת לחלוק עלינו את השוין לאמר בן עזאי הלא כיון דב"ש וכו' למאן דמפרש: (ל) ד"ה הואיל וכו' בחזקתה הם:

א) הדברים נראים שעין שרבינו היה גורס מחלוקת דר' אילא ור' זירא על משנה דנפל הבית עליו ועל אשתו ועי' בשמ"ק כאן שכ' דעיקר הגירסא הוא כגירסת דידן ואף שרשב"ם ז"ל לא גרס כן ע"ש ונראה שנ"ל ואף דהגמ"ה לא גרס כן וכוון לדברי רבינו כאן.

מתני' נָפַל הַבַּיִת עָלָיו וְעַל אִשְׁתּוֹ, יוֹרְשֵׁי הַבַּעַל אוֹמְרִים: אִשָּׁה מֵתָה *רִאשׁוֹן וְאַחַר כָּךְ מֵת הַבַּעַל, יוֹרְשֵׁי (א) אִשָּׁה אוֹמְרִים: בַּעַל מֵת רִאשׁוֹן וְאַחַר כָּךְ מֵתָה אִשָּׁה — בֵּית שַׁמַּאי אוֹמְרִים: יַחֲלוֹקוּ; וּבֵית הִלֵּל אוֹמְרִים: אנְכָסִים בְּחֶזְקָתָן, כְּתוּבָּה — בְּחֶזְקַת יוֹרְשֵׁי הַבַּעַל, נְכָסִים הַנִּכְנָסִין וְהַיּוֹצְאִין עִמָּהּ — בְּחֶזְקַת יוֹרְשֵׁי הָאָב.§

גמ'

מתני' נָפַל הַבַּיִת עָלָיו וְעַל אִשְׁתּוֹ. וְאֵין לָהּ בָּנִים מִמֶּנּוּ. יוֹרְשֵׁי הַבַּעַל. אָבִיו אוֹ אָחִיו, אוֹ בָּנָיו מֵאִשָּׁה אַחֶרֶת. אִשָּׁה מֵתָה רִאשׁוֹנָה. וְאֵין לְיוֹרְשֵׁי אִשָּׁה כְּלוּם בְּכָל נְכָסֶיהָ, שֶׁהֲרֵי הַבַּעַל מֵת אַחֲרוֹן וְיָרַשׁ אֶת אִשְׁתּוֹ קוֹדֶם מוֹתוֹ. יוֹרְשֵׁי הָאִשָּׁה. קְרוֹבֶיהָ מִמִּשְׁפַּחַת אָבִיהָ (וְאַחֲרֵי כֵן מֵתָה הִיא, וִירֵשׁוּהָ בְּכָל נְכָסֶיהָ). נִכְסֵי צֹאן בַּרְזֶל. וְהִיא נְדוּנְיָא דְּהַנְעָלַת לֵיהּ וְנִכְתְּבָה בִּכְתוּבָּה. וּמָנֶה וּמָאתַיִם וְתוֹסֶפֶת, וְנִכְסֵי מְלוֹג שֶׁלָּהּ. ב"ש אוֹמְרִים יַחֲלוֹקוּ. שֶׁהֲרֵי מָמוֹן מוּטָּל בְּסָפֵק הוּא. וְי"מ בִּיבָמוֹת בְּ"הַחוֹלֵץ" (ד' לח:) דְּאַכְּתוּבָּה לָא פְּלִיגֵי ב"ש אֶלָּא אַשְּׁאָרָא. וּב"ה אוֹמְרִים נְכָסִים בְּחֶזְקָתָן. בַּגְּמָ' מְפָרֵשׁ בְּחֶזְקַת מִי. הִלְכָּךְ, לָאו לְקַמֵּיהּ קָאֵי, אֶלָּא ה"ג: וּכְתוּבָּה בְּחֶזְקַת יוֹרְשֵׁי הַבַּעַל. וְהָנֵי נְכָסִים דְּקָאָמְרִי ב"ה — הֵן נִכְסֵי צֹאן בַּרְזֶל שֶׁהִכְנִיסָה מִבֵּית אָבִיהָ וּשְׁמָאָן בִּכְתוּבָּתָהּ, וְאַחֲרָיוּתָם עָלָיו, אִם פִּיחֲתוּ — פִּיחֲתוּ לוֹ, וְאִם הוֹתִירוּ — הוֹתִירוּ לוֹ. וּכְתוּבָּה בְּחֶזְקַת יוֹרְשֵׁי הַבַּעַל. מָנֶה וּמָאתַיִם וְתוֹסֶפֶת. *שֶׁמָּמוֹן הַבַּעַל רָאוּי לִיתֵּן א) לָהּ, הִלְכָּךְ מִסָּפֵק לֹא תּוֹצִיאֶנּוּ מֵחֶזְקַת הַבַּעַל וּמֵחֶזְקַת יוֹרְשָׁיו. נְכָסִים הַנִּכְנָסִים וְיוֹצְאִים עִמָּהּ. הֵן נִכְסֵי מְלוֹג שֶׁנָּפְלוּ מִבֵּית הָאָב, וְאֵין אַחֲרָיוּתָן עָלָיו. בְּחֶזְקַת יוֹרְשֵׁי הָאָב. שֶׁמֵּאָבִיהָ בָּאוּ לָהּ.

גמ'

נפל הבית עליו ועל אשתו כו' ב"ה אומרים נכסים בחזקתן. תימה: למ"ד בגמרא בחזקת יורשי האשה, אמאי לא חשיב להו בהדי נכסים הנכנסים והיוצאין עמה? ולמ"ד בחזקת יורשי הבעל אמאי לא תני לה בהדי כתובה? ואיכא למימר דלא שוו בטעמייהו, (ב) כדפרישית בסמוך. **ובית** הלל אומרים נכסים בחזקתן. קשיא לר"י: מ"ש דהכא אמר נכסים בחזקתן, ומפרש בגמ': בחזקת יורשי האשה, ואילו בסיפא תנן: נפל הבית עליו ועל אמו אלו ואלו מודים שיחלוקו. ואמאי? הוה ליה למימר (ג) כמו התם: נכסים בחזקתן — דהיינו בחזקת יורשי האם, כדפי' בגמרא! ותירץ: דהאי תנא ס"ל ירושת הבעל דרבנן, ולכך לא הוי אלא בחזקת יורשי האשה. ואפילו ס"ל נמי דאורייתא, יש לחלק ולומר: כיון דירושת הבעל אינה משום קורבה — הוי בחזקת האשה. אבל גבי נפל הבית עליו ועל אמו — הוו נמי בחזקת הבן, משום קורבה. מיהו קשה לר' אלחנן: דהא ר"ע איירי בסמוך בההיא דנפל הבית עליו ועל אמו, ואילו ר"ע אית ליה ירושת הבעל דאורייתא, לעיל בפ' "יש נוחלין" (דף קיא:), וגם בפרק "שור שנגח ד' וה'" (ב"ק דף מב:)! מיהו, מצי למימר(ד) ברישא דנפל הבית עליו ועל אמו — לאו ר"ע קאמר לה. והא דקאמר "מודה אני" — היינו אפי' סבירא להו כב"ש, אבל מ"מ לא קתני לה ברישא. ועוד קשה לו: לטעם דמחמת קורבה (ה) לה, למה יהא יותר בחזקת הבן מבחזקת שאר יורשי האם? והלא הם באים מחמת קורבה אלו כמו אלו! ור"י תירץ: דגבי הבעל יש לחשוב יותר בחזקת האשה, לפי שכמו שדרך האשה (ו) מתה קודם בעלה — כך דרך הבעל למות קודם האשה ולא יירשנה, ואין זה פורענות, ולכך לא סמכה דעתה כולי האי. אבל גבי בן ואם, דאם מת לפני האם הוי פורענות, להכי תקינו הכא גבי נפל הבית עליו ועל אמו שיהיו (ז) בחזקתה, לפי שהוא עתיד ועומד לירש את אמו יותר ממה שהוא עתיד הבעל לירש את אשתו. **ובית** הלל אומרים נכסים בחזקתן. קשיא לר"י: למ"ד בגמרא בחזקת יורשי הבעל, למה ליה טעמא דחזקתן? תיפוק ליה שאינם יכולין להיות בחזקת יורשי האשה, לפי שהיא צריכה שבועה על כתובתה, ואין אדם מוריש שבועה לבניו, כדאמרי רב ושמואל בפ' "כל הנשבעין" (שבועות דף מח.), וקי"ל כוותייהו! ובשלמא לב"ש דאמר יחלוקו, (ח) שתלי בחזקת יורשי האשה — אין להקשות כלום דאין אדם מוריש שבועה לבניו, דהא אית להו לב"ש כל העומד לגבות כגבוי דמי, והוי כמו שמוחזקין בממון, ואז אדם מוריש שבועה לבניו, כדאמרינן בפרק "כל הנשבעין" (שם:). וגם לר"א [דאמר] בחזקת יורשי האשה — ליכא לאקשויי מידי, דהא אית ליה בפרק "כל הנשבעין" (שם.) דאדם מוריש שבועה לבניו, ופליג ארב ושמואל. אבל ר' יוחנן דהכא — מסתמא לא פליג ארב ושמואל דהתם! ומצינו למימר — כגון שפטרה משבועה, אבל לא משמע הכי. אבל י"ל דהיא הנותנת, (ט) משום שהנכסים בחזקת הבעל ואינם בחזקת יורשי האשה — לא(י) יוכל להוריש שבועה לבניה, ולא יטלו יורשי האשה כלום. אבל אם היו בחזקת יורשי האשה — אז הוה אמרי' שיש לה הכל, דהא כיון שהיו מוחזקין בממון — שבועה כזו יכולה להוריש לבניה כממון, ולא אמרינן אין אדם מוריש שבועה לבניו. דהא לב"ש נמי, הואיל והיא מוחזקת בממון מטעם דכל העומד לגבות וכו' — לא אמרינן אין אדם מוריש שבועה לבניו. אבל ליכא לשנויי: כגון שייחד לה קרקע בד' מצרנהא, דפטורה משבועה, כדאמרי' בריש "אע"פ" (כתובות דף נד.), דא"כ כי מקשה מכמה *(ברייתות) בפ' "כל הנשבעין" (שבועות דף מח.) ופריך נמי מברייתא דמוקי(כ) כב"ש — לישני ליה: כגון שייחד לה ארעא בד' מצרנהא, מ"ר. ובשם הר"ר שמשון מ"כ שמעתי, דלא שייך הכא טעמא דאין אדם מוריש שבועה לבניו, דהא אין טעונה שבועה אלא משום דחיישינן דלמא מתפיס לה צררי, והיינו כגון שהלך למ"ה דאז מתפיס לה צררי, אבל נפל עליו כו' שהוא לפתע פתאום — ליכא למיחש להתפסת צררי. ואין נראה לר"י, כי למה אין לחוש שתפסה מחיים, כדאמרי' ב"אלמנה ניזונית" (כתובות נו. ושם): אלמנה שתפסה מטלטלין למזונותיה — מה שתפסה תפסה. ואמרינן דהיינו למזונותיה, אבל לכתובה — מפקינן מינה. ומיירי כגון שתפסה מחיים, דאמרי' בפרק "הכותב" (שם פה.): (ל) התפיסה לאחר מיתה לאו כלום היא. ולמה אין לנו לחוש לתפיסה מחיים? ואמרינן נמי ב"השולח" (גיטין ד' לה. ושם): רב לא מגבי כתובה לארמלתא, דחיישא לצררי. **נכסים** בחזקתן. ביבמות פרק "החולץ" (דף לח.) ובכתובות פרק "האשה שנפלו" (דף פ: ושם)(מ): מתה, מה יעשו בכתובה ובנכסים הנכנסים והיוצאים עמה? ב"ש אומרים: יחלוקו יורשי הבעל עם יורשי האב, וב"ה אומרים: נכסים בחזקתן. ופי' רש"י: כי היכי דפליגי הכא אמוראי בגמרא הוו פליגי התם, ו"בחזקתן" היינו למר כדאית ליה ולמר כדאית ליה. ואין נראה לר"ת, דלא דמיא כלל מתני' דהתם להך דהכא, דהא התם לא פליגי ב"ש אלא אנכסי מלוג ולא אכתובה, כדדייק התם בגמרא, מדקתני "יורשי הבעל עם יורשי האב", א"כ יורשי האב ודאי דהיינו בנכסי מלוג, אבל בכתובה — ב"ש מודו לב"ה. ואילו הכא פליגי ב"ש אפי' בכתובה, מדקתני "יחלוקו" סתמא, ולא קתני "עם יורשי האב" כי התם. והיינו טעמא, דלא דמיא כלל דהכא לדהתם, (נ) דהא ודאי אין כח ליורשי הבעל, דהא מיד כשמת הויא לה כמו שגבתה כבר כתובתה, והויא לה ספק דאימור מתה ראשונה, ולכך יחלוקו. אבל התם כשמת הבעל — קם היבם תחתיו, וזקוקה לו, ולא הויא כמי שגבתה כתובתה, דעד אחר חליצה אין לה כלום. ולהכי יש להו כח ליורשי הבעל, ומודו כולי עלמא שהנכסים שלו בחזקת יורשי הבעל, דלא פליגי אלא בנכסי מלוג, אבל בכתובה ובנכסי צאן ברזל — לא, שלא נתנה כתובתה לגבות מחיים. אבל הכא אית להו דיחלוקו מטעם דשטר העומד לגבות כגבוי דמי, ולכך אין לחלק בין נכסי צאן ברזל לכתובה. ועוד אמר, דע"כ לא פליגי התם בחזקת מי כי הכא, דא"כ תקשה לך למ"ד הכא בחזקת יורשי האשה — א"כ התם נמי הוו נכסי צאן ברזל יותר בחזקת יורשי האשה לב"ש, דלא פליגי בהא. ונכסי מלוג יחלוקו — א"כ הוו נכסי צאן ברזל יותר בחזקת האשה מנכסי מלוג. ואדרבה, יותר הם בחזקת הבעל מנכסי מלוג, כדתנן ביבמות ריש פרק "אלמנה לכהן גדול" (דף סו.): עבדי צאן ברזל יאכלו בתרומה, עבדי נכסי מלוג לא יאכלו בתרומה. אלמא, מוחזקין יותר נכסי צאן ברזל בחזקת הבעל מנכסי מלוג. א"כ היכי מצי למימר דבשל מלוג יחלוקו יורשי הבעל, ובשל צאן ברזל יהיו כולם לגמרי בחזקת יורשי האשה? וליכא לאקשויי, למאי [דפרישית] (ס) דהתם הוו נכסים בחזקת יורשי הבעל — אמאי לא עריב ותני להו: נכסים וכתובה בחזקת יורשי הבעל, וכן למ"ד בגמ' נכסים בחזקת יורשי הבעל, אמאי לא עריב ותני נכסים (ע) וכתובת אשה בחזקת יורשי הבעל? דאיכא למימר דלא שווינהו בטעמייהו, דנכסי צאן ברזל אינם כל כך בחזקת יורשי הבעל כמו כתובה, לפי שנכסי צאן ברזל הביאה מביתה, אבל כתובה מנה ומאתים הוא נותן. ואפי' כשאינה זקוקה ליבם — הכתובה בחזקת יורשי הבעל. ולמ"ד (פ) בחזקת יורשי האשה בגמרא — לא שייך הכא למיתני בהדי נכסי מלוג, דלא שוו לגמרי בטעמייהו, דאלו בחזקת הבעל יותר ואלו בחזקת האשה, כדפרי' לעיל בסמוך. מ"ר. *נפל הבית עליו ועל אמו אלו ואלו מודין שיחלוקו. שאלו לרבינו שמואל: למה יחלוקו? הוה לן למימר שיורשי האם הם ודאי בחלקו האחד, (צ) שיש לה בנים אחרים, והבן זה הוא ספק כי שמא מת קודם אמו, והוה ליה ספק וודאי, ואין ספק מוציא מידי ודאי, כדאמר ביבמות פרק "החולץ" (ד' לח. ושם): ספק ויבם שבאו לחלוק בנכסי סבא, בא ספק ואמר: ההוא גברא בר מיתנא, ופלגא דידיה. ויבם אמר: את ברא דידי, ולית לך ולא מידי. הוי יבם ודאי, וספק ספק, ואין ספק מוציא מידי ודאי. ופירש רש"י שם: דלהכי קרו ליה ליבם ודאי, לפי שהוא ודאי בפלגא אחד — יש להיות ודאי בכל הנכסים. וא"כ ה"נ, אמאי לא אמרינן הכי? ותירץ רבינו שמואל: דהכא מיירי שאין לה לאם בנים אחרים, אלא יורשי האם היינו אחיה, שאם *מת הבן אחריה אין להם כלום, ולכך הם ספקות אלו כמו אלו. ואין נראה לר"י ולר"ת ולריב"א, דהא אפי' יש לה בנים — אין לנו לחשוב זה (ק) ספק ודאי, מדקאמר לקמן (ד' קנט.) גבי נפל הבית עליו ועל אביו והיתה עליו כתובת אשה ובעל חוב כו' מאי לאו יורשי האב (ר) כו'. ופירש רבינו שמואל: בני מורישיו — אחי יורשי האב — אחי הבן. אלמא, אע"ג דיש בנים אחרים לאב לא הוי אמרי' (ש) ספק ודאי, שאין לנו לחושבן ודאי בכל הנכסים לפי שהוא ודאי בחלק אחד! ועוד קשה לרבי: מדתנן בפ"ק דב"מ (דף ב.): זה אומר כולה שלי וזה אומר חציה שלי, מי שאמר חציה שלי — ישבע שאין לו פחות [מרביע ויטלנו, וזה ישבע שאין לו פחות מג' רביעים] ויטלנו. אמאי לא הוי הכל שלו, כיון שהוא ודאי בזה החצי — יטול הכל, דהוי ספק וודאי, ואין ספק כו'? ועוד קשה לר"י: מדאמר לעיל פרק "בית כור" (דף קו.): שני אחין שחלקו

קם א מיי' פ"ה מהל' נחלות הל' ו סמג עשין צו טוש"ע אה"ע סי' צ סעיף ו:

רבינו גרשום

היה לו לגבות מן המוכר ולא יותר. ומשני מאי גובה נמי חצי שבח ולעולם יחלוקו: נפל הבית עליו ועל אשתו יורשי הבעל אומרים האשה מתה ראשון. ואין לה כתובה דהבעל יורש אשתו וממונא בחזקת בעל קאי. ויורשי האשה אחיה אומרים הבעל מת ראשון. ב"ש אומרים יחלוקו בין עיקר הכתובה מאתים או מנה ובין התוספת דהיינו נכסי צאן ברזל שקבל עליו באחריות ובין הנכסים הנכנסים והיוצאין עמה כגון נכסי מלוג הכל יחלוקו שמוטל בספק הוא אם הוא יורש או היא: וב"ה אומרים נכסים בחזקתן. כלומר העמד הנכסים על מי שהיה מחזיק בהן העיקר א) כתובה מאתים או מנה וכתובה דהיינו תוספת בחזקת יורשי הבעל משום דבחזקת הבעל קיימי קודם דלא ניתנה כתובה לגבות מחיים: ונכסים הנכנסין והיוצאין עמה בחזקת יורשי האב של אשה משום דבחיי הבעל היתה אשתו מוחזקת בהן בנכסי מלוג שלה שהבעל לא קבלן באחריותו:

נ"ל משניות

שייך לעמ"ב

גי' רש"ל מתה האם אחיה אין

א) נ"ל ליתן להם הלכך מספק לא תוציאם מחזקת כו'. יעב"ץ]:

רש"ל מוחק זה

נ"ל ראשונה

הגהות הב"ח

(א) במשנה יורשי האשה: (ב) תוס' ד"ה נפל וכו' ועל אשתו וכו' בטעמייהו כדאפרש בסמוך: (ג) ד"ה ובית הלל וכו' הוה ליה למימר נמי התם: (ד) בא"ד מיהו מצי למימר דרישא: (ה) בא"ד לטעם דמחמת קורבה למה כצ"ל ותיבת לה נמחק: (ו) בא"ד שדרך האשה שתמות קודם וכו' הוי פורענות. נ"ב הכי איתא ר"פ י"נ: (ז) בא"ד בחזקתו לפי שהוא עתיד: (ח) ד"ה ובית הלל וכו' שתלי בחזקת יורשי האשה אין להקשות כלום מההיא דאין אדם: (ט) בא"ד אבל י"ל דהיא הנותנת למשום. נ"ב תימה לפי דעת התוס' א"כ לריש לקיש משום בר קפרא דיחלוקו קשה מההיא דאין אדם מוריש שבועה לבניו דמסתמא לא פליג ארב ושמואל וכמו שכתבו התוס' אליבא דר' יוחנן ועוד דהא אנן קי"ל כריש לקיש משום בר קפרא דיחלוקו וקי"ל כרב ושמואל דאין אדם מוריש כו' וא"כ קשיא הלכתא אהלכתא ולפי' הר' שמשון אתי שפיר: (י) בא"ד לא תוכל להוריש שבועה וכו' הוה אמרינן שיש להם הכל דהא כיון וכו' יכולה להוריש לבניה דהא לבית שמאי נמי הואיל והיא מוחזקת בממון לא אמרינן אין אדם מוריש שבועה לבניו אבל ליכא לשנויי: (כ) בא"ד ופריך נמי מברייתא דמוקי לה כב"ש. נ"ב כלומר אמאי דחיק נפשיה לשנויי בכמה גווני ולבסוף משני נמי על ברייתא אחת הא מני ב"ש היא דאמר שטר העומד לגבות כו' לישני לכולהו בשינויא חדא כגון שייחד כו' אלא בע"כ דלא ניחא כלל לשנויי כגון שייחד כו': (ל) בא"ד דתפיסה דלאחר מיתה לאו כלום היא וכו' לא מגבי כתובה: (מ) ד"ה נכסים וכו' האשה שנפלו שניהו מתה מה יעשו בכתובתה: (נ) בא"ד דהכא לדהתם ודאי אין כח וכו' מיד כשמת הבעל הויא לה: (ס) בא"ד למאי דפרישית התם אי הוו: (ע) בא"ד נכסים וכתובה בחזקת יורשי הבעל דאיכא למימר דלא שוו בטעמייהו וכו' שנכסי צאן ברזל הביאה האשה מביתה: (פ) בא"ד ולמ"ד בגמרא בחזקת יורשי האשה לא שייך הכא למיתני בהדי נכסים הנכנסים והיוצאין עמה דלא שוו לגמרי: (צ) ד"ה נפל וכו' כשיש לה בנים וכו' דלפי שהוא ודאי: (ק) בא"ד לחשוב זה הספק ודאי כדקאמר לעיל גבי נפל. נ"ב זהו לפי גירסת ר"ח ור"ת דסוגיא זו קבועה לעיל: (ר) בא"ד מאי לאו יורשי האב בני דמסיק מאי יורשי האב אחי ופירש רבינו שמואל אחי הבן אלמא כצ"ל ותיבות בני מורישיו אחי יורשי האב נמחק: (ש) בא"ד הוא הוה אמרינן דהוי ספק:

א) עי' לקמן בסוגיא ונ"ע ואולי דל"ל על מי שהיה מחזיק בהן: וכתובה. דהיינו מאתים או מנה ותוספת בחזקת יורשי וכו'.

אֶלָּא הָא מַנִּי? ר' מֵאִיר הִיא, דְּאָמַר: אָדָם מַקְנֶה דָּבָר שֶׁלֹּא בָּא לָעוֹלָם. אָמַר רַב יַעֲקֹב מִנְּהַר פְּקוֹד מִשְּׁמֵיהּ דְּרָבִינָא, תָּא שְׁמַע: א) א שִׁטְרֵי חוֹב הַמּוּקְדָּמִין פְּסוּלִין, ב וְהַמְאוּחָרִין כְּשֵׁרִין; וְאִי סָלְקָא דַּעְתָּךְ "דְּאִיקְנֵי" קָנָה וּמָכַר, "דְּאִיקְנֵי" קָנָה וְהוֹרִישׁ – לָא מִשְׁתַּעְבֵּד, מְאוּחָרִין אַמַּאי כְּשֵׁרִין? "דְּאִיקְנֵי" הוּא! הָא מַנִּי? רַבִּי מֵאִיר הִיא, דְּאָמַר: אָדָם מַקְנֶה דָּבָר שֶׁלֹּא בָּא לָעוֹלָם. אָמַר רַב מְשַׁרְשְׁיָא מִשְּׁמֵיהּ דְּרָבָא, תָּא שְׁמַע: ב) לְשֶׁבַח קַרְקָעוֹת כֵּיצַד? הֲרֵי שֶׁמָּכַר שָׂדֶה לַחֲבֵירוֹ וְהִשְׁבִּיחָהּ, וּבָא בַּעַל חוֹב וּטְרָפָהּ, כְּשֶׁהוּא גּוֹבֶה – גּוֹבֶה אֶת הַקֶּרֶן מִנְּכָסִין מְשׁוּעְבָּדִין, וְאֶת הַשֶּׁבַח מִנְּכָסִין בְּנֵי חוֹרִין; וְאִי סָלְקָא דַּעְתָּךְ "דְּאִיקְנֵי" קָנָה וּמָכַר, "דְּאִיקְנֵי" קָנָה וְהוֹרִישׁ – לָא מִשְׁתַּעְבֵּד, בַּעַל חוֹב אַמַּאי גּוֹבֶה שִׁבְחָא? הָא מַנִּי? ר' מֵאִיר הִיא, דְּאָמַר: אָדָם מַקְנֶה דָּבָר שֶׁלֹּא בָּא לָעוֹלָם. אִם תִּמְצָא לוֹמַר: "דְּאִיקְנֵי" קָנָה וּמָכַר, "דְּאִיקְנֵי" קָנָה וְהוֹרִישׁ, לָא מִשְׁתַּעְבֵּד – הָא לָא מִשְׁתַּעְבֵּד. אִם תִּמְצָא לוֹמַר: ג מִשְׁתַּעְבֵּד, לָוָה וְלָוָה וְחָזַר וְקָנָה, מַהוּ? (א) לְקַמָּא מִשְׁתַּעְבֵּד אוֹ לְבַתְרָא מִשְׁתַּעְבֵּד? אֲמַר רַב נַחְמָן: הָא מִילְּתָא אִיבַּעְיָא לָן, וּשְׁלַחוּ מִתָּם: רִאשׁוֹן קָנָה. רַב הוּנָא אָמַר: יַחֲלוֹקוּ. וְכֵן תָּנֵי רַבָּה בַּר אֲבוּהּ: יַחֲלוֹקוּ. אֲמַר רָבִינָא, מַהֲדוּרָא קַמָּא דְּרַב אַשִׁי אֲמַר לָן: רִאשׁוֹן קָנָה, מַהֲדוּרָא בַּתְרָא דְּרַב אַשִׁי אֲמַר לָן: יַחֲלוֹקוּ. ד וְהִלְכְתָא: יַחֲלוֹקוּ. מֵיתִיבֵי: לְשֶׁבַח קַרְקָעוֹת כֵּיצַד? ה הֲרֵי שֶׁמָּכַר שָׂדֶה לַחֲבֵירוֹ וְהִשְׁבִּיחָהּ, וּבָא בַּעַל חוֹב וּטְרָפָהּ, כְּשֶׁהוּא גּוֹבֶה – גּוֹבֶה אֶת הַקֶּרֶן מִנְּכָסִין מְשׁוּעְבָּדִין, וְאֶת הַשֶּׁבַח מִנְּכָסִין בְּנֵי חוֹרִין; וְאִם אִיתָא, חֲצִי שֶׁבַח מִבָּעֵי לֵיהּ! מַאי גּוֹבֶה נַמִּי דְּקָתָנֵי – ו חֲצִי שֶׁבַח.§

מתני'

רשב"ם

אֶלָּא הָא מַנִּי ר"מ כו'. וְכִי מִיבָּעֵי לָן – לְרַבָּנַן הוּא דְּמִיבָּעְיָא לָן, כְּדַאֲמָרַן לְעֵיל. הַמּוּקְדָּמִים. שֶׁנִּכְתְּבוּ בְּיוֹם ט"ו בְּנִיסָן, וְכָתַב בְּתוֹךְ הַשְּׁטָר בְּאֶחָד בְּנִיסָן. פְּסוּלִין. דְּאָתֵי לְמִיטְרַף לָקוֹחוֹת שֶׁל ט"ו יָמִים רִאשׁוֹנִים דְּנִיסָן שֶׁלֹּא כַּדִּין, שֶׁהֲרֵי הַהַלְוָאָה הָיְתָה בְּט"ו בְּנִיסָן, וְהוּא יִטְרוֹף לָקוֹחוֹת דְּט"ו קוֹדֶם. וּמִיהוּ, אִם הַהַלְוָאָה הָיְתָה בְּאֶחָד בְּנִיסָן בִּפְנֵי עֵדִים, וְקָנוּ מִיָּדוֹ לְהִשְׁתַּעְבֵּד נִכְסֵי לֹוֶה לַמַּלְוֶה, וְלֹא כָּתְבוּ אֶת הַשְּׁטָר עַד ט"ו בְּנִיסָן, וְכָתְבוּ בּוֹ בְּאֶחָד בְּנִיסָן – כִּי הַאי מוּקְדָּם כָּשֵׁר, כִּדְאָמַר לְהוּ רַבָּה בַּר שֵׁילָא לְהָנָךְ דְּכָתְבֵי אַקְנַיְיתָא: אִי יָדְעִיתוּ הַהוּא יוֹמָא דְּאַקְנֵיתוּ בּוֹ – לְחַיֵּי, וְאִי לָא – כְּתִיבוּ יוֹמָא דְּקַיְימִיתוּ בֵּיהּ. לְקַמָּן בְּ"גֵּט פָּשׁוּט" (דף קעב.). הַמּוּקְדָּמִין פְּסוּלִין. כִּדְפְרִישִׁית, שֶׁהִקְדִּים זְמַן הַכָּתוּב בַּשְּׁטָר לְיוֹם כְּתִיבָתוֹ. א"נ, שֶׁנִּכְתַּב הַשְּׁטָר בְּאֶחָד בְּנִיסָן וְכֵן כָּתוּב בּוֹ "בְּאֶחָד בְּנִיסָן לָוָה פְּלוֹנִי מִפְּלוֹנִי", וְהוּא לֹא לָוָה מִמֶּנּוּ כְּלוּם עַד ט"ו בְּנִיסָן – גַּם זֶה מוּקְדָּם, וּפָסוּל. שֶׁאֵין לוֹ לִטְרוֹף אֶלָּא מִזְּמַן הַהַלְוָאָה וְאֵילָךְ, וּדְלָא כְּאַבַּיֵּי דְּאָמַר: עֵדָיו בַּחֲתוּמָיו זָכִין לוֹ, בְּ"שְׁנַיִם אוֹחֲזִין" (ב"מ דף יג.). וְהַמְאוּחָרִים כְּשֵׁרִין. לָוָה בְּנִיסָן וְלֹא נִכְתַּב עַד תִּשְׁרֵי. אִי נַמִּי, כְּתָבוּהוּ בַּיּוֹם שֶׁלָּוָה, אַךְ אִיחֵר הַזְּמַן בְּתוֹךְ הַשְּׁטָר וְכָתַב בּוֹ בְּתִשְׁרֵי – כְּשֵׁרִין, שֶׁמָּחַל לוֹ הַשִּׁעְבּוּד עַד תִּשְׁרֵי, וְלֹא יִטְרוֹף לָקוֹחוֹת אֶלָּא מִתִּשְׁרֵי וְאֵילָךְ. מְאוּחָרִין אַמַּאי כְּשֵׁרִין. כְּשֶׁלָּוָה בְּנִיסָן וְנִכְתַּב בְּתִשְׁרֵי? וַהֲלֹא שֶׁמָּא קָנָה זֶה (ב) אֵלּוּ נְכָסִים בֵּין נִיסָן לְתִשְׁרֵי וְלֹא אִשְׁתַּעְבְּדוּ לַמַּלְוֶה, דְּהָא "דְּאִיקְנֵי" הוּא בִּשְׁעַת הַלְוָאָה, וְהַטּוֹרֵף יָבֹא לִטְרוֹף מִתִּשְׁרֵי וְאֵילָךְ שֶׁלֹּא כַּדִּין מִן הַלָּקוֹחוֹת שֶׁקָּנוּ מִן הַלֹּוֶה נְכָסִים הַקְּנוּיִין לוֹ מִנִּיסָן וְעַד תִּשְׁרֵי! אֶלָּא שְׁמַע מִינָּהּ "דְּאִיקְנֵי" מִשְׁתַּעְבֵּד, וְהִלְכָּךְ מְאוּחָרִים כְּשֵׁרִים, דְּלֵיכָּא לְמֵיחַשׁ לְהָכִי. הָא מַנִּי ר"מ הִיא. וְהִלְכָּךְ מְאוּחָרִים כְּשֵׁרִין, שֶׁאִם כָּתַב בְּתוֹךְ הַשְּׁטָר שׁוּם אַחֲרָיוּת (ג) – כָּתַב "דִּקְנָאִי וּדְעָתִיד אֲנָא לְמִיקְנֵי", שֶׁאֵין כּוֹתְבִין אַחֲרָיוּת לַחֲצָאִין, וְלֵיכָּא לְמֵיחַשׁ לְמִידֵּי. וְגַם אִם לֹא נִכְתַּב בּוֹ אַחֲרָיוּת – לֵיכָּא לְמֵיחַשׁ כְּלָל, דְּהָא לְר' מֵאִיר לָא טָרֵיף מִמְּשַׁעְבְּדֵי, בִּ"שְׁנַיִם אוֹחֲזִין". וּמִיהוּ, אִם כָּתַב בְּהוּ "דִּקְנָאִי" וְלָא כְּתִיב בְּהוּ "דַּאֲקְנֵי" – בְּהָא וַדַּאי מוֹדֶה ר' מֵאִיר דִּמְאוּחָרִין פְּסוּלִין, כְּקוּשְׁיָין דִּלְעֵיל, דִּלְמָא אָתֵי לְמִטְרַף קַרְקָעוֹת שֶׁקָּנָה בֵּין זְמַן הַלְוָאָה לִזְמַן כְּתִיבַת הַשְּׁטָר שֶׁלֹּא כַּדִּין. מִיהוּ, לָא שְׁכִיחָא מִילְּתָא לִכְתּוֹב אַחֲרָיוּת לַחֲצָאִין, וְהִלְכָּךְ לֹא חָשׁ לְאַקְשׁוּיֵי טְפֵי. לְשֶׁבַח קַרְקָעוֹת כֵּיצַד. בְּמַסֶּ' גִּיטִּין (דף מח:) תְּנַן: אֵין מוֹצִיאִין לַאֲכִילַת פֵּירוֹת וּלְשֶׁבַח קַרְקָעוֹת וְלִמְזוֹן הָאִשָּׁה וְהַבָּנוֹת מִנְּכָסִים מְשׁוּעְבָּדִים, מִפְּנֵי תִּיקּוּן הָעוֹלָם. וְהָשְׁתָּא מְפָרֵשׁ לְשֶׁבַח קַרְקָעוֹת כֵּיצַד. וּבִ"שְׁנַיִם אוֹחֲזִין" (דף יד:) מִיתְנְיָא: הֲרֵי שֶׁגָּזַל שָׂדֶה מֵחֲבֵירוֹ כו'. וּמְשַׁנֵּי: לָא תְּרוֹצֵי קָא מְתָרְצַתְּ לֵיהּ? תָּרֵיץ נַמִּי בְּבַעַל חוֹב. וּכְדִמְתָרְצָא הָתָם מִיתְנְיָא הָכָא. וּבָא בַּעַל חוֹב וְטָרְפָהּ. כְּשֶׁהִיא מְשׁוּבַּחַת בְּזִיבּוּל וַחֲרִישָׁה וּזְרִיעָה. כְּשֶׁהוּא גּוֹבָה. הַלּוֹקֵחַ מִן הַמּוֹכֵר. בַּעַל חוֹב שֶׁבַח מְנָא לֵיהּ. וַהֲלֹא זֶה הַשֶּׁבַח, הַלּוֹקֵחַ שֶׁלָּקַח שָׂדֶה זוֹ אַחַר הַלְוָאַת הַמַּלְוֶה הִשְׁבִּיחוֹ, וּדְאַקְנֵי קְרִינָא בֵּיהּ בִּשְׁעַת הַלְוָאָה! וְאת"ל כו'. בָּעְיָא בְּאַפֵּי נַפְשָׁהּ הִיא. הָא לֹא קָנָה. וְלֵיכָּא לְמִיבָּעֵי אִי בַּתְרָא קָנֵי אִי קַמָּא קָנֵי, כִּדְלְקַמָּן, שֶׁהֲרֵי לֹא קָנָה לֹא זֶה וְלֹא זֶה. וְאִם תִּמְצָא לוֹמַר דְּאִיקְנֵי קָנָה וּמָכַר מִשְׁתַּעְבֵּד. לָוֶה וְכָתַב לַמַּלְוֶה "שִׁעְבַּדְתִּי לָךְ כָּל נְכָסַי דִּקְנָאִי וּדְאִיקְנֵי", וְחָזַר וְלָוָה מֵאַחֵר, וְכָתַב לוֹ כְּמוֹ שֶׁכָּתַב לוֹ לָרִאשׁוֹן, וְאח"כ קָנָה נְכָסִים וּמְכָרָן, אוֹ שֶׁמֵּת וְהוֹרִישָׁם לַיּוֹרְשִׁים, וּבָאוּ שְׁנֵי הַנּוֹשִׁים לִטְרוֹף אוֹתָן הַנְּכָסִים, הַדִּין עִם מִי? לְקַמָּא מִשְׁתַּעְבֵּד – שֶׁהֲרֵי כָּתוּב בִּשְׁטָר מוּקְדָּם, אוֹ לְבַתְרָא מִשְׁתַּעְבֵּד – דְּלָא חָלִים "דְּאִיקְנֵי" לִתְפּוֹס עַד שֶׁיָּבוֹאוּ הַנְּכָסִים בָּעוֹלָם, וְכִי קָנָה הָנֵי נְכָסִים אַחֲרֵי כֵן – הָא הָדַר בֵּיהּ מִקַּמָּא, וְיִקְנֶה בַּתְרָא. יַחֲלוֹקוּ. כָּל אֶחָד לְפִי מְעוֹתָיו, דִּבְבַת אַחַת נִשְׁתַּעְבְּדוּ לָהֶם. שֶׁהֲרֵי אַחַר ב' הַהַלְוָאוֹת קְנָאָהּ, וּבְאוֹתָהּ הָעֵת שֶׁקְּנָאָהּ – מִיָּד נִשְׁתַּעְבְּדוּ לִשְׁנֵיהֶן, שֶׁאֵין קְדִימָה לְאֶחָד מֵהֶן. מַהֲדוּרָא בַּתְרָא. כְּשֶׁחָזַר לִימּוּדוֹ פַּעַם שְׁנִיָּה. נִמְצָא בִּתְשׁוּבַת רַב הָאי וּבְפר"ח: רַב אַשִׁי חָיָה שִׁשִּׁים שָׁנָה, וּבְכָל שָׁנָה מְחַזֵּר לִימּוּדוֹ בִּשְׁנֵי חָדְשֵׁי הַכַּלָּה נִיסָן וְתִשְׁרֵי, וְלִכְשֶׁהִגִּיעוּ שְׁלֹשִׁים שָׁנָה סִיֵּים כָּל לִימּוּדוֹ וְכֵן עָשָׂה בִּשְׁלֹשִׁים שָׁנִים אַחֲרוֹנִים. וּמַהֲדוּרָא קַמָּא הַיְינוּ שְׁלֹשִׁים שָׁנִים רִאשׁוֹנִים, וּמַהֲדוּרָא בַּתְרָא הֵן שְׁלֹשִׁים שָׁנִים אַחֲרוֹנִים. וְאִם אִיתָא חֲצִי שֶׁבַח מִיבָּעֵי לֵיהּ. שֶׁכֵּיוָן שֶׁמָּכַר הַלֹּוֶה שָׂדֵהוּ וְכָתַב לוֹ אַחֲרָיוּת עָלָיו, וְאַחֲרֵי כֵן הִשְׁבִּיחָן הַלּוֹקֵחַ – נִמְצָא הַמַּלְוֶה וְהַלּוֹקֵחַ שְׁנֵיהֶן נוֹשִׁין בַּלֹּוֶה, וְנִמְצָא הַשֶּׁבַח קְנוּי לַלֹּוֶה אַחַר שִׁעְבּוּד שְׁנֵיהֶן, לַמַּלְוֶה בְּחוֹבוֹ, וְלַלּוֹקֵחַ בְּכֶסֶף מִקְנָתוֹ. לְפִיכָךְ חוֹלְקִין הַשֶּׁבַח כְּדִין לָוָה וְלָוָה וְחָזַר וְקָנָה. הִלְכָּךְ אֵין לַמַּלְוֶה בְּכָל מָקוֹם אֶלָּא חֲצִי הַשֶּׁבַח. וּמְשַׁנֵּי: מַאי גּוֹבֶה נַמִּי (ד) חֲצִי שֶׁבַח. וְשִׁינּוּיָא דְּסָמְכָא הוּא. מֵהָא שָׁמְעִינַן דְּהָא דְּאָמַר שְׁמוּאֵל בִּ"שְׁנַיִם אוֹחֲזִין" (ב"מ דף יד:): בַּעַל חוֹב גּוֹבֶה אֶת הַשֶּׁבַח – לָא סְבִירָא לָן כְּוָותֵיהּ, אֶלָּא גּוֹבֶה חֲצִי שֶׁבַח, וְכֵן הֲלָכָה. וְאִי קַשְׁיָא: דְּהָכָא בָּעֵי שְׁמוּאֵל: "דְּאִיקְנֵי" מַהוּ? וְהָתָם קָאָמַר: בַּעַל חוֹב גּוֹבֶה אֶת הַשֶּׁבַח, דְּהַיְינוּ "דְּאִיקְנֵי"! אִיכָּא לְמֵימַר דְּאַלִּיבָּא דְּר' מֵאִיר קָאָמַר. אִי נַמִּי, מִיבָּעֵי לָן לְרַבָּנַן מַאי, וְאִיהוּ פָּשִׁיט מִנַּפְשֵׁיהּ "דְּאִיקְנֵי" קָנָה, וּסְבָרָא דְּנַפְשֵׁיהּ קָאָמַר.

מתני'

תוספות

מיהו למ"ד אין גובה, אע"ג דמלוה לפרוע מדידהו — אין כופין, כדמוכח ב"הכותב" (כתובות דף פו.). אבל כי שבק להון אחריות נכסים, אע"פ דפריעת בע"ח מלוה — כופין, כדמוכח בכל מקום דנזקקין ליתומים גדולים. (ה) והיכא דאמרי "לא ניחא לן למעבד מלוה" אמרינן בכתובות (שם) דמכין אותו עד שתצא נפשו, כמו במצות עשה, כגון עשה סוכה ועשה לולב.

המוקדמים פסולים. אומר ר"י: דפסולים הוו לגמרי, דאפי' מבני חרי לא גבי, אע"פ שלוה מודה. וראיה — מדקאמר ריש לקיש ב"איזהו נשך" (ב"מ דף עב. ושם ד"ה שטר) דהך משנה מתוקמא כר' מאיר, דאמר: שטר שיש בו רבית קונסין (ו), ואין גובה בו לא את הקרן ולא את הרבית. היינו אפי' לוה מודה. ואפי' מבני חרי לא גבי התם, דהא תניא בתוספתא (פ"ה דב"מ): המוליא שטר חוב שיש בו רבית — יקרענו, בא לב"ד — יקרעוהו. והדר תני הך משנה(ז) דהכא — משמע פסולים לגמרי. אך י"ל דשאני התם, דמשעת כתיבה הוא דעבד ליה שומא, אבל הכא לא עבד ליה שומא. וכי האי גוונא דחי בפרק "המניח את הכד" (ב"ק דף ל: ושם). מיהו, לישנא דפסולין משמע פסולין לגמרי, שלא לגבות מבני חרי.

גובה את הקרן מנכסים משועבדי' ושבח מבני חורין. וא"ת: כיון שיש לו נכסים ללוה שיגבה ממנו הלוקח — א"כ לא יקח הבעל חוב ממנו, לימא ליה לוקח: מקום הנחתי לך לגבות ממנו! וי"ל: דאיירי כגון שאין לו למוכר נכסים אחרים אלא משועבדים, ולכך טורף הימנו המשועבדים, ולכשיחזור ויקנה נכסים בני חורין — יחזור זה לוקח ויטרוף מבני חרי. ג) ואפי' "דאיקני" קנה ומכר משתעבד, (ח) משתעבד כבר לוקח לב"ח כל שעבודו. א"נ י"ל: כגון שעשאו לוה למלוה קרקע זה אפותיקי, דהשתא לא מצי למימר ליה: הנחתי לך מקום לגבות ממנו ד).

אם תמצי לומר משתעבד לוה ולוה כו'. וה"נ הוה מצי למיבעי (ט) היכא דאמר "איקני" ולא מכר והוריש, לוה ולוה, ואפי' תמצא לומר "דאיקני" קנה ומכר לא משתעבד. אלא מדסליק מיניה נקט בעיא.

מאי גובה דקתני נמי חצי שבח. בתר הכי גרסינן בכל הספרים ישנים: שלחו מתם בן שלוה כו' עד סוף הסוגיא: לאו יורשי האב אתי (י) הבן כו', ואחר כך משנה דנפל הבית עליו ועל אמו וגמרא דיליה, ואחר כך בעו מיניה מרב ששת בן מהו שירש את אמו בקבר. וכן הגירסא בפירוש רבינו חננאל, וכן גרס רבינו תם, וכן הגירסא ישרה דגמרא, ד"שלחו מתם" שייכא על המשנה דנפל הבית עליו ועל אביו, דמייתי עלה ההיא משנה לבסוף. וגמרא דבעו מיניה מרב ששת — היא שייכא על משנה דנפל הבית עליו ועל אמו דמייתי לה עלה. אבל בספרים שלנו גרסינן ההיא דשלחו מתם על משנת נפל הבית עליו ועל אמו, כמו שפירש רבינו שמואל. והוא פי' (כ) גר' ר"ח נראה לו יותר, וכן גרס רבינו תם.

נפל

עין משפט נר מצוה

קנה א מיי' פכ"ג מהל' מלוה ולוה הל' א סמג עשין צד טוש"ע ח"מ סי' מג סעיף ז:

קנו ב מיי' שם הל' ב טוש"ע שם סעי' יג:

קנז ג מיי' שם פי"ח הל' א סמג עשין צד טוש"ע ח"מ סי' קיא סעיף כ וסי' קיב סעיף א:

קנח ד מיי' שם פ"כ הל' ד ופכ"א הל' א סמג שם טוש"ע ח"מ סי' קד סעיף ו:

קנט ה ו מיי' שם פכ"א הלכה א סמג עשין צד טוש"ע ח"מ סי' קטו סעיף א:

רבינו גרשום

הלואה אבל דאיקני לא: אלא הא מני. מתני' דמשמ' דאיקני קנה בעל חוב ומצוה לפרוע חובת אביהן: ר' מאיר היא דאמר אדם מקנה דבר שלא בא לעולם. כי תיבעי לך אליבא דרבנן דאיקני קנה והוריש אי משתעבד אי לא: המוקדמין. שנכתבו קודם הלואה: פסולין. דאתי למיטרף לקוחות שלא כדין: והמאוחרין כשרין. ואמאי כשרין הואיל דאיקני קנה ומכר לא משתעבד הא נפיק מיניה חורבא דאתי למיטרף לקוחות שלא כדין כגון שאם לוה הימנו בניסן וקנה נכסים באייר וכתב לו שטר בסיון וכתב לו דאיקני ומכר בתמוז אותן נכסין שקנה באייר אחר שלוה ויוציא זה את שטרו שנכתב שבסיון לוה פלוני לפלוני ויאמר שאותן נכסים שקנה באייר קודם הלואה קנאם ומשועבד לו ואינו כן ואתי למיטרף שקנו נכסים שלא כדין אם כן אמאי מאוחרין כשרין אלא לאו ש"מ דמשו"ה כשרין דאקני וקנה ומכר משתעבד והשתא לא טריף לקוחות שלא כדין דמשועבד לו ותפשוט לך אליבא דרבנן מהכא דאיקני קנה ומכר משתעבד. לעולם מהכא לא תפשוט לרבנן לעולם קסברי קנה ומכר לא משתעבד וטעמא מאי המאוחרין כשרין דמשתעבד הא מני ר' מאיר היא: ת"ש. דתנן במס' גיטין אין מוציאין לאכילת פירות ולשבח קרקעות ולמזון אשה והבנות מנכסים משועבדין מפני תיקון העולם. ואמרי' לשבח קרקעות כיצד. הרי שמכר שדהו לחבירו והשביחה ובא בעל חוב של מוכר וטרפה מן הלקוחות עם השבח מפני שהיתה משועבדת לו: כשהוא גובה. הלוקח מן המוכר: גובה את הקרן מנכסים משועבדים. לפי שכתב לו אחריות השדה מה שמכר לו: ושבח גובה מנכסים בני חורין. האי שבח שהשביח לוקח הואיל שהיתה הקרקע משועבדת למלוה דמי כאילו השביחו ליה וטריף ליה מלוה: ואי ס"ד דאיקני כו' הואיל דלא משתעבד בעל חוב אמאי גובה שבח. והא דאיקני הוא דכשלוה הימנו אכתי לא הוה האי קרקע משובחת ואמאי גובה. אלא ש"מ דאיקני קנה ומכר משתעבד משום הכי גובה עם השבח ותיפשוט לך מיהא כו'. הא מני ר"מ היא כי תיבעי לך אליבא דרבנן: הא לא משתעבדי אליבא דרבנן. ואם תימצי לומר משתעבד הא קא מיבעי לי לוה ממון מזה וכתב לו דאיקני וחזר ולוה משני וכתב ליה דאיקני ואחר שלוה משני חזר וקנה ומכר מאי לקמא משתעבד הואיל דהקנה לו מעיקרא ואין לשני במקום ראשון כלום או לבתרא משתעבד הואיל דסמוך לקנינו קנה ומכר: מהדורא קמא דרב אשי. כשהיינו למדין לפניו בבחרותו והיינו יושבים סביב לו: מהדורא בתרא. בזקנותו כשהחזיר לו תלמודו: אמר לנו יחלוקו. הואיל דלשניהן כתב דאיקני ואחר כך קנה ומכר: מיתיבי. למאן דאמר יחלוקו לשבח קרקעות כיצד הרי שמכר שדה לחבירו והשביחה והרי היא יוצאה מתחת ידו שטרפה בעל חוב של מוכר דכתב ליה דאיקני ולזה הלוקח שמכר לו השדה כתב לו נמי דאיקני שאם טורף ממנו השדה א) שישתעבד לו דאיקני דהיינו כגון לוה וחזר ולוה ושוב קנה דהרי השבח שהשביח לוקח דמי כאילו השביחו לוה ומכרו ללוקח שברשות המלוה השביחו שהיתה משועבדת לו. וקתני כשהוא גובה הלוקח מן המוכר גובה הקרן מנכסים משועבדים ואת השבח מנכסים בני חורין דמשמע דכל השבח. גבה ממנו ואם איתא דהיכא דכתב לתרוייהו מלוין יחלוקו אי הכי אמאי גובה הלוקח השבח כולו ממוכר חצי שבח בלבד היה לו לגבות ממנו דהאי שבח שהשביח לוקח דמי כמו שהשביחו מוכר ומכרו ללוקח והיינו דאיקני ומכר. ולוקח גופיה כמלוה הוא דהא כתב לו דאיקני ולמלוה נמי כתב לו דאיקני והאי שבח מכר הוא ואם איתא דיחלוקו אמאי טורף האי בעל חוב השבח כולו חציו בלבד היה לו לטרוף מן השבח והלוקח דכמלוה הוא היה לו לתפוש נמי חצי מן השבח לעצמו וחצי האחר שטרף לו בע"ח היה

א) נראה דצ"ל השדה והשבח שישתעבד לו דאיקני הוא דהיינו וכו'.

מסורת הש"ס

א) ב"מ יז. עב. סנהדרין דף לב. ר"ה דף ב. ת. שביעית פ"י מ"ה. לקמן דף קעא: ב) [ב"מ יד: ע"ש ודף עב:] ג) גי' רש"א ואפי' כתב לו דאיקני וקנה ומכר ומשתעבד כבר לקח הבע"ח: ד) [ועי' היטב תוס' ב"מ יד: ד"ה תריץ וכו' מה שכתבו סוגיא דהכא בקושיא]:

הגהות הב"ח

(א) גמ' לקמא משתעבד או לבתרא. נ"ב וקשה מאי קא מיבעיא ליה פשיטא דלקמא משתעבד דאי לבתרא מאוחרין אמאי כשרין וי"ל דלא [והשאר חסר]: (ב) רשב"ם ד"ה מאוחרין אמאי וכו' שמא קנה זה הלוה אלו נכסים וכו' שקנו מן הלוה הני נכסים: (ג) ד"ה הא מני וכו' שום אחריות כך כתב: (ד) ד"ה ומשני מאי גובה נמי דקתני חצי: (ה) תום' ד"ה (בע"א) מלוה וכו' ליתומים גדולים וכדאמרינן בכתובות לא ניחא לי למיעבד מלוה מאי ואמרינן מכין אותו: (ו) ד"ה המוקדמים וכו' קונסין אותו ואין גובה וכו' והיינו אפילו וכו' לא גבי דהא תניא כצ"ל ותיבת התם נמחק: (ז) בא"ד והדר תני הך משנה דהתם משמע דהכא נמי פסולים לגמרי: (ח) ד"ה גובה את הקרן וכו' ואפי' דאיקני קנה ומכר משתעבד מכל מקום כבר כל שעבודו דבעל חוב על הלוקח אי נמי יש לומר כצ"ל ונ"ב פי' את"ל דאיקני קנה ומכר לא משתעבד ל"ק מידי אלא אפי' את"ל דאיקני קנה ומכר משתעבד נמי ל"ק דאיכא למימר דמאחר דבשעה שלוה לא היה לו שום קרקע [אלא משעבדי] אם כן כבר חלה כל שעבודו דבע"ח על אותה הקרקע ושוב לא מצי לחותו לטרוף ממשועבדי' דבתריה ואין להקשות אמאי לא פירשו התוס' דלאחר שטרף בע"ח קרקע מן הלוקח קנה המוכר קרקעות ומכרן דאיכא למימר דא"כ גם השבח יגבה מהנהו משעבדי דגם השבח היה קלוב כיון שכבר טרף הבע"ח קודם שלקח זה הקרקע וכן פירשו התוס' להדיא בפ"ק דב"מ דף י"ד וע"ש שלא הזכירו כי אם דמיירי שעשאו אפותיקי ולא ס"ל תירוץ הראשון דתוס' דהכא: (ט) ד"ה אם תמצי לומר וכו' וה"נ הוה מצי למיבעי אפילו אם תמצי לומר דאיקני קנה ומכר לא משתעבד היכא דאמר דאיקני ולוה וחזר וקנה ולא מכר והוריש מדסליק מיניה נקט בעיא כצ"ל: (י) ד"ה מאי וכו' יורשי האב אתי הבן כצ"ל ותיבת הבן נמחק: (כ) בא"ד פירוש דגרס ר"ח:

מתני' נָפַל הַבַּיִת עָלָיו וְעַל אָבִיו. עַל רְאוּבֵן וְעַל יַעֲקֹב אָבִיו, וְאֵין יָדוּעַ מִי מֵת קוֹדֶם. עָלָיו וְעַל מוֹרִישָׁיו. עַל רְאוּבֵן וְעַל מוֹרִישָׁיו, כְּגוֹן אֲחֵי רְאוּבֵן אוֹ אֲחֵי יַעֲקֹב אָבִיו שֶׁאֵין לָהֶם קָרוֹב יוֹתֵר מֵרְאוּבֵן, וּרְאוּבֵן רָאוּי לְיוֹרְשָׁן. וְהָיְתָה עָלָיו. עַל רְאוּבֵן, כְּתוּבַּת אִשָּׁה אוֹ בַּעַל חוֹב, וְאֵין לוֹ מִמַּה לִפְרוֹעַ.

אומֵר: בַּחוֹל אָמְרוּ, וְקַל וָחוֹמֶר לַשַּׁבָּת. כַּיּוֹצֵא בוֹ, זָכִין לְגָדוֹל וְאֵין זָכִין לְקָטָן, דִּבְרֵי ר' אֱלִיעֶזֶר; רַבִּי יְהוֹשֻׁעַ אוֹמֵר: בְּגָדוֹל אָמְרוּ, קַל וָחוֹמֶר לְקָטָן. רַבִּי יְהוּדָה אוֹמֵר, רַבִּי אֱלִיעֶזֶר אוֹמֵר: בְּשַׁבָּת — דְּבָרָיו קַיָּימִין, מִפְּנֵי שֶׁאֵינוֹ יָכוֹל לִכְתּוֹב, אֲבָל לֹא בַּחוֹל; רַבִּי יְהוֹשֻׁעַ אוֹמֵר: בְּשַׁבָּת אָמְרוּ, קַל וָחוֹמֶר בַּחוֹל. כַּיּוֹצֵא בוֹ, זָכִין לְקָטָן וְאֵין זָכִין לְגָדוֹל, דִּבְרֵי רַבִּי אֱלִיעֶזֶר; ר' יְהוֹשֻׁעַ אוֹמֵר: לְקָטָן אָמְרוּ, קַל וָחוֹמֶר לְגָדוֹל.§ **מתני'** [א]נָפַל הַבַּיִת עָלָיו וְעַל אָבִיו, אוֹ עָלָיו וְעַל מוֹרִישָׁיו, וְהָיְתָה עָלָיו כְּתוּבַּת אִשָּׁה וּבַעַל חוֹב, יוֹרְשֵׁי הָאָב אוֹמְרִים: הַבֵּן מֵת רִאשׁוֹן וְאח"כ מֵת הָאָב, וּבַעֲלֵי הַחוֹב אוֹמְרִים: הָאָב מֵת רִאשׁוֹן וְאח"כ מֵת הַבֵּן — ב"ש אוֹמְרִים: יַחֲלוֹקוּ, וּבֵית הִלֵּל אוֹמְרִים: [א]נְכָסִים בְּחֶזְקָתָן.§

גמ' תְּנַן הָתָם: [ב]הַמַּלְוֶה אֶת חֲבֵירוֹ בִּשְׁטָר — גּוֹבֶה מִנְּכָסִים מְשׁוּעְבָּדִים, עַל יְדֵי עֵדִים — גּוֹבֶה מִנְּכָסִים בְּנֵי חוֹרִין. בָּעֵי שְׁמוּאֵל: "דְּאִיקְנֵי" וְקָנָה, מַהוּ? אַלִּיבָּא דְּרַבִּי מֵאִיר [ג]דְּאָמַר: אָדָם מַקְנֶה דָּבָר שֶׁלֹּא בָּא לָעוֹלָם — לָא תִּיבָּעֵי לָךְ, דְּוַדַּאי קָנָה, אֶלָּא כִּי תִּיבָּעֵי לָךְ — אַלִּיבָּא דְּרַבָּנַן דְּאָמְרִי: אֵין אָדָם מַקְנֶה דָּבָר שֶׁלֹּא בָּא לָעוֹלָם. אֲמַר רַב יוֹסֵף: תָּא שְׁמַע, [ד]וַחֲכָמִים אוֹמְרִים: זֶה הָיָה פִּיקֵּחַ שֶׁמָּכַר לוֹ אֶת הַקַּרְקַע, מִפְּנֵי שֶׁהוּא יָכוֹל לְמַשְׁכְּנוֹ עָלָיו. אֲמַר לֵיהּ רָבָא: מִינֵּיהּ קָאָמַר? [ה]מִינֵּיהּ — [ב]אֲפִילּוּ מִגְּלִימָא דְּעַל כַּתְפֵּיהּ! כִּי קָא מִבַּעְיָא לָן [ו]"דְּאִיקְנֵי" — קָנָה וּמָכַר, "דְּאִיקְנֵי" — קָנָה וְהוֹרִישׁ, מַאי? אֲמַר רַב חָנָא, תָּא שְׁמַע: נָפַל הַבַּיִת עָלָיו וְעַל אָבִיו, עָלָיו וְעַל מוֹרִישָׁיו, וְהָיְתָה עָלָיו כְּתוּבַּת אִשָּׁה וּבַעַל חוֹב, יוֹרְשֵׁי הָאָב אוֹמְרִים: הַבֵּן מֵת רִאשׁוֹן וְאח"כ מֵת הָאָב, וּבַעֲלֵי חוֹבוֹת אוֹמְרִים: הָאָב מֵת רִאשׁוֹן כו'; וְאִי סָלְקָא דַּעְתָּךְ "דְּאִיקְנֵי" קָנָה וּמָכַר, "דְּאִיקְנֵי" קָנָה וְהוֹרִישׁ — לָא מִשְׁתַּעְבֵּד, נְהִי נַמִי דְּאָב מִית בְּרֵישָׁא, "דְּאִיקְנֵי" הוּא! אֲמַר לְהוּ רַב נַחְמָן: זְעֵירָא חַבְרִין תַּרְגְּמָהּ — [ז][ג]מִצְוָה עַל הַיְתוֹמִים לִפְרוֹעַ חוֹבַת אֲבִיהֶן. מַתְקִיף לָהּ רַב אַשִׁי: מִלְוֶה עַל פֶּה הוּא, [ח]וְרַב וּשְׁמוּאֵל דְּאָמְרִי תַּרְוַיְיהוּ: [ט]מִלְוֶה עַל פֶּה — אֵינוֹ גּוֹבֶה לֹא מִן הַיּוֹרְשִׁין וְלֹא מִן הַלָּקוֹחוֹת!

אֶלָּא

רשב"ם

יוֹרְשֵׁי הָאָב אוֹמְרִים הַבֵּן מֵת רִאשׁוֹן. בְּנָפַל הַבַּיִת עָלָיו וְעַל אָבִיו קָאֵי, שֶׁיּוֹרְשֵׁי יַעֲקֹב, כְּגוֹן בְּנֵי יַעֲקֹב שִׁמְעוֹן וְלֵוִי אֲחֵי רְאוּבֵן, אוֹ אֲפִילּוּ חֲנוֹךְ וּפַלּוּא בְּנֵי רְאוּבֵן שֶׁגַּם הֵם יוֹרְשֵׁי יַעֲקֹב, אוֹמְרִים: הַבֵּן מֵת רִאשׁוֹן, דְּהַיְינוּ רְאוּבֵן מֵת רִאשׁוֹן, וּמִלָּא חֲבוּהּ דְּאָב קָאָתֵינָא, כִּדְאָמְרִינַן בַּגְּמָרָא, וְלֹא זָכָה רְאוּבֵן בְּהָנֵי נִכְסֵי כְּלָל, וְנִירַשׁ אָנוּ כָּל נִכְסֵי יַעֲקֹב. וּלְעִנְיַן נָפַל הַבַּיִת עָלָיו וְעַל מוֹרִישָׁיו שַׁיָּיךְ לְמִיתְנֵי: יוֹרְשֵׁי מוֹרִישָׁיו אוֹמְרִים: הַבֵּן מֵת רִאשׁוֹן. ב"ש אוֹמְרִים יַחֲלוֹקוּ. כִּדְמְפָרֵשׁ טַעֲמָא בִּיבָמוֹת בְּ"הַחוֹלֵץ" דְּאַף עַל גַּב דְּיוֹרְשֵׁי הָאָב וַדַּאי יוֹרְשִׁין בְּהַאי מָמוֹן, וּבַעַל חוֹב סָפֵק, וְקָאָתֵי סָפֵק וּמוֹצִיא מִידֵי וַדַּאי – קָסָבְרֵי בֵּית שַׁמַּאי: שְׁטָר הָעוֹמֵד לִגְבּוֹת כִּגְבוּי דָּמֵי, וְתַרְוַיְיהוּ וַדַּאי חֲשִׁיבֵי. וּב"ה סָבְרֵי נְכָסִים בְּחֶזְקָתָן. בְּחֶזְקַת יוֹרְשֵׁי הָאָב. שֶׁהֲרֵי הֵם יוֹרְשִׁים וַדַּאי, אוֹ מִיַּעֲקֹב אוֹ מֵרְאוּבֵן, וּכְמוּחְזָקִין דָּמוּ, שֶׁהֲרֵי יַעֲקֹב מוּחְזָק בִּנְכָסָיו הָיָה וְאֵלּוּ בָּאִים מִכֹּחוֹ. וּבַעַל חוֹב סָפֵק, וְאֵין סָפֵק מוֹצִיא מִידֵי וַדַּאי. **גמ'** תְּנַן הָתָם. לְקַמָּן בְּ"גֵט פָּשׁוּט". הַמַּלְוֶה אֶת חֲבֵירוֹ בִּשְׁטָר. אֲפִילּוּ לֹא נִכְתַּב בּוֹ אַחֲרָיוּת – גּוֹבֶה מִנְּכָסִים מְשׁוּעְבָּדִים. אִם אֵין לַלֹּוֶה נְכָסִים בְּנֵי חוֹרִין – גּוֹבֶה מַלְוֶה מִן הַלָּקוֹחוֹת, דְּאָמַר בְּ"שְׁנַיִם אוֹחֲזִין" (ב"מ דף יד.): לְרַבָּנַן, אַחֲרָיוּת שֶׁלֹּא נִכְתַּב בַּשְּׁטָר טָעוּת סוֹפֵר הוּא, וּכְמִי שֶׁנִּכְתַּב בּוֹ דָּמֵי. דְּלָא שָׁדֵי אִינִישׁ זוּזֵי בְּכַדִּי, וּלְכָךְ נִתְכַּוֵּין הַמַּלְוֶה שֶׁיִּכְתּוֹב בַּשְּׁטָר אַחֲרָיוּת, אֶלָּא שֶׁשָּׁכַח הַסּוֹפֵר וְטָעָה. וּסְתָם שְׁטָר קָלָא אִית לֵיהּ, וְלָקוֹחוֹת הוּא דְּאַפְסִידוּ אַנַּפְשַׁיְיהוּ, שֶׁלָּקְחוּ קַרְקַע מִן הַלֹּוֶה וְלֹא הִנִּיחוּ לוֹ בְּנֵי חוֹרִין כְּדֵי לִגְבּוֹת מֵהֶן מַלְוֶה אֶת חוֹבוֹ. בָּעֵי שְׁמוּאֵל. הַכּוֹתֵב לַחֲבֵירוֹ: מְשַׁעְבֵּד אֲנִי לְךָ בְּחוֹבְךָ כָּל נְכָסִים שֶׁאֶקְנֶה, מַהוּ? וְהַיְינוּ שֶׁכּוֹתְבִין בִּשְׁטָרוֹת "דִּקְנָאִי וּדְעָתִיד אֲנָא לְמִיקְנֵי". מַהוּ. מִי טָרֵיף מִלָּקוֹחוֹת נְכָסִים שֶׁקָּנָה הַלֹּוֶה אַחַר כְּתִיבַת הַשְּׁטָר וּמְכָרָן לְאֵלּוּ? אַלִּיבָּא דְּר"מ. גַּבֵּי הָאוֹמֵר לְאִשָּׁה: הֲרֵי אַתְּ מְקוּדֶּשֶׁת (א) לִכְשֶׁיָּמוּת אִישֵׁךְ, לִכְשֶׁתָּמוּת אֲחוֹתֵךְ, לְאַחַר שֶׁתִּתְגַּיְּירִי כו' – לָא תִּיבָּעֵי לָךְ, דְּוַדַּאי קָנָה. דְּכֵיוָן דְּפֵירוֹת דֶּקֶל דַּעֲדַיִין לֹא בָּאוּ לָעוֹלָם קָנָה – כ"ש דְּמִשְׁתַּעְבְּדֵי לֵיהּ קַרְקָעוֹת, דְּאָתוּ לְעָלְמָא אֶלָּא שֶׁעֲדַיִין לֹא קְנָאָן לֹוֶה בְּשָׁעָה שֶׁשִּׁעְבֵּד. אֶלָּא כִּי תִּיבָּעֵי לָךְ אַלִּיבָּא דְּרַבָּנַן. מַאי? מִי שָׁאנֵי שִׁעְבּוּד מִקִּנְיָן? וְטַעֲמָא כִּדְפָרֵישִׁית. א"נ, אַלִּימוּהוּ רַבָּנַן לְשִׁעְבּוּד יוֹתֵר מִקִּנְיָן, דְּלֹא תִּנְעוֹל דֶּלֶת בִּפְנֵי לֹוִין, אוֹ לָא? א"ר יוֹסֵף ת"ש. דִּתְנַן בְּפֶ' "שְׁנֵי דַּיָּינֵי גְזֵירוֹת" בִּכְתוּבּוֹת (דף קי.): הַמּוֹצִיא שְׁטַר חוֹב עַל חֲבֵירוֹ, וְהַלָּה הוֹצִיא שְׁטָר שֶׁכָּתוּב בּוֹ שֶׁמָּכַר לוֹ אֶת הַשָּׂדֶה מַלְוֶה לַלֹּוֶה, אַחַר שֶׁנִּכְתַּב הַשְּׁטָר חוֹב שֶׁהוּא מוֹצִיא עָלָיו. אַדְמוֹן אוֹמֵר: יָכוֹל הַלֹּוֶה לִטְעוֹן: אִילּוּ חַיָּיב הָיִיתִי לְךָ הָיָה לְךָ לִפְרוֹעַ אֶת שֶׁלְּךָ מִמֶּנִּי, וְלֹא הָיָה לְךָ לִמְכּוֹר לִי קַרְקַע בִּשְׁבִיל צוֹרֶךְ מָעוֹת. וַחֲכָמִים אוֹמְרִים זֶה. הַמַּלְוֶה הָיָה פִּיקֵּחַ, שֶׁמָּכַר לוֹ לַלֹּוֶה אֶת הַקַּרְקַע, שֶׁהוּא יָכוֹל עַתָּה לְמַשְׁכְּנוֹ בְּעַד חוֹבוֹ, וְלֹא יָכוֹל לִדְחוֹתוֹ וְלוֹמַר: אֵין לִי לִפְרוֹעַ כְּלוּם. (ב) וְהִנֵּה זֶה הַקַּרְקַע "דְּאִיקְנֵי" הֲוָה, שֶׁלְּאַחַר שֶׁנִּכְתַּב הַשְּׁטָר חוֹב קְנָאוֹ הַלֹּוֶה זְמַן מְרוּבֶּה, וְהִנֵּה זֶה הַמַּלְוֶה חוֹזֵר וְגוֹבֶה בְּחוֹבוֹ, אַלְמָא: "דְּאִיקְנֵי" וְקָנֵי – מִשְׁתַּעְבֵּד לַמַּלְוֶה. **אמר** לֵיהּ רָבָא מִינֵּיהּ. בִּתְמִיָּה, מִקַּרְקַע שֶׁקָּנָה הַלֹּוֶה עַצְמוֹ וְאֵינָהּ מְשׁוּעְבֶּדֶת לְשׁוּם אָדָם, הֵיאַךְ אַתָּה מֵבִיא רְאָיָה? מִינֵּיהּ פְּשִׁיטָא שֶׁיִּגְבֶּה הַמַּלְוֶה, וַאֲפִילּוּ מִגְּלִימָא דְּעַל כַּתְפֵּיהּ, דְּהָא לָא קָמִבַּעְיָא לָן. אֶלָּא הֵיכָא דִּכְתַב "דְּאִיקְנֵי" וְקָנָה וְאַחֲרֵי כֵן שִׁעְבְּדוֹ לְאַחֵר, מִיבַּעְיָא לָן אִי אַלִּים תְּנָאֵיהּ שֶׁכָּתַב לוֹ "דְּאִיקְנֵי" לִטְרוֹף מִלָּקוֹחוֹת אוֹ מִיּוֹרְשִׁין שֶׁאַחַר כְּתִיבַת שְׁטָרוֹ שֶׁקָּדַם לָהֶן, אוֹ לָא. נְהִי נַמִי דְּאָב מָיֵית בְּרֵישָׁא. וְיָרַשׁ הַבֵּן, כִּדְקָאָמַר בַּעַל חוֹב – "דְּאִיקְנֵי" הוּא, שֶׁקְּנָאוֹ הַבֵּן אַחַר כְּתִיבַת הַשְּׁטָר וְהוֹרִישׁוֹ לְיוֹרְשָׁיו, וַאֲפִילּוּ הָכִי גּוֹבֶה אוֹתוֹ בַּעַל חוֹב. אַלְמָא: "דְּאִיקְנֵי" וְקָנָה וְהוֹרִישׁ – מִשְׁתַּעְבֵּד! מִצְוָה עַל הַיְתוֹמִין כו'. וְלֹא מִשּׁוּם שֶׁכָּתַב לוֹ "דְּאִיקְנֵי" הוּא. וְגַבֵּי קָנָה וּמָכַר לָא מִשְׁתַּעְבֵּד, אֶלָּא גַּבֵּי יוֹרְשִׁים מִשּׁוּם מִצְוָה. וַאֲפִילּוּ לֹא כָּתַב לוֹ "דְּאִיקְנֵי" – מִשְׁתַּעְבֵּד יוֹרֵשׁ לַמַּלְוֶה, מִשּׁוּם מִצְוָה עַל הַיְתוֹמִים. א"כ מִלְוֶה עַל פֶּה הוּא. וְאַמַּאי טָרֵיף מִמְּקַרְקְעֵי דְּיַתְמֵי? וְהָא רַב וּשְׁמוּאֵל דְּאָמְרֵי תַּרְוַיְיהוּ. לְקַמָּן בְּ"גֵט פָּשׁוּט": מִלְוֶה עַל פֶּה אֵינוֹ גּוֹבֶה מִן הַיּוֹרְשִׁין, וְכִי אָמְרִינַן מִצְוָה עַל הַיְתוֹמִין – הנ"מ מִלְוֶה בִּשְׁטָר. וּשְׁמוּאֵל גּוּפֵיהּ הוּא דְּקָמִבַּעְיָא לֵיהּ הָא בָּעְיָא, וְאִם כֵּן קַשְׁיָא דִּידֵיהּ אַדִּידֵיהּ. וּמִיהוּ, לְקַמָּן פָּסְקִינַן הִלְכְתָא: מִלְוֶה עַל פֶּה גּוֹבֶה מִן הַיּוֹרְשִׁין, שֶׁלֹּא תִּנְעוֹל דֶּלֶת בִּפְנֵי לֹוִין.

אֶלָּא

תוספות

נפל הבית עליו ועל אביו כו' בית שמאי אומרים יחלוקו וב"ה אומרים נכסים בחזקתן. דסבירא להו לבית הלל: כיון דמחוסר גויינא, אפילו מת האב תחלה — הוו בחזקת היורשין. ובית שמאי לטעמייהו, דאית להו: כל העומד לגבות כגבוי דמי, ולכך הוי כאילו הוא מוחזק בכך. **אמר** רב יוסף ת"ש זה היה פיקח כו'. לא הוה מצי להביא ראיה מרב נחמן דאמר (לעיל קכה.): יתומים שגבו קרקע בחובת אביהם — בעל חוב גובה אותה מהם, דהיינו טעמא — מדרבי נתן. ועוד, אפילו היה יכול להביא ראיה — מתני' עדיפא ליה. [י] **דאיקני** קנה ומכר מהו. אליבא דר"מ, דקאמר: אדם מקנה דבר שלא בא לעולם — לא קמבעיא ליה, כדמפרש בסמוך. וא"ת: אימור דאמר רבי מאיר כגון פירות דקל דעבידי דאתו, הני לא עבידי דאתו שיקנה נכסים וימכור! ויש לומר: דמודי ר' מאיר בהא שהשעבוד חל ממילא, אע"פ שלגבי קנין לא היה לו להועיל כאן. (ג) דהא גבי "דאיקני" נמי אמרינן לעיל דמהני אפילו לרבנן דרבי מאיר, אף על פי שסבורים דאין אדם מקנה דבר שלא בא לעולם, משום דאלים כח השעבוד. הכי נמי אלים לרבי מאיר, לענין דמהני אע"ג דלא עבידי דאתו. [כ][**דאיקני** קנה ומכר] כו'. (ד) הקשה רבינו שמואל: תיפשוט ליה מדידיה, מדאמר שמואל בפרק קמא דב"מ (דף יד:): בעל חוב גובה את השבח, פירוש(ה): שהשביח הלוקח. ואין לומר כמו שפי' דאליבא דרבי מאיר איירי, דהא שמואל לית ליה דר' מאיר, דהא פסיק בפ' "אע"פ" (כתובות דף נט.) כרבי יוחנן הסנדלר, דאמר: אין אדם מקדיש דבר שלא בא לעולם! ויש לומר: דשמואל דסבירא ליה כר' מאיר הכא, דאלים כח השעבוד שיועיל אע"פ שלא בא לעולם, אע"ג דבקנין לא סבר ליה כוותיה מטעם דפי' לעיל, דהכא מיבעיא ליה לרבנן. **מצוה** על היתומים לפרוע חובת אביהן. וכופין (ו) כאן. ומיהו, אין כופין במקום שלא הניח להם אחריות נכסים. אבל הניח להם כופין, דהא נזקקין ליתומים, ובמלוה בשטר. והכי נמי משמע בסמוך [ל] כדפרישית, מדקאמר: מלוה על פה אינו גובה מן היורשים — משמע דאי למאן דאמר גובה מן היורשין חייב לפרוע, ומלוה על היתומים לפרוע חובת אביהן. (ז) והך דהכא אינו כי ההיא (כתובות דף נא:) דגבי קטינא דארעא, דהתם מלוה בעלמא דלא כפייה, דמיירי בדלא שבק להון אחריות נכסים. והכא בדין בעי למימר, דאף על גב דלא [מ]משתעי בשטר, כיון דמנכסי דידיה מיפרע — כופין היתומים למאן דאמר מלוה על פה גובה מן היורשים. מיהו

רבינו גרשום

אומר בחול אמרו. חכמים דדבריו קיימין דמצי למיכתב אין כתיבה מעכבת קל וחומר לשבת דאין יכול לכתוב דאין כתיבה מעכבת: כיוצא בו זכין לגדול. הואיל ואית ליה יד אין יד מעכבת בו: ר' יהושע אומר לגדול אמרו וכו' כסוגיא דבחול אמרו: נפל הבית עליו ועל אביו או עליו ועל מורישיו. אותן שאר קרובים שמורישין לו ירושתו כגון דודו או אחיו או אשתו: והיתה עליו. על אותו בן לפרוע כתובת אשה ובעל חוב: יורשי האב. כגון בניו של אב או אחיו של אב: אומרים הבן מת ראשון. ואין לו בנים לבן וחזרה ירושתו לאביו ואחר כך מת האב: ובעלי חוב אומרים האב מת ראשון ואח"כ מת הבן ועליכם לפרוע חובותיו מנכסיו המגיעין לחלקו של בן: ב"ש אומרים. הואיל וממון המוטל בספק הוא חולקין ויפרעו החצי: וב"ה אומרין נכסים בחזקתן. בחזקת יורשי האב ולא יפרעו כלום: תנן התם כו' גובה מנכסים משועבדים. מה שמכר או מה שממשכן שוב [אחר] שלוה משום דמלוה בשטר אית ליה קלא וידעי דמשתעבדי ליה בנכסיו: בעי שמואל הא ודאי פשיטא ליה דהנהו נכסים דישנן תחת יד של לוה בשעה שלוה מן המלוה כולן משועבדים לו. אבל הא מיבעי ליה אי כתב ליה בשטריה וכל אותן נכסים דאיקני עדיין כל זמן שהחוב בידו משתעבדי ליה מהו מי אמרינן כיון דלא הוי בידיה בשעת הלואה לא משתעבדי או דילמא כיון דאתני ליה משתעבדי ליה נמי: כי תיבעי לך אליבא דרבנן דאמרי אין אדם מקנה דבר שלא בא לעולם. מי אמרי' כי אמרי רבנן אין אדם מקנה דבר שלא בא לעולם כגון פירות דקל דליתנייהו בעולם והוא מקני ליה השתא ומשום הכי לא קנה אבל מקרקעי איתנהו בעלמא ולהיכא דכתב [דאקני] ודאי קנה משום כשאקנם יהיו משועבדות לך דהשתא לא מקני ליה מעכשיו וקני או דילמא לא שנא: אמר רב יוסף ת"ש. דתנן במס' כתובות מי שהוציא שטר על חבירו שחייב לו מנה והלה מוציא שטר שמכר לו שוב את השדה אדמון אומר יכול לטעון הלוה אילו הייתי חייב לך כשמכרת לי שוב שדה ונתתי לך

דמים היה לך לתופשן בשביל חובך שאתה אומר ולא היה לך ליתן לי השדה ולא שטר מכירה אבל כשנתת לי שטר המכירה והשדה הדבר מוכרח שלא הייתי חייב לך כלום שכבר פרעתי לך קודם לכן. וחכמים אומרים אין יכול לטעון כך דזה פיקח היה שמכר לו קרקע להכי מכר לו את הקרקע שאם יאמר זה אין לי ממה לפרוע חובך יכול למשכנו הקרקע שמכר לו לתפשו עד שיגבה חובו אלמא דסבירא להו לרבנן דמה שקנה שוב אחרי ההלואה יכול למשכנו ותפשוט לך מיהא אפי' לרבנן דאי כתב לו דאקנאי ודקנינא דמשתעבד נמי מאי דקני שוב: [illegible] פיה קאמרת דיכול למשכנו מה שקנה שוב הא פשיטא לי דמיניה גבה אפי' מגלימא דעל כתפיה אע"ג דלא כתב ליה דאיקני. אלא כי קמבעיא לן היכא דכתב ליה דאיקני [illegible] בעל חוב לאפקינהו מידא דלקוחות או מן יורשין הואיל וכתב ליה דאיקני אי לא: ת"ש ממתני' נפל הבית על אביו ועליו כו' בעל חוב אומר האב מת ראשון [illegible] ואי ס"ד דאי כתב דאיקני וקנה ומכר וקנה והוריש לא משתעבד לבעל חוב מאי קטעני בעלי חוב נהי נמי דכדקאמרי דאב מת ברישא ג"כ לא יגבו כלום [illegible] לו מאביו הורישן ליורשיו קודם שהספיק בעל חוב לתבוע חובו דלאלתר מת אלא לאו ש"מ מדקתני מתני' בעל חוב אומר האב מת ראשון ואחר כך מת [illegible] דאיקני אע"ג דקנה והוריש משועבד ומתני' רבנן היא: אמר להו רב נחמן. לעולם מיהא ליכא למישמע מינה דאי קנה והוריש אי משתעבדי אי לא. דהכי [illegible] לו נכסים לבן וחייבין אתם לפרוע חובנו לאו משום האי טעמא דקנה והוריש משתעבד אלא משום דמצוה על היתומין לפרוע חובת אביהם ולא מן הדין [illegible] משתעבדין ודמי כמאן דלא איכתב והאי דקא תבעי יורשין לאו משום דינא הוא אלא משום מצוה: מתקיף לה רב אשי. הואיל דדמי כמאן דלא איכתוב להיכא [illegible] עבד לו (ולא לעולם) אמאי מצי למטען בעל חוב וכתובת אשה האב מת ראשון ואח"כ מת הבן. והא מלוה על פה אינה גובה לא מן היורשין ולא מן הלקוחות [illegible] דירשו הנהו נכסי דהוו כשעת

עין משפט נר מצוה

קנב א מיי' פ"א מהל' נחלות הל' ח סמג עשין פב טוש"ע ח"מ סי' רפ סעיף יב:

קנג ב מיי' פי"א מהל' מלוה ולוה הל' ח סמג עשין צד טוש"ע ח"מ סי' קיב סעי' א ועי' בב"י:

קנד ג מיי' שם הלכה ח סמג שם טוש"ע ח"מ סי' קז סי' א:

מסורת הש"ס

א) [לקמן דף קנט.] יבמות לח. [לקמן דף קנח:] ב) [לעיל דף קלג.] ג) [לעיל דף סג.] ד) כתובות קי. ה) [ב"ק יא:] ו) [לעיל מד:] ז) כתובות צא: ח) קדושין יג: [ב"ב קעה.] ט) [ערכין כב.] ...

הגהות הב"ח

(א) רשב"ם ד"ה אליבא דר"מ וכו' מקודשת לי לכשימות: (ב) ד"ה וחכמים וכו' לפרוע כלום והנה זה הקרקע: (ג) תוס' ד"ה דאיקני וכו' כאן יועיל הכא גבי דאיקני וקנה נמי אמרינן: (ד) ד"ה דאיקני וכו' הקשה רבינו שמואל. נ"ב בסוף דף זה ממש וע"ש: (ה) בא"ד פירוש השבח שהשביח הלוקח ואין לומר כמו שפירש הוא דאליבא: (ו) ד"ה מצוה וכו' וכופין כדמוכח כאן: (ז) בא"ד חובת אביהן הכא כצ"ל ותיבת והך נמחק:

א)אאָמְרוּ לוֹ: מַעֲשֶׂה בְּאִמָּן שֶׁל בְּנֵי רוֹכֵל שֶׁהָיְתָה חוֹלָה, וְאָמְרָה: (א) תְּנוּ כְּבֵינָתִי לְבִתִּי, וְהִיא בִּשְׁנֵים עָשָׂר מָנֶה, וּמֵתָה, וְקִיְּמוּ אֶת דְּבָרֶיהָ! אָמַר לָהֶן: בְּנֵי רוֹכֵל תְּקַבְּרֵם אִמָּן.§ **גמ'** ב)תַּנְיָא, אָמַר לָהֶן רַבִּי ג)אֱלִיעֶזֶר לַחֲכָמִים: (ב) מַעֲשֶׂה בְּמָרוֹנִי אֶחָד שֶׁהָיָה בִּירוּשָׁלַיִם, וְהָיוּ לוֹ מִטַּלְטְלִין הַרְבֵּה וּבִיקֵּשׁ לִיתְּנָם בְּמַתָּנָה, אָמְרוּ לוֹ: אֵין לָהֶם תַּקָּנָה עַד שֶׁיַּקְנֶה עַל גַּב קַרְקַע. (ג) הָלַךְ וְלָקַח בֵּית סֶלַע אֶחָד סָמוּךְ לִירוּשָׁלַיִם, וְאָמַר: צְפוֹנוֹ לִפְלוֹנִי וְעִמּוֹ מֵאָה צֹאן וּמֵאָה חָבִיּוֹת, וּדְרוֹמוֹ לִפְלוֹנִי וְעִמּוֹ מֵאָה צֹאן וּמֵאָה חָבִיּוֹת. וּמֵת, וְקִיְּמוּ חֲכָמִים אֶת דְּבָרָיו! אָמְרוּ לוֹ: ד)מִשָּׁם רְאָיָה? מָרוֹנִי בָּרִיא הָיָה.§ "אָמַר לָהֶן: בְּנֵי רוֹכֵל תְּקַבְּרֵם אִמָּן" וכו'.§ (ד) מַאי טַעֲמָא קָא לָיְיט לְהוּ? אָמַר רַב יְהוּדָה אָמַר שְׁמוּאֵל: מְקַיְּימֵי קוֹצִים בְּכֶרֶם הָיוּ, וְרַבִּי ה)אֱלִיעֶזֶר לְטַעְמֵיהּ, דִּתְנַן: ו)הַמְקַיֵּים קוֹצִים בְּכֶרֶם — רַבִּי ז)אֱלִיעֶזֶר אוֹמֵר: קִידֵּשׁ, וַחֲכָמִים אוֹמְרִים: בלֹא קִידֵּשׁ אֶלָּא דָּבָר שֶׁכָּמוֹהוּ מְקַיְּימִין. (ה) ח)בִּשְׁלָמָא כַּרְכּוֹם חֲזֵי, אֶלָּא קוֹצִים לְמַאי חֲזֵי? אָמַר רַבִּי חֲנִינָא: מַאי טַעֲמָא דְּר' ט)אֱלִיעֶזֶר? שֶׁכֵּן בַּעֲרַבְיָא מְקַיְּימִין קוֹצִים בַּשָּׂדוֹת לִגְמַלֵּיהֶן. אָמַר רַבִּי לֵוִי: גקוֹנִין קִנְיָן מִשְּׁכִיב מְרַע אֲפִי' בְּשַׁבָּת, וְלֹא לָחוּשׁ לְדִבְרֵי ר' י)אֱלִיעֶזֶר, דאֶלָּא שֶׁמָּא תִּטְרוֹף דַּעְתּוֹ עָלָיו.§

מתני' רַבִּי כ)אֱלִיעֶזֶר אוֹמֵר: בְּשַׁבָּת — דְּבָרָיו קַיָּימִין, מִפְּנֵי שֶׁאֵין יָכוֹל לִכְתּוֹב, אֲבָל לֹא בַּחוֹל; רַבִּי יְהוֹשֻׁעַ אוֹמֵר: בְּשַׁבָּת אָמְרוּ, הקַל וָחוֹמֶר בַּחוֹל. כַּיּוֹצֵא בּוֹ, זָכִין לְקָטָן וְאֵין זָכִין לְגָדוֹל, דִּבְרֵי רַבִּי אֱלִיעֶזֶר; רַבִּי יְהוֹשֻׁעַ אוֹמֵר: ולְקָטָן אָמְרוּ, קַל וָחוֹמֶר לְגָדוֹל.§ **גמ'** מַתְנִי' מַנִּי? רַבִּי יְהוּדָה הִיא; דְּתַנְיָא: רַבִּי מֵאִיר אוֹמֵר, ר' אֱלִיעֶזֶר אוֹמֵר: בַּחוֹל — דְּבָרָיו קַיָּימִין, מִפְּנֵי שֶׁיָּכוֹל לִכְתּוֹב, אֲבָל לֹא בְּשַׁבָּת; רַבִּי יְהוֹשֻׁעַ אוֹמֵר

רשב"ם

בְּנֵי רוֹכֵל. שֵׁם אֲבִיהֶן. שֶׁהָיְתָה חוֹלָה וְאָמְרָה תִּינָּתֵן כְּבֵינָתִי לְבִתִּי. אִם מַתְּנַת שְׁכִיב מְרַע בְּלֹא שִׁיּוּר הָיְתָה, אִיכָּא לְמֵימַר דְּמוֹדֶה ר"א בִּמְצַוֶּה מֵחֲמַת מִיתָה דְּלָא בָּעֵי קִנְיָן, וְהוּא דְּמִית, דְּהָא לָא מִיבָּעֵי לְאוֹקוּמֵי מַעֲשֶׂה דִּבְנֵי רוֹכֵל בִּמְצַוֶּה מֵחֲמַת מִיתָה. וְאִם מַתְּנַת שְׁכִיב מְרַע בְּמִקְצָת הָיְתָה, וּמִיבָּעֵי לָן לְאוֹקוּמֵי בִּמְצַוֶּה מֵחֲמַת מִיתָה, כִּדְאוֹקִימְנַן לְעֵיל, דְּהָא מַתְּנַת שְׁכִיב מְרַע בְּמִקְצָת כּוּלֵּי עָלְמָא מוֹדִים דְּלָא מִיקַנְיָא בַּאֲמִירָה, וְאִם כֵּן ע"כ פָּלֵיג ר"א אֲפִילּוּ בִּמְצַוֶּה מֵחֲמַת מִיתָה. אָמַר לָהֶן אֵין מְבִיאִין רְאָיָה מִבְּנֵי רוֹכֵל. דִּרְשָׁעִים הָיוּ, וְהַלְוַאי שֶׁתְּקַבְּרֵם אִמָּם. כִּדְמְפָרֵשׁ טַעֲמָא בַּגְּמָרָא. וּקְנָסָא הוּא דִּקְנָסוּם רַבָּנַן לְקַיֵּים מַתְּנַת אִמָּם לְבִתָּהּ בְּלֹא קִנְיָן. **גמ'** בְּמָרוֹנִי. עַל שֵׁם מְקוֹמוֹ. וּבִיקֵּשׁ לִיתְּנָם. שֶׁהָיָה שְׁכִיב מְרַע לְדִבְרֵי ר"א, וּמְקַבְּלֵי מַתָּנָה לָא הָווּ גַּבֵּיהּ, כִּדְמְפָרֵשׁ בְּקִדּוּשִׁין. וְהָתָם פָּרֵיךְ עֲלָהּ טוּבָא. אָמְרוּ לֵיהּ אֵין לָהֶם תַּקָּנָה. לִזְכּוֹת בָּהֶן הַמְקַבֵּל מַתָּנָה לְפוּס מַאי דְּלָא סָמְכָא דַּעְתָּן עַד שֶׁיַּקְנֶה כו'. הָכִי מְפָרֵשׁ בְּפ"ק דְּקִדּוּשִׁין. וְהָתָם מְפָרֵשׁ שַׁפִּיר. וְלָקַח בֵּית סֶלַע. שֶׁאֵינוֹ רָאוּי לִזְרִיעָה, וּקְנָאוֹ בְּזוֹל לְשֵׁם כֵּן, עַל מְנָת לְהַקְנוֹת (ו) לוֹ. מָרוֹנִי בָּרִיא הָיָה. בִּשְׁעַת מַתָּנָה, וְאח"כ מֵת. מְקַיְּימֵי קוֹצִים. קרדונ"ש. בְּכֶרֶם. דְּכה"ג אַשְׁכַּחַן בְּמַסֶּכֶת כִּלְאַיִם דְּמַאֲכַל בְּהֵמָה הָוֵי כִּלְאַיִם בְּכֶרֶם, מִשּׁוּם "לֹא תִזְרַע כַּרְמְךָ כִּלְאָיִם", וַאֲפִילּוּ מְקַיֵּים לוֹקֶה, דְּדָרְשִׁי' בְּמוֹעֵד קָטָן (דף ב:) "כִּלְאַיִם שָׂדְךָ לֹא". שֶׁכֵּן בַּעֲרַבְיָא כו'. וְרַבָּנַן בָּתַר רוּבָּא דְּעָלְמָא אָזְלִי, שֶׁאֵין מְקַיְּימִין שָׂדוֹת לִגְמַלֵּיהֶן. קוֹנִין מִשְּׁכִיב מְרַע אֲפִי' בְּשַׁבָּת. לָא שְׁנָא הֵיכָא שֶׁצָּרִיךְ קִנְיָן, כְּגוֹן שֶׁשִּׁיֵּיר, לָא שְׁנָא בִּמְחַלֵּק כָּל נְכָסָיו. דְּכֵיוָן דְּתָלֵי טַעֲמָא מִשּׁוּם שֶׁמָּא תִּטְרוֹף דַּעְתּוֹ עָלָיו, דְּלָא סָמְכָא דַּעְתֵּיהּ שֶׁתִּתְקַיֵּים צַוָּאָתוֹ בַּאֲמִירָה, הִלְכָּךְ כְּדֵי לְהָפִיס דַּעְתּוֹ קוֹנִין אֲפִילּוּ בְּשַׁבָּת בְּכָל מַתְּנָתוֹ, בֵּין שֶׁשִּׁיֵּיר וְצָרִיךְ קִנְיָן, בֵּין בְּלֹא שִׁיֵּיר, וּבַאֲמִירָה סַגִּי. וְאע"ג דְּקִנְיָן דָּמֵי לְמִקָּח וּמִמְכָּר, שֶׁהֲרֵי קוֹנִין בְּכֵלָיו שֶׁל קוֹנֶה, שֶׁמַּקְנֶה סוּדָרוֹ כְּדֵי לִקְנוֹת בּוֹ הַמַּתָּנָה. וְלֹא לָחוּשׁ לְדִבְרֵי ר' אֱלִיעֶזֶר. מַה שֶּׁקּוֹנִין — לָאו דְּצָרִיךְ קִנְיָן כְּר"א, דְּהָא קַיְימָא לָן כְּרַבָּנַן דְּדִבְרֵי שְׁכִיב מְרַע כִּכְתוּבִין וְכִמְסוּרִין. אֶלָּא לְהָפִיס דַּעְתּוֹ, כְּדֵי שֶׁלֹּא תִּטְרוֹף דַּעְתּוֹ — קוֹנִין, דְּהַשְׁתָּא סָמְכָא דַּעְתֵּיהּ. **מתני'** רַבִּי אֱלִיעֶזֶר אוֹמֵר. אִם בְּשַׁבָּת חִילֵּק נְכָסָיו — אָז תִּקְּנוּ חֲכָמִים שֶׁיְּהוּ דְּבָרָיו קַיָּימִין בְּלֹא קִנְיָן וּכְתִיבָה, שֶׁלֹּא תִּטְרוֹף דַּעְתּוֹ, שֶׁמִּן הַדִּין אֵין יָכוֹל לִקְנוֹת וְלִכְתּוֹב בְּשַׁבָּת. אֲבָל לֹא בַּחוֹל. שֶׁיֵּשׁ תַּקָּנָה בְּקִנְיָן וּכְתִיבָה, וְלָמָּה תִּטְרוֹף דַּעְתּוֹ? בְּשַׁבָּת אָמְרוּ. שֶׁדְּבָרָיו קַיָּימִין, אע"ג דְּלֵיכָּא לְמֵימַר מִגּוֹ דְּיָכוֹל (ז) לִקְנוֹת וְלִכְתּוֹב כִּי לָא עָבֵיד נָמֵי קָנֵי. וְקַל וָחוֹמֶר בַּחוֹל, דְּכָל הָרָאוּי לְבִילָּה אֵין בִּילָּה מְעַכֶּבֶת בּוֹ. זָכִין לְקָטָן. הוֹאִיל וְאֵין לוֹ יָד לִזְכּוֹת לְעַצְמוֹ מָמוֹן שֶׁנּוֹתְנִין לוֹ — תִּקְּנוּ חֲכָמִים שֶׁיְּהֵא אַחֵר זוֹכֶה וּמְקַבֵּל לְצָרְכּוֹ. וְאֵין זָכִין לְגָדוֹל. שֶׁהֲרֵי יָכוֹל לִזְכּוֹת בְּעַצְמוֹ. ר' יְהוֹשֻׁעַ אוֹמֵר לְקָטָן אָמְרוּ. מִשּׁוּם דְּזָכִין לוֹ שֶׁלֹּא בְּפָנָיו, וְכ"ש לְגָדוֹל שֶׁיֵּשׁ לוֹ יָד לְקַבֵּל וְלִזְכּוֹת. וְשָׁלִיחַ נָמֵי מָצֵי מְשַׁוֵּי, וְהִלְכָּךְ כ"ש דְּזָכִין לְאָדָם שֶׁלֹּא בְּפָנָיו. **גמ'** קַל וָחוֹמֶר לְשַׁבָּת. דְּכֵיוָן דְּאֵין יָכוֹל לִכְתּוֹב עָשׂוּ לוֹ תַּקָּנָה לִקְנוֹת דְּבָרָיו בַּאֲמִירָה בְּעָלְמָא, כְּדֵי שֶׁלֹּא תִּטְרוֹף.
מתני'

תוספות

אמרו לו מעשה דבני רוכל כו'? לימא להו דשבת הוה. ע"כ דברי ר"ת. ועוד הקשה ר"י: מדאמרי' בגיטין בסוף פ"ק (דף יד: ושם) גבי "הולך מנה לפלוני" כו' ומוקי לה התם בשכיב מרע, וקאמר ר"י הנשיא משום ר' יעקב שאמר משום רבי מאיר כר' אליעזר, (ח) דבחול צריך קנין. ואי גרסי' הכא "רבי אליעזר" — הא אית ליה לר"מ בגמ' דרבי אליעזר אומר בחול דבריו קיימין, ולא הצריך קנין. והתם בחול איירי, מדקאמר "הולך מנה לפלוני" — דמשמע בחול. אלא ש"מ דגרס "רבי אלעזר", ואית ליה בין בשבת בין בחול צריך קנין, ופליג אדרבי אליעזר ורבי יהושע דבסמוך. וגרסי': ולא לחוש לדברי רבי אלעזר. וכן בפ"ק דקדושין (דף כו:) גבי בעיא דלבורין. ולקמן בגמ' גבי המקיים קוצים בכרם גרס "רבי אלעזר", וכן בשבת פרק "חבית" (דף קמד:) דמייתי לה ההוא דהמקיים קוצים בכרם. והר"ר יצחק בר מאיר הקשה מן התוספתא (פ"י), דקתני התם: המסוכן שחלק נכסיו על פיו, בין בחול בין בשבת — דברי המת יעשו. אבל בריא — עד (ט) שיקנו בכסף ובשטר ובחזקה. ר"א אומר: נכסים שיש להם אחריות נקנים בכסף ובשטר ובחזקה, ושאין להם אחריות אין נקנים אלא במשיכה. אמר ר' אליעזר: מעשה במרוני אחד שהיה בירושלים והיו לו מטלטלין הרבה כו'. במה דברים אמורים — בחול, אבל בשבת לא יעשה, ואם עשה — עשוי. ר' יהושע אומר: בחול אמרו, קל וחומר בשבת, דברי ר"מ. ורבי יהודה אומר: רבי אליעזר אומר: במה דברים אמורים — בשבת, אבל בחול לא יעשה, ואם עשה — עשוי. רבי יהושע אומר: בשבת אמרו, קל וחומר בחול. אלמא משמע דכולה רבי אליעזר קתני לה! ואור"י: דלא קשיא מידי, ד"במה דברים אמורים" דתוספתא — אמתני' דהכא קאי, ולא אמילתא דרישא דר' אלעזר דתוספתא, אלא אמילתא דרבנן קאמר, דאמרי דלא בעי קנין. והכי פירושא: דאם עשה עשוי, ולא אמרינן דאין קנין לאחר מיתה. דכיון שאין יכול לעשות אלא בקנין — מודו כ"ע שיועיל זה הקנין לאחר מיתה, והוי כאילו פירש: מהיום אם לא יחזור בו לאחר מיתה. וה"ק: לא יעשה בלא קנין, ואם עשה בקנין — מה שעשה עשוי, ולכתחילה נמי יכול לעשותה בקנין. **כבינתי** לבתי. פי' רבינו שמואל: ל)נוסק"א בלע"ז, שחוגרת בה צוארה. ואין נראה לר"י, מדאמר בשבת פרק "במה אשה יוצאה" (דף סב.): ולא תצא בכוליאר. וקאמרי' בגמרא: מאי בכוליאר — אמר רב: מכבנתא, (י) היינו כבינתי דהכא. ופי' רש"י התם נושקא. ולמה אסור לצאת בו בשבת? והלא אינו עשוי אלא דרך מלבוש, ושלפא ומחוי נמי לא שייך ביה כיון שתגלה בשרה! ועוד אמרי' ביומא פרק "אמר להם הממונה" (דף כה.) גבי כהנים, תנא: היו עומדים בכוליאר, פירוש עומדין בעיגול. ע"כ נראה לר"י כפירוש הערוך, מ)שפירש: בכוליאר הוא כעין עטרה, ומ"מ יש בה שום דבר חד, כדאמרי' בשילהי דשבת (דף קנו:) דשקלה למכבנתא ויהבא בעיני דחיויא. וכבינתי דהכא אין לפרש נוסק"א, אפילו תחלק בין מכבנתא דשבת לכבינתי דהכא, דהא כתיב בישעי' (ג) "ובתי הנפש והלחשים", ופי' רש"י שם: "בתי הנפש" — נושקא, שהיא כנגד (כ) שהנפש נתון שם. וכתוב נמי "והרדידים" ומתרגמינן: כבינתי. ועוד תנן במס' כלים (פכ"ט מ"א): והסגום והרדיד כו', ופירש בערוך נ)דהיינו רדידים, וקרוי בלשון ישמעאל ריד"א, והוא לעיף דק שהאשה מתכסה בה ראשה, "ותכס בצעיף ותתעלף" מתרגם בתרגום ירושלמי: רדידא (בראשית לח). **קונין** מש"מ ואפי' בשבת. במצוה מחמת מיתה, או בכותב כל נכסיו אתי שפיר, דשייך התם טירוף דעת. כי אע"פ שהקנין אינו מעלה ומוריד — מ"מ מלטער על הדבר. וה"ה נמי בכותב מקצת, אע"פ שסבור הוא עדיין לחיות, שהרי אינו יכול לחזור בו, ומשייר לנפשו — מ"מ שייך ביה טירוף דעת, כדפי' רבינו שמואל. ואפי' בשבת נמי מותר להקנות, כדאמר ב"הזורק" (גיטין עז: ושם): ההוא ש"מ דכתב לה גיטא לדביתהו, למחר תקיף ליה עלמא טובא. אמר רבא: מי איכא דוכתא ס)דלינסבא גיטא ותיזל איהי ותיחוד ותפתח כו'. והיכי קא קניא ליה? הא אקנייה רשותא בשבת אסור! אלא ש"מ בש"מ הקילו, וא"כ מותר להקנות גם הכא. ותדע דבש"מ הקילו, דהא תקשה: היכי הוה מצי לגרש בשבת? והתניא בתוספתא דבילה: ע)אין מגרשין בשבת! אלא בש"מ הקילו[פ]. *זכין לגדול ואין זכין לקטן. וא"ת: למה אין זכין לקטן? הלא זכין לאדם שלא בפניו! וי"ל: כיון דזכיה מטעם שליחות, מאן דמצי משוי שליח — יש לו זכיה, ומאן דלא מצי משוי שליח — אין לו זכיה[צ]. ומאן דאית ליה זכין לקטן ואין זכין לגדול, ס"ל: כיון דגדול יכול לקנות — לא תקון ליה רבנן זכיה כמו בקטן.
נפל

מסורת הש"ס

א) נדה דף מה. סנהדרין דף נה:: ב) נדה דף נב. יבמות דף קה:: ג) חולין דף כו: נדה דף נב. יבמות דף יב: כתובות דף לו.: ד) גיטין דף יד:: ה) [צ"ל חמשא בשיתא: ו) [צ"ל יוצא דופן (דף מו.): ז) [ועי' תוס' נדה נב: ד"ה הלכה ותוס' שם מט. ד"ה ואב"א ר' שמעון]: ח) [וע"ע תוס' חולין כו: ועי' תוס' כתובות לו. ד"ה עד]:

עין משפט נר מצוה

קמא א ב מיי' פכ"ט מהל' מכירה הל' יג יד סמג עשין פב טוש"ע ח"מ סי' רלה ס"י:

קמב ג מיי' פ"ד מהל' אישות הלכה ז ועיין בהשגות ובמגיד משנה סמג עשין מח טוש"ע אה"ע סי' מג סעיף ב:

קמג ד מיי' פ"א מהל' יבום הל' טז סמג עשין כא טוש"ע אה"ע סי' קסז סעיף א ב:

קמד ה ו מיי' שם הל' יז טוש"ע שם סעי' ג ד:

קמה ז ח מיי' פ"ד מהל' אישות הל' ז סמג עשין מח טוש"ע אה"ע סי' קנה ס"ב:

קמו ט מיי' פ"ג מהל' זכיה ומתנה הל' א סמג עשין פב טוש"ע ח"מ סי' רמח סעיף א:

גמרא

וּלְטַעֲמִיךְ, זַבִּין שָׁוֵי חַמְשָׁא בְּשִׁיתָא, הָכִי נַמִי דִּזְבִינֵיהּ זְבִינֵי? אֶלָּא, קִים לְהוּ לְרַבָּנַן דְּיָנוּקָא מִקַּרְבָא דַּעְתֵּיהּ גַּבֵּי זוּזֵי, וְאִי אָמְרַתְּ זְבִינֵיהּ זְבִינֵי, אזִמְנִין דִּמְקַרְקְשִׁי לֵיהּ זוּזֵי, אָזֵיל מְזַבֵּין לְכוּלְּהוּ נִכְסֵי דַּאֲבוּהּ; אֲבָל גַּבֵּי מַתָּנָה, אִי לָאו דַּהֲוָה לֵיהּ הֲנָאָה מִינֵּיהּ לָא הֲוָה יָהֵיב לֵיהּ מַתָּנָה, באָמְרוּ רַבָּנַן: תֶּיהֱוֵי מַתְּנָתוֹ מַתָּנָה, (א) דְּלַעֲבִידוּ לְהוּ מִילֵּי. אָמַר רַב נַחְמָן אָמַר שְׁמוּאֵל: בּוֹדְקִין גלְקִדּוּשִׁין, לְגֵרוּשִׁין, וְלַחֲלִיצָה וּלְמֵיאוּנִין. וְלִמְכּוֹר בְּנִכְסֵי אָבִיו — עַד שֶׁיְּהֵא בֶּן עֶשְׂרִים. וְכֵיוָן דִּבְדַקְנָא לְקִדּוּשִׁין, לְגֵרוּשִׁין לָמָּה לִי? לָא נִצְרְכָא אֶלָּא לְיִבּוּם, דִּתְנַן: א)דבֶּן תֵּשַׁע שָׁנִים וְיוֹם אֶחָד שֶׁבָּא עַל יְבִמְתּוֹ — קְנָאָהּ, וְאֵין נוֹתֵן גֵּט עַד שֶׁיַּגְדִּיל. הלַחֲלִיצָה — לְאַפּוּקֵי מִדְּר' יוֹסֵי, ב)דְּאָמַר: "אִישׁ" כָּתוּב בַּפָּרָשָׁה, אֲבָל אִשָּׁה — בֵּין גְּדוֹלָה וּבֵין קְטַנָּה, קָא מַשְׁמַע לָן ודְּמַקְּשִׁינַן אִשָּׁה לְאִישׁ, דְּלָא כְּר' יוֹסֵי. זוּלְמֵיאוּנִין — לְאַפּוּקֵי מִדְּרַבִּי יְהוּדָה, ג)דְּאָמַר: עַד שֶׁיִּרְבֶּה שָׁחוֹר, קָא מַשְׁמַע לָן חדְּלָא כְּרַבִּי יְהוּדָה. וְלִמְכּוֹר בְּנִכְסֵי אָבִיו עַד שֶׁיְּהֵא בֶּן עֶשְׂרִים — לְאַפּוּקֵי מִמַּאן דְּאָמַר בֶּן שְׁמֹנֶה עֶשְׂרֵה. וְהִלְכְתָא: תּוֹךְ זְמַן כְּלִפְנֵי זְמַן. וְהִלְכְתָא כְּגִידֵּל בַּר מְנַשֶּׁה. וְהִלְכְתָא כְּמָר זוּטְרָא. וְהִלְכְתָא כְּאַמֵּימָר. וְהִלְכְתָא כְּרַב נַחְמָן אָמַר שְׁמוּאֵל בְּכוּלְּהוּ.§

מתני' ד)הַמְחַלֵּק נְכָסָיו עַל פִּיו — ר' אֱלִעָזָר אוֹמֵר: אֶחָד טבָּרִיא וְאֶחָד מְסוּכָּן, נְכָסִים שֶׁיֵּשׁ לָהֶן אַחֲרָיוּת — נִקְנִין בְּכֶסֶף וּבִשְׁטָר וּבַחֲזָקָה, וְשֶׁאֵין לָהֶן אַחֲרָיוּת — אֵין נִקְנִין אֶלָּא בִּמְשִׁיכָה. (ב) אָמְרוּ

רשב"ם

א"ל וּלְטַעֲמִיךְ. דְּתָלֵית טַעֲמָא בְּמִידֵּי דְּאִית לֵיהּ רַוְוחָא וְהֶפְסֵדָא. זַבִּין שָׁוֶה ה) אַרְבַּע בְּחָמֵשׁ. דְּאִית לֵיהּ רַוְוחָא טוּבָא. ה"נ דִּזְבִינֵיהּ זְבִינֵי. בִּתְמִיָּה. וְהָא לָא פְּלוּג רַבָּנַן בִּמְכִירַת פָּחוֹת מִבֶּן עֶשְׂרִים שֶׁאֵינוֹ יוֹדֵעַ בְּטִיב מַשָּׂא וּמַתָּן מִידֵּי, אֶלָּא (ג) כּוּלְּהוּ תַּקּוּן דְּלָא לֶיהֱוֵי זְבִינֵי! אֶלָּא. הַיְינוּ טַעֲמָא דִּמְכִירָה — קִים לְהוּ לְרַבָּנַן כו' זִימְנִין דִּמְקַרְקְשֵׁי כו'. הִלְכָּךְ, בְּכוּלְּהוּ מְכִירוֹת תַּקּוּן דְּלָא לֶיהֱוֵי זְבִינֵי. אִי לָאו דְּאִית לֵיהּ הֲנָאָה. גְּדוֹלָה מִינֵּיהּ, לָא הֲוָה יָהֵיב לֵיהּ כו'. דְּלִיעַבְדָן מִילֵּי. לִגְמוֹל לוֹ חֶסֶד וּלְהֵיטִיב לוֹ בְּכָל עִנְיָנִין. בּוֹדְקִין לְקִדּוּשִׁין. אַע"פ שֶׁהוּא בֶּן י"ג שָׁנִים וְיוֹם אֶחָד, וְהָאִשָּׁה בַּת י"ב שָׁנִים וְיוֹם אֶחָד — לָא סָמְכִינַן אַשָּׁנִים לְאַחֲזוּקִינְהוּ כִּגְדוֹלִים וּבְנֵי שֵׂעָר לְהֵחָשֵׁב קִדּוּשֵׁיהֶן וַדַּאי, אַף לְהָקֵל, כְּגוֹן לְבַטֵּל קִדּוּשֵׁי שֵׁנִי שֶׁקִּידֵּשׁ אַחֲרָיו בְּלֹא גֵט. אֶלָּא בּוֹדְקִין אַחֲרָיו, אִם הֵבִיא שְׂעָרוֹת — אָז יֵחָשְׁבוּ קִדּוּשֵׁי וַדַּאי. וּלְגֵירוּשִׁין. לְקַמֵּיהּ מְפָרֵשׁ. וְלַחֲלִיצָה. כִּדְמְפָרֵשׁ לְקַמֵּיהּ, דְּמִשּׁוּם אִשָּׁה נָקַט לָהּ, שֶׁלֹּא תַּחֲלוֹץ עַד שֶׁתַּגְדִּיל וְתָבִיא סִימָנֵי שֵׂעָר. וּלְמֵיאוּנִין. אִם הֵבִיאָה שְׂעָרוֹת לֹא תְּמָאֵן. עַד שֶׁיְּהֵא בֶּן עֶשְׂרִים. אַע"ג דְּאַיְיתֵי שְׂעָרוֹת מִי"ג. וְכִי מֵאַחַר דִּבְדַקְנָא לֵיהּ. לְהַאי גַּבְרָא בִּשְׁעַת קִדּוּשִׁין, וְנִמְצָא גָּדוֹל, לָמָּה צָרִיךְ בְּדִיקָה בִּשְׁעַת גֵּירוּשִׁין? אֶלָּא לְיִבּוּם. דְּמִבֶּן תֵּשַׁע קְנָאָהּ בְּבִיאָה, וְאֵין יָכוֹל לְגָרֵשׁ עַד שֶׁיָּבִיא שְׁתֵּי שְׂעָרוֹת. לְאַפּוּקֵי מִדְּר' יוֹסֵי. דְּמִשּׁוּם חֲלִיצָה "אִישׁ" לָא אִיצְטְרִיךְ, דְּמִגֵּירוּשִׁין שָׁמְעִינַן לָהּ. ה"ג: עַד שֶׁיִּרְבֶּה הַשָּׁחוֹר קמ"ל דְּלָא כְּרַבִּי יְהוּדָה. וּבְמַסֶּכֶת נִדָּה מְפָרֵשׁ: עַד שֶׁיִּרְבּוּ הַשְּׂעָרוֹת וְיִהְיוּ שׁוֹכְבוֹת, וְנִרְאֶה כְּמוֹ שֶׁהִרְבָּה הַשָּׁחוֹר. וְלֹא גָּרַס "עַל הַלָּבָן". וּלְר' יְהוּדָה אֵין בּוֹדְקִין, דְּהָא לְאַחַר הֲבָאַת שְׂעָרוֹת מְמָאֶנֶת עַד שֶׁיִּרְבֶּה וְיִהְיוּ שׁוֹכְבוֹת. וְהִלְכְתָא כְּגִידֵּל בַּר מְנַשֶּׁה. דְּבֶן י"ג הַיּוֹדֵעַ בְּמַשָּׂא וּמַתָּן מוֹכֵר בְּנִכְסֵי אָבִיו אֲפִי' מְקַרְקְעֵי. דְּאִילּוּ מִטַּלְטְלֵי — אֲפִילּוּ פָּעוֹטוֹת כְּבָר שֵׁית מוֹכְרִין. כְּמָר זוּטְרָא. דִּלְעֵדוּת מִטַּלְטְלֵי מֵעִיד בֶּן י"ג שֶׁאֵינוֹ יוֹדֵעַ בְּטִיב מַשָּׂא וּמַתָּן, אֲבָל בְּעֵדוּת קַרְקַע לֹא. וְהִלְכְתָא כְּאַמֵּימָר. דְּמַתְּנַת בֶּן י"ג שֶׁאֵינוֹ יוֹדֵעַ בְּטִיב מַשָּׂא וּמַתָּן הָוְיָא מַתְּנָתוֹ מַתָּנָה, וְאַע"ג דִּמְכִירַת נְכָסָיו לֹא הָוְיָא מְכִירָה. וְהִלְכְתָא כְּרַב נַחְמָן אָמַר שְׁמוּאֵל בְּכוּלְּהוּ. קִדּוּשִׁין וְגֵירוּשִׁין חֲלִיצָה וּמֵיאוּנִין, דְּלָא סָמְכִינַן אַשָּׁנִים עַד שֶׁנִּבְדּוֹק סִימָנִין. וְלִמְכּוֹר בְּנִכְסֵי אָבִיו — עַד שֶׁיְּהֵא בֶּן עֶשְׂרִים וְיָבִיא סִימָנִים מִי שֶׁאֵינוֹ יוֹדֵעַ בְּטִיב מַשָּׂא וּמַתָּן, דְּטְפֵי מֵעֶשְׂרִים לֹא *אַמְטוּ רַבָּנַן לְהַמְתִּין לְחָכְמָתוֹ. וְאִם לֹא הֵבִיא שֵׂעָר בְּעֶשְׂרִים נַחְזִיקֶנּוּ כְּקָטָן עַד רוֹב שְׁנוֹתָיו אִם לֹא נִמְצְאוּ בּוֹ סִימָנֵי סָרִיס. וְאִיכָּא לְמֵימַר דַּוְקָא בְּנִכְסֵי אָבִיו, אֲבָל בִּנְכָסִים שֶׁנִּתְּנוּ לוֹ בְּמַתָּנָה, אוֹ שֶׁקָּנָה מִטַּלְטְלִין שֶׁאֵינָם יְרוּשַּׁת אֲבוֹתָיו — הָנְהוּ מוֹכֵר פָּחוֹת מִבֶּן עֶשְׂרִים, כְּדִין מִטַּלְטְלִין.

*צ"ל אמרו. רש"ל

מתני' ר' אֱלְעָזָר אוֹמֵר אֶחָד בָּרִיא וְאֶחָד מְסוּכָּן כו'. ר' אֱלְעָזָר סְבִירָא לֵיהּ (ד) לְעִנְיַן שְׁכִיב מְרַע אֵינָם כִּכְתוּבִין וְכִמְסוּרִין כְּלָל, אֶלָּא כְּבָרִיא בְּעָלְמָא, וְצָרִיךְ קִנְיָן כִּשְׁאָר מַתְּנַת בָּרִיא. וְאַע"ג דְּמִית — לֹא קָנָה מְקַבֵּל מַתָּנָה בְּלֹא קִנְיָן. וַאֲפִי' מְצַוֶּה מֵחֲמַת מִיתָה נַמִי לְר"א בָּעֵי קִנְיָן, שֶׁהֲרֵי מַעֲשֶׂה שֶׁל אִמָּן שֶׁל בְּנֵי רוֹכֵל אוֹקִימְנַן לְעֵיל (דף קנא:) בִּמְצַוֶּה מֵחֲמַת מִיתָה, וַאפ"ה פָּלֵיג ר"א וְאָמַר לְהוּ לַחֲכָמִים: בְּנֵי רוֹכֵל תְּקַבְּרֵם אִמָּם, וְשֶׁלֹּא כַּדִּין קִיְּימוּ דְּבָרֶיהָ, כִּי אִם לְקוֹנְסָן. וְאֶחָד מְסוּכָּן. וְאַף עַל גַּב דְּלָא שַׁיֵּיר מִידֵּי — לָא מִיקְנֵי בַּאֲמִירָה כְּלָל. וְנִרְאֶה בְּעֵינַי דְּכֵיוָן דְּלָא מַפְלִיג ר"א בֵּין שְׁכִיב מְרַע לְבָרִיא לְעִנְיַן הֵיכָא דְּמִית (ה) — הוּא הַדִּין הֵיכָא דְּעָמַד אֵינוֹ חוֹזֵר, אִם קָנוּ מִיָּדוֹ, לְר' אֶלְעָזָר. בְּנֵי

תוספות

ולטעמיך זבין שוי חמשא בשיתא. וא"ת: גם בגדולים נמי, אין ממכרו מכר בכה"ג, דהוי ליה בטול מקח ומחזיר אונאה! וי"ל: דלאו דוקא נקט חמשא בשיתא. אי נמי דוקא, ואתי שפיר למה שמפרש ר"ת דאין אונאה לקרקעות. אי נמי, כגון שאמר בפירוש: יודע אני שאינו שוה כל כך. אי נמי, לא יתבטל לגמרי כיון דליכא יותר משתות.

בודקין לקדושין ולגירושין. הך בדיקה אחר שהגיע (ו) לכלל שנים. אבל מקמי שנים — הוו שערות שומא בעלמא, כדאמרינן בנדה פרק ו)("בא סימן") (דף נב וקס). וגם מהניא הך בדיקה לענין שאם פשטה ידה וקבלה קדושין מאחר, אי משכחינן בתר הכי סימנים — בתראי לא הוו קדושין, ואי לא משכחי סימנים — הוי ספיקא, דחיישינן שמא נשרו, בספיקא דאורייתא כי הכא, כדאמר בפ' "בא סימן". וליכא למימר (ז) דאם פשטה ידה וקבלה קדושין מאחר חיישינן לקדושי [שניהם] וכדשמואל דאמר בפ' "עשרה יוחסין" (קדושין דף עט:): קדשה אביה בדרך וקדשה היא עצמה בעיר — חוששין לקדושי [שניהם]. דהתם לא קאמר הכי אלא ביומא דמשלם שית, שבאותו יום נגרה. אבל הכא, שהגיע כבר לגדלות מזמן גדול — לא.

ולגירושין. שאם לא ימצאו שערות — לא יהיו גירושין, דלא סמכינן אחזקה להקל. וכן לחליצה ולמיאון. ואע"ג דגבי מיאון אמרי' בפ' "בא סימן" (דף מח: וקס): קטנה שהגיעה לכלל שנותיה אינה צריכה בדיקה, דחזקה הביאה סימנין — היינו היכא דלא בדקנא, אבל היכא דבדקנא ולא אשכחינן — יכולה למאן, ולא חיישינן שמא נשרו, כיון שלא בעל, כדאמרי' בפ' "בא סימן" (ד' נב.). מיהו, בזמן הזה לא בקיאין בהכרת גומות ז).

וכי מאחר דבדקנוה לקדושין לגירושין למה לי כו'. וא"ת: ומאי קושיא? וכי חובה הוא לבדוק לקדושין? אבל לגירושין צריך הוא לבדוק אם הוא גדול לגרש. ועוד: דהוה ליה למימר האי לישנא: למאי הלכתא בדקינן לגירושין? דממה נפשך היא מגורשת, שאם היה קטן בשעת קדושין — אפי' גירושין לא בעי, ואם היה גדול עכשיו — הוא (ח) גדול בשעת גירושין, ואם היה ספיקא — הא ספיקא דאורייתא לחומרא, דחיישינן שמא נשרו, כדאמרי' בפ' "בא סימן" (שם)! ודוחק לומר דבודקין לקדושין, דהיינו אם לא מצאו שערות לא תהא מקודשת, דלא חיישינן שמא נשרו. דהויא אז מילתא דשמואל בהכי דלא כהלכתא.

לחליצה לאפוקי מדר' יוסי. וא"ת: אימא דלענין איש מיירי, דהתם אפי' ר' יוסי מודה! וי"ל: דמשמע לי' דמיירי בין באיש בין באשה, דומיא דלגיטין ולקדושין דמיירי בין באיש בין באשה.

לאפוקי מדר' יהודה כו'. ואם תאמר: מנא ליה לאפוקי מדרבי יהודה? דלמא בבדיקה דרבי יהודה איירי? ויש לומר: דומיא דבדיקות דלעיל, דהוי ב' שערות. מיהו, צריך עיון אי קאמר ר' יהודה למילתיה גבי מיאון דוקא, או לא.

עד שירבה שחור על הלבן. פי' רבינו שמואל דלא גרסינן "על הלבן". ור"י אומר דגרסינן שפיר, דעל הלבן — היינו על הבשר שהוא לבן, ואיידי שהזכיר שחור בשיער — הזכיר בשר בלשון לבן ח).

רבי אלעזר אומר אחד בריא ואחד מסוכן כו'. הכי גרים רבינו תם: ר' אלעזר, ולא "ר' אליעזר". והוא ר' אלעזר בן שמוע. דאי גרים "ר' אליעזר" היה קשה מדתני בתר הך בבא פלוגתא דר' אליעזר ורבי יהושע גבי קנין דשכיב מרע בבבא אחריתי, ואי גרס "ר' אליעזר" בתרוייהו — א"כ ליערבינהו וליתנינהו: המחלק נכסיו על פיו רבי אליעזר אומר אחד בריא כו', בד"א — בחול, אבל בשבת — דבריו קיימין, ר' יהושע אומר כו'. אלא מדפלגינהו לתרי בבי — שמע מינה הראשון הוא ר' אלעזר בן שמוע. ועוד ראיה, דקאמר בגמרא: א"ר לוי קונין מש"מ ואפילו בשבת, ולא לחוש לדברי ר' אלעזר כו'. ואי גרס "ר' אליעזר" — הא אית ליה בסמוך דבשבת דבריו קיימין בלא קנין. ועוד: מאי האי דקאמר אמרו

רבינו גרשום

ולטעמיך. דמקשת הכי מי מצי זבין שפיר בנכסי אביו. דזבן שוה ד' בה' ה"נ דזביניה זביני. אלא לא אזיל כלל משום האי טעמא דזבין שפיר ולא משום דלא אתו לידיה דלא מצי למיהב מתנה אלא מאי טעמא אין מכירתו מכירה אע"ג דזבין שפיר דגזרינן האי דזבין שפיר אטו האי דלא זבין שפיר דכי היכי דהאי אין מכירתו מכירה הכי נמי אידך דקים להו לרבנן כו': מילי. הנאה וגמילות חסד: אמר רב נחמן אמר שמואל בודקין לגיטין ולקדושין ולחליצה ולמיאונין. אי הוה בן י"ג שנה ויום אחד: (ולמכור בנכסי אביו. לא מצי למיזבן): ואם בת היא לחליצה ולמיאונין בודקין אם היא בת י"ב שנה ויום אחד: ולמכו' בנכסי אביו. לא מצי למזבן עד שיהא בן עשרים והביא שתי שערות: וכיון דבדקינא. ליה לקדושין דגדול היה כשקדשה כל שכן דלגירושין הוי גדול: לא נצרכה אלא לקדושי יבם. דבן תשע קנאה והויא אשתו ואם דעתו לגרשה אינו רשאי עד שיגדל: איש כתיב בפרשת יבמים. ככה יעשה לאיש ומקשי' אשה לאיש דזה וזה עד שיגדילו: לאפוקי מדר' יהודה דאמר. עד מתי הבת ממאנת עד שתביא ב' שערות. ר' יהודה אמר עד שירבה שחור כו' קמ"ל דהלכה כת"ק דר' יהודה: תוך זמן כלפני זמן. ואין מכירתו מכירה: והלכתא כגידל בר מנשה. כדשלח ליה רבא: והלכת' כמר זוטרא. דאמר לא אמרינן דעדותן עדות אלא במטלטלין: והלכתא כרב נחמן אמר שמואל בכולהו. דאמר בודקין לגירושין כו': **פיסקא** המחלק נכסיו על פיו. כגון שכ"מ שאינו צריך לקנין ולא כתיבה ולא משיכה אלא בדבור בעלמא: ר' אליעזר אומר אחד בריא ואחד מסוכן. המחלק על פיו: נכסים שיש להן אחריות. כלומר ר' אליעזר לא סבירא ליה דדברי שכיב מרע ככתובין וכמסורין דמי וצריכין כל חיזוקין כבריא: אמרו

הגהות הב"ח

(א) גמ' מתנתו מתנה כי היכי דלעבידו להו מילי: (ב) שם במשנה אלא במשיכה וחכמים אומרים אלו ואלו נקנין באמירה אמרו לו מעשה: (ג) רשב"ם ד"ה ה"נ וכו' אלא בכולהו תקון: (ד) ד"ה רבי אלעזר וכו' ר' אלעזר ס"ל לדברי שכיב מרע: (ה) ד"ה ואחד מסוכן כו' ה"ה היכא דעמד. נ"ב ותימה א"כ אמאי נקט במעשה דמרוני ומת הא אפילו בלא מת נמי כמו שהקשו תוס' דף קנא ע"ב ודוחק לומר דנקט מת לאורויי דשכיב מרע היה דלאין זה ראיה וכמו שהשיבו לו מאם ראיה מרוני בריא היה ונראה בעיני דנקט ומת לאורויי דמצוה מחמת מיתה היה ולכך אם עמד חוזר ואע"ג דקנו מיניה ואשמועינן דבעי קנין אפילו במצוה מחמת מיתה וכדאוקימנ' לעיל בגמ' דמעשה דבני רוכל מצוה מחמת מיתה הי' ומה שפי' רשב"ם בסמוך איכא למימר דמודה ר"א במצוה מחמת מיתה אינו אלא לפי תשובת אמרו לו [דלא הוה סלקא] אדעתייהו דר"א מצריך קנין אפי' במצוה מחמת מיתה כל כמה דלא השיב ר"א ממעשה דמרוני לפי זה ודאי [יש להקשות מאי ...]: (ו) תוס' ד"ה בודקין וכו' שהגיע לכלל שנים וכו' ומהניא הך בדיקה וגם מהני: (ז) בא"ד וליכא למימר לשמואל דאם פשטה וכו' דהתם לא קאמר שמואל הכי: (ח) ד"ה וכי מאחר וכו' שכבר הוא גדול:

קלא א מיי' פ"ב מהל' אישות הל' יא סמג עשין כ טוש"ע אה"ע סי' קלה סעיף יב וסי' קעב סעיף ו בהג"ה:
קלב ב מיי' פ"ו מהל' יבום וחליצה הל"ב סמג עשין נא טוש"ע אה"ע סי' קעב סעיף א:
קלג ג מיי' פ"ב מהל' אישות הל' יב סמג עשין ל טוש"ע אה"ע סי' קנה סעיף יב:
קלד ד מיי' שם ועיין בהשגות ובמגיד משנה טוש"ע שם סעיף יג:
קלה ה מיי' פכ"ט מהל' מכירה הל' יז סמג עשין פב טוש"ע ח"מ סי' רלה סעיף יד:
קלו ו מיי' שם הל' יב טוש"ע שם סעיף א וסעיף ח:
קלז ז ח מיי' פ"ט מהל' עדות הל' ח סמג לאוין ריד טוש"ע ח"מ סי' לה סעיף ג:
קלח ט י מיי' פכ"ט מהל' מכירה הל' ו סמג עשין פב טוש"ע ח"מ סי' רלה סעיף א:
קלט כ מיי' פ"ט מהל' עדות הלכה ז סמג לאוין ריד טוש"ע ח"מ סי' לה סעיף א:
קמ ל מיי' פכ"ט מהל' מכירה הל' יד סמג עשין פב טוש"ע ח"מ סי' רלה סעיף י:

*נ"י במטלטלי *במקרקעי

לאו מי איתמר עלה כו'. הכא נמי הוה מצי לשנויי בפחות מזמן מכר, והיה יודע בטיב משא ומתן, והיו רוצים לבודקו אם הביא שתי שערות אם לאו. שאם הוא קטן — הרי כפעוטות, שאין ממכרן ממכר במקרקעי, כדאמרינן בסמוך. אלא שפיר קא משני. **הכי** גרים ר"ת. דזימנין דאתו מחמת בריאותא וזימנין דאתו מחמת כחישותא. והכי גרסי' ב"הבא רבה" (יבמות דף לו.*) בכל הספרים. וכך נראה יותר, דכי אתו לקמיה דרבי חייא משמע שעדיין לא הביאו שתי שערות, ולכך אמר להבריאם או להכחישם כדי להביא שערות. ולא כספרים דגרסי: זימנא דנתרי מחמת בריותן. **מקחה** מקח וממכרה ממכר. לאו דוקא נקט מקחה מקח, דהא פשיטא. אלא איידי דנקט ממכרה ממכר, נקט נמי מקחה מקח.

לא אמרו אלא במטלטלי אבל מקרקעי לא. אין לפרש לעדות קרקע, דמאי שנא למטלטלי? ועוד, דהכא לא שייכא שום שטות. אלא נראה לפרש דהיינו עדות — שיאמרו: כך וכך היתה שוה זו הקרקע. דכיון דמיקרבא דעתיה לגבי זוזא (ד) ישום אותה *יותר משוויה. אבל מטלטלים — לא ישום אותם *יותר משווים, דמיקרבא דעתיה נמי לגבי מטלטלי. וגם אין הפסד *במקרקעי כמו *במטלטלי.

היינו דקאתו ואמרו ליה: מהו לבודקו; אלא אי אמרת מבן עשרים, כי בדקו ליה מאי הוי? והא א)תנן: אבן עשרים שלא הביא שתי שערות — יביאו ראיה שהוא בן עשרים, והוא הסרים ב)לא חולץ ולא מיבם! לאו איתמר עלה, אמר ר' שמואל בר רב יצחק אמר רב: ג)והוא שנולדו בו סימני סרים? אמר רבא: דיקא נמי, דקתני: והוא הסרים, שמע מינה. וכי לא נולדו לו סימני סרים, עד כמה? תני ר' חייא: ד)עד רוב שנותיו. (א) כי אתא לקמיה דרבי חייא, אי כחיש — אמר להו: ליברי, ואי אברי — אמר להו: ליכחוש, דהני סימני זמנין דאתו מחמת כחישותא, וזמנין דאתו מחמת בריותא. ב)איבעיא להו: תוך זמן כלפני זמן, או כלאחר זמן? (אמר) רבא אמר רב נחמן: ה)תוך זמן כלפני זמן; רבא בר רב שילא אמר ר"נ: תוך זמן כלאחר זמן. והא דרבא ג)לאו בפירוש איתמר אלא מכללא איתמר, דההוא תוך זמן (ג) דאזיל זבין נכסי ואתא לקמיה דרבא, אמר להו: לא עשה ולא כלום; מאן דחזא סבר: משום דתוך זמן כלפני זמן, ולא היא, התם שטותא יתירתא חזא ביה, דהוה קא משחרר להו לעבדיה. שלח ליה גידל בר מנשיא ד)לרבא, ילמדנו רבינו: תינוקת בת ארבע עשרה שנה ויום אחד יודעת בטיב משא ומתן, מהו? שלח ליה: ו)אם יודעת בטיב משא ומתן — מקחה מקח וממכרה ממכר. ולישלח ליה: תינוק! ה)מעשה שהיה כך היה. ולישלח ליה: תינוקת בת שתים עשרה שנה ויום אחד! מעשה שהיה כך היה. (והא דרבא לאו בפירוש איתמר אלא מכללא איתמר, ד)ההוא פחות מבן עשרים דאזל זבין נכסי [אבוהו, כגידל בר מנשיא,] אתא לקמיה דרבא. אמרו ליה קרוביה: זיל אכול תמרי ושדי ביה קשייתא בי רבא, עבד הכי; אמר להו: זביניה לאו זביני. כי קא כתבו ליה שטרא, אמרו ליה לקוחות, זיל אימא ליה לרבא: מגלת אסתר בזוזא, שטרא דמר בזוזא? אזל א"ל; אמר להו: זביניה זביני. אמרו ליה קרוביה: לקוחות אגמרוהו! אמר להו: מסברי ליה סבר, (ג) כיון דמסברי ליה וסבר — מידע ידע, והאי דעבד הכי — חוצפא יתירא הוא דהוה ביה. אמר רב הונא בריה דרב יהושע: ז)ולעדות — עדותו עדות. אמר מר זוטרא: ח)לא אמרן אלא למטלטלי, אבל למקרקעי לא. א"ל רב אשי למר זוטרא: מ"ש מטלטלי? ט)דזביניה זביני; אלא מעתה, הא דתנן: ו)י)הפעוטות — מקחן מקח וממכרן ממכר במטלטלין, ה"נ דעדותן עדות! א"ל: התם כ)בעינא "ועמדו שני האנשים", וליכא. אמר אמימר: ל)ומתנתו מתנה. א"ל רב אשי לאמימר: השתא, ומה זביני דמקבל זוזי אמרת דלא, דלמא מוזיל ומזבין — כל שכן מתנה דלא מטי ליה ולא מידי! א"ל:

ולטעמיך

רש"ל מ"ז רש"ל | דברים יט | תורה אור

היינו דאמרו ליה מהו לבודקו. שאם לא ימצאו בו שערות יחזיקוהו כקטן עד עשרים, כדמפרש ואזיל. ודוקא לענין למכור בנכסי אביו תרתי בעינן, שמונה עשרה שנים ושערות. אבל לענין עונשים ומצות — מבן י"ג חשיב גדול אם הביא שערות. יביאו ראיה. קרובי האלמנה, כדי לפטרה מזיקת היבם, להתירה לשוק בלא חליצה ויבום. והוא הסרים כו'. והרי הוא סרים, ולא חולץ ולא מיבם. כדאמר ביבמות דלא קרינא ביה "להקים לאחיו שם", וכל שאינו עולה ליבום אינו עולה לחליצה. אלמא, מבן עשרים ואילך, אע"ג דלא אייתי שערות — כגדול מחזיקין ליה, ומפני שהוא סרים לא אייתי שערות. והוא שנולדו בו סימני סרים. סימנין המפורשין ביבמות (דף פ:). דכיון דאיכא תרתי — חשבינן ליה כגדול. אבל בן עשרים שלא הביא שערות, ואין בו סימני סרים — חשבינן ליה כקטן עד רוב שנותיו, כדמפרש ואזיל. ואי נולדו בו סימני סרים מקמי דליהוי בן עשרים, ושערות נמי לא אייתי — אכתי לא סמכינן למיחשביה סרים עד דליהוי בן עשרים ויהא בו סימני סרים, דאיכא תרתי. וכי לא נולדו בו סימני סרים. ושערות נמי לא הביא, עד כמה נחזיקהו כקטן? רוב שנותיו. ל"ו שנים, שהן רוב שבעים, כדכתיב: "ימי שנותינו בהם שבעים שנה" (תהלים צ). הני סימנים זימנין כו'. פירוש הוי, ואלדלקמיה קאי, כי אתו לקמיה דר' חייא כו'. בחישותא. כשהנער כחוש בבשרו. כי אתו לקמיה. המתעכבין יותר מדאי להביא שערות. אבחשוהו. דלמא מחמת בריאותא נתרו להו. תוך זמן. שנת שמונה עשרה גופיה למר, ושנת עשרים גופיה למר, והביא שערות. כלפני זמן. שאין מכירתו מכירה בנכסי אביו. דההוא תוך זמנו. שמכר בנכסי אביו. ולא היא. מהכא לא פשטינן ליה. דקא משחרר להו לעבדיה. וזהו איבוד ממון בחנם, שאין לו בה הנאה. אית דגרסי: מקחה מקח וממכרה ממכר במטלטלין. ולא מבעיא בת ארבע עשרה, אלא אפי' כבת שב וכבת שית, כדתנן: הפעוטות כו' ומוקים להו בגיטין כבר שית וכבר שבע, אלא מעשה שהיה כך היה. ולא נהירא, דמאי אתא לאשמועינן? מתני' היא: הפעוטות מקחן מקח כו', ואפילו אין יודעין יפה בטיב משא ומתן, דהא כבר שית כבר שבע מוקמית לה! ונראה בעיני דבמקרקעי מיירי, ולא גרסינן "במטלטלין". והכי מפרש לה: שלח ליה רב גידל בר מנשיא לרב, ילמדנו רבינו: תינוקת בת י"ד שיודעת בטיב משא ומתן מהו למכור בנכסי אביה, אע"ג דלא הויא בת עשרים? מהכא שמעינן דעד השתא איירינן בשאין יודע כל כך בטיב משא ומתן, ואפילו הכי מבן עשרים ואילך מוכר בנכסי אביו, הואיל ואינו שוטה ממש. אבל בפחות מבן עשרים — בעינן חכמה יתירה למכור בנכסי אביו. ה"ג: שלח ליה אם יודעת בטיב משא ומתן מקחה מקח וממכרה ממכר. ולישלח ליה בתינוק כו'. והא דרבא לאו בפירוש כו'. לא גרסינן הכא כלל. וה"ג: ההוא פחות מבן עשרים שמכר בנכסי אביו, בחזקת יודע בטיב משא ומתן, כגידל בר מנשיא, אתא לקמיה דרבא. כדי לחזור בו, ולומר שאינו יודע בטיב משא ומתן. אמרו ליה קרוביה. לאותו יתום. זיל אכול תמרי. והשלך גרעינים לפני רבא, ויהיה סבור שאתה שוטה, ויחזיר לך נכסיך. כי כתבו ליה שטרא. פסק דין שיחזירו לו נכסיו. אמרו ליה לקוחות כו'. הורוהו דבר חכמה שיאמר לפני רבא, ויחשב חכם בעיניו ויודע בטיב משא ומתן, ולא יפסידו לקוחות מקחם. מגילת אסתר. שהוא דבר גדול, רגיל סופר לכתוב בזוזא, ובשביל שטר קטן שכותב לי שואל לי זוז? בתמיה. אמרו ליה. קרובים לרבא. לקוחות אגמרוהו. לומר כן להאי, אך אינו יודע כלום. אמר להו כיון דמסברי ליה. דבר חכמה, ויודע להבין — חכם הוא, וממכרו ממכר. והאי דשדא קשייתא — חוצפא בעלמא הוא דעבד, ולא מתוך שטות. א"ר (זירא) [הונא] ולעדות מעיד. אע"פ שאמרנו בפחות מכ' שאינו יודע בטיב משא ומתן אינו מוכר בנכסי אביו, אבל לעדות — נאמן הוא להעיד מה שראה ושמע מבן י"ג ואילך שהביא שתי שערות, הואיל ואינו שוטה. אלא במטלטלי. בעדות מטלטלי. מ"ש. עדות מטלטלי דנאמן. משום דזביניה זביני. במטלטלי, אע"פ שאינו יודע בטיב משא ומתן, דהיינו פעוטות — ה"נ דעדותו במטלטלי הויא עדות. אלא מעתה הא דקתני הפעוטות כו'. ומוקמינן לה בגיטין: כבר שית כבר שבע. ועמדו שני האנשים. בעדות מוקמינן לה במסכת שבועות (דף ל.), ובעינן אנשים ולא קטנים. אמר אמימר ומתנתו. של בן י"ג ויום אחד הויא מתנה, אע"פ שאינו יודע בטיב משא ומתן, ואין מכירת קרקעותיו מכירה. השתא ומה זביני דקשקיל זוזי. דדרך חכמה היא זאת, אפילו הכי תקינו רבנן דלא ליהוי זביני עד שיהא בן עשרים, הואיל ואינו בקי בטיב משא ומתן. מתנה שהוא דרך שטות מיבעי, דתקון רבנן דלא ליהוי מתנה? א"ל

רבינו גרשום

אלא למאן דאמר בן כ' מצי זבין בנכסי אביו ולא קודם לכן. ואי האי דבני ברק היה בן כ' למה ליה לבודקו בשערות והתנן בן כ' שנה שלא הביא ב' שערות וקנו ממנו כלום בנכסי אביו יביאו ראיה שהוא מבן כ' ומכירתו מכירה אלמא אי הוה בן כ' אע"ג דלא הביא ב' שערות מכירתו מכירה. ומסיים (הברייתא) [המשנה] והוא סרים. כלומר מאחר שלא הביא עד כ' סרים הוא ולא חולץ ולא מייבם משום דכל העולה לייבום עולה לחליצה והא סרים אינו עולה לייבום משום אשר לא יבנה את בית אחיו כתיב. וקשיא לרבא דאמר מבן כ' דאי בר הכי הוא לא צריך ליבדקיה בשערות. לעולם אימא לך דצריך למיבדק בן כ' אם הביא שתי שערות אי לא והכא טעמא מאי קתני הכי יביאו ראיה שהוא בן כ' ותו לא לאו מי איתמר עלה דההיא (ברייתא) [משנה] אמאי דתנא והוא סרים לא חולץ. א) ואמאי קאמר יביאו ראיה שהוא בן כ' ותו לא. אמר שמואל והוא שנולדו לו סימני סרים קודם כ' שנה מאותן סימנים דקאמרי' במס' יבמות (דף פ ע"ב) אין בשרו מעלה הבל ואינו עושה כיפה ומשום הכי אינו צריך לבדוק בתר סימנים ומכירתו מכירה. אבל [לא] נולדו לו סימני סרים צריך למיבדק בתר סימנים אע"ג דאיהו כ'. דיקא נמי (דהא ברייתא) דבנולדו לו סימני סרים מיירי מדקתני והוא הסרים קא מיירי ומש"ה לא בדקינן בסימנים. וכי לא נולדו לו סימני סרים ולא הביא ב' שערות והוא כבן כ' עד כמה שנים מצפין לשערות דאמרי' קטן הוא דאין מכירתו מכירה. תני ר' חייא עד רוב שנותיו דהיינו ל"ו שנה כדכתיב ימי שנותינו בהם שבעים שנה וגו'. אבל כשיגיעו רוב שנותיו מכירתו מכירה אע"ג דלא הביא והכי דייקינן. הלכך אליבא דרבא עד כ' בעי דיביא ב' שערות והוא מבן כ' מכירתו מכירה. אבל אי לא הביא אפי' עבר כ' אין מכירתו מכירה עד רוב שנותיו. והכי נמי פחות מבן כ' אם הביא אין מכירתו מכירה עד שיהיה בן כ'. ואם נולדו לו סימני סרים עד כ' אין מכירתו מכירה למעלה מכ' מכירתו מכירה. וה"נ דריש אליבא דרב הונא לפי ענין מילתא כי האי גוונא אם הוא בן י"ח והביא ב' שערות מכירתו מכירה. אם לא הביא עד רוב שנותיו ג) ואם הביא קודם י"ח אין מכירתו מכירה. ואם הביא סימני סרים קודם י"ח מכירתו מכירה לאחר י"ח: כי אתא לקמיה דר' חייא. האי יותר מבן כ' עד שלא הביא שערות. אמר להו כו': איבעיא להו. למר כדאית ליה ולמר כדאית ליה אם הביא ב' שערות בתוך הזמן בשנת כ' או בי"ח ומכר מהו מי אמרי' תוך זמן כלפני זמן. כי היכי דלפני זמן אע"ג דהביא אין מכירתו מכירה ה"נ האי או דלמא כלאחר זמן דמי כי היכי דלאחר כ' אם הביא מכירתו מכירה ה"נ האי בתוך הזמן הואיל והביא מכירתו מכירה. וה"נ איבעיא להו אליבא דמ"ד בן י"ח: (רבה ב"ר שילא) [רבא] אמר תוך זמן כלפני זמן ואין מכירתו מכירה אע"ג דהביא ב' שערות דההוא תוך זמנו שמכר בנכסי אביו ג) לא עשה כלום משום דתוך זמן הוא. והיינו מכללא ולא בפירוש

בפירוש אמרה. ולא היא התם טעמא מאי אמר תוך זמן כלפני זמן ולא עשה כלום משום דשטותא יתירתא הוא דחזה ביה דהוה משחרר ליה לעבדיה ומש"ה אמר דקטן הוא דעשה מעשה קטן ושוטה ואי לאו הכי ודאי הוה אמר תוך זמן כלאחר זמן ואם הביא ב' שערות מכירתו מכירה: יודעת בטיב משא ומתן. אם מכרה במקרקעי שלה ולא בשל אביה מהו מי הויא מכירה אי לא. במטלטלי לא איצטריך למיבעי דפשיטא ליה דמשהיא בת ט' שנה ויום אחד מוכרת במטלטלין אם יודעת בטיב משא ומתן כדקתני מתני' הפעוטות כבן ט' כבן עשר מקחן מקח וממכרן ממכר במטלטלין: ולשלח ליה בתינוק. היודע בטיב משא ומתן אם יכול למכור מקרקעי שלו אי לא: מעשה שהיה כן היה. שתינוקת מכרה וה"ה לתינוק: ולשלח ליה בת י"ב שנה ויום אחד. דכבר בוגרת היא מאי שנא בת י"ד שנה ויום אחד: והא דרבא. דאמר לעיל מאימת קטן מוכר בנכסי אביו מבן כ': לאו בפירוש כו' דההוא פחות מבן כ'. מדקאמר פחות מבן כ' שנה שמעי' מינה דיותר מבן י"ח שנה היה: וקא זבין נכסי דאבוה אתא לקמיה דרבא. דקא בעי למיהדר ביה משום דפחות מבן כ' שנה מכר. השיאוהו קרוביו עצה שיעשה שטות לפני רבא כדי שיתראה עליו שוטה שאין יודע בטיב משא ומתן: עבד הכי. דשדא קשייתא קמיה. אמר להו לאו זביניה זביני. דשוטה הוא: כי כתבו ליה שטר. אפסק דין דזביניה לאו זביני: אמרו לו לקוחות. לאותו שמכר: זיל אימא ליה לרבא. לימדו ליה הן דבר חכמה שיעמוד לפניו שיתראה לפניו כחכם כדי שיחזור בו ויאמר ממכרו ממכר. למדוהו לומר לו מגילת אסתר שהיא גדולה אין נותנין לסופר שכותבה אלא זוזא ושטרא דאיהו קטן רוצה הסופר לטול בו זוז: אמר להו זביניה זביני. הואיל ויודע כל כך בטיב משא ומתן: א"ל קרוביה. לרבא הא טענה לקוחות אגמרוהו כי היכי דליתחזי חכם ואיהו לא ידע לאסוקי אדעתיה למימר הכי: אמר להו. ודאי דעת יש לו דכל אינש דמסברו ליה וסבר כלומר כל אדם שמלמדין אותו והוא מאזין ודאי מידע ידע וחכם הוא ומכירתו מכירה. והאי דעבד הכי דשדא קשייתא חוצפא יתירא דהויא ביה. השתא דייקינן מהא הלכתא דפשיטא דמקחו מקח וממכרו ממכר במטלטלין שלו ולא במקרקעי שלו. אע"ג דהביא ב' שערות שוטה הוי. והוא דידעי פעוטות בטיב משא ומתן. בן י"ג שנה ויום אחד והביא שערות ויודע בטיב משא ומתן מוכר במקרקעי שלו ובמטלטלי של אביו. מן י"ח שנה ולמעלה לרבא אם הביא ב' שערות ויודע בטיב משא ומתן מוכר בנכסי אביו. ואם הוא בן עשרים ולא הביא שערות ואינו יודע בטיב משא ומתן אין מוכר בנכסי אביו. ואם לא נולדו לו סימני סרים והוא בן כ' ולא הביא שערות אע"פ שיודע בטיב משא ומתן אין מוכר בנכסי אביו עד רוב שנותיו. והכי נמי מפרשי' אליבא דמאן דאמר עד י"ח לפי ענינו: אמר רב הונא בריה דרב יהושע. אע"ג דפחות מבן כ' אם הביא שערות ואין יודע בטיב משא ומתן אינו רשאי למכור בנכסי אביו לענין עדות עדותו עדות לכל דבר. ולא אמרו דעדותו עדות אלא למטלטלי דמצי נמי לזבוני במטלטלי אביו [פחות] מבן כ'. אבל למקרקעי לא מצי לזבוני עד שיביא שערות ויודע בטיב משא ומתן לא מצי לאסהודי לאחרינא במקרקעי: אלא מעתה. דאמרת שמשום הכי מצי לאסהודי משום דמצי לזבוני א"כ פעוטות דמצי זביני כדתנן ה"נ דעדותן עדות. הא לא הוי אלא בן (תשיסר) [שית ושבע]. הא לא מצית אמרת לגבי עדות אנשים בעינן כדכתיב ועמדו שני האנשים בעדים הכתוב מדבר וליכא דתינוקות הן. ולעולם גבי עדותן עדות במטלטלין אבל לא במקרקעי: אמר אמימר. אע"ג דאינו יכול למכור בנכסי אביו עד כ' שנה וכדאוקמת' הלכתא אפ"ה אי יהיב מתנה מנכסי אביו מתנתו מתנה: ומה זביני דמקבל זוזי אמרת לא. מתנה דבחנם הוא לא כ"ש: א"ל

א) נראה דל"ל ולא קאמר יביאו וכו'. ב) נ"ל עד רוב שנותיו אין מכירתו מכירה. ג) נ"ל ואתא לקמיה דרבא ואמר דלא עשה כלום.

א) נדה דף מז: יבמות דף פ. ודף לו.: ב) נדה דף מה.: ג) [ברכות ע. וש"נ]: ד) נ"ל לרב וכן גי' רשב"ם. יעב"ץ: ה) [עירובין סה: וש"נ]: ו) כתובות ע. גיטין דף נט. ודף סה.:

הגהות הב"ח (א) גמ' עד רוב שנותיו (כי אתא לקמיה דרבי חייא וכו' מחמת בריותא) תא"מ ונ"ב זו גירסת ר"ת אבל גירסת רשב"ם כך הוא הני סימנין זימנין דנתרי מחמת כחישותא וזימנין דנתרי מחמת בריותא כי אתו לקמיה דר' חייא אי כחיש א"ל ליברי ואי איברי א"ל לכחוש איבעיא להו כו': (ב) שם דההוא תוך זמן דאתא לקמיה דרבא כצ"ל ותיבת דאזיל זבין נכסי נמחק: (ג) שם וכיון דמסברי ליה סבר: (ד) תוס' ד"ה לא אמרו כו' ישום אותה יותר משוויה נ"ב נראה דעיקר הטעם כיון דמקרבא דעתיה לגבי זוזא אינו בקי בשומת קרקע כי אינו נותן דעתו כי אם במאי דמקרבא דעתיה והלכך אפשר לומר דישום אותה ביותר משוויה או בפחות משוויה [וטעם דיותר] משוויה הוא לפי שכתבו עוד וגם אין הפסד כו' דכונתם מחמת [שמטלטלים נחסרין] מדי יום יום לא ישום אותם יותר משוויים משא"כ במקרקעי דכיון שאין בהם [חסרון אפשר דישום אותם יותר משוויים]:

תורה אור

הָכִי קָאָמַר לֵיהּ רַבִּי יוֹחָנָן לְר' שִׁמְעוֹן בֶּן לָקִישׁ: בִּשְׁלָמָא לְדִידִי דְּאָמִינָא רְאָיָה בְּקִיּוּם הַשְּׁטָר, הַיְינוּ דְּמַשְׁכַּחַתְּ לָהּ דְּנָחְתִי לָקוֹחוֹת לַנְּכָסִים, אֶלָּא לְדִידָךְ דְּאָמְרַתְּ רְאָיָה בְּעֵדִים, הֵיכִי מַשְׁכַּחַתְּ לָהּ דְּנָחְתִי לָקוֹחוֹת בַּנְּכָסִים? אָמַר לֵיהּ: מוֹדֵינָא לָךְ בְּעַרְעָר דִּבְנֵי מִשְׁפָּחָה א דְּלָאו עַרְעָר הוּא, מַאי קָאָמְרִי? קָטָן הָיָה — *ב חֲזָקָה אֵין הָעֵדִים חוֹתְמִין עַל הַשְּׁטָר אֶלָּא אִם כֵּן נַעֲשָׂה גָּדוֹל. אִיתְּמַר: קָטָן מֵאֵימָתַי מוֹכֵר בְּנִכְסֵי אָבִיו? רָבָא אָמַר רַב נַחְמָן: בֶּן שְׁמוֹנֶה עֶשְׂרֵה שָׁנָה, וְרַב הוּנָא בַּר חִינָּנָא אָמַר רַב נַחְמָן: (א) ג מִבֶּן עֶשְׂרִים שָׁנָה. (ב) (וְהָא דְּרָבָא *לָאו בְּפֵירוּשׁ אִיתְּמַר אֶלָּא מִכְּלָלָא אִיתְּמַר.) מְתִיב ר' זֵירָא: *מַעֲשֶׂה בִּבְנֵי בְּרַק בְּאֶחָד שֶׁמָּכַר בְּנִכְסֵי אָבִיו וּמֵת, וּבָאוּ בְּנֵי מִשְׁפָּחָה וְעִרְעֲרוּ לוֹמַר קָטָן הָיָה בִּשְׁעַת מִיתָה, וּבָאוּ וְשָׁאֲלוּ אֶת רַבִּי עֲקִיבָא: מַהוּ לְבוֹדְקוֹ? אָמַר לָהֶם: אִי אַתֶּם רַשָּׁאִין לְנַוְּולוֹ; וְעוֹד, סִימָנִין עֲשׂוּיִין לְהִשְׁתַּנּוֹת לְאַחַר מִיתָה; בִּשְׁלָמָא לְמַאן דְּאָמַר בֶּן שְׁמוֹנֶה עֶשְׂרֵה שָׁנָה, הַיְינוּ

הָכִי קָאָמַר לֵיהּ רַבִּי יוֹחָנָן לְרֵישׁ לָקִישׁ בִּשְׁלָמָא לְדִידִי דְּאָמִינָא רְאָיָה בְּקִיּוּם הַשְּׁטָר. וְאַפְּכִינָא נַמִי מַתְנִי' דְּלְרַבָּנַן אֵין צָרִיךְ לְקַיְּימוֹ כֵּיוָן דְּמוֹדֶה שֶׁכְּתָבוֹ – הַיְינוּ דְּמַשְׁכַּחַתְּ לְהוּ נִכְסֵי בִּידָא דְּלָקוֹחוֹת, וְאָתוּ יוֹרְשִׁין וְקָמְעַרְעֲרֵי, כִּדְאָמַר לְעֵיל: הָכִי נַמִי מִסְתַּבְּרָא מִדְּקָתָנֵי דְּאָמַר לְהוּ אִי אַתֶּם רַשָּׁאִין לְנַוְּולוֹ כו'. הִלְכָּךְ, שֶׁמָּא קִיְּימוּ שְׁטָר, אוֹ אֲפִילּוּ לֹא קִיְּימוּ, כֵּיוָן דְּמוֹדוּ בְּנֵי מִשְׁפָּחָה בִּשְׁטָר שֶׁכְּתָבוֹ נוֹתֵן – אֵין צָרִיךְ לְקַיְּימוֹ, וְהוּחְזְקוּ לָקוֹחוֹת בַּנְּכָסִים. אֶלָּא לְדִידָךְ דְּאָמְרַתְּ רְאָיָה בְּעֵדִים. וּלְדִידָךְ לָא מִתְהַפְּכָא מַתְנִי', וְכֵיוָן דְּאָמְרִי רַבָּנַן הַמּוֹצִיא מֵחֲבֵירוֹ עָלָיו הָרְאָיָה, דְּהַיְינוּ מְקַבֵּל מַתָּנָה – נִכְסֵי בִּידָא דְּלָקוֹחוֹת הֵיכִי מַשְׁכַּחַתְּ לַהּ? הָא לֵית לְהוּ עֵדִים שֶׁגָּדוֹל הָיָה! לָאו עִרְעוּר הוּא. וּמִן הַדִּין הוּחְזְקוּ לָקוֹחוֹת בַּנְּכָסִים. נַעֲשָׂה גָּדוֹל. נוֹתֵן וּמְקַבֵּל וְעֵדִים, כּוּלָּם גְּדוֹלִים וּכְשֵׁרִים. וּמַסְקָנָא דִּשְׁמַעְתָּא: מוֹדֶה בִּשְׁטָר שֶׁכְּתָבוֹ אֵין צָרִיךְ לְקַיְּימוֹ, כִּדְשְׁמוּאֵל וּכְר' יוֹחָנָן, לָא שְׁנָא הֵיכָא דְּאִיהוּ מֵרַע לֵיהּ לִשְׁטָרָא לְמֵימַר "שְׁטַר פַּסִּים הוּא" "שְׁטַר אֲמָנָה הוּא", לָא שְׁנָא הֵיכָא דְּעֵדִים מֵרְעִי לֵיהּ לוֹמַר "אֲנוּסִין הָיִינוּ", דְּהָא אַפְּכִינָא נַמִי הָכָא לְהַהִיא דִּכְתוּבּוֹת לְעֵיל, דְּאֵין נֶאֱמָנִין לְפָסְלוֹ כו'. קָטָן. הַיּוֹרֵשׁ נִכְסֵי אָבִיו שֶׁמֵּת. מֵאֵימָתַי מוֹכֵר בְּנִכְסֵי אָבִיו. בְּקַרְקְעוֹתָיו, וְתֶהֱוֵי מְכִירָתוֹ מְכִירָה. דְּאִילּוּ גַּבֵּי מִטַּלְטְלֵי תְּנַן (גיטין דף נט): הַפָּעוֹטוֹת מִקָּחָן מִקָּח וּמִמְכָּרָן מִמְכָּר בְּמִטַּלְטְלִין. וּמְפָרְשִׁינַן הָתָם: כְּבַר שִׁית כְּבַר שֶׁבַע, כָּל חַד לְפוּם חוּרְפֵּיהּ. וּמִשּׁוּם כְּדֵי חַיָּיו תַּקִּינוּ לֵיהּ רַבָּנַן בְּמִטַּלְטְלִין דְּתֶהֱוֵי מְכִירָה לִמְזוֹנוֹתָיו, אֲבָל בְּמְקַרְקְעֵי לָא. בֶּן שְׁמוֹנֶה עֶשְׂרֵה. וְיוֹם אֶחָד, דְּפָסְקִינַן לְקַמָּן: תּוֹךְ זְמַן כִּלְפְנֵי זְמַן. וְאַע"פ שֶׁאֵינוֹ יוֹדֵעַ בְּטִיב מַשָּׂא וּמַתָּן יָפֶה. כִּדְמוֹכַח לְקַמָּן בַּת י"ד שֶׁיּוֹדַעַת בְּטִיב מַשָּׂא וּמַתָּן מוֹכֶרֶת, וּכְגוֹן שֶׁהֵבִיאָה שְׁתֵּי שְׂעָרוֹת, כִּדְמוֹכַח לְקַמָּן.

אלא לדידך דאמרת ראיה בעדים נכסי ביד לקוחות היכי משכחת לה. דיביאו היורשין עדים שהיה קטן, (ג) ואם לא יוכלו למצוא, מאי מערערים היורשין? פסק רבינו שמואל, דקי"ל כרבי יוחנן ושמואל דאית להו הכא: מודה בשטר שכתבו אין צריך לקיימו. ואין נראה לר"י, אלא נראה לו דקי"ל כרב נחמן, דאית ליה בפרק שני דכתובות (דף יט. ושם): מודה בשטר שכתבו צריך לקיימו. דכוותיה קיימא לן בדיני, וכן פסק רבינו חננאל.

איתמר קטן אימתי מוכר בנכסי אביו. הכי גרסינן בספרים ישנים, וגם רבינו תם גריס כך: רבא אמר רב נחמן בן שמנה עשרה, רב הונא בר *חילבא אמר רב נחמן: בן עשרים. וגרסינן בתרה: והא דרבא לאו בפירוש איתמר אלא מכללא איתמר, דההוא (ד) דפחות מבן עשרים דזבין בנכסי דאבוה כו' עד אמר להו רבא: מדאסברוהו וסבר מידע הוי ידע, והא דעבד הכי חולפא יתירא הוה ביה. פירוש: הגיע זמנו למכור בנכסי אביו, ומתחלה היה סבור רבא שהיה שוטה, ולכך לא הוה מקחו מקח וממכרו ממכר. ולבסוף כיון דראה דאסברוהו וסבר — אם כן אינו שוטה לגמרי, כיון שהגיע זמנו למכור — יכול למכור. וא"ת: תקשה דרבא אדרבא, דהכא קאמר: בן שמנה עשרה, ואילו בגיטין פ' "התקבל" (דף סה.) גבי ג' מדות בקטן כו' קאמר רבא: ולמכור בנכסי אביו עד שיהא בן עשרים! ואומר ר"י: דנראה דגרסינן בההיא ד"התקבל": "רבה", חבירו של רב יוסף, שהיה רגיל לעשות מדות, כמו ההיא דסוף "המצניע" (שבת דף צה:) דחמש מדות בכלי חרס, דגרס התם "רבה" מדאמר ליה *(רב אסי: רבי) אתה אומר כן, דאילו רבא לא עלה לארץ ישראל כמו רבה. ומיהו, אין זו ראיה כל כך, כי גם רבא מצינו שהיה עושה מדות, דאמר רבא בגיטין פ' "הזורק" (דף עט.): שלש מדות בגיטין, ואמר רבא נמי פרק קמא דחולין (דף יז:) שלש מדות בסכין. אך לכאורה משמע דגרסינן התם "רבה" מכח הך קושיא דהכא כדפרישית. (ה) ואי גריס התם "רבה" — א"ש טפי בהכי הא דקאמר בג' מדות בקטן: הגיעו לעונת נדרים נדריהן נדר והקדשן הקדש, וכנגדן בקטנה חולצת. ואם כן משמע דאית ליה לרבה קטנה חולצת, ואילו בפ' "יוצא דופן" (נדה מו. ושם) אמר רבא: קטנה שהגיעה לכלל שנותיה — אינה צריכה בדיקה, חזקה הביאה סימנים. ומסיק התם: דוקא קאמר רבא לענין מיאון, אבל לחליצה — בעיא בדיקה. ואי גרס התם "רבה" — אתי שפיר. ורבינו שמואל תירץ שם: וכנגדו בקטנה חולצת — דהיינו בת (ו) שנים עשרה שנים ויום אחד, שהקטנה היא אז גדולה. ולא נהירא, דאם כן לא הוה ליה למימר ו"כנגדו בקטנה", אלא: וכנגדו חולצת. אלא משמע: שכנגדו קטנה שהגיעה לעונת נדרים, שהיא בת עשתי עשרה שנה ויום אחד. ורבינו תם תירץ: דודאי רבא סבר לה כדפסיק בפ' "מצות חליצה" (יבמות קה: ושם) ולקמן בשמעתין, דלחליצה בעי גדולה. ובגיטין איירי רבא אליבא דר' יוסי, דאמר קטנה חולצת. דאמרינן בפ' "מצות חליצה": לדברי ר' יוסי קטנה חולצת משהיא כפעוטות. רבא אמר: משתגיע לעונת נדרים. משמע דלדברי ר' יוסי קאמר, ואיהו סבירא ליה התם כמ"ד התם: והלכתא משתביא שתי שערות. ולספרים דגרסי כן בדרבא "עד שיהא בן עשרים" — הוי אתי שפיר ההיא דגיטין פ' "התקבל" (דף סה.). אך אותה גירסא אינה נראית כלל, שצריך למחוק הספרים דגרסי "והא דרבא לאו בפירוש איתמר אלא מכללא איתמר", שהרי הוא כתוב אחר שלא גידל בר מנשיא כו'. ופירש רבינו שמואל: (ז) היינו טעמא דאסברוהו ליה וסבר — אם כן חכם גדול היה וידע בטיב משא ומתן. משום דחייש לעובדא דגידל בר מנשיא אייתי ליה בתר הכי. ואין נראה כלל, וכי בשביל שהוא היה יודע לסבור זה היה חשוב חכם יודע בטיב משא ומתן? על כן נראה יותר גירסת ספרים ישנים. **מוכר** בנכסי אביו. פי' רבינו שמואל*: דדוקא בנכסי אביו, אבל בנכסים שקנה ושנתנו לו במתנה — יוכל למכור. וכן פי' רב אלפס, דבנכסים שקנה אין אנו חוששין אם מוכרן. והא דאמרינן לקמן: למקרקעי אין עדותן עדות — פירוש לשום קרקעות, כמו שאפרש בסמוך, דהיינו (ח) דדעתיה מיקרבא לגבי זוזי, ואינו בקי בשומא. ורבינו תם פירש: דהוא הדין נכסים שקנה אינו יכול למכור, מטעם דמיקרבא דעתיה לגבי זוזי. ומה שהקשה ר"י: שמא כשהוא שוטה זבין וכשהוא שוטה זבן — לאו קושיא היא, דטעמא לא משום שטות הוא, אלא משום דמיקרבא דעתיה לגבי זוזי. **מתיב** רבי זירא מעשה כו' באחד שמכר בנכסי אביו. פירוש: בזמן שהיה לו למכור, למר כדאית ליה ולמר כדאית ליה. דמסתמא קודם לכן לא מכר. והא סוגיא כמ"ד לעיל נכסי ביד לוקח הוו קיימי, ולהכי קאמר: כי בדקי ליה מאי הויא כו'. אבל למ"ד בחזקת יורשים הוו — לא הוה ליה למימר כי האי לישנא, אלא הוה ליה למימר: אמאי צריך בדיקה? פשיטא דגדול הוה. ולפי זה אין הוכחה גמורה דבזמן מכירה מכר. וריב"ם פירש: בשלמא למאן דאמר בן שמנה עשרה, ונכסי ביד לקוחות הוו קיימי, ואתו יורשים וקא מערערי לומר קטן היה. והיו צריכים להביא ראיה שהיה קטן, ולא מצאו עדים שהיה פחות משמנה עשרה. שאם מצאו — לא היו צריכים יותר, אפילו הביא שתי שערות לא עשה ולא כלום. אבל מצאו עדים שהיה פחות מבן עשרים, והיו רוצים לומר שמא לא הביא שתי שערות עדיין ועודנו קטן. אבל אם לא מצאו עדים שהעידו שהיה פחות מבן עשרים שנה — היינו מחזיקין אותו כגדול, דחזקה אין העדים חותמים על השטר אלא אם כן נעשה גדול, בן כ'. דליכא למימר דלא היו מחזיקים ליה בן כ' לפי שהיה סריס — הא ליכא למימר, דאם כן מאי פריך: אלא למאן דאמר בן כ' כי בדקי מאי הוי? טובא וטובא הוי, שאם אינו יודע בן כמה שנים הוא, דע"י חזקה דאין עדים חותמים אלא אם כן נעשה גדול בן עשרים לא הוה משוינן ליה סריס! אלא שמע מינה דעל ידי אותה חזקה משוינן ליה סריס. והשתא פריך שפיר: בשלמא למאן דאמר בן שמנה עשרה — היינו דקאמרי מהו לבודקו, אלא למאן דאמר בן עשרים כי בדיק ליה כו'. והאי קושיא אתיא להאי דאסיקנא לעיל: נכסי ביד לקוחות הוו קיימי, כדפרי' לעיל. מיהו, למאן דאמר בחזקת היורשים הוו קיימי — מצי למפרך שפיר: בשלמא למאן דאמר בן שמנה עשרה — היינו (ט) דקאמר מה לי לבודקו, שלאחר שהביא עדים שהוא בן שמנה עשרה היו היורשים טוענים שלא הביא שתי שערות עדיין וקטן היה, אפילו בן שמנה עשרה, ואין המכר כלום. אלא למאן דאמר בן עשרים, אפילו לא הביא שתי שערות היה גדול, ואין היורשים יכולים לטעון כלום. אבל הגמרא נקט לישנא למאי דאסיקנא דנכסי בחזקת לקוחות קיימי.

לאו

קנח א מיי' פכ"ט מהל' מכירה הלכה טז סמג עשין פב טוש"ע ח"מ סי' רלה סעיף ג:
קנט ב מיי' שם הלכה ט ופכ"ד מהל' מלוה ולוה הלכה ה סמג שם טוש"ע שם בהג"ה וסי' מו סעיף לח:
קס ג מיי' פכ"ט מהל' מכירה הלכה יג סמג עשין פב טוש"ע ח"מ סי' רלה סעיף ט:

רבינו גרשום

בשלמא לדידי דאמינא ראיה בקיום השטר. דאע"ג דמודה בשטר שכתבו צריך לקיימו היינו דמשכחת דנכסי בידא דלקוחות ובני משפחה היו מערערין להחזיק בהן והלקוחות קיימו שטרן ונחתו בנכסי: אלא לדידך דאמרת ראיה בעדים היכי משכחת לה דנחתי לקוחות לנכסי. והא אולי בתר עדים ולא אשכחן אלא ש"מ ראיה בקיום השטר. וריש לקיש אמר לעולם ראיה בעדים והכא טעמא מאי אזלינן בתר קיום השטר דמודינא לך דערער דבני משפחה לאו ערעור הוא. דמאי קאמרי קטן הוה לאו מילתא היא דחזקה אין עדים חותמין על השטר אא"כ נעשה המוכר או הנותן גדול: אתמר קטן אימתי מוכר בנכסי האב. דאמרי' מכירתו מכירה: [רבא] אמר רב נחמן בן כ' שנה ורב הונא אמר בן י"ח שנה. קס"ד מאן דאמר בן י"ח שנה צריך שיביא שתי שערות ולמאן דאמר בן כ' אע"ג דלא הביא ב' שערות מכירתו מכירה. בשלמא למאן דאמר מבן י"ח מכירתו מכירה בנכסי אביו ולא קודם האי קטן נמי דבני ברק מבן י"ח שנה היה ואיצטריך לבודקו בשערות.

[כתובות יט. סנהדרין כט:]

[ברכות ט. וש"נ]

[לעיל קנד.]

[לקמן קנו. סוף ד"ה והלכתא כר"נ ע"ש]

הגהות הב"ח

(א) גמ' בן עשרים כצ"ל ואות מ"ס נמחק: (ב) שם תיבות והא דרבא לאו בפירוש איתמר אלא מכללא איתמר נמחק: (ג) תוס' ד"ה אלא וכו' שהיה קטן וגם כשלא יכלו למצוא למה היו מערערים היורשים לבודקו כו' פסק: (ד) ד"ה איתמר וכו' דההוא פחות מבן עשרים דזבין וכו' וכיון שהגיע: (ה) בא"ד כדפרישית ותו דאי גריס התם רבה א"ש טפי בהכי והא דקאמר ג' מדות: (ו) בא"ד דהיינו בת שתים עשרה: (ז) בא"ד ופי' רבינו שמואל נמי היינו טעמא דכיון דאסברוהו ליה וכו' ומשום דשייך לעובדא דגידל בר מנשיא: (ח) ד"ה מוכר וכו' דהיינו מטעם דדעתיה מיקרבא: (ט) ד"ה מתיב וכו' היינו דקאמרי מהו לבודקו שלאחר שהביאו הלקוחות עדים:

קכז א טוש"ע ח"מ סי' קמ סעיף ג:

בשלמא לדידי דאמינא ראיה בעדים, כיון דאמר לקוחות איתו עדים ולא אשכחו — היינו דקא אתו ואמרו ליה: מהו לבודקו; אלא לדידך דאמרת ראיה בקיום השטר, למה להו לבודקו? לקיימו שטרייהו ולוקמו בנכסי! מי סברת: נכסי בחזקת בני משפחה קיימי, וקא אתו לקוחות ומערערי? נכסי בחזקת לקוחות קיימי, וקא אתו בני משפחה וקא מערערי. הכי נמי מסתברא, מדקאמר להו: אי אתם רשאים לנוולו, ואישתיקו; אי אמרת בשלמא בני משפחה קא מערערי, משום הכי אישתיקו, אלא אי אמרת לקוחות קא מערערי, אמאי שתקי? לימרו ליה: אנן זוזי יהבינן ליה, ליננוול ולינוול! אי משום הא לא איריא, הכי קאמר להו: חדא, דאי אתם רשאים לנוולו; ועוד, וכי תימרו זוזי שקל, ליננוול ולינוול — סימנים עשויין להשתנות לאחר מיתה. (ת"ש), שאל רבי שמעון בן לקיש את רבי יוחנן, זו ששנויה במשנת בר קפרא: הרי שהיה אוכל שדה ובא בחזקת שהיא שלו, וקרא עליו אחד ערער לומר: "שלי היא", והוציא זה את אונו לומר: "שמכרתה לי" או "שנתתה לי במתנה", אם אמר: "איני מכיר בשטר זה מעולם" — [א]יתקיים השטר בחותמיו. אם אמר: "שטר פסים הוא זה", או שטר אמנה, שמכרתי לך ולא נתת לי דמים", אם יש עדים — הלך אחר עדים, ואם לאו — הלך אחר השטר; לימא, ר' מאיר היא, דאמר: מודה בשטר שכתבו אינו צריך לקיימו, ולא רבנן? אמר ליה: לא, שאני אומר: דברי הכל — מודה בשטר שכתבו אינו צריך לקיימו. והא מיפלג פליגי! [א]דתנן: [ב]אין נאמנין לפוסלו, דברי ר' מאיר, וחכמים אומרים: נאמנין! אמר ליה: אי עדים אלימי ומרעי שטרא, איהו כל כמיניה? אמר ליה, והלא משמך אמרו: יפה ערערו בני משפחה! אמר ליה: זו אלעזר אמרה, אני לא אמרתי דבר זה מעולם. אמר רבי זירא: אם יכפור רבי יוחנן ברבי אלעזר תלמידו, יכפור ברבי ינאי רבו? דאמר רבי ינאי אמר רבי: מודה בשטר שכתבו (אינו) צריך לקיימו, ואמר ליה רבי יוחנן: רבי, לא משנתנו היא זו? וחכמים אומרים: המוציא מחבירו עליו הראיה, אין ראיה אלא בקיום השטר! ברם נראין דברי רבינו יוסף, דאמר רבינו יוסף אמר רב יהודה אמר שמואל: זו דברי חכמים, אבל רבי מאיר אומר: מודה בשטר שכתבו שצריך לקיימו. (א) ומאי "דברי הכל"? דרבנן לגבי רבי מאיר דברי הכל היא. והא איפכא תנן, וחכמים אומרים: המוציא מחבירו עליו הראיה! איפוך. והא תניא: אין נאמנין לפוסלו, דברי רבי מאיר, וחכמים אומרים: נאמנין! איפוך. והא רבי יוחנן ראיה בעדים קאמר! איפוך. לימא, ליפוך נמי תיובתא? לא, הכי

בשלמא לדידי דאמינא ראיה. דאמרי רבנן במתני' המוציא מחבירו עליו הראיה – היינו ראיה בעדים שבריא היה, ויגבה מתנתו מיד היורשין – ה"נ בקשו לקוחות לעשות כך, ולבקש עדים כדי לטרוף מקמן מיד היורשין, וכיון דלא אשכחו כו'. לקיימו שטרייהו. ומסתמא אין העדים חותמין על השטר אא"כ נעשה גדול. בחזקת לקוחות הוו קיימי. והחזיקו בהן קודם ערעור. ואתו יורשין וקא מערערי. ואמרי: קטן היה, ושלא כדין תפסתם. דהתם גבי יורשין לא שייך קיום שטריה. היינו דשתקי. כדי שלא לינוול קרובם. לינוול ולינוול. אין אנו חוששין בבשתו, שאינו קרובנו, והפסדנו מרובה. ה"ג: זו ששנויה כו'. ואסיפא קאי, לימא ר"מ היא כו'. שטר פסים. שפייסת ממני לכתוב לך שטר מכירה, להחזיקך בעשיר לוקח קרקעות. שטר אמנה. האמנתיך למסור לך שטר מכירה קודם שקבלתי הדמים. שאני אומר לדברי הכל כו'. כדמפרש לקמיה, דכי פליגי רבנן ואמרי מודה בשטר שכתבו שצריך לקיימו – הני מילי היכא דאיכא עדים דמרעי ליה לשטרא ופוסלין חתימת עצמן – ה"ז פסול גדול, הלכך אע"ג דמודה לוה שכתבו – צריך לקיימו. אבל בהך דבר קפרא, דלוה גופיה קפסיל ליה ולא עדים, כיון דמודה שכתבו – לאו כל כמיניה למימר שטר פסים הוא, והכל מודים שא"צ לקיימו. אי עדים אלימי כו'. דהתם אמרי עדים: פסולי עדות היינו. איהו כל כמיניה. בתמיה, וכי יש כח ביד הלוה לומר "איני חייב כלום" והכא לא אמרי': הפה שאסר הוא הפה שהתיר, דכיון דאמר לוה: כתבתי שטר זה, אלא שטר פסים או שטר אמנה הוא. ד"מה לי לשקר" במקום עדים לא אמרינן. דאנן סהדי דלאו שטר אמנה הוא, דעדים אשטר אמנה ופסים לא חתמי, דלא ניתן ליכתב כדאמר בפרק ב' דכתובות (דף יט.), והלכך לא מהימן למימר שטר אמנה הוא. והלא אמרו משמך כו'. ריש לקיש קא"ל לר' יוחנן: היכי מצית למימר דלדברי הכל מודה בשטר שכתבו א"צ לקיימו, אף על גב דאיהו נמי פסיל ליה משום שטר אמנה או שטר פסים, דלאו כל כמיניה לאורועיה איהו כל זמן דעדים גופייהו לא מרעי ליה? והלא משמך אמרו: יפה ערערו בני משפחה! אע"ג דמודו בני משפחה בשטר שכתב נותן מתנה, כיון דאמרי קטן היה – נאמנין, עד שיתקיים השטר בחותמיו. אלמא מודה בשטר שכתבו לדידך צריך לקיימו! ויכפור בר' ינאי. בתמיה, והלא לר' ינאי רבו א"ר יוחנן בהדיא צריך לקיימו! ברם נראין דברי רבינו יוסף. ר' זירא קא"ל. ואתא לתרוצי דמאי דא"ר יוחנן לריש לקיש לעיל "שאני אומר לדברי הכל א"צ לקיימו" – היינו טעמא: דס"ל לר' יוחנן דמתהפכינן מתניתין ר"מ לרבנן, דס"ל לרבנן א"צ לקיימו, כדמפרש ואזיל. והאי דקא"ר יוחנן "לדברי הכל א"צ לקיימו" – לאו דווקא, אלא משום דאליבא דרבנן קאמר דא"צ לקיימו, חשיב ליה כלדברי הכל. זו דברי חכמים. מתני' דמוכח א"צ לקיימו. נמי תיובתא. דקאמר לעיל: איתיביה ר' יוחנן לר"ש בן לקיש וכו' – ליפוך, והשתא צריך לומר "איתיביה ריש לקיש לר' יוחנן", דמהא שמעינן דמתניתין ראיה בעדים קאמר! הכי

ואם תאמר: למה יש לנו לומר שהוא קטן, כיון שהגיע לכלל שנותיו? והא אמרינן בנדה פרק "בא סימן" (דף מח.): קטנה שהגיעה לכלל שנותיה — אינה צריכה בדיקה, חזקה הביאה סימנים! וי"ל: שאמר שהיה זה גדול שהגיע לכלל שנותיו, ולא היו לו סימני גדלות, ולהכי איכא לספוקי שמא קטן היה עדיין. **אלא** לדידך דאמרת (ג) בקיום השטר לקיימו שטרייהו ולוקמו בנכסייהו. דמסתמא, כיון שאמת היה שמכר — היו מוצאים עדים לקיים שטרם. אלא ש"מ שהיו צריכין לבקש עדים שהיה גדול בשעת המכר, וכרבנן, דאמרי המוציא מחבירו עליו הראיה. וא"ת: ומאי קושיא? עד כאן לא קאמרי רבנן ראיה בקיום השטר אלא משום דסבירא להו כרבי נתן, דאמר דאזלינן בתר השתא, דאם בריא הוא עתה — יש לנו לומר שאז היה בריא. אבל הכא לא שייכא שום חזקה! וי"ל, דאיכא למימר: חזקה שאין עדים חותמים על השטר אא"כ נעשה גדול, מהניא כי ההיא חזקה דבתר השתא אזלינן. **בחזקת** לקוחות הוו קיימי. והיורשים היו רוצים להוציאן מידן, והיו רוצים לבודקו אם הוא קטן. והשתא ניחא הא דקאמר להו: סימנין עשויין להשתנות לאחר מיתה. שאפילו לא תמצאו לו סימנים — איכא למימר שנשרו לאחר מיתה. **זוזי** יהבינן לינוול ולינוול. אבל יורשים אינם רשאים לנוולו בשביל הירושה, דלא מידי יהבי. ועוד, שהוא קרובם. **אי** עדים אלימי ומרעי שטרא כו'. לעיל בפ' "חזקת הבתים" (דף מח: ושם ד"ה אמר) הבאתי שם הך מילתא גבי "מודעא היו דברינו" וכו'. **והלא** משמך אמרו יפה ערערו בני משפחה. מטעם קיום השטר, ולא מטעם עדים. **ברם** נראין דברי רבינו יוסף כו'. (ג) והא דפריך לעיל ריש לקיש לר' יוחנן ממשנת בר קפרא, וא"ל ר' יוחנן: שאני אומר מודה בשטר שכתבו א"צ לקיימו — לא אמר דבר זה מעולם. וכולה סוגיא דלעיל ליתא לפי מסקנא זו. וכה"ג איכא ביבמות בפ' "החולץ" (דף לה: ושם ד"ה כ"ע) דפריך ליה ר' יוחנן לריש לקיש, ולמסקנא מעמיד מחלוקתם בענין אחר, גבי החולץ למעוברת. וכן בפ"ק דחגיגה (דף ז.) גבי הראיון, ובנדה פ' "המפלת" (דף כד.) גבי פניו מוסמסים. וכי א"ל ר' יוחנן לר' ינאי לעיל: רבי, לא משנתנו היא זו — לא הקשה ממילתא דרבנן, אלא הזכיר לו המשנה, דפלוגתא דרבנן ורבי מאיר היא בהא. [וע"ע תוס' בכורות ד: ד"ה אלא].

אלא

רבינו גרשום

בשלמא לדידי דאמינא. דמייתי ראיה בעדים הכא נמי עבדי הני דבדקו בתר עדים אם כשמכר קטן היה אי לא ולא אשכחן משום הכי אזלו ושאילו מהו לבודקו: אלא לדידך דאמרת ראיה בקיום השטר. אמאי אזלי לקוחות למישאל מהו לבודקו יקיימו שטרייהו דבידייהו דליתו סהדי דמכירין חתימת ידי העדים ובודאי אותן החתומין על השטר לא חתמו א) אא"כ היה גדול ובתר הכי לוקמי לקוחות בנכסייהו אלא ש"מ מדלא עבדי הכי דלא אזלינן בתר קיום השטר אלא בתר עדים וקשיא לר"ל. אמר לך ר"ל לעולם בתר קיום השטר אזלינן ודקא קשיא לך הכא אמאי לא אזלינן בתר קיום השטר אלא בתר עדים. מי סברת דנכסים שמכר שעדיין בידא דמשפחה הוו ואתו לקוחות וקא מערערי אי הוי עובדא הכי מצית למפרך שפיר. לאו הכי הוי עובדא אלא נכסי הוו כבר ביד לקוחות (דלקוחות הוה) ולא מצו בני משפחה למיזל בתר קיום השטר ומאי הוי זכותייהו קיום השטר. ובני משפחה אינהו קא מערערי דקטן הוה ומשום הכי אזלי מעיקרא בתר עדים כי לא אשכחו אמרי מהו לבודקו: ה"נ מסתברא. דבני משפחה הוי מערערי ולא לקוחות: מדקאמר להו אי אתם רשאים לנוולו ואשתיקו. משום דמשפחתו הוה לא היו רוצים לנוולו: לקוחות אמאי משתקי. מצי למימר ליה הואיל דזוזי יהיבנא ליה בהא ארעא לינוול ולינוול אלא ש"מ דנכסים בידא דלקוחות הוו ובני משפחה מערערי. אמר לך ר' יוחנן לעולם אכתי קשיא ליה לר"ל ונכסים בידא דיורשין הוי קיימי והא דקא מייתי ראיה מהכא. אי משום הא לא אריא דהכי קאמר להו: במשנת בר קפרא. שהיה שונה בה: והוציא זה. המוחזק בשדה: את אונו. כח שלו שטר מכירה שהיה בידו: יתקיים השטר בחותמיו. שיעידו שנים עליהן שהוא כתב ידן ולא מחזקינן לעדים בשקרי דחתימי מילי דשקר: ואם אמר. המערער: שטר פסים הוא. שפייסתני בשעה שהיית רוצה לישא אשה שאכתוב לך שטר ששדה מכורה לך בעבור אותו [שטר] יהיו סבורין כך שאתה עשיר וקונה נכסי' ומעולם שוב לא החזרתה אותו לי ולא שלך היא השדה: או שטר אמנה הוא. שמכרתי לך שדה זו על מנת שאאמין לך הדמים עד זמן שקבענו ומעולם לא נתת לי דמים: ואם יש לו עדים. שכן הוא כמו שמערער אומר הלך אחר עדים: ג) והוא מודה בשטר שכתבו לזה אינו צריך לקיימו עוד לאותו מוחזק ולא ישלם למערער כלום: לימא. דבר קפרא ששנה משנה זו לפלוגתא אמרה לשמעתא ואליבא דר' מאיר דאמר הואיל ומודה הוא האי מערער באותו שכתב אין צריך לקיימו ומקוים ועומד הוא ומשום הכי אמר הלך אחר השטר: והא מיפלגי. במודה בשטר שכתב אם צריך לקיימו אי לא כדמפרש לעיל: אין נאמנין לפוסלו דברי ר' מאיר. משום דמודה בשטר שכתבו אינו צריך לקיימו: וחכ"א דנאמנין וצריך לקיימו אלמא דבפלוגתא אמר בר קפרא לשמעתיה: א"ל ר' יוחנן. לדברי הכל אמרה לשמעתיה דמודה בשטר שכתבו אין צריך לקיימו ואזלינן בתר השטר. והתם טעמא מאי אמור רבנן דמודה בשטר שחתמוהו צריך לקיימו משום דעדים אלימי אינון דמצי לאורועי שטרא שהם חתמוהו ונאמנין הן לפוסלו אבל הכא להיכא דמערער מודה שכתבו ואמר שטר פסים הוא שטר אמנה הוא אפי' רבנן מודו דלאו כל כמיניה לאורועי שטרא ומשום הכי אינו צריך לקיימו והלך אחר השטר: א"ל. ריש לקיש לר' יוחנן והיכי מצית למימר דלדברי הכל אמרה לשמעתיה ולאו כל כמיניה לאורועי שטרא: והלא משמך אמרו יפה ערערו. ואמאי יפה ערערו. והלא כיון ג) שהוא מודה שאותן בני משפחתן כתבו הא איכא למימר לאו כל כמינייהו לאורועי שטרא ולומר קטן היה ואמאי יפה ערערו: א"ל. לעולם מודה בשטר שכתבו אין צריך לקיימו דלאו כל כמיניה לאורועי שטרא וזו ששמעת משמי אלעזר תלמידי אמרה ולא משמי אמרה: אם יכפור ר' יוחנן בר' אלעזר תלמידו יכפור בר' ינאי רבו. בתמיה גרסי': דאמר ר' ינאי מודה בשטר שכתבו (אין) צריך לקיימו דלאו כל כמיניה לאורועי שטרא: ואמר [ליה] ר' יוחנן רבי לא משנתנו היא זו. דמודה בשטר שכתבו צריך לקיימו דקתני וחכ"א המוציא מחבירו עליו הראיה ואין ראיה אלא בקיום השטר דאע"ג דהאי נותן מתנה מודה בשטר שכתבו אפ"ה איצטריך לקיימו למקבל. אלמא דס"ל לר' יוחנן מודה בשטר שכתבו צריך לקיימו לרבנן והדרא קושיין לדוכתה דלימא בר קפרא כר' מאיר ולא כרבנן: ברם נראין דברי רבינו יוסף. תירוץ הוא דקא מתרץ והכי מתפרש לעולם אימא לך בר קפרא כחכמים אמרה לשמעתיה דנראין דברי רבינו יוסף אמר רב יהודה אמר שמואל זו דברי חכמים דאמרי עליו הראיה ששכיב מרע היה מאי טעמא משום דכיון דמודה הוא בשטר שכתבו אין צריך למקבל לקיימו לפיכך צריך זה הנותן להביא ראיה ששכיב מרע היה. אבל ר' מאיר היה אומר המוציא מחבירו עליו הראיה דקסבר מודה בשטר שכתבו צריך לקיימו ועל זה המוציא להביא ראיה וכרבנן היה משנת בר קפרא: והא איפכא. שמעינן להו במתני' דר' מאיר סבר עליו להביא ראיה לשכיב מרע וחכ"א המוציא וכו' דר' מאיר סבר מודה בשטר שכתבו אין צריך לקיימו ואכתי כר"מ אמרה לשמעתיה ולא כרבנן: איפוך. ותני ליה רבינו יוסף: והתניא וכו' וחכ"א כו' נאמנין. דמשמע מודה שכתבו צריך לקיימו ואכתי קשיא: איפוך. הכי נאמנין דברי ר' מאיר וחכ"א אין נאמנין דאין צריך לקיימו והשתא איתרצא משנת בר קפרא אליבא דחכמים: ומקשי' דר' יוחנן אדר' יוחנן. דאמר לעיל אין ראיה אלא בקיום השטר דסבירא ליה מודה בשטר שכתבו צריך לקיימו והאמר ר' יוחנן ראיה [בעדים]: איפוך. הכי ר' יוחנן אמר ראיה בקיום השטר וריש לקיש אמר ראיה בעדים. ומקשי' הואיל דמהפכת למילתייהו ליבעי נמי להפך ההיא תיובתא דמותיב ר' יוחנן לריש לקיש וליפוך הכי איתיביה ריש לקיש לר' יוחנן דאמר ראיה בקיום השטר מעשה בבני ברק כו' לא תיפוך לתיובתא דר' יוחנן מקשי ליה לריש לקיש והכי מותיב לה ר' יוחנן לריש לקיש

בשלמא

א) [נ"ל דתניא:] ב) [כתובות יח:]

הגהות הב"ח

(א) גמ' שצריך לקיימו (ומאי דברי הכל דרבנן לגבי ר"מ דברי הכל היא) תא"מ ונ"ב לפי פי' התוספות לא גרסי' ליה: (ב) תוס' ד"ה אלא לדידך דאמרת ראיה בקיום וכו' וי"ל כיון דאיכא למימר הכא חזקה שאין: (ג) ד"ה ברם וכו' והא דפריך. נ"ב נראה דקשה להו מאי פריך ר"ל לר"י לימא ר"מ היא כו' הלא למאי דמיתהפכא רבנן היא ולא ר"מ וא"כ למה השיב ר"י שאני אומר ד"ה מודה בשטר שכתבו א"צ לקיימו וקאמר נמי אי עדים אלימי וכו' לימא דלרבנן בכל דוכתא אמרי' דמודה בשטר שכתבו א"צ לקיימו ע"כ צריך לפרש דכולה סוגיא דלעיל ליתא וא"ה לדרבי יוחנן בכל דוכתא א"צ לקיימו כחכמים דס"ל מודה בשטר שכתבו א"צ לקיימו והא דהוצרך תלמודא להפך דברי ר"י ולא קא משני דרבי יוחנן אליבא דרבי מאיר קאמר אלמא דס"ל לתלמודא דרבי יוחנן [אליבא דחכמים קאמר] א"כ אף למאי דמיתהפכא נמי קשיא היאך אמר רבי יוחנן ראיה בקיום השטר והלא הלכה כחכמים דא"צ לקיימו וי"ל [הא דקאמר ראיה בקיום השטר היינו] אם אינו מודה שכתבו ופלוגתייהו אש"מ דעלמא קאי ולא אפלוגתא דרבי מאיר וחכמים דמתניתין [והשאר חסר]:

א) עי' בתוס' כאן בד"ה אלא וי"ל דאיכא למימר חזקה שאין עדים וכו' וי"ל דרבינו ג"כ כוון בזה לתרץ הקושיא. ב) ואם לאו הלך אחר השטר. והוא מודה וכו' כצ"ל. ג) נראה דצ"ל והלא כיון שאותן בני המשפחה מודים שהוא כתבו הא איכא למימר וכו'.

רְאָיָה בְּמַאי? רַב הוּנָא אָמַר: רְאָיָה בְּעֵדִים; רַב חִסְדָּא וְרַבָּה בַּר רַב הוּנָא אָמְרִי: רְאָיָה בְּקִיּוּם הַשְּׁטָר. רַב הוּנָא אָמַר [א]רְאָיָה בְּעֵדִים, קָא מִיפַּלְגִי בִּפְלוּגְתָּא דְּר' יַעֲקֹב וְרַבִּי נָתָן, (סִימָן: מַנִּיחַ) רַבִּי מֵאִיר כְּרַבִּי נָתָן, וְרַבָּנַן כְּרַבִּי יַעֲקֹב; רַב חִסְדָּא וְרַבָּה בַּר רַב הוּנָא אָמְרִי רְאָיָה בְּקִיּוּם הַשְּׁטָר, קָא מִיפַּלְגִי [א)]בְּמוֹדֶה בִּשְׁטָר שֶׁכְּתָבוֹ צָרִיךְ לְקַיְּימוֹ, דְּר"מ סָבַר: מוֹדֶה בִּשְׁטָר שֶׁכְּתָבוֹ — אֵינוֹ צָרִיךְ לְקַיְּימוֹ, וְרַבָּנַן סָבְרִי: [ב]מוֹדֶה בִּשְׁטָר שֶׁכְּתָבוֹ — צָרִיךְ לְקַיְּימוֹ. וְהָא אִיפְּלִיגוּ בָּהּ חֲדָא זִימְנָא! [ב)]דְּתַנְיָא: אֵין נֶאֱמָנִין לְפוֹסְלוֹ, דִּבְרֵי רַבִּי מֵאִיר, וַחֲכָמִים אוֹמְרִים: [ג]נֶאֱמָנִין! צְרִיכָא, דְּאִי אִיתְּמַר הַהִיא, בְּהַהִיא קָאָמְרִי רַבָּנַן, מִשּׁוּם דְּאַלִּימֵי עֵדִים וּמַרְעֵי שְׁטָרָא, אֲבָל הָכָא, הוּא דְּלָאו כָּל כְּמִינֵּיהּ — אֵימָא לָא; וְאִי אִיתְּמַר בְּהָא, בְּהָא קָאָמַר ר' מֵאִיר, אֲבָל בְּהַךְ אֵימָא מוֹדֶה לְהוּ לְרַבָּנַן, צְרִיכָא. וְכֵן אָמַר רַבָּה: רְאָיָה בְּעֵדִים. א"ל אַבַּיֵי: מַאי טַעֲמָא? אִי נֵימָא, מִדְּכוּלְּהוּ כְּתִיב בְּהוּ "כַּד הֲוָה מְהַלֵּךְ עַל רַגְלוֹהִי בְּשׁוּקָא", וּבְהָא לָא כְּתִיב בָּהּ — שְׁמַע מִינָּהּ שְׁכִיב מְרַע הָוֵי. אַדְּרַבָּה, מִדְּכוּלְּהוּ כְּתִיב בְּהוּ: "כַּד קְצִיר וּרְמֵי בְּעַרְסֵיהּ", וְהָא לָא כְּתִיב בָּהּ — שְׁמַע מִינָּהּ בָּרִיא הָוֵי! אִיכָּא לְמֵימַר הָכִי וְאִיכָּא לְמֵימַר הָכִי, [ג)]אוֹקֵי מָמוֹנָא בְּחֶזְקַת מָרֵיהּ. וּבִפְלוּגְתָּא, דְּרַבִּי יוֹחָנָן אָמַר: רְאָיָה בְּעֵדִים, וְר' שִׁמְעוֹן בֶּן לָקִישׁ אָמַר: רְאָיָה בְּקִיּוּם הַשְּׁטָר. אֵיתִיבֵיהּ רַבִּי יוֹחָנָן לְרַבִּי שִׁמְעוֹן בֶּן לָקִישׁ: [ד)][ד]מַעֲשֶׂה בִּבְנֵי בְרַק בְּאֶחָד שֶׁמָּכַר בְּנִכְסֵי אָבִיו וּמֵת, (א) וּבָאוּ בְּנֵי מִשְׁפָּחָה וְעִרְעֲרוּ לוֹמַר: קָטָן הָיָה בִּשְׁעַת מִיתָה, וּבָאוּ וְשָׁאֲלוּ אֶת רַבִּי עֲקִיבָא: מַהוּ לְבוֹדְקוֹ? אָמַר לָהֶם: [ה]אִי אַתֶּם רַשָּׁאִים לְנַוְּולוֹ; וְעוֹד, סִימָנִין עֲשׂוּיִין לְהִשְׁתַּנּוֹת לְאַחַר מִיתָה; בִּשְׁלָמָא

רְאָיָה בְּמַאי. בֵּין לְרַבָּנַן בֵּין לְר"מ קָבָעֵי. וּמִשּׁוּם דְּאִיכָּא לְפָרְשָׁהּ בִּתְרֵי גַּוְונֵי כִּדְלְקַמָּן, קָבָעֵי הָכִי. רְאָיָה בְּעֵדִים. כִּדְמְפָרֵשׁ לְקַמֵּיהּ. ר"מ כְּר' נָתָן וְרַבָּנַן כְּר' יַעֲקֹב. ר"מ אָזֵיל בָּתַר הַשְׁתָּא כְּר' נָתָן, וּמַתְנִיתִין כְּגוֹן שֶׁהוּא בָּרִיא עַכְשָׁיו. וְהָכִי קָאָמַר מַתְנִי': אָמַר שכ"מ הָיִיתִי וְעַכְשָׁיו אֲנִי בָּרִיא, וְחוֹזְרַנִי בִּי. וְהֵן אוֹמְרִים בָּרִיא הָיִיתָ — עָלָיו לְהָבִיא רְאָיָה בְּעֵדִים שֶׁשְּׁכִיב מְרַע הָיָה. וחכ"א: הַנּוֹתֵן מוּחְזָק הוּא בַּנְּכָסִים, וְעַל הַמְקַבֵּל מַתָּנָה שֶׁהוּא מוֹצִיא מֵחֲבֵירוֹ — עָלָיו הָרְאָיָה, בְּעֵדִים שֶׁיָּבִיא שֶׁבָּרִיא הָיָה. רְאָיָה בְּקִיּוּם הַשְּׁטָר. רְאָיָה שֶׁאָמְרוּ חֲכָמִים הַמּוֹצִיא מֵחֲבֵירוֹ עָלָיו הָרְאָיָה — בְּקִיּוּם הַשְּׁטָר קָאָמְרִי רַבָּנַן, שֶׁצָּרִיךְ לְקַיֵּים שְׁטָרוֹ, שֶׁלֹּא יוּכַל נוֹתֵן לִטְעוֹן וְלוֹמַר מְזוּיָּף הוּא. וְכֵיוָן דְּנִתְקַיֵּים שֶׁלֹּא ע"פ הַנּוֹתֵן, דְּאֵין כָּאן הַפֶּה שֶׁאָסַר הוּא הַפֶּה שֶׁהִתִּיר, שֶׁהֲרֵי לֹא נִתְקַיֵּים ע"פ הַנּוֹתֵן דְּנֵימָא מִיגּוֹ — יָבֹא בַּעַל הַשְּׁטָר וְיִזְכֶּה בְּמַתְּנָתוֹ. דְּכ"ע אָזְלִינַן בָּתַר הַשְׁתָּא כְּרַבָּה וְרַבִּי נָתָן, וְכֵיוָן דְּבָרִיא הוּא עַכְשָׁיו — זָכָה בַּעַל הַשְּׁטָר. אַךְ יְקַיֵּים שְׁטָרוֹ, שֶׁלֹּא יוּכַל נוֹתֵן לְפָסְלוֹ. אֲבָל רְאָיָה דְּר"מ — רְאָיָה בְּעֵדִים הִיא, כִּדְמְפָרֵשׁ: עָלָיו לְהָבִיא רְאָיָה שֶׁשכ"מ הָיָה, דִּבְרֵי ר"מ. בְּמוֹדֶה. לֹוֶה בִּשְׁטָר שֶׁכְּתָבוֹ וְאֵינוֹ מְזוּיָּף, אֶלָּא שֶׁטּוֹעֵן: פְּרַעְתִּיו, אוֹ: שכ"מ הָיִיתִי, אוֹ: שְׁטַר אֲמָנָה אוֹ שְׁטַר פַּסִּים הוּא. צָרִיךְ הַמַּלְוֶה לְקַיְּימוֹ. ע"פ אֲחֵרִים, שֶׁלֹּא יוּכַל לֹוֶה לְפָסְלוֹ בְּמִיגּוֹ, קָמִיפַּלְגִי. ר"מ סָבַר א"צ לְקַיְּימוֹ. דִּסְתָם שְׁטָרוֹת הֲרֵי הֵם כְּשֵׁרִים, וּבִשְׁטָרוֹת לָא נֵימָא הַפֶּה שֶׁאָסַר הוּא הַפֶּה שֶׁהִתִּיר לְפָסְלוֹ. וְהָכִי קָאָמַר מַתְנִי': צָרִיךְ לְהָבִיא רְאָיָה בְּעֵדִים שֶׁשכ"מ הָיָה, דִּבְרֵי ר"מ. מֵאַחַר שֶׁמּוֹדֶה הוּא בַּשְּׁטָר שֶׁכְּתָבוֹ, וְנִתְקַיֵּים הַשְּׁטָר בְּכָךְ, דְּאָזְלִינַן בָּתַר הַשְׁתָּא שֶׁהוּא בָּרִיא כְּר' נָתָן. וחכ"א: הַמּוֹצִיא מֵחֲבֵירוֹ, שֶׁהוּא בַּעַל הַשְּׁטָר, צָרִיךְ לְהָבִיא רְאָיָה — קִיּוּם הַשְּׁטָר, שֶׁיִּתְקַיֵּים בְּחוֹתְמָיו. דְּהוֹדָאַת נוֹתֵן שֶׁטּוֹעֵן כְּתַבְתִּיו — לָא מְהַנְּיָא מִידֵּי, דְּהָא קָאָמַר: שכ"מ הָיִיתִי, וְהַפֶּה שֶׁאָסַר הוּא הַפֶּה שֶׁהִתִּיר. וְהִלְכָּךְ צָרִיךְ בַּעַל הַשְּׁטָר לְקַיְּימוֹ וְיִזְכֶּה בְּמַתְּנָתוֹ, דְּאָזְלִינַן בָּתַר הַשְׁתָּא שֶׁהוּא בָּרִיא, כְּר' נָתָן. וּמִתְּרֵי לִישָּׁנֵי וּמִתְּרֵי אֲמוֹרָאֵי שָׁמְעִינַן דְּאָזְלִינַן בָּתַר הַשְׁתָּא כְּרַבָּה וְר' נָתָן, כִּדְפְרִישִׁית. וְהָא אִיפְּלִיגוּ בָּהּ חֲדָא זִימְנָא. בְּמוֹדֶה בַּשְּׁטָר שֶׁכְּתָבוֹ צָרִיךְ לְקַיְּימוֹ. דְּתַנְיָא. בְּפֶרֶק ב' דִּכְתוּבּוֹת. אֵין נֶאֱמָנִין כו'. דִּתְנַן הָתָם: הָעֵדִים שֶׁאָמְרוּ "כְּתַב יָדֵינוּ הוּא זֶה אֲבָל אֲנוּסִים הָיִינוּ, קְטַנִּים הָיִינוּ, פְּסוּלִים הָיִינוּ" — הֲרֵי אֵלּוּ נֶאֱמָנִין, שֶׁהַפֶּה שֶׁאָסַר הוּא הַפֶּה שֶׁהִתִּיר. וְתַנְיָא בַּגְּמָרָא: אֵין נֶאֱמָנִין לְפָסְלוֹ, דִּבְרֵי ר"מ, וּפָלֵיג אַמַּתְנִי' דְּלָא חָיֵישׁ לְהַפֶּה שֶׁאָסַר גַּבֵּי שְׁטָרוֹת, דְּלָא נֶחְשְׁדוּ יִשְׂרָאֵל עַל כָּךְ. וּמְפָרֵשׁ הָתָם בְּמַסְקָנָא טַעֲמָא, דְּקָסָבַר ר"מ מוֹדֶה בִּשְׁטָר שֶׁכְּתָבוֹ לֹוֶה שֶׁא"צ מַלְוֶה לְקַיְּימוֹ. (ג) וְכֵיוָן שֶׁאָמַר לֹוֶה "אֲנִי כְּתַבְתִּיו" — תּוּ לָא מְהֵימְנֵי עֵדִים לְמִפְסְלֵיהּ, שֶׁהֲרֵי אֵין לְךָ קִיּוּם גָּדוֹל מִזֶּה שֶׁהַלֹּוֶה מוֹדֶה שֶׁכְּתָבוֹ. דְּמִסְתָּמָא לֹא נַעֲשָׂה בִּפְסָלוּת, וּכְמוֹ שֶׁכָּתַב יָדוֹ יוֹצֵא מִמָּקוֹם אַחֵר דָּמֵי, דִּתְנַן הָתָם: אֵין נֶאֱמָנִין, דְּאֵין כָּאן הַפֶּה שֶׁאָסַר. וַחכ"א נֶאֱמָנִין. דְּאע"ג דְּמוֹדֶה לֹוֶה שֶׁכְּתָבוֹ — צָרִיךְ לְקַיְּימוֹ. וְכֵיוָן שֶׁאֵינוֹ מִתְקַיֵּים כִּי אִם ע"פ עֵדִים הַלָּלוּ, שֶׁאוֹמְרִים כְּתַב יָדֵינוּ הוּא זֶה — הָא קָאָמְרֵי נַמִי קְטַנִּים הָיִינוּ, וְנֶאֱמָנִים, דְּהַפֶּה שֶׁאָסַר הוּא הַפֶּה שֶׁהִתִּיר. בְּהַהִיא קָאָמְרִי רַבָּנַן. דְּאע"ג שֶׁמּוֹדֶה לֹוֶה שֶׁכְּתָבוֹ — לָא חָשִׁיב כְּקִיּוּם, כֵּיוָן דְּעֵדִים עַצְמָן פּוֹסְלִין חֲתִימָתָן, מִשּׁוּם דְּאַלִּימֵי עֵדִים לְאוֹרוּעֵי שְׁטָרָא, וְלָא מְהַנְּיָא הוֹדָאַת לֹוֶה. אֲבָל בְּמַתְנִי' אֵימָא: לָאו כָּל כְּמִינֵּיהּ לְאוֹרוּעֵי שְׁטָרָא וּלְמֵימַר שכ"מ הָיָה, כֵּיוָן דְּמוֹדֶה שֶׁכְּתָבוֹ, וְעֵדִים לָא קָא פָּסְלֵי חֲתִימָתָן. אֵילֵימָא. הַיְינוּ טַעֲמַיְיהוּ דְּרַבָּנַן, מִדְּכוּלְּהוּ מַתְּנוֹת בָּרִיא כְּתִיב בְּהוּ "כַּד מְהַלֵּךְ עַל רַגְלוֹהִי בְּשׁוּקָא" וְהַאי לָא כְּתִיב בֵּיהּ — ש"מ שכ"מ הָיָה, וְהִלְכָּךְ אָמְרֵי רַבָּנַן: הַמּוֹצִיא מֵחֲבֵירוֹ, דְּהַיְינוּ מְקַבֵּל מַתָּנָה, עָלָיו לְהָבִיא רְאָיָה שֶׁבָּרִיא הָיָה, דְּמִסְתָּמָא י"ל שֶׁשכ"מ הָיָה. אִיכָּא לְמֵימַר הָכִי כו'. רַבָּה הוּא דְּקָא מְשַׁנֵּי לְאַבַּיֵי הָכִי: הַיְינוּ טַעֲמַיְיהוּ דְּרַבָּנַן, מִשּׁוּם דְּאִיכָּא לְמֵימַר הָכִי וְהָכִי, וּמְסַפְּקָא לָן אִם מַתְּנַת בָּרִיא הוּא אִם מַתְּנַת שכ"מ — הִלְכָּךְ אוֹקֵי מָמוֹנָא בְּחֶזְקַת מָרֵיהּ, בְּחֶזְקַת נוֹתֵן. וְהִלְכָּךְ, הַמּוֹצִיא מֵחֲבֵירוֹ, דְּהַיְינוּ בַּעַל הַשְּׁטָר — עָלָיו לְהָבִיא רְאָיָה בְּעֵדִים שֶׁבָּרִיא הָיָה, לְהוֹצִיא הַמָּמוֹן מֵחֶזְקַת הַנּוֹתֵן. וּבִפְלוּגְתָּא. דְּרַב הוּנָא וְרַב חִסְדָּא, פְּלִיגֵי ר' יוֹחָנָן ור"ל. בִּבְנֵי בְרַק. מָקוֹם. וְעָמְדוּ עָלָיו בְּנֵי מִשְׁפָּחָה. וְקס"ד הָשְׁתָּא: נִכְסֵי בְּחֶזְקַת יוֹרְשִׁין קַיְימֵי, וְלֹא בָּאוּ עֲדַיִין לְיַד לָקוֹחוֹת, וְאָתוּ לָקוֹחוֹת וְקָא מְעַרְעֲרוּ לְהוֹצִיא מִן הַיּוֹרְשִׁין, לְפִי שֶׁקְּנָאוּם מִן הַמֵּת. וְהַיּוֹרְשִׁין עוֹרְרִין, וּמְשִׁיבִין דָּבָר לַלָּקוֹחוֹת, וְאוֹמְרִים: קָטָן הָיָה קְרוֹבֵנוּ בִּשְׁעַת מִיתָה. וְקי"ל לְקַמָּן (דף קנה.) דְּאֵינוֹ יָכוֹל לִמְכּוֹר בְּנִכְסֵי אָבִיו עַד שֶׁיְּהֵא בֶּן עֶשְׂרִים, וְלֹא נוֹצִיא הַנְּכָסִים מֵחֶזְקָתֵנוּ. וְהַלָּקוֹחוֹת לֹא מָצְאוּ עֵדִים שֶׁיֹּאמְרוּ גָּדוֹל הָיָה, וּלְכָךְ הוּצְרְכוּ לְבוֹדְקוֹ. וּכְשֶׁלֹּא יוּכְלוּ לְבוֹדְקוֹ וְגַם הָעֵדִים לֹא מָצְאוּ — הִפְסִידוּ. דְּר"ע כְּרַבָּנַן, דְּאָמְרִי: הַמּוֹצִיא מֵחֲבֵירוֹ עָלָיו הָרְאָיָה בְּעֵדִים שֶׁבָּרִיא הָיָה. וה"נ, עַל הַלָּקוֹחוֹת לְהָבִיא רְאָיָה שֶׁגָּדוֹל הָיָה. בָּאוּ. לָקוֹחוֹת וְשָׁאֲלוּ אֶת ר"ע. עֲשׂוּיִין לְהִשְׁתַּנּוֹת. וַאֲפִי' אִם דּוֹמִין עַתָּה לְסִימָנֵי גָּדוֹל, י"ל אִילּוּ הָיָה קַיָּים — הֲוָה שׁוּמָא.

---

*ונראה לר"י לפרש: ל"ש דבקעה (ג) רה"ר לטומאה אלא שלא עברו עליה ימות הגשמים. פי': על הטומאה, שנודע שלא עברו עליו ימות הגשמים משעבר שם, ולא ידע אם בימות החמה נכנס או בימות הגשמים נכנס. שאם בא לשאול לפנינו — יש לנו לחושבה רה"ר, דבתר השתא אזלינן. אבל אם עברו עליה בימות הגשמים, פי': שלא נודע לו אם בימות החמה או בימות הגשמים נכנס, ומשבאה ספיקא עברו עליה ימות הגשמים — אפילו הוא בא לשאול בימות החמה הוי רה"י לטומאה, דליכא למימר בתר השתא אזלינן, כיון שקרוב היה לימות הגשמים יותר. ורשות היחיד לכאן ולכאן הכי פירושא: לגבי (ד) שם טומאה כמו לגבי שבת. והשתא ניחא דמייתי הכא הך מילתא אי אזלינן בתר השתא, דאיירי נה בהך שמעתא.

ראיה במאי כו' רב חסדא ורבה בר רב הונא אמרי ראיה בקיום השטר. פירש רבינו שמואל דבין לר"מ ובין לרבנן בעי: ראיה במאי? ואין נראה, דהא פשיטא לר"מ דהוי ראיה בעדים. וכן פירש רבינו שמואל אחר כן, דלר"מ הוה ראיה בעדים.

וכן אמר רבה ראיה בעדים. תימה: אמאי מוקי רבה למתני' ראיה בעדים, דמוקי רבנן כר' יעקב, ור"מ כר' נתן? והא איהו גופיה ס"ל כר' נתן, ולוקמא בקיום שטרות וכולהו כרבי נתן! מיהו, אי אשכחן בשום מקום דאית ליה מודה בשטר שכתבו א"צ לקיימו — הוה אתי שפיר. דאי הוה מוקי לפלוגתייהו נמי בקיום שטרות — הוה להו רבנן דלא כוותיה. א"נ, יש לומר דמשמע ליה ראיה דרבנן דומיא דראיה דר"מ, דהיינו בעדים.

ועוד סימנין עשויין להשתנות לאחר מיתה. וא"ת: לאי דס"ד שהלקוחות היו בודקין אותו אם היה גדול אם לאו, היאך יכול להיות שאם נראה קטן בחייו שיראה גדול לאחר מיתה? ופירש ר"ת: שבחייו היו השערות לבנות והוו שומא, ועכשיו הושחרו לאחר מיתה ונראות כסימנים. ואין נראה, דלא אשכחן בשום מקום (ה) בשערות שהם סימן חילוק בין לבנות לשחורות. ואומר ר"י: דשמא בחייו לא היו גומות, ומחמת מיתה יש שם גומות, כדאמרי' בנדה: גומות אע"פ שאין שערות, בפ' "בא סימן" (דף נב. ושם). ואם

רבינו גרשום

הגהות הב"ח

עין משפט נר מצוה

קכא א מיי' פ"ח מהל' זכיה ומתנה הלכה כז סמג עשין פב טוש"ע ח"מ סי' רנא סעיף ב:

קכב ב ג מיי' פ"כ מהל' אבות הטומאה הלכה ו:

מסורת הש"ס

א) [קדושין עט: גיטין כח.] ב) קדושין עט: : ג) טהרות פ"ו מ"ז שבת דף ו: : ד) [ב"ק נג. ב"מ קיז:]

(א) אֲמַר רַבָּה: הֲרֵי מֵת, וַהֲרֵי קִבְרוֹ מוֹכִיחַ עָלָיו. אֲמַר לֵיהּ אַבָּיֵי: אהָשְׁתָּא, וּמַה סְפִינָה שֶׁרוּבָּן לְאַבֵּד — נוֹתְנִין עֲלֵיהֶן חוּמְרֵי חַיִּים וְחוּמְרֵי מֵתִים, חוֹלִין, א)שֶׁרוֹב חוֹלִין לְחַיִּים — לֹא כָּל שֶׁכֵּן! אֲמַר רַב הוּנָא בְּרֵיהּ דְּרַב יְהוֹשֻׁעַ: כְּמַאן אָזְלָא הָא שְׁמַעְתָּא דְּרַבָּה? כְּרִ' נָתָן; דְּתַנְיָא: ב)מִי מוֹצִיא מִיַּד מִי? הוּא מוֹצִיא מִידֵיהֶן בְּלֹא רְאָיָה, וְהֵן אֵין מוֹצִיאִין מִיָּדוֹ אֶלָּא בִּרְאָיָה, דִּבְרֵי רַבִּי יַעֲקֹב; רַבִּי נָתָן אוֹמֵר: אִם בָּרִיא הוּא — עָלָיו לְהָבִיא רְאָיָה שֶׁהָיָה שְׁכִיב מְרַע, אִם שְׁכִיב מְרַע הוּא — עֲלֵיהֶן לְהָבִיא רְאָיָה שֶׁבָּרִיא הָיָה. אָמַר רַבִּי אֶלְעָזָר: וּלְטוּמְאָה — כְּמַחֲלוֹקֶת; דִּתְנַן: ג)בבִּקְעָה, בִּימוֹת הַחַמָּה — רְשׁוּת הַיָּחִיד לְשַׁבָּת וּרְשׁוּת הָרַבִּים לְטוּמְאָה, בִּימוֹת הַגְּשָׁמִים — רְשׁוּת הַיָּחִיד לְכָאן וּלְכָאן. (ב) אָמַר רָבָא: גלֹא שָׁנוּ אֶלָּא שֶׁלֹּא עָבְרוּ (ג) עָלָיו יְמוֹת הַגְּשָׁמִים, אֲבָל עָבְרוּ עָלָיו יְמוֹת הַגְּשָׁמִים — רְשׁוּת הַיָּחִיד לְכָאן וּלְכָאן.§ "וַחֲכָמִים אוֹמְרִים: הַמּוֹצִיא מֵחֲבֵירוֹ עָלָיו הָרְאָיָה" וכו'.§

רְאָיָה

רשב"ם

אָמַר רַבָּה הֲרֵי. אָנוּ רוֹאִין שֶׁהוּא מֵת. וּבָתַר הַשְׁתָּא אָזְלִינַן, (ד) וְהֶעֱמַדְנוּ עַל חֶזְקַת מִיתָתוֹ, וְיֵשׁ לָנוּ לוֹמַר שֶׁמִּתּוֹךְ אוֹתוֹ חוֹלִי מֵת, וְקָנָה הַמְקַבֵּל מַתָּנָה. **א"ל אַבָּיֵי.** מַאן לֵימָא לָךְ דְּמֵהַהוּא חוֹלִי אִיפְּטַר לְבֵית עוֹלָמֵיהּ? וַהֲלֹא רוֹב חוֹלִים לְחַיִּים, וְחָזַר בּוֹ, וְאַחֲרֵי כֵן חָלָה וּמֵת. **הַשְׁתָּא וּמַה סְפִינוֹת.** הַטּוֹבְעוֹת בַּיָּם, שֶׁרוּבָּן לֵיאָבֵד, וְאַפ"ה נוֹתְנִין עָלָיו חוּמְרֵי חַיִּים וְחוּמְרֵי מֵתִים, כְּדִתְנַן בְּפֶ' "כָּל הַגֵּט" (גיטין ד' כח:): אֲבָל עִיר שֶׁכְּבָשָׁהּ כַּרְכּוֹם, וּסְפִינָה שֶׁאָבְדָה בַּיָּם — נוֹתְנִין עָלָיו חוּמְרֵי חַיִּים וְחוּמְרֵי מֵתִים, בַּת כֹּהֵן לְיִשְׂרָאֵל בַּת יִשְׂרָאֵל לְכֹהֵן שְׁתֵּיהֶן אֵין אוֹכְלוֹת בִּתְרוּמָה. **חוֹלִים שֶׁרוֹב חוֹלִים לְחַיִּים.** כְּדִתְנַן (גיטין שם.): הַמֵּבִיא גֵּט מִמְּדִינַת הַיָּם, וְהִנִּיחוֹ זָקֵן אוֹ חוֹלֶה (ה) נוֹתְנִין לָהּ בְּחֶזְקַת שֶׁהוּא קַיָּים — לֹא כָּל שֶׁכֵּן דְּנֵימָא עָמַד וְחָזַר בּוֹ. וּמִיהוּ, (רָבָא) [רַבָּה] לָא הֲדַר בֵּיהּ, וְקַיְ"ל כְּוָותֵיהּ. דִּשְׁמַעְתֵּיהּ כְּרַבִּי נָתָן אָזְלָא, דְּקַיְ"ל כְּוָותֵיהּ, כִּדְאָמְרִי' בְּעָלְמָא (ב"מ ד' קיז:): ר' נָתָן דַּיָּינָא הוּא וְנָחֵית לְעוּמְקָא דְּדִינָא. **מִי מוֹצִיא מִיַּד מִי.** מַתָּנָה שֶׁאֵין כָּתוּב בָּהּ לֹא לְשׁוֹן מַתְּנַת בָּרִיא וְלֹא לְשׁוֹן מַתְּנַת שְׁכִיב מְרַע, כִּי מַתְנִי', זֶה אוֹמֵר בָּרִיא הָיִיתָ וְזֶה אוֹמֵר שְׁכִיב מְרַע הָיִיתִי. **הוּא מוֹצִיא מִידֵיהֶן.** וְנוֹתֵן עוֹמֵד בִּנְכָסָיו וְזוֹכֶה בָּהֶן, דְּהַעֲמֵד נְכָסִים עַל חֶזְקָתָן. וְיַד בַּעַל הַשְּׁטָר שֶׁבָּא לִתְבּוֹעַ נְכָסָיו שֶׁל זֶה – עַל הַתַּחְתּוֹנָה, דְּלָא אָזְלִינַן בָּתַר הַשְׁתָּא. (ו) כִּדְאַבָּיֵי, דְּרוֹב חוֹלִים לְחַיִּים, דְּאִיכָּא לְמֵימַר דַּהֲדַר בֵּיהּ. **וְהֵם אֵין מוֹצִיאִין מִיָּדוֹ.** אא"כ מְבִיאִין רְאָיָה בְּעֵדִים שֶׁבָּרִיא הָיָה. **אִם בָּרִיא הוּא.** בִּשְׁעַת הַעֲמָדָה בַּדִּין עָלָיו וכו', דְּאָזְלִינַן בָּתַר הַשְׁתָּא. **אָמַר ר"א וּלְעִנְיַן טוּמְאָה.** דְּקַיְ"ל סְפֵק טוּמְאָה בִּרה"י סְפֵיקוֹ טָמֵא, וּבִרה"ר סְפֵיקוֹ טָהוֹר. וְקַיְ"ל נַמִּי דְּבִקְעָה בִּימוֹת הַחַמָּה רְשׁוּת הָרַבִּים לְטוּמְאָה, וּבִימוֹת הַגְּשָׁמִים רְשׁוּת הַיָּחִיד לְטוּמְאָה, כְּדִתְנַן כו'. **כְּמַחֲלוֹקֶת.** כִּי הֵיכִי דְּנֶחְלְקוּ ר' יַעֲקֹב וְר' נָתָן בְּמַתָּנָה סְתָם, אִי אָזְלִינַן בָּתַר הַשְׁתָּא אוֹ בָּתַר חֶזְקַת נְכָסִים – הָכִי נַמִּי אִפְלִיגוּ גַּבֵּי טוּמְאָה, שֶׁאִם בָּא אָדָם לְבֵ"ד וְנִשְׁאַל עַל שֶׁנִּכְנַס לְבִקְעָה וְאֵין יוֹדֵעַ מָתַי נִכְנַס אִי בִּימוֹת הַחַמָּה וְטָהוֹר, אִי בִּימוֹת הַגְּשָׁמִים וְטָמֵא – חָזֵינַן: אִם עַתָּה כְּשֶׁנִּשְׁאַל יְמוֹת הַחַמָּה הֵן – טָהוֹר הוּא, דְּאָזְלִינַן בָּתַר הַשְׁתָּא לְר' נָתָן. וְאִם יְמוֹת הַגְּשָׁמִים הוּא – טָמֵא, דְּבָתַר הַשְׁתָּא אָזְלִינַן. וּלְרַבִּי יַעֲקֹב דְּאָזֵיל בָּתַר חֲזָקָה – הַעֲמֵד טָהוֹר עַל חֶזְקָתוֹ, וְטָהוֹר, עַד שֶׁיָּבֹאוּ עֵדִים וְיָעִידוּ שֶׁבִּימוֹת הַגְּשָׁמִים נִכְנַס. **דִּתְנַן בִּקְעָה כו'.** מְסוּיֶּיגֶת בְּגָדֵר סָבִיב, ורה"י הִיא לְשַׁבָּת. וַאֲפִי' הִיא קַרְפֵּף יוֹתֵר מִבֵּית סָאתַיִם (ז) – לִזְרוֹק בְּתוֹכוֹ מֵרה"ר חַיָּיב, וּלְטַלְטֵל אָסוּר. **רה"ר לְטוּמְאָה.** דְּלָאו מְקוֹם סְתִירָה הוּא. אֲבָל בִּימוֹת הַגְּשָׁמִים שֶׁיֵּשׁ שָׁם זְרָעִים – אֵין נִכְנָסִים לְתוֹכָהּ, וְהָוֵי מְקוֹם סְתִירָה, וּסְפֵק טוּמְאָה טָמֵא. **אָמַר רָבָא לֹא שָׁנוּ כו'.** מִילְּתָא בְּאַפֵּי נַפְשָׁהּ הִיא. וְהַמְפָרֵשׁ דְּמִילְּתֵיהּ דְּר"א אַדְּרָבָא קָאֵי – אֵינוֹ אֶלָּא טוֹעֶה, דְּרָבָא בַּתְרָא הוּא, וְא"ל לִדְחוֹק מִילְּתֵיהּ דְּרַבִּי אֶלְעָזָר וּלְהַעֲמִידָהּ עַל פֵּירוּשׁ רָבָא. **לֹא שָׁנוּ.** דְּבִקְעָה בִּימוֹת הַחַמָּה רה"ר לְטוּמְאָה. **אֶלָּא שֶׁלֹּא עָבְרוּ.** עַל בִּקְעָה זוֹ יְמוֹת הַגְּשָׁמִים מִשֶּׁגְּדָרוּהָ. אֲבָל עָבְרוּ עָלֶיהָ יְמוֹת הַגְּשָׁמִים – תּוּ לָא פָּקַע מִינָּהּ שֵׁם רה"י אֲפִילּוּ מִשֶּׁיַּגִּיעוּ יְמוֹת הַחַמָּה, וְתֶיהֱוֵי לְעוֹלָם רה"י לְכָאן וּלְכָאן. וּסְבָרָא מַעַלְיָיתָא הִיא, אוֹ חוּמְרָא דְּרַבָּנַן הוּא. ור"ח פֵּירֵשׁ דְּרָבָא פְּלִיג אַדְּר' אֶלְעָזָר, וְהָכִי כָּתַב: וְרָבָא חוֹלֵק עַל רַבִּי אֶלְעָזָר. וּפֵי' נַמִּי: לֹא שָׁנוּ דְּבִקְעָה כו' אֶלָּא בִּזְמַן שֶׁלֹּא עָבְרוּ עַל זוֹ הַטּוּמְאָה שֶׁהָיְתָה עַתָּה בַּבִּקְעָה, יְמוֹת הַגְּשָׁמִים. אֲבָל עָבְרוּ עַל זוֹ הַטּוּמְאָה יְמוֹת הַגְּשָׁמִים – רה"י הִיא לְכָאן וּלְכָאן.

רְאָיָה

תוספות

השתא ומה ספינה שרובן לאבד כו'. הקשה הר"ר יצחק בר' מאיר: אמאי לא פריך ליה מדתנן בגיטין (דף כח. ושם): הניחו זקן או חולה — (ח) בחזקת שהוא קיים, ואוכלת אשתו בתרומה, ולא אמרי' דלמא מת! ואינה קושיא, דהתם לא מת לבסוף. אבל הכא מת לבסוף, ולא הוי לנו לומר שעמד, אי לא משום דמדמינן ליה לספינה המטורפת בים, דהוי כמו שסופן לאבד במים — ואפ"ה חשבינן להו בחזקת שהם חיים עדיין. א"נ, מההיא משנה לא היה יכול להוכיח אלא שהוא בחזקתו כמו שהניחו. אבל מהך משנה יש להוכיח שניצול מחליו, כמו בני הספינה (ט) המטולים בים שנצולו מן המים.

כמאן אזלא הא שמעתא דרבה כר' נתן. וא"ת: אמאי לא קאמר כר"מ? דרבה גופיה מוקי לקמן ר' נתן כר"מ דמתני'! וי"ל: דמשום דר' נתן ד)דיינא הוא, ונחית לעומקא דדינא. ומטעם זה פי' רבינו שמואל דהלכה כרבה. אי נמי, דמתני' לא מוכחא בהדיא (י) שהוא בחזקת בריא עתה, אבל ממילתיה דרבי נתן משמע הכי בהדיא. **והן** אין מוציאין מידו אלא בראיה. וא"ת: פשיטא, כיון שהוא מוציא מידם בלא ראיה שהן אין מוציאין מידו בלא ראיה! וי"ל: דהא קמ"ל, דהא בראיה — מוציאין, אע"פ שאין השטר מוכיח שהיה בריא.

רבי נתן אומר אם בריא הוא עליו להביא ראיה כו'. אומר ר"י: דהך סוגיא דהכא לית ליה כההיא סוגיא דפ' בתרא דקדושין (דף עט.) דקאמר התם: קדשה אביה בדרך ונתקדשה היא עצמה בעיר, והרי היא בוגרת. רב אמר: הרי היא בוגרת לפנינו, ושמואל אמר: חוששין לקדושי שניהם. וקאמר התם: לימא כתנאי, מי מוציא מיד מי — הוא מוציא מידם בלא ראיה כו'. לימא רב דאמר כרבי נתן, ושמואל דאמר כרבי יעקב? אמר לך שמואל: אנא דאמרי אפי' כרבי נתן, עד כאן לא קאמר ר' נתן התם אלא דכולי עלמא בחזקת בריאים קיימין, [והאי] דמפיק נפשיה מחזקת בריאים — עליו להביא ראיה. אלא הכא — מי מפיק נפשיה מחזקה? וא"כ, ה"נ איזו ראיה מייתי מר' נתן לרבה? התם היינו טעמא — דכ"ע בחזקת בריאים קיימי, אבל הכא אין לנו לומר שהיה בחזקת שכיב מרע שלא עמד, דשמא עמד. ומסיפא נמי, דקתני: אם שכיב מרע הוא עליהן להביא ראיה שהיה בריא — אינו ראיה, דהתם היינו טעמא — דאוקי ממונא אחזקיה, ובדרבה דהכא איכא חזקת ממון לגבי יורשים. אלא לאו ש"מ דלית לה להך סוגיא סברא דהתם.

בימות הגשמים רשות היחיד לכאן ולכאן. פי' רבינו חננאל: דבימות הגשמים אין בני אדם נכנסין בתוכה מפני רוב הגשמים. ואין נראה, שאין זה מחמת מילוי מים, אלא מפני התבואה. כדקתני בתוספתא (פ"ז דטהרות) שהביא רבינו חננאל, (כ) דקתני: אלו ימות החמה — משתעקר התבואה ממקומה. והא דקתני סיפא: (ל) את ימי הגשמים משתרד רביעה שניה — לאו היינו מפני רוב המים, אלא שמשם ואילך גדלים הזרעים, ודריסת הרגל מזקת להם. כדתניא בס"פ "מרובה" (ב"ק דף פא.): מהלכים בשבילי הרשות משתרד רביעה שניה, שמשם ואילך דריסת הרגל מזקת לזרעים ולתבואה.

רשות היחיד לשבת ורשות הרבים לטומאה. בפ"ק דשבת (דף ו:) פליגי בה אמוראי, איכא מאן דמוקי לה בבקעה שהוקפה מארבע (מ) רוחות. רה"ר לטומאה — שאפי' חצר שנכנסים בה בזו ויוצאין בזו אמרי' בעירובין (דף ח.) דהוי רשות הרבים לטומאה, כ"ש בקעה שהולכים בה תדיר. ואיכא דמוקי לה בלא הוקפה והוי כרמלית, ואמאי קרי לה רשות היחיד — לפי שאינה רה"ר.

אמר רבא לא שנו אלא שלא עברו עליה ימות הגשמים. פי' רשב"ם: שעברו עליה ימות הגשמים משנגדרה הבקעה, (נ) ואפ"ה בימות החמה חשיבא רשות היחיד. ואין נראה כלל, כי איזו סברא היא דכיון שנגדרה ועברו עליה ימות הגשמים הויא רשות היחיד אפי' בימות החמה, וקודם שעברו ימות הגשמים לא תהיה רשות היחיד? ועוד: דלא מצי לאוקומא למילתיה דרבא דהכא אלא למ"ד בפ"ק דשבת (שם) והוא שיש לה גדר מד' רוחותיה. ועוד: אמאי קאמר רבא למילתיה הכא יותר מכל שאר מקומות שבגמרא שהביא הך משנה? ופי' רבינו חננאל דלענין טומאה קאי, וה"ק: לא שנו אלא שלא עברו על טומאה זו ימות הגשמים, ואז אם נכנס בימות החמה — הוי רשות הרבים. אבל אם עברו על טומאה זו ימות הגשמים, אפילו נכנס בה בימות החמה ובא לשאול בימות החמה — הוי רשות היחיד. גם על פירוש זה (קשה) תמיה גדולה היא: למה יחשב רשות היחיד, כיון דנכנס בימות החמה ובא לשאול בימות החמה? ודוחק לומר דחומרא דרבנן היא. ועוד תקשה: למה אומר רבא דבריו בכאן יותר מבשאר מקומות דמייתי הך משנה? וי"ל: דהא נמי לא קשיא היא, כדפירש רבינו חננאל דרבא חולק אדר"א, ולא כתב יותר. ונראה (ס) *דחולק בענין זה, מדאמר רבא אם עברו עליה ימות הגשמים הוי רה"י, אפילו בא לשאול בימות החמה ונכנס בימות החמה — א"כ לא אזיל בתר השתא, בתר שעת שאילה. ושמא כדברי ר' יוחנן רוצה לומר, כדאיתא בירושלמי עלה בפרק "מי שמת", אמר ר' יוחנן: נטמא בספק בקעה בין בימות החמה בין בימות הגשמים — מחלוקת ר"מ וחכמים. בא לשאול בימות [החמה — נשאלין לו בימות החמה, בימות הגשמים — נשאלין לו בימות הגשמים. א"ר יוחנן(ע): ובלבד ימים הסמוכים לגשמים] *ותנן בתוספתא: ואלו הן ימות החמה — משתעקר התבואה מתוכה, ימות הגשמים — משתרד רביעה שניה.

למדמחלק בענין זה א"כ כו' כצ"ל רש"א

[נ"ל ותניא בתוספתא דטהרות פ"ז]

רבינו גרשום

אמר רבא. בתר השתא אזלינן דמסתבר כדאמר מקבל והרי מת והרי קברו מוכיח עליו שלא עמד מחליו: אמר ליה אביי. היכי מצית אזל בתר השתא: ומה ספינה. שטבעה בים שרובן של אנשים שהיו בה לאיבוד ואפ' הכי נותנין עליו חומרי חיים שאין משיאין נשותיהם דחיישי' שמא השליכן לחוץ במקום רחוק כשהן חיים וחומרי מתים שאם כהנים היו אותן שטבעו נשיהן ועבדיהן אין אוכלין תרומה בחזקת שהן חיין דאיכא למימר מתו: חולים שרוב חולין לחיים לא כ"ש. שנותנין עליו חומרי חיים ואיכא למימר דנתרפא וקם מחליו וחזר מאותה מתנה: כמאן אזלא הא שמעתא דרבא דאזיל בתר השתא: כר' נתן כדתניא. לא כתב בה כשנותן מתנת שכיב מרע הוא. הוא אומר שכיב מרע היה ועמד וחזר והוא אומר בריא היה: מי מוציא מיד מי. הוא שכיב מרע מוציא מידן בלא ראיה שנכסין הן ברשותו ובחזקתו ונכסים בחזקתן קיימי והן אין מוציאין בלא ראיה שבריא היה כשנתן לו דברי ר' יעקב: ר' נתן אומר אם בריא היה כו'. אלמא דבתר השתא אזלינן ודיינינן לי' שבריא הוא אי לא מייתי ראיה דשכיב מרע הוה: אמר ר' אלעזר א)מחלוקת ר' יעקב במחלוקת ר' יעקב ור' נתן כדאיירינן לענין טומאה. דתנן הבקעה מסוגית סביב. בימות החמה רשות היחיד לשבת אם יותר מבית סאתים אין מטלטלין בה אלא בארבע והזורק מרשות הרבים חייב חטאת מפני שיש לה מחיצות. רשות הרבים לטומאה הואיל והתבואה בימות החמה כבר היא קצורה אין מונעין בני אדם לעבור דרך עליה. ודמיא כרה"ר לענין טומאה דכל ספק טומאה ברה"ר ספיקו טהור. דכתיב ונסתרה והיא נטמאה. אף ספק טומאה שיש בבקעה ספיקו טהו'. ובימות הגשמים רשות היחיד לכאן ולכאן בין לשבת בין לטומאה. לפי שהיא זרועה ומונעין ממנה דריסת רגל. ואמר רבא לא שנו דבקעה בימות החמה רשות היחיד לשבת ורשות הרבים לטומאה אלא שלא עברו עליה שוב ימות הגשמים. ב) אע"ג דהשתא ימות החמה רשות היחיד לכאן ולכאן בין לגבי טומאה בין לגבי שבת דלא אזלי בתר השתא. וכו' יעקב סבירא ליה דלא אזיל בתר השתא ות"ק כר' נתן: וחכמים אומרים המוציא מחבירו עליו הראיה הואיל דנתן (דבעל מתנה) מוחזק הוא על המקבל להביא ראיה שבריא היה:

ראיה

הגהות הב"ח

(א) גמ' אמר רבה הרי מת. נ"ב כך הוא גירסת התוס' והרא"ש ולא כאלפסי דגורס רבא עי' באשר"י: (ב) שם אמר רבא לא שנו. נ"ב ל"ג ואמר רבא אלא אמר רבא ואותו שמפרש דמילתיה דר"א אדרבא קאי גורס ואמר רבא ורשב"ם דחה אותו: (ג) שם שלא עברו עליה וכו' אבל עברו עליה ימות הגשמים: (ד) רשב"ם ד"ה אמר רבה וכו' והעמדנוהו על חזקת: (ה) ד"ה חולין וכו' נותן לה בחזקת שהוא קיים לא כ"ש דנימא דלמא עמד וחזר בו: (ו) ד"ה הוא מוציא וכו' וכדאביי וכו' ואיכא למימר: (ז) ד"ה דתנן וכו' לזורק לתוכו מרשות הרבים: (ח) תוס' ד"ה השתא וכו' זקן או חולה נותן לה בחזקת שהוא קיים ואוכלת אשתו בתרומה בחזקת שהוא קיים ולא אמרינן וכו' ולא היה לנו לומר: (ט) בא"ד בני הספינה המטולטלים בים: (י) ד"ה כמאן וכו' בהדיא דהוא: (כ) ד"ה בימות וכו' שהביא רבי' חננאל אלו הן ימות כצ"ל ותיבת דקתני נמחק: (ל) בא"ד והא דקתני סיפא ימות כצ"ל ותיבת את נמחק: (מ) ד"ה רשות וכו' מארבע רוחותיה ורשות הרבים: (נ) ד"ה אמר וכו' משנגדרה הבקעה ולהכי אפי' בימות החמה חשיבא: (ס) בא"ד ונראה לפרש לחולק: (ע) בא"ד ובלבד ימים הסמוכים לגשמים ונראה לר"י כצ"ל ותיבות ותנן בתוספתא ואלו הן ימות החמה משתעקר התבואה מתוכה ימות הגשמים משתרד רביעה שניה נמחק:

א) נראה דצ"ל מחלוקת ר' יעקב ור' נתן כאן כמחלוקת ר' יעקב ור"נ דאיירינן לענין טומאה כצ"ל ועי' היטב בש"ס כאן שנדפס בדפוס ווין בסוף ס' הרב המאירי על מס' שבת. ב) נ"ל אבל עברו עליה ימות הגשמים אע"ג השתא וכו'.

עין משפט נר מצוה

סבור מיניה: הני מילי לאחר, אבל לעצמו לא; אמר להו רב חסדא, כי אתא רב הונא מכופרי פירשה: א בין לעצמו בין לאחרים. ההוא דקנו מיניה, אתא לקמיה דרב הונא, אמר: מאי איעבד לך, דלא אקנית כדמקנו אינשי. ההיא מתנתא דהוה כתוב בה "בחיים ובמות" — רב אמר: הרי היא כמתנת שכיב מרע, ושמואל אמר: הרי היא כמתנת בריא. רב אמר: הרי היא כמתנת שכיב מרע; מדכתיב בה "במות" — אחר מיתה קאמר ליה, והאי דכתיב "בחיים" — סימן בעלמא, דחיי. ושמואל אמר: הרי היא כמתנת בריא; מדכתיב בה "בחיים" — מחיים קאמר, והאי דכתב ו"במות" — כמאן דאמר "מעתה ועד עולם". אמרי נהרדעי: ב הלכתא כוותיה דרב. אמר רבא: ואי כתיב בה "מחיים" — קנה. אמר אמימר: ג לית הלכתא כוותיה דרבא. אמר ליה רב אשי לאמימר: פשיטא, דהא אמרי נהרדעי הלכתא כוותיה דרב! מהו דתימא "מחיים" מודי רב, קא משמע לן. ההוא דאתא לקמיה דרב נחמן לנהרדעא, שדריה לקמיה דר' ירמיה בר אבא לשום טמיא, אמר: הכא אתרא דשמואל, היכי נעביד כוותיה דרב! ההיא דאתאי לקמיה דרבא, עבד לה רבא כשמעתיה, הוה קא טרדא ליה, אמר ליה לרב פפא בריה דרב חנן ספריה: זיל כתוב לה, וכתוב בה: *שוכר עליהן או מטען. אמרה: ליטבע ארביה! אטעויי קא מטעית לי! אמשינהו למניה דרבא במיא, ואפי' הכי לא איפרק מטיבעא.§ **מתני'** לא כתב בה שכיב מרע, הוא אומר שכיב מרע הייתי, והן אומרים בריא היית — צריך להביא ראיה ששכיב מרע היה, דברי ר"מ; וחכ"א: ד המוציא מחבירו עליו הראיה.§ **גמ'** ההוא מתנתא דהוה כתב בה: "כד הוה קציר ורמי בערסיה", ולא כתב בה "ומגו מרעיה איפטר לבית עולמיה", אמר

רשב"ם

סבור מיניה הני מילי. דאין לאחר קנין כלום, שאם כתב וזיכה לראשון וכתב וזיכה לאחר - דראשון קנה לגמרי, וכגון שמת שכיב מרע. אבל לעצמו - יכול לחזור בו, אם יעמוד מחליו - לא קנה ראשון, שלא היה קנין אלא מחמת מיתה. **אמר להו רב חסדא.** בין לאחר בין לעצמו. ולא דמיא לדרב יהודה אמר שמואל, דאמר: בידוע שלא היה קנין אלא מחמת מיתה, דהתם כתב וקנו, אבל הכא - זיכה וכתב וקנו, דכל כך - ודאי לייפות את כחו. **ההוא** דקנו מיניה. כתב וזיכה וקנו מיניה, ורצה לחזור בו כשעמד מחליו. כדמקנו אינשי. שכיב מרע הנותנין לאחר מיתה לדעת שיחזרו בהן אם יעמדו - שכותבין או מקנין, או כותבין ומקנין. אבל אתה כתבת וזכית והקנית, דהא ודאי שמואל מודי בין לעצמו בין לאחר. והשתא שמעינן מד' מילי דאמר שמואל בשמעתין, דקיימא לן כוותיה בדיני: מתנת שכיב מרע בדלא שייר, שיש בה קנין בלא זיכה לו את השטר - לא ידענא מאי אידון בה, ולא קנה מקבל מתנה אפי' מת הנותן, דשמא לא גמר להקנותו אלא בשטר, ואין שטר לאחר מיתה. אבל אם ייפה את כחו בכתיבת השטר או בצוואה, דכתב בה "וקניינא מיניה מוסיף על מתנתא דא" - קני המקבל מתנה, שבזה לא נאמר לא גמר להקנותו אלא בשטר כו'. והוא שמת הנותן, אבל אם עמד - חוזר, דבידוע שלא היה קנין אלא מחמת מיתה. ומדרב יהודה אמר שמואל דאוקימנא במייפה את כחו שמעינן ליה להא. ושכיב מרע שאמר "כתבו ותנו מנה לפלוני" ומת - כותבין ונותנין לאחר מיתה, כדאוקימנא לשמואל במייפה את כחו. אבל בלא ייפוי - לא קנה, דאין שטר לאחר מיתה. ואם כתב וזיכה השטר למסרו לזה לראיה, וכתב וזיכה לזה - השני קנה, והדר ביה מראשון. והוא שמת, ואם עמד - חוזר, דכל מתנת שכיב מרע בכל הנכסים בלא ייפוי כח בשטר, אם עמד - חוזר. הלכך שני נמי קנה, דהדר ביה מקמא. אבל אם כתב וזיכה והקנה - קאמר שמואל דקנה קמא לגמרי, בין לעצמו בין לאחר, ואם עמד - אינו חוזר. **ההיא מתנתא.** מתנת שכיב מרע במקצת שכתוב בה קנין, וקונה לדברי הכל, בין עמד בין לא עמד. דהוה כתוב בחיי ובמותי. מתנה זו אני מקנה לך בחיים ובמות. וליכא לאוקמה במתנת בריא, דהיכי לימא רב: הרי היא כמתנת שכיב מרע למיקני לאחר מיתה? והלא אין שטר לאחר מיתה. רב **אמר** הרי היא במתנת שכיב מרע. למיקני לאחר מיתה, ואם עמד - חוזר. וכ"ש אם מתנת שכיב מרע בכל שהוא, בלא שיור, דלא קני אלא עד לאחר מיתה. **סימנא** לחיים. כלומר, במות דוקא הוא, ומחיים לאו דוקא, אלא לסימן טוב, לפי שהזכיר מיתתו, שלא רצה לפתוח פיו לשטן, כלומר: המקום יצילני מחולי זה ולא אמות. **הרי היא** כמתנת בריא. כאילו לא כתב בה "במות". ואפי' אם עמד - אינו חוזר, ואפי' במתנה בלא שיור. דהכא לא לימא שמואל: לא ידענא מאי אידון בה, דנימא אין שטר לאחר מיתה - דהא כתב בה מחיים. מחיים קנה. דמשמע, דוקא מעתה התחיל לקנות. דהא **אמרי** נהרדעי הלכתא כוותיה דרב. גבי "בחיים ובמות", וה"ה היכא דכתב "מחיים". **קא** משמע לן. דלא שאני לרב בין "בחיים" ל"מחיים" - סימנא לחיים. **ההוא** דאתא לקמיה דר"נ. דהוה כתוב בשטר דידיה "בחיים ובמות". **לשום** טמיא. מקום. **אתריה** דשמואל. ואע"ג דהלכתא כרב - לאו (א) אורחא למידן כרב באתריה דשמואל, זיל עביד ליה התם כרב. בשמעתיה. דהוה כתיב ביה "מחיים", וקנה בעל השטר והאשה הפסידה. **וקטרדא** ליה. לומר: לא יפה דנתני. **א"ל** לספריה זיל כתוב לה. שהדין עמה, וכתוב בסוף השטר משנה השנויה בב"מ ב"השוכר את האומנין" (דף עה:): שוכר עליהן או מטען. וסימן היה בתוך השטר, שלדחות האשה ולהטעותה נתכוין, להיפטר ממחלוקתה. והיא הבינה בדברים, וקללתו. **ליטבע** ארביה. תיטבע ספינתו(ב). **אטעויי** קמטעית לי. בתמיה. **אמשינהו** למניה. שדאום במים, להתקיים קללתה בכך. **לא איתפרק** מעונשה. ד"אל תהי קללת הדיוט קלה בעיניך". ומהא שמעינן דבין "בחיים" בין "מחיים" - סימנא לחיים. **מתני'** לא כתוב בה שכיב מרע. "כדקציר ורמי בערסיה". וגם לשון מתנת בריא לא נכתב בה: "כד מהלך על רגלוהי בשוקא", שזהו לשון מתנת בריא כדאמרינן בגמרא. ובמתנה בלא שיור מיירי, דאמרן ביה דאינה מתנה, שאם עמד חוזר. **הוא אומר** שכיב מרע הייתי. וחוזרני בי. **בריא** היית. ולא תחזור. **צריך.** הנותן להביא ראיה שכשכיב מרע היה באותה שעה, וכל זמן שלא יביא ראיה - זכה המקבל מתנה, דברי ר' מאיר. ובגמרא מפרש ראיה במאי, וטעמא מאי. **וחכמים אומרים** כו'. בתרי גווני מיפרשי טעמייהו דרבנן בגמרא. **המוציא** מחבירו עליו הראיה. דהיינו מקבל מתנה, ונותן הוי מוחזק בנכסים. **גמ'** מגו מרעיה **איפטר** כו'. כך היו רגילין לכתוב מתנת שכיב מרע הנכתבות לאחר מיתתן, להודיע שהנכסים הללו נתונין לזה המקבל בצוואת שכיב מרע, ומתוך אותו חולי נפטר, שלא עמד בינתים ולא חזר בו.

אמר

ב"מ עה:

תוספות

ועוד, דמה שפירש דסיפא דמתני' לא מיירי כעין רישא — אין נראה כלל, דא"כ (ג) דקתני רישא: שייר קרקע כל שהוא מתנתו מתנה — אפי' לא שייר נמי, כיון דע"י קנין. ובסיפא דקתני: לא שייר אין מתנתו מתנה — אפילו שייר נמי, כיון דליכא קנין! על כן נראה יותר כדפרישית. וגם מה שפירש *ר"ת דמשנתנו מיירי אליבא דרב בלא קנין, משמע שרוצה לומר דמתנת שכיב מרע שכתוב בה קנין — היינו אפילו בקנין לחוד. וגם פירש דהא קיימא לן כרב, כיון דשמואל אמר לא ידענא מה אידון בה, אע"ג דבעלמא קיימא לן כשמואל בדיני. וקשה אמאי דפסיק לעיל דמתנת שכיב מרע במקצת בעיא קנין, ומשני: מתניתין בדקנו מיניה. א"כ מאי אירייא שייר? אפי' לא שייר נמי, דאין נראה כלל שיחלוק רב על פסק הלכה שפסקנו לעיל: מתנה דשכיב מרע במקצת בעיא קנין. ועוד, דאמרי' בגיטין פ' "התקבל" (דף סו.): מכלל דרב הונא סבר מתנת שכיב מרע לא בעיא קנין, והא קיימא לן דבעיא קנין! ומאי קושיא אי פליג רב הונא על פסק הלכה זה וסבר ליה כרב רביה דהכא? דהא בשבת פ' "מפנין" (ד' קכח.) פריך על רב הונא מרב רביה, דקאמר התם: והא רב הונא תלמידיה דרב הוה, ורב אית ליה מוקצה. ועוד: דאמרי בי רב הכא, ו"אמרי בי רב" היינו רב הונא, כמו שמפרש ר"ת בסוף פ"ק דסנהדרין (דף יז: ושם ד"ה אלא). וגם רש"י סובר כן דהיינו רב הונא, היכא דלא מוכח שהוא רב המנונא.

לא כתב בה שכיב מרע כו'. וה"ה נמי דלא כתב בה לשון בריא "כדמהלך על רגלוהי בשוקא". אלא משום דקתני: צריך להביא ראיה שהוא שכיב מרע — נקט האי לישנא.

ולא כתב ביה מגו מרעיה איפטר לבית עולמיה. והיורשים היו טוענין שעמד, ואף על פי שלא היו טוענין שחזר בו. דודאי, כיון שעמד — מסתמא ודאי חזר בו, אע"פ שלא אמר בפירוש. והכי משמע בגיטין פרק "מי שאחזו" (דף עב: ושם) דאמר רב הונא התם: גיטו כמתנתו, מה מתנתו אם עמד חוזר — אף גיטו חוזר. ופריך ליה, מדתנן: "הרי זה גיטך מהיום אם מתי מחולי זה" והלך ועמד בשוק וחלה ומת, אם מחמת החולי הראשון מת — הרי זה גט, ואם לאו — אינו גט. ואם אמרת אם עמד חוזר — הרי זה עמד. ומאי קושיא? דנהי דעמד, והלא לא חזר בו! אלא ש"מ, דאפי' לא פירש שחזר בו — יש לנו לומר שחוזר בו. ועוד קאמר התם (דף עג.) א"ר אלעזר: שכיב מרע שניתק מחולי אל חולי — מתנתו מתנה. ודוקא ניתק, אבל עמד — אין מתנתו מתנה, אע"פ שלא חזר בו.

השתא

עין משפט נר מצוה

קיח א מיי' פ"ט מהל' זכיה ומתנה הלכה טז סמג עשין פב טוש"ע ח"מ סי' רנ סעיף יב:

וגי' רש"א ר"ח ע"ש

קיט ב ג מיי' שם פ"ח הלכה יט סמג עשין פב טוש"ע ח"מ סי' רנא סעיף א:

קכ ד מיי' שם פ"ט הל' כב סמג עשין פב טור (וש"ע) ח"מ סי' רנא (ס"ב):

רבינו גרשום

הני מילי. דאין לאחר קנין כלום היכא דיהיב לאחר שהקנה לראשון: אבל לעצמו. דבעי מיהדר ביה לא דוודאי מצי למיהדר ביה: פירשה בין לעצמו בין לאחר. אין לאחר קנין כלום: ההוא. גברא שכיב מרע דיהב מתנה לחד וקנו מיניה ולאחר קנין בעי למיהדר ביה: דלא אקנית כדקני אינשי. דלא איבעי לך לאקנויי בקנין והשתא אין לאחר קנין כלום אפי' לעצמו כדאמ' לעיל: האי מתנה דהוה כתוב בה בחיי ובמותא מקנינא ליה האי מתנתא כלומר בין יחיה בין ימות לאחר מיתה הוא דקני אבל אי עמד חוזר והאי דכתב בה בחיים כדאמר לחיים שלא רצה להזכיר את עצמו מיתה שלא יפתח אדם פה לשטן ולא משום דליקני ליה מחיים. מחיים הוא דקאמר ליה דתיחול למיקני והאי דכתוב ביה כו': הלכתא כותי' דרב. דהאי דקאמר מחיים סימן לחיים: אמר רבא אי כתב בה מחיים א)סימן לחיים. אי כתב בה בחיים ובמות קנה. (והכי) דהכי משמ' מחיים מתחיל להגמר למיקנה אבל אי כתוב בה מחיים ודאי סימן לחיים קאמר. פשיטא דהא אמרי נהרדעי הלכתא כותיה דרב דממילא איכא למישמע מינה דלית הלכתא כותי' דרבא. מהו דתימא בחיים ובמות מודי רב דקנה קמ"ל דלא: ההוא דאתא לקמיה דרב נחמן. דהוה כתיב מתנתא בחיים ובמות: הכא אתרא דשמואל היא. ולא בעינא להתיר דבריו דגברא רבא הוא: לשום טמיא. מקום דליעבד ליה התם כדרב. דלא קנה [אלא] לאחר מיתה דהאי דקאמר מחיים סימן לחיים הוא: עבד ליה כשמעתיה. דאי כתוב בה בחיים קנה: הוה קא טרדא ליה. דקאמרה לי' והא הלכתא כרב דלא קנה והיתה רוצה שיכתוב לה פסק דין שלא קנה: זיל כתוב לה. בקלף אחד: שוכר עליהן או מטען. כלומר כתוב לה דברים בעלמא הואיל דמיטרדא לי כדי שתהא סבורה דזכותה אתה כותב לה כדי שתדחה מעלינו משום דהוה עסוק בההיא משנה בבבא מציעא משום הכי נקט האי לישנא דמטען משום דמטעה לה בדברים בעלמא. והרגישה שמטעה אותה וקללתו שתטבע ספינתו וממונו: אמשינהו. שדא מלבושיו במיא כדי שיתקיים בם קללתה ולא הועיל: [מתני'] לא כתב בה. שכיב מרע היה שנתנה לה. הוא אמר שכיב מרע הייתי. כשנתתי לך וברשותי לחזור: והוא. המקבל אמר בריא היית ומתנת בריא נתתה ואי אתה רשאי לחזור: צריך להביא ראיה לנותן. ששכיב מרע היה דברי ר' מאיר. ואין מתנתו מתנה. וחכמים אומרים המוציא מחבירו עליו הראיה ועל המקבל להביא ראיה שבתורת בריא יהבא ניהליה: כדקציר ורמי בערסיה. יהב פלוני שכיב מרע לפלוני והיו היתומים אומרים לאחר כך עמד מחליו וחזר בו והמקבל אומר מאותו חולי נפטר. ושלי היא דבמתנת שכיב מרע נתנה:

אמר

א) מלשון רבינו כאן משמע שהיה גורס בדברי רבא להיפך דאי כתיב בה בחיים ובמות ופלוגתא דרב ושמואל הוא אם כתוב בה מחיים והדבר צ"ע.

הגהות הב"ח

(א) רשב"ם ד"ה אתריה וכו' לאו אורחא ארעא למיזן: (ב) ד"ה ליטבע וכו' ספינתו בנהר הס"ד: (ג) תוס' ד"ה (בכך הקודם) שלהו וכו' דא"כ קשה מדקתני רישא שייר קרקע כל"ל והד"א עם ד"ה כתב וד"ה מתנת:

קטז א מיי' פ"ח מהל' זכייה ומתנה הלכה יא סמג עשין פב טוש"ע ח"מ סי' רנ סעיף יז:

קיז ב ג ד מיי' שם פ"ט הלכה טו עז סמג שם טוש"ע שם סעיף יג:

בְּיָדוּעַ שֶׁלֹּא הָיָה קִנְיָן אֶלָּא מֵחֲמַת הַמִּיתָה! וְאַחֲוֵי לֵיהּ בְּיָדֵיהּ, וְאִשְׁתִּיק. כִּי קָם, אֲמַר רַב נַחְמָן בַּר יִצְחָק לְרָבָא: מַאי אַחֲוֵי לָךְ? אֲמַר לֵיהּ: בִּמְיַפֶּה אֶת כֹּחוֹ. הֵיכִי דָמֵי מְיַפֶּה אֶת כֹּחוֹ? א)אֲמַר רַב חִסְדָּא: א"וְקַנֵּינָא מִינֵּיהּ מוֹסִיף עַל מַתַּנְתָּא דָא". פְּשִׁיטָא, כָּתַב לָזֶה וְכָתַב לָזֶה — הַיְינוּ דְּכִי אֲתָא רַב דִּימִי אֲמַר: ב)דַּיְיתִיקֵי מְבַטֶּלֶת דַּיְיתִיקֵי; כָּתַב וְזִיכָּה לָזֶה, כָּתַב וְזִיכָּה לָזֶה — רַב אָמַר: רִאשׁוֹן קָנָה, וּשְׁמוּאֵל אָמַר: בשֵׁנִי קָנָה; רַב אָמַר רִאשׁוֹן קָנָה — הֲרֵי הִיא כְּמַתְּנַת בָּרִיא. וּשְׁמוּאֵל אָמַר שֵׁנִי קָנָה, גהֲרֵי הִיא כְּמַתְּנַת שְׁכִיב מְרַע. וְהָא אִפְלִיגוּ בָּהּ חֲדָא זִימְנָא, בְּמַתְּנַת שְׁכִיב מְרַע שֶׁכָּתוּב בָּהּ קִנְיָן! צְרִיכָא, דְּאִי אִיתְּמַר בְּהָא — בְּהָא קָאָמַר רַב, מִשּׁוּם דְּקָנוּ מִינֵּיהּ, אֲבָל בְּהָא דְּלָא קָנוּ מִינֵּיהּ — אֵימָא מוֹדֶה לֵיהּ לִשְׁמוּאֵל; וְאִי אִיתְּמַר בְּהָא — בְּהָא קָאָמַר שְׁמוּאֵל, אֲבָל בְּהָךְ — אֵימָא מוֹדֶה לֵיהּ לְרַב, צְרִיכָא. בְּסוּרָא מַתְנוּ הָכִי. בְּפוּמְבְּדִיתָא מַתְנוּ הָכִי: אָמַר רַב יִרְמְיָה בַּר אַבָּא, שְׁלַחוּ לֵיהּ מִבֵּי רַב לִשְׁמוּאֵל: יְלַמְּדֵנוּ רַבֵּינוּ, שְׁכִיב מְרַע שֶׁכָּתַב כָּל נְכָסָיו לַאֲחֵרִים וְקָנוּ מִיָּדוֹ, מַהוּ? שְׁלַח לְהוּ: דאֵין אַחַר קִנְיָן כְּלוּם. סְבוּר

רש"י בְּיָדוּעַ שֶׁלֹּא הָיָה קִנְיָן אֶלָּא מֵחֲמַת מִיתָה. הִלְכָּךְ חוֹזֵר בּוֹ. הָא אִם מֵת — קָנָה הַמְקַבֵּל מַתָּנָה, וְלָא אָמְרִינַן שֶׁמָּא לֹא גָּמַר לְהַקְנוֹתוֹ אֶלָּא בִּשְׁטָר, וְאֵין שְׁטָר לְאַחַר מִיתָה. וְקַשְׁיָא אַדִּשְׁמוּאֵל, דְּאָמַר: לֹא יָדַעְנָא מַאי אֵידוּן בָּהּ בְּמַתְּנַת שְׁכִיב מְרַע שֶׁיֵּשׁ בָּהּ קִנְיָן, דְּהַיְינוּ הַךְ. וְהָכָא אָמַר קָנָה אַחַר מִיתָה! אַחֲוֵי לֵיהּ בְּיָדֵיהּ. שֶׁיּוֹדֵעַ תֵּירוּץ בַּדָּבָר. א"נ, רָמַז לוֹ כְּעֵין יִיפּוּי כֹּחַ, לוֹמַר דְּמוֹקְמִי' לְהַהוּא דְּאָמַר קָנָה בִּמְיַיפֶּה אֶת כֹּחוֹ. וְקַנֵּינָא מִינֵּיהּ מוֹסִיף עַל מַתַּנְתָּא דָא. כְּכָל מַה דִּכְתוּב וּמְפוֹרָשׁ לְעֵיל, בְּמָנָא דְּכָשֵׁר לְמִקְנְיָא בֵּיהּ, שָׁרִיר וְקַיָּים. כְּלוֹמַר, וְקַנְיָא מִינֵּיהּ קִנְיָן גָּמוּר לְהוֹסִיף וּלְיַיפּוֹת כֹּחוֹ, לְבַד הַמַּתָּנָה שֶׁנָּתַן בְּעַל פֶּה. וְלִישָּׁנָא יְתֵירָא לְיַיפּוֹת כֹּחַ הוּא. כָּתַב לָזֶה וְכָתַב לָזֶה. שְׁכִיב מְרַע שֶׁכָּתַב כָּל נְכָסָיו לִרְאוּבֵן בְּמַתְּנַת שְׁכִיב מְרַע, לא"ש בְּעַל פֶּה וְלא"ש בִּכְתָב, לְבָרֵר מַתְּנָתוֹ. וְחָזַר וּכְתָבוֹ אוֹ נְתָנוֹ לְשִׁמְעוֹן, אֲבָל לֹא מָסַר לָהֶן אֶת הַשְּׁטָר. דַּיְיתִיקֵי. שֶׁל שֵׁנִי מְבַטֵּל דַּיְיתִיקֵי שֶׁל רִאשׁוֹן. דִּשְׁכִיב מְרַע יָכוֹל לַחֲזוֹר בּוֹ, הִלְכָּךְ אַחֲרוֹן קָנָה, שֶׁהֲרֵי חָזַר בּוֹ מֵרִאשׁוֹן. דַּיְיתִיקֵי — לְשׁוֹן מַתְּנַת שְׁכִיב מְרַע, דְּאָמְרִי': דָּא תְּהֵא לְמֵיקַם וּלְמֶיהֱוֵי, דְּדִבְרֵי שְׁכִיב מְרַע כִּכְתוּבִים וְכִמְסוּרִין דָּמוּ. כָּתַב וְזִיכָּה לָזֶה. כָּתַב כָּל נְכָסָיו לִרְאוּבֵן וּמָסַר לוֹ אֶת הַשְּׁטָר לִרְאָיַית זְכוּתוֹ. וְיֵשׁ לְשׁוֹנוֹת אֲחֵרִים, וְלֹא יָשְׁרוּ בְּעֵינַי. רַב אָמַר רִאשׁוֹן קָנָה. דְּהָא זִיכָּה כְּקִנְיָן חָשֵׁיב לֵיהּ, וַהֲרֵי הִיא כְּמַתְּנַת שְׁכִיב מְרַע שֶׁכָּתוּב בָּהּ קִנְיָן, דְּאַרְכְּבֵיהּ אַתְּרֵי רִיכְשֵׁי, וַאֲפִי' אִם עָמַד אֵינוֹ חוֹזֵר. וּשְׁמוּאֵל אָמַר שֵׁנִי קָנָה. כְּדִין מַתְּנַת שְׁכִיב מְרַע בְּכָל נְכָסָיו שֶׁאֵין בָּהּ קִנְיָן, וְאִם עָמַד — חוֹזֵר. וְאָמְרִי' לְעֵיל: כָּל שֶׁאִם עָמַד חוֹזֵר — חוֹזֵר בְּמַתְּנָתוֹ, וְהִלְכָּךְ שֵׁנִי קָנָה. וְהָא אִיפְלִיגוּ בָּהּ חֲדָא זִימְנָא. לְעֵיל, בְּמַתְּנַת שְׁכִיב מְרַע שֶׁכָּתוּב בָּהּ קִנְיָן, דְּרַב אָמַר: אַרְכְּבָהּ אַתְּרֵי רִיכְשֵׁי, וּשְׁמוּאֵל אָמַר כו'. דְּסָבַר רַב דַּאֲפִי' לְעַצְמוֹ נַמִי לֹא קָנָה, דְּאֵינוֹ יָכוֹל לַחֲזוֹר בּוֹ — הִלְכָּךְ הָכָא רִאשׁוֹן נַמִי קָנָה. אֲבָל בְּהַךְ. בָּתְרַיְיתָא, דְּלָא קָנוּ מִינֵּיהּ, סד"א דְּלָא הָוֵי זִיכָּה יִיפּוּי כֹּחַ כְּקִנְיָן, וְאֵימָא מוֹדֶה (א) לִשְׁמוּאֵל (דְּשֵׁנִי קוֹנֶה, דְּאֵין כָּאן לֹא יִיפּוּי כֹּחַ) וְלֹא הוֹרָעַת כֹּחַ דִּשְׁמוּאֵל, דְּנֵימָא: לֹא יָדַעְנָא מַאי אֵידוּן בָּהּ, כִּדְאָמַר לְעֵיל. דְּהָא אֵין כָּאן קִנְיָן, דְּנֵימָא: לֹא גָּמַר לְהַקְנוֹתוֹ אֶלָּא בִּשְׁטָר, וְאֵין שְׁטָר לְאַחַר מִיתָה. בְּסוּרָא מַתְנוּ הָכִי. אִית דִּמְפָרְשִׁי: אַדִּלְעֵיל קָאֵי, אַפְּלוּגְתָּא קַמַּיְיתָא דְּמַתְּנַת שְׁכִיב מְרַע שֶׁכָּתוּב בָּהּ קִנְיָן, וְאָמַר רַב אַרְכְּבָהּ אַתְּרֵי רִיכְשֵׁי וּשְׁמוּאֵל אָמַר כו'. וַאֲתָא לְמֵימַר: בְּסוּרָא מַתְנוּ הָכִי כִּדִלְעֵיל, וְקַשְׁיָא לְהוּ הָא דְּאָמַר רַב יְהוּדָה אָמַר שְׁמוּאֵל. אֲבָל בְּפוּמְבְּדִיתָא מַתְנוּ הָכִי וכו' וְלָא קַשְׁיָא לְהוּ מִידֵּי הָא דְּאָמַר רַב יְהוּדָה אָמַר שְׁמוּאֵל, דְּהָשְׁתָּא נַמִי מוֹדֵי שְׁמוּאֵל דְּאִם מֵת הָוֵי קִנְיָן, כִּדְדַיְיקִינַן נַמִי מִמִּילְּתֵיהּ דְּרַב יְהוּדָה. וְלָאו מִילְּתָא הִיא, דְּהָשְׁתָּא נַמִי קַשְׁיָא הַךְ אַדְּרַב יְהוּדָה, דְּהָכָא קָאָמַר: אֵין לְאַחַר קִנְיָן כְּלוּם, בֵּין לְאַחֵר בֵּין לְעַצְמוֹ, וַאֲפִי' אִם עָמַד אֵינוֹ יָכוֹל לַחֲזוֹר בּוֹ. וּלְעֵיל אָמַר רַב יְהוּדָה אָמַר שְׁמוּאֵל: בְּיָדוּעַ שֶׁלֹּא הָיָה קִנְיָן אֶלָּא מֵחֲמַת מִיתָה, וְיָכוֹל לַחֲזוֹר בּוֹ. אֶלָּא אַהַךְ דְּסָלֵיק מִינֵּיהּ קָאֵי, דִּפְלִיגֵי רַב וּשְׁמוּאֵל בְּכָתַב וְזִיכָּה לָזֶה וְכָתַב וְזִיכָּה לָזֶה. וְכֵן פר"ח: בְּסוּרָא מַתְנוּ הָכִי לִפְלוּגְתָּא דְּרַב וּשְׁמוּאֵל דְּכָתַב וְזִיכָּה לָזֶה, כְּדַאֲמָרַן. בְּפוּמְבְּדִיתָא מַתְנוּ: שְׁלַחוּ מִבֵּי רַב לִשְׁמוּאֵל יְלַמְּדֵנוּ רַבֵּינוּ כָּתַב וְזִיכָּה לָרִאשׁוֹן וְקָנוּ מִיָּדוֹ מַאי? שְׁלַח לְהוּ: כֵּיוָן שֶׁזִּיכָּה לוֹ וְקָנוּ מִינֵּיהּ — קָנָה, וְאֵין יָכוֹל לַחֲזוֹר בְּמַתְּנָתוֹ, וְכ"ש לְהַקְנוֹתוֹ לְאַחֵר. וְאֵין אוֹמְרִים בָּזֶה שֶׁמָּא לֹא גָּמַר לְהַקְנוֹתוֹ אֶלָּא בִּשְׁטָר, דְּהָא זִיכָּה לוֹ וְקָנוּ מִינֵּיהּ. כֵּיוָן דְּכוּלֵּי הַאי [עֲבַד] — לֹא הָוֵי אֶלָּא לְיַיפּוֹת כֹּחוֹ, וְקָנָה. סְבוּר

תוספות ורמי דרב אדרב כו'. ומשני: דרב אדרב לא קשיא, התם דקנו מיניה בתוך השטר, ולכך יש ייפוי כח בתוך השטר — אין כאן ייפוי כח יותר. אבל לא קנו מיניה בתוך השטר — אין כאן ייפוי כח יותר. ומה שהביא רבינו שמואל ראיה דה"ה בלא שטר, מדפריך עלה בסמוך מדרב יהודה אמר שמואל: שכיב מרע כו' — לאו ראיה היא, דאיכא למימר דהכי פריך: ומי אמר שמואל שמא לא גמר להקנותו אלא בשטר כו'? והא אמר שמואל: שכיב מרע שכתב כל נכסיו, אע"פ שקנו מידו, אם עמד — חוזר, אבל אם מת — אינו חוזר. ואע"ג דליכא קנין בשטר, מ"מ היה לנו לחשבו לשמואל גרעון כח, דהא אפי' לרב דאית ליה דקנין בשטר הוי ייפוי כח, היה סבור כאן שהוא גרעון כח, שיוכל לחזור בו אם עמד — כל שכן שמואל שסובר לעיל דקנין בשטר גרעון כח, שהיה לו לסבור גם כאן גרעון כח יותר ממה שהוא סבור לעיל, ואפי' לא עמד יחזור בו. כמו רב שסובר כאן גרעון כח יותר ממה שסובר למעלה, [קל וחומר לשמואל דלא גרע] רס"ל אבל דוחק הוא לומר דשמואל לא מפליג בין הקנה לו לכתב קנין בשטר, וטעמא דמתני' משום ייפוי כח, כדפרישית לעיל. ולפי זה נראה לי, דכל הך שמעתתא אין צריך להעמיד כלל בכתב כל נכסיו כפי' רבינו שמואל וכפי' רבינו חננאל, אלא יכלו להעמידה בטוב במתנת שכיב מרע, [בין] במקלתה בין בכולה. דעל כרחך בכולה נמי איירי, מדפריך עלה משכיב מרע שכתב כל נכסיו לאחרים וכו'. וכל קושיות שפירש רבינו שמואל להעמידה במתנת שכיב מרע בכולה — אינם קושיות לפי זה. אלא יש לפרש דבמתנת שכיב מרע בכולה ובמקלת מיירי שפיר. (ב) ומאי דקיימא לן כשמואל — יש ללמוד שאין לכתוב במתנת שכיב מרע קנין. ומה שכתב הגאון בתקון שטרות "קנו מיניה בכל לשון של זכות" — נראה שהיה צריך לכתוב שם שום ייפוי כח, או "אף קנו ממנו" דמשמע טפי ייפוי כח, או שמא צריך לכתוב "וקנינא מיניה מוסיף על מתנתא דא"ג). **כתב** וזיכה לזה וכתב וזיכה לזה. פירש רבינו שמואל: זיכה — שמסר לו את השטר. וקשה לרבינו יצחק בר מאיר: דא"כ, הא דקאמר כתב לזה וכתב לזה — היינו בלא מסירה, והיכי קאמר עלה דייתיקי מבטלת דייתיקי? והתנן לעיל בפרק "יש נוחלין" (דף קלה:): נמצאת דייתיקי קשורה לו על יריכו, וזכה בה אחד מן היורשים — אינה כלום! ועוד, דאי במסירה — [לא] היה אמר רב שאינו יכול לחזור בו רס"ל השכיב מרע, דאל"כ תקשה לך מדאמר בסוף פ"ק דבבא מציעא (דף יח.): דייתיקי מתנה ושוברין הרי זה לא יחזיר, שאני אומר כתובים היו ונמלך עליהם שלא ליתנם. ודייק בגמ' (דף יט.): טעמא דלא אמר "תנו", הא אמר "תנו" — נותנין. ורמינהי: דייתיקי ואפותיקי, אע"פ ששניהם מודים — לא יחזיר לא לזה ולא לזה! ומוקי לה למתני' התם דבשכיב מרע יהבינן ניהליה, [דקאמר הא אמר תנו נותנין] — לית ליה פסידא, רס"ל דבתרייתא זכי, דהא הדר ביה מקמייתא. ולמה אין לנו לחוש דילמא יהבה לזה מתחלה ומסרה, דהשתא לא מצי תו הדר ביה? על כן נראה לפרש: כתב וזיכה — דלאו היינו מסר, שאפי' מסר לו יכול לחזור בו. אלא זיכה — היינו שזיכה בו את הנכסים, וכתב לו בשטר שזיכה לו ע"י אחר, אם מטלטלים הם, ואם מקרקעי — א"ל: חזק וקני. והזכות כתב בתוך השטר. ופריך: והא איפליגו בה חדא זימנא, שהרי הזיכוי בתוך השטר במקום הקנין עומד, ואית ליה לרב לעיל דהוי כמתנת בריא, ואינו יכול לחזור בו! ומיהו, משמואל לא קשיא מידי, שהרי הוא אומר כאן דשני קנה, ואילו לעיל קאמר דאין שטר לאחר מיתה, ולא קנה כלל. אבל מרב פריך שפיר. ומשני: אי איתמר בההיא — בההיא קאמר רב משום דקנו מיניה, פי': הקנין כתוב בתוך השטר. אבל בהא דלא קנו מיניה וכו'. ואי איתמר בהא — בהא קאמר שמואל וכו'. למילתא דשמואל אין צריך כאן שום צריכותא, דודאי שמואל לא סבירא ליה הכא כמו לעיל, דהא לרב גרידא הוא דצריך לאקשויי הכי.

*רס"ל הל"ח **שלחו** ליה מבי רב כו' קנו מידו מהו. פי': שכתבו קנין בשטר עם הזיכוי. שלח (ג) ליה: אין אחר הקנין כלום, ואין יכול לחזור בו. ואפי' לעצמו נמי אינו יכול לחזור בו, כדמפרש רב הונא. ורבינו יעקב פירש סוגיא זו בענין אחר, ומיירו רב ושמואל אפי' היכא שאין כתוב הקנין בשטר, אלא קנין בעלמא. ומתני' דקתני: שייר קרקע כל שהוא מתנתו מתנה — היינו בקנין, וסיפא דקתני: לא שייר קרקע כל שהוא אין מתנתו מתנה — מיירי בלא קנין. ולא מיירי סיפא דומיא דרישא. וההיא דכתב וזיכה — היינו *מסתמא, כפי' רבינו שמואל, שזיכוי זה במקום קנין עומד. והא דקאמרי' לעיל: דייתיקי מבטלת דייתיקי בכתב לזה ולזה — היינו כשלא כתב לו לשם שטר, אלא לשם צוואה בעלמא. והשתא לא תקשה מידי מההיא דסוף פ"ק דבבא מציעא, דהתם איירי בדייתיקי של צוואה, דסתם דייתיקי דצוואה היא. ואין נראה, דלשון דייתיקי לא משמע אלא שטר גמור, שנתנו לשם שטר של אותה מתנה. דהכי משמע לישנא ד"כתובים היו ונמלך עליהם שלא ליתנם". ועוד

גי' רש"א מסר כפי' ר"ח

רבינו גרשום

שלא היה קנין אלא מחמת מיתה. וטעמא דעמד משום הכי חוזר הא לא עמד אלא מת הוי קנין וקנה אלמא דסבירא ליה דשטר לאחר מיתה [הוי] שטר וקשיא דשמואל אדשמואל: ואחוי ליה. רמז לו שישתוק שהוא יתרצה לו: אמר ליה. האי אחוי לי בידו משום הכי אמר שמואל דקנה לאחר מיתה במיפה את כחו אבל היכא דלא ייפה את כחו אין שטר לאחר מיתה: וקנינא מיניה מוסיף על מתנתא. היינו דאמר אף כתובו כלומר דמשמע דמחיים הקנה לו: כתב לזה שדה זו וחזר וכתב לזה אותה שדה עצמה היינו דייתיקי מבטלת דייתיקי. כלומר שני קנה ראשון לא קנה שחזר בו: כתב וזיכה לזה. שא"ל לך וזכה בה לפני: וכתב וזיכה אותה שדה עצמ' [לאחר] מהו מי אמרינן דכקנין דמי אותה זכיה וקני אי לא קנה: רב אמר ראשון קנה. דארכביה אתרי ריכשי מאחר שכתב וזיכה לזה אין לשני במקום ראשון כלום: ושמואל אמר שני קנה. משום דשמא ראשון לא גמר להקנות אלא בשטר ואין שטר לאחר מיתה והואיל דכתב לשני וחזר מראשון לא הוי מתנה ולא קני ראשון: והא אפליגו בה חדא זמנא לעיל (בין) רב ושמואל א) בההיא דלעיל קאמר רב ארכבוה אתרי ריכשי. משום דקנו מיניה וכתבו לו קנין אבל בהא דכתב וזיכה לו דלא קנו מיניה דההיא זכי' לאו כקנין דמי אימא מודה ליה לשמואל דשני קנה ולא ראשון קמ"ל דלא: בהא קאמר שמואל. דשני קנה משום דלא קנו לראשון: בסורא מתנו הכי כדאמר לעיל: קנו מידו בלא כתיבה וחזר ונתנו לאחר מהו. מי אמרינן דחזר מראשון וקני שני ולא ראשון או דילמא הואיל דהקנה לראשון אין לשני כלום: שלח ליה אין לאחר קנין כלום. וראשון קנה שני לא קנה דהא דקאמר לעיל לא ידענא מאי אידון בה שמא לא גמר להקנותו אלא בשטר ואין שטר לאחר מיתה ב). אבל הקנה לו בעל פה דקנין מחיים הוה אין לאחר קנין כלום:

א) נראה דצ"ל דאי איתמר בהא. בההוא דלעיל בהא קאמר רב וכו'. ב) נראה דצ"ל ואין שטר לאחר מיתה היינו היכא דלוה לכתוב שטר ג"כ אבל הקנה לו בע"פ וכו'.

א) לעיל דף קלו.: ב) שם דף קלה:: ג) גי' רש"ל והא דכתב והל"ת:

הגהות הב"ח

(א) רשב"ם ד"ה אבל בהך וכו' מודה ליה לשמואל וכו' לא ייפוי כח דרב ולא הורעת כח דשמואל: (ב) תום' ד"ה (בע"א) מתנת כו' ולמאי דקיימא לן כשמואל: (ג) ד"ה שלחו וכו' שלח להו אין אחר הקנין:

רס"ל מ"ז

א) כתובות דף נה: ב) לעיל דף קכה: גיטין דף ט: ג) לעיל דף קנא: ד) גי' רש"ל וגי' רש"א א"כ אף לדידיה תנו דמתני' היינו כתבו ותנו דכה"ג: ה) גי' רש"ל שייך:

קטו א ב מיי' פ"ח מהל' זכייה ומתנה הלכה יוד יא סמג עשין פב טוש"ע ח"מ סי' רנ סעיף ט וסעיף יז:

א)אִיתְּמַר: מַתְּנַת שְׁכִיב מְרַע שֶׁכָּתוּב בָּהּ קִנְיָן – בֵּי רַב מִשְּׁמֵיהּ דְּרַב אָמְרִי: אַרְכְּבֵיהּ אַתְּרֵי רִיכְשֵׁי, וּשְׁמוּאֵל אָמַר: לָא יָדַעְנָא מַאי אֵדוּן בָּהּ. בֵּי רַב מִשְּׁמֵיהּ דְּרַב אָמְרִי: אַרְכְּבֵיהּ אַתְּרֵי רִיכְשֵׁי, הֲרֵי הִיא כְּמַתְּנַת בָּרִיא, הֲרֵי הִיא כְּמַתְּנַת שְׁכִיב מְרַע; הֲרֵי הִיא כְּמַתְּנַת בָּרִיא – שֶׁאִם עָמַד אֵינוֹ חוֹזֵר, הֲרֵי הִיא כְּמַתְּנַת שְׁכִיב מְרַע – שֶׁאִם אָמַר הַלְוָאָתוֹ לִפְלוֹנִי – הַלְוָאָתוֹ לִפְלוֹנִי. וּשְׁמוּאֵל אָמַר: לָא יָדַעְנָא מַאי אֵדוּן בָּהּ, אשֶׁמָּא לֹא גָּמַר לְהַקְנוֹתוֹ אֶלָּא בִּשְׁטָר, וְאֵין שְׁטָר לְאַחַר מִיתָה. וְרָמֵי דְּרַב אַדְּרַב, וְדִשְׁמוּאֵל אַדִּשְׁמוּאֵל; דִּשְׁלַח רָבִין מִשְּׁמֵיהּ דְּרַבִּי אַבָּהוּ, הֱווּ יָדְעִי שֶׁשָּׁלַח ר' אֶלְעָזָר לַגּוֹלָה מִשּׁוּם רַבֵּינוּ: ב)שְׁכִיב מְרַע שֶׁאָמַר "כִּתְבוּ וּתְנוּ מָנֶה לִפְלוֹנִי" וּמֵת – אֵין כּוֹתְבִין וְנוֹתְנִין, שֶׁמָּא לֹא גָּמַר לְהַקְנוֹתוֹ אֶלָּא בִּשְׁטָר, וְאֵין שְׁטָר לְאַחַר מִיתָה; וְאָמַר רַב יְהוּדָה אָמַר שְׁמוּאֵל, הִלְכְתָא: כּוֹתְבִין וְנוֹתְנִין; קַשְׁיָא דְּרַב אַדְּרַב, קַשְׁיָא דִּשְׁמוּאֵל אַדִּשְׁמוּאֵל! דְּרַב אַדְּרַב לָא קַשְׁיָא: הָא דְּקָנוּ מִינֵּיהּ, הָא דְּלָא קָנוּ מִינֵּיהּ; דִּשְׁמוּאֵל אַדִּשְׁמוּאֵל לָא קַשְׁיָא: בבִּמְיַפֶּה אֶת כֹּחוֹ. יְתֵיב רַב נַחְמָן בַּר יִצְחָק אֲחוֹרֵיהּ דְּרָבָא, וִיתֵיב רָבָא קַמֵּיהּ דְּרַב נַחְמָן קָא בָּעֵי מִינֵּיהּ, מִי אֲמַר שְׁמוּאֵל: שֶׁמָּא לֹא גָּמַר לְהַקְנוֹתוֹ אֶלָּא בִּשְׁטָר וְאֵין שְׁטָר לְאַחַר מִיתָה? וְהָא ג)אָמַר רַב יְהוּדָה אָמַר שְׁמוּאֵל: שְׁכִיב מְרַע שֶׁכָּתַב כָּל נְכָסָיו לַאֲחֵרִים, אַף עַל פִּי שֶׁקָּנוּ מִיָּדוֹ – עָמַד חוֹזֵר,

בְּיָדוּעַ

רשב"ם

מַתְּנַת שְׁכִיב מְרַע שֶׁכָּתוּב בָּהּ קִנְיָן בֵּי רַב אָמְרִי אַרְכְּבֵיהּ כו'. עַל כָּרְחָךְ בְּכוֹתֵב כָּל נְכָסָיו פְּלִיגִי רַב וּשְׁמוּאֵל. דְּאִי בְּמַתְּנַת שְׁכִיב מְרַע בְּמִקְצָת שֶׁכָּתַב בָּהּ קִנְיָן פְּלִיגִי – בְּהֶדְיָא הו"ל לְמֵימַר: מַתְּנַת שְׁכִיב מְרַע בְּמִקְצָת כו'. וְעוֹד, הָא תְּנַן מַתְנִי' סְתָמָא: שִׁיֵּיר קַרְקַע כָּל שֶׁהוּא מַתְּנָתוֹ מַתָּנָה, וְלָא מַפְלִיג (א) בֵּין כָּתַב בִּשְׁטָר קִנְיָן בֵּין לֹא כְּתָבוֹ בְּתוֹכוֹ, וְהֵיאַךְ אָמַר שְׁמוּאֵל: לָא יָדַעְנָא מַאי אֵידוּן בָּהּ, וְלֹא קָנֵה? הָא כֵּיוָן דִּכְתִיב בָּהּ קִנְיָן, וּמַתְּנַת מִקְצָת הִיא – עַל כָּרְחָךְ קָתָנֵי מַתְנִי' הֲרֵי הִיא מַתָּנָה! וְכֵן פר"ח. וְעוֹד: הָא פָּסְקָנָא לְדִבְרֵי הַכֹּל הִלְכְתָא דְּמַתְּנַת שְׁכִיב מְרַע בְּמִקְצָת בָּעְיָא קִנְיָן, וַהֲרֵי הִיא מֵעַתָּה כְּמַתְּנַת בָּרִיא לְגַמְרֵי, וְאֵינוֹ יָכוֹל לַחֲזוֹר בּוֹ אֲפִילּוּ כְּשֶׁעוֹמֵד. וְאִם אֵין בָּהּ קִנְיָן – אֵינָהּ כְּלוּם, וַאֲפִילּוּ אִם מֵת לֹא קָנָה. וְלָא הֲוָה לֵיהּ לַגְּמָרָא לְקוֹבְעָהּ אַחַר הֶפְסֵק. וְעוֹד, מִדְּרָמֵינַן עֲלָהּ לְקַמָּן מִדְּרַב יְהוּדָה אָמַר שְׁמוּאֵל: שְׁכִיב מְרַע שֶׁכָּתַב כָּל נְכָסָיו כו', מִכְּלָל דְּהָא נַמִי בְּכוֹתֵב כָּל נְכָסָיו מַיְירֵי. שֶׁכָּתוּב בָּהּ קִנְיָן. וְהוּא הַדִּין אִם אֵין כָּתוּב קִנְיָן בְּתוֹךְ הַשְּׁטָר. אוֹ אֲפִילּוּ אֵין כָּאן הַשְּׁטָר כְּלָל, אֶלָּא שְׁכִיב מְרַע שֶׁהִזְכִּיר צַוָּואַת שְׁכִיב מְרַע כְּשֶׁחִילֵּק כָּל נְכָסָיו, וְגַם הִקְנָה אוֹתָם בְּקִנְיָן סוּדָר לִמְקַבֵּל מַתָּנָה. אֲבָל אוֹרְחָא דְּמִלְּתָא נָקַט, שֶׁדֶּרֶךְ לִכְתּוֹב הַצַּוָּואוֹת וְהַקִּנְיָינִין בַּשְּׁטָר, כְּדֵי שֶׁלֹּא תִּשְׁתַּכַּח הַצַּוָּואָה. וַאֲפִי' לִשְׁמוּאֵל דְּאָמַר: לָא יָדַעְנָא מַאי אֵידוּן בָּהּ, שֶׁמָּא לֹא גָּמַר לְהַקְנוֹתוֹ אֶלָּא בִּשְׁטָר – ה"ה אִם לֹא נִכְתַּב הַקִּנְיָן בְּתוֹךְ הַשְּׁטָר, וּכְדְבָעֵינָן לְפָרוּשֵׁי בְּסָמוּךְ. וּרְאָיָה לַדָּבָר מֵהָא דְּרָמֵינַן עֲלָהּ בְּסָמוּךְ מֵהָא דְּאָמַר רַב יְהוּדָה אָמַר שְׁמוּאֵל: שְׁכִיב מְרַע שֶׁכָּתַב כָּל נְכָסָיו, אע"פ שֶׁקָּנוּ מִיָּדוֹ כו' – וְהַיְינוּ בְּקִנְיָן בְּעָלְמָא, בְּלֹא כְּתִיבָה בִּשְׁטָר, מַיְירֵי. אַרְכְּבֵיהּ אַתְּרֵי רִיכְשֵׁי. כְּמוֹ "רוֹכְבֵי הָרֶכֶשׁ" (אסתר ח), "הַמֶּרְכָּבָה לָרֶכֶשׁ" (מיכה א), כְּלוֹמַר, הִטִּיל שְׁתֵּי כּוֹחוֹת לְצוֹרֶךְ מַתָּנָה זוֹ; ע"י שֶׁכָּתַב בָּהּ "כִּדְקָנֵיר וְרָמֵי בְּעַרְסֵיהּ" וְכָל לְשׁוֹן שְׁכִיב מְרַע – נָתַן בָּהּ כֹּחַ שְׁכִיב מְרַע, כִּדְמְפָרֵשׁ לְקַמֵּיהּ. וְע"י קִנְיָן שֶׁכָּתוּב בָּהּ, שֶׁאֵינוֹ צָרִיךְ בְּצַוָּואַת שְׁכִיב מְרַע אֶלָּא בְּמַתְּנַת בָּרִיא – נָתַן לוֹ כֹּחַ מַתְּנַת בָּרִיא, שֶׁאִם עָמַד אֵינוֹ חוֹזֵר. דְּכֵיוָן דְּדִבְרֵי שְׁכִיב מְרַע כִּכְתוּבִין וְכִמְסוּרִין דָּמוּ, וּלְעִנְיַן מִיקְנָא לְאַחַר מִיתָה לֹא צָרִיךְ קִנְיָן – הִלְכָּךְ לְיַיפּוֹת כֹּחוֹ שֶׁל מְקַבֵּל מַתָּנָה הִקְנָה בְּקִנְיָן, כְּדֵי שֶׁלֹּא יוּכַל לַחֲזוֹר בּוֹ, אֲפִילּוּ אִם יַעֲמוֹד מֵחָלְיוֹ. שֶׁאִם אָמַר הַלְוָאָתוֹ לִפְלוֹנִי. בְּזֹאת הַמַּתָּנָה, אִם נָתַן לוֹ הַלְוָאָה שֶׁחַיָּיב לוֹ אִישׁ אַחֵר, אע"ג דְּלֵיכָּא מַעֲמַד שְׁלָשְׁתָּן – קָנָה. דְּקַיְימָא לָן [גִּיטִּין] (דף יג.): "מָנֶה לִי בְּיָדְךָ, תְּנֵהוּ לִפְלוֹנִי" בְּמַעֲמַד שְׁלָשְׁתָּן קָנָה, לֹא שְׁנָא מִלְוֶה וְלֹא שְׁנָא פִּקָּדוֹן. וְהָכָא קָנֵי בְּצַוָּואַת שְׁכִיב מְרַע, וְאע"ג דְּלֵיכָּא בְּמַעֲמַד שְׁלָשְׁתָּן. לָא יָדַעְנָא מַאי אֵידוּן בָּהּ. דִּלְמָא לֹא קָנָה כְּלָל אֲפִילּוּ אִם מֵת. דְּכֵיוָן דַּהֲוָה קָנֵי בַּאֲמִירָה בְּעָלְמָא בְּצַוָּואַת שְׁכִיב מְרַע, הוֹאִיל וְלֵיכָּא שִׁיּוּר נְכָסִים – לָמָּה לִי תּוּ לְאַקְנוּיֵי בְּסוּדָר? הִלְכָּךְ אִיכָּא לְמֵימַר מֵיהֲדַר הָדַר, וְעָקַר מִמֶּנָּה כֹּחַ מַתְּנַת שְׁכִיב מְרַע, וְאֵינוֹ רוֹצֶה שֶׁיִּקְנֶה בַּאֲמִירָה בְּעָלְמָא אֶלָּא בְּקִנְיָן סוּדָר, וּמַה הוּא מַקְנֶה לוֹ בְּהַאי קִנְיָן – מַתְּנַת שְׁכִיב מְרַע הוּא מַקְנֶה לוֹ, דְּהַיְינוּ לְאַחַר מִיתָה, וְאֵין שְׁטָר לְאַחַר מִיתָה אֶלָּא אִם כֵּן *הִקְנָה לוֹ מֵחַיִּים. א"נ, אֵין הַקִּנְיָן כָּתוּב בַּשְּׁטָר וְגַם הַשְּׁטָר לֹא נִכְתַּב כְּלָל, אֶלָּא שֶׁצִּוָּה וְנָתַן מֵחַיִּים כָּל נְכָסָיו בְּצַוָּואַת שְׁכִיב מְרַע וּמַקְנֶה בְּסוּדָר – אֵין קִנְיָן תּוֹפֵס, שֶׁלֹּא נִתְכַּוֵּין לְהַקְנוֹת אֶלָּא לְאַחַר מִיתָה. דְּמִיַּד כְּשֶׁמֵּת נָפְלוּ נְכָסִים קַמֵּי יוֹרְשִׁין, וְתוּ לָא חָיְילָא מַתְּנָתוֹ. אֵין כּוֹתְבִין וְנוֹתְנִין. לְאַחַר שֶׁמֵּת, שֶׁמָּא לֹא גָּמַר לְהַקְנוֹת לוֹ בְּעַל פֶּה אֶלָּא עַד שֶׁיִּכְתּוֹב הַשְּׁטָר, וּשְׁטָר שֶׁנִּכְתַּב לְאַחַר מִיתָה לָאו כְּלוּם הוּא. דִּלְעִנְיַן שְׁטָר לֹא אָמוּר רַבָּנַן דִּבְרֵי שְׁכִיב מְרַע כִּכְתוּבִין וְכִמְסוּרִין דָּמוּ, אֶלָּא לְעִנְיַן מַתְּנַת מָמוֹן, דְּאִי אָמַר "תְּנוּ" – נוֹתְנִין אַף לְאַחַר מִיתָה. הִלְכְתָא כּוֹתְבִין וְנוֹתְנִין. דִּלְיַיפּוֹת כֹּחוֹ שֶׁל מְקַבֵּל מַתָּנָה נָוֶה לִכְתּוֹב. קַשְׁיָא דְּרַב אַדְּרַב קַשְׁיָא דִּשְׁמוּאֵל אַדִּשְׁמוּאֵל. דִּלְעֵיל אָמַר רַב: בָּתַר אוּמְדָּנָא דְּיִיפּוּי כֹּחוֹ שֶׁל מְקַבֵּל מַתָּנָה אָזְלִינַן, וּשְׁמוּאֵל אָמַר: אֵין שְׁטָר לְאַחַר מִיתָה, וְהָכָא קָאָמַר אִיפְּכָא. הָא דְּקָנוּ מִינֵּיהּ. כִּדְאָמְרַן, שֶׁכָּתוּב בָּהּ קִנְיָן, וְה"ה לְקִנְיָן בְּלֹא כְּתִיבָה. וְכֵיוָן דְּאַקְנֵי בְּקִנְיָן – לְיַיפּוֹת כֹּחוֹ הוּא דַּעֲבַד. בִּמְיַיפֶּה אֶת כֹּחוֹ. כִּדְלְקַמָּן: "וְקָנִינָא מִינֵּיהּ מוֹסִיף עַל מַתָּנָה דָּא" – יִיתּוּר לָשׁוֹן לְיַיפּוֹת כֹּחוֹ הוּא. וְה"נ בְּצַוָּואָתוֹ שֶׁאָמַר "כִּתְבוּ וּתְנוּ" פֵּירֵשׁ שֶׁיִּכְתְּבוּ בַּשְּׁטָר הַהוּא יִיפּוּי כֹּחַ דְּקִנְיָן, דְּמוֹסִיף עַל מַתְּנָתָא.

בְּיָדוּעַ

נ"א מסר

תוספות

דאין נראה לומר דקמשמע לן ברישא דאין מעמד שלשתן מועיל בשטר, אם ד)(לא תימא ד"תנו" במתני' היינו "כתבו", וכי) האי גוונא שלא בא השטר לעולם לא ה)מהני מעמד שלשתן. ועל כרחך צריכין אנו לומר: הא כדאיתא והא כדאיתא; רישא קמ"ל דאין גט לאחר מיתה, וסיפא קמ"ל דין של מעמד שלשתן בממון. ואע"ג דדייק התם בגמרא דסיפא איירי בבריא דומיא דרישא, אלמא משמע שיש לנו לדמות אהדדי – היינו טעמא בבריא, דבעי לאוקומא בחד גוונא דאיירי בחד גברא, אבל אינם דומות לגמרי אהדדי. *[הגה"ה]. ועוד י"ל: דמצי לאוקומא רישא דגט שחרור במעמד שלשתן, כיון דאוקי מתניתין בהכי. ואשמועינן ברישא, דאע"ג דאמר "תנו גט לאשתי במעמד שלשתן", שאשתו רוצה בכך, וכן העבד – לא קנו בכך. אפילו אם תמצי לומר שלענין זכות נייר השטר הוי ממון, ואהני ליה מעמד שלשתן – לענין שכתוב בתוכו לא מהני. ואע"ג ד"תן" כ"זכי" דמי – הכא לא יזכה בו העבד, דאיכא לאוקמא דמיירי שאינו באותה שעה ברשות הנפקד, ואן בעינן מיד ליד. א"נ, שאין הנפקד רוצה לזכות לעבד, וזוכה בעל כרחו במעמד שלשתן במתנה, אבל לא בגט שחרור, כדפרישנא לעיל ב"המוכר את הספינה" (דף עו.) שמועיל מעמד שלשתן בעל כרחו של נפקד. מיהו, אין נראה להעמיד רישא בפלוגתא דאמוראי, דאיכא דמוקי לה במעמד שלשתן ואיכא דמוקי לה ב"כתבו ותנו". אלא ודאי בסיפא הוא דפליגי, ולא הוי סיפא דומיא דרישא מכל וכל, כדפרישית לעיל. ולא גרסי' נמי בהך סיפא "זה", דאפילו בסתם מנה מיירי מתניתין, כדאיתא בפ"ק דגיטין (דף יג. ושם). **מתנת** שכיב מרע שכתוב בה קנין. פירש רבינו שמואל: דמיירי בשכתב לו כל נכסיו. וה"ה בלא שטר, אלא שהקנה לו(ב), אמרי' דאין קנין לאחר מיתה לשמואל. והביא ראיה מדפריך לה לקמן מהא מילתא דשמואל דאמר: שכיב מרע שכתב כל נכסיו לאחרים, אע"פ שקנו לו כו'. ואין נראה לרבינו יצחק בר מאיר, דא"כ מתני' דקתני: שכיב מרע ששייר קרקע כל שהוא מתנתו מתנה – במאי מיירי לרב? אי שלא בקנין – אמאי מתנתו מתנה? והא קי"ל לעיל דבעי קנין. ואי בקנין, א"כ סיפא דקתני: לא שייר קרקע כל שהוא אין מתנתו מתנה – והא אית ליה לרב הכא דמתנתו מתנה בקנין! ועוד, דלשמואל דאמר אין גט לאחר מיתה – הוא הדין נמי דאין קנין לאחר מיתה, א"כ מתני' דקתני: שייר קרקע כל שהוא מתנתו מתנה – היינו בקנין, איך יועיל לשמואל כלום? הלא שמא לא גמר להקנותו אלא לאחר מיתה! ודוחק הוא להעמיד משנתנו במייפה כחו, וכגון שאמר, (ג) דבסמוך לא משמע הכי. ועוד קשה: מדפסיק גמרא דהלכתא מתנת שכיב מרע במקצת בעיא קנין ואם עמד אינו חוזר, משמע: הא בכולה, אם עמד – חוזר, ואפילו ע"י קנין. והא ליתא לרב, דאית ליה דקנין אלים כל כך בכל נכסיו כמו במתנת בריא! ועוד קשיא: דוחק גדול הוא שהגמרא אינו אומר אלא שטר, והוא אמר דה"ה נמי קנין בלא שטר. ועוד, דלספרים דגרסינן לקמן: וכגון דכתב ליה "וקנינא מיניה מוסיף על מתנתא" – דמשמע שבתוך השטר כתב לו כן. מיהו, יש ספרים דגרסי' לקמן: כגון דא"ל "וקנינא מיניה" כו'. ונראה לר"י לפרש דמיירי בשטר דוקא. והיינו טעמא דרב: שסובר שלכך כתב לו קנין בתוך השטר – לאלומי כחו יותר, שאפי' בכל נכסיו אם עמד אינו חוזר, כיון שכתב לו בתוך השטר. ושמואל סבר דשטר זה אינו אלא מגרע כחו, כי אע"פ שיש בו קנין – אין בו בכך ייפוי כח, אלא יש לנו לומר שלא גמר להקנותו אלא בשטר כו'.

ורמי

רבינו גרשום

שכתוב בו קנין כו'. קרקע זו נתן לפלו' ולפלו' והקנה לו. ארכביה אתרי ריכשי. כלומר כוחות וחזוקין מחזקינן ליה: שאם עמד אינו חוזר. הואיל שכתוב בו קנין: שאם אמר הלואתי לפלו' וכתבו קנין אע"ג דלא הוה במעמד שלשתן קנה. אבל בבריא בעינן מעמד שלשתן: ושמואל אמר לא ידענ' היכי אידון בה. הואיל שכתב בו קנין דשמא לא גמר להקנותו אלא באותו שטר שכתוב בו קנין ואין שטר כו': משום רבינו. זה רב: ואין שטר לאחר מיתה ורב אמר לעיל ארכביה אתרי ריכשי. דרב אדרב לא קשיא הא דקנו מיניה משום הכי ארכבוה אתרי ריכשי. משום דקנין מחיים הוא ולא לאחר מיתה ולא הוי שטר לאחר מיתה דקנין מחיים הוה אבל אי לא קנו מיניה אלא אמר כתבו ותנו מנה לפלו' ולא הספיקו לכתוב וליתן עד שמת אין כותבין ואין נותנין ומשום דאין שטר לאחר מיתה: והכא דקאמר דנותנין במיפה את כחו קאמר להו אף כתובו והבו. מדקאמר אף כתובו משמע דמתנה מחיים הואי ולהכי אמר אף כתובו כדי ליפות את כחו שהוא נמי שטר אבל היכא דלא מיפה את כחו לא קנה דשמא לא גמר להקנותו אלא בשטר ואין שטר לאחר מיתה: מי אמר שמואל הכי שמא לא גמר להקנותו אלא בשטר כו' והא אמר רב יהודה אמר שמואל כו'.

הגהות הב"ח

(א) רשב"ם ד"ה מתנת ש"מ וכו' בין כתב בשטר קנין. נ"ב פי' אע"פ דמיירי בדקנו מיניה מ"מ לא מפליג בין כתב הקנין בתוך השטר בין לא כתבו בתוך השטר: (ב) תוס' ד"ה מתנת וכו' אלא שהקנה לו נמי אמרינן: (ג) בא"ד וכגון שאמר וקנינא כו' דבסמוך לא משמע וכו' דדוחק גדול וכו' על מתנתא לא דמשמע:

עין משפט
נר מצוה

קח א מיי' פ"ח מהלכות זכיה ומתנה הלכה כג סמג עשין פב טוש"ע חו"מ סי' רנ סעיף ז:
קט ב מיי' שם הלכה יד סמג שם טוש"ע שם סעיף ב:
קי ג מיי' פ"ו מהלכות גירושין הל' כח ופ"ט הל' ב יב יד כב סמג עשין נ טוש"ע אה"ע סי' קמא סעיף נח:
קיא ד מיי' פ"ו מהלכות עבדים הל' א סמג עשין פז טוש"ע יו"ד סי' רמז סעיף עו:
קיב ה ו ז מיי' פ"י מהל' זכיה הל' א סמג עשין פב טוש"ע חו"מ סי' רנג סעיף יח:
קיג ח מיי' שם פ"ח הל' יד סמג שם טוש"ע חו"מ סי' רנ סעיף ד:
קיד ט מיי' שם הלכה כג כד טוש"ע שם סעיף ז:

מסורת הש"ס

א) [כתובות נא.]: ב) [לעיל ז. וש"נ]: ג) לעיל קמו:: ד) [לקמן קנב.]: ה) לקמן קנו: [גיטין יז:]: ו) גיטין יג.: ז) [גיטין סו.]:

וְכִי קָיְימָא הֲוַת הָדְרָא בָּהּ. זִימְנָא חֲדָא חָלְשָׁא, שְׁלַחָה לֵיהּ: תָּא קְנֵי, שְׁלַח: לָא בָּעֵינָא. שְׁלַחָה לֵיהּ: תָּא קְנֵי כָּל הֵיכָא דְּבָעֵית. אֲזַל שַׁיְּירָהּ וְקָנוּ מִינָּהּ. כִּי קָיְימָא הֲדָרָא בָּהּ, אֲתַאי לְקַמֵּיהּ דְּרַב נַחְמָן. שְׁלַח לֵיהּ: תָּא. לָא אֲתָא, אֲמַר: מַאי אֵיתֵי? הָא שַׁיְּירָהּ וְקָנוּ מִינָּהּ. שְׁלַח לֵיהּ: אִי לָא אָתֵית, [א]מְחֵינָא לָךְ בְּסִילְוָא דְּלָא מַבַּע דָּמָא. אֲמַר לְהוּ לְסָהֲדֵי: הֵיכִי הֲוָה מַעֲשֶׂה? אָמְרוּ לֵיהּ, אֲמַרָה הָכִי: וַוי דְּקָא מִיתָה הַךְ אִיתְּתָא! אֲמַר לְהוּ: [א]א"כ הֲוָה מְצַוֶּה מֵחֲמַת מִיתָה, וּמְצַוֶּה מֵחֲמַת מִיתָה – חוֹזֵר. אִיתְּמַר: מַתְּנַת שְׁכִיב מְרַע בְּמִקְצָת – (א) אֲמַרוּהָ רַבָּנַן קַמֵּיהּ דְּרָבָא מִשְּׁמֵיהּ דְּמָר זוּטְרָא בְּרֵיהּ דְּרַב נַחְמָן דַּאֲמַר מִשְּׁמֵיהּ דְּרַב נַחְמָן: הֲרֵי הִיא כְּמַתְּנַת בָּרִיא, וַהֲרֵי הִיא כְּמַתְּנַת שְׁכִיב מְרַע; הֲרֵי הִיא כְּמַתְּנַת בָּרִיא – שֶׁאִם עָמַד אֵינוֹ חוֹזֵר, וַהֲרֵי הִיא כְּמַתְּנַת שְׁכִיב מְרַע – דְּלָא בָּעֲיָא קִנְיָן. אֲמַר לְהוּ [ב]רָבָא: לָאו אָמֵינָא לְכוּ, לָא תִּיתְלוּ בּוּקֵי סְרִיקֵי בְּרַב נַחְמָן? הָכִי אָמַר רַב נַחְמָן: הֲרֵי הִיא כְּמַתְּנַת בָּרִיא וּבָעֲיָא קִנְיָן. אֵיתִיבֵיהּ רָבָא לְרַב נַחְמָן: [ג]שִׁיֵּיר קַרְקַע כָּל שֶׁהוּא – מַתְּנָתוֹ קַיֶּימֶת; מַאי לָאו דְּלָא קָנוּ מִינֵּיהּ? לָא, דְּקָנוּ מִינֵּיהּ. אִי הָכִי, אֵימָא סֵיפָא: לֹא שִׁיֵּיר קַרְקַע כָּל שֶׁהוּא – אֵין מַתְּנָתוֹ קַיֶּימֶת; וְאִי דְּקָנוּ מִינֵּיהּ, אַמַּאי אֵין מַתְּנָתוֹ קַיֶּימֶת? א"ל, הָכִי [ד]אָמַר שְׁמוּאֵל: שכ"מ שֶׁכָּתַב כָּל נְכָסָיו לַאֲחֵרִים, [ב]אע"פ שֶׁקָּנוּ מִיָּדוֹ – עָמַד חוֹזֵר, בְּיָדוּעַ שֶׁלֹּא הָיָה (ב) מְצַוֶּה אֶלָּא מֵחֲמַת מִיתָה. אֵיתִיבֵיהּ רַב מְשַׁרְשְׁיָא לְרָבָא: מַעֲשֶׂה [ה]בְּאִמָּן שֶׁל בְּנֵי רוֹכֵל שֶׁהָיְתָה חוֹלָה, וְאָמְרָה: תִּנָּתֵן כְּבֵינָתִי לְבִתִּי, וְהוּא בִּשְׁנֵים עָשָׂר מָנֶה, וּמֵתָה, וְקִיְּימוּ (ג) דְּבָרֶיהָ! הָתָם בִּמְצַוָּה מֵחֲמַת מִיתָה. אֵיתִיבֵיהּ רָבִינָא לְרָבָא: [ו][ג]הָאוֹמֵר "תְּנוּ גֵּט זֶה לְאִשְׁתִּי [ד]וּשְׁטַר שִׁחְרוּר זֶה לְעַבְדִּי" וּמֵת – לֹא יִתְּנוּ לְאַחַר מִיתָה, [ה]"תְּנוּ מָנֶה לִפְלוֹנִי" וּמֵת – יִתְּנוּ לְאַחַר מִיתָה; וּמִמַּאי דְּלָא קָנוּ מִינֵּיהּ? דּוּמְיָא דְּגֵט, מַה גֵּט לָאו בַּר קִנְיָן, אַף הַאי נַמִי דְּלָא קָנוּ מִינֵּיהּ! הָתָם נַמִי [ו]בִּמְצַוֶּה מֵחֲמַת מִיתָה. רַב הוּנָא בְּרֵיהּ דְּרַב יְהוֹשֻׁעַ אָמַר: מְצַוֶּה מֵחֲמַת מִיתָה בְּעָלְמָא בָּעֲיָא קִנְיָן, וְכִי תַּנְיָא הָנֵי מַתְנְיָיתָא – [ז]בִּמְחַלֵּק כָּל נְכָסָיו, דְּהַהִיא מַתְּנַת שְׁכִיב מְרַע שַׁוְיוּהָ. [ח]וְהִלְכְתָא: [ז]מַתְּנַת שְׁכִיב מְרַע בְּמִקְצָת בָּעֲיָא קִנְיָן, וְאַע"ג דְּמֵת; [ט]מְצַוֶּה מֵחֲמַת מִיתָה לָא בָּעֲיָא קִנְיָן, וְהוּא דְּמֵת; עָמַד חוֹזֵר, וְאַף עַל גַּב דְּקָנוּ מִינֵּיהּ. אִיתְּמַר

כי הות קיימא הדרא בה. כדתנן: לא שייר קרקע כל שהוא – אין מתנתו מתנה. תא וקני כל היכא דבעית. בא עמה אלי וקנה השדה בקנין גמור בכל ענין שתרצה, שלא אוכל לחזור. אתא ושייר וקנו מינה. לא רצה לקבל כל השדה, אלא שייר לעצמה מעט, דהוה ליה מתנה (ד) מקלת ועל ידי קנין, דקים לן לקמן דלא מלית הדרא בה אלא אם כן מצוה מחמת מיתה, דמגלי דעתיה דמחמת מיתה קיהיב, ואי קאי – הדר ביה. בסילווא דלא מבע דמא. קוץ שמכאיב ואין יציאת דם ניכר בו, דהיינו נידוי. אמרו ליה. העדים. אמרה. (ה) כששילחה בשביל אחיה. ווי כי מיתה חד איתתא. ולא תרצה את אחיה, שאינו רוצה לבא אלי. א"כ מצוה מחמת מיתה היא. וכל מצוה מחמת מיתה – חוזר, בין במתנה במקלת בין במתנה בלא שיור. ואפילו קנו מידו, אי קאי מחליו – הדר בכולהו, בידוע שלא היה קנין אלא מחמת מיתה, הואיל והיה מתאונן על מיתתו בעת צוואתו. והכי פסקינן לקמן. איתמר מתנת שכיב מרע במקצת. שלא היה בה קנין, והיא אותה מתנה ששנינו: שייר קרקע כל שהוא מתנתו מתנה, שאם עמד אינו חוזר. דכיון דהוי בה שיור – כך היה דעתו, שאם יעמוד לא יחזור, ולכך שייר לעצמו מה ששייר. והרי היא כמתנת שכיב מרע. שאין בה שיור, דלא בעיא קנין, ואם מת – קנה, ואם עמד – אינו חוזר. ובעיא קנין. וכיון דקנו מיניה – אם עמד אינו חוזר, דאיכא קנין ושיור. וכל שכן דאם מת – קנה. אבל בלא קנין – אפילו מת לא קנה, וכ"ש אם עמד חוזר. והכי פסקינן לקמן. איתיביה רבא לרב נחמן. מתני': שייר קרקע כל שהוא כו' דהיינו מתנת שכיב מרע במקלת. אימא סיפא אם לא שייר קרקע כל שהוא אין מתנתו מתנה. אם יעמוד מחליו. ואם מת – קנה. ואי דקנו מיניה אמאי לא הויא מתנתו מתנה. שאם יעמוד לא יחזור. בידוע שלא היה קנין אלא מחמת מיתה. הואיל ולא שייר, ואע"פ שלא צוה מחמת מיתה בהדיא. רוכל. שם אדם. כבינתי. בית נפש, נושק"א בלע"ז. והוא לשון כבולות דרחלות במסכת שבת (דף נד.), שמכבנין אותן למילת. וקיימו חכמים את דבריה. אע"פ דמתנת מקלת בלא קנין הואי, דמדקתני "דבריה" משמע דברים בלא קנין הואי. התם במצוה מחמת מיתה. שהזכירה דמדאגת מיתה היא מחלקת. דמצוה מחמת מיתה לא בעי קנין היכא דמת, בין איכא שיור בין ליכא שיור. והכי פסקינן לקמן. מתנת

מתה וקיימו חכמים את דבריה. פי': אלמא מתנת שכיב מרע במקלת לא בעי קנין. וא"ת: לפי סברתו של מקשה, אמאי נקט מתה? אפילו בלא מתה נמי, כיון דמתנת שכיב מרע במקלת אינו חוזר, דהוי כמתנת בריא! וכן יש להקשות בהך דלקמן ד"תנו מנה לפלוני" ומת, כי לפי סברת המקשה אמאי נקט "ומת"? כי אין נראה לומר שיחלוק רבא במה שאומר הרי היא (ו) מתנת בריא, ולא יסבור שאם עמד אינו חוזר, אלא דבעי קנין – דהא שמעינן ליה לרב נחמן דאית ליה לעיל (דף קמח:) דמתנת שכיב מרע במקלת אינו יכול לחזור, גבי שכיב מרע שכתב כל נכסיו לאחרים רואין אם כמחלק מת כו'! וי"ל: דהוה מצי למימר "וליטעמיך". ובהרבה מקומות בגמ' (ז) י"ל "וליטעמיך" ואינו אומר. ועוד יש לומר: כיון דסובר המקשה דלא בעי קנין – הוא הדין נמי שסובר שיכול לחזור בו. אי הוה כמתנת בריא – הוי כמתנת בריא לגמרי, ומנין לנו לחלק בזה? תנו גט לאשתי ושטר שחרור לעבדי ומת לא יתנו לאחר מיתה. הכי גרסינן: "תנו גט". ולא גרסי' "תן גט זה", ד"תן גט זה" – משמע שנתנו לו כבר, אבל "תנו" משמע שעדיין לא נתנו, אלא שמצוה להם ליתנו לו על ידי שליחות. ואי גרסי' "תן" – סתם לן תנא כר' מאיר, דאמר בפרק קמא דגיטין (דף יג:): חוב הוא לעבד שיוצא מתחת יד רבו לחירות, הלכך לא (ח) קנה לו השליח. אי נמי, י"ל: דמתוקמא כרבנן דאמרי זכות הוא לו, ומיירי כגון שמרצה לו ליתנו לו, ולא נטלו עד לאחר מיתה. אי נמי, נטלו לאלתר ולא זכה בשביל העבד. דהא דאמרינן בפ"ק דגיטין (דף יג. ושם ד"ה האומר): כל האומר "תנו" כזכי – היינו כשנתנו מיד ליד. והא דקתני "תן גט זה" אשמועינן חידוש, שאף על פי שעשאו מחיים, והגט בעין, ומינה שלוחים כבר לתת הגט – כיון שניתן לאחר מיתה אינו גט, דאין גט לאחר מיתה. מיהו, אין נראה לר"י לגרוס "זה". דאם כן היכי מצי דייק בגמרא דפ"ק דגיטין (שם:) על הך משנה דלא מיתוקמא הך משנה בשכיב מרע, דאי בשכיב מרע לא הוה ליה למיתני "תנו" אלא "כתבו"? ואי תנא "זה" לאשמועינן חידוש דלא יתנו לאחר מיתה – אפילו הוה מתוקמא מתניתין בשכיב מרע [לא ה"ל (ט) למיתני "כתבו"] כיון דמיירי שהגט הוא בעין. ואין נראה לומר דדייק מדהוה ליה למיתני "כתבו גט זה לאשתי ותנו שטר שחרור זה לעבדי" דהוי שמעי' דבשכיב מרע איירי, מדתני "כתבו" ומדתני "תנו שטר שחרור זה לעבדי" אשמועינן חידוש. דהא אין לו לתנא להשמיענו חידוש במה שהיה לו לשנות שני עניינים, שהרי יש לו לקצר ולשנות ולערב הכל יחד, ולא להאריך. וא"ת: מאי קא משמע לן דאין גט לאחר מיתה? הא כבר תנן ליה בפרק "מי שאחזו" (גיטין דף עב.) דאין גט לאחר מיתה, ואמרינן נמי בריש כתובות (דף ב: ושם): אי אשמועינן דאין גט לאחר מיתה – הא תנא ליה כו'! וי"ל: דמתניתין דהכא איצטריך, שאף על פי שמינה שליח בחייו ולאחר מיתה נמי עומד השליח במקומו (י) ויכול לגרש, ששלוחו של אדם כמותו – קמ"ל, דלא ידעינן הא ממשנה ד"מי שאחזו" (גיטין שם). ומההיא ד"מי שאחזו" שמעינן שאף על פי שנתן לה גט מחיים – אין גט לאחר מיתה. וא"ת: (כ) על הך דדייק בגיטין על הך משנה דהכא איירי בבריא, מדקאמר "תנו" ולא אמר "כתבו", ומנין לנו לדקדק דמיירי בבריא מדלא קאמר "כתבו"? דלמא הא דתנן "תנו" לאשמועינן דאפ"ה אין כופין היורשין לשחרר, ולא אתא כרבנן דפליגי עליה דרבי בברייתא דירושלמי בפ"ק דגיטין, דקתני התם: "תנו שטר שחרור זה לעבדי" ומת, רבי אומר: לא זכה, וחכמים אומרים: זכה, וכופין את היורשין לקיים דברי המת. אמר ר' זירא: בשתם חולקים, מה אנו קיימים? אם באומר "שחררו" – אף רבי מודה, ואם באומר "כתבו ותנו" – אף רבנן מודו. אלא כן אנו קיימים, באומר "תנו", רבי אומר: האומר "תנו" כאומר "כתבו ותנו", רבנן אומרים: האומר תנו כאומר "שחררו". וי"ל: דלא נחתא מתניתין לאשמועינן דמצוה לקיים דברי המת דתשמע אם כופין היורשים אם לאו, דלא נחתא אלא לאשמועינן שלא יתנו שלוחים שבמקומו גט לאחר מיתה.

תנו מנה לפלוני ומת יתנו לאחר מיתה. אומר ר"י: דלמאן דמוקי בגמרא הך משנה בשכיב מרע – אתי שפיר (ל) והוי סיפא דומיא דרישא. והשתא מיירי כולה מתניתין בענין אחד, [ומחלק] בין צוואת שכיב מרע בשטר לצוואת ממון, דבשטר אין מועיל צוואתו לאחר מיתה כמו בממון. ואע"פ שלא דמו לגמרי, לפי שהשטר שרוצה ליתן לאחר מיתה אין בעולם, והמנה בעולם, מכל מקום כיון דבשעת מיתה שניהם בעולם – דמו אהדדי קצת. אבל למאן דמוקי לה התם בבריא ובמעמד שלשתן, קשה, דהשתא לא הוי רישא דומיא דסיפא (מ)! דאין

הגהות הב"ח

(א) גמרא איתמר מתנת ש"מ במקלת אמר רבא אמר רב נחמן ה"ה כמתנת בריא ובעיא קנין אמרוה רבנן קמיה דרבא משמיה דמר זוטרא: (ב) שם בידוע שלא היה קנין אלא מחמת מיתה: (ג) שם וקיימו חכמים את דבריה: (ד) רשב"ם ד"ה אתא ושייר וכו' במקלת וכו' דמגלי דעתיה דמדאגת מיתה: (ה) ד"ה אמרה כששלחה: (ו) תום' ד"ה מתה וכו' כי אין נראה לומר שיחלוק רבא במה שאומר הרי היא כמתנת בריא. נ"ב וא"כ שפיר קתני מתה ומת בהני מתני' הא ליתא דהא שמעינן ליה לר"נ כו' ולפחות מיירי היכא דליכא קנין ויש להקשות לאיזה צורך דחו תוספות סברא [זו מהא דר"נ ממתני' דשייר קרקע] כל שהוא מתנתו מתנה שמעינן שפיר דבמקלת אם עמד אינו חוזר לפחות היכא דליכא קנין וי"ל דמתני' איכא למדחי ולמימר דקא מיירי במת והיכא דליכא קנין ובמקלת מתנתו קיימת טפי מבכולה ואין להקשות היכי ס"ד לפרש כן אליבא דרבא הלא מדפריך [רבא לר"נ מהא דשייר] קרקע כו' וממאי דאהדר ליה ר"נ שמעינן דמתני' איירי בעמד ואינו חוזר במתנת מקלת די"ל דרב משרשי' [והשאר חסר]: (ז) בא"ד ובהרבה מקומות בגמ' הוה מצי למימר וליטעמיך ואינו אומר וכו' לאי הוה: (ח) ד"ה תנו גט וכו' הלכך לא זכה לו השליח וכו' אי נמי נטלו לאלתר ואפילו הכי לא זכה בשביל העבד וכו' כל האומר תן כזכי: (ט) בא"ד אפילו הוה מתוקמא מתני' בשכיב מרע לא הוה ליה למימר כתבו ואין נראה לומר כצ"ל ותיבות כיון שמיירי שהגט הוא בעין נמחק: (י) בא"ד עומד השליח במקומו וסד"א דיכול לגרש וכו' קמ"ל דלא ידעינן: (כ) בא"ד וא"ת הא דדייק בגיטין על הך משנה דאיירי בבריא כצ"ל ותיבת דהכא נמחק: (ל) ד"ה תנו מנה וכו' אתי שפיר דהוי סיפא דומיא דרישא השתא: (מ) בא"ד (הנמשך לדף קנב) דאין נראה לומר דקא משמע לן ברישא דאין מעמד שלשתן מועיל בשטר אם לא דאף לדידיה תנו דמתניתין היינו כתבו וכי האי גוונא שלא בא השטר לעולם לא שייך מעמד שלשתן ועל כרחך וכו' וסיפא קמ"ל דין של מעמד שלשתן בממון ואע"ג דלא הוי רישא דומיא דסיפא אין לחוש דה"כ למאן דמוקי לה בשכיב מרע לא הוי רישא דומיא דסיפא מכל וכל שהשטר אינו בעולם כשמצוה ליתן והמנה הוא כבר בעולם ואע"ג דדייק התם בגמ' דסיפא איירי בבריא דומיא דרישא אלמא משמע שיש לנו לדמות אהדדי היינו טעמא דבעי לאוקמא בחד גוונא בבריא משום דאית לן למימר דאיירי בחד גברא אבל אינם דומות לגמרי אהדדי כצ"ל ועל תיבות דאין נראה לומר נ"ב פי' אין נראה לומר דקמ"ל ברישא דאין מעמד שלשתן מועיל בשטר כשהוא בעין דלמה לא יועיל כשהשטר בעין אם לא שתאמר דאף למאן דמוקי לה בבריאה [illegible] משמע כמ"ש התוספות לעיל בתחלת [illegible] הא נמי ליתא דהשתא נמי קשה א"כ [illegible] מעמד ג' ועל כרחך וכו' דאע"ג כו' [illegible] כתבו מיהו אין נראה כו' שסתרו [illegible] כל כדפי' לעיל והוא התירוץ שהגהתי לעיל: [illegible]

רבינו גרשום

לא בעינא. שאת חוזרת בך כשאת עומדת: אתא. רב דימי עביד לה דשיירה וקנו מינה לרב דימי: כי קמת. ההיא איתתא הדרא בה ותבעתיה לדינא: הא שיירא הא קנאי. כלומר החזקתי א) בחופה שעשית לי ששיירה לעצמה כי היכי דתסמוך עלה והקנתה לי בקנין: בסילוא דלא מבע דמא. כלומר בנידוי: ווי דקא מתה ההיא אתתא. מחמת חוליה הקשה וכסבורה היא למות להכי מקנת לו: א"ל אם כן [הוי] מצוה מחמת מיתה וכל היכא דמצוה מחמת מיתה חוזר אע"ג דשייר דהא דקתני במתני' דשייר קרקע כל שהוא מתנתו מתנה היכא דיהיב ליה סתמא ולא היה סבור למיתה דאיכא למימר דמתנת בריא הוא אבל היכא דמצוה מחמת מיתה דסבורה היתה למות ועמדה אע"פ ששיירה חוזרת: שנתן מנכסיו מקצתן. ומקצתן שייר שאם יעמוד יסמוך עליהן: דלא בעיא קנין. משום דדברי שכיב מרע ככתובין וכמסורין דמי: הכי אר"נ הרי היא כמתנת [בריא] ובעי קנין. אע"פ ששייר במקצת ועמד דלהיכא אמרינן דברי שכיב מרע ככתובין וכמסורין דמי אע"פ בלא שייר היכא דמיית אבל היכא דעמד אע"פ ששייר בעיא קנין: מאי לאו דלא קנו מיניה. ואפי' הכי קתני מתני' דמתנתו מתנה וקשיא לרבה דאמר משמיה דרב נחמן בעי קנין: לא. מתני' בדקנו מיניה משום הכי מתנתו מתנה: אי הכי. דמוקמת למתני' בדקנו מיניה אימא סיפא כו' ואי דקנו מיניה אמאי אין מתנתו מתנה והא קנו מיניה. אלא ש"מ בדלא קנו מיניה עסקי' מתניתין ואכתי קשיא לרבה: אמר ליה. לעולם מתני' בדקנו מיניה היא ולגבי סיפא משום הכי אין מתנתו מתנה דהכי אמר שמואל שכ"מ שכתב כל נכסיו לאחרים ולא שייר כלום אע"פ שקנו כו': איתיביה רב משרשיא לרבה. דאמר היכא דשייר קרקע כל שהוא אפי' הכי קנין בעי: האומר תנו גט זה לאשתי לא יתנו לאחר מיתה דאין גט לאחר מיתה. האומר תנו מנה לפלוני ומת יתנו לאחר מיתה. אלמא דכיון דשייר קנה וקשיא לרבה דאמר בעי קנין: אמר ליה. לעולם בעי קנין אע"ג דשייר ואם עמד חוזר להיכא דלא קנו והכא טעמא מאי יתנו לאחר מיתה אע"ג דלא קנו. דמצוה מחמת מיתה הוא ומת אבל היכא דלא מצוה מחמת מיתה הוא בעי קנין: כבינתי. בתי נפש והוא (מט"ז) [בי"ב] מנה משקלה: וקיימו חכמים את דבריה. הואיל דשייר אע"ג דלא קנו מיניה: אמר ליה ה"נ כו' אבל עמד חוזר הואיל דלא קנו (לא): בעי קנין אע"פ ששייר ואם עמד לא קני וחוזר. והא דתניא כל הני מתני' דקתני שייר קרקע כל שהוא מתנתו מתנה אע"ג דלא קני והא נמי דקתני באומר תנו מנה לפלוני ומת יתנו לאחר מיתה אע"ג דלא קני. והוא מעשה באמן של בני רוכל דבלא קנין קיימו חכמים את דבריה במחלק את נכסיו שאמר לפלוני כך ולפלוני כך וכך. ומשום הכי ודאי לא בעי קנין דלא שייר כלום וכדאמר לעיל אם כמחלק אם מת קנו כולם. אבל אם עמד ולא קנו אע"ג דשייר חוזר. והלכך מתנת שכיב מרע שנתן מקצת נכסיו ומקצת שייר בעי קנין: ב) מיניה מצי יורשין לביטולינהו ולמימר במתנה דמתנת בריא בלא קנין דמי וחוזר שכתוב

א) אולי צ"ל בחופה שעשתה לי ששיירה לעצמה וכו'. ב) אולי צ"ל ואם לא קנו מיניה מצי יורשין לירתינהו ולהחזיק במתנה דכמתנת בריא וכו'.

כותבין שטר למוכר ואע"פ שאין לוקח עמו; כיון שהחזיק זה בקרקע — נקנה שטר כל מקום שהוא; וזו היא ששנינו: נכסים שאין להן אחריות נקנין עם הנכסים שיש להן אחריות בכסף ובשטר ובחזקה. בהמה איקרי נכסי, דתנן: המקדיש נכסיו והיתה בהן בהמה ראויה לגבי מזבח — זכרים (א) עולות, ונקבות ימכרו לצרכי זבחי שלמים. עופות איקרי נכסי, דתנן: המקדיש נכסיו והיו בהן דברים הראויין לגבי מזבח: יינות, שמנים ועופות. תפלין איקרי נכסי, דתנן: המקדיש נכסיו — מעלין לו תפלין. איבעיא להו: ספר תורה מאי? (ב) כיון דלא מזדבן, דאסור לזבוניה — לאו נכסי הוא, או דלמא כיון דמזדבן ללמוד תורה ולישא אשה — נכסי הוא? תיקו. (סימן: זוטרא אימיה דעמרם מתרתי אחוותא רב טובי ורב דימי ורב יוסף) אימיה דרב זוטרא בר טוביא (ג) כתבינהו לנכסה לרב זוטרא בר טוביא, דבעיא לאנסובי ליה לרב זביד. אינסיבא וגרשה, אתיא לקמיה דרב ביבי בר אביי, אמר: משום אנסובי, והא אינסיבא. אמר ליה רב הונא בריה דרב יהושע: משום דאתו ממולאי אמריתו מילי מולייתא? אפילו למאן דאמר מברחת קני, הני מילי היכא דלא גליא דעתה, אבל הכא — גליא דעתה דמשום אינסובי הוא, והא אינסיבא ואיגרשה. אימיה דרמי בר חמא באורתא כתבתינהו לנכסה לרמי בר חמא, בצפרא כתבתינהו לרב עוקבא בר חמא. אתא רמי בר חמא לקמיה דרב ששת, אוקמיה בנכסי; אזל רב עוקבא בר חמא קמיה דרב נחמן, אוקמיה בנכסי. אתא רב ששת לקמיה דרב נחמן, אמר ליה: מאי טעמא אוקמיה מר לרב עוקבא בר חמא? אי משום דהדרא בה — והא שכיבא! אמר ליה, הכי אמר שמואל: כל שאילו עמד חוזר, חוזר במתנתו. אימור דאמר שמואל — לעצמו, לאחר מי אמר? אמר ליה, בפירוש אמר שמואל: בין לעצמו בין לאחר. אימיה דרב עמרם חסידא הוה לה מלוגא דשטראי, כי קא שכבא אמרה: ליהוי לעמרם ברי; אתו אחוה לקמיה דרב נחמן, אמרו ליה: והא לא משך! אמר להו: דברי שכיב מרע ככתובין וכמסורין דמו. אחתיה דרב טובי בר רב מתנה כתבתינהו לנכסה לרב טובי בר רב מתנה בצפרא, לפניא אתא רב אחדבוי בר רב מתנה בכה לה, אמר לה, השתא אמרי: מר צורבא מרבנן ומר לאו צורבא מרבנן! כתבתינהו ניהליה; אתא לקמיה דרב נחמן, אמר ליה, הכי אמר שמואל: כל שאילו עמד חוזר, חוזר במתנתו. אחתיה דרב דימי בר יוסף הוה לה פיסקתא דפרדיסא, כל אימת דהות חלשא הוה מקניא ליה ניהליה, וכי

רשב"ם

כותבין שטר למוכר אף על פי שאין כו'. דאינו חוב אלא למוכר, וכיון שהוא רוצה (ד) – יכתוב לו. כיון שהחזיק זה בקרקע כו'. מסקנא דמילתא דרב הונא היא: אם קדם מוכר וכתב לו את השטר ואח"כ מכר לזה את השדה, כיון שהחזיק הלוקח בשדה נקנה לו השטר בכל מקום, (ה) דאין אדם יכול לעכבו. דלדעת כן מכר לו את השדה – שיזכה הלוקח בשטר הנכתב לו לשמו, וכשהחזיק בשדה נקנה לו השטר, כדתנן: נכסים שאין להן אחריות כו'. אלמא שטר מיקרי נכסים שאין להן אחריות. דתנן. במסכת שקלים בפ"ד (משנה ז): המקדיש נכסיו והיה בהן בהמה הראויה על גבי המזבח, זכרים ונקבות, רבי אליעזר אומר: זכרים ימכרו לצרכי עולות, ונקבות ימכרו לצרכי זבחי שלמים, ודמיהם יפלו עם שאר נכסים לבדק הבית. ר' יהושע אומר: זכרים עצמן כו', ובמס' תמורה (דף לא:) מפרש פלוגתייהו. יינות שמנים כו'. גם זו שנויה במסכת שקלים. דתנן. במס' ערכין: המקדיש נכסיו – מעלין לו תפילין. כלומר, אף תפילין הקדש, ומעלין לו בדמים ופודן בשוויהן. אלמא, מדחל עלייהו הקדש – מיקרי נכסי, שהרי נכסיו הקדיש. ספר תורה. מי מיקרי נכסי? כתפילין דמו, או דלמא תפילין היינו טעמא – דהוי מלבוש, אבל ספר – מצוה היא ולא נכסי, ואע"פ שיכול למכרו לא מיקרי נכסי? תיקו. משום דקבעי לאינסובי לרב זביד. וכן פירשה לו בהדיא, כדמוכח בסיפא, דגליא דעתה משום דבעיא לאינסובי היא נותנתן לזה, דאין זה אלא להבריח מבעלה. ואיגרשה. ותבעה נכסה מבנה. והא אינסיבא. והפסידה, דקנה בנה. ולא אהני גלויי דעתה אלא להכי, שאילו לא היתה ניסת לרב זביד – לא תתקיים המתנה. אבל השתא דאינסיבא – נתקיימה המתנה. ממולאי. דאביי אביו ממשפחת בית עלי, כדאמרינן (ר"ה דף יח.): אביי (ל) ורבה ממשפחת בית עלי קאתו. וזהו שם מקומן, (ו) בבראשית רבה: ר' מאיר אזל לממלא, ראה אותן שהם שחורי ראש כו'. מילי מולייתא. בעלי מומין, שאין בהן ממש. כמו: שקל מוליא ושדא בגלא – גבשושית (לעיל דף נד.). אפילו למאן דאמר מברחת קני. יש מפרשים: היינו גבי ההוא מעשה דאימיה דרב שמואל בר אבא מאקרוקניא בפרק "החובל" (ב"ק דף פח.). ולאו מלתא היא, דהתם בחיי בעלה כתבה נכסי מלוג שלה לבנה לזכות בהן אחר מיתת בעלה. והכי מפרשינן לה: אפי' לרבנן דפליגי אדרשב"ג בכתובות בפרק "האשה שנפלו לה נכסים" (דף עט.) ואמרי: רצה – משחק בה, ומעכב המתנה לעצמו, וקנה הכל. ולעיל פרישית לה. הני מילי. דאמרי רבנן: רצה משחק בה וקנה – היכא דיהבה סתמא, ולא גליא דעתה דמשום אינסובי הוא, ולא נודע שלהבריח מתכוונת. אבל הכא גליא דעתה דמשום אינסובי. מברחת מבעלה, ולדעת כן שיחזרו לה אחר גירושין, והרי אינסיבא ואיגרשא – הכא מודו רבנן דלא קני, אלא יחזרו לה נכסים. כדאמרינן נמי התם: עד שתכתוב "מהיום ולכשארצה", דכיון דגליא דעתה – כמאן דכתבה ליה הכי דמי. אימיה דרמי בר חמא כו'. ומסקנא: אחרון קנה, משום דהדרא בה מראשון. ובפרק "מי שהיה נשוי" בכתובות (דף צד:) איכא (ז) מעשה אחרינא: אימיה דרמי בר חמא בצפרא כתבתינהו לנכסי לרמי בר חמא, לאורתא כתבתינהו לרב עוקבא. אתא רמי בר חמא לקמיה דרב ששת אוקמיה בנכסי, אתא רב עוקבא בר חמא לקמיה דרב נחמן אוקמיה בנכסי. ומסקנא: שודא דדייני, ולהקדמה לא חיישינן, הואיל וביום אחד נכתבו. מיהו, ההוא מיבעיא לן לאוקמא במתנת בריא, והא דהכא בשכיב מרע. ובשכיב מרע, לא שנא ביום אחד לא שנא בשני ימים – אחרון קני, דהא הדר ביה מקמייה. והא מתה. דבשלמא אם לא מתה – תנן: לא שייר קרקע כל שהוא – אין מתנתו מתנה, וכמו שחוזרה מן הראשון כשנתנה לשני, תחזור בה מן השני נמי אם תרצה. אבל עכשיו שמתה – תתקיים מתנה ראשונה, ויקנה ראשון, שהרי היא נתנה במתנת שכ"מ ודבריה ככתובין וכמסורין כשמתה, ולא אמרינן דייתיקי מבטלת דייתיקי והכי סבירא ליה. כל שאילו עמד כו'. וזאת האשה, מאחר שאם עמדה היתה חוזרת – הועילה חזרתה מן הראשון אע"פ שמתה, וקנה שני. וכן הלכה. אימור דאמר שמואל לעצמו. היכא דחזר בו החולה ושייר לעצמו ולא נתנה לאחרים – הויא חזרתו חזרה אע"ג דמית. אבל הכא דחזר בו מראשון ונתן לאחר – שמא לאו חזרה גמורה היא. מלוגא דשטרי. כרך של שטרות, אי נמי: נרתק מלא שטרות. הוי לעמרם בני. כגון שקנו מידה. אי נמי בלא קנין, וכגון דלא שיירה מידי. והא לא משך. רב עמרם האי מלוגא דשטרי בחייה. השתא אמרי. כולי עלמא שאחי שנתת לו מתנה הוי צורבא מרבנן. הכי אמר שמואל כל שאילו עומד חוזר כו'. ובתרא קני. פיסקתא. כמו פיסקא, (ח) חתיכת קרקע.

כי

תוספות

איבעיא להו ספר תורה מאי. ואם תאמר: מאי קמיבעיא ליה? על כרחך הוא בכלל נכסים שאין להם אחריות דנקנין במשיכה, או (ט) נכסים שיש להם אחריות שנקנין בכסף בשטר בחזקה, דמי נפיק מביניא? ואומר ר"י: דאע"ג דהוי לענין קנייה כנכסים שאין להם אחריות, מ"מ לאו הוי בכלל נכסים, לפי שאינו יכול למכרו אלא ללמוד תורה ולישא אשה, כדאמר בפרק בתרא דמגילה (דף כז.). מ"ר.

אפילו למאן דאמר מברחת קנה כו'. צריך לומר דמיירי במקצת נכסים, דאי בכל נכסים — פשיטא דלא קנה, כדמוכח בפרק "האשה שנפלו" (כתובות דף עט.) דלא פליגי אלא במקצת נכסים, אבל בכל נכסים לא פליגי. גליא דעתה דמשום אינסובי הוא והא אינסיבא ואיתגרשה. וכן גורס ר"ח. ואינו נראה לר"י, דהא משמע דהוי טעמא משום דמיגרשא, אבל אם היתה תחת בעלה — קנה. ואילו בפ' "האשה שנפלו" (שם וע"ש) משמע דאפי' כשהיא תחת בעלה לא קנינהו (י) לוקח. דפריך התם: וכי מאחר דלא קנינהו לוקח — ליקניניהו בעל! ומשני: תקנתא דרבנן שעשאוהו כגון שמכרתם. מיהו י"ל, דמכל מקום נהי דלא קני בעל ולוקח — מכל מקום ברשות המקבל מתנה הם, עד שתתגרש. מ"ר.

מתה

מסורת הש"ס

א) לעיל עז: לקמן קסז:: ב) שקלים פ"ד מ"ז זבחים קג. תמורה כ. לא: ג) שקלים פ"ד מ"ח: ד) ב"ק קב. ערכין כג: ה) מגילה כז. ו) לעיל קלז: מ"ק קט. יבמות טו. כתובות פה. [עירובין כה:] ז) כתובות פה: [וע"ש בתוס'] ח) [בשאלתות פ' ויחי איתא בצפרא] ט) [שם איתא באורתא] י) [עי' תוס' לעיל ס. ד"ה איתא אבל] כ) [לקמן קנו. גיטין יג. טו.] ל) ר"ה יח. ורבה:

עין משפט נר מצוה

צו א מיי' פי"א מהלכות זכיה ומתנה הלכה טו סמג עשין פב טוש"ע חו"מ סי' רמה סעיף יא:
צח ב מיי' פ"ה מהלכות ערכין הלכה ז סמג עשין קלא:
צט ג מיי' פ"ה מהלכות זכיה ומתנה הל' טו סמג עשין פב טוש"ע חו"מ סי' רמה סעיף יא:
ק ד מיי' פ"ה מהלכות ערכין הלכה ח סמג עשין קלא:
קא ה מיי' פ"ו מהל' זכיה ומתנה הל' טו סמג עשין פב טוש"ע חו"מ סי' רמה סעיף יא:
קב ו מיי' פ"ה מהלכות ערכין הלכה ג סמג עשין קלא:
קג ז ח מיי' פ"י מהלכות ס"ת הלכה ב סמג עשין כה טוש"ע יו"ד סי' ער סעיף א:
קד ט מיי' פי"א מהלכות זכיה ומתנה הל' טו סמג עשין פב טוש"ע חו"מ סי' רמה סעיף יא:
קה י מיי' פ"ו שם הלכה יב ועי' בכ"מ משנה סמג לאוין פא טוש"ע אה"ע סי' צ סעיף ז:
קו כ ל מיי' פ"ט מהל' זכיה ומתנה הלכה טו סמג עשין פב טוש"ע חו"מ סי' רנ סעיף יג:
קז מ מיי' פ"י מהלכות זכיה ומתנה הל' א סמג עשין פב טוש"ע חו"מ סי' רנג סעיף כ:

רבינו גרשום

מתנה: וזו היא ששנינו נכסים שאין להם אחריות. כגון השטרות כו'. אלמא דשטר איקרי נכסי: דתנן המקדיש כל נכסיו והיה בהן בהמה הראויה לגבי המזבח זכרים ונקבות. ר"א אומר זכרים א) יקרבו עולות ונקבות ימכרו לזבחי שלמים והשאר יהיה לבדק הבית. ר' ב) יהודה אומר אלו ואלו ימכרו בדמים ויפלו עם שאר בדק הבית. אלמא דבהמה איקרי נכסי: ויינות שמנים ועופות ר' אליעזר אומר ימכרו לחייבי אותו מין ויפלו עם שאר נכסים לבדק הבית: מעלין לו תפילין. נוטלין אותן ממנו ויהיו (אותו) הקדש: ספר תורה. ולא אמר בהדיא מי איקרי נכסי: כתבתינהו לנכסה דהיתה מברחת מבעלה דקא בעיא לאנסובי לרב זביד. ובסוף איגרשה והיתה רוצה להחזיר בהן: אמר משום אנסובי. דקא בעיא הברחה והא אנסיבא ולא מציא למהדרה בה: אפי' למאן דאמר מברחת שכתבה כל נכסיה קני. המקבל הני מילי דקני היכא דלא גליא דעתה דמשום אנסובי הוא דכתבן לו: הא אנסיבא ואיגרשה וכיון דאגרשה דמי כמאן דלא אנסיבא דלהיכא אמרינן דקני היכא דלא מיגרשה אבל הא דאיגרשה הדרא בה: הדר כתבתינהו לנכסה לרב עוקבא דתרוייהו היו בניה. אמר ליה מאי טעמא עבדת הכי. דאוקמת להו ביד שני: אי משום דכיון דהדרא. ויהבתינהו לרב עוקבא אהדרה מראשון ושני קנה: והא מתה. וכיון דמתה אינה חוזרת דלהיכא אמרינן דהויא חוזרה היכא דלא מתה ולא הויא מתנה אבל הואיל ומתה גמרה בלבה לראשון וקנה: חוזר במתנה. ואע"ג דמתה הא איתתא נמי מצי למיהדר בה. אימר דאמר שמואל דמצי למיהדר. היכא דלעצמו הדר כלומר לצרכו לכדי חייו אבל דיהבתינהו לאחריני לא הוי חזרה וראשון קנה: א"ל כו'. בין לאחר אע"ג דמת שני קנה ולא ראשון: מלוגא דשטרות. כריכות הרבה של שטרות: מר לאו צורבא מרבנן הוא. דלא יהבא ליה מידי: חוזר במתנתו. ושני קנה:

לא

הגהות הב"ח

(א) גמ' זכרים ימכרו לצרכי עולות ונקבות ימכרו: (ב) שם ס"ת מאי (כיון דלא וכו' נכסי הוא) תא"מ ונ"ב ס"א נמחק כל זה: (ג) שם כתבתינהו לנכסה לרב זוטרא וכו' אינסיבא ואיגרשה אתיא: (ד) רשב"ם ד"ה כותבין כו' וכיון שהוא רוצה כותבין לו: (ה) ד"ה כיון וכו' בכל מקום שהוא דאין: (ו) ד"ה ממולאי וכו' שם מקומן כדאיתא בבראשית: (ז) ד"ה אימיה וכו' מעשה אחרינא אימיה דרמי בר חמא. נ"ב ע"ל בפרק חזקת דף ל"ה בפי' ר"ש: (ח) ד"ה פיסקתא כמו פיסקא. נ"ב ע"ל בדף סח ע"ב ודף קמג ע"ב: (ט) תוס' ד"ה איבעיא להו וכו' במשיכה או בכלל נכסים שיש להם: (י) ד"ה גליא וכו' לא קננהו לא בעל ולא מקבל מתנה דפריך התם וכו' ומשני תקנתא דרבנן שעשאוהו כנכסים שאין ידועים לבעל מיהו י"ל.

א) לפנינו הגי' שם במשנה זכרים ימכרו לצרכי עולות ונקבות ימכרו לצרכי זבחי שלמים ודמיהן יפלו עם שאר נכסים לבדק הבית. ב) שם הגי' ר' יהושע אומר זכרים עצמן יקרבו עולות ונקבות ימכרו לצרכי זבחי שלמים ויביאו בדמיהן עולות ושאר נכסים יפלו לבדק הבית.

צה א ב מיי' פ"ו מהל' זכייה ומתנה הל' יב סמג עשין פב ולאוין פא טוש"ע אה"ע סי' ל ס"ו:
צו ג ד ה ו ז ח מיי' שם פי"א הלכה טו סמג עשין פב טוש"ע חו"מ סי' רמח סעיף יא:

אָמַר לֵיהּ: אֲנַן מִשּׁוּם דְּלָאו כְּרוּת גִּיטָּא מַתְנִינַן לָהּ. אָמַר רָבָא אָמַר רַב נַחְמָן: חֲמִשָּׁה — עַד שֶׁיִּכְתְּבוּ כׇּל נִכְסֵיהֶם, וְאֵלּוּ הֵן: שְׁכִיב מְרַע, עַבְדּוֹ, אִשְׁתּוֹ, וּבָנָיו, מַבְרַחַת. שְׁכִיב מְרַע, דִּתְנַן:[א] שְׁכִיב מְרַע שֶׁכָּתַב כׇּל נְכָסָיו לַאֲחֵרִים וְשִׁיֵּיר קַרְקַע כׇּל שֶׁהוּא — מַתְּנָתוֹ קַיֶּימֶת, לֹא שִׁיֵּיר קַרְקַע כׇּל שֶׁהוּא — אֵין מַתְּנָתוֹ קַיֶּימֶת. עַבְדּוֹ, דִּתְנַן: [ב]הַכּוֹתֵב כׇּל נְכָסָיו לְעַבְדּוֹ — יָצָא בֶּן חוֹרִין, שִׁיֵּיר קַרְקַע כׇּל שֶׁהוּא — לֹא יָצָא בֶּן חוֹרִין. אִשְׁתּוֹ, דְּאָמַר רַב יְהוּדָה אָמַר שְׁמוּאֵל: [ג]הַכּוֹתֵב כׇּל נְכָסָיו לְאִשְׁתּוֹ — לֹא עֲשָׂאָהּ אֶלָּא אַפּוֹטְרוֹפָּא. בָּנָיו, דִּתְנַן: [ד]הַכּוֹתֵב כׇּל נְכָסָיו לְבָנָיו, וְכָתַב לְאִשְׁתּוֹ קַרְקַע כׇּל שֶׁהוּא — אִבְּדָה כְּתוּבָּתָהּ. מַבְרַחַת, [ה]דְּאָמַר מָר: [א]מַבְרַחַת צְרִיכָה שֶׁתִּכְתּוֹב כׇּל נְכָסֶיהָ. [ב]וּבְכוּלְּהוּ — (א) מִטַּלְטְלֵי הָוֵי שִׁיּוּר, לְבַר מִכְּתוּבָּה, דְּאַמְּקַרְקְעֵי תַּקִּינוּ רַבָּנַן, מִמִּטַּלְטְלֵי לָא תַּקּוּן רַבָּנַן. אַמֵּימָר אָמַר: מִטַּלְטְלֵי דִּכְתִיבִי בִּכְתוּבָּה וְאִיתְנְהוּ בְּעֵינַיְיהוּ — הָוֵי שִׁיּוּר. [ג]אָמַר "נְכָסַי לִפְלָנְיָא" — [ד]עַבְדָּא אִיקְּרֵי נְכָסֵי, דִּתְנַן: [ו]הַכּוֹתֵב כׇּל נְכָסָיו לְעַבְדּוֹ — יָצָא בֶּן חוֹרִין. [ה]אַרְעָא אִיקְּרֵי נְכָסֵי, דִּתְנַן: [ז]נְכָסִים שֶׁיֵּשׁ לָהֶן אַחֲרָיוּת נִקְנִין בְּכֶסֶף וּבִשְׁטָר וּבַחֲזָקָה. [ו]גְּלִימָא אִיקְּרֵי נְכָסֵי, דִּתְנַן: [ח]וְשֶׁאֵין לָהֶן אַחֲרָיוּת — אֵין נִקְנִין אֶלָּא בִּמְשִׁיכָה. [ז]זוּזֵי אִיקְּרֵי נְכָסֵי, דִּתְנַן: [ט]וְשֶׁאֵין לָהֶן אַחֲרָיוּת נִקְנִין עִם נְכָסִים שֶׁיֵּשׁ לָהֶן אַחֲרָיוּת, בְּכֶסֶף וּבִשְׁטָר וּבַחֲזָקָה. כִּי הָא [י]דְּרַב פַּפָּא הָווּ לֵיהּ תְּרֵיסַר אַלְפֵי זוּזֵי בֵּי חוֹזָאֵי, אַקְנִינְהוּ נִיהֲלֵיהּ לְרַב שְׁמוּאֵל בַּר אַחָא אַגַּב אַסֵּיפָּא דְּבֵיתֵיהּ, כִּי אֲתָא, נְפַק לְאַפֵּיהּ עַד תָּווֹךְ. [ח]שְׁטָרָא אִיקְּרֵי נְכָסֵי, [כ]דְּאָמַר רַבָּה בַּר יִצְחָק: שְׁנֵי שְׁטָרוֹת הֵן, אָמַר "זְכוּ בְּשָׂדֶה (ב) זֶה לִפְלוֹנִי וְכִתְבוּ לוֹ אֶת הַשְּׁטָר" — חוֹזֵר בִּשְׁטָר וְאֵינוֹ חוֹזֵר בְּשָׂדֶה, "עַל מְנָת שֶׁתִּכְתְּבוּ לוֹ אֶת הַשְּׁטָר" — חוֹזֵר בֵּין בִּשְׁטָר בֵּין בְּשָׂדֶה; וְרַב חִיָּיא בַּר אָבִין אָמַר רַב הוּנָא: שְׁלֹשָׁה שְׁטָרוֹת הֵן, תְּרֵי — הָנֵי דַּאֲמָרַן, אִידָּךְ — אִם קָדַם מוֹכֵר וְכָתַב אֶת הַשְּׁטָר, כְּאוֹתָהּ שֶׁשָּׁנִינוּ:
כּוֹתְבִין

דַּאֲנַן מִשּׁוּם דְּלָאו כְּרוּת גִּיטָּא מַתְנִינַן לָהּ. עֶבֶד גָּמַר "לָהּ" "לָהּ" מֵאִשָּׁה, דְּבָעֵינַן גֵּט כְּרִיתוּת. וְכֵיוָן דְּיֵשׁ לְבַעַל הָעֶבֶד זְכוּת בַּשְּׁטָר שֶׁכָּתוּב בּוֹ, שֶׁשִּׁיֵּיר קַרְקַע וּמִטַּלְטְלֵי לְעַצְמוֹ – לֹא הִקְנָה לוֹ הַשְּׁטָר לְגַמְרֵי, שֶׁגַּם זְכוּת הָאָדוֹן כָּתוּב בּוֹ, הִלְכָּךְ לָא קָרֵינָא בֵּיהּ גֵּט כְּרִיתוּת. כְּעִנְיָן זֶה פֵּירֵשׁ רַבֵּינוּ חֲנַנְאֵל וְרַבּוֹתַי שֶׁבְּלוּתִי"ר. וְגַם יֵשׁ לְפָרֵשׁ כָּךְ: לְעוֹלָם עַבְדָּא כִּי מְקַרְקְעֵי דָּמֵי. (ג) וְגַבֵּי גֵּט אַמַּאי חָשְׁבִינַן אֲפִי' מִטַּלְטְלִין שִׁיּוּר אֵצֶל עֶבֶד – הַיְינוּ טַעֲמָא, מִשּׁוּם דִּכְרִיתוּת גָּמוּר בָּעֵינַן, וְכֵיוָן שֶׁזֶּה שִׁיֵּיר מִטַּלְטְלִין – מַאן לֵימָא לָן דְּלֹא הָיָה בְּדַעְתּוֹ לְשַׁיֵּיר הָעֶבֶד בִּכְלַל הַמִּטַּלְטְלִין, אַחֲרֵי שֶׁלֹּא פֵּירֵשׁ מָה הֵן הַמִּטַּלְטְלִין שֶׁשִּׁיֵּיר. וְאַע"ג דִּבְדוּכְתָּא אַחֲרִינָא עַבְדָּא כִּמְקַרְקְעֵי דָּמֵי, מִיהוּ גַּבֵּי כְּרִיתוּת – לָאו כְּרִיתוּת הוּא. **אָמַר רָבָא א"ר** נַחְמָן חֲמִשָּׁה. נוֹתְנֵי מַתָּנָה הֵן, שֶׁאֵין דִּינָן חָלוּק מִנּוֹתְנֵי מִקְצָת עַד שֶׁיִּכְתְּבוּ כׇּל נִכְסֵיהֶם, וְאָז דִּינָן חָלוּק מִמְּשַׁיֵּיר קְצָת מִמֶּנּוּ. וּכְגוֹן שֶׁלֹּא שִׁיְּירוּ כְּלוּם, אֲפִי' בְּמִטַּלְטְלִין, כִּדְמַסִּיק בְּסֵיפָא, לְבַר מִכְּתוּבַּת אִשָּׁה – בִּמְקַרְקְעֵי הָוֵי שִׁיּוּר וְלֹא מִטַּלְטְלֵי. וְאֵלּוּ הֵן שְׁכִיב מְרַע עַבְדּוֹ אִשְׁתּוֹ וּבָנָיו מַבְרַחַת. וְהַשְׁתָּא מְפָרֵשׁ לְהוּ וְאָזֵיל, שְׁכִיב מְרַע כו'. וְכוּלְּהוּ כְּבָר מְפוֹרָשִׁים בְּפֶרֶק זֶה וּבְ"יֵשׁ נוֹחֲלִין" לְבַד מִמַּבְרַחַת, וּלְקַמָּן בְּסָמוּךְ אֲפָרְשֶׁנָּה. בָּנָיו דִּתְנַן הַכּוֹתֵב נְכָסָיו לְבָנָיו וְכָתַב לְאִשְׁתּוֹ קַרְקַע כׇּל שֶׁהוּא **אִבְּדָה** כְּתוּבָּתָהּ. אֲבָל שִׁיֵּיר לֹא אִבְּדָה, דְּמִגּוֹ דְּנָחְתָא אַהַאי שִׁיּוּרָא בִּשְׁבִיל כְּתוּבָּתָהּ – נָחְתָא נַמִי אַכּוּלְּהוּ נִכְסֵי, כִּדְאָמַר בְּ"יֵשׁ נוֹחֲלִין": הַהוּא דְּפַלְגִינְהוּ לְנִכְסֵיהּ לְאִתְּתֵיהּ וְלִבְנֵיהּ שִׁיֵּיר חַד דִּיקְלָא וכו'. וְאַסְקִי' הָתָם: מִגּוֹ דְּנָחֲתָא אַדִּיקְלָא נָחֲתָא נַמִי אַכּוּלְּהוּ נִכְסֵי. מַבְרַחַת דְּאָמַר מָר כו'. כְּלוֹמַר, אִשָּׁה אַלְמָנָה שֶׁיֵּשׁ לָהּ נְכָסִים וְדַעְתָּהּ לִינָּשֵׂא, וְרוֹצָה לְהַבְרִיחַ נְכָסֶיהָ מִבַּעְלָהּ שֶׁלֹּא יְהֵא זַכַּאי בִּנְכָסֶיהָ, וְאִם תִּתְאַלְמֵן אוֹ תִּתְגָּרֵשׁ יַחְזְרוּ לָהּ נְכָסֶיהָ. וְאִם לֹא הוֹצִיאַתָן מֵרְשׁוּתוֹ קוֹדֶם נִשּׂוּאִין – יִזְכֶּה בָּהֶן בַּעַל. וְאָמְרִינַן בִּכְתוּבּוֹת: צְרִיכָה שֶׁתִּכְתּוֹב כׇּל נְכָסֶיהָ לְאַחֵר סְתָם, כֵּיוָן דְּלֹא שִׁיְּירָהּ מִידֵּי – אֲנַן סָהֲדֵי דְּלֹא נָתְנָה לָזֶה אֶלָּא בִּשְׁבִיל שֶׁרוֹצָה לִינָּשֵׂא, וְלִכְשֶׁתִּרְצֶה יַחְזְרוּ לָהּ. אֲבָל אִם שִׁיְּירָה כׇּל שֶׁהוּא – קָנָה הַמְקַבֵּל מַתָּנָה, וְלֹא יַחְזְרוּ לָהּ כׇּל הַנְּכָסִים עוֹלָמִית. וְזֶה הַדָּבָר אֵינוֹ כָּתוּב בַּגְּמָרָא כָּךְ, אֶלָּא מִכְּלָלָא שָׁמְעִינַן לָהּ. דְּאָמְרִינַן בִּכְתוּבּוֹת בְּפֶרֶק "הָאִשָּׁה שֶׁנָּפְלוּ לָהּ נְכָסִים" (דף עט.), אָמַר רַב חֲנִילָאִי בַּר אִידִי אָמַר שְׁמוּאֵל: אֲנִי מוֹרֶה הוֹרָאָה, אִם יָצָא שְׁטָר מַבְרַחַת לְיָדִי – אֶקְרָעֶנּוּ. וְיָהֵיב טַעֲמָא – דְּלָא שָׁבֵיק אִינִישׁ לְנַפְשֵׁיהּ וְיָהֵב לַאֲחֲרִינֵי. מֵיתִיבִי: הָרוֹצָה שֶׁתַּבְרִיחַ נְכָסֶיהָ מִבַּעְלָהּ כֵּיצַד הִיא עוֹשָׂה? כּוֹתֶבֶת שְׁטָר פַּסִּים לַאֲחֵרִים, דִּבְרֵי רשב"ג, וַחֲכָמִים אוֹמְרִים: רָצָה, מְשַׂחֵק בָּהּ, עַד שֶׁתִּכְתּוֹב "מֵהַיּוֹם וּלְכְשֶׁאֶרְצֶה". טַעֲמָא – דְּכָתְבָה לֵיהּ הָכִי, הָא לֹא כָּתְבָה הָכִי – קַנְיִנְהוּ לוֹקֵחַ. אָמַר ר' זֵירָא: לָא קַשְׁיָא; הָא – בְּכוּלָּן, הָא – בְּמִקְצָתָן. שָׁמְעִינַן מֵהָכָא: הֵיכָא דְּכָתְבָה כּוּלָּן לֹא קָנָה לוֹקֵחַ. וְאַף בַּעַל לֹא קָנָה, כִּדְמַשְׁנֵי הָתָם: עֲשָׂאוּם כִּנְכָסִים שֶׁאֵינָן יְדוּעִין לַבַּעַל אַלִּיבָּא דר"ש. אֲבָל הֵיכָא דְּלֹא כָּתְבָה כּוּלָּן – צְרִיכָה שֶׁתִּכְתּוֹב "מֵהַיּוֹם וּלְכְשֶׁאֶרְצֶה", לֹא קָנָה לוֹקֵחַ. וּבְכוּלְּהוּ. הָנֵי חֲמִשָּׁה, מִמִּטַּלְטְלֵי הָוֵי שִׁיּוּר. שֶׁאִם שִׁיֵּיר מִטַּלְטְלִין – כְּשִׁיֵּיר קַרְקַע דָּמֵי. וְאִיתְנְהוּ בְּעֵינַיְיהוּ הָוֵי שִׁיּוּר. שֶׁהֲרֵי אִשָּׁה גּוֹבָה כְּתוּבָּתָהּ מֵהֶם, כִּדְאָמַר אַמֵּימָר בְּפֶרֶק "אע"פ" בִּכְתוּבּוֹת (דף נה.): מִטַּלְטְלֵי וְאִיתְנְהוּ בְּעֵינַיְיהוּ – בְּלֹא שְׁבוּעָה. וְאִיכָּא לְמֵימַר דְּאָזְדָא אַמֵּימָר לְטַעְמֵיהּ, דְּהָא הָכָא אַמֵּימָר נַמִי קָאָמַר לָהּ. פִּסְקֵי הֲלָכוֹת הֵן שֶׁפּוֹסֵק הַגְּמָ': שְׁכִיב מְרַע שֶׁאָמַר "נִכְסַיי לִפְלָנְיָא", א"נ, בְּבָרִיא שֶׁהִקְנָה בְּסוּדָר וְאָמַר "נִכְסַיי לִפְלָנְיָא". וּבָא הַגְּמָרָא לְפָרֵשׁ אֵיזוֹ דָּבָר קָרוּי מָמוֹן. וְהוּא הַדִּין אִם אָמַר בִּלְשׁוֹן לַעַ"ז "אוֹיי"ר", אוֹ בְּלָשׁוֹן שֶׁמְּכַנִּין הַמָּמוֹן – דִּין "נִכְסַיי לִפְלוֹנִי" נוֹהֵג בּוֹ. **עַבְדָּא** מִקְרֵי נִכְסֵי. כְּמוֹ כֶּסֶף וְזָהָב, וַהֲרֵי הוּא בִּכְלַל הַמַּתָּנָה. דִּתְנַן. בְּקִדּוּשִׁין. נְכָסִים שֶׁיֵּשׁ לָהֶם אַחֲרָיוּת. וְהַקַּרְקָעוֹת – אַחֲרָיוּת כׇּל מִלְוֶה וְחוֹב וּכְתוּבָּה נִסְמָכִין עֲלֵיהֶן, לְפִי שֶׁאֵין גְּזֵלָה שׁוֹלֶטֶת בָּהֶן וְאֵינָן אוֹבְדִין, וְקָתָנֵי בָּהֶן לְשׁוֹן נְכָסִים. וְשֶׁאֵין לָהֶם אַחֲרָיוּת. הַיְינוּ מִטַּלְטְלִין. וְאַרֵישָׁא קָאֵי, דְּמִיקְרוּ נְכָסִים, וּכְמַאן דְּמִיתְנֵי "נְכָסִים שֶׁאֵין לָהֶם אַחֲרָיוּת". נִקְנִין עִם נְכָסִים שֶׁיֵּשׁ לָהֶן אַחֲרָיוּת. שֶׁאִם מָכַר אָדָם אוֹ נָתַן לַחֲבֵירוֹ מִטַּלְטְלִין וְקַרְקָעוֹת, הֶחֱזִיק בַּקַּרְקָעוֹת – קָנָה מִטַּלְטְלִין. **כִּי הָא** דְּרַב **פַּפָּא**. כְּלוֹמַר, וּמִנַּיִין לָנוּ דִּנְכָסִים שֶׁאֵין לָהֶם אַחֲרָיוּת הַנִּקְנִין עִם נְכָסִים שֶׁיֵּשׁ לָהֶן אַחֲרָיוּת, מַיְירֵי נַמִי בְּמָעוֹת? (ד) וּמְנָלַן דְּמָעוֹת נַמִי נִקְנוּ עַל יְדֵי קַרְקָעוֹת? וַהֲלֹא אֵין מַטְבֵּעַ נִקְנֵית בַּחֲלִיפִין, וְעַל יְדֵי קַרְקָעוֹת מְנָלַן? כִּי הָא דְּרַב פַּפָּא כו' אַקְנִינְהוּ נִיהֲלֵיהּ לְרַב שְׁמוּאֵל הַהוֹלֵךְ שָׁם, בְּקִנְיַן סוּדָר. **אַגַּב אַסֵּיפָּא** דְּבֵיתֵיהּ. שֶׁהִקְנָה לוֹ בְּסוּדָר קַרְקַע כְּנִיסַת בֵּיתוֹ, וְאַגַּבּוֹ הִקְנָה לוֹ הַמָּעוֹת בְּתוֹרַת הַרְשָׁאָה הַמְפוֹרֶשֶׁת בְּבָבָא [קַמָּא] (דף ע.). אִי נַמִי, הָלַךְ וְהֶחֱזִיק הַקַּרְקַע וְהִקְנָה לוֹ הַמָּעוֹת כׇּל מָקוֹם שֶׁהֵן. אַלְמָא מָעוֹת מִיקְרֵי נִכְסֵי. עַד (ה) תָּווֹךְ. מָקוֹם. וְיֵשׁ מְפָרְשִׁין: חֲצִי הַדֶּרֶךְ, וּמְפָרְשִׁין נַמִי שֶׁלֹּא יַחֲזִיק בָּהֶן לְעַצְמוֹ. וְלֹא הִיא, דְּכֵיוָן דִּכְתַב בְּהַרְשָׁאָה "וְכׇל מַאן דְּמִתְמְעֵי לֵיהּ מִן דִּינָא קַבְּלִתִּי בֵּין לִזְכוּת בֵּין לְחוֹבָה" – מִינָּהּ שָׁמְעִינַן דִּשְׁלִיחַ שַׁוְויֵהּ, הָכִי מְפָרֵשׁ בְּבָבָא [קַמָּא] (שם). זְכוּ בְּשָׂדֶה זוֹ. הִקְנָה לָהֶן בְּסוּדָר לְצוֹרֶךְ פְּלוֹנִי. חוֹזֵר בִּשְׁטָר. מִיִּיפּוּי כֹּחַ דִּשְׁטָר יָכוֹל לַחֲזוֹר בּוֹ, כׇּל זְמַן שֶׁלֹּא נִמְסַר הַשְּׁטָר לְאוֹתוֹ פְּלוֹנִי. **וְאֵינוֹ** חוֹזֵר בְּשָׂדֶה. אַחֲרֵי שֶׁכְּבָר זָכוּ בְּקִנְיָן אוֹ בַּחֲזָקָה, וְזָכִין לְאָדָם שֶׁלֹּא בְּפָנָיו. שְׁלֹשָׁה. עִנְיְנֵי שְׁטָרוֹת הֵן. וְלֹא בָּא לַחֲלוֹק אֶלָּא לְהוֹסִיף. **אִם** קָדַם מוֹכֵר וְכָתַב שְׁטָר. מְכִירָה, לִהְיוֹת מְזוּמָּן לַלּוֹקֵחַ, כׇּל שָׁעָה שֶׁיִּרְצֶה לְמׇכְרוֹ לְשָׂדֵהוּ לֹא יְהֵא עִיכּוּב בְּמָעוֹתָיו בִּשְׁבִיל כְּתִיבַת הַשְּׁטָר, וּלְכָךְ קָדַם וְהִכְתִּיבוֹ. וְהוּא יָכוֹל לַעֲשׂוֹת כֵּן, כְּאוֹתָהּ שֶׁשָּׁנִינוּ:
כּוֹתְבִין

אמר ליה אנן משום דלאו כרות גיטא מתנינן לה. שכן השיב רב נחמן לרבא. אבל רב אשי לא היה אומר מסברא דנפשי'. וה"נ משמע בפ"ק דגיטין (דף ט. ושם) דפריך התם דרב נחמן אדרב נחמן, ומשני: משום דלאו כרות גיטא. אלמא משמע דרב נחמן גופיה הוא דקאמר הכי. ר"ת.

ואלו הן שב"מ וכו'. והא דלא חשיב הא דתניא לעיל בפרק "יש נוחלין" (דף קלב.): הכותב כל נכסיו לאשתו ויצא (ו) עליה שטר חוב, ר' אליעזר אומר: תקרע כתובתה כו'. ו"כל נכסיו" קאמר התם, וקאמר התם נמי בתר הכי: דניחא לה דתיפוק קלא עלה דכתב ניהלה לכולהו נכסי — איכא למימר דכולהו נכסים לאו דוקא, שאין צריך אלא יותר מכתובתה. א"נ, בפלוגתא לא קא מיירי. ואע"ג דשטר מברחת נמי איכא פלוגתא בכתובות (דף עט.), כמו שהביא רבינו שמואל — מכל מקום היכא דגליא דעתה דמשום אנסובי הוא — מודו כולי עלמא, כדקאמר לקמן. **מטלטלין** ואיתנהו בעינייהו הוי שיור. פירוש: שייחדה לכתובה, כדאמר אמימר בפ' "אע"פ" (שם נה.) כדפי' רבינו שמואל. ולא דמיא להא דאמר לעיל בפרק "יש נוחלין" (דף קלב:): מטלטלי קאמרת? מטלטלי לא קאמינא. פי': דמטלטלין לא הוי שיור לכתובה. דהכא מיירי במטלטלין שייחדם לכתובה, וכדפירש רבינו שמואל, ואותו ודאי הוי שיור.

כי הא דרב **פפא** הוו ליה תריסר אלפי כו'. פירשתי לעיל בפרק "המוכר את הספינה" (דף עז:), וגם ההיא ד"שני שטרות הם" פירשתי שם.

איבעיא

רבינו גרשום

כמטלטלי הוא. אלמא דבהדיא הוא דכמטלטלי דמי: אמר ליה לעולם מהא ליכא למשמע מינה דכמטלטלי דמי. דהכא מאי עשו מטלטלי שיור שלא יצא לבן חורין לאו משום הואיל דשייר מטלטלי איכא למימר איהו הוא. אנן כרות גיטא בעינן כלומר גט שחרור כרות בעינן וספר כריתות שכרות לגמרי ולא משייר כלום וכיון דשייר משום הכי קתני ולא יצא בן חורין ולאו משום דאתי למידק מיניה דלהוי כמטלטלי ולעולם אימא לך כמקרקעי דמי: אמר רב נחמן ה' דברים הן. שאין מעשיהן מעשה עד שיכתבו כל נכסיהן: אלו הן כו' לא עשאה אלא אפטרופא. שיחלקו לה כבוד ואם שייר קרקע כל שהוא שלא כתב לה הכל שלה דאיכא למימר מדשייר הקנה לה הכל והאי שיור לצורך היורשין שייר: אבדה כתובתה. במחלק לפניה והיא שותקת דכיון דלא שייר לעצמו כלום וכתב לה קרקע כל שהיא והיא שתקה אבדה כתובתה: מברחת. כגון בתולה או אלמנה שרצתה להנשא והיו לה נכסים וכתבתן לאחר כדי להבריח מבעלה שלא יקנה אותן עמה על מנת כן אם תנשא שיהיו כולן שלו ואם לאו שיחזרו לה הנכסים לצרכה ולא לאותו מקבל מתנה. שהיא תכתוב לו כל נכסיה דאי שיירה כלום ונישאת יגבה בעלה מידו דאיכא למימר מדשיירה הא שיירה נמי כל הנכסים ולא נתנתן לו. ואיכא דאמרי אי נתנה כל נכסיה לו אם תתאלמן יכולה לחזור בהן דכידוע דלא נתנה לו אלא כדי להבריחן מבעלה. ואי שיירה שלא כתבה הכל אמרינן דקנה האי דכתבה לו הואיל דשיירה. ובכולהו הני חמשה דאמר אי שיירי מטלטלי הוי שיור ואיבדו לבד מכתובת האשה דאע"ג דשייר מטלטלי לא הוי שיור ולא כלום היא ולא אבדה כתובתה. א) הואיל וכתב לה קרקע כל שהוא דמחלה. אפי' שייר מטלטלי ואיתנייהו בעינייהו כמקרקעי דמי והוי שיור הואיל ואיתנייהו בעינייהו ולא אבדה כתובתה דהאי דשתקה דסמכה דעתה למיגבי מינייהו: שכיב מרע שאמר כל נכסיי לפלוני. עבדא איקרי נכסי דתנן כו': אסיפא דביתיה. בקצת סוף ביתו: עד תוך. עד אותו מקום מרוב שמחה שהביא לו: ב' שטרות. כלומר משני ענינים הן השטרות. אם אמר זכו בשדה זו לפלוני: ואינו חוזר בשדה. משום דהשתא לא תלי הזכיה בשטר דמעיקרא קאמר זכו וזכין לו לאדם שלא בפניו. ואם אמר על מנת שתכתבו לו את השטר זה דהשתא תלי הזכיה גם בשטר חוזר בזה ובזה. כל דלא אתא לידיה דמקבל מתנה

א) נראה דחסר כאן וצ"ל דאמקרקעי תקינו רבנן: הואיל וכתב לה וכו'.

מסורת הש"ס

א) [לעיל קמו: פאה פ"ג מ"ז: ב) [לעיל קמט:] וש"נ]: ג) [לעיל קלא: קמה. גיטין יז.]: ד) פאה שם לעיל קלב: ה) כתובות עט. [ועי' רשב"ם]: ו) [לעיל קמו: וש"נ]: ז) קדושין כו.: ח) שם: ט) לעיל עז: ב"מ מו. ב"ק קד. ע"ש: כ) קדושין כז. ע"ש לעיל עז. ע"ש:

הגהות הב"ח

(א) גמ' ובכולהו ממטלטלי הוי שיור לבר מכתובה דמקרקעי תקינו: (ב) שם זכו בשדה זו לפלוני: (ג) רשב"ם ד"ה דאנן משום וכו' מקרקעי דמי וכ"ת גבי גט אמאי: (ד) ד"ה כי הא דרב פפא וכו' מיירי נמי במעות דמעות כל"ל ותיבת ומנלן נמחק: (ה) ד"ה עד תוך מקום. נ"ב והכי איתא בפרק בנות כותים דף ל"ג רב פפא איקלע לתווך כו': (ו) תוס' ד"ה ואלו וכו' ויצא עליו שטר חוב ר' אליעזר אומר תקרע מתנתה והעמוד על כתובתה וחכמים אומרים תקרע כתובתה כו' וכל נכסיו:

מסורת הש"ם

א) קדושין כו. לעיל כז. פאה פ"ג מ"ו: ב) [עי' תוס' מנחות לט. ד"ה שירי גרדומיו]: ג) חולין קלה.: ד) [חולין קלז: עירובין יד: וש"נ]: ה) לעיל סח.: ו) [לעיל קמט: וש"נ]: ז) [צ"ל כל נכסיו לעבדו]:

וְאָמַר רַב דִּימִי בַּר יוֹסֵף אָמַר ר' אֶלְעָזָר: [א]עָשׂוּ מִטַּלְטְלִין שִׁיּוּר אֵצֶל עֶבֶד, [ב]וְלֹא עָשׂוּ מִטַּלְטְלִין שִׁיּוּר אֵצֶל כְּתוּבָּה! הָתָם בְּדִין הוּא דְּלָא לִיתְנֵי קַרְקַע, וְאַיְּידֵי דִּתְנָא רֵישָׁא, [א]רַבִּי עֲקִיבָא אוֹמֵר: קַרְקַע כָּל שֶׁהוּא חַיֶּיבֶת בְּפֵאָה וּבְבִכּוּרִים, וְלִכְתּוֹב עֲלֵיהֶם פְּרוֹזְבּוֹל, וְלִקְנוֹת עִמָּהֶם נְכָסִים שֶׁאֵין לָהֶם אַחֲרָיוּת בְּכֶסֶף וּבִשְׁטָר וּבַחֲזָקָה, מִשּׁוּם הָכִי קָתָנֵי קַרְקַע. [ב]וְכָל הֵיכָא דְּתָנֵי "כָּל שֶׁהוּא" לֵית לֵיהּ שִׁיעוּרָא? וְהָא תְּנַן, [ג]רַבִּי דּוֹסָא בֶּן הָרְכִּינָס אוֹמֵר: חָמֵשׁ רְחֵלוֹת גּוֹזְזוֹת מָנֶה (א) מָנֶה וּפְרָס — חַיָּיבוֹת בְּרֵאשִׁית הַגֵּז, וַחֲכָמִים אוֹמְרִים: [ג]חָמֵשׁ רְחֵלוֹת גּוֹזְזוֹת כָּל שֶׁהֵן; וְאָמְרִינַן, [ד]וְכַמָּה כָּל שֶׁהֵן? אָמַר רַב: [ד]מָנֶה וּפְרָס, וּבִלְבַד שֶׁיְּהוּ מְחוּמָּשׁוֹת! הָתָם בְּדִין הוּא דְּלָא לִיתְנֵי כָּל שֶׁהוּא, וְאַיְּידֵי דְּקָאָמַר תַּנָּא קַמָּא שִׁיעוּרָא רַבָּה אֲמַר אִיהוּ נַמִי שִׁיעוּרָא זוּטְרָא, קָרֵי לָהּ "כָּל שֶׁהוּא".§ פְּשִׁיטָא, אֲמַר (ב) "מִטַּלְטְלַי לִפְלָנְיָא" — [ה]כָּל מָאנֵי תַּשְׁמִישְׁתֵּיהּ קָנֵי, לְבַר מֵחִטֵּי וּשְׂעָרֵי. [ו]"כָּל מִטַּלְטְלַי לִפְלָנְיָא" — אֲפִי' חִטֵּי וּשְׂעָרֵי, וַאֲפִילּוּ רֵיחַיִם הָעֶלְיוֹנָה קָנָה, לְבַר מֵרֵיחַיִם הַתַּחְתּוֹנָה. [ז]"כָּל דְּמִטַּלְטֵל" — אֲפִי' רֵיחַיִם הַתַּחְתּוֹנָה קָנֵי. אִיבַּעְיָא לְהוּ: עַבְדָּא כִּמְקַרְקְעָא אוֹ [ח]כְּמִטַּלְטְלָא דָּמֵי? אֲמַר לֵיהּ רַב אַחָא בְּרֵיהּ דְּרַב אָוְיָא לְרַב אַשִׁי, תָּא שְׁמַע: [ה]הַמּוֹכֵר אֶת הָעִיר — מָכַר בָּתִּים, שִׁיחִין וּמְעָרוֹת, וּמֶרְחֲצָאוֹת, וּבֵית הַבַּדִּין, וּבֵית הַשְּׁלָחִין, אֲבָל לֹא אֶת הַמִּטַּלְטְלִין; וּבִזְמַן שֶׁאָמַר: "הִיא וְכָל מַה שֶּׁבְּתוֹכָהּ", אֲפִילּוּ הָיוּ בָּהּ בְּהֵמָה אוֹ עֲבָדִים — הֲרֵי כּוּלָּן מְכוּרִין; אִי אָמְרַתְּ בִּשְׁלָמָא כְּמִטַּלְטְלָא דָּמֵי, מִשּׁוּם הָכִי לָא מִיזְדַּבַּן בְּרֵישָׁא, אֶלָּא אִי אָמְרַתְּ כִּמְקַרְקְעָא דָּמֵי, אַמַּאי לָא מִיזְדַּבַּן? וְאֶלָּא מַאי? כְּמִטַּלְטְלָא דָּמֵי, מַאי אֲפִי'! [אֶלָּא] מַאי אִית לָךְ לְמֵימַר? שָׁאנֵי מִטַּלְטְלָא דְּנָיֵיד מִמִּטַּלְטְלָא דְּלָא נָיֵיד; אֲפִי' תֵּימָא כִּמְקַרְקְעָא דָּמֵי, שָׁאנֵי מְקַרְקְעָא דְּנָיֵיד מִמְּקַרְקְעָא דְּלָא נָיֵיד. א"ל רָבִינָא לְרַב אַשִׁי, תָּא שְׁמַע: [ו]הַכּוֹתֵב [ז](לְעַבְדּוֹ כָּל נְכָסָיו) — יָצָא בֶּן חוֹרִין, שִׁיֵּיר קַרְקַע כָּל שֶׁהוּא — לֹא יָצָא בֶּן חוֹרִין; ר' שִׁמְעוֹן אוֹמֵר: לְעוֹלָם הוּא בֶּן חוֹרִין — עַד שֶׁיֹּאמַר "כָּל נְכָסַי נְתוּנִין לִפְלוֹנִי עַבְדִּי חוּץ מֵאֶחָד מֵרִבּוֹא שֶׁבָּהֶן"; וְאָמַר רַב דִּימִי בַּר יוֹסֵף אָמַר רַבִּי אֶלְעָזָר: עָשׂוּ מִטַּלְטְלִין שִׁיּוּר אֵצֶל עֶבֶד, וְלֹא עָשׂוּ מִטַּלְטְלִין שִׁיּוּר אֵצֶל כְּתוּבָּה; וַאֲמַר לֵיהּ רָבָא לְרַב נַחְמָן: מַאי טַעְמָא? עַבְדָּא מִטַּלְטְלָא הוּא, וּמִטַּלְטְלָא לְמִטַּלְטְלָא הָוֵי שִׁיּוּר, וּכְתוּבַּת אִשָּׁה מְקַרְקְעָא הוּא, וּמִטַּלְטְלָא לִמְקַרְקְעָא לָא הָוֵי שִׁיּוּר. אֲמַר

רשב"ם

וְאָמַר רַב דִּימִי אָמַר רַבִּי אֶלְעָזָר עָשׂוּ כו'. אע"ג דְּקָתָנֵי: שִׁייֵּר קַרְקַע כָּל שֶׁהוּא לֹא יָצָא בֶּן חוֹרִין – הוּא הַדִּין אִם שִׁייֵּר מִטַּלְטְלִין כָּל שֶׁהוּא, דְּעַבְדָּא נַמִי כְּמִטַּלְטְלֵי דָּמֵי, שֶׁהֲרֵי אֵינוֹ מְחוּבָּר לַקַּרְקַע וְקָרוּ לֵיהּ בְּנֵי אָדָם מִטַּלְטְלֵי. אַלְמָא, אע"ג דְּקָתָנֵי קַרְקַע – לָאו דַּוְקָא, אֶלָּא הוּא הַדִּין לְמִטַּלְטְלֵי. וּמַתְנִיתִין נַמִי, מִטַּלְטְלֵי כְּדֵי פַּרְנָסָתוֹ כִּמְקַרְקְעֵי כְּדֵי פַּרְנָסָתוֹ דָּמֵי. וְלֹא עָשׂוּ מִטַּלְטְלֵי שִׁיּוּר אֵצֶל כְּתוּבָּה. דִּתְנַן גַּבֵּי דְּהַהִיא בְּמַסֶּ' פֵּאָה. וּבְפִרְקִין דִּלְעֵיל (דף קלב.) מַיְיתִינַן לָהּ וּפָרְשִׁינַן לָהּ: הַכּוֹתֵב נְכָסָיו לְבָנָיו וְכָתַב לְאִשְׁתּוֹ קַרְקַע כָּל שֶׁהוּא – אִבְּדָה כְּתוּבָּתָהּ. וְאִית דְּמוֹקֵי לָהּ הָתָם בְּשׁוֹתֶקֶת. וּפֵירֵשׁ רַב נַחְמָן: כֵּיוָן שֶׁעֲשָׂאָהּ שׁוּתֶּפֶת בֵּין הַבָּנִים אִבְּדָה כְּתוּבָּתָהּ, דִּבְהַהִיא קַרְקַע כָּל שֶׁהוּא שֶׁשִּׁייֵּר לָהּ, שֶׁלֹּא נָתַן לְבָנָיו – מָחֲלָה כְּתוּבָּתָהּ. וְדַוְקָא קַרְקַע כָּל שֶׁהוּא, אֲבָל שִׁייֵּר לָהּ וְכָתַב לָהּ מִטַּלְטְלִין כָּל שֶׁהוּא – לֹא אִבְּדָה כְּתוּבָּתָהּ. דִּכְתוּבָּה עִיקָּרָהּ גּוֹבָה מִמְּקַרְקְעֵי וְלֹא מִמִּטַּלְטְלֵי, (ג) בְּמַסֶּכֶת כְּתוּבּוֹת, הִלְכָּךְ אַמְּקַרְקְעֵי סָמְכָה דַּעְתָּהּ. וּלְכָךְ לֹא עָשׂוּ מִטַּלְטְלִין שִׁיּוּר לִכְתוּבָּתָהּ, דְּאִם שִׁייֵּר לָהּ הַבַּעַל מִטַּלְטְלִין וְנָתַן לָהּ כְּשֶׁחִילֵּק נְכָסָיו לְבָנָיו, וְכָתַב לְאִשְׁתּוֹ מִטַּלְטְלִין כָּל שֶׁהוּא – לֹא אִבְּדָה כְּתוּבָּתָהּ. אֲמַר לֵיהּ רַב יוֹסֵף לְאַבַּיֵי. לְעוֹלָם אֵימָא לָךְ: כָּל הֵיכָא דְּתָנֵי קַרְקַע – דַּוְקָא הוּא. וְהָכָא גַּבֵּי עֶבֶד, הַיְינוּ טַעְמָא דְּלָאו דַּוְקָא, דִּבְדִין הוּא דְּלָא אִיבָּעֵי לֵיהּ לְמִיתְנֵי מְקַרְקְעֵי, אֶלָּא מִטַּלְטְלֵי הֲוָה לֵיהּ לְמִיתְנֵי בְּהֶדְיָא. וְאַיְּידֵי דְּקָתָנֵי רֵישָׁא. בְּמַסֶּכֶת פֵּאָה, ר' עֲקִיבָא אוֹמֵר: קַרְקַע כָּל שֶׁהוּא חַיֶּיבֶת בְּפֵאָה וּבְבִכּוּרִים, וְלִכְתּוֹב עָלָיו פְּרוֹזְבּוֹל, וְלִקְנוֹת עִמָּהֶן נְכָסִים שֶׁאֵין לָהֶם אַחֲרָיוּת בְּכֶסֶף בִּשְׁטָר וּבַחֲזָקָה; דְּהָנֵי כּוּלְּהוּ דַּוְקָא מְקַרְקְעֵי וְלֹא מִטַּלְטְלֵי – תָּנָא נַמִי סֵיפָא קַרְקַע, אַף ע"ג דְּהוּא הַדִּין בְּסֵיפָא לְמִטַּלְטְלֵי. וּמִשּׁוּם סִידּוּרָא דְּכָל שֶׁהֵן מַתְנוּ גַּבֵּי הֲדָדֵי. וּבְוִידּוּי לָא גָּרְסִי' בְּסֵדֶר הַמִּשְׁנָה. דִּבִשְׁלָמָא גַּבֵּי פֵּאָה – "פְּאַת שָׂדְךָ" כְּתִיב קַרְקַע כָּל שֶׁהוּא. גַּבֵּי בִּכּוּרִים כְּתִיב "רֵאשִׁית פְּרִי הָאֲדָמָה אֲשֶׁר נָתַתָּה לִּי". וְלִכְתּוֹב עָלֶיהָ פְּרוֹזְבּוֹל – הָכִי תַּקּוּן רַבָּנַן, אִם יֵשׁ לוֹ לַלֹּוֶה קַרְקַע – כּוֹתְבִין פְּרוֹזְבּוֹל לַמַּלְוֶה לִגְבּוֹת חוֹבוֹ בַּשְּׁבִיעִית, דְּדָמֵי כְּמַאן דְּאִית לֵיהּ מַשְׁכּוֹן, דִּמְקַרְקְעֵי דְּלֹוֶה מִשְׁתַּעְבֵּד לֵיהּ, וְגַבֵּי מַשְׁכּוֹן לָא מְשַׁמְּטָא שְׁבִיעִית, דְּלָא קָרֵינָא בֵּיהּ "לֹא יִגּוֹשׂ" הוֹאִיל וְאִית לֵיהּ מַשְׁכּוֹן, וְלֹא רָצוּ בֵּית דִּין לַעֲקוֹר תַּקָּנַת שְׁבִיעִית מִן הַתּוֹרָה. וְלִקְנוֹת עִמָּהֶן נְכָסִים שֶׁאֵין לָהֶם אַחֲרָיוּת – מִקְּרָאֵי נָפְקָא לַן בְּקִדּוּשִׁין. אֶלָּא וִידּוּי מַעֲשֵׂר, אע"ג דִּכְתִיב בֵּיהּ (דברים כו): "הַשְׁקִיפָה מִמְּעוֹן קָדְשְׁךָ וגו' וְאֵת הָאֲדָמָה אֲשֶׁר נָתַתָּה לָנוּ" [וגו'] – אֲפִי' אֵין לוֹ קַרְקַע יִתְוַדֶּה, דְּהַאי "לָנוּ" אַכָּל יִשְׂרָאֵל קָאֵי, כִּדְתְנַן בְּמַסֶּכֶת מַעֲשֵׂר שֵׁנִי (פ"ה מי"ד): מִכָּאן אָמְרוּ יִשְׂרָאֵל וּמַמְזֵרִים מִתְוַדִּין אֲבָל לֹא גֵּרִים וַעֲבָדִים מְשׁוּחְרָרִים, שֶׁאֵין לָהֶם חֵלֶק בָּאָרֶץ. אַלְמָא, אֲפִי' אֵין לוֹ קַרְקַע, אֶלָּא שֶׁיְּהָא רָאוּי הוּא וַאֲבוֹתָיו לִיטּוֹל חֵלֶק בָּאָרֶץ. וַאֲמַר לֵיהּ אַבַּיֵי לְרַב יוֹסֵף. דְּאַקְשֵׁי לְעֵיל: לְמ"ד כְּדֵי פַּרְנָסָתוֹ, "כָּל שֶׁהוּא" תְּנַן. וְכָל הֵיכָא דִּתְנַן "כָּל שֶׁהוּא" מִי לָא בָּעֵינַן שִׁיעוּרָא? וְהָתְנַן. בְּפֶרֶק "רֵאשִׁית הַגֵּז". חָמֵשׁ רְחֵלוֹת גּוֹזְזוֹת כָּל אַחַת וְאַחַת מִשְׁקַל מָנֶה וּפְרָס. לִיטְרָא וַחֲצִי לִיטְרָא, חַיֶּיבֶת בְּרֵאשִׁית הַגֵּז, דִּבְרֵי ר' דּוֹסָא. וּמֵ"חָמֵשׁ צֹאן עֲשׂוּיוֹת" נָפְקָא לְהוּ לְבֵית הִלֵּל דְּבָעֵינַן חָמֵשׁ, וַחֲכָמִים אוֹמְרִים: ה' רְחֵלוֹת וכו'. אָמַר רַב מָנֶה וּפְרָס. בֵּין חֲמִשְׁתָּן. וּבִלְבַד שֶׁיְּהוּ מְחוּמָּשׁוֹת – כָּל אַחַת יֵשׁ בָּהּ גְּמַר חוֹמֶשׁ שֶׁל מָנֶה וּפְרָס. אֲבָל בָּצִיר מֵהָכִי כְּמַאן דְּלֵיתֵיהּ דָּמֵי. שִׁיעוּרָא רַבָּה. מָנֶה וּפְרָס לְכָל אַחַת, תָּנָא סֵיפָא נַמִי שִׁיעוּרָא זוּטָא. אֲבָל מַתְנִי' דְּקָתָנֵי "כָּל שֶׁהוּא" – דַּוְקָא הוּא, וְהִלְכָּךְ לָא מְכַוְּונַן שְׁמַעְתָּא דְּסָבֵי. אָמַר. שְׁכִיב מְרַע "מִטַּלְטְלֵי לִפְלָנְיָא". וְהוּא הַדִּין לְבָרִיא עַל יְדֵי קִנְיָן. לְבַר מֵחִטֵּי וּשְׂעָרֵי. וְהוּא הַדִּין לְבַר מִבְּהֶמוֹתָיו. כֵּן נִרְאֶה בְּעֵינַי. אֲפִי' רֵיחַיִם הָעֶלְיוֹנָה. שֶׁרְגִילִין לִיטְּלָהּ מִשָּׁם כְּדֵי לְתַקְּנָהּ. אֲבָל רֵיחַיִם הַתַּחְתּוֹנָה – בִּמְקוֹמָהּ מְתַקְּנִין אוֹתָהּ. כָּל דְּמִטַּלְטֵל. כָּל שֶׁיְּכוֹלִין לְטַלְטְלוֹ, שֶׁאֵינוֹ מְחוּבָּר לַקַּרְקַע מַמָּשׁ, וְאע"פ שֶׁאֵין רְגִילִין לְטַלְטְלוֹ. אִיבַּעְיָא לְהוּ עַבְדָּא כְּמִטַּלְטְלֵי דָּמֵי. נְהִי וַדַּאי דְּעַבְדָּא כִּמְקַרְקְעֵי דָּמֵי לְעִנְיַן שְׁבוּעָה וְקִנְיָן בְּכֶסֶף וּבִשְׁטָר וּבַחֲזָקָה, (ד) דְּכָל מִילֵּי דְּאוֹרַיְיתָא דִּין מְקַרְקְעֵי יֵשׁ לָהֶם מִ"וְהִתְנַחַלְתֶּם", אֲבָל לְעִנְיַן לְשׁוֹן בְּנֵי אָדָם – מִיקְּרוּ לְהוּ מִטַּלְטְלֵי, וְיֶשְׁנָן בִּכְלַל מַתְּנַת מִטַּלְטְלֵי שֶׁהֲרֵי מִטַּלְטְלֵי הוּא, אוֹ לָא? הַיְינוּ דְּלָא אִזְדַּבַּן לֵיהּ בְּרֵישָׁא. בְּמַאי דְּקָתָנֵי בְּרֵישָׁא דְּמַתְנִיתִין, הֵיכָא דְּמָכַר אֶת הָעִיר סְתָמָא, וְלֹא אָמַר לוֹ "הִיא וְכָל מַה שֶּׁבְּתוֹכָהּ" – לָא קָחֲשֵׁיב אֶלָּא מְקַרְקְעֵי, אֲבָל עֲבָדִים וּמִטַּלְטְלִין לֹא נִמְכְּרוּ. אַלְמָא עַבְדָּא כְּמִטַּלְטְלֵי דָּמֵי. וּפָרְכִינַן: אֶלָּא מַאי עַבְדָּא כְּמִטַּלְטְלֵי דָּמֵי. א"כ מַאי "אֲפִי'" דְּקָתָנֵי סֵיפָא: מָכַר אֶת הַמִּטַּלְטְלִין וַאֲפִי' עֲבָדִים. וְאִי כְּמִטַּלְטְלֵי דָּמֵי אַמַּאי קָאָמַר "אֲפִילּוּ", דְּמַשְׁמַע דְּאֵינוֹ דּוֹמֶה כָּל כָּךְ לְמִטַּלְטְלִין? אֶלָּא מַאי אִית לָךְ לְמֵימַר. אַמַּאי קָמִפַּלְגֵי בֵּין לְמִטַּלְטְלִין לְמִיתְנֵי "אֲפִי'" מִשּׁוּם דְּשָׁאנֵי בֵּין מִטַּלְטְלֵי דְּנָיְידֵי דְּהַיְינוּ עֲבָדִים, לְמִטַּלְטְלֵי דְּלָא נָיְידֵי, וְהִלְכָּךְ קָתָנֵי בְּהוּ "אֲפִילּוּ". ה"נ בְּרֵישָׁא, אִיכָּא לְמֵימַר דְּעַבְדָּא כִּמְקַרְקְעֵי דָּמֵי, וְהַאי דְּלָא מִיזְדַּבְּנֵי בִּכְלַל הָעִיר – דְּשָׁאנֵי לְהוּ לִבְנֵי אָדָם בֵּין מְקַרְקְעֵי דְּנָיֵיד לִמְקַרְקְעֵי דְּלָא נָיֵיד, וְכֵיוָן דְּעִיר מָכַר, דְּהַיְינוּ מְקַרְקְעֵי דְּלָא נָיֵיד – לָא אַסֵּיק אַדַּעְתֵּיהּ לִמְכּוֹר אֶלָּא מְקַרְקְעֵי דְּלָא נָיֵיד, דְּהַיְינוּ דּוּמְיָא דְּעִיר. אֲבָל הֵיכָא דְּאָמַר סְתָמָא "מְקַרְקְעֵי לִפְלָנְיָא" – עֲבָדִים בִּכְלָל, וְהֵיכָא דְּאָמַר סְתָמָא "מִטַּלְטְלֵי לִפְלָנְיָא" – לְעוֹלָם אֵימָא לָךְ דְּאֵינוֹ בִּכְלָל. עָשׂוּ מִטַּלְטְלֵי שִׁיּוּר. דְּכִי הֵיכִי דְּקָתָנֵי: שִׁייֵּר קַרְקַע כָּל שֶׁהוּא לֹא יָצָא לְחֵירוּת, הָכִי נַמִי אִם שִׁייֵּר מִטַּלְטְלֵי כָּל שֶׁהוּא לֹא יָצָא לְחֵירוּת. וַאֲמַר לֵיהּ רָבָא לְרַב נַחְמָן מַאי טַעְמָא. וְהֵשִׁיב לוֹ רַב נַחְמָן: עַבְדָּא מִטַּלְטְלֵי. דְּכֵיוָן דְּשִׁייֵּר מִטַּלְטְלִין לְעַצְמוֹ – אִיכָּא לְמֵימַר דְּעַבְדּוֹ שִׁייֵּר לְעַצְמוֹ, שֶׁהוּא מִטַּלְטְלִין, וְלֹא יָצָא לְחֵירוּת. אַלְמָא כְּמִטַּלְטְלֵי דָּמֵי! א"ל רַב אַשִׁי לְרָבִינָא. לְעוֹלָם אֵימָא לָךְ כִּמְקַרְקְעֵי, וְהַאי עָשׂוּ מִטַּלְטְלִין שִׁיּוּר אֵצֶל הָעֶבֶד – לָאו הַיְינוּ טַעְמָא כִּדְרַב נַחְמָן דְּאָמַר עַבְדָּא מִטַּלְטְלֵי הוּא, אֶלָּא כִּדְפָרֵישִׁית טַעְמָא. דְּאֵנַן

תוספות

קרקע כל שהוא חייבת בפאה כו'. לעיל בשלהי "לא יחפור" (דף כז.) פירשתי לה. וכל היכא דתני כל שהוא לית ליה שיעורא והא תנן כו'. ואע"ג דקרקע כל שהוא חייב בפאה היינו כל שהוא דוקא, כדאמרינן לעיל בפרק "לא יחפור" (דף כז. ושם: ד"ה במטה) — היינו משום דמסתבר טפי הכי. ובקדושין פ"ק (דף כו.) הארכתי שם בדיני "כל שהוא". וכמה כל שהוא אמר רב מנה ופרם. ואם תאמר: מאי מקשה ליה? והלא ודאי הוא חולק על רב דלעיל! וי"ל, דהכי קאמר: מי פליג על רב בכל הני? מנה ופרם. שיעור דרבנן ור' דוסא לא ידעינן מנא (ה) ליה. ואיידי דקאמר תנא קמא שיעורא רבה אמרי אינהו שיעורא זוטא. והא דתנן (כלים פ"ה מ"א): תנור תחלתו ארבעה וסופו כל שהוא, ואמרינן (חולין דף קכד.): מאי "כל שהוא" — טפח, איכא (ו) למימר דאיידי דנקט שיעורא רבה נקיט נמי שיעורא זוטא. עבדא כמקרקעי דמי או כמטלטלי דמי. לענין מילי דרבנן מיבעי ליה. אבל במלתא דאורייתא — פשיטא דאיתקוש לקרקעות, כדפי' לעיל בפרק "המוכר את הבית" (דף סח.) על הך מילתא. אמר

עין משפט נר מצוה

צא א מיי' פ"ז מהלכות עבדים הלכה א סמג עשין פז טוש"ע יו"ד סי' רסז סעיף נז:

צב ב מיי' פ"ו מהלכות זכייה ומתנה הלכה י סמג עשין פב טוש"ע אה"ע סי' קו סעיף ב:

צג ג ד מיי' פ"י מהל' בכורים הלכה יג סמג עשין קמג טוש"ע יו"ד סי' שלג סעיף ט:

צד ה ו ז ח מיי' פי"א מהל' זכייה ומתנה הלכה יב יג יד סמג עשין פב טוש"ע חו"מ סי' רמח סעיף י:

הגהות הב"ח

(א) גמרא גוזזות מנה ופרס מנה ופרס חייבות: (ב) שם פשיטא אמר מטלטלאי לפלניא וכו' כל מטלטלאי לפלניא וכו' כל מטלטלאי דמטלטל אפי' ריחים התחתונה קני: (ג) רשב"ם ד"ה ולא עשו וכו' ולא ממטלטלי כדאמר במס' כתובות: (ד) ד"ה איבעיא להו וכו' דלכל מילי דאורייתא (ה) תוס' ד"ה מנה וכו' מנא להו הס"ד (ו) ד"ה ואיידי וכו' איכא נמי למימר דאיידי:

רבינו גרשום

שייר: אמר ר' אלעזר עשו מטלטלין שיור אצל העבד. דאי שייר מטלטלין כל שהן איכא למימר דהעבד שייר ולא יצא בן חורין אלמא אע"ג דקתני קרקע לאו דוקא קרקע ואם שייר מטלטלין ה"נ דהוי שיור בקרקע. והא משנה הכותב כל נכסיו לעבדו בפאה היא: ולא עשו מטלטלין שיור אצל כתובה. דקיי"ל כתובה ממקרקע גביא ותנן הכותב כל נכסיו לבניו וכתב לאשתו קרקע כל שהוא אבדה כתובתה דחלק לפניה לבניו והיא שותקת. אם שייר לעצמו קרקע שלא כתב הכל לבניו ואע"פ שכתב לה עם בניו קרקע כל שהוא לא אבדה כתובתה דהאי דשתקה סמכה דעתה לגבות מההוא קרקע דשייר לעצמו. אבל אי לא שייר לעצמו אלא מטלטלין אבדה כתובתה דלא מצי למימר האי דשתקי דאהנהו מטלטלי סמכה דעתאי דאין כתובה נגבית אלא מן הקרקע והיינו דקאמר ר' אלעזר לא עשו מטלטלי שיור אצל בניו כדי שתהא גובה מהן: אמר ליה לעולם אימא לך כל היכא דתני קרקע הכי דוקא ולא מטלטלי נינהו. ודקשיא לך ממשנה זו ומדרב דימי בר יוסף הא לא קשיא דבדין הוא דלא ליבעי ליה למיתני קרקע גבי עבד כלל אלא איידי דאיצטריך ליה למיתני בסיפא קרקע דלא סגי בלאו הכי תנא ליה ברישא ולא משום דוקא. דתנן ר' עקיבא אמר כו'. ולעולם מתני' דקתני קרקע הכי דוקא ולא הוי מטלטלי שיורי. ומקשי' אליבא דרב יוסף דמתקיף לעיל (מאי שונה) למאן דתני כדי פרנסתו כל שהוא לית ליה שיעורא רבה והתנן חמש רחלות גוזזות מנה ופרס. כלומר כל אחת גוזזת משקל מנה ופרס דהיינו משקל ליטרא וחצי חייב בראשית הגז. וחכ"א חמש רחלות גוזזות כל שהוא. ואמרי' מאי כל שהוא ואמר רב מנה ופרס דבין כולן גוזזות משקל ליטרא ומחצה ובלבד שיהו מחומשות שלא תהא בהמה ובהמה גוזזת פחות מחומש של מנה ופרס אלמא אע"ג דקתני כל שהוא אית ליה שיעורא כדאמר מנה ופרס וגבי מתני' אע"ג דקתני קרקע כל שהוא אית ליה שיעורא וקשיא לרב יוסף. ומשני לעולם כל היכא דקתני קרקע כל שהוא הכי דוקא והכא טעמא מאי משוה ליה שיעורא איידי דתנא ליה רישא שיעורא רבה חמש רחלות גוזזות מנה ופרס תנא נמי סיפא שיעורא זוטא ולא משום דוקא: שכיב מרע שאמר מטלטלי נתונין לפלוני יהבינן ליה כל מאני תשמישתא. כגון כל תשמישי הבית: לבר מחטי ושערי. דלאו לתשמישי הבית דמיין: אבל אי אמר כל מטלטלי. כל מה שיש לו המטלטל: אפי' ריחים העליונים. דמטלטלי הוא לבר מריחים התחתונה. דקביעא בקרקע הוא ולאו מיטלטל. אבל אי אמר כל דמיטלטל כלומר כל דמצי למיטלטל אפי' ריחים התחתונה משום דאפשר לחופרה מן הקרקע ותהא מיטלטל: איבעיא להו עבדא כמקרקע. ואי אמר כל מקרקעי לפלוני יהיבנא ליה אפי' עבדא: אי כמטלטלי דמי. ואי אמר כל מטלטלי לפלוני יהבינן ליה עבדא: ת"ש כו'. הנהו כולהו בקרקעות הוו: בית השלחין. מקוה מים שמשקה ממנו בית השלחין: מאי אפי'. הכי צריך ליה למיתני ובזמן שאמר הוא וכל מה שבתוכו היו בה בהמה ועבדים הרי אלו מכורים אלא לאו מדקאמר אפי' מכלל דלאו כמטלטלי דמי: אלא מאי אית לך למימר. הא דקתני ליה גבי מטלטלי וקתני אפי'. משום דשאני מטלטלי דנייד כגון עבדים ובהמה דניידי ממטלטלי דלא ניידי משום הכי קתני (כו') אפי' מטלטלי דניידי כגון עבדים: אפי' תימא כו' מקרקעי דלא ניידי. ומשום הכי לא קתני גבי מקרקעי דמקרקעי דנייד הוא ומשום הכי קתני אפי': מאי טעמא עבדא כמטלטלי

"שִׁיֵּיר קַרְקַע כָּל שֶׁהוּא — מַתְּנָתוֹ קַיֶּימֶת". וְכַמָּה "כָּל שֶׁהוּא"? אָמַר רַב יְהוּדָה אָמַר רַב: קַרְקַע כְּדֵי פַּרְנָסָתוֹ, וְרַב יִרְמְיָה בַּר אַבָּא אָמַר: מִטַּלְטְלִין כְּדֵי פַּרְנָסָתוֹ. אָמַר רַבִּי זֵירָא: כַּמָּה מְכַוְּונָן שְׁמַעֲתָתָא דְּסָבֵי! קַרְקַע טַעֲמָא מַאי? דְּאִי קָאֵי סָמֵיךְ עֲלַיהּ, [א]מִטַּלְטְלֵי נַמִי, אִי קָאֵי סָמֵיךְ עִילָּוַיְיהוּ. מַתְקִיף לָהּ רַב יוֹסֵף: וּמַאי כַּוּוֹנְתָּא? מַאן דְּאָמַר: מִטַּלְטְלִין — קַרְקַע תְּנַן! מַאן דְּאָמַר: כְּדֵי פַּרְנָסָתוֹ — [ב]כָּל שֶׁהוּא תְּנַן! אֲמַר לֵיהּ אַבַּיֵי: וְכָל הֵיכָא דְּתָנֵי קַרְקַע, קַרְקַע דַּוְקָא? וְהָא תְּנַן: [א)][ג]הַכּוֹתֵב כָּל נְכָסָיו לְעַבְדּוֹ — יָצָא בֶּן חוֹרִין, שִׁיֵּיר קַרְקַע כָּל שֶׁהוּא — לֹא יָצָא בֶּן חוֹרִין; ר' שִׁמְעוֹן אוֹמֵר: לְעוֹלָם הוּא בֶּן חוֹרִין, עַד שֶׁיֹּאמַר: "כָּל נְכָסַי נְתוּנִין לִפְלוֹנִי עַבְדִּי חוּץ מֵאֶחָד מֵרִבּוֹא שֶׁבָּהֶן"; וְאָמַר

כַּמָּה מְכַוְּונָן. כַּמָּה יָפֶה כִּוְּונוּ, שֶׁפֵּירְשׁוּ "כָּל שֶׁהוּא" – כְּדֵי פַּרְנָסָתוֹ, לְמָר בִּמְקַרְקְעֵי וּלְמָר אֲפִי' (א) בְּמִטַּלְטְלֵי. דִּמְקַרְקְעֵי. כְּדֵי פַּרְנָסָתוֹ, טַעְמָא מַאי הָוֵי שִׁיּוּר, לְהַקְנוֹת הַמַּתָּנָה שֶׁנָּתַן מִקְּלָת? מִשּׁוּם דְּכִי קָאֵי מֵחָלְיוֹ סָמֵיךְ עֲלַיְיהוּ. וְהִלְכָּךְ נָתַן לְדַעַת כֵּן, שֶׁאֲפִילּוּ אִם יַעֲמוֹד מֵחָלְיוֹ – תִּתְקַיֵּים הַמַּתָּנָה, וְהוּא יִתְפַּרְנֵס מִמַּה שֶּׁשִּׁיֵּיר. מִטַּלְטְלֵי נַמִי כו'. מַאי כַּוּוֹנְתָּא. וַהֲלֹא אֵינָן מְכוּוָּנוֹת יָפֶה, דִּלְמ"ד מִטַּלְטְלֵי כו'. קַרְקַע דַּוְקָא. בִּתְמִיָּה, וְהָתְנַן בְּמַסֶּכֶת פֵּאָה. הַכּוֹתֵב נְכָסָיו לְעַבְדּוֹ יָצָא בֶּן חוֹרִין. שֶׁהֲרֵי הָעֶבֶד בִּכְלַל נְכָסִים, וְנִמְצָא שֶׁהִקְנָה לָעֶבֶד אֶת גּוּפוֹ עִם שְׁאָר נְכָסִים. שִׁיֵּיר קַרְקַע כָּל שֶׁהוּא. כְּגוֹן שֶׁאָמַר "חוּץ מִקַּרְקַע כָּל שֶׁהוּא" – לֹא יָצָא בֶּן חוֹרִין. שֶׁהָעֶבֶד הוּקַּשׁ לְקַרְקָעוֹת, דִּכְתִיב: "וְהִתְנַחַלְתֶּם" (ויקרא כה), וְהַאי "קַרְקַע כָּל שֶׁהוּא" אִיכָּא לְמֵימַר שֶׁעַל הָעֶבֶד הוּא אוֹמֵר. וְנִמְצָא שֶׁאֵינוֹ בֶּן חוֹרִין, וְגַם הַנְּכָסִים לֹא קָנָה. וְה"ה אִם אָמַר "חוּץ מִמִּטַּלְטְלִין כָּל שֶׁהוּא", כִּדְמְפָ' ר' אֶלְעָזָר לְקַמֵּיהּ, שֶׁעָשׂוּ הַמִּטַּלְטְלִין שִׁיּוּר אֵצֶל הָעֶבֶד, דְּדִלְמָא הַאי עֶבֶד הוּא הַמִּטַּלְטְלִין שֶׁשִּׁיֵּיר, דְּעַבְדָּא מִיטַּלְטֵל. אֲבָל אִם אָמַר "כָּל נְכָסַיי נְתוּנִים לְךָ חוּץ מִשָּׂדֶה פְּלוֹנִי" – הֲרֵי הוּא בֶּן חוֹרִין, שֶׁהָעֶבֶד אֵינוֹ בִּכְלַל אוֹתוֹ שָׂדֶה שֶׁפֵּירֵשׁ. רַבִּי שִׁמְעוֹן אוֹמֵר לְעוֹלָם הוּא בֶּן חוֹרִין. אִם שִׁיֵּיר קַרְקַע כָּל שֶׁהוּא. דְּשִׁיֵּיר קַרְקַע וְלֹא עֶבֶד, עַד שֶׁיִּהְיֶה הַשִּׁיּוּר שֶׁשִּׁיֵּיר סְתָם, וְיֹאמַר "כָּל נְכָסַיי נְתוּנִים לִפְלוֹנִי עַבְדִּי, חוּץ מֵאֶחָד מֵרִבּוֹא שֶׁבָּהֶן", שֶׁהַהוּא "אֶחָד מֵרִבּוֹא" – אַעֶבֶד קָאֵי, וְאֵינוֹ מְשׁוּחְרָר. וְדֶרֶךְ כָּבוֹד כָּתַב לְעַבְדּוֹ כָּךְ, ומ"מ לֹא קָנָה כְּלוּם.

ומוקי התם טעמא משום דמצוה לקיים דברי המת. ומיירי שהושלש מתחלה לכך, כי היכי דלא תקשה ממעשה דאיסור גיורא, דהכא לא אמרינן מצוה לקיים דברי המת ואע"ג דהוה ביד שליש. אלא היינו טעמא — משום דלא הושלש לו מתחלה לכך. וקשה על זה הפירוש מהא דאמרינן בגיטין פרק "השולח" (דף מ.): "פלונית שפחתי עשתה לי קורת רוח" — כופין את היורשים כו', משום דמצוה לקיים דברי המת. והתם לא הושלש ביד שליש מידי! וצריך לומר: דגבי שחרור יש לנו לומר יותר מצוה לקיים דברי המת מבשאר דברים. והשתא נמי אתי שפיר, דלא תקשה מהא דאמרי' לקמן (דף קנא:): האומר "תנו גט לאשתי" כו' אבל האומר "תנו מנה לפלוני" ומת — יתנו לאחר מיתה, ודייק מינה: מתנת שכ"מ במקצת לא בעי קנין. דלא הוה מצי למימר טעם משום דמצוה לקיים דברי המת, דלא אמרי' הכי אלא כשהושלש מתחלה לכך. וא"ת: על הך משנה דגיטין (דף יג.) דמייתי לקמן: אבל אמר "תנו מנה לפלוני" ומת — יתנו לאחר מיתה, אמר רב עלה בסוף פ"ק (שם) בגמרא: והוא שמונחין בקרן זוית. איכא דמוקי לה התם למשנה בבריא ובמעמד שלשתן, ואיכא דמוקי לה התם בשכיב מרע. ואמאי לא מוקי לה למתני' התם כשהושלש מתחלה לכך ומשום מצוה לקיים דברי המת? ואי משום דכיחידאה לא הוי מוקמי התם ואע"ג דקי"ל הכי, כדאמר בפ"ק דגיטין (דף טו.), וכדאשכחן נמי בפ' "כל הגט" (שם דף ל.) דלא מוקי שמואל מתני' דפרק "כל הגט" דהמלוה מעות את הכהן ואת הלוי כר' יוסי, משום דכיחידאה לא מוקמי, אע"ג דס"ל בפ"ק דבבא מציעא (דף יב.) כוותיה. ורבנן פליגי עליה דר"מ (ג) דמצוה לקיים דברי המת בספ"ק דגיטין (דף יד:), אע"ג דר' יוסי פליג עליה בכתובות (דף סט:) מ"מ חולקין רבנן על ר"מ בספ"ק דגיטין (שם) גבי "הולך מנה לפלוני". אך מההיא דר' יוסי בפ"ק דבבא מציעא אין ראיה כל כך, דאיכא לדחויי דכיחידאה לא מוקמינן, משום דר' יוסי הוי יחידאה היכא דפליג במסכת בכורות בפרק "הלוקח עובר פרתו" (דף יח), ולא פסיק שמואל הלכה כוותיה אלא בהא דבבא מציעא פ"ק, משום דסתמא עניים גופייהו ניחא להו כדאיתא התם, (ג) ולהכי מודה נמי איהו במתני' ד"כל הגט". ויש שהם מתרלים שם בשם ר"ת, דלא אמר התם מצוה לקיים דברי המת כיון שראוי לינתן מחיים ולא לינתן לאחר מיתה, להכי לא שייך בה מצוה לקיים דברי המת. תדע, דהוי דומיא דגט ושטר שחרור, שאינו ראוי לינתן אלא מחיים. ואין נראה לר"י, דהא אפי' בדבר דשייך מחיים אמרי' בסוף פ"ק דגיטין, בברייתא ד"הולך מנה לפלוני" והלך ובקשו ולא מצאו, דמשמע התם דאפילו בדבר דשייך לינתן מחיים קאמר מצוה לקיים דברי המת. מיהו, יש לדחות ולומר שהמשלח צוה ליתנם לו לאחר מותו, דמוקמינן לה נמי בשכיב מרע, שעיקר צואתו אינו אלא לאחר מיתה. א"נ י"ל: דלא ס"ל לרב התם בהך מימרא מצוה לקיים דברי המת, אלא ס"ל כשמואל, דמסיק התם בכתובות פרק "מציאת האשה" כר' יוסי, דלית ליה מצוה לקיים דברי המת. ואע"ג דפריך על רב יוסף בסוף ההוא פרק: והא קי"ל מצוה לקיים דברי המת, ולא פריך עליה דרב הכי — משום דלא הוה ידע לשנויי עלה מידי. ואין זו תימה אי סבר לה בהא כשמואל. ואע"ג דפריך התם עלה דרב: והא קי"ל התם דברי שכ"מ כו' — משום (ד) דליכא מאן דפליג בה. ועוד י"ל: דלא משתמע לי' לאוקמא מתני' דהתם שהושלש מתחלה לכך, מדקתני: "תנו מנה לפלוני", ולא קתני "תן מנה זה לפלוני", דהוה משמע שהושלש מתחלה [לכך] ואע"ג דבגמ' בסוף פרקין דגיטין גבי "הולך מנה לפלוני", קתני סתם: מצוה לקיים דברי המת, ולא קתני "זה" — היינו משום דמשמע ליה שפיר כשהושלש בלא "זה", דבאותה שעה אמר לו להוליך. מ"ר. ועוד היה מפרש ר"ת: דלא שייך הכא בשמעתין מצוה לקיים דברי המת, משום דכל דאיתיה בירושה — איתיה במתנה מצוה לקיים דברי המת*, וכל דליתיה בירושה כו' כדאמר גבי מתנת שכיב מרע. מיהו, לא דמי למתנת שכיב מרע שהיא כעין ירושה, דיש לנו יותר לדמותה לירושה, כדאמר לעיל. ועוד: דכי היכי דמפרש גמרא דמתנת שכ"מ אינה בגר — ה"ל למימר נמי טעמא דמצוה לקיים דברי המת אינו בגר. מיהו, יש לדחות, דפשיטא ליה דלא שייך בגר, כיון דליתיה בירושה פשיטא ליה שכיון שמת — בטל, ואין לו שום זכות להוריש, ואיך יקיימו דבריו? מיהו, כדפירשנו לעיל ניחא טפי. מ"ר. ועוד היה אומר ר"י: דלא אמרי' מצוה לקיים דברי המת אלא באומר לו פה אל פה, ורבא לא אזל לגביה. וחזר בו ר"י כדקאמר ב"השולח" (גיטין דף מ:): "עשיתי פלוני עבדי בן חורין" כו' א"ר יוחנן: וכולן בשטר. וא"כ הא דקתני בתר הכי: "אעשנו בן חורין" רבי אומר: זכה, וחכ"א: לא זכה, אלא כופין את היורשים כו' — מיירי נמי בשטר, ולא פה אל פה. דאי א"ל, [ליורשים לעשותו בן חורין] — למה לי שטר?* וכן פי' ר"ח. **שייר** קרקע כל שהוא. ולא פירש איזו קרקע, אלא חוץ ממקרקעי סתם כל שהוא, וי"ל: גופו של עבד שייר, דעבדא כמקרקעי דמי, ומטלטלין נמי עשו שיור, דאם אמר נמי "חוץ ממטלטלין כל שהוא" — שייר בגופו של עבד, וקרקע דתנן איידי, (ה) כדקאמר גמרא. ובגמרת א"י בפ"ג דפאה: ור' יוסי בשם ר' אלעזר: שייר מטלטלין ולא עשה כלום, אני אומר: גופו של עבד שייר. ובמסקנא מפרש: משום דלאו כרות גיטא מתנינן לה. דכיון שיש לבעל העבד זכות בשטר, שכתוב בו שייר קרקע לעצמו — לא הקנה לו שטר לגמרי, שגם זכות האדון כתוב בו, הלכך לא קרינא ביה "ספר כריתות". וטעמא דר"ש דאמר לעולם הוא בן חורין — משום דחשיב ליה כרות גיטא בהכי, כיון שלא שייר בגוף העבד. מיהו, מתחלה היה סבור דטעמא דת"ק — משום דשייר בגוף העבד. וכן בפ"ק דגיטין (דף ח:) דמוקי פלוגתייהו בפלגינן דבורא, מתחלה היה סבור כן, דלת"ק משום שייר בגוף העבד ולר"ש לא שייר, דפלגינן דבורא, והעבד קנוי לעצמו. ושם פירש רבינו חננאל: מתחלה סובר ת"ק כיון ששייר קרקע כל שהוא סתם, אין יכול לברר העבד הנכסים שהקנה לו רבו, ולא קנה בנכסים, דאמר: יד בעל השטר על התחתונה, וכיון שבנכסים לא קנה — עצמו נמי לא קנה. ור"ש סבר: אע"ג דלא קנה בנכסים — עצמו קנה, דפלגינן דבורא, עד שיאמר "חוץ מאחד מרבוא", דאיכא למימר גופו של עבד שייר. וכן פירש בגמרת א"י, לשון רבינו חננאל*. והתוספתא נראה דבשבוש מיתניא, דמאי בא ר"ש להשמיענו, דאפילו היכא שאומר "חוץ מעיר פלונית"? וכי בשביל שהזכיר מה שמוציא יש לו להיות פחות בן חורין? דכל שכן [שהוא משוחרר] כשאומר סתם, דיד בעל השטר על התחתונה, וסמי תוספתא מקמי ירושלמי. ומיהו, אין נראה לשבש התוספתא(ו). (ז) **שייר** קרקע כל שהוא **לא יצא** בן חורין *ור"ש **אומר אפילו אמר** כל נכסיי קנוי לך חוץ מעיר **פלונית** חוץ משדה פלונית זכה בנכסים קנה **עצמו** בן חורין. פירוש: אפילו הזכיר בהדיא מה שמוציא מן השחרור, דאז יש לנו לומר שלא שחרר העבד — אפ"ה קנה נכסים, ונשתחרר. דפלגינן דבורא, דאית לן למימר: מאותה שדה או מאותה עיר הדר ביה, אבל מן העבד לא הדר ביה. מכלל דרבנן דפליגי עליה אית להו דלא פלגינן דבורא, ומדהדר בנכסים — הדר נמי בעבד. א"נ, מדשייר בנכסים — שייר נמי בעבד. ובפ"ק דגיטין (דף ח:) מייתי לה נמי להך דהכא, למימרא דפלגינן דבורא, ולא כפרש"י דהתם, אלמא לא שייר כלל מן העבד אלא מן הנכסים, ובהא פליגי רבנן עליה, ובפלוגתייהו בפ"ק (שם.) גבי ר"מ אומר עכו כא"י לגיטין. אבל אין להקשות על פירוש רבינו שמואל שפירש ששייר העבד משום דהוי מקרקעי, מדאמר עשו מטלטלים שיור אצל עבד — דהא ודאי אמת הוא, דהוי מטלטלים כמו מקרקעי. מ"ר.
קרקע

רבינו גרשום

כדי פרנסתו שאם יעמוד מחליו שיהא לו על מה להסמך: אפי' אם (אמר) שייר מטלטלי כדי פרנסתו קני: כמה מכוון שמעתתא דסבי. ר' יהוד' ור' ירמיה: מקרקעי מאי טעמא א): אמר שייר קרקע כל שהוא תנן ולא כדי פרנסתו קרקע דוקא ולא מטלטלי: והתנן הכותב כל נכסיו לעבדו. במתנה יצא בן חורין משום דהעבד עצמו בכלל נכסיו הוא וכתבו לעצמו מתנה. אם שייר קרקע כל שהוא ב) כתב לעבד לא יצא בן חורין. דאיכא למימר אותו עצמו שייר דעבדים הוקשו לקרקעות דכתי' והתנחלתם וגו': חוץ מאחד מרבוא שבהן. הואיל ושייר בסתמא איכא למימר דעבד שייר. אבל אי שייר קרקע איכא למימר קרקע ממש

א) נראה דחסר כאן וצ"ל מקרקעי מ"ט אמר דמתנתו קיימת וכו': שייר קרקע וכו'. ב) אולי צ"ל אם שייר קרקע כל שהוא בהמתנה שכתב להעבד וכו'.

פט א ב מיי' פ"ח מהל' זכייה ומתנה הלכה טו סמג עשין פב טוש"ע חו"מ סי' רנ סעיף ד:
צ ג מיי' פ"ז מהלכות עבדים הלכה א סמג עשין פו טוש"ע יו"ד סי' רסז סעיף נז:

א) [לקמן קנ.] גיטין ח: מב. פאה פ"ג מ"ח.

הגהות הב"ח

(א) רשב"ם ד"ה כמה וכו' במטלטלי דמקרקעי וכו' שנתן במקצת וכו' סמיך עליה והלכך כצ"ל והד"א: (ב) תוס' ד"ה (בע"א) דקא כו' פליגי עליה דר"מ דאמר מצוה לקיים וכו' לא מוקמינן היינו משום וכו': (ג) בא"ד ולהכי מודה נמי. נ"ב פירוש שמואל מודה כו': (ד) בא"ד דליכא מאן דפליג. נ"ב פי' באמוראים ליכא מאן דפליג מא"כ במצוה לד"ה דפליג שמואל אבל בתנאים ודאי איכא רבי אליעזר דפליג בדברי ש"מ לקמן בדף קנו במשנה: (ה) ד"ה שייר וכו' דתנן איידי דרישא כדקאמר: (ו) בא"ד אין נראה לשבש התוספתא אלא כמו שפי' בפנים עכ"ה הס"ד: (ז) ד"ה שייר נמחק תחלת הדבור וצריך להתחיל ור' שמעון אומר וכו' אבל מן העבד לא הדר ביה אבל רבנן פליגי עליה ואית להו דלא פלגינן וכו' ובפ"ק דגיטין גבי ר"מ אומר עכו כארץ ישראל מייתי לה נמי להך דפלגינן דבורא אליבא דרבי שמעון ולא כפי' רש"י דהתם דלא שייר כלל מן העבד אלא מן הנכסים ובהא פליגי רבנן עליה כדפרישית אבל אין להקשות על פי' כצ"ל:

רש"ל כ' דהך לקיים דברי המת הוא סוף דבור והך וכל דליתי' בירושה הוא דבור חדש [לא נמצא במהרש"ל]

מהרש"א כ' דהך ל"ל שטר הוא סוף דבור והך וכן פירש ר"ח הוא שייך לתחלת דבור הסמוך

לשון ר"ח ור"י פי' דאף מתחלה סבר דת"ק לא איירי דוקא בשייר סתם דשמא שייר בגוף העבד אלא אפי' שייר דבר מבורר ופירש מה ששייר אפ"ה פליג ת"ק וכן מוכח מהתוספתא ר"ש אומר כל נכסיי נתונים לפלוני עבדי חוץ מאחד מריבוא שבהן לא אמר כלום חוץ מעיר פלונית משדה פלונית אע"פ שאין שם אלא אותה שדה ואותה העיר זכה העבד זה בנכסים וקנה עצמו בן חורין וכו' זכה בנכסים אם יש לו שאר נכסי וקנה עצמו לחורין בכל ענין כן פי' רבינו שמשון בפ"ג דפאה ומדאמר ר"ש בחוץ מעיר פלונית או חוץ משדה פלונית דיצא בו לחירות מכלל דשמע לרבנן דאף בכה"ג לא יצא לחירות והכי פליגי כצ"ל והשאר עד לשבש התוספתא הוא הג"ה:

ור"ש אומר וכו' ופי' רבינו שמואל דדלמא הוא העבד ששייר ואין נראה לר"י דהא תניא בהדיא בתוספתא ר"ש אומר אפי' אמר כל נכסי וכו' כצ"ל וכ"ה בת"י. רש"ח.

"יֶהֱנֶה בָּהֶן", מַהִי? דְּנֶיהֱוֵי כּוּלְּהוּ מַתָּנָה קָאָמַר, אוֹ דִּלְמָא לִיתְהַנֵּי מִינַּיְיהוּ מִידֵי קָאָמַר? "יֵרָאֶה בָּהֶן", מַהוּ? "יַעֲמוֹד בָּהֶן", מַהוּ? "יִשָּׁעֵן בָּהֶן", מַהוּ? [א]תֵּיקוּ. אִיבַּעְיָא לְהוּ: מָכַר כָּל נְכָסָיו, מַהוּ? אָמַר רַב יְהוּדָה אָמַר רַב: [ב]אִם עָמַד אֵינוֹ חוֹזֵר. וְזִימְנִין אָמַר רַב יְהוּדָה אָמַר רַב: אִם עָמַד חוֹזֵר. וְלָא פְּלִיגִי: [ג]הָא דְּאִיתְנְהוּ לְזוּזֵי בְּעֵינַיְיהוּ, הָא דְּפָרְעִינְהוּ בְּחוֹבוֹ. אִיבַּעְיָא לְהוּ: שְׁכִיב מְרַע שֶׁהוֹדָה, מַהוּ? ת"ש: דְּאִיסּוּר גִּיּוֹרָא הֲוָה לֵיהּ תְּרֵיסַר אַלְפֵי זוּזֵי בֵּי רָבָא. רַב מָרִי בְּרֵיהּ, הוֹרָתוֹ שֶׁלֹּא בִּקְדוּשָּׁה וְלֵידָתוֹ בִּקְדוּשָּׁה הֲוַאי, וּבֵי רַב הֲוָה. אֲמַר רָבָא: הֵיכִי נִיקְנִינְהוּ רַב מָרִי לְהָנֵי זוּזֵי? אִי בִּירוּשָּׁה — [ד]לָאו בַּר יְרוּשָּׁה הוּא; אִי בְּמַתָּנָה — מַתְּנַת שְׁכִיב מְרַע כִּירוּשָּׁה שַׁוְיוּהָ רַבָּנַן, [ה]כָּל הֵיכָא דְּאִיתֵיהּ בִּירוּשָּׁה אִיתֵיהּ בְּמַתָּנָה, כָּל הֵיכָא דְּלֵיתֵיהּ בִּירוּשָּׁה לֵיתֵיהּ בְּמַתָּנָה; אִי בִּמְשִׁיכָה — לֵיתְנְהוּ גַּבֵּיהּ; אִי בַּחֲלִיפִּין — (א) [ו]אֵין מַטְבֵּעַ נִקְנֶה בַּחֲלִיפִּין; אִי אַגַּב קַרְקַע — לֵית לֵיהּ אַרְעָא; אִי בְּמַעֲמַד שְׁלָשְׁתָּן — אִי שָׁלַח לִי לָא אָזִילְנָא. מַתְקִיף לָהּ רַב אִיקָא בְּרֵיהּ דְּרַב אַמִּי: אַמַּאי? [ז]וְלוֹדֵי אִיסּוּר דְּהָלֵין זוּזֵי דְּרַב מָרִי נִינְהוּ, וְלִיקְנִינְהוּ בְּאוֹדִיתָא! אַדְּהָכִי נְפַק אוֹדִיתָא מִבֵּי אִיסּוּר. אִיקְפַּד רָבָא, אֲמַר: קָא מַגְמְרִי טַעֲנָתָא לְאֶינָשֵׁי וּמַפְסְדִי לִי.

שַׁיֵּיר

רשב"ם

יֶהֱנֶה. יִרְאֶה. **הָא דְּאִיתְנְהוּ בְּעֵינַיְיהוּ.** חוֹזֵר. דִּלְהָכִי שַׁבְקִינְהוּ, (א) אִם אֶעֱמוֹד מֵחָלְיִי — אַחֲזִירֵם. דְּפָרְעִינְהוּ בְּחוֹבֵיהּ. אִם עָמַד אֵינוֹ חוֹזֵר. **אִיבַּעְיָא** לְהוּ שְׁכִיב מְרַע שֶׁהוֹדָה. וְאָמַר בְּחָלְיוֹ: שָׂדֶה וּמָעוֹת הַלָּלוּ שֶׁל פְּלוֹנִי הֵן. וְאע"פ שֶׁהָיִינוּ מוּחְזָקִים בִּנְכָסִים הַלָּלוּ שֶׁאֵינָן שֶׁל אוֹתוֹ פְּלוֹנִי, שֶׁהָיִינוּ יוֹדְעִין שֶׁהֵן שֶׁל זֶה הַמּוֹדֶה בָּהֶם לַאֲחֵרִים. מִי אָמְרִינַן שֶׁהוּא אוֹמֵר כֵּן שֶׁלֹּא לְהַשְׁבִּיעַ אֶת בָּנָיו, אוֹ דִּלְמָא כֵּיוָן דְּאוֹדֵי — אוֹדֵי? ת"ש כו'. וּמַסְקָנָא דְּהוֹדָאָתוֹ הוֹדָאָה. וְאע"ג דְּאָמְרִינַן בְּסַנְהֶדְרִין בְּפֶרֶק "דִּינֵי מָמוֹנוֹת תִּנְיָינָא" (דף כט:): הַהוּא דַּהֲווּ קָרֵי לֵיהּ עַכְבְּרָא דְּשָׁכֵיב אַדִּינָרֵי. כִּי קָשָׁכֵיב אֲמַר: פְּלָנְיָא וּפְלָנְיָא מַסְּקוּ בִּי זוּזֵי. אֲתוּ תַּבְעִינְהוּ לַיּוֹרְשִׁים כו'. וּמַסְקָנָא: אָדָם עָשׂוּי שֶׁלֹּא לְהַשְׁבִּיעַ אֶת בָּנָיו, וּפְטוּרִין מִלְּשַׁלֵּם. וְהָכָא אָמְרִינַן דְּאָזְלִינַן בָּתַר הוֹדָאַת פִּיו! נִרְאֶה בְּעֵינַי: דְּהָתָם הַיְינוּ טַעֲמָא, כֵּיוָן שֶׁעוֹשֶׂה עַצְמוֹ עֶבֶד לֹוֶה לְאִישׁ מַלְוֶה — וַדַּאי לְהַחֲזִיק עַצְמוֹ כְּעָנִי הָיָה עוֹשֶׂה. אֲבָל כֵּיוָן שֶׁהַמָּמוֹן בְּעַיִן, וְהוּא מוֹדֶה שֶׁל פְּלוֹנִי הוּא — י"ל שֶׁהִפְקִידוֹ אֶצְלוֹ מִקּוֹדֶם לָזֶה הַשְּׁכִיב מְרַע, אוֹ הִקְנָה לוֹ הַשְּׁכִיב מְרַע ע"י אַחֵר, וַהֲרֵי הוּא חָפֵץ שֶׁיָּבֹא לְיָדוֹ. **דְּאִיסּוּר.** הוּא אִיסּוּר גִּיּוֹרָא, שֶׁבָּא עַל רָחֵל בַּת מָר שְׁמוּאֵל קוֹדֶם שֶׁנִּתְגַּיֵּיר, וְנִתְעַבְּרָה הֵימֶנּוּ בְּגֵיוּת אֶת רַב מָרִי בַּר רָחֵל, וּבְתוֹךְ כָּךְ נִתְגַּיֵּיר, וְאח"כ נוֹלַד רַב מָרִי. וַהֲוָה לֵיהּ הוֹרָתוֹ שֶׁלֹּא בִּקְדוּשָּׁה וְלֵידָתוֹ בִּקְדוּשָּׁה. וְהִיא מִבְּנוֹת שְׁמוּאֵל שֶׁנִּשְׁבּוּ, כִּדְאִיתָא בִּכְתוּבּוֹת (דף כג.). **אָמַר רָבָא בְּמַאי** קָנֵי לְהוּ כו'. וְהִלְכָּךְ אֲנִי זוֹכֶה בָּהֶן, דְּנִכְסֵי הַגֵּר דִּינָן כְּהֶפְקֵר, וַהֲרֵי הֵן בְּיָדִי, וְהִנְנִי קוֹדֵם וְזוֹכֶה. **גֵּר לָאו בַּר אוֹרוּתֵי הוּא.** דְּרַחֲמָנָא אַפְקְרֵיהּ לְזַרְעֵיהּ דְּגוֹי. דְּלֵיתֵיהּ בִּירוּשָּׁה. כְּגוֹן רַב מָרִי, לֵיתֵיהּ נַמִי בְּדִין מַתְּנַת שְׁכִיב מְרַע. לֵיתְנְהוּ גַּבֵּיהּ. אֵין הַמָּעוֹת בְּבֵיתוֹ שֶׁל אִיסּוּר, שֶׁיּוּכַל לִיתְּנָם לוֹ בְּיָדוֹ. **אֵין מַטְבֵּעַ נִקְנֶה בַּחֲלִיפִּין.** כִּדְבָעָא מִלְּיָעָא בְּ"הַזָּהָב" (דף מו.). **אִי אַגַּב** קַרְקַע. כִּדְאָמְרִי' בְּפ"ק דְּקִדּוּשִׁין (דף כו.), וְנָפְקָא לָן מִקְּרָא דִּ"לְכֶסֶף וְלַזָּהָב וגו' עִם עָרֵי מְצוּרוֹת אֲשֶׁר בִּיהוּדָה". **אִם בְּמַעֲמַד** שְׁלָשְׁתָּן. אֲנִי וְאִיסּוּר וְרַב מָרִי כְּיַחַד, נִפְקָד וּמַפְקִיד וּמְקַבֵּל מַתָּנָה. **לָא אָזְלִינָא.** בָּתַר אִיסּוּר, פֶּן אַפְסִיד. **אַמַּאי.** לֹא תִּמְלָא עִנְיָן שֶׁיּוּכַל רַב מָרִי לִזְכּוֹת? (ב) וַהֲלֹא יוֹדֶה אִיסּוּר שֶׁהֵן שֶׁל רַב מָרִי, וְיִזְכֶּה בָּהֶן! **אַדְּהָכִי וְהָכִי נְפַק אוֹדִיתָא.** מִתּוֹךְ שֶׁנֶּאֱמַר בְּבֵית הַמִּדְרָשׁ יָצָא הַקּוֹל, וְלִימְּדוּהוּ לִטְעוֹן כֵּן. כָּל אֵלּוּ הַדְּבָרִים שֶׁאָמַר רָבָא הֲלָכוֹת הֵן.

בַּמֶּה

תוספות

שכיב מרע שהודה מהו. פירש רבינו שמואל: דמיבעיא ליה אם אומר כן שלא להשביע את בניו, או דלמא כיון דאודי אודי. והא דאמר בפרק "זה בורר" (סנהדרין דף כט:) דאדם עשוי שלא להשביע את בניו — התם מיירי שמחזיק עצמו עבד לוה לאיש מלוה, עשוי שלא להשביע את בניו. אבל גבי פקדון אינו עושה — ודאי [שלא] להשביע את בניו, אלא מודה. ואין נראה לומר, דאדרבה, כ"ש הוא, שיותר יש לנו לומר שאומר אמת במלוה, כיון שמשעבד עצמו, אבל גבי פקדון — עושה שלא להשביע את בניו! ועוד: איזו ראיה מביא מאיסור גיורא שהודאתו היתה ודאי אמת כדי ליתן, דלא שייך כאן מידי שלא להשביע את בניו! ונראה לר"י לפרש (ג) כן: שכיב מרע שהודה מהו? מי שהודה שיש לפלוני מנה בידו, אע"פ שאנו מוחזקים בו שאין לו — מי אמרינן דקני במתנת שכיב מרע ואם עמד חוזר, או דלמא קני לגמרי ואם עמד אינו חוזר? ופשיט מההוא מעשה דאיסור גיורא דקני לגמרי במתנת בריא על ידי הודאתו. דאי במתנת שכיב מרע — היאך קנה? והא אמרינן: כל מאן דאיתיה בירושה איתיה במתנת שכיב מרע כו' — א"כ במתנת בריא היא, ואם עמד — אינו חוזר. וכן משמע מתוך פירוש ר"ח, דפירש: לודי איסור דהנהו דמים דרב מרי בריה, וקני להו באודיתא דאבוה. ועוד יש מפרשים: שכיב מרע שהודה מהו? פי': שהודה שיש לו פקדון ביד אחרים, והקנהו לזה, מי מהני להקנותו באמירה בעלמא או לא? ופשיט ליה מעובדא דאיסור דקני באמירה בעלמא. וה"ה נמי בבריא הוה מצי למיבעי, אלא אפילו בשכיב מרע דמקני באמירה בעלמא לא פשיטא ליה אי קני אי לא. מיהו, אי קני בשכיב מרע — לא הוה שמעינן דקני בבריא, אבל אי לא הוה קני בשכ"מ — כ"ש בבריא. מ"ר, וראשון עיקר.

רב מרי בריה הורתו שלא בקדושה כו'. וביבמות פרק "החולץ" (דף מה: ושם) אמרינן: אכשריה (ד) לרב מרי בר רחל ומנייה בפורסי דבבל, ואע"ג דכתיב "מקרב אחיך" כו', כיון דאמו מישראל — "מקרב אחיך" קרינן ביה, וזה ודאי היה גר. ויוכל להיות שהוא אותו שבכאן בנו של איסור. מיהו, בפרק "מי שהחשיך" (שבת דף קנד. ושם ד"ה ואמרי) רב מרי בר רחל ישראל גמור היה, דקאמר התם: רבה, אבוה דרב מרי בר רחל. וצ"ל דתרי רב מרי בר רחל הוו. מיהו, מה שפירש רבינו שמואל דרב מרי בר איסור גיורא, שבא על בת שמואל קודם שנתגייר, והורתו שלא בקדושה — שנשבית, כדאמרינן בכתובות (דף כג.) — אין נ"ל, דהא אמרינן בירושלמי שאמרה אמת במה שאמרה "נשביתי וטהורה אני", וה"נ משמע בגמרא שלנו, דאמר ליה ר' יוחנן לרב שמן בר אבא: זיל איטפל בקרובתך. על כן נראה דהא דאמרינן בעלמא [ב)]רב מרי ברה דבת שמואל — אחר הוה, ושמא הוא שנזכר אביו בפרק "מי שהחשיך" (שבת דף קנד.). ומה שקורא אותו על שם אמו — לפי שרוצה ליחסו אחר שמואל, כדאשכחן: [ג)]רבנא עוקבא ורבנא נחמיה בני ברתיה דרב, וכן רבי שמעון בן פזי, ואבא שאול בן אמא מרים (כתובות פז.). **כל** (ה) **דאיתיה בירושה איתיה** במתנת שכיב מרע. נראה לי דאם היו לגר בנים — איתא במתנת שכיב מרע, אע"ג דהמקבל גר, דליתיה בירושה. דעל הנותן הוא דאיכא קפידא, ולא על המקבל. וראיה לדבר, בפרק "נושאין על האנוסה" (יבמות דף לט.) שיש בן מוכר את אביו, דמוקי [ד)][רבי יוחנן] בשכיב מרע. וכן [משכיב מרע] שכתב כל נכסיו לעבדו חוזר בנכסים ואינו חוזר בעבד, ואם מת ולא חזר — קנה העבד הכל, כדאיתא בפ"ק דגיטין (דף ט.) ועבד ליתיה בירושה. **ואי אגב** קרקע לית ליה **ארעא.** וה"נ הוה יכול איסור להודות שיש לו קרקע כדפרישית לעיל בפרק "חזקת הבתים" (דף מד: ד"ה דלא). אלא שפיר קאמר לקמן דליקנינהו ניהליה באודיתא, שהודה שהמעות עצמן של רב מרי. **מגמרי** טענתייהו **לאינשי** ומפסדי מנאי. ואם תאמר: הא דאמרינן בפ"ק דקדושין (דף יז: ושם): הלוה מעות מן הגוי שנתגיירו בניו — לא יחזיר לבניו, ואם החזיר — אין רוח חכמים נוחה הימנו. והא תניא: רוח חכמים נוחה הימנו! ל"ק: כאן — שהיתה הורתו ולידתו שלא בקדושה, כאן — שהיתה הורתו שלא בקדושה ולידתו בקדושה. ואם כן היה לו לרבא להחזיר! ותירץ ר"ת: דהתם, כיון שעשה לו הגוי חסד שהלוה לו — יעשה עמו חסד ויתן לבניו, אבל כאן שלא עשה עמו חסד כשהפקידם אצלו — אין צריך להחזיר לבניו. וה"ר יצחק ב"ר מאיר פי': דכיון דלא קתני בהדיא בברייתא: ואם לא החזיר אין רוח חכמים נוחה הימנו — לא הוה חייש לה רבא. ואין נראה כלל, דהא מדקתני אם החזיר רוח חכמים נוחה הימנו — מכלל דאם לא החזיר אין רוח חכמים נוחה הימנו, וקתני לה לכולהו בדי במסכת שביעית (פ"י משנה ט): המחזיר חוב בשביעית רוח חכמים נוחה הימנו, [ה)]והמלוה מעות מן הגר והחזיר לבניו — רוח חכמים נוחה הימנו. וקתני נמי התם: כל המטלטלין נקנין במשיכה, ואם קיים דבריו שלא במשיכה — רוח חכמים נוחה הימנו. ואמר עלה ב"הזהב" (ב"מ דף מח. ושם) דאם לא קיים דבריו — אין רוח חכמים נוחה הימנו, מכלל דכולהו בדי שמעינן מכלל הן לאו[ו)]. **דקא** מגמרי **טענתא לאינשי** כו'. יש תימה: למה לא קיים רבא את דבריו? והא קיימא לן: מצוה לקיים דברי המת! ועוד, הא דקיימא לן לקמן (דף קנא:) ובכל דוכתי דדברי שכיב מרע ככתובין וכמסורין דמו, תיפוק ליה דמצוה לקיים דברי המת למאן דאית ליה, דהיינו ר' מאיר. ומתנת שכיב מרע נמי לא קניא אלא לאחר מיתה! ותירץ הר"ר יצחק ב"ר מאיר: דלא אמרינן מצוה לקיים דברי המת אלא היכא דאמר "תנו מנה זה לפלוני", אבל היכא דאמר "מנה זה לפלוני" ולא אמר "תנו" — כל כי האי גוונא לא הוה אמרי' מצוה לקיים דברי המת. מיהו קשיא: מדמייתו חכמים ראיה לר' אליעזר דדברי שכיב מרע נקנים באמירה מההוא דאמן של בני רוכל שקיימו חכמים את דבריה (לקמן דף קנו:), אלמא דדברי שכיב מרע ככתובין וכמסורין דמו(ו). ואין ראיה היא, דלמא היינו טעמא דמצוה לקיים דברי המת! ואין לחלק בין היכא דאמר "תנתן כבינתי לבתי" להיכא דאמר "תנו". ועוד קשיא מהא דאמר בגיטין בפ' "התקבל" (דף סה: ושם): גניבא יוצא בקולר הוה, כי נפיק אמר "הבו ארבע מאה זוזי לר' אבינא מחמרא דנהר פניא" כו'. ולא אמרינן התם מצוה לקיים דברי המת, ואע"ג דאפי' באומר כשהיה בריא אמרי' ליה הכי, כדמוכח בפרק קמא דגיטין (דף טו.)! ועוד קשה מהא דפרק "השולח" (שם דף מ.) גבי "פלונית שפחתי עשתה לי קורת רוח" כו', דאמרינן התם מצוה לקיים דברי המת. מיהו, מזה אין קשיא כלל, כמו שאפרש בסמוך. ור"י תירץ: דלא אמרינן מצוה לקיים דברי המת אלא היכא שהוא ביד שליש, כי הא (ז) דתנן "שקל לבני" כו', וכי הסיא דמס' כתובות פרק "מציאת האשה" (דף סט: ושם): המשליש מעות לבתו — יעשה שליש מה שהושלש בידו,

ומוקי

מסורת הש"ס

א) [ב"מ מו.] ב) [כתובות עז. ועוד טובא] ג) [לעיל נח: חולין לב.] ד) מהרש"א כתב דט"ס הוא וצ"ל ר"י ר"נ ר"י בעל התוספות: ה) [צ"ל והלוה] ו) [וע"ע תוס' קדושין יח. ד"ה כאן]

עין משפט נר מצוה

פג א מיי' פ"ט מהלכות זכייה ומתנה הל' ד סמג עשין פב טוש"ע חו"מ סי' רנג סעיף ב ולא קנה:

פד ב ג מיי' שם הלכה כא סמג עשין פב טוש"ע חו"מ סי' רנ סעיף ג:

פה ד מיי' פ"א שם הל' ו ופ"ט הל' ז ועי' בהשגות ובמ"מ ופ"ו מהל' נחלות הלכה י סמג עשין פב טוש"ע חו"מ סי' רנו סעיף א וסי' ערה ס"א וסי' רפג ס"א:

פו ה מיי' פ"ט מהלכות זכייה ומתנה הלכה ז ועי' בהג"ל סמג שם טוש"ע חו"מ סי' רנו ס"א:

פז ו מיי' פ"ו מהלכות מכירה הלכה א סמג שם טוש"ע חו"מ סי' רג סעיף א:

פח ז מיי' פ"ט מהלכות זכייה ומתנה הל' ט סמג שם טוש"ע חו"מ סי' רנ סעיף ג וסי' רנה סעיף ב:

הגהות הב"ח

(א) רשב"ם ד"ה הא וכו' שבקינהו אמר אם אעמוד מחליי אחזור הס"ד: (ב) ד"ה אמאי וכו' לזכות בהו והלא: (ג) תוס' ד"ה שכיב מרע וכו' ונראה לר"י לפרש שכיב כצ"ל ותיבת כן נמחק: (ד) ד"ה רב מרי וכו' אכשריה רבא לרב מרי: (ה) ד"ה כל היכא דאיתיה וכו' דמוקי רבי בשכיב מרע וכן מי שכתב כל נכסיו לעבדו ועמד חוזר: (ו) ד"ה דקא מגמרי וכו' וכמסורין דמו ומאי ראיה היא דילמא: (ז) בא"ד כי הא דתניא האומר תנו שקל לבני כו' וכי ההיא:

רבינו גרשום

דיחסין וירש לשון ירושה הן. אם אמר שכיב מרע יהנה מהם. דמשמע דמתהנה בהן בכל ענין כמו בנכסיו של עצמו. מי אמרי' דלשון מתנה הוא או לא והכי נמי יראה דמשמע יראה כבנכסיו ממש וה"נ ישען כלומר יסמך בהן כנכסיו וה"נ יעמוד דמשמע יעמוד כבנכסיו: מכר כל נכסיו ולא שייר כלום ועמד מהו. מי אמרי' דמצי למיהדר בהו דלהכי זבנינהו מחמת מיתתו דאי מיית ליה הוו מכורין אבל השתא כשעמד אין מכירתו מכירה. או דילמא מכירה שאני ממתנה ואינה חוזרת: הא דאיתנהו זוזי בעינייהו. שלא הוציאן על דעת כן מכרן שאם יעמוד יחזור בהן. אבל פרעינהו לזוזי בחובו על דעת כן מכרן דגמר ומקני ליה מיד ומכירתו מכירה ולא יחזור: שכיב מרע שהודה. שאמר כך וכך אני חייב לפלוני ומת מהו. מי אמרי' דודאי חייב להן וקנו בעלי חובין שהודה להם או דילמא להכי קאמר הכי שאם יעמוד מחליו שלא יחשבו בני אדם שהוא עשיר שמשל אחרים הוא ולא קני: ת"ש דאיסור הוה גר. ונכסי הגר כשמת ואין לו יורש כל המחזיק בהן זכה: והורתו שלא בקדושה. דאכתי לא הוה גר אביו: ולידתו בקדושה. לאחר שנתגייר וגזרינן לידתו [בקדושה] אטו הורתו שלא בקדושה ולא יורש הוא שלא היתה הורתו בקדושה: ליתנהו גבי איסור הני זוזי. דמצי למשכינהו: לית ליה קרקע. לאיסור. אי שלח לי לא אזילנא ליה. כי היכי דליקנו במעמד שלשתן: אדהכי והכי נפק אודיתא מבי איסור. שהודה שאותן זוזין דרב מרי הן. ותפשוט לך מהכא שכיב מרע שהודה קני מדאתקיף רב איקא הכי: אמר גמרינהו טענתא לאינשי ומפסדי לי. דהשתא החזקתי בהן ושלי הוא אלמלא לא לימדו לעשות הודאה:

איבעיא להו: בית לאחד ודיוטא לאחד, מהו? מי הוי שיור או לא? אם תמצא לומר: בית לאחד ודיוטא לאחד לא הוי שיור, "חוץ מדיוטא" מהו? אמר רבא אמר רב נחמן, אם תמצא לומר: בית לאחד ודיוטא לאחד לא הוי שיור – א"חוץ מדיוטא" הוי שיור; ואליבא דרב זביד, דאמר: א)שאם רצה להוציא בה זיזין – מוציא; אלמא, כיון דשייר דיוטא – מקום זיזין נמי שייר. (הכא נמי, כיון דאמר "חוץ מפירותיו" – מקום פירי שייר.) אמר רב יוסף בר מניומי אמר רב נחמן: שכיב מרע שכתב כל נכסיו לאחרים – ברואין: אם במחלק, מת – קנו כולן, עמד – חוזר בכולן; אם בנמלך, מת – קנו כולן, עמד – אינו חוזר אלא באחרון. (א) ודלמא עיוני קא מעיין והדר יהיב! סתמיה דשכיב מרע מידק דייק והדר יהיב. אמר רב אחא בר מניומי אמר רב נחמן: גשכיב מרע שכתב כל נכסיו לאחרים ועמד – אינו חוזר, חיישינן שמא יש לו נכסים במדינה אחרת. ואלא מתני' דקתני: לא שייר קרקע כל שהוא – אין מתנתו קיימת, היכי משכחת לה? אמר רב חמא: (ב) דבאומר "כל נכסי". מר בר רב אשי אמר: (ג) הבמוחזק לן דלית ליה. איבעיא להו: חזרה במקצת הוי חזרה בכולה או לא? תא שמע: כולן לראשון ומקצתן לשני – ושני קנה, ראשון לא קנה; מאי לאו בשמת? לא, בשעמד. הכי נמי מסתברא, מדקתני סיפא: ב)מקצתן לראשון וכולן לשני – ראשון קנה, שני לא קנה; אי אמרת בשלמא בשעמד – משום הכי שני לא קנה. אלא אי אמרת בשמת, תרווייהו ליקנו! א"ל רב יימר לרב אשי: ותהוי נמי בשעמד; אי אמרת בשלמא חזרה במקצת הויא חזרה בכולה – היינו דשני מיהת קנה. אלא אי אמרת חזרה במקצת לא הויא חזרה בכולה – ניהוי כמחלק, ולחד מינייהו לא ליקנו! יוהלכתא: חזרה במקצת הויא חזרה בכולה; רישא – משכחת לה חבין שמת בין שעמד, סיפא – לא משכחת לה אלא כשעמד. טאיבעיא להו: ג)הקדיש כל נכסיו ועמד, מהו? מי אמרינן: כל לגבי הקדש גמר ומקני, או דלמא כל לגבי נפשיה לא גמר ומקני? הפקיר כל נכסיו, מהו? מי אמרינן: כיון דאף לעניים כעשירים גמר ומקני, או דלמא כל לגבי נפשיה לא גמר ומקני? חילק כל נכסיו לעניים, מאי? מי אמרינן: צדקה ודאי מגמר גמר ומקני, או דלמא כל לגבי נפשיה לא גמר ומקני? יתיקו. (ד) (ל"א: הקדיש כל נכסיו, מהו? הפקיר כל נכסיו, מהו? כחילק כל נכסיו לעניים, מהו? תיקו.) אמר רב ששת: ל"יטול", ו"יזכה", ו"יחזיק" ו"יקנה" – כולן לשון מתנה הן. במתניתא תנא: מאף "יחסין" ו"ירת" בראוי ליורשו, ד)ור' יוחנן בן ברוקא היא. איבעיא להו: יהנה

תוספות

חיישינן שמא יש לו נכסים במקום אחר. ואע"ג דאמרי' לעיל איפכא להקל, וניחוש דלמא עיוני עיין והדר יהיב – היינו טעמא דמסתבר למימר עיוני עיין, הואיל וכבר חלקם. שכיב

רשב"ם

איבעיא להו בית לאחד. במתנת בריא, ודיוטא לאחד, (ה) הוי מקום שיור? מי איכא להאי בעל דיוטא שיור מקום בחצר להוצאת זיזין או לא? אם תמצי לומר לא הוי שיור לאחריני, אבל לעצמו הוי שיור, כגון דאמר ליה: בית אני מוכר לך חוץ מדיוטא העליונה. או דלמא ליכא שיור? ואליבא דרב זביד. דכי א"ל סתמא "בית זה אני מוכר לך" – לא קנה דיוטא העליונה, כדתנן ב"המוכר את הבית" (לעיל דף סא.): לא מכר את הגג בזמן שיש לו מעקה גבוה י' טפחים, דהיינו דיוטא. וכי א"ל "חוץ" – לטפויי מילתא קאתי, ושייר לו מקום בחצר להוצאת זיזין מן הדיוטא לחצר של לוקח. אם במחלק. שמשעה ראשונה שהתחיל לחלק היה בדעתו לחלק כל נכסיו, ולא לשייר כלום. אם מת קנו כולן. כדין כל מתנת שכ"מ שאין צריכה קנין אם מת. אם בנמלך. שלא היה בדעתו לחלק כל נכסיו, אלא אחר שחילק שתק ולא רצה לחלק עוד, חזר ונמלך בעצמו לחלק כל הנותר. אלא באחרון. בלבד, דלא הוי בה שיור. אבל קמאי קנו, כדקתני מתניתין: שייר קרקע כל שהוא – מתנתו מתנה. ניחוש. דלמא האי דשתיק וחישב בין מתנה למתנה – לא הוי כנמלך, אלא עיוני מעיין מה יתן לכל אחד. ומעיקרא היה בדעתו לחלק את הכל. ויחזור בו כשיעמוד מחליו, ואמאי קנו קמאי? סתמא דשכיב מרע. עיוני קמעיין בלבו מה יתן לכל אחד קודם שיבואו לפניו, ואין לו לשתוק בין זה לזה, ומדשתק – נמלך הוי. אמר רב נחמן שכיב מרע שכתב כל נכסיו. הידועין, ולא נמצא לו שיור, ועמד – אינו חוזר כו'. באומר כל נכסי. לא חילק שדותיו וכרמיו לכל אחד בפני עצמו, אלא לשון זה כתב: "כל נכסיי אני נותן לפלוני ופלוני", דכל היכא דאיתנהו נתונין הן (ו) במתנה, ואין כאן שיור. ובפר"ח גרס: כל נכסיי אלו הן. ולא נהירא. במוחזק. שאנו מוחזקין בו שאין לו עוד נכסים. איבעיא להו חזרה במקצת. שכיב מרע שכתב כל נכסיו לאחד, וחזר בו במקצת, ונתן שוב לאחר, שהרי יכול לעשות כן, כדאמרינן: דייתיקי מבטלת דייתיקי בפירקין דלעיל (דף קלה:): מי הויא חזרה בכל הנכסים שנתן לראשון, דגלי דעתיה שמתחרט בראשון, ומה שנתן לשני – מתנה במקצת היא, דאיכא שיור, והויא מתנה, ואתו יורשין ומפקי מיד ראשון כל המותר. או לא הויא חזרה, אלא מה שנתן לשני – קנה שני, והמותר קנה ראשון. ואם יעמוד מחליו – יחזור בשניהן, שהרי לא שייר לעצמו כלום. ת"ש דתניא כולן לראשון. במתנת שכ"מ, ומקצתן נתן לשני, שחזר במקצת. שני קנה. מה שנתן לו, ממה נפשך, ל"ש מת ול"ש עמד. דהא מתנת שכ"מ במקצת היא, והויא מתנה, שהרי שייר לעצמו מותר נכסים שנתן לראשון, שהרי ראשון לא קנה. מאי לאו בשמת. וקתני: הראשון לא קנה. אלמא, חזרה במקצת הויא חזרה בכולהו. דאי לא הויא חזרה – תרווייהו ליקנו בכל הנכסים. ומשני: לא. לעולם לא הויא חזרה. וברייתא – כשעמד. הלכך, שני קנה, דמתנה במקצת לא מצי הדר ביה, כדקתני מתני'. אבל בראשון, שניתנו לו כל הנכסים בלא שיור – אם עמד חוזר, כדתנן במתני'. ולקמן פרכינן: אי כשעמד – תרווייהו לא ליקנו, ואפי' שני. דכיון דחזרה במקצת לא הויא חזרה בכולהו – גבי שני ליכא שיור, דהא לא הדר ביה מראשון אלא במה שנתן לשני, ובין שניהן נתן הכל ולא שייר לעצמו כלום. ומהכא פשטינן במסקנא: חזרה במקצת הויא חזרה בכולה. הלכך, בין שמת בין שעמד – שני קנה, שהרי חזר בו מראשון לגמרי, ושייר לעצמו שיור נכסיו שנתן לראשון וחזר בו מהן, ומתנה במקצת שמה מתנה. ה"נ מסתברא. דבשעמד עסקינן. דקתני: מקצתן לראשון, (ז) וחזר בו, ונתן כולו לשני – ראשון קנה, שהיה בה שיור, והויא מתנה, כדקתני מתני' דמתנת שכ"מ במקצת מתנה גמורה היא. שני לא קנה כלל, דלא שייר לעצמו כלום, והלכך אם עמד – חוזר. אי אמרת בשלמא בשעמד היינו דשני מיהא לא קנה. כדתנן: לא שייר קרקע כל שהוא – אין מתנתו מתנה. אלא אי אמרת בשמת תרווייהו נמי ליקנו. כדין מתנת שכ"מ שקונה אחר מיתה היכא דליכא שיור, ואם עמד חוזר. דאילו מתנה במקצת, בין מת בין עמד – מתנה גמורה היא. אלא לאו בשעמד, ומדסיפא בשעמד – רישא נמי בשעמד. א"ל רב יימר לרב אשי ותהוי נמי. רישא בשעמד, אפ"ה תפשוט דחזרה במקצת הויא חזרה בכולה. דאי אמרת בשלמא חזרה במקצת הויא חזרה (ח) – היינו דשני קנה, דאיכא שיור נכסים לשכ"מ שחוזר בו ממה שנתנו לראשון, וראשון לא קנה. אלא אי אמרת לא שמה חזרה, אלא מה שלא נתן לשני נשאר ביד ראשון – תרווייהו נמי לא ליקנו, שהרי בין שניהם נתן כל הנכסים, ולא שייר לעצמו קרקע כל שהוא. בין שמת בין שעמד. שני קנה, דהא הדר ביה מראשון, ואיכא שיור טובא. ראשון לא קנה, דהא הדר ביה. ואפי' מת לא יקנה ראשון, דהא קי"ל דייתיקי מבטלת דייתיקי, מה לי חוזר בו מראשון ונותן לשני, מה לי חוזר בו ומעכב לעצמו וליורשיו. סיפא לא משכחת לה אלא בשעמד. הלכך ראשון קנה, דמתנה מקצת הוא ואיכא שיור. שני לא קנה, דלא הוה במתנתו שיור. דאי בשמת תרווייהו ליקנו. איבעיא להו. שכיב מרע שהקדיש כל נכסיו בלא שיור, ואח"כ עמד מחליו, מי מלי הדר ביה? מי חמיר ממתנת הדיוט, דנימא דגמר והקדיש הכל בלב שלם בין יחיה בין ימות. ואת"ל דגבי הקדש הכל מוקדש, ואפילו עמד. הפקיר כל נכסיו מהו. מי לימא כוונתו לשמים ואקני לגמרי, לכל מי שיבוא ויזכה, או לא? א"נ, כיון דהפקיר ממונו – הוליאו מדעתו לגמרי ואינו חפץ בחזרתו, שאינו רוצה ליהנות עוד ממנו. ואת"ל גבי הפקר, דאינו חושש בזה הממון, הואיל והפקירו ולא דקדק לחלקו לאוהביו. חילק נכסיו לעניים מהו. מי לימא יד עניים כיד הקדש, ואם עמד אינו חוזר, או לא? תיקו. א"ר ששת. שכ"מ שאמר "יזכה פלוני בנכסיי" או "יטול" או "יחזיק" או "יקנה" – כולן לשון מתנה, וקנה. דלשון מתנה בעינן, כדאמרינן לעיל (דף קמז:): ידור פלוני בבית זה – לא אמר ולא כלום, עד דאמר "תנו" או "יטול" ו"יקנה" או "יחסין" ו"ירת" אם הוא ראוי ליורשו, כגון בן בין הבנים. ור' יוחנן בן ברוקה היא. דאמר בפירקין דלעיל (דף קל.): דבריו קיימין, וקי"ל כוותיה, דפסקינן התם הלכה כמותו. יהנה

רבינו גרשום

בעיא מתנינן לי' ואדריש לקיש דאמר ריש לקיש כו' משום דלטפויי מלתא קאתי: איבעיא להו מכר בית לאחד ודיוטא לאחר מהו. מי אמרינן דהוי שיור בחצר ומצי האי שני להוציא בה זיזין וגזוזטראות: אמר לראשון חוץ מדיוטא אני מוכר לך. הוי שיור בגוף החצר דלטפויי קאתי: שכיב מרע שכתב כל נכסיו לאחרים. ולא שייר כלום: רואין אם כמחלק. שיהיה שדה זו לפלוני א) וכן מכל נכסיו ואם מת קנו כולן ואם עמד מחליו חוזר בכולן אפי' מראשון דלא אמרי' מה שנתן לאחרון הוי שיור לקמאי משום דאמר מעיקרא הוה סדור בלבו מה שיהא נותן לכל חד ואילו היה יכול לומר לכולן בדבור אחד היה עושה אלא שאי אפשר לקרות שתי שמות כאחת ולא הוי אחרון שיור יותר מראשון דלכולן רצה לומר בדבור אחד אלא שאי אפשר הלכך אם עמד חוזר בכולן אפי' מראשון: אם בנמלך. שנתן שדה אחת לפלוני וקודם שהיה נותן לאחד היה ממתין ומימלך מעצמו ואחר כך נותן וכן בכולן. ודאי הוי שיור ואם עמד אינו חוזר אלא באחרון בלבד דלא שייר מאחרון כלום. ומקשי' ואמאי קנו כולהו לבר מאחרון וניחוש דלמא האי דמימלך השתא עיוני מעיין ומחשב האיך סידר בלבו מעיקרא לכל אחד איזו שדה לזה ואיזו לזה ולהכי שתק עד דאידכר ולא משום דמשייר הלכך ליהוי חוזר בכולן. ומשני לעולם אינו חוזר אלא באחרון בלבד וכל אחרונה הוי שיור לראשונה הואיל דנמלך. ודקא אמרת ניחוש דלמא עיוני מעיין ודאי לא מעיין השתא בשעת דבור דסתמא שכיב מרע מידק דייק ברישא מאי דבעי למיעבד והדר יהיב בשעה אחת לכל מאן דבעי אלא האי כיון דמתמלך וממתין שעה בין נתינה לנתינה ש"מ שיורי שייר ואינו חוזר אלא באחרון בלבד דלא שייר לו כלום: שמא יש לו נכסים במדינת הים. ושייר לעצמו: היכי משכחת לה. הא מצינן למימר שמא נכסים יש לו במדינת הים ושיירו ואמאי אין מתנתו מתנה: באומר כל נכסי לו. דהשתא לא משייר ליה כלום בעולם. והא דאמר רב נחמן שכיב מרע שכתב כל נכסיו עמד אינו חוזר משום דכל נכסין שבכאן משמע שכתב לו ולא אותן שבמדינת הים: ומר בר רב אשי (משמיה) אמר מתני' במוחזק. שמוחזק הוא שאין לו נכסים במדינת הים שלא היה שם מעולם ומשום הכי לא שייר ואין מתנתו מתנה. ולעולם כדקאמר רב נחמן: איבעיא להו. שכיב מרע שכתב כל נכסיו לאחד וחזר וכתב מאותן הנכסים עצמן מקצתן לאחר שרשאי הוא לעשות כן כדאמר דייתיקי מבטל דייתיקי: מאי. מי אמרינן כיון דחזר במקצת כמאן דחזר בכולהו דמי ואין לו לראשון כלום. או דלמא במאי דחזר חזר במאי דלא חזר לא חזר וקני במאי דלא חזר: ת"ש כתב כולן נכסים לראשון ומקצתן של אותן נכסים כתב לשני. דחזר במקצת מראשון. שני קנה דלא חזר במתנתו: ראשון לא קנה. אפי' במאי שלא חזר: מאי לאו בשמת. אותו שכיב מרע עסקינן ושמעת מיניה דחזורה במקצת הויא חזרה בכולה: לא בשעמד. לעולם לא הויא חזרה בכולה והכא מאי טעמא ראשון לא קנה הואיל שכתב לו כל נכסיו דלא שייר לעצמו כלום וכיון דעמד לא קנה ושני קנה משום דלא כתב לו אלא מקצת אבל אם מת לא הויא חזרה בכולה: הכי נמי מסתברא. דברייתא בשעמד הוא: מדקתני סיפא. דהך ברייתא כתב מקצתן לראשון וכולן הנכסים שנשתיירו לשני ראשון קנה משום דשייר. שני לא קנה דלא שייר לעצמו כלום: אלא אי אמרת בשמת תרווייהו ליקני. כדאמרינן לעיל אם כמחלק מת קנו כולם והא מחלק הוא. אלא ש"מ בשעמד ואכתי לא שמעת מינה דחזורה במקצת הויא חזרה בכולה: אמר ליה רב יימר לרב אשי ותיהוי נמי ברייתא זו בשעמד. ואפי' הכי איכא למידק מינה דחזורה במקצת הויא חזרה בכולה: אי אמרת בשלמא כו' היינו דשני מיהת קונה. דהואיל דחזרה במקצת מראשון הוה כחזרה בכולה וברשותיה דנותן קיימי והוא לא נתן לשני אלא מקצתן הרי שייר מקצת שלא נתן לעצמו משום הכי קנה שני: אלא אי אמרת לא הויא חזרה בכולה. תרוייהו לא ליקני ראשון לא ליקני שכתב לו כל נכסיו ולא שייר לעצמו כלום ושני לא ליקני הואיל דחזרה במקצת לא הויא חזרה בכולה ולא נשתייר לעצמו כלום דאותו מקצת מראשון נתן לשני והשאר היו ברשות ראשון ולא ברשות נותן. אלא לאו ש"מ דמשום הכי קתני רישא שני קנה דחזרה במקצת הויא חזרה בכולה ונשתייר לו מקצת. והכי הלכתא דחזרה במקצת הוי חזרה בכולה. ורישא דהך ברייתא מתוקמא שפיר בין בשמת בין בשעמד. דאם מת הואיל שנתן כולן לראשון ומקצתן לשני שני ודאי קנה ראשון לא קנה. דכי היכי דחזר במקצת שנתן לשני חזר נמי בכל מה שנשתייר לו לראשון בין בשעמד ראשון לא קנה דהא כתב לו כל נכסיו בלא שיור ושני קנה שכשחזר במקצת מראשון חזר בכולן וכשנתן מקצת לשני שייר לעצמו מקצת האחר: סיפא לא משכחת לה. דראשון קנה שני לא קנה: אלא בשעמד. ולא משום טעמא דחזרה אלא משום דלראשון שייר ולשני לא שייר דאי בשמת תרווייהו ליקני: הקדיש כל נכסיו מהו מי אמרינן. הואיל דלא שייר כלום חוזר בו כדין מתנת הדיוט. או דלמא אינו חוזר ולא דיינינן ליה כהדיוט וכך מפרשי' הפקיר וחילק: אם תמצי לומר הפקיר לא ידע ממאן ליתבע. חילק מהו: כולן לשון מתנה הוא. וקנה. בראוי ליורשו דיחסין

א) נראה דצ"ל אם כמחלק שיהיה שדה זו לפלוני ושדה זו לפלוני וכך מכל נכסיו וכו'.

עין משפט נר מצוה

עז א מיי' פכ"ד מהל' מכירה הל' טז ועי' במ"מ טוש"ע ח"מ סי' ריב סעיף ג:

עח ב מיי' פ"ח מהל' זכייה ומתנה הל' כא סמג עשין פב טוש"ע ח"מ סי' רנ סעיף יא:

עט ג ד ה מיי' שם הל' כ ועיין בהשגות ובמ"מ טוש"ע שם ס"י:

פ ו ז ח מיי' שם פ"ט הל' יז סמג שם טוש"ע ח"מ שם סעיף יב:

פא ט י כ מיי' שם הל' יט טוש"ע שם סעיף ג וחוזר בכולן:

פב ל מיי' שם הל' ג וסמג שם טוש"ע ח"מ סי' רנג סעיף ב:

מסורת הש"ס

א) [לעיל סג: סד.] ב) נדרים מג: ג) [עי' תוס' לקמן קעד: ד"ה שכיב] ד) [לעיל קל.]

הגהות הב"ח

(א) גמרא אלא באחרון ניחוש דלמא עיוני: (ב) שם באומר כל נכסי. נ"ב ס"א באומר נכסי אלו: (ג) שם במוחזק לן דלית ליה. נ"ב גם מכאן ראיה למה שכתבו תוספות לעיל דף מד ע"ב דאפשר שיש אדם שאין לו קרקע ע"ש: (ד) שם לא גמר ומקני תיקו איבעיא להו הקדיש כל נכסיו כצ"ל ותיבת ל"א נמחק: (ה) רשב"ם ד"ה איבעיא וכו' לאחר הס"ד ואח"כ מ"ה מי הוי שיור כצ"ל ותיבת מקום נמחק: (ו) ד"ה באומר וכו' במתנת שכיב מרע ואין כאן: (ז) ד"ה ה"נ וכו' וחזר ונתן כולן לשני. נ"ב פי' וכולן מה ששייר ולא נתן לראשון נתן הכל לשני וכן פירשו הרי"ף והרא"ש להדיא: (ח) ד"ה א"ל רב יימר וכו' חזרה בכולה היינו דשני:

א) לעיל קמז. [וש"נ]: ב) לעיל סג. סד.: ג) [עי' מהר"ם גירסא אחרת ברשב"ם בזה]: ד) [ליתא לפנינו אלא בתוס' גיטין יג: ד"ה במעמד]:

א) שכיב מרע שאמר "תנו הלואתי לפלוני" — הלואתו לפלוני, ואף על גב דליתיה בבריא! רב פפא אמר: הואיל ויורש יורשה. רב אחא בריה דרב איקא אמר: הלואה איתא בבריא, וכדרב הונא אמר רב. א)דאמר רב הונא אמר רב: "מנה לי בידך תנהו לפלוני", במעמד שלשתן — קנה. איבעיא להו: דקל לאחד ופירותיו לאחר, מהו? מי שייר מקום פירי, או לא שייר? אם תמצי לומר: לאחר ב)לא הוי שיור, (א) לעצמו חוץ מפירותיו, מהו? אמר רבא אמר רב נחמן, אם תמצי לומר: דקל לאחד ופירותיו לאחר לא הוי שיור — דקל לאחד ושייר פירותיו לפניו — ג)שייר מקום פירי, מאי טעמא? כל לגבי נפשיה בעין יפה משייר. אמר ליה ר' אבא לרב אשי: אנן אדרבי שמעון בן לקיש מתנינן לה. ב)דאמר רבי שמעון בן לקיש: המוכר בית לחבירו, ואמר לו "על מנת שדיוטא העליונה שלי" — דיוטא העליונה שלו.

איבעיא

הלואתי לפלוני. ממון שחייב לי פלוני במלוה על פה אני נותן לפלוני, ויפרעם לו הלוה במקומי – נתקיימו הדברים, ותהא הלואתו לפלוני. ואע"ג דבבריא ליתיה, דאינו יכול להקנות לחבירו מלוה על פה, דלהוצאה ניתנה, ואין קנין תופס אלא בדבר שהוא בעין אא"כ מלוה בשטר, וכגון שמסר לו השטר. א"נ, במעמד שלשתן, כדאמר [בגיטין] (דף יג.). ומשני: הואיל ויורש יורשה. לזו המלוה כאילו ברשותו היא, ואמרינן לקמן (דף קמט.): מתנת שכיב מרע כירושה שויוה רבנן. הלכך, כיון דאיתיה בירושה – איתיה במתנת שכיב מרע. **במעמד שלשתן קנה.** מתלת הלכתא בלא טעמא הוא. ולפי שהדבר נהוג הוא בין הסוחרים והחנונים – תקנו את הדבר לקנות באמירה במעמד שלשתן, לפי שאין קנין מועיל בדבר שאין בעין. ומוקמינן לה התם בין במלוה בין בפקדון. ואע"ג דאסיקנא דמילתא דליתא בבריא ליתא בשכיב מרע – אפי' הכי, מטבע, דקי"ל ב"הזהב" (ב"מ מו.) דאין מטבע נקנה בחליפין, אפ"ה אם נתנו במתנת שכיב מרע – קנה, מהאי טעמא ד"הלואתי לפלוני". **איבעיא להו דקל לאחד כו'.** אית דמוקמי לה בבריא, ובא להודיענו דיני מכירה מה שייר לעצמו. ולא נהירא לי, דא"כ (ב) מה ענין בעיא זו בזו השמועה ובזה הפרק? ב"המוכר את הספינה" איבעי לן למיבעיא, בשמעתא דהקונה שני אילנות (לעיל דף פא.). ועל כרחין בשכיב מרע מוקמינן ליה, ואמתניתין קאי, דקתני בשכיב מרע: שייר קרקע כל שהוא – מתנתו מתנה. ואיבעיא להו אם נתן דקל לאדם אחד, ונמלך, וחזר ונתן פירותיו לאחר. ואמרינן לקמן, א"ר נחמן: שכיב מרע שכתב כל נכסיו, אם נמלך, מת – קנו כולן, אם עמד – אינו חוזר אלא באחרון בלבד דלא הוה ביה שיור, אבל קמאי דהוה בה שיור – קנו. והכא מי אמרינן שייר מקום פירי – כשנתנו הדקל לראשון בלא פירות שייר לעצמו מקום הפירות, ענפי האילן שבו גדילין הפירות. וכשנתן לשני את הפירות – עדיין מקום הפירות שייר לעצמו, ואילן המחובר כקרקע דמי, וקורא אני עליו "שייר קרקע כל שהוא", והויא מתנתו מתנה בין באילן בין בפירות, ואם עמד אינו חוזר. והוא דאיכא קנין, כדפסקינן לקמן (דף קנא:) במתנת שכיב מרע במקצת. **או לא הוי שיור.** וכשנתן הדקל לראשון – כולו נתן, וליכא שיור קרקע. ואמרינן לקמן: כמה כל שהוא? רב יהודה אמר: מתקרקעי כדי פרנסתו. **שייר לעצמו.** הפירות, מהו? מי שייר מקום הפירות, ולכשייבש האילן יקוץ ענפיו? כך כתוב בספרים: אמר רבא א"ר נחמן אם תמצי לומר דקל לאחד ופירות לאחר לא הוי שיור, שייר פירותיו לפניו שייר מקום פירי, מאי טעמא כל לגבי נפשיה כי משייר בעין יפה משייר. ולא נהירא לי האי לישנא, משום (ג) דלא מיתני עליה הך סוגיא דלקמן: א"ל אנן אדריש לקיש מתנינן ליה. הלכך לישנא אחרינא הכתוב בספרים עיקר, דגרסינן בהו: חוץ מפירותיו מהו? דהוה דומיא דרב זביד וריש לקיש. (ד) ג)והיינו פירוש לשון אחרון: דקל לאחד ופירותיו לאחר, מי הוי שיור מקום הפירות באילן וקנה ראשון, דהא איכא שיור קרקע כל שהוא. או לא, וכשנתן לו את הדקל – הכל נתן גם מקום לימוח פירות? את"ל לא הוי שיור, "חוץ מפירותיו" מהו? מי אמרינן: כיון דמעיקרא הדקל לבדו בלא פירות נתן לו, ולא הוזקק לומר בו לישנא יתירא "חוץ מפירותיו", אלא לשייר מקום לעצמו אמר, ואיכא שיור קרקע כל שהוא ומתנתו מתנה. **א"ר נחמן אם תמצי לומר כו'.** "חוץ מפירותיו" הוי שיור, דכל לשון מיותר לשייר קצת מן המתנה לעצמו בא. ואליבא דרב זביד, דתנן ב"המוכר את הבית" (לעיל דף סא:): לא מכר היציע ולא את הגג בזמן שיש לו מעקה עשרה טפחים – דהיינו נמי דיוטא העליונה. ואמרינן בגמרא (שם סג.) אמר ריש לקיש: זאת אומרת המוכר בית לחבירו ואמר לו "על מנת שהדיוטא העליונה שלי" – הדיוטא העליונה שלו. ואמרינן: למאי הלכתא אהני תנאי דע"מ – לשייר לעצמו מקום בחצר שלפני הבית, אם רצה להוציא זיזין מדיוטא עליונה שהיא שלו בחצר הלוקח – מוציא, ולא יעכב בעל החצר על המוכר, ואליבא דרב זביד כו', כלומר, וכדפרשה רב זביד למילתיה דריש לקיש, דאהני יתורא דע"מ להוציא זיזין, לשיורי ליה מקום בחצר. הכי נמי אהני יתור לשון ד"חוץ מפירותיו" לשייר מקום באילן. **אנן אדריש לקיש מתנינן.** להאי איבעיא להו, ולהך מילתא דרב נחמן דאם תמצי לומר, כדמפרש לקמן ואזיל, ובמתנת בריא, ומינה תפשוט לשכיב מרע. ולאו גבי דקל איבעיא, אלא לגבי דיוטא, כדמפרש ואזיל. **דיוטא.** היא עלייה העליונה שעל גג הבית.

איבעיא

שכיב מרע שאמר כו' הלואתו לפלוני אע"ג דליתא בבריא. בקנין (ה), שאין הלואה בעין. ונהי דיכול להקנות אגב קרקע, אי גרסינן "מסיק" מדרב פפא (לעיל דף עז: ושם), מ"מ כיון דליתא בבריא בקנין, דלא מצי להקנות [בלא] דבר אחר עם ההלואה — לא חשיב איתא בבריא, דהא דירת בית כמו כן יכול להקנות על ידי הבית, ופירות דקל ע"י הדקל — שיקנה לו הבית לדור בו כך וכך שנים, והדקל לאכול פירותיו כך וכך שנים. אלא בענין שיוכל להקנותו בענין זה ששכיב מרע מקנהו בדבורו יוכל בריא להקנותו בקנין חליפין או במכירה. והלואה אין יכול למכור, כי אינה בעין. ומשני: הואיל ויורש יורשה, ומתנת שכיב מרע כירושה. ואע"ג דיורש יורש נמי דירת הבית [ופירות דקל] — היינו לפי שיורש גם הבית והדקל, אי נמי, במעמד שלשתן. אבל מה שיוכל להקנות אגב קרקע — לא חשיב איתיה בבריא, דהא דירת בית ופירות דקל יכול להקנות אגב הבית והדקל, כדפרי'. ותימה לי: לימא איתא בבריא בהודאה, כדמוכח לקמן (דף קמט.) דשכיב מרע שהודה קנה בלא טעם דשכיב מרע, מדקני בגר! (ו) ונראה לי דהא לא חשיב איתא בבריא, כיון דליתא כענין שהוא בשכיב מרע, בלשון מתנה וקנין. והא דקאמר: הואיל ויורש יורשה — לא בעי למימר מטעם דאיתא בבריא, אלא כיון שיורש יורשה — יש כח לשכיב מרע ליתן, דברשותו הויין, דמתנת שכיב מרע כירוש. ותדע דעל טעם זה דהואיל ויורש — לא נקט "איתא בבריא הואיל ויורש יורשה", ועל מעמד שלשתן — נקט "איתא בבריא במעמד שלשתן", כמו שכתוב בכל הספרים ובפירוש רבינו חננאל. ואין נראה לחלק בין הודאת פקדון להודאת מלוה. **שכיב** מרע שאמר הלואתי לפלוני כו' ואע"ג דליתא בבריא. ומה שרגילין לכתוב הרשאה גבי מלוה, פי' לעיל בפ' "המוכר את הספינה" (דף עז: סד"ה ר"פ). וגם שאין נראה פירוש רש"י שפירש בכתובות (דף נה: ד"ה מתנת ושם) (ז) דטעם משום דאין מטבע נקנה בחליפין. וגם אין נראה עוד לפרש כפי' ה"ר חיים: דליתא בבריא — שיכול למחול שטר חוב אם מכרו, משא"כ בשכיב מרע, כדאמר לעיל (דף קמז:). כל זה פירשנו לעיל, בפרק "המוכר את הספינה". **תנהו** לפלוני במעמד שלשתן קנה. ומה שמפרש רבינו תם שמועיל בעל כרחו של נפקד, פי' לעיל בפ' "המוכר את הספינה" (דף פה. ד"ה ה"ג). וגם מה שמפרש שמעמד שלשתן (ח) אין בגוי, פירשנו בפרק שני דקדושין (דף מח.)ד). **איבעיא** להו דקל לאחד ופירותיו לאחר מהו מי שייר מקום פירי כו'. פי' רבינו שמואל דאשיור דשכיב מרע קאי, דתנן במתניתין דאם שייר קרקע כל שהוא מתנתו מתנה. ואין נראה לר"י, דהא לקמן, על משנת שייר קרקע כל שהוא, הוה ליה למיבעי הך בעיא. ועוד, דשיעורא דשיור הוי כדי פרנסתו, כדאמר בסמוך. ועוד, מה יש לחוש בשיור קרקע? הא אפילו (ט) מטלטלין לקמן אמרינן דהוו שיור! על כן נראה לר"י, דאלעיל קאי: "ידור פלוני בבית זה" — לא אמר כלום, משום דהוי דבר שלא בא לעולם. וקא מיבעיא ליה: כי אמר דקל לאחד ופירותיו לאחר, ושייר מקום לימוח הפירות, מי אמרינן לא הוי שיור לענין שיחשבו הפירות דבר שלא בא לעולם. או שמא נתן גם לבעל הפירות מקום לימוח הפירות, וא"כ זכה במקום לימוח הפירות, ולא הוו הפירות דבר שלא בא לעולם — שהרי כבר זכה במקום הפירות שבא לעולם. ואם תמצא לומר לאחר לא הוי שיור, לעצמו מאי? פי': ששייר לעצמו, מי אמרינן שזה לא היה עושה — שיקנה למקבל מתנה גוף הדקל, ולגבי דידיה הוו הפירות דבר שבא לעולם, או דלמא אפילו הכי הוו (י) דבר שלא בא לעולם, שלא שייר מקום פירי אפילו לעצמו. וכן תניא לעיל בפרק "המוכר את הבית" (דף סג.): בן לוי שאמר לישראל "שדה זה אני מוכר על מנת שמעשר ראשון שלי" — מעשר ראשון שלו. ופריך: והא אין אדם מקנה דבר שלא בא לעולם! משמע דשייך אין אדם מקנה כו' אפי' לעצמו. ואע"ג דאמר לעיל דסתם מוכר או נותן אילן דמשייר קרקע — הכא בשכיב מרע אין לו לומר דשייר קרקע ולא מקום פירי אלא פירות בלבד. ועוד: הרי נתן כל האילן, ואיך יש לנו לומר ששייר מקום פירי? ומסיק: דלעצמו הוי שיור, דמאן דלנפשיה משייר — בעין יפה משייר. ויש ספרים דגרסי: חוץ מפירותיו מהו. והיא היא, היינו שנתן הדקל במתנת שכיב מרע, ושייר פירותיו לעצמו. **אנן** אדרבי שמעון בן לקיש מתנינן לה כו' עד ואם תמצי לומר לאחר לא הוי שיור לעצמו מהו. ואע"ג דר"ל איירי לעצמו, מ"מ כיון ד"בחוץ" מיירי — הכא קמבעיא לו מה יאמר ריש לקיש בזה. דב"על מנת" פשיטא ליה ודאי דמשייר, אבל בהא קא מיבעיא ליה.

חיישינן

עין משפט נר מצוה

עד א מיי' פ"י מהלכות זכייה ומתנה הלכה ב סמג עשין פב טוש"ע ח"מ סי' רנג סעיף כ:
עה ב מיי' פכ"ג מהל' מכירה הלכה ד טוש"ע ח"מ סימן רע סעיף ז וסעיף ט:
עו ג מיי' שם טוש"ע שם סעיף י:

הגהות הב"ח

(א) גמ' אם תמצי לומר לאחר לא הוי שיור שייר לעצמו מהו (חוץ מפירותיו מהו) תא"מ ונ"ב גירסת הספרים את"ל לאחר לא הוי שיור שייר לעצמו מהו אמר רבא כו' ורשב"ם גורס דקל לאחד ופירותיו לאחד מהו את"ל לאחר לא הוי שיור חוץ מפירותיו מהו אמר רבא א"ר נחמן את"ל דקל לאחד ופירותיו לאחר לא שייר מקום פירי חוץ מפירותיו שייר מקום פירי ואליבא דרב זביד דאמר שאם רצה להוציא בה זיזין מוציא אלמא כיון דדיוטא שייר מקום זיזין נמי שייר הכי נמי כיון דאמר חוץ מפירותיו מקום פירות שייר: (ב) רשב"ם ד"ה איבעיא להו וכו' דא"כ מפני מה קבעה לבעיא זו בזו השמועה וכו' קמאי דהוה בהו שיור וכו' כשנתן הדקל לראשון וכו' המחובר בקרקע כקרקע דמי: (ג) ד"ה שייר לעצמו וכו' דלא מיתני עליה הך סוגיא דלקמן. נ"ב נראה דקשיא ליה דלפי גירסא זו גם בההיא סוגיא דלקמן גרסינן ואת"ל לאחר לא הוי שיור לעצמו מהו מאי קא מיבעיא ליה הא ריש לקיש מיירי בלעצמו וכמו שהקשו התוספות ומה שתירצו דקא מיבעיא ליה מה יאמר ר"ל בחוץ כו' לא נתיישב לרשב"ם דא"כ אמילתא דר"ל ה"ל לקבוע בעיא זו דמה יאמר ר"ל בחוץ בלאו בעיא [קמייתא] ולכך נ"ל עיקר דגרסי' חוץ מפירותיו מהו דהשתא גם הך בעיא איירי בלאחריני אלא דקמייתא מיירי בלאו לישנא יתירא ובתרייתא [בלישנא יתירא וכן לקמן] בכה"ג דתרתי קא מיבעיא ליה בבית לאחד ודיוטא לאחר חדא בלאו לישנא יתירא ואחריני בלישנא יתירא: (ד) בא"ד דומיא דרב זביד ור"ל והכי פירוש לשון: (ה) תוס' ד"ה שכיב מרע וכו' בקנין כיון שאין הלואה וכו' בדבר כבר מה פלא גם דליתא בבריא בקנין גרידא דלא מצי להקנות אלא ע"י דבר אחר: (ו) בא"ד מדקני בגר וכו' ונראה לחלק בין הודאה פקדון להודאה מלוה וכו' לי דהא לא חשיב וכו' כיון דליתא כענין שהוא בשכיב מרע בלשון מתנה וקנין והא דקאמר הואיל ויורש יורשה וכו' לא נקט וכו' ובפי' ר"ח הס"ד: (ז) ד"ה שכיב מרע וכו' דלעשו משום וכו' דליתא בבריא מפני שיכול: (ח) ד"ה תנהו וכו' שלמתן וכו' אין בגויס: (ט) ד"ה איבעיא וכו' אפילו במטלטלין לקמן אמרינן דהוי שיור: (י) בא"ד אפילו הכי הוו הפירות דבר שלא וכו' אפי' לעצמו והכי מוכח לעיל בפרק המוכר את הבית דהמניא בן לוי וכו' שדה זו אני:

רבינו גרשום

שכיב מרע שאמר תנו הלואתי לפלוני. כלומר חוב שחייב לי פלוני תהא של פלוני הרי הוא שלו וקנה לאלתר: אע"ג דליתא בבריא. דבריא שאמר כן לא קנה כו' אלא במעמד שלשתן: אמר רב פפא לעולם מילתא דליתא בבריא ליתא נמי בשכיב מרע. והכא כשאמר הלואתי לפלוני טעמא מאי קנה הואיל ויורש שלו יורשה לאלתר בלא אמירה אם לא נתנה לזה הואיל וכל כך היא בחזקתו הלואתו שיורש שלו יורשה אע"ג דהיא ברשות לזה משום הכי יש לו כח לומר הלואתי לפלוני וקנה אבל בבריא ליתא דאין ירושה אלא לאחר מיתה: רב אחא בריה דרב איקא אמר. הא מילתא דשכיב מרע דאמר הלואתי לפלוני איתא בבריא ענין הלואה כרב הונא וכו' קנה. אלמא דאיתא בבריא: איבעיא לן. הא מילתא פשיטא לן שכיב מרע שכתב כל נכסיו ושייר קרקע כל שהוא אף על גב דעמד מתנתו מתנה דסמיך נפשיה על ההוא קרקע וגמר ומקנה. אבל הא קמיבעיא לן דקל נתן לאחד ופירותיו לאחר מי אמרינן להיכא דנתן דקל לזה ושייר הפירו' ואמר תנו לאידך הפירות מי אמרי' הואיל שכשנתן הדקל שייר הפירות וקנה ראשון דבההוא שיור דשייר הפירות סמכה דעתיה א) דאין חוזר ועמד שיחזור על הפירות שנתן לאחרון דבההוא שעתא שנתן ב) הפירות לא שייר לו הפירות ומש"ה מתנתו שנתן לראשון מתנה מעליא היא. או דלמא הואיל דלא שייר בגוף הדקל לא הוי שיור ואין מתנתו מתנה ואם עמד חוזר בעל המתנה אפי' בדקל שנתן לראשון: אם תמצי לומר לא הוי שיור. הואיל דלא שייר בגוף הדקל ואפי' ראשון לא קנה. הא קא מיבעי לי אם אמר דקל לפלוני חוץ מפירותיו מהו. מי אמרינן אע"ג דאי אמר בסתמא דקל זה לפלוני לא קא יהיב ליה פירי והשתא דקאמר חוץ מפירותיו לטפויי מלתא קא אתי ובדקל גופיה קא משייר מקום הפירות ומתנה שנתן לראשון מתנה מעליא היא הואיל ששייר בגוף הדקל. או דלמא לא שנא דאין זה שיור ואין מתנתו מתנה: חוץ מפירותיו ודאי הוה שיורו שיור ומתנתו מתנה אליבא דרב זביד דאמר בפרק המוכר את הבית אמר ריש לקיש זאת אומרת המוכר בית לחבירו על מנת שדיוטא העליונה שלו שייר לעצמו דיוטא העליונה. אמר רב זביד למאי הלכתא דאע"ג דלא אמר הכי על מנת לא מכר את הדיוטא משום דלא שייכא כלל לבית ואמאי אמר חוץ לטפויי מלתא קאתי שאם רצה להוציא בה בחצר (זיזין) שמכר לו עם הבית זיזין וגזוזטרא לדיוטא שלו יוצא. הכי נמי להיכא דקאמר דקל זה לפלוני ודאי לא קנה פירות דבסתמא לא קנה ולא נתנו לו אלא לקצוץ ממנו נופין יבשין וכיון דהוסיף ואמר חוץ מפירותיו ודאי לטפויי מלתא קאתי דבגוף דקל שיורי שייר ומתנתו מתנה. ל"א איבעיא להו דקל לאחד ופירותיו לאחר מהו מי שייר לעצמו מקום פירי בגוף הדקל ומתנתו מתנה (שיור) או לא. אם תמצא לומר לא שייר ואין מתנתו מתנה הואיל דלא שייר בגוף הדקל משום דנותן בעין יפה נותן. הא קא מיבעי לי נתן דקל לאחד ושייר פירותיו לעצמו מאי. מי אמרי' כל לגבי נפשיה כי משייר לעצמו בעין יפה משייר הואיל ושייר פירות שייר בדקל מקום פירות ומתנתו מתנה או לא: אמר רבא אם תמצי לומר כו': א"ל ר' אבא. הא מילתא דרב זביד דפשיטא לכו הא אנן בלשון

בעיא

א) נראה לצ"ל דלא יחזור ויעמוד שיחזור וכו'. ב) צ"ל דבההיא שעתא שנתן הדקל הא שייר לו הפירות וכו'.

לְתְפִלָּתוֹ שֶׁל כֹּהֵן גָּדוֹל. וְרָבָא אָמַר רַב נַחְמָן: מַתְּנַת שְׁכִיב מְרַע מִדְּרַבָּנַן בְּעָלְמָא הִיא, שֶׁמָּא תִּטָּרֵף דַּעְתּוֹ עָלָיו. וּמִי אֲמַר רַב נַחְמָן הָכִי? וְהָא (א) אֲמַר רַב נַחְמָן, אע"ג דְּאָמַר שְׁמוּאֵל: א)אהַמּוֹכֵר שְׁטַר חוֹב לַחֲבֵירוֹ וְחָזַר וּמְחָלוֹ — מָחוּל, וַאֲפִילּוּ יוֹרֵשׁ מוֹחֵל, במוֹדֶה שְׁמוּאֵל, שֶׁאִם נְתָנוֹ בְּמַתְּנַת שְׁכִיב מְרַע דְּאֵינוֹ יָכוֹל לְמוֹחֲלוֹ; אִי אָמְרַתְּ בִּשְׁלָמָא דְּאוֹרַיְיתָא — מִשּׁוּם הָכִי אֵינוֹ יָכוֹל לִמְחוֹל, אֶלָּא אִי אָמְרַתְּ דְּרַבָּנַן הִיא, אַמַּאי אֵינוֹ יָכוֹל לִמְחוֹל? גאֵינָהּ שֶׁל תּוֹרָה וַעֲשָׂאוּהָ כְּשֶׁל תּוֹרָה. אָמַר רָבָא אָמַר רַב נַחְמָן: דשְׁכִיב מְרַע שֶׁאָמַר "יָדוּר פְּלוֹנִי בְּבַיִת זֶה", "יֹאכַל פְּלוֹנִי פֵּירוֹת דֶּקֶל זֶה" — לֹא אָמַר כְּלוּם, עַד שֶׁיֹּאמַר: "תְּנוּ בַּיִת זֶה לִפְלוֹנִי וְיָדוּר בּוֹ", "תְּנוּ דֶּקֶל זֶה לִפְלוֹנִי וְיֹאכַל פֵּירוֹתָיו". לְמֵימְרָא, דְּסָבַר ר"נ: מִילְּתָא דְּאִיתָא בְּבָרִיא אִיתָא בִּשְׁכִיב מְרַע, דְּלֵיתָא בְּבָרִיא לֵיתָא בִּשְׁכִיב מְרַע? וְהָא אָמַר רָבָא אָמַר רַב נַחְמָן: שְׁכִיב

רשב"ם

לִתְפִלָּתוֹ שֶׁל כֹּהֵן גָּדוֹל. שֶׁהָיָה מִתְפַּלֵּל בְּיוֹם הַכִּפּוּרִים שֶׁתְּהֵא שָׁנָה זוֹ גְּשׁוּמָה וּשְׁחוּנָה. וְעַתָּה לְפִי הָעִנְיָן שֶׁיִּרְאֶה בְּרֹאשׁ הַשָּׁנָה יִתְפַּלֵּל בְּיוה"כ. מַתְּנַת שְׁכִיב מְרַע. שֶׁקּוֹנָה בַּאֲמִירָה בְּעָלְמָא – אֵינָהּ מִן הַתּוֹרָה, וּקְרָאֵי דִּלְעֵיל עֵצָה טוֹבָה קמ"ל, שֶׁיְּצַוֶּה לְבֵיתוֹ בִּשְׁעַת מִיתָתוֹ מַה שֶּׁיֵּשׁ לוֹ לְצַוּוֹת, הֵן עַל יְדֵי קִנְיָן הֵן ע"י דִּבּוּר, כְּגוֹן דְּבָרִים שֶׁאֵין צְרִיכִין קִנְיָן, שֶׁאָדָם מוֹדִיעַ לִבְנֵי בֵּיתוֹ מִי חַיָּיב לוֹ כְּלוּם, וּמָמוֹנוֹ וַחֲפָצָיו בְּיַד מִי (ב) וְהֵיכָן מוּפְקָדִין. אֶלָּא מִדְּרַבָּנַן בְּעָלְמָא קוֹנָה, גְּזֵירָה שֶׁמָּא עַד שֶׁיָּבֹאוּ עֵדִים לִקְנוֹת תִּטָּרֵף דַּעְתּוֹ שֶׁל חוֹלֶה קוֹדֶם שֶׁיָּבֹאוּ, וְלֹא יוּכַל לְהַקְנוֹת, וְנִמְצֵאת צַוָּאָתוֹ בְּטֵלָה. וְקַשְׁיָא לִי: מַה בְּכָךְ אִם תִּבָּטֵל? מֵאַחַר שֶׁאֵינוֹ קוֹנֶה בַּאֲמִירָה – תִּבָּטֵל וְתִבָּטֵל! וְלִישָּׁנָא אַחֲרִינָא מְפָרְשִׁינַן, וְנִרְאֶה בְּעֵינַי, דִּלְהָכִי תַּקּוּן רַבָּנַן שֶׁיִּקְנוּ דְּבָרָיו בַּאֲמִירָה, שֶׁאִם אֵין דְּבָרָיו נִקְנִין – חָיְישִׁינַן שֶׁמָּא תִּטָּרֵף דַּעְתּוֹ בְּחָלְיוֹ מִתּוֹךְ צַעַר, שֶׁהוּא יוֹדֵעַ שֶׁלֹּא יְקַיְּימוּ בָּנָיו צַוָּאָתוֹ. מִי אָמַר רַב נַחְמָן הָכִי. דְּמִדְּרַבָּנַן הִיא וְלֹא מִדְּאוֹרַיְיתָא. הַמּוֹכֵר שְׁטַר חוֹב. שֶׁחַיָּיב לוֹ לֹוֶה לַמַּלְוֶה מָמוֹן, וּמָסַר לוֹ הַמַּלְוֶה אֶת הַשְּׁטָר לְיַד לוֹקֵחַ, וּמְכָרוֹ לוֹ, וְכָתַב לוֹ "קְנֵי לָךְ (ג) וְכָל שִׁעְבּוּדֵיהּ". אִי נַמִּי – כִּדְפָסְקִינַן הָתָם הִלְכְתָא: אוֹתִיּוֹת נִקְנוֹת בִּמְסִירָה, בְּפֶרֶק "הַמּוֹכֵר אֶת הַסְּפִינָה" (לעיל עז.). וְחָזַר. הַמּוֹכֵר וּמָחַל לַלֹּוֶה. מָחוּל. דְּלֹא מָכַר לוֹ רִאשׁוֹן לַשֵּׁנִי אֶלָּא כָּל זְכוּת שֶׁתָּבֹא לְיָדוֹ, וְלָא עֲדִיף הַאי לוֹקֵחַ מִמַּלְוֶה דְּאָתֵי מֵחֲמָתֵיהּ דְּמַלְוֶה. וּמִיהוּ, מְעוֹתָיו יַחֲזִיר לוֹ מוֹכֵר לַלּוֹקֵחַ, דְּהָא הִלְכְתָא הִיא דְּדָיְינִינַן דִּינָא דְּגַרְמֵי, וְזֶה הִפְסִיד מְעוֹתָיו כְּשׂוֹרֵף שְׁטָרוֹתָיו שֶׁל חֲבֵירוֹ, דְּקַיְימָא לָן ב) דְּחַיָּיב מֵהַהוּא עוּבְדָא דְּכַפְיֵיהּ רַפְרָם לְרַב אַשִׁי וְאַגְבֵּי מִינֵּיהּ כִּי כְּשׁוּרָא לְגַלְמֵי. וַאֲפִילּוּ יוֹרֵשׁ. שֶׁל מַלְוֶה, מוֹחֵל. וּסְבָרָא הוּא, דְּלָא אַלִּים כֹּחַ שֶׁל לוֹקֵחַ בַּמֶּה שֶׁנִּמְסַר לוֹ שְׁטַר הַמַּלְוֶה אֶלָּא לִזְכּוֹת בַּחוֹב הַכָּתוּב (ד) בִּמְקוֹם הַמַּלְוֶה אוֹ הַיּוֹרֵשׁ, אַף לֹא נֶעֱקַר שִׁעְבּוּדוֹ מִן הַמַּלְוֶה, וְקָרֵינָא בֵּיהּ "עֶבֶד לֹוֶה לְאִישׁ מַלְוֶה", וְיָכוֹל לִמְחוֹל שִׁעְבּוּדוֹ. מוֹדֶה שְׁמוּאֵל שֶׁאִם נְתָנוֹ. הַמַּלְוֶה לְאִישׁ אַחֵר בְּמַתְּנַת שְׁכִיב מְרַע. וּכְגוֹן שֶׁחִלֵּק כָּל נְכָסָיו. אִי נַמִּי, עַל יְדֵי קִנְיָן, כְּדִין כָּל מַתְּנַת שְׁכִיב מְרַע בְּמִקְצָת. אִי נַמִּי, בְּלֹא קִנְיָן, דְּכֵיוָן דִּמְסָרוֹ לוֹ בְּחַיָּיו – אֵין לְךָ קִנְיָן גָּדוֹל מִזֶּה. וּמִיהוּ, אִם עָמַד – חוֹזֵר אִם מַתְּנַת שְׁכִיב מְרַע (ה) בְּמִקְצָת הוּא, כִּדְפָסְקִי' לְקַמָּן. דְּאֵינוֹ יָכוֹל לִמְחוֹל, דְּדִבְרֵי שְׁכִיב מְרַע כִּכְתוּבִין וְכִמְסוּרִין דָּמוּ, וַאֲלִימֵי מִמַּתְּנַת בָּרִיא, וְאֵין הַיּוֹרֵשׁ יָכוֹל לִמְחוֹל. וּמְשַׁנֵּי: אֵינָהּ שֶׁל תּוֹרָה. אֶלָּא מִדְּרַבָּנַן הִיא. וַעֲשָׂאוּהָ כְּשֶׁל תּוֹרָה. וּמִשּׁוּם טֵירוּף דַּעְתּוֹ, כִּדְאָמְרַן לְעֵיל. **א"ר נחמן** שְׁכִיב מְרַע שֶׁאָמַר יָדוּר פְּלוֹנִי בְּבַיִת זֶה **יֹאכַל פְּלוֹנִי** פֵּירוֹת דֶּקֶל זֶה **לֹא אָמַר** כְּלוּם. שֶׁהַדִּירָה אֵין בָּהּ מַמָּשׁ לְהַקְנוֹתָהּ, וּפֵירוֹת דֶּקֶל נַמִּי – אֵין אָדָם מַקְנֶה דָּבָר שֶׁלֹּא בָּא לָעוֹלָם. וְכֵיוָן דְּמַתְּנַת בָּרִיא אֲפִי' בְּקִנְיָן סוּדָר לָא קָנֵי, דְּמִילֵּי לָא מִיקְנוּ אֶלָּא א"כ הִקְנָה לוֹ הַחֵפֶץ, כְּגוֹן דֶּקֶל לְפֵירוֹתָיו וּבַיִת לָדוּר – מַתְּנַת שְׁכִיב מְרַע נַמִּי לָא קָנְיָא. דְּמִילְּתָא דְּלֵיתָא בְּבָרִיא לֵיתָא בִּשְׁכִיב מְרַע. שֶׁאֵין שְׁכִיב מְרַע חָמוּר מִן הַבָּרִיא, אֶלָּא דַּאֲמִירָתוֹ בִּמְקוֹם קִנְיָן שֶׁל בָּרִיא הוּא, וְהֵיכָא דְּאֵין קִנְיָן (ו) מוֹעֶלֶת בְּבָרִיא – אֲמִירָה בִּשְׁכִיב מְרַע לָא מְהַנְיָא מִידֵּי. הִלְכָּךְ אֵין מוֹעִיל עַד שֶׁיֹּאמַר "תְּנוּ בַּיִת זֶה לִפְלוֹנִי" כו'. **לְמֵימְרָא** דְּסָבַר רַב נַחְמָן כו'. לָא אַלִּים כֹּחַ הַשְּׁכִיב מְרַע יוֹתֵר מִן הַבָּרִיא, אֶלָּא שֶׁאֲמִירָתוֹ קוֹנָה כְּקִנְיָן סוּדָר דְּבָרִיא.

הַלְוָאָתִי

תוספות

לתפלתו של כהן גדול. שיתפלל שאם חמה – לא תהיה חמה יותר מדאי, ואם קרירא – לא תהיה קרירא יותר מדאי.

המוכר שטר חוב לחבירו וחזר ומחלו מחול כו'. פי' רבינו שמואל: דלמאן דדאין דינא דגרמי – הוה מוחל צריך להחזיר ללוקח מה שנתן לו. ואור"י: א"צ להחזיר אלא מעות שנתנו בו הלקוחות, ולא כל השטר. וראיה לדבר – מדאמר בפרק "החובל" (ב"ק פט: ושם): אלא הא דתניא: וכן היא שחבלה בבעלה לא הפסידה כתובתה, ואמאי לא הפסידה? תזבין לה לכתובתה לבעלה בטובת הנאה, דהאי חבלה דאי מחלה לה (ז) גבי בעל – ליכא קפידא! ומוקי לה כרבי מאיר. ומשמע: דוקא גבי בעל יכולה למכור, אבל לגבי אחריני – לא תוכל למכור כי האי גוונא, פן תמחלנה לבעלה. והיאך תמחלנה לרבי מאיר, דאית ליה ב"הגוזל קמא" (שם ק.) דינא דגרמי? ע"כ נראה, אפי' למאן דאית ליה דינא דגרמי – היינו דוקא לענין שיש לה לשלם מה שנתנו בה הלקוחות, ולא כל דמי הכתובה שהפסידתם. והא דאמר ב"הגוזל קמא" (שם דף צח:): מאן דדאין דינא דגרמי מגבי שטרא מעליא, גבי שורף שטרותיו של חבירו, וכן בפ' "הכותב" (כתובות דף פו.) על הך מלתא דשמואל – לאו דוקא נקט "שטרא מעליא", שהרי לא תחזיר אלא מה שנתנו בה הלוקחין. אלא משום דנקט לעיל התם "ניירא בעלמא קלאי מינך" – נקט בתר הכי "שטרא מעליא". ועוד ראיה מרב נחמן, דאית ליה ב"הגוזל בתרא" (ב"ק קטז:) דינא דגרמי, גבי ההוא גברא דאחווי אכריא דחבריה, אתא לקמיה דרב נחמן חייביה כו'. ואילו בפרק "הכותב" (כתובות פה: ושם פו. ד"ה תיזיל) אמר: קריבתיה דרב נחמן זבינתה לכתובתה בטובת הנאה ואיגרשא ושכיבא, אתו לקוחות וקתבעי לה לברתה כו'. אמר רב נחמן: מאן לימא לה דתיזיל ולימחלה לכתובתה לגבי אבוה, והדר תירתה מיניה. ומה תרויח לרב נחמן? והא איהו גופיה אית ליה ב"הגוזל בתרא" דינא דגרמי, ואם כן צריכה להחזיר לו כל הדמים, ומה תרויח בזה? אלא שמע מינה שתרויח בזה שלא היתה צריכה להחזיר להם אלא מה שנתנו בה. ג)ואם תאמר: מכל מקום הפסידתם הרבה, שהרי גרושה היתה, והיה להם ללקוחות אז לגבות כתובתה מן הגרושה! ואומר רבי: דשמא קטנה היתה, ולא היו יכולים אז לגבות ממנה כלום. ומכל מקום מחילתה מחילה כיון שהגיעה לפעוטות, כדאמר ב"הנזקין" (גיטין דף נט.) דמתנתה מתנה. עוד קשה לי: רב נחמן איך השיאה עצה למחול כתובת אמן? והא אמר בפרק "לא יחפור" (לעיל כב: ושם) דגרמא בנזקין אסור. פי', אע"ג דפטור הוא – איסורא מיהא איכא. וכל שכן למאן דדאין דינא דגרמי כמו רב נחמן, דאיכא איסור יותר כשמורה לה למחול, דאפילו בגרמא בניזקין שפטור לגמרי אסור, וכ"ש דינא דגרמי שיש מחייבין, שאסור! ואומר ר"י: דכיון שהיה לה הפסד לדבר – שרי. וגם שלא היו מפסידין כלל בדבר, שמחזרת להם מה שנתנו בה. ועוד ראיה, מדאמר בפרק שני דקדושין (דף מז:): "התקדשי לי בשטר חובי" או שהיה לו מלוה ביד אחרים ד)(וקדשה) עלייהו, רבי מאיר אומר: מקודשת, וחכמים אומרים: אינה מקודשת. ומסקנא דמילתא דפליגי בדשמואל, דאמר שמואל: המוכר שטר חוב לחבירו וחזר ומחלו – מחול. מאן דאמר אינה מקודשת – אית ליה דשמואל, דלא סמכה דעתה, כי שמא ימחול. ואם צריך להחזיר כל הדמים – למה ימחול? ושפיר סמכה דעתה! ועוד, דקאמר התם בתר הכי, דסמכה דעתה דלא שביק נפשה ויהיב לאחריני. הוה ליה למימר שיתחייב לשלם הכל אם ימחול! ומיהו, יש לדחות, כי שמא היה לה בושת לבוא לב"ד ולתבוע מבעלה מה שמחלה, ולכך לא סמכה דעתה בכך יותר. ועוד ראיה, ממה דאמר בפרק קמא דבבא מציעא (דף יט: ושם) גבי מלא שובר, בזמן שהאשה מודה – יחזיר לבעל. וליחוש שמא כתבה ליתן בניסן ולא נתנה אלא עד תשרי, ואזלה וזבנתה לכתובתה בטובת הנאה מניסן עד תשרי, ומפיק ליה לשובר דכתיב בניסן, ואתי למיטרף לקוחות שלא כדין! ואמר רבא: שמע מינה איתא לדשמואל, דאמר שמואל המוכר שטר חוב לחבירו כו'. פי': ואם כן – לא טריף שלא כדין, שהרי יכולה היא למחול לבעלה. ותימה: למאן דדאין דינא דגרמי, איך (ח) יטרוף שלא כדין? והלא אם תמחול לבעלה – יחזרו עליה הלקוחות ויגבו ממנה הכל! על כן נראה שאין צריכה להחזיר להם אלא מה שנתנו בה. ומיהו קשה לי: מ"מ יטרוף לקוחות שלא כדין, שהרי יחזרו עליה ממה שנתנו בה לכל הפחות! ואומר ר"י: דבדבר מועט כזה אין לחוש, דאין כאן טריפה שלא כדין. ועוד הוה קשיא לי: דהא הוה מצי התם למיפרך מגרושה שכתבה ליתן בניסן ולא נתנה עד תשרי, ואזלה וזבנא לכתובה דמניסן ועד תשרי, ומפיק ליה לשובר דכתיב בניסן, ואתי למיטרף לקוחות שלא כדין. וכיון שהיא גרושה – א"כ מוכרת כתובתה בדמים יקרים, ואם כן הפסידה הרבה ללקוחות, וטורף בעלה שלא כדין – שהרי לא תוכל למחול מה שהפסידתם! ואי הוה מוקי לה להאי ברייתא כמאן דלא דאין דינא דגרמי – הוה אתי שפיר, אך לא היינו יכולים עוד להביא ממנה ראיה. מיהו, לפי מה שפי' ר"י בפ"ק דבבא מציעא, דבגרושה ליכא למיחש הכי – הוה א"ש. וכן הוא עיקר, כמו שפי' שם, דלא הוי מצי למיפרך מגרושה. וא"ת: מאי האי דקאמר בפ"ק דבבא מציעא (דף כ.): ש"מ איתא להא דשמואל דאמר המוכר שטר חוב כו'? ניחוש דלמא כתבה ליתן בניסן ולא נתנה עד תשרי, והלכה והכניסתה לבעלה, שאז אינה יכולה למחול, דידו כידה, כדאמר ב"הכותב" (כתובות פה:)! וי"ל דמיירי שיודעין שאין לה בעל. **אלא** אינה כשל תורה כו'. מה שפירש רבינו יעקב שאין להוכיח מכאן דמכר שטר חוב ה)אל מן התורה – פירשנו לעיל בפרק "המוכר את הספינה" (דף עו: ד"ה קני).

שכיב מרע שאמר ידור פלוני בבית זה **יאכל** פלוני פירות דקל זה **לא אמר** כלום **למימרא** דסבר רב נחמן מילתא דליתא **בבריא**. שאינו יכול להקנות הדירה, לדבר שאין בו ממש הוא. ופירות הדקל – דאין אדם מקנה דבר שלא בא לעולם.

שכיב

עין משפט נר מצוה

ע א מיי' פ"ו מהלכות מכירה הל' יא ועיין בהשגות ובמגיד משנה סמג עשין פב טוש"ע חו"מ סי' סו סעיף כג:

עא ב מיי' פ"ט מהלכות זכייה ומתנה הלכה ב ועיין בהשגות ובכ"מ סמג שם טוש"ע חו"מ סס סעי' כז וסי' רנג סעיף כ וברב אלפס כתובות דף קט:

עב ג מיי' שם הלכה ב ועיין בכ"מ ופ"ח הלכה ב סמג שם וברב אלפס שם:

ענ ד מיי' שם פ"י הל' טו טוש"ע חו"מ סי' רנג סעיף כה:

רבינו גרשום

הלכך לא קשיין אהדדי: לתפלתו של כהן גדול. דאי חמים ההוא יומא בידוע שכל השנה מחוממת וצריך לבקש רחמים שתהא גשומה ואי קריר צריך לבקש רחמים שאם גשומה תהא שחונה: אמר רבא אמר רב נחמן מתנת שכיב מרע מדרבנן היא. דקניא באמירה וכל מתנה דאשכחן באוריית' בבריא מיירי. ומה שיכול ליתן למי שאינו יורש באמירה רבנן תקינו להו למיעבד כל רעותיה דאי לא מצי למיעבד שמא תטרוף דעתו עליו מחמת צער. איכא דאמרי להכי לא בעי לא קנין ולא כתיבה ולא משיכה אלא באמירה בעלמא דזימנין דמתרמי דמית בשבת ולא מצי למיעבד קנין ולא משיכה ולא כתיבה ותטרוף דעתו עליו ושכיב ולא פקיד להכי תקינו דבאמירה סגי: ומי אמר רב נחמן הכי. דמדרבנן הויא מתנת שכיב מרע: והאמר רב נחמן אע"ג דאמר שמואל המוכר שטר חוב לחבירו וחזר לאחר מכיר' ומחלו. לבעל חובו [מחול] דנייר בעלמא הוא דזבין ליה ומלוה ליתה בעינה דלהוצאה נתנה. אבל זוזי דיהיב לוקח בשביל שטר מהדר ליה ללוקח: אפי' יורש של מוכר מצי מחיל החוב. הואיל דיורש הוא: מודה שמואל שאם נתנו. לשטר חוב במתנת שכיב מרע לשום אדם שאין יורש יכול למחול דמתנה אלימא ממכר: אי אמרת בשלמא [דאורייתא] משום הכי. אלימא מתנה ממכר: אלא אי אמרת מדרבנן. אמאי אלימא מתנה ממכר. ש"מ מדאורייתא וקשיא דרב נחמן אדרב נחמן. ומשני לעולם אימא לך מדרבנן ולא מדאורייתא ומשום הכי אינו יכול למחול דעשאוה כשל תורה ואלמוה רבנן (כתיבתי) [מתנתו] כמדאורייתא משום גזירה שמא תטרוף דעתו עליו: לא אמר כלום. דאין זה זכיית מתנה כדאמר לקמן יטול ויזכה ויחזיק ויקנה כולן לשון מתנה הם. אבל היכא דאמר ידור ויאכל פירותיו לא עד שיאמר תנו בית זה לפלוני וידור בו. והאי דאמר ידור ויאכל לאו דוקא הוא דכיון דאמר תנו לחוד קנה קאמר אלא אגב דאמר ברישא ידור ויאכל קתני סיפא נמי ידור ויאכל: למימרא דקסבר רב נחמן. דאמר ידור ויאכל אין לשון קנית מתנה היא משום דמלתא דלשון קניה הוא (דאיתא) בבריא איתיה בשכיב מרע. דבריא אמר תנו היינו לשון מתנה (היינו) ה"נ שכיב מרע אבל אמר בריא ידור לא הוי לשון מתנה וליתיה נמי בשכיב מרע: והאמר רב נחמן שכיב

מסורת הש"ס

א) ב"ק פט. ב"מ כ. כתובות פה: פו. קדושין מח. ב) [כתובות פו.] ג) [רש"ל מחקו] ד) [נ"ל והרכס] ה) ר"מ גורס אינו חל.

הגהות הב"ח

(א) גמרא אמר רב נחמן אע"ג. נ"ב גי' רשב"ם א"ר נחמן אמר שמואל כו' ומודה שמואל כו' אבל בתוס' גורסין אע"ג כו' ע"ש סוף דף ע"ו: (ב) רשב"ם ד"ה מתנת וכו' ביד מי וכו' ולישנא אחרינא מפרשין וכו' שיקנו דבריו באמירה. נ"ב וכך מפורש לקמן בדף קנ"ו ע"ב דקאמר ולא תחוש לדברי ר"א אלא חוזר בו דעתו עליו: (ג) ד"ה המוכר כו' קני לך איהו וכל: (ד) ד"ה ואפי' כו' הכתוב בו במקום: (ה) ד"ה מודה שמואל וכו' אם נתנו במתנת שכיב מרע בכולה הוה כדפסקינן: (ו) ד"ה א"ר נחמן וכו' דאין קנין מועיל בבריא אמירה בשכיב מרע נמי לא מהניא: (ז) תוס' ד"ה המוכר וכו' דלא מחלה לה לגבי בעל ליכא קפידא ומוקי לה כר"מ: (ח) בא"ד ותימה למאן דאין וכו' איך הוא יטרוף וכו' דמכל מקום.

דּוֹמֶה שֶׁיֵּשׁ לִי בֵּן, עַכְשָׁיו שֶׁאֵין לִי בֵּן – נְכָסַי לִפְלוֹנִי; הָיָה חוֹלֶה וּמוּטָּל בַּמִּטָּה, וְאָמְרוּ לוֹ: נְכָסָיו לְמִי? אָמַר לָהֶן: דּוֹמֶה שֶׁאִשְׁתִּי מְעוּבֶּרֶת, עַכְשָׁיו שֶׁאֵין אִשְׁתִּי מְעוּבֶּרֶת – נְכָסַי לִפְלוֹנִי, וְנוֹדַע שֶׁיֵּשׁ לוֹ בֵּן אוֹ שֶׁהָיְתָה אִשְׁתּוֹ מְעוּבֶּרֶת – [א]אֵין מַתְּנָתוֹ מַתָּנָה; לֵימָא, ר' שִׁמְעוֹן בֶּן מְנַסְיָא הִיא וְלָא רַבָּנַן? אֲפִי' תֵּימָא רַבָּנַן, "דּוֹמֶה" שָׁאנֵי. וּדְקָאָרֵי לָהּ מַאי קָאָרֵי לָהּ? מַהוּ דְּתֵימָא: צַעֲרֵיהּ הוּא דְּקָא מְדַבֵּר, קָא מַשְׁמַע לָן. א"ר זֵירָא אָמַר רַב: מִנַּיִן לְמַתְּנַת שְׁכִיב מְרַע שֶׁהִיא מִן הַתּוֹרָה? (במדבר כז) שֶׁנֶּאֱמַר: °"וְהַעֲבַרְתֶּם אֶת נַחֲלָתוֹ לְבִתּוֹ", יֵשׁ לְךָ הַעֲבָרָה אַחֶרֶת שֶׁהִיא כָּזוֹ, וְאֵי זוֹ? זוֹ מַתְּנַת שְׁכִיב מְרַע. רַב נַחְמָן אָמַר רַבָּה בַּר אֲבוּהּ, מֵהָכָא: (שם) °"וּנְתַתֶּם אֶת נַחֲלָתוֹ לְאֶחָיו", יֵשׁ לְךָ נְתִינָה אַחֶרֶת שֶׁהִיא כָּזוֹ, וְאֵי זוֹ? זוֹ מַתְּנַת שְׁכִיב מְרַע. וְרַב נַחְמָן, מַאי טַעְמָא לָא אָמַר מִ"וְּהַעֲבַרְתֶּם"? הַהוּא מִיבְּעֵי לֵיהּ לְכִדְרַבִּי; דְּתַנְיָא, [א]רַבִּי אוֹמֵר: בְּכוּלָּן נֶאֶמְרָה בָּהֶן נְתִינָה וְכָאן נֶאֶמְרָה הַעֲבָרָה, אֵין לְךָ שֶׁמַּעֲבִיר נַחֲלָה מִשֵּׁבֶט לְשֵׁבֶט אֶלָּא בַּת, הוֹאִיל וּבְנָהּ וּבַעְלָהּ יוֹרְשִׁין אוֹתָהּ. וְר' זֵירָא, מַאי טַעְמָא לָא אָמַר מִ"וּנְתַתֶּם"? אוֹרְחֵיהּ דִּקְרָא הוּא. רַב מְנַשְּׁיָא בַּר יִרְמְיָה אָמַר, מֵהָכָא: (מ"ב כ) °"בַּיָּמִים הָהֵם חָלָה חִזְקִיָּהוּ לָמוּת וַיָּבֹא אֵלָיו יְשַׁעְיָהוּ בֶן אָמוֹץ הַנָּבִיא וַיֹּאמֶר אֵלָיו כֹּה אָמַר ה' צַו לְבֵיתְךָ כִּי מֵת אַתָּה וְלֹא תִחְיֶה" – בְּצַוָּאָה בְּעָלְמָא. רָמִי בַּר יְחֶזְקֵאל אָמַר, מֵהָכָא: (שמואל ב יז) °"וַאֲחִיתֹפֶל רָאָה כִּי לֹא נֶעֶשְׂתָה עֲצָתוֹ וַיַּחֲבֹשׁ אֶת הַחֲמוֹר וַיֵּלֶךְ אֶל בֵּיתוֹ אֶל עִירוֹ וַיְצַו אֶל בֵּיתוֹ וַיֵּחָנַק" – בְּצַוָּאָה בְּעָלְמָא. ת"ר, שְׁלֹשָׁה דְּבָרִים צִוָּה אֲחִיתוֹפֶל אֶת בָּנָיו: אַל תִּהְיוּ בְּמַחֲלוֹקֶת, וְאַל תִּמְרְדוּ בְּמַלְכוּת בֵּית דָּוִד, וְיוֹם טוֹב שֶׁל עֲצֶרֶת בָּרוּר – זִרְעוּ חִטִּים. מָר זוּטְרָא אָמַר: בָּלוּל אִיתְּמַר. אָמְרֵי נְהַרְדְּעֵי מִשְּׁמֵיהּ דְּר' יַעֲקֹב: לֹא בָּרוּר – בָּרוּר מַמָּשׁ, וְלֹא בָּלוּל – בָּלוּל מַמָּשׁ, אֶלָּא אֲפִילּוּ בָּלוּל וְרוּחַ צְפוֹנִית מְנַשַּׁבְתּוֹ – זֶה הוּא בָּרוּר. אֲמַר לֵיהּ רַבִּי אַבָּא לְרַב אָשֵׁי: אֲנַן אַדְּרַב יִצְחָק בַּר אַבְדִּימִי מַתְנִינַן לָהּ, [ב]דְּאָמַר רַב יִצְחָק בַּר אַבְדִּימִי: מוֹצָאֵי יוֹם טוֹב הָאַחֲרוֹן שֶׁל חַג הַכֹּל צוֹפִין לְעָשָׁן הַמַּעֲרָכָה, נָטָה כְּלַפֵּי צָפוֹן – עֲנִיִּים שְׂמֵחִים וּבַעֲלֵי בָתִּים עֲצֵבִין, מִפְּנֵי שֶׁגִּשְׁמֵי שָׁנָה מְרוּבִּין וּפֵירוֹת מַרְקִיבִין; נָטָה כְּלַפֵּי דָּרוֹם – עֲנִיִּים עֲצֵבִים וּבַעֲלֵי בָתִּים שְׂמֵחִין, מִפְּנֵי שֶׁגִּשְׁמֵי שָׁנָה מוּעָטִין וּפֵירוֹת מִשְׁתַּמְּרִין; נָטָה כְּלַפֵּי מִזְרָח – הַכֹּל שְׂמֵחִין; כְּלַפֵּי מַעֲרָב – הַכֹּל עֲצֵבִין. וּרְמִינְהִי: מִזְרָחִית – לְעוֹלָם יָפָה, מַעֲרָבִית – לְעוֹלָם קָשָׁה, רוּחַ צְפוֹנִית – יָפָה לַחִטִּים בְּשָׁעָה שֶׁהֵבִיאוּ שְׁלִישׁ, וְקָשָׁה לַזֵּיתִים בְּשָׁעָה שֶׁיָּנִיצוּ, וְרוּחַ דְּרוֹמִית – קָשָׁה לַחִטִּין בְּשָׁעָה שֶׁהֵבִיאוּ שְׁלִישׁ, וְיָפָה לַזֵּיתִים בְּשָׁעָה שֶׁיָּנִיצוּ; וְאָמַר רַב יוֹסֵף, וְאִיתֵּימָא מָר זוּטְרָא, וְאִיתֵּימָא רַב נַחְמָן בַּר יִצְחָק, [ג]וְסִימָנָךְ: שֻׁלְחָן בַּצָּפוֹן וּמְנוֹרָה בַּדָּרוֹם, הַאי מְרַבֵּי דִּידֵיהּ וְהַאי מְרַבֵּי דִּידֵיהּ! לָא קַשְׁיָא: [ד]הָא לָן וְהָא לְהוּ. תַּנְיָא, אַבָּא שָׁאוּל אוֹמֵר: יוֹם טוֹב שֶׁל עֲצֶרֶת בָּרוּר – סִימָן יָפֶה לְכָל הַשָּׁנָה כּוּלָּהּ. אֲמַר רַב זְבִיד: הַאי יוֹמָא קַמָּא דְּרֵישׁ שַׁתָּא, אִי חֲמִים – כּוּלָּהּ שַׁתָּא חֲמִימָא, אִי קְרִיר – כּוּלָּהּ שַׁתָּא קְרִירָא. לְמַאי נָפְקָא מִינָּהּ?

לתפלתו

רשב"ם

דומה. כלומר, כמדומה הייתי שיש לי בן, עכשיו שנודע לי שאין לי בן. אין מתנתו מתנה. דאילו היה יודע שיש לו בן, או שאשתו מעוברת – לא היה נותן. דלמא צעריה קמדבר. ולא תלה טעם מתנתו במיתת בנו, אלא כמתאונן על בנו שמת. ולפי שבן ראוי לירש נכסי אביו, וזה אין לו בן לירש, ומתוך כך נזכר לצער מיתת בנו בשעת חילוק נכסיו. וליכא אומדן דעתיה כל כך, דאיכא למימר רבי שמעון בן מנסיא היא ולא רבנן, דליכא הכא אומדן דמוכח כל כך, קמ"ל דדוקא קאמר, וכדמפרש ותולה מתנתו במיתת בנו דמי, ודברי הכל היא. מנין למתנת שכיב מרע. שקונה בדבור בלא קנין סודר. כגון מצוה מחמת מיתה, דפסקינן לקמן (דף קנא:) דלא בעי קנין אפילו במקצת והוא דמית. אי נמי, שכיב מרע שחלק כל נכסיו בלא שיור, ומית. שנאמר והעברתם את נחלתו. דהוה מצי למכתב: איש כי ימות ובן אין לו – נחלתו לבתו וכו', "והעברתם" יתירא הוא. ורבינו חננאל פי': מדכתיב "את נחלתו" "את" רבויא הוא. ולא נהירא, דהא אמרינן לקמן: ההיא מיבעי ליה לכדתניא ר' אומר כו', (א) "והעברתם" דריש ולא דריש "את", אלמא לעיל נמי דריש אידך מלשון העברה. ואית דמפרשי: מדשני קרא בדבוריה, דמצי למכתב "ונתתם" כדכתיב באידך. ולא נהירא נמי האי לישנא, דהא "ונתתם" נמי חשבינן מיותר באותה סוגיא, דהכי הוה ליה למכתב: איש כי ימות ובן אין לו נחלתו לבתו, ואם אין לו בת נחלתו לאחיו. וכן כולם. הלכך כל "והעברתם" "ונתתם" מיותרים הם, כן נראה בעיני. שהיא כזו. *ברשות [נ"א כירושת] הבת, שהיא בלא קנין. ונתתם את נחלתו כו'. קרא יתירא הוא, דמצי למכתב: ואם אין לו בת (ונתתם) נחלתו לאחיו, וכן כולן. הואיל ובנה או בעלה. שהן משבט אחר, יורשין אותה. והכי אתא קרא לאשמועינן: והעברתם את נחלתו משבטו – על ידי בתו שתירשנו, ושמא תינשא אחרי כן לאיש משבט אחר, ותמות ויירשנה. צו לביתך. אלמא צוואת שכיב מרע בעלמא קונה. שלשה דברים צוה אחיתופל. הכי הוה קים להו. ואל תמרדו במלכות בית דוד. שלא אירע לו יפה. ויום טוב של עצרת. דהיינו שבועות, אם תראהו ברור – נאה, ולא יום המעונן – זרעו חטים, שמצליחין באותה שנה. "כעצם השמים לטוהר" (שמות כד) מתרגמי': לבְרירו. בלול. מעורב, יום המעונן. ורוח צפונית מנשבת בו. שמפזרת את העבים, כדכתיב (איוב לז): "מצפון זהב יאתה" – רוח צפונית מאיר את היום כזהב. אנן אדרב יצחק בר אבדימי מתנינן לה. סימני תבואות אם יצליחו אם לאו – אדרב יצחק סמכינן, ולא אסימני עצרת, בשביל שבחג נידונין על המים. כלפי צפון. רוח דרומית מנשבת בו ומטהו כלפי צפון. ופירותיהן מרקיבין. ומתוך שאינן יכולין להשמר – נמכרין בזול. כלפי דרום. רוח צפון מנשבת בו. מפני שגשמי שנה מועטין. ובאותם הגשמים מתברכין הפירות הנזרעין, ושאוצרות משתמרין ונמכרין ביוקר – הרי ריוח לעשירים ועצב לעניים. למזרח כולן שמחים. שמערבית ממטרת כמדה, ופירות אינן ביוקר. כולן עצבין. שמזרחית מונעת מטר ומביאה בצורת ויוקר גדול, ופירות קרקע אינן לוקחים. אלמא מזרחית קשה ומערבית יפה. ורמינהי. מהך ברייתא דקתני איפכא. בשעה שהביאו שליש. דאין צריכין למטר. שולחן בצפון. כדכתיב (שמות כו): "והשלחן תתן על צלע צפון", והמנורה בדרום כדכתיב (שם): "ואת המנורה נכח השלחן". האי מרבי דידיה כו'. כל אחד מגדל את שלו; לחם חטין על השלחן בצפון – וצפונית יפה לחטים, שמן זית מדליקין במנורה שבדרום – ודרומית יפה לזיתים. הא לן. לבני בבל השוכנים במצולה, וארצנו מלוחלחת ואינה צריכה למטר כל כך – לדידן מיתנייא ברייתא בתרייתא שמערבית קשה, לפי שממטרת יותר מדאי לבני בבל, ומזרחית יפה. וברייתא קמייתא דמתנייא איפכא – להו, לבני א"י שארצם גבוהה, וצריכין למטר הרבה. כולה שתא חמימא. כלומר, רוב השנה.

לתפלתו

תוספות

מנין למתנת שכיב מרע שהיא מן התורה כו'. לאו מן התורה דוקא קאמר, דהא רב נחמן גופיה אית ליה לקמן דאינה כשל תורה ועשאוה כשל תורה, אלא אסמכתא בעלמא הוא דקאמר. והא דקאמר: מאי טעמא לא אמר מ"והעברתם" — הכי פי': מאי טעמא לא מפיק אסמכתא דידיה מן "והעברתם". וכי האי גוונא איכא בפרק קמא דמועד קטן (דף ה.) גבי ציון שהוא מדרבנן, ופריך התם: והא ה) (מהכא נפקא) והא מיבעי ליה לכדתניא כו', ועל כרחך ציון מדרבנן היא, כדאמר בפ' "דם הנדה" (נדה נז.).

הכל צופין לעשן המערכה כו'. בפרק קמא דיומא (דף כא:) פריך לה מדתנן: לא נצחה הרוח עשן המערכה. ומשני לה שפיר.

לא קשיא הא לן והא להו. פי' רבינו שמואל: דרוח מזרחית מונעת את המטר. וקשה: דאמר לעיל בפרק "לא יחפור" (דף כה:): "ורחב מים במולק" — זו רוח מזרחית, משמע שמביאה מים! על כן נראה לפרש דמביאה מים, אלא שבא"י יפה ובבבל קשה, שהארץ מלוחלחת מליאה מים. ומה שפי' כלפי מערב הכל עצבין לפי שמזרחית מונעת מטר — לא היה לו לפרש כן. אלא, לפי שמביאה מים יותר מדאי.

לתפלתו

עין משפט נר מצוה

סט א מיי' פ"ח מהלכות זכייה ומתנה הלכה ז סמג עשין פב טוש"ע ח"מ סי' רנג סעיף ה:

מסורת הש"ס

א) לעיל קמ: ב) יומא כא: ג) לעיל כה: מנחות פו: ד) [ברכות נ:] ה) [צ"ל להכי הוה לאחיו] ו) ועי' תוס' סוטה לב: סד"ה ורכיב:

הגהות הב"ח

(א) רשב"ם ד"ה שנאמר והעברתם וכו' ר' אומר כו' והתם והעברתם דריש:

רבינו גרשום

בתר אומדנא והאי דקאמר כתבו דלכתבו ויתנו לה ולאו משום מוכחא מלתא כי התם: אמר להם דומה שיש לי בן. במדינת הים שיירשני ועכשיו שאין לי שמת נכסי לפלוני: לימא ר' שמעון בן מנסיא היא. דאזיל בתר אומדנא משום הכי אין מתנתו מתנה הכי נמי אומדן דעתו הוא (שאילו היה יודע) שאילו היה לו בן לא היה נותנו לו ולהכי אין מתנתו מתנה: ולא רבנן. דפליגי עליה דר' שמעון בן מנסיא: אפי' תימא רבנן. אע"ג דאמרו לעיל מתנתו מתנה הכא מודו דאין מתנתו מתנה דשאני התם דקאמר דומה. כלומר דומה לי עד עכשיו שיש לי בן ועכשיו שאתם שואלין נכסי למי לדבריכם כמדומה שאין בן ועכשיו אם כן הוא נכסי לפלוני. והואיל דלא שמע בפירוש שמת [אלא] לפי דבריהן אמר נכסי לפלוני. לא עקר נכסיו מבנו דלא הקנה לפלוני אלא לפי דבריהם להכי אין מתנתו מתנה. אבל הכא דשמע בפירוש שמת ומעצמו כתבן לו יש לומר ודאי מתנתו מתנה דיש לומר קודם לכן גמר בדעתו ליתנם לזה. אבל הכא דקאמר דומה לא נראה שבדעתו היה ליתנם לו קודם לכן ולא מסיק א) ולא גמר: ודקארי לה. דקאמר ולא רבנן: מאי קארי לה. וכי לא היה יודע להיכא דקאמר דומה שאני דאפי' רבנן מודו דלא הויא מתנה. לעולם אימא לך כדמעיקרא דרבי שמעון ולא רבנן דלא שאני הכא דקאמר דומה דהא דקאמר דומה לאו משום דלא מקני ליה דודאי היה יודע דלית ליה בן וגמר ומקני ליה והאי דקאמר הכי דומה צעריה הוא דקא מדכר. כלומר כמדומה הייתי שכשאצא מן העולם שהייתי מניח בן שיירשני ועכשיו שגרם עון שהוא יודע שאין לו בן נכסי לפלוני ולא לפי דבריהן קאמר ולהכי אין מתנתו מתנה דאזלינן בתר אומדנא שאילו היה יודע שהיה לו בן לא היה נותן ור' שמעון היא ולא רבנן כדאמרי' מעיקרא ולהכי קארי לה. ולא היא לא אמרינן צעריה מדכר אלא שאני היכא דקאמר דומה ואפי' רבנן היא: מנין למתנת שכיב מרע שהיא מן התורה. דבלא קנין וכתיבה ומשיכה קנה בדבור בעלמא: שנאמר והעברתם את נחלתו לבתו. דאיבעי ליה למימר ונתתם את נחלתו כדכתב באידך אלא מאי קמ"ל הא קמ"ל דיש לך העברה אחרת לאינש דעלמא שהיא כזו כלומר והעברתם יורשת באמירה בעלמא ומעברת לנחלה משאר קרובים בלא קנין וכתיבה ולא משיכה ה"נ מתנת שכיב מרע דאפי' במקום בת ובן רשאי ליתן מתנה לאחר באמירה בעלמא: ונתתם את נחלתו לאחיו. דמצי למימר ותהיה נחלתו: שהיא כזאת. כי היכי דהא סגי באמירה לזה כך ולזה כך ה"נ שכיב מרע באמירה סגיא אפי' במקום אחים: אורחיה דקרא הוא. דקאמר ונתתם דבלאו הכי אי אפשר ולא אתי לדרשא: צו לביתך. בצואה בדבור בעלמא: אל תמרדו במלכות בית דוד. שלא אירע לו יפה: של עצרת. של שבועות: ברור. שאינו יום מעונן: זרעו חטין. אותה שנה שמצליחין: בלול אתמר. כלומר יום מעונן: ורוח צפונית מנשבת בו. שמפזרת את העבים ושותה המטר הרי זה ברור ואותה שנה מצליחין החטין: אמר ליה ר' אבא לרב אשי. אותו סימן של שנה שאתם שונין בעצרת של שבועות אינו סימן. ב) של גשמי שנה בדר' יצחק מתנינן לה דאמר מוצאי יו"ט האחרון צופין לעשן המערכה. נטה תמרתו כלפי צפון דרוח דרומית מדחה אותו כלפי צפון קשה לחטים: עניים שמחים. כלומר משום שלא יכולין העשירים לאצר פירותיהן מפני שמרקיבין ונותנין אותו בזול לעניים: נטה כלפי דרום. שרוח צפונית שכנגדו מדחה אותו שהוא יפה לחטים כדאמר באידך ברייתא דלקמן: פירותיהן משתמרין. שלא ירקבו: נטה למזרח. שרוח מערבית יפה לחטין מדחה אותו כולם שמחין. מפני שגשמי שנה מרובין ויהיה שובע גדול ופירותיהן משתמרין שלא ירקבו: למערב כולן עצבין. מפני שרוח מזרחית שקשה לחטים מנשבת בו יהי' גשמי שנה ג)מועטים ופירותיהן מרקיבים: מדקתני כולן שמחים אלמא דרוח מערבית מנשבת בו ויפה להן ומדקתני נמי למערב כולן עצבי' אלמא דרוח מזרחית מנשבת בו דקשה היא. ורמינהי רוח מזרחית לעולם יפה מערבית לעולם קשה. אלמא דאיפכא מסתברא וקשיין אהדדי: רוח צפונית יפה לחטין. וקשיא לעיל דאמר נוטה כלפי דרום עניים עצבין דהתבואה מועטת ומשתמרת: רוח דרומית קשה לחטים. וקשיא לעיל דאמר נוטה כלפי צפון עניים שמחים דהתבואה מרובה ומרקיבין: שולחן בצפון. דרוח צפונית יפה לחטין שעושין מהן לחם הפנים שמניחים על השולחן: ומנורה בדרום. דרוח דרומית יפה לזיתים שמשמן זית עושים נרות: רוח צפון שהשולחן שם מרבה חטים. ורוח דרומית שהמנורה שם מרבה זיתים: לא קשיא הא לן. לבני בבל דיתבי במצולה דלא צריכי מים הוי כדקתני בברייתא שניה ורוח מזרחית שאינה (מנשבת) [מגשמת] כל כך יפה להם ורוח מערבית שהגשמים מרובין קשה להן: והא דקתני בברייתא ראשונה יפה להן שא"י גבוהה מכל הארצות ויבישה היא להכי נוטה למזרח כולן שמחין שרוח מערבית שולטת שגשמין מרובין. נוטה למערב כולן עצבין לפי שרוח מזרחית שולטת שגשמים מועטין

הלכך

א) נראה דצ"ל ולא מסיק אדעתיה ולא גמר בלבו להקנות: ב) נראה דצ"ל אלא אנן סימן של גשמי שנה כדרב יצחק וכו'. ג) לשון זה צ"ע ואולי דצ"ל מפני שגשמי שנה מרובין יותר מדאי ופירותיה מרקיבים כצ"ל ועי' בתוס' ד"ה לא.

סד א טוש"ע אה"ע סי' ל סעיף ה בהגה"ה:
סה ב ג ד ה מיי' פ"ו מהל' זכייה ומתנה הלכה כא כב כג טוש"ע אה"ע סי' נ סעיף ג:
סו ו מיי' שם פ"ח הל' טו סמג עשין פב טוש"ע ח"מ סי' רנ סעיף ד:
סז ז מיי' שם הלכה יד טוש"ע שם סעיף ב:
סח ח ט י מיי' פ"ב מהל' גירושין הל' יב סמג עשין נ טוש"ע אה"ע סי' קמא סעיף טז:

אֲמַרָה לֵיהּ: (א) מַן יָהֵיב לָן מִכּוֹתָבוֹת דִּירִיחוֹ וְאָכַלְנָא בֵּיהּ! נְפַל עֲלָהּ חוּרְבָּה וּמֵתָה; אָמְרוּ חֲכָמִים: אהוֹאִיל וְלֹא נִכְנַס אַחֲרֶיהָ אֶלָּא לְבוֹדְקָהּ, מֵתָה — אֵינוֹ יוֹרְשָׁהּ. § "סִבְלוֹנוֹת מוּעָטִין שֶׁתִּשְׁתַּמֵּשׁ בָּהֶן בְּבֵית אָבִיהָ" וכו'. § יָתֵיב רָבִין סָבָא קַמֵּיהּ דְּרַב פַּפָּא וְיָתֵיב וְקָאָמַר: בבֵּין שֶׁמֵּתָה הִיא וּבֵין שֶׁמֵּת הוּא, הֲדַר הוּא — סִבְלוֹנוֹת הָדְרִי, מַאֲכָל וּמִשְׁתֶּה לָא הָדַר; גהֲדָרָא בָּהּ אִיהִי — הָדְרָא אֲפִילּוּ כִּישָּׁא דְּיַרְקָא. אֲמַר רַב הוּנָא בְּרֵיהּ דְּרַב יְהוֹשֻׁעַ: דוְשָׁמִין *לָהֶן דְּמֵי בָּשָׂר בְּזוֹל. עַד כַּמָּה בְּזוֹל? העַד תִּילְתָּא. §

מתני' *ושְׁכִיב מְרַע שֶׁכָּתַב כָּל נְכָסָיו לַאֲחֵרִים *וְשִׁיֵּיר קַרְקַע כָּל שֶׁהוּא — מַתְּנָתוֹ קַיֶּימֶת, זלֹא שִׁיֵּיר קַרְקַע כָּל שֶׁהוּא — אֵין מַתְּנָתוֹ קַיֶּימֶת. §

גמ' מַאן תַּנָּא דְּאָזְלִינַן בָּתַר אוּמְדָּנָא? אֲמַר רַב נַחְמָן: רַבִּי שִׁמְעוֹן בֶּן מְנַסְיָא הִיא; דְּתַנְיָא: *הֲרֵי שֶׁהָלַךְ בְּנוֹ לִמְדִינַת הַיָּם, וְשָׁמַע שֶׁמֵּת בְּנוֹ וְעָמַד וְכָתַב כָּל נְכָסָיו לְאַחֵר, וְאַחַר כָּךְ בָּא בְּנוֹ — מַתְּנָתוֹ מַתָּנָה; רַבִּי שִׁמְעוֹן בֶּן מְנַסְיָא אוֹמֵר: אֵין מַתְּנָתוֹ מַתָּנָה, *(שֶׁאִלְמָלֵא) הָיָה יוֹדֵעַ שֶׁבְּנוֹ קַיָּים — לֹא הָיָה כּוֹתְבָן. רַב שֵׁשֶׁת אֲמַר: ר' שִׁמְעוֹן שְׁזוּרִי הִיא; *דְּתַנְיָא, *בָּרִאשׁוֹנָה הָיוּ אוֹמְרִים: חהַיּוֹצֵא בְּקוֹלָר וְאָמַר "כִּתְבוּ גֵּט לְאִשְׁתִּי" — הֲרֵי אֵלּוּ יִכְתְּבוּ וְיִתְּנוּ. חָזְרוּ לוֹמַר: טאַף הַמְפָרֵשׁ וְהַיּוֹצֵא בְּשַׁיָּירָא; רַבִּי שִׁמְעוֹן שְׁזוּרִי אוֹמֵר: יאַף הַמְסוּכָּן. וְרַב נַחְמָן מַאי טַעֲמָא לָא מוֹקִים לָהּ כְּרַבִּי שִׁמְעוֹן שְׁזוּרִי? שָׁאנֵי הָתָם, דַּאֲמַר "כִּתְבוּ". וְרַב שֵׁשֶׁת מ"ט לָא מוֹקִים לָהּ כְּרַבִּי שִׁמְעוֹן בֶּן מְנַסְיָא? אוּמְדָּנָא דְּמוּכָח שָׁאנֵי. מַאן תַּנָּא לְהָא דְּתָנוּ רַבָּנַן: *הֲרֵי שֶׁהָיָה חוֹלֶה וּמוּטָּל בְּמִטָּה, וְאָמְרוּ לוֹ: נְכָסֶיךָ לְמִי? וְאָמַר לָהֶן:

דּוֹמֶה

רש"י

אֲמָרָה לֵיהּ. דֶּרֶךְ שְׂחוֹק. מַאן יָהֵיב לָן מִכּוֹתָבוֹת דִּירִיחוֹ. שֶׁהֵן מְתוּקִים, וְנֶאֱכַל עִם הַצְּנוֹן שֶׁהוּא חַד. שֶׁכֵּן הָיָה דַּרְכָּן לֶאֱכוֹל תְּמָרִים עִם הַצְּנוֹן, שֶׁזֶּה חַד וְזֶה מָתוֹק, וּמְתַקֵּן זֶה אֶת זֶה. וּלְפִי שֶׁהֵבִינָה שֶׁלְּנַסּוֹתָהּ נִתְכַּוֵּין הֱשִׁיבַתּוּ דֶּרֶךְ שְׂחוֹק כָּךְ. וְלִלִּישָּׁנָא דְּאָמְרִי' שֶׁנָּטַל עִמּוֹ כּוֹתֶבֶת, אָמְרָה: כּוֹתָבוֹת דִּירִיחוֹ אֲנִי מֵרִיחַ, וְלֹא לְגוֹן. יְרִיחוֹ נִקְרֵאת עִיר הַתְּמָרִים, וְהַיְינוּ כּוֹתָבוֹת. נָפְלָה עָלֶיהָ חוּרְבָּה וּמֵתָה. וּבָא הַבַּעַל לִפְנֵי ב"ד וְהָיָה רוֹצֶה לִירַשׁ אֶת אִשְׁתּוֹ. וְאָמְרוּ חֲכָמִים: הוֹאִיל וְלֹא נִכְנַס עִמָּהּ לָבֹא עָלֶיהָ, אֶלָּא לְבוֹדְקָהּ וּלְגָרְשָׁהּ, וּמֵתָה בְּתוֹךְ כָּךְ – אֵינוֹ יוֹרְשָׁהּ. אִית דְּגָרְסִי הָכִי, וּמוֹקֵי לָהּ בַּאֲרוּסָה. וְלָא נְהִירָא לִי, דַּאֲפִילּוּ בָּא עָלֶיהָ בִּימֵי אֵירוּסִין קוֹדֶם הַכְנָסָתָהּ לַחוּפָּה – לָא יָרֵית לָהּ, כִּדְתָנֵי *חָנָן בַּר אַמִּי: אִשְׁתּוֹ אֲרוּסָה לֹא אוֹנֵן כו', מֵתָה אֵינוֹ יוֹרְשָׁהּ, דְּאֵין הַבַּעַל יוֹרֵשׁ אֶת אִשְׁתּוֹ עַד שֶׁתִּכָּנֵס לַחוּפָּה, כִּדְנָפְקָא לָן (לעיל דף קט:) יְרוּשַּׁת הַבַּעַל מִ"שְּׁאֵרוֹ הַקָּרוֹב אֵלָיו מִמִּשְׁפַּחְתּוֹ וְיָרַשׁ אוֹתָהּ" – דְּהַיְינוּ לְאַחַר שֶׁנִּכְנְסָה לַחוּפָּה. הִלְכָּךְ בִּנְשׂוּאָה מוֹקְמִינַן לָהּ, וְהָכִי גָּרְסִי': וְאָמְרוּ חֲכָמִים הוֹאִיל וְנִכְנַס אַחֲרֶיהָ לְבוֹדְקָהּ, מֵתָה אֵינוֹ יוֹרְשָׁהּ. דְּכֵיוָן דְּהָיָה בְּדַעְתּוֹ לְגָרְשָׁהּ אִם יִמְצָאֶנָּה בַּעֲלַת מוּם, וּבְתוֹךְ כָּךְ מֵתָה קוֹדֶם שֶׁנִּתְפַּיְּיסוּ – אֵינוֹ זוֹכֶה בִּירוּשָּׁהּ. וּמֵהָכָא שָׁמְעִינַן מִי שֶׁמֵּתָה אִשְׁתּוֹ מִתּוֹךְ קְטָטָה, שֶׁיֵּשׁ בְּדַעְתּוֹ לְגָרְשָׁהּ – שׁוּב אֵינוֹ יוֹרְשָׁהּ, כִּדְאָמְרִי' בְּמַסֶּ' גִּיטִּין (דף יח.): מִשֶּׁנָּתַן עֵינָיו לְגָרְשָׁהּ שׁוּב אֵין לַבַּעַל פֵּירוֹת. וְיָתֵיב וְקָאָמַר בֵּין שֶׁמֵּת הוּא בֵּין שֶׁמֵּתָה הִיא וַהֲדַר בָּהּ. אִיהוּ, וּמְגָרֵשׁ לָהּ. סִבְלוֹנוֹת הָדְרִי. כְּגוֹן סִבְלוֹנוֹת שֶׁאֵין עֲשׂוּיִן לִיבָּלוֹת, שֶׁשָּׁלַח סְתָם. אֲבָל אוֹכְלָא וּמִשְׁתְּיָא שֶׁשָּׁלַח בְּבֵית חָמִיו – לָא הָדְרִי מִסְתָּמָא, אִם אָכַל מִסְּעוּדַת חָתָן שָׁם בְּדִינָר, דְּהַיְינוּ עֲשׂוּיִן לִיבָּלוֹת, הִלְכָּךְ מְחוּלִּין כִּדְתַנְיָא לְעֵיל.* אֲבָל אִם פֵּירֵשׁ "עַל מְנָת שֶׁיַּחְזְרוּ לִי" – הָדְרִי, לָא שְׁנָא סִבְלוֹנוֹת מְרוּבִּין וְלָא שְׁנָא סִבְלוֹנוֹת מוּעָטִין, כִּדְמְפָ' בְּמַתְנִי'. אֲבָל אִי הָדְרָא בָּהּ אִיהִי – אֲפִי' כִּישָּׁא דִּירְקָא הָדְרָא – אֲגוּדָּה שֶׁל יָרָק. אֲבָל קִדּוּשִׁין לָא הָדְרִי, כִּדְאָמְרִי' לְעֵיל: גְּזֵירָה שֶׁמָּא יֹאמְרוּ כו'. וְשָׁמִין לָהֶן הַבָּשָׂר בְּזוֹל. כְּשֶׁיַּחְזְרוּ לוֹ אוֹכֶל וּמַשְׁקֶה שֶׁהֶאֱכִילָם וְהִשְׁקָם – יְשׁוּמוּ בְּזוֹל, כִּדְמְפָ' לְקַמֵּיהּ, לִפְחוֹת שְׁלִישׁ מִדָּמָיו. שֶׁבְּעִנְיָן זֶה שָׁמִין כָּל מַחֲזִירִין אוֹכָלִים הַנֶּאֱכָלִים מִתְּחִלָּה שֶׁלֹּא לְדַעַת חֲזָרָה, שֶׁאִילּוּ הָיָה יוֹדֵעַ שֶׁצָּרִיךְ לְהַחֲזִיר לֹא הָיָה אוֹכֵל מִשֶּׁלּוֹ. וּמִיהוּ, בְּזוֹל מִיהָא מַחֲזִיר. וְה"נ אָמְרוּ (ב"ק דף כ.) גַּבֵּי אָכְלָה מִתּוֹךְ הָרְחָבָה מְשַׁלֶּמֶת מַה שֶּׁנֶּהֱנֵית – דְּמֵי עָמִיר בְּזוֹל, אוֹ דְּמֵי שְׂעוֹרִים בְּזוֹל. וְכֵן (כתובות דף לד:) גַּבֵּי הִנִּיחַ לָהֶם אֲבִיהֶם פָּרָה שְׁאוּלָה שְׁחָטוּהָ וַאֲכָלוּהָ – מְשַׁלְּמִין דְּמֵי בָשָׂר בְּזוֹל. וּמֵהָכָא פַּשְׁטִינַן לְכָל בְּזוֹל, דְּהַיְינוּ כָּל הַדָּמִים חָסֵר שְׁלִישׁ; כָּל זוּזָא חָשְׁבִינַן וְאָמְרִי' לְשַׁלּוּמֵי בְּאַרְבָּעָה דַּנְקֵי – אַרְבַּע מָעוֹת, דְּהַיְינוּ שְׁנֵי חֶלְקֵי דִּינָר. שֶׁהֲרֵי שֵׁשׁ מָעָה כֶּסֶף דִּינָר, וְדַנְקָא הִיא מָעָה. **מתני'** שְׁכִיב מְרַע שֶׁכָּתַב כָּל נְכָסָיו לַאֲחֵרִים. וְה"ה אִם חִילֵּק עַל פִּיו בְּלֹא כְּתִיבָה, שֶׁאָמַר "נְכָסַיי לִפְלוֹנִי", (ב) כִּדְתַנְיָא לְקַמָּן (דף קנו:) בְּאִמָּן שֶׁל בְּנֵי רוֹכֵל שֶׁמֵּתָה, וְקִיְּימוּ חֲכָמִים אֶת דְּבָרֶיהָ. וּכְגוֹן שֶׁהָיוּ עֵדִים שֶׁהָיָה שְׁכִיב מְרַע כְּשֶׁכָּתַב אוֹ נָתַן מַתָּנָה זוֹ, אוֹ שֶׁכָּתַב בִּשְׁטָר "כַּד קְצִיר וּרְמֵי בְּעַרְסֵיהּ", כִּדְאָמְרִי' לְקַמָּן בַּגְּמָרָא. שִׁיֵּיר קַרְקַע כָּל שֶׁהוּא. כְּשִׁיעוּר הַמְפוֹרָשׁ בַּגְּמָ'. מַתְּנָתוֹ מַתָּנָה. דְּמַתְּנַת שְׁכִיב מְרַע בְּמִקְצָת, אִם עָמַד מֵחָלְיוֹ – אֵינוֹ חוֹזֵר. וּכְגוֹן שֶׁכָּתוּב בּוֹ קִנְיָן, כִּדְפַסְקִינַן לְקַמָּן בַּגְּמָרָא: וְהִלְכְתָא מַתְּנַת שְׁכִיב מְרַע בְּמִקְצָת בָּעֵי קִנְיָן, אע"ג דְּמִית. וּמְצַוֶּה מֵחֲמַת מִיתָה (ג) בְּמִקְצָת לָא בָּעֵי קִנְיָן. וְהוּא דְּמִית, [אֲבָל אִם] עָמַד – חוֹזֵר, אע"ג דְּקָנוּ מִינֵּיהּ, הוֹאִיל וּמִדַּאֲגַת מִיתָה נָוֶה מַתָּנָה זוֹ. מַתְּנָתוֹ מַתָּנָה. הוֹאִיל וְשִׁיֵּיר לְעַצְמוֹ הֲרֵי הִיא כְּמַתְּנַת בָּרִיא. הִלְכָּךְ, בֵּין עוֹמֵד מֵחָלְיוֹ בֵּין מֵת – מַתְּנָתוֹ קַיֶּימֶת, דְּשֶׁלֹּא מִדַּאֲגַת מִיתָה נָתַן. **לא** שִׁיֵּיר קַרְקַע כָּל שֶׁהוּא אֵין מַתְּנָתוֹ מַתָּנָה. וְאִם עָמַד – חוֹזֵר, אֲפִי' קָנוּ מִיָּדוֹ. שֶׁנִּרְאִין הַדְּבָרִים שֶׁמֵּחֲמַת מִיתָה נָתַן, וע"מ שֶׁאִם לֹא יָמוּת לֹא יִתְקַיֵּים מַתָּנָה. דְּמִדְּלָא שִׁיֵּיר מִידֵּי, אָמְרִי' (ד) לָאו אַדַּעְתָּא דְּהָכִי יָהֵב לֵיהּ, שֶׁאִם יַעֲמוֹד מֵחָלְיוֹ יָמוּת בָּרָעָב וְיִצְטָרֵךְ לַבְּרִיּוֹת. אֲבָל אִם מֵת מִיהָא מַתְּנָתוֹ מַתָּנָה, בֵּין שִׁיֵּיר בֵּין לֹא שִׁיֵּיר, כִּדְמוּכַח בַּגְּמָ': אָמַר רַב נַחְמָן שְׁכִיב מְרַע שֶׁכָּתַב כָּל נְכָסָיו לַאֲחֵרִים, רוֹאִין; אִם כִּמְחַלֵּק מֵת קָנוּ כּוּלָּן כו'. וַאֲפִי' לֹא קָנוּ מִיָּדוֹ – קָנוּ כָּל הַנְּכָסִים לְאַחַר מִיתָתוֹ הֵיכָא דְּלָא שִׁיֵּיר מִידֵּי, דְּדִבְרֵי שְׁכִיב מְרַע כִּכְתוּבִין וְכִמְסוּרִין דָּמוּ. וְטַעֲמָא מְפָרֵשׁ בַּגְּמָ'. וְדַוְקָא שְׁכִיב מְרַע שֶׁכָּתַב כָּל נְכָסָיו סְתָם וְלֹא נָוֶה מֵחֲמַת מִיתָה, וְלֹא הִזְכִּיר דִּבְרֵי מִיתָה בִּשְׁעַת צַוָּאָה. אֲבָל מְצַוֶּה מֵחֲמַת מִיתָה, אֲפִי' שִׁיֵּיר קַרְקַע כָּל שֶׁהוּא וְקָנוּ מִינֵּיהּ – אֵין מַתְּנָתוֹ מַתָּנָה, אֶלָּא אִם עָמַד – חוֹזֵר, כִּדְפַסְקִינַן לְקַמָּן בַּגְּמָרָא, וּכְדְפָרֵישִׁית. **גמ'** מַאן תַּנָּא. דִּסְבִירָא לֵיהּ דְּאָזְלִינַן בָּתַר אוּמְדָּנָא דְּדַעְתָּא דְּנוֹתֵן מַתָּנָה, אע"פ שֶׁלֹּא פֵּירֵשׁ – כְּמִי שֶׁפֵּירֵשׁ דָּמֵי? דְּקָתָנֵי: הֵיכָא דְּלָא שִׁיֵּיר קַרְקַע כָּל שֶׁהוּא אָמְדִינַן דַּעְתֵּיהּ שֶׁנִּתְיָיאֵשׁ מִן הַחַיִּים, וּלְהָכִי לָא שִׁיֵּיר, וְאַדַּעְתָּא דְּהָכִי יָהֵב, שֶׁאִם יָמוּת – תִּתְקַיֵּים הַמַּתָּנָה, וְאִם יַעֲמוֹד – תַּחֲזוֹר לוֹ, וְלֹא תִּתְקַיֵּים הַמַּתָּנָה. וְעָמַד וְכָתַב נְכָסָיו לַאֲחֵרִים. כְּשֶׁשָּׁמַע שֶׁמֵּת בְּנוֹ, אַף לֹא פֵּירֵשׁ שֶׁבִּשְׁבִיל מִיתַת בְּנוֹ הוּא עוֹשֶׂה, אֶלָּא סְתָם נָתַן. מַתְּנָתוֹ מַתָּנָה. אַחֲרֵי שֶׁלֹּא פֵּירֵשׁ וְתָלָה בְּמִיתַת בְּנוֹ, דְּלָא אָזְלִינַן בָּתַר אוּמְדַּן דַּעְתֵּיהּ. וּמַתְנִי' ר"ש בֶּן מְנַסְיָא הִיא, דְּקָתָנֵי (ה) הָכָא: לֹא שִׁיֵּיר – אֵין מַתְּנָתוֹ מַתָּנָה, דְּאָמְדִינַן דַּעְתֵּיהּ שֶׁאִילּוּ הָיָה יוֹדֵעַ שֶׁיַּעֲמוֹד מֵחוֹלִי זֶה לֹא הָיָה נוֹתֵן כָּל נְכָסָיו. הַיּוֹצֵא בְּקוֹלָר. לֵיהָרֵג, וְאֵין דַּעְתּוֹ מְיוּשֶּׁבֶת עָלָיו כָּל כָּךְ, וּכְשֶׁאָמַר "כִּתְבוּ" – ע"מ לָתֵת לְאִשְׁתּוֹ אָמַר, אֶלָּא מִתּוֹךְ טִרְדּוֹ וְדַאֲגָתוֹ שָׁכַח וְלֹא אָמַר "תְּנוּ". הַמְפָרֵשׁ. מִיַּבָּשָׁה לַיָּם. **אַף** הַמְסוּכָּן. קָרוֹב לְמִיתָה, שֶׁדַּעְתּוֹ שֶׁיִּכְתְּבוּ וְיִתְּנוּ, דִּלְפְטוֹר אֶת אִשְׁתּוֹ מִן הַיִּיבּוּם נִתְכַּוֵּין. **שָׁאנֵי** הָתָם דְּאָמַר כִּתְבוּ. גַּלֵּי דַּעְתֵּיהּ שֶׁרוֹצֶה לָתֵת גֵּט, דְּאִי לָאו לְגָרְשָׁהּ – כְּתִיבַת גֵּט מַה צּוֹרֶךְ? **אוּמְדָּנָא** דְּמוּכָח שָׁאנֵי. שֶׁכָּל זְמַן שֶׁהָיָה בְּנוֹ קַיָּים לֹא נָתַן עַד שֶׁשָּׁמַע שֶׁמֵּת. אֲבָל חוֹלֶה, כֵּיוָן דְּרוֹב חוֹלִין לְחַיִּים, וְהוּא לֹא נָוֶה מֵחֲמַת מִיתָה – לֵיכָּא אוּמְדָּנָא דְּמוּכַח כּוּלֵּי הַאי.

דּוֹמֶה

תוספות

נכנס אחריה לחורבה לבודקה. פי' רבינו יעקב: דבארוסה מיירי, (ו) ובא לראות אם היא תותרנית אם לאו, ואם אינה תותרנית — ישאנה. ואמרו חכמים: הואיל ולא נכנס אחריה אלא לבודקה, ולא לשם נישואין נכנס, ולכן אם מתה — לא יירשנה. אבל אם לא נכנס אחריה לבודקה — היה יורשה. וכגון שהחורבה שלו, כדאמר בכתובות פרק "נערה" (דף מח: ושם): לעולם היא ברשות האב, היה לו חצר בדרך ונכנסה עמו — יורשה, דחצר דידיה לנשואין. ולפירוש זה לא היתה תותרנית, אלא כותבות היו בחיקו כמו שאמרה, או היתה יודעת שצנון היה, ולכך אמרה מאן יהיב לן מכותבות לאכול עם הצנון. ורבינו שמואל פירש: שנשאה כבר ונמצאת תותרנית, שהיה בדעתו לגרשה. ומיהו קשיא, דלא הוה ליה למימר: הואיל ולא נכנס אחריה אלא לבודקה, אלא הוה ליה למימר: הואיל ונכנס אחריה לבודקה! ומה שפי' רבינו שמואל מכח הך דהכא, שאם היה בדעתו לגרשה שוב אין לו פירות — לאו ראיה היא, כדפרישית, שהרי לאו נשואה היתה. ומההיא דגיטין (דף יח.) נמי אין ראי', דהא בין ר' יוחנן ור"ל דפרק שני דגיטין (דף יז:) לא סבירא להו הכי, אלא לרבי יוחנן מוליאין פירות משעת *[נתינה, ולר"ל משעת כתיבה. ולמאי דמפרש ר"י התם] אית ליה לר"ל משעת חתימה, דהא איכא נמי בין ר' שמעון ורבנן פירי משעת כתיבה עד שעת חתימה. **מיכלא** ומשתיא לא הדרי סבלונות הדרי. מוהרי הדרי, והיינו סבלונות. ותרי גווני מוהרי, כדפי' רשב"ם לעיל. **מאן** תנא דאזיל בתר אומדנא כו'. ל"ע אי שייכא הך מילתא בדברים שבלב אינם דברים. ובפרק שני דקדושין (דף מט: ושם) הארכתי בה. **רבי** שמעון שזורי היא. וה"ה היה יכול לומר רבנן דידיה. אלא לרבי שמעון ומחלוקתו קאמר. אי נמי, משום דר' שמעון שזורי אית ליה טפי דאזלינן בתר אומדנא יותר מדרבנן דידיה, להכי נקט ר' שמעון שזורי.

מנין

רבינו גרשום

אמרה ליה אין ודאי אני מריחה כמוך: מאן יהיב לן מכותבות של יריחו. תמרים ואכילנא מיניה אותו צנון. ואמרו חכמים הואיל ונכנס אחריה לבודקה ולא לדבר אחר לא אמרינן בא עליה שוב ואשתו גמורה היא ואינו יורשה. ואיכא דאמרי נשואה היתה הואיל ונכנס אחריה לבודקה על דעת כן [נכנס] שדעתו נוטה בה לגרשה אם היא תותרנית אינו דין שיורשה הואי דגמר בלבו בחייה לגרשה ומתה לאלתר דיינינן ליה כמאן דגרשה ואינו יורשה: סבלונות הדרי. וכל תכשיטין ששלח לה כדי להביאם עמה: מאכל ומשתה. ששגר למחר מקדושין לא הדרי הואיל ואכל שם בדינר: הדרא בה היא. אע"פ שאכל שם בדינר הדר כל מאכל ומשתה ואפי' כישא דירקי אגודה של ירק: ושמין לו דמי בשר בזול. כלומר אם אכל שם אין מחזירין לו כל הבשר והמאכל כשיעור אותן דמים שהיה שוה כששילח לשם אלא כל זוז שנתן לה במאכל מחשבין ליה ד' דנקי. הזוז מחלקין לו' חלקים ד' חלקים תחזור לו וב' חלקי' מנכה לו היינו שליש מנכה: **פיסקא** שכיב מרע שכתב כל נכסיו לאחרים ושייר קרקע כל שהוא. לעצמו שלא כתב כולו אע"פ שעמד מתנתו מתנה דאמרינן הואיל ששייר קרקע אמדינן דעתיה למימר דלהכי שייר דלסמוך עילויה שיתפרנס ממנה אי קאים ולא תחזור לו עולמית מה שנתן. אבל לא שייר קרקע כלל אין מתנתו מתנה ואם עמד חוזר במה שנתן. ובתר אומדן דעתא אזלינן במתני': מאן תנא דמתני' דאזיל בתר אומדנא: רבי שמעון בן מנסיא אומר אין מתנתו מתנה. דאומדן דעת הוא. שאילו היה יודע שבנו קיים לא היה נותן ומתני' ר' שמעון בן מנסיא היא: רב ששת אמר מתני' ר' שמעון שזורי היא. דאזיל בתר אומדנא. היוצא בקולר ליהרג ואמר כתבו גט לאשתי שלא תפול ליבם אע"ג דלא אמר כתבו ותנו הרי זה יכתבו ויתנו. מה שאין כן בשאר אינש דעלמא אמר כתבו לחוד אין כותבין ונותנין משום שמא משחק הוא בה אבל זה שהוא בסכנה גמר ומקנה לה אע"ג דלא אמר תנו דהאי דלא אמר תנו משום שהיה בהול בצרתו ולא הספיק לומר תנו שהיו מוליכין אותו בקולר וכן במפרש בים שאמר כתבו והיוצא בשיירא במדבריות בארץ מרחקים שאינו יודע אם יחזור אם לאו אע"ג דלא אמר תנו יהבינן לה דגמר בדעתי' למימר ומשום טרדא לא אמר: ר' שמעון שזורי אומר אף המסוכן. שמסוכן בחליו שאין יודע אם יחיה אם לאו אם אמר כתבו כותבין ונותנין לאלתר דאזיל בתר אומדנא דהאי לא רצה לשחק בה והאי דלא אמר תנו שהוא טרוד בחליו. ר' שמעון מוסיף על ת"ק הוא ולא פליג עליה אלמא דר' שמעון שזורי אזיל בתר אומדנא. ורב נחמן דמוקי מתני' כר' שמעון בן מנסיא מ"ט לא מוקים כר' שמעון שזורי שאני התם דלאו אומדן דעת הוא אלא בפירוש גלוי דעת הוא דכיון דאמר כתבו ודאי רוצה שיתנו לה. והאי דלא אמר ותנו מרוב פחד וטרוד ולאו ארעתיה. אבל גבי ר' שמעון בן מנסיא ודאי איכא אמדות דעת שאילו היה יודע שבנו קיים לא היה כותבו. ורב ששת דמוקי כר"ש שזורי מ"ט לא מוקים לה כר"ש בן מנסיא. אמר לך רב ששת אומדנא דמוכח שאני. כלומר התם מוכחא מלתא ומפורסמת היא להיכא דשמע שמת בנו וכתב כל נכסיו לאחר ואחר כך בא בנו אין מתנתו מתנה דודאי מוכחא מלתא ולא אומדנא היא שאילו היה יודע שבנו קיים לא היה כותבן והתם שאני. אבל הכא גבי ר' שמעון שזורי דקאמר כתבו גט לאשתי דמסוכן הוא ולאו מוכחא מלתא כולי האי האי דאמר כתבו דלדעת כן אמר כתבו דליתנו דאזלינן

בתר

הגהות הב"ח

(א) גמרא מאן יהיב וכו' עליה חורבה: (ב) רשב"ם ד"ה שכיב מרע וכו' כדתנן לקמן: (ג) ד"ה מתנתו וכו' מחמת מיתה לא בעי כצ"ל ותיבת במקצת נמחק: (ד) ד"ה לא שייר וכו' אמרינן ודאי לאו אדעתא: (ה) ד"ה מתנתו וכו' דקתני היכא דלא שייר: (ו) תוס' ד"ה נכנס וכו' דבארוסה מיירי ונכנס אחריה לראות אם היא תותרנית לא ישאנה ואם אינה וכו' יורשה דסתם חצר דידיה:

[יבמות כט: ע"ש]
[כתובות לד: ב"ק ל. קיב ב"מ מב.]
[פאה פ"ג מ"ז לקמן קנ.]
לעיל קלב. [תוספתא כתובות פ"ד]
[נ"ל שאלמלי עי' תוס' מגילה כח.]
גיטין יג: סה: חולין עה: [מנחות ל: טבול יום פ"ד מ"ה]
[דף קמה.]
[תוספתא לכתובות פ"ד]
לקמן קנא:
[גי' רש"ל וגי' רש"א כתיבה ולר"ל משעת נתינה ולמאי דמפכת אית ליה]
נ"ל דתנן

*וְאָמַר ר' יְהוֹשֻׁעַ בֶּן לֵוִי: כָּל יְמֵי עָנִי רָעִים וְהָא אִיכָּא שַׁבָּתוֹת וְיָמִים טוֹבִים! *כִּדְשְׁמוּאֵל, דְּאָמַר שְׁמוּאֵל: אשִׁנּוּי וֶסֶת – תְּחִלַּת חוֹלִי. כְּתִיב בְּסֵפֶר בֶּן סִירָא: כָּל יְמֵי עָנִי רָעִים, בֶּן סִירָא אוֹמֵר: אַף לֵילוֹת. בְּשֵׁפֶל גַּגִּים גַּגּוֹ, מִמְּטַר גַּגִּים לְגַגּוֹ; בְּרוּם הָרִים כַּרְמוֹ, מֵעֲפַר כַּרְמוֹ לִכְרָמִים.§

מתני' הַשּׁוֹלֵחַ סִבְלוֹנוֹת לְבֵית חָמִיו, שָׁלַח שָׁם מֵאָה מָנֶה וְאָכַל שָׁם סְעוּדַת חָתָן אֲפִילּוּ בְּדִינָר – אֵינָן נִגְבִּין, לֹא אָכַל שָׁם סְעוּדַת חָתָן – הֲרֵי אֵלּוּ נִגְבִּין. בשָׁלַח סִבְלוֹנוֹת מְרוּבִּין שֶׁיַּחְזְרוּ עִמָּהּ לְבֵית בַּעְלָהּ – הֲרֵי אֵלּוּ נִגְבִּין, סִבְלוֹנוֹת מוּעָטִין שֶׁתִּשְׁתַּמֵּשׁ בָּהֶן בְּבֵית אָבִיהָ – אֵין נִגְבִּין.§

גמ' אָמַר רָבָא: דַּוְקָא דִּינָר, אֲבָל פָּחוֹת מִדִּינָר – לָא. פְּשִׁיטָא, דִּינָר תְּנַן! מַהוּ דְּתֵימָא, הוּא הַדִּין דַּאֲפִילּוּ פָּחוֹת מִדִּינָר, וְהַאי דְּקָתָנֵי דִּינָר – אוֹרְחָא דְּמִילְּתָא קָתָנֵי, קָא מַשְׁמַע לָן. "אָכַל" תְּנַן, שָׁתָה מַאי? הוּא תְּנַן, שְׁלוּחוֹ מַאי? "שָׁם" תְּנַן, שִׁגֵּר לוֹ מַאי? תָּא שְׁמַע, דְּאָמַר רַב יְהוּדָה אָמַר שְׁמוּאֵל: מַעֲשֶׂה בְּאָדָם אֶחָד שֶׁשִּׁגֵּר לְבֵית חָמִיו מֵאָה קְרוֹנוֹת שֶׁל כַּדֵּי יַיִן וְשֶׁל כַּדֵּי שֶׁמֶן וְשֶׁל כְּלֵי כֶּסֶף וְשֶׁל כְּלֵי זָהָב וְשֶׁל כְּלֵי מֵילַת, וְרָכַב בְּשִׂמְחָתוֹ, וְהָלַךְ וְעָמַד עַל פֶּתַח בֵּית חָמִיו, וְהוֹצִיאוּ כּוֹס שֶׁל חַמִּין וְשָׁתָה, וּמֵת. וְזוֹ הֲלָכָה הֶעֱלָה רַבִּי אַחָא שַׂר הַבִּירָה לִפְנֵי חֲכָמִים לְאוּשָׁא, וְאָמְרוּ: סִבְלוֹנוֹת הָעֲשׂוּיִן לִיבָּלוֹת – אֵין נִגְבִּין, וְשֶׁאֵין עֲשׂוּיִן לִיבָּלוֹת – נִגְבִּין; שְׁמַע מִינַּהּ אֲפִילּוּ שָׁתָה. שָׁמְעַתְּ מִינַּהּ אֲפִילּוּ פָּחוֹת מִדִּינָר? אָמַר רַב אַשִׁי: מַאן לֵימָא לָן דְּלָא שָׁחְקִי לֵיהּ מַרְגָּנִיתָא דְּשַׁוְיָא אַלְפָּא זוּזֵי וְאַשְׁקְיֵהּ? שָׁמְעַתְּ מִינַּהּ אֲפִילּוּ שִׁגְּרוּ לוֹ. דִּלְמָא כָּל פֶּתַח בֵּית חָמִיו כְּבֵית חָמִיו דָּמֵי. אִיבַּעְיָא לְהוּ: מַהוּ *שֶׁיְּשַׁלֵּשׁ? שֶׁבַח סִבְלוֹנוֹת, מַהוּ? כֵּיוָן דְּאִי אִיתְנְהוּ לְדִידֵיהּ הָדְרִי – בִּרְשׁוּתֵיהּ שְׁבוּחַ, אוֹ דִּלְמָא כֵּיוָן דְּאִי אָבְדִי אוֹ מִגַּנְבִי בָּעֵי שַׁלּוּמֵי לֵיהּ – בִּרְשׁוּתָא דִּידָהּ שְׁבוּחַ? תֵּיקוּ. בָּעֵי רָבָא: סִבְלוֹנוֹת הָעֲשׂוּיִן לִיבָּלוֹת וְלֹא בָּלוּ, מַהוּ? תָּא שְׁמַע: וְזוֹ הֲלָכָה הֶעֱלָה רַבִּי אַחָא שַׂר הַבִּירָה לִפְנֵי חֲכָמִים בְּאוּשָׁא, וְאָמְרוּ: סִבְלוֹנוֹת הָעֲשׂוּיִן לִיבָּלוֹת – אֵין נִגְבִּין, וְשֶׁאֵין עֲשׂוּיִן לִיבָּלוֹת – נִגְבִּין; מַאי לָאו אע"ג דְּלָא בָּלוּ? לָא, גדְּבָלוּ. תָּא שְׁמַע: סִבְלוֹנוֹת מוּעָטִין שֶׁתִּשְׁתַּמֵּשׁ בָּהֶן וְהִיא בְּבֵית אָבִיהָ – אֵין נִגְבִּין! תַּרְגְּמָהּ רָבָא: בְּיִיבָא וְסִבַּכְתָּא. אָמַר רַב: יְהוּדָה אָמַר רַב: מַעֲשֶׂה בְּאָדָם אֶחָד שֶׁשִּׁגֵּר לְבֵית חָמִיו יַיִן חָדָשׁ וְשֶׁמֶן חָדָשׁ וּכְלֵי פִשְׁתָּן חָדָשׁ בָּעֲצֶרֶת. מַאי קָא מַשְׁמַע לָן? אִיבָּעֵית אֵימָא: חֲשִׁיבוּתָא דְּאֶרֶץ יִשְׂרָאֵל קמ"ל; וְאִיבָּעֵית אֵימָא: דְּאִי טָעֵין – טַעֲנָתֵיהּ טַעֲנָה. אָמַר רַב יְהוּדָה אָמַר רַב: מַעֲשֶׂה בְּאָדָם אֶחָד שֶׁאָמְרוּ לוֹ אִשְׁתּוֹ תּוּתְרָנִית הִיא, וְנִכְנַס אַחֲרֶיהָ לְחוּרְבָּה לְבוֹדְקָהּ; אָמַר לָהּ: רֵיחַ צְנוֹן אֲנִי מֵרִיחַ בַּגָּלִיל, אָמְרָה

רשב"ם

וְאָמַר ר' יְהוֹשֻׁעַ בֶּן לֵוִי. כְּתִיב: "כָּל יְמֵי עָנִי רָעִים". וְהָא אִיכָּא שַׁבָּתוֹת וְיָמִים טוֹבִים, שֶׁיֵּשׁ לוֹ מָנוֹת וּמְזוֹנוֹת שֶׁהָיוּ מְחַלְּקִין לַעֲנִיִּים מֵעֶרֶב שַׁבָּת לְעֶרֶב שַׁבָּת! אֶלָּא כִּשְׁמוּאֵל אַתָּה קוֹרֵא לְאַשְׁמוּעִי'. וְכוּלָּהּ ר' יְהוֹשֻׁעַ קָאָמַר לָהּ. שִׁינּוּי וֶסֶת. (א) חוֹק. כְּמוֹ עָנִי, שֶׁכָּל יְמוֹת הַחוֹל אוֹכֵל פַּת חֲרֵיבָה, וּבְשַׁבָּת אוֹכֵל בָּשָׂר. הָכִי גָּרְסִי': תְּחִלַּת חוֹלִי – מִתּוֹךְ כָּךְ מַתְחִיל לַחֲלוֹת. וְאִית דְּגָרְסִי: חוֹלִי מֵעַיִים. כְּתִיב בְּסֵפֶר בֶּן סִירָא. שְׁלֹמֹה כָּתַב: "כָּל יְמֵי עָנִי רָעִים", אֲבָל בַּלֵּילוֹת כְּשֶׁיָּשֵׁן – יֵשׁ לוֹ מְנוּחָה. וּבֶן סִירָא אוֹמֵר: אַף הַלֵּילוֹת אֵין לוֹ מְנוּחָה, כִּי בְּשֵׁפֶל גַּגִּים גַּגּוֹ, וְנִמְלָא דֶּלֶף טוֹרְדוֹ כְּיוֹם סַגְרִיר. מֵעֲפַר כַּרְמוֹ לִכְרָמִים. זֶבֶל (ב) וְאַשְׁפָּה שֶׁהֵבִיא לְכַרְמוֹ נִשְׁפָּךְ לִכְרָמִים אֲחֵרִים, שֶׁהוּא בְּמָקוֹם רָעוּעַ בֶּהָרִים וּבִסְלָעִים, בְּמָקוֹם שֶׁאֵין עָשִׁיר חָפֵץ בּוֹ – נוֹפֵל לְמַטָּה, בִּכְרָמִים שֶׁל עֲשִׁירִים, שֶׁהֵם בְּמָקוֹם טוֹב וּמִדְרוֹן וְנוֹחַ לַעֲסוֹק בָּהֶן.

מתני' הַשּׁוֹלֵחַ סִבְלוֹנוֹת. מִנְהַג חֲתָנִים לְאַחַר קִדּוּשִׁין, לְמָחֳרָת שׁוֹלֵחַ לְבֵית חָמִיו לִכְבוֹד אִשְׁתּוֹ תַּכְשִׁיטִין וּמִינֵי פֵּירוֹת וְכַדֵּי יַיִן וְכַדֵּי שֶׁמֶן, וּפְעָמִים אוֹכֵל שָׁם עִמָּהּ. אֵינָן נִגְבִּין. אִם מֵת הוּא אוֹ שֶׁמֵּתָה הִיא, אוֹ שֶׁחָזַר בּוֹ וְרוֹצֶה לְגָרְשָׁהּ. שֶׁמֵּחֲמַת חִיבַּת שִׂמְחַת אֲכִילָה שֶׁאָכַל וְשָׁתָה וְשָׂמַח עִמָּהֶן – מָחַל סִבְלוֹנוֹת הָעֲשׂוּיִן לִיבָּלוֹת. אֲבָל אֵין עֲשׂוּיִן לִיבָּלוֹת – הָדְרִי, אע"פ שֶׁאָכַל וְשָׁתָה עִמָּהֶן, כִּדְתַנְיָא בַּגְּמָ'. וּבְסִבְלוֹנוֹת סְתָם מַיְירֵי, דְּהָא לְקַמָּן מַפְלִיג בְּסִבְלוֹנוֹת שֶׁשָּׁלַח כְּדֵי שֶׁיָּבִיאוּ עִמָּהּ לְבֵית בַּעְלָהּ לְסִבְלוֹנוֹת שֶׁשָּׁלַח כְּדֵי שֶׁתִּשְׁתַּמֵּשׁ בְּבֵית אָבִיהָ, וְהָנֵהוּ לָא תָּלוּ בַּאֲכִילַת חָתָן – מִכְּלָל דְּרֵישָׁא בִּסְתָם סִבְלוֹנוֹת, וְהָנֵהוּ תְּלוּיִין בִּסְעוּדַת חָתָן, אִם אָכַל עִמָּהֶן – מְחוּלִּין, וְאִם לָאו – נִגְבִּין. שָׁלַח סִבְלוֹנוֹת מְרוּבִּין. וּפֵירֵשׁ: כְּדֵי שֶׁיָּבִיאוּ עִמָּהּ לְבֵית בַּעְלָהּ. וְה"ה לִמְוּעָטִים אִם שְׁלָחָן לְכָךְ, אֶלָּא אוֹרְחָא דְּמִילְּתָא נָקַט, מְרוּבִּים רָגִיל לִשְׁלוֹחַ וּלְפָרֵשׁ כְּדֵי שֶׁיָּבִיאוּ עִמָּהּ לְבֵית בַּעְלָהּ, וּמוּעָטִין – כְּדֵי שֶׁתִּשְׁתַּמֵּשׁ בָּהֶן בְּבֵית אָבִיהָ.

גמ' אָמַר רָבָא דַּוְקָא. אָכַל שָׁם סְעוּדַת חָתָן בְּדִינָר תְּנַן אֵין נִגְבִּין, אֲבָל פָּחוֹת מִדִּינָר – לֹא מָחַל מִידֵּי. אוֹרְחָא דְּמִילְּתָא קָתָנֵי. שִׁיעוּר אֲכִילַת אָדָם בְּדִינָר, כִּדְאָמְרָן:* עַד זוּזָא אָכְלֵי בְּכַרְסֵיהּ. הוּא תְּנַן. דְּקָתָנֵי: אִם אָכַל שָׁם, דְּמַשְׁמַע הוּא עַצְמוֹ. שִׁיגְּרוּ לוֹ. לֶחָתָן מִן סְעוּדָתָם בְּבֵיתוֹ, מַאי? וְרָכַב בְּשִׂמְחָתוֹ. מִתּוֹךְ שִׂמְחַת הוֹן רַב שֶׁשָּׁלַח לְבֵית חָמִיו שָׁתָה עַל סוּסוֹ, וּמֵת אַחַ"כ קוֹדֶם נִשּׂוּאִין. בְּאוּשָׁא. כְּשֶׁהָיְתָה סַנְהֶדְרִין לְשָׁם. דְּאוּשָׁא הִיא אַחַת מֵעֶשֶׂר גָּלְיוֹת שֶׁגָּלְתָה סַנְהֶדְרִין, כִּדְאִיתָא בְּמַסֶּ' רֹאשׁ הַשָּׁנָה (דף לא.). סִבְלוֹנוֹת הָעֲשׂוּיִן לִיבָּלוֹת. קוֹדֶם נִשּׂוּאִין – אֵין נִגְבִּין, דְּהָנֵהוּ מְחוּלִּין בִּסְעוּדַת חָתָן בְּדִינָר, כִּדְפָרֵישִׁית בְּמַתְנִי'. וְשֶׁאֵין עֲשׂוּיִין לִיבָּלוֹת. כְּגוֹן תַּכְשִׁיטֵי זָהָב וָכֶסֶף. ה"ג: ש"מ אֲפִי' פָּחוֹת מִדִּינָר. וְתַקְשֵׁי לְרָבָא. מַאן לֵימָא לָן דְּלָא שְׁחִיקִי לֵיהּ מַרְגָּנִיתָא. בְּכוֹס הַחַמִּין, שֶׁכֵּן דֶּרֶךְ הַשָּׂרִים שׁוֹתִין אוֹתוֹ לִרְפוּאָה. אֲפִי' שִׁיגְּרוּ נַמִּי. שֶׁהֲרֵי שָׁתָה כְּשֶׁהוּא רוֹכֵב סוּסוֹ לִפְנֵי פֶּתַח בֵּית חָמִיו. כְּבֵית חָמִיו דָּמֵי. אֲבָל שִׁגְּרוּ לוֹ בְּבֵיתוֹ אִיבַּעְיָא לָן. שֶׁבַח סִבְלוֹנוֹת מַהוּ. הֵיכָא דְּהָדְרִי סִבְלוֹנוֹת, מִי הָדְרִי שֶׁבַח שֶׁהִשְׁבִּיחוּ? כְּגוֹן שָׁלַח לְבֵית חָמִיו צֹאן וּבָקָר, וְיָלְדוּ. בָּעֵי רָבָא סִבְלוֹנוֹת הָעֲשׂוּיִם לִיבָּלוֹת. דַּאֲמַרַן דְּלָא הָדְרִי. אִם לֹא בָּלוּ בִּשְׁעַת חֲזָרָה, אוֹתָן שֶׁאֵין עֲשׂוּיִן לִיבָּלוֹת מִי הָדְרִי עִמָּהֶן אוֹ לָא? תָּא שְׁמַע סִבְלוֹנוֹת מוּעָטִין שֶׁתִּשְׁתַּמֵּשׁ בָּהֶן וְהִיא בְּבֵית אָבִיהָ אֵין נִגְבִּין. בִּשְׁלָמָא הַךְ קַמַּיְיתָא, כֵּיוָן דְּקָתָנֵי עֲשׂוּיוֹת לִיבָּלוֹת – מָצֵית לְאוֹקְמָהּ בִּדְבָלוּ. אֲבָל הָכָא מִילְּתָא דִּפְסִיקָא קָתָנֵי: שֶׁתִּשְׁתַּמֵּשׁ בָּהֶן בְּבֵית אָבִיהָ, אע"פ שֶׁיֶּשְׁנָן בְּעַיִן. וּמִיהוּ, הֲוָה מָצֵי לְתָרוּצֵי (כְּשֶׁאֵין עֲשׂוּיִן לִיבָּלוֹת אוֹ) כְּשֶׁעֲשׂוּיִן לִיבָּלוֹת וּבָלוּ. אֶלָּא רְבוּתָא אַשְׁמוּעִי', אֲפִי' כְּשֶׁעֲשׂוּיִן לִיבָּלוֹת וְלֹא בָּלוּ. כְּגוֹן בְּיִיבָא וְסִיבַכְתָּא. מִינֵי לְעִיפִים וְקִישּׁוּרֵי נָשִׁים, שֶׁהֵן דָּבָר מוּעָט, וּמָחֵיל לְהוּ לְגַמְרֵי, לָא שְׁנָא בָּלוּ וְלָא שְׁנָא לֹא בָּלוּ. אֲבָל תַּכְשִׁיטִין חֲשׁוּבִין תִּיבָּעֵי לָךְ. מָצָאתִי גִּירְסָא בְּפר"ח* שֶׁאֵינָהּ בַּסְּפָרִים שֶׁלָּנוּ. הָא דְּאָמַר רָבָא: דַּוְקָא דִּינָר, כְּלוֹמַר שֶׁאִם אָכַל בְּבֵית חָמִיו מַה שֶּׁשָּׁוֶה דִּינָר, אוֹ שָׁתָה יַיִן, אֲבָל פָּחוֹת מִדִּינָר – לֹא. וַעֲלָהּ קָאָמְרִי': מַהוּ שֶׁיְּשַׁלֵּשׁ בְּסִבְלוֹנוֹת. וְעָלְתָה בְּתֵיקוּ. פֵּירוּשׁ: אִם שָׁלַח סִבְלוֹנוֹת בְּק' מָנֶה וְאָכַל בְּבֵית חָמִיו בְּכָל הַסִּבְלוֹנוֹת. וְהַשְׁתָּא דְּאָכַל בַּחֲצִי דִּינָר יִזְכּוּ לַחֲצִי הַסִּבְלוֹנוֹת, וְהוּא הַדִּין לִשְׁלִישׁ וְלִרְבִיעַ? וְזֶהוּ פֵּירוּשׁ "מַהוּ שֶׁיְּשַׁלֵּשׁ בְּסִבְלוֹנוֹת", וְעָלְתָה בְּתֵיקוּ. כֵּלִים מִפִּשְׁתָּן חָדָשׁ. שִׁבְחָא דא"י. שֶׁמְּמַהֶרֶת לְבַשֵּׁל פֵּירוֹתֶיהָ בָּעֲצֶרֶת. דְּאִי טָעֵין טַעֲנָתֵיהּ טַעֲנָה. אִי הָדְרִי סִבְלוֹנוֹת, וְטָעֵין: יַיִן וְשֶׁמֶן שָׁלַחְתִּי לָךְ בָּעֲצֶרֶת – לֹא הוּחְזַק בִּשְׁאֵר בְּכָךְ, וְהָדְרִי לֵיהּ. שֶׁאָמְרוּ לוֹ אִשְׁתּוֹ תּוּתְרָנִית הִיא. חוֹלִי הוּא, שֶׁאֵינָהּ יְכוֹלָה לְהָרִיחַ, וּמוּם שֶׁבַּסֵּתֶר הוּא. וּתְנַן בְּ"הַמַּדִּיר" בִּכְתוּבּוֹת (דף עב:): הַמְקַדֵּשׁ אֶת הָאִשָּׁה ע"מ שֶׁאֵין בָּהּ מוּמִין וְנִמְצְאוּ עָלֶיהָ מוּמִין – אֵינָהּ מְקוּדֶּשֶׁת. כְּנָסָהּ סְתָם וְנִמְצְאוּ בָּהּ מוּמִין – תֵּצֵא שֶׁלֹּא בִּכְתוּבָּה כו', עַד וְהַכ"א: בַּמֶּה דְּבָרִים אֲמוּרִים – בְּמוּמִין שֶׁבַּסֵּתֶר כו'. וְזֶה הָאִישׁ לֹא קִבֵּל עָלָיו אֶת הַמּוּמִין, וְאִם קִדְּשָׁהּ סְתָם וּכְנָסָהּ סְתָם וְנִמְצְאוּ בָּהּ מוּמִין – תֵּצֵא בְּלֹא כְּתוּבָּה. וּמִיהוּ, גֵּט בָּעֲיָא, כִּדְמְפָרֵשׁ בַּגְּמָרָא בְּפֶרֶק "הַמַּדִּיר". נִכְנַס אַחֲרֶיהָ לְחוּרְבָּה לְבוֹדְקָהּ. שָׁם, וְנָשָׂא עִמּוֹ בְּתוֹךְ חֵיקוֹ צְנוֹן, לְנַסּוֹתָהּ אִם תָּרִיחַ. וְיֵשׁ מְפָרְשִׁים: כּוֹתֶבֶת נָטַל בְּתוֹךְ חֵיקוֹ, וְלֹא צְנוֹן, וְקָרוֹב לַגָּלִיל הָיָה מַעֲשֶׂה. אָמַר לָהּ רֵיחַ צְנוֹן אֲנִי מֵרִיחַ בַּגָּלִיל. לְנַסּוֹתָהּ אִם תָּרִיחַ. שֶׁמִּתּוֹךְ דְּבָרֶיהָ נִיכָּר אִם תָּרִיחַ. וְעַל הַצְּנוֹן שֶׁבְּתוֹךְ חֵיקוֹ אָמַר. וּלְלִישָּׁנָא דִּמְפָרֵשׁ שֶׁכּוֹתֶבֶת הָיָה עִמּוֹ, לְכָךְ אָמַר לָהּ רֵיחַ צְנוֹן, לָדַעַת אִם תְּשִׁיבֵנוּ דָּבָר לֵאמֹר: רֵיחַ כּוֹתֶבֶת אֲנִי מְרִיחָה, וְלֹא רֵיחַ צְנוֹן.

אָמְרָה

תוספות

סבלונות העשוין ליבלות אין נגבין. והא דתנא: מרובין שתביא עמה מבית אביה לבית בעלה הרי אלו נגבין – היינו אין עשוין לבלות, ומועטין היינו עשוין לבלות. א"נ, במועטות בעינן דוקא שאין עשוי לבלות, אבל במרובים – אפי' בבלות נמי נגבין.

איבעיא להו מהו *שתשלש. פי': אמילתא דרבא קאי, דאמר: דוקא אכל דינר, אבל פחות מדינר לא. וקא אמר: אם אכל פחות מדינר, מהו שתגבה לפי מה שאכל, אם אכל חצי דינר – תגבה החצי? ולישנא ד"תשלש" – כמו: משלשין בממון ואין משלשין במכות (מכות דף ה.). מ"ר.

תרגמה רבא בייבא. פי' רבינו שמואל: דה"ה דהוה מצי לשנויי: לא, והוא דבלו. ור"י אומר: דבשלמא בברייתא איירי בבלו, אלא מתני' דלא איירי בבלו – לא מיתוקמא בבלו.

רבינו גרשום

שינוי וסת. שאוכל יותר ממה שהוא רגיל מזיק לו למעיו: א) אותו שגגו נמוך משאר גגות וכרמו גבוה משאר כרמים ימיו רעים: **פיסקא** השולח סבלונות לבית חמיו. כעין שרגילין לעשות חתנים למחרת של קדושין שולח החתן סבלונות שלו דורון לבית חמיו כגון בהמות וכדי יין וכדי שמן ועושה סעודה ואוכל עמהן. אם שלח שם אפי' שוה מאה מנה ואכל שם סעודת חתן אפי' שוה דינר בלבד ומתה היא או הדרא בה אין נגבין שעל דעת סעודה שלח ואגב שאכל שם סעודת חתן בדינר מחל לו הכל. לא אכל שם סעודת חתן בדינר לא חשיב וגובין הכל: שלח שם סבלונות מרובין. מלבושים ותכשיטין כסף וזהב על מנת שתביאם עמה לבית בעלה בשעת חופה: הרי אלו נגבין. אפי' אכל שם בדינר דלא עביד אינש דמחיל כולי האי: סבלונות מועטין. מלבושין שאין יקרין שתשמש בהן בעודה בבית אביה: אין נגבין. אפי' לא אכל שם בדינר דמחיל לה הואיל דמועטין: אמר רבא דוקא כשאכל שם שוה דינר אין נגבין אבל פחות מדינר נגבין המותר: אורחא דמילת' היא דעד דינר רגילי אינשי למיכל בסעודה כדאמרי' לעיל עד זוזי אתי בכרסיה והוא הדין דאפי' פחות מדינר קמ"ל דוקא דינר דבדינר מחיל ולא בבציר: אכל בדינר תנן. אין נגבין: שתה בדינר ולא אכיל מאי. מי אמרינן שתיה בכלל אכילה וכאכל דמי או דלמא כמו שלא אכל דמי ונגבין: אכל שם סעודת חתן [תנן] אכל שם שלוחו ולא הוא מאי. נגבין או אין נגבין: אם אכל שם בבית חמיו תנן שיגרו לו בביתו מסעודתם שוה דינר מאי. מי אמרי' בבית חמיו דוקא דאין נגבין אבל בבית לא או דלמא לא שנא: כוס של חמין. מזוג בחמין: שתה ומת. הכי אירע לו ולא משום כישוף: זו הלכה של מעשה העלה ר' אחא כו' סבלונות העשוין ליבלות אין נגבין כגון בהמות וכדי יין דלמישחט ומיכל קיימי דאסוחי אסח דעתי' מינייהו: שאין עשוין ליבלות. כגון כלי כסף וכלי זהב וכלי מילת נגבין. דהכי אמרי' לעיל: ש"מ אפי' פחות מדינר. דהאי כוס של חמין לא היה שוה דינר ואפ"ה אמרו חכמים דאין נגבין: אמר רב אשי. מהא ליכא למשמע מינה דמאן לימא לן דלא שחקו בההוא כוס מרגניתא שויא אלפא זוזי דהכי רגילי אינשי לשחוק מרגניתא במשקה משום רפואה: ש"מ אפי' שגרו לו. נמי אין נגבין משום דהוציאו לו לחוץ כוס של חמין: איבעיא להו. הא פשיטא לן דסבלונות העשוין ליבלות אם אכל שם בדינר אין חוזרין. שבח סבלונות מהו. אם לא אכל שם בדינר דנגבין הסבלונות העשוין ליבלות אם השביחו כגון ששלח בהמות לבית חמיו וילדו מהו חוזר אותו שבח או לא. מי אמרינן אותן עצמן ששלח הדרי אבל שבח דלא שלח הוא כגון הוולדות לא הדרי או דלמא כיון דמכח אותן ששלח באין הדרי: בעי רבא. אם אכל שם בדינר ונשתיירו שם מסבלונות העשוין ליבלות ולא בלו כגון שנשתיירו עדיין בהמות בחיים מהו חוזר או לא מי אמרינן הואיל דלא בלו בעינייהו קיימא וחוזרין או דלמא הואיל ועשוין ליבלות כמאן דבלו דמיין ואין חוזרין: ת"ש סבלונות מועטין שתשמש בהן בבית אביה. כגון מלבושין שאין יקרים כל כך ולובשת אותן תדיר בכל יום הרי אלו אין נגבין. ש"מ סבלונות העשוין ליבלות אע"פ שלא בלו אין נגבין: תרגמה רבא. לעולם אימא לך סבלונות העשוין ליבלות אע"ג דלא בלו (אין) נגבין והכא טעמא מאי בייבא וסבכתא עסקי' בקישוריה ובמפה שעל ראשה ולאו דבר חשוב הוא ובמתנה יהב לה: מעשה כו' מאי אתא לאשמועי'. אם שגר אם לא שגר: שבחא דארץ ישראל. שמבכרת פירותיה כל כך בעצרת: ואי בעית אימא. הא קמ"ל דאי טעין ואמר החתן בעצרת שלחתי סבלונות יין חדש ושמן חדש לאו גוזמא היא דארץ ישראל מבכרת פירותיה היא: אשתך תותרנית. מטומטרית שאינה מריח שום ריח ומום שבסתר הוא דמותר לגרשה. איכא דאמרי ארוסה היתה. אמרה

א) נראה דצ"ל אף לילות שגגו נמוך וכו' משאר כרמים ולכן ימיו ולילותיו רעים.

סב א מיי' פ"ד מהל' דעות הלכה כא:

סג ב ג מיי' פ"ו מהל' זכייה ומתנה הלכה כא כב טור וש"ע אה"ע סי' נ סעיף ג:

[ועי' גירסת ר"ח שכתב הרשב"ם ד"ה מצאתי]

סנהדרין קא.

שם כתובות קי: נדרים לז:

הגהות הב"ח

(א) רשב"ם ד"ה שינוי ווסת וכמו עני כצ"ל ותיבת חוק נמחק: (ב) ד"ה מעפר וכו' זבל שהביא כצ"ל ותיבת ואשפה נמחק וכ"ב אשפה הוא המקום שמניחים הזבל לשם כדלעיל דף עח ע"ב:

[בכרי"ף והרא"ש איתא ששילם:]

[לעיל קמה.]

רש"ל מ"ז

[וכן גירסת הערוך ערך סבלונות]

עין משפט נר מצוה

נח א מיי' פ"ז מהלכות זכייה ומתנה הלכה ה טור אה"ע סי' ס:

נט ב מיי' שם הלכה ז טור שו"ע שם:

ס ג מיי' שם הלכה ד טור שו"ע שם:

סא ד מיי' שם הלכה ג:

גמרא

וְאֵין הַשְּׁבִיעִית מְשַׁמַּטְתָּה, וְאֵין הַבְּכוֹר נוֹטֵל בָּהּ פִּי שְׁנַיִם.§ נִגְבֵּית בְּבֵ"ד, מַאי טַעֲמָא? כְּמִלְוֶה דָּמְיָא. וְאֵין בָּהּ מִשּׁוּם רִבִּית — דְּלָאו אַדַּעְתָּא דְּהָכִי יָהֵב לֵיהּ. וְאֵין הַשְּׁבִיעִית מְשַׁמַּטְתָּה — דְּלָא קָרֵינָא בֵּיהּ "לֹא יִגּוֹשׂ". וְאֵין הַבְּכוֹר נוֹטֵל פִּי שְׁנַיִם — דַּהֲוָה לֵיהּ רָאוּי, וְאֵין הַבְּכוֹר נוֹטֵל בָּרָאוּי כְּבַמּוּחְזָק. אָמַר רַב כָּהֲנָא, [א]כְּלָלָא דְּשׁוּשְׁבִינוּתָא: הֲוָה בְּמָתָא — אִיבָּעֵי לֵיהּ לְמֵיתָא. (א) שְׁמַע קַל טַבְלָא — אִיבָּעֵי לֵיהּ לְמֵיתָא. לָא שְׁמַע קַל טַבְלָא — אִיבָּעֵי לֵיהּ לְאוֹדוּעֵיהּ, (ב) תַּרְעוֹמֶת אִית לֵיהּ, שַׁלּוּמֵי מְשַׁלֵּם. וְעַד כַּמָּה? אֲמַר אַבַּיֵי: [ב]נָהֲגוּ בְּנֵי גְּנָנָא, עַד זוּזָא — (ג) אַיְתָא א)בְּכַפֵּיהּ אָכְלֵיהּ בְּכָרֵסֵי', עַד אַרְבָּעָה — מְשַׁלֵּם פַּלְגָא, מִכָּאן וְאֵילָךְ — אִינִישׁ אִינִישׁ כַּחֲשִׁיבוּתֵיהּ. תָּנוּ רַבָּנַן: [ג]עָשָׂה עִמּוֹ בְּפוּמְבֵּי, וּבִקֵּשׁ לַעֲשׂוֹת עִמּוֹ בְּצִנְעָא — יָכוֹל לוֹמַר לוֹ: בְּפוּמְבֵּי אֶעֱשֶׂה עִמְּךָ, כְּדֶרֶךְ שֶׁעָשִׂיתָ עִמִּי; [ד]עָשָׂה עִמּוֹ בִּבְתוּלָה, וּבִקֵּשׁ לַעֲשׂוֹת עִמּוֹ בְּאַלְמָנָה — יָכוֹל לוֹמַר לוֹ: בִּבְתוּלָה אֶעֱשֶׂה עִמְּךָ, כְּדֶרֶךְ שֶׁעָשִׂיתָ עִמִּי. עָשָׂה עִמּוֹ בִּשְׁנִיָּה, וּבִקֵּשׁ לַעֲשׂוֹת עִמּוֹ בָּרִאשׁוֹנָה — יָכוֹל לוֹמַר לוֹ: לִכְשֶׁתִּשָּׂא אִשָּׁה אַחֶרֶת אֶעֱשֶׂה עִמְּךָ. עָשָׂה עִמּוֹ בְּאַחַת, וּבִקֵּשׁ לַעֲשׂוֹת עִמּוֹ בִּשְׁתַּיִם — יָכוֹל לוֹמַר לוֹ: בְּאַחַת אֶעֱשֶׂה עִמְּךָ, כְּדֶרֶךְ שֶׁעָשִׂיתָ עִמִּי. תָּנוּ רַבָּנַן: עַתִּיר נְכָסִין עַתִּיר פּוּמְבֵּי — זֶה הוּא בַּעַל הַגָּדוֹת, עַתִּיר סְלָעִים עַתִּיר תְּקוֹעַ — זֶהוּ בַּעַל פִּלְפּוּל, עַתִּיר מֹשַׁח עַתִּיר כְּמָם — זֶהוּ בַּעַל שְׁמוּעוֹת, ב)הַכֹּל צְרִיכִין לְמָרֵי חִטַּיָּא — גְּמָרָא. ג)אָמַר רַבִּי זֵירָא אָמַר רַב, מַאי דִּכְתִיב: °"כָּל יְמֵי עָנִי רָעִים" (משלי טו) — זֶה בַּעַל גְּמָרָא, "וְטוֹב לֵב מִשְׁתֶּה תָמִיד" — זֶה בַּעַל מִשְׁנָה. רָבָא אָמַר: אִיפְּכָא. וְהַיְינוּ דְּאָמַר רַב מְשַׁרְשְׁיָא מִשְּׁמֵיהּ דְּרָבָא, מַאי דִּכְתִיב: °"מַסִּיעַ אֲבָנִים יֵעָצֵב בָּהֶם (קהלת י) בּוֹקֵעַ עֵצִים יִסָּכֶן בָּם"? "מַסִּיעַ אֲבָנִים יֵעָצֵב בָּהֶן" — אֵלּוּ בַּעֲלֵי מִשְׁנָה, "בּוֹקֵעַ עֵצִים יִסָּכֶן בָּם" — אֵלּוּ בַּעֲלֵי גְמָרָא. רַבִּי חֲנִינָא אָמַר: "כָּל יְמֵי עָנִי רָעִים" — זֶה שֶׁיֵּשׁ לוֹ אִשָּׁה רָעָה, "וְטוֹב לֵב מִשְׁתֶּה תָמִיד" — זֶה שֶׁיֵּשׁ לוֹ אִשָּׁה טוֹבָה. רַבִּי יַנַּאי אָמַר: "כָּל יְמֵי עָנִי רָעִים" — זֶה אִיסְטְנִיס, "וְטוֹב לֵב מִשְׁתֶּה תָמִיד" — זֶה שֶׁדַּעְתּוֹ יָפָה. רַבִּי יוֹחָנָן אָמַר: "כָּל יְמֵי עָנִי רָעִים" — זֶה רַחֲמָן, "וְטוֹב לֵב מִשְׁתֶּה תָמִיד" — זֶה אַכְזָרִי. וְרַבִּי יְהוֹשֻׁעַ בֶּן לֵוִי אָמַר: "כָּל יְמֵי עָנִי רָעִים" — זֶה שֶׁדַּעְתּוֹ קְצָרָה, "וְטוֹב לֵב מִשְׁתֶּה תָמִיד" — זֶה שֶׁדַּעְתּוֹ רְחָבָה.

וְאָמַר

רשב"ם

וְאֵין שְׁבִיעִית מְשַׁמַּטְתָּה. אִם עָבְרָה שְׁבִיעִית בֵּינְתַיִים, קוֹדֶם שֶׁחָזַר זֶה וְנָשָׂא גַּם הוּא אִשָּׁה. וְאֵין בְּכוֹר נוֹטֵל פִּי שְׁנַיִם. הֵיכָא דְּחוֹזֶרֶת לָאֶמְצַע, כִּדְתַנְיָא לְעֵיל. נִגְבֵּית בְּבֵ"ד מ"ט מִפְּנֵי שֶׁהִיא כְּמִלְוֶה. ה"ג לָהּ. וּבִסְפָרִים כָּתוּב: נִגְבֵּית בְּבֵ"ד וְחוֹזֶרֶת בְּעוֹנָתָהּ, מ"ט מִפְּנֵי שֶׁהִיא כְּמִלְוֶה. דִּלְדַעַת כֵּן הִלְוָוהוּ שֶׁיַּחֲזִיר לוֹ בְּעוֹנַת שִׂמְחָתוֹ, וּפֵרָעוֹן הוֹלֵךְ אַחַר קְבִיעוּת זְמַן שֶׁקָּבַע לוֹ הַמַּלְוֶה. דְּלָאו אַדַּעְתָּא דְּרִבִּית יָהֵיב לֵיהּ. שֶׁאִם רָצָה פּוֹחֵת לוֹ, אֶלָּא מִתּוֹךְ שִׂמְחַת רֵיעוּת הִרְבָּה בְּדוֹרוֹן. דְּלָא קָרֵינָא בֵּיהּ לֹא יִגּוֹשׂ. שֶׁאֵינוֹ יָכוֹל לְדָחֲקוֹ בְּבֵ"ד בַּשְּׁבִיעִית, שֶׁהֲרֵי לֹא הִגִּיעַ זְמַנּוֹ עַד שֶׁיִּשָּׂא הוּא אִשָּׁה וְיַחֲזִיר לוֹ אָז, דְּאֵינָהּ נִגְבֵּית אֶלָּא בְּבֵ"ד בְּעוֹנָתָהּ, כִּדְאָמְרִינַן בְּמַסֶּכֶת מַכּוֹת (דף ג:): הַמַּלְוֶה אֶת חֲבֵירוֹ לְעֶשֶׂר שָׁנִים — אֵין שְׁבִיעִית מְשַׁמַּטְתּוֹ. אַף זֶה, לֹא הִגִּיעַ זְמַנּוֹ עַד לְאַחַר שְׁבִיעִית, הִלְכָּךְ בַּשְּׁבִיעִית — אַכַּתִּי לָא מְטָא זִמְנֵיהּ שֶׁיּוּכַל לְנוֹגְשׂוֹ, דַּעֲדַיִין לֹא נָשָׂא אִשָּׁה. דַּהֲוֵי לֵיהּ רָאוּי. וּפָסְקִינַן הִלְכְתָא בְּפֶרֶק "יֵשׁ נוֹחֲלִין" (לעיל דף קכה:): אֵין הַבְּכוֹר נוֹטֵל פִּי שְׁנַיִם בְּמִלְוֶה, בֵּין שֶׁגָּבוּ קַרְקַע בֵּין שֶׁגָּבוּ מָעוֹת. הֲוָה בְּמָתָא. אוֹתוֹ שֶׁעָלָיו לְהַחֲזִיר שׁוֹשְׁבִינוּת הֲוָה בָּעִיר כְּשֶׁנָּשָׂא שׁוֹשְׁבִינוֹ אִשָּׁה וְלֹא בָּא לְשִׂמְחָתוֹ. אִיבָּעֵי לֵיהּ לְמֵיתֵי. וְנִגְבֵּית בְּבֵ"ד. קוֹל טַבְלָא. (ד) אשקלנ"א בְּלַעַ"ז, שֶׁהָיוּ מַשְׁמִיעִין קוֹל לָבֹא לִשְׂמוֹחַ עִם הֶחָתָן. אִיבָּעֵי לֵיהּ לְאוֹדוּעֵי. וּמִדְּלָא אוֹדְעֵיהּ — תַּרְעוֹמוֹת אִית לֵיהּ עֲלֵיהּ, כִּדְמְפָרֵשׁ וְאָזֵיל, אֲבָל שַׁלּוּמֵי מִיהָא מְשַׁלֵּם. עַד כַּמָּה. דְּהָא וַדַּאי צָרִיךְ לְנַכּוֹת דְּמֵי אֲכִילָתוֹ, שֶׁהֲרֵי לֹא אָכַל עִמּוֹ. עַד זוּזָא (ה) כו'. זוּזָא הָיָה אוֹכֵל, הִלְכָּךְ זוּזָא פּוֹחֵת מִדְּמֵי שׁוֹשְׁבִינוּתוֹ. אִית דְּגָרְסִי: עַד זוּזָא אַיְיתֵיהּ בְּכַפֵּיהּ אָכְלֵי בְּכָרֵסֵיהּ בְּבִטְנוֹ, כְּמוֹ בֵּית הַכּוֹסוֹת. אִי נַמִי: בְּכָרֵסֵיהּ. עַד אַרְבַּע. אִם נִתְחַיֵּיב ד' זוּזִים מִשּׁוֹשְׁבִינוּתוֹ. מְשַׁלֵּם פַּלְגָא. דְּכֵיוָן דְּמֵבִיא ד' — רְגִילִין לְהַאֲכִילוֹ בְּרֶיוַח עַד שְׁנֵי זוּזִים, וְכֵיוָן דְּלֹא אָכַל — יִפְחוֹת שְׁנַיִם מִן הַד'. כַּחֲשִׁיבוּתֵיהּ. לְפִי מַה שֶּׁהוּא חָשׁוּב, וּמֵבִיא הַרְבֵּה וּרְגִילִין (ו) לְכַבְּדוֹ בְּמִינֵי מַעֲדַנִּים — יִפְחֲתוּ לוֹ מִדְּמֵי שׁוֹשְׁבִינוּתוֹ כְּפִי מַה שֶּׁהָיָה אוֹכֵל. עָשָׂה עִמּוֹ בְּפוּמְבֵּי. בְּגָלוּי, שִׂמְחָה מְפוּרְסֶמֶת. וְזֶה שֶׁחָזַר וְנָשָׂא גַּם הוּא אִשָּׁה — בִּקֵּשׁ לַעֲשׂוֹת חוּפָּתוֹ בִּצְנִיעוּת, אוֹ לְפִי שֶׁעֵת צָרָה הִיא, אוֹ שֶׁרוֹצֶה לְמַעֵט סְעוּדָּתוֹ וְאֵינוֹ חוֹשֵׁשׁ לְהַרְבּוֹת אוֹכְלִין. בְּפוּמְבֵּי אֲנִי עוֹשֶׂה עִמְּךָ. בְּשִׂמְחָה יְתֵירָה אֲנִי חָפֵץ, כְּמוֹ שֶׁעָשִׂיתִי לְךָ, וְכֵן כָּל הָנָךְ דִּמְפָרֵשׁ וְאָזֵיל. לִכְשֶׁתִּשָּׂא אִשָּׁה אַחֶרֶת. לֹא אֲשַׂמֵּחֲךָ יוֹתֵר מִמַּה שֶּׁשִּׂמַּחְתַּנִי, שֶׁאֵינִי חָפֵץ בְּשִׂמְחָה יְתֵירָה. ת"ר עָתִיר בְּנִכְסִין. עָשִׁיר מִשָּׂדוֹת וּכְרָמִים וְזֵיתִים הַנִּרְאִין לַבְּרִיּוֹת, וְגַם עָתִיר פּוּמְבֵּי — עוֹשֶׁר הַגָּלוּי, כְּגוֹן רוֹב בְּהֵמוֹת שֶׁהַכֹּל יוֹדְעִים בָּהֶן. זֶהוּ בַּעַל אַגָּדָה. שֶׁדּוֹרֵשׁ בְּכָל מָקוֹם בָּרַבִּים בְּבָתֵּי מִשְׁתָּאוֹת, שֶׁדּוֹרֵשׁ דְּבָרִים טוֹבִים וְהַכֹּל נֶאֱסָפִין לִשְׁמוֹעַ, וְיֵשׁ לוֹ קוֹל חָכְמָה. וּבָא לְהַשְׁמִיעָנוּ שֶׁמִּתּוֹךְ שֶׁאֵין הַגָּדוֹת צְרִיכוֹת עִיּוּן — יָכוֹל לִדְרוֹשׁ בְּכָל מָקוֹם. עָתִיר סַלְעִין. שׁוּלְחָנִי שֶׁמִּשְׂתַּכֵּר תָּמִיד בְּמִינֵי מַטְבְּעוֹת. עָתִיר תְּקוֹעַ. יֵשׁ מְפָרְשִׁין: שֶׁיֵּשׁ לוֹ בָּתִּים הַרְבֵּה וּמִשְׂתַּכֵּר בָּהֶן תָּדִיר, וּמִיקְרֵי הָכִי עַל שֵׁם "וַיַּעֲקֹב תָּקַע אֶת אָהֳלוֹ" (בראשית לא). וְלִי נִרְאֶה — כִּדְאָמְרִינַן בִּמְנָחוֹת (דף פה:): תְּקוֹעַ אַלְפָא לְשֶׁמֶן. עִיר הִיא, וּמִשָּׁם הָיוּ מְבִיאִים שֶׁמֶן לִמְנָחוֹת. וְדִימָה לְמַטְבְּעוֹת וּלְשֶׁמֶן אֶת הַפִּלְפּוּל, עַל שֵׁם שֶׁמַּרְוִיחַ יוֹם יוֹם תָּדִיר בְּפִלְפּוּלוֹ טְעָמִים הַרְבֵּה, כִּסְחַר הַמַּטְבְּעוֹת וְטַעֲמֵי הַשֶּׁמֶן שֶׁמְּבִיאִין מִתְּקוֹעַ. עָתִיר מֹשַׁח. "אַנְשֵׁי מִדּוֹת" (במדבר יג) מְתַרְגְּמִינַן: אֱינָשֵׁי מִשְׁחָן. עָתִיר בְּדָבָר הַמָּדוּד, כְּגוֹן תְּבוּאָה, שֶׁאֵין מִשְׂתַּכְּרִין בָּהּ תָּדִיר, אֶלָּא מַכְנִיסִין אוֹתָהּ לָאוֹצָר, וְלִכְשֶׁתַּגִּיעַ עֵת מְכִירָה אָז יִמְכְּרֶנָּה וְיִשְׂתַּכֵּר. וְהַיְינוּ נַמִי "עָתִיר כְּמָס", כְּמוֹ "כָּמוּס עִמָּדִי חָתוּם בְּאוֹצְרוֹתָי" (דברים לב) — דָּבָר שֶׁמַּכְנִיסִין לָאוֹצָר. זֶהוּ בַּעַל שְׁמוּעוֹת. שֶׁיּוֹדֵעַ הֲלָכוֹת וּמֵימְרוֹת הָאֲמוֹרָאִין, וְלִכְשֶׁיַּגִּיעַ עֵת הוֹרָאָה — יְגַלֶּה שְׁמוּעוֹתָיו. תַּלְמוּד. סוּגְיַית גְּמָרָא וְתֵרוּצֵי מִשְׁנָיוֹת וּבָרַיְיתוֹת. וְזֶהוּ עִיקַּר הַתַּלְמוּד, שֶׁאִם לֹא הַתַּלְמוּד — אֵין לְמֵדִין הֲלָכָה מִתּוֹךְ מִשְׁנָה, כִּדְאָמְרִינַן: הַתַּנָּאִים מְבַלֵּי עוֹלָם (סוטה דף כב.). זֶה בַּעַל תַּלְמוּד. שֶׁמֵּמִית עַצְמוֹ לְכַוֵּין הֲלָכוֹת וּלְתָרֵץ הֲוָיוֹת. רָבָא אָמַר אִיפְּכָא. "כָּל יְמֵי עָנִי רָעִים" — זֶה בַּעַל מִשְׁנָה, שֶׁאֵינוֹ יָכוֹל לְהוֹרוֹת הֲלָכָה מִתּוֹךְ מִשְׁנָתוֹ, וְגַם כִּי כְּשֶׁחֲלוּקוֹת זוֹ עַל זוֹ אֵינוֹ יָכוֹל לְתָרֵץ. "וְטוֹב לֵב" — זֶה בַּעַל הַתַּלְמוּד, שֶׁיּוֹדֵעַ מִשְׁנָיוֹת עַל עִיקָּרָם וּבָקִי בְּטַעְמֵיהֶם, וְיֵשׁ בְּיָדוֹ כֹּחַ לְהוֹרוֹת הֲלָכָה לְמַעֲשֶׂה. יֵעָצֵב. לְשׁוֹן "בְּעִצָּבוֹן תֹּאכְלֶנָּה" (בראשית ג). זֶה בַּעַל מִשְׁנָה. שֶׁשּׁוֹנֶה מִשְׁנָיוֹת כָּל הַיּוֹם, וְאֵין לוֹ אֶלָּא צַעַר, שֶׁמִּתְקַשֶּׁה בְּטַעֲמֵיהֶן וְאֵינוֹ יוֹדֵעַ לְפָרֵשׁ. יִסָּכֶן. לְשׁוֹן חֲמִימוּת, כְּמוֹ "וַתְּהִי לַמֶּלֶךְ סוֹכֶנֶת" (מלכים א א), כְּלוֹמַר שֶׁנֶּהֱנֶה מֵהֶן. זֶה אִיסְטְנִיס. מִי שֶׁדַּעְתּוֹ קָלָה וְלִבּוֹ ד) נִמְאָס בְּכָל דָּבָר מְגוּנֶּה שֶׁהוּא רוֹאֶה. יָפָה. שֶׁסּוֹבֵל הַכֹּל, דְּאֵינוֹ מַזִּיק לוֹ שׁוּם לִכְלוּךְ וְשׁוּם דְּבַר מִיאוּס. קְצָרָה. כְּמוֹ עַצְלָן וְקַפְּדָן, עֵינוֹ רָעָה בְּשֶׁלּוֹ וּבְשֶׁל אֲחֵרִים. זֶה רַחֲמָן. כַּמָּה (ז) עֲנִיִּים הוּא רוֹאֶה וְכַמָּה מְאוֹרָעוֹת שֶׁלִּבּוֹ דּוֹוֶה תָּדִיר עֲלֵיהֶן.

וְאָמַר

תוספות

ואין השביעית משמטתה. דלא קרי ביה "לא יגוש". מכאן היה מביא ר"ת ראיה דקיימא לן כלישנא בתרא דפרק קמא דמכות (דף ג: ושם ד"ה א"ד) דאמר רב יהודה אמר שמואל: המלוה את חבירו לעשר שנים — אין שביעית משמטתו. ואע"ג דאתי לידי "לא יגוש" — השתא מיהא לא קרינן ביה "לא יגוש". דהכי נמי משמע הכא, דכיון דלא קרינא ביה בשושבינות — (ח) לא שייך ביה למימר דשביעית משמטתה. ועל ידי כן מגיה ר' יעקב מה שיסד הפייט ר' אליהו הזקן: "זמן עשר כסף כי ילונו בחלי ימיו יעזבנו", (ט) ולישנא קמא דפרק קמא דמכות (שם) אית ליה דהמלוה לחבירו לי' שנים שביעית משמטתו. ואין ר"ת פוסק כן, אלא כלישנא בתרא, דאית ליה אין שביעית משמטתו, (י) ומגיה: "זמן עשר כסף כי ילונו ולא במשפט בחלי ימיו יעזבנו". ואין נראה לר"י ראיה מכאן, דלא שייכא כלל שושבינות למלוה, שהרי מכמה דברים הם חלוקים זה מזה, כדמשמע הכא. והכא הכי פירושו: אין שביעית משמטתו דלא קרינא ביה "לא יגוש" — ושמא לעולם לא יבא לידי "לא יגוש", שיכול לומר לו: בבתולה אני עושה עמך. או שמא לא ישא אשה. אבל מלוה, שלבסוף בא לידי "לא יגוש" — שביעית משמטתה.

ואין הבכור נוטל פי שנים דהוה ליה ראוי כו'. ואפילו למאן דאמר לעיל בפ' "יש נוחלין" (דף קכד:): מלוה לא הוי ראוי — שושבינות מיהא הוי ראוי, כי שמא לא יפרע לו לעולם.

עשה עמו באחת ובקש לעשות עמו בשתים. פי': שיפרע לו בשתי נשים, בכל אחת חצי, שרוצה לישא זו אחר זו — יכול לומר: באחת אני עושה עמך כדרך שעשית עמי, ולא אטרח בשתים. והר"ר יצחק בר מרדכי פירש דגרסינן איפכא: עשה עמו בשושבינות בשתי נשים, ובקש שיעשה עמו באשה אחת — יכול לומר לו: כשתשא אשה אחרת אביא לך בשתים, פי': ולא אתן לך הכל בזאת האשה. ומיהו, גירסת הספרים אתי שפיר, כדפרישית.

סבלונות

רבינו גרשום

קודם זמן שושבינות נמי: ואין בה משום רבית. אם החזיר לו זה יותר דלאו לשם רבית יהיב ליה אלא לשם מתנה: דלא קרינן ביה לא יגוש. דהיכא דמצי למתבעיה כל זימנא אם לא קבע לו זמן קרינן ביה לא יגוש ושביעית משמטתו. אבל הא הואיל ואין נגבית אלא בעונתה לית ביה משום לא יגוש. ואין הבכור נוטל פי שנים בה. בשושבינות שחזרה לאחר מיתת האב שהיו חייבין לאביו: הוה במתא. כשנשא חבירו אשה והיה חייב להחזיר לו שושבינות ואיבעי לי' למיתי לחופתו והלכך אף דלא אתא אפי' הכי חייב לשלוח לו סבלונות משום דנגבית בב"ד. ואי לא ידע דעבד חופה כגון דהוה בשוקי בראי אך דשמע קל טבלא שמקרקשין בזוג סימן שיתקבצו לחופה איבעי ליה למיתי. ואי לא אתא אפי' הכי חייב להחזיר לו: לא שמע. שהוא רחוק הרבה משכונתו: איבעי ליה שיודיעו. שיבא: תרעומת אית ליה. גביה שלא זימנו לסעודתו אבל מיהו שלומי לישלם סבלונותיו. אבל הואיל שלא אכל שם צריך לנכות לו מן השושבינות: ועד כמה. צריך שינכה לו: אמר אביי נהגו בני גננא עד זוזא שוה בכריסיה. כלומר שוה זוז אוכל אדם כשהוא אוכל לחופה ואם נתן לו זה ד' זוזי לשושבינותו ועכשיו כשמחזיר לו סבלונותיו ולא אכל לחופתו משלם פלגא ב' זוזין וב' זוז ינכה לו משום שאם היה מאכילו לשובע לא היה אוכל פחות מב' זוזין והאי דאמר עד זוזא אתא בכריסיה היינו היכא דלית מאכל כל כך כי אם לצמצם: מיכן ואילך. כלומר יתר על כן שאם שושבינו זה אדם חשוב ולא זמנו לסעוד בחופתו והיה חייב לזה בשושבינו ד' זוז ינכה לו מאותו דורון ג' זוז משום דאם היה הוא שם היו משימין לפניו כפי חשיבותו (ד' זוזי ינכה לו מאותו). ולא היה שוה פחות מג' זוז והרביעי יחזור לו: עשה עמו. בשושבינו: בפומבי. בפרהסיא דכולה עלמא הביא עמו לשמחו. ועשה עמו אידך חופתו בצנעא מפני (שהוא למד או מפני) אימת בני אדם ובקש שיפרע לו שושבינות בצנעא בלא קול יכול לומר לו זה לא אשלם כי אם בפומבי אני רוצה לשמוח עם אנשים הרבה בחופתו כמו ששמחתי עמו דבצניעות לא הוי שמחה כלום. וכל הני דלקמן מצי למימר הכי: באחת. כשנשא אשה אחת בקש שיפרע לו כשהוא נושא שתים כאחת לא הויא כל כך שמחה בשתי צרות אלא יכול לומר כשתשיא לבנך או לאחיך בתולה אחת או אשה ראשונה אפרע לך שאני רוצה לשמוח עמך כמו ששמחתני אתה: עתיר נכסי. זה הוא עשיר נכסים וכרמים שבחוץ: עתיר פומבי. זה שיש לו רוב בהמות ויוצאין לרעות בחוץ ויש להן קול עושר. זהו בעל אגדה שיכול לדרוש בכ"מ בפני רבים בבית הכנסת ובבית המשתה ויש לו [שם] שהוא חכם: עתיר סלעין. שיש לו כסף וזהב ומשתכר בה: עתיר תקוע. זה שיש לו בתים הרבה ומשכירן ומביאין לו שכירותו ואין לו קול עושר כל כך: זהו בעל פלפול. שיושב בביתו ומוסיף מפלפולו על שמועתו ששמע דתקוע היינו בתים כדכתיב ויעקב תקע את אהלו: עתיר משה. שהוא עשיר בדבר המדוד כגון איפות של חטים ואינו מרויח בהן אלא בביתו אצורין: עתיר כמם. זהו שיש לו פקדונות של כסף וזהב ואינו מרויח בהם אלא בבית אצורים. ששומע מפי רבו ויודע מה ששומע ואינו מחודד כל כך שידע לחדש דבר מדעתו: הכל צריכין למרי חטיא. שאין אדם יכול לחיות בלא חטה. זה בעל גמרא שאין אדם יכול להורות איסור והיתר ולא לדין כי אם בעל גמרא שיודע לפרש ולחקור הכל: זה בעל תלמוד. שעוסק כל היום בהויות ותירוצים ובעל משנה אינו טורח שאין בה קושיות: רבא אמר איפכא. ימי עני רעים זה בעל משנה שהכל סתום במשנה. בעל תלמוד פשוט לו הכל שרואה הקושיות ותירוצים וראיות שמסייעות זו לזו: יעצב בהן זה בעל משנה. שאינו יודע לפרש סתומות שבמשנה: יסכן בם. מתחמם בהם ומתהנה זה בעל תלמוד שמאזין ומבחין מה שבתוכו: שדעתו קצרה. רגזן: הרחמני. שדואג בצער כל אדם: אסתנים. דאנינא דעתיה:

שינוי

מסורת הש"ס

א) ס"א בכיסי': ב) [ברכות סד.] הוריות יד. ג) סנהדרין ק: ד) [נ"ל נמאס. יעבץ]:

הגהות הב"ח

(א) גמ' שמע קל טבלא. נ"ב פירוש שהיה קרוב לעיר: (ב) שם איבעי ליה לאודועיה לא אודעיה תרעומת אית ליה עליה שלומי: (ג) שם אייתיה בכפיה. נ"ב ס"א אייתי בכיסי' אכליה בכריסיה: (ד) רשב"ם ד"ה קול טבלא שתולין בקרש אחד זוג ענבל אשקלנ"א בלע"ז: (ה) ד"ה עד זוזא אכליה בכרסיה זוזא היה אוכל: (ו) ד"ה כחשיבותיה וכו' ורגילין משום חשיבות לכבדו במיני: (ז) ד"ה זה רחמן כמה עניים הוא רואה: (ח) תום' ד"ה ואין השביעית וכו' בשושבינות לא יגוש לא שייך ביה למימר: (ט) בא"ד בחלי ימיו יעזבנו לפסק כלישנא קמא דפ"ק דמכות דלאית ליה וכו': (י) שם ומגיה זמן עשר. נ"ב פי' שלא במשפט הוא שיעזבנו בחלי ימיו והשמפט היא שאין השביעית משמטתה ונקט לישנא דקרא אבל לא היתה כוונת ר"ת להגיה ולתקן את דברי רבינו אליהו:

"תְּנוּ לִי בַּעְלִי וְאֶשְׂמַח עִמּוֹ", הָכָא נַמִי [א]נֵימָא: "תְּנוּ לִי שׁוֹשְׁבִינִי וְאֶשְׂמַח עִמּוֹ"! אָמַר רַב יוֹסֵף: הָכָא בְּמַאי עָסְקִינַן — [ב]כְּגוֹן שֶׁשָּׂמַח עִמּוֹ ז' יְמֵי מִשְׁתֶּה, וְלֹא הִסְפִּיק לְפוֹרְעוֹ עַד שֶׁמֵּת. לֵימָא: "תְּנוּ לִי בַּעְלִי וְאֶשְׂמַח עִמּוֹ" תַּנָּאֵי הִיא? דְּתַנְיָא: הַמְאָרֵס אֶת הָאִשָּׁה — [ג]בְּתוּלָה גּוֹבָה מָאתַיִם, וְאַלְמָנָה מָנֶה; מָקוֹם שֶׁנָּהֲגוּ לְהַחֲזִיר קִדּוּשִׁין — מַחֲזִירִין, מָקוֹם שֶׁנָּהֲגוּ שֶׁלֹּא לְהַחֲזִיר קִדּוּשִׁין — אֵין מַחֲזִירִין, דִּבְרֵי רַבִּי נָתָן. רַבִּי יְהוּדָה הַנָּשִׂיא אוֹמֵר, בֶּאֱמֶת אָמְרוּ: מָקוֹם שֶׁנָּהֲגוּ לְהַחֲזִיר — מַחֲזִירִין, מָקוֹם שֶׁנָּהֲגוּ שֶׁלֹּא לְהַחֲזִיר — אֵין מַחֲזִירִין. רַבִּי יְהוּדָה הַנָּשִׂיא הַיְינוּ תַּנָּא קַמָּא! אֶלָּא לָאו, "תְּנוּ לִי בַּעְלִי וְאֶשְׂמַח עִמּוֹ" אִיכָּא בֵּינַיְיהוּ, וְחַסּוּרֵי מִחַסְּרָא וְהָכִי קָתָנֵי: הַמְאָרֵס אֶת הָאִשָּׁה — בְּתוּלָה גּוֹבָה מָאתַיִם, וְאַלְמָנָה מָנֶה; בד"א — דַּהֲדַר בֵּיהּ אִיהוּ. אֲבָל מֵתָה, מָקוֹם שֶׁנָּהֲגוּ לְהַחֲזִיר — מַחֲזִירִין, מָקוֹם שֶׁנָּהֲגוּ שֶׁלֹּא לְהַחֲזִיר — אֵין מַחֲזִירִין; וְדַוְקָא שֶׁמֵּתָה הִיא, אֲבָל מֵת הוּא — אֵין מַחֲזִירִין, מַאי טַעְמָא? יְכוֹלָה הִיא שֶׁתֹּאמַר: "תְּנוּ לִי בַּעְלִי וְאֶשְׂמַח עִמּוֹ". וַאֲתָא רַבִּי יְהוּדָה הַנָּשִׂיא לְמֵימַר, בֶּאֱמֶת אָמְרוּ: בֵּין מֵת הוּא וּבֵין מֵתָה הִיא, מָקוֹם שֶׁנָּהֲגוּ לְהַחֲזִיר — מַחֲזִירִין, מָקוֹם שֶׁנָּהֲגוּ שֶׁלֹּא לְהַחֲזִיר — אֵין מַחֲזִירִין, וְלָא מָצְיָא אָמְרָה: "תְּנוּ לִי בַּעְלִי וְאֶשְׂמַח עִמּוֹ"! לָא, דְּכוּלֵּי עָלְמָא — יְכוֹלָה שֶׁתֹּאמַר: "תְּנוּ לִי בַּעְלִי וְאֶשְׂמַח עִמּוֹ", וּדְמִית הוּא — כ"ע לָא פְּלִיגִי. כִּי פְּלִיגִי — שֶׁמֵּתָה הִיא, וְהָכָא בְּקִדּוּשִׁין לְטִיבּוּעִין נִיתְּנוּ קָא מִיפַּלְגִי, רַבִּי נָתָן סָבַר: [א]קִדּוּשִׁין לָאו לְטִיבּוּעִין נִיתְּנוּ, וְר' יְהוּדָה הַנָּשִׂיא סָבַר: קִדּוּשִׁין לְטִיבּוּעִין נִיתְּנוּ. וְהָא מָקוֹם שֶׁנָּהֲגוּ לְהַחֲזִיר — מַחֲזִירִין קָתָנֵי! הָכִי קָאָמַר: וְסִבְלוֹנוֹת, וַדַּאי מָקוֹם שֶׁנָּהֲגוּ לְהַחֲזִיר — מַחֲזִירִין. וְהָנֵי תַּנָּאֵי כְּהָנֵי תַּנָּאֵי; דְּתַנְיָא: קִדְּשָׁהּ בְּכִכָּר — בְּתוּלָה גּוֹבָה מָאתַיִם, וְאַלְמָנָה מָנֶה, דִּבְרֵי רַבִּי מֵאִיר; רַבִּי יְהוּדָה אוֹמֵר: בְּתוּלָה גּוֹבָה מָאתַיִם, וְאַלְמָנָה מָנֶה, וּמַחֲזֶרֶת לוֹ אֶת הַשְּׁאָר; רַבִּי יוֹסֵי אוֹמֵר: קִדְּשָׁהּ בְּעֶשְׂרִים — נוֹתֵן לָהּ שְׁלֹשִׁים חֲצָאִין, קִדְּשָׁהּ בִּשְׁלֹשִׁים — נוֹתֵן לָהּ עֶשְׂרִים חֲצָאִין. בְּמַאי עָסְקִינַן? אִילֵימָא שֶׁמֵּתָה, מִי אִית לָהּ כְּתוּבָּה? וְאֶלָּא שֶׁמֵּת הוּא, אַמַּאי מַחֲזֶרֶת לוֹ אֶת הַשְּׁאָר? וְנֵימָא: "תְּנוּ לִי בַּעְלִי וְאֶשְׂמַח עִמּוֹ"! וְאֶלָּא בְּאֵשֶׁת יִשְׂרָאֵל שֶׁזִּינְּתָה; וּבְמַאי? אִי בְּרָצוֹן, מִי אִית לָהּ כְּתוּבָּה? וְאֶלָּא בְּאוֹנֶס, מִישְׁרָא שַׁרְיָא לֵיהּ! וְאֶלָּא, בְּאֵשֶׁת כֹּהֵן שֶׁנֶּאֶנְסָה, וּבְקִדּוּשִׁין לְטִיבּוּעִין נִיתְּנוּ קָמִיפַּלְגִי, רַבִּי מֵאִיר סָבַר: קִדּוּשִׁין לְטִיבּוּעִין נִיתְּנוּ, וְר' יְהוּדָה סָבַר: לָאו לְטִיבּוּעִין נִיתְּנוּ. וְרַבִּי יוֹסֵי מְסַפְּקָא לֵיהּ אִי לְטִיבּוּעִין נִיתְּנוּ אִי לָא, וְהִלְכָּךְ, קִדְּשָׁהּ בְּעֶשְׂרִים — נוֹתֵן לָהּ שְׁלֹשִׁים חֲצָאִין, קִדְּשָׁהּ בִּשְׁלֹשִׁים — נוֹתֵן לָהּ עֶשְׂרִים חֲצָאִין. אָמַר רַב יוֹסֵף בַּר מַנְיוּמִי אָמַר רַב נַחְמָן: בְּכׇל מָקוֹם שֶׁנָּהֲגוּ לְהַחֲזִיר — מַחֲזִירִין, וְתַרְגּוּמָא: נְהַרְדְּעָא. שְׁאָר בָּבֶל מַאי? רַבָּה וְרַב יוֹסֵף דְּאָמְרִי תַּרְוַיְיהוּ: מוֹהֲרֵי הָדְרֵי, קִדּוּשֵׁי לָא הָדְרֵי. אָמַר רַב פָּפָּא, הִלְכְתָא: בֵּין שֶׁמֵּת הוּא בֵּין שֶׁמֵּתָה הִיא [ב)]וְהָדַר בֵּיהּ הוּא — [ד]מוֹהֲרֵי הָדְרֵי, קִדּוּשֵׁי לָא הָדְרֵי; הָדְרָא בָּהּ אִיהִי — אֲפִי' קִדּוּשֵׁי נַמִי הָדְרֵי. אַמֵּימָר אָמַר: [ה]קִדּוּשֵׁי לָא הָדְרֵי, גְּזֵירָה שֶׁמָּא יֹאמְרוּ קִדּוּשִׁין תּוֹפְסִין בַּאֲחוֹתָהּ. רַב אַשִׁי אָמַר: גִּיטָּהּ מוֹכִיחַ עָלֶיהָ. וְהָא דְּרַב אַשִׁי [ג)]בְּדוּתָא הִיא, דְּאִיכָּא דְּשָׁמַע בְּהָא וְלָא שָׁמַע בְּהָא. § "שֶׁהַשּׁוֹשְׁבִינוּת נִגְבֵּית בְּבֵית דִּין" ת"ר, [ו]חֲמִשָּׁה דְּבָרִים נֶאֶמְרוּ בְּשׁוֹשְׁבִינוּת: נִגְבֵּית בְּבֵית דִּין, וְחוֹזֶרֶת בְּעוֹנָתָהּ, וְאֵין בָּהּ מִשּׁוּם רִבִּית, וְאֵין

רשב"ם

תְּנוּ לִי בַּעְלִי. כְּלוֹמַר, אֲנִי מְזוּמֶּנֶת לְהַשְׁלִים תְּנָאֵי קִדּוּשַׁי, דְּהַיְינוּ נִשּׂוּאִין, וְאֵין הָעִיכּוּב תָּלוּי בִּי. אָמַר רַב יוֹסֵף. בְּעָלְמָא אָמְרִי' "תְּנוּ לִי שׁוֹשְׁבִינִי וְאֶשְׂמַח עִמּוֹ" כִּדְקָאָמְרַתְּ. אֲבָל הָכָא בְּמַאי עָסְקִינַן — כְּגוֹן שֶׁשָּׂמַח וְאָכַל עִם הַמֵּת בְּחוּפָּתוֹ אוֹתוֹ שֶׁחַיָּיב לוֹ הַשּׁוֹשְׁבִינוּת, וְנִתְחַיֵּיב הַשּׁוֹשְׁבִין מִיָּד לְפָרְעוֹ אַחֲרֵי שֶׁשָּׂמַח עִמּוֹ. אֶלָּא שֶׁמֵּת, וְיִיבֵּם אָחִיו אֶת אִשְׁתּוֹ. וְשׁוֹשְׁבִינוּת זוֹ רְאוּיָה הִיא, וְתַחֲזוֹר לְאֶמְצַע. דֶּרֶךְ שׁוֹשְׁבִינוּת — אוֹכֵל עִמּוֹ, וְאַח"כ מֵבִיא הַדּוֹרוֹן. לֵימָא תְּנוּ לִי בַּעְלִי וְאֶשְׂמַח עִמּוֹ תַּנָּאֵי הִיא. לְמָר מַחֲזִירִין קִדּוּשִׁין אִם מֵת הָאָרוּס, וּלְמָר אֵין מַחֲזִירִין. בְּתוּלָה גּוֹבָה מָאתַיִם. אִם מֵת אוֹ גֵּירְשָׁהּ. וּבִדְכָתַב לָהּ מִן הָאֵירוּסִין. דְּהֵיכָא דְּלָא כָּתַב לָהּ — בָּעְיָא הִיא בִּכְתוּבּוֹת (דף פט:), וְלָא אִיפְּשִׁיטָא. מָקוֹם שֶׁנָּהֲגוּ לְהַחֲזִיר קִדּוּשִׁין מַחֲזִירִין. לְקַמֵּיהּ מְפָרֵשׁ לָהּ וְאָזֵיל. ר' יְהוּדָה הַנָּשִׂיא אוֹמֵר כו'. לְקַמָּן פָּרֵיךְ עֲלָהּ. דַּהֲדַר בֵּיהּ אִיהוּ. חוֹזֵר בָּהּ, וְרוֹצֶה לְגָרְשָׁהּ. הִלְכָּךְ תִּטּוֹל כְּתוּבָּתָהּ מִלְּבַד קִדּוּשִׁין. וְהוּא הַדִּין אִם מֵת הוּא, כִּדְמְפָרֵשׁ וְאָזֵיל. וּמִשּׁוּם דְּמִיבָּעֵי לֵיהּ לְפָרוּשֵׁי בְּאַנְפֵּי נַפְשֵׁיהּ טַעֲמָא דְּמֵת הוּא, מִשּׁוּם "תְּנוּ לִי בַּעְלִי וְאֶשְׂמַח עִמּוֹ", נָקַט הָכָא לִישָּׁנָא דַּהֲדַר בֵּיהּ אִיהוּ. דְּמִית הוּא כּוּלֵּי עָלְמָא לָא פְּלִיגֵי. דְּאֵינָהּ מַחֲזֶרֶת קִדּוּשִׁין, דְּמָצְיָא אָמְרָה: "תְּנוּ לִי בַּעְלִי וְאֶשְׂמַח עִמּוֹ", כִּדְאוֹקְמָהּ רַב יוֹסֵף בַּר אַבָּא לְבָרַיְיתָא דִּלְעֵיל. לְטִיבּוּעִין נִיתְּנוּ. שֶׁאִם תָּמוּת וְלֹא יִזְכֶּה לִישָּׂאֶנָּה — יִהְיוּ אֲבוּדִין, וְלֹא יַחְזְרוּ לוֹ. וּפָרְכִינַן: וְהָא מָקוֹם שֶׁנָּהֲגוּ לְהַחֲזִיר מַחֲזִירִין קָתָנֵי. בְּמִילְּתֵיהּ דְּר' יְהוּדָה הַנָּשִׂיא, וְהֵיכִי מוֹקְמַתְּ לָהּ לְדִידֵיהּ דִּלְטִיבּוּעִין נִיתְּנוּ? הָכִי קָאָמַר. רַבִּי יְהוּדָה. סִבְלוֹנוֹת וַדַּאי. בְּהַהוּא מוֹדֵינָא לָךְ דִּבְמִנְהָגָא תַּלְיָא מִילְּתָא. וְהוּא תַּכְשִׁיטִים שֶׁשּׁוֹלֵחַ לַאֲרוּסָתוֹ לְאַחַר שֶׁקִּדְּשָׁהּ. אֲבָל קִדּוּשִׁין — וַדַּאי לְטִיבּוּעִין נִיתְּנוּ. וְהָנֵי תַּנָּאֵי. דִּלְקַמָּן, כִּי הָנֵי תַּנָּאֵי דִּלְעֵיל דִּפְלִיגֵי בְּקִדּוּשִׁין לְטִיבּוּעִין נִיתְּנוּ. בְּכִכָּר. כֶּסֶף, הַיְינוּ כ"ה מָנֶה. בְּתוּלָה גּוֹבָה כו'. לְקַמָּן מִיפָּרְשָׁא כּוּלָּהּ. בְּתוּלָה גּוֹבָה מָאתַיִם זוּז. דְּהַיְינוּ שְׁנֵי מָנִין, וְהַיְינוּ חֲמִשִּׁים שֶׁקֶל כְּמוֹהַר הַבְּתוּלוֹת, מִלְּבַד קִדּוּשִׁין — תִּטּוֹל כְּתוּבָּתָהּ. כִּכָּר. כ"ה מָנִים. מָנֶה — כ"ה שְׁקָלִים. שֶׁקֶל — ד' דִּינָר, דְּהַיְינוּ ד' זוּזִים. ר' יְהוּדָה אוֹמֵר בְּתוּלָה גּוֹבָה מָאתַיִם. מִן הַכִּכָּר שֶׁל קִדּוּשִׁין, וּמַחֲזֶרֶת הַשְּׁאָר לַאֲרוּסָהּ. רַבִּי יוֹסֵי אוֹמֵר. לְקַמֵּיהּ מְפָרֵשׁ לָהּ. אִילֵימָא שֶׁמֵּתָה. הִיא, וּמִשּׁוּם הָכִי קָאָמַר ר' יְהוּדָה מַחֲזֶרֶת לוֹ אֶת הַשְּׁאָר — דְּקִדּוּשִׁין לָאו לְטִיבּוּעִין נִיתְּנוּ. אֶלָּא בְּשֶׁמֵּת הוּא. וְהִלְכָּךְ גּוֹבָה כְּתוּבָּתָהּ כְּדִין אַלְמָנָה. וְאַמַּאי קָמַחֲזֶרֶת לְר' יְהוּדָה אֶת הַשְּׁאָר? וְהָא אוֹקִימְנָא לְעֵיל: יְכוֹלָה הִיא שֶׁתֹּאמַר "תְּנוּ לִי בַּעְלִי וְאֶשְׂמַח עִמּוֹ"! שֶׁזִּינְּתָה. תַּחַת אָרוּס [שֶׁלָּהּ] וּבָאָה לִגְבּוֹת כְּתוּבָּתָהּ כְּשֶׁיְּגָרְשֶׁנָּה בַּעְלָהּ. מִישְׁרָא שַׁרְיָא לֵיהּ. כִּדְנָפְקָא לָן בְּסוֹטָה (דף ב.) מִ"וְהִיא לֹא נִתְפָּשָׂה" — אֲסוּרָה, הָא נִתְפְּשָׂה — מוּתֶּרֶת. וְאִם בָּא לְגָרְשָׁהּ שֶׁלֹּא כַּדִּין לָמָּה תַּחֲזִיר [לוֹ] אֶת הַשְּׁאָר? שֶׁנֶּאֶנְסָה. וַאֲסוּרָה לוֹ, כִּדְנָפְקָא לָן (כתובות דף נא:) מִ"וְהִיא לֹא נִתְפָּשָׂה"; הָא יֵשׁ לָךְ אַחֶרֶת, אע"פ שֶׁנִּתְפְּשָׂה — אֲסוּרָה, וְאֵיזוֹ — זוֹ אֵשֶׁת כֹּהֵן. וְכֵיוָן דְּלָא פָּשְׁעָה — לֹא הִפְסִידָה כְּתוּבָּתָהּ לְד"ה. אֲבָל בְּקִידּוּשֶׁיהָ פְּלִיגֵי. ר' יוֹסֵי מְסַפְּקָא לֵיהּ. וַהֲווּ קִדּוּשִׁין מָמוֹן הַמּוּטָּל בְּסָפֵק, וְחוֹלְקִין. וּמַחֲזֶרֶת לוֹ אֶת הַחֵצִי, אוֹ חוֹשֶׁבֶת בִּכְתוּבָּתָהּ וְתִטְרוֹף מִמֶּנּוּ מוֹתַר כְּתוּבָּתָהּ. הִלְכָּךְ, קִידְּשָׁהּ לְאַלְמָנָה בְּכ' שְׁקָלִים דְּהַיְינוּ שְׁמוֹנִים זוּזִים — הַמ' זוּזִים צְרִיכָה לְהַחֲזִיר לוֹ, וְחוֹשֶׁבֶת בִּכְתוּבָּתָהּ, וְהוּא נוֹתֵן לָהּ ל' חֲצָאֵי שְׁקָלִים, דְּהַיְינוּ ס' זוּז — הֲרֵי נִתְקַבְּלָה הָאַלְמָנָה ק' זוּז, דְּהַיְינוּ מָנֶה בִּכְתוּבָּתָהּ. קִדְּשָׁהּ בְּל' שְׁקָלִים. דְּהַיְינוּ מֵאָה וְעֶשְׂרִים זוּז — חֶצְיָים תַּחְשׁוֹב בִּכְתוּבָּתָהּ, דְּהַיְינוּ ס' זוּז. וְאַרְבָּעִים הַחֲסֵרִים לָהּ הוּא יִתֵּן — עֶשְׂרִים חֲצָאֵי שֶׁקֶל, דְּהַיְינוּ מ' זוּז. נִרְאֶה בְּעֵינַי דְּהָ"ג: אָמַר רַב יוֹסֵף בַּר מַנְיוּמִי אָמַר רַב נַחְמָן בְּכׇל מָקוֹם שֶׁנָּהֲגוּ לְהַחֲזִיר מַחֲזִירִין. הֵיכָא דְּמֵתָה אִשָּׁה. מוֹהֲרֵי הָדְרֵי. שֶׁשּׁוֹלֵחַ אַחַר קִדּוּשִׁין, וְהֵן סִבְלוֹנוֹת, הָדְרֵי בְּמִיתַת הָאִשָּׁה. וְנִרְאֶה בְּעֵינַי דְּתַרְתֵּי גַּוְונֵי נִינְהוּ, מוֹהֲרֵי וְסִבְלוֹנוֹת, דְּהָא גַּבֵּי סִבְלוֹנוֹת נַמִי הָכִי פָּסְקִינַן לָהּ לְקַמָּן גַּבֵּי מַתְנִי' דְּסִבְלוֹנוֹת, וְתַרְתֵּי זִימְנֵי לָמָּה לִי? וי"ל דְּמוֹהַר הוּא מָמוֹן שֶׁמַּקְדִּים לָהּ עַתָּה בִּימֵי אֵירוּסִין, שֶׁיְּהֵא כּוֹתֵב בִּכְתוּבָּתָהּ כְּשֶׁתִּנָּשֵׂא לוֹ, וּלְהָכִי מִיקְרֵי מוֹהַר. גְּזֵירָה שֶׁמָּא יֹאמְרוּ. קִדּוּשֵׁי טָעוּת הָיוּ, וּלְכָךְ חָזְרוּ, וְנִמְלְאוּ קִדּוּשִׁין תּוֹפְסִין בַּאֲחוֹתָהּ וּמוּתֶּרֶת לוֹ. אִיכָּא דְּשָׁמַע. בַּהֲחָזָרַת קִדּוּשִׁין. וְלָא שָׁמַע בְּהָא. בְּגֵט. הִלְכָּךְ קִדּוּשִׁין לָא הָדְרֵי. וְחוֹזֶרֶת בְּעוֹנָתָהּ. כְּשֶׁיִּשָּׂא זֶה אִשָּׁה — יַחֲזִיר לוֹ שׁוֹשְׁבִינוּתוֹ, וְלֹא קוֹדֶם. וְאֵין בָּהּ מִשּׁוּם רִבִּית. אִם הִרְבָּה לוֹ בְּדוֹרוֹן יוֹתֵר. וְאֵין

תוספות

ורבי יהודה הנשיא אומר באמת אמרו מקום שנהגו להחזיר קדושין כו'. ל"ג הכא "קדושין", דלקמן מוקי לה בסבלונות.

[ד)]**ורבי** יהודה סבר באמת אמרו כו'. ואין לומר: דלמא ר' יהודה סבר (דכמת) היא יכולה לומר כו', דתנא בתרא לטפויי קא אתי.

נותן לה שלשים חצאים. שכך היו רגילין לעשות חשבון מחלאי סלעים, כדקאמר לקמן בפ' "גט פשוט" (דף קסו:): ספ"ל מלמעלה וקפ"ל מלמטה כו', ומפרש רבינו יעקב: ספ"ל — ס' פלגי, קפ"ל — ק' פלגי.

ורבי יוסי מספקא ליה קדושין אי לטיבועין נתנו אי לאו לטיבועין נתנו. וא"ת: ולמה חולקין? הוה ליה למימר: המוציא מחבירו עליו הראיה, כדין כל ממון המוטל בספק, כרבנן דסומכוס! ולעיל ב"המוכר את הבית" (דף סב: ד"ה איתמר) פירשתי לה.

מסורת הש"ס

א) [כתובות עו:]: ב) פי' או הדר: ג) [עי' מ"ש על הגליון פסחים יא.]: ד) גי' רש"א מה"ד ולא מגיה אמרה:

עין משפט נר מצוה

נג א ב מיי' פ"ז מהל' זכייה ומתנה הל' ט י טוש"ע אה"ע סי' ס:

נד ג מיי' פ"י מהלכות אישות הל' יא ופי"א הלכה א סמג עשין מח טוש"ע אה"ע סימן נד סעיף ו וסי' סו סעיף ו:

נה ד מיי' פ"ו מהלכות זכייה ומתנה הל' כא סמג עשין מח טור שו"ע אה"ע סי' נ סעיף ג:

נו ה מיי' שם הלכה יח טוש"ע שם סעיף א:

נז ו מיי' פ"ז מהלכות זכייה הל' יג טוש"ע אה"ע סי' ס:

רבינו גרשום

ואמר רב יוסף לא שנו. דמחזיר אלא כשמתה היא אבל מת הוא דהיא תפסה אין מחזירין ליורשיו מאי טעמא יכולה היא כו' הכי נמי יכול לומר האי תנו לי שושביני שאשמח עמו ואם לאו לא אחזיר: הכא במאי עסקינן. דלא מצי למטען הכי בשכבר שמח עמו האי דמת ולא הספיק לפורעו עד שמת והואיל דכבר שמח עמו מחזיר אע"ג דמת: המארס את האשה. וכתב לה עיקר כתובה מן האירוסין: במה דברים אמורים. דגביא: דהדר ביה הבעל. מן הקדושין ונתן גט בדידה מותרינן למימר תנו בעלי ואשמח עמו הא לאו הכי לא אחזיר הקדושין. אבל בדידיה לא איתרינן למימר תנו לי אשתי ואשמח עמה הא לאו הכי לא אחזיר הקדושין משום דהוא לא תפיס ברשותיה הקדושין: ואתא ר' יהודה למימר כו' ולא מציא אמרה תנו לי בעלי ואשמח עמו. אלמא דבפלוגתא דתנאי היא: א) וכשמת הוא כולי עלמא לא פליגי דיכולה לומר תנו לי בעלי כו' אפי' לר' יהודה ואין מחזירין. כי פליגי (בין) ר' נתן ור' יהודה הנשיא שמתה היא ובקדושין לטיבועין נתנו אי הדרי אי לא הדרי הוא דמיפלגי. ר' נתן סבר קדושין לאו לטיבועין נתנו משום הכי מקום שנהגו להחזיר מחזירין דלא נתנו לטיבועין. ור' יהודה הנשיא סבר קדושין לטיבועין נתנו משום הכי מקום שנהגו שלא להחזיר אין מחזירין. משום דאכתי לאו תירוצא מקשינן ליה לאלתר אכתי איכא למיפרך לתרוייהו והא מקום שנהגו כו' ור' יהודה היינו ת"ק דר' נתן. ומתרץ לעולם ר' יהודה סבירא ליה קדושין לטיבועין נתנו מפיק טעמא מסיפא מקום שנהגו שלא להחזיר אין מחזירין ודקא קשיא רישא והא מקום שנהגו להחזיר מחזירין. רבי יהודה רישא מתרץ לה בסבלונות. מתנות שמשגו לה חתן זולת הקדושין והכי קאמר סבלונות ודאי באמת אמרו מקום שנהגו להחזיר סבלונות מחזירין אזלינן בתר מנהג אבל קדושין לא הדרי ואי קשיא לך הא סיפא נמי דמוקמת בקדושין לר' יהודה קתני מקום שנהגו כו' הא לא קשיא ההוא תנא שנהגו לאו דוקא אלא דאיידי דאצטריך למתני רישא דסבלונות מנהגא תנא בסיפא נמי מנהגא. ור' נתן נמי דאמר קדושין לאו לטיבועין נתנו מפיק טעמא מרישא מקום שנהגו להחזיר מחזירין וסיפא מוקי לה בסבלונות ונהגו דרישא לאו דוקא: והני תנאי. דפליגי בקדושין אי לטיבועין נתנו: כי הני תנאי דתניא קדשה בככר. ששים מנה וכתב לה כתובה מן האירוסין: בתולה גובה מאתים ואלמנה מנה. לבד מן הככר שנתקדשה [דר"מ]. אלמא דסבר ר' מאיר דקדושין לטיבועין ניתנו: ר' יהודה אומר בתולה גובה מאתים. מן ההוא ככר והנשאר מן הככר מחזרת. אלמא דסבר דקדושין לאו לטיבועין נתנו לפיכך פורע לה מן הקדושין עצמן. טעמא דר' יוסי מפרש לקמן: במאי עסקי'. ברייתא דגבייא כתובה: אי בשמתה. והא הבעל יורש את אשתו: אלא

שמת הוא ואמאי אמר ר' יהודה מחזרת לו את השאר והא מציא למימר תני בעלי ואשמח עמו. אלא ודאי דלא מת הוא ובמאי עסקי' דגביא כתובתה בשזינתה: משרא שריא ליה. ואמאי גובה כלום הואיל דהיא תחת בעלה: אלא באשת כהן שנאנסה. דאפי' באונס אסיר' לי' דעשאה זונה: ר' מאיר סבר קדושין לטיבועין נתנו. וגובה כתובתה לבד הקדושין: ור' יהודה סבר כו'. אלמא דפלוגתא דתנאי היא: ור' יוסי מספקא ליה אי לטיבועין נתנו אי לא. הלכך ממון המוטל בספק הוא וחולקין דאי פשיטא לן דלטיבועין נתנו היכא דקדשה בעשרים צריך לפרוע לה עוד לאלמנה בכתובה מנה לבד מן הקדושין ואי נמי פשיטא לן דלאו לטיבועין נתנו להיכא דקדשה בכ' סלעים צריך שיתן לה עוד חמש על אותם עשרים דהיינו מנה כתובת אלמנה והכי נמי מפרש להיכא דקדשה [בל' סלעים] דאי לטיבועין נתנו נותן לה עוד לבר מקדושין כתובה מנה אי לאו לטיבועין נתנו תחזיר לו היא ה' סלעים שהן על כ"ה של כתובה. אבל השתא דמספקא ליה אי לטיבועין אי לא חולקין הקדושין בשוה בינו ובינה דאי קדשה בכ' סלעים תעכב י' בידה חצי קדושין וי' שנשתיירו הן שלו לפיכך נותן לה עוד ל' חצאי סלע שהן ט"ו סלעים על י' סלעים שלו שנשתיירו בידה הרי כ"ה סלעים והיינו שיעור כתובה מנה. וה"נ להיכא דקדשה בל' סלעים חציין תטול היא לעצמה משום ספק וחצין הן של בעל ועוד צריך שיתן לה עוד כ' חצאי סלעים דהיינו י' סלעים על אותן ט"ו סלעים של קדושין שנשארו לו בידה הרי כ"ה סלעים שיעור כתובה מנה: א"ר נחמן ב) בכל מקום שנהגו להחזיר קדושין דמי. כלומר סתם עיירות של בבל שאין ידוע אם שלא נהגו בהם להחזיר אם לאו אם עומדות הן אותן עיירות וסמוכות לעיר שנהגו בה להחזיר מחזירין כמו כן אותן עיירות: ותרגומא נהרדעא. הן סתם עיירות אם סמוכה לנהרדעא עיר שמחזירין בה תדון כל נהרדעא כמוה. שאר בבל חוץ מנהרדעא מאי. כלומר היאך נוהגין: מוהרי הדרי. היינו סבלונות תכשיטין שנותן לה לאחר קדושין נהגו להחזיר אם מתה או שנגרשה. קדושי לא הדרי: אמימר אמר אפילו הדרא בה היא קדושי לא הדרי. דאי הדרי דמי להו לבני אדם (דחשיב) כאילו מעולם לא קדשה ויאמרו בני אדם מותר לו לישא אחותה וטעו הואיל דקדשה אסור לו אחותה משום ואשה אל אחותה לא תקח אבל השתא כל זמן שקדושיה בידה לא אתו למיטעי: רב אשי אמר אפי' אי הדרי קדושי לא אתי למטעי דמכל מקום אף על גב דהדרי קדושי גט היא צריכה מפני הקדושין. וגיטה מוכיח עליה שהיתה אשתו ואסור באחותה: ודרב אשי בדותא היא. דאי מהדרא קדושי. איכא דשמע דמהדרי קדושי וסבר דדמי כאילו לא נתקדשה כלל. ולא שמע בגט שנתן ואתי למטעי: וחוזרת בעונתה. בעת שישא זה אשה יפרע לו ולא קודם מפני שהיא כמלוה דכי היכי דמלוה לא מצי תבע בבי דינא

קודם

שמת

א) נראה דצ"ל לא דאם מת הוא דכולי עלמא כו'. ב) נ"ל בכל מקום כו' וכן הגיה הת"ח בפנים וכ"ה בדפו"י ועי' בד"ס.

מג א ב מיי' פ"ט מהל' נחלות הלכה ו סמג עשין פב טוש"ע חו"מ סי' קעז סעיף א וסי' רפט סעיף ה:
מד ג מיי' שם הלכה יא טוש"ע שם סי' קעז סעיף ז:
מה ד מיי' שם ופי"ח מהל' איסורי ביאה הל' ד סמג שם וסי' מח טוש"ע שם ועוש"ע אה"ע סי' לד סעיף ג:
מו ה מיי' פ"ט מהל' נחלות הלכה יא סמג עשין צ טוש"ע חו"מ סי' קעז סעיף ו:
מז ו ז טוש"ע שם ס"ב:
מח ח מיי' שם הל' יד ועי' בהשגות ובמגיד משנה וסמג שם טוש"ע חו"מ סי' ר סעיף ד ה:
מט ט מיי' פ"ז מהלכות זכייה ומתנה הלכה ב ויג סמג עשין שם טוש"ע אה"ע סי' נ ס"ח:
נ כ מיי' שם הלכה טו טור אה"ע סי' ס:
נא ל מיי' פ"ט מהלכות נחלות הל' יד ועיין בה"מ סמג עשין צו טור חו"מ סי' רפ ס"ה:
נב מ מיי' שם הל' יג ועי' בהג"ה טוש"ע שם סעיף ז:

מתני' אַחִין הַשּׁוּתָּפִין שֶׁנָּפַל אֶחָד מֵהֶן לְאוּמָּנוּת — נָפַל לָאֶמְצַע; חָלָה וְנִתְרַפֵּא — נִתְרַפֵּא מִשֶּׁל עַצְמוֹ.§ **גמ'** תָּנָא: הַאי אוּמָּנוּת — לְאוּמָּנוּת הַמֶּלֶךְ. תָּנוּ רַבָּנַן: א אֶחָד מִן הָאַחִין שֶׁמִּינּוּהוּ גַּבַּאי אוֹ פּוֹלְמוּסְטוֹס, אִם מֵחֲמַת הָאַחִין — לָאַחִין, אִם מֵחֲמַת עַצְמוֹ — לְעַצְמוֹ. אִם מֵחֲמַת אַחִין לָאַחִין, פְּשִׁיטָא! לָא צְרִיכָא, ב דַּחֲרִיף טְפֵי. מַהוּ דְּתֵימָא: חוּרְפֵיהּ גָּרֵים לֵיהּ, קָא מַשְׁמַע לָן. תָּנוּ רַבָּנַן: ג אֶחָד מִן הָאַחִין שֶׁנָּטַל מָאתַיִם זוּז לִלְמוֹד תּוֹרָה אוֹ לִלְמוֹד אוּמָּנוּת, יְכוֹלִין הָאַחִין לוֹמַר לוֹ: אִם אַתָּה אֶצְלֵנוּ — יֵשׁ לְךָ מְזוֹנוֹת, אִם אֵין אַתָּה אֶצְלֵנוּ — אֵין לְךָ מְזוֹנוֹת. וְלֵיתְבוּ לֵיהּ כָּל הֵיכָא דְּאִיתֵיהּ! מְסַיֵּיעַ לֵיהּ לְרַב הוּנָא, א) דְּאָמַר רַב הוּנָא: ד בִּרְכַּת הַבַּיִת בְּרוּבָּה. וְלֵיתְבוּ לֵיהּ לְפִי בִּרְכַּת הַבַּיִת! (א) ה הָכִי נַמִי.§ ו "חָלָה וְנִתְרַפֵּא — נִתְרַפֵּא מִשֶּׁל עַצְמוֹ".§ שְׁלַח רָבִין מִשְּׁמֵיהּ דְּר' אֶלְעָא: ז לֹא שָׁנוּ אֶלָּא שֶׁחָלָה בִּפְשִׁיעָה, אֲבָל בְּאוֹנֶס — נִתְרַפֵּא מִן הָאֶמְצַע. הֵיכִי דָּמֵי בִּפְשִׁיעָה? ח כִּדְרַבִּי חֲנִינָא, ב) דְּאָמַר רַבִּי חֲנִינָא: הַכֹּל בִּידֵי שָׁמַיִם חוּץ מִצִּנִּים פַּחִים, שֶׁנֶּאֱמַר: ° "צִנִּים פַּחִים בְּדֶרֶךְ עִקֵּשׁ שׁוֹמֵר נַפְשׁוֹ יִרְחַק מֵהֶם".§ (משלי כב) **מתני'** ט הָאַחִין שֶׁעָשׂוּ מִקְצָתָן שׁוּשְׁבִינוּת בְּחַיֵּי הָאָב, חָזְרָה שׁוּשְׁבִינוּת — חָזְרָה לָאֶמְצַע, שֶׁהַשּׁוּשְׁבִינוּת י נִגְבֵּית בְּבֵית דִּין. אֲבָל כ הַשּׁוֹלֵחַ לַחֲבֵירוֹ כַּדֵּי יַיִן וְכַדֵּי שֶׁמֶן — אֵין נִגְבִּין בְּבֵ"ד, מִפְּנֵי שֶׁהֵן גְּמִילוּת חֲסָדִים.§ **גמ'** וּרְמִינְהִי: ל שָׁלַח לוֹ אָבִיו שׁוּשְׁבִינוּת, כְּשֶׁהִיא חוֹזֶרֶת — חוֹזֶרֶת לוֹ; מ נִשְׁתַּלְּחָה לְאָבִיו שׁוּשְׁבִינוּת, כְּשֶׁהִיא חוֹזֶרֶת — חוֹזֶרֶת מִן הָאֶמְצַע! אָמַר רַבִּי אַסִּי א"ר יוֹחָנָן: כִּי תְּנַן נַמִי מַתְנִיתִין, נִשְׁתַּלְּחָה לְאָבִיו תְּנַן. וְהָא "אַחִין שֶׁעָשׂוּ מִקְצָתָן שׁוּשְׁבִינוּת" קָתָנֵי! תְּנֵי: "לְמִקְצָתָן". וְהָא "חָזְרָה שׁוּשְׁבִינוּת" קָתָנֵי! ה"ק: חָזְרָה לִגְבּוֹת — נִגְבֵּית מֵאֶמְצַע. רַבִּי אַסִּי אָמַר, לָא קַשְׁיָא: כָּאן בִּסְתָם, כָּאן בִּמְפָרֵשׁ; כִּדְתַנְיָא: שָׁלַח לוֹ אָבִיו שׁוּשְׁבִינוּת, כְּשֶׁהִיא חוֹזֶרֶת — חוֹזֶרֶת לוֹ; שָׁלַח אָבִיו שׁוּשְׁבִינוּת סְתָם, כְּשֶׁהִיא חוֹזֶרֶת — חוֹזֶרֶת לָאֶמְצַע. וּשְׁמוּאֵל אָמַר: הָכָא בְּיָבָם עָסְקִינַן, ג) שֶׁאֵינוֹ נוֹטֵל בָּרָאוּי כִּבְמוּחְזָק. מִכְּלָל דְּאִידָךְ מְשַׁלֵּם? (ב) לֵימָא: "תְּנוּ לִי שׁוּשְׁבִינִי וְאֶשְׂמַח עִמּוֹ"! מִי לָא תַנְיָא: ד) מָקוֹם שֶׁנָּהֲגוּ לְהַחֲזִיר קִדּוּשִׁין — מַחֲזִירִין, מָקוֹם שֶׁנָּהֲגוּ שֶׁלֹּא לְהַחֲזִיר — אֵין מַחֲזִירִין; וְאָמַר רַב יוֹסֵף בַּר אַבָּא אָמַר מָר עוּקְבָא אָמַר שְׁמוּאֵל: לֹא שָׁנוּ אֶלָּא שֶׁמֵּתָה הִיא, אֲבָל מֵת הוּא — אֵין מַחֲזִירִין, מ"ט? יְכוֹלָה הִיא שֶׁתֹּאמַר: תְּנוּ

תורה אור

מתני' הָכִי גָּרְסִינַן בְּסֵדֶר הַמִּשְׁנָה: אַחִין הַשּׁוּתָּפִין שֶׁנָּפַל אֶחָד מֵהֶן לְאוּמָּנוּת. אוּמָּנוּת הַמֶּלֶךְ. שֶׁמֵּחֲמַת אָבִיו נָפַל לְאוּמָּנוּת זוֹ, שֶׁכֵּן מִנְהַג הַמֶּלֶךְ, מַעֲמִיד מִבַּיִת זוֹ מוֹכֵס חֹדֶשׁ אֶחָד וּמִבַּיִת זוֹ חֹדֶשׁ אֶחָד, וְכֵן מִכָּל בָּתֵּי הָעִיר. נָפַל לָאֶמְצַע. כָּל זְמַן שֶׁקָּנוּ בִּתְפוּסַת הַבַּיִת הָרֶיוַח לָאֶמְצַע, שֶׁהִרְוִיחַ זֶה בְּאוּמָּנוּתוֹ. חָלָה. בִּפְשִׁיעָה, כִּדְמְפָרֵשׁ בַּגְּמָרָא. **גמ'** תָּנָא אוּמָּנוּת הַמֶּלֶךְ. וְטַעֲמָא כִּדְפָרֵישִׁית. אֲבָל אוּמָּנוּת אַחֶרֶת שֶׁנָּפַל בָּהּ מֵעַצְמוֹ — הָרֶיוַח שֶׁלּוֹ. אוֹ פּוֹלְמוּסְטוֹס. שׁוֹטֵר. וְרַבֵּינוּ חֲנַנְאֵל פֵּי': פּוֹלְמוּסְטוֹס — לוֹחֵם מִלְחָמוֹת בִּלְשׁוֹן יָוָן. מֵחֲמַת אַחִין. כְּמִנְהַג הָעִיר לָקַחַת מִכָּל בַּיִת שׁוֹטֵר אֶחָד לְפִי הַזְּמַן הַקָּבוּעַ, אוֹ לְחֹדֶשׁ אוֹ לְשָׁנָה. מֵחֲמַת עַצְמוֹ. מֵחֲמַת חֲשִׁיבוּתוֹ וּמֵחֲמַת חֲרִיפוּתוֹ. בִּרְכַּת הַבַּיִת בְּרוּבָּהּ. שֶׁאִילּוּ הָיָה דָּר עִמָּהֶן הָיָה הַבַּיִת מִתְבָּרֵךְ בִּגְלָלוֹ. וְלֵיתְבוּ לֵיהּ. קְצָת מְזוֹנוֹת, וִיפַחֲתוּ לוֹ לְפִי חֶסְרוֹן בִּרְכַּת הַבַּיִת בִּגְלָלוֹ, שֶׁאֵין דָּר עִמָּהֶם. צִנִּים פַּחִים. לִישָּׁנָא דִּקְרָא. "צִנִּים פַּחִים בְּדֶרֶךְ עִקֵּשׁ" — הַצִּנָּה וְהַקּוֹר פַּח וּמוֹקֵשׁ בְּדֶרֶךְ עִקֵּשׁ, כִּי בְּיָדוֹ הַדָּבָר תָּלוּי לְהִשָּׁמֵר מִן הַצִּנָּה. וְיֵשׁ מְפָרְשִׁים: "צִנִּים פַּחִים" — קוֹר וָחוֹם. **מתני'** ה"ג: הָאַחִין שֶׁעָשׂוּ מִקְצָתָן שׁוּשְׁבִינוּת בְּחַיֵּי הָאָב. שֶׁשָּׁלַח הָאָב אֶת אֶחָד מִבָּנָיו לִשְׂמוֹחַ אֶת הֶחָתָן, וּבְיָדוֹ דּוֹרוֹנוֹת. שֶׁכֵּן דֶּרֶךְ שׁוּשְׁבִינוּת: נוֹטֵל דּוֹרוֹן לְשִׂמְחַת חוּפַּת חֲבֵירוֹ וְאוֹכֵל עִמּוֹ, וְזֶה יַחֲזִיר לוֹ כְּמוֹ כֵן כְּשֶׁיִּשָּׂא אִשָּׁה, כִּדְתַנְיָא לְקַמָּן (דף קמה:): ה' דְּבָרִים נֶאֶמְרוּ בְּשׁוּשְׁבִינוּת. "רֵעֶה דָוִד" (ש"ב טו) מְתַרְגְּמִינַן: שׁוּשְׁבִינָא דְּדָוִד. חָזְרָה שׁוּשְׁבִינוּת. כְּשֶׁיַּחֲזוֹר זֶה הַבֵּן וְיִשָּׂא אִשָּׁה, וְזֶה יַחֲזִיר שׁוּשְׁבִינוּתוֹ — חָזְרָה לָאֶמְצַע. נִגְבֵּית בְּבֵ"ד. כְּדִין מִלְוָה אֲבִיהֶם. וּבַגְּמָ' פָּרֵיךְ עֲלָהּ, וּמְשַׁנֵּי לָהּ: נִגְבֵּית בְּבֵית דִּין כְּדִין מִלְוָה. אֲבָל הַשּׁוֹלֵחַ לַחֲבֵירוֹ. בְּלֹא חוּפָּה. אִי נַמִי בְּחוּפָּתוֹ, וְאֵינוֹ הוֹלֵךְ לֶאֱכוֹל שָׁם וְלִשְׂמוֹחַ עִמּוֹ בְּחוּפָּתוֹ — אֵין זֶה דִּין שׁוּשְׁבִינוּת, אֶלָּא מַתָּנָה בְּעָלְמָא וּגְמִילוּת חֶסֶד, וְאֵינָהּ נִגְבֵּית בְּבֵ"ד. **גמ'** וּרְמִינְהִי שָׁלַח לוֹ אָבִיו שׁוּשְׁבִינוּת. כְּלוֹמַר שָׁלַח עַל יָדוֹ וּלְצָרְכּוֹ, שֶׁהוּא יֹאכַל וְיִשְׂמַח עִמּוֹ. דְּהָא לְקַמָּן מַפְלִיג בֵּין שָׁלַח אָבִיו שׁוּשְׁבִינוּת לְשָׁלַח לוֹ אָבִיו שׁוּשְׁבִינוּת. חוֹזֶרֶת לוֹ. לְאוֹתוֹ הַבֵּן, וְלֹא לָאֶמְצַע כִּדְקָתָנֵי מַתְנִיתִין, וְקַשְׁיָא לְמַתְנִיתִין. דִּסְבִירָא לֵיהּ לְהַאי תַּנָּא דְּכֵיוָן דְּשָׁלַח הָאָב עַל יַד זֶה הַבֵּן — חָפֵץ הוּא שֶׁלּוֹ לְבַדּוֹ יַחֲזִיר שׁוּשְׁבִינוּת, וְלֹא לִשְׁאָר בָּנָיו. חוֹזֶרֶת מִן הָאֶמְצַע. דְּמִלְוָה עַל הַיְּתוֹמִים לִפְרוֹעַ חוֹבַת אֲבִיהֶן. נִשְׁתַּלְּחָה לְאָבִיו תְּנַן. כִּדְמְתָרֵץ לָהּ וְאָזֵיל. (ג) וְ"חוֹזֶרֶת לָאֶמְצַע" דְּמַתְנִיתִין — הַיְינוּ חוֹזֶרֶת מִן הָאֶמְצַע, כִּדְמְפָרֵשׁ וְאָזֵיל. אֲבָל הֵיכָא דְּשָׁלַח אָבִיו שׁוּשְׁבִינוּת ע"י בְּנוֹ לַאֲחֵרִים — מוֹדֶה תַּנָּא דְּמַתְנִי' דְּחוֹזֶרֶת לְאוֹתוֹ הַבֵּן לְבַדּוֹ, כַּבָּרַיְיתָא. חָזְרָה. לִגְבּוֹת. רַבִּי אַסִּי אָמַר. לְעוֹלָם מַתְנִי' כִּדְקָתָנֵי, שֶׁהָאָב שָׁלַח שׁוּשְׁבִינוּת לַאֲחֵרִים, וּכְשֶׁהִיא חוֹזֶרֶת חוֹזֶרֶת לָאֶמְצַע וכו'. וּבָרַיְיתָא דְּקָתָנֵי חוֹזֶרֶת לְאוֹתוֹ הַבֵּן לְבַדּוֹ — לָא קַשְׁיָא; מַתְנִי' — בִּסְתָם, שֶׁשָּׁלַח סְתָם ע"י אֶחָד מִבָּנָיו וְלֹא פֵּירֵשׁ דִּלְדַעַת בֵּן זֶה שָׁלַח, הִלְכָּךְ חוֹזֶרֶת לָאֶמְצַע. אֲבָל הַבָּרַיְיתָא — בִּמְפָרֵשׁ הַשּׁוּשְׁבִינוּת תַּחֲזוֹר לְאוֹתוֹ הַבֵּן, הִלְכָּךְ חוֹזֶרֶת לוֹ, וְאֵינָהּ חוֹזֶרֶת לָאֶמְצַע. כִּדְתַנְיָא שָׁלַח לוֹ אָבִיו שׁוּשְׁבִינוּת. כְּלוֹמַר, נָתַן לוֹ אָבִיו מָעוֹת וּשְׁלָחוֹ לַעֲשׂוֹת שׁוּשְׁבִינוּת. כְּשֶׁחוֹזֶרֶת — חוֹזֶרֶת לוֹ לְבַדּוֹ. אֲבָל שָׁלַח אָבִיו שׁוּשְׁבִינוּת סְתָם, וְלֹא יִיחֵד לְאֶחָד מִבָּנָיו, אַף עַל פִּי שֶׁעַל יְדֵי אֶחָד מִבָּנָיו שָׁלַח — אֵינָהּ חוֹזֶרֶת לוֹ לְבַדּוֹ, אֶלָּא לָאֶמְצַע. וּשְׁמוּאֵל אָמַר. לְעוֹלָם כִּדְקָתָנֵי בָּרַיְיתָא, דְּהָאָב הַשּׁוֹלֵחַ שׁוּשְׁבִינוּת עַל יַד אֶחָד מִבָּנָיו — חוֹזֶרֶת לְאוֹתוֹ הַבֵּן לְבַדּוֹ. וּמַתְנִיתִין דְּקָתָנֵי: חוֹזֶרֶת לָאֶמְצַע — ה"מ שֶׁמֵּת הַבֵּן שֶׁנִּשְׁתַּלְּחָה שׁוּשְׁבִינוּת עַל יָדוֹ, (ד) וְרוֹצֶה הָיָה לַחֲזוֹר לוֹ אֶלָּא שֶׁמֵּת, וְיִיבֵּם אֶחָד מִן הָאַחִים אֶת אִשְׁתּוֹ. וְרַחֲמָנָא אָמַר "יָקוּם עַל שֵׁם אָחִיו" לְנַחֲלָה, וְדִינוֹ הָיָה לִיטּוֹל הַשּׁוּשְׁבִינוּת בִּמְקוֹם אָחִיו אִי לָאו דְּקַרְיֵיהּ רַחֲמָנָא "בְּכוֹר", כִּדְכְתִיב: "וְהָיָה הַבְּכוֹר" וגו', וְאֵין הַבְּכוֹר נוֹטֵל בָּרָאוּי כִּבְמוּחְזָק, וְאָמְרִינַן לְקַמָּן דְּאֵין בְּכוֹר נוֹטֵל פִּי שְׁנַיִם. הִלְכָּךְ חוֹזֶרֶת לָאֶמְצַע לְכָל הָאַחִין. וּמַקְשָׁה גְּמָרָא: מִכְּלָל דְּאִידָךְ. אוֹתוֹ שֶׁנִּשְׁתַּלְּחָה לוֹ שׁוּשְׁבִינוּת עַל יְדֵי זֶה הַבֵּן שֶׁמֵּת, בָּעֵי שַׁלּוֹמֵי? בִּתְמִיָּה, וְכִי יֵשׁ לוֹ לְשַׁלֵּם שׁוּשְׁבִינוּת לְיוֹרְשֵׁי שׁוּשְׁבִינוֹ שֶׁמֵּת? וַהֲלֹא יָכוֹל לוֹמַר: תְּנוּ לִי שׁוּשְׁבִינִי וְאֶשְׂמַח עִמּוֹ וְאוֹכֵל בְּחוּפָּתוֹ, כְּמוֹ שֶׁשָּׂמַח גַּם הוּא וְאָכַל בְּחוּפָּתִי, וְכֵיוָן שֶׁמֵּת — נִפְטַרְתִּי מִלְּשַׁלֵּם. שֶׁכֵּן מִנְהַג שׁוּשְׁבִינוּת לְהָבִיא דּוֹרוֹן וְלֶאֱכוֹל עִמּוֹ בְּחוּפָּתוֹ. מָקוֹם שֶׁנָּהֲגוּ לְהַחֲזִיר קִדּוּשִׁין. אַחַר מִיתַת הָאִשָּׁה בִּימֵי אֵירוּסִין, כִּדְמְפָרֵשׁ וְאָזֵיל.

תנו

ברכת הבית ברובה. פי' רבינו חננאל: נר לאחד נר למאה. ויש מפרשים: דמזלא דבי תרי עדיף. ה) וקשה, מדפריך בסמוך: ליתבו לפי ברכת הבית. וכי ידעינן כמה הוי וכמה נתברך הבית בגללו? ואומר רבינו תם: אין הכי נמי, יכולין לידע כמה הוציאו בשנה ראשונה, וכמה הוציאו בזו. ואין נראה לר"י, שהרי אין כל השנים שוים במזל אחד ו).

חלה ונתרפא כו'. ותניא בתוספ' (פ"י): במה דברים אמורים — ברפואה שיש לה קצבה, אבל רפואה שאין לה קצבה — הרי היא בכלל מזונות, ויתרפא מן האמצע. וכן בכתובות (דף נב:) גבי אלמנה, אומר: רפואה שיש לה קצבה — הרי היא בכלל כתובה, ושאין לה קצבה — הרי היא כמזונות. (ה) ובאונס דהכא אין חילוק בין אין לה קצבה ליש לה קצבה, כן תירץ הר"י.

אבל חלה באונס נתרפא מן האמצע. ולא דמי להא דתנן לעיל (דף קלט.): אין הקטנים נזונים על הגדולים. (ו) הכא הוי באקראי בעלמא, אבל התם — לעולם כן הוי, שהקטנים מפסידים יותר מזונות.

הכל בידי שמים חוץ מצנים פחים. פירוש: אריא וגנבי הבאים על האדם — הכל נגזר בידי שמים, אבל צנים פחים — מזה לא נגזר עליו, כלו' יכול לשמור. אבל ודאי, אם רוצה לאבד עצמו באש או בנהר — יכול לאבד עצמו אע"פ שלא נגזר כלום. ולא דמי להא דאמר: ז) הכל בידי שמים חוץ מיראת שמים. דהתם מיירי במדות של אדם מה יהיה — גבור או חלש, עשיר או עני, ארוך או קצר, [חכם או טפש] כדאיתא בנדה בפרק "כל היד" (דף טז: ושם). אבל הכא מיירי במאורעות הבאות על האדם.

חוץ מצנים פחים. דהיינו קור וחום, כדמשמע בריש מסכת ע"ז (דף ג: ושם). והא דאמרינן ב"המקבל" (בבא מציעא דף קז:): "והסיר ה' ממך כל חולי" — זו צינה, הכי פירושו: שיתן לך דעת לשמור מן הצינה, ליתן לך בגד ללבוש. ח) ובירושלמי אמר שאנטונינוס היה לו לילך בדרך, אמר ליה לרבי: צלי עלי. אמר ליה: יהא רעוא דתשתזיב מן צנתא. אמר ליה: דא צלותא? בתמיה. יתיר חד כסו וצנתא אזלא. א"ל: יהא רעוא דתשתזיב מן שרבא. אמר ליה: הא ודאי צלותא, דכתיב "ואין נסתר מחמתו".

האחין שעשו למקצת שושבינות. שכך היה מנהג, כשהאב היה עושה חופה לבנו היו שושבינים מביאין דורונות לכבוד החופה ונותנין לבנו, ועל האב היה לפרוע כשהיו נושאים גם הם נשים. ולכך חוזרת מן האמצע, שהרי היה על האב לפרוע.

ורבי

א) [כתובות קג.]: ב) ב"מ קז: ע"ז ג: כתובות ל. ע"ש: ג) [מבואר בבכורות נב.]: ד) [תוס' פסחים פ"ג]: ה) [ב"מ קה.]: ו) [וע"ע תוס' כתובות קג. ד"ה ברכת]: ז) [ברכות לג:]: ח) [עי' תוס' כתובות ל. ד"ה הכל ובע"ז ג: ד"ה שומר כתבו דבר זה בשם מדרש רבה פ' מצורע פ' טז]:

הגהות הב"ח

(א) גמ' ברכת הבית אין הכי נמי: (ב) שם נימא תנו לי שושביני: (ג) רשב"ם ד"ה נשתלחה וכו' ואזיל וחזרה לאמצע: (ד) ד"ה ושמואל וכו' על ידו ורצוי היה לחזור לו וכו' דאין הבכור נוטל בה פי שנים: (ה) תום' ד"ה חלה וכו' ובאונס דהכא אין חילוק. כ"כ פי' הא דמחלק בתוספתא בין יש לה קצבה לאין לה מיירי באונס דהכא במתני' דמוקי לה רבין בפשיעה אין חילוק בין אין לה קצבה ליש לה קצבה דבכל גווני משל עצמו והכי איתא בפסקי תוספות ועי' בטור חו"מ סימן קע"ז: (ו) ד"ה אבל וכו' דהכא הוי באקראי וכו' כן הוא שהקטנים:

רבינו גרשום

המשלח אין נגבין בבית דין מפני שלשום גמילות שילחו לו ולא לשום תשלומין ואם מחזיר לא' מן היורשין לא יחלקו בשוה אלא כל הקודם זכה דאינה במלוה: ורמינהו שלח לו אביו שושבינות. דאמר לאחד מבניו לך תהוי שושבינו של פלוני והוליך לו דורונות ולא הספיק להחזיר לו עד שמת האב כשהיא חוזרת חוזרת לו ולא לאמצע. וקשיא למתני' דקתני יחלקו לאמצע: נשתלחה לאביו תנן. שהשושבינות ששלחו לו לאביו אשה שושבינות אחרים או שושבינות שנשא האב אשה אחרת ושילחו לו ולא הספיק לשלם להם עד שמת האב וצריכין היורשין לפרוע שהרי נגבית בבית דין כשהיא חוזרת כשפורעין היתומים פורעין בשוה. קתני מידת כשהיא חוזרת חוזרת לו ולא לאמצע וקשיא למתני': כי תנן נמי מתני' חוזרה לאמצע כשנשתלחה לאביו תנן לפי שכשהן חוזרין ופורעין בשביל אביהן חוזרין לאמצע ופורעין בשוה ולעולם כדקתני ברייתא: והא עשו מקצתן שושבינות קתני. דמשמע שהן עשו לאחרים שלחו דורונות ועכשיו כשהיא חוזרת חוזרת לאמצע ואבתי' קשיא ברייתא למתני': אימא הכי ולעולם כדקתני ברייתא ומתני' תריץ ליה הכי שעשו שושבינות למקצתן שמקצת אחין נשאו אשה ועשו להן אחרים שושבינות דהיינו נשתלחה לאביו שושבינות כשהיא חוזרת נגבית מן האמצע. ולעולם מתני' כברייתא ולא קשיא ברייתא למתני'. והא חזרה שושבינות קתני מתני'. דמשמע דאחין הללו עשו

רבינו גרשום

דכתב לה: במעמד שלשתן. הנותן והמקבל ובעל חוב: קנה. בלא שטר ובלא משיכה ולא ידעינן טעמא מאי: פיס' האחין השותפין. שלא חלקו ירושת אביהן שנפל אחד מהן לאומנות המלך: נפל לאמצע. מה שמרויח באותו אומנות יחלק עם אחיו וזו היא אומנות המלך שהיו מתחילין מבית שבראש המבוי למנות בעל הבית גבאי מנת המלך מן בני העיר ומה שמרויח באותו ממון הוא שלו בשכר שמקבצו והקרן נותן לאוצר המלך והחדש או שנה יהיה זה גבאי והחדש אחר שכנו הקרוב הסמוך לו וכן הולכין בסדר הבתים לכל בית חודש וכשהגיע לבית זה של אחין הללו ומינו אחד מהן השכר לאמצע: חלה ונתרפא. אין מתרפא מתפוסת הבית בשחלה בפשיעה אלא מחלקו מתרפא. תנא לאומנות המלך כדאמרן: פולמוסטוס. שוטר: אם מחמת אחין. שהמוזמן בא על בית אביהן ולא מחמת זה של אחין מינוהו והשכר לאמצע שהבית גורם ובתפוסת הבית דמי. ואם מחמת עצמו שהיו יודעים שיש באחד מן האחין זריז מאד כבה בתים ונתנוהו לזה בשביל חריפותו השכר לעצמו: מהו דתימא חורפיה הוא דקא גרים ליה. שבירוהו מן האחים ודמי כמאן דלא בשבילו קמ"ל דהשכר לאמצע הואיל דבית האחין הוא: שנטל מאתים זוז. מתפוסת הבית ומבקש שיתנו לו מזונות מתפוסת הבית יכולים לעכב בידו ולומר לו אם את כו'. אמאי ליתבו ליה מזונות כל היכא דאית ליה. מדלא יהבינן לו. מסייע ליה לרב הונא דאמר ברכת הבית ברובה. כלומר נר לאחד נר למאה שאם היו ה' אחין והיו מופרשין זה מזה כל אחד ואחד להוצאתו מסתפקים בב' פשיטים ליום ועכשיו כשהם בהוצאה אחת די להם ח' פשיטים ומשום הכי אין נותנין לו הוצאתו בכל מקום שהוא דנמצאו מפסידין שאר אחין. ומקשי' וליתבו ליה כל היכא דאיתא. כפי ברכת הבית שיתן כפי חלקו המגיעו מאותן ח'. ומשני אין הכי נמי דליתבו ליה: צנים פחים. שלא שמר עצמו מן הצנה הנופחת: פיס' האחין שעשו מקצתן שושבינות בחיי אביהן. ששיגר אביהן ב' או ג' מהן ועמהן דורונות לחתן ואוכלין עמו ושמחין עמו היינו שושבינות וכן נמי כשישאו הן נשים זה שהוא עכשיו חתן יביא כן לחופתן להם דורונות וישמח עמהן ואם עשו אחין הללו מקצתן שושבינות בחיי אביהן ששלח אביהן על ידן הדורונות לחתן ואחר מיתת אביהן נשאו נשים שני אחין הללו ובא זה לשלם להם הדורונות ששלחו לו אעפ"י שלהם שילם בעד הדורונות חזרה לאמצע. שיש בהן חלק לכל האחין מפני שאלמלא לא אלו הדורונות היו נגבות על פי בית דין. דדמי כמי שהיה חייב לאביהן מלוה מה מלוה נגבית בבית דין והיא של כל האחין בשוה אף אלו דורונות שמחזיר יחלקו בשוה לפי שאותו אחין ממון אביהן הוליכו אבל השולח לחבירו כדי יין וכדי שמן לא לשם חתן אלא לשם סבלונות ולא הספיק להחזיר לו עד שמת שושבינות לאחרים ועכשיו שילמו להן שושבינות והוי לאמצע. אימא חזרה לגבות מהן שהן האמצע ולעולם כברייתא: ורב אשי אמר. לא צריך לתרוצי מתני' כדמתרצת ולא קשיא כאן בסתם כאן במפרש שלח לו אביו שושבינות (דלא) אמר בפירוש את תהא שושבינות לפלוני משמע שמה שיחזור לו שלך יהא ובהכי מיירי ברייתא דכמתנה מחיים דמי משום הכי כשהיא חוזרת חוזרת לו. (בסתם לא גרס' לו) אלא מתני' מיירי ששלח אביו שושבינות סתם דלא אמר לאחד את תהא שושבינות ולכן כשהיא חוזרת חוזרת לאמצע: ושמואל אמר לעולם הכי עיקר כדקתני בברייתא והכא במתני' ביבם עסקינן משום הכי כגון ששלח אביו בשבילו שושבינות ומת אביו ונשא הבן אשה לאחר כך ולא הספיק אידך להחזיר לו עד שמת ונפלה ארוסתו לפני אחד מן האחין ליבום ואותו המשלם חייב להחזיר לו דורון אע"פ שמת חזרה לאמצע ולא ליבם בלבד לפי שיבם אינו נוטל בראוי כבמוחזק ושושבינות זה ראוי היה ולא החזיק בה בחייו: ומקשי' מכלל דאידך המשלם בעי שלומי אע"פ שמת שושבינו ואמאי למימר להו תנו לי שושביני שמת ואשמח עמו ואחזור לו שושבינות ואי לא לא אחזור לשום מי לא תניא. דהכי מצי טעין: דתניא מקום שנהגו להחזיר קדושין. כשמת אחד מהן הארוס או הארוסה מחזירין:

ואמר

אודייני — הַשָּׂכָר לָאֶמְצַע; וְהָא אוּדַיְינֵי דְּמֵחֲמַת עַצְמוֹ *[הוּא]! אשָׁאנֵי א)אוּדַיְינֵי, דִּלְנְטִירוּתָא הוּא דַּעֲבִידָא, וַאֲפִילּוּ קְטַנִּים נַמִּי מָצוּ מְנַטְּרִי לָהּ.§ "אָמְרוּ: רְאוּ מַה שֶּׁהִנִּיחַ אַבָּא, הֲרֵי אָנוּ עוֹשִׂין וְאוֹכְלִין — הִשְׁבִּיחוּ לְעַצְמָן".§ רַב סָפְרָא שְׁבַק אֲבוּהּ זוּזֵי, שְׁקַלִינְהוּ, עֲבַד בְּהוּ עִיסְקָא; אֲתוּ אַחֵי תְּבָעוּהוּ בְּדִינָא קַמֵּיהּ דְּרָבָא, אֲמַר לְהוּ: ברַב סָפְרָא גַּבְרָא רַבָּה הוּא, לָא שָׁבֵיק גִּירְסֵיהּ וְטָרַח לְאַחֲרִינֵי.§ "הָאִשָּׁה שֶׁהִשְׁבִּיחָה אֶת הַנְּכָסִים — הִשְׁבִּיחָה לָאֶמְצַע".§ אִשָּׁה בְּנִכְסֵי יַתְמֵי מַאי עֲבִידְתָּהּ? אֲמַר רַבִּי יִרְמְיָה: גבְּאִשָּׁה יוֹרֶשֶׁת. פְּשִׁיטָא! מַהוּ דְּתֵימָא: כֵּיוָן דְּלָאו דַּרְכָּהּ לְמִטְרַח, אַף עַל גַּב דְּלָא פָּרֵישׁ — כְּמוֹ דְּפָרֵישׁ דָּמֵי, קָמַשְׁמַע לָן.§ "וְאִם אָמְרָה: רְאוּ מַה שֶּׁהִנִּיחַ לִי בַּעְלִי, הֲרֵינִי עוֹשָׂה וְאוֹכֶלֶת — הִשְׁבִּיחָה לְעַצְמָהּ".§ פְּשִׁיטָא! מַהוּ דְּתֵימָא: כֵּיוָן דְּשַׁבְחָא לַהּ מִילְּתָא, דְּאָמְרִי: קָא טָרְחָא קַמֵּי יַתְמֵי — אַחוּלֵי אַחְלָה, קָא מַשְׁמַע לָן. ב)אֲמַר רַבִּי חֲנִינָא: דהַמַּשִּׂיא אִשָּׁה לִבְנוֹ גָּדוֹל בְּבַיִת — קְנָאוֹ. הוְדַוְקָא גָּדוֹל, וְדַוְקָא ובְּתוּלָה, וְדַוְקָא אִשְׁתּוֹ זרִאשׁוֹנָה, וְדַוְקָא חשֶׁהִשִּׂיאוֹ רִאשׁוֹן. טפְּשִׁיטָא, יִיחֵד לוֹ אָבִיו בַּיִת וַעֲלִיָּיה — בַּיִת קָנָה, עֲלִיָּיה לֹא קָנָה; יבַּיִת וְאַכְסַדְרָה, מַהוּ? כשְׁנֵי בָתִּים זֶה לִפְנִים מִזֶּה, מַהוּ? תֵּיקוּ. מֵיתִיבֵי: יִיחֵד לוֹ אָבִיו בַּיִת וּכְלֵי בַיִת — לכְּלֵי בַיִת קָנָה, בַּיִת לֹא קָנָה! אָמַר רַבִּי יִרְמְיָה: מכְּגוֹן שֶׁהָיָה אוֹצָרוֹ שֶׁל אָבִיו מוּנָּח שָׁם. נְהַרְדְּעֵי אָמְרִי: אֲפִילּוּ שׁוֹבְכָא דְּיוֹנֵי. רַב יְהוּדָה וְרַב פַּפִּי אָמְרִי: אֲפִילּוּ נעֲצִיצָא דְּהַרְסָנָא. מָר זוּטְרָא אַנְסְבֵיהּ לִבְרֵיהּ, וּתְלָא לֵיהּ סַנְדְּלָא. רַב אַשִׁי נַסְבֵיהּ לִבְרֵיהּ, וּתְלָא לֵיהּ אַשִּׁישָׁא דְּמִשְׁחָא. ג)אֲמַר מָר זוּטְרָא: הָנֵי תְּלָת מִילֵּי שַׁוְינְהוּ רַבָּנַן ד)כְּהִלְכְתָא בְּלָא טַעְמָא: חֲדָא — הָא; אִידָךְ — ה)דְּאָמַר רַב יְהוּדָה אָמַר שְׁמוּאֵל: הַכּוֹתֵב כָּל נְכָסָיו לְאִשְׁתּוֹ — לֹא עֲשָׂאָהּ אֶלָּא אַפּוֹטְרוֹפָּא; אִידָךְ — ו)דְּאָמַר רַב: ס"מָנֶה לִי בְּיָדְךָ, תְּנֵהוּ לִפְלוֹנִי", בְּמַעֲמַד שְׁלָשְׁתָּן — קָנָה.§

מתני'

רש"י

אודייני. בּוֹר וְכִיסּוּיוֹ, וְשׂוֹכְרִין אוֹתוֹ לְהַשְׁקוֹת שָׂדוֹת מִמֵּימָיו. **מֵחֲמַת עַצְמוֹ הוּא.** שֶׁמְּשַׁמְּרִין אוֹתוֹ הַגְּדוֹלִים, וּצְרִיכִין לַעֲמוֹד עַל גַּבָּיו, פֶּן יִהְיֶה הֶפְקֵר לְכָל שׁוֹאֲבֵי מַיִם. **דִּלְנְטִירוּתָא עֲבִידָא.** אֵינָן צְרִיכִין לְהוֹצִיא מִשֶּׁלָּהֶן כְּלוּם עָלָיו, אֶלָּא לְשָׁמְרוֹ, וְגַם הַקְּטַנִּים יְכוֹלִין לְשָׁמְרוֹ. **עָבַד** (א) **בְּהֶן עִיסְקָא.** וְחָשֵׁיב לֵיהּ שֶׁבַח נְכָסִים מֵחֲמַת נְכָסִים, הוֹאִיל וְאֵין צָרִיךְ טוֹרַח כָּל כָּךְ אֶלָּא לִקְנוֹת וְלִמְכּוֹר. **לָא שָׁבֵיק גִּירְסֵיהּ וְטָרַח לְאַחֲרִינֵי.** וּכְמִי שֶׁאָמַר "רְאוּ מַה שֶּׁהִנִּיחַ לָנוּ אַבָּא" דָּמֵי. וְשָׁמְעִי' מֵהָכָא דְּכָל הֵיכָא דְּמַאן דְּהוּא כְּמוֹ רַב סָפְרָא, אע"ג דְּלָא אָמַר "לְעַצְמִי אֲנִי עוֹשֶׂה" — כְּמַאן דְּאָמַר דָּמֵי, וְהִשְׁבִּיחַ לְעַצְמוֹ. **אִשָּׁה מַאי עֲבִידְתָּהּ.** אוֹ תִּטּוֹל כְּתוּבָּתָהּ וְתֵלֵךְ לָהּ, אוֹ תִּטְרַח קַמֵּי יַתְמֵי וְתִהְיֶה נִיזּוֹנֶת, וּמַעֲשֵׂה יָדֶיהָ שֶׁלָּהֶן. וְאֵין לָהּ לְהִשְׂתַּכֵּר בְּמָמוֹן הַיּוֹרְשִׁים! **בְּאִשָּׁה יוֹרֶשֶׁת.** כְּגוֹן שֶׁנָּשָׂא רְאוּבֵן בַּת שִׁמְעוֹן, (ב) וּמֵתוּ, וְיָרְשׁוּ בְּנֵי רְאוּבֵן וּבַת שִׁמְעוֹן אֶת נִכְסֵי יַעֲקֹב אֲבִי אֲבִיהֶן. אוֹ כְּגוֹן בַּת בֵּין הַבָּנוֹת, אוֹ בַּת הַבֵּן בֵּין הַבָּנִים — דִּינָהּ כְּדִין הָאַחִין. אוֹ שֶׁאָמַר בַּעְלָהּ: תִּטּוֹל אִשְׁתִּי כְּאֶחָד מִן הַבָּנִים. אִם הִשְׁבִּיחָה אֶת הַנְּכָסִים, פֵּירְשָׁהּ — לְעַצְמָהּ, לֹא פֵּירְשָׁהּ — הַשֶּׁבַח לָאֶמְצַע. וְאַלְמָנָה שֶׁאָמְרָה בְּב"ד "רְאוּ מַה שֶּׁהִנִּיחַ לִי בַּעְלִי, הֲרֵינִי עוֹשָׂה וְאוֹכֶלֶת" — הִשְׁבִּיחָה לְעַצְמָהּ. וְהוּא דְּלָא שָׁקְלָא מְזוֹנֵי, דְּאִי שָׁקְלָא מְזוֹנֵי — הָא תְּנַן: ז) אַלְמָנָה נִיזּוֹנֶת מִנִּכְסֵי יְתוֹמִין וּמַעֲשֵׂה יָדֶיהָ שֶׁלָּהֶן. הִלְכָּךְ, אִשָּׁה שֶׁמֵּת בַּעְלָהּ וְהִנִּיחַ נְכָסִים מוּעָטִין שֶׁאֵין בָּהֶן כְּדֵי כְּתוּבָּתָהּ, אִם אָמְרָה "רְאוּ מַה שֶּׁהִנִּיחַ לִי בַּעְלִי", וְנִתְעַצְּלוּ ב"ד אוֹ יוֹרְשִׁין לְהַשְׁבִּיעָהּ עַל כְּתוּבָּתָהּ, אֲפִילּוּ הִשְׁבִּיחָה אֶלֶף כִּכָּר — הִשְׁבִּיחָה לְעַצְמָהּ. אֲבָל אִם הִשְׁבִּיחָה הַנְּכָסִים סְתָם — תִּטְרוֹף כְּתוּבָּתָהּ, וְהַמּוֹתָר לַיּוֹרְשִׁין, וְאַעַ"פ שֶׁלֹּא נִשְׁתַּיֵּיר מִבַּעְלָהּ אֲפִילּוּ רְבִיעַ כְּתוּבָּתָהּ. **אַחוּלֵי אַחְלָה.** וְחָזְרָה בָּהּ מִמַּה שֶּׁאָמְרָה תְּחִלָּה "הֲרֵינִי עוֹשָׂה וְאוֹכֶלֶת", קָא מַשְׁמַע לָן. **קְנָאוֹ.** הַבֵּן לְאוֹתוֹ הַבַּיִת. תַּקָּנַת חֲכָמִים הִיא. וְהִלְכְתָא בְּלָא טַעֲמָא, כִּדְלְקַמָּן. וּבְמַסֶּ' גִּיטִּין[א] מוֹקְמִינַן לָהּ ח) — כְּגוֹן שֶׁיֵּשׁ לְאָבִיו בָּעִיר בַּיִת אַחֵר לָדוּר בּוֹ. **וְדַוְקָא גָּדוֹל כו'.** דִּבְכִי הַאי גַּוְונָא חָבִיב לֵיהּ טְפֵי, וְגָמַר וּמַקְנֵי לֵיהּ. **יִיחֵד לוֹ בַּיִת וַעֲלִיָּיה.** כְּלוֹמַר יִיחֵד לוֹ הָאָב לִבְנוֹ בַּיִת שֶׁיֵּשׁ עֲלִיָּיה עַל גַּבָּיו. **אַכְסַדְרָה.** לִפְנֵי הַבַּיִת, וּפוֹתְחִין בּוֹ חַלּוֹנוֹת, וְדֶרֶךְ אַכְסַדְרָה נִכְנָסִים לַבַּיִת. **שְׁנֵי בָתִּים כו'.** אִם תִּמְצָא לוֹמַר בַּיִת וְאַכְסַדְרָה קָנָה — הַיְינוּ מִשּׁוּם דְּאַכְסַדְרָה מְשׁוּעְבָּד לַבַּיִת, אֲבָל שְׁנֵי בָתִּים זֶה לִפְנִים מִזֶּה מַהוּ? **אוֹצָרוֹ בְּתוֹכוֹ.** הִלְכָּךְ בַּיִת לֹא קָנָה, דְּכֵיוָן דְּמִשְׁתַּמֵּשׁ הָאָב בַּבַּיִת — לֹא הוֹצִיאוֹ מֵחֶזְקָתוֹ, וְלֹא מַקְנֵי לֵיהּ לִבְנוֹ. **עֲצִיצָא דְּהַרְסְנָא.** כְּלִי מָלֵא דָּגִים מְטוּגָּנִים בְּשֶׁמֶן. **אַשִּׁישָׁא דְּמִשְׁחָא.** כּוֹס מָלֵא שֶׁמֶן. **שַׁוְינְהוּ רַבָּנַן.** הֵם תִּקְנוּ אֶת הַדְּבָרִים כָּךְ, אַף עַל פִּי שֶׁאֵינוֹ דִּין תּוֹרָה, כִּי (ג) מִדָּה וּמִדָּה הֵם. **חֲדָא הָא.** הַמַּשִּׂיא אִשָּׁה לִבְנוֹ. וְתַקָּנַת חֲכָמִים הִיא לִכְבוֹד הֶחָתָן, שֶׁגְּנַאי הַדָּבָר לָשֵׂאת אִשָּׁה וְאֵין מָקוֹם לָדוּר בּוֹ. **אַפּוֹטְרוֹפָּא.** דְּאָמְדֵי סָהֲדֵי דְּלֹא עָקַר נַחֲלַת הַבָּנִים. וְלֹא נִתְכַּוֵּין אֶלָּא שֶׁיְּכַבְּדוּהָ הַבָּנִים, מִתּוֹךְ שֶׁאוֹכְלִין עַל יָדָהּ. **בְּמַעֲמַד שְׁלָשְׁתָּן.** נִפְקָד וּמַפְקִיד וּמְקַבֵּל מַתָּנָה. **קָנָה.** כָּךְ תִּקְנוּ חֲכָמִים, לְפִי שֶׁהַדָּבָר תָּדִיר הוּא בֵּין הַבְּרִיּוֹת, וְלֹא הִזְקִיקוּ חֲכָמִים לְהַקְנוֹת בְּקִנְיָן וּבְעֵדִים.

תוספות

דאי הוו אמרי גדולים "ראו מה שהניח לנו אבינו" — היו אוהבי הקטנים או קרוביהם משכירים להם פועלים משל אביהם בשבילם, ומדלא אודעינהו — אחולי אחילו גבייהו. וכעובדא דמרי בר איסק (ב"מ דף לט:) דא"ל אחוה: לפלוג לי נמי מפרדיסי ובוסתני דשתל, ואמר ליה רב חסדא: שפיר קאמר לך, דתנן: הניח גדולים וקטנים כו' השבח לאמצע — לא שתלם בעצמו, אלא השכיר פועלים ממעות הירושה, ואותו האח נמי היה מוצא קרובים דהוי שתלי ליה. וכן אחי דרב ספרא היו מוצאין שישתכרו במעותיהן, דאין טורח למכור ולקנות, אי לאו דהוי כאומר להן "ראו". ופריך מאודייני, דמחמת עצמו הוא, שלא היו מוצאין שיעשה להם אותה שמירה, לפי שצריך לעמוד שם זמן מרובה. ומשני, דקטנים גופייהו מנטרי, ואם היו מודיעין להם — היו עושין. ועוד יש פירוש רבינו תם, ופירוש ריב"ם, ולא ישרו בעיני ר"י. **אודייני.** פי' בקונטרס: בור וכסויו. ואין נראה לרבינו תם. אלא מפרש שהוא כלי גבוה, שעומדים עליו שומרי שדות וכרמים לראות מעליו למרחוק, וגם הוא ראוי לישן עליו, כדאמרינן בפרק בתרא דמועד קטן (דף כז.): ישן על גבי מטה או על גבי ספסל או על גבי אודייני. ויש ספרים שכתוב בהן "אידווני", כמו: דוי להכא ולהכא (תמיד דף כו: ושבת לה.). **באשה** יורשת. פירש בקונטרס: כגון ראובן שנשא בת שמעון אחיו, ומת יעקב אביהם, ואחר כך מתו ראובן ושמעון, שאז יורשין בני ראובן ובת שמעון מאביהן. וקצת קשה לישנא ד"ראו מה שהניח לי בעלי" — דמשמע דירשה מבעלה, ולא מיעקב. ופירש ריב"ם: אשה יורשת — שנשא ראובן בת שמעון אחיו ומת, והיו לו לראובן אחים קטנים או בני אחים קטנים דהוו יתמי, והרי היא יורשת את בעלה עם הקטנים, שהיא במקום אביה. ומיהו קשה(ד): דקאמרי' בסמוך דטרחא קמי יתמי, דמשמע בני בעלה! על כן נראה לר"י כפירוש הקונטרס, דכיון שבעל אוכל פירות ירושתה כל ימי חייו כדין — שייך שפיר "ראו מה שהניח לי בעלי". אי נמי כלשון אחר שפירש בקונטרס, שאמר הבעל: תטול האשה כאחד מן הבנים.

ואם אמרה ראו מה שהניח לי בעלי. פירש בקונטרס: וכיון דאמרה הכי — לית לה מזוני. ואין נראה לרשב"א. דדוקא אם מכרה כתובתה או ט)לקחה כתובתה בבית דין — אין לה מזונות. אבל זו שלא לקחה כלום מכתובתה, אלא נכסי מלוג שלה, או מה שירשה או מה שנתן לה בעלה כאחד מן הבנים — לא הפסידה מזונות. דאפי' מכרה מקצת כתובתה אמרינן בפרק "אלמנה" (כתובות דף צח.) דלית דחש ליה לדר' שמעון דאמר: מקצת כסף ככל כסף, ולא הפסידה מזונות — כ"ש נכסי מלוג, דלא שייכי כלל לכתובתה. וגם מה שפירש, שאם נתעצלו בית דין להשביעה מה שהשביחה לעצמה — לא ידע רשב"א מנליה, דלעולם הויא בחזקת יורשים עד שישביעוה ב"ד, דאין לה כח לגבות כתובתה אלא בבית דין, והכא מיירי דוקא באשה יורשת. **בית** ואכסדרה מהו. דנהי דעלייה לא קנה, אכסדרה שייכא טפי לגבי בית. ואם תמצא לומר לא קנה, משום דאין בו תשמיש בית — שני בתים זה לפנים מזה מהו? דכבית אחד דמי. ולפירוש הקונטרס הוה ליה להקדים בעיא דשני בתים לבית ואכסדרה.

כהלכתא בלא טעמא. קצת טעם יש, דכיון שפינה את הבית — סמכא דעתיה דבן. וגם אין לו אנה לדור, סברא הוא שנתנו לו. וכן הכותב כל נכסיו לאשתו או לבנו — מסתמא לא ליתן לה נתכוין, אלא לכבדה, שלא היה מניח בניו בולא כלום. ובמעמד שלשתן לא רצו חכמים להטריח להביא עדים ולעשות קנין, דמסתמא כיון שאמר לו במעמד שלשתן — הקנה לו לגמרי. ונראה לר"י, דבמעמד שלשתן, אם חזר ומחלו — אינו מחול, ומפורש בכמה מקומות. **הניח** בנים גדולים עד במעמד שלשתן קנה. עד כאן שיטת ר"א ז"ל.

ברכת

עין משפט נר מצוה

לד א מיי' פ"ט מהלכות נחלות הלכה ב ועי' בהשגות ובמ"מ סמג עשין פב טוש"ע חו"מ סי' רפז סעיף א עי' מ"מ כ"מ ל"מ:

לה ב מיי' שם הלכה ה טוש"ע שם סעיף ב:

לו ג מיי' שם הלכה ג טוש"ע שם סעיף א:

לז ד ה ו ז ח מיי' פ"ו מהלכות זכייה ומתנה הלכה טו סמג עשין פב טוש"ע אה"ע סי' נח סעיף א:

לח ט י מיי' שם הל' טז טוש"ע שם סעיף ג [ולא קנה]:

לט כ מיי' שם טוש"ע שם סעיף ד [וקנה אחד]:

מ ל מ מיי' שם הל' טו טוש"ע שם סעיף ב:

מא נ מיי' שם טוש"ע שם סעיף א:

מב ס מיי' פ"ו מהלכות מכירה הלכה ז ופ"ג מהל' זכייה ומתנה הל' ג סמג עשין פב טוש"ע ח"מ סי' סו סעיף יט וסי' קכו סעיף א:

רבינו גרשום

אודייני. בור וכסויו השכר לאמצע. והאי אודייני דמחמת עצמן הוא. שצריך תמיד לנקות הבור ולכסותו שלא יפול בו זבל כדי שיקנו בני אדם מים נקיים יותר ברצון ואעפ"כ שהגדולים טורחין בו הן בעצמן ומנקין אותו ומשמרין אותו השכר לאמצע: שאני אודייני. משום הכי השכר לאמצע דלנטורי עבידא אפי' קטן מצי מנטר בהן ולכסותו שיהא נקי ומצו למימר להו קטנים לגדולים מלאכה כזאת אנו יכולין לעשותה אבל שאר נכסים אם שבחו מחמת עצמן השכר לעצמן: ואמר רבא רב ספרא גברא רבה הוא לא שבק גרסתיה וטרח לאחריני: ומסתמא אע"ג דלא אמר להו ראו מה שהניח לנו אבינו משמע מינה דלצרכו קא טרח או אחריני וסתמא כמאן דפריש להו דמי וכל השכר לאמצע: מתני' וכן האשה שהשביחה לאמצע: ש"מ דיורשת היא עם הבנים או עם הבנות כאחד ואמאי וכי אשה מאי עבידתה להיות יורשת נכסי בעלה. אמר ר' ירמיה באשה יורשת עסקינן כגון שנשא שמעון בת ראובן אחיו ולא היו לראובן כי אם בנות ושמעון שנשאה לא היה לו יורש ומת ראובן ואח"כ מת שמעון בלא יורש ונמצא שנפלה ירושת שמעון לבנות ראובן עם אשתו יורשת בנכסי בעלה מפני שבעלה דודה הוא. ואם אמרה לאחיותיה ראו מה שהניח (לנו אבינו) [לי בעלי] הריני משבחת לעצמי השביחה לעצמה: פשיטא. הואיל דיור' היא לאמצע השביחה דדינה כדין אחים. אצטריך סלקא דעתך אמינא לאו אורחא היא למיטרח לאחריני ואע"ג דלא פירשה דהוא לעצמה אלא בסתמא עשתה כמאן דפירשה דמי קמשמע לן דלא:

ואם אמרה ראו מה שהניח לי בעלי כו'. פשיטא. א) מה לי היא משאר יורשין דמפרשי' הואיל דיורשת היא: מהו דתימא אחולי אחלה גבייהו. אע"ג דקאמרה ראו מה שהניח לי כו' קמ"ל הואיל דאמרה ראו כו' דלא אחילה להו והשביחה לעצמה: בבית קנאו. לאותו בית דאיכא למימר משום דהשיאו לשם גמר ונתנו לו אע"ג דלא כתב ליה מתנה דהלכה למשה מסיני הוא כדאמר לקמן: ודוקא כשהנושא בנו גדול. משום דקרוב ליה דעתיה טפי ובתולה משום דאיכא שמחה טפי מאלמנה ובההיא שמחה גמר למיתן ליה: הא פשיטא לי ייחד לו בית ועלייה היתה על גבי בית בית קנה עלייה לא קנה. משום דבית לחוד ועלייה לחוד דעלייה לא משתעבד לבית לכלל. או דלמא תמצי לומר עלייה לא קנה דלא שייכא גבי בית. בית ואכסדרה מהו. מי אמרינן כיון דשייכא בהדי בית קונה דדרך אכסדרה נכנסין לבית וקנה או דלמא בבית אשתמש באכסדרה לא אשתמש ולא קנה. וכן נמי שני בתים זה לפנים מזה משום דחיצון משועבד לפנימי מהו מי אמרינן כיון דבפנימית ישתמש בחיצונה לא קנה או דלמא כיון דיש דרך לפנימית על החיצונה כמאן דאשתמש בה ובתרוייהו קנה תיקו: וכלי בית. תשמישי בית: כלי בית קנה בית לא קנה. וקשיא לר' חנינא דאמר לעיל דבית קני: כגון שהיה אוצרי פירותיו של אביו. צבורין באותו בית ולא מייחד ליה לגמרי משום הכי לא קנה: ותלא ליה סנדלא. בבית שיהא עומד בחזקתו ומשום דלא ליקני לביתיה: אשישא דמשחא. פך של שמן דלא ליקני נמי: עציצא. כלי שמשימין ציר לקרבי דגים: שוינהו רבנן כהלכתא. שיהו עיקר כהלכה למשה מסיני. ולא מטעמא שלא נתנו טעם בדבר חדא האי דאמרן. המשיא אשה לבנו גדול בבית קנאו לא ידעי' מאי טעמא קנאו בלא שטר מתנה ובלא קנין. לא עשאה אלא אפטרופא. שיהו נוהגין לה בנין כבוד ולא ידעינן טעמא מאי לא תקנה כיון

דכתב

א) נראה דצ"ל פשיטא הואיל ויורשת היא מה לי היא משאר יורשין דמהני אם פירשו:

מסורת הש"ס

א) כתב הת"ח שלגירסת הרמב"ם פ"ט מהלכות נחלות ל"ג שאני אודייני וכו' אלא ה"ג אלא אסיפא איתמר והכי איתמר לא שנו אלא ששבחו נכסים מחמת עצמן אבל שבחו נכסים מחמת נכסים השבח לאמצע: ב) [גיטין עז.]: ג) [שם]: ד) [עי' פרש"י שם]: ה) לעיל קלג: [ולקמן קנ:] גיטין עז: ו) קדושין מח. גיטין יג. עז. [ולקמן קמח. בכל מקומות אלו איתא א"ר הונא א"ר]: ז) [כתובות נה:]: ח) [בגמ' דגיטין לא נמצא אלא ברש"י עז. שם ד"ה בבית בית מיוחד שאינו דר בו אלא עשאו לו לבית חתנות עכ"ל וכ"כ הב"י אה"ע סימן נט]: ט) [צ"ל תבעה]:

הגהות הב"ח

(א) רשב"ם ד"ה עבד בהו עסקא וכו' וא"צ טורח. נ"ב עי' בב"מ דף סח ע"ב מבואר לישב בחנות הוא טורח קל יותר מזה וא"כ פשיטא דהוה כמו מחמת נכסים וק"ל: (ב) ד"ה באשה יורשת כגון שנשא ראובן בת שמעון אחיו ומת יעקב אביהם ואח"כ מתו ראובן ושמעון וירשו בני ראובן ובת שמעון וכו' ואלמנה שאמרה. נ"ב כלומר וסיפא דתני אם אמרה ראו כו' לא קאי אאשה יורשת אלא הכי פירושו ואלמנה כו' דאל"כ מאי האי דקאמרה ראו מה שהניח לי בעלי וכו' וכמו שהקשו התוס': (ג) ד"ה שווינהו וכו' מדה ומדה הם. נ"ב לא קאי אלא אמשיא אשה לבנו והכותב כל נכסיו לאשתו דהנך תלוים במדת האדם: (ד) תוס' ד"ה באשה וכו' ומיהו קשה דקאמרי'. נ"ב והרי"ף כתב וז"ל כגון ראובן שנשא בת שמעון אחיו ומת שמעון והניח בנות ומת ראובן בלא בנים נמצאת אשת ראובן יורשת בעלה עם אחיותיה בנות שמעון עכ"ל דלפי זה שייך שפיר לישנא דיתמי:

הגהות הגר"א

[א] רשב"ם ד"ה קנאו. מוקמינן. נ"ל ומוקמינן. ור"ל בסמוך (כמ"ש ייחד לו כו' כגון שהיה אוצרו כו' אפי' כו') ומ"ש ובמסכת גיטין קאי אלמעלה (דגם שם איתא דהוי הלכתא בלא טעמא. ובדפוס ישן הגירסא ברשב"ם "כדלקמן ובמסכתא מוקמינן" וא"ש ג"כ כנ"ל.

עין משפט
נר מצוה

מסורת הש"ס

תורה אור

וְאִם הֵבִיא חֲמִשִּׁים בִּכְלִי אֶחָד וַחֲמִשִּׁים בִּכְלִי אֶחָד – יָצָא; אִם הֵבִיא – אִין, לְכַתְּחִלָּה – לָא; וְאִי סָלְקָא דַּעְתָּךְ כָּל כִּי הַאי גַּוְונָא פַּלְגָא וּפַלְגָא הוּא, אֲפִילּוּ לְכַתְּחִלָּה נַמִי! הָכִי הַשְׁתָּא? הָתָם אֲנַן סָהֲדֵי דְּהַאי גַּבְרָא מֵעִיקָּרָא לְקָרְבָּן גָּדוֹל קָא מְכַוֵּין, וְהַאי דְּקָאָמַר בִּשְׁנֵי כֵלִים – דְּיָדַע דְּלָא אֶפְשָׁר לְאַתּוּיֵי בִּכְלִי אֶחָד, כַּמָּה דְּאֶפְשָׁר לְאִיתּוּיֵי מַיְיתִינַן. א) וְהִלְכְתָא כְּוָותֵיהּ דְּרַב יוֹסֵף בְּשָׂדֶה, עִנְיָן, וּמֶחֱצָה. הַהוּא דְּשָׁדַר פִּיסְקֵי דְשִׁירָאֵי לְבֵיתֵיהּ, אָמַר רַבִּי אַמִי: א הָרְאוּיִין לְבָנִים – לַבָּנִים, רְאוּיִין לְבָנוֹת – לַבָּנוֹת. וְלָא אֲמָרַן אֶלָּא דְּלֵית לֵיהּ כַּלָּתָא, אֲבָל אִית לֵיהּ כַּלָּתָא – ב לְכַלָּתֵיהּ שָׁדַר; וְאִי בְּנָתֵיהּ לָא נְסִיבָן, ג לָא שָׁבֵק בְּנָתֵיהּ וּמְשַׁדֵּר לְכַלָּתֵיהּ. הַהוּא דַּאֲמַר לְהוּ: "נִכְסַיי לְבָנַיי", הֲוָה לֵיהּ בְּרָא וּבְרַתָּא; מִי ד קָרוּ אֱינָשֵׁי לִבְרָא "בָּנַיי", (וְלִסְלוּקֵי לִבְרַתָּא מֵעִישּׂוּר קָאָתֵי.) אוֹ דִּלְמָא לָא קָרוּ אֱינָשֵׁי לִבְרָא "בָּנַיי", וְלִמְשׁוּכָהּ לִבְרַתָּא בְּמַתָּנָה קָאָתֵי? אֲמַר אַבַּיֵי, ה ת"ש: °"וּבְנֵי דָן חוּשִׁים". א"ל רָבָא, דִּלְמָא כִּדְתָנָא דְּבֵי חִזְקִיָּה: שֶׁהָיוּ מְרוּבִּין כְּחוּשִׁים שֶׁל קָנֶה! אֶלָּא אֲמַר רָבָא: °"וּבְנֵי פַלּוּא אֱלִיאָב". רַב יוֹסֵף אֲמַר: °"וּבְנֵי אֵיתָן עֲזַרְיָה". הַהוּא דַּאֲמַר לְהוּ: "נִכְסַאי לְבָנַאי", הֲוָה לֵיהּ בְּרָא וּבַר בְּרָא; קָרוּ אֱינָשֵׁי לְבַר בְּרָא "בְּרָא", אוֹ לָא? רַב חֲבִיבָא אֲמַר: קָרוּ אֱינָשֵׁי לְבַר בְּרָא "בְּרָא"; מָר בַּר רַב אַשִׁי אֲמַר: ו לָא קָרוּ אֱינָשֵׁי לְבַר בְּרָא "בְּרָא". תַּנְיָא כְּוָותֵיהּ דְּמָר בַּר רַב אַשִׁי: ז הַמּוּדָּר הֲנָאָה מִבָּנִים – מוּתָּר בִּבְנֵי בָנִים.§

(רש"ל מ"ז; בראשית מו; במדבר כו; דה"א ב)

מתני' כ) ח הִנִּיחַ בָּנִים גְּדוֹלִים וּקְטַנִּים, הִשְׁבִּיחוּ גְּדוֹלִים אֶת הַנְּכָסִים – הִשְׁבִּיחוּ לָאֶמְצַע; אִם אָמְרוּ: "רְאוּ מַה שֶּׁהִנִּיחַ אַבָּא, הֲרֵי אָנוּ עוֹשִׂין וְאוֹכְלִים" – הִשְׁבִּיחוּ לְעַצְמָן. ט וְכֵן הָאִשָּׁה שֶׁהִשְׁבִּיחָה אֶת הַנְּכָסִים – הִשְׁבִּיחָה לָאֶמְצַע; אִם אָמְרָה: "רְאוּ מַה שֶּׁהִנִּיחַ לִי בַּעֲלִי, הֲרֵי אֲנִי עוֹשָׂה וְאוֹכֶלֶת" – הִשְׁבִּיחָה לְעַצְמָהּ.§ **גמ'** אָמַר רַב חֲבִיבָא בְּרֵיהּ דְּרַב יוֹסֵף בְּרֵיהּ דְּרָבָא מִשְּׁמֵיהּ דְּרָבָא: י לֹא שָׁנוּ אֶלָּא שֶׁשָּׁבְחוּ נְכָסִים מֵחֲמַת נְכָסִים, אֲבָל שָׁבְחוּ נְכָסִים מֵחֲמַת עַצְמָן – הִשְׁבִּיחוּ לְעַצְמָן. אִינִי? וְהָא אָמַר ר' חֲנִינָא: אֲפִילּוּ לֹא הִנִּיחַ לָהֶם אֲבִיהֶם אֶלָּא
אוּדַיְינֵי

רש"י

הֲרֵי זֶה שֶׁפֵּירֵשׁ מֵאָה עִשָּׂרוֹן בִּשְׁנֵי כֵלִים, כְּגוֹן זֶה שֶׁאָמַר "לָךְ וּלְבָנַיִךְ". וְלָא קָתָנֵי חֲמִשִּׁים בִּכְלִי (א) וַחֲמִשִּׁים בִּכְלִי אֶלָּא דִּיעֲבַד, אֲבָל לְכַתְּחִלָּה לָא, אֶלָּא מֵבִיא שִׁשִּׁים בִּכְלִי אֶחָד וְאַרְבָּעִים בִּכְלִי אֶחָד, וְקַשְׁיָא לְרַב יוֹסֵף דְּאָמַר: מֶחֱצָה! וּפָרֵיךְ: הָתָם אֲנַן סָהֲדֵי דִּלְקָרְבָּן גָּדוֹל קָא מְכַוֵּין. לְאַתּוּיֵי בִּכְלִי אֶחָד, וְהַאי דְּקָאָמַר שְׁנֵי כֵלִים וְלָא קָאָמַר מֵאָה עִשָּׂרוֹן לְהָבִיא בִּכְלִי אֶחָד – מִשּׁוּם דְּיָדַע דְּלָא אֶפְשָׁר לְאַתּוּיֵי בִּכְלִי אֶחָד יוֹתֵר מִשִּׁשִּׁים עִשָּׂרוֹן. דִּתְנַן בְּפֶרֶק "הַמְּנָחוֹת וְהַנְּסָכִים" (מנחות דף קג:): מִתְנַדֵּב אָדָם מִנְחָה שֶׁל שִׁשִּׁים עִשָּׂרוֹן וּמֵבִיא בִּכְלִי אֶחָד, וְאִם אָמַר "הֲרֵי עָלַי ס"א" – מֵבִיא ס' בִּכְלִי אֶחָד וְאֶחָד בִּכְלִי אֶחָד, שֶׁכֵּן הַצִּבּוּר מְבִיאִין בְּיוֹם טוֹב הָרִאשׁוֹן שֶׁל חַג שֶׁחָל לִהְיוֹת בְּשַׁבָּת שִׁשִּׁים וְאֶחָד, דַּיּוֹ לַיָּחִיד שֶׁיְּהֵא פָּחוֹת מִן הַצִּבּוּר אֶחָד. א"ר שִׁמְעוֹן: וַהֲלֹא אֵלּוּ לַכְּבָשִׂים וְאֵלּוּ לַפָּרִים, וְאֵינָן נִבְלָלִין זֶה עִם זֶה. אֶלָּא עַד שִׁשִּׁים יְכוֹלִין לִבְלוֹל כו'. וְהִלְכְתָא כְּוָותֵיהּ דְּרַב יוֹסֵף בְּשָׂדֶה כו'. מִשּׁוּם דִּבְכוּלֵּי גְּמָרָא רַבָּה וְרַב יוֹסֵף הִלְכְתָא כְּרַבָּה, אִיצְטְרִיךְ לְמֵימַר דְּהִלְכְתָא כְּרַב יוֹסֵף בְּהָנֵי תְּלָת. בְּשָׂדֶה. בְּפֶרֶק "הַשּׁוּתָּפִין" (לעיל דף יב:) גַּבֵּי הַהוּא גַּבְרָא דִּזְבַן אַרְעָא אַמְּצְרָא דְּבֵי נָשָׁא, וּתְלָת מִילֵּי קָאָמַר רַב יוֹסֵף הָתָם. עִנְיָן. בְּפֶרֶק "יֵשׁ נוֹחֲלִין": קִנְיָן אֵימָתַי חוֹזֵר? רַב יוֹסֵף אָמַר: כָּל זְמַן שֶׁעֲסוּקִים בְּאוֹתוֹ עִנְיָן, וְאִית דְּגָרַס: קִנְיָן. וּמֶחֱצָה. הַיְינוּ הַךְ דְּא"ר יוֹסֵף: קַנְאִי פַּלְגָא. פִּיסְקֵי דְשִׁירָאֵי. חֲתִיכוֹת מְעִיל, וּסְתָם שֶׁלֹּא לְחַלֵּק לִבְנֵי בֵּיתוֹ. הָרְאוּיִן לְבָנִים. מַלְבּוּשֵׁי זָכָר. לְכַלָּתֵיהּ שָׁדַר. וְלֹא לִבְנוֹתָיו. וְדַוְקָא דְּאִינְסִיבָא בְּנָתֵיהּ, שֶׁאֵינָהּ מוּטֶּלֶת עָלָיו. (ב) יְרוּשַׁלְמִי בְּפ' "שְׁנֵי דַיָּינֵי גְזֵירוֹת": מִי שֶׁשָּׁלַח לִמְדִינַת הַיָּם, וְאָמַר: יִתְּנוּ אֵלּוּ לְבָנָיו – בְּנוֹתָיו בִּכְלָל, וְאִם בִּשְׁעַת מִיתָה אָמַר "אֵלּוּ לְבָנַי" – אֵין הַבָּנוֹת בִּכְלָל. הַהוּא דַּאֲמַר לְהוּ. בִּשְׁעַת מִיתָה. נִכְסַיי לְבָנַיי. וְלֹא הָיָה לוֹ אֶלָּא בֵּן אֶחָד זָכָר, וְגַם בָּנוֹת הָיוּ לוֹ. וּבָעֵי גְּמָרָא: מִי קָרוּ אֱינָשֵׁי לִבְרָא יְחִידָאָה "בָּנַיי" לְשׁוֹן רַבִּים, וְא"כ כָּל נְכָסָיו נָתַן לִבְנוֹ וְאֵין הַבָּנוֹת בִּכְלָל. אוֹ לָא, וְיַחְלְקוּ הַבָּנוֹת עִמּוֹ? וּבְנֵי דָן חוּשִׁים. אַלְמָא בֵּן אֶחָד קָרֵי לְשׁוֹן רַבִּים. כְּחוּשִׁים שֶׁל קָנֶה. שֶׁגְּדֵלִים הַרְבֵּה בְּיַחַד, בְּלַעַ"ז טרוק"ש. אִי נַמִי, עֲלֵי קָנִים אוֹ קִשְׁרֵי הַקָּנִים קְרוּיִן כֵּן. וּבַר בְּרָא. בֵּן שֶׁל אוֹתוֹ בֵּן, אוֹ שֶׁל אַחֵר שֶׁמֵּת. מִי קָרוּ אֱינָשֵׁי לְבַר בְּרָא בְּרָא. וּלְפִיכָךְ אָמַר "נִכְסַיי לְבָנַיי" לְשׁוֹן רַבִּים, וְיַחְלְקוּ בֵּינֵיהֶם. אוֹ לָא קָרוּ לֵיהּ בְּרָא, וְהַאי דְּקָאָמַר לְשׁוֹן רַבִּים – הַיְינוּ כְּדַאֲמָרַן לְעֵיל "וּבְנֵי פַלּוּא אֱלִיאָב". מוּתָּר בִּבְנֵי בָנִים. אֲבָל לְעִנְיַן פְּרִיָּה וּרְבִיָּה חֲשִׁיבֵי כְּבָנִים, בְּפֶרֶק "הַבָּא עַל יְבִמְתּוֹ" (יבמות דף סב:). **מתני'** הִשְׁבִּיחוּ הַגְּדוֹלִים אֶת הַנְּכָסִים. סְתָם, בְּעוֹדָן בִּתְפוּסַת הַבַּיִת. הִשְׁבִּיחוּ לָאֶמְצַע. וְיִטְּלוּ קְטַנִּים כִּגְדוֹלִים, וּכְדִמְפָרֵשׁ בַּגְּמָרָא שֶׁשָּׁבְחוּ הַנְּכָסִים מֵחֲמַת נְכָסִים. וְאִם אָמְרוּ גְּדוֹלִים לַקְּטַנִּים. בִּפְנֵי עֵדִים, אוֹ אָמְרוּ לְבֵית דִּין, אוֹ בַּצִּבּוּר: רְאוּ מַה שֶּׁהִנִּיחַ לָנוּ אַבָּא, וּמְזוּמָּנִים אָנוּ לַחֲלוֹק, וּמַה שֶּׁנַּשְׁבִּיחַ – נַשְׁבִּיחַ מֵחֶלְקֵנוּ. וְנִתְעַצְּלוּ ב"ד לַחֲלוֹק – אָז הִשְׁבִּיחוּ לְעַצְמָן. וְכֵן הָאִשָּׁה. שֶׁמֵּת בַּעְלָהּ. וּבַגְּמָרָא מוֹקֵי לָהּ בְּאִשָּׁה יוֹרֶשֶׁת. וְאִם אָמְרָה רְאוּ מַה שֶּׁהִנִּיחַ לִי בַּעְלִי הֲרֵינִי עוֹשָׂה וְאוֹכֶלֶת (ג) הִשְׁבִּיחָה לְעַצְמָהּ. וְהוּא דְּלָא שָׁקְלָה מְזוֹנֵי. דְּאִי שָׁקְלָה מְזוֹנֵי – לָא, דִּתְנַן: אַלְמָנָה נִזּוֹנֶת מִנִּכְסֵי יְתוֹמִין, וּמַעֲשֵׂה יָדֶיהָ שֶׁלָּהֶן (כתובות דף צה:). **גמ'** לֹא שָׁנוּ. דְּהִשְׁבִּיחוּ לָאֶמְצַע. אֶלָּא שֶׁשָּׁבְחוּ נְכָסִים מֵחֲמַת נְכָסִים. לֹא טָרְחוּ וְלֹא הוֹצִיאוּ מִשֶּׁלָּהֶם כְּלוּם, אֶלָּא מִנִּכְסֵי אֲבִיהֶן שָׂכְרוּ פּוֹעֲלִים וְהִשְׁבִּיחוּ הַנְּכָסִים. מֵחֲמַת עַצְמָן. שֶׁחָפְרוּ וְנָטְעוּ וְשָׂכְרוּ מִשֶּׁלָּהֶם וְלֹא מִשֶּׁל אֲבִיהֶם – אָז הַשֶּׁבַח לְעַצְמָן.
אוּדַיְינֵי

תוספות

אם הביא דיעבד אין לכתחלה לא. תימה לר"י: דמאי קשיא ליה? וכי אין פשוט לו באומר "נכסי לשני בני אדם" שיהיו שוים? ואפי' הכי במנחה לכתחלה לא, וא"כ ע"כ משום דלקרבן גדול קא מכוין! ואור"י, דהכי פריך: דהא סברא היא שלא תטול אשתו אלא כאחד מן הבנים, ואפ"ה קאמר רב יוסף דנוטלת מחצה. א"כ ה"נ, אע"פ שמסברא יש לנו לומר דלקרבן גדול קא מכוין – לא היה לנו ללכת אחר הסברא. **תא** שמע ובני דן חושים. וא"ת: דכיון דקרו אינשי לברא "בניי", א"כ למה הוצרך לומר "נכסיי לבניי"? פשיטא שהוא לבנו! וי"ל: דאצטריך, שאם מלא דייתיקי או מתנה – שלא יהיה בה כלום. **שהיו** לו בנים כחושים של קנה. ואע"פ שכשירד למצרים עדיין לא היו לו בנים כל כך – מ"מ נקרא כן על שם העתיד. כדדריש "אשר שם שַׁמות" – אל תקרי שַׁמות, אלא שֵׁמות (ברכות דף ז:). **והשביחו** גדולים השבח לאמצע. פירש ריב"ם דה"ה גדולים וגדולים, אלא אורחא דמילתא נקט. ולא דמי ליורד לתוך שדה של חבירו ונטעה שלא ברשות (ד), [או] לשותף שהוא כיורד ברשות. דשותף אינו מוחל טרחו לחברו, אבל אחין מחיל אהדדי. **ואם** אמר ראו מה שהניח כו'. פירש רבינו שמואל: ראו מה הניח לנו אבינו, ומזומנים אנו לחלוק, ומה שנשביח – נשביח מחלקנו. משמע שרוצה לומר שאינו משביח אלא מחלקו המגיעו, ואין לו אלא שבח המגיע לחלקו. ואין נראה, מדאמר: רב ספרא שבק אבוה זוזי, שקלינהו רב ספרא – משמע דשקלינהו לכולהו. ועוד: אם לא לקח אלא המגיע לחלקו, מה היה יכול לתבעו? הא אמר ב"איזהו נשך" (ב"מ דף סט. ושם) דזוזי כמאן דפליגי דמי! ועוד: כשיחלקו, אם מגיע חלק האחד לחלקו – אם כן נמצא שלא היה השבח שלו! על כן נראה לר"י כפירוש ריב"ם: דשבח שהשביח מכל הנכסים הוי שלו. ולא דמי ליורד לתוך שדה של חבירו שלא ברשות, שאין לו אלא שכר טרחו עם היציאה, או [שותף, דהוי כיורד ברשות ונוטל כאריס – היינו משום] דיכולים להרויח זה כמו זה ולא מחלי. אבל הכא, אם הגדולים לא ירויחו – (ה) הקטנים לא ירויחו בהם. וכן צריך לומר גבי דרב ספרא, דקטנים היו ולא היו יכולין להרויח, ולהכי כיון דגברא רבה הוא ולא שבק גירסי' וטרח לאחריני, אע"פ שלא אמר "ראו" – כאילו אמר "ראו", ומחלי ליה הקטנים. והא דאמר בריש "אלו מציאות" (שם דף כב:) גבי תמרי דזיקא, דיתמי לאו בני מחילה נינהו, הכא דאין מפסידין, ולא בא בידם הריוח – מחלי שפיר. (ו) **בתוספתא** גרסינן: אם אמרו יתומים [בפני ב"ד] ראו מה שהניח כו'. ולא ידע ר"י אמאי נקט גבי בנים בפני ב"ד. אי משום דגלי אדעתיה דלא מחל להם – אפי' בפני עדים נמי גלי דעתיה! ושמא להכי צריך בפני ב"ד – כדי שיתעצמו בדבר לתקן להם שיטריח בשבילם, ומדלא תקנו להם – ודאי לא מצאו להם תקנה לחלק, ומחלו הכל. ורב ספרא נמי ידוע היה לב"ד, אף על פי שלא אמר. ומיהו, רשב"ם פי' דה"ה בפני עדים.

השביחו לעצמן. ואע"ג דב"המפקיד" (שם דף מ. ושם) בעובדא דמרי בר איסק, אמרינן דכיון דשלא ברשות נחת, דהא אין מורידין קרוב לנכסי קטן, השבח לאמצע – הכא לית לן למימר הכי, דהתם איכא למיחש שמא יחזיק הקרוב בנכסי קטן שאינו כאן, אבל הכא – ליכא למיחש, שהקטנים עם הגדולים ביחד אין יכולין להחזיק זה על זה. **לא** שנו אלא ששבחו נכסים מחמת נכסים. פירש בקונטרס: שלא טרחו ולא הוציאו משלהם כלום, אלא מנכסי אביהם שכרו פועלים. ומחמת עצמם – היינו שכרו פועלים משלהם. משמע שרוצה לומר, דטעמא דכיון דשכרו משל אביהם – הוי לאמצע,
דאי

עין משפט נר מצוה

כט א מיי' פ"ו מהלכות זכיה ומתנה הל' יד סמג עשין פב טוש"ע חו"מ סי' רמז סעיף א:

ל ב ג מיי' שם טוש"ע שם סעיף ב:

לא ד ה ו מיי' שם פי"א הלכה א סמג שם טוש"ע שם סעיף ג:

לב ז מיי' פ"ט מהלכות נדרים הל' כג סמג לאוין רמב טוש"ע יו"ד סי' ריז סעיף מו:

לג ח ט י מיי' פ"ט מהל' נחלות הל' ב ג ועיין בהשגות ובמ"מ סמג עשין נו טוש"ע ח"מ סי' רפז סעיף א:

רבינו גרשום

לוג אחד בס' עשרון נבללין בס"א אין נבללין: לכתחלה לא יצא. והא הכא כיון דאמר הרי עלי מנחה להביא בשני כלים ומשמע דכולן אין מחזיקן בכלי אחד ויתן חציין בכלי אחד וחציין בכלי אחר ואפ"ה לא יצא לכתחלה אלא א"כ הביא ס' בכלי אחד הכא נמי להיכא דאמר סתם נכסיי לך ולבניך אמאי תטול פלגא ותיובתא דרב יוסף: הכי השתא התם. כיון דאמר הרי עלי מנחה עשרון להביא בשני כלים משום קרבן גדול איכוין ואילו אפשר להביא כולן בכלי שרת אחת כך היתה רצונו והאי דקאמר בשני כלים כו'. בשדה. דאמר מעלינן ליה כנכסי דבי מריון: ענין. דאמר מענין לענין א) ומחצה הכא. דשדר פסקי שיראין לביתיה. חתיכות של מעיל לאנשי ביתו ולא היה לו אשה. מה שיש בהם הראוי לבנים לבנים כו': לכלתיה שדר. שמכבד אדם כלתו משום חביבות בנו: לברא יחידא בניי אי לא. או דלמא לתרויהון בשוה: ובני דן חושים. דאפי' לחד ברא קרי בניי: שהיו מרובים כחושים של קנה. כלומר רוב בנים היו לו כאותן שרטוטין של קנים שיש בקנים שהן ארוכות. ואית דאמרי כחושים של קנים כעלים של קנה שהן קליפות הרבה זו ע"ג זו: מותר בבני בנים. דלא נקראו בני בנים בנים: **פיס'** הניח בנים גדולים וקטנים. והניח להם נכסים: השביחו גדולי' את הנכסי'. שלקחו מתפוסת הבית שמן הנכסים עצמן השביחו האחרים השבח לאמצע הוא שעדיין לא חלקו את נכסיהן. אבל אם אמרו הגדולים לקטנים שהודיעום ואמרו ראו מה שהניח לנו אבא הרי אנו עושין ומשביחין לעצמנו ואוכלין השבח לעצמן: לא שנו. דהשביחו לאמצע: אלא ששבחו נכסים מחמת נכסים. שנפלו מתפוסת הבית ושכרו פועלין להשביחן אבל שבחו מחמת עצמם שהם שבחו וחפרו משלהן אין השבח לאמצע אלא לעצמן: איני. דאם השביח מחמת עצמן אין השכר לאמצע: והאמר ר' חנינא אפי' לא הניח להן אביהן אלא אודייני

א) נ"ל שעסוקין באותו ענין לעיל דף קיז.

מסורת הש"ס

א) לעיל דף קיז: ב) בבא מציעא לט:

הגהות הב"ח

(א) רשב"ם ד"ה (בע"א) האומר וכו' בכלי אחד וחמשים בכלי אחד אלא דיעבד: (ב) ד"ה לכלתיה וכו' ירושלמי. נ"ב גם הרי"ף הביאו: (ג) ד"ה ואם אמרה וכו' השביחה לעצמה. נ"ב רשב"ם ז"ל לשיטתו אזיל שפירש בגמ' דאשה יורשת כגון שנשא ראובן כו' דלפי זה הא דתנן אם אמרה ראו כו' לאו באשה יורשת קמיירי אלא מילתא באנפי נפשה היא והכי פירושו ואלמנה שאמרה בב"ד ראו כו' ומיירי בהניח לה נכסים מועטים ואמרה ראו מה שהניח לי בעלי כו' אפי' השביחה אלף ככר השביחה לעצמה והיינו דוקא דלא שקלה מזוני כו' אבל באשה יורשת ודאי כשפירשה השביחה לעצמה אע"פ שנזונת מתפוסת הבית ומה שלא פי' רשב"ם להך בבא מיירי נמי באשה יורשת היינו משום דתני ראו מה שהניח לי בעלי וכמו שהקשו התוספות: (ד) תום' ד"ה והשביחו וכו' שלא ברשות ולא לשותף: (ה) ד"ה ואם וכו' הקטנים לא ירויחו. נ"ב עיין באשר"י שנתן טעם גם לגדולים וגדולים: (ו) ד"ה בתוספות ר"ח גרסינן אם אמרו בפני ב"ד ראו מה כצ"ל:

וכרכיש בה רישיה בי מדרשא. אזל לגביה, א"ל: אילו א"ל "קני כחמור", מי קני? דאיתמר: "קני כחמור" — [א]לא קנה. [א)]"את וחמור" — רב נחמן אמר: [ב]קנה מחצה, ורב המנונא אמר: לא אמר כלום, ורב ששת אמר: קנה הכל. אמר רב ששת: מנא אמינא לה? דתניא, רבי יוסי אומר: אין לך מר בקישות אלא פנימי שבו, לפיכך כשהוא תורם — מוסיף על החיצון שבו ותורם; אמאי? "את וחמור" הוא! שאני התם, דמדאורייתא תרומה מעלייתא היא; [ב)]דאמר רבי אילעא: מנין לתורם מן הרע על היפה שתרומתו תרומה? שנאמר: (במדבר יח) "ולא תשאו עליו חטא בהרימכם את חלבו ממנו", ואם אינו קדוש — נשיאות חטא למה? מכאן לתורם מן הרע על היפה שתרומתו תרומה. אמר ליה רב מרדכי לרב אשי, מתיב רב אויא תיובתא: [ג)]מעשה בחמש נשים ובהן שתי אחיות, וליקט אחד כלכלה של תאנים, ושלהן היתה, ושל שביעית היתה, ואמר: "הרי כולכן מקודשות לי בכלכלה זאת", וקבלה אחת מהן ע"י כולן — אמרו חכמים: [ג]אין אחיות מקודשות; אחיות הוא דאין מקודשות, הא נכריות מקודשות; [ד]ואמאי? "את וחמור" היא! אמר ליה: היינו [ד)]דחזאי רב הונא בר אויא בחלמא דמותיב רב אויא תיובתא, לאו מי אוקימנא [ה]דאמר: "הראויה מכם לביאה תתקדש לי"? ההוא דאמר לה לדביתהו: "נכסיי ליך ולבניך", אמר רב יוסף: [ו]קנתה מחצה. ואמר רב יוסף: מנא אמינא לה? דתניא, [ה)]רבי אומר: (ויקרא כד) "והיתה לאהרן ולבניו" — [ז]מחצה לאהרן מחצה לבניו. אמר ליה אביי: בשלמא התם — אהרן בר חלוקה הוא, להכי פרט ביה רחמנא למשקל פלגא, אשה לאו בת ירושה היא, דיה שתטול כאחד מן הבנים! איני? והא עובדא הוה בנהרדעא ואגביה שמואל פלגא, בטבריא — ואגביה רבי יוחנן פלגא! ותו, כי אתא רב יצחק בר יוסף אמר: [ח]ההוא דמי כלילא דשדו דבי מלכא אאבולי ואאיסטרוגי, אמר רבי: ניתבו אבולי פלגא ואיסטרוגי פלגא! הכי השתא? התם מעיקרא כי הוו כתבי — אאבולי הוו כתבי, ואיסטרוגי הוו מסייעי בהדייהו, וידע מלכא דהוו קא מסייעי; השתא, (רש"ל) [מאי דקא כתבי] אאבולי ואאיסטרוגי — למימרא דהני פלגא והני פלגא. מתיב רבי זירא: [ט]האומר "הרי עלי מנחה מאה עשרון להביא בשני כלים" — מביא ששים בכלי אחד וארבעים בכלי אחד, ואם

רשב"ם

וכרכיש. הודה לדבריי. קני כחמור מי קנה. כמו שהחמור לא קנה — כן הוא לא קנה. הכא נמי, כי היכי דבנים העתידים לבא בעולם לא קנו — איהו נמי לא קנה. את וחמור. את ובהמה זו תקנו נכסיי. קנה מחצה. דהכי אמר ליה: אתה וחמור תקנו שניכם, הוא מחצה ואתה מחצה, ולא אבד האיש חלקו בשביל החמור, שלא תלאן זה בזה. לא קנה ולא כלום. דכיון דבקנין אחד שיתף שניהם — לא נגמרה בדעתו להקנות לזה בלא זה כלום, וכיון דחמור לא קנה — איהו נמי לא קנה. רב ששת אמר קנה הכל. אדם יודע שאין חמור קונה, וגמר בדעתו שמי שיוכל לקנות משניהם — יקנה. כשהוא תורם. קישות אחד מחמשים, איכא למיחש דלמא איכא מר בפנימי שבזה טפי מאידך, ואין כאן אחד מחמשים במתוק, ונמצא תורם מן המר על המתוק. הלכך, כשהוא תורם — מוסיף על המתוק כדי כבילה מקישות אחרת, ותורם קישות וכבילה על הארבעים ותשע, ואיכא השתא מתוק בתרומה טובא, ונמצא תורם מן המתוק על המתוק. ואמאי את וחמור הוא. שאמר: קישות זה יהא תרומה על אלו. וכיון דיש בה מר ומתוק, כי היכי דמר לא חייל בה תרומה, ולא מבטל שם טבל מן המ"ט, הכי נמי המתוק לא יחול עליו שם תרומה! אלא מאי אית (א) למימר — המתוק קנה הכל ופטר מטבל את המ"ט. ולעיל נמי, "את וחמור" אף על גב דחמור לא קנה — הוא קנה הכל, כי היכי דהכא דמר לא קנה ומתוק קנה הכל! ומשני: שאני תרומה. דמר נמי תרומה מעלייתא הוא כמתוק, ואין כאן "את וחמור", ושניהן קונין זה כזה. לא תשאו. על התרומה חטא, אם תרימו את חלבו מן היפה. הא אם תרימו מן הרע — תשאו עליו חטא, שלא עשית מצוה מן המובחר. נשיאות חטא למה. אלא יחזור ויתרום מן היפה. מעשה בחמש נשים. בפ' "האיש מקדש". והתם מפרש לה רב שפיר. אמר רב: שמע מינה ממתניתין ארבעה, ונקט בידיה תלת. שמע מינה: המקדש בפירות שביעית מקודשת. וש"מ: קדשה בגזל אינה מקודשת ואפילו בגזל דידה, מדקתני: שלהן היתה ושל שביעית היתה, טעמא — דשביעית, דהפקר הוא, הא דשאר שני שבוע — לא. וש"מ: אשה נעשית שליח לחבירתה ואפי' במקום שנעשית לה צרה, שהרי קבלה אחת על ידי כולן, ונתקדשה היא וחברותיה בכלכלה זו, ונעשו צרות זו לזו. אין אחיות מקודשות. דקדושין שאין מסורין לביאה לא הוו קדושין כלל, ואפי' בחדא מינייהו. ואמאי. נכריות מקודשות? והא "את וחמור" הוא, הרי מקדש בכלכלה זו כולן, חמש נכריות ואחיות, וכי היכי דאחיות לא קנו — נכריות נמי לא יקנו! אלא שמע מינה, מה שיש בידו כח לקנות — יקנה הכל, כרב ששת. היינו דחזאי רב הונא בר אויא בחלום. ומשום דאמרת לי דמותיב רב אויא תיובתא נתקיים חלומי. מיהו, לאו קושיא הוא, דלאו מי אוקימנא כו'? בתמיה. הראויה מכם. ואין אחיות בכלל. ואביי הוא דמוקי לה הכי בקדושין. וקי"ל כרב נחמן, דאמר ד"את וחמור" — קנה מחצה, והמזכה לעובר לכשיולד — קנה, כרב נחמן. בפירוש רבינו חננאל. קני פלגא. כנגד הבנים, היא מחצה והם מחצה. והיתה לאהרן וגו'. בלחם הפנים כתיב. "אהרן" — זה כהן גדול, מחצה לכהן גדול ומחצה למשמרת כהנים. והך ברייתא במסכת יומא בפרק ראשון (דף יז:) דתנן התם גבי כהן גדול: מקריב חלק בראש ונוטל חלק בראש, ותניא בגמרא: ונוטל חלה אחת משתי חלות של עצרת, ארבע או חמש מששה לחם הפנים. רבי אומר: לעולם חמש, שנאמר: "והיתה לאהרן ולבניו" — מחצה לאהרן ומחצה לבניו. והתם מפרש למה אינו נוטל שש, דהאיכא י"ב חלות, שתים מערכות שש המערכת. ומכאן אנו למדין דהמזכיר יחיד אצל מרובין לענין מתנה — נוטל כנגד המרובין. חלוקה הוא. בכלל שאר כהנים. אע"ג דלא גלי ביה קרא, שלא כתב אהרן אלא "והיתה לכהנים" — היה חולק עמהן. דמי כלילא. כתר מלכות. דשדו בי קיסר. הטילו על אלו לעשותה. אבולי ואיסטרטיגי. עשירים ושרים, כדגרסינן (במגילה דף טו.) במרדכי והמן: זה בא בפרוזבולי וזה בא בפרוזבוטי. "גלידים" ו"מלך פלשתים" (שמואל א יד. מלכים א ד) מתרגמינן איסטרטיגי. ואיסטרטיגי פלגא. אע"ג דאבולי עשירים יותר. אבולי הוו כתיבי. בכתב של מלך ליתן הכל, אלא שאיסטרטיגי מסייעי להו פורתא. השתא דקא כתבי כו'. להוסיף על מה שהיו רגילין ליתן נכתבו עמה. מתיב ר' זירא. לרב יוסף. האומר הרי עלי מנחה מאה עשרון להביאם בשני כלים מביא ששים בכלי אחד ומ' בכלי אחד כו' הרי

תוספות

רב נחמן אמר קנה מחצה. והלכתא כרב נחמן. והא דאמר בפ"ב דקדושין (דף נא.): וליטעמיך אימא סיפא, מעשה בחמש נשים כו' עד: "את וחמור" הוא, ו"את וחמור" לא קנה — לאו משום דהלכתא הכי, אלא הכי בעי למימר: ותקשה למאן דאמר לא קנה, וכי היכי דלדידיה צריך לתרוצה — הכי נמי צריך לתרוצה לרבא.

אין לך מר בקישות אלא פנימי שבו. תימה: כיון דבכל קישואין הפנימי מר והחיצון מתוק, למה לא יתרום מזה על זה? והלא החיצון יפטור החיצון, והפנימי יפטור הפנימי, ולמה צריך להוסיף על החיצון? ונראה לר"י: דר' יוסי דהכא לא איירי בשכל הקישואין מרים, אלא אותה שתורם נמצאת מרה. וקאי אהא דתנן במסכת תרומות (בפ"ג משנה א), ומייתי לה ב"האשה רבה" (יבמות דף פט. ושם): התורם קישות ונמצאת מרה, אבטיח ונמצא סרוח — תרומה, ויחזור ויתרום. ור' יוסי פליג, וסבר דאין צריך לחזור ולתרום, אלא מוסיף מן החילון על החילון. דאפי' אותה שנמצאת מרה — אין החילון מר כל כך שלא יהא עליו תורת אוכל. והכי משמע בהדיא בירושלמי על ההיא משנה דהתורם קישות, דקאמר: בשלמא אבטיח ונמצא סרוח — תרומה ויחזור ויתרום, דספק גמור הוא אם היה סרוח בשעת הפרשה אם לאו, אלא קישות ונמצאת מרה — אמאי הוי תרומה? הא ודאי דהיתה מרה גם בשעת הפרשה ולמה היא תרומה כלל? ומשני: עשאוה ספק אוכלין, דאוכל גמור הוא מן התורה, ולכך היא תרומה. והכי נמי אמרינן הכא, דמדאורייתא תרומה מעליא הוא, אלא דקנסי ליה משום דהוה ליה למטעמיה, כדאמרי' ב"האשה רבה" (שם) ועשאוה ספק אוכל, ולכך יחזור ויתרום. ובתר הכי מייתי בירושלמי ההיא דר' יוסי דהכא, דאין לך מר בקישות אלא פנימי שבו. וקא בעי התם: וכי בדבר שיכול ליבדק נחלקו? ומשני: על עיקר בדיקתה נחלקו, דתנא קמא סבר: יש מרירות הרבה בחילון, וראוי לעשותו ספק אוכלין. ור' יוסי סבר: אין בו מרירות כל כך, ואין ראוי לעשותו ספק אוכלין, ולכך לא יחזור ויתרום. הרי משמע בהדיא דרבי יוסי פליג אמתניתין דהתורם קישות.

אם

רבינו גרשום

קירקיש בה רישא. כלומר דהכי עיקר דלית חולק לטליא: אמר לו זהו הטעם דאילו אמר לו קנה כחמור. ממון שלי מי קני כחמור הא חמור לאו בר קניה הוא וכי היכי דחמור לא קנה איהו נמי לא קנה הכי נמי להיכא דאמר ליה זיל קני כחד מינייהו ואינהו לאו בני קניה נינהו דאכתי לא אתו לעלמא דקיימא לן המזכה לעובר לא קנה האי בר קשישא נמי לא קנה להכי דיטול לחודיה בלא דידהו ויחלוקו בשוה והיינו טעמא דלית ליה חולק: אי אמר ליה קני את וחמור רב נחמן אמר קנה מחצה. דהכי קאמר את דבר קנין את קנה חצי וחמור לאו בר קנין הוא אינו קונה: ורב המנונא אמר לא קנה ולא כלום. דדימה קנינו לחמור כלומר כי היכי דחמור לא קנה כלום הכי נמי את לא תהא קונה כלום: רב ששת אמר קנה הכל. הכי קסבר בשלמא חמור לאו בר קנין הוא ואינו קונה כלום אבל את דבר קנין את קנה הכל חלקו וחלק חמור: אמר רב ששת מנא אמינא לה. דקנה הכל: דתניא ר' יוסי אומר אין לך בקישות מר אלא פנימי שבתוכו לפיכך כשהוא תורם מוסיף על התרומה חצי קישות אחד בלבד הואיל ויש מר בתוכו ואינו כולו מתוק נמצא תורם מן הרע על היפה דאין ברירה לפיכך מוסיף עליו עוד חצי קישות כדי שיהא זה חצי חיצון במקום המר שבאותו קישות של תרומה דחשיב כאילו כולו מתוק. ואמאי מתוקנין לדבריך דאמרת את וחמור לא קנה כלום הכא נמי האי מר שבתוך קישות זה של תרומה כחמור הוא מה חמור אינו קונה האי מר נמי אינו פוטר כלום. ולימא כי היכי דהאי מר אינו פוטר כלום החיצון המתוק נמי לא פטר ולא תהא תרומה אלא מדקא מוסיף ותורם והוי תרומה אע"ג דיש מר בתוכה ש"מ דאת וחמור קנה הכל. ומשני לעולם אימא לך את וחמור לא קנה כלום והכא מאי טעמא מתוקנין בתוספת דמדאורייתא אפי' תרם מן הרע על היפה תרומתו תרומה כדר' אילעא וכו' אבל החמירו רבנן משום חביבת המצוה דלא יתרום אלא מן היפה על היפה ולא דמי כלום לאת וחמור: הא מותיב רב אויא תיובתא. דאת וחמור קנה הכל: וליקט איש אחד כלכלה של תאנים. של נשים הללו היו תאנים: ושלהן. ושל שביעית היתה. דהפקר הוו וכל המחזיק בהפקר קנה להכי הוי יכול לקדש בהן: הא נכריות שהיו בין חמש נשים מקודשות. ואמאי מקודשות אפי' הנכריות והא את וחמור הוא כי היכי דאחיות לא הוי מקודשות (ביחד) לאותו איש הכי נמי נכריות לא ליהוי מקודשות אלא ש"מ מדמקודשות נינהו ש"מ דאת וחמור קני הכל ותיובתא דר' המנונא: אמר ליה היינו דחזאי לרב אויא אמש בחלום. משום דמשתעי השתא במאי דאותיב רב אויא. ולא אוקימנא בהא דמשום הכי נכריות מקודשות כגון דאמר הראויה מכם לביאה תתקדש למעוטי אחיות דאינן ראויות לו לביאה דלא דמיין לאת וחמור דלא קנה הכל דמנו דחמור לא קנה איהו נמי לא קנה: ר' אומר והיתה לאהרן ולבניו. גבי לחם הפנים כתיב דמצי למכתב והיתה לכהנים והיה נוטל אהרן כאחד מבניו אלא מדגלי ביה קרא והיתה לאהרן ש"מ לטפויי מילתא הוא דמחצה לאהרן ומחצה לבניו: אבל האי איתתא לאו בת חלוקה. לירת עם בניו השתא דקאמר נכסיי לך ולבניך דיה שתטול כאחד מבניה דלא שקלא פלגא. והא הוה עובדא דאמר לה ש"מ נכסיי לך ולבניך ואגבי שמואל פלגא לאתתא: אבולי ואסטרטיגי. שהשליך על בני העיר ועל בני חצר סתם שיקנו לו כתר. אבולי בני העיר. אסטרטיגי חצרנים. ואמר רבי ניתבו אבולי פלגא ואסטרטיגי פלגא ה"נ לגבי הא אתתא מאי שנא: מי דמי התם. גבי אבולי ואסטרטיגי מעיקרא אבולי לחודייהו שהן עשירים הוו כתיבי ליתן המס ואסטרטיגי סיוע במקצת בעלמא הוו מסייעי בהדייהו השתא וכו': ששים בכלי אחד. דהכי דינא דקי"ל לוו

מסורת הש"ס

א) [קדושין נא.] ב) לעיל פד: ב"מ נו. יבמות פט: קדושין מו: [תמורה ה.] ג) קדושין נ: ד) [מנחות מז. פד: בכורות ה. ע.] ה) ע"ז י: סנהדרין כח. [יומא יז:]

עין משפט נר מצוה

כב א מיי' פכ"ג מהל' מכירה הלכה יב סמג עשין פב טוש"ע חו"מ סי' רי סעיף ג:

כג ב מיי' שם טוש"ע שם סעיף ג:

כד ג ד ה מיי' פ"ט מהל' אישות הלכה ב סמג עשין מח טוש"ע אה"ע סי' מא סעיף ג:

כה ו מיי' פי"א מהל' זכייה ומתנה הלכה ה סמג עשין פב טוש"ע חו"מ סי' רמז סעיף ב:

כו ז מיי' פ"ד מהלכות תמידין הלכה יג:

כז ח עי' בטוש"ע חו"מ סי' קסג סעיף ו בהג"ה וסי' קסח סעיף ב בהג"ה מענין מסים:

כח ט מיי' פי"ו מהל' מעשה קרבנות הל"ו:

הגהות הב"ח

(א) רשב"ם ד"ה ולמאי וכו' אית לך למימר:

עין משפט נר מצוה

יח א ב ג מיי' פ"ב מהל' נחלות הלכה ה סמג עשין כז טור ש"ע חו"מ סי' רעו סעיף ה [וברב אלפס במכלתין פ"ח דף ריח:].

יט ד מיי' שם הלכה ב טוש"ע שם סעיף ג [וברב אלפס שם]:

כ ה מיי' פכ"ב מהלכות מכירה הלכה י ופ"ח מהל' זכיה הלכה ה סמג עשין פב טור ש"ע חו"מ סי' רי סעיף א וסי' רנג סעיף כו:

כא ו מיי' פכ"ב מהל' מכירה הל' י סמג שם טור וש"ע חו"מ סי' רי סעיף ח:

גמרא

דְּהוּא מָיֵית בְּרֵישָׁא, וְאֵין הַבֵּן יוֹרֵשׁ אֶת אִמּוֹ בַּקֶּבֶר לְהַנְחִיל לָאַחִין מִן הָאָב. לְמֵימְרָא, דְּהוּא מָיֵית בְּרֵישָׁא? וְהָא הֲוָה עוּבְדָא וּפִרְכֵּס תְּלָתָא פִּרְכּוּסֵי! אֲמַר מָר בַּר רַב אַשִׁי: א)מִידֵי דַּהֲוָה אַזְנַב הַלְּטָאָה שֶׁמְּפַרְכֶּסֶת. מָר בְּרֵיהּ דְּרַב יוֹסֵף מִשְּׁמֵיהּ דְּרָבָא אָמַר: לוֹמַר, אשֶׁמְּמַעֵט בְּחֵלֶק בְּכוֹרָה. וְדַוְקָא בֶּן יוֹם אֶחָד, באֲבָל עוּבָּר – לָא, מַאי טַעְמָא? °"וְיָלְדוּ לוֹ" אָמַר רַחֲמָנָא; (דברים כא) דְּאָמַר מָר בְּרֵיהּ דְּרַב יוֹסֵף מִשְּׁמֵיהּ דְּרָבָא: גבֵּן שֶׁנּוֹלַד לְאַחַר מִיתַת אָבִיו – אֵינוֹ מְמַעֵט בְּחֵלֶק בְּכוֹרָה, מַאי טַעְמָא? "וְיָלְדוּ לוֹ" אָמַר רַחֲמָנָא, וְהָא לֵיכָּא. בְּסוּרָא מַתְנוּ הָכִי. בְּפוּמְבְּדִיתָא מַתְנוּ הָכִי, אָמַר מָר בְּרֵיהּ דְּרַב יוֹסֵף מִשְּׁמֵיהּ דְּרָבָא: דבְּכוֹר שֶׁנּוֹלַד לְאַחַר מִיתַת אָבִיו – אֵינוֹ נוֹטֵל פִּי שְׁנַיִם, מַאי טַעְמָא? "יַכִּיר" אָמַר רַחֲמָנָא, וְהָא לֵיתָא דְּיַכִּיר. וְהִלְכְתָא כְּכָל הָנֵי לִישָּׁנֵי דְּאָמַר מָר בְּרֵיהּ דְּרַב יוֹסֵף מִשְּׁמֵיהּ דְּרָבָא. אָמַר רַבִּי יִצְחָק אָמַר רַבִּי יוֹחָנָן: הַמְזַכֶּה לְעוּבָּר – לֹא קָנָה. וְאִם תֹּאמַר: מִשְׁנָתֵינוּ – ב)ההוֹאִיל וְדַעְתּוֹ שֶׁל אָדָם קְרוֹבָה אֵצֶל בְּנוֹ. ג)אֲמַר לֵיהּ שְׁמוּאֵל לְרַב חָנָא בַּגְדָּתָאָה: פּוֹק אַיְיתִי לִי בֵּי עֲשָׂרָה, וְאֵימַר לָךְ בְּאַפַּיְיהוּ: הַמְזַכֶּה לְעוּבָּר – קָנָה. וְהִלְכְתָא: הַמְזַכֶּה לְעוּבָּר – לֹא קָנָה. הַהוּא דַּאֲמַר לִדְבֵיתְהוּ: נִכְסַי לִבְנֵי דְּיֶהֱווּ לִי מִינֵּיךְ, אֲתָא בְּרֵיהּ קַשִּׁישָׁא אֲמַר לֵיהּ: הַהוּא גַּבְרָא מַאי תֶּיהֱוֵי עֲלֵיהּ? אֲמַר לֵיהּ: זִיל קְנֵי כְּחַד מִבְּרָא; והָנָךְ – וַדַּאי לָא קָנוּ, דְּאַכַּתִּי לֵיתְנְהוּ. הַאי, אִית חוֹלֵק לְטַלְיָא בִּמְקוֹם בְּנַיָּא, אוֹ לֵית לֵיהּ חוֹלֵק לְטַלְיָא בִּמְקוֹם בְּנַיָּא? רַבִּי אָבִין וְרַבִּי מְיָישָׁא וְרַבִּי יִרְמְיָה דְּאָמְרִי: אִית חוֹלֵק לְטַלְיָא בִּמְקוֹם בְּנַיָּא; רַבִּי אַבָּהוּ וְרַבִּי חֲנִינָא בַּר פַּפִּי וְרַבִּי יִצְחָק נַפָּחָא דְּאָמְרִי: לֵית חוֹלֵק לְטַלְיָא בִּמְקוֹם בְּנַיָּא. אֲמַר לֵיהּ רַבִּי אַבָּהוּ לְרַבִּי יִרְמְיָה: ד)הִלְכְתָא כְּוָותָן אוֹ הִלְכְתָא כְּוָתַיְיכוּ? אֲמַר לֵיהּ: פְּשִׁיטָא דְּהִלְכְתָא כְּוָותָן, דְּקַשִּׁישְׁנָא מִינַּיְיכוּ, וְלָאו הִלְכְתָא כְּוָותַיְיכוּ, דְּדַרְדְּקֵי אַתּוּן. אֲמַר לֵיהּ: מִידֵי בְּקַשִּׁישׁוּתָא תַּלְיָא מִילְּתָא? בְּטַעֲמָא תַּלְיָא מִילְּתָא. וְטַעֲמָא מַאי? ה)זִיל לְגַבֵּיהּ דְּרַבִּי אָבִין דְּאַסְבַּרְתָּהּ נִיהֲלֵיהּ,

וְכַרְכֵּישׁ

תוספות

דהוא מיית ברישא. והיינו טעמא, כדאמר בפ"ק דערכין (דף ז.): דאיידי דזוטרא חיותיה – עיילא ליה טיפתא דמלאך המות ומחתכא ליה לסימנין. והא דאמר בפרק "בהמה המקשה" (חולין דף עד.): השוחט הבהמה ומצא בה בן תשעה חי כו' – היינו דוקא כששחטה או הרגה, שאז היא מתה תחלה, כדאמרי' בפ"ק דערכין ז)(דף ז. ושם). והא דאמר (א) ב"השוחט" (חולין דף לח:) דמתה אמו והדר ילדתה – היינו מתה על ידי אדם, אי נמי על ידי מלאך המות וכגון שנעקר הולד לצאת, דאז אין הולד מת, כדמשמע בפ"ק דערכין (דף ז. ושם). וא"ת: כיון דבהריגה או נעקר לצאת היא מייתא ברישא ולא הולד – א"כ אמאי נקט בן יום אחד? עובר נמי נוחל ומנחיל! וי"ל: דבן יום אחד פסיקא ליה, אבל בעובר לא פסיקא ליה למיתני נוחל ומנחיל.

ופרכס תלתא פרכוסי. ולית דגרס: עד תלתא פרסי. פירוש: מהלך שלש פרסאות.

בכור שנולד אחר מיתת האב אין נוטל בחלק בכורה מאי טעמא יכיר בעינן. קשה לר"י: דאמאי לא מפיק ליה מ"וילדו לו" דלעיל? דבפ' "יש בכור" (בכורות דף מז. ושם ד"ה וילדו) דריש ליה נמי גבי בכור, דדריש מיניה: בכור שילא דרך דופן – אין נוטל בחלק בכורה! ויש לומר: אי לא דידעינן בכור מקרא אחרינא – לא הוה מוקי האי קרא בפשוט אלא בבכור. וכן בפ' "יש נוחלין" (לעיל דף קכז.) דמפיק מ"וילדו לו בנים" דטומטום אין ממעט בחלק בכורה, ומ"והיה הבן הבכור" מפיק דבכור טומטום אין נוטל פי שנים – התם נמי, אי לאו דידעינן בכור מקרא אחרינא – לא הוה מוקמי קרא ד"וילדו לו בנים" בפשוט, אלא בבכור. והשתא אתי שפיר, דלא תקשי: אמאי לא נימא דיוצא דופן אינו ממעט בחלק בכורה מ"וילדו לו", כדממעטינן בבכורות מיניה דאין בכור יוצא דופן נוטל פי שנים? אלא ודאי, כל כמה דליכא תרי קראי – לא מוקמי אלא אבכור, ולא אפשוט.

והלכתא המזכה לעובר לא קנה. פירש ריב"ס: דבירושה הבאה מאיליה יכול להיות דהלכה כר' יוסי, דאמרינן בפרק "אלמנה" (יבמות דף סז. ושם ד"ה אוכלין) דהודו לו חכמים לרבי יוסי, דמסתבר טעמיה. אף על פי שלא חזרו בהם נראה דהלכתא כוותיה, כיון דמסתבר טעמיה.

רב

רשב"ם

לְהַנְחִיל מָמוֹנוֹ לְאָחִיו מִן הָאָב. וְלָא בְּהֶדְיָא תְּנַן לָהּ, אֶלָּא מִדּוּקְיָי' דְּהַךְ דִּתְנַן לְקַמָּן (דף קנח:): נָפַל הַבַּיִת עָלָיו וְעַל אִמּוֹ כו'. דְּמַשְׁמַע דְּאִם מֵת קוֹדֶם אִמּוֹ – אֵין יוֹרְשֵׁי הַבֵּן יוֹרְשִׁין מָמוֹן הָאֵם. וּבְ"יֵשׁ נוֹחֲלִין" נַמִי דָּיְיקִינַן לָהּ מִמַּתְנִי' דְּהָאִשָּׁה אֶת בְּנָהּ וְהָאִשָּׁה אֶת בַּעְלָהּ, מָה הָאִשָּׁה אֶת בַּעְלָהּ – אֵין הַבַּעַל יוֹרֵשׁ אֶת אִשְׁתּוֹ בַּקֶּבֶר, אַף הָאִשָּׁה אֶת בְּנָהּ – אֵין הַבֵּן יוֹרֵשׁ אֶת אִמּוֹ בַּקֶּבֶר לְהַנְחִיל לְאָחִיו מִן הָאָב. אֲבָל אִילּוּ מֵתָה אֵם תְּחִלָּה, וְאַחַר כָּךְ מֵת עוּבָּר – הָיָה מַנְחִיל לָאַחִין מִן הָאָב, דִּלְעוֹלָם אֵימָא לָךְ דְּעוּבָּר יוֹרֵשׁ. וּפִרְכֵּס. הָעוּבָּר, אַחַר יְצִיאַת נַפְשָׁהּ. וּמְשַׁנֵּי: מִידֵי דַּהֲוָה אַזְנַב הַלְּטָאָה. שֶׁמְּפַרְכֶּסֶת אַחַר שֶׁחֲתָכוּהָ מִן הַלְּטָאָה, וְאֵין בָּהּ חִיּוּת. מָר בְּרֵיהּ דְּרַב יוֹסֵף מִשְּׁמֵיהּ דְּרָבָא אָמַר. לְעוֹלָם אֵימָא לָךְ: זִימְנִין דְּהִיא מָיְיתָא בְּרֵישָׁא וְאַחַר כָּךְ עוּבָּר, וּמַנְחִיל הָעוּבָּר לָאַחִין מִן הָאָב, דְּעוּבָּר יוֹרֵשׁ הוּא. וְאַף עַל גַּב דְּתֵירֵץ רָבָא לְעֵיל: שָׁאנֵי הָתָם דְּמֵעִיקָּרָא רַפּוּיֵי מְרַפְּיָיא בִּידַיְיהוּ, וְאָתָא לְמֵימַר דְּעוּבָּר אֵינוֹ יוֹרֵשׁ – שִׁיטַת גְּמָרָא הוּא זֶה: אָזֵיל הָכָא וְקָא מַדְחֵי לֵיהּ, וְאָזֵיל הָכָא וְקָא מַדְחֵי לֵיהּ. וּלְעוֹלָם הַךְ מִשְׁנָה דְּבֶן יוֹם אֶחָד נוֹחֵל וּמַנְחִיל לָאו לְמַעוּטֵי עוּבָּר מִדִּין יְרוּשָּׁה, אֶלָּא לְמַעוּטֵי דְּאֵינוֹ מְמַעֵט בְּחֵלֶק בְּכוֹרָה, וּכְדִמְפָרֵשׁ וְאָזֵיל, שֶׁבָּא לוֹמַר דְּבֶן יוֹם אֶחָד מְמַעֵט בְּחֵלֶק בְּכוֹרָה. כְּגוֹן, יַעֲקֹב שֶׁמֵּת וְהִנִּיחַ שְׁנֵי בָנִים, רְאוּבֵן וְשִׁמְעוֹן, וְהִנִּיחַ שְׁנֵים עָשָׂר מָנֶה – רָאוּי הַבְּכוֹר לִיטּוֹל פִּי שְׁנַיִם כְּאֶחָד מִן אֶחָיו, וְיִטּוֹל רְאוּבֵן שְׁמֹנָה מָנִים וְשִׁמְעוֹן אַרְבָּעָה מָנִים. נוֹלַד לֵוִי בְּחַיֵּי יַעֲקֹב, וּמֵת יַעֲקֹב בּוֹ בַּיּוֹם אַחֲרֵי לֵידַת לֵוִי – נִמְצָא נוֹטֵל רְאוּבֵן שִׁשָּׁה, וְשִׁמְעוֹן שְׁלֹשָׁה, וְלֵוִי שְׁלֹשָׁה. וּמֵת לֵוִי בּוֹ בַּיּוֹם אַחֲרֵי מִיתַת אָבִיו, דַּהֲוָה לֵיהּ בֶּן יוֹם אֶחָד, וּמַנְחִיל לְאָחִיו שְׁלֹשָׁה מָנִים הָרְאוּיִן לוֹ, וּבְחֶלְקוֹ לֹא יִטּוֹל רְאוּבֵן חֵלֶק בְּכוֹרָה כְּנֶגֶד שִׁמְעוֹן – שֶׁהֲרֵי מִכֹּחַ אָחִיו לֵוִי הוּא יוֹרֵשׁ. נִמְצָא רְאוּבֵן נוֹטֵל שִׁבְעָה מָנִין וָחֵצִי וְשִׁמְעוֹן ד' מָנִין וָחֵצִי, נִמְצָא שֶׁמִּיעֵטוֹ לֵידַת לֵוִי לִרְאוּבֵן חֲצִי מָנֶה מֵחֶלְקַת בְּכוֹרָתוֹ. וְדַוְקָא בֶּן יוֹם אֶחָד, אֲבָל אִם הָיָה לֵוִי עוּבָּר כְּשֶׁמֵּת אָבִיו יַעֲקֹב וְאַחַר כָּךְ נוֹלַד לֵוִי – אֵינוֹ מְמַעֵט בְּחֵלֶק בְּכוֹרָה אֶלָּא בְּחֵלֶק פְּשִׁיטוּת. כֵּיצַד? מֵת אָבִיו נוֹטֵל רְאוּבֵן מִן הַשְּׁנֵים עָשָׂר מָנִים אַרְבָּעָה מָנִים בְּחֵלֶק בְּכוֹרָה כְּאִילּוּ אֵין הָעוּבָּר בָּעוֹלָם, שֶׁהֲרֵי לֹא הִנִּיחַ יַעֲקֹב בָּנִים יְלוּדִים אֶלָּא רְאוּבֵן וְשִׁמְעוֹן. וּשְׁמֹנָה מָנִים הַנּוֹתָרִים יַחְלְקוּ בֵּין שְׁלָשְׁתָּן, רְאוּבֵן וְשִׁמְעוֹן וְלֵוִי, כָּל אֶחָד יִטּוֹל שְׁלֹשׁ מָנִים חָסֵר שְׁלִישׁ. וְגַם אִם יַחֲזוֹר וְיָמוּת לֵוִי – יִטּוֹל אָחִיו בְּחֶלְקוֹ. נִמְצָא רְאוּבֵן נוֹטֵל אַרְבָּעָה מָנִים שֶׁל חֵלֶק בְּכוֹרָה, וּשְׁלֹשָׁה מָנִים חָסֵר שְׁלִישׁ חֵלֶק פְּשִׁיטוּתוֹ, וּמֶחֱצִית שֶׁל חֵלֶק לֵוִי דְּהַיְינוּ מָנֶה וּשְׁלִישׁ – סַךְ הַכֹּל ח' מָנִין. וְאִם הָיוּ עֲשָׂרָה אַחִין – יַחְלְקוּ חֵלֶק לֵוִי לַעֲשָׂרָה חֲלָקִים, וְחֵלֶק בְּכוֹרָה לֹא יָזוּז מִקַּדְמוּתוֹ. וְיָלְדוּ לוֹ בָּעֵינַן. כְּשֶׁנּוֹלְדוּ לָאָב בְּחַיָּיו אָמַר רַחֲמָנָא לָתֵת לוֹ פִּי שְׁנַיִם חֵלֶק בְּכוֹרָה עַל אֶחָיו שְׁכֶם אֶחָד, אֲבָל עוּבָּר הַנּוֹלָד לְאַחַר מִיתָתוֹ שֶׁל אָב לָא קָרֵינָא בֵּיהּ "וְיָלְדוּ לוֹ", וּלְגַבֵּי חֵלֶק בְּכוֹרָה כְּמַאן דְּלֵיתָא דָּמֵי, וְיִטּוֹל הַבְּכוֹר חֵלֶק בְּכוֹר גָּדוֹל לְפִי חֶשְׁבּוֹן אוֹתָן אַחִין הַנּוֹלָדִים בְּחַיֵּי אָבִיו. בְּכוֹר הַנּוֹלָד לְאַחַר מִיתַת הָאָב. כְּגוֹן יָלְדָה תְּאוֹמִים, אוֹ הָיוּ לְיַעֲקֹב נָשִׁים הַרְבֵּה, וְנוֹלַד רְאוּבֵן אַחַר מִיתָתוֹ מִלֵּאָה, וְיוֹסֵף מֵרָחֵל. יַכִּיר בָּעֵינַן. וְכֵיוָן דְּנוֹלַד בְּחַיָּיו, אֲפִילּוּ לֹא רָאָהוּ אָבִיו וְלֹא הִכִּירוֹ מִיָּמָיו, הוֹאִיל וְרָאוּי לְהֶיכֵּרָא – אֵין הֶיכֵּרָא מְעַכֶּבֶת בּוֹ, כִּדְר' זֵירָא דְּכָל הָרָאוּי לְבִילָּה כו' (לעיל דף פא:). בפר"ח. וא"ת מִשְׁנָתֵינוּ. דְּאִיתְיְדַע רַב נַחְמָן לְרַב הוּנָא דִּלְעֵיל: הָאוֹמֵר "אִם יָלְדָה אִשְׁתִּי" כו'. קְרוֹבָה אֵצֶל בְּנוֹ. וְגָמַר וּמַקְנֶה בְּכָל לִבּוֹ. אֲבָל לְעוּבָּר אַחֵר – לֹא קָנָה. בַּגְדָּתָאָה. דְּמִן בַּגְדָּד, עִיר שֶׁנּוֹלַד בָּהּ. וּבִכְתָבֵי רַב שְׁרִירָא הִיא נִזְכֶּרֶת. בֵּי עֲשָׂרָה. לְפַרְסוּמֵי לְמִילְּתָא. וְהִלְכְתָא הַמְזַכֶּה לְעוּבָּר לֹא קָנָה. כְּרַבִּי יוֹחָנָן. וּכְגוֹן שֶׁאֵינוֹ בְּנוֹ, אֲבָל הַמְזַכֶּה לְעוּבָּר שֶׁבִּמְעֵי אִשְׁתּוֹ – קָנָה, דְּדַעְתּוֹ שֶׁל אָדָם קְרוֹבָה אֵצֶל בְּנוֹ. נִכְסַי לִבְרִי דִּיהֲוֵי לִיךְ מִינַּאי. וְלֹא הָיְתָה אִשְׁתּוֹ מְעוּבֶּרֶת, הִלְכָּךְ לֹא קָנָה, כִּדְלְקַמָּן. דְּכָה"ג לָא אָמְרִינַן דַּעְתּוֹ שֶׁל אָדָם קְרוֹבָה אֵצֶל בְּנוֹ, אֶלָּא הֵיכָא דִּמְזַכֶּה לְעוּבָּר שֶׁנִּתְעַבְּרָה אִשְׁתּוֹ כְּבָר. וְשׁוּב מָצָאתִי כֵּן בְּפר"ח. בְּרֵיהּ קַשִּׁישָׁא. מֵאִשְׁתּוֹ רִאשׁוֹנָה. יִקְנֶה כְּאֶחָד מִן הַבָּנִים הָעֲתִידִים לְהִוָּלֵד מֵאִשָּׁה זוֹ. אִית חוֹלֵק לְטַלְיָא בִּמְקוֹם בְּנַיָּא. דְּאַף עַל גַּב דִּבְנַיָּא לֹא קָנוּ בְּכֹחַ מַתָּנָה זוֹ אֲפִילּוּ חֵלֶק אֶחָד, דְּהָא לֵיתְנְהוּ אֲפִילּוּ עוּבָּר דְּנֵימָא דַּעְתּוֹ שֶׁל אָדָם קְרוֹבָה אֵצֶל בְּנוֹ, וְלֹא יִקְנוּ אֶלָּא בְּתוֹרַת יְרוּשָּׁה בְּמִיתַת אֲבִיהֶם – אפ"ה בְּרֵיהּ טַלְיָא קָנָה בְּכֹחַ מַתָּנָה זוֹ חֵלֶק אֶחָד מִלְּבַד חֶלְקוֹ שֶׁיּוֹרֵשׁ עִם אֶחָיו. אִית חוֹלֵק לְטַלְיָא כְּנֶגֶד אֶחָד מֵהֶן. אִילּוּ קָנֵי. דְּה"ק: וְיִקְנֶה כְּחַד מִבְּרָא דְּיֶהֱוֵי לָהּ מִינַּאי, וְאַף עַל פִּי שֶׁלֹּא יִקְנוּ – רוֹאִין כַּמָּה בָּנִים יִהְיוּ לָהּ, אִם הֵן שְׁלֹשָׁה בָּנִים מִלְּבַד הַקַּשִּׁישׁ – חוֹלְקִין בְּאַרְבָּעָה חֲלָקִים, וְיִטּוֹל זֶה חֵלֶק אֶחָד מֵהֶן. וְחוֹזְרִין וְחוֹלְקִים שְׁלֹשָׁה חֲלָקִים הַנּוֹתָרִים לְאַרְבָּעָה, וְיִטּוֹל כָּל אֶחָד חֵלֶק אֶחָד בְּתוֹרַת יְרוּשָּׁה. טַלְיָא. תִּינוֹק גָּדוֹל, כִּדְאָמַר בְּפֶרֶק "הַמּוֹכֵר אֶת הַסְּפִינָה" (לעיל דף נא:) דְּאָמַר ז) רַב נַחְמָן: נְהִירְנָא כִּי הֲווּ מְטַיְּילִין טַלְיָא וְטַלְיְתָא כְּבַר שַׁב סְרֵי בְּשׁוּקָא וְלָא הֲווּ חָטְאוּ. בִּמְקוֹם בְּנַיָּא. כְּשֶׁיִּירְשׁוּ הַבָּנִים אֶת אֲבִיהֶן – אִית חוֹלֵק לְטַלְיָא עִמָּהֶם, לְבַד יְרוּשָּׁתוֹ כִּדְפָרִישִׁית. לֵית חוֹלֵק לְטַלְיָא. אֶלָּא חֵלֶק יְרוּשָּׁה בִּלְבַד. כִּדְמְפָרֵשׁ לְקַמֵּיהּ, דְּ"קְנֵי כַּחֲמוֹר" הוּא, דְּקָאָמַר לֵיהּ: קְנֵי כְּאֶחָד מִן הַבָּנִים שֶׁיִּהְיוּ לִי, וְכִי הֵיכִי דְּאִינְהוּ לֹא קָנוּ, שֶׁהֲרֵי לֹא הָיוּ עֲדַיִין אֲפִילּוּ עוּבָּר בִּשְׁעַת מַתָּנָה – אִיהוּ נַמִי לֹא קָנָה, שֶׁנִּתְלֵית מַתָּנָתוֹ בְּמַתְּנַת הַבָּנִים.

וְכַרְכֵּישׁ.

רבינו גרשום

והא הוה עובדא. דמתה אמו ואח"כ פרכס העובר ג' פרכוסי אלמא דבתר הכי חיי: [מידי דהוה]. שדומה חיותו לזנב הלטאה שמחותכת ומפרכסת וההוא חיותי אינו חיות: מר בריה דרב יוסף משמיה דרב' אמר. הא דקתני מתני' תינוק יום אחד נוחל ומנחיל הכי מפרש לה לומר שממעט בחלק בכורה. שאם היו ט' אחין וזה התינוק נחלק הנכסים בי"א חלקים ונוטל הבכור פי שנים דאי ליתא להאי לא היו מחלקין אלא לי' חלקים ונוטל הבכור ב' חלקים ואם מת האי תינוק יחלקו חלקו בשוה בינהן: אבל עובר אינו ממעט. שלא היה כלום ולעולם המזכה לעובר קנה: מאי טעמא. אינו ממעט: וילדו לו בנים. בחייו ממעטי: בכור הנולד לאחר מיתת האב. כגון שילדה תאומים וניכר הבכור שיצא תחלה: כהני תלת לישני דרבא. חדא לומר שממעט בחלק בכורה והני תרתי: ואם תאמר משנתינו. האמר אם ילדה אשתו זכר יטול מנה ילדה נקבה נוטל מאתים דמשמע המזכה לעובר קנה. משנתינו היינו טעמא הואיל ואדם קרוב אצל בנו: אייתי לי עשרה. כדי לפרסומי מילתא דידיה: אמר ליה זיל קני כחד מינייהו. כשנולדו וירשו את אביהן ויחלקו את ירושתן אי האי נסיב טפי אי לאו ולדברי הכל המזכה לעובר לא קנה: ר' אבין ורבי מיאשה ורבי ירמיה אמרו אית חלק לטליא. לבחור זה במקום בניא דיהוי ליה כלומר מעכשיו זיכה לו חלק אחד מנכסיו כאחד מן הבנים שיהי' לו ויחלקו המותר ויטול גם הוא חלקו עמהן ומתחלה יטול אחד קודם חלוקה שאם יהי' לו הבנים ג' לבד מטליא יטול הוא א)רוב הנחלה תחלה ומן המותר יטול כאחד מהם: ר' אבהו ור' יצחק נפחא ור' חנינא לית חולק טפי לטליא. האי בר קשישא לית ליה שום חלק טפי במקום בניא אלא יטול כאחד מהן ולא שום חלק יותר: אמר ליה. ר' ירמיה: פשיטא דהל' כוותן דאנן קשישן מנייכו. אלא מאי קא סברת דהלכתא כוותיכו לא דרדקי אתון: מידי בקשישא תליא מילתא בטעמא תליא מילתא. וטעמא דילן מסתבר טפי. וא"ל ר' ירמיה ואימא לי טעמא מאי לית חלק לטליא. אמר ליה ר' אבהו זיל לגבי דר' אבין כו'

קורקיש

מסורת הש"ס

א) [ערכין ז. נדה מד: חולין כח.], ב) [לעיל קלט:], ג) יבמות סז: כתובות ז. [זבחים עב.:], ד) [לעיל סה.], ה) [נדה מב:], ו) [נ"ל ר' יוחנן:], ז) [ע"ש הפי' שכתבו תוס' נדה מד. ד"ה איהו ע"ש]:

הגהות הב"ח

(א) תוס' ד"ה דהוא וכו' והא דאמר בפרק השוחט דמתה אמו:

א) [לעיל קמא:]: ב) ערכין ז. נדה מד.: ג) [לאויר העולם]: ד) [צ"ל ובן יום אחד]:

וְלֵימָא לֵיהּ: דְּאָמַר "לִכְשֶׁתֵּלֵד"! רַב הוּנָא לְטַעְמֵיהּ, דְּאָמַר רַב הוּנָא: א אַף "לִכְשֶׁתֵּלֵד" — לֹא קָנָה, דְּאָמַר רַב נַחְמָן: הַמְזַכֶּה לְעוּבָּר לֹא קָנָה, "לִכְשֶׁתֵּלֵד" — קָנָה; וְרַב הוּנָא אָמַר: אַף "לִכְשֶׁתֵּלֵד" — לֹא קָנָה; וְרַב שֵׁשֶׁת אָמַר: אֶחָד זֶה וְאֶחָד זֶה — קָנָה. אָמַר רַב שֵׁשֶׁת: מְנָא אָמֵינָא לַהּ? דְּתַנְיָא: ב גֵּר שֶׁמֵּת וּבִזְבְּזוּ יִשְׂרָאֵל נְכָסָיו, וְשָׁמְעוּ שֶׁיֵּשׁ לוֹ בֵּן אוֹ שֶׁהָיְתָה אִשְׁתּוֹ מְעוּבֶּרֶת — חַיָּיבִין לְהַחֲזִיר. הֶחֱזִירוּ הַכֹּל, וְאַחַר כָּךְ שָׁמְעוּ שֶׁמֵּת בְּנוֹ אוֹ שֶׁהִפִּילָה אִשְׁתּוֹ, הֶחֱזִיק בַּשְּׁנִיָּה — קָנָה, וּבָרִאשׁוֹנָה — לֹא קָנָה; וְאִי סָלְקָא דַּעְתָּךְ עוּבָּר לָא קָנֵי, לָמָּה לְהוּ אַחְזוּקֵי בַּשְּׁנִיָּה? הָא אַחֲזִיקוּ לְהוּ חֲדָא זִימְנָא! אָמַר אַבָּיֵי: א) יְרוּשָּׁה הַבָּאָה מֵאֵילֶיהָ שָׁאנֵי. רָבָא אָמַר: שָׁאנֵי הָתָם, דְּרִפּוּיֵי מְרַפְּיָאן בִּידַיְיהוּ מֵעִיקָּרָא. מַאי בֵּינַיְיהוּ? אִיכָּא בֵּינַיְיהוּ: שֶׁשָּׁמְעוּ בּוֹ שֶׁמֵּת וְלֹא מֵת, וְאַחַר כָּךְ מֵת. תָּא שְׁמַע: ב) תִּינוֹק בֶּן יוֹם אֶחָד נוֹחֵל וּמַנְחִיל; בֶּן יוֹם אֶחָד — אִין, עוּבָּר — לָא! הָא אָמַר רַב שֵׁשֶׁת: ג נוֹחֵל בְּנִכְסֵי הָאֵם לְהַנְחִיל לָאַחִין מִן הָאָב. וְדַוְקָא בֶּן יוֹם אֶחָד, ד אֲבָל עוּבָּר — לָא, מַאי טַעְמָא? דְּהוּא

רשב"ם

וְלֵימָא (א). רַב הוּנָא: מַתְנִי' — דְּאָמַר "אִם תֵּלֵד אִשְׁתִּי זָכָר תְּנוּ לֵיהּ מָנֶה לִכְשֶׁתֵּלֵד", דְּלָא זָכֵי לֵיהּ כְּלוּם עַד שֶׁיִּוָּלֵד, וְאֵין זֶה מְזַכֶּה לְעוּבָּר דְּאָמְרִינַן לְעֵיל דְּלֹא קָנָה. וּמְשַׁנֵּי: רַב הוּנָא דְּאָמַר אֵינִי יוֹדֵעַ מִי שְׁנָאָהּ, וְלָא אוֹקְמָהּ כְּשֶׁתֵּלֵד — לְטַעְמֵיהּ, דְּאָמַר רַב הוּנָא: אַף הַמְזַכֶּה לְעוּבָּר בְּכִה"ג דְּאָמַר "לִכְשֶׁתֵּלֵד", כְּלוֹמַר "נְכָסַיי לְהַאי דְּמִיעַבְּרָא לִכְשֶׁיִּוָּלֵד" — לֹא קָנָה. דְּכֵיוָן דְּבִשְׁעַת הַקְנָאָה עוּבָּר הוּא וְאֵינוֹ יָכוֹל לִזְכּוֹת — לֹא יִקְנֶה לִכְשֶׁיִּוָּלֵד, ע"י אֲמִירָה דְּאָמַר "לִכְשֶׁתֵּלֵד". לִכְשֶׁתֵּלֵד קָנָה. אע"ג דְּפָלֵיג ר"נ בְּהַמּוֹכֵר פֵּירוֹת דֶּקֶל לַחֲבֵירוֹ, דְּאָמַר: אַף מִשֶּׁבָּאוּ לָעוֹלָם יָכוֹל לַחֲזוֹר בּוֹ, דְּאֵין אָדָם מַקְנֶה דָּבָר שֶׁלֹּא בָּא לָעוֹלָם — הָכָא גַּבֵּי עוּבָּר מוֹדֵי, דְּחָשֵׁיב לֵיהּ כְּיֶשְׁנוֹ בָּעוֹלָם, וְגַם הַנְּכָסִים שֶׁנּוֹתֵן לוֹ הֲרֵי הֵן בָּעוֹלָם. אֶלָּא שֶׁצָּרִיךְ לְתַקֵּן לְשׁוֹנוֹ, וְלוֹמַר: נְכָסַיי לְהַאי עוּבָּר לִכְשֶׁתֵּלֵד, דְּאָז רָאוּי לִקְנוֹת לְגַמְרֵי. וּבִזְבְּזוּ. הֶחֱזִיקוּ כָּל אִישׁ וְאִישׁ מַה שֶּׁמָּצָא "בָּזְזוּ אִישׁ לוֹ". חַיָּיב לְהַחֲזִיר. כֵּיוָן דְּאִשְׁתּוֹ מְעוּבֶּרֶת — עוּבָּר יוֹרֵשׁ הָוֵי. אַלְמָא, הַמְזַכֶּה לְעוּבָּר קָנָה. אוֹ שֶׁהִפִּילָה אִשְׁתּוֹ. וְחָזְרוּ יִשְׂרָאֵל וְהֶחֱזִיקוּ בִּנְכָסָיו. הֶחֱזִיק בַּשְּׁנִיָּה. אַחַר שֶׁמֵּת הַבֵּן אוֹ הָעוּבָּר — קָנָה, דְּהַשְׁתָּא לֵיכָּא עוֹד שׁוּם יוֹרֵשׁ. בָּרִאשׁוֹנָה לֹא קָנָה. דְּאִיגַּלַּאי מִילְּתָא שֶׁהָיָה לוֹ בֵּן אוֹ עוּבָּר. וְאע"ג דְּסוֹף סוֹף מֵת הָעוּבָּר בַּבֶּטֶן, וְלֹא יָצָא לַאֲוִיר הָעוֹלָם — כְּיוֹרֵשׁ גָּמוּר חָשֵׁיב לֵיהּ, וּמָרַע לְחֶזְקַת מַחֲזִיקֵי רִאשׁוֹנָה. אַלְמָא: עוּבָּר יוֹרֵשׁ, כְּרַב שֵׁשֶׁת. וְרָבָא אָמַר. לְעוֹלָם אֵימָא לָךְ: לָא שְׁנָא הַמְזַכֶּה לְעוּבָּר, לָא שְׁנָא יְרוּשָּׁה הַבָּאָה מֵאֵילֶיהָ — לֹא קָנָה כְּלָל. וְשָׁאנֵי הָתָם גַּבֵּי הַמַּחֲזִיק בָּרִאשׁוֹנָה, הַאי דְּלֹא קָנָה — לָאו מִשּׁוּם עוּבָּר הוּא, דְּהָא אֵין עוּבָּר יוֹרֵשׁ. אֶלָּא מֵעִיקָּרָא, כְּשֶׁהֶחֱזִיקוּ — רִפּוּיֵי מְרַפְּיָין בִּידַיְיהוּ. כְּשֶׁמֵּת הַגֵּר וּבִזְבְּזוּ נְכָסָיו וְהֶחֱזִיקוּ — לֹא נִתְכַּוְּונוּ לְהַחֲזִיק לְגַמְרֵי, דְּהָא מְסַפְּקָא לְהוּ אִם יֵשׁ לוֹ יוֹרְשִׁין אִם לָאו, כְּמוֹ שֶׁהוֹכִיחַ סוֹפוֹ עַל תְּחִלָּתוֹ, שֶׁשָּׁמְעוּ לְבַסּוֹף שֶׁהָיָה לוֹ בֵּן, אוֹ אִשְׁתּוֹ מְעוּבֶּרֶת, וְשֶׁמָּא לֹא תַּפִּיל. וּלְכָךְ לָא הָוְיָא חֶזְקָתוֹ חֲזָקָה אא"כ חָזְרוּ וְהֶחֱזִיקוּ אַחַר מִיתַת הַבֵּן וְהָעוּבָּר. וּלְעוֹלָם אֵימָא לָךְ עוּבָּר אֵינוֹ יוֹרֵשׁ, וְגַם הַמְזַכֶּה לוֹ לֹא קָנָה. מַאי בֵּינַיְיהוּ. בֵּין לְאַבָּיֵי בֵּין לְרָבָא חֲזָקָה רִאשׁוֹנָה לָאו כְּלוּם הִיא, מַה לִּי מִשּׁוּם דְּעוּבָּר יוֹרֵשׁ לְאַבָּיֵי, מַה לִּי מִשּׁוּם דְּרִפּוּיֵי מְרַפְּיָא לְרָבָא, מַאי נָפְקָא לָן מִינַּהּ? אִיכָּא בֵּינַיְיהוּ שֶׁשָּׁמְעוּ בּוֹ שֶׁמֵּת וְלֹא מֵת וְאח"כ מֵת. לְשׁוֹנוֹת רַבִּים שָׁמַעְתִּי, וְלֹא יָשְׁרוּ בְּעֵינַי. אָמְנָם כֵּן צָרִיךְ לְפָרֵשׁ: אִיכָּא בֵּינַיְיהוּ בֵּין אַבָּיֵי לְרָבָא בְּכה"ג גֵּר שֶׁמֵּת, וּבִזְבְּזוּ יִשְׂרָאֵל נְכָסָיו וְהֶחֱזִיקוּ, וְאח"כ שָׁמְעוּ שֶׁאִשְׁתּוֹ מְעוּבֶּרֶת, וְשָׁמְעוּ אַחֲרֵי כֵן שֶׁמֵּת הָעוּבָּר, וַעֲדַיִין הָיוּ מוּחְזָקִין. א"נ, שֶׁהֶחֱזִיקוּ אַחַר שֶׁשָּׁמְעוּ בּוֹ שֶׁמֵּת, וְלֹא הָיָה מֵת כְּשֶׁשָּׁמְעוּ, אֶלָּא אח"כ מֵת. לְאַבָּיֵי דְּאָמַר עוּבָּר יוֹרֵשׁ מִשּׁוּם דְּהָוֵי יְרוּשָּׁה הַבָּאָה מֵאֵילֶיהָ, הַמַּחֲזִיקִים רִאשׁוֹנָה קוֹדֶם מִיתַת עוּבָּר לֹא הֶחֱזִיקוּ, אֶלָּא מַחֲזִיקֵי אַחַר מִיתָתוֹ. וּלְרָבָא, דְּתָלֵי טַעְמָא בְּרִפּוּיֵי, הַמַּחֲזִיקִים רִאשׁוֹנָה שֶׁשָּׁמְעוּ בּוֹ שֶׁמֵּת — הָוְיָא חֶזְקָתָן חֲזָקָה. וְאע"פ שֶׁנּוֹדַע לְבַסּוֹף שֶׁעֲדַיִין לֹא מֵת, מ"מ לָא מְרַפְּיָא בִּידֵיהֶם, כֵּיוָן שֶׁשָּׁמְעוּ בּוֹ שֶׁמֵּת, וְהָעוּבָּר לֹא יָצָא לַאֲוִיר הָעוֹלָם וְלֹא זָכָה לִירַשׁ, דִּלְרָבָא אֵינוֹ יוֹרֵשׁ עַד שֶׁיֵּצֵא לַאֲוִיר. ג) וְהַמַּחֲזִיק בַּשְּׁנִיָּה אַחַר מִיתַת הָעוּבָּר — לָא הָוֵי חֶזְקָתָן חֲזָקָה. כֵּן נִרְאֶה בְּעֵינַי, וְעִיקָּר. לָשׁוֹן קְצָרָה: אִיכָּא בֵּינַיְיהוּ שֶׁשָּׁמְעוּ בּוֹ שֶׁמֵּת הָעוּבָּר וְאח"כ הֶחֱזִיקוּ, וְהוּא לֹא מֵת, אֶלָּא אח"כ מֵת, וּבָאוּ אֲחֵרִים לְהַחֲזִיק. לְרָבָא — חֶזְקָתוֹ רִאשׁוֹנָה לָא מְרַפְּיָא, שֶׁהֲרֵי שָׁמְעוּ שֶׁמֵּת וְנִתְכַּוְּונוּ לְהַחֲזִיק לְגַמְרֵי, וְקָנוּ, דְּסוֹף סוֹף הָעוּבָּר לֹא יָצָא לַאֲוִיר הָעוֹלָם וְלֹא יִירַשׁ מִידֵי. וּלְאַבָּיֵי — אַחֲרוֹנִים קָנוּ. ת"ש. דִּתְנַן בְּמַסֶּ' נִדָּה בְּפֶ' "יוֹצֵא דּוֹפֶן" (דף מד.): תִּינוֹק בֶּן יוֹם אֶחָד מְטַמֵּא בִּנְגָעִים כו' עַד נוֹחֵל וּמַנְחִיל. וּפָרְכִינַן בַּגְּמָרָא: נוֹחֵל מִמַּאן — מֵאָבִיו, מַנְחִיל לְמַאן — לָאַחִין מִן הָאָב. אַחִין, אִי בָּעוּ — מִינֵּיהּ לֵירְתוּ, אִי בָּעוּ — מֵאֲבִיהֶם לֵירְתוּ, וּמַאי נָפְקָא לָן מִינֵּיהּ בְּהַאי תִּינוֹק? אֲפִי' כִּי לֹא בָּא לָעוֹלָם הָיְתָה יְרוּשָּׁה נוֹפֶלֶת לִפְנֵי אֵלּוּ הָאַחִין! וּמְשַׁנִּינַן: אָמַר רַב שֵׁשֶׁת נוֹחֵל בְּנִכְסֵי הָאֵם לְהַנְחִיל לָאַחִין מִן הָאָב. דְּמִינֵּיהּ קָא יָרְתִי. כְּגוֹן רָחֵל שֶׁיָּלְדָה אֶת יוֹסֵף, וּמֵתָה רָחֵל בַּיּוֹם שֶׁנּוֹלַד יוֹסֵף, וְיָרַשׁ אֶת אִמּוֹ, שֶׁהֲרֵי בֶּן יוֹם אֶחָד וּמַנְחִיל לִרְאוּבֵן וְשִׁמְעוֹן בְּנֵי יַעֲקֹב שֶׁהֵן אֶחָיו מֵאָבִיו. דְּמִינֵּיהּ דְּיוֹסֵף יָרְתִי, וְלֹא מֵרָחֵל, שֶׁהֲרֵי אֵינָהּ אִמָּם. הָכִי אִיתָא בְּמַסֶּכֶת נִדָּה. וְהָכָא הָכִי הוּא דְּפָרְכִינַן, תָּא שְׁמַע: תִּינוֹק בֶּן יוֹם אֶחָד נוֹחֵל וּמַנְחִיל, בֶּן יוֹם אֶחָד — אִין, עוּבָּר — לָא. אַלְמָא עוּבָּר אֵינוֹ יוֹרֵשׁ יְרוּשָּׁה דְּמִמֵּילָא, וְכָל שֶׁכֵּן דְּהַמְזַכֶּה לְעוּבָּר לֹא קָנָה, וְקַשְׁיָא לְרַב שֵׁשֶׁת! וּמְשַׁנֵּי, א"ר שֵׁשֶׁת: נוֹחֵל כו'. וְהַאי שִׁינּוּיָא בְּמַסֶּכֶת נִדָּה אִיתֵיהּ מִשּׁוּם קוּשְׁיָא אַחֲרִיתִי, כְּדְפָרֵישִׁית לְעֵיל. וְנִרְאֶה בְּעֵינַי דְּהָכִי גָּרְסִינַן: וְהָאָמַר רַב שֵׁשֶׁת נוֹחֵל בְּנִכְסֵי הָאֵם כו'. הִלְכָּךְ, כֵּיוָן דְּהַהוּא יוֹמָא דְּאִתְיְלִיד מֵתָה אִמּוֹ — מִשּׁוּם הָכִי דָּיְיקִינַן: דַּוְקָא בֶּן יוֹם אֶחָד שֶׁנּוֹלַד וְיָצָא לַאֲוִיר הָעוֹלָם וְאח"כ מֵתָה אִמּוֹ, וְאח"כ מֵת הוּא, וְהוֹרִישׁ לְאָחִיו מִן הָאָב. אֲבָל עוּבָּר — לֹא, אֵינוֹ יָכוֹל לִירַשׁ אִמּוֹ בְּעוֹדֶנּוּ בְּבִטְנָהּ לְהַנְחִיל

תוספות

בן יום אחד נוחל ומנחיל אבל עובר לא אמר רב ששת כו'. הקשה רבינו אפרים: דלפרוך ליה מרישא דהך משנה, דקתני רישא בפרק "יוצא דופן" (נדה דף מג: ושם): בן יום אחד מאכיל בתרומה ופוסל מן התרומה. דוקא בן יום אחד, אבל עובר — לא, אלמא המזכה לעובר לא קנה. וקשיא לרב ששת, דהשתא לא מצי לשנויי כדמשני אסיפא! ועוד קשה לר"י על ההיא ד"יוצא דופן", דקאמר התם: מאי איריא בן יום אחד? אפי' עובר נמי פוסל! ואמר רב ששת: הכא בכהן שיש לו שתי נשים, אחת גרושה ואחת שאינה גרושה, ויש לו בנים משאינה גרושה ובן ד)אחד מהגרושה, דפוסל בעבדי אביו מלאכול בתרומה. ולאפוקי מדר' יוסי דאמר עובר נמי פוסל — קמ"ל: בן יום אחד אין, אבל עובר לא. ולמה לי למנקט ב' נשים? לוקמה באשה אחת גרושה ויש לו בן ממנה, דוקא בן יום אחד פוסל, אבל עובר — לא, ואכלי העבדים בשביל כל המשפחה כולה, לרבנן דר' יוסי, כדאמרינן ביבמות בפרק "אלמנה" (דף סז. ושם)! ונראה לר"י: דסבר רב ששת דלרבנן דר' יוסי נמי עובר אית ליה זכייה. וטעמא דעובר אינו פוסל — משום דסמוך מיעוטא דמפילות למחצה דנקבות, והוו להו זכרים מיעוטא, ולמיעוטא לא חיישינן כדחייש רבי יוסי. ולהכי אוקי התם בכהן שיש לו שתי נשים ויש לו בנים משאינה גרושה, דכיון דיש לו בנים — לא פוסל עובר אע"ג דיש לו זכייה, דלא חיישינן למיעוטא דזכרים, כדפרישית. אבל אם אין לו בנים — פוסל עובר גם לרבנן, דאית ליה זכייה, דבין הוא זכר בין היא נקבה — הרי הן שלה. ופליג רב ששת אשמואל, דאמר בפרק "אלמנה" (שם) דלרבנן אוכלין בשביל כל המשפחה. דסבר שמואל דלרבנן לית ליה זכייה לעובר. והשתא ניחא הא דקאמר לעיל רב ששת: מנא אמינא לה? דתניא גר שמת כו', ולא דחי דהך ברייתא כר' יוסי. דרבנן נמי לא פליגי, אלא דלא חיישי למיעוטא, כדפרישית. ואם תאמר: לעיל דאמר: החזיק בשניה קנה, בראשונה לא קנה, אמאי לא קנה המחזיק בראשונה, כיון דלסוף הפילה? דהא בפרק "אלמנה" (שם דף סז. ושם) אמרינן דזכרים הוי מיעוטא משום מיעוטא דמפילות, ואין לעובר שסופו להיות נפל חלק בעבדים! וי"ל: דהתם תלינן שמא כבר בשעת אכילת העבדים מת העובר בבטן, ולית ליה זכייה.

נוחל בנכסי האם להנחיל לאחין מן האב. תימה: דמה עלה על דעת המקשה? דהא ע"כ צריך לומר כדמשני רב ששת: נוחל בנכסי האם. דאי לאו הכי — תקשה ליה, דאחים, אי בעו — מיניה לירתו, אי בעו — מאבוה לירתו, דהכי דייק בפרק "יוצא דופן"! וי"ל: דודאי ידע המקשה שפיר דנוחל בנכסי האם קאמר, אלא שהיה סובר דהיא מייתא ברישא. ורב ששת משני דהוא מיית ברישא. ולא הוצרך רב ששת לומר נוחל בנכסי האם, אלא לפי שלא פירש המקשה — מפרש לה רב ששת. ובפ"ק דערכין (דף ז. ושם) דפריך לשמואל מרב ששת, דאמר דהוא מיית ברישא — הוה מצי למימר דשמואל סובר כמו מקשה דהכא, דהיא מייתא ברישא. אע"ג דשמואל סובר כרב ששת דאמר: המזכה לעובר קנה, לקמן בסמוך, מ"מ אין צריך לתרץ כרב ששת, דיכול לתרץ כמר בריה דרב יוסף שאין ממעט בחלק בכורה, אלא דניחא ליה להעמיד שמואל כרב ששת. ועוד י"ל: דמעיקרא ס"ד דנוחל בנכסי האב, וכגון שלא היה לו אלא העובר לבד, והקנה נכסיו לאחרים אם לא ירשנו זה. וקתני דדוקא בן יום אחד נוחל מאביו כדי להנחיל ליורשין מאביו, אבל עובר — לא. וה"נ הוה מצי לשנויי בפרק "יוצא דופן" (נדה דף מד. ושם). א"נ, י"ל: דהמקשה סבר כמר בריה דרב יוסף, לומר שממעט בחלק בכורה בלא דרשה ד"וילדו לו", דדוקא בן יום אחד ממעט בכורה, אבל עובר לא.

עין משפט נר מצוה

יד א טוש"ע חו"מ סי' רי סעיף א ועי' בהגהות מיי' פכ"ב מהל' מכירה סי' ח:

טו ב מיי' פ"ב מהלכות זכיה ומתנה הל' יח סמג עשין פב טוש"ע חו"מ סי' ערה סעיף ל:

טז ג מיי' פ"א מהלכות נחלות הלכה יג ועיין בהשגות ובמגיד משנה סמג עשין כז טור ושו"ע חו"מ סי' רעו סעיף ה [וברב אלפס פרק ח דמכלתין דף ריא:]:

יז ד שם בהג"ה [וברב אלפס שם]:

רבינו גרשום

ומקשי' ואכתי לוקים ליה לסיפא בעובר ואימא דאמר לכשתלד אשתי. כל מה שתלד יטול דמשמע לכשתלד דכבר ילדה יטול שוב יזכה בו ולא עכשיו ואמאי לא תירצה רב הונא הכי לסיפא דמתני'. ומשני רב הונא נמי סבירא ליה דאפי' אם אמר לכשתלד לא קנה כיון דהוה קנין במתנה קודם שיבא לעולם ומשום הכי אמר משנתינו איני יודע מי שנאה: מנא אמינא לה. דהמזכה לעובר לא קנה: או שאשתו מעוברת חייבין להחזיר הכל. אע"ג דאכתי לא בא עובר לאויר העולם יקנה בנכסי אביו אלמא המזכה לעובר קנה: מי שהחזיק בשניה. לאחר שאין לו בן קנה משום דנכסי הגר הרי הן כמדבר מי שהחזיק בהן זכה: אמר אביי. לעולם בעלמא המזכה לעובר לא קנה והכא משום הכי בראשונה לא קנה דנחלה הבאה ליה לעובר מאיליה שאני דזכה בה דיורש הוא: רבא אמר. לעולם בעלמא המזכה לעובר לא קנה והכא אמאי החזיק בראשונה לא קנה משום דמעיקרא כשהחזיקו בהן חזקה רעועה הואי ורפוי הוה מרפי בידייהו דלא הוו ידעי אם אית ליה בן או לא להכי מי שהחזיק בשניה כשידעו ודאי שאין לו בן החזיק: מאי בינייהו. בין אביי לרבא מכדי בין למר בין למר עובר לא קנה ותרוייהו סברי דמי שהחזיק בשניה קנה בראשונה לא קנה: איכא בינייהו. דאותם שהחזיק בשניה שמעו בו בבנו שמת והחזיק בנכסים ועדיין לא היה מת ואחר כך מת ובאו אחרים לאחר שהחזיקו אלו ותפשו הנכסים קודם שמת זה ושוב מת. אביי סבר הואיל ששמעו בו שמת אע"ג דלא מת והחזיקו בהם אחרים כיון דאחר כך מת אותה חזקה של אחרים לא הויא חזקה משום דקמאי חזקה גמורה החזיקו. א) ורבא ס"ל כיון דבשעתא שהחזיקו בהן אחרים אכתי לא מת והחזיקו אחרים אע"ג דשוב מת הני בתראי קנו קמאי לא קנו משום דמעיקרא אע"ג דשמעו בו שמת כיון דלא מת חזקה רעועה היתה ורפוי היתה מרפיא בידייהו אע"ג דשוב מת קנו בתראי. ובחזקה שניה פליגי בין אביי ובין רבא אבל בחזקה ראשונה לדברי הכל חייבין להחזיר הואיל ששמעו שיש לו בן או שאשתו מעוברת: ת"ש. אי מזכה לעובר קנה אי לא קנה: תינוק בן יום אחד נוחל. ממון של אבותיו ומנחיל דהרי הוא כגדול לכל ירושתו: אבל עובר לא. אינו נוחל ומנחיל וקשיא לרב ששת. אמר לך רב ששת לעולם קנה והכא מתני' הכי מיפרשא בן יום אחד נוחל בנכסי האם להנחיל ממון לאחים מן האב דוקא כשהיה התינוק בן יום אחד שנולד בשחרית ומתה אמו בערבית דהוי חי יום אחד. אבל עובר שבמעי אמו אם מתה אמו לא אמרינן דהוא חי במעי אמו בתר מיתת אמו ונוחל את אמו להנחיל את האחין מן האב משום דעובר מיית ברישא מן אימיה:

והא

הגהות הב"ח

(א) רשב"ם ד"ה ולימא ליה רב הונא וכו' ולא אוקמה לכשתלד:

א) נראה דלדעת רבינו דהיכא דהפילה אח"כ מודה אביי דלמפרע לא הי' בר ירושה כיון שלא הי' עומד להוולד והלכך אותם שהחזיקו בהם אז קנו.

דתניא: "המבשרני במה נפטר רחמה של אשתי, אם זכר יטול מנה — ילדה זכר נוטל מנה, "אם נקבה מנה" — ילדה נקבה נוטל מנה, ילדה זכר ונקבה — אין לו אלא מנה. והא "זכר ונקבה" לא אמר! דאמר נמי "אם זכר ונקבה נמי יטול מנה". אלא למעוטי מאי? למעוטי נפל. ההוא דאמר לה לדביתהו: נכסי להאי דמעברת; אמר רב הונא: הוי מזכה לעובר, [א]והמזכה לעובר לא קנה. איתיביה רב נחמן לרב הונא: האומר "אם ילדה אשתי זכר יטול מנה" — ילדה זכר נוטל מנה! אמר ליה: משנתינו איני יודע מי שנאה. (א) ולימא ליה: רבי מאיר היא, דאמר: [א]אדם מקנה דבר שלא בא לעולם! אימור דשמעת ליה לרבי מאיר — לדבר [ב]שישנו בעולם, לדבר שאינו בעולם מי שמעת ליה? ולימא ליה: רבי יוסי היא, דאמר: עובר קני! דתנן: [ג][ב]עובר פוסל ואינו מאכיל, דברי רבי יוסי! שאני [ד]ירושה הבאה מאיליה. ולימא ליה: רבי יוחנן בן ברוקה היא, דאמר: לא שנא ירושה ולא שנא מתנה! דתנן, [ה]רבי יוחנן בן ברוקה אומר: אם אמר על מי שראוי ליורשו — דבריו קיימין! אימור דשמעת ליה לרבי יוחנן בן ברוקה — לדבר שישנו בעולם, לדבר שאינו בעולם מי אמר? ולימא ליה: רבי יוחנן בן ברוקה היא, וסבר לה כרבי יוסי! מי יימר דסבר לה. ולימא ליה: ב"מבשרני"! אי הכי, דקתני סיפא: ואם אין שם יורש אלא הוא — יורש הכל; אי ב"מבשרני" יורש מאי עבידתיה? ולימא ליה: בשילדה! אי הכי, דקתני סיפא: ואם אמר "כל מה שתלד אשתי יטול" — הרי זה יטול; "כל שתלד"? "כל שילדה" מיבעי ליה! ולימא

ה"ג: המבשרני במה נפטר רחמה של אשתי אם ילדה זכר יטול מנה ילדה זכר נוטל מנה ואם נקבה מנה ילדה נקבה נוטל מנה ילדה זכר ונקבה אין לו אלא מנה. והא זכר ונקבה לא קאמר. דאמר נמי זכר ונקבה יטול מנה. ואלא למעוטי מאי. למעוטי נפל. והכי פירושו: המבשרני מה תלד אשתי, אם יבשרני שילדה זכר – יטול המבשר מנה. לפיכך אם ילדה זכר – יטול המבשר מנה כדאמר הכא. אבל על בשורת הבת לא יטול כלום, דהא לא קאמר. ואם כה יאמר: אם נקבה מנה, כלומר, אם יבשרני שילדה אשתי נקבה יטול מנה. ואירע מעשה שילדה נקבה – נוטל המבשר מנה. אבל על בשורת זכר לא יטול כלום, דהא לא קאמר אב מידי. ונראה בעיני דגרסינן בה הכי: "אם זכר מנה אם נקבה מנה", ילדה זכר – נוטל מנה, ילדה נקבה – נוטל מנה. והשתא אתי שפיר הך דפרכינן לבסוף: אלא למעוטי מאי? לפי שכל ענייני בשורת לידה פירש, בין לידת זכר בין לידת נקבה בין לידת תאומים. ואם אירע מעשה שילדה זכר ונקבה תאומים – אין לו למבשר אלא מנה. ופרכינן: והא זכר ונקבה לא אתני אב, ועל לידת תאומים לא אסיק האב אדעתיה, ולא אמר שיטול המבשר כלום אלא על זכר לבדו או נקבה לבדה! ומשני, דאמר נמי: אם יבשרני זכר ונקבה ביחד, ותנא כי רוכלא לא חשיב ואזיל. ואלא למעוטי מאי. כיון דבכל בשורות יטול המבשר מנה – לא [ו](פירש) לא זכר ולא נקבה ולא תאומים, [ז](הוה) ליה למימר: המבשרני במה נפטר רחמה של אשתי – יטול מנה! למעוטי נפל. מה שפירש האב "אם זכר אם נקבה" למעוטי אם יבשר: הפילה אשתך, דלא יטול כלום. דסתם זכר ונקבה היינו בר קיימא, ולא מת. והמזכה לעובר. על ידי אחר – לא קנה עד שיולד, ואפילו היכא דאמר "נכסיי להא עובר כשיולד", דאמר רב הונא לקמן: אף לכשתלד לא קנה. איתיביה ר"נ לרב הונא. ממתני' דתנן: האומר "אם ילדה אשתי" כו' דהיינו מזכה לעובר. איני יודע מי שנאה. לא מצינו לא יחיד ולא רבים. ולימא ליה ר"מ היא דאמר אדם מקנה דבר שלא בא לעולם. ואמאי קאמר רב הונא "איני יודע מי שנאה"? הא איהו גופיה ס"ל כר"מ, כדאמר ביבמות בפרק "האשה שהלך בעלה למדה"י" (דף צג.) דאמר ר"נ בר יצחק: רב הונא כרב, ורב כר' ינאי, ור' ינאי כר' חייא, ור' חייא כרבי, ורבי כר"מ, ור"מ כר"א בן יעקב, ור"א בן יעקב כר"ע, דאמר: אדם מקנה דבר שלא בא לעולם. ומפרש התם: רב הונא – דאיתמר: המוכר פירות דקל לחבירו, אמר רב הונא: עד שלא באו לעולם – יכול לחזור בו, ור"נ אמר: אף משבאו לעולם יכול לחזור בו כו'. רבי מאיר – דתנן: האומר לאשה "הרי את מקודשת לי לאחר שאתגייר", "לאחר שתתגיירי" כו' – אינה מקודשת, רבי מאיר אומר: מקודשת. ומתניתין נמי קס"ד דה"ה גבי עובר, דכי היכי דאדם מקנה דבר שלא בא לעולם ה"נ מקנה לעובר שלא בא לעולם. אימור דשמעת ליה לר"מ [ח]בדבר שישנו בעולם. בשעת קנין, אלא שעדיין לא הגיע זמנו לקנות, כדקתני: "הרי את מקודשת לאחר שאתגייר", "לאחר שתתגיירי" כו' – האשה הנקנית לו הרי היא בעולם, אלא שעדיין לא נתגיירה, ולא הגיע זמנה לקנות. אבל עובר אינו בעולם, ולא קני מידי, ולהכי איני יודע מי שנאה. ולימא ליה ר' יוסי היא. ואהא דאמינא כרבנן, ואמאי קאמר "איני יודע מי שנאה". ר' יוסי היא דאמר עובר קנה. חלק בעבדי אביו. דתנן בפרק "אלמנה" ביבמות: בת ישראל שנישאת לכהן ומת והניחה מעוברת – לא יאכלו עבדיה בתרומה, מפני חלקו של עובר. כדמפרש התם דעובר במעי זרה זר הוא. שהעובר פוסל ואינו מאכיל, דברי ר' יוסי. כלומר: שהעובר שנתעברה ישראלית מכהן בעלה שמת, פוסל את העבד מלאכול בתרומה מפני חלקו. דעובר במעי זרה – זר הוא, ולא קרינא ביה "יליד ביתו הם יאכלו בלחמו", דאינו ילידו של כהן לקרות כהן עד שיצא לאויר העולם. ואינו מאכיל את אמו ישראלית שעיברתו מכהן, דקי"ל התם שאוכלת בתרומה בשביל בנה כהן כאילו בעלה כהן חי, כדכתיב: "ויליד ביתו הם יאכלו בלחמו", אבל עובר – לא, דס"ל לרבי יוסי עובר במעי זרה זר הוא, כדמפרש התם. שמעינן מיהא דעובר יש לו חלק במעי אמו בעבדי אביו שמת, מדפסיל להו באכילת תרומה. אלמא – מזכה לעובר קנה, הואיל ויורש ממילא בנכסי אביו! ומשני: ירושה הבאה מאיליה שאני. ויש לה כח לתפוס. אבל להקנות לו אדם – לא קנה. דתנן. ב"יש נוחלין": רבי יוחנן בן ברוקה אומר: אם אמר "איש פלוני יירשני" על מי שראוי ליורשו במקצת, כגון בן בין הבנים, וקס"ד דבעובר בין הבנים קאמר, דהיינו ראוי ליורשו לכשיולד – דבריו קיימין. אלמא: המוריש לעובר קנה, דהיינו מזכה לעוברו. ולעיל נמי במזכה לעובר שלו מיירי, שהוא ראוי ליורשו. במי שישנו בעולם. כגון בן בין הבנים. אבל עובר בין הבנים – לא. וסבירא ליה כרבי יוסי. דעובר יורש. ואיכא למימר דאיירי רבי יוחנן בעובר בין הבנים, דהיינו ראוי ליורשו במקצת, כרבי יוסי דעובר יורש. מי יימר דס"ל. לרבי יוחנן בן ברוקה, כרבי יוסי? והלכך לא נודע מי שנאה. ולימא ליה. דמתני' איירי במבשרני כי המבשר ישנו בעולם, ונוקי למתני' שהמבשר יטול מנה ולא העובר, דהמזכה לעובר לא קנה! מאי עבידתיה. דמבשר, לירש כלום. ולימא ליה בשילדה. כשאמר האב "אם ילדה זכר תנו לו מנה", כבר נולד בשעת אמירה. הלכך יטול מנה, דלא איירי במזכה לעובר.

ולימא.

נכסי להאי דמעברת. בשכיב מרע איירי, מדקאמר עלה: ולוקמה כר' יוחנן בן ברוקה. ורבי יוחנן בן ברוקה בשכיב מרע איירי, מדקא בעי לעיל (דף קלא.) עליה: בבריא היאך? ואע"ג דדברי שכיב מרע ככתובין וכמסורין דמו — לא מהני מידי, כיון דבבריא לא מהני אפילו ע"י קנין. ואע"ג דאמר לקמן (דף קמח.): שכ"מ שאמר הלואתו לפלוני — הלואתו לפלוני, אע"ג דליתיה בבריא אפילו בקנין, דאי איתיה בבריא בקנין — אם כן הוי שכיב מרע ובריא שוין, מ"מ הכא ליתא בשכ"מ כיון דליתא בבריא בקנין, דכולהו לא בחדא מחתא מחתינהו.

איתיביה רב נחמן לרב הונא. ואם תאמר: אדפריך רב נחמן לרב הונא, תקשי ליה לנפשיה, דאית ליה לקמן: המזכה לעובר לא קנה! וי"ל: דהוא מוקי מתניתין לכשתלד. דסבירא ליה לקמן: לכשתלד קנה. אי נמי, רב נחמן איירי בעובר שאינו בנו, ומוקי מתניתין בבנו, דדעתו של אדם קרובה אצל בנו, כר' יוחנן לקמן. וכן פסקו רבינו חננאל ורשב"ס וה"ג, דבבנו — המזכה לעובר קנה.

דתנן העובר פוסל ואין מאכיל. פירש רשב"ס: פוסל — עבדי אביו מלאכול בתרומה, דעובר במעי אמו זר. ואינו מאכיל — את אמו, דילוד מאכיל, ושאינו ילוד אינו מאכיל. ורש"י פירש ביבמות (דף סז.) בענין אחר: פוסל את אמו כהנת — אם הוא זר, ואינו מאכיל את אמו — אם הוא כהן במעי זרה, דעובר במעי זרה זר הוא. ולהאי פירוש לא מוכח הכא מידי. אבל אין לפרש כלל: פוסל עבדי אביו — אם הוא זר במעי כהנת, ואינו מאכיל עבדי אביו — אם הוא כהן במעי זרה. דחדא מילתא היא, דהא פשיטא דכיון דאם הוא כהן אינו מאכיל — כ"ש אם הוא ישראל, ולא הוה ליה למיתני "פוסל" אלא: אינו מאכיל.

ולימא ליה ר' יוחנן בן ברוקה היא. תימה: דאמאי נקט רבי יוחנן בן ברוקה? דאפילו רבנן מודו דבלשון מתנה מועיל! ויש לומר: דכיון דראוי ליורשו, והוא לא הזכיר לשון מתנה — אם כן בירושה קאמר.

יב א מיי' פכ"ב מהל' מכירה הל' י ופ"ח מהל' זכיה ומתנה הלכה ה סמג עשין פב טוש"ע חו"מ סי' רי סעיף א:
יג ב מיי' פ"ח מהלכות תרומות הלכה א ב:

רבינו גרשום

המבשרני במה נפטר רחמה של אשתי. כלומר מי שיבא לי לבשר מה ילדה אשתי מבכרת אם יאמר שילדה זכר יטול המבשר מנה וכן יעשה ילדה זכר יטול מנה. ואם יאמר לי ילדה נקבה יטול כמו כן מנה ילדה נקבה נוטל מנה. ואי איתרמי דילדה זכר ונקבה ביחד ואמר לו אשתך ילדה זכר ונקבה אין לו אלא מנה אע"ג דהתנה לו לזכר ונקבה מנה ואמאי יהיב ליה בבשורת לידת זכר ונקבה ביחד [והא זכר ונקבה] לא קאמר דיטול המבשר כלום ואמאי נוטל מנה. אין דאמר נמי אם מבשרני דילדה זכר ונקבה ביחד יטול מנה משום הכי מיתוקמא הך ברייתא כי האי גוונא. אי הכי כדאוקמת דאמר לזכר ולנקבה יטול מנה. אי הכי למעוטי מאי. כלומר מה הניח הברייתא במשמע שהמבשר לו שלא יטול. למעוטי נפל. דאם מבשר לו דהפילה אשתו אין לו כלום דמסתמא דהמבשרני בבן של קיימא קאמר: איתיביה רב נחמן לרב הונא. ממתני' דקתני האומר אם ילדה אשתי זכר יטול מנה ילדה זכר יטול מנה אלמא דהמזכה לעובר קנה: אמר ליה רב הונא לעולם המזכה לעובר לא קנה. ומתני' איני יודע מי שנאה דסתמא היא ולא סבירא לן כוותיה: ולימא ליה ר' מאיר שנאה דאמר אדם מקנה דבר שלא בא לעולם: למי שאינו בעולם. כגון עובר זה לא אמר ר' מאיר: ולימא ליה ר' יוסי שנאה במס' יבמות דתנן העובר פוסל. כגון בת כהן שנישאת לישראל ונתעברה ממנו ומת בעלה לאחר שנתעברה לא קרינן ביה ובת כהן כי תהיה אלמנה וגו' מלחם אביה תאכל דהא יש לה זרע ופוסל עבדיה שלא יאכלו בתרומה משום דעובר זה שהוא ישראל יש לו חלק בעבדים אלמא דעובר שלא בא לעולם קנה עבדים. אלמא המזכה לעובר קנה: ואינו מאכיל. בתרומה כגון בת ישראל שנשאת לכהן ונתעברה ממנו ומת בעלה לאחר שמת אינה אוכלת משום דיצאה מרשותו ואע"ג דנתעברה ממנו לא אמרינן שתהא זוכה לאכול כמו שנולד הבן ואין מאכיל לעבדים משום דילוד מאכיל ושאינו ילוד אינו מאכיל. ומשני לעולם משנתינו. איני יודע מי שנאה והכא לגבי דר' יוסי שאני דירושה הבאה מאליה היא שאין מזכה לו אדם אלא מעצמה נופלת לו ירושת אבות הלכך קנה בעבדים אבל היכא דאביו קיים וא"ל נכסיי להאי דמעברת לא קנה דמזכה לעובר הוא: ולימא ליה ר' יוחנן בן ברוקה היא דאמר. אם אמר על מי שראוי ליורשו דבריו קיימין והאי עובר נמי ראוי ליורשו הוא: ולימא ליה ר' יוחנן בן ברוקה היא וסביר' לי' כר' יוסי. ולהכי קאמר סביר' ליה ר' יוחנן ב"ב כר' יוסי דאם תקשי אימר דא"ר יוחנן ב"ב במי שישנו בעולם במי שאינו בא לעולם לא אמר איכא לתרוצי דסבירא ליה כר' יוסי דאמר דעובר פוסל אע"ג דליתיה בעולם דעובר קנה. ואם תאמר נחלה הבאה מאליה שאני איכא לתרוצי דר' יוסי סבירא ליה כר' יוחנן דאמר אם אמר על מי שראוי ליורשו דבריו קיימים אע"ג דלאו נחלה הבאה מאליה היא. ומשני לעולם משנתינו אינו יודע מי שנאה ודקאמר ולימא כר' יוחנן וסבירא ליה כר' יוסי מי יימר דסבירא ליה דלמא לא סבירא ליה. והדרא קושיא לדוכתה אימר דאמר ר' יוחנן בן ברוקה כו': ולימא ליה ר' הונא לרב נחמן הא דמותבת לי ממתני' האומר אם ילדה אשתי כו' לא קשיא לי דהאי דקאמר מתני' ילדה זכר יטול מנה לא אמר לעובר אלא המבשרני יטול מנה דלמבשר זוכה ולא לעובר והאי תנא דהמבשרני היא ואמאי אמר איני יודע מי שנאה: לא מיתוקמא מתני' כתנא דמבשרני דכי אוקמת רישא במבשרני הכי איבעי לאוקמי סיפא ולא אפשר משום דקתני סיפא אם אין שם יורש אלא הוא אותו טומטום יורש את הכל ואי במבשרני מיתוקמא מאי עבידתיה דמבשר גבי ירושה אלא ש"מ לא מתוקמא רישא כי אם בעובר דכי היכי דסיפא לא מיירי אלא בעובר רישא נמי בעובר. וש"מ דעובר קנה ולהכי אמר אינו יודע מי שנאה: ולימא ליה רב הונא לרב נחמן משנתינו לא משמע כדקסברת עד הכא אלא הכי משמע אם ילדה אשתו זכר הוא יטול מנה ומשמע דבשעת זכייה כבר בא לעולם לא מצית למימר הכי דאם כן סיפא דקתני כל מה שתלד אשתי משמע להבא ואם כדבריך כל מה שילדה מיבעי למתני כדמוקמת לרישא אלא משום קושיא זו לא מצי למימר הכי. ולהכי קאמר איני יודע מי שנאה.

א) [לעיל עט: וש"נ]: ב) [גיטין יג. לעיל עט:]: ג) יבמות סז.: ד) [לקמן קמב.]: ה) לעיל קל.: ו) [צ"ל יפרש]: ז) [צ"ל והוה]: ח) בס"י אית' במי:

הגהות הב"ח

(א) גמ' ולימא ליה ר"מ היא. נ"ב ר"מ גופיה ס"ל אף לדבר שאינו בעולם דהיינו לאחר שאתגייר אלא דרב הונא לא פסק כר"מ אלא לדבר שישנו בעולם [ולהכי פריך] ולימא ליה ר"מ היא ומשני דר"מ נמי לא ס"ל אלא לדבר שישנו בעולם דלאחר שאתגייר נמי דבר שישנו בעולם היא וכ"כ מהרש"ל:

אלא לאביי מאי ניזון כבת? ולטעמיך, לרבא מאי יורש כבן? אלא ראוי לירש ואין לו, ה"נ — ראוי לזון ואין לו.§ "האומר אם ילדה אשתי זכר" וכו'.§ למימרא, דבת עדיפא ליה מבן, והא א)אמר ר' יוחנן משום רשב"י: כל שאינו מניח בן ליורשו — הקב"ה מלא עליו עברה, שנאמר: °"והעברתם את נחלתו לבתו", ואין העברה אלא עברה, שנאמר: °"יום עברה היום ההוא"! לענין ירושה — בן עדיף ליה, לענין הרווחה — בתו עדיפא ליה. ושמואל אמר: הכא במבכרת עסקינן, וכדרב חסדא, דאמר רב חסדא: בת תחלה — סימן יפה לבנים. איכא דאמרי: דמרביא לאחהא, ואיכא דאמרי: דלא שלטא ביה עינא בישא. אמר רב חסדא: ולדידי בנתן עדיפן לי מבני. ואיבעית אימא: הא מני? ר' יהודה היא. הי רבי יהודה? אילימא רבי יהודה ד"בכל", ב)דתניא: °"וה' ברך את אברהם בכל" — רבי מאיר אומר: שלא היה לו בת, רבי יהודה אומר: שהיתה לו בת ו"בכל" שמה; אימור דשמעת ליה לרבי יהודה — ברתא נמי לא חסריה רחמנא לאברהם, דעדיפא מבן מי שמעת ליה? אלא הא רבי יהודה, ג)דתניא: אמצוה לזון את הבנות, וק"ו לבנים דעסקי בתורה, דברי ר"מ; רבי יהודה אומר: מצוה לזון את הבנים, וק"ו לבנות דלא ליתזלן. אלא הא דתניא: ילדה זכר ונקבה — הזכר נוטל ששה דינרין, והנקבה נוטלת שני דינרין, ד)במאי? אמר רב אשי, אמריתה לשמעתא קמיה דרב כהנא: במסרס, דאמר: "זכר תחלה — מאתים, נקבה אחריו — ולא כלום. נקבה תחלה — מנה, זכר אחריה — מנה", וילדה זכר ונקבה, ולא ידעינן הי מינייהו נפק ברישא; זכר שקיל מנה ממה נפשך, אידך מנה הוה ה)ממון המוטל בספק וחולקין. והא דתניא: ילדה זכר ונקבה — אין לו אלא ו)מנה, היכי משכחת לה? אמר רבינא: ב"מבשרני"; דתניא

במדבר כז | ישעיה נח | בראשית כד

אלא לאביי. דאמר: אינו נוטל כלום לא עם בנים ולא עם בנות, מאי ניזון כבת? ולטעמיך מאי יורש כבן. דקתני רישא? והלא על כרחך יורש כבן ואין לו מבעי ליה לפרושי! סיפא נמי לא שנא. למימרא דבת עדיפא ליה מברא. דיהיב לה לנקבה מאתים זוז, דהיינו שני מנין. שנאמר. "ובן אין לו והעברתם את נחלתו לבתו". לענין נחלה בן עדיף ליה. דיקרא שם המת על נחלתו. אבל הבת מסבת נחלה ממטה למטה אחר. בתו עדיפא. שאינה יכולה לחזר אחר מזונותיה כזכר. ושמואל אמר. מתני' במבכרת, דבת עדיפא ליה, כדמפרש טעמא לקמן ואזיל. דמרביא. מגדלת. א"ר חסדא לדידי בנתן עדיפן לי. אית דמפרשי לדרב חסדא במבכרת, כשמעתין. אך הלשון מדקאמר "לדידי" — אינו מוכיח כך. ונראה בעיני שלא נתקיימו לו בנים כי אם בנות, לכך מתאוה היה לבנות. ולא נתיישב לי יפה דעתו של רב חסדא. הא מני ר' יהודה היא. מתניתין ר' יהודה שחפץ בהרווחה דבת, כדמפרש לקמיה, דלא ליתזלו. ה"ג: דתניא מצוה לזון את הבנות כו'. ברייתא היא בכתובות בפרק "נערה שנתפתתה". מצוה לזון משום "ומבשרך לא תתעלם". ומיהו, חובה הוא דליכא, כדתנן התם: אינו חייב במזונות בתו, ואין מחייבין אותו לזון בניו ובנותיו, כדאמרינן התם, דאמרינן ליה: יארוד ילדה ושדיא אבני מתא שדיא. דעסקי באורייתא. ולא ליתזלו. פירוש הוא, ואינו מן הברייתא. זכר נוטל ששה דינר. של זהב, דהיינו מנה וחצי. לפי שהמנה כ"ה סלעים, שהן מאה זוז דינרי כסף, ודינר זהב נמכר בכ"ה דינר כסף, כדתנן בבבא קמא בפרק "שור שנגח ד' וה'" (דף לו.) במשנה. נמצא הששה דינר מאה וחמשים זוז, שהן מנה וחצי. נוטלת שני דינר. של זהב, דהיינו חצי מנה. במסרס. שסירס תנאיו זה למפרע מזה, שהתנה על לידת תאומים: אם יצא הזכר תחלה ואח"כ הנקבה — יטול הזכר מאתים והנקבה לא תטול כלום. וחזר וסירס תנאו, להתנות על לידת מפרע, אם נקבה תחלה — מנה, ואחר כך זכר מנה. זכר נוטל מנה ממה נפשך. אפי' נולד אחרון. המוטל בספק. אם זכר נולד תחלה יטלנו כו', ואם נקבה תחלה — תטלנו, הלכך חולקין, נמצא הזכר נוטל ששה דינר זהב. היכי משכחת לה. דמדקתני "אין לו אלא מנה" משמע דסלקא דעתך אמינא (א) דאף על גב דקאמר יטלו שני מנין — אפילו הכי אין לו אלא מנה, והיכי משכחת לה דאיכא למימר הכי? במבשרני. לא התנה לתת לזכר ולנקבה כלום, אלא למבשר, כדמפרש ואזיל. ה"ג

אלא לאביי מאי ניזון כבת. וא"ת: מאי קושיא היא לאביי? נימא דברייתא סברה דטומטום לא הוה בריה אלא ספק, ולהכי ניזון כבת. ואליבא דמתניתין דוקא קאמר אביי, דאפי' כבת לא שקיל, משום דמתניתין סברה כרבן שמעון בן גמליאל דבריה הוי, כדמוכח סיפא, ולהכי מוקי רישא נמי כרבן שמעון בן גמליאל! וי"ל: דגמרא רוצה ליישב דברי אביי אפילו כרב חסדא, דאית ליה בבכורות (דף מא: ושם) דטומטום הוי ספק לדברי הכל. והא דקאמר רבן שמעון בן גמליאל: אין קדושה חלה עליו — היינו דוקא קדושת פיו שאמר "אם זכר עולה ואם נקבה שלמים", (ג) וטעמא — משום דסבר שלא נתכוין אלא לזכר הידוע בודאי, ולנקבה הידועה בודאית, ולא לטומטום. והא דקאמר התם עלה בגמרא: אפילו בקדושה אימא לא מיתפיס — משום דקסבר ולדות קדשים בהוייתן הן קדושים. ואי ספיקא הוי ולא בריה — כי קדשי בהוייתן מאי הוי? כיון דהוי זכר גמור או נקבה, למה לא יקדש בהווייתה? ההיא סוגיא כרבי [יוסי] דאית ליה בסוף "הערל" (יבמות דף פג. ושם) דבריה הוא. אבל לרב חסדא קדושת אמו חלה עליו, וראוי לעולה אם הוא זכר, ונקבה לזבחי שלמים. ואביי גופיה איירי בבכורות (דף מב: ושם) על מלתא דריש לקיש, דאמר: טומטום דאדם הוי ספק לכולי עלמא. ואפשר דאביי סבר הכי. דאם איתא דסבר אביי דפליגי תנאי בטומטום, אי הוה בריה או ספק — טפי הוה ליה לאוקומי מתני' רישא כרבנן וסיפא כרבן שמעון בן גמליאל, כמו שהעמיד רבא, ממה שדחק לומר דוחין אותו ואין לו. (ג) ועוד איכא למימר, דלישנא דמתני' דקתני: דוחין אותו — דמשמע דהוי ספק, ולהכי לא מצי לשנויי דמתניתין אתיא כמאן דאמר דטומטום הוי בריה. וא"ת: מכל מקום מאי פריך לאביי מברייתא? נימא דמתניתין כרבן שמעון בן גמליאל דאמר דדעת אדם אזכר ודאי הידוע ואנקבה ידועה ודאית, וברייתא כרבנן דפליגי התם ארבן שמעון בן גמליאל, וסברי דקדושת פיו חלה על טומטום כשמתנה על זכר ונקבה! ויש לומר: דנראה לגמ' דסבר אביי דאפי' רבנן דפליגי התם ארבן שמעון בן גמליאל — מודו הכא, דאין דעתו של אדם קרובה להקנות אלא לזכר ולנקבה ודאי. ודוקא גבי הקרבה הוא דפליגי, כיון דטומטום ראוי להקרבה — דעתו נמי אטומטום. דאי הוי סבר אביי דפליגי נמי הכא — לא היה דוחק מתני' לפרש: דוחין אותו ואין לו, דטפי הוה מסתבר לאוקומי בתרי תנאי מלפרש הכי. אלא ודאי סבר אביי דכ"ע מודו הכא. ורבא פליג עליה, וסבר דפליגי רבנן נמי הכא, ומוקי רישא כרבנן. אבל אין לומר דלרבא נמי אתיא רישא דדוחין אותו ויש לו אפי' כרבן שמעון בן גמליאל, אע"ג דאין דעתו של אדם אלא על זכר ידוע ועל נקבה ידועה, מ"מ רישא דאיירי בתנאי בית דין במזון הבנות שאני. דאם כן, מה היה לו להזכיר רבן שמעון בן גמליאל? הוי לו לחלק בהדיא אותן חלוקים, ולומר דלא דמיא רישא לסיפא! אלא ודאי אין לחלק, דחכמים לא תקנו אלא לפי דעת האדם דמתנה כך, כדמשמע לישנא דמתני' (כתובות דף נג.): לא כתב לה חייב מפני שהוא תנאי בית דין, ולכך חייב כאילו כתב לה. והכי משמע בריש "נערה" (שם דף מג.) דלפי דעת אדם תקנו מזון הבנות, דקאמר התם: לענין זילותא — אלמנתו עדיפא ליה, לענין הרווחה — בתו עדיפא ליה.

ולטעמיך לרבא מאי יורש כבן. תימה: מאי קושיא היא לרבא? לימא ד"יורש כבן" — היינו מה שיתר על מזון הבנות עד שיבגרו, ואותו המותר יהיה לטומטום כמו לבנים, כדאמר לעיל: בשלמא לרבא יורש כבן בנכסים מועטים! וי"ל: דלישנא ד"יורש כבן" משמע דיורש גמור הוא כבן בשאר נכסים, ואפילו ישאר שם הרבה. **לדידי** בנתן עדיפן לי מבני. פי' בקונטרס: שלא נתקיימו לו בנים. ואין נראה, דהרבה בנים היו לו, כדאשכחן (לעיל ז.) ר"נ בר ר"ח (לעיל ז:), מר ינוקא ומר קשישא בני ר"ח (ע"ז יא:), רב חנן בר ר"ח, וכן רב מרי ורב פנחס בני ר"ח ב"הגוזל בתרא" (ב"ק דף קיז.). ז)אלא נראה לר"י, דלהכי קאמר "בנתן עדיפן לי מבני" — לפי שהיו חתניו גדולי הדור, ח)רבא ט)(ורב מרי בר חמא) ומר עוקבא בר חמא. **בת** היה לו ובכל שמה. וא"ת: ולמה לא השיאה ליצחק, למ"ד בפרק "ארבע מיתות" (סנהדרין דף נח:) דבן נח מותר באחותו? וי"ל: דשמא קטנה היתה, ולא רצה עדיין להשיאה ליצחק. אי נמי, מהגר היתה לו ולא משרה, ולכך לא רצה להשיאה ליצחק. **זכר** נוטל ששה ונקבה שנים היכי משכחת לה. דליכא למימר דמיירי כגון שאמר: ילדה זכר נוטל ששה, ונקבה שנים. דא"כ הוה ליה למנקט כמו במשנתינו: ילדה זכר נוטל מאתים ונקבה מנה.

אידך מנה הוי ממון המוטל בספק. לרבנן דאמרי (ב"ק מו.): המוציא מחבירו עליו הראיה — הוי הכל בחזקת הזכר, שהוא יורש לאחר מיתה. אי נמי, אפילו כרבנן, ואיכא לאוקומה בחיי האב, שאין הזכר מוחזק יותר מן הנקבה.

נכבסי

יא א מיי' פ"ז מהלכות מתנות עניים הלכה טז ופי"ב מהלכות אישות הלכה יד טו סמג עשין מח טור ושו"ע יו"ד סי' רנא סעיף ג וטוש"ע אה"ע סי' עא סעיף א:

רבינו גרשום

הפתחים וניזון כבת בנכסים מרובין כדרבא דיש לו: אלא לאביי. דאמר אין לו מאי ניזון כבת הא משמע דשקיל. אמר לך אביי ולטעמיך דרבא מי ניחא מאי יורש כבן דמשמע דשקיל והא לא שקיל מידי. אלא כי היכי דמתרצת לרבא ראוי לירש הוא האי טומטום כדקתני מתני' ואם אין שם יורש אלא הוא יורש הכל ואין לו במקום יורשין משום דספיקא הוא ועוד דנכסים מועטין. לדידי נמי ראוי היה ליזון ואין לו. במקום בנות שדוחות אותו אצל הזכרים: מדקתני אם ילדה נקבה יטול מאתים מכלל דבת עדיפא ליה מברא והאמר ר' יוחנן כו' אלמא דברא עדיף. ומשני לענין נחלה ברא עדיף שקם תחתיו אבל לענין הרווחה כשנותן מתנה הרווחה דבת עדיפא ולה יהיב טפי משום דיתבה בבית כדכתיב כל כבודה בת מלך פנימה. אבל בן מצי למיזל ולמרווח בכל מקום משום הכי יהיב לבת טפי מבן: ושמואל אמר. משום [הכי] יהיב לה מאתים דאמה מבכרת היא וניחא ליה שתלד בת יותר מבן כרב חסדא כו': דמרביא אחי. כלומר שגדלתן: ואיכא דאמרי דלא שלטה בה עינא [בישא]. הואיל דאי' לה בת מעיקרא לא לימרו אינשי כמה בנין אתילדו ליה להאי: ואי בעית אימא מתני' דקתני דברתא עדיפא ר' יהודה היא. א)ר' יהודה דעסקי באורייתא. לאו מן הברייתא אלא מפרש לברייתא. וה"נ כי [היכי] דלא ליתזלי לחזר אחר מזונות: אלא הא דתניא ילדה אשתו זכר ונקבה. זכר נוטל ו' דינרים של זהב דהיינו ק"נ דינרין של כסף לפי שהדינר של זהב קונין בכ"ה דינרין של כסף ומשקל דינר זהב שקול כשני דינרי של כסף. לפי שדינר של זהב שקול ה' פשיטי למשקל הברזל ודינר של כסף הוא ב' פשיטים וחצי למשקל ברזל לפי חשבון זה היה הזהב נמכר בי"ב משקלות של כסף שהן כ"ד דינרין של כסף ואותו דינר (של) כ"ה שמותר נכנס בהכרע המשקלות ומותיר ונישום ו' דינרי של זהב הן ק"נ של כסף ועוד מן הפסוקים של מלכים ודברי הימים מקניית דוד לארונה אנו למידים שהזהב היה נמכר בימי דוד בי"ב משקל של כסף: ונקבה נוטלת ב' דינרין. זהב דהיינו ג' דינרין: היכי משכחת לה. כלומר היכי מיתרצי האי מלתא דעבדין הכי והיכי מפרשי' לה לאו משום קשיא מתנינן לה אלא משום דקא בעי פירושא: במסרס. כלומר שמהפך דבריו כי האי גוונא דליכא למישמע מאי קאמר שמערב דבריו זו בזו דאמר הכי אם ילדה אשתי נקבה אם זכר תחלה יטול מאתים. ונקבה אחרי' ולא כלום ואם ילדה אשתו נקבה תחלה תטול מנה ואחריה זכר יטול מנה. ואי תתרמי מלתא בילדה תאומים זכר ונקבה ולא ידעו הי מינייהו אתיליד ברישא דאי בבריא לן דזכר אתיליד ברישא היה נוטל מאתים כדאמר מעיקרא. ואם נקבה נוטלת מנה השתא דמספקא לן זכר יטול מנה ממה נפשך דהכי קאמר אפי' ילדה זכר אחר נקבה יטול מנה. ואידך מנה מהנהו מאתים דזכר הוו להו ממון המוטל בספק. דמספקא לן דאם נקבה תחלה נוטלת מנה כמו שאמר. ואם נקבה אחר זכר אינה נוטלת כלום ואם זכר תחלה היה נוטל כל המאתים הלכך חד מנה יטול זכר ממה נפשך ומאידך מנה שקיל פלגא משום חצי מנה מספק דהיינו ב' דינר של זהב שהן ג' דינר של כסף: ואלא הא דתניא ילדה זכר ונקבה אין לו אלא מנה היכי משכחת לה. והיכי מתרמי והיכי מפרשי לה דלא קשיא להך דלעיל: אמר רבא משכחת לה במבשרני כו'.

המבשרני

א) נ"ל אלא הא ר' יהודה דתניא מצוה לזון וכו' דעסקי באורייתא וכו'.

מסורת הש"ס

א) לעיל קטז: ב) [תוספ' דקודשין פ"ה] לעיל טז: [ושם לא אמר רבי יהודה ובכל שמה וכן בע"י ליתא להנך שתי תיבות]: ג) כתובות מט. [תוספתא כתובות פ"ד ע"ש]: ד) ס"א היכי משכחת לה: ה) [ב"ק לה: וש"נ] ו) [דינרין היכי משכחת לה כ"ה בס"א]: ז) [ושם איתא רב מרי בריה דרב פנחס בריה דרב חסדא ועי' קדושין לב:]: ח) [כדאיתא לעיל יב: וברכות מד.]: ט) [נ"ל ורמי בר חמא]:

הגהות הב"ח

(א) רשב"ם ד"ה היכי משכחת וכו' דסלקא דעתך אמינא דיש לו שני מנין וקמ"ל דאע"ג דאיכא למימר יטלו שני מנין: (ב) תוס' ד"ה אלא וכו' וטעמא משום דסבר. נ"ב פי' רשב"ג: (ג) בא"ד ועוד איכא למימר. נ"ב חוזר אקושיא דלעיל:

בַּת אִשְׁתּוֹ מַהוּ שֶׁתְּמַעֵט בַּנְּכָסִים? אַלְמְנָתוֹ מַהוּ שֶׁתְּמַעֵט בַּנְּכָסִים? אַלְמְנָתוֹ וּבַת אֵי זֶה מֵהֶן קוֹדֶמֶת? אֲמַר לֵיהּ: זִיל הָאִידָּנָא וְתָא לְמָחָר. כִּי אֲתָא, אֲמַר לֵיהּ: פְּשׁוֹט מִיהַת חֲדָא, א)דְּאָמַר רַבִּי אַבָּא אָמַר רַבִּי אַסִי: עָשׂוּ אַלְמָנָה אֵצֶל הַבַּת כְּבַת אֵצֶל הָאַחִין בִּנְכָסִים מוּעָטִין, מַה בַּת אֵצֶל אַחִין — הַבַּת נִיזּוֹנֶת וְהָאַחִין יִשְׁאֲלוּ עַל הַפְּתָחִים, אַף אַלְמָנָה אֵצֶל הַבַּת — אאַלְמָנָה נִיזּוֹנֶת וְהַבַּת תִּשְׁאַל עַל הַפְּתָחִים.§ "אַדְמוֹן אוֹמֵר: בִּשְׁבִיל שֶׁאֲנִי זָכָר הִפְסַדְתִּי"? וכו'.§ ב)מַאי קָאָמַר? אֲמַר אַבַּיֵי, הָכִי קָאָמַר: בִּשְׁבִיל שֶׁאֲנִי זָכָר, וְרָאוּי אֲנִי לַעֲסוֹק בַּתּוֹרָה הִפְסַדְתִּי? אֲמַר לֵיהּ רָבָא: אֶלָּא מֵעַתָּה, מַאן דְּעָסֵיק בַּתּוֹרָה הוּא דְּיָרֵית, דְּלָא עָסֵיק בַּתּוֹרָה לָא יָרֵית?! אֶלָּא אֲמַר רָבָא, הָכִי קָאָמַר: בִּשְׁבִיל שֶׁאֲנִי זָכָר, וְרָאוּי אֲנִי לִירַשׁ בִּנְכָסִים מְרוּבִּין — הִפְסַדְתִּי בִּנְכָסִים מוּעָטִין?§

מתני' בהִנִּיחַ בָּנִים וּבָנוֹת וְטוּמְטוּם, בִּזְמַן שֶׁהַנְּכָסִים מְרוּבִּין — הַזְּכָרִים דּוֹחִין אוֹתוֹ אֵצֶל נְקֵבוֹת, נְכָסִים מוּעָטִין — הַנְּקֵבוֹת דּוֹחוֹת אוֹתוֹ אֵצֶל זְכָרִים. גהָאוֹמֵר: "אִם ג)תֵּלֵד אִשְׁתִּי זָכָר יִטּוֹל מָנֶה", יָלְדָה זָכָר — יִטּוֹל מָנֶה; (א) "נְקֵבָה מָאתַיִם", יָלְדָה נְקֵבָה — נוֹטֶלֶת מָאתַיִם; "אִם זָכָר מָנֶה, אִם נְקֵבָה מָאתַיִם", וְיָלְדָה זָכָר וּנְקֵבָה — זָכָר נוֹטֵל מָנֶה, נְקֵבָה נוֹטֶלֶת מָאתַיִם; יָלְדָה טוּמְטוּם — אֵינוֹ נוֹטֵל. אִם אָמַר "כָּל מַה שֶׁתֵּלֵד אִשְׁתִּי יִטּוֹל" — ה"ז יִטּוֹל; וְאִם אֵין שָׁם יוֹרֵשׁ אֶלָּא הוּא — יוֹרֵשׁ אֶת הַכֹּל.§ **גמ'** דּוֹחִין אוֹתוֹ, וְשָׁקֵיל כְּבַת? הָא קָתָנֵי סֵיפָא: יָלְדָה טוּמְטוּם — אֵינוֹ נוֹטֵל! אָמַר אַבַּיֵי: דּוֹחִין אוֹתוֹ וְאֵין לוֹ. וְרָבָא אָמַר: דדּוֹחִין אוֹתוֹ וְיֵשׁ לוֹ, וְסֵיפָא — אֲתָאן לְרַבָּן שִׁמְעוֹן בֶּן גַּמְלִיאֵל, ד)(דְּתַנְיָא) ה)יָלְדָה טוּמְטוּם וְאַנְדְּרוֹגִינוֹס — רַבָּן שִׁמְעוֹן בֶּן גַּמְלִיאֵל אוֹמֵר: האֵין קְדוּשָּׁה חָלָה עֲלֵיהֶן. מֵיתִיבֵי: טוּמְטוּם יוֹרֵשׁ כְּבֵן וְנִיזּוֹן כְּבַת; בִּשְׁלָמָא לְרָבָא, יוֹרֵשׁ כְּבֵן — בִּנְכָסִים מוּעָטִין, וְנִיזּוֹן כְּבַת — בִּנְכָסִים מְרוּבִּין, אֶלָּא

דמיתסרא גוביינא, ואי מינסבא לית לה. אבל לאלמנה אצל הבנים או אצל בנות — לא רצו חכמים לתקן דין נכסים מועטים אצל האלמנה, שלא רצו לעקר (ה) דין ירושה מן הבנים אצל האלמנה. והשתא מיבעי ליה, כשיש בנים ובנות, שיש כבר דין נכסים מועטין בשביל בנות, אם ממעטא נמי אלמנה. (הג"ה. וכן כתוב בתוס': ומיזון האלמנה עם הבנות. או דלמא כיון דאי מינסבא לית לה מזוני — השתא נמי לית לה, אלא הכל יהיה לבנות. ואי ממעטא — מ"מ לא מיזון האלמנה עמהן אלא (ו) עד שיגברו הבנות. ע"כ. הג"ה). והא דקאמר בסמוך דאלמנה אצל הבת אלמנה ניזונת והבת תשאל על הפתחים — היינו שיש שם בנים עם הבנות, שיש כאן דין נכסים מועטים אצל בנות. אבל אי ליתנהו לבנים — לא תטול האלמנה כלום יותר [מהבת] (הג"ה. ולכאורה היה נראה לפרש דאי ממעטין — אין לבנים כלום, כיון שאין שם עודף על מזונות אלמנה ובנות עד שיגברו הבנות. אבל אי לאו ממעטין — ניזונות שלשתם. אבל בתוס' כתוב כאשר כתבתי בפנים. ע"כ. הג"ה). ואור"י שכן משמע בירושל', כדקאמר התם: אלמנה ובנות — שתיהן שוות, אלמנה ובנים — שניהם שוים. פירוש: לענין מזונות אין האלמנה דוחה את הבנות, ולא בנות דוחות את האלמנה. ופעמים שהאלמנה דוחה את הבנות ע"י הבנים. וכשם שדוחה האלמנה את הבנות ע"י הבנים, כך דוחה את הבנים על ידי בנות כו'. ויש לדקדק על לשון הירושלמי. ומ"מ משמע שרוצה לומר כן.

אלא מעתה מאן דעסיק באורייתא הוא דירית. ואף על פי דאמרינן לקמן (דף קמא.): מצוה לזון את הבנות, וק"ו הבנים העוסקין באורייתא — היינו לענין מצוה, אבל לענין דינא — אין לחלק בין עסקי באורייתא ללא עסקי ז).

אלא

בַּת אִשְׁתּוֹ מַהוּ. אע"ל בַּעַל חוֹב מְמַעֵט, ה"מ דְּאע"ג דְּאִילוּ מָיֵית — אִית לֵיהּ. אֲבָל בַּת אִשְׁתּוֹ, דְּל"ל אִי מָיְיתָא, מִי מְמַעֲטָא? אַלְמְנָתוֹ וּבַת. וְאֵין כָּאן אֶלָּא מְזוֹן אַחַת מֵהֶן, וּשְׁתֵּיהֶן תּוֹבְעוֹת מְזוֹנוֹת בִּתְנַאי כְּתוּבָּה. הִלְכָּךְ, כֵּיוָן דְּתַרְוַיְיהוּ בְּתַקַּנְתָּא דְּרַבָּנַן אָכְלִי, אֵיזוֹ תִּקְדּוֹם? תִּפְשׁוֹט מִיהָא חֲדָא. אַלְמָנָתוֹ וּבַת. מַאי קָאָמַר. מַאי יִפּוּי כֹּחַ יֵשׁ לַזָּכָר בִּמְזוֹנוֹת בִּמְקוֹם אַחֵר יוֹתֵר מִנְּקֵבָה, דְּקָאָמַר: בִּשְׁבִיל שֶׁאֲנִי זָכָר וּזְכוּתִי גָּדוֹל הִפְסַדְתִּי? מַאן דְּעָסֵיק כו'. כְּלוֹמַר, מִי שֶׁיֵּשׁ לוֹ שְׁנֵי בָנִים, אֶחָד עוֹסֵק בַּתּוֹרָה וְאֶחָד אֵינוֹ עוֹסֵק — וְכִי אִבֵּד זְכוּתוֹ בִּירוּשָּׁתוֹ בִּשְׁבִיל שֶׁאֵינוֹ עוֹסֵק? (ג)וְיָפֶה כֹּחִי בִּנְכָסִים מְרוּבִּין. שֶׁאֲנִי יוֹרֵשׁ הַכֹּל, אֲפִילּוּ מֵאָה מָנֶה, וְאֵין לַנְּקֵבָה כִּי אִם מְזוֹנוֹת. **מתני'** וְטוּמְטוּם. אָטוּם, אֵינוֹ נִיכָּר בּוֹ לֹא זַכְרוּת וְלֹא נַקְבוּת, וְסָפֵק זָכָר סָפֵק נְקֵבָה הוּא, (ג) וְאִיכָּא לְמ"ד נַמִי סָפֵק בְּרִיָּה הוּא. וְדוֹחִין אוֹתוֹ, וְאֵין לוֹ לֹא כְּזָכָר וְלֹא כִּנְקֵבָה. הַזְּכָרִים דּוֹחִין אוֹתוֹ. לִיזּוֹן וְלֹא לִירַשׁ, דְּאָמְרִי לֵיהּ: אַיְיתֵי רְאָיָה דְּזָכָר אַתְּ וְתִירַשׁ עִמָּנוּ, לֵךְ אֵצֶל נְקֵבוֹת. וּמִיהוּ, אִיכָּא לְמ"ד בַּגְּמָרָא דַּאֲפִילּוּ כִּנְקֵבוֹת לָא שָׁקֵיל, דְּאֵינוֹ לֹא זָכָר וְלֹא נְקֵבָה. וְהַאי דְּנָקַט לִישָּׁנָא דִּזְכָרִים דּוֹחִין — הַיְינוּ מִשּׁוּם דְּבָעֵי לְמִישְׁקַל בַּזְּכָרִים, לִהְיוֹת יָדוֹ עַל הָעֶלְיוֹנָה, וְאִינְהוּ דָּחוּ לֵיהּ מִינַּיְיהוּ, לוֹמַר: לֵךְ אֵצֶל נְקֵבוֹת, אע"פ שֶׁגַּם (ד) הֵנָּה יִדְחוּהוּ. הָאוֹמֵר אִם יָלְדָה כו'. מְחַלֵּק נְכָסָיו הָיָה, וּמְצַוֶּה לְקַיֵּים דִּבְרֵי הַמֵּת. א"נ, בָּרִיא וְזִיכָּה לוֹ ע"י אַחֵר. וְאע"ג דְּאָמַר רַב הוּנָא הַמְזַכֶּה לְעוּבָּר לֹא קָנָה — הָא פָּרְכִינַן לָהּ מִמַּתְנִי' בַּגְּמָרָא, וְלָא מְתָרֵץ לֵיהּ. הָאוֹמֵר יָלְדָה אִשְׁתִּי זָכָר יִטּוֹל מָנֶה. אוֹתוֹ הַזָּכָר לִכְשֶׁיּוּלַד. וְאֵירַע הַמַּעֲשֶׂה שֶׁיָּלְדָה זָכָר — נוֹטֵל כִּדְקָאָמַר אָבִיו. נְקֵבָה מָאתַיִם. וּבַגְּמָ' פָּרֵיךְ: לְמֵימְרָא דִּבְרַתָּא עֲדִיפָא לֵיהּ מִבְּרָא? ה"ג: אִם זָכָר מָנֶה אִם נְקֵבָה מָאתַיִם וְיָלְדָה זָכָר וּנְקֵבָה זָכָר נוֹטֵל מָנֶה נְקֵבָה נוֹטֶלֶת מָאתַיִם. יֵשׁ מְפָרְשִׁים שֶׁיָּלְדָה שְׁנֵיהֶן כְּאֶחָד, הַזָּכָר וְהַנְּקֵבָה, וְיִטּוֹל הַזָּכָר מָנֶה וְהַנְּקֵבָה תִּטּוֹל מָאתַיִם, כִּדְקָאָמַר הָכָא: אִם זָכָר מָנֶה אִם נְקֵבָה מָאתַיִם. וְלָאו מִלְּתָא הִיא, שֶׁהֲרֵי לֹא אָמַר הָכָא "אִם יָלְדָה זָכָר וּנְקֵבָה", וְלֹא אַסֵּיק אַדַּעְתֵּיהּ בְּלֵידַת תְּאוֹמִים. אֶלָּא הָכִי קָאָמַר: אִם זָכָר מָנֶה, אִם נְקֵבָה מָאתַיִם. דְּמַשְׁמַע — אִם זָכָר לְבַדּוֹ בְּלֹא נְקֵבָה, אוֹ נְקֵבָה בְּלֹא זָכָר. וְכֵיוָן דְּהָכִי הוּא — לֹא יִטּוֹל כְּלוּם הַבֵּן וְהַבַּת אִם נוֹלְדוּ תְּאוֹמִים, כִּדְאָמְרִינַן בַּגְּמָרָא: וְהָא זָכָר וּנְקֵבָה לָא קָאָמַר, שֶׁמָּא לֹא הָיָה חָפֵץ בְּלֵידַת תְּאוֹמִים. א"נ, אֵין לֵידַת תְּאוֹמִים בִּכְלַל "אִם זָכָר אִם נְקֵבָה", דְּמַשְׁמַע: אִם זָכָר לְבַדּוֹ אִם נְקֵבָה לְבַדָּהּ. אֶלָּא ה"פ: הָאוֹמֵר "אִם זָכָר יָלְדָה אִשְׁתִּי יִטּוֹל אוֹתוֹ הָעוּבָּר מָנֶה, אִם נְקֵבָה יָלְדָה אִשְׁתִּי תִּטּוֹל מָאתַיִם", וְיָלְדָה זָכָר וּנְקֵבָה, כְּלוֹמַר זָכָר אוֹ נְקֵבָה, כִּדְקָאָמַר הָכָא — זָכָר נוֹטֵל מָנֶה אִם יִוָּלֵד זָכָר, נְקֵבָה נוֹטֶלֶת מָאתַיִם אִם יִהְיֶה הָעוּבָּר נְקֵבָה. וְלַאֲשְׁמוּעִינַן אַתָּא, שֶׁאִילּוּ לֹא פֵּירֵשׁ אֶלָּא אֶחָד מֵהֶם כִּדְקָתָנֵי רֵישָׁא, אוֹ זָכָר בְּלֹא נְקֵבָה אוֹ נְקֵבָה בְּלֹא זָכָר, וְיָלְדָה אִשְׁתּוֹ מַה שֶּׁלֹּא אָמַר — לֹא יִטּוֹל הָעוּבָּר כְּלוּם. אֶלָּא הַשְׁתָּא שֶׁגִּילָּה דַּעְתּוֹ עַל לֵידַת זָכָר וְעַל לֵידַת נְקֵבָה — כָּל מַה שֶׁתֵּלֵד הָאִשָּׁה יִטּוֹל, בֵּין זָכָר בֵּין נְקֵבָה. וּמִיהוּ, אִם יָלְדָה זָכָר וּנְקֵבָה תְּאוֹמִים — לֹא יִטְּלוּ כְּלוּם, כִּדְמוֹכַח בַּגְּמָרָא, וּכְדְפָרֵישִׁית לְעֵיל. כֵּן נִרְאֶה בְּעֵינַי, וְעִיקָּר. יָלְדָה טוּמְטוּם אֵינוֹ נוֹטֵל. דִּבְרִיָּה בִּפְנֵי עַצְמָהּ חָשֵׁיב לֵיהּ, לֹא זָכָר וְלֹא נְקֵבָה, כִּדְמְפָרֵשׁ בַּגְּמָרָא. ה"ז יִטּוֹל. הַטּוּמְטוּם. וְאִם אֵין שָׁם יוֹרֵשׁ אֶלָּא הוּא. אוֹתוֹ הַטּוּמְטוּם. יוֹרֵשׁ אֶת הַכֹּל. וְאַף עַל גַּב דִּבְרִיָּה הוּא, ה"מ הֵיכָא דְּאִיכָּא בָּנִים וּבָנוֹת וְדוֹחִין אוֹתוֹ בָּנִים אֵצֶל בָּנוֹת וְהַבָּנוֹת אֵצֶל בָּנִים, וְאֵין לוֹ לֹא כְּבֵן וְלֹא כְּבַת, כִּדְקָאָמַר אַבַּיֵי בַּגְּמָרָא מִשּׁוּם דִּבְרִיָּה הוּא. אֲבָל הֵיכָא דְּלֵיכָּא יוֹרֵשׁ אֶלָּא הוּא, לָא נָפֵיק מִכְּלַל "בֵּן אֵין לוֹ" — עַיֵּין עָלָיו, "אִם אֵין לוֹ בַּת" — עַיֵּין עָלֶיהָ. א"נ, מִשּׁוּם דְּקָרֵינָא בֵּיהּ "הַקָּרוֹב אֵלָיו מִמִּשְׁפַּחְתּוֹ וְיָרַשׁ אוֹתָהּ". **גמ'** וְשָׁקֵיל כְּבַת. בִּתְמִיָּה. דְּקָתָנֵי: דּוֹחִין אוֹתוֹ אֵצֶל נְקֵבוֹת, וּמַשְׁמַע דְּשָׁקֵיל מְזוֹנוֹת כְּבַת נְקֵבָה. וְהָא קָתָנֵי סֵיפָא. גַּבֵּי הָאוֹמֵר "אִם יָלְדָה אִשְׁתִּי" כו' — יָלְדָה טוּמְטוּם אֵינוֹ נוֹטֵל לֹא כְּבֵן וְלֹא כְּבַת. דִּבְרִיָּה הוּא, וְאֵינוֹ לֹא זָכָר וְלֹא נְקֵבָה. וְה"ה לְעִנְיַן יְרוּשָּׁה! אָמַר אַבַּיֵי דּוֹחִין אוֹתוֹ. אֵצֶל נְקֵבוֹת, וְאֵין לוֹ עִם נְקֵבוֹת, שֶׁגַּם הֵן יִדְחוּהוּ אֵצֶל זְכָרִים. רָבָא אָמַר דּוֹחִין אוֹתוֹ וְיֵשׁ לוֹ. מִמָּה נַפְשָׁךְ, דְּסָפֵק זָכָר סָפֵק נְקֵבָה הוּא, וְיִטּוֹל כַּפָּחוּת שֶׁבָּהֶן, דְּלָאו בְּרִיָּה הוּא. וְסֵיפָא דְּקָתָנֵי: נְכָסִין מוּעָטִין נְקֵבוֹת דּוֹחִין אוֹתוֹ אֵצֶל זְכָרִים — עַל כָּרְחִין דּוֹחִין אוֹתוֹ וְאֵין לוֹ קָאָמַר. וְסֵיפָא דְּמַקְשֵׁת לִי מִינָּהּ דְּחָשֵׁיב לֵיהּ בְּרִיָּה — אֲתָאן לְרשב"ג דִּתְנַן בְּמַסֶּכֶת תְּמוּרָה בְּפֶרֶק "כֵּיצַד מַעֲרִימִין": כֵּיצַד מַעֲרִימִין עַל הַבְּכוֹר? מַבְכֶּרֶת שֶׁהָיְתָה מְעוּבֶּרֶת, אוֹמֵר: מַה שֶּׁבְּמֵעֶיהָ שֶׁל זוֹ, אִם זָכָר — עוֹלָה, אִם נְקֵבָה — שְׁלָמִים, יָלְדָה שְׁנֵי זְכָרִים — אֶחָד מֵהֶם יִקְרַב עוֹלָה, וְהַשֵּׁנִי יִמָּכֵר לְחַיָּיבֵי עוֹלָה, ו) וּדְמֵיהֶן חוּלִּין. יָלְדָה שְׁתֵּי נְקֵבוֹת — אַחַת מֵהֶן תִּקְרַב שְׁלָמִים, וְהַשְּׁנִיָּה תִּמָּכֵר לְחַיָּיבֵי שְׁלָמִים, וּדְמֶיהָ חוּלִּין. יָלְדָה טוּמְטוּם וְאַנְדְּרוֹגִינוֹס, רַבָּן שִׁמְעוֹן בֶּן גַּמְלִיאֵל אוֹמֵר: אֵין קְדוּשָּׁה חָלָה עֲלֵיהֶן. דִּבְרִיָּה הוּא, דְּאֵינוֹ לֹא זָכָר וְלֹא נְקֵבָה, וְהִלְכָּךְ לֹא יָחוּל עֲלֵיהֶן קְדוּשַּׁת שְׁלָמִים וְעוֹלָה בְּמְעֵי אִמָּן, וְלֹא קְדוּשַּׁת בְּכוֹר בְּפְטִירַת רֶחֶם. דְּלָא קָרֵינָא בֵּיהּ "הַזָּכָר תַּקְדִּישׁ". וּמַתְנִיתִין נַמִי דְּקָתָנֵי: יָלְדָה טוּמְטוּם אֵינוֹ נוֹטֵל — לְרשב"ג הוּא, דְּחָשֵׁיב לֵיהּ בְּרִיָּה. מֵיתִיבֵי טוּמְטוּם יוֹרֵשׁ כְּבֵן וְנִיזּוֹן כְּבַת. מִי שֶׁמֵּת וְהִנִּיחַ נְכָסִים. יוֹרֵשׁ כְּבֵן כו'. כִּדְמְפָרֵשׁ וְאָזֵיל. בִּשְׁלָמָא לְרָבָא. דְּחָשֵׁיב לֵיהּ סָפֵק, הָכִי פֵּירוּשָׁהּ: בִּזְמַן שֶׁהַנְּכָסִים מוּעָטִין יוֹרֵשׁ כְּבֵן, כְּאֶחָד מִן הַבָּנִים, שֶׁלֹּא יִטּוֹל כְּלוּם. דְּכֵיוָן דְּסָפֵק הוּא — לֹא עָדִיף מִבָּנִים דְּשׁוֹאֲלִין עַל הַפְּתָחִים, שֶׁהַנְּקֵבוֹת דּוֹחוֹת אוֹתוֹ אֵצֶל הַזְּכָרִים, וְאֵין לוֹ. דְּאָמְרִי לֵיהּ: אַיְיתֵי רְאָיָה דִּנְקֵבָה אַתְּ, וּשְׁקוֹל כָּמוֹנוּ. וְנִיזּוֹן כְּבַת בִּנְכָסִים מְרוּבִּין. מִמָּה נַפְשָׁךְ, שֶׁהַזְּכָרִים דּוֹחִין אוֹתוֹ אֵצֶל הַנְּקֵבוֹת, וְיֵשׁ לוֹ מְזוֹנוֹת מִמָּה נַפְשָׁךְ, כִּרְבָא.

אֶלָּא

רבינו גרשום

ממעט: אם תמצא לומר [בת אשתו] כיון אף על גב דאינסבא אית לה וממעטא. אלמנתו מהו שתמעט מי אמרינן כיון דאילו אינסבא לית לה מזוני לא ממעט. או דלמא כיון דהשתא אית לה מזוני ממעט. אם תמצא לומר כיון דאית לה מזוני (לא) ממעטא [אלמנתו] ובת אם אין שם אלא כדי שיעור מזונות של אחת איזו קודמת. מי אמרינן הואיל ובת אע"ג דמינסבא אית לה קודמת לאלמנה. או דלמא כיון דהשתא כי הדדי נינהו. וכ"ז שלא נשאו קרובה דעתו דבעל טפי לאשתו מבתו בדין הוא דקדמה: פשוט מינייהו חדא. מכל הני בעיין דלעיל: אלמנתו תזון. משום דניחא לבעל שלא תזלזל אלמנתו והני נכסין מועטין נינהו: מאי קאמר. כלומר מאי חשיבות לבן כאן הכא בנכסים מועטין יותר מבת שהבן מתרעם כלומר מפני חשיבותי הפסדתי. אמר אביי לא בשביל שיהא לו כח בנכסים מועטין יותר מבת קאמר אלא מפני שראוי לעסוק בתורה קאמר: **פיס'** זכרים דוחין אותו אצל הנקבות. שלא יירש עמהן דאיכא למימר נקבה היא: נקבות דוחות אותו אצל הזכרים. שלא יזון אלא ישאל על הפתחים כשאר אחין דאיכא למימר זכר הוא: מדקתני רישא דמתני' דוכרים דוחין אותו אצל נקבות מכלל דשקיל במזונות כבת. והא קתני בהא מתני' האומר אם ילדה אשתי זכר יטול מנה ילדה זכר נוטל מנה ואם נקבה כו' ילדה טומטום אינו נוטל כלום. אלמא דלא שקיל כלל: אמר אביי הא דקתני זכרים דוחין אותו אצל הנקבות. לאו משום דשקיל מזונות אלא דוחין אותו אצלן ולא יהבי ליה כלום דכי אזיל הכא מדחי ליה ואי אזיל הכא מדחי ליה ואין לו כלום: לעולם אימא לך רישא דוחין אותו לנקבות ויש לו מזונות. וסיפא דקתני ילדה טומטום אין לו כלום אתאן לרשב"ג דתנן במס' תמורה בפ' כיצד מערימין על הבכור מבכרת שהיתה מעוברת אומר מה שבמעיה של זו אם זכר עולה ואם נקבה זבחי שלמים ילדה זכר ונקבה הזכר יקרב עולה ונקבה שלמים ילדה שני זכרים אחד מהן יקרב עולה והשני ימכר לחייבי עולה ודמי' חולין ילדה שתי נקבות אחת מהן תקרב שלמים והשנייה תמכר לחייבי שלמים ודמיה חולין ילדה טומטום ואנדרוגינוס רשב"ג אומר אין קדושה חלה עליהן ולא יתן כלום. הכי נמי משום הכי אינו נוטל כלום. מאי טעמא מצי להתנות על בכור כל זמן שהוא במעי אמו משום דאין הבכור מתקדש אלא בשעת לידתו בפטר רחם. בשלמא רבא דאמר דוחין אותו ויש לו משום הכי קתני הכא דיורש כבן בנכסים מועטין. והבן בנכסי' מועטין אין לו אלא ישאל על הפתחים ה"נ האי טומטום יורש באותה ירושה של בן דישאל על הפתחים

עין משפט נר מצוה

ו א מיי' פי"ט מהלכות אישות הלכה כא סמג עשין מח טוש"ע אה"ע סי' נג סעיף ז וסימן קיב סעיף טז:

ז ב מיי' פ"ה מהלכות נחלות הלכה ב סמג עשין נו טוש"ע ח"מ סי' רפ סעיף ח וע"ש בהג"ה וסעיף ט:

ח ג מיי' פ"ח מהלכות זכיה ומתנה הלכה ו סמג עשין פב טוש"ע חו"מ סי' רי סעיף א וסי' רנג סכ"ו וסכ"ז:

ט ד מיי' פ"ה מהלכות נחלות הלכה ב סמג עשין נו טור שו"ע סי' רפ סעיף ט:

י ה מיי' פט"ו מהלכות מעשה הקרבנות הל"ח:

מסורת הש"ס

א) כתובות מג. ע"ש:ב) שם קח.: ג) נ"ל ילדה רש"ל: ד) [נ"ל דתנן ועי' תוס' יבמות פג: ד"ה לא לכל]: ה) תמורה כד: ו) [ודמיו חולין]: ז) [וע"ע תוס' כתובות קח: ד"ה אמר רבא]:

הגהות הב"ח

(א) במשנה יטול מנה אם נקבה: (ב) רשב"ם ד"ה מאן וכו' שאינו עוסק הס"ד ואח"כ מ"ה בשביל שאני זכר ויפה כחי בנכסים: (ג) ד"ה וטומטום וכו' ספק נקבה הוא ודוחין אותו ויש לו כנקבה ואיכא למאן דאמר לאו ספק הוא אלא בריה הוא: (ד) ד"ה הזכרים וכו' שגם הם ידחוהו: (ה) תד"ה (בע"א) מי וכו' דין ירושה מן הבנים. נ"ב פי' אלא שניהם נזונים יחד: (ו) שם בהג"ה עד שיגברו הבנות. נ"ב כך היה כתוב פי' בגליון וכך כונת בעל ההג"ה שמלא כך הפירוש בתוספות ישנים ואח"כ כתב ולכאורה היה נראה כו' והוא מן ההג"ה הראשונה.

שָׁקְלִי לְהוּ בָּנוֹת לְכוּלְּהוּ? אֶלָּא אָמַר רָבָא: אמוֹצִיאִין לָהֶן מְזוֹנוֹת לַבָּנוֹת עַד שֶׁיִּבָּגְרוּ, וְהַשְּׁאָר לַבָּנִים. א)פְּשִׁיטָא, מְרוּבִּין וְנִתְמַעֲטוּ — בכְּבָר זָכוּ בָּהֶן יוֹרְשִׁין. מוּעָטִין וְנִתְרַבּוּ מַאי? גבִּרְשׁוּת יוֹרְשִׁין קַיְימִי, הִלְכָּךְ בִּרְשׁוּת יוֹרְשִׁין שְׁבוּח, אוֹ דִּלְמָא סַלּוּקֵי מְסַלְּקִי יוֹרְשִׁין מֵהָכָא? תָּא שְׁמַע, ב)דְּאָמַר רַבִּי אַסִּי אָמַר רַבִּי יוֹחָנָן: דיְתוֹמִין שֶׁקָּדְמוּ וּמָכְרוּ בִּנְכָסִים מוּעָטִין — מַה שֶּׁמָּכְרוּ מָכְרוּ. יְתֵיב רַבִּי יִרְמְיָה קַמֵּיהּ דְּרַבִּי אַבָּהוּ וְקָא בָּעֵי מִינֵּיהּ: אַלְמְנָתוֹ מַהוּ שֶׁתְּמַעֵט בַּנְּכָסִים? מִי אָמְרִינַן: כֵּיוָן דְּאִית לָהּ מְזוֹנֵי — מְמַעֲטָא, אוֹ דִּלְמָא כֵּיוָן דְּאִילּוּ מִנַּסְבָא לֵית לָהּ, הָשְׁתָּא נַמִּי לֵית לָהּ? האִם תִּמְצָא לוֹמַר: כֵּיוָן דְּאִילּוּ מִנַּסְבָא לֵית לָהּ הָשְׁתָּא נַמִּי לֵית לָהּ, בַּת אִשְׁתּוֹ מַהוּ שֶׁתְּמַעֵט בַּנְּכָסִים? מִי אָמְרִינַן: כֵּיוָן דְּכִי מִנַּסְבָא נַמִּי אִית לָהּ — וּמְמַעֲטָא, אוֹ דִּלְמָא כֵּיוָן דְּאִילּוּ מֵתָה לֵית לָהּ — וְלָא מְמַעֲטָא? וְאִם תִּמְצָא לוֹמַר: כֵּיוָן דְּאִילּוּ מֵתָה לֵית לָהּ וְלָא מְמַעֲטָא, בע"ח מַהוּ שֶׁיְּמַעֵט בַּנְּכָסִים? מִי אָמְרִינַן: כֵּיוָן דְּכִי מָיֵית נַמִּי אִית לֵיהּ — מְמַעֵט, אוֹ דִּלְמָא כֵּיוָן דִּמְחַסְּרִי גּוּבַיְינָא וְלָא מְמַעֵט? וְאִיכָּא דְּבָעֵי לָהּ לְאִידָּךְ גִּיסָא: בע"ח מַהוּ שֶׁיְּמַעֵט בַּנְּכָסִים? בַּת

שקלי להו בנות לכולהו. בתמיה. דכיון דקרית להו מועטין — א"כ לא יטלו בהן כלום הבנים, דהא תנא במתני' גבי נכסים מועטין: הבנים ישאלו על הפתחים! והשאר לבנים. והאי דקתני ישאלו על הפתחים — היינו משהוציאו אותו השאר בהוצאת מזונות. מכאן ואילך, הבנות יזונו עד שיבגרו, והבנים ישאלו על הפתחים. **פשיטא** מרובין ונתמעטו. בשעת מיתה היו מרובין, ועכשיו הוקירו מזונות או נתקלקלו הנכסים וחסרו, ואין בהן כדי מזון אלו ואלו עד שיבגרו. כבר זכו בהן יורשין. בשעת מיתת אביהן, וקרינא בהו נכסים מרובים. ויקחו הבנות חלקן המגיעם כפי שומא של שעת מיתת אביהן, והבנים יירשו חלקם שהיה מגיעם באותה שעה, וכל מה שחסרו הנכסים — חסרו לבנות ולבנים, לכל אחד כפי חלקו הראוי לו. ונתרבו. שהוזלו מזונות. מהו. מי מטי רווחא לבנים, ויטלו מותר נכסים העודף מכדי מזונות בנות עד שיבגרו? יתומים שקדמו. קודם שהעמידו בנות בדין, ומכרו אפילו בנכסים מועטין. מה שמכרו מכרו — דאין מוציאין למזון האשה והבנות מנכסים משועבדים, וכ"ש בנכסים מרובין, כדאמר בכתובות: האחים שעבדו — מוציאין לפרנסה ואין מוציאין למזונות. ש"מ, כיון שאם מכרו — מכירתן מכירה — יש להן תפיסת יד בנכסים, ואם נתרבו — יש להן חלק בהן, וזכותם בהן עומדת. **אלמנתו** מהו שתמעט בנכסים. מי שמת והניח בנים ובנות, והניח נמי אלמנתו, וצריכה נמי מזונות כל ימי מיגר ארמלותה, ואין כאן נכסים אלא כדי מזון הבנים והבנות עד שיבגרו. מי אמרינן: כיון דאית לה מזוני — ממעטא, ולא מיקרו נכסים מרובין. ומפרישין מהנכסים מזון האשה והבנות עד שיבגרו, והמותר לבנים, דהא מועטין נינהו, ולאחר שיוציאו המותר — ישאלו על הפתחים. או דלמא: כיון דאילו מינסבא לבעל לית לה מזוני — לא ממעטא, וכמאן דליתא דמיא, ומוציאין מן הנכסים לבנות כדי מזונן עד שיבגרו, וכל השאר יירשו הבנים כדין נכסים מרובין. דהא אלמנה לא ממעטא להו, וקרינן בהו "הבנים יירשו והבנות יזונו". ומחלק הבנות לא תזון האלמנה עמהם. והיינו דאיכא בין ממעטא ללא ממעטא, דאי ממעטא — הבנים ישאלו והאלמנה תזון, ואי לא ממעטא — יזונו יחד האלמנה והבנים. אבל הבנות אין להן להפסיד במזונותיהם כלל, בין ממעטא בין לא ממעטא, דהא בין בנכסים מרובין בין בנכסים מועטין תנן: הבנות יזונו. אי נמי, היכא דלא ממעטא — מיקרו נכסים מרובין. ואף על פי שנתעכבה היום או למחר מלינשא — הרי הוא כמרובין ונתמעטו, דאמרינן: כבר זכו בהן יורשין, ויזונו שלשתן יחד, בנים ובנות ואלמנה. כן נראה שיטה זו בעיני. **בת אשתו.** מי שקיבל עליו בשעת נשואין לזון בת אשתו מאיש אחר חמש שנים, ומת, ומוטל על היורשין לזונה. כיון דאף על גב דמינסבא **אית** לה מזוני. עד חמש שנים מן היורשין, שהרי חוב הוא שנתחייב לה אביהן — ממעטא, ויזונו היא והבנות, והבנים ישאלו. **לא ממעטא.** ומיקרו מרובין בשעת מיתה ונתמעטו אחרי כן, וכבר זכו יורשין. והבנות יזונו עד בגר, ואותה הבת תזון עמהן. בעל חוב מהו שימעט. אם אין נכסים אלא כדי החוב ומזון הבנות, מי אמרינן דממעט, והבנות יזונו והבנים ישאלו על הפתחים. או לא ממעט, ויזונו בנים ובנות עד שעת טריפת בעל חוב. וכשיטרוף, אם יש מותר — יזונו בנות עד בגר, ואם לאו — יפסידו.

יתומים שקדמו ומכרו בנכסים מועטין. פי' בקונטרס: שקדמו ומכרו קודם שעמדו בדין לגבות לבנות נכסים מועטין. ומיהו, לר"י נראה: דאפי' כבר תפסו הבנות או הגבו להם ב"ד, אם מכרו אחים — מכור. וכן משמע ביבמות בפרק "אלמנה" (דף סז:) דקאמר התם, רבי ישמעאל ברבי יוסי אומר משום אביו: הבת מאכלת, והבן אינו מאכיל. מ"ט בן דאין מאכיל — מפני חלקו של עובר, בת נמי לא תאכיל מפני חלקו של עובר! א"ר אסי: הכא בנכסים מועטין עסקינן, וכגון דאיכא בן בהדה דהאי בת. דממ"נ, אי ההיא דמיעברא ביה בן הוא — לא עדיף מהאי דקאי, ואי בת היא — אמאי קא אכלה בתקנתא דרבנן? כל כמה דלא נפקא לאויר העולם — לא תקינו ליה רבנן. ופריך: במאי אוקימתה — בנכסים מועטין, והאמר רבי אסי א"ר יוחנן: יתומים שקדמו ומכרו בנכסים מועטין כו'. ומאי קושיא? ולוקמה כגון שתפסו כבר הבנות, או שהגבו להם ב"ד, דאין יכולין למכור! אלא משמע דלעולם יכולין למכור. וקצת יש לדחות, דנהי דיכולין ב"ד לגבות חלק של בת עומדת, חלק של עובר שיש לחוש שמא היא בת — אין יכולין לגבות, כיון שלא יצאת לאויר העולם, ואותו חלק יכולין האחין למכור. ומיהו, אין נראה לדחות כן. ועוד ראיה: דאמר בפ' "הנושא" (כתובות דף קג.) אמר ר"נ: יתומים שקדמו ומכרו מדור האלמנה — לא עשו ולא כלום. ומ"ש מדרבי אסי א"ר יוחנן יתומים שקדמו ומכרו בנכסים מועטין מה שמכרו מכרו? התם לא תפס' מחיים, הכא תפסה מחיים. משמע כיון דלא תפסי מחיים, אע"ג דתפסי לאחר מיתה — לא היה מועיל כלום, אלא מה שמכרו מכרו. והא דאמר בפ' "נערה" (שם דף נג.) רשב"א אומר: נכסים שיש להן אחריות מוציאין לבנים מן הבנים, ולבנות מן הבנות כו', אבל לא לבנים מן הבנות בנכסים מועטין. מ"מ, אע"ג דאין מוציאין, אם מכרו — מכרו. והשתא אתי שפיר, דבכל ענין משמע. דפשיטא דמועטין ונתרבו זכו בהם יורשין אפילו כבר תפסו וגבו להם ב"ד, דאי לאו הכי — אכתי הוה ליה למיבעי במועטין ונתרבו וכבר תפסו או הגבו להם ב"ד מאי? ואם תאמר: כיון דבנכסים מועטין נמי מה שמכרו מכרו אפילו כבר תפסו, מה חילוק יש בין נכסים מרובין לנכסים מועטין? דבנכסים מרובין נמי נראה שאין מותרין למכור ולהפקיע מזונות! וי"ל: דיש חילוק, דבנכסים מרובין יכולין למכור לצורך גדול, אבל בנכסים מועטין — אין יכולין למכור כלל לכתחלה. ועוד: דמרובין ונתמעטו יזונו הבנים עם הבנות, ובנכסים מועטין לא יזונו כלל. **מה** שמכרו מכרו. וא"ת: דהכא אמרינן דבין מרובין ונתמעטו ובין מועטין ונתרבו זכו בהם היורשים. ובפרק "מי שהיה נשוי" (כתובות דף צא. ושם) גבי כתובת בנין דכרין, אמר: פשיטא מרובין ונתמעטו — כבר זכו בהן יורשין. פירוש: יורשי כתובה הגדולה. מועטין ונתרבו מאי? ת"ש: דהנהו בני לרצור מועטין ונתרבו הוו, אתו לקמיה דרב עמרם, אמר להו: זילו פייסינהו, ואי לא כו', עד דאתו לקמיה דר"נ, אמר: כשם שמרובין ונתמעטו כבר זכו בהם יורשין — כך מועטין ונתרבו זכו בהן יורשין. ופירש בקונטרס: זכו בהן יורשין של כתובה הקטנה. ופליג ר"נ ארב עמרם, דאמר זילו פייסינהו, דמשמע לבני קטנה אמר לפיים בני הגדולה, דאי לבני הגדולה אומר — לא הוה שייך לשון פיוס, כיון דמן הדין שקלי בני הקטנה בנחלה גמורה דאורייתא! ולא קשיא מידי, דהכא יד הבנים לעולם על העליונה, כדי להעמיד נחלה דאורייתא. ועוד: דהכא לא פקע כח היתומים מעולם, כדקאמר: מה שמכרו מכרו. ולר"י נראה: דהא דקאמר התם ר"נ כו' מועטים ונתרבו זכו בהם יורשין — היינו יורשי כתובה הגדולה, ויטלו אלו כתובת אמם ואלו כתובת אמם, מדלא קאמר "כבר זכו בהן יורשין". וקשיא: דא"כ התם אזלינן לעולם בתר תקנתא דרבנן שתתקיים כתובת בנין דכרין, והכא אזלינן בתר מעיקרא! וי"ל: דהתם לא מיעקרא כולי האי נחלה דאורייתא, דהרי מ"מ כולן יורשין, אע"פ שאין נוטלין בשוה. אבל הכא — מיעקרא לגמרי. **מי אמרינן כיון דאילו מינסבא** לית לה **לא ממעטא.** תימה לר"י: היאך טועה לומר כן? והא בת נמי, אי מינסבא לית לה, כדתנן: ג)"דתהון מתזן עד דתלקחן לגוברין". ומאי קאמר נמי: בע"ח מיחסר גוביינא? בת נמי מיחסרא גוביינא, ואי מתה נמי לית לה, כמו בת אשתו! ועוד: אי באלמנה שייך נכסים מועטין — מה שיעור יהיה? דבשלמא בבנות יש שיעור למ"ד עד שיבגרו, אבל באלמנה לא שייך בגרות, ועד מתי יהיו נכסים מועטין? ונראה לפרש: דודאי אם אין כאן אלא אלמנה אבל הבנים — שניהם שוין בנכסים. וכן אם אין כאן אלא אלמנה ובנות. דלא תקנו (א) נכסים מועטים אלא לבנות שהן יוצאי יריכו והם בנות ירושה במקום שאין בנים, ואע"ג דמיחסרא

מסורת הש"ס

א) כתובות נא.: ב) סוטה כא: כתובות קג. יבמות סז: : ג) [כתובות נב:]:

עין משפט נר מצוה

ב א מיי' פי"ט מהלכות אישות הלכה יז סמג עשין מח טוש"ע אה"ע סי' קיב סעיף א:
ג ב מיי' שם הלכה יט טוש"ע שם סעיף יג:
ד ג ד מיי' שם טוש"ע שם סעיף יד:
ה ה ו ז מיי' שם הלכה כ טוש"ע שם סעיף טו וע"ש:

הגהות הב"ח

(א) תום' ד"ה מי אמרי' וכו' דלא תקנו דין נכסים:

רבינו גרשום

שקלי להו בנות. מיד בתמיה ולית לבנים כלום והא יש בנכסים הללו הרבה יותר משיעור מזונות לבנות עד שיבגרו: אלא אמר רבא מוציאין מהן. מיד שיעור מזונות לבנות עד שיבגרו והשאר יהיו לבנים למזונות: יתומין שקדמו ומכרו בנכסים מועטין מה שמכרו מכרו. ואין גובין מהן השתא מה שמכרו בנכסים מועטין זכו בהן כל שכן במועטין ונתרבו: שוב יתיב קבעי אלמנתו שהיורשין חייבין לזונה ואי ליכא אלא סיפוק הבנות וסיפוק אלמנה דאם לא הוי מינסבא איכא מיעוט נכסים דלית בהו עד שיבגרו וממעטא לגבייהו ואמרינן נכסין מועטין הן. והבנים ישאלו על הפתחים: מי אמרינן כיון דאית לה מזונות ממעטא. וישאלו על הפתחים. או דלמא כיון דבידה לאינסובי אימת דבעי. וכי מנסבא לית לה מזוני מיורשין ה"נ השתא חשבינן לה כמאן דמינסבא ולא ממעטא: בת אשתו. שקבל עליו לזונה ה' שנים כשנשא אמה והשתא מת הבעל ויורשין חייבין במזונותיה עד סוף ה' שנים מהו שתמעט בנכסים. דלא הויין מרובין: מי אמרינן. אע"ג דאי מינסבא אית לה ה' שנים מזונות כמו שקיבל ממעטא או דלמא כיון דאלו מתה לית ליה מזונות השתא נמי לא ממעטא: בעל חוב של אביהן מהו שימעט. כשמחשבין החוב שיש לו לקבל הוו נכסים מועטין. מי אמרי' אע"ג דאילו מת בעל חוב אית ליה יורשין שגובין במקומו וממעט. או דילמא כו': איכא דבעי להך גיסא. שמקדים במאוחר תחלה: בעל חוב מהו שימעט בנכסים. מי אמרינן כיון שמחוסר גוביינא לא ממעט או דילמא כיון דאילו מת נמי אית להיורשין נמי

א א ב מיי' פ"ט מהל' אישות הל' יז סמג עשין מח ט טוש"ע אה"ע סי' קיב סעיף יא:

וְהַיּוֹרֵשׁ אֶת אִשְׁתּוֹ! אָמַר לֵיהּ רָבָא: וְהַשְׁתָּא דִּשְׁלַח מִי יָדְעִינַן? א)הָאָמַר ר' יוֹסֵי בְּר' חֲנִינָא: בְּאוּשָׁא הִתְקִינוּ, הָאִשָּׁה שֶׁמָּכְרָה (א) נִכְסֵי מְלוֹג בְּחַיֵּי בַעְלָהּ וּמֵתָה — הַבַּעַל מוֹצִיא מִיַּד הַלָּקוֹחוֹת! אֶלָּא אָמַר רַב אַשִׁי: בַּעַל — שַׁוְיוּהוּ רַבָּנַן כְּיוֹרֵשׁ וְשַׁוְיוּהוּ רַבָּנַן כְּלוֹקֵחַ, וְהֵיכָא דְּטָבָא לֵיהּ עֲבַדוּ לֵיהּ; גַּבֵּי יוֹבֵל שַׁוְיוּהוּ רַבָּנַן כְּיוֹרֵשׁ מִשּׁוּם פְּסֵידָא דִּידֵיהּ, גַּבֵּי דְּר' יוֹסֵי בְּר' חֲנִינָא שַׁוְיוּהוּ רַבָּנַן כְּלוֹקֵחַ מִשּׁוּם פְּסֵידָא דִּידֵיהּ, גַּבֵּי דְּרַבִּין מִשּׁוּם פְּסֵידָא דְּאַלְמָנָה שַׁוְיוּהוּ רַבָּנַן כְּיוֹרֵשׁ. וְהָא גַּבֵּי דְּר' יוֹסֵי בְּר' חֲנִינָא דְּאִיכָּא פְּסֵידָא לַלָּקוֹחוֹת, וְשַׁוְיוּהוּ רַבָּנַן כְּלוֹקֵחַ! הָתָם אִינְהוּ אַפְסִידוּ אַנַּפְשַׁיְיהוּ, כֵּיוָן דְּאִיכָּא בַּעַל, לָא אִיבָּעֵי לְהוּ לְמִיזְבַּן מֵאִיתְּתָא דְּיָתְבָא תּוּתֵי גַבְרָא.§

הדרן עלך יש נוחלין

מִי ב)שֶׁמֵּת וְהִנִּיחַ בָּנִים וּבָנוֹת, אבִּזְמַן שֶׁהַנְּכָסִים מְרוּבִּין — הַבָּנִים יִירְשׁוּ וְהַבָּנוֹת יִזּוֹנוּ, נְכָסִים מוּעָטִין — הַבָּנוֹת יִזּוֹנוּ וְהַבָּנִים יִשְׁאֲלוּ עַל הַפְּתָחִים; אַדְמוֹן אוֹמֵר: בִּשְׁבִיל שֶׁאֲנִי זָכָר הִפְסַדְתִּי? אָמַר רַבָּן גַּמְלִיאֵל: רוֹאֶה אֲנִי אֶת דִּבְרֵי אַדְמוֹן.§ **גמ'** וְכַמָּה מְרוּבִּין? אָמַר רַב יְהוּדָה אָמַר רַב: כְּדֵי שֶׁיִּזּוֹנוּ מֵהֶן אֵלּוּ וְאֵלּוּ שְׁנֵים עָשָׂר חֹדֶשׁ. כִּי אֲמַרִיתָא קַמֵּיהּ דִּשְׁמוּאֵל, אֲמַר: זוֹ דִּבְרֵי רַבָּן גַּמְלִיאֵל בַּר רַבִּי, אֲבָל חֲכָמִים אוֹמְרִים: בכְּדֵי שֶׁיִּזּוֹנוּ מֵהֶן אֵלּוּ וְאֵלּוּ עַד שֶׁיִּבָּגְרוּ. אִיתְּמַר נַמִי: כִּי אֲתָא רָבִין אָמַר ר' יוֹחָנָן, וְאָמְרִי לָהּ אָמַר רַבָּה בַּר בַּר חָנָה אָמַר רַבִּי יוֹחָנָן: כָּל שֶׁיִּזּוֹנוּ מֵהֶן אֵלּוּ וְאֵלּוּ עַד שֶׁיִּבָּגְרוּ — הֵן מְרוּבִּין, פָּחוֹת מִכָּאן — הֲרֵי אֵלּוּ מוּעָטִין. וְאִי לֵיכָּא לְאֵלּוּ וְאֵלּוּ עַד שֶׁיִּבָּגְרוּ, שָׁקְלִי

והיורש את אשתו. פי' בקונטרס: ואי הוי לוקח מחיים — גם לאחר מיתה לא פקע, והוי לוקח. ואין נראה, דהא מחיים אין לו אלא פירות! ונראה לר"י לפרש: דמבעיא ליה אם בעל יורש הוי או לוקח הוי בין מחיים בין לאחר מיתה, מדלא מפליג מידי. ופשיט מדרבין, דלכל הפחות הוי יורש לאחר מיתה, כדקאמר: מתה הבת — אלמנתו מזונת מנכסיו, אע"פ שהבעל יורשה. אבל מחיים אין להוכיח מדבריו דהוי יורש אע"ג דקאמר: נשאת הבת — אלמנתו נזונת, דהא אפילו הוי לוקח מחיים קאמר שפיר דנזונת, שתוכל למכור הגוף מחיים והפירות לאחר מיתה, כיון דבעל יורש הוי לכל הפחות לאחר מיתה. ולהכי קא"ל אביי: ואי לאו דשלח רבין לא הוה ידעינן דהוי יורש לאחר מיתה? והתנן, אלו שאין חוזרים ביובל: הבכורה והיורש את אשתו, אלמא דיורש הוי לאחר מיתה. **גבי** יובל שויוהו רבנן כיורש. לאו דוקא נקט "שויוהו רבנן", דהא כיון דאית ליה דאינה חוזרת ביובל — אית ליה דירושת הבעל דאורייתא. דהכי אמר בבכורות (ד' נב:), וכן פי' בקונטרס. אלא "שויוהו רבנן" — בעי למימר: הניחוהו להיות יורש, ולא עשאוהו לוקח. **התם** אינהו אפסידו אנפשייהו כו' תימה: דבפרק "מי שהיה נשוי" (כתובות ד' צה:) אמר אביי: "נכסי לך ואחריך לפלוני", ומכרה ומתה — הבעל מוציא מיד הלקוחות, ו"אחריך" מיד בעל, ולוקח מיד "אחריך", ואוקימנא בידא דלוקח. ופריך התם: מאי שנא מהא דתנן דיעשו פשרה ביניהם? ומשני: התם אית להו פסידא לכולהו, הכא לוקח הוא דאית ליה פסידא. פי': וכיון דאיכא פסידא דלוקח — שויוהו רבנן (ג) בעל כיורש, ואין מוציא מיד לוקח. והשתא האמר הכא דאיהו דאפסיד אנפשיה, דלא ה"ל למיזבן מאתתא דיתבא תותי גברא, לפי שהבעל יוציא מידו! וכ"ת: התם לא אפסיד אנפשיה, שהוא סבור שלא יטול הבעל ממנו, לפי ש"אחריך" יוציא מידו — מ"מ הרי יודע דיחזרו חלילה, ויצטרכו לעשות פשרה, ויהיה הבעל! ואור"י: דהתם לא אפסיד אנפשיה, לפי שסבור שיעשה פשרה עם "אחריך" ולא יגבה הבעל כלום. וא"ת: מ"ש מהא דאמר התם לעיל: "נכסי לך ואחריך לפלוני" ענודה וניסת — בעל לוקח הוי ואין ל"אחריך" במקום בעל כלום. אלמא, אע"ג דאיכא פסידא ל"אחריך" הוי בעל לוקח! וי"ל: דמתנה שאני, דאין כל כך פסידא אם לא יקבל במתנה. וא"ת: דאמר בריש "המפקיד" (ב"מ ד' לה. ושם) שמו לה לאשה ואכסיבא, או שמו מינה (ד) ואגסיבא — בעל לוקח הוי ולא מיהדר כו', אע"ג דאיכא פסידא ללוה לא מיהדר ליה ארעא אע"פ דשומא הדרא לעולם! וי"ל: כיון דבדין לא הדר, אלא משום "ועשית הישר והטוב" לא חשיב כל כך פסידא. עוד מקשים, דאמר ב"החובל" (ב"ק ד' פט. ושם): כי אתו רב פפא ורב הונא בריה דרב יהושע מבי רב אמרו: תקנת אושא מתני' היא: העבד והאשה פגיעתן רעה, אחרים שחבלו בהם חייבים והם שחבלו באחרים פטורין. ואי ס"ד ליתא לתקנת אושא תזבין נכסי מלוג ותיתיב ליה! משמע: הא איתא לתקנת אושא לא ליתיב ליה ולא מידי, ואמאי? הא לא תקנו רבנן דהוי לוקח אלא היכא דליכא פסידא לאחריני, אבל הכא איכא פסידא דנחבלים! וי"ל: דהוה מצי למפרך "ולטעמיך", אלא דבלאו הכי פריך שפיר. ולרשב"א נראה דלא קשה מידי, דהא כיון דתקינו רבנן דבעל מוציא מיד הלקוחות לטובתו היכא דליכא פסידא לאחריני — לא פלוג, ותקנו דבכ"מ שאשה מוכרת הבעל מוציא, אפילו במקום שחבלה באחרים דאיכא פסידא דאחריני. כיון דלא שכיחא מלתא שיהא פסידא דאחריני, לכך לא פלוג רבנן, ובכל מקום מוציא.

וְהַיּוֹרֵשׁ אֶת אִשְׁתּוֹ. מְפָרֵשׁ הָתָם: קָסָבַר יְרוּשַּׁת הַבַּעַל דְּאוֹרַיְיתָא. וְאִי לוֹקֵחַ הָוֵי מִשָּׁעָה שֶׁנִּשֵּׂאת — אֲפִילּוּ לְאַחַר מִיתָה לָא נָפְקָא מִכְּלַל מִקָּח וּמִמְכָּר, וְתֶהְדַּר בַּיּוֹבֵל! בְּאוּשָׁא הִתְקִינוּ. שֶׁגָּלְתָה סַנְהֶדְרִין לְשָׁם, כִּדְמְפָרֵשׁ בְּר"ה (ד' לא.). הָאִשָּׁה שֶׁמָּכְרָה נִכְסֵי מְלוֹג בְּחַיֵּי בַעְלָהּ. שֶׁאִם יָמוּת בַּעְלָהּ יִזְכֶּה בָּהֶן, וְאִם תָּמוּת הִיא וְיִירָשֶׁהָ בַּעַל — יַפְסִידוּ. וְנִכְסֵי מְלוֹג הֵן נְכָסִים שֶׁנָּפְלוּ לָהּ מִבֵּית אָבִיהָ, אוֹ שֶׁהִכְנִיסָה קַרְקָעוֹת שֶׁלֹּא נִשּׁוֹמוּ בִּכְתוּבָּתָהּ, וְלֹא קִיבֵּל בַּעַל עָלָיו אַחֲרָיוּת, וְאוֹכֵל פֵּירוֹתֵיהֶן בְּחַיֶּיהָ כְּתַקָּנַת חֲכָמִים תַּחַת פִּרְקוֹנָהּ. וּלְהָכִי מִיקְרֵי מְלוֹג — שֶׁמּוֹלְגָן וּמְחַסְּרָן בַּעַל, שֶׁאוֹכֵל הַפֵּירוֹת כִּמְלִיגַת הָרֹאשׁ. אִי אָמְרַתְּ בִּשְׁלָמָא לוֹקֵחַ שַׁוְיוּהוּ רַבָּנַן, מִשָּׁעָה שֶׁנְּשָׂאָהּ, מִשּׁוּ"ה מַפֵּיק, דְּלוֹקֵחַ רִאשׁוֹן הָוֵי. אֶלָּא אִי אָמְרַתְּ בַּעַל בְּנִכְסֵי אִשְׁתּוֹ יוֹרֵשׁ הָוֵי מִשְּׁעַת נִשּׂוּאִין — אַמַּאי מַפֵּיק? לָמָּה תִּקְנוּ בְּאוּשָׁא שֶׁהַבַּעַל מוֹצִיא? וַהֲלֹא הָאִשָּׁה שֶׁהִיא מוֹרֶשֶׁת אוֹתוֹ מָכְרָה, וְאֵין כֹּחַ בַּיּוֹרְשִׁין לִירַשׁ מַה שֶּׁמָּכַר אֲבִיהֶן! אֶלָּא וַדַּאי מִדְּתִקְּנוּ שֶׁהַבַּעַל מוֹצִיא, כָּךְ הָיָה עִיקַּר תַּקָּנַת אוּשָׁא — שֶׁיְּהֵא הַבַּעַל לוֹקֵחַ בִּנְכָסֶי' מִשָּׁעָה שֶׁנְּשָׂאָהּ, וְהִלְכָּךְ מוֹצִיא, שֶׁהֲרֵי קָדַם מִקָּחוֹ לְמִקְחָן שֶׁל לָקוֹחוֹת. **אֶלָּא אָמַר רַב אַשִׁי** כו'. לְתָרֵץ עַל כָּל אֵלּוּ הַדְּבָרִים, שֶׁיֵּשׁ מְקוֹמוֹת שֶׁעֲשָׂאוּהוּ כְּיוֹרֵשׁ, וְיֵשׁ מְקוֹמוֹת שֶׁעֲשָׂאוּהוּ כְּלוֹקֵחַ. **וְהֵיכָא דְּטָבָא לֵיהּ** כו'. כִּדְמְפָרֵשׁ וְאָזֵיל. **גַּבֵּי יוֹבֵל** כו' **מִשּׁוּם פְּסֵידָא דִּידֵיהּ.** דְּלֹא תֶּהְדַּר בַּיּוֹבֵל לְמִשְׁפַּחַת אִשְׁתּוֹ. **גַּבֵּי דְּרַבִּין.** אע"ג דְּאִיכָּא פְּסֵידָא דִּידֵיהּ — חָיְישֵׁי' לִפְסֵידָא דְּאַלְמָנָה, שֶׁמֵּאַחַר שֶׁקָּדַם תְּנַאי מְזוֹנוֹתֶיהָ לַנִּשּׂוּאִין — לֹא טוֹב לָנוּ לְהַפְסִידָהּ בְּיָדַיִם. **דְּאִיכָּא פְּסֵידָא דְּלָקוֹחוֹת.** אַמַּאי לָא חָיְישִׁינַן, כִּי הֵיכִי דְּחָיְישִׁינַן לִפְסֵידָא דְּאַלְמָנָה? **דְּיָתְבָא תּוּתֵי גַבְרָא.** וְרָאוּי לְיוֹרְשָׁהּ כְּשֶׁתָּמוּת, וַאֲלוּ הֶעֱרִימוּ לְהוֹצִיאָם מִיָּדוֹ — הִלְכָּךְ יַפְסִידוּ. וּלְעִנְיַן שְׁמַעְתָּא דְּשְׁאִילְתָּא, פֵּי' רַבֵּינוּ חֲנַנְאֵל, וְרוֹאֶה אֲנִי אֶת דְּבָרָיו: לְוָותָה וְאָכְלָה וְעָמְדָה וְנִיסֵּת — מִסְתַּבְּרָא דְּכְיוֹרֵשׁ הָוֵי, מִשּׁוּם פְּסֵידָא דְּמַלְוֶה. וְכֵן סוּגְיָא דִּשְׁמַעְתָּא, דְּכָל הֵיכָא דְּאִיכָּא פְּסֵידָא, כְּגוֹן פְּסֵידָא דְּאַלְמָנָה, דְּלֵיכָּא לְמֵימַר אִיהוּ דְּאַפְסִיד אַנַּפְשֵׁיהּ — שַׁוְיוּהוּ רַבָּנַן כְּיוֹרֵשׁ.

הדרן עלך יש נוחלין

מִי שֶׁמֵּת. מְרוּבִּין. מְפָרֵשׁ בַּגְּמָרָא. **וְהַבָּנוֹת יִזּוֹנוּ.** מְזוֹנוֹת וּפַרְנָסַת נִשּׂוּאִין, עַד דְּתִבָּגְרָן אוֹ עַד דְּתִנָּסְבָן לְגוּבְרִין, כִּדְתְנַן בִּכְתוּבּוֹת (ד' נב: נג.). **יִשְׁאֲלוּ.** יַחְזְרוּ עַל הַפְּתָחִים. **בִּשְׁבִיל שֶׁאֲנִי זָכָר הִפְסַדְתִּי.** בִּתְמִיָּה. (ב) וּבַגְּמָ' מְפָרֵשׁ מַאי קָאָמַר. אֶלָּא לֹא אַפְסִיד, וְנִזּוֹנִים יַחַד. **אָמַר רַבָּן גַּמְלִיאֵל** כו'. וְהָכִי הִלְכְתָא כְּאַדְמוֹן, דְּאָמַר בְּפֶ' בַּתְרָא דִּכְתוּבּוֹת: כָּל מָקוֹם שֶׁאָמַר ר"ג רוֹאֶה אֲנִי אֶת דִּבְרֵי אַדְמוֹן — הֲלָכָה כְּמוֹתוֹ. **גמ' כְּדֵי שֶׁיִּזּוֹנוּ.** פַּרְנָסָה וּמְזוֹנוֹת. **אֵלּוּ וְאֵלּוּ.** בָּנִים וּבָנוֹת. **כִּי אֲמַרִיתָא.** אַחַר פְּטִירָתוֹ שֶׁל רַב, וּבָאתִי לִלְמוֹד קַמֵּיהּ דִּשְׁמוּאֵל. **עַד שֶׁיִּבָּגְרוּ.** שֶׁכָּךְ הִתְנָה לָהֶן אֲבִיהֶן: עַד דְּתִבָּגְרָן אוֹ תִּנָּסְבָן, כִּדְאָמַר בִּכְתוּבּוֹת. **וְאִיפְּכָא מוּעָטִין,** וְיִזּוֹנוּ הַבָּנוֹת עַד שֶׁיִּבָּגְרוּ, וְהַמּוֹתָר לַבָּנִים כִּדְמְפָרֵשׁ וְאָזֵיל. שָׁקְלִי

הדרן עלך יש נוחלין

מי שמת. והבנות יזונו. מה שהזכיר רשב"ם בהדי מזונות פרנסה — אין נראה לריב"ן. דהא מזונות היינו אכילה ושתיה, ופרנסה היינו מלבושין וצרכי הנשואין. ותרי מילי נינהו, כדאמר [בפ' "מציאת האשה"] (כתובות ד' סח:): מוציאין לפרנסה ואין מוציאין למזונות, וקתני נמי: הבנות נזונות ומתפרנסות, וכן בכמה דוכתי משמע דתרי מילי נינהו. **אמר** ר"ג רואה אני את דברי אדמון. בכתובות (ד' קט.) אמר: כ"מ שאמר ר"ג רואה אני את דברי אדמון — הלכה כמותו. א"ל רבא לרב נחמן: אפי' בברייתא כו'? מכל הסיא סוגיא משמע דהלכה כאדמון. ותימה: דהכא בגמרא כולה שמעתא כרבנן דאדמון, ולא כהלכתא. דא"ר ג)(יוסי) א"ר יוחנן: יתומים שקדמו ומכרו בנכסים מועטין וכו'. ובעיא נמי דר' ירמיה מר' אבא(ה) הויא אליבא דרבנן. ואמר נמי בסוטה (ד' כא:): היכי דמי רשע ערום? א"ר ג)(יוסי) א"ר יוחנן — זה המשיא עצה למכור בנכסים מועטין. ור"ח וה"ג ורב אלפס פסקו כרבנן דאדמון, משום דשמעתין דהכא כוותייהו אזלא. ור"ת אומר דאדמון לא פליג ארבנן, אלא שמתמיה על התקנה שתקנו בנכסים מועטין, אבל מ"מ כרבנן ס"ל. ולא משמע הכי, מדקאמר ר"ג: רואה אני את דברי אדמון. [ועיין תוספות כתובות קח: סד"ה אדמון].

רבינו גרשום

אלמא בעל בנכסי אשתו יורש הוי: נכסי מלוג. להכי קרי נכסי מלוג שכיון שלא קבל עליו הבעל אחריות מתחסרין והולכין כמו שמולגין את הראש שמתחסר השער להכי מקרי נכסי מלוג. אי אמרת בשלמא לוקח הוי משום הכי מפיק דקדם שעבוד לקיחתו משעה שהכניסה לו והלקוחות לא קנו עדיין אלא אי אמרת כיורש הוי הלא הוא אינו יורש בנכסי אשתו אלא לאחר מיתת אשתו והלקוחות קדם שעבודן קודם מיתתה אלא לאו ש"מ משום הכי מוציא הבעל בנכסי אשתו דלוקח הוי. אלמא אע"ג דשלח רבין באגרתיה הבעל יורש הוי ליכא למשמע מיניה והשתא מצינן למשמע דלוקח הוי: משום פסידא דידיה דלא תיפוק מידיה ביובל ירושת אשתו דאי דיינינן ליה בלוקח נפקא מיניה ביובל כשאר לקוחות. לגבי רבי יוסי ב"ר חנינא טבא עבדי ליה לבעל. דשוינהו כלוקח משום פסידא דידיה הוי דאי אמרת יורש הוי אם כן קדמה קניית לקוחות מירושתו שאין ירושה אלא לאחר מיתה אבל כי משוינן ליה לוקח קדמה קנייתו למכירתה משום הכי מוציא מיד הלקוחות גבי רבין דשלח באגרתיה דיורש הוי משום פסידא דאלמנה דתהוי נזונת מנכסי יורשין שויוהו רבנן כיורש כי היכי דתיקום שטר שעבוד כתובתה מירושתו של בעל שיורש הבת של זו דאי אמרינן דבעל כלוקח הוי אינה נזונת דאין מוציאין למזון האשה והבנות מנכסים משועבדים ללוקח מפני התקן העולם. ומקשי' משום דפסידא דאלמנה אמרת שויוהו רבנן כיורש הא גבי מילתא דרבי יוסי ב"ר חנינא דאיכא פסידא ללוקח דבעל מוציא מידו ושויוהו רבנן לבעל כלוקח. ואי משום השתא דפסידא איבעי רבנן לשויוהו כיורש דהשתא לא קא מפסדי לקוחות דשעבודן הוי קדים מירושת הבעל. התם שאני הוא ובדין הוא דליפסדו מדידהו דהלקוחות הוא דאינהו דאפסידו אנפשייהו דלא איבעי להו למיזבן כו'. אבל גבי אלמנה מאי הוי לה למיעבד משום הכי שויוהו רבנן כיורש דלא תפסיד אלמנה במזונותיה:

הדרן עלך יש נוחלין

פ"ט מי שמת כו' בזמן שהנכסים מרובין הבנים יירשו. שיהא הממון בחזקתם: והבנות יזונו. מן הנכסים עד שינשאו ונוטלות עישור נכסים: כדי שיזונו אלו ואלו כל סיפוקן בין בפרנסה בין במזונות עד שיבגרו עד שיביאו שערות הבנות לי"ב שנה ויום א' והבנים לי"ג שנה ויום א' ואי ליכא כדי שיזונו אלו ואלו עד שיבגרו אלא יש בהם כדי מזונות של י' שנים. שקלי

הגהות הב"ח

(א) גמ' נכסי מלוג. (ב) רשב"ם ד"ה בשביל וכו' בתמיה אלא לא אפסיד ומזונים יחד והגמ' מפרש מאי קאמר הס"ד: (ג) תוס' ד"ה התם וכו' [illegible] בעל כיורש וכו' [illegible]: (ד) בא"ד או שמו מינה ואגסיבא [illegible]: (ה) ד"ה אמר וכו' מר' אבא נמי הויא אליבא.

א) כתובות נ. [illegible] ב"מ לה. [illegible] ב) כתובות קח: ג) [צ"ל ר' אסי]

תלמוד בבלי

הוצאת קוֹרֵן ירושלים

— מהדורת נאה —

מסכת בבא בתרא
דף קלט: עד דף קנט:

COMMENTARY BY

Rabbi Adin Even-Israel Steinsaltz

EDITOR-IN-CHIEF

Rabbi Dr Tzvi Hersh Weinreb

EXECUTIVE EDITOR

Rabbi Joshua Schreier

•

STEINSALTZ CENTER

KOREN PUBLISHERS JERUSALEM

Please note that the number ranges that appear at the bottom of each daf of the Vilna pages indicate the corresponding pages of the Koren Talmud Bavli translation and commentary.

תלמוד בבלי

— מהדורת נאה —

בבא בתרא חלק ז

Steinsaltz Center

KOREN